Magill's
Cinema
Annual
2004

Magill's Cinema Annual 2 0 0 4

23rd Edition
A Survey of the Films of 2003

Christine Tomassini, Editor

**Jim Craddock and Michael J. Tyrkus,
Contributing Editors**

A VideoHound® Reference

GALE®

THOMSON

™

GALE

Detroit • New York • San Diego • San Francisco • Cleveland • New Haven, Conn. • Waterville, Maine • London • Munich

Magill's Cinema Annual 2004

Project Editor
Christine Tomassini

Editorial
Jim Craddock
Michael J. Tyrkus

Editorial Support Services
Wayne Fong

Manufacturing
Evi Seoud
Rhonda Williams

Product Design
Tracey Rowens

For permission to use material from this product, submit your request via Web at http://www.gale-edit.com/permissions, or you may download our Permissions Request form and submit your request by fax or mail to:

Permissions Department
The Gale Group, Inc.
27500 Drake Rd.
Farmington Hills, MI 48331-3535
Permissions Hotline:
248-699-8006 or 800-877-4253, ext. 8006
Fax: 248-699-8074 or 800-762-4058

While every effort has been made to ensure the reliability of the information presented in this publication, Gale does not guarantee the accuracy of the data contained herein. Gale accepts no payment for listing; and inclusion of any organization, agency, institution, publication, service, or individual does not imply endorsement of the editors or publisher. Errors brought to the attention of the publisher and verified to the satisfaction of the publisher will be corrected in future editions.

ISBN 1-55862-460-0
ISSN: 0739-2141

Printed in the United States of America
10 9 8 7 6 5 4 3 2 1

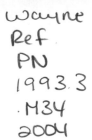

Table of Contents

Preface

Magill's Cinema Annual 2004 continues the fine film reference tradition that defines the VideoHound series of entertainment industry products published by Gale. The twenty-second annual volume in a series that developed from the 21-volume core set, *Magill's Survey of Cinema*, the *Annual* was formerly published by Salem Press. Gale's ninth volume, as with the previous Salem volumes, contains essay-reviews of significant domestic and foreign films released in the United States during the preceding year.

The *Magill's* editorial staff at Gale, comprising the VideoHound team and a host of *Magill's* contributors, continues to provide the enhancements that were added to the *Annual* when Gale acquired the line. These features include:

- More essay-length reviews of significant films released during the year

- Obituaries and book review sections

- Trivia and "fun facts" about the reviewed movies, their stars, the crew, and production

- Quotes and dialogue "soundbites" from reviewed movies, or from stars and crew about the film

- More complete awards and nominations listings, including the

American Academy Awards®, Golden Globe, New York Critics Awards, Los Angeles Film Critics Awards, and others (see the User's Guide for more information on awards coverage)

- Box office grosses, including year-end and other significant totals

- Publicity taglines featured in film reviews and advertisements

In addition to these elements, the *Magill's Cinema Annual 2004* still features:

- An obituaries section profiling major contributors to the film industry who died in 2003

- An annotated list of selected film books published in 2003

- Nine indexes: Directors, Screenwriters, Cinematographers, Editors, Art Directors, Music Directors, Performers, Subject, and Title (now cumulative)

Compilation Methods

The *Magill's* editorial staff reviews a variety of entertainment industry publications, including trade magazines and newspapers, as well as online sources, on a daily and weekly basis to select significant films for review in *Magill's Cinema Annual*. *Magill's* staff and other contributing reviewers, including film scholars and university faculty, write the reviews included in the *Annual*.

Magill's Cinema Annual: A VideoHound Reference

The *Magill's Survey of Cinema* series, now supplemented by the *Annual*, is the recipient of the Reference Book of the Year Award in Fine Arts by the American Library Association.

Gale, an award-winning publisher of reference products, is proud to offer *Magill's Cinema Annual* as part of its popular VideoHound® product line, which includes *VideoHound's Golden Movie Retriever* and *The Video Source Book*. Other Gale film-related products include the *St. James Film Directors Encyclopedia*, *The St. James Women Filmmakers Encyclopedia* and the *Contemporary Theatre, Film, and Television* series.

Acknowledgments

Thank you to Judy Hartman, GGS Information Services, for her typesetting expertise, and Wayne Fong for his invaluable technical assistance. The *VideoHound* staff is thanked for its contributions to this project, especially Carol Schwartz for her generosity, hard work, and goodwill, as well as Peter Gareffa for his guidance and direction. Also, the following producers, distributors, and publicists were gracious enough to provide screeners and other materials that helped in the writing of some of the reviews in this edition: Susan Norget and Anne Crozat of Susan Norget Public Relations and Marketing; Sophie Gluck of Sophie Gluck and Associates; Brooke Travis of Weber Shandwick/Rogers Cowan; Rodrigo Barando of Kino International; the publicity office of Samuel Goldwyn Films; and the Press Office of the Film Society of Lincoln Center.

The Year in Film: An Introduction

The Lord of the Rings: The Return of the King ruled over all in a busy year for movies. The box office champ ($364 million) pleased critics, audiences, and the Academy (winning every award for which it was nominated, 11 in all), as well as many other award-giving bodies. The only people left unhappy may be Tolkien purists and Christopher Lee for the exclusion of Lee's scenes as Saruman. Undoubtedly, these scenes will show up in the extras-laden Special Edition DVD, if the disposition of the first two chapters is any indication. Executives at New Line might be somewhat upset to see the lucrative trilogy come to an end, as well. There has been talk of making *The Hobbit*, but that would have to wait at least until after Peter Jackson finishes his next project, a remake of *King Kong*. Regardless of the destiny of any further Tolkien adaptations, *The Lord of the Rings* can truly be considered an artistic, commercial, and cinematic success, and *The Return of the King* a fitting and triumphant final chapter.

The complete success of *King* is even more impressive when compared to the disappointing conclusion of *The Matrix* trilogy. While both sequels did well at the box office (*Reloaded* grossed over $281 million and *Revolutions* grossed $139 million), they were greeted with less-than-enthusiastic critical and audience acceptance. Anticipation and expectations were high before the May release of *Reloaded*, but nearly everyone was disappointed with its labyrinthine plotting and overwhelming digital effects. This disappointment dampened excitement for *Revolutions*, which barely recouped its $110 million budget domestically. Both sequels suffered from the Wachowski Brothers' over-reaching to top an original that was *so* original that it may have set the bar too high.

Lord of the Rings and *The Matrix* were not the only franchise trilogies to conclude their runs in 2003, just the most anticipated. The *American Pie* gang (most of them) ended their run with *American Wedding* by sending Jim and Michelle to the altar and everyone (however reluctantly) into adulthood. Robert Rodriquez concluded two successful franchises, *El Mariachi* and *Spy Kids* with, respectively, *Once*

Upon a Time in Mexico and *Spy Kids 3-D*. Both featured Rodriguez's longtime collaborator Antonio Banderas, but *Mexico* had the extra bonus of Johnny Depp, complementing nicely his award-winning (Screen Actors Guild Best Actor) appearance in the surprise hit *Pirates of the Caribbean: The Curse of the Black Pearl*. Other third installments included Arnold's pre-gubenatorial return from the future in *Terminator 3: Rise of the Machines* and another spoof of horror and sci-fi hits in *Scary Movie 3*, although both left open the possibility of further chapters. In fact, viewers of *Terminator*, pondering hints dropped in the film about future events, may demand it.

As one might imagine, these weren't the only sequels to show up at the multiplex in 2003. Besides the above-mentioned titles, some 14 others bowed, with varying degrees of success. Martin Lawrence and Will Smith revisited the action that jump-started their movie careers with *Bad Boys 2*, Jackie Chan and Owen Wilson reteamed in *Shanghai Knights,* Angelina Jolie once again donned the English accent and skimpy outfits of her *Lara Croft* character with *Lara Croft Tomb Raider: The Cradle of Life*, and Reese Witherspoon started a busy year with *Legally Blond 2: Red White and Blonde*. With *Charlie's Angels: Full Throttle* also showing up during the blockbuster season, the sequel seemed a genre dominated by women, until you consider the horror franchise builders *Final Destination 2, Jeepers Creepers 2,* and the showdown that would make pro wrestling jealous, *Freddy vs. Jason,* which was so successful, a sequel is already in the works.

Horror also played host to another increasing trend: remakes. *Texas Chansaw Massacre* led the parade that included *Cheaper by the Dozen* (admittedly not a horror film, unless you hate children), *Freaky Friday, The Italian Job,* and *Love Don't Cost a Thing,* an African-American remake of the 80s teen comedy *Can't Buy Me Love. Down with Love,* while not exactly a remake, took much of the look, style, and plot from frothy early 60s Doris Day—Rock Hudson comedies like *Pillow Talk.* The filmmakers classified *Love* as an homage. Another homage brought long-dormant filmmaker

Quentin Tarantino back to the national consciousness. His ultra-violent *Kill Bill: Vol. 1* paid tribute to everything from grindhouse Kung-Fu chop-socky to Japanese samurai movies to biker flicks to the Spaghetti Westerns of Sergio Leone. *Kill Bill* also added fuel to the continuing debate over violence in the media, but then again, his films have always had that effect.

Kevin Costner hadn't really disappeared, but in 2003 he did something he hadn't done in a while: direct a movie that both critics and audiences could (and did) embrace. His *Open Range* also helped revitalize the Western, along with Ron Howard's *The Missing* and Anthony Minghella's *Cold Mountain*. *Range* and *Missing* could additionally credit the presence of rugged vets Robert Duvall and Tommy Lee Jones, respectively, while *Mountain* boasted the award-winning (Academy, Screen Actors Guild, and Golden Globe Best Supporting Actress) performance of Renee Zellweger, a strong lead performance from Jude Law, and an old-time epic feel.

That epic feel is part of another long-forgotten genre that resurfaced in 2003. *Master and Commander: The Far Side of the World* brought back the sea-faring adventure, along with the aforementioned *Pirates of the Caribbean: The Curse of the Black Pearl*, and the Pixar animation favorite *Finding Nemo*. *Master and Commander* received an Academy Award for cinematography, while *Nemo* won for Best Animated Feature. *Pirates*, following 2002's *The Country Bears*, continued Disney's trend of adapting all of its amusement park rides into movies, along with the Eddie Murphy vehicle *Haunted Mansion*.

The people who adapt Marvel Comics into movies had a busy year, successfully bringing back all of the original mutants (and adding some new ones) for *X2: X-Men United*; introducing the Oedipal and glandular *Hulk*; and debuting the blind, crusading superhero *Daredevil* a disappointing outing that did nothing to brighten Ben Affleck's difficult year, but did bring us the lovely Jennifer Garner as nemesis/love interest Elektra.

Affleck's trials and tribulations began with the unrelenting media scrutiny of his rocky relationship with *Gigli* co-star Jennifer Lopez, continued with said film's brutal critical excoriation and subsequent boxoffice nosedive, and didn't improve with the so-so reception for *Daredevil* and the John Woo-helmed *Paycheck*. Even the *Project Greenlight* film *The Battle of Shaker Heights* added to his aggravation, although the series did make for some compelling TV at times. The *Shaker Heights* experience did nothing to harm its young star, Shia LeBeouf, whose work there and in the engaging film *Holes* tabbed him as a young actor of immense talent with a bright future.

As a counterpoint to the summertime bombast, another comics adaptation tended toward the mundane and uncelebrated. Robert Pulcini and Shari Springer Berman's adapta-

tion of Harvey Pekar's autobiographical comic *American Splendor* garnered critical raves for Paul Giamatti's portrayal of Pekar, as well as a Writers Guild and Los Angeles Film Critics award for Berman and Pulcini's adapted screenplay. The New York and Los Angeles Film Critics also named *American Splendor* as their Best Film of the year. Indeed, in a different year (read: one not including the juggernaut final chapter of the *Lord of the Rings* saga), *Splendor* and films such as *Mystic River* and *Lost in Translation* would have made for an interesting race for the Best Picture Oscar.

As it was, *Mystic River*, Clint Eastwood's masterful tale of childhood abuse and the tragedy it wrought on the adult lives of its victims, and *Lost in Translation*, Sofia Coppola's subdued, funny, and charming story of lonely Americans in Tokyo, divided up (along with *American Splendor*) just about all the awards that were left in the *King*'s wake. Bill Murray (*Lost in Translation*) and Sean Penn (*Mystic River*) split the major Best Actor awards, with Penn winning the Oscar, Golden Globe (Drama), and National Board of Review nods, and Murray taking home hardware from the Golden Globes (Comedy or Musical), Independent Spirit, L.A. Film Critics, National Society of Film Critics, and New York Film Critics. Tim Robbins garnered Supporting Actor nods for his work in *River* from the Academy, the Golden Globes, and the Screen Actors Guild. Sofia Coppola's work as screenwriter and director was rewarded with a Best Picture, Best Screenplay, and Best Director award at the Independent Spirits, as well as Best Original Screenplay from the Academy, Writers Guild, and the Golden Globes.

Other women who made an impact in 2003 were Patricia Clarkson, who won critical praise (and a few awards) for her work in *The Station Agent* and *Pieces of April*; Renee Zellweger in *Cold Mountain*; Diane Keaton for *Something's Gotta Give*; and perhaps most impressive, Charlize Theron, for her bracing transformation for the role of serial killer Aileen Wournos in the chilling *Monster*. Theron received the Best Actress Award from the Academy, the Golden Globes, Independent Spirits, National Society of Film Critics, and the Screen Actors Guild for the role.

Some actresses impressed through sheer volume of work during the year. Marcia Gay Harden (*Mona Lisa Smile*, *Mystic River*, and *Casa de los Babys*), Cate Blanchett (*The Missing*, *Veronica Guerin*, and the omnipresent *Lord of the Rings*), Rachel Weisz (*Confidence*, *Runaway Jury*, and *Shape of Things*), Darryl Hannah (*Kill Bill: Vol. 1*, *Casa de los Babys*, and *Northfork*), and Gabrielle Union (*Bad Boys 2*, *Cradle 2 the Grave*, and *Deliver Us from Eva*) all appeared in three films in 2003. That's quite a busy publicity tour schedule. Not many of the men could keep up, but a few tried. Colin Farrell had major parts in *SWAT*, *The Recruit*, and *Daredevil*, and a smaller role in *Veronica Guerin*. Christopher Walken showed up in *The Rundown*, *Poolhall Junkies*, *Kangaroo Jack*, and *Gigli*, which brings us back to Mr. Affleck (*Daredevil*, *Gigli*, and *Paycheck*), who might consider taking some time off. There are plenty of others who appeared in two movies, but they are starting to become too numerous to mention here.

In 2003, the Hollywood trend of "Bigger is Better" continued, with seemingly more "event" movies than ever. Whether this was a result of some franchises (*Lord of the Rings*, *The Matrix*) offering up long-anticipated chapters, the studios trying to stem the tide of declining boxoffice with big-ticket extravaganzas that scream for the big-screen treatment (such as Tom Cruise's *The Last Samurai*), or a combination of both, it's not a trend that will go away soon. But there was another trend this past year. Plenty of smaller, more personal, independently-produced and highly-regarded fare was available for those willing to seek it out. Some examples include *House of Sand and Fog*, with Ben Kingsley, Jennifer Connolly, and an award-winning performance from Shohreh Aghdashloo; *In America*, Jim Sheridan's semi-autobiographical tale of recent immigrants trying to get by, which was co-written with his daughters; the frightening (especially if you're a parent) tale of teenage rebellion and experimentation *Thirteen*, which featured powerful performances by Holly Hunter, Evan Rachel Wood, and Nikki Reed (who also co-wrote the screenplay, based on her own experiences); and Canada's *Barbarian Invasions*, the Oscar winner for Best Foreign Film, which explores the healing of a relationship between an estranged son and his dying father. *Seabiscuit* is a movie which straddled that line, a big summer release that garnered rave reviews, but limited audience attention after a strong first

few weeks. Maybe the boxoffice wasn't there, or they weren't available in wide enough release, or maybe they got lost in the rush to crown the *King*, but that doesn't mean they aren't worth a second (or first) look.

Off-screen, 2003 saw the world lose more Classic Hollywood royalty with the deaths of Bob Hope, Katharine Hepburn, and Gregory Peck. Hollywood also mourned the loss of longtime screen favorites Hume Cronyn, Donald O'Connor, Charles Bronson, Art Carney, Alan Bates, William Marshall, Buddy Hackett, Robert Stack, Richard Crenna, Penny Singleton, Buddy Ebsen, Jack Elam, and John Ritter, as well as stellar behind-the-camera talents Elia Kazan, John Schlesinger, the controversial Leni Reifenstahl, and legendary cinematographer Conrad L. Hall. These and other celebrated talents who passed in 2003 are profiled in the Obits section at the back of this book.

We look forward to another year in film, as, we suppose, do you. We also look forward to bringing you the next edition of *Magill's Cinema Annual*, and invite your comments, suggestions, and questions. Please send them to:

Jim Craddock
Project Editor, *Magill's Cinema Annual*
Gale
27500 Drake Road
Farmington Hills, MI 48331-3535
Phone: 248-699-4253
Toll-Free: 800-347-GALE (4253)
Fax: 248-699-8062

Contributing Reviewers

Laura Abraham
Freelance Reviewer

Michael Adams
Graduate School, City University of New York

Vivek Adarkar
Long Island University

Michael Betzold
Freelance Reviewer

David L. Boxerbaum
Freelance Reviewer

Beverley Bare Buehrer
Freelance Reviewer

Peter N. Chumo II
Freelance Reviewer

Beth Fhaner
Freelance Reviewer

David Flanagin
Freelance Reviewer

Jill Hamilton
Freelance Reviewer

Eric Monder
Freelance Reviewer

Michael J. Tyrkus
Freelance Reviewer

James M. Welsh
Salisbury State University

Hilary White
Freelance Reviewer

User's Guide

Alphabetization

Film titles and reviews are arranged on a word-by-word basis, including articles and prepositions. English leading articles (A, An, The) are ignored, as are foreign leading articles (El, Il, La, Las, Le, Les, Los). Other considerations:

Acronyms appear alphabetically as if regular words.

Common abbreviations in titles file as if they are spelled out, so *Mr. Death* will be found as if it was spelled *Mister Death*.

Proper names in titles are alphabetized beginning with the individual's first name, for instance, *Veronica Guerin* will be found under "V."

Titles with numbers, for instance, *200 Cigarettes*, are alphabetized as if the numbers were spelled out, in this case, "Two-Hundred." When numeric titles gather in close proximity to each other, the titles will be arranged in a low-to-high numeric sequence.

Special Sections

List of Awards. An annual list of awards bestowed upon the year's films by the following associations: Academy of Motion Picture Arts and Sciences, Directors Guild of America Award, Golden Globe Awards, Los Angeles Film Critics Awards, National Board of Review Awards, National Society of Film Critics Awards, New York Film Critics Awards, the Screen Actors Guild Awards, and the Writer's Guild Awards.

Obituaries. Profiles major contributors to the film industry who died in 2003.

Selected Film Books of 2003. An annotated list of selected film books published in 2003.

Indexes

Film titles and artists are arranged into nine indexes, allowing the reader to effectively approach a film from any one of several directions, including not only its credits but its subject matter.

Directors, Screenwriters, Cinematographers, Editors, Art Directors, Music Directors, and *Performers* indexes are arranged according to artists appearing in this volume, followed by a list of the films on which they worked.

Subject Index. Films may be categorized under several of the subject terms arranged alphabetically in this section.

Title Index. The title index is a cumulative alphabetical list of films covered in the twenty-two volumes of the *Magill's Cinema Annual*, including the films covered in this volume. Films reviewed in past volumes are cited with the year in which the film was originally released; films reviewed in this volume are cited with the film title in bold with a bolded Arabic numeral indicating the page number on which the review begins. Original and alternate titles are cross-referenced to the American release title in the Title Index. Titles of retrospective films are followed by the year, in brackets, of their original release.

Sample Review

Each *Magill's* review contains up to sixteen items of information. A fictionalized composite sample review containing all the elements of information that may be included in a full-length review follows the outline below. The circled number preceding each element in the sample review designates an item of information that is explained in the outline on the next page.

(1) **Title:** Film title as it was released in the United States.

(2) **Foreign or alternate title (s):** The film's original title or titles as released outside the United States, or alternate film title or titles. Foreign and alternate titles also appear in the Title Index to facilitate user access.

(3) **Taglines:** Up to ten publicity taglines for the film from advertisements or reviews.

(4) **Box office information:** Year-end or other box office domestic revenues for the film.

(5) **Film review:** A signed review of the film, including an analytic overview of the film and its critical reception.

(6) **Reviewer byline:** The name of the reviewer who wrote the full-length review. A complete list of this volume's contributors appears in the "Contributings Reviewers" section which follows the Introduction.

(7) **Principal characters:** Listings of the film's principal characters and the names of the actors who play them in the film.

(8) **Country of origin:** The film's country or countries of origin.

(9) **Release date:** The year of the film's first general release.

(10) **Production information:** This section typically includes the name(s) of the film's producer(s), production company, and distributor; director(s); screenwriter(s); cinematographer(s) (if the film is animated, this will be replaced with Animation or Animation direction, or it will not be listed);

editor(s); art director(s); production designer(s); music composer(s); and other credits such as visual effects, sound, costume design, and song(s) and songwriter(s).

(11) **MPAA rating:** The film's rating by the Motion Picture Association of America. If there is no rating given, the line will read, "Unrated."

(12) **Running time:** The film's running time in minutes.

(13) **Reviews:** A list of citations of major newspaper and journal reviews of the film, including publication title, date of review, and page number.

(14) **Film quotes:** Memorable dialogue directly from the film, attributed to the character who spoke it, or comment from cast or crew members or reviewers about the film.

(15) **Film trivia:** Interesting tidbits about the film, its cast, or production crew.

(16) **Awards information:** Awards won by the film, followed by category and name of winning cast or crew member. Listings of the film's nominations follow the wins on a separate line for each award. Awards are arranged alphabetically. Information is listed for films that won or were nominated for the following awards: American Academy Awards®, British Academy of Film and Television Arts, Directors Guild of America, Golden Globe, Los Angeles Critics Association Awards, National Board of Review Awards, National Society of Film Critics Awards, New York Critics Awards, Writers Guild of America, and others.

① The Gump Diaries
② (Los Diarios del Gump)

③ *Love means never having to say you're stupid.*
— Movie tagline

 Box Office: $10 million
④

⑤ In writer/director Robert Zemeckis' *Back to the Future* trilogy (1985, 1989, 1990), Marty McFly (Michael J. Fox) and his scientist sidekick Doc Brown (Christopher Lloyd) journey backward and forward in time, attempting to smooth over some rough spots in their personal histories in order to remain true to their individual destinies. Throughout their time-travel adventures, Doc Brown insists that neither he nor Marty influence any major historical events, believing that to do so would result in catastrophic changes in humankind's ultimate destiny. By the end of the trilogy, however, Doc Brown has revised his thinking and tells marty that, "Your future hasn't been written yet. No one's has. Your future is whatever you make it. So make it a good one."

In *Forrest Gump,* Zemeckis once again explores the theme of personal destiny and how an individual's life affects and is affected by his historical time period. This time, however, Zemeckis and screenwriter Eric Roth chronicle the life af a character who does nothing but meddle in the historical events of his time without even trying to do so. By the film's conclusion, however, it has become apparent that Zemeckis' main concern is something more than merely having fun with four decades of American history. In the process of re-creating significant moments in time, he has captured on celluloid something eternal and timeless—the soul of humanity personified by a nondescript simpleton from the deep South.

The film begins following the flight of a seemingly insignificant feather as it floats down from the sky and brushes against various objects and people before finally coming to rest at the feet of Forrest Gump (Tom Hanks). Forrest, who is sitting on a bus-stop bench, reaches down and picks up the feather, smooths it out, then opens his traveling case and carefully places the feather between the pages of his favorite book, *Curious George.*

In this simple but hauntingly beautiful opening scene, the filmmakers illustrate the film's principal concern: Is life a series of random events over which a person has no control, or is there an underlying order to things that leads to the fulfillment of an individual's destiny? The rest of the film is a humorous and moving attempt to prove that, underlying the random, chaotic events that make up a person's life, there exists a benign and simple order.

Forrest sits on the bench throughout most of the film, talking about various events of his life to others who happen to sit down next to him. It does not take long, however, for the audience to realize that Forrest's seemingly random chatter to a parade of strangers has a perfect chronological order to it. He tells his first story after looking down at the feet of his first bench partner and observing, "Mama always said that you can tell a lot about a person by the shoes they wear." Then, in a voice-over narration, Forrest begins the story of his life, first by telling about he first pair of shoes he can remember wearing.

The action shifts to the mid-1950's with Forrest as a young boy (Michael Humphreys) being fitted with leg braces to correct a curvature in his spine. Despite this traumatic handicap, Forrest remains unaffected, thanks to his mother (Sally Field) who reminds him on more than once occasion that he is no different from anyone else. Although this and most of Mrs. Gump's other words of advice are in the form of hackneyed cliches, Forrest whose intelligence quotient is below normal, sincerely believes every one of them, namely because he instinctively knows they are sincere expressions of his mother's love and fierce devotion.

⑥ —*John Byline*

 CREDITS

Forrest Gump: Tom Hanks ⑦
Forrest's Mother: Sally Field
Young Forrest: Michael Humphreys

⑧ **Origin:** USA
Language: English, Spanish ⑨
Released: 1994
Production: Liz Heller, John Manulis; New Line Cinema; released by Island Pictures
Directed by: Scott Kalvert ⑩
Written by: Bryan Goluboff
Cinematography by: David Phillips
Music by: Graeme Revell
Editing: Dana Congdon
Production Design: Danny Nowak
Sound: David Sarnoff
Costumes: David Robinson
MPAA rating: R ⑪
Running time: 102 minutes ⑫

 REVIEWS

Entertainment Weekly. July 15, 1994, p. 42. ⑬
The Hollywood Reporter. June 29, 1994, p. 7.
Los Angeles Times. July 6, 1994, p. F1.
New York Times Online. July 15, 1994.

QUOTES

⑭ Forrest Gump (Tom Hanks): "The state of existence may be likened unto a receptacle containing cocoa-based confections, in that one may never predict that which one may receive."

 TRIVIA

⑮ Hanks was the first actor since Spencer Tracy to win back-to-back Oscars for Best Actor. Hanks received the award in 1993 for his performance in *Philadelphia.* Tracy won Oscars in 1937 for *Captains Courages* and in 1938 for *Boys Town.*

AWARDS AND NOMINATIONS

⑯ **Academy Awards 1994:** Film, Actor (Hanks), Special Effects, Cinematography
Nomination:
Golden Globes 1994: Film, Actor (Hanks), Supporting Actress (Field), Music

Agent Cody Banks

Save the World. Get the Girl. Pass Math.
—Movie tagline

 Box Office: $47.8 million

Agent *Cody Banks* combines the adventure of saving the world from the bad guys with the adventure of trying to ask a girl out. For 15-year-old Cody Banks (Frankie Muniz of TV's *Malcolm in the Middle*), asking the girl out is the much more difficult task.

This Seattle boy would be just another high schooler, but when he was 13, Cody was secretly recruited by the CIA. He was told he was going away to summer camp, but it was really a secret CIA training camp. Thus, he has remarkable abilities, but thus far, no mission to test them out. In the opening sequence, we see Cody's skills when he chases down a runaway car with a young boy in it. Armed only with his skateboard, Cody races after the car, dodging obstacles like a construction site. At the last minute—just before the car hits a train—Cody gets the car stopped. When the mother turns to thank him, he has disappeared.

In real life, Cody is much less suave. He tries to talk to a girl in one of his classes and stammers so much that the girl asks, "Are you, by any chance, in special ed?" Cody is put to the test when he learns that he is to be on assignment. His duty: to get close to Natalie Connors (Hilary Duff of TV's *Lizzie McGuire*), the lovely daughter of scientist Dr. Connors (Martin Donovan).

Dr. Connors has developed some nanobots—microscopic robots that eat anything they come into contact with (except, inexplicably, the glass containers they come in.) The slightly dense Connors expects that his nanobots will help the world by cleaning up the oil from oil spills. His sponsors, Brinkman (Ian McShane) and Molay (Arnold Vosloo), naturally have a more fiendish plan in mind. They want to take the nanobots, put them in ice cubes ("Everyone uses ice cubes!" they offer by way of explanation) and use them to knock out military parts, leaving countries defenseless. How they plan to distribute these ice cubes is left unsaid. Are they just going to go up to military facilities selling the tainted ice cubes from the back of their truck?

Cody's job is to get to know Natalie so that she will invite him to her birthday. He will then break into Dr. Connors' lab, get info, and save the world. To this aim, the CIA enrolls him in Natalie's prestigious prep school and signs him up for every one of her classes. "Isn't that a little creepy?" asks Cody. "This is the CIA, creepy is what we do," is the reply.

Cody is more like a stalker than potential boyfriend to Natalie. She, too, wonders if he's in special ed. Cody is so bad with women that he needs to be tutored by the powers that be at the CIA, including his trainer, Ronica Miles (Angie Harmon). Ronica is a strange addition to the film. She's ultra curvaceous and wears clothes to accent that fact, even when it doesn't seem wise. For example, when she's trying to break into the bad guy's mountain top hideaway, she wears a skintight silver jumpsuit. If she's trying to blend in, perhaps this wasn't the best choice. It's hard to tell exactly what having this mature sex object for Cody is supposed to signify but it seems kind of yucky. There's a scene where Cody and Ronica are sparring and they end up rolling around on the floor and landing in several compromising positions.

Eventually, Cody's "lessons" seem to kick in and Cody makes a good impression on Natalie when he takes a driver's ed car and drives it like a maniac. He also impresses her by beating up a bunch of bullies by using his suave CIA moves. Only in a screenplay written by men (five of them to be exact) would a girl be impressed by fighting and wild driving.

Another major portion of the movie is the array of James Bond-like gadgets that a Q-like character (*Saturday Night Live*'s Darrell Hammond) gives him for his mission. Cody's cell phone projects holographic images. His watch can shock people. And his glasses are X-ray specs. But best are the transportation devices. At CIA headquarters, people get around by using Segway Human Transporters, which actually exist. There are also one-person helicopters and skateboards that turn into snowboards. The bad guy's hideout seems like an old set from a Bond flick. It boasts cavernous rooms and a PA system broadcasting a calm female voice who says things like "T minus three hours until distribution sequence" and "Authorize level 4." Does the same woman always do these?

There are some clever things in the movie. Cody's parents (Cynthia Stevenson and Daniel Roebuck) are so clueless that they don't even notice that he's been working for the CIA. When Cody's chores threaten to interrupt his mission, the CIA sends out a team to clean out his hamster cage, mow the lawns and clean up the house. "We have dust bunnies on the second floor!" radio the uptight operatives to one another.

And there are some not so clever things in the movie. The saving the world concept and predictable foreign bad guys are concepts that have gone dreary. And the nanobot technology doesn't make much sense. If they eat through everything, why don't they continue to eat everything they see, infinitely? And there are a couple of poo jokes. Someone farts when the CIA operatives are in a crowded van, then in the next scene somebody has to pick up dog poo and hide it in their coat. And the climatic ending is seemingly interminable. Cody and co. are trying to escape from the baddies' mountaintop lair just before it's set to blow up. It's also being eaten by escaped nanobots. Cody and his friends keep being set to escape, but a door won't open or something. The setbacks are so numerous that they become tedious.

Critics thought the film was a *Spy Kids* rip-off but some of them thought that it was all right anyway. Scott Brown of *Entertainment Weekly* wrote "One has to wonder whether tutoring tweens in the objectification of women (including Angie Harmon as Cody's den mother-cum-dominatrix boss) is acceptable collateral damage." Dave Kehr of the *New York Times* wrote, "This Frankenfilm comes lumbering out of the laboratory of the Danish director Harold Zwart, any trace of personality surgically removed and replaced by a fully road-tested cliché." And Megan Lehmann of the *New York Post* called the film "illogical, thrown-together claptrap." Kevin Thomas of the *Los Angeles Times* enjoyed the film and wrote, "Well-designed and displaying plenty of technical finesse, *Agent Cody Banks* may be targeted at teens but even their grandparents might consider it fun."

—Jill Hamilton

CREDITS

Cody Banks: Frankie Muniz
Natalie Connors: Hilary Duff
Ronica Miles: Angie Harmon
CIA Director: Keith David
Mrs. Banks: Cynthia Stevenson
Molay: Arnold Vosloo
Dr. Connors: Martin Donovan
Mr. Banks: Daniel Roebuck
Brinkman: Ian McShane
Earl: Darrell Hammond

Origin: USA
Released: 2003
Production: David C. Glasser, Dylan Sellers, David Nicksay, Guy Oseary, Maverick Films; Splendid Pictures, James Wong; released by MGM
Directed by: Harald Zwart
Written by: Scott M. Alexander, Ashley Edward Miller, Zack Stentz, Larry Karaszewski
Cinematography by: Denis Crossan
Music by: John Powell
Sound: Larry Sutton
Music Supervisor: Julianne Jordan
Editing: Jim Miller
Art Direction: Kevin Humenny
Costumes: Suzanne McCabe
Production Design: Rusty Smith
MPAA rating: PG
Running time: 95 minutes

REVIEWS

Chicago Sun-Times Online. March 14, 2003.
Entertainment Weekly. March 21, 2003, p. 88.
Los Angeles Times Online. March 14, 2003.
New York Times Online. March 14, 2003.
USA Today Online. March 14, 2003.
Variety Online. March 2, 2003.
Washington Post. March 14, 2003, p. WE43.

Alex & Emma

Is it love . . . or are they just imaging things?
—Movie tagline

 Box Office: $14.2 million

Director Rob Reiner, who brought us *When Harry Met Sally,* one of the best modern romantic comedies, delivers a disappointing and predictable take on the genre with *Alex & Emma.* Originally titled *Loosely Based on a True Love Story,* this formulaic romantic comedy was inspired by Russian novelist Fyodor Dostoevsky and his experience while writing *The Gambler.* Heavily in debt after gambling away his advance, Dostoevsky hired a stenographer to help him finish *The Gambler,* and the two fell in love and got married.

In *Alex & Emma,* the likeable Luke Wilson stars as Alex Sheldon, a Boston writer who is in debt to a pair of Cuban loan sharks for $100,000 that they plan to collect in 30 days. Luckily for Alex, he has a publisher (played by Reiner himself) who wants to pay him $125,000 for a new manuscript. Alex simply has to write his novel within 30 days . . . at a time when he is facing a major creative block.

After the mob torches Alex's laptop, he decides to hire stenographer Emma Dinsmore (Kate Hudson) to take dictation and assist him with his looming deadline. As Alex proceeds to dictate his laughably bad novel, Emma takes every opportunity to make suggestions and edit his writing. Naturally, the two dislike each other and quarrel constantly.

The present-day action is interspersed with scenes from Alex's novel. Set in the 1920s and evoking the stories of F. Scott Fitzgerald, Alex's book creates a world of opulent summer homes, white linen suits, and beautiful, wealthy people. Wilson, in a dual role, also plays the novel's protagonist, Adam, an impoverished writer who takes a summer job along the coast of Maine as a tutor to the children of Polina (Sophie Marceau), a wealthy French widow. Although

Polina is about to marry her clueless, rich fiancé (David Paymer), Adam lusts after the gorgeous Frenchwoman. Marceau perfectly portrays Polina as an object of fantasy, the elusive, glamorous beauty who is forever out of reach to someone like Adam. In actuality, it's apparent that Polina is nothing but a superficial, manipulative gold digger.

Hudson appears in Alex's novel-in-progress as an attractive, innocent au pair, setting up the requisite love triangle. As the story shifts, Hudson's character changes nationalities, giving the actress an opportunity to show her versatility by demonstrating three different accents, including Swedish, German, and Spanish. Although a glimmer of comic relief shines through Hudson's performance as the changeable au pair, the scenes ultimately feel forced and too broad. One critic likened Hudson's use of the different accents to "a tired Vaudeville routine."

Alex & Emma quickly becomes tedious as it cuts back and forth between reality and fiction. The scenes of the two main characters crafting a novel suffer from the claustrophobic setting, and the sequences from the novel itself seem lacking in any genuine emotion. The main problem with the film is that both the present day and period scenes are downright dull. You know it's just a matter of time before Alex/Adam realizes that the love of his life is not his fantasy woman viewed from a distance, but the young woman who's been there all along. In the meantime, the audience is forced to endure this annoying snooze-fest. With a weak script and non-existent chemistry between the leads, there is nothing to recommend about this lifeless romance. The director and the actors have all done better work.

Reviewers were unanimous in their negative criticism of *Alex & Emma.* In his review for the *Los Angeles Times,* Kenneth Turan comments that the movie "is not a particularly comic or romantic film about the writing of a truly tedious novel. This is double trouble with a vengeance." *Variety* reviewer Todd McCarthy calls the movie "a desperately slight romantic comedy marked by contrived romance and little comedy." Many critics bemoaned the fact that Reiner was associated with this film as its director. Jeffrey M. Anderson, writing in the *San Francisco Examiner* says, "I'd like to think that, besides [Reiner's] two acting scenes that bookend the movie, he wasn't even on the set at all. It would explain a lot."

When audience members got up to walk out of the theater midway through a screening of *Alex & Emma,* I knew that this romantic comedy was beyond hope. I only wish I could have left at the halfway mark, too, but I stayed until the bitter end. One thing is certain, though: Reiner and the rest of the talented cast are sure to find future projects more worthy of their talents.

—*Beth Fhaner*

Alex/Adam: Luke Wilson
Emma/Yiva/Elsa/Eldora/Anna: Kate Hudson
Polina Delacroix: Sophie Marceau
John Shaw: David Paymer
Croupier: Francois Giroday
Wirschafter: Rob Reiner
Grandmother: Cloris Leachman
Polina's father: Rip Taylor

Origin: USA
Released: 2003
Production: Rob Reiner, Alan Greisman, Todd Black, Elie Samaha, Jeremy Leven; Franchise Pictures, Escape Artists; released by Warner Bros.
Directed by: Rob Reiner
Written by: Jeremy Leven
Cinematography by: Gavin Finney
Music by: Marc Shaiman
Sound: Robert Eber
Editing: Robert Leighton, Alan Edward Bell
Art Direction: Helen Harwell
Costumes: Shay Cunliffe
Production Design: John Larena
MPAA rating: PG-13
Running time: 96 minutes

 REVIEWS

Chicago Sun-Times Online. June 20, 2003.
Entertainment Weekly. June 27, 2003, p. 112.
eye Weekly. June 19, 2003.
Los Angeles Times Online. June 20, 2003.
New York Times Online. June 20, 2003.
People. June 30, 2003, p. 34.
San Francisco Chronicle. June 20, 2003, p. D5.
San Francisco Examiner Online. June 20, 2003.
USA Today Online. June 20, 2003.
Variety Online. June 16, 2003.
Washington Post. June 20, 2003, p. WE44.

QUOTES

Alex (Wilson) to Emma (Hudson): "I'm a brilliant novelist."

 TRIVIA

The film was originally titled *Loosely Based on a True Love Story,* which is a take on the true story of Fyodor Dostoevsky, who fell in love with his stenographer while he was writing *The Gambler.*

Alias Betty (Betty Fisher and Other Stories) (Betty Fisher et Autres Histoires)

Crimes of passion are not always between lovers.
—Movie tagline

Motherhood assumes many forms of insanity; apparently, our mothers aren't always what they seem to be. *Alias Betty* tears that childhood fear wide open and elaborates on the frailty of the maternal nature.

Artfully condensed into 103 minutes, *Alias Betty* suspends the viewer over the following questions: What if my child was stolen, what if my child died, and which is worse? What if my mother steals a child for me and convinces me that this is a good thing, what faith could I place in wits—huh?

Based on *The Tree of Hands* by English novelist Ruth Rendell, *Alias* feels edgy in places and complacent in others. True to classic French cinema it weaves Parisian plots to a refreshing point of convolution, without being too specific or terribly deep. This is choice perspective for thriller-noir.

To set the tone, director Claude Miller (*The Accompanist*) states the meaning of bad blood (porphyry) before presenting the awkward reunion between gaunt Betty Fisher (Sandra Kimberlaine) and her beautiful, crazed mother, Margot (Nicole Garcia). Betty has spent her whole life writing her way out of the pain of having suffered her mother's often-abusive mental condition as a child and has become a successful novelist and mother herself. Margot has agreed to stay on medication. Their confidence in each other at this reunion is "iffy" at best.

Meanwhile, in one of the neighborhoods in the outer rings of Paris, Carole (Mathilde Seigner), while not an undeserving mother, seems to have no affinity with motherhood itself. Her son, Jose (Alexis Chatrian), seems born from the restlessness and boredom of poverty. At present, Carole busies herself devising phony real estate schemes with her equally sleazy ex-boyfriend and possibly the father of her son, Alex (Edouard Bear), and co-habitating with her gentle African lover Francois (Luck Mervil).

One of these sons has to die. Betty's son Joseph (Arthur Setbon)—because she cares—falls from a window. One month later, as Betty emerges from the miasma of her grief, her universe collides with Carol's because Margot, improvising as loving caregiver, kidnaps Carole's son and presents him to Betty as a new son. An extra, a spare, Jose is "the same sort of boy" as Margot points out to Betty, and judging by signs of abuse on his body, probably not terribly missed. Though she tries, Betty's too weak to refuse.

The film is fairly serious and brave throughout, but in the face of the absurdity of the various plots, not without humor. Margot, in a remarkable performance by Garcia, is the source of it all. She represents the sins of the mother and the heart of this story, which is about the conundrum a mother's negligence creates in the minds of children, even when they are grown and parents themselves.

The end, while not a conventionally happy one, is quite satisfying. Miller narrates the story tandem to the novel's grace, taking irrational behavior and making it seem perfectly sane, imbuing each scene with the precious quality that made *A Tree of Hands* a good read in the first place and making the most of Betty's own sensitivity as a writer to bestow original meaning to her own turn at the timeless tale of mother-daughter conflict.

—*Laura Abraham*

CREDITS

Betty Fisher: Sandrine Kiberlain
Margot Fisher: Nicole Garcia
Carole Novacki: Mathilde Seigner
Jose Novacki: Alexis Chatrian
Alex Basato: Edouard Baer
Joseph Fisher: Arthur Setbon
Francois: Luck Mervil
Edouard: Stephane Freiss

Origin: France, Canada
Language: French
Released: 2001
Production: Yves Marmion, Annie Miller; Go Films, Les Films de la Boissiere; released by Wellspring Media
Directed by: Claude Miller
Written by: Claude Miller
Cinematography by: Christophe Pollock
Sound: Claude La Haye
Editing: Veronique Lange
Art Direction: Jean-Pierre Kohut Svelko
Costumes: Jacqueline Bouchard
MPAA rating: Unrated
Running time: 101 minutes

REVIEWS

Boxoffice. November, 2002, p. 153.
Los Angeles Times Online. October 4, 2002.
New York Times Online. September 13, 2002.
San Francisco Chronicle. November 8, 2002, p. D5.
Sight and Sound. June, 2002, p. 36.
Variety. September 10, 2001, p. 65.
Washington Post. November 8, 2002, p. WE37.

QUOTES

Margot (Nicole Garcia) complains to daughter Betty (Sandrine Kiberlain): "You don't have a TV? I'm lost without a TV!"

All the Real Girls

Love is a puzzle. These are the pieces.
—Movie tagline
Boy Meets Girl. Boy Loses Girl.
—Movie tagline

In an interview with the *Long Beach Press-Telegram*, *All the Real Girls* actor and co-writer Paul Schneider said about his film's non-Hollywood love story, "I always ask people if the movie was awkward enough for them. Because if people know what they're going to say in love, are they really in love? If they're comfortable and not confused and awkward, are they really putting their hearts out there? I would venture to say not. What about love is studied and conventional and smooth? Nothing."

The driving force behind the film was Schneider's film school buddy, David Gordon Green, who directed and wrote this film. The two first met at the North Carolina School of Arts and continued to be friends after school. Green first got notice with the film *George Washington*, the 2001 off-kilter indie that scored a lot of good reviews. Now a mere 27-years-old, Green is garnering more good reviews for his second feature. The film won an award for "Emotional Truth" from juries at the Sundance Film Festival.

Part of that emotional truth comes from that awkwardness that Schneider was hoping to capture on film. As Paul (Schneider) and Noel (Zooey Deschanel) wallow their way through an adolescent relationship, the audience is as confused as the would-be lovers as to where the relationship is going. In one scene in which Noel tells Paul some upsetting news, it's hard to tell if she's trying to break up with him or tell him she loves him. It's just like a real life lovers talk in which it's hard to tell if you're having a "good" talk or a "bad" one.

Noel, the little sister of Paul's best buddy, Tip (Shea Wingham, sporting a big Elvis pompadour) has returned from several years away at an all-girls boarding school. Paul, who is in his early twenties, has been whiling away the years in their small North Carolina mill town. He's held some odd jobs but his main interest has been chasing the town's eligible women, sleeping with them, then dumping them. Paul and Tip consider themselves to be cold ladies men and call themselves "partners in crime." Tip is none too happy that Paul's next conquest looks like it's going to be his little sister.

But Paul's feelings for Noel surprise him. He wants to behave differently in this relationship. The movie starts with Noel and Paul's first kiss. The two inch together, and Noel asks why Paul never kisses her. After some discussion, they decide that Paul will kiss her on one particular part of her body, her hand. With utmost tenderness, Paul brushes off the spot, doublechecks with Noel to make sure that it's indeed the correct spot, then lightly kisses it. It's quickly obvious that this isn't going to be the kind of romance where the two share a big passionate kiss as Paul rescues Noel—at the altar!—just before she marries the wrong man.

Paul is attracted to Noel's passion. She plays an instrument, can discuss the pretensions of boarding school and engages him in the kind of metaphysical discussions that people of a certain age really like. "I had a dream that you grew a garden on a trampoline and I was so happy I invented peanut butter." Is this stuff supposed to be deep and symbolic of greater truths or is Green just trying to show how people in love think everything is meaningful? It's hard to say. *All the Real Girls* is somewhat inscrutable. It's the kind of movie that, when the film seems like it might have ended, the audience sits there blinking, unsure if it is over or not. It could have ended where it does, but it could have just as easily ended somewhere else in the movie.

A regular Hollywood movie would have the focus be the obstacle of Tip in Noel and Paul's relationship, but this is no regular movie. Tip's anger over the relationship gets some play, but he gets over it, and the movie keeps going on. When Paul and Noel finally have sex, a regular movie would have that be a beautiful high point of the film. But here the sex is ordinary, maybe even less so. Noel stares at the ceiling and it seems a lot less passionate than their meandering conversations. In a regular movie, Paul would be a wholly good guy, but here he is more ambiguous. He's nice to Noel but he has issues with his mother (Patricia Clarkston). At one point, his mother misses a job because Paul forgets to bring the car home in time. As his mother accuses him, Paul is unconcerned. He is too interested in his own issues to care about what his mother is telling him.

Green takes his time telling what little story there is. Characters have long, unfocused conversations where they may say something interesting and they may not. Cinematographer Tim Orr follows the slow lead with almost static shots of the mill, of the old houses, of a reflection of the town in a pond. There are amateur actors mixed in with the professionals in the film, which gives it more of an offbeat, less polished feel.

The best part of this movie is Deschanel. She's received good notices for her work in her previous films (*The Good Girl, Almost Famous*), but this was the first time she had the starring role. She has a natural style that works really well in this film. Deschanel is particularly good in her conversations with Paul. She has a timing that makes them seem a lot like real conversations—she sounds like she's just coming up with her lines spontaneously. In an interview, Schneider reports that the actress had a lot to do with how the character turned out. Previously they had been basing her character on women they knew in college, but threw all that away when Deschanel came in for an audition. "We realized we weren't smart enough to create somebody as complex as Zooey. We pretty much had to go back to the drawing board and flesh out the character. Zooey just blew us away."

Critics liked the film, though some had reservations. A.O. Scott of the *New York Times* wrote, "The movie has the oddity and directness of a pop song before it has been discovered and played to death. Watching it is like happening on a demo recording by an unknown band on a low-watt college radio station—a song not quite like anything you've heard before, and not quite finished, which you want to hear again even before it has ended." Megan Lehmann of the *New York Post* wrote, "It's the little things that resonate in this tender and sincere tale of first love." Kenneth Turan of the *Los Angeles Times* wrote, "Green embodies the cinematic equivalent of the 'slow food' movement: He's never in a hurry, never afraid of stillness, determined to avoid razzle-dazzle no matter what it takes." Jan Stuart of *Newsday* wrote, "*All the Real Girls* is wildly uneven: dialogue of enormous grace and vitality alternates with moments of strained lyricism." And Mike Clark of *USA Today* wrote, "*Girls* isn't fabulous, but you do feel its characters really have connected. Meanwhile, we wish Green well as we wish maybe he'd speed it up—just a little."

—Jill Hamilton

CREDITS

Paul: Paul Schneider
Noel: Zooey Deschanel
Elvira Fine: Patricia Clarkson
Bo: Maurice Compte
Leland: Benjamin Mouton
Tip: Shea Whigham
Bust-Ass: Danny McBride

Origin: USA
Released: 2003

Production: Jean Doumanian, Lisa Muskat; released by Sony Pictures Classics
Directed by: David Gordon Green
Written by: Paul Schneider, David Gordon Green
Cinematography by: Tim Orr
Music by: David Wingo, Michael Linnen
Sound: Christof Gebert
Editing: Zene Bakel, Steven Gonzales
Art Direction: Jeffrey Barrows
Costumes: Erin Aldridge Orr
Production Design: Richard Wright
MPAA rating: R
Running time: 108 minutes

 REVIEWS

Entertainment Weekly. February 21, 2003, p. 128.
Los Angeles Times Online. February 14, 2003.
New York Times Online. February 9, 2003.
New York Times Online. February 9, 2003.
USA Today Online. February 14, 2003.
Variety Online. January 28, 2003.

 TRIVIA

The film received a Special Jury Prize at the 2003 Sundance Film Festival for "emotional truth."

AWARDS AND NOMINATIONS

Nomination:
Ind. Spirit 2004: Actress (Deschanel).

Amen

In the guise of irony, the latest political thriller from Costa-Gavras, *Amen*, tries to have it both ways: stirring the conscience of its audience with its timeliness and, at the same time, allowing its audience the vicarious experience of total power. As a period piece in the assured hands of a veteran politically-conscious filmmaker—Costa-Gavras's 17th feature in 44 years—*Amen*, based on the behemothic, ponderous play, *The Deputy* by Rolf Hochhuth, is about the revolt of conscience as experienced by the film's two protagonists in response to the unspeakable atrocities of the Nazi Holocaust. Both Kurt Gerstein (Ulrich Tukur), the central character, a chemical scientist working for the Reich, and

Riccardo Fontana (Mathieu Kassovitz), a young Italian Jesuit priest, who joins him in his just cause, are men caught up in forces well beyond their individual power to control.

Curiously, despite the film's ostensible liberal-minded political agenda, its impact lies in the opposite direction. For one, Costa-Gavras keeps us at a distance from the human aspects of the horror he is dealing with, unlike the play, which offers monologues from some of the victims. Secondly, he represents Nazi villainy for the most part through the ambivalent refinement of a subsidiary character known only as the Doctor (Ulrich Muhe), a SS officer in charge of keeping the machinery of extermination well-oiled. Instead of hating the Doctor, we marvel at this blend of power and congeniality. At the very end, the film too seems to be taking his side, both Gerstein and Fontana having met untimely ends.

The film follows the narrative structure of the play somewhat faithfully. Hochhuth's Doctor, however, is far more of a sadist, and a revolting one at that. In the stage directions, which often run to several pages, Hochhuth describes him as standing "in sharp contrast . . . to anything that has been learned about human beings." To Gerstein, the Doctor makes a present, obtained from Auschwitz, of the brain tissue of Jewish twins. In the film, he is far more muted as a character, functioning as Gerstein's devilish alter ego, one who has made his peace with the powers that be, both political and religious, while Gerstein remains struggling with his conscience. Towards the end of the film, when it becomes certain that the Allies will triumph, the Doctor sees himself as deserving the refuge of the Vatican. In his own eyes, he has always been a devout Catholic. The Church too burnt people in order to purify them, he reasons; the only difference with the gas chambers under his supervision was one of scale. Ironically, owing to an astute performance, the Doctor emerges as the film's only original plot element, since the Holocaust and its horrors have become all too familiar to film audiences, especially after Steven Spielberg's monumental *Schindler's List* (1993).

Thus, for the most part, *Amen*, despite its distinguished literary source, cannot help but appear a retreaded effort. Costa-Gavras's all too serious portrayal of the real-life Gerstein, whose accounts served to authenticate the Holocaust, results in dramatic scenes, but his film is totally lacking in the suspense one would expect from a political thriller.

The film, in charting Gerstein's attempts to make the German people, and the Allies, aware of what is taking place, resembles Roland Joffe's *The Killing Fields* (1984), an account of how reporter Sidney Schanberg brought the genocide in Cambodia to the notice of the world. Unlike its illustrious predecessor, however, *Amen* espouses no political idealism. It does not end on a note of triumph. The victory, if any, is that of the universality of human conscience. If we cannot prevent such tragedies, the film seems to say, we can at least make sure they are authenticated.

We are introduced to Gerstein at a conference on diseases, where he presents a method of purifying water so as to prevent the spread of typhus. As a "specialist in purification," no pun intended, Gerstein's expertise is commissioned by the SS to overcome a problem about which he is kept in the dark. In Poland, he is taken to visit a "special" camp by the suave Doctor. Here, Gerstein witnesses the use of a chemical, Zyklon B, which he himself invented as a pesticide. First, he sees the crystals being poured down a chute, then he's allowed to peek into the chamber to observe their effect. Costa-Gavras doesn't allow us to see what Gerstein sees. Instead, we see him overcome by the horror of it all. On the train ride back, he becomes physically sick.

The man of conscience that he is, Gerstein decides to approach the Swedish consulate in Berlin. To a Secretary, he provides an eyewitness account of "something horrifying." "Whole families are being exterminated!" he pleads, then adds how he will never forget the sight of children clinging to their mothers in those final moments. The Secretary of course is in no position to promise any course of action.

What becomes clear at this point is that Gerstein believes in the basic goodness of his countrymen, and in that of the Allies, most notably the U.S. and Britain. If the German people are informed, he reasons, they will rise against the atrocity. This is also where the film takes on a contemporary resonance. The genocides in Iraq, Rwanda, Bosnia and Afghanistan spring to mind as tragedies that could have been averted by world intervention, but instead were allowed to run their course owing to the deadlock created by international diplomacy.

Gerstein encounters similar inaction. When he speaks to Pastor Wehr (Pierre Franckh) about how "the Church must alert all Christians," the Pastor tells him to resign from the SS. All the Church can do, at this stage, according to the Pastor, is to act in a "thoughtful" and "responsible" manner that, in other words, amounts to doing nothing at all. Another representative of the Church tells Gerstein: "Our pastors are behind Hitler. Nobody will believe you!"

As one put in charge of storing the Zyklon crystals, all Gerstein can do is make sure large stocks are deemed unusable. Gerstein also comes to the conclusion that he has to see the Pope. At the Vatican, the Cardinal (Michel Duchaussoy) will hear none of it, and tells Gerstein to leave. "Only His Holiness can stop this!" Gerstein pleads, but to no avail. Behind Gerstein's back, the Cardinal remarks mockingly, "The SS defending the Jews! They think we're idiots!"

A witness to that meeting, Riccardo Fontana (Mathieu Kassovitz), a young Jesuit priest who will now take on the role of the film's second protagonist, approaches Gerstein. He claims his father, the Count Fontana (Ion Caramitru) is close to the Pope. At a dinner, Riccardo tells Tittman (Angus MacIness), an American envoy, about the exterminations. Tittman, who has heard such "rumors," advises Riccardo, "Don't say thousands if you want to be believed.

Say a few hundred!" When Riccardo does get to see the Pope (Marcel Iures), the latter has a ready answer: "I know the sufferings of the world, Riccardo. My heart bleeds."

As Gerstein gets promoted to Head of Sanitation Services by Himmler, his duties require him to visit camps in Czechoslovakia to make sure the supply of the required chemicals proceeds apace. Even so, Gerstein keeps up his efforts at seeking diplomatic inroads, hoping the Allies can be made to bomb the railway lines leading to the camps. The reason the Allies refrain from doing so becomes evident in the conversation between Riccardo and the American Ambassador (Taylor Richard Durden), who tells him simply that only the Allies winning the war can stop the genocide. He adds that diverting Allied resources towards saving Jews "will suit Hitler just fine." Similarly, the final word from the Church is that "if the Holy Father intervenes, the Germans will invade the Vatican."

The final section of the film focuses on how Gerstein and Riccardo are driven to follow the dictates of conscience, each in his own way. Gerstein, using the influence of a friend in the transport ministry, obtains a pass to see the Pope, a meeting arranged by the Count. The Cardinal however intervenes and tells Gerstein that the Pope does not want to say anything that the German will consider an act of hostility. "Nothing can stop this now," Gerstein muses aloud to Riccardo, on his way back to Berlin.

As Italian Jews are rounded up in Rome, Riccardo, by wearing the Star of David, passes himself off as one and gets onto a freight car. Gerstein then forges Himmler's signature, from his letter of promotion, onto a document ordering Riccardo to be freed. When the Doctor discovers the forgery, after eavesdropping on Gerstein and Riccardo, he orders the latter to be put to death. Gerstein however is allowed to return to his duties at the Institute, as a personal favor by the Doctor.

When the Allies triumph, Gerstein writes his memoirs—the basis for the events we have seen enacted—before we hear he has hung himself in his cell. The film's final scene has the Doctor approaching a member of the Catholic clergy, who promises him asylum in Argentina.

As would be expected, critics have recognized the film's serious intent, but have proven reluctant to overlook its basic flaw as a political thriller. Jack Mathews in the *Daily News* puts it best when he writes that our "knowing his (Gerstein's) efforts were futile turns the movie into a kind of obscene tease." He also goes on to question the film's premise, which grows out of Gerstein's belief that "if the German people knew of the Holocaust, they'd stop it." A. O. Scott in the *New York Times* has an altogether different take on Gerstein's moral dilemma. He finds that "Gerstein's predicament, horrifying as it is, also bears an element of black, Kafkaesque absurdity: his only hope of halting the crime in which he is implicated is to continue in his complicity."

—*Vivek Adarkar*

CREDITS

Kurt Gerstein: Ulrich Tukur
Riccardo Fontana: Mathieu Kassovitz
Pope Pius XII: Marcel Iures
The Doctor: Ulrich Muhe
The Cardinal: Michel Duchaussoy
Count Fontana: Ion Caramitru

Origin: France
Released: 2002
Production: Claude Berri; Renn Productions, TF-1 Films, KC Medien, Canal Plus; released by Kino International
Directed by: Constantin Costa-Gavras
Written by: Constantin Costa-Gavras, Jean-Claude Grumberg
Cinematography by: Patrick Blossier
Music by: Armand Amar
Sound: Pierre Gamet, Dominique Gaborieau
Editing: Yannick Kergoat
Art Direction: Maria Miu
Costumes: Edith Vesperini
Production Design: Ari Hantke
MPAA rating: R
Running time: 130 minutes

REVIEWS

Boxoffice. September, 2002, p. 142.
Los Angeles Times Online. January 31, 2003.
New York Daily News Online. January 24, 2003.
New York Post Online. January 24, 2003.
New York Times Online. January 19, 2003, p. 37.
New York Times Online. January 24, 2003, p. 37.
Newsday Online. January 24, 2003.
Sight and Sound. August, 2002, p. 37.
Variety. March 4, 2002, p. 37.

American Splendor

Ordinary life is pretty complex stuff.
—Movie tagline

 Box Office: $5.6 million

From the earliest days of the cinema there were two schools of thought regarding the proper function of a film: simply to document human life and events as did Lumiere; or to create fiction and fantasy, to take viewers to imaginary places, first in the manner of Georges Méliès and later with the sophistication and special effects of the *Star Wars* and *Lord of the Rings* trilogies. In a year when the third installment of *Lord of the Rings* caught the fancy of the Motion Picture Academy, *American Splendor,* in its own understated way, reminded viewers of that other time-honored alternative, demonstrating how an ordinary life could be presented interestingly. A disclaimer at the end of the film advises viewers, "This film is a dramatization based on certain facts. Some of the names have been changed and some of the events and characters have been fictionalized for dramatic purposes." Having said that, however, the film most certainly concentrates on the life and "artistic" career of Harvey Pekar.

At the same time, this film attempts to demonstrate the truth of its central figure's mantra: "Life is pretty complex stuff." At issue here is the life of Harvey Pekar, who has worked for over 30 years as a file clerk at a V.A. hospital in Cleveland, Ohio. In his spare time he has been creating autobiographical underground comics that prompted *Entertainment Weekly* to describe Pekar as "an original, ambitious thinker who invented a new form of literature." Taking a partly documentary approach, the filmmakers interview Pekar, while at the same time throwing out "all the rules of nonfiction and dramatic re-creation, animation, and live action, to reconstitute, paraphrase, interpret, and riff on Pekar's life and art." In the process, Lisa Schwarzbaum believed that "a new movie form [was] born." Dennis and Joan West, who interviewed the filmmakers for *Cineaste,* agreed: "By way of homage to Pekar's chosen medium, the film of *American Splendor* likewise makes stylistic forays into comic-book esthetics, including animated sequences and illustrated frames, in order to create a complex hybrid of a film, one that celebrates the blurred boundaries between comics and film, documentary and fiction."

The story begins in 1975 with the less than promising statement: "From the streets of Cleveland comes . . . ," but what follows seems less than "splendid." In fact, Harvey Pekar appears to be a loser. His wife holds a Ph.D. and has plans to leave him, while Harvey is a file clerk afflicted with "voice troubles" to the extent that he can't even argue effectively with the wife because a doctor has advised him not to talk for a few months. All he can do is squawk and squeal in an irritating way. The "real" Harvey introduces the character at work: "Here's me, or the guy playing me, anyway." That guy would be Paul Giamatti, but two other actors also represent Pekar in the film: Daniel Tay plays the boy Harvey, trick-or-treating, and Donal Logue plays the stage actor who represents Harvey in the theater adaptation of *American Splendor.* Add to this the graphic representations, drawn by at least three different artists, all capturing different moods and nuances.

In 1962 Harvey meets the pioneering underground cartoonist Robert Crumb at a yard sale. They share an interest in jazz and comics and hang out together. At the time Crumb is working as a greeting card illustrator but he also sketches out comic book ideas in his spare time. He later travels to San Francisco and becomes famous for his work in counter-culture comics. Crumb returns to Cleveland in 1975 after Harvey's second wife has left him. Meanwhile, as the film is turning Harvey, himself, into a comic book character by giving him thought bubbles, he comes to this conclusion, which he shares with Crumb: "I could write comic books that are different from anything being done." Crumb reads sample storylines illustrated with Harvey's stick figures. "You're turning yourself into a comic hero," Crumb jokes, but he agrees to take the material and illustrate Harvey's life. Thus the comic *American Splendor* is born and Harvey takes his first steps on the road towards celebrity.

It's not that he makes a living at it "like Bob Crumb," but Harvey has a talent for taking the mundane and the ordinary and making it interesting, while at the same time making himself seem interesting. After his second wife has divorced him, Harvey starts corresponding with Joyce, who runs a comic store in Wilmington, Delaware. She first writes Harvey because she needs a copy of *American Splendor* No. 8, which Harvey sends to her. It turns out that they both like Theodore Dreiser's novel *Jennie Gerhardt,* which gives them something in common besides comic books. Joyce is borderline dysfunctional and, besides selling comics, teaches state prisoners how to write. Harvey invites her to visit him in Cleveland, meets her train, then takes her to a restaurant for some "yuppie food," which makes her throw up. Despite the heaves, it's a match made in heaven. "I think we should just skip the courtship thing and get married," Joyce says, and that is exactly what happens.

Meanwhile, Harvey's fame grows. *American Splendor* is made into a play in California. David Letterman invites Harvey to appear on national television in order to make fun of him, but because Harvey is an American original, the audience loves him, and he is invited back, again, and again. Joyce has an attack of depression, then social conscience, and decides she needs to visit Israel. Right after she leaves, Harvey discovers a lump that is diagnosed as cancer. Harvey's battle with cancer becomes a fresh idea for a book, *Our Cancer Year.* Harvey recovers, more secure in his celebrity than ever. Even Harvey's pal, Toby, whom Joyce considers to be "borderline autistic," becomes famous. After driving to Toledo to see *The Revenge of the Nerds* (1984), Toby, a paradigm nerd, becomes an MTV star. Harvey lives in a world that is kind to non-entities.

American Splendor was made by Robert Pulcini and Shari Springer Berman, a husband-and-wife team, who shared the responsibilities of directing and writing. Harvey Pekar is represented in three broad dimensions in this documentary/biopic hybrid: as he is drawn by such comic artists as Robert Crumb; as interpreted on the screen by actor Paul Giamatti (in what Owen Gleiberman called a "hilarious and touching performance"); and, finally, as himself, functioning both as narrator and subject. If the "real" Harvey is asked to stand up, that proves not to be a problem. The "real" Harvey is also seen in the Letterman interviews, except for his last, when Harvey seems determined to self-destruct by not only attacking Letterman but the owner of Letterman's network (General Electric) and even Letterman's audience.

American Splendor placed fourth in Lisa Schwarzbaum's Ten Best list for 2003, but even higher for her *Entertainment Weekly* colleague Owen Gleiberman, who listed it first, praising co-directors Shari Springer Berman and Robert Pulcini for having made "a film that cracks open into a comic book that morphs into a documentary, only to snap back into the most boisterous, tender, and crazily exquisite movie of the year." In fact, it made the top ten lists for more than 200 critics, was nominated for five Independent Spirit Awards, and was named best picture of 2003 by the National Society of Film Critics.

Berman and Pulcini push the envelope of documentary filmmaking by melding it with fiction, as Xan Brooks noted in *Sight and Sound,* inviting "the real Pekar to narrate the story being enacted by his fictional alter ego (played by Paul Giamatti)," eventually permitting not only Pekar to share the soundstage with the actor playing him, but also the real Joyce Brabner and her alter ego (Hope Davis), and the real Toby Radloff and his alter ego (played by Judah Friedlander). "Standard biography is no match for such a man" as Harvey Pekar, who is "at once author and character, hero and victim, his life and his art the result of a perpetual two-way osmosis."

Though not perhaps the stuff of Academy Awards (despite its nomination for best adapted screenplay), *American Splendor* impressed the mainline critics, including Roger Ebert, who called it "plain brilliant" (Ebert's diction was perfect for an absolutely accurate assessment). The film won the Grand Jury prize at the Sundance Film Festival in 2003 and also won the 2003 Cannes Film Festival International Critics Award. "The wonderful thing about the *American Splendor* comic books is that they really play with structure and form," Robert Pulcini explained in his *Cineaste* interview. "We thought we had the license to do anything we wanted, because the comic books are so free form. We felt that in order to stay true to the spirit of the comic books, we had to find a really interesting structure." Obviously, they succeeded brilliantly, and for that reason *American Splendor* was recognized as a uniquely original American documentary about an American original Everyman.

—James M. Welsh

Harvey Pekar: Paul Giamatti
Joyce Brabner: Hope Davis
Real Harvey: Harvey Pekar
Real Joyce: Joyce Brabner
Mr. Boats: Earl Billings
Robert Crumb: James Urbaniak
Toby Radloff: Judah Friedlander
Stage Actor Harvey: Donal Logue
Stage Actress Joyce: Molly Shannon
Fred: James McCaffrey
Interviewer: Shari Springer Berman
Bob the Director: Robert Pulcini

Origin: USA
Released: 2003
Production: Ted Hope; HBO Films, Good Machine; released by Fine Line Features
Directed by: Shari Springer Berman, Robert Pulcini
Written by: Shari Springer Berman, Robert Pulcini
Cinematography by: Terry Stacey
Music by: Mark Suozzo
Sound: Whit Norris
Music Supervisor: Linda Cohen
Editing: Robert Pulcini
Costumes: Michael Wilkinson
Production Design: Therese DePrez
MPAA rating: R
Running time: 101 minutes

 REVIEWS

Boxoffice. April, 2003, p. 81.
Chicago Sun-Times Online. August 22, 2003.
Entertainment Weekly. August 22, 2003, p. 109.
Los Angeles Times Online. August 15, 2003.
New York Times Online. August 15, 2003.
People. August 25, 2003, p. 34.
USA Today Online. August 15, 2003.
Vanity Fair. August, 2003, p. 64.
Variety Online. January 22, 2003.
Washington Post. August 22, 2003, p. WE33.

AWARDS AND NOMINATIONS

L.A. Film Critics 2003: Film, Screenplay
N.Y. Film Critics 2003: Actress (Davis)
Natl. Soc. Film Critics 2003: Film, Screenplay
Writers Guild 2003: Adapt. Screenplay
Nomination:
Oscars 2003: Adapt. Screenplay

Golden Globes 2004: Support. Actress (Davis)
Ind. Spirit 2004: Actor (Giamatti), Director (Pulcini, Berman), Film, Screenplay, Support. Actor (Friedlander).

American Wedding (American Pie 3)

Forever hold your piece.
—Movie tagline
This time they're going all the way.
—Movie tagline

 Box Office: $104.4 million

American Wedding is the third installment in the popular series of sex comedies that began four years ago with *American Pie,* a movie that was sweet, raunchy, and very funny. Jesse Dylan (Bob Dylan's son) assumes the directorial reins for the newest film, which does not come close to matching the freshness of the first but is not quite a dismal retread, as was the second. This third outing is marginally better than *American Pie 2* only because writer Adam Herz at least had the good sense to give the characters a new plot. Awkward, nerdy Jim (Jason Biggs) and the outwardly demure but truly sex-hungry Michelle (Alyson Hannigan), both fresh out of college, get engaged, and all the wedding preparations provide fodder for the sex-related humor this series specializes in. Only our nostalgia for the first movie and a residual fondness for a few of the characters, however, sustain our interest amidst an ever-increasing reliance on gross and downright ugly shtick.

Herz has stripped away many of the characters from the first two films (or else the actors wisely chose not to return)—Shannon Elizabeth's Nadia, Chris Klein's Oz, Natasha Lyonne's Jessica, Tara Reid's Vicky, and Mena Suvari's Heather. Given how little he has to do beside stand around and be a part of Jim's increasingly shrinking group of friends, Thomas Ian Nicholas's Kevin also might as well have been written out. It should be noted, however, that, even in the second film, most of these characters, especially the women, had become superfluous. The original film was the rare teen sex comedy that gave equal weight to the female characters and the male, but, as the series has progressed (or regressed?), the boys have taken center stage.

The other major trend in the series is the growing dominance of Steve Stifler (Seann William Scott). In the original, he is one of the large ensemble; in the second film, his obnoxious, frat-boy behavior looms large; but he so dominates the third film that it might as well be subtitled *The Steve Stifler Show*. Not only does Stifler steamroll everyone else, but he has become louder, more obnoxious, and more profane than ever. Some audiences clearly love watching his unbridled, sex-crazed shenanigans, and, admittedly, how much one likes *American Wedding* will depend on how much one enjoys watching Stifler run amok. He is all id let loose on American suburbia, but even a little goes a long way, and just because a character says "fuck" in practically every sentence does not make him amusing or quirky—it just means he swears a lot.

The only thing that makes Stifler watchable is his attempt to impress Cadence (January Jones), Michelle's sister, by pretending to be a gentleman. Competing for her affections with Finch (Eddie Kaye Thomas), the cultured intellectual of the group, Stifler tries his hardest to control his naturally base instincts. It is almost as if the filmmakers were acknowledging how grating this character has become and thought it would be fun to see him struggle with good manners. The joke actually works, at least for a while, just because it makes Stifler do something different.

It is too bad that Cadence herself is a dull character. With the absence of the previous group of girls, the film could use a sharp female presence in addition to Michelle, but Cadence is very underwritten. No one expects psychological complexity in an *American Pie* film, but she is nothing more than the beautiful object of desire for Finch and Stifler. Likewise, the usually funny Fred Willard joins the cast as Harold, Michelle's father, but he is not given much to do beyond looking shocked at the high jinks around him while sizing up Jim as a potential son-in-law.

Given all of these shortcomings, *American Wedding* has a few great moments. The opening, in which an uneasy Jim is set to propose to Michelle in a fancy restaurant, is hilarious. When she misinterprets his stammerings as a request to spice up their sex life, she slides under the table to pleasure him orally. Jim has left the engagement ring at home, so his always supportive dad (Eugene Levy) races to the restaurant, where he takes all of his son's expressions of ecstasy as signs of nervousness. After Jim's dad delivers a slew of double entendres ("Hope you didn't blow your wad on this [ring], son," "You look like you're ready to burst," "I cannot believe my son is gonna pop the question"), Jim is finally exposed with his pants down, and Michelle crawls out. Cheerfully raunchy, embarrassing, and yet ultimately goodhearted toward its hapless characters, this is a classic *American Pie* scene. It is also a great beginning that the rest of the film rarely matches and a reminder of how much fun Jim's dad and Michelle are.

Granted, the reserved exterior masking the soul of a nympho may make Michelle a one-joke character, as is the helpful but clueless dad. But they also exude a goofy, sincere charm that the one-note Stifler lacks. Despite her kinkiness,

for example, Michelle wants a beautiful, traditional wedding, and Jim's eagerness to please her is actually quite touching (he even takes dance lessons from Stifler to prepare for the big day) and reminiscent of the heart that made the first film such a treat.

One would think that a movie about an impending wedding would focus on the couple, especially the bride, but the screenplay downplays Jim and Michelle so that Stifler can run the show. An inadvertent visit to a gay bar results in Stifler being hit on (the doofus cannot figure out where he is) and then engaging in a weird, overly long dance-off with a burly guy named Bear (Eric Allen Kramer), who later helps Stifler arrange the bachelor party. This episode involves Jim walking into his home with his future in-laws when his buddies are cavorting with two buxom strippers, one dressed as a cop in leather and one barely dressed as a maid. Kevin is tied to a chair, and Finch is trying to smear chocolate syrup over his body for the girls to lick off. Finally, after the attempt to hide the girls fails and everyone is exposed, Stifler somehow turns the disaster around by claiming it was all an elaborate scheme designed to make Jim look like a hero by rescuing Kevin. This episode may be stupid and preposterous, but it does have a gleeful comic energy lacking in much of the movie.

Indeed, a lot of the so-called humor in *American Wedding* falls flat, revolving around desperate, lame attempts to match the infamous but good-natured sex-with-a-pie scene in the original. At the engagement party, a dog licks the cream of a smashed cake off Stifler's crotch, and Jim's attempt to pull the dog off him only makes the situation worse when a second dog runs in and they all look like they are having an orgy. Another pointless joke finds Jim shaving his pubic hair to please Michelle, only to have it fly onto the wedding cake.

But the film's absolute low point—maybe the low point of any film this year—begins with a dog swallowing the wedding ring and Stifler having to wait for the creature to relieve itself. Once Stifler scoops up the mess, Michelle's mother, Mary (Deborah Rush), mistakes the brown gob for a truffle, and he must eat it himself so she will not, thus leaving him with excrement all over his teeth. Later, he arranges a secret rendezvous with Cadence in a closet, and he accidentally has sex with Jim's senile grandmother instead (she was put there because she is a big pain to have around). It is clear that we are supposed to think it is funny for Stifler to humiliate himself constantly, but watching this annoying egomaniac getting his comeuppance in disgusting ways is just as bad as enduring his awful behavior in the first place.

If Stifler's repugnant antics represent *American Wedding* at its worst, then Michelle's odd combination of innocence and lewdness fuels the film's brightest moments. When Michelle asks Jim's father for advice on writing her vows and she refers to making love as "boning," it is clear that, in her own lovable way, this is just as acceptable a term. It is too bad there is not more of Michelle; she is, after all, the most appealing character in the film (as well as in the whole series), and Hannigan is the rare actress who can be radiant, dorky, and funny all at the same time.

The film concludes with the wedding, which is actually played fairly straight as a sweet ending to the trilogy (the dance lessons pay off, and Michelle is very pleased with Jim's newfound ability). For a coda, we are also treated to the last-minute cameo appearance of Stifler's mom (Jennifer Coolidge), Finch's erotic obsession from the previous two movies. She and Finch end up together in a bubble bath, but the joke, like so many in *American Wedding*, feels obligatory. It is a tired ending for a franchise whose original comic inspiration has long since gone stale.

—*Peter N. Chumo II*

REVIEWS

Chicago Sun-Times Online. August 1, 2003.
Entertainment Weekly. August 8, 2003, p. 52.
Los Angeles Times Online. August 1, 2003.
New York Times Online. August 1, 2003.
People. August 11, 2003, p. 33.
USA Today Online. August 1, 2003.
Variety Online. July 30, 2003.
Washington Post. August 1, 2003, p. WE39.

QUOTES

Michelle's dad Harold (Fred Willard) sneers at Jim (Jason Biggs): "As the future protector of my first-born, you're off to a bad start."

CREDITS

Jim Levenstein: Jason Biggs
Michelle Flaherty: Alyson Hannigan
Steve Stifler: Seann William Scott
Paul Finch: Eddie Kaye Thomas
Cadence Flaherty: January Jones
Jim's dad: Eugene Levy
Kevin Myers: Thomas Ian Nicholas
Harold Flaherty: Fred Willard
Jim's Mom: Molly Cheek
Bear: Eric Allen Kramer
Mary Flaherty: Deborah Rush
Stifler's mom: Jennifer Coolidge
Grandma: Angela Paton
Head Coach: Lawrence Pressman
Fraulein Brandi: Amanda Swisten
Officer Krystal: Nikki Schieler Ziering

Origin: USA
Released: 2003
Production: Warren Zide, Craig Perry, Chris Moore, Adam Herz, Chris Bonder; released by Universal Pictures
Directed by: Jesse Dylan
Written by: Adam Herz
Cinematography by: Lloyd Ahern II
Music by: Christophe Beck
Sound: Cameron Hamza
Music Supervisor: John Bissell
Editing: Stuart Pappe
Art Direction: Greg Weimerskirch
Costumes: Pamela Withers-Chilton
Production Design: Clayton Hartley
MPAA rating: R
Running time: 96 minutes

And Now Ladies and Gentlemen

Well-loved veteran French filmmaker Claude Lelouch's crime musical, *And Now, Ladies and Gentlemen,* is such an unique generic mix that only Lelouch's mastery at blending song and cinema could have allowed him to pull it off. Anyone who lived through the emergence of film as an international art, beginning in the mid-1960s, will remember the peculiarly Gallic charm of Lelouch's *A Man and A Woman* (1966). His latest can be seen as a valentine fashioned for those who fell in love with that bonbon, as well as those who fell in love to it. For that select group, the film would take its place in their memories as an experience to be cherished, and more importantly, one that cannot be repeated.

Lelouch not only tackles this antinomy head-on, but he dramatizes it, showing how the new can prove an enemy of romance. The songs that his chanteuse-heroine sings, often rendered in their entirety, are mostly old standards. But Lelouch is even prepared to go further and advance an obscurantist proposition that what true love really needs is belief in the primitive and the timeless. That he's unable to establish a link between that level of "spiritual romance" and his unique blend of song and cinema, reveals Lelouch to be as romantic as his two leads.

Coming as it does soon after Pedro Almodovar's runaway box-office hit from Spain, *Talk to Her* (2002), *And Now* cannot help but strike audiences as a lighter version of Almodovar's fable of parallel lives rendered tragic by the workings of fate. What prevents Lelouch's tale from seeming more than sentimental fluff in comparison is his dramatic vision, which confines itself to the world of the dream, and the lost dream at that. Almodovar, while prone to the surreal and the fantastic, remains steeped in his gritty social realism. Lelouch, on the other hand, situates his tale in the hazy recesses of memory within the minds of his two leads. But Lelouch is also slyly drawing upon his select audience's memories. There is an unabashed self-tribute where the heroine sings the well-known theme song from *A Man and A Woman*.

This could explain why, even though Lelouch features scenes set in Paris, surely one of the world's most romantic cities, we don't see very much of that city in the film. Instead, we do see the high seas from the deck of a racing yacht, and we are treated to breathtaking aerial vistas of cities in Morocco. Clearly, Lelouch presents these physical settings as imbued with the aura of a dream, one in which Valentin (Jeremy Irons), a clever, thieving scoundrel, and Jane (Patricia Kaas), a beautiful, itinerant jazz singer, find themselves, while sharing the same psychopathological affliction.

But if the film itself were to be seen as a memory, then its narrative could be understood as both dream and reality. It is the battle between these two opposing realms that sustains the film's surface lyricism. If Lelouch has anything to do with it, it is clear who is going to win this little war.

And Now therefore opens not with an introductory scene, but with a nodal one. In tight close-ups, we see Jane's face and that of a female gypsy, both locked into a profane ritual. We don't have a clue as to where they are, except for the percussive sound in the background that has a North African feel to it. As a lady friend behind her translates, Jane is told by the gypsy that she has an incurable ailment, and that she needs to perform a ritual of penance by the graveside of a female mystic, who in turn will cure her from beyond the grave.

With the flap of a filmic wing, Lelouch cuts to a jewel heist that has been planned, and is now being executed singlehandedly by Valentin. At a Bulgari store in London, Valentin poses as a police inspector with news of a planned robbery. He tells the manager not to offer resistance, since the police have it all covered. We then see Valentin, disguised as a stumbling, bumbling old thief, enter the store with a briefcase, which is promptly filled with choice items. The clerk is then told to count to a hundred, but before he can get to fifty, we see Valentin speed away on a motorcycle.

As if in celebration of the ease and sophistication of this seemingly perfect crime, Lelouch cuts to intimate shots of Jane performing in a night club in Paris, singing a duet with a black female singer about the joys of being "together again." This sets into motion the narrative trajectory that will in fact bring together Jane and Valentin, as far removed as their respective fields of endeavor might appear.

In the next sequence, Valentin, now disguised as an aging dowager, reappears at a Bulgari store in Paris and, with the aid of Francoise (Allesandra Martines), an agile

brunette serving as accomplice, robs it blind of a priceless necklace belonging to the Czarina of Russia. All this is juxtaposed and underscored by Jane's singing. For her effort, Francoise is rewarded with a Cadillac convertible—that she accepts—along with Valentin's overtures of intimacy—that she rejects.

Lelouch is now ready to introduce the plot element of the so-called temporary amnesia that we will see progressively crippling the lives of Valentin and Jane. The former is seen navigating a racing yacht, hoping to buy it from its owner, the sporty Thierry (Thierry L'Hermitte), who is beside him. In their conversation, overheard by Francoise, Valentin absent-mindedly mentions a jewelry store. When Francoise later reminds him of this, he looks taken aback by his own mental debility. Similarly, Jane is stopped by the police because she is driving around in circles. She explains she was lost in the music being played by an orchestra nearby. We hear the orchestra, but the policemen do not. Later we learn that just as Valentin sometimes doesn't remember where he is, Jane forgets the lyrics to the songs she is singing.

The parallel aspect of their independent lives becomes all too clear at this moment. Jane breaks off with a trumpet player, a situation we cannot readily identify with, since we haven't been privy to their relationship. Valentin discovers that Francoise has been in love with Thierry, so he takes off by himself to "circle the world" in a yacht that he christens *Ladies and Gentlemen.* Jane, after another of her "attacks," leaves for Morocco to get away from it all. Valentin, knocked unconscious on the high seas, also finds himself on Moroccan shores.

Even with such twists and turns, and more serious ones to come, Lelouch never lets the reality quotient sustaining his love story drop below the level of the dream. Even the doctor in the city of Fez speaks in a romantic, forlorn tone, first to Jane and then to Valentin, about how memories are "what's left of dreams." In fact, it is the doctor who tells Valentin about a café singer who is suffering from the same kind of "blackouts," only she hears orchestras.

For a while, the film appears to have hit a plane of dramatic stasis, since now nothing seems to be keeping Lelouch's two romantic leads apart, except the nature of their ailment. Valentin, for example, cannot remember making love to Jane, even though she describes the act, which we see enacted. Jane is told that her blackouts could in fact be "black holes," that is, she will see the person she's talking to framed by night when it is in fact day. We see her struck by just this effect at a time when she feels closest to Valentin.

Once Valentin and Jane meet, the film returns us to the nodal scene with which it began. This time, as the gypsy gives her instructions, we see Valentin looking on. To liven up the proceedings, Lelouch manufactures a subplot revolving around the Countess Falconetti (Claudia Cardinale in a cameo as an aging virago), who is staying at the same luxury hotel as Jane and Valentin. When she reports the theft of her jewels, the local police inspector is all too ready to blame Valentin. As he and Jane trudge along the dusty mountainous path to the shrine of Lalla Chaffia they are being watched by the police. Before he can pray at the shrine, which is supposed to grant all wishes, Valentin is arrested, but Jane is able to pray for him.

Not that that prevents things from getting darker. Valentin, after being tortured, is diagnosed with a brain tumor. If only to get operated upon, he confesses to the theft of the Countess's jewels. He is however set free when the Countess herself is found to be the culprit. Cured by surgery, Valentin takes it upon himself to pay back all those from whom he has stolen.

The film's climax shows Jane using her cell phone to surprise Valentin, who is standing on a pier a few feet away, with his back to her. He has come there to cheer on Thierry who is racing his yacht. Jane tells Valentin she's speaking from Paris. She then gets a rude shock when she sees Francoise come rushing up and embrace Valentin, who responds by hugging her tightly. Jane then turns away with tear-filled eyes. Valentin eventually catches up with her in the Paris club where she is singing, and the film ends on a note of romantic triumph.

Lelouch's curious mix of generic elements seems to have left most American critics unmoved. A. O. Scott, writing in the *New York Times,* is at least prepared to take the film on its own terms, as a "jet-set fantasy . . . [that] is a nice enough place to visit." Kevin Thomas of the *Los Angeles Times* would appear to be in a minority, as he perceives in the film "a swooningly lyrical vision," one able to "evoke a sense of mortality, of the fickleness of fate, and even of spiritual longing."

—Vivek Adarkar

Valentin: Jeremy Irons
Jane Lester: Patricia Kaas
Francoise: Alessandra Martines
Thierry: Thierry Lhermitte
Boubou: Ticky Holgado
David: Yvan Attal
Countess Falconetti: Claudia Cardinale
Police Inspector: Amidou
Dr. Lamy: Jean-Marie Bigard

Origin: France, Great Britain
Language: English, French
Released: 2002

Production: Claude Lelouch; Les Films 13, France 2 Cinema, Gemka, L&G Productions Ltd.; released by Paramount Classics
Directed by: Claude Lelouch
Written by: Claude Lelouch, Pierre Uytterhoeven, Pierre Leroux
Cinematography by: Pierre William Glenn
Music by: Michel Legrand
Sound: Harald Maury
Editing: Helene De Luze
Art Direction: Johann George
Costumes: Pierre Bechir
MPAA rating: PG-13
Running time: 126 minutes

Boston Globe Online. August 8, 2003.
Chicago Sun-Times Online. August 22, 2003.
Entertainment Weekly. August 15, 2003, p. 52.
Los Angeles Times Online. August 1, 2003.
New York Times Online. August 1, 2003.
Variety Online. May 26, 2002.
Washington Post. August 8, 2003, p. C5.

Police Inspector (Amidou): "I don't check alibis. Only the innocent don't have alibis."

Anger Management

Feel the Love.
—Movie tagline
Let the Healing Begin.
—Movie tagline

 Box Office: $134.4 million

Even to someone who is not an admirer of Adam Sandler's movies, the idea of pairing the goofy comic actor with Jack Nicholson might sound intriguing enough to encourage a trip to the movie theater (or at least the video store), if only for the curiosity factor. Although fairly popular with audiences, very few of Sandler's movies have been widely lauded in critical circles, while the reverse can be said for Nicholson. A rare exception was Sandler's turn in Paul

Thomas Anderson's *Punch Drunk Love* (2002), which ironically did not meet with the success of typical Sandler fare. Produced by Sandler, *Anger Management* is a return to the formulaic storytelling of his prior hits, yet the addition of Nicholson results in a movie that manages to move a notch above the likes of *The Waterboy* thanks to his manic performance. Still, the film misses many genuine opportunities for greater depth, believability, and a more sophisticated edge.

Sandler plays David Buznik, a relatively tame and meek (some might even say boring) character who contrasts sharply with many of the actor's previous roles. The plot's complications begin when David runs into unexpected and inexplicable trouble on an airplane. In a humorous scene that becomes so bizarre that it borders on the absurd, a flight attendant accuses David of yelling and becoming hostile when he very mildly makes an inquiry about a set of headphones he'd requested. When he touches her arm, she accuses him of physical assault. The entire situation is made even more ridiculous by the fact that David obsessively avoids conflict and virtually any kind of public emotional display. He does not even defend himself when a judge orders him to complete an anger management program under the care of well-known therapist Dr. Buddy Rydell, played by Nicholson.

When David arrives for therapy, he immediately recognizes Buddy as the man who had been sitting next to him on the plane. Thinking that surely Buddy will be his ally, David strikes up a deal that if he will stay for one session, Buddy will sign his release papers, relieving him of any further sessions. That deal falls apart when David later loses his cool (mildly) as Buddy keeps pressing him about "who he is," even though David has tried to answer by describing his job, his interests, and his hobbies. Buddy then decides that David may need a couple more sessions because of his outburst; he also assigns David an accountability partner, Chuck (John Turturro), who is very high-strung and violent.

Chuck soon gets David into trouble at a local bar by picking a fight in which David accidentally strikes a blind man and hits a barmaid in the face. Back in court, with David now facing prison time, Buddy walks in and accepts all responsibility for David's care. David is thankful until he realizes that Buddy is moving in with him so he can watch his every step. It soon begins to seem that Buddy may really be the one needing therapy as he takes over David's life.

David begins to see signs of Buddy's temper when Buddy throws a plate of food across the room when David cooks him the wrong breakfast. He suspects there is something wrong with Buddy and at this point begins to fear him, a fear that worsens when Buddy informs him that he will be accompanying him to work. On the way to work, David becomes frustrated because he gets stuck in traffic and knows he is going to be late. To calm David down, Buddy tells David to pull over and asks him to sing "I Feel Pretty." With people screaming and cursing at David, David gives in to

Buddy and the two sing a lovely version of the tune, truly one of the funniest moments in the film.

After a few days of "therapy", David receives a phone call at his house for Buddy. He learns that Buddy's mother, who lives in Boston, is going to have minor surgery. David sees this as an opportunity to get rid of his crazy therapist and tells Buddy that the surgery is serious, so he should go see her. Buddy, in shock, begins to cry for his mother. David feels bad for lying and tells Buddy that it was a joke, that indeed his mother was going to have surgery, but it was minor. Buddy does decide to go to Boston, but he insists that David come along so that he can continue monitoring him.

While in Boston, the two go out for dinner at a restaurant, where Buddy sets David up for trouble. Buddy tells David to go up to a beautiful young woman and ask her if he could buy her a drink, just to boost his self-confidence. After initially refusing since he has a girlfriend, David goes up to the girl and is immediately rejected. Buddy has him go back to her and say something inappropriate, explaining that if David is rejected a second time, he will relieve him of his therapy. Motivated by the thought of ridding himself of Buddy, David agrees and to his surprise, the girl asks him to sit down. Unfortunately, Buddy disappears while they are talking, so David goes home with the girl. While at the girl's house, he discovers the young woman is quite batty herself.

When David returns to New York, his girlfriend Linda (Marisa Tomei) tells him that she thinks they need a break so that David can have space to figure out what he wants to do with their relationship. Though he is troubled by the suggestion, David goes along with it. Soon he discovers that Buddy is moving in on Linda behind his back, but Buddy protests that he is just trying to keep Linda from other men. However, when Buddy later returns from a date with Linda, he tells David that they have fallen in love.

Some time passes and David hears that Buddy is going to take Linda to a Yankees game, where he evidently intends to propose to her. David begins to feel the courage rise as he knows that he can't live without Linda. This sets up the climax, where David finds out the real origins of and reasons for his recent odyssey into the madness that is apparently Buddy's life and psychiatric method.

The ending of the story, in which Sandler's character experiences a big, emotional revelation in front of a large group of people who cheer/help him along, is almost a staple of Sandler's movies. In the too-sweet, over-the-top sentimental moments like this, *Anger Management* suffers some of the weaknesses of previous Sandler outings. And although the conflicts throughout the movie are amusing, one has to wonder why David and Linda seem to be the only sane people around, undermining the credibility of the plot somewhat. Sandler often seems out of place and uncomfortable in the character of David, precisely because David is so reserved and subdued, a personality to which he is not particularly well-suited. Jack Nicholson, on the other hand, steals the show as Buddy, who alternates between angry outbursts and calm, thoughtful friendliness. His lively, manic performance makes the movie much more interesting than it would have been without him, and he has a knack for bringing out humor in moments that wouldn't have been as funny if played differently. Overall, the pairing of Nicholson and Sandler was an inspired idea, but it might have been even more entertaining with the right execution and with a little more mania on the part of Sandler himself.

—*David Flanagin*

CREDITS

Dave Buznik: Adam Sandler
Dr. Buddy Rydell: Jack Nicholson
Linda: Marisa Tomei
Lou: Luis Guzman
Andrew: Allen Covert
Judge Daniels: Lynne Thigpen
Frank Head: Kurt Fuller
Nate: Jonathan Loughran
Stacy: Krista Allen
Gina: January Jones
Galaxia/Security Guard: Woody Harrelson
Chuck: John Turturro
Kendra: Heather Graham
Panaman Amanana/Arnie Shankman: John C. Reilly
Sam: Kevin Nealon
Blindman: Harry Dean Stanton
Himself: Bobby Knight (Cameo)
Himself: John McEnroe (Cameo)

Origin: USA
Released: 2003
Production: Jack Giarraputo, Barry Bernardi; Revolution Studios, Happy Madison Productions; released by Sony Pictures Classics
Directed by: Peter Segal
Written by: David Dorfman
Cinematography by: Donald McAlpine
Music by: Teddy Castellucci
Sound: Thomas Causey
Music Supervisor: Michael Dilbeck
Editing: Jeff Gourson
Art Direction: Domenic Silvestri
Costumes: Ellen Lutter
Production Design: Alan Au
MPAA rating: PG-13
Running time: 101 minutes

REVIEWS

Chicago Sun-Times Online. April 11, 2003.
Los Angeles Times Online. April 11, 2003.
New York Times Online. April 11, 2003.
People. April 21, 2003, p. 35.
Rolling Stone. May 1, 2003, p. 62.
USA Today Online. April 11, 2003.
Variety Online. April 10, 2003.
Washington Post. April 11, 2003, p. WE44.

QUOTES

Dr. Buddy Rydell (Jack Nicholson): "Sarcasm is anger's ugly cousin."

Anything But Love (Standard Time)

Billie Golden (Isabel Rose) fancies herself a bit of a movie star, in the style of old school musical heroines. She's a lounge singer and dresses herself as a leading lady from 1940s or 50s movies. For a first date, she thinks nothing of copping Audrey Hepburn's *Breakfast at Tiffanys* look. For Billie, this doesn't just mean wearing a black dress—it's the exact dress, the same hairstyle, the works.

As Billie is to an old style movie star, *Anything But Love* is to an old romantic movie musical. It looks like it, sounds like it and has some of the charm, but it's not quite as good as the original. Still, for fans of old time movies where a girl's main problem is deciding which suitor to marry, *Anything But Love* offers a good time. It's a nice homage to the genre and has a bit of its own fun.

From the opening of *Anything But Love*, it's all played with utter seriousness. The opening credits appear over a shot of a hand leafing through sheet music. It could be straight from 1950. For anyone who grew up watching those old movies, it's a comforting sight. And the stylistic touches signal that we're going to enter a fantasy world—not in the sense of dragons and such—but where a girl with a big heart and a lot of moxie (and in these types of films it would indeed be referred to as moxie) will surely find happiness.

The glamorous heights that Billie aspires to contrast with the reality of her pretty dull life. She lives in Queens with her mother, Laney Golden (Alix Korey, an actual renowned cabaret singer who, oddly, never sings in the film), who spends a lot of time nagging Billie to get a real job and find a good husband. Laney is the kind of woman who easily spouts off such remarks as, "You're so greasy you should come with a bottle of Dawn." Billie moonlights at the Skylark Lounge, an airport lounge, where she sings standards to a tiny crowd of mildly interested patrons. The owner, Sal (Victor Argo), is a friend of the family who's known them since the days when Laney and Billie's dad performed together in an act of their own.

The plucky Billie finally gets a break when she runs into Greg Ellenbogen (Cameron Bancroft), the most popular guy from Billie's high school. Billie, of course, had a huge crush on him and was, in turn, largely ignored by him. Greg is now a successful corporate lawyer. It's unbelievable to Billie that Greg would want to go out with her, and she is thrilled when he asks her on a date.

Although things go well for a while, signs pop up that he might not be "the one." For one thing, he sold out his dreams. Before he was a corporate lawyer, he did more personally fulfilling public interest work. He views Billie's singing similarly, as something that should be given up to pursue something more serious. Woe be it to the man in a film who dismisses a woman's vocation as a "hobby." Also, there's the matter of his name. Is the romantic lead in a movie musical really going to be named Ellenbogen? I mean, in this film, the heroine is Billie Golden—this is the sign of a screenwriter who pays attention to names.

The screenwriters in question are Robert Cary, who also directed, and Rose, who portrays Billie. In a way, it's sort of obvious that this project was something that Rose willed into being because she is somewhat unlikely as the star. She plays the role with the right emotions and all that, but she doesn't have the look of a star, or at least the kind that would head up a romantic movie. She doesn't have a movie star's beauty and lacks the kind of star quality that would make up for it. Still, for Rose, seeing *Anything But Love* hit the screens had to be a big treat.

Billie is ready to join Greg and be set up in the suburbs as a well-kept wife, but she's having some doubts. These are expressed in a fun fantasy sequence in which she dances to mod, 1960s-style music with a couple of the other firm wives, and eventually becoming indistinguishable from them—bland, tastefully dressed arm candy. The dance was choreographed by Cary, once a dancer himself.

Complicating matters, or perhaps fixing them, is one Elliot Shepard (Andrew McCarthy), a grumpy piano player. After taking an immediate dislike to Billie (warning sign #1 of future love) at an audition, he sabotages her by playing poorly. The two keep running into to each other and, to guide the plot along, Billie starts taking piano lessons from him. The two bond over their shared passion for music and start sitting a lot closer to each other on the piano bench. Of course, this sets up the dilemma: should Billie pick Elliot, who's poor but a passionate artist, or Greg, who's rich but a big bore?

McCarthy, who amazingly doesn't look a day older than he did in his 1980s heyday, is suitably scruffy. The one annoying tic about his performance is that he's constantly adjusting and readjusting his baseball cap. It's supposed to be a cute bond between him and Billie—she says "wear it frontwards or backwards" when they meet and again later when they reunite—but it seems more like the man is suffering from some sort of itchy scalp condition. A lot less of this would have made his character seem more desirable and less like he needed to be fumigated. Otherwise, McCarthy seems to be taking his role seriously and honestly seems passionate over Billie. Even though Rose doesn't really have the elusive kind of star quality that this role needs, she still fits well enough in the part. It's easy to believe her as the kind of person who owns more vintage formals than pants. Eartha Kitt shows up as herself at just the right moment to offer opportune advice. After years in show business, she is still a leonine presence.

Critics didn't feel like swooning much over *Anything But Love,* but it did have its fans. Lisa Schwarzbaum gave the film a C+ in *Entertainment Weekly* and wrote, "The frustration of this good-hearted, off-key warble of an indie . . . is that the filmmaking pales when compared with the classic elements of the 1950s and early '60s romantic musical to which it pays homage." Dave Kehr of the *New York Times* described it as "anything but unpredictable," but added, "it is a pleasant, good-natured picture that struggles, gallantly, if vainly, to recapture the style and sensibility of a studio musical on the severely limited budget of an independent film." Kevin Thomas of the *Los Angeles Times* called the film "a charmer" that succeeds, "because it dares to take its people and their dreams seriously, with a gently humorous affection, instead of merely sending them up, and because it is clearly taking place in the Manhattan of here and now and not in some vague time warp."

—Jill Hamilton

CREDITS

Billie Golden: Isabel Rose
Elliot Shepard: Andrew McCarthy
Greg Ellenbogen: Cameron Bancroft
Laney Golden: Alix Korey
Sal: Victor Argo
Marcy: Ilana Levine
TJ: Sean Arbuckle
Herself: Eartha Kitt

Origin: USA
Released: 2002
Production: Aimee Schoof, Isen Robbins; released by Samuel Goldwyn Films

Directed by: Robert Cary
Written by: Isabel Rose, Robert Cary
Cinematography by: Horacio Marquinez
Music by: Andrew Hollander, Steven Lutvak
Music Supervisor: Janice Ginsberg
Editing: Robert Reitano
Costumes: Sarah Beers
Production Design: Cecil Gentry
MPAA rating: PG-13
Running time: 99 minutes

 REVIEWS

Boxoffice. December, 2003, p. 28.
Chicago Sun-Times Online. November 21, 2003.
Entertainment Weekly. Novembe 28, 2003, p. 102.
Los Angeles Times Online. November 14, 2003.
New York Times Online. November 14, 2003.
Variety Online. November 19, 2002.

Anything Else

In any relationship, one person always does the heavy lifting.
—Movie tagline

 Box Office: $3.2 million

I t has been 26 years since Woody Allen broke new ground with *Annie Hall,* a seriocomic take on love and relationships that established him as a major filmmaker and remains to this day one of his two or three defining films. Jason Biggs and Christina Ricci, who star in his latest movie, *Anything Else,* were not yet born when *Annie Hall* won four major Oscars, nor was much of the audience for which his latest film seems intended. So perhaps Allen thought that, with the passage of time, now would be the right moment to revisit some of his old themes and narrative techniques for a new generation. From a protagonist who addresses the audience directly, and a narrative structure that freely moves back and forth in time, to a relationship clouded by anxiety and doubt, *Anything Else* evokes the spirit of Allen's classic nervous romance in many ways. While it does not come close to matching *Annie Hall*'s originality, it is nonetheless funny, smart, and very entertaining—a witty throwback to the relationship comedy that is Allen's forte.

The advertising for *Anything Else,* however, downplayed the fact that this is a quintessential Woody Allen film,

focusing, instead, on the costars of the film. Young moviegoers who can easily recognize Biggs and Ricci are probably unfamiliar with much of Allen's work, and the attempt to appeal to a new generation may be his way to broaden his audience after several recent less-than-stellar box office showings. Yet even before the story begins, *Anything Else* is unmistakably an Allen film, from the familiar black title cards at the beginning accompanied by a jazz-infused soundtrack to the beautiful opening shot of Allen's beloved Central Park. (This is Allen's first wide-screen film since *Manhattan,* and the compositions, courtesy of cinematographer Darius Khondji, are lovely.) Peppered with a wide array of cultural references, from Humphrey Bogart to Tod Browning's *Freaks* to Dostoyevsky's *Notes from Underground,* the literate dialogue is also a welcome return to the intelligence at the heart of Allen's best screenplays.

Biggs plays Jerry Falk, the hero of the film, a young comedy writer going through a difficult relationship with Ricci's Amanda, the woman he loves beyond all reason despite the pain she causes him. An insecure, neurotic actress, she thinks she is too fat despite the fact that Jerry and every other man find her incredibly sexy. She is a spontaneous, mercurial woman who starts eating a sliver of cheesecake, then the whole cake, and finally a complete meal just before meeting her boyfriend for the special anniversary dinner he has planned. Ricci can be sexy and innocent at the same time, and even when Amanda is manipulative and flatout dishonest, there is an underlying sweetness that is seductive. It is easy to understand why Jerry would tolerate so much from this difficult woman, who also looks great lounging around the apartment in her underwear even as she obsesses over her imaginary weight problem.

While Allen himself appears in the film as Jerry's mentor, David Dobel, Biggs nonetheless plays the typically Allenesque role, even adopting some of the nerdy, stammering mannerisms of Allen, although not to the degree that Kenneth Branagh did in *Celebrity.* Biggs is surprisingly effective at adapting his insecure *American Pie* persona for a more intellectual part.

Jerry's main problem is that, as much as he loves Amanda, she recoils when he tries to make love to her or even touch her. They have not had sex for six months, and, while Jerry is constantly frustrated and going crazy, he hangs on because he loves her and he hates to sleep alone. He also has a problem cutting ties with people who are no good for him. The screenplay adopts a loose time structure, employing flashbacks to fill us in on the Jerry-Amanda relationship. We see, for example, their first meeting and the instant attraction they feel, despite the fact that each is in a relationship with someone else. They bond over classic jazz and especially the music of Billie Holiday—seemingly sure signs of compatibility in an Allen film. Their initial meeting is quite funny, as it is played out against the utter dismay of Jerry's devoted girlfriend, who can see immediately that her man is smitten with Amanda. On their first afternoon alone together, Amanda sums it up when she purrs, "You must really have a crush on me. I would say it's fatal."

But life with Amanda quickly became a nightmare. If their sexual problem did not pose enough of a challenge, Amanda's mother, Paula (Stockard Channing), comes to live with them for a while, even though their apartment is small and Jerry barely has room to work on his novel. Paula is a neurotic handful herself—she wants to turn herself into a nightclub singer and asks Jerry to write some witty in-between-song banter, even though he hardly has time for his own writing. Unfortunately, Paula comes off as a one-joke, shrewish annoyance. An extra burden on Jerry's shoulders, she is more pathetic than amusing. In her best scene, she brings home a young boyfriend with a stash of cocaine—a reference to a great scene in *Annie Hall* but without that film's hilarious payoff.

Trying to find a solution to his own problem, Jerry spontaneously checks into a hotel room with Amanda to spark up their sex life, an ill-fated attempt that leads to some of the film's brightest gags. Instead of a night of passion, he gets a night of misery; Amanda's throat swells up, and she has a hard time breathing. Then, during their trip to the emergency room, the doctor ends up touching her everywhere—something poor Jerry does not even get to do.

The most refreshing aspect of the film is the reworking of Allen himself from his usual role as leading man to supportive friend and confidant (as if he had the Tony Roberts role in *Annie Hall* or the Michael Murphy role in *Manhattan*). Finding life's wisdom in old jokes (a parallel to *Annie Hall*'s opening monologue), Dobel is constantly giving Jerry advice during their walks through Central Park. He expounds on a variety of topics dear to his heart, from man's isolation in a godless universe to the rising threat of anti-Semitism and the need to be prepared for another Holocaust. In one of the film's funniest scenes, he buys Jerry a rifle and urges him to put together a survivalist kit. Dobel is paranoid, intellectual, and very witty, and of course a prototypical Allen character, but, having liberated himself from playing the romantic lead, Allen allows himself to be edgy and crazy. He even gets physical for a change; after two burly thugs take Dobel's coveted parking space and taunt him, he smashes up their car—a violent scene that is nonetheless hilarious because it is something we would never expect the usually mild-mannered nebbish to do.

In another departure for an Allen character, Dobel casts a critical eye on psychoanalysis (a practice Allen has been closely linked to), heaping on it the same bemused scorn Allen usually reserves just for religion. Jerry's sessions with his analyst bear out Dobel's skepticism—the doctor just sits there, barely saying a word as Jerry searches in vain for help. But the big joke is that Dobel himself may be as unreliable (or even more so) as the psychiatrists that he is quick to criticize as "charlatans" who presume to give everyone else

the big answers to life's questions. Dobel yearns to be a comedy writer but is stuck in a teaching job and never seems any closer to achieving his dream.

Dobel is in essence Jerry's true therapist and even urges Jerry to spy on Amanda when he suspects her of infidelity. When Jerry stakes out her acting class and discovers that she is indeed cheating, the aftermath makes him feel worse. In her most earnest voice, Amanda claims that she cheated to see if she could even be aroused anymore and in essence did it for both of them. More befuddled than ever, Jerry heeds her absurd pleas to stay with her.

Jerry is also saddled with an agent named Harvey (Danny DeVito), who works solely for him (at a whopping 25 percent cut) and who Jerry should cut loose but feels guilty letting go. A throwaway role that does not add much to the film, Harvey is just one more example of Jerry's inability to cut the ties that hold him down. When, at Dobel's urging, Jerry finally lets him go, Harvey practically has a heart attack in a crowded restaurant.

In the turning point of the story, Dobel persuades Jerry to forsake everyone and everything in New York City to join him as a team to write for TV in California—the idea of quintessential New Yorker Allen urging his young alter ego to leave the Big Apple for California is yet another inspired bit of comedy tweaking the familiar Allen persona.

As Jerry breaks up with Amanda, she simultaneously breaks up with him, telling him that she met someone else and would rather leave than cheat on him. Then Dobel splits from Jerry, backing out of the California trip because he shot a state trooper over an anti-Semitic comment and now has to go into hiding. Jerry never finds out if this outlandish story is true, but leaves for California anyway. On his way to the airport, he happens to glimpse, in the film's final comic twist, Amanda with her new boyfriend, the emergency room doctor.

At film's end, Jerry looks back on all the advice Dobel has given him and recalls his mentor's admonition, "Whenever you write, strive for originality, but if you have to steal, steal from the best." This finally is what Allen has done in *Anything Else*. Having previously paid homage to Bergman in *Interiors* and Fellini in *Stardust Memories*, Allen now pays homage to himself, stealing from one of his classics to create a charming, bittersweet romance full of funny one-liners. While it does not reach new heights, *Anything Else* occupies a comfortable middle ground in the Allen canon and is a welcome reminder of a time when angst-filled relationships moved him to create his most enduring works.

—*Peter N. Chumo II*

CREDITS

Jerry Falk: Jason Biggs

Amanda: Christina Ricci
David Dobel: Woody Allen
Paula: Stockard Channing
Harvey: Danny DeVito
Bob: Jimmy Fallon
Connie: Erica Leerhsen
Dr. Reed: David Conrad
Brooke: KaDee Strickland
Ray Polito: Adrian Grenier

Origin: USA
Released: 2003
Production: Letty Aronson; Gravier Productions, Perdido; released by Dreamworks Pictures
Directed by: Woody Allen
Written by: Woody Allen
Cinematography by: Darius Khondji
Sound: Gary Alper
Editing: Alisa Lepselter
Art Direction: Tom Warren
Costumes: Laura Jean Shannon
Production Design: Santo Loquasto
MPAA rating: R
Running time: 108 minutes

REVIEWS

Chicago Sun-Times Online. September 19, 2003.
Entertainment Weekly. September 26, 2003, p. 76.
Los Angeles Times Online. September 19, 2003.
New York Times Online. September 19, 2003.
People. September 29, 2003, p. 33.
USA Today Online. September 19, 2003.
Variety Online. August 27, 2003.
Washington Post. September 19, 2003, p. WE43.

Assassination Tango

No one is more dangerous than the man who lives two lives.
—Movie tagline

 Box Office: $1 million

Robert Duvall has had a long and distinguished career spanning four decades, from *To Kill a Mockingbird* to *Apocalypse Now* to *Tender Mercies* (and a best actor Oscar) and *The Apostle.* He's generally played hard-bitten tough guys with gentle hearts, and his sympathetic role as the last of a breed of range riders in *Open Range* displayed all his best qualities as an actor: his understated, believable compassion and humanity wrapped up in a quirky, unforgettable character.

In addition to his acting efforts, Duvall wrote and directed *Angelo, My Love* in 1984, and received Oscar nominations and acclaim in 1997 for his portrayal of a Southern preacher in *The Apostle,* his second writing and directing effort. Fortunately, his third try at writing and directing, *Assassination Tango,* was a mere blip on the radar screen when it opened in the spring of 2003. The movie came and went in near-record time, and few people saw it, luckily for Duvall—the film is a flat-out embarrassment for a man with such a distinguished career.

Unfortunately, to begin with, the title *Assassination Tango* is rather misleading. This film is about tango dancing . . . and about a hit man who commits an assassination, but the two topics have nothing to do with each other. The assassination plot is just a device to get Duvall's lead to Buenos Aires so he can see a lot of tango dancers.

This is a vanity project with a capital "V." While it's true that Duvall himself is a devotee (he dances the tango every day), his assumption that other people will be interested in watching tango dancers and listening to inane discussions about the dance betrays a lack of perspective about the topic. It would have been better, actually, if Duvall had made a documentary about the tango—then at least the movie would have provided exactly what was expected, and tango afficionados could have seen it while others stayed away.

Instead, we get a weak thriller interspersed with disconnected and inconsequential tango sequences. There is nothing thrilling about the thriller—one of the most mundane plots ever written. Duvall plays John Anderson, a hit man for a New York gangster named Frankie (Frank Gio). John's been around the block a few times, but he has recently settled down with Maggie (Kathy Baker), a teacher who doesn't know about John's real line of work. John's smitten with Maggie's ten-year-old daughter and is making big plans for her birthday.

But Frankie has a job for John in Argentina, with money too good to pass up. About the best thing in this awful film is that Frankie doesn't have to convince John to come out of retirement and do one last hit—that old crime-film chestnut doesn't come out of the fire. John's only real concern is that the job is airtight and he can get back in time for the kid's birthday. Frankie assures him it's a quick three-day in-and-out, but, of course, when John arrives in Buenos Aires he's informed that the target—a former general wanted dead by victims of his inhumane misdeeds during an earlier period of military rule—won't be back from the countryside for three weeks.

This gives Duvall plenty of time to spend watching tango dancers. Although his character professes to be a dancer, he swears he's never seen tango performed like this, and he lurks in theaters and clubs. Soon enough he latches onto an attractive young dancer, Manuela (Luciana Pedraza). She takes him to her sister for a tango lesson, there's a conversation in a coffee shop, and then, apparently, the assassin and the dancer engage in an affair, although we never see any sex. It is at this point in the vanity project that the vanity becomes inexcusable: Pedraza is Duvall's real-life girlfriend, and this is her first film role.

It's not that Pedraza is so bad, though she certainly lacks dramatic intensity. (In fact, she's better than Duvall.) It's just that now the picture is complete: Duvall has written, directed, and starred in a movie that gives him an excuse to cast his girlfriend as the leading lady and do the tango with her. Notice, however, that all their tango sequences are done in slow motion; the suspicion is that they're actually not that proficient a pair of dancers.

The other dancers, including a number of the best tango dancers in Argentina, *are* good, and they are a pleasure to watch. But their performances would have been much more fun to watch if they weren't serving as filler for a slow, creaky plot in which nothing much is happening. The choreography is by Miguel Angel Zotto, one of the top tango dancers in the world, but Duvall doesn't even direct most of the tango sequences in a compelling way. Instead of sweeping us into the dance, his camera remains static and distant.

Worse yet, he indulges himself further with a dinner-club conversation about the dance with one of tango's top female performers. In Spanish, she tells us, apropos of nothing, that the tango "is life, is love, is hate . . . is everything." Duvall's John cracks an obscure joke about a tango man whose last dance before he died was called "Adios, Muchachos." His tango expert in turn grabs her breasts and advises him to grab his testicles because that is apparently the only proper response to raising this subject, which seems to be taboo.

It's unclear whether Duvall has actually written much dialogue, especially his own. His character constantly interrupts, mutters, repeats questions, and makes inane asides and comments. Apparently Duvall is trying for some kind of conversational realism, but he goes overboard, instead making the conversations almost unintelligible and always annoying. His talk with Pedraza's Manuela in the cafe is one of the most awkward romance-igniters ever filmed. Instead of cleverly flirting, they ask blunt, insipid questions: "Are you married? Do you cheat?" When Manuela makes it clear she is available, John simply mumbles, "Wow," and then asks to drink her coffee. You'd think there might be chemistry between these two, but instead there is only clumsy awkwardness.

Unfortunately, the limp and murky assassination plot is unable to provide any sort of excitement. John has been hired to avenge the death of a couple's son at the hands of the much-hated general. Orchestrating the plot is Miguel (Ruben Blades), whose relationship to the enterprise isn't at all clear. John also makes contact with a mobster who runs a boxing gym—above a tango studio, of course—and who is his link with Frankie. This guy implies that Miguel can't be trusted, so John switches rooms and, sure enough, his former room is raided.

John, Miguel, and others discuss the plot several times in stilted, unnecessary scenes. John climbs to a platform overlooking the villa where the general is to be shot while taking 6 o'clock tea in his garden. John goes there repeatedly to check out the range; you'd think a hit man might be concerned about appearing over and over again at the crime scene, but not in this movie. In the end, however, John decides something is amiss, and he dons an unconvincing disguise, shoots the general's guard, and walks into the garden and kills his target point-blank.

It's never made clear who was double-crossing him, or what role Miguel played, but now John can't trust his handlers and he's not sure how to get out of the country. He hides out in his room, but goes back to his old room to get a pair of riding boots he bought for his girlfriend's daughter, almost gets caught, and then, back in his room, he berates himself: "Why did I do that? I could have just bought another pair." It's pretty embarrassing dialogue.

Just when you think Duvall may have finally cooked up some real suspense and there might be some action scenes concerning his escape, John simply boards a ferry to Montevideo, Uruguay, clears customs with only a minor skirmish, and boards a plane home, where he reunites with Frankie and reconnects with Maggie and her daughter. There's a resounding thud covered up by another tango danced for the closing credits.

Assassination Tango is a sad affair. Duvall's direction is amateurish, his writing is wretched, and his acting is an embarrassment. He looks ridiculous with slicked-back gray hair tied into a small ponytail and walks with a pronounced bowlegged and ungainly gait, making him look like a cowboy trying to play a suave mobster. He doesn't utter a dramatic or memorable line throughout the entire film, instead filling the soundtrack with blabbering and mumbled ad-libs. No other director in the world would have tolerated such a performance.

Scene after scene is clumsily shot, puzzlingly framed, and ineffectively edited. It's hard to believe an accomplished professional could produce something this awful. During the tango sequences, the plot doesn't just stall, it stops completely while we watch some dancing. There is no connection between the tango dancers and the assassination, nothing to join together the two disparate threads of the title.

Somehow Duvall convinced Francis Ford Coppola's American Zoetrope Studios to produce this sorry excuse for a movie. Reputation may go a long way, but Duvall ends up looking like a silly old man indulging his whims at the audience's expense. Had the screenplay not been written by an established star, the script would have been rejected; meanwhile many promising young writers with great ideas can't get a foot in Hollywood's door. It's unfair. Hopefully, few people will notice what happened here, for *Assassination Tango* is the cinematic equivalent of vanity publishing; only the "author" and his immediate family and friends should have to witness this debacle.

—*Michael Betzold*

CREDITS

John J. Anderson: Robert Duvall
Miguel: Ruben Blades
Maggie: Kathy Baker
Manuela: Luciana Pedraza
Orlando: Julio Oscar Mechoso
Whitey: James Keane
Frankie: Frank Gio
Jenny: Katherine Micheaux Miller

Origin: USA
Released: 2003
Production: Robert Duvall, Rob Carliner; American Zoetrope; released by United Artists
Directed by: Robert Duvall
Written by: Robert Duvall
Cinematography by: Felix Monti
Music by: Luis Bacalov
Sound: Ben Cheah
Music Supervisor: Charlie Feldman
Editing: Stephen Mack
Costumes: Beatriz di Benedetto
Production Design: Stefania Cella
MPAA rating: R
Running time: 114 minutes

 REVIEWS

Boxoffice. November, 2002, p. 126.
Chicago Sun-Times Online. April 4, 2003.
Entertainment Weekly. April 4, 2003, p. 77.
Los Angeles Times Online. March 28, 2003.
New York Times Online. March 28, 2003.
Vanity Fair. April, 2003, p. 162.
Variety Online. September 10, 2002.
Washington Post. April 4, 2003, p. C5.

Bad Boys 2

 Box Office: $138.3 million

Whatever may have been the merits of 1995's *Bad Boys,* starring Will Smith and Martin Lawrence, *Bad Boys II* follows the worst path that a sequel can take. For that matter, it follows the worst path *any* movie can take, substituting meaningless action and violence for story and then mistaking superficial character conflict for development. While the movie is often visually "slick," as a whole it is little more than a tedious, loud, often irritating conflagration of mayhem, mean-spiritedness, and morbid gore. As many sequels do, *Bad Boys II* opened to big business, but ultimately the movie failed to become the blockbuster its makers hoped it would be (the movie was made on a budget of $130 million). Almost universally disliked by critics, the movie is the quintessential "mindless" action flick, the kind of movie that is made for the sole purpose of capitalizing on the popularity of its predecessor. Even though the movie runs a painfully dragged-out 146 minutes, there is only minimal plot to speak of (and almost no exposition), though there is certainly a lot of movement and a lot of talk. Characters are neither likeable nor developed; even action scenes, which seem to exist simply for their own sake, are so clumsily constructed that they make little sense. As critic Roger Ebert put it, "The movie has a carelessness that shows contempt for the audience." Indeed, *Bad Boys II* is characterized throughout by a lack of respect—respect for the characters, respect for an engaging storyline, respect for human life, and respect for the intelligence of the audience.

Will Smith and Martin Lawrence play Mike Lowrey and Marcus Burnett, respectively, two Miami cops who are supposed to be best friends but who never really get along with each other throughout the entire movie. Gabrielle Union plays Marcus' sister Sydney (Syd), a DEA agent from New York who's visiting the family in Miami but is really there doing undercover work. Unbeknownst to Marcus, Mike and Syd became involved romantically when Mike recently traveled to New York. Even though Marcus has been going to counseling to help him deal with stress (the movie never makes the exact reasoning clear) and lauds the positive effect it has supposedly had on him, Mike is unwilling to risk his partner's wrath by telling him about his relationship with Syd. Apparently this plot line is supposed to bring some sort of character development to the chaotic and shallow story, but it serves to do little other than make the movie longer than it already is. The relationship between Mike and Syd receives only cursory screen time and is transparently superficial. Plus, Syd is the only likeable and halfway sympathetic character of the three, so one is hard-pressed to care about her relationship with Mike.

The three of them wind up entangled in the same case, an attempt to root out and stop a nasty drug supplier, Hector "Johnny" Tapia (Jordi Mollà), a cruel and crazy Latin evil-doer who is making big plans to move to a mansion in Cuba. Tapia's operation uses a mortuary as a cover, moving money by hiding it in caskets and transporting drugs by hiding them in cadavers (a "brilliant" idea someone came up with apparently so the movie could have one of its most morbid and unnecessarily stomach-churning scenes). Tapia has eluded capture by the Miami police for years, which is why the DEA covertly sends its New York agents to snag him without letting the local cops in on their plans. Mike and Marcus discover the DEA's presence and Syd's involvement when they just happen to witness her fleeing from a gang of hit men after a planned meeting with Tapia's men goes awry.

A long car chase ensues as Syd tries to get away from the hit men, Mike and Marcus in hot pursuit to save her. Subscribing to the belief that a good action movie can't go without a huge car chase scene that at least attempts to outdo all other car chase scenes, the filmmakers turn this sequence into one of the longest and most ridiculous parts of the movie. Speeding through heavy traffic, the hunted, the hunters, and the rescuers cause huge car pile-ups. Seemingly every car that gets in the way ends up flipping over or being crushed. At one point, after the hit men commandeer a trailer carrying new cars, Mike and Marcus are shocked to see the bad guys dropping automobiles onto the freeway right in front of them. Evidently this sequence is supposed to be a "wow 'em" scene for those select viewers who enjoy watching rampant destruction, but ultimately the scene stretches on for so long, and so many cars are destroyed, that eventually it loses all of its shock value. Additionally, the sequence is symptomatic of a disturbing pattern running throughout the film; obviously all the crashed and destroyed cars are carrying passengers, prompting one to wonder how many people would have died in all the mayhem. Yet Mike and Marcus show virtually no regret—and definitely no restraint—in the face of all the destruction, injury, and certain death to which they are contributing. "This is sick," Marcus says at one point, though the sentiment seems merely obligatory. "It's about to get sicker," Mike replies. Unfortunately, these words seem applicable to the film itself.

The simplistic plot of the movie becomes bewilderingly muddled as Mike and Marcus track down the men who tried to kill Syd. When the duo finds the men in an old house, a bloody shootout leaves all but one dead. Yet, inexplicably, Mike and Marcus learn nothing from the survivor and the movie never attempts to explain who these people were or why they were trying to kill the DEA agents. The entire sequence seems included simply as an excuse for another pointless shootout and more gratuitous bloodletting.

The bloodshed and gore continues to worsen when Mike and Marcus infiltrate Tapia's house, disguised as exterminators, to wire the place. While they are there, a meeting between Tapia and the Russian club owner turns ugly when Tapia has the Russian's closest associate chopped into bits and brought before him in a leaking trash can (once again, there's no clear reason for this, except maybe to show how wicked and dangerous Tapia can be). Mike doesn't see the chopped-up body but he does come across the blood-splattered kitchen where the slaughter took place and there he finds a solitary finger that was inadvertently left behind. Meanwhile, in the attic laying wires, Marcus witnesses two rats having sex and is amazed that "they [do it] like us!" Unfortunately, the audience must witness it, too.

Just as Mike predicted earlier, it gets "sicker." After making a connection between Tapia and the mortuary, Mike and Marcus hit the road in pursuit of a van carrying corpses. The scene turns into yet another senseless display of morbidity, presented as humor, when corpses fall out of the vehicle, only to be run over (and even decapitated) by Mike's Ferrari. Later, when the two cops sneak into the mortuary to find evidence, the viewer is treated to shots of slit-open cadavers, the top third of a head falling off into the floor, and Marcus climbing onto a gurney alongside a naked female corpse in order to hide from mortuary workers. They do in fact discover money and drugs, but that plot point is swallowed in the "humor" of the scene.

When Mike and Marcus take pictures and videos from their discovery to their captain (Joe Pantoliano), he is disgusted and vows that it is time to bring Tapia down. The captain subsequently enlists the aid of a S.W.A.T. team to stop a shipment of money to Tapia, but soon thereafter, Tapia kidnaps Syd and takes her to Cuba. "This shit just got real," Mike proclaims. Never mind, of course, all the other people who have died up to this point—evidently none of what has transpired so far really mattered to Mike since it did not touch him personally. What happens next is so predictable (and by this point, so tedious) that it could have come straight out of a dozen other action movies. Mike, Marcus, Syd's DEA partners, and apparently every other available cop heads to Cuba to rescue Syd. In the process, Tapia's extravagant mansion is leveled and Tapia himself is killed—blown up, actually.

The basic plot of *Bad Boys II* is so simplistic and over-used that the story could have been told in a ninety-minute movie, but the filmmakers chose to compensate for the weak story by moving erratically from place to place (figuratively and literally) and attempting to fill in the gaps with ugly, morbid humor, chaotic and meaningless violence, and superficial bickering posing as genuine character development. Supposedly Mike and Marcus are best friends, but Marcus truly seems to despise Mike (he threatens to break up their partnership, he calls Mike a "dog" when he learns of the relationship between Mike and his sister, and he accuses

Mike of always trying to "take over" when he visits the family). The premise that the two are actually friends is not borne out in the story, as Marcus never really acts like he enjoys Mike's company. Along the same lines, neither Marcus nor Mike is particularly likeable. They both seem psychotic at times, and they are very rarely humorous even when the filmmakers expect the audience to laugh at or with them. The inclusion of Sydney is likewise a ploy to cover up the weaknesses in the plot and to pretend that there is actual depth to the characters or their superficial development.

One of the most disturbing things about *Bad Boys II,* however, is its pervasive lack of respect for human life. As previously mentioned, Mike and Marcus hardly seem to be ethical or moral enough to serve as police officers, and in reality, they would have lost their badges many times over for their persistent disregard for the life and safety of people around them. Nothing seems sacred to them, and they learn nothing through their experiences. They are neither heroes nor anti-heroes—though, in a movie like this, one should not expect the sophistication necessary to include anti-heroes. Yet their attitudes are just part of a pattern that characterizes the entire film, most blatantly obvious in the ultra-destructive car chases and the scenes with the human corpses. What is amazing is that the filmmakers clearly thought these elements were either entertaining or humorous. The nature of the movie suggests that the filmmakers were not trying to do anything meaningful; there is no underlying theme to the violence, and the morbid humor is not genuine dark humor, which certainly has its place in cinema. It is all simply too clumsy, too chaotic, too thin, and definitely too long.

—David Flanagin

Production: Jerry Bruckheimer; released by Columbia Pictures
Directed by: Michael Bay
Written by: Ron Shelton, Jerry Stahl
Cinematography by: Amir M. Mokri
Sound: Peter J. Devlin
Music Supervisor: Kathy Nelson, Bob Badami
Editing: Mark Goldblatt, Roger Barton, Thomas A. Muldoon
Art Direction: Bradford Ricker, J. Mark Harrington, David Lazan
Costumes: Deborah L. Scott, Carol Ramsey
Production Design: Dominic Watkins
MPAA rating: R
Running time: 146 minutes

REVIEWS

Chicago Sun-Times Online. July 18, 2003.
Entertainment Weekly. July 25, 2003, p. 49.
Los Angeles Times Online. July 18, 2003.
New York Times Online. July 18, 2003.
People. July 28, 2003, p. 29.
USA Today Online. July 18, 2003.
Variety Online. July 13, 2003.
Washington Post. July 18, 2003, p. WE31.

QUOTES

Mike (Will Smith) to Marcus (Martin Lawrence): "We ride together. We die together."

CREDITS

Det. Marcus Burnett: Will Smith
Det. Mike Lowrey: Martin Lawrence
Sydney "Syd" Burnett: Gabrielle Union
Captain Howard: Joe Pantoliano
Theresa Burnett: Theresa Randle
Hector "Johnny" Tapla: Jordi Molla
Alexei: Peter Stormare
Floyd Poteet: Michael Shannon
Roberto: Jon Seda
Det. Mateo Reyes: Yul Vazquez
TNT Leader: Henry Rollins
Det. Marco Vargas: Jason Manuel Olazabel
Carlos: Otto Sanchez

Origin: USA
Released: 2003

Bad Santa

He doesn't care if you're naughty or nice.
—Movie tagline

 Box Office: $59.5 million

Willie T. Soke (Billy Bob Thornton) makes an especially disturbing image of Santa as he sits tossing them back in O'Hara's Pub, dressed in his shabby red suit, his fleecy white beard abandoned to expose his stubbled, haggard face. As his voiceover explains, however, his father taught him to crack safes, not celebrate Christmas. So what's Willie doing playing Santa Claus to hundreds of hopeful children at the local shopping mall? What's he doing besides drinking alcohol and insulting the kids? He and his elf pal Marcus (Tony Cox) are planning to rob the store after it closes. Their m.o. has Marcus foiling the alarm system while Willie cracks the safe. In one night the pair clear over $100,000 dollars, enough to float them through the year until next Christmas, when they pull the same scam again at another shopping mall.

Willie dreams of using his money to open a bar on a nice warm beach somewhere, say Miami, but it appears that every year he drinks away his profits and when Marcus calls with the next Santa job he's forced to go. This year the duo is working in Chamberlain's department store in Phoenix, where they have been hired by store manager Bob Shipetska (John Ritter) but are being watched over by the chain-smoking, orange-eating head of security Gin Slagel (Bernie Mac).

One day, while doing his usual haphazard job of asking kids what they want for Christmas, Willie finds a most unappealing little boy (Brett Kelly) on his lap. In serious need of a handkerchief, the overweight kid barely manages to get his request to Santa before being scooted along for the next child. After his grueling day, Willie sets off for the nearest bar to find his own form of Christmas cheer. There he finds a comely bartender, Sue (Lauren Graham) who, because her father was Jewish, has "always had a thing for Santa." It's not long before these two are "celebrating" Christmas in the back seat of a car in the parking lot. When they emerge from their revelry, however, Willie is attacked by a nut job (Ajay Naidu) who is off his medication. Luckily for Willie, that snot-nosed little kid is there to help him.

The next day at work Bob catches Willie having sex with a woman in a dressing room, but is too tentative to do much about it himself. Heck, this guy has to spell all the naughty words he'll need to describe Willie's actions when he alerts Gin. It soon becomes obvious, though, that Gin may not be the upstanding person one would want their head of security to be.

When Willie returns to his motel room after work that day he is surprised to find the police there. Looking for a place to hide, without blowing the next robbery, Willie makes his way back to The Kid's house. The Kid, who is obviously starved for affection, is delighted to have Santa staying with him. He lives in a comfortable up-scale home in the suburbs with his permanently zoned-out grandmother (Cloris Leachman). As The Kid explains, his mother is dead and his father is off exploring mountains until next year. This is an opportunity Willie can't pass up and he robs the family's safe and takes their car.

As it becomes more and more obvious that Willie is an emotional cripple, it also becomes more obvious that The Kid has built his own emotional walls, too. For example, he seems impervious to everything: the taunting of bullies, Santa's swearing and abuse, the neglect of his grandmother, or even the fact that he hasn't had a Christmas gift in two

years. The reason for this last fact is that The Kid's father isn't really climbing mountains, he is in prison serving 3-6 years for embezzlement.

Willie soon finds the pathetic kid slowly worming his way into his deadened heart (which is also being mended by the attentions of bartender Sue). For example, even after he has thoroughly trashed and eaten all the candy in The Kid's prized Advent calendar while drunk, Willie tries to make amends by taping it back together and substituting everything from candy corn to aspirin for the chocolate he has so thoughtlessly eaten. But for Willie, er, excuse me, Santa, the Kid is more than willing to put up with anything.

Needless to say, anything that eventually touches Willie's heart will also eventually cause him to change his mind about the kind of life he leads. But just as Willie tries to back out, Gin catches on to everything and demands a half of the take, and Marcus turns on Willie, forcing him to finish the job.

What happens to Gin and Willie and Marcus is best left for the movie to tell, and what's so startling about this blacker than black comedy is how well it tells the story. What could have been an incredibly distasteful entry in the Christmas film register is actually a wickedly funny, and sharply told story . . . although it probably won't be to everyone's taste.

One good indicator that *Bad Santa*'s pedigree may not be from Hollywood central is that its executive producers are Joel and Ethan Coen. Known for such quirky films as *Raising Arizona* and *O Brother, Where Art Thou*, the Coen Brothers are not known for catering to mainstream demands. Envisioning a character such as those the curmudgeonly Wallace Berry used to play in the 1930s crossed with Walter Matthau's equally curmudgeonly Coach Buttermaker from *The Bad News Bears*, the Coens, who also came up with the general idea for the movie, sum it up as "A bad Santa suddenly changes." (And by the way, from the publicity it would seem that the film's title should be said in the same tone of voice one would use when admonishing one's dog after it had pooped on the rug: "Bad Santa!")

Like the Coens, director Terry Zwigoff is also known for films that are a little off-center. His cult-hit *Ghost World* and offbeat documentary *Crumb* would seem to indicate his connection to characters—both real and fictional—who themselves are a little off-center, a little on the edges of society, but who, once they are known better, reveal great heart underneath their unconventional exteriors.

It's hard to believe that this deranged and stubbornly funny, take-no-prisoners comedy comes from the minds of John Requa and Glenn Ficarra who co-wrote 2001's *Cats & Dogs*. How did their PG credentials ever indicate they could so sharply tell such a subversive Christmas tale? And sharply told it is. Listen to the music of the dialogue, the poetry of the voiceovers. They are works of art.

With the seeds of the story coming from the Coen Brothers, an appropriately twisted vision provided by director Zwigoff, and an incredibly irreverent follow through from Requa and Glenn, it only remains for the actors to bring this wicked vision to the screen.

Great credit must go to Billy Bob Thornton who, although he has a history of playing unsavory characters, outdoes himself here. In an uncompromising way, Zwigoff presents Willie as a pretty nasty character right from the start. We have no sympathy for this drunken, unkempt, mean-spirited loser in a slovenly Santa suit. Even though a voiceover tells us of his crummy childhood and dispirited life, it doesn't make us like him any better. Willie hates himself and we're inclined to do likewise. It is to Thornton's credit that even while disliking the main character we're compelled to follow his story.

Similarly off-putting is The Kid as played by Brett Kelly, whose appropriately pathetic name (Thurman Merman) remains unknown until near the end of the film. Kelly almost lost the chance to appear in the film when he couldn't make a call-back audition because he came down with a case of highly contagious chicken pox. Luckily the filmmakers were so impressed with Brett's first audition that they waited for him. It paid off. Brett is wonderful as a boy who is miraculously oblivious to Willie's flaws because he is so desperate for affection. Who better than Santa to fill his needs? And who better than Brett to play Santa's stalker, who will eventually change him through sheer persistence and not through lovability and sincerity?

The casting, even in smaller parts, also helps to make *Bad Santa* the prize that it is. Tony Cox's diminutive stature hides a prodigious planning ability and more than a little mean streak. Lauren Tom's mail-order bride greediness, Lauren Graham's Sue being introduced to The Kid as "Mrs. Santa's sister" when she's brought home for a bit of naughtiness, and Bernie Mac's theft of a shoplifting kid's MP3 player as his version of justice all have the ring of an uncompromising but twisted reality. Even Cloris Leachman's hilariously comatose grandmother with a penchant for making sandwiches hits just the right notes.

Special mention, though, should be given to John Ritter's store manager. While it is just a small part, a timid man afraid of angering anyone, it is expertly played by Ritter, a long-time friend of Thornton's since their *Sling Blade* days, who gives his last performance here. The film is dedicated to him.

Bad Santa is an unorthodox gem. Occasionally the editing seems a little jumpy, but that can be explained by the fact that Zwigoff had to make cuts to the film in order to avoid an NC-17 rating. It does, however, make one wonder what was cut. (It's also said that Zwigoff wants nothing to do with the "happy" ending that the studio requested.)

This film is one of those rare comedies in which the laughter originates within the characters themselves and not from the external gags they have to perform. We recognize that Willie is in an existential hell of his own making, but that doesn't mean he can't have one wicked sense of humor about it all.

Bad Santa takes our expectations about Christmas movies, twists them fearlessly and irreverently, and the result is one very funny movie that is bound to generate more than its share of contention and outright offense. But if sometimes Christmas brings out the "bah, humbugs" in you then this movie might be just the medicine you're looking for.

—*Beverley Bare Buehrer*

CREDITS

Willie T. Stokes: Billy Bob Thornton
Marcus: Tony Cox
Sue: Lauren Graham
The Kid: Brett Kelly
Bob Chipeska: John Ritter
Gin Slagel: Bernie Mac
Lois: Lauren Tom
Grandma: Cloris Leachman

Origin: USA
Released: 2003
Production: Bob Weinstein, John Cameron, Sarah Aubrey; Triptych Pictures; released by Dimension Films
Directed by: Terry Zwigoff
Written by: Glenn Ficarra, John Requa
Cinematography by: Jamie Anderson
Music by: David Kitay
Sound: Marc Weingarten, Lee Orloff
Music Supervisor: Rachel Levy
Editing: Robert Hoffman
Art Direction: Peter Borck
Costumes: Wendy Chuck
Production Design: Sharon Seymour
MPAA rating: R
Running time: 91 minutes

REVIEWS

Chicago Sun-Times Online. November 26, 2003.
Entertainment Weekly. November 28, 2003, p. 101.
Los Angeles Times Online. November 26, 2003.
New York Times Online. November 26, 2003.
People. December 1, 2003, p. 29.
Rolling Stone. December 11, 2003, p. 213.
USA Today Online. November 26, 2003.
Variety Online. November 17, 2003.
Washington Post. November 26, 2003, p. C1.

AWARDS AND NOMINATIONS

Nomination:
Golden Globes 2004: Actor—Mus./Comedy (Thornton).

The Barbarian Invasions (Les Invasions Barbares)

A provocative new comedy about sex, friendship, and all the other things that invade our lives.
—Movie tagline

Canadian intellectual filmmaker Denys Arcand's bittersweet comedy, *The Barbarian Invasions,* is built around a brilliant premise: that socialist thought can offer no spiritual sustenance. Arcand, however, swathes this idea with his own brand of sophisticated film storytelling, which he first introduced in *The Decline of the American Empire* (1986). In fact, many of the characters in *Invasions* are from that earlier film, and are also played by the same actors. This menagerie of the worldly-wise revolves around the film's central character, Remy (Remy Girard), a middle-aged historian fighting a losing battle with cancer. But Remy's socialist fervor has a nationalist tinge. He would rather meet his end in Montreal than seek better treatment in the U.S. "I voted for Medicare," he barks, "and now I must endure the consequences!"

But whether he's prepared to accept it or not, life for Remy has come to a grinding halt. His devoted son, Sebastien (Stephane Rousseau), a nondescript yuppie, employed as a successful stock market expert in London, is called to be by his side. It so happens that Remy hates him, calling him a "puritanical capitalist," and lumping him together with all the other "barbarians" in the film's title, whom he detests and fears at the same time.

On one level, Remy's plight, in the film's discursive scheme, finds its objective correlative in one bit of recent history, which the film presents with rare documentary footage. That historical nodal point occurs when the second plane hit the World Trade Center. We see it approaching from behind the camera and striking the building perpendicularly. Arcand, however, falls short of using that traumatic moment to throw light on the interaction between the political and the personal and thus he ends up exploiting it in a near-sensationalistic manner.

Furthermore, what gets discounted as part of the background to Arcand's filmic fiction is the barbarian ability, in this particular instance, to use the very technologies and apparatuses of civilization against the civilized, whereas the barbarians in previous epochs, the ones that Remy keeps referring to, could only use their own brand of force. Yet Remy, and therefore Arcand, does not seem to perceive this distinction.

Arcand's intellectual hodgepodge would have made for dreary viewing indeed if Remy had not emerged as such a colorful character, clean-shaven head and all. The antithesis of anyone's image of a senior professor, Remy finds all his knowledge culminating in erotic license. Once happily married, he now brags of a string of mistresses. Gathered by Remy's hospital bedside, yet apparently having long since given up on him and his lecherous ways, are his still attractive ex-wife, the dark-haired and congenial Louise (Dorothee Berryman), and two ex-mistresses, including the slightly jowly Diane (Louise Portal) and the plump Dominique (Dominique Michel).

Despite its supporting cast of intelligent characters, the narrative axis of the film is structured around the eventual reconciliation between father and son. Sebastien feels his first duty, upon his arrival with beautiful girlfriend Gaelle (Marina Hands) in tow, is to find a private room for his father in the congested hospital laboring under Canada's socialized public health system. However, before he can do that, he has to accompany Remy in a special ambulance to Baltimore for tests, for which he's prepared to bear the costs. On the way to Baltimore and back, each conversation that Sebastien has on his cell phone with his office in London rankles Remy, and, at first, when Sebastien admits that he's there because of Louise, Remy retorts, "Go to hell!"

When the two return to Montreal, Sebastien lets Remy have his own laptop, so that he can look at a streaming video of his daughter, Sylvaine (Isabelle Blais), who is sailing the Pacific. Her affection moves Remy to no end. Meanwhile, Sebastien, in his efforts to get a private room, is given the runaround not just by the hospital administration, but by the union concerned. Eventually, he realizes that it is only bribery that works. However, the little bonding that could have taken place between father and son at this stage is shattered when Remy ends up losing the laptop. This puts Sebastien in a tizzy since he cannot now access his e-mail.

It is at this point that Arcand interjects the World Trade Center footage. Remy, historian that he is, appears to remain unmoved by this barbaric event. He rants to the Catholic nurse, Sister Constance (Johanne Marie Tremblay), that the genocide of 200 million that took place on the American continent, beginning in the 16th Century at the hands of the Spaniards, has not been memorialized in even "the tiniest holocaust museum."

The next section of the film is then set into motion as Remy is visited by Claude (Yves Jacques) and Claude's homosexual lover, Alessandro (Toni Cecchinato). Claude in *Decline* was a struggling graduate student. Here, he is well ensconced as the Director General of the Canadian University Institute of Rome. Soon to join Remy is the paunchy and jovial Pierre (Pierre Curzi), a former colleague from *Decline*, who has traded in his bohemian ways in order to settle down with the much younger and very beautiful Ghislaine (Mitsou), with whom he now has two babies. These well-wishers provide cheer, but they remain helpless to do anything about Remy's physiological pain, which seems to strike all of a sudden.

That task is again left to Sebastien, who is told that the only thing that can help is heroin which, in its pure form, is 800 per cent stronger than morphine. The quest for this illegal substance brings Sebastien into contact with the film's most interesting character under forty: the darkly attractive Natalie (Marie-Josee Croze), Diane's estranged daughter, a drug addict who makes a living as a proofreader. Sebastien drives her through the night streets to a seedy part of town. While waiting alone in the car as she goes off to score, he is accosted by Inspector Levac (Roy Dupuis), who he had approached earlier for the same purpose. Levac assures Sebastien that he does not have to fear arrest. It seems there are too many neoimmigrants who have taken to dealing in such contraband. "The Lebanese, the Iraqis, the Turks . . . ," Levac says, then adds, "It's a regular invasion." Remy, however, benefits from this invasion, as Natalie instructs him to inhale the vapor off a foil while she heats the thick brown powder on it from below. The next morning, Remy is back to his ebullient self. He tells his surprised doctor that he needs no painkillers.

To the amused audience by his bedside, Remy holds forth on the autoerotic fantasies of his life. Foremost among them is the Italian actress Ines Orsini, portraying the Portugese saint Maria Goretti in a film on the saint's life. The scene Remy cannot forget is when she lifts her thick black skirts as she walks into the water on a beach. Arcand shows us the actual black-and-white footage. Orsini, we learn, was later replaced during the years by the likes of Francoise Hardy, Julie Christie and Chris Evert.

When alone with Natalie, Remy ruefully confesses his regrets: He could have written books, instead he chased women. In a moment alone with Gaelle, the latter admits to Remy how she has no faith in love, that the very concept is just "pop song philosophy," that being the child of a broken home, she came to know first hand what love can lead to.

There is also a brief digression in which Gaelle, who works for an auction house in London, looks at religious artifacts in the basement of a Catholic church in Montreal. She finds nothing of value as an antique for the world market. Presumably, this scene is intended to show the decay of religion taking place around Remy.

Wisely, Arcand provides a counterpoint to the hospital room Remy seems to be trapped in. Sebastien accompanies him to Pierre's house in the country. On the way, Remy gets him to stop beside a lake. There, Remy is left alone to contemplate from his wheelchair the tranquil beauty of nature.

The final section of the film shifts the action to Pierre's house, where the incurable Remy, aided by his entourage of friends, will meet his end peacefully. After scenes of erudite conversation and bonhomie, father and son finally come together. Remy tells Sebastien that his wish is for him to "have as fine a son as you." Soon Remy decides he's ready for the end. What seems to solidify Remy's acceptance is a freshly received streaming video from Sylvaine in which she tearfully admits, "You'll always be with me!" After being administered a set of euthanasic injections by Natalie, whom he calls his "guardian angel," Remy closes his eyes for the last time. Arcand cuts to the black and white footage of Orsini wading into the water.

In an epilogue of sorts, Sebastien helps Natalie, who is undergoing rehab, to start a new life in the apartment that houses Remy's favorite tomes. He then flies back to London, comforted by the loving Gaelle at his side.

Whatever its drawbacks, critics are bound to be impressed by the film's wit and intelligence. Writing in the *New York Times* at the time of the film's screening at the New York Film Festival, A. O. Scott observed that Arcand "has a sense of history that is as acute as it is playful." Scott goes on to note that the film's "humor is broad and its emotions large and accessible. But it is also, at the same time, a sophisticated and rigorous analysis of recent history." He compares *The Barbarian Invasions* to "a long, sloppy party, full of food, wine, maudlin moments and endless conversation."

—*Vivek Adarkar*

CREDITS

Remy: Remy Girard
Sebastien: Stephane Rousseau
Nathalie: Marie Josee Croze
Gaelle: Marina Hands
Louise: Dorothee Berryman
Sister Constance: Johanne-Marie Tremblay
Dominique: Dominique Michel
Diane: Louise Portal
Claude: Yves Jacques
Pierre: Pierre Curzi

Origin: Canada, France
Language: French
Released: 2003

Production: Denise Robert, Daniel Louis; Cinemaginaire Inc., Pyramide Productions; released by Miramax Films
Directed by: Denys Arcand
Written by: Denys Arcand
Cinematography by: Guy Dufaux
Music by: Pierre Aviat
Sound: Patrick Rousseau
Editing: Isabelle Dedieu
Art Direction: Caroline Adler
Costumes: Denis Sperdouklis
Production Design: Francois Seguin
MPAA rating: R
Running time: 110 minutes

REVIEWS

Boxoffice. November, 2003, p. 83.
Entertainment Weekly. November 28, 2003, p. 101.
Los Angeles Times Online. November 21, 2003.
New York Times Online. October 17, 2003.
New York Times. November 18, 2003, p. AR15.
People. December 1, 2003, p. 32.
Rolling Stone. November 27, 2003, p. 103.
USA Today Online. November 21, 2003.
Variety Online. May 21, 2003.

QUOTES

Remy (Remy Girard): "My son is an ambitious capitalist prude whereas all my life I've been a hedonistic socialist lecher."

AWARDS AND NOMINATIONS

Oscars 2003: Foreign Film
Cannes 2003: Actress (Croze), Screenplay
Natl. Bd. of Review 2003: Foreign Film
Nomination:
Oscars 2003: Orig. Screenplay
Golden Globes 2004: Foreign Film.

Basic

Deception is their most dangerous weapon.
—Movie tagline

 Box Office: $26.5 million

In the hurricane-soaked jungles of Panama, a Ranger training team is six hours overdue. When a helicopter is sent out to search for them they spot three survivors below. One is wounded and being carried by a second, but both are being chased and shot at by a third. By the time the helicopter rescues them, the third man is dead and only the wounded man, Kendall (Giovanni Ribisi) and his rescuer, Dunbar (Brian Van Holt) are alive.

In order to find out what happened and where the other Rangers are, camp commander Styles (Tim Daly) has provost marshal Julia Osborne (Connie Nielsen) investigate the incident. Unfortunately Kendall is incapacitated by his wounds and Dunbar isn't talking. Consequently Styles calls in an old friend of his, Tom Hardy (John Travolta). Tom was in the army with Styles but has since moved on to the DEA. Currently, however, he is under suspension because he is suspected of taking bribes from a drug lord. But did he?

Styles knows Tom is a first-rate interrogator and hopes he can get the truth from Dunbar before he is scheduled to be transported in six hours. (Or at least that's what we're led to believe.) Eventually Hardy gets Dunbar to tell what happened, but pieces of the puzzle seem missing. When Kendall finally wakes up, Hardy and Osborne get his side of the story, but it doesn't jive with Dunbar's.

On some things both stories agree. Both say that Sergeant West (Samuel L. Jackson) was an abusive bastard, that they saw West dead, that West really had it in for Pike, and that in some way drugs were involved. After that, not much meshes. So who's lying and who's telling the truth? And does it make any difference that Kendall is the son of one of the Joint Chiefs of Staff, that father and son hate each other, and that Kendall Jr. is a gay drug user? Or that drug charges in the army carries a 20 year sentence. Wouldn't Dad be proud?

The problem is, each time Hardy and Osborne interrogate these two men the story backtracks over itself and constantly shifts. The audience never knows who really is doing what to whom and why, and at some point may even stop caring. A well-conceived, complex plot with a well-earned and understandable payoff is a glory to behold. But a plot that is needlessly convoluted, where one senses many plot holes that one can't quite put one's finger on because the story has cheated so many times, and where the conclusion seems to come out of left field, leaves one feeling betrayed.

Obviously the blame for this twisting muddle must be firmly laid at the feet of scriptwriter James Vanderbilt. Although the script for *Basic* was the subject of some heated bidding, it is Vanderbilt's debut screenplay. Actually, it is his second sold, but his first produced. It attempts to combine the *Rashomon*-like device of showing reality from several different perspectives, as was done successfully in *Courage Under Fire*, with a military investigation mystery like *A Few Good Men* and Travolta's own *The General's Daughter*. The problem is, *Rashomon*-type films only work when they give us a deeper insight into the relativity of personal experience and truth and mystery films only work when there's a good payoff. *Basic* does neither.

That's not to say *Basic* doesn't have great pacing. Tension steadily builds as we try to follow the twists and the turns of the mystery, but at some point we realize that even the characters we've been following aren't who they say they are (and this happens several times) and the plot twists seem thrown in for no reason other than to confuse the audience since they have no relationship to the actual storyline.

For some *Basic* may be ingeniously inventive, but for many it will just be annoyingly evasive. Unlike, say, *The Usual Suspects* or *Memento*, *Basic*'s changeable storyline probably won't hold up under a second viewing . . . or a third or a fourth because it may take more than that just to straighten out all the red herrings and blind alleys. *Basic*'s tagline reads, "Deception is their most dangerous weapon." but the film's plot deceptions may also be dangerously fatal to audiences.

Screenwriter Vanderbilt should not be held responsible for this mess all on his own. Some blame should be laid at the feet of director John McTiernan. Perhaps best known for his work directing *Die Hard* and *The Hunt for Red October*, more recently his career seems to be sliding since the film before this one was the futuristic fiasco *Rollerball*.

Blame might also be spread out to include John Travolta. An interesting actor, Travolta can play both good guy and bad. He can seem all bonhomie one minute and can quickly show menace behind that boyish smile the next. His cinematic charm seems to belie a quicksilver edge of evil. He's hard to read, which could play well into this chameleon of a plot, but instead it just adds to the confusion and sense of manipulation.

Teaming Travolta with Connie Nielsen (*Gladiator*) may also have been a mistake. The actress seems badly cast, too delicate and pretty for a military interrogator. There is virtually no chemistry between Hardy and Osborne as they move from open hostility, to underlying sexual attraction, to respect. But we don't even know if we can trust their feelings about each other at any given point in the movie because we've been lied to so often.

Teaming Travolta with Samuel L. Jackson, however, seemed like a great idea since they've been terrifically teamed together before in *Pulp Fiction*. In *Basic*, Jackson does little more than scream and act abusively and sadistically, and unfortunately he and Travolta are paired for just a few minutes of screen time at the most. Very disappointing.

By the end of the film, one may begin to wonder, what's the point of all the confusion? Of working so hard to try and figure out the mystery? There are no truths to be found here, no insights into the relativity of reality. We just feel manipulated.

—*Beverley Bare Buehrer*

CREDITS

Tom Hardy: John Travolta
Sgt. Nathan West: Samuel L. Jackson
Capt. Julia Osborne: Connie Nielsen
Levi Kendall: Giovanni Ribisi
Raymond Dunbar: Brian Van Holt
Pike: Taye Diggs
Castro: Christian de la Fuente
Mueller: Dash Mihok
Col. Bill Sykes: Timothy Daly
Nunez: Roselyn Sanchez
Pete Vilmer: Harry Connick Jr

Origin: USA
Released: 2003
Production: Michael Tadross, Mike Medavoy, Arnie Messer, James Vanderbilt; Intermedia Films, Phoenix Pictures; released by Columbia Pictures
Directed by: John McTiernan
Written by: James Vanderbilt
Cinematography by: Steve Mason
Music by: Klaus Badelt
Sound: Tom Nelson
Editing: George Folsey Jr.
Art Direction: Gary Kosko
Costumes: Kate Harrington
Production Design: Dennis Bradford
MPAA rating: R
Running time: 95 minutes

REVIEWS

Chicago Sun-Times Online. March 28, 2003.
Entertainment Weekly. April 4, 2003, p. 78.
Los Angeles Times Online. March 28, 2003.
New York Times Online. March 28, 2003.
People. April 7, 2003, p. 34.
Variety Online. March 22, 2003.
Washington Post. March 28, 2003, p. WE42.

QUOTES

Tom (John Travolta) to Julia (Connie Nielsen): ". . . I'm still a little drunk from earlier today. So if I skip over the witty banter and move straight into coming on to you, I hope you don't take offense."

The Battle of Shaker Heights (Project Greenlight's The Battle of Shaker Heights)

When you're 17, every day is war.
—Movie tagline

The revolution will not be televised!
—Movie tagline

Winning the grand prize on *Project Greenlight*, the Matt Damon and Ben Affleck-produced HBO reality show in which a script wins a $1 million budget and a distribution deal with Miramax, can be both a blessing and curse. Forget the funding, the filmmakers must subject themselves to being filmed as they make the movie. All the petty squabbles, temper tantrums, and generally bad behavior make it to the small screen for viewer analysis.

Winning the 2003 competition gave scriptwriter Erica Beeney the kind of exposure that she probably never would have gotten otherwise, but it wasn't without a cost. In the series, viewers followed as Beeney's script went through the painful process of going from one person's specific vision to a committee-made film. It was changed, manhandled, and went through the usual Hollywood torture chamber. Viewers were aware that the directors, Kyle Rankin and Efram Potelle, were selected separately from Beeney, and presumably didn't have as good an idea of how the film should look. Fans of the series found their own heroes and villains. Kenneth Turan of the *Los Angeles Times* called the directors "snarky" and Lou Lumenick of the *New York Post* wrote that the duo "direct rather heavy-handedly . . . with egos out of all proportion to their talents"; Elvis Mitchell of the *New York Times* referred to producer Chris Moore as a "military strongman." Usually when we watch a film, we don't know that the producer demanded drastic cuts or ate three bagels a day.

It seems unlikely that people who hadn't seen *Project Greenlight* would be interested in this film. After all, the previous *Project Greenlight* picture, *Stolen Summer*, was notably bad, and right now, the *Greenlight* endorsement is not exactly a positive. And those who did see the series and were interested in how the film turned out might be disappointed since they built up an expectation of how the film would look. It's somewhat akin to how movie adaptations of a book often aren't popular with the book's readers—the readers are too aware of what was left out. As Turan of the *Los Angeles Times* noted, "As *Project Greenlight* fans know, *Shaker*

Heights started out with a darker subplot. The lopping off of that story is the reason *Shaker Heights* is only 78 minutes long, but nothing that remains on screen makes us regret its absence." Again, this is not usually the kind of stuff we know before going into a film.

The final product contains vague remnants of the darker subplot. Kelly Ernswiler (Shia LaBeouf), is a bitter teen in Shaker Heights, Ohio, a suburb of Cleveland. The one thing that seems to give him pleasure is participating in war game exercises. But even there, Kelly, a bright, witty, kid, can't seem to succeed. He upsets his fellow war gamers when he veers from the script, concocting surprise ambushes and the like. His home life is no better. His father, Abe (William Sadler), is a recovering addict who is constantly bringing in homeless addicts to stay in the Ernswiler house. Kelly describes him as "a VH1 documentary without the music." Kelly has no sympathy for his father and hasn't forgiven him for not being present during much of the teen's childhood. When his father mentions how long he's been sober, Kelly replies, "Big deal. I've been sober my whole life." His mother, Eve (Kathleen Quinlan of *Apollo 13*), is a painter who hires other people to make paintings for her.

School isn't much better. Kelly is bored with his classes and horrified when his history teacher gives what the teen views as a whitewashed version of the civil war. Kelly speaks out in class, which doesn't endear him to the teacher or the other students. The one bright spot in Kelly's life is his new friendship with Bart Bowland (Elden Henson), a guy from the war games. Bart's wealthy family is charmed by Kelly's fast wit and clever lines and they serve as a bit of a surrogate family. Kelly is at the Bowland house a lot, mostly hoping to see Tabby (Amy Smart), a beautiful Yale art student. She's out of Kelly's league, but with typical moxie, he gives it a try. When he walks in on her while she's painting, he asks her about her work. "I'm playing with diffusion," she answers. "Well, when you're done with it, please put it away," he replies cheekily. Tabby is intrigued by Kelly and his sharp tongue but not as intrigued as he imagines her to be.

Judging from what made it to the screen, perhaps Miramax was right in suggesting that the drama be lessened and the comedy strengthened. The drama that remains is the weak point of the film. Scenes in which emotions are ratcheted up tend to play like drama school readings. In one scene, Eve shouts at her son, "When are you going to stop being angry? I want to be angry!" And there's not all that much of a plot. Kelly wants a girl he can't have. Kelly fights with his parents. Kelly wants to get revenge on a mean bully.

But what makes this film an off-kilter treat is LaBeouf's Kelly. Like Max in *Rushmore*, Kelly is an odd guy, an offbeat hero. His witty lines don't carry the same punch in print, but in the film, LaBeouf makes them work. He tosses off hilarious asides like other people pepper their speech with "you know." When his guidance counselor asks him, "How am I going to get through to you?" Kelly answers, "Well, advertising executives often use sexuality to appeal to my demographic." Kelly doesn't seem to know how to deal with life except to keep talking and joking. He's really a fun character to watch.

The casting of the Kelly character was ideal. LaBeouf, so different here than he was as the quiet hero of *Holes*, is restless and too smart for his own good. Other casting decisions worked too. Smart is suitably mysterious as the unattainable Tabby. She seems just interested enough in Kelly to keep him encouraged but never really accepts him. And Elden Henson as Bart was an interesting choice. He has the looks of a not-so intelligent thuggish kind of guy and he seems like he'd usually be chosen for bully roles. It's odd that he's playing the loyal friend, but it works and it's nice to see someone play so well against type.

It's a shame that *Project Greenlight* ruined *The Battle of Shaker Heights* for so many people, because it's quite an entertaining movie. It's original, funny, and has a great lead performance. It's the kind of film that might do better on video as word of mouth spreads.

Critics generally hailed LaBeouf's performance but didn't care for the rest of the film. Michael Atkinson of the *Village Voice* explained: "The movie is neither a pure character study nor a plot-driven bildungsfilm, but an awkward hybrid, albeit one warm with textured relationships. The characters talk like smart, unpredictable people, and Kelly Ernswiler is one of a kind." Mitchell of the *New York Times* complained that "after about an hour, it's as if you were sitting through one of those smarmy 80's teenage comedies with Jon Cryer that make up the programming on those third-tier Cinemax offshoots." Turan of the *Los Angeles Times* summed up: "If you're looking for a low-rent amateurish combination of *Tadpole*, *The Good Girl*, and *Igby Goes Down*, this film has your number."

—*Jill Hamilton*

Kelly Ernswiler: Shia LaBeouf
Bart Bowland: Elden (Ratliff) Henson
Tabby Bowland: Amy Smart
Lance: Billy Kay
Sarah: Shiri Appleby
Eve Ernswiler: Kathleen Quinlan
Abe Ernswiler: William Sadler
Harrison Bowland: Ray Wise
Miner Weber: Anson Mount
Maurice/German Soldier: Philipp Karner

Origin: USA
Released: 2003

Production: Chris Moore, Jeff Balis; LivePlanet; released by Miramax Films
Directed by: Kyle Rankin, Efram Potelle
Written by: Erica Beeney
Cinematography by: Thomas Ackerman
Music by: Richard (Rick) Marvin
Sound: Mike Florimbi
Music Supervisor: Pete Soldinger
Editing: Richard Nord
Costumes: Bega Metzner
Production Design: Lisa K. Sessiona
MPAA rating: PG-13
Running time: 85 minutes

Chicago Sun-Times Online. August 29, 2003.
Entertainment Weekly. September 5, 2003, p. 56.
Los Angeles Times Online. August 22, 2003.
New York Times Online. August 22, 2003.
People. September 8, 2003, p. 39.
Variety Online. August 22, 2003.
Washington Post. August 28, 2003, p. WE35.

Below

Six hundred feet beneath the surface terror runs deep.
—Movie tagline

When director David Twohy released *Below,* he already had some fans waiting. His independent thrillers, 1996's *The Arrival* and 2000's *Pitch Black,* impressed some viewers for being a cut above the usual action fare. Also promising was the fact that one of the writers, along with Twohy and Lucas Sussman, was Darren Arononfsky from the acclaimed *Pi* and *Requiem for a Dream.* (Twohy himself first made his name in Hollywood as a writer on such films as *G.I. Jane, Waterworld* and *The Fugitive.*) Was *Below* a successful follow-up to their earlier films? Depends on who you ask.

In interviews for the film, Twohy said that he had been studying the work of Jacques Tourneur, who directed 1942's noir classic *Cat People.* In that film, the viewers are left to imagine things on their own, instead of having them spelled out for them on-screen. Atmosphere plays as big a role as actual events. Unfortunately, Twohy focuses so heavily on atmosphere that there's barely any action. Things do happen, but they don't seem particularly interesting and it's difficult to understand why the characters are having such reaction to them. In one scene a copy of *Macbeth* suddenly appears, but it's hard to tell why this should be a big deal. It's not good when movies over-explain what's going on, but it's also not good when things are so unexplained that scenes are not even comprehensible. Twohy relies way too heavily on creating an atmosphere and not heavily enough on taking advantage of that atmosphere.

The film takes place on a United States submarine, the USS Tiger Shark, in World War II. The crew is riled up when they rescue three people from a hospital ship that had been sunk. One of them, nurse Claire (Olivia Williams) is a "skirt." This both excites the men who have not seen a woman in a while and spooks them, since having a woman on board a sub is supposed to be bad luck. Claire starts poking around and starts feeling like something strange is going on onboard. Odell (Matt Davis) thinks that maybe she might be right. Or maybe he just has a crush on her. Claire seems to have the idea that the sub might be haunted. So wispy is the story though that even by the end of the film, no one will be quite sure whether there actually was a ghost, or whether the guys below just didn't get enough oxygen. This isn't so much intriguing ambiguity as it is bad storytelling.

Spooky things start happening. The trouble is, the things aren't that spooky. Well, there is one thing that is spooky. When one character looks into a mirror, he watches his reflection and notices that the reflection is just a fraction slower in repeating his movements. It's creepy and inventive. But that is but one moment in the film. The rest of the thrills are none too thrilling. The lights, they flicker. The sub makes weird sounds. Could it be someone typing out a Morse code message or is it just some seaweed? And when the crew is trying to be completely quiet so that a nearby German boat doesn't detect them, someone's record player suddenly starts playing "Sing, Sing, Sing." Maybe if it played the new Justin Timberlake record, it would be more horrifying, but are we supposed to find "Sing, Sing, Sing" scary?

The crew faces various dangers. A German boat shoots at them, then later comes back with a big hook to try to find their sub. The Germans' depth charges hit the sub. The periscope gets damaged and the control tower is hit. Parts of the sub get flooded and there's less oxygen. As the oxygen runs out, the hydrogen level increases. At first, these conditions can cause hallucinations. Later, they cause death. The crew is led by Lieutenant Brice (Bruce Greenwood), who starts acting nuttier as the dangers mount. Brice had taken over after the previous leader mysteriously died. Or was he killed? Is the ghost onboard the ghost of the old captain? After all, *Macbeth* was one of his favorite plays.

It's almost as though this is half a movie. Twohy is good at creating atmosphere and it would have been great if he could have found a partner who was strong on plot to fill out the rest of the movie. The look of the film, for example, is great. Twohy captures that soda-fountain clean-cut look that we imagine soldiers of the 1940s to have. He's got their appearance down and their slang is right on. And Twohy

makes good use of the sounds that the crew might hear on a sub. Whales go by the boat and make mysterious noises that creep out the crew. And a sonar machine makes an eerie blip, blip, blip noise. But all of this needs to be fleshed out with a clearer and stronger plot. Twohy gives too much implication and not enough payoff. A satisfying plot twist involving Lt. Brice near the end of the film is clever, but it's too little too late.

Critics disagreed on the film, though it had more detractors than fans. Roger Ebert of the *Chicago Sun-Times* wrote, "*Below* has ambitions to be better than average, but doesn't pull itself together and insist on realizing them." Manohla Dargis of the *Los Angeles Times* wrote, "If *Below* had been released in 1943—the year of its story—it would have come in at an agile 70 minutes instead of a protracted 104." Jan Stuart of *Newsday* liked the film more and wrote, "Twohy knows how to inflate the mundane into the scarifying, and gets full mileage out of the rolling of a stray barrel or the unexpected blast of a phonograph record." And Dave Kehr of the *New York Times* wrote of Twohy, "His films are distinguished by a clean, classic direction of action; a sophisticated sense of the relationships between people under stress; and a camera style that keeps the viewer intrigued without calling attention to itself. . . . *Below* may not mark Mr. Twohy's emergence into the mainstream, but his promise remains undiminished."

—Jill Hamilton

CREDITS

Lt. Brice: Bruce Greenwood
Ensign O'Dell: Matthew Davis
Claire Paige: Olivia Williams
Lt. Loomis: Holt McCallany
Coors: Scott Foley
Weird Wally: Zach Galifianakis
Stumbo: Jason Flemyng
Kingsley: Dexter Fletcher
Chief: Nicholas Chinlund
Hoag: Andrew Howard
Pappy: Christopher Fairbank

Origin: USA
Released: 2002
Production: Sue Baden-Powell, Darren Aronofsky, Eric Watson; Protozoa Pictures; released by Dimension Films
Directed by: David N. Twohy
Written by: David N. Twohy, Darren Aronofsky, Lucas Sussman
Cinematography by: Ian Wilson
Music by: Graeme Revell
Sound: Peter Lindsay

Editing: Martin Hunter
Art Direction: Fred Hole
Costumes: Elizabeth Waller
Production Design: Charles Lee
MPAA rating: R
Running time: 103 minutes

REVIEWS

Chicago Sun-Times Online. October 18, 2002.
Entertainment Weekly. October 18, 2002, p. 23.
Entertainment Weekly. October 18, 2002, p. 91.
Los Angeles Times Online. October 11, 2002.
New York Times Online. October 11, 2002.
Variety Online. October 6, 2002.
Washington Post. October 18, 2002, p. WE36.

Bend It Like Beckham

Who wants to cook Aloo Gobi when you can bend a ball like Beckham?
—Movie tagline

A winning comedy.
—Movie tagline

 Box Office: $25.3 million

Gurinder Chadha's frothy, ultralight social comedy from England, *Bend It Like Beckham,* is sprinkled with subtle exotic touches, reminiscent of the filmmaker's previous noteworthy work; here, however, her narrative strains credulity, and draping it in the most lavish saris cannot conceal its slightness. In this, Chadha seems to have come under the generic pressure that has resulted in family entertainment for homesick elitist Indians by filmmakers far less talented than her. What redeems her effort here is its refreshing casting, which includes a bravura performance by a newcomer in the lead.

The film revolves around Jess (Parminder Nagra), born Jasminder, who is between school and college, and escapes the constraints of a male-dominated orthodox family by lapsing into fantasies of becoming a soccer star, and playing alongside Manchester United's Most Valuable Player, David Beckham. Jess is convinced that no one "can cross the ball and bend it like Beckham." Her elder sister, the coquettish Pinky (Archie Panjabi), is about to be married off and their mother, Mrs. Bhamra (Shaheen Khan), wants Jess to follow suit. Her father, Mr. Bhamra (Anupam Kher), a stalwart

Sikh, calls Jess "son," and is slowly won over to her playing in a girls' soccer team.

The matriarch in Mrs. Bhamra wants Jess to learn North Indian cooking, and start behaving in a more feminine manner. She is shocked at the sport of soccer requiring Jess to run around "bare-legged" in shorts, and that too in front of men. For Mrs. Bhamra, that will only bring "shame upon the family." Jess's father, once an ace bowler in cricket, recalls how he was discriminated against when he came to England from Uganda. He would like to spare Jess the racial discrimination, which he's convinced still exists at the higher levels of all sport in England.

What makes Jess appealing as a character is that despite her British accent and westernized outlook, she's a dutiful daughter first and rebel second. Thus, at the start of the film, the tomboyish Jess is quite content to merely kick the ball around with the guys in the neighborhood park, and pour her heart out to a giant poster of Beckham in her bedroom. In real life, she feels most comfortable with Tony (Ameet Chana), who is also an admirer of Beckham, but who has a crush on him as well.

What changes everything is Jess's prowess with the ball being noticed by Jules (Keira Knightley, who looks like a blonde Winona Ryder), and who changes Jess's life by urging her to try out for the local girls' soccer team. Jess doesn't even know there is such a thing as a local girls' soccer team.

When Jess is accepted into the team, after having passed muster in the eyes of its coach, Joe (Jonathan Rhys Meyers), it creates complications in Jess's life, but none that are not easily resolved. Jess is finally convinced she would be right in lying to her parents, since Pinky has been lying all along and carrying on with her fiance behind everyone's back. The liberation that Pinky finds in forbidden sex, Jess finds in forbidden sport.

Chadha keeps the action moving at a sprightly pace, so that even when the scenes are repetitive, they don't last for very long. In the film's scheme of things, the slightest complication can catapult into a major disaster. When Pinky's prospective mother-in-law (Harvey Virdi) sees Jess embracing the short-haired Jules in jubilation on a sidewalk, she thinks Jess is carrying on with a strange man in public, and the wedding is called off. Off it remains for weeks, until the in-laws come calling again because their son is in love with Pinky.

The climactic event the film builds towards is the regional final, to which an American sports scout has been invited and which, coincidentally, falls on the day of Pinky's wedding. On the emotional front, a triangle develops between Jules, Joe, and Jess, with its foreseeable misunderstandings and resolutions.

As could be foreseen, Jess is able to sneak away from the wedding, with Tony's help and her father's blessings, and score big in the game of games. Chadha doesn't exploit the nail-biting suspense in soccer; she merely cuts to the chase to show Jess being able to "cross the ball and bend it like Beckham." The American scout selects both Jess and Jules for scholarships to a college in California. In the final scene, as the two girls take leave of their families at the airport, and Jess is kissing Joe goodbye, she looks up to see David Beckham arriving just then, a sight that to her is like a benediction.

By and large, critics have forgiven the film's air of a TV sitcom by perceiving it as a colorful, exotic domestic comedy. But A. O. Scott in the *New York Times* compares it to the films of Hanif Kureishi and Mira Nair and finds it "a step backward," one that lacks their depiction of the "South Asian diaspora (as) a vortex of contradiction and confusion."

—Vivek Adarkar

CREDITS

Jesminder "Jess" Bhamra: Parminder K. Nagra
Juliette "Jules" Paxton: Keira Knightley
Joe: Jonathan Rhys Meyers
Mrs. Bhamra: Shaheen Khan
Mr. Bhamra: Anupam Kher
Pinky: Archie Panjabi
Paula Paxton: Juliet Stevenson
Alan Paxton: Frank Harper
Mel: Shaznay Lewis

Origin: Great Britain, Germany
Released: 2002
Production: Deepak Nayar, Gurinder Chadha; Kintop Pictures, Road Movies, Roc Media; released by Fox Searchlight
Directed by: Gurinder Chadha
Written by: Gurinder Chadha, Paul Mayeda Berges, Guljit Bindra
Cinematography by: Jong Lin
Music by: Craig Preuss
Sound: John Hayes
Music Supervisor: Liz Gallacher
Editing: Justin Krish
Art Direction: Mark Scruton
Costumes: Ralph Holes
Production Design: Nick Ellis
MPAA rating: PG-13
Running time: 112 minutes

REVIEWS

Boxoffice. August, 2002, p. 56.
Chicago Sun-Times Online. March 12, 2003.

Entertainment Weekly. March 21, 2003, p. 85.
Los Angeles Times Online. March 12, 2003.
New York Times Online. March 12, 2003.
People. March 31, 2003, p. 30.
Sight and Sound. May, 2002, p. 38.
Vanity Fair. March, 2003, p. 130.
Variety. April 1, 2002, p. 32.

QUOTES

Mrs. Bhamra (Shaheen Khan) is horrified daughter Jess (Parminder K. Nagra) is playing soccer: "She shouldn't be running around showing her bare legs to men."

AWARDS AND NOMINATIONS

Nomination:
Golden Globes 2004: Film—Mus./Comedy
Writers Guild 2003: Orig. Screenplay.

Better Luck Tomorrow

Never underestimate an overachiever.
—Movie tagline
Who do you want to be?
—Movie tagline

Box Office: $3.8 million

Better Luck Tomorrow is an odd combination of genres. It's part teen film—a centerpiece of the plot is a nerdy smart guy's crush on a pretty cheerleader—and part gangster film. The odder thing is that it works. The teen and gangster parts flow easily into one another and seem part of the same whole.

What *Better Luck Tomorrow* also does well is showcase a group of Asian-American actors without having them fall into all the usual clichés. Not one of them seems to know martial arts and never once do they show themselves to be violin prodigies. They do, however, embody the stereotype of Asian-American as scholastic overachiever.

Ben (Parry Shen) is a serious student, one of the top in his class of his Orange County suburban high school. He looks to everything as to whether or not it will look good on his college applications. Anything, however tedious, is worth doing if it will improve his apps. He lives a controlled, routine life. He chooses one vocabulary word a day and repeats it all day in hopes of getting a perfect verbal score on his SATs. He shoots free throws every day and keeps a precise journal on his percentage of baskets. He has a big crush on his lab partner, Stephanie (Karin Anna Cheung) but she prefers her smooth boyfriend, Steve (John Cho).

Daric (Roger Fan) is an even better student than Ben. Ben is in a lot of clubs, but Daric is the president of all of them. After Ben gets a spot on the J.V. basketball team, Daric writes a piece of bad journalism for the school paper claiming that Ben is the "token Asian" on the team. To Ben's chagrin, he gets a group of boosters, who bring signs to the games, insisting that Ben be put in the game. In disgust, Ben quits the team.

Daric approaches Ben with a deal. If Ben completes a cheat sheet for an exam the next day, he'll earn $50. In the first of many not-particularly wise decisions, Ben accepts. Soon Ben is making pretty good money and has recruited his equally smart buddy, Virgil (Jason Tobin). Virgil is gifted academically, but he's a loose cannon who is disturbingly hyper. Also in the cheating circle is Han (Sung Kang), Virgil's cousin who's been a longtime participant in petty crime.

The cheat sheets are so successful that the group branches out into drugs and various other scams. In a voiceover, Ben says that since the teens keep their grades up, they are assumed to be good kids. Claiming to have a study group, for example, lets them stay out half the night. And indeed, no matter how elaborate Ben's criminal activities become, he makes sure that they don't interfere with his academics and extracurricular. Even when Ben and his buddies are dealing drugs and stealing computer parts, they make sure to be involved with beach cleanup days, charity car washes and jobs interpreting for Spanish-speaking patients at the hospital.

As Ben and his buddies get deeper into crime, they gain a reputation as being part of "the Chinese mafia." They make more money than they can spend and try to buy whatever it will buy them, including drugs and prostitutes. Ben starts stressing out over his time commitments. After all, if he's dealing drugs all day, he can't get to his homework until 1 a.m. He starts snorting cocaine to give him extra energy.

Ben decides the crime has to stop when he wakes up with a bloody nose. He quits the group and goes back to his orderly life of studying and lusting after Stephanie. But, like in nearly all gang crime films, he gets wrangled into doing one last deal involving Steve, the same Steve that's Stephanie's boyfriend. It's hard to tell what, exactly, this last scam entails, but it doesn't end well, especially for Steve. But then the audience knows that Ben's going to end up in big trouble at some point. The first minutes of the film show Ben and Virgil frantically digging up a body after they hear a beeper sounding from underground. The film rewinds to four months earlier and explains how it could come to all this.

The movie is good at capturing the unfocused energy of youth. There's a need to escape the stifling boredom of suburbia but no one knows quite what they should do. Several characters express disappointment at having such perfect lives. Ben, for one, yearns to participate in activities simply because they would not look good on his college applications. There are no parents in the film and few grown-ups. The grown-ups who are there are clueless and ineffectual, like a droning science teacher (played by Jerry Mathers of *Leave It To Beaver*) who shows his students a film called, *The Amoeba*.

Director Justin Lin (who also co-wrote and co-produced the film) has a fresh interesting style. When Steve and Ben are having a talk at a batting cage, Lin's camera shows the point of view of the ball. When a new character is introduced, Lin flashes a quick succession of snapshots of the person, while Ben explains what they're like. He's a fan of using slow and fast motion in interesting and inventive ways. He's also good at getting performances out of his actors. Usually in gang comedies, there are a few guys who are just there to provide more bulk to the gang. But every guy in Ben's gang comes across as having a complex personality. And Stephanie, who in a normal teen movie would be no more than an object of lust, actually gets to have a personality and conflicted emotions. Ben comes across as a regular grade-chasing guy. He is not cool or charismatic and he doesn't become so during the movie. It makes the story stronger that he's such an unnoticeable, dull guy.

Even though his story is, in many ways, a dark one, Lin manages to keep the mood light. Virgil is one of the biggest sources of comic relief. When he gets mad at his cousin Han, he angrily hurls a pink stuffed animal at him, yelling, "You're dead!" The actor who plays Virgil has a long, almost equine face that is interesting to watch. He's also a good physical comedian, which serves him well since Virgil is constantly in motion, doing things like falling over skateboards.

Critics liked the film. Elvis Mitchell of the *New York Times* called it "a paranoid, bildungsroman of a black comedy." Roger Ebert of the *Chicago Sun-Times* wrote, "*Better Luck Tomorrow* is not just a thriller, not just a social commentary, not just a comedy or a romance, but all of those in a clearly seen, brilliantly made film." Merle Bertrand of *Film Threat* wrote, "*Better Luck Tomorrow* is a rare high school dramedy with some heft to it. Smartly photographed and edited, it manages to walk the difficult tightrope strung between the typically loopy coming of age film and a simmering disaster in the making."

—*Jill Hamilton*

CREDITS

Ben: Parry Shen
Virgil: Jason J. Tobin
Daric: Roger Fan

Han: Sung Kang
Steve: John Cho
Stephanie: Karin Anna Cheung

Origin: USA
Released: 2002
Production: Julie Asato, Ernesto M. Foronda, Justin Lin; Hudson River Film Company, Cherry Sky Films, Day O Productions, Trailing Johnson Productions; released by Paramount Pictures, MTV Films
Directed by: Justin Lin
Written by: Justin Lin, Ernesto M. Foronda, Fabian Marquez
Cinematography by: Patrice Lucien Cochet
Music by: Michael J. Gonzales
Sound: Curtis X. Choy
Music Supervisor: Ernesto M. Foronda
Editing: Justin Lin
Costumes: Sandi Lieu
Production Design: Yoojung Han
MPAA rating: R
Running time: 98 minutes

REVIEWS

Chicago Sun-Times Online. April 11, 2003.
Entertainment Weekly. April 18, 2003, p. 49.
Los Angeles Times Online. April 6, 2003.
Los Angeles Times Online. April 11, 2003.
New York Times Online. April 11, 2003.
People. April 21, 2003, p. 36.
USA Today Online. April 11, 2003.
Variety. January 21, 2002, p. 36.
Washington Post. April 18, 2003, p. C1.

QUOTES

Stephanie (Karin Anna Cheung): "You know how you make decisions that lead to other decisions but you don't remember why you made those decisions in the first place."

Beyond Borders

Where hope survives.
—Movie tagline

Box Office: $4.4 million

As Martin Campbell's misguided effort to illuminate the plight of the needy in places like Cambodia and Ethiopia, *Beyond Borders* makes the mistake of unnecessarily glamorizing the whole affair, putting star power over story, romance over social awareness. Certainly star Angelina Jolie has proved her dedication to such causes as Goodwill Ambassador for the United Nations High Commissioner for Refugees (UNHCR) and by adopting her son Maddox while on location in Cambodia for the filming of *Beyond Borders*. The problem lies not in a lack of compassion from the filmmakers or actors, but in the execution of an unrealistic and melodramatic portrait of the issue which manages to trivialize the crisis that refugees face worldwide.

Jolie is awkward in the role of Sarah Jordan, a shallow socialite who believes she is actually saving the world by attending swanky charity fundraisers where the self-congratulatory wealthy write checks and sip expensive champagne. In a flashback to 1984, Sarah and her new husband, Henry (Linus Roache), are attending a posh, London ball that is crashed by the unorthodox but passionate doctor Nick Callahan (Clive Owen). The doctor, with the most noble of intentions, parades around a starving Ethiopian boy, Jojo (Keelan Anthony), in an attempt to shame the rich Londoners. Sarah is both inspired by and smitten with the handsome do-gooder and finds herself struggling with a desire to travel to Ethiopia and help children like Jojo, who is treated more like an object by the doctor than a real live child.

Henry, of course, is less than thrilled at the prospect of his wife running away to dangerous places to help starving kids. Still, a determined Sarah raises money for supplies and food and follows the hotheaded doctor to Ethiopia, where she is greeted with disdain and coldness. Even after she saves a local child from being eaten by a vulture, Nick believes her presence there is a token gesture and mocks her attempts at charity. Making the story less believable is that Sarah manages to perform her heroic deeds in the desert completely clad in pristine white while the dirty and fly-ridden huddled masses look on.

Though they are from very different worlds and constantly at odds, it is clear Nick and Sarah have a mutual attraction and form a growing bond over their shared desire to save these children. It is exactly this juxtaposition of starving children and budding romance that is so objectionable, especially when it is the romance that takes center stage.

Several years later, Sarah is still in her shaky marriage and has had a son, but she has become increasingly involved in the plight of the refugees through her job at the United Nations. Nick, for his part, continues his efforts, traveling deeper and deeper into such dangerous territory as Cambodia. It is there, amid the whizzing bullets of warring rebels, that Sarah finds herself once again drawn to Nick and the two finally consummate their relationship. Sarah feels she is entitled to the tryst because Henry had been unfaithful to her, but she heads back to London shortly thereafter, leaving the altruistic doctor free to carry on his work. The final scenes take place in Chechnya, where Nick has been kidnapped and a desperate Sarah, who now also has a daughter, travels to save him despite warnings from her concerned sister Charlotte (Teri Polo).

Although both leads are most capable actors, both have done far better work and neither can overcome the melodramatic drivel they are forced to wade through to get to each other and save the refugees. The relentless selflessness and pig-headedness of Owen's character wear thin as do Jolie's wide-eyed concern and sadness. There is also a disturbing lack of chemistry between them in their single love scene, a necessary element in reinforcing this make-believe romance. The disturbing footage of famine and war victims—some computer-enhanced, some actual land-mine victims—adds little credibility to this far-fetched story. *Beyond Borders* focuses too much on the romance of its glamorous leads and too little on the actual plight of victims of war and starvation around the world.

—*Hilary White*

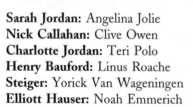

CREDITS

Sarah Jordan: Angelina Jolie
Nick Callahan: Clive Owen
Charlotte Jordan: Teri Polo
Henry Bauford: Linus Roache
Steiger: Yorick Van Wageningen
Elliott Hauser: Noah Emmerich
Kat: Kate Ashfield
Joss: Jamie Bartlett
Lawrence Bauford: Timothy West
Mrs. Bauford: Kate Trotter
Colonel Gao: Burt Kwouk

Origin: USA
Released: 2003
Production: Dan Halstead, Lloyd Phillips; Mandalay Pictures, Camelot; released by Paramount Pictures
Directed by: Martin Campbell
Written by: Caspian Tredwell-Owen
Cinematography by: Phil Meheux
Music by: James Horner
Sound: Pud Cusack
Editing: Nicholas Beauman
Art Direction: Leslie Tomkins
Costumes: Norma Moriceau
Production Design: Wolf Kroeger
MPAA rating: R
Running time: 127 minutes

REVIEWS

Chicago Sun-Times Online. October 24, 2003.
Entertainment Weekly. October 31, 2003, p. 51.
Los Angeles Times Online. October 24, 2003.
New York Times Online. October 24, 2003.
People. November 3, 2003, p. 33.
San Francisco Examiner Online. October 24, 2003.
USA Today Online. October 24, 2003.
Variety Online. October 19, 2003.
Washington Post. October 24, 2003, p. WE35.

AWARDS AND NOMINATIONS

Nomination:
Golden Raspberries 2003: Worst Actress (Jolie).

Big Fish

An adventure as big as life itself.
—Movie tagline

Box Office: $65.4 million

"**M**ake him stop," is Will Bloom's (Billy Crudup) desperate plea to his mother Sandra (Jessica Lange). He has gone through his entire life listening to his father, Edward (Albert Finney), tell tall tales time after time after time to anyone and everyone. He tells them around Will's cub scout campfire, to Will's prom date, and at Will's wedding reception. Every time Edward starts in, Will closes up. While some find Edward's stories amusing and colorful, as Will says, "No one loves them after hearing them 1,000 times."

What kind of stories does Edward tell? Well, there's the story about how he bravely knocked on the door of the town witch (Helena Bonham Carter) and looked into her beclouded glass eye and saw how he was going to die. With this knowledge he now approaches the rest of his life fearlessly knowing he is safe until then. Because of this, Edward has many stories about his life of phenomenal achievements. For the young Edward (Ewan McGregor) there's not a school sport he doesn't excel in, there's not a job or business he doesn't try that he doesn't master, there's not a science fair he doesn't win, and if a building is burning in town, Edward will be the one rushing in to rescue the family dog.

So courageous is he that when a giant comes to town and begins eating dogs, sheep, and entire cornfields it is

Edward who volunteers to "talk" to him in order to get him to leave. Obviously in Edward's good-natured tale he'll befriend the giant and travel with him to new adventures one of which takes him through the town of Spectre where everyone's happy and barefoot including the local poet Norther Winslow (Steve Buscemi) who went missing several years ago and has been happily working on his latest poem for 12 years. Eventually they land with a circus run by Amos Calloway (Danny DeVito) where the giant Karl (Matthew McGrory) becomes a side-show attraction and where Edward will see the woman he is going to marry, Sandra (played as a young girl by Alison Lohman). Of course she disappears before he can find out who she is, but Amos promises to tell Edward one fact about her a month in exchange for his free labor. So Edward scrubs the back of the fat man, picks up elephant poop, and even allows himself to be shot out of a cannon and all for mere tidbits of information: her favorite flowers are daffodils, she likes music, she's going to college . . . but never her name. Never, that is, until Edward saves Amos' life one night after the circus owner has turned into a wolf. Armed with his potential wife's name and her location Edward sets off to woo her with fields of daffodils and skywriting airplanes. Just as she is within his grasp, he is drafted. He gets his tour of duty reduced by applying for hazardous missions including parachuting in to destroy a communist power plant where he is saved by Ping and Jing, conjoined twins—two heads and torsos, but only two legs—who see in Edward a chance to escape their plight singing to party members and soldiers and become, perhaps, great Western lounge singers.

For Will, though, it all begins with Edward's fantastic tale of the day his son was born. Seems Edward was fishing in the river using his golden wedding band as bait in order to catch "The Beast," a fish that couldn't be caught. And just as he catches the fish and fights to retrieve his wedding ring, Will pops out of his mother. And when he says pops out, he really means pops out, the newborn sliding across the hospital floor like a slippery hockey puck.

These are the kinds of stories that drive Will crazy. He knows his father was really in Wichita selling novelties the day he was born so why not tell the truth? In adulthood, Will is a UPI news correspondent in Paris. He collects and writes about facts, and his father's flagrant disregard of the truth is driving a wedge between them. As a travelling salesman, Edward was often absent from Will's life, and when he was home, his stories made him so popular that Will was often overshadowed by his father's tales. Even when Edward tells the story of his son's birth, Will feels like nothing more than a footnote. Consequently, they haven't spoken for three years.

And then the phone rings in Will's Paris home. His father is dying. Now is the time to go home, re-open communication with his father, and find out the truth behind all the embellished stories that are all Will knows of his father's life. They are, in Will's words, "strangers who know each other very well." But when he confronts his dying father with, "Show me who you are for once." His father calmly replies, "I've been myself since the day you were born, and if you can't see that then it's your fault not mine."

Perhaps there is more of Edward in these fabrications than Will or even we in the audience realize. "Not everything your father says is a complete fabrication," his mother tells him. But why does he do it? Is it worth the alienation of a son? Mark Twain once said that the truth should never get in the way of a good story, and this is advice Edward Bloom has taken to heart since he obviously prefers the past he has created in his imagination to the ordinary facts of his life. In fact, his inventiveness has actually transformed his ordinary life into one that is much grander . . . at least in his own mind.

Edward sees himself as the proverbial "big fish in a little pond" as he grows up in the small town of Ashton. "You think this town is too small for you?" he asks the giant Karl. "Well, it's too small for a man of my ambition. I love every square inch of it. But I can feel the edges closing in on me. A man's life can only grow to a certain size in a place like this." This reference is yet another fish allusion mentioned in the film: goldfish will grow to the size of the bowl they live in. Edward is a character whose imagination is too great for the small goldfish bowl in which he exists. Consequently, he goes on adventures with more enthusiasm and delight than anyone could imagine.

Edward is a character from that great southern tradition: the colorful storyteller, and screenwriter John August has done a faithful job of bringing Daniel Wallace's whimsical book *Big Fish: A Novel of Mythic Proportions* to the screen. But it is a story that is more than just a chance to tell tall tales. It is also a wonderful love story and a poignant father-son tale. By eloquently and seamlessly combining these three elements, the ending of *Big Fish* is deeply satisfying emotionally. Of course this would not be true if we didn't connect with the characters. In *Big Fish* every character, those in the real world as well as those in the surreal one, is consistently and delightful eccentric . . . with the possible exception of Edward's all-too-rooted-in-reality son, Will. But that's the point. We end up seeing Will's life as a little impoverished by the fact that he can't take delight in his father or his tales. He can't seem to realize that there are emotional truths that are just as valid as literal truths, and that they may even be more enriching.

Billy Crudup's Will, therefore, does come off as seeming a bit too hard on his father, but then we in the audience haven't been exposed to the repetitiveness of his stories the way Will has. So to some extent Will is an outsider even to the viewer. It is hard to understand his hard-nosed attitude when we can see the magic of his father's stories but then they are new to us but not to Will. Maybe if we had heard the droning on and on over the years we, too might see

Edward as a self-centered blowhard, a man who couldn't tell the truth if his life—or relationship with his son—depended upon it. But to our delight, we haven't, and Edward—both in the form of Albert Finney and Ewan McGregor who looks startlingly like the young Finney when he starred in *Tom Jones*—comes across instead as optimistically confident, cheerful, and charming. While most of the women have little to do in the film, Steve Buscemi is positively goofy in the best sense of the word. Watching him rob a bank, dance with the camera, or read Norther's latest epic poem ("The grass so green, the sky is blue, Spectre is really great"), leaves the viewer charmed by his silliness.

Big Fish is a magnificently realized movie. From production designer Dennis Gassner's extraordinarily fanciful sets to Philippe Rousselot's remarkable cinematography, Edward's adventures are totally captivating. But no small measure of credit has to go to director Tim Burton and his trademark imaginative blending of stories and sets. *Edward Scissorhands, Batman,* and *Ed Wood* are hard acts to beat, but with *Big Fish* Burton does go beyond anything he has done before. Perhaps the director made a connection with this story that hit very close to home. Burton was very distanced from his own parents (both of whom are deceased). As a new father himself, *Big Fish* may be an attempt to heal that wound.

Burton seems to invest an inordinate amount of love, inventiveness, quirkiness and humor into *Big Fish*. There's not a speck of real menace or cynicism to break the mystical bond between story and audience. Daniel Wallace's touching story and Burton's fanciful directing are perfectly wedded in *Big Fish*. Not since *O Brother, Where Art Thou?* has such an amiable story been so imaginatively told. *Big Fish* is one of those rare movies that can enchant and entertain, be inspiring and thoughtful at the same time without ever going over the top. It almost seems fragile in its whimsical beauty and its sense of wonder.

—*Beverley Bare Buehrer*

CREDITS

Edward Bloom (young): Ewan McGregor
Edward Bloom (senior): Albert Finney
Will Bloom: Billy Crudup
Sandra Bloom (senior): Jessica Lange
Sandra Bloom (young): Alison Lohman
Jenny/Witch: Helena Bonham Carter
Dr. Bennett: Robert Guillaume
Norther Winslow: Steve Buscemi
Amos Calloway: Danny DeVito
Josephine: Marion Cotillard
Don Price: David Denman

Mildred: Missi Pyle
Karl the Giant: Matthew McGrory
Beaman: Loudon Wainwright III

Origin: USA
Released: 2003
Production: Richard D. Zanuck, Bruce Cohen, Dan Jinks; released by Columbia Pictures
Directed by: Tim Burton
Written by: John August
Cinematography by: Philippe Rousselot
Music by: Danny Elfman
Sound: Petur Hliddal
Editing: Chris Lebenzon
Art Direction: Richard Johnson
Costumes: Colleen Atwood
Production Design: Dennis Gassner
MPAA rating: PG-13
Running time: 125 minutes

REVIEWS

Boxoffice. December,2003, p. 14.
Boxoffice. January, 2004, p. 37.
Chicago Sun-Times Online. December 24, 2003.
Entertainment Weekly. December 12, 2003, p. 55.
Los Angeles Times Online. December 10, 2003.
New York Times Online. December 10, 2003.
People. December 15, 2003, p. 29.
Rolling Stone. December 11, 2003, p. 213.
Variety Online. November 20, 2003.
Washington Post. December 26, 2003, p. WE41.

QUOTES

Old Edward Bloom (Albert Finney): "Most men they'll tell you a story straight true. It won't be complicated but it won't be interesting either."

AWARDS AND NOMINATIONS

Nomination:
Oscars 2003: Orig. Score
Golden Globes 2004: Film—Mus./Comedy, Song ("Man of the Hour"), Support. Actor (Finney), Orig. Score.

Biker Boyz

Survival of the fastest.
—Movie tagline

 Box Office: $21.7 million

It was difficult to find a review of *Biker Boyz* that didn't make a comparison with the street drag-race movie, *The Fast and the Furious*. It's easy to see why. Both movies should be prefaced with a big old "Don't try this at home" warning. Both have guys (mostly) illegally racing on L.A.-area streets. Both feature a world where it is cool to show up in a crowded parking lot and start doing doughnuts. And both were inspired by articles. The idea for *Biker Boyz* came from an article by Michael Gougis about middle-class African-American bike racers that appeared in the Los Angeles newsweekly, *New Times*. The article detailed the lives of a group of generally upstanding citizens who also happened to have a need for speed.

Both films also have male bonding up the wazoo. Both have lame pseudo-philosophical dialogue. (A favorite in *Biker Boyz* is "Burn rubber, not your soul," whatever that means.) And both feature buxom babes who are largely relegated to the arduous task of waving the start flag at the beginning of races. (One scribe, Jeff Stark of *Salon,* wrote, "There is more than one scene with a woman whose breasts might hop out of their harness and run away to star in another movie."

What *Biker Boyz* has on *The Fast and the Furious* is a stellar cast. There's Laurence Fishburne, Derek Luke (the star of *Antwone Fisher*), Orlando Jones (*Drumline*), Eriq La Salle, and Lisa Bonet. And then there's also Kid Rock, which if not stellar casting, is at least novel. (A common question upon hearing the cast roll was "What is Laurence Fishburne doing in a movie like that?" Surely it wasn't for the change to say lines like, "I am the king of Cali, baby! Me! Smoke!" The answer is that Fishburne happens to be a fan of motorcycle racing himself. Or maybe it was the money.) *Biker Boyz* also tries to give itself more substance. Instead of a lame plot about smuggling, writers Craig Fernandez and Reggie Rock Bythewood, wrote one about father and son bonding. This is also one of the downfalls of *Biker Boyz*.

What *The Fast and the Furious* has on *Biker Boyz,* besides spelling skill, is fastness and furious-ness. *The Fast and the Furious* was about the dumbest movie on the block, but that thing was exciting. The camera angles were quick, the action new and different, and the music helped propel the whole thing along. *Biker Boyz* doesn't have nearly the same thrill. It rarely takes advantage of the inherent thrills in bike racing and misses a lot of chances for action. You'd

thing that a movie about bike racing would be full of bike racing, but there's really not as much as there could be.

Instead, *Biker Boyz* fills its space with its human interest story. Yawn. The difference between the two films is illustrated in the first few scenes of *Biker Boyz*. There is a motorcycle race, and instead of playing it up for all the adrenaline possible, director Bythewood shows the race from an angle in front of the bikes. So the bikes speed by and we get no sense of their speed. By filming it in the wrong way, Bythewood erases all the visceral sense of speed. Also in the early parts of the movie, there's a funeral. The funeral lasts more than a few seconds. This is violating a major tenet of action movies: thou shalt not show the consequences of death, and thou shalt definitely not slow down the action. People should die, then be whisked quickly away, offscreen. No one's saying that that's the right thing to do, but that's how it is.

It would seem admirable that *Biker Boyz* is trying to up the psychological element in the story, but the results don't turn out well. The relationship issues get in the way of the action and they're not compelling enough to replace the action. It's doubtful anyway that people showing up to see some Biker Boyz give too much of a hoot about a boy bonding with a father figure and such.

Kid (Luke) is in the biking gang, "The Black Knights." He wants to be a racer but is only a "prospect," or fledgling driver. His disapproving father, Tariq (La Salle) is the obsequious mechanic for alpha racer, Smoke (Fishburne). (As *Salon* writer Stark succinctly put it, "There will never be a good movie with a character named 'Smoke.'") At a race, Smoke's opponent spins out of control and kills Tariq. Kid drops out of sight for few months and then emerges to start racing. For reasons not particularly illuminated in the script, he despises Smoke and wishes only to beat him in a race. In this world, the winner of races gets a large purse—up to $5000—and the loser's helmet. If someone beats Smoke, the undefeated champion, then they can also claim his title as the King of Cali.

Kid, who is something of a biking hustler, gives up his hustling ways to go legit and form his own gang, the Biker Boyz. They wear really cheesy matching outfits with bandanas over their mouths. But in the context of this movie, this is considered to be cool. The whole thing is leading up to a race between Smoke and cocky upstart, Kid. To fill time, there's a subplot where Dogg (Kid Rock) is being a jerk and trying to challenge Smoke. That story just kind of fizzles away.

Side characters include Soul Train (Jones) as Smoke's number two man by night and attorney by day, and Kid's girlfriend, Tina (Meagan Goode). Queenie (Lisa Bonet) is Smoke's longtime girlfriend. Bonet seems really out of it in this role. Maybe it's acting, but she appears to be listening to another movie in her head as her body is present in this one. There is also Kid's sassy, sexy mother (do black women in movies ever get to be anything but sassy and sexy?), Anita

(Vanessa Bell Calloway). Anita is a tough-talking lady who tries to reign in her son's wild ways by saying snappy things like, "You know what we call bikers in the E.R.? Organ donors!"

But the centerpiece of the movie is a secret that comes out about Smoke and Kid. They are actually father and son. This leads to some Oedipal, alpha male fighting but ultimately tender words. Kid learns from his new daddy figure such helpful life lessons as, "The difference between men and boys is the lessons they learn." *Biker Boyz* is too tender to be a good action movie and not tender enough to be a strong movie about emotions. That said, there is exactly one stunt that is good in the movie. In one sequence, Kid and his biker friends go joyriding and they drag their steel soled shoes on the ground, kicking up a spray of sparks. Then they do wheelies all together while speeding down the street. If they could have had more things like this peppered throughout the movie maybe even things like the repetition of the "Burn rubber, not your soul" clunkers could have even been tolerable.

Most critics weren't wowed by the film. Christy Lemire of the *Associated Press* wrote, "Remarkably, for a movie that's about racing, *Biker Boyz* is neither fast nor furious." Wesley Morris of the *Boston Globe* called it "a lethargic piece of black edu-tainment." And Stephen Holden of the *New York Times* wrote that the film "imagines itself a leaner, hipper, African-American-slanted answer to *The Fast and the Furious,* but it has little of the visceral energy of its forerunner and none of its adolescent sense of grandeur." Gene Seymour of *Newsday* liked it a bit more and wrote, "*Biker Boyz* is the kind of movie Howard Hawks would have made if he'd lived long enough to feel the heat of hip-hop's impact on the culture at large."

—*Jill Hamilton*

Origin: USA
Released: 2003
Production: Erwin Stoff, Stephanie Allain, Gina Price-Bythewood; 3 Arts Productions; released by Dreamworks Pictures
Directed by: Reggie Rock Bythewood
Written by: Reggie Rock Bythewood, Craig Ferandez
Cinematography by: Greg Gardiner
Music by: Camara Kambon
Sound: Susumu Tokunow
Music Supervisor: John Houlihan
Editing: Terilyn Shropshire, Caroline Ross
Art Direction: Michael Atwell
Costumes: Rita S. McGhee
Production Design: Cecilia Montiel
MPAA rating: PG-13
Running time: 111 minutes

REVIEWS

Chicago Sun-Times Online. January 31, 2003.
Entertainment Weekly. February 7, 2003, p. 53.
Los Angeles Times Online. January 31, 2003.
New York Times Online. January 31, 2003.
USA Today Online. January 31, 2003.
Variety Online. January 29, 2003.
Washington Post. January 31, 2003, p. WE40.

QUOTES

Anita (Vanessa Bell Calloway) to son Kid (Derek Luke): "Do you know what we call bikers in the ER? Organ donors."

CREDITS

Smoke: Laurence "Larry" Fishburne
Kid: Derek Luke
Soul Train: Orlando Jones
Motherland: Djimon Hounsou
Queenie: Lisa Bonet
Stuntman: Brendan Fehr
Wood: Larenz Tate
Dogg: Kid Rock
Primo: Rick Gonzalez
Tina: Meagan Good
Half & Half: Salli Richardson
Anita: Vanessa Bell Calloway
Tariq/Slick Will: Eriq La Salle
Max: Titus Welliver
T.J.: Kadeem Hardison
Chu Chu: Terrence DaShon Howard
Donny: Tyson Beckford

Blue Car

Ready or not . . . the future comes just the same.
—Movie tagline
Sometimes it takes a journey to find yourself.
—Movie tagline

In the dour coming-of-age drama *Blue Car,* young Agnes Bruckner makes a nuanced, thought-provoking debut as Megan Denning, an unhappy teenaged girl buffeted by severe family trauma and adolescent confusion. Former television soap opera actress Karen Moncrieff wrote and directed this first-time effort, which won notice at the 2002 Sundance Festival and was picked up by Miramax. David

Strathairn co-stars as Megan's enigmatic English teacher, Mr. Auster. Both performances are subtle and unnerving, but the depressing script fails to provide any surprises.

There have been a slew of movies about older male teachers and their female teenage students, from *Lolita* to *To Sir With Love,* and on and on. From the beginning, there's little doubt about which way this script is heading. Auster thinks he spots a poet's soul and talent in Megan—or so it seems—and he invites her to begin meeting him in his classroom at lunchtime to work on some poetry. Megan's feelings about these meetings are telegraphed by a scene in which her little sister Lily (a scene-stealing Regan Arnold) asks why she is getting dressed up for school and wearing her mom's blouse. But other than her upgrade in attire, Megan provides no verbal or visual clues that she might be attracted to Mr. Auster. At their lunch hour meetings, there is no hanky-panky, and at first the teacher seems almost disinterested in her, but Mr. Auster is emotionally abusive in a more subtle way. He wants to make her tell him her secrets. He tells Megan that all good poets must touch their deepest nerves and bare their souls, and he begins prying into the most painful part of her life, the moment when her father left the family behind by driving off in the family's blue sedan. Megan has written a poem called "Blue Car," which betrays her own feeling that she is somehow to blame for her father's abrupt departure.

Since her dad walked away, Megan's home life has been pretty miserable. Her frazzled mother, Diane (Margaret Colin), is working long hours and going to school after work; it seems that she's also courting her boss. Diane expects Megan to take care of Lily, but Lily is uncooperative and depressed, and she often plays Megan against her mom, so that Diane scolds Megan. Lily is sullen and given to cutting her flesh with scissors. Megan nurses Lily's wounds and tries to comfort her, but she also tells her that she looks just like her dad, and this seems to send Lily into a deeper funk. Lily also blames herself for their father's absence. She eventually stops eating and is hospitalized after fainting during Mass, where she suddenly starts speaking about being an angel.

The tragedy that befalls Lily is the worst thing about *Blue Car.* It is a terribly insidious plot device that is handled with gross manipulation of sentiment and then abruptly left behind; life goes on as if nothing much has occurred. Moncrieff conveys emotions in hackneyed "indie" fashion—with extreme close-ups, plaintive and uninspiring folk-pop dirges on the soundtrack, and trite shots of faces framed and reflected in windows and mirrors. This is a movie that fairly screams out about how sensitive and deep it is trying to be. Yet, for all its laudable efforts to transcend stock movie roles and make its characters achingly real, its plot is nothing but a set-up.

The plot turns around Megan's efforts to raise money to go to Florida to attend a national poetry tournament at the urging of Mr. Auster. Unwilling to accept his financial help,

Megan instead turns to theft and deceit, but all her efforts are thwarted or wasted. She destroys most of her life in her attempt to get to the contest and win. This chance at victory feels like a shot at redemption to her, and Mr. Auster's thinly measured praise is the only bright spot in her worsening life.

Moncrieff doesn't sugar-coat family relations. Diane Denning isn't shown in a very positive light; she's a weary, impatient mother given to rages and to accusing Megan of being ungrateful. For her part, Megan is also brash and bitter, verbally hitting her mother right where it hurts. It's clear that everyone in the family is trying to assess blame for the father's departure. One of the strengths of *Blue Car* is its nasty, no-holds-barred family arguments, but that's also one of its weaknesses. How many people want to go to the movies to land smack-dab in mean-spirited feuding and name-calling? Too many scenes are almost embarrassing, as if we're voyeurs peeking in on family matters.

There's a fine balance between world weariness and realism and making a movie that has all the love and sweetness sucked out of it. *Blue Car*'s characters are so lacking in human goodness and optimism and so dreadfully full of weaknesses and shallowness that it's hard to feel much sympathy for them. Even with Bruckner's brilliant performance, the movie stacks up the details of her victimization like a court indictment, and then has her squandering all that potential sympathy by acting dishonestly out of her desperation. After all the nastiness and despair, the patch-it-back-together epilogue seems dreadfully inane and lacking in credibility.

Much-needed comic relief is provided about two-thirds through the film with the appearance of a new character, Pat (A. J. Buckley), the older brother of Megan's best friend, Georgia (Sarah Buehler). He is a foul-mouthed braggart and thief, and he gives the film a life—here finally is someone with a sense of humor. But even he is quickly revealed to be a betrayer, and yet another person Megan can't trust. The plot in this movie stacks the deck; the only relief that Megan can find in this landscape of despair, the only person who seems to treat her decently, is Mr. Auster. He and his poetry contest are the only means by which she can become self-confident and escape the world that seems to be closing in on her.

The slowly developing relationship between Auster and Megan, however trite, is masterfully handled, mostly because of the two actors' fine performances. Strathairn is excellent in presenting a rather parched, desperate soul who is adept at revealing just enough of himself to suck in his young pet. He seems an eminently decent man, tortured by the near-insanity of his wife (Frances Fisher) and generous to a fault with his time. But he's also a skilled manipulator, making himself indispensable to his student in subtle ways. Strathairn also conveys the desperation of a needy man trying to keep his worst impulses in check.

The best things about *Blue Car* are scenes in which much is conveyed by omission. After Megan begins to call on Mr. Auster for emotional support to deal with her family tragedies, she asks, "Why are you so nice to me?" One look at Strathairn's tortured face and the answer is clear, and Megan quickly says something else, knowing she shouldn't be asking the question. Until the end of the film, Moncrieff tries to maintain suspense about where the relationship is headed, but she also constantly undermines it. She makes Megan so vulnerable that it will be hard for her to resist throwing herself in Auster's arms, and there is something terribly manipulative about that.

Bruckner is fantastic at portraying the ordinariness and opaqueness of a teenage girl. Her character is not glamorous and doesn't have a strong personality; she is quiet, determined, confused, and looks and acts just like a normal teenaged girl, not an older actress trying to play one. There are moments when her pain is palpable, and her performance during the expected climactic scene with Strathairn is both mesmerizing and deeply disturbing. In fact, it is Bruckner and Strathairn who make this otherwise trite movie rather special.

It's a shame these two bold and groundbreaking performances are undermined by the leadenness of a script that plods along and a movie that wallows in its own "independent" anti-cinematic moods. There are ways to be dark without draining a film's characters of appeal, and there are ways to be cost-conscious without making the product look cheesy, but Moncrieff hasn't managed to pull them off. The discerning will notice, for example, that the Florida beach scenes go quickly from sun to fog and back to sun, and that there are mountains in the background—because it was shot in California. Low-budget films don't have to eschew humor, surprise, and creativity in order to be authentic, but *Blue Car* is like a trip through a feminist purgatory, where all the situations are tawdry, the lighting is dark, and the soundtrack is plaintive. It's not inspiring, just depressing, and while it's wonderfully acted, it never comes alive.

—*Michael Betzold*

Meg: Agnes Bruckner
Auster: David Strathairn
Diane: Margaret Colin
Lily: Regan Arnold
Delia: Frances Fisher
Pat: A.J. Buckley
Georgia: Sarah Beuhler

Origin: USA
Released: 2003
Production: Peer J. Oppenheimer, Amy Sommers, David Waters; released by Miramax Films
Directed by: Karen Moncrieff

Written by: Karen Moncrieff
Cinematography by: Rob Sweeney
Music by: Stuart Spencer-Nash
Sound: Mark Ferrell
Editing: Toby Yates
Costumes: Kristan Andrews
Production Design: Kristan Andrews
MPAA rating: R
Running time: 96 minutes

 REVIEWS

Boxoffice. April, 2002, p. 176.
Chicago Sun-Times Online. May 16, 2003.
Los Angeles Times Online. May 2, 2003.
New York Times Online. May 2, 2003.
People. May 19, 2003, p. 40.
San Francisco Chronicle. April 27, 2003, p. O1.
Variety. January 21, 2002, p. 34.

AWARDS AND NOMINATIONS

Nomination:
Ind. Spirit 2004: Actress (Bruckner), First Screenplay.

Boat Trip

Singles Cruise. Double Trouble.
—Movie tagline

Box Office: $8.6 million

It's difficult to tell who *Boat Trip* was made for. It's a movie about a gay (male) cruise that features excessive shots of a buxom (female) Swedish tanning team. With its ample lineup of racy jokes it's not a family film. The frequent boob shots and crude humor isn't going to make it a popular rerun on the Lifetime Channel. And the amount of Cuba Gooding Jr. fans who have managed to stick with him through films like *Snow Dogs* probably isn't enough to earn the film's catering budget back. Any uber-hetero guy who would be yukking it up over double entendres like a hot woman getting a massage urging her masseur to "give it to me harder—harder!" probably isn't going to be the type to suggest to his buddies that they should check out the new film about a gay cruise.

Despite being about gay people, *Boat Trip* doesn't seem to be made for them either. Before the film even came out, gay groups protested the film for its heavy reliance on stereotypes. The many gay jokes in the film tend to be of the variety that gay guys like disco and listen to a lot of Liza Minnelli. This is old stuff. Anyone looking to be versed in the current state of gay humor for mainstream America would do better to tune in a couple minutes of *Will and Grace* or even *Frasier*.

Boat Trip seems like a low-grade Farrelly Brothers film, and there is a Farrelly connection there. Director and co-writer Mort Nathan was one of the writers on their 1996 film *Kingpin*. He's a longtime TV guy with shows like *Benson, The Golden Girls,* and *Archie Bunker's Place* to his credit. Maybe that's why *Boat Trip* seems like some sort of twisted late night version of *The Love Boat*.

Jerry (Gooding) is wallowing in self-pity after his proposal to Felicia (Viveca A. Fox) is met with the news that she is seeing her car detailer. While out cruising for chicks yet again, his friend, Nick (*Saturday Night Live*'s Horatio Sanz, a low-rent John Belushi), sees an old homely buddy with a gorgeous babe on his arm. The secret, the friend reveals, is going on a cruise. The women, you see, can't leave. It's a sure thing. Nick immediately decides that he and Jerry must take a cruise to score some action. And "action" is exactly the way the crude Nick would describe it.

Their plans to get some ladies is foiled when they annoy their travel agent and he secretly books them on the Socrates Club, a gay cruise. In a scene that shows Nathan's typical disregard for sense, Jerry and Nick spend several minutes boarding the ship, walking all around the decks and through lobbies, talking about how they are going to meet so many women. They don't notice that, of all the passengers roaming around, not one is a woman. Doesn't it seem like they were so ready to enjoy the ladies, they might spend a moment or two bothering to ogle potential conquests? Once they find out that they are on a gay cruise, they—in fine intolerant fashion—are so horrified that they actually want to jump off the ship. It doesn't cross their minds that they could enjoy the cruise anyway.

The filmmakers seem to be equally uncomfortable with the idea of spending time on an all-gay cruise, so they quickly hustle some women onto the scene. Jerry meets Gabriella (Roselyn Sanchez of *Rush Hour 2*), the cruise's dance instructor. She claims to be happy to be on the gay cruise so she won't have to risk having yet another bad experience with a straight guy. She reveals that she's happy that she can just be "her" without having to worry about her make-up or clothing. (Nonetheless, this doesn't deter her from wearing tons of makeup and barely-there clothing anyway.) She tells Jerry that she's fine having a sex-free cruise, but confesses that if things get too bad she might have one of the gay guys service her. For stupid plot reasons, Jerry takes this to mean that he should pretend to be gay. Why he

can't just present himself as he is, is another thing that doesn't occur to him.

And, get this, Nick has to pretend that he's gay, too. In a moment of despair, Nick shoots a flare gun into the air and accidentally shoots down a helicopter. This is played for laughs, especially when—ha-ha—Nick sneaks away and doesn't report the incident to anyone. Despite Nick's lack of common decency, the passengers manage to be rescued anyway and end up on the boat. They are the aforementioned Swedish tanning team. Inga (Playboy Playmate of the Year Victoria Silvstedt) tells a panting Nick that they are happy to be on a gay cruise so that they can train by exposing sensitive parts of their body to the sun without dealing with leering men. Posing as gay, Nick gets his jollies by spreading suntan lotion all over the women. Inga admits that she would easily go to bed with Nick, if only he weren't gay.

Inga's not the only one who inexplicably has the hots for the rotund and boorish Nick. An old queen, Lloyd (Roger Moore, yes, 007), also has a thing for Nick. He's always suggestively leering over the sweaty guy. At one point, the poor older actor actually has to lick a sausage and coo, "Would you care for a bite of my sausage? In England, we call them bangers . . ."

The most interesting plot turn involves Nick spending a drunken evening with some new poker buddies and ending up in one of their beds. In the morning, he thinks something has happened and decides that he's gay. The filmmakers can't accept this kind of resolution though, and have Nick discover that he did not have gay sex. He decides immediately that he is not gay after all. In fact he is so not-gay that later he will be willing to hike miles in snowy Swedish mountains in order to see Inga again.

Jerry's situation unfolds in predictable beats. He gets close to Gabriella, they have sex, then she learns he was lying to her. As any good movie girlfriend would do, she has a brief snit, but will eventually take him back. At least she, unlike many other movie girlfriends, threatens him with a stern "Don't you ever, ever lie to me again." Yeah, that ought to do it. Of course, there are some complications. Jerry's wedding to the wrong woman first has to be interrupted at the exact point when the minister asks, "Is there anyone here who can offer any reason . . ." Jerry then has to skydive onto Gabriella's ship to propose to her, when a simple meeting at her next pier would do.

Boat Trip is quite racy, and earns its R rating. There are a lot of visual sexual gags and lots of pseudo-naughty dialogue. When the guys mistake the ship's Hole in One club for a golf club, Moore's Lloyd comments, "Some of the chaps do swing some very large clubs." Members of the Swedish tanning team are constantly saying things like, "Now we are laying down to sleep on our hot tight bodies." To the movie's credit, it doesn't stick to just one kind of humor, and every now and then a clever line gets through. When Nick is forced to make a quick decision, he says to himself, "Can't . . . think. Took too much shop in high school."

To cover his hide, Nathan shoves in a scene in which Nick decides that maybe gay people are okay after all. In the clunker of a scene, Nick has a heart to heart with Hector (Maurice Godin), the lisping super-gay guy next door and learns that "We are all God's children."

Boat Trip was supremely unpopular with critics. Wesley Morris of the *Boston Globe* wrote, "There is some concern that *Boat Trip* . . . might be harmful to gay men. This is not entirely true. *Boat Trip* is bad for everybody." Of Gooding, Carla Meyer of the *San Francisco Chronicle* wrote, "Flouncing and preening, the actor works so hard to sell the movie's penile, puerile jokes, his strain so evident, that it borders on sad." Elvis Mitchell of the *New York Times* wrote, "If *Boat Trip* were screened on a cruise ship, most of the passengers would be dog-paddling back to shore." And Roger Ebert of the *Chicago Sun-Times* wrote, "it is dim-witted, unfunny, too shallow to be offensive, and way too conventional to use all of those people standing around in the background wearing leather and chains and waiting hopefully for their cues."

—*Jill Hamilton*

CREDITS

Jerry: Cuba Gooding Jr.
Nick: Horatio Sanz
Gabriella: Roselyn Sanchez
Felicia: Vivica A. Fox
Hector: Maurice Godin
Lloyd: Roger Moore
Sonya: Lin Shaye
Inga: Victoria Silvstedt
Malcolm: Richard Roundtree
Brian's boyfriend: Will Ferrell
Brian: Artie Lange
Captain: Bob Gunton
Sheri: Jennifer Gareis

Origin: USA
Released: 2003
Production: Brad Krevoy, Andrew Sugerman, Gerhard Schmidt, Frank Huebner; Motion Picture Corporation of America, Apollomedia, Gemini Film Productions, International West Pictures; released by Artisan Entertainment
Directed by: Mort Nathan
Written by: Mort Nathan, William Bigelow
Cinematography by: Shawn Maurer
Music by: Robert Folk
Sound: Jacob Goldstein
Music Supervisor: Michelle Kuznetsky, Mary Ramos
Editing: John Axness

Art Direction: Uli Hanisch
Costumes: Tim Chappel
Production Design: Charles Breen
MPAA rating: R
Running time: 95 minutes

REVIEWS

Chicago Sun-Times Online. March 21, 2003.
Entertainment Weekly. March 28, 2003, p. 49.
Los Angeles Times Online. March 21, 2003.
New York Times Online. March 21, 2003.
Variety Online. March 20, 2003.
Washington Post. March 21, 2003, p. WE38.

AWARDS AND NOMINATIONS

Nomination:
Golden Raspberries 2003: Worst Actor (Gooding), Worst Director (Nathan).

The Bread, My Sweet (A Wedding for Bella)

In Italian a good man is a piece of bread.
—Movie tagline

The Bread, My Sweet is as innocent and sweet as its title suggests, but this independent film about a man fulfilling his dying godmother's wish falters because of amateurish scripting and the mannered work of the supporting cast. In the lead, Scott Baio gives a surprisingly deep and convincing performance as Dominic, a Pittsburgh trade company raider by day but an Italian biscotti bakery owner by night. Dominic promises his surrogate mother Bella (Rosemary Prinz) an upstairs neighbor who has just learned she has only six months left to live, that he will marry her daughter, Lucca (Kristin Minter).

The problem for Dominic is that he doesn't love Lucca and the lack of feeling seems to be mutual. Dominic forces his family, including his mentally disabled brother, Eddie (Billy Mott), to keep Bella's illness a secret, but word gets out and Dominic is forced to act upon Bella's request. After some persuasion, Lucca agrees to the marriage, with the condition that after Bella dies, the union will be dissolved.

Bella is overjoyed at the prospect of the nuptials (she has been saving money for it ever since Lucca was born), and she gets happily involved in the preparations. Unfortunately, Bella's health deteriorates and she dies soon after the ceremony. As Dominic mourns for Bella, he starts to reassess his career as a shark-like broker. Soon, he decides to devote himself entirely to the small bakery business and give up the corporate life. Then Dominic and Lucca reevaluate their relationship, choosing not to break up after all.

There is much potential for comedy in Melissa Martin's screenplay. At least two plot devices stem from previous screwball farces: Dominic juggling his wildly different jobs recalls *Live a Little, Love a Little* (1968) with Elvis Presley; and Dominic and Lucca maintaining a false front to appease the elderly woman comes right out of *La Cage aux Folles* (1978) and its remake, *The Bird Cage* (1996). But Martin, who also directed, creates a sentimental mood, making the situations as realistically dramatic as possible. After all, the story is loosely based on a real-life romance and the actual history surrounding the Enrico Biscotti Company in Pittsburgh (where the film was shot). Martin is also clearly inspired by other films, including romantic stories much more fanciful than *The Bread, My Sweet*, including *Moonstruck* (1987), *Like Water for Chocolate* (1992), *Chocolat* (2001), and *My Big Fat Greek Wedding* (2002). Not coincidentally, all these films bring food and ethnic heritage into the foreground and find sensuous associations between food and love. On the plus side, Martin never makes her characters as stereotyped or silly as the Italian family in *Moonstruck* or the Greek family in *My Big Fat Greek Wedding*, but neither does she make them as engaging or entertaining. In a typical scene, Dominic's godfather, Massimo (John Seitz), launches into "La Donna e Mobile," but the "spontaneous" moment is strained and overly cute, not unlike the kind of Hollywood bit the film is seemingly trying to avoid.

Yet even the dramatic devices seem forced and phony, mainly due to the screenplay as well as Rosemary Prinz's showy performance as Bella. Prinz makes her feature film debut with a theatrical style more suited to her work on the stage and her role on the television soap opera *As the World Turns*. The scene in which Bella opens an old coffee can and takes out the money she's been saving for Lucca's wedding is the stuff of formulaic tearjerkers and so old-hat it might not even be allowed on *As the World Turns!* Prinz also overplays her light moments, including when trying on outfits in a "wedding preparation" montage that could have been concocted for *My Best Friend's Wedding* (1997). If *The Bread, My Sweet* wants to play its situations for drama, Bella's exacting attitude and guilt-tripping methods should be shown as the source of the immigrant family's chilling dysfunction, not as comic relief.

The lead actors try hard to keep the story from getting too cutesy—or too melodramatic. Scott Baio (best remembered for his teen heartthrob roles on TV's *Happy Days* and *Charles in Charge*) and Kristin Minter (the sassy clerk on *E.R.*) show they are skilled at portraying characters very different from those of their TV personas. Their scenes together are likable and credible. The supporting players seem to follow in Rosemary Prinz's declamatory footsteps: John Seitz's galvanic Massimo would have been portrayed years ago by Nehemiah Persoff; Billy Mott plays Eddie as if rehearsing an Actor's Studio workshop exercise; and the extras who populate the corporate-trade offices look highly self-conscious, as if they had never been in a movie before.

As Melissa Martin's directorial debut, *The Bread, My Sweet* shows some promise in that the film technique is generally adequate, but Martin will have to work harder as a writer and control her actors more if she she wants to engage her viewers or make a lasting contribution to film.

—Eric Monder

CREDITS

Dominic: Scott Baio
Lucca: Kristin Minter
Bella: Rosemary Prinz
Massimo: John Seitz
Eddie: Billy Mott
Pino: Shuler Hensley

Origin: USA
Released: 2001
Production: Melissa Martin, William C. Hulley, Adrienne Wehr; Buon Sibo, Who Knew Productions; released by Panorama Entertainment
Directed by: Melissa Martin
Written by: Melissa Martin
Cinematography by: Mark Knobil
Music by: Susan Hartford
Editing: Chuck Aikman
Production Design: Paul Bucciarelli
MPAA rating: PG-13
Running time: 105 minutes

REVIEWS

Chicago Sun-Times Online. November 8, 2002.
New York Times Onlne. October 24, 2003.
San Francisco Chronicle. April 18, 2003, p. I5.
Variety Online. May 24, 2001.

QUOTES

Bella (Rosemary Prinz) to Dominic (Scott Baio): "Three years ago, I didn't know your name. Now, you are my son."

Bringing Down the House

Everything he needed to know about life, she learned in prison.
—Movie tagline

 Box Office: $132.5 million

P retty much all you need to know about *Bringing Down the House* is there in the print ads for the film. It shows Steve Martin with eyes wide, looking a bit worried. His hands are clasped conservatively in front of him. The object of Martin's worry seems to be Queen Latifah, who is resplendent in two-tone blue fingernails and a bust line that seems to be pushing her purse aside. Eugene Levy is in the background looking like the usual square guy that he plays. The ad is topped by the pull quote, "Side-splitting, knee-slapping, belly-aching laughs." Besides sounding quite painful, the quote is attributed to that noted film critic Mose Persico of Entertainment Spotlight. Entertainment Spotlight is that well-known, er, web site? Newspaper? Public access cable show? In case that's not recommendation enough, there's also a blurb from Richard Reid of Northwest Cable News. Reid apparently said the film was "In-your-face funny and loaded with laughs." No word yet on what writers from the magazine Cat Fancy thought of the film.

From all this we can glean that the film is probably about Queen Latifah upsetting the ordered world of Martin and Levy. We can surmise that her sassy ways will upset, but ultimately save the lives of the two uptight white guys. From the dearth of decent rave reviews, we can also figure out that all of this doesn't happen in a very humorous manner.

Those who want to get the gist of the rest of the movie without actually having to go through the trouble of actually seeing the film, can get by with just seeing the trailer. This trailer is like a *Cliff Notes* for the film. Every salient plot point and joke is in there in quick, condensed form. Info that can be gleaned from the film include the major subplot that Levy's character is attracted to Queen Latifah's "cocoa goddess" self, that Latifah's character represents herself in a major way and that Martin's character will get back with his wife. And that's pretty much the whole thing.

It's all held together by one main joke, which is basically, "Don't those black people talk funny?" The stance that the movie takes is that white people speak correctly and the black people don't know how to talk properly. The humor is escalated, according to writer Jason Filardi, when the white people try to—snick, snick—talk like black people. Thus we have Eugene Levy saying, "Swing it you cocoa goddess,"

"You got me straight trippin', boo" and the like. This happens over and over so we can appreciate the full humor of it.

Filardi and director Adam Shankman (*The Wedding Planner*) set up a pretty contrived plot in order to let those laughs flow. Peter Sanderson (Martin) is a tax lawyer who is continually choosing work over his kids, Sarah (Kimberly J. Brown) and Georgey (Angus T. Jones), and his ex-wife, Kate (Jean Smart). He's the kind of guy who will interrupt a heart-to-heart talk with a family member to take a call on his cell phone. In a sitcom-worthy plot element, Peter has to win the big client, rich Mrs. Arness (Joan Plowright), to succeed at his job.

Peter has been corresponding via e-mail with Lawyergirl, who he believes to be a tall blonde attorney. He sets up a date with her, and when she arrives at the door, he is shocked when she turns out to be . . . black. That the movie takes it as completely normal that Peter would be horrified by his date being this large black woman could have been the most racist moment in the film, but there's actually something later that tops it.

Charlene Morton (Latifah) turns out to be a convict who wants Martin to expunge her record of the armed robbery crime that she says she didn't commit. Peter refuses and kicks her out, but for vague plot reasons, she ends up staying at his house. This creates havoc in his life because, well, just because. His neighbor (Betty White) is a relative of one of the partners in his firm and if she mentions that Peter is harboring a black person, why that would cost him his job. Additionally, Peter must hide his relationship with Charlene from Mrs. Arness. Thus, when Peter and Charlene are talking at his country club and Mrs. Arness walks in, it's panic time. Peter comes up with a scheme in which he pretends that Charlene is his nanny. Why he can't just say she's a client and be done with it is never adequately explained. Is it a career-breaker to simply be seen talking to a black person?

Racist jokes are still a tricky area and *Bringing Down the House* tries to be lighthearted and inoffensive about its jokes. And mainly the jokes are pretty tame. It's the underlying assumptions that offend. For example, as Charlene lives with the Sanderson family she starts helping them all out. She teaches the son to read and cooks fabulous meals. When Peter needs help wooing his ex-wife back, she is more than happy to help him there, too. After a drunken evening, the two stumble into the living room and Charlene starts giving him pointers. The scene involves Peter grabbing Charlene's ample chest and dry humping her. It's one thing to help the kids out with their homework, but letting dad practice on your chest is a little beyond the call of duty. Roger Ebert of the *Chicago Sun-Times* made the point that any other movie would have had Charlene and Peter falling in love. Instead, Charlene is pawned off on the unappealing Howie Rottman (Levy). Charlene and Peter are the ones who have the chemistry. Would them falling in love be too subversive? In a neighborhood where you're not even allowed to have black guests who aren't nannies or maids, perhaps it is.

That said, the scene between Charlene and Peter is the funniest one in the film. Martin is truly at his best as Latifah eggs him on to be sexy. She urges him on to talk nastily and say out loud what he would want to do to his ex-wife. Martin screws on his supposedly sexy face and says primly, "I'm going to have sexual intercourse with you!" Other failed attempts include, "I'm going to give you an aromatherapy massage!"

Scenes like this show just how good Martin can be. He throws himself into the role, even doing some serviceable hip-hop dancing, and is such a likable actor, it just makes you wish he was in some other, better movie. Martin is a wonderful comic performer and his presence alone is enough to make this a better movie-watching experience than it should be. Queen Latifah is also a formidable presence. Latifah, who was executive producer on the film, reportedly helped tone down some of the more racist aspects of the film, but there was a lot more to be done. This is a film that forces her to dress in a maid's uniform, be called dismissively "Jemina" and be asked "What did you just say?" after she speaks. When she says she read law books in prison, Peter says with surprise, "And with comprehension!" Imagine, a black person who can read with comprehension. Still, Latifah has enough force that she comes out with her pride intact. White is good as the cheerfully offensive neighbor. After hearing Latifah speak, she pops her head out her window and says quizzically, "I thought I heard negro."

Critics (from known publications, at least) didn't care for the movie so much. Manohla Dargis of the *Los Angeles Times* wrote, "Charlene sasses Sanderson every which way, but somehow the joke is usually on her." Lou Lumenick of the *New York Post* wrote, "There's a certain predictability and pulling of punches that makes one yearn for the wild and crazy comedies of the early '80s, when Martin and his comic muse, director Carl Reiner would have turned this premise into something truly subversive." James Hill of BET.com wrote that the film "ends up being a one-joke movie that constantly asks you, 'Hey, isn't it funny when White people try to act Black?'" And Elvis Mitchell of the *New York Times* wrote, "High-school cafeteria soup had more flavor than this bland, tepid throwback."

—*Jill Hamilton*

Peter Sanderson: Steve Martin
Charlene Morton: Queen Latifah
Howie Rottman: Eugene Levy
Kate: Jean Smart
Georgey Sanderson: Angus T. Jones
Sarah Sanderson: Kimberly J. Brown
Mrs. Arness: Joan Plowright
Ashley: Missi Pyle
Widow: Steve Harris
Todd Gendler: Michael Rosenbaum
Mrs. Kline: Betty White

Origin: USA
Released: 2003
Production: David Hoberman, Ashok Amritraj; Hyde Park Entertainment; released by Touchstone Pictures
Directed by: Adam Shankman
Written by: Jason Filardi
Cinematography by: Julio Macat
Music by: Lalo Schifrin
Sound: David MacMillan
Music Supervisor: Michael McQuarn
Editing: Jerry Greenberg
Art Direction: Jim Nedza
Costumes: Pamela Ball Withers
Production Design: Linda DeScenna
MPAA rating: PG-13
Running time: 105 minutes

REVIEWS

Chicago Sun-Times Online. March 7, 2003.
Entertainment Weekly. March 14, 2003, p. 44.
Los Angeles Times Online. March 7, 2003.
New York Times Online. March 7, 2003.
People. March 17, 2003, p. 35.
USA Today Online. March 7, 2003.
Variety Online. February 23, 2003.
Washington Post. March 7, 2003, p. WE39.

QUOTES

Georgey (Angus T. Jones), reading girlie magazine: "Dad, what's a rack?" Peter (Steve Martin), snatching magazine away replies: "It's a country."

Brother Bear

Nature Calls.
—Movie tagline

 Box Office: $84.9 million

The most lasting imprint that *Brother Bear* will likely leave on the world of film is that it marked what Disney Studios was calling the last of its movies made (for the foreseeable future) with the traditional 2-D style of animation. The studio was switching to the computer animation that proved so popular (and lucrative) in films like *Finding Nemo*.

Brother Bear wasn't much of a success at the box office, but, as many critics pointed out, that wasn't because of its animation style. Kenneth Turan of the *Los Angeles Times,* praised the "richness and fluidity" of the film's visuals, while noting that "this irreplaceable technique has, through no fault of its own, become joined at the hip to a sensibility so conventional and overly familiar it practically has moss growing on it."

And it doesn't help matters that the (many) screenwriters—Tab Murphy, Lorne Cameron, David Hoselton, Steve Bencich, and Ron. J. Friedman—didn't come up with a particularly inspired script. It's not the animation style that makes this film so stodgy and lackluster, it's the content. Just because they're working in an old format doesn't mean they can only use old ideas. It's too bad that this "last" big hand-drawn animated feature had to be so weak. When faced with a choice between tired yet good-looking movies like this vs. witty original movies that leap off the screen like *A Bug's Life,* it's a pretty obvious choice.

To try to keep up with some of the hip factor that delighted parents as much as kids in films like *Toy Story* or *Shrek, Brother Bear* adds a few modern touches. The thing is, these touches are miserable failures. For one thing, there's the music by Phil Collins. Note to filmmakers: Having a parent-appeasing song by the eels in *Shrek* was hip. Having music by Phil Collins is not. Next is having Dave Thomas and Rick Moranis give voice to a pair of moose, Rutt and Tuke. The two *SCTV* veterans use the same voices that they used for their Canadian beer-drinking characters Bob and Doug MacKenzie. Said routine dates from the 1970s and nary a "take off, hoser" is replaced with fresher material. Again, not hip. It's not even close, and perhaps approaching a category of being negatively hip. Finally, there are the voices. The story involves three brothers who lived in prehistoric times. They talk like modern guys and say things like "Dude." It's beyond anachronistic.

When they're not calling each other "dude," Kenai (Joaquin Phoenix) and his older brothers, Denahi (Jason Raize) and Sitka (D. B. Sweeney), live their lives as part of a tribe that lived 10,000 years ago in some sort of cold part of the earth where there are mountains, bears and northern lights. Kenai is getting ready for the big ceremony in which the tribe's shaman, Tanana (Joan Copeland), will give him his totem. The totem, a wood figure carved by Tanana, represents the principle that will guide a person's life. When a boy learns to live his life by the principles of his totem, he will then become a man. Kenai hopes to get an exciting one like his older brothers. Sitka has the eagle to represent guidance and Denahi has the wolf to represent wisdom. Kenai is disappointed to receive a bear to represent love. Dude, that's lame. We sense that a lesson will be learned.

When Kenai fails to tie up properly a basket of fish, a bear steals the catch. Ignoring his love totem, Kenai chases after the bear to kill it, but soon finds himself in danger. His brothers rush to save him, but in the resulting loud and scary fight, Sitka ends up dead. (And what better way to begin a fine Disney movie for little kids than a fight, loud noises, and the scary death of a close family member?) To add a touch more violence to the proceedings, Kenai then kills the bear.

In some sort of weird supernatural event involving a combination of the northern lights, his brother Sitka's spirit, and all the ancestors, Kenai ends up becoming a bear himself only to discover that Denahi, who doesn't realize what has happened, is chasing him. Kenai also discovers that, while he can't communicate with humans, he can now talk with animals, including the most-annoying Koda (voiced by Jeremy Suarez of *Jerry Maguire*). Koda is that animated cliché, the cheery sidekick that won't leave and won't shut up. To add to the misery of the long-suffering parents in the audience, Koda has the additional annoying trait of being way too cute and perky.

Koda and Kenai start hanging out together because Koda thinks he can help Kenai find the place where the lights meet the mountain. Kenai puts up with Koda because he knows that if the small bear can help him find his way to the mountain, he can change back to human form. Along the way, they have barely entertaining adventures, a few (very few) laughs and help each other escape danger. Koda teaches Kenai the ways of the bear and Kenai serves as a big brother figure to Koda, who could use an older bear around since his mom seems to be missing.

There are some things that work in the film. The movie's idea that ancestors live in the sky in animal form and actively watch their descendants is fun to contemplate. And the movie does look quite nice. Particularly good are the views of the dramatic lights in the sky which look appropriately otherworldly.

But the good in *Brother Bear* is far outweighed by what doesn't work. It's not funny enough. The moose are supposed to provide the laughs for the film and they're not up to the task. The movie's not character-driven enough. Phoenix is a very good actor, but his Kenai lacks any kind of hook—he's just not an interesting guy. As Roger Ebert would say, we don't care about him. And *Brother Bear* doesn't seem timeless enough. A movie about an ancient culture could have a timeless dignity, but tarting up the dialogue with current slang ruins that whole angle.

Only a fraction of critics liked *Brother Bear*. Turan of the *Times* wrote, "*Brother Bear* does have a satisfying ending and it's nice to see a G-rated movie without bathroom humor, but there is too much formula and not enough reason to pay attention here." Mark Caro of the *Chicago Tribune* wrote, "The journey is diverting in a Saturday-morning kind of way, but it doesn't compare to, say, *Finding Nemo,* where the stakes are higher, the laughs harder, the emotions deeper." Rob Blackwelder of *Spliced Wire* wrote, "*Brother Bear* isn't a bad movie, but it is obviously a product of minimal inspiration." Stephen Holden of the *New York Times* wrote, "This self-conscious, self-important film has the machine-tooled, market-tested gloss of an A-list Disney product straining to conquer the world the way *The Lion King* did nearly a decade ago."

—*Jill Hamilton*

CREDITS

Kenai: Joaquin Rafael (Leaf) Phoenix (Voice)
Koda: Jeremy Suarez (Voice)
Denahi: Jason Raize (Voice)
Rutt: Rick Moranis (Voice)
Tuke: Dave Thomas (Voice)
Sitka: D.B. Sweeney (Voice)
Tanana: Joan Copeland (Voice)
Tug: Michael Clarke Duncan (Voice)
Old Denahi: Harold Gould (Voice)
Old Lady Bear: Estelle Harris (Voice)

Origin: USA
Released: 2003
Production: Studio Ghibli; Walt Disney Pictures; released by Buena Vista
Directed by: Aaron Blaise, Robert Walker
Written by: Tab Murphy, Lorne Cameron, David Hoselton, Steve Bencich, Ron J. Friedman
Music by: Phil Collins, Mark Mancina
Editing: Tim Mertens
Art Direction: Robh Ruppel
MPAA rating: G
Running time: 85 minutes

REVIEWS

Entertainment Weekly. October 31, 2003, p. 55.
Los Angeles Times Online. October 25, 2003.
New York Times Online. October 24, 2003.
People. November 3, 2003, p. 33.
USA Today Online. October 24, 2003.
Variety Online. October 19, 2003.

Nomination:
Oscars 2003: Animated Film.

Bruce Almighty

In Bruce We Trust?
—Movie tagline
He's got the power.
—Movie tagline
The guy next door just became the man upstairs.
—Movie tagline

 Box Office: $233.2 million

B ruce Nolan (Jim Carrey) is a television reporter for Channel 7 in Buffalo, N.Y., and although he is quite successful doing his humorous human-interest stories, he feels the job is lightweight and longs to be the next Walter Cronkite. He desperately wants to trade his job of covering stories like the creation of Buffalo's biggest cookie for that of the soon-to-be-vacant anchor desk. Unfortunately for Bruce, he has competition for the job in the form of the shallow and condescending Evan Baxter (Steven Carell), another reporter at the station.

Bruce is assigned to cover the 156th anniversary of the famous Niagara Fall's tourist boat, "The Maid of the Mist," in a live feed during sweeps week. And, again unfortunately for Bruce, during that story he finds out that he has been passed over for the anchor job, which has been given to Evan. It's just too much for Bruce. He has an on-air melt down and signs off his story with the ultimate no-no, dropping an F-bomb on the air.

Of course this gets Bruce fired, but that is only the beginning of the downward spiral of his day. Out in the parking lot he sees some punks picking on a homeless man and he intervenes, but this just gets Bruce beaten up and his car vandalized.

At home, Bruce complains to his live-in girlfriend Grace Connelly (Jennifer Aniston). She tries to make him feel better with platitudes like, "everything happens for a reason," but Bruce won't accept that fatalistic philosophy. This brings Grace to ask Bruce if he actually believes God has singled him out for punishment, but Bruce believes that God isn't picking on him, He's ignoring him. "I'm not being a martyr," Bruce says, "I'm being a victim."

Poor Bruce. "I'm not OK with a mediocre job, a mediocre apartment, a mediocre life," he tells Grace, who, by extension must obviously be his mediocre girlfriend, and then storms out to his mediocre car to drive around the mediocre city of Buffalo. Railing at God as he drives, he begs for a signal . . . and he gets a few. But Bruce is so busy being negative, he is oblivious as he drives by the "caution ahead" sign and the truck bearing a load of "stop" signs, and he ends up crashing his car.

The next day, Bruce's pager goes off but he ignores the request for a return phone call. It goes off again and again, and he throws it out his apartment window where it lands in the street and is run over by a car. But when he hears the totally demolished pager go off yet again, he is curious, picks it up, and calls the number listed on it. A highly personalized, taped message eventually leads Bruce to a large, seemingly empty warehouse bearing the sign "Omni Presents." There he meets a man (Morgan Freeman) who seems to be the janitor, but who tells him that he is, in fact, God.

"You've been doing a lot of complaining about me and quite frankly I'm tired of it," God tells Bruce, and to teach him a lesson God gives Bruce his powers while his Almightiness takes a little vacation. (Great exchange: "God doesn't take vacations, does he?" Bruce asks. "Ever hear of the Dark Ages?" God replies.) There are only two things Bruce can't do: tell anyone he's God, and mess with people's free will.

Well, once Bruce is finally convinced that the janitor was indeed God and that he does indeed have divine powers, what does he do? A few parlor tricks (dividing his bowl of tomato soup like the Red Sea) and a lot of personal revenge. For starters, remember that gang bully? When Bruce meets him again he demands an apology, but the thug says he'll only do that when a monkey crawls out his butt. Guess what. With all that power, the only things Bruce can think of to do are those things that will entertain him, advance his career or work things to his advantage. In other words, Buffalo now has a god who is selfish, impulsive, and incredibly short-sighted. (When he "lassoes" the moon and pulls it closer for a romantic evening with Grace—whose breasts he secretly enlarged without her consent—he never once considers the consequences of this act: a tsunami in Japan.)

God Bruce, of course, gets his job back by manipulating events so that all his lightweight pieces become stop-the-presses stories. A mundane piece on police dogs has one of them digging up the body of Jimmy Hoffa . . . and Bruce is there, camera in hand, to cover it. At a chili cook-off, a meteor suddenly crashes just behind Bruce while he is on camera. Soon he has the title "Mr. Exclusive."

Two of the things Bruce does with his power, however, provide two of the funniest parts of the movie. In one, Grace's large dog, who insists on urinating on a chair in the apartment, is taught to actually use the bathroom toilet, including flushing and putting the seat down. Seeing that dog reading the newspaper in the john or exiting the room, oblivious to the toilet paper stuck to the bottom of its paw, is quite funny. Kudos to the trainer who rescued that canine thespian from an animal shelter.

Just about everyone agrees, however, that the funniest scene in the entire movie has Bruce sabotaging his anchor rival Evan by causing him to experience a series of embarrassing vocal anomalies, including a lot of jibberish on his first night on the air. Steven Carell (one of the correspondents on television's *The Daily Show with John Stewart*) steals the scene.

With Bruce gaining fame as Mr. Exclusive and Even making a fool of himself on camera, it's not long before Bruce gets his shot at the anchor desk. Everything seems to be going great for him, except for that strange buzzing in his brain and the fact that his success is ruining his relationship with Grace.

As for that buzzing, well, Bruce is hearing people's prayers, and there are more of them than he can possibly handle. As a result he tries to organize them: folders are too cumbersome and post-it-notes too overwhelming, so Bruce gets modern. He turns them into e-mail on Yahweh.com. Answering them, however, takes too much time so he just sets his computer to automatically answer "yes" to all of them. This benevolence will come back to haunt him. For example, one result is that there are so many lottery winners that everyone wins a disappointing $17. Between this and a power outage caused by that meteor, and people reading Doomsday prophecies into what has been happening, the people in Buffalo begin to riot.

It would seem like the perfect time to be reading the news from the anchor desk, but no matter how much Bruce intercedes, he can't keep the power on. "It's not so easy, this God business, is it?" God asks a frustrated Bruce. It certainly isn't, when we all-too-human humans are given way too much power, to go along with all our selfishness and short-sightedness. As the real, all-knowing God tells Bruce, "Since when does anyone have a clue about what they want?" And this includes Bruce. He only thought he knew what he wanted, but in the end he truly wants what he has just lost.

In *Bruce Almighty* Jim Carrey again teams with director Tom Shadyac (*Ace Ventura* and *Liar, Liar*), and with his crazy energy and that mischievous grin, he is a likeable enough actor in parts like this. But it is a part he has, more or less, done before: basically an ineffectual loser who suddenly finds himself out of his element and bumbling his way to winning whatever needs to be won, usually a woman.

Similarly, Jennifer Aniston is well cast as Bruce's down-to-earth girlfriend. She is cute and funny and overflowing with common sense, a real everywoman, but unfortunately her character is often nothing more than a springboard for Carrey's antics.

Undoubtedly, though, the best casting was Morgan Freeman as God. He is perfect. His quiet elegance and strength, his non-threatening seriousness that seems laced with a twinkle of good humor, his dignity and presence, his wisdom and patience all contribute to what virtually everyone hopes God is really like. This is a God who suffers human frailty without ever being truly mean to us. He understands. Of all the cinema Gods—Rex Ingram, George Burns, Richard Pryor, Whoopi Goldberg, Alanis Morrisette, Peter O'Toole, etc.—Morgan Freeman is by far the best.

Bruce Almighty created quite a bit of buzz back in 2000 when its screenplay was picked up on speculation by Universal for an unusual $1 million. Written by Steven Koren (*Superstar*), Mark O'Keefe (TV's *Jesse* and *NewsRadio*), and Steve Oedekerk (*Ace Ventura: When Nature Calls, Patch Adams*), the story is high concept, intentionally broad, more than a bit schmaltzy, and very predictable. It can also be very entertaining and appeals to the soft spot in all but the most jaded hearts. Audiences always complain that they want more "nice" films, well, here's one . . . and although many critics pan its corniness, audiences have loved it.

There have been other movies based on the premise of divine intervention in a person's life to show them what is truly of value. In fact, *It's a Wonderful Life*, from which *Bruce* often borrows, is actually playing on a TV set in background at one point. And like that predecessor, *Bruce* is not concerned much with religion per se. It is a basically secular movie that tries not to alienate anyone with its spiritual references.

It is a funny film with honest and heartfelt messages: Be appreciative of the gifts we are given (Bruce has an amazingly effortless ability to make people laugh but he thinks it's more important to be serious); don't just hope God will intervene on your behalf, try to figure things out for yourself; it's important to help other people, we can't just think of ourselves; and finally, the true source of power lies within us.

If after seeing this movie you agree that only telegrams should send messages and not movies, if you think this kind of movie is just too mawkish and trite, if you think the ending is annoyingly goody-goody, you should at least be able to thank God for Bruce's dog and Morgan Freeman. And if not, for God's sake, stop being so negative . . . you just never know who's listening.

—*Beverley Bare Buehrer*

Bruce Nolan: Jim Carrey
Grace Connelly: Jennifer Aniston
God: Morgan Freeman
Debbie: Lisa Ann Walter
Jack Keller: Philip Baker Hall
Susan Ortega: Catherine Bell

Ally Loman: Nora Dunn
Evan Baxter: Steven Cavell

Origin: USA
Released: 2003
Production: Tom Shadyac, James D. Brubaker, Michael Bostick, Jim Carrey, Steve Koren; Spyglass Entertainment, Shady Acres, Pit Bull; released by Universal Pictures
Directed by: Tom Shadyac
Written by: Steve Oedekerk, Steve Koren, Mark O'Keefe
Cinematography by: Dean Semler
Music by: John Debney
Sound: Jose Antonio Garcia
Music Supervisor: Jeff Carson
Editing: Scott Hill
Art Direction: Jim Nedza
Costumes: Judy Ruskin
Production Design: Linda DeScenna
MPAA rating: PG-13
Running time: 101 minutes

REVIEWS

Chicago Sun-Times Online. May 23, 2003.
Entertainment Weekly. May 30, 2003, p. 89.
Los Angeles Times Online. May 23, 2003.
New York Times Online. May 23, 2003.
People. June 2, 2003, p. 33.
USA Today Online. May 23, 2003.
Variety Online. May 23, 2003.
Washington Post. May 23, 2003, p. WE35.

QUOTES

Bruce (Jim Carrey): "Behind every great man . . . is a woman rolling her eyes."

Bubba Ho-Tep

The King of Rock vs. The King of the Dead.
—Movie tagline
You know the legends. . . . Now learn the truth.
—Movie tagline

 Box Office: $1.2 million

The makers of *Bubba Ho-Tep* must have known going in that they would already have a built-in audience for whatever they'd come up with. It would not be a big audience—this is not the same group that would be waiting for the next Meg Ryan romantic comedy or Tom Cruise epic. This is a group familiar with stuff that flies below the radar, B-grade stuff like *Evil Dead* and the *Phantasm* series. This group may be small, but it's fiercely loyal. An appearance by genre star Bruce Campbell at a theater near a university in Irvine, California, was standing room only. The university appearance was smart marketing. *Bubba Ho-Tep* is the kind of stuff that plays well with college audiences—the kind of audiences that don't mind seeing a movie with a weird name. (According to the movie: "Bubba: male from the southern United States. Ho-Tep: Relative of one of the Egyptian dynasties.")

Bubba Ho-Tep is filled with the work of heroes of this genre. The film was based on a short story by Joe R. Landsdale, the Nacogdoches, Texas-based "mojo story-teller." The so-called "Steven King of Texas" is known for writing horror fiction that's filled with pop-culture references. His God of the Razor character, probably his best known, combines elements of the Excalibur story and Jack the Ripper. Director Don Coscarelli, who also wrote the movie story, is the guy responsible for such cult films as the *Phantasm* series and *Beastmaster*. And who better to star in such a film than Campbell, *Evil Dead* star and a guy who described himself in his offbeat autobiography, *If Chins Could Kill,* as king of the second tier film circuit?

If all of this wouldn't automatically make it into a cult film—and it certainly does—the plot alone would. Elvis Presley (Campbell) is alive and well in the Shady Rest Convalescent Home in Mud Creek, Texas. After breaking his hip, he can't walk very well and he suffers from the discomfort of a strange growth on his nether regions. In a voiceover, Elvis is plenty happy to explain his presence at Shady Rest: He was busy being Elvis when he got fed up with it all—the fame, the drugs, the Colonel. He found an Elvis impersonator named Sebastian Haff and made a deal to trade places with him. The two signed a contract that they could trade back whenever they wanted. The contract was subsequently burned up in a barbecue accident, but Elvis didn't much mind. He was happy with his new, calmer lifestyle. He quietly toured the country as Sebastian Haff, Elvis impersonator. (The movie doesn't explain what happened to all the Elvis money, but as might already be apparent, it's not exactly a documentary.) Things get complicated when the real Haff goes and overdoses. And when Elvis breaks his hip while onstage, he has to live in the rest home. Here, he's willing to tell the real story of who he is, but no one seems very eager to believe him. His nurse (Ella Joyce) first thinks his story is funny, then she becomes annoyed by it. He notes bitterly, "When you get old, everything you do is either useless or sadly amusing."

There is one guy that does believe him. The guy down the hall, Jack (the always-excellent Ossie Davis), readily accepts his story. It figures, though, since Jack thinks he's John F. Kennedy. "But Jack . . . you're black," says Elvis, cautiously. "They dyed me this color. What better way to hide the truth than that?" replies Jack indignantly. The two seem to accept each other's stories. After all, what other choice do they have?

It's difficult to believe, but the story actually gets stranger. Two seemingly unrelated issues—that the rest home has a cockroach problem and that various residents are dying off—turn out to be part of something bigger. The cockroaches are actually ancient Egyptian scarabs. They mutate into giant cockroaches, then into a big scary mummy that, inexplicably wears a cowboy hat and boots. That would explain the name of the movie. That the movie had a negligible budget might also explain the odd attire. What better way to give your monster a distinguishable feature when you don't have any money to spend?

The monster invades the home at night to suck the souls out of the residents. He needs to suck up a lot of souls because older people's souls are not as nourishing as younger ones. JFK knows this because he's been studying up on it. He's also looking for more clues by trying to interpret the hieroglyphics that the monster has written on the restroom walls. Why would a killer mummy spend his off time writing notes in bathroom stalls? Why not? What else is he going to do? As the two oldsters continue to study the case, they discover that a bus carrying items for an Egyptian exhibition has crashed nearby. A mummy from the exhibition fell into a pond that's right near the rest home.

The movie finds the premise of these two going off to fight a mummy to be pretty darned hilarious. Thus we have lots of lines like this from Elvis, "I think you know what we're getting at, Mr. President, we're going to kill us a mummy." Or Elvis describing a scarab as "the size of a peanut butter and banana sandwich." These two famous guys break out a walker and a wheelchair and set out to battle the evil.

The story is certainly the most showy aspect of the film, but the part of the movie that works the best is actually more subtle. Campbell and Davis take their performances seriously and, improbably, turn this crazy film into a gentle meditation on aging. Elvis spends a lot of time ruminating on the details of his life. He pines for his daughter, Lisa Marie, and wishes he had handled things differently. He mourns for his old agile body and a time when he was taken seriously. He regrets that he made so many bad movies. The two men are desperate to have a purpose and to feel like they're living useful lives.

Most critics liked the film well enough, though there were dissenters. Roger Ebert of the *Chicago Sun-Times* wrote, "It does sort of work in one way: It has the damnedest ingratiating way of making us sit there and grin at its harebrained audacity, laugh at its outhouse humor, and be somewhat moved (not deeply, but somewhat) at the poignancy of these two old men and their situation." Megan Lehmann of the *New York Post* wrote, "The cheap effects make the lumbering mummy-in-a-cowboy-hat hilariously unscary, and the final showdown is a creakily staged hoot. It's a credit to the actors, particularly the superb Campbell, that completely preposterous material can be made strangely touching." Kevin Thomas of the *Los Angeles Times* called the film a "limp spoof" and wrote that Coscarelli "fails to come up with enough incidents and action to make this overly leisurely picture the zany fun it means to be." Elvis Mitchell of the *New York Times* wrote, "When *Ho-Tep* requires that extra charge of magic or technique to lift it, the picture stalls out; finally it is neither scary enough nor funny enough."

—*Jill Hamilton*

CREDITS

Elvis: Bruce Campbell
Jack Kennedy: Ossie Davis
Nurse: Ella Joyce
Administrator: Reggie Bannister
Bubba Ho-Tep: Bob Ivy
Kemosabe: Larry Pennell
Callie: Heidi Marnhout

Origin: USA
Released: 2003
Production: Don Coscarelli, Jason R. Savage; Silver Sphere; released by Vitagraph
Directed by: Don A. Coscarelli
Written by: Don A. Coscarelli
Cinematography by: Adam Janeiro
Music by: Brian Tyler
Sound: Paul Bucca
Editing: Donald Milne, Scott J. Gill
Costumes: Shelley Kay
Production Design: Daniel Vecchione
MPAA rating: R
Running time: 92 minutes

REVIEWS

Boxoffice. April, 2003, p. 98.
Chicago Sun-Times Online. October 17, 2003.
Entertainment Weekly. October 17, 2003, p. 62.
Los Angeles Times Online. February 26, 2003.
Los Angeles Times Online. October 3, 2003.
New York Times Online. September 26, 2003.
Variety Online. June 26, 2002.

Buffalo Soldiers

Steal all that you can steal . . .
—Movie tagline
A story so outrageous you couldn't make it up.
—Movie tagline

Reviewers have described *Buffalo Soldiers* as a dark, satirical military-service comedy in the tradition of Mike Nichols's *Catch-22* (1970) and Robert Altman's *M*A*S*H** (1970), but it has more in common with such smug, semi-coherent films from the same year as *Getting Straight* and *The Strawberry Statement*. *Buffalo Soldiers* wants to explore the dangers, both to society and the soldiers themselves, inherent in a peacetime military and to celebrate the mindless recklessness the soldiers get up to when bored by their duties. As a result, it seems to be shaking its finger at the exploits of its protagonists while giggling at the sight of boys having a good time. Whatever its intentions, the film's constant shifts in tone and the holes riddling the narrative doom it to failure.

Ray Elwood (Joaquin Phoenix) has joined the army only as an alternative to six months in jail. As a supply corporal at a base near Stuttgart, West Germany, in 1989, Elwood continues his criminal activity, selling such supplies as stain removers to the Germans and drugs to his fellow soldiers. A hands-on entrepreneur, Elwood processes his own heroin. When some Stinger missiles fall into his hands, he hopes to trade them for narcotics worth $5 million. Reviewers, many of whom liked the film, have compared Elwood to military literature's most famous hustler, *Catch-22*'s Milo Minderbinder. In his magnificent 1961 novel, Joseph Heller intends Minderbinder as a satirical treatment of the soiled innocence of the American entrepreneur who will do anything to accomplish his ends, ignoring all ethical issues and moral consequences. Elwood, however, is just a bored hoodlum doing what he does best. Any satirical aim is missing.

Elwood is able to get away with anything because his commanding officer, Colonel Wallace Berman (Ed Harris), is a very dim bulb. Berman cares only about currying favor with a visiting general (Dean Stockwell) to increase his chances for promotion and thereby satisfy his restless, unhappy wife (Elizabeth McGovern). Mrs. Berman, of course, is having an affair with Elwood. *Buffalo Soldiers* revels in the clichés of military drama and comedy. It's *Sergeant Bilko* with profanity and a high body count.

Elwood's Cold War paradise threatens to erupt, however, with the arrival of a new top sergeant, Robert E. Lee (Scott Glenn), a veteran of three tours of duty in Vietnam. The character's name is good for a mild chuckle and also shows how the mighty have fallen when Lee turns out to be less no-nonsense than psychotic. After Lee's arrival, the film should become a tug of war between the two antagonists, but instead, with the exception of dating Lee's daughter (Anna Paquin) to get back at him, Elwood offers little resistance. Since it's obviously a foregone conclusion that Elwood will prevail, there is little dramatic tension. The plot runs its course with Lee doing bad things to Elwood and the miscreant surviving. It's all rather pointless.

Writer-director Gregor Jordan has said in interviews that his portrait of Elwood was influenced by anti-heroic films such as *Catch-22, Cool Hand Luke* (1967), Brian de Palma's *Scarface* (1983), and *Ferris Bueller's Day Off* (1986). Elwood does seem to owe a debt to the hero of John Hughes' benign high-school comedy because he thinks he's so cute. Achieving a balance between Bueller's rather smug adorableness, Luke Jackson's naive resistance to authority, Yossarian's antipathy to losing his identity (and his life) in the military, and Tony Montana's self-destructive violent ambition would have been an achievement, but alas, the result is dumbed-down anarchism.

The most interesting thing about *Buffalo Soldiers* is its checkered history. It had its debut at the 2001 Toronto International Film Festival only to see its release delayed first because of the September 11 terrorist attacks and then the war with Iraq. This is clearly no time for a satirical treatment of the military, even if the film is set in the past. Ridley Scott's *Black Hawk Down* (2001) was made around the same time but presents an entirely different view of the military. While everyone in Scott's army is clean-cut and heroic, everyone in Jordan's army is corrupt, evil, or stupid. The Berlin Wall is about to fall, yet many of the soldiers do not even know in what country Berlin lies or whether they are in East or West Germany. While this interpretation of America's intellectually passive youth is no doubt accurate, it is nonetheless depressing in this context. When the film was shown at the 2003 Sundance Film Festival, a spectator threw a bottle that hit the back of Anna Paquin's seat. The perpetrator claimed not to be throwing at the actress but at the screen because of what was taken to be the film's anti-Americanism.

Buffalo Soldiers is appalling not because it is unpatriotic or violent—not that there's anything wrong with either—but because it is so unrelentingly bad. Satire, particularly the literary black comedy associated with John Barth, J. P. Donleavy, Thomas Pynchon, and Heller, engages the intellect, but there's nothing intellectually stimulating about this film. It's just one crude joke and gratuitous scene after another: A soldier's death after hitting his head on the edge of a table during an indoor football game sets the tone. Elwood is not at all moved by the man's death yet is amused by the failure of everyone else in the room to notice it. A tank crew high on Elwood's drugs goes on an accidentally destructive rampage during which two innocent soldiers are immolated, and it's supposed to be funny.

Why are these deaths and the many robberies, beatings, and murders later in the film not investigated by anyone? Why are there so few officers on this base? Why can't there be one token competent person? Why does Berman have to be such a cartoon? The soldiers who don't know where Berlin is aren't the only dummies here.

And what does the title mean? The term buffalo soldiers is associated with the African-Americans who served in the U.S. Army in the West following the Civil War, but this has nothing to do with what is going on in the film. The Robert O'Connor novel upon which it is based indicates the title comes from a Bob Marley song, but this tune does not appear on the soundtrack.

The only positive aspect is some of the performances. Phoenix's expressive eyes alternate between fear and a twinkle. He has the skills to enliven Elwood but is let down by the script, as are McGovern and Paquin, whose roles are plot devices more than characters. The underrated and underused (in major films) Glenn has, as always, considerable presence, but he's played this dangerous loony before. Harris's odd blend of stiffness and the mannered is perfect for Berman, and he imbues the colonel with a hint of pathos. The most notable performance is by Stockwell—speaking of underrated and underused—whose general, surrounded by sycophants, dominates his one scene. Stockwell demonstrates the type of relaxed authority sorely needed by the filmmakers themselves. The audience is left feeling embarrassed for these worthy performers being adrift in such a mess.

Jordan said in an interview with the *New York Times* that Miramax's Harvey Weinstein, notorious for taking films away from directors and cutting them extensively, never suggested altering his film. Even Harvey "Scissorhands" must have seen *Buffalo Soldiers* as a hopeless cause. Why Weinstein took on this project and bothered to release it during a period of especially conservative patriotism is another matter.

Stanley Kramer, director of such maudlin, ham-fisted trifles as *The Defiant Ones* (1958), *Inherit the Wind* (1960), and *Guess Who's Coming to Dinner* (1967), used to complain that reviewers did not consider his films objectively because they disagreed with his liberal message, ignoring that there is a big difference between a film's intended theme and the way this theme is presented. *Buffalo Soldiers* is a muddled message delivered very ineptly, without any clear social or political intent. Regardless of their political views, most viewers are likely to be disgusted and depressed by this sordid amalgam of easy, ironic, and stupid gags. Novelist O'Connor's pregnant stepdaughter was killed in the attack on the World Trade Center. The real world can be much more repulsive than bad films.

—*Michael Adams*

CREDITS

Ray Elwood: Joaquin Rafael (Leaf) Phoenix
Sgt. Robert Lee: Scott Glenn
Robyn Lee: Anna Paquin
Col. Wallace Berman: Ed Harris
Stoney: Leon Robinson
General Lancaster: Dean Stockwell
Mrs. Berman: Elizabeth McGovern
Knoll: Gabriel Mann
Sgt. Saad: Shiek Mahmud-Bey
Garcia: Michael Pena
Hicks: Glenn Fitzgerald
Col. Marshall: Brian Delate
Col. Armstrong: Jimmie Ray Weeks

Origin: USA, Great Britain, Germany
Released: 2001
Production: Rainer Grupe, Ariane Moody; FilmFour, Odeon Pictures, Good Machine, Grosvenor Park; released by Miramax Films
Directed by: Gregor Jordan
Written by: Gregor Jordan, Eric Weiss, Nora MacCoby
Cinematography by: Oliver Stapleton
Music by: David Holmes
Sound: Martin Muller
Editing: Lee Smith
Art Direction: Christoph Simons
Costumes: Odile Dicks-Mireaux
Production Design: Steven Jones-Evans
MPAA rating: R
Running time: 98 minutes

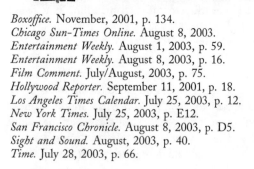

REVIEWS

Boxoffice. November, 2001, p. 134.
Chicago Sun-Times Online. August 8, 2003.
Entertainment Weekly. August 1, 2003, p. 59.
Entertainment Weekly. August 8, 2003, p. 16.
Film Comment. July/August, 2003, p. 75.
Hollywood Reporter. September 11, 2001, p. 18.
Los Angeles Times Calendar. July 25, 2003, p. 12.
New York Times. July 25, 2003, p. E12.
San Francisco Chronicle. August 8, 2003, p. D5.
Sight and Sound. August, 2003, p. 40.
Time. July 28, 2003, p. 66.

USA Today. July 25, 2003, p. E6.
Variety. September 24, 2001, p. 25.
Washington Post. August 8, 2003, p. C1.

QUOTES

Ray Elwood (Joaquin Phoenix): "War is hell, but peace—peace is boring."

Bulletproof Monk

A power beyond measure requires a protector without equal.
—Movie tagline

 Box Office: $23.3 million

B efore *Bulletproof Monk* hit the screens in 2003, it was first a comic. The mini-series, which came out in 1999, was never particularly popular, but nonetheless someone thought that it was movie-worthy material. Perhaps it was the fact that noted Hong Kong action film director, John Woo, was one of the producers that made the studio greenlight this film. Perhaps it was that studios seem to find it difficult to refuse to make any movie that involves a comic book. It's hard to believe it was the pairing of Seann William Scott (best known as Stifler from the *American Pie* films) and Chow Yun-Fat (*Crouching Tiger, Hidden Dragon* and several Woo films) would whet the studio execs' appetites. Oddly, the best thing going for the film is the pairing between the longtime Asian star and young Scott. The two have a bit of chemistry that makes the film more tolerable than it deserves to be.

In the opening minutes of the film, it's obvious that director Paul Hunter, who has done several Nike ads as well as videos like the Michael Jackson "You Rock My World," is trying to cash in on the good will generated by *Crouching Tiger, Hidden Dragon.* Two monks stand on a rickety bridge that hangs precariously over a deep canyon. They fight and launch into the kinds of leaps and spins that can only be done with the assistance of a computer program or a bunch of stagehands with wires. The difference between *Crouching Tiger* and this movie, though, is that in the newer film, the actors' illogical leaps into the air don't have the beauty and grace that they did in the earlier film. Instead, the fighters just seem to be leaping just because they can. And it looks more fake, too.

From the beginning of the film, there are several bad signs. The opening scene takes place in Tibet in 1943, at the Temple of Sublime Truth. The name does not bode well for an intelligent movie. Then after fighting, the monks suddenly start talking to each other in English. Why? No apparent reason. Maybe the subtitling budget ran out. Maybe the filmmakers figured that there's only so much reading an action movie can stand. The older monk says that after 60 years of guarding the Scroll of Ultimate Truth, he is finally going to take a vacation. Moments later he is shot by a group of Nazis who are also after the scroll. As he dies, he huskily whispers to the Monk With No Name (Chow-Yun Fat), "You . . . must . . . protect the scroll."

It seems that every 60 years a new monk is chosen to guard this scroll. While on duty, said monk will not age a day and will be given special powers of protection. Why the big deal about the scroll? If someone reads the scroll, they will have so much power that they can rule the world. Why the monks don't just destroy the scroll and be done with it is not discussed. But then, as A. O. Scott of the *New York Times* put it, "There are, generally speaking, two kinds of people in the modern film audience: those who care about defending the Scroll of the Ultimate Truth and those who don't."

Flash forward 60 years and the Monk needs to find a replacement. For some reason, he is in an unnamed United States city. (Many critics made note of the fact that the filmmakers had a poorly disguised Toronto standing in as the city.) He meets Kar (Scott), a pickpocket who is the most disciplined youth he has ever met. This must be the guy. Kar steals the scroll from Monk and Monk starts following him. Monk watches as Kar is abducted by a group of subterranean thugs led by a Brit called Funktastic (Patrick Hagerty), who looks a lot like Billy Idol. The bad guys demand a cut of Kar's pickpocketing take and, cue music, they start fighting. This provides an opportunity for Monk to observe Kar's smooth fighting moves, plus gives the filmmakers the fight that they need to show every 15 minutes or so. It's also a chance for Kar to meet the foxy Bad Girl/Jade (Jaime King, the Revlon spokeswoman formerly known as James King).

Monk sees "potential" in Kar and starts sort of stalking him. He shows up in his apartment and takes over Kar's bed. He says stuff like, "Knowing others means you're wise; knowing yourself means you're enlightened," and "Water which is too pure has no fish." He helps hone Kar's fighting style, which the youth learned from operating the projector at a run-down theater that only shows old Chinese action films. "It's not about power," says Monk sagely, "It's about grace." Unfortunately, the teacher and pupil stuff was all done far more entertainingly in *The Karate Kid.*

Kar warms to the Monk and starts helping him keep the scroll away from evil Nazi, Struker (Karel Roden) and his granddaughter, Nina (Victoria Smurfit). Struker had been at the Nazi raid in 1943 and has been chasing the scroll ever since. Now in his 80s and confined to a wheelchair, the over-

acted character wants the scroll because it will give him eternal life. Nina is just as cold-hearted as he is. After someone calls her a "crazy bitch," she replies cooly, "I'm not crazy, but I am a bitch." Her character also provides someone with whom Jade can get into a climactic girl fight.

Writers Ethan Reiff and Cyrus Voris try to add a light touch to the action, but their sense of humor is flat. (One might argue that they don't do such a hot job with the action either.) When Jade and Kar are rushing off to save the world, one says, "If we don't come out alive, that would really suck." Or maybe the writers were writing it as romantic banter—it's hard to say. A repeated joke has to do with a koan that Monk gives Kar having to do with the difference in the amount of hot dogs in packages and hot dog buns. This old joke is a staple of low-level standup comedians.

What's good about the movie is Chow Yun-Fat. Even when he's in really stupid scenes like the one in which he is running through a building in slow motion while being shot, he manages to bring a certain dignity to the proceedings. He brings a depth to the role which, almost certainly, was not written into it. Scott's action hero is not that far away from the happy-go-lucky teen guy roles of his earlier films, except this time his muscles are bigger.

Mostly, critics didn't like the film, but it did have a few fans. A. O. Scott wrote, "Whether the weary, patient amusement Mr. Chow registers as he trips over his English lines belongs to the actor or the lama he plays is hardly relevant; his charisma is infinite, and he finds a perfect foil in the slack-jawed manic Mr. Scott. They seem to be having a very good time, and why should they be the only ones?" Kenneth Turan of the *Los Angeles Times* wrote, "It putters along in its standard way, throwing in enough acceptable fighting to keep the die-hards happy but, even with over-use of computerized effects, never doing enough to take our breath away." Lisa Schwarzbaum of *Entertainment Weekly* wrote, "Junky *Monk* . . . is as ungainly in its jammed-together East-meets-West as Steven Seagal in a yoga pose."

—*Jill Hamilton*

CREDITS

Monk With No Name: Chow Yun-Fat
Kar: Seann William Scott
Jade/Bad Girl: Jaime (James) King
Strucker: Karel Roden
Nina: Victoria Smurfit
Mr. Kojima: Mako
Master Monk: Roger Yuan
Mr. Funktastic: Patrick Hagerty

Origin: USA
Released: 2003

Production: Charles Roven, Terence Chang, John Woo, Douglas Segal; Lion Rock, Lakeshore Entertainment, Mosaic Media Group, Flypaper Press; released by MGM
Directed by: Paul Hunter
Written by: Ethan Reiff, Cyrus Voris
Cinematography by: Stefan Czapsky
Music by: Eric Serra
Sound: John J. Thomson
Music Supervisor: Anita Camarata
Editing: Robert K. Lambert
Art Direction: T. Arrinder Grewal
Costumes: Delphine White
Production Design: Deborah Evans
MPAA rating: PG-13
Running time: 103 minutes

REVIEWS

Boxoffice. March, 2003, p. 14.
Chicago Sun-Times Online. April 16, 2003.
Los Angeles Times Online. April 16, 2003.
New York Times Online. April 16, 2003.
People. April 28, 2003, p. 35.
USA Today Online. April 16, 2003.
Variety Online. April 14, 2003.
Washington Post. April 16, 2003, p. C1.

QUOTES

Monk With No Name (Chow Yun-Fat): "All you have to do is believe." Kar (Seann William Scott): "Whatever, man."

Cabin Fever

Terror . . . in the flesh.
—Movie tagline

Box Office: $21 million

There's a fine line between parodying a thing and just copying it. *Cabin Fever* is right on that line. Writer-director-producer Eli Roth along with Randy Pearlstein, who co-wrote the story, obviously know their horror films. They reference heaps of films like *Night of the Living Dead, Evil Dead,* and *Texas Chainsaw Massacre.* The filmmakers added more authenticity by hiring frequent David Lynch composer Angelo Badalamenti (and Nathan Barr) to add an eerie score (Roth was a former assistant to Lynch.) The question is, is it to good purpose; or does it just show that these guys have spent a lot of time watching horror films? And is being well versed in the horror genre minutia something one can truly have intellectual pride about?

Peppering the film with so many elements that we've seen before gives *Cabin Fever* a bit of a tired feeling. For example, when the requisite car-full of happy-go-lucky teens head for a remote area for a fun vacation, we know it's not going to be the fun romp they expect. We know their vehicle is going to break down. We know that they will stop at a gas station and/or store populated by strange and unhelpful locals. All of this does indeed happen. The locals at the store in *Cabin Fever* include a big old guy who seems to be a big ol' racist and a little boy who likes to bite people. Part of what is horrifying about horror films is that they present new or unexpected things to be scared about.

The teens who will most likely be doomed to some horrible fate cover the usual territory. There is the sexy couple in a perpetual clinch, Marcy (Cerina Vincent) and Jeff (Joey Kern, who was in another bad film, *The Grind*). There is nice guy Paul (Rider Strong, channeling Judd from the San Francisco version of *The Real World*) who lusts after his longtime friend, Karen (Jordan Ladd). Karen knows Paul's feelings and likes to tease him with hints that they could be more to each other. Finally there is Bert (James DeBello) who is pretty much a jerk and nothing beyond that. When he sets up a BB gun to start shooting squirrels, one of his buddies asks him why he would do such a senseless thing. "Because they're gay," replies Bert, who gets no female counterpart.

The kids are doing the usual teens-in-horror-movie activities such as smoking, drinking and having sex, when a weird man (Arie Verveen), who is apparently dying, shows up at their door begging for help. The man is covered in welts and seems to be suffering from a bad disease. While standing on their porch he vomits blood. Somehow they end up fighting him, and eventually setting him on fire. This adds to some of the film's typically lame and funny-for-the-wrong-reason dialogue: "He asked for our help! We set him on fire!"

Sick guy, who by now has become Dead guy, falls into the town's reservoir. Roth follows the path from the reservoir, through the pipes, through the forest and into the faucet that is dispensing water . . . right on the teen's spaghetti. The first victim is good girl Karen. Once her crowd figures out what's probably happening with her, they are quick to lock her in a shed. They kindly chain her up so she doesn't do anything like break out to try to get them. Guess her boyfriend Paul isn't really so nice after all. After going to all the trouble of shackling her and isolating her, and whatnot, one character goes in there, touches her, and swabs her bloody mouth. If they are going to do that, why not just plop her on the comfy couch in the cabin?

Others start checking themselves for the telltale bloody welts. Despite the film's flaws, it does have a good sense of nightmare fodder. When Marcy is in the tub shaving her legs, she feels a slight tug on the razor. She glances down. Her legs are covered in bloody welts! What makes no sense is that she continues to shave them. I mean, besides the pain, when your legs are bloody shreds already, is a close shave going to improve their appearance much?

Another creative horror moment is when Paul finds the rotting dead guy floating in the reservoir. As he peaks in for a closer look, he falls into the water and ends up in a terrified embrace with the corpse. Later when a sick Bert drives desperately into town, he hits a deer. The deer isn't killed and is stuck to the windshield, kicking wildly. There are also fun things like a severed bloody foot found in a yard and a character getting a screwdriver in the ear. There is an equally delightful moment in which a dog chews out the insides of a character's body.

The film first premiered to a receptive audience at the Sundance Film Festival, but despite *Cabin Fever*'s pedigree, critics weren't impressed. Owen Gleiberman of *Entertainment Weekly* gave the film a C+ and wrote, "*Cabin Fever* is being marketed as a terror-ific sleeper, but a zombie movie that's this full of clichés really is a kind of meatloaf. It's the fright-flick equivalent of comfort food." Roger Ebert of the *Chicago Sun-Times* wrote, "By the end, we've lost all interest. The movie adds up to a few good ideas and a lot of bad ones, wandering around in search of an organizing principle." Stephen Holden of the *New York Times* wrote that Roth "has cooked up a tempting teens-in-the-woods bloodbath that suggests a *Blair Witch Project* with the blanks filled in, the camera stabilized with an evocative score (by Nathan Barr) whose shivery texture is spiced with the sounds of buzzing flies." Manohla Dargis of the *Los Angeles Times* concluded that Roth and Pearlstein "choke up on the occasional belly laugh in *Cabin Fever*, but they're so busy selling their jokes and their film-geek smarts they never figure out how to scare us."

—*Jill Hamilton*

CREDITS

Karen: Jordan Ladd
Paul: Rider Strong
Bert: James DeBello
Marcy: Cerina Vincent
Jeff: Joey Kern
The Hermit: Arie Verveen
Deputy Winston: Giuseppe Andrews
Justin: Eli Roth

Origin: USA
Released: 2003

Production: Lauren Moews, Eli Roth, Sam Froelich, Evan Astrowsky; Black Sky Entertainment, Deer Path Films, Down Home Entertainment, Tonic Films; released by Lions Gate Films
Directed by: Eli Roth
Written by: Eli Roth, Randy Pearlstein
Cinematography by: Scott Kevan
Music by: Nathan Marr
Sound: Brian Best
Editing: George Folsey Jr., Ryan Folsey
Costumes: Paloma Candelaria, Katrina Migliore
Production Design: Franco-Giacomo Carbone
MPAA rating: R
Running time: 94 minutes

REVIEWS

Boxoffice. September, 2003, p. 117.
Chicago Sun-Times Online. September 12, 2003.
Entertainment Weekly. September 19, 2003, p. 64.
Los Angeles Times Online. September 12, 2003.
New York Times Online. September 12, 2003.
USA Today Online. September 12, 2003.
Variety Online. April 29, 2003.
Washington Post. September 12, 2003.

Calendar Girls

They dropped everything for a good cause.
—Movie tagline

*C*alendar Girls writers Juliette Towhidi and Tim Firth and director Nigel Cole (2000's *Saving Grace*) have hit upon the formula for little Brit/Irish picture success. It's old folks + nakedness = art house breakout hit. It worked with men in *Waking Ned Devine* and *The Full Monty,* and here their twist is that the naked people are women. It's getting hard to find a film from those parts in which an oldster actually keeps their clothes on. The most groundbreaking thing about *Calendar Girls* is not that its middle-aged stars are naked, but that they are the stars of the film in the first place. If women of a certain age appear in a film, usually they are peripheral characters or played for laughs. It's almost revolutionary that these older women are not only allowed to take center stage, but are also allowed to have real emotions and be sexual (although perhaps the success of *Something's Gotta Give* will help to change that.)

Calendar Girls is based on a true story that made the news worldwide as one of those amusing human interest stories that buffers the effect of all the "real" news. In 1999, a group of women at the Rylstone Women's Institute decided to take off their tasteful floral dresses for a charitable calendar. The calendar featured the women strategically placed behind homemade jars of jam and other foodstuffs.

In the film version, Chris (Helen Mirren) and Annie (Julie Walters) are best friends whose youthful selves are housed in middle-aged bodies. They attend meetings of their local Women's Institute and find themselves getting the giggles over the dull-as-dirt speaker topics of broccoli and rugs. It's a kick to see these two ladies have such a wicked sense of fun.

Chris stands by Annie as Annie's lovely husband, John (John Alderton), is diagnosed with leukemia and subsequently dies from it. The rebellious Chris decides that the best way to pay tribute to John is to raise money through the Women's Institute to buy a comfortable sofa for the hospital's family waiting room. The previous year, the Women's Institute, or WI, raised money by publishing a calendar featuring photos of bridges, but it only raised a measly 75 pounds. The current proposal, to put out a calendar of picturesque churches looks like it will have the same dismal earnings.

Spurred by a cheesecake calendar she spots in a mechanic's shop, Chris decides the best way to earn money would be to have the women in the WI pose for their own cheesecake calendar. After all, she reasons, John would have approved. One of his final pieces of writing compared women to flowers and said that they are most beautiful in their final stages. (In the pompousness-deflating wit that's typical of the film, John added "And then they go to seed.")

If the filmmakers could have maintained the mood and sentiment present in the first part of the film, *Calendar Girls* would have been the better for it. It's light and funny as Chris and Annie try to convince their friends that it would be a good idea to be naked in front of the camera. After all, these are women whose undergarments most likely involve wire and thick cotton. Some of it is a little overplayed. When the women do the photo shoot, they are too nervous to have the male photographer actually take the picture, so he's only allowed to set up the shot. If they're going to be naked for all the world to see, it seems strange that the one person they wouldn't let see them is the photographer.

But the overall good humor of the proceedings override some of the moments that aren't so believable. Some of the best scenes involve the reactions of Chris's son, Jem (John-Paul MacLeod) to her shenanigans. In one scene, Chris has disrobed to show the ladies of the WI how their bodies will be obscured by other objects in the photographs. At the most inopportune moment, teenaged Jem and his friend walk in. A look of quiet horror spreads over her son's face, and he backs out of the room. Reactions from other women's family members are less dramatic, but just as humorous. After the calendar comes out, one wealthy older woman is having breakfast with her husband. Without looking up from his newspaper, he blandly comments, "You're nude in

the Telegraph, Dear. Could you pass the bacon?" The writers also work some issues in there, too. The women struggle with body images and a society that sees an older woman's body as either invisible or repulsive. One very private woman, Ruth (Penelope Wilton), decides to do the calendar as a form of personal liberation after she discovers that her husband has been cheating on her.

Things bog down in the movie after the calendar comes out. It seems like the writers are casting about for something else to do with the film and they end up creating manufactured drama. (Actually earlier in the film, they manufactured drama as well. In the film, the powers-that-be in the local WI are dead set against the idea of a pinup calendar. In real life, everyone thought it was a fine idea.) In the second half of the film, all the things that were quirky and British and charming are lost as the women and their calendar become a success. Chris gets drunk on the fame and starts neglecting her kind husband, Rod (Ciaran Hinds), and ignoring Jem's mounting personal problems. Annie objects to Chris's raw ambition, feeling that she is more excited about the fame than in honoring John's memory.

Most tiresome are the scenes in which "the girls" head to Hollywood. Here, we have the obligatory scenes in which they find themselves in a fabulously luxurious hotel room, ride a limo down Sunset Blvd. and appear on Jay Leno's show. (Elvis Mitchell of the *New York Times* noted Leno's ubiquitousness in movies lately, referring to his "monthly film appearance" and wondering how Leno found the time to perform his day job.) The regular-folks-arrive-in-Hollywood has been done so many times, there is little need to waste the film.

Things improve when the girls get back to their native Knapely, England, but it's too little, too late. By that time, the film has lost its momentum. The returned charm in the final scenes only serves to show how far the film veered from its original charm. What *Calendar Girls* does have going for it, however, are its actors, especially Mirren and Walters. The two are totally believable as longtime best friends. They handle their roles with an easy, knee-jerk humor and large senses of fun. The laughing attacks that they suffer at their dreary WI meetings seem totally natural. It's also fun to watch the lived-in faces of the actors playing their fellow WI cohorts, including Annette Crosbie and Celia Imrie.

Critics were largely fond of the film, although many managed to work the word "trifle" into their reviews. Manohla Dargis of the *Los Angeles Times* wrote, "*Calendar Girls* is closer in texture and consistency to individually wrapped American cheese than good, tangy English cheddar. But even humble plastic-wrapped cheese has its virtues and so does this film." The *Boston Globe*'s Wesley Morris feels that "the story has the complexity of a People magazine cover story, and the accompanying photography is even more flattering," but he had compliments for Mirren, calling her an "easy, breezy presence" with "a sparkling comedic sensibility." And Roger Ebert of the *Chicago Sun-Times* described seeing the film at the Locarno Film Festival with 12,000 other people: "The story was so straightforward and universal that it played perfectly well, got laughs in all the rights places, and left at least 10,000 of us pleased, if not overwhelmed."

—*Jill Hamilton*

CREDITS

Chris Harper: Helen Mirren
Annie Clark: Julie Walters
John Clark: John Alderton
Cora: Linda Bassett
Jessie: Annette Crosbie
Lawrence: Philip Glenister
Rod: Ciaran Hinds
Celia: Celia Imrie
Marie: Geraldine James
Ruth: Penelope Wilton
Eddie: George Costigan
Richard: Graham Crowden
Frank: John Fortune
Himself: Jay Leno (Cameo)

Origin: Great Britain
Released: 2003
Production: Nick Barton, Suzanne Mackie; Harbour Pictures; released by Touchstone Pictures
Directed by: Nigel Cole
Written by: Juliette Towhidi, Tim Firth
Cinematography by: Ashley Rowe
Music by: Patrick Doyle
Sound: Tim Fraser
Music Supervisor: Liz Gallacher
Editing: Michael Parker
Art Direction: Mark Raggett
Costumes: Frances Tempest
Production Design: Martin Childs
MPAA rating: PG-13
Running time: 108 minutes

REVIEWS

Boxoffice. November, 2003, p. 83.
Chicago Sun-Times Online. December 19, 2003.
Entertainment Weekly. January 9, 2004, p. 61.
Los Angeles Times Online. December 19, 2003.
New York Times Online. December 19, 2003.
People. January 12, 2004, p. 33.
Sight and Sound. November, 2003, p. 37.

USA Today Online. December 19, 2003.
Variety Online. August 10, 2003.

AWARDS AND NOMINATIONS

Nomination:
Golden Globes 2004: Actress—Mus./Comedy (Mirren).

Camp

A Comedy About Drama.
—Movie tagline
You can't fit in when you stand out.
—Movie tagline

Box Office: $1.6 million

As a child growing up, Todd Graff, the writer and director of *Camp,* attended the arts camp, Stagedoor Manor, in Loch Shedrake, New York. The camp boasts a host of famous alumni like Robert Downey Jr. and Mary Stuart Masterson. According to the *Los Angeles Times,* Graff recalls being "blown away by his memory of Jennifer Jason Leigh's performance as Laura in *[The] Glass Menagerie.* At age 12."

The camp, full of talented youngsters who can't seem to fit in in the outside world, was the inspiration for *Camp*'s Camp Ovation. In this film, Graff pays homage to a place where 10 year-olds belt out world-weary versions of "Ladies Who Lunch" and an "honest to goodness straight boy" is as rare as an exotic bird. The film is also an homage to the countless summer camp movies that are a vacation mainstay. Like those movies, *Camp* faithfully begins with the kids getting ready for camp and ends with the last day of camp. Lives have changed, kisses have been exchanged, and lessons learned. The good thing about *Camp* is that it has all those usual elements but has the added oomph of better jokes, more open sexuality, and a host of show-stopping song and dance numbers.

Before arriving at *Camp,* Michael (Robin De Jesus) is getting turned away from his prom for showing up in a dress. As he's subsequently getting beaten up by a group of his peers, he gets a faraway look in his eyes. He's imagining himself in a different place—Camp Ovation. Meanwhile, things aren't going much better for Ellen (Joanna Chilcoat). She tries to bribe her brother to take her to her prom, but her brother refuses, calling her a loser.

Once they arrive at Camp Ovation, they are both delighted to meet Vlad (Daniel Letterle), the sole straight guy at camp. Vlad, who plays a sincere version of the Rolling Stones' "Wild Horses" on his guitar for his audition, is a guy who looks like he has it all. He seems like a nice guy and boasts a charming smile and a buff body. He starts showing interest in insecure Ellen and helps her blossom. His roommate Michael immediately develops a huge crush on him. Vlad, who is the type who wants to please everyone, is not above flirting with Michael and leading him on.

Vlad, whose secret shame is that he has obsessive compulsive disorder that causes him to translate people's words into number sequences, is so eager to please that he gets into romantic entanglements with some of the other campers as well. After Dee (Sasha Allen) suggests that Vlad may be less straight than he imagines, he immediately tries to prove otherwise by engaging her in a make-out session. For her part, Dee goes along because she is looking to be something other than a "fag hag." And when the mean camp sexpot, Jill (Alana Allen) invites him over for a "wonderful surprise," he is more than happy to oblige her, too.

In his own way, Vlad also seduces the visiting guest counselor Bert (musician Don Dixon). Bert, who hasn't written anything since his sole Broadway hit in 1989, has turned into a bitter alcoholic who rages against Times Square being turned into a theme park. Put off by the kids' enthusiasm, he tells them they aren't going to survive in the real world and warns them that they'll become the kind of people who collect obscure original cast recordings. When Bert passes out in yet another drunken stupor, Vlad finds sheets of music in Bert's room. It's material that Bert has been working on. Vlad makes copies and he and the other kids secretly learn the music, then give Bert a surprise performance. It's corny and, as many critics noted, relies a lot on the Judy and Mickey let's-put-on-a-show ethic, but that stuff was popular for a reason. It works. And this does too. Bert doesn't suddenly have an epiphany and give up drinking, but he does get a bit of renewed hope.

Meanwhile, Camp Ovation has plenty of other drama going on too. One involves Jenna (Tiffany Taylor), a girl whose parents force her to get her jaw wired shut so that she can lose some weight. The jokes grows old fast, but it pays off in the end when she gives a stunning rendition of "Here's Where I Stand." Over in Jill's room, Jill's tiny and worshipful roommate Fritzi (Anne Kendrick) is having troubles of her own. At first Jill treats Fritzi like a slave and has the grateful girl bring her iced tea and the like. But when she discovers Fritzi washing her underwear, she severs the relationship. The wronged Fritzi sets her considerable energy to sabotaging Jill. One such trick involves doctoring Jill's drink with Woolite. As Jill is onstage trying to sing "Ladies Who Lunch" while vomiting, Fritzi shows up in full costume and takes the stage. It is she who belts out the aforementioned show-stopping version of the song. Her conviction is all the more strange because she's such a tiny and young girl singing such an adult song.

Entertainment references abound in *Camp*. One character describes something as "so *Stella Dallas*," Similarly, a kid has a framed photo in his room that, of course, everyone knows is Stephen Sondheim. The casual way that Graff assumes this kind of knowledge is one of the most charming things about the film. As the kids travel to camp on a bus, they pass the time by enthusiastically singing, "Losing My Mind" from *Follies*. When the sports counselor tries to ingratiate himself to a fresh-faced, freckled boy, the boy laughs and says, "We have a sports counselor?" And when the serious dance teacher gives a speech trying to scare the kids about the rigors of training, one unimpressed boy listens, then comments mildly, "We've all seen *Fame*."

Graff has written several other films like *Dangerous Minds* and *The Beautician and the Beast*, but this is his first time as director. To give the film a more realistic feel, he recruited nonprofessional actors, including some from Stagedoor Manor. The actors' lack of experience doesn't hurt the film and, indeed, gives it a certain realism. And they are universally wonderful during the song and dance numbers. There are many moments when the performances are out and out showstoppers. These are some talented kids and it's a pleasure to watch them shine. With a tiny budget, unknown actors and a shooting schedule of only 23 days, it would be easy for *Camp* to be a bad film. But there is so much heart, humor, and obvious affection for these kinds of kids that *Camp* is a joy to watch.

Critics found flaws in the film, but generally liked it in spite of them. Glenn Whipp of the *Los Angeles Daily News* wrote, "*Camp* is a little rough around the edges—Graff, the first time director, has trouble juggling characters, resisting formula and keeping the whole thing moving forward—but its awkwardness ends up being part of its charm." Stephen Holden of the *New York Times* wrote, "*Camp* may be rickety, formulaic, overacted, and totally wobbly, but its spark of enthusiasm is so infectious that you have to love it for its faults." Kenneth Turan of the *Los Angeles Times* wrote that the film "has a good deal of the appeal, and the drawbacks, of a high school play. It can be pokey and overly earnest and its dramatics are not always polished, but, on the other hand, would you want them to be?"

—*Jill Hamilton*

CREDITS

Vlad: Daniel Letterle
Ellen: Joanna Chilcoat
Michael: Robin De Jesus
Jenna: Tiffany Taylor
Dee: Sasha Allen
Jill: Alana Allen
Fritzi: Anna Kendrick

Bert: Don Dixon

Origin: USA
Released: 2003
Production: Katie Roumel, Christine Vachon, Pamela Koffler, Danny DeVito, Michael Shamberg; Jersey Films, Killer Films, Laughlin Park Pictures; released by IFC Films
Directed by: Todd Graff
Written by: Todd Graff
Cinematography by: Kip Bogdahn
Music by: Stephen Trask
Sound: Robert Larrea
Music Supervisor: Linda Cohen
Editing: Myron Kerstein
Costumes: Dawn Weisberg
Production Design: Dina Goldman
MPAA rating: PG-13
Running time: 114 minutes

REVIEWS

Boxoffice. April, 2003, p. 79.
Entertainment Weekly. August 1, 2003, p. 62.
Los Angeles Times Online. July 25, 2003.
New York Times Online. May 11, 2003.
New York Times Online. July 25, 2003.
Rolling Stone. August 7, 2003, p. 78.
Variety Online. January 22, 2003.
Washington Post. August 8, 2003, p. WE42.

QUOTES

Vlad (Daniel Letterle): "Have you ever experimented with heterosexuality?" Michael (Robin De Jesus): "What? You mean sleep with a straight guy? What for?"

AWARDS AND NOMINATIONS

Nomination:
Ind. Spirit 2004: Debut Perf. (Kendrick).

Capturing the Friedmans

Who do you believe?
—Movie tagline

Box Office: $3.1 million

A t first it looks as though *Capturing the Friedmans* is going to cover familiar terrain. It's about a crime committed long ago, jail time served, and a seemingly nice family that is charged with unspeakable crimes. If *Capturing the Friedmans,* produced by HBO Documentary Films, followed the path typical of countless TV newsmagazines, we would see lots of evidence pointing to a different verdict, probably that the family was framed. In this film nothing is that clear. For one thing, the guilt or innocence of the accused parties is never established. (At a question and answer session after a screening of the film at the 2003 Sundance Film Festival—where it won the documentary Grand Prize—director Andrew Jarecki was asked whether he thought his subjects were guilty or not; he said he didn't know.) So murky is the evidence on each side that the movie becomes something more than a crime mystery. It becomes a character study and portrait of a dysfunctional family falling apart.

Capturing the Friedmans is also oddly voyeuristic. Ironically, the film focuses on someone who's a voyeur himself. In 1987, Arnold Friedman was a popular teacher in Great Neck, New York. In addition, the award-winning instructor taught computer and piano classes after school. The father of three kids, David, Seth and Jesse, he also liked to look at mail-order pictures of young boys having sex. While dealing with the subject of child porn, the film ends up showing vague images of it. This coupled with the close and intimate look at the family is disturbing and unsettling.

Arnold Friedman was an early convert to home movies. He would take lots of pictures of everything, and his son David followed the tradition. The family grew so accustomed to having the cameras rolling that, in addition to filming birthdays and holidays, they would also record family fights and uncomfortable events. As oldest child David faced the prospect of his father and his youngest brother, Jesse, being jailed on child molestation charges, he made a recording of himself in his underwear talking about his anguish over the situation. In this video diary, he tells the camera, "This is private. If you're not me, then you really shouldn't be watching this because this is supposed to be a private situation between me and me. So turn it off, don't watch this, this is private." Still, we watch.

Jarecki, the founder of Moviefone, stumbled upon the story. He was working on a documentary about the clowns that entertain at children's parties in New York City and interviewed the town's top clown, David Friedman. He delved deeper into David's story and discovered that his family had been involved in a major child molestation case in 1987.

After Arnold was busted for possession of child pornography in a post office sting operation, the police started questioning his after-school computer students about the possibility that they had been molested by the teacher. Arnold and his son Jesse were eventually charged with over 200 counts of child molestation. Reportedly in after-school computer classes in the family's basement, Arnold showed the kids lewd videogames, abused them, and son Jesse violently participated. According to the evidence that the film presents, the prosecution's case was not terribly strong. For one thing, there was never any physical evidence found. For another, it seems that the police were leading the children to say the things that they wanted to hear. One of the alleged victims only was able to remember various episodes of the abuse after sessions of hypnosis. The film presents authorities that remind us hypnosis is not a good tool for retrieved abuse memories and can, in fact, plant them in the brain. A couple of kids, now adults, remember trying to agree with the police version of what went on in the Friedmans' basement just so that they could be done with the questioning.

Jarecki paints the situation as one of mass hysteria. One of the parents, whose child reported no molestation, was harshly accused of being in denial by the parents of children who allegedly had been abused. And in the wealthy community, there was a strange sense of one-upmanship among the victims. If one child was abused seven times, then another was surely abused eight times.

Just when it seems pretty clear that the Friedmans' were the victims of overzealous persecution, Jarecki reveals information that makes the situation a lot more murky. Arnold, as harmless as he seems, is indeed a pedophile. After all, he did have the child pornography, and he later admits to abusing his brother as a boy (his brother has no recollection of these events). In a letter to a sex crimes expert, Friedman reveals that he did "cross the line" at some points in his life and have sexual contact with boys.

Through it all, his greatest ally is his son, David, who steadfastly believes in his father's innocence. David worships his father and can't fathom that he would have this other side to him. In fact, in a telling moment, when told of his father's confession to having had intimate contact with boys, David tries to rationalize it to the interviewer by questioning what that even means. Maybe intimate contact didn't mean any actual touching.

To tell his story, Jarecki had hours and hours of family home videos at his disposal. Thus we can watch the uncomfortable specter of the family rallying around Arnold as they shun his wife and their mother, Elaine. Because Elaine is not convinced of her husband's innocence, the sons band together and ostracize her. The camera captures screaming fights in which horrible things are said. We see the family the night before Arnold is set to go to jail. To deal with it, they try to keep things light and clown around for the camera.

At the end of the film, it's difficult to decide what might and might not be true. The testimonies are often completely contradictory. In one instance, Jesse's attorney says that Jesse

finally admitted that as a boy, his father molested him. In an interview with Jesse, he says that the attorney told him to lie and say that was true so that his case would be stronger. As Roger Ebert of the *Chicago Sun-Times* put it, "By the end of *Capturing the Friedmans*, we have more information, from both inside and outside the family, than we dreamed would be possible. We have many people telling us exactly what happened. And we have no idea of the truth. None."

Critics found the film to be compelling. Owen Gleiberman of *Entertainment Weekly* gave the film an A and called it, "gripping, moving and tragic." Elvis Mitchell of the *New York Times* appreciated how Jarecki "finds a way to show that denial and hope often grow from the same vine. Lives are built around the way they're harvested—and this talented director has a feel for the soil." Lou Lumenick saw the film as "reality footage of a clan that makes the Osbournes seem positively normal."

—*Jill Hamilton*

CREDITS

Origin: USA
Released: 2003
Production: Andrew Jarecki, Marc Smerling; Hit the Ground Running Films; released by Magnolia Pictures
Directed by: Andrew Jarecki
Cinematography by: Adolfo Doring
Music by: Andrea Morricone
Sound: John Gurrin
Editing: Richard Hankin
MPAA rating: Unrated
Running time: 107 minutes

REVIEWS

Boxoffice. August, 2003, p. 29.
Chicago Sun-Times Online. June 6, 2003.
Entertainment Weekly. June 6, 2003, p. 54.
Los Angeles Times Online. June 13, 2003.
New York Times Online. May 30, 2003.
People. June 16, 2003, p. 40.
Variety Online. January 26, 2003.
Washington Post. June 13, 2003, p. WE33.

AWARDS AND NOMINATIONS

Sundance 2003: Feature Doc
Nomination:
Oscars 2003: Feature Doc.
Directors Guild 2003: Feature Doc. (Jarecki).

Carnage

With its ghoulish title and images of death, *Carnage* invites expectations of a horror film (incidentally, it has nothing to do with the 1983 horror flick of the same title), but director Delphine Gleize has more lofty ideas in mind for this meditative art house mood piece. In her feature debut, Gleize (who also wrote the screenplay) creates a complex study of several people who are linked by the death of an Andalusian bull, Romero, killed in the bullring by Victor (Julien Lescarret), a young matador. Victor himself is gored before he is able to slay the beast, and, while Victor lands in the hospital, Romero is carved up in a factory.

Later, Carlotta (Chiara Mastroianni), an insecure actress, sells one of Romero's bones to the parents of an epileptic girl, Winnie (Raphaelle Molinier), as a gift for her dog. A philandering scientist, Jacques (Jacques Gamblin), makes use of Romero's eyes while neglecting his pregnant wife, Betty (Lio). A taxidermist receives Romero's horns as a gift from her mother. An elegant woman, Alicia (Angela Molina), dines on Romero at a fancy restaurant after a nearby diner allows her to have the last serving for the evening.

The members of this motley group cross paths with one another as their stories unfold: for example, Alicia turns out to be the mother of Winnie's school teacher, a young woman who is intrigued with her pupil's prescience and insight. Ultimately, the ties among the individuals create a sense of hope for most of these alienated souls.

Clearly, director Gleize wants to lay bare a societal network using an unexpected and unlikely connecting device. In a way, Gleize claims the same territory as playwrights Arthur Schnitzler (*Reigen*) and John Guare (*Six Degrees of Separation*). Some of *Carnage*'s critics found other comparisons. Rex Roberts stated in *Film Journal International* that "like Peter Greenaway, [Gleize] is fascinated by the lurid beauty of putrefaction and dissipation; like Atom Egoyan, she creates an alternate reality that floats above (or lurks below) the ordinary, one in which the alienated and desperate find succor and redemption." Peter Keough of *The Boston Phoenix* noted, "Gleize demonstrates an appreciation of synchronicity, fate, and human folly akin to that of Robert Altman in his *Nashville* days or Krzysztof Kieslowski circa *La double vie de Véronique*." A. O. Scott of the *New York Times* saw *Carnage* as "part of a tendency in European filmmaking—and also in some independent American pictures like *Sliding Doors* and *13 Conversations About One Thing*—toward replacing linear narrative with chains of association and coincidence."

The difference between the 28-year-old French director and these other writers and directors is that mysticism and magical realism play significant roles here. For viewers, *Carnage*'s New Age elements will either prove irksome or wondrous, but everyone should be prepared for the languid story pace and oblique character definitions. The way *Carnage* dwells so much on quirky characters without really delineating those characters makes even Altman's *Three Women* seem conventional by comparison.

Still, patient viewers will be rewarded with individually lovely moments and haunting, beautifully composed shots. Alicia's fateful moment on a nocturnal city street evokes Italian opera. Jacques's eye-opening confrontation with a man in a bear suit evokes a surreal ballet (more grotesque surrealism occurs in the hospital scenes with Victor's trio of bumbling doctors). And Carlotta's exploration of her inner self during a series of group encounter sessions takes place in an otherworldly setting—an indoor swimming pool that would make the great Russian formalist Vsevolod Meyerhold proud. Cinematographer Crystel Fournier and set designer Andre Fonsny construct rich and intricate scenes, making memorable use of the Cinemascope frame, while Gleize's mise-en-scene and technique with her actors indicates supreme assurance (particularly for a first-time feature).

Although *Carnage* fits in with the recent trend of multilingual, multistory European films (e.g. *Code Unknown*), the film references Luis Bunuel more than anyone or anything else (both Rex Roberts and Peter Keough make this observation in their reviews): making Romero an "Andalusian" bull (*Un Chien Andalou*); the casting of Angela Molina (the femme fatale from *That Obscure Object of Desire*) and Catherine Deneuve's daughter, Chiara Mastroianni, (several decades after Deneuve's appearance in *Belle de Jour*); and the occasional moments of outright absurdism and surrealism. The major difference (for good or for bad) is that Bunuel was usually darker in his humor and less humanistic in his themes. *Carnage*'s hopeful, "upbeat" denouement hardly compares to a typical Bunuel film, with the possible exception of his little-seen *Sunrise*. In that film, however, the final positive image at least promotes a populist political message. *Carnage* offers little political critique or commentary. Still, *Carnage* impresses as a work of art, however flawed or unfathomable.

—*Eric Monder*

CREDITS

Carlotta: Chiara Mastroianni
Alicia: Angela Molina
Jeanne: Lucia Sanchez
Luc: Bernard Sens
Rosie: Esther Gorintin
Jacques: Jacques Gamblin

Paco: Feodor Atkine
Lucie: Marilyne Even
Alexis: Clovis Cornillac
Winnie: Raphaelle Molinier
Betty: Lio

Origin: France, Spain, Belgium, Switzerland
Language: French, Spanish
Released: 2002
Production: Jerome Dopffer; France 3 Cinema, StudioCanal, Balthazar Productions, Oasis Producciones, Need Productions; released by Wellspring Media
Directed by: Delphine Gleize
Written by: Delphine Gleize
Cinematography by: Crystal Fournier
Music by: Eric Neveux
Sound: Pierre Andre
Editing: Francois Quiquere
Art Direction: Andre Fonsny
MPAA rating: Unrated
Running time: 130 minutes

 REVIEWS

New York Times Online. September 5, 2003.
Variety Online. May 18, 2002.
Village Voice Online. September 3, 2003.
Washington Post. October 17, 2003, p. WE47.

Casa de los Babys

Six Women. One Dream.
—Movie tagline

Independent filmmaker John Sayles's fourteenth film deals with six diverse American women who languish in a South American hotel nicknamed "Casa de los Babys" while waiting to adopt children. As he explores each woman's distinct personality and the unique motives each has for adopting a foreign child, Sayles also explores the social and political aspects of what cross-cultural adoption involves.

These issues include the local radicals and their negative views of the rich American interlopers; the South Americans, including the hotel owner, who make a living off such foreign guests while still disliking them; the poor, desperate mothers who give up their babies for adoption; the plight of the many abandoned children roaming the streets; and the problems the women themselves have with wading through the red tape involved in the adoption process, which some-

times makes it seem as if the locals are, as one of the women puts it, "making us pay for our babies with the balance of trade." The combination of emotional, social, and political issues make for a richly textured, though sometimes, unsatisfying movie where many topics are never fully explored.

A talented female cast embodies the characters of Nan (Marcia Gay Harden), an abrasive and unlikable soul who, although wealthy, steals toiletries in droves from the maid's cart; Jennifer (Maggie Gyllenhaal), an infertile young women hoping that a baby will save her troubled marriage; Leslie (Lili Taylor), who has trouble being in a lasting relationship; Gayle (Mary Steenburgen), an amiable recovering alcoholic and born-again Christian; fitness fanatic Skipper (Daryl Hannah), who has had multiple miscarriages; and Eileen (Susan Lynch), an Irish Catholic immigrant. The women bond over their common desire and current plight of waiting for the adoptions to go through as the days turn into weeks. While they wait, sometimes patiently, sometimes not, we watch them sunbathe, eat, fight, chat, and otherwise interact with each other and the locals, while overhearing their revealing conversations.

We slowly learn about each woman's unique heartache and what ultimately brought them to this place in search of a child. The blonde and fit Skipper heartbreakingly reveals to another woman that she named each of her three children after she miscarried. One of the movie's highlights is the quietly effective monologues of the Irish Eileen (also in Sayles's *The Secret of Roan Inish*) and a local Latina maid Asuncion (Vanessa Martinez) who speak of their personal battles and forge an undeniable connection between them although neither can understand the other's language. Representing the other side of the coin is the tough-talking, cynical Nan who feels that she is being taken advantage of and callously demands that her adoption be moved to the fore, no matter what the cost. Interestingly, Sayles doesn't completely discount Nan's point of view—don't trust anyone and everything has a price—but tempers it with that of the more optimistic characters.

Presiding over the hotel is owner Senora Munoz (Rita Moreno) who is used to playing host to scores of women just like Sayles's sextet. Although she secretly loathes them, such women are the crux of her business as well as that of her brother, a lawyer who handles such adoptions. Munoz's son (Pedro Armandariz), however, bears an outwardly hostile attitude toward such women, deeming them capitalist exploiters even while his own relatives thrive off them. Such conflicts are at the heart of Sayles's story where nothing is easily explained or justified.

The cast is uniformly excellent, with especially moving performances from the young Gyllenhaal, Hannah, Lynch, Harden, Martinez, and Moreno. It's an understated, character-driven piece played with the appropriate restraint and emotional resonance by each of the players. There is no overly sentimental melodrama to ruin the essence of the essentially moving story about the women who want and a people who are in need. Though a scant 96 minutes, Sayles perhaps tries to pack too much in and the various subplots merely distract from the engaging leads, who themselves must compete for ample screen time. While perhaps not the best of Sayles's socially aware films, he has hit an emotional chord using the unique subject matter of the adoption industry. Sayles makes clear the importance of this subject in the program notes: "The debate over nature vs. nurture is central to many of our most vital scientific, social, and literary movements. Nowhere does it get to a more personal airing than in the phenomenon of adoption and nowhere within that phenomenon than in adoption between cultures." Filmed entirely in Mexico, the South American country that it is supposed to represent remains unnamed.

—*Hilary White*

CREDITS

Jennifer: Maggie Gyllenhaal
Nan: Marcia Gay Harden
Skipper: Daryl Hannah
Eileen: Susan Lynch
Gayle: Mary Steenburgen
Leslie: Lili Taylor
Senora Munoz: Rita Moreno
Asuncion: Vanessa Martinez

Origin: USA
Released: 2003
Production: Lemore Syvan, Alejandro Sprintgall; released by IFC Films
Directed by: John Sayles
Written by: John Sayles
Cinematography by: Mauricio Rubinstein
Music by: Mason Daring
Sound: Judy Karp
Editing: John Sayles
Costumes: Mayes C. Rubes
Production Design: Felipe Fernandez del Paso
MPAA rating: R
Running time: 95 minutes

REVIEWS

Boxoffice. November, 2003, p. 98.
Chicago Sun-Times Online. October 3, 2003.
Entertainment Weekly. October 3, 2003, p. 52.
Los Angeles Times Online. September 19, 2003.
New York Times Online. September 19, 2003.
USA Today Online. October 3, 2003.
Variety Online. August 25, 2003.

QUOTES

Leslie (Lili Taylor): "You don't need to understand the words to watch TV—stupidity is the universal language!"

Chaos

Coline Serreau's clever comedy-thriller from France, *Chaos,* proposes a novel solution to the problem of Arab immigrants, whose ranks within that country's borders have been swelling by the millions: This sprightly, thrill-a-minute ride seems to say, very simply, "If you can't get rid of them, exploit 'em!" *Chaos* does this admirably by combining its ethnically-oriented ideological slant with a rousing feminist subtext.

Serreau's originality, as writer-director, lies in the fact that her film has a heroine as well as a shadow heroine. Helene Vidal (Catherine Frot, a Helen Hunt lookalike), is the disgruntled Parisian housewife propelling the film's narrative as its protagonist, but the character celebrated by the narrative thrust is the darkly attractive Noemie/Mallika (Rachida Brakni), the siren with two names. It is the latter who provides the film with its pulsating drive. Helene is always seen rushing around, but with no real objective other than to play "catch-up" with her yuppie, workaholic husband, Paul (Vincent Lindon). Then there's her rarely seen boss, whom she assuages through faxes when she cannot be at work as a lawyer. It is only after her path crosses that of the beleaguered Noemie that her life takes on meaning through female bonding.

The film opens with a quick close-up of Helene's face reflected cameo-like in a mirror. A mere instant is all that is allowed to check her appearance as she and Paul scurry about getting ready for a dinner party. In the cramped elevator, they stand back to back. As their car speeds down a nighttime street, Noemie comes running toward them head on in the blinding glare. She begs to be let in, but instead of helping her, Paul orders Helene to roll up the window, which she does. The men pursuing Noemie smash her face against the windshield, then kick her mercilessly. Paul waits until the men have disappeared, then gets out to wipe the blood off Noemie's face, gets back in the car, and starts off. Helene wants to call the police on her cell phone, but Paul points to the blood on the windshield and vows not to get involved. "But what about the girl?" asks Helene. "What girl?" he responds.

We then see the blood on the windshield being sprayed by the automatic jets of a car wash during the title sequence. When the eddies clear, Paul and Helene are revealed staring ahead from the front seat, complicit yet cleansed of responsibility.

Then, as if to affirm its omniscient perspective and its curious generic mix, the film launches into a sequence of domestic comedy. Mamie (Line Renaud), Paul's aging mother, is seen wearily carrying her bags as she gets down from a train. Inside the apartment, as they hear her voice on the intercom, Paul gestures to Helene to indicate that he isn't there. The poor old woman, on her annual trip to the city, leaves her customary gift of walnut oil with Helene at the door, hoping Paul will find time to visit her at her hotel. As she reaches the foot of the stairwell, she looks struck by doubt and hides, silently looking on as Paul rushes out. Similarly, Helene finds herself leaving a kettle for Fabrice (Aurelien Wiik), her independent young son, at the door of his apartment after he gets his girlfriend Florence (Chloe Lambert) to tell his mother that he's not in. When Helene is out on the street, she, too, stops and spies on Fabrice and Florence as they come out of the building. As things turn out, it is Noemie, the outsider, who will override these generational rifts and bring all four members of the family together.

When Helene wakes up screaming one night, her conscience spurs her to care for the comatose Noemie, who regains consciousness in a state of total paralysis. "My life's a mess. So is yours," Helene confides to the girl, who can still hear. "I'd like you to live." When she starts spending more time at Noemie's bedside than at home, an irate Paul curses her for reneging on her wifely duties, such as accompanying him to parties and keeping his linen suits pressed.

Noemie, who is unable to speak and making a slow recovery, is plagued by a gang of pimps led by the bald, nefarious Pali (Wojtek Pszoniak) and his sidekick, the much younger Touki (Ivan Franek). First Touki appears, wanting Noemie to sign a transfer by proxy, but Helene is able to chase him away. Out on the road, she even knocks him out cold by sneaking up on him and bringing a wooden plank down on his head. But when Helene is away devoting attention to the amorally confused Fabrice, Pali poses as Noemie's uncle and almost succeeds in kidnapping the mute girl, but Helene, after a breakneck chase, manages to save Noemie and whisks her away to Mamie's house in the country.

The shock of the events leads Noemie to regain her speech. The bond between her and Helene becomes cemented as the girl recounts her past, starting with her childhood in Marseilles. From this point on, the film gathers its ideological momentum as it becomes Noemie's film. Rapid scenes follow in an extended flashback as Noemie tells Helene how her father, a construction worker, abandoned the family after moving to Paris when she was just a little girl by the name of Mallika. A stepfather then looked after her, her sister Zora, and her brothers. As a teenager, she was a conscientious student, determined to make her way in the world. However, when she found out that her stepfather was planning to take her to Algiers in order to sell her into marriage, she had no recourse but to run away. She was soon reduced to begging, then was picked up by Touki, who promised to look after her. Instead, she was locked up for two months with seven other girls in a secluded mansion where she was raped repeatedly, beaten senselessly, and turned into a heroin addict. Then she was released to work the streets. At 18, she was taken to Paris so she could earn more money for Touki.

In the big city, her intelligence was recognized by Pali, who trained her to play the stock market and taught her the ways of the Internet. While she made a lot of money for him by way of startups, she saw none of the dough. The experience, however, allowed her to devise a three-stage plan to get what she wanted from the highest echelons of male orthodoxy.

Her first target was Blanchet (Jean-Marie Stehle), an ailing, old, divorced multimillionaire. After intentionally spilling her drink on him at a cocktail party, she seduced him with her exotic charms. The second stage of her plan involved a series of faked orgasms, after which, she merely took off. As planned, Blanchet went insane with longing to the point that when he reappeared, in the third stage, he was prepared to leave her all his fortune. Using the Internet, she moved the money to a Swiss bank in Basel. When Blanchet died soon after, Pali and Touki came after their cut. It was at this point that she ran into Paul and Helene in the scene at the start of the film.

The stage is thus set for Noemie to repay Helene's favor. She first has to get Helene out of the jam with the police for whisking her out of hospital. She then has to get even with Paul for not offering her refuge. When Helene calls Paul from Marseilles to say she's returning home, the police have his phone tapped. Paul in turn flies to Marseilles to warn Helene of what awaits her. Helene and Noemie suspect the worst when they see him at the airport just as they're about to leave. "The cops must have sent him!" Noemie reasons and tells Helene to hide while she puts her three-step plan into action against Paul.

Helene watches as Noemie bumps into Paul, keeling over helplessly. During the second stage, she spies on the two inside a toilet stall as Noemie fakes her orgasm. Helene then reunites with Paul and returns to Paris, pretending to be ignorant of Noemie's presence on the same flight. Inspector Marsat (Michel Lagueyrie) meets Helene and Paul as they arrive, but he reveals that it is the gang of pimps he is after. Meanwhile, we see lavish consumer goods being delivered to Noemie's brothers and stepmother in Marseilles. Noemie's plan is to take away her kid sister, Zora (Hajar Nouma), before she's sold into marriage.

In the film's final section, Serreau adopts the frantic pace that has animated the lives of Noemie and Helene.

Back in Paris, Paul goes insane with longing for Noemie, who gets the currently solitary Fabrice to fall for her as well. Keeping the men at bay, Noemie hatches a plan to get back at Touki and Pali by having them double-cross each other and, in the process, get arrested by Marsat. In the bloody showdown, watched by Helene and Noemie through binoculars, Pali shoots Touki dead before Marsat rounds up the gang. Noemie then keeps a rendezvous with Paul, only to drive him to Mamie's place. She then calls at the Vidal apartment to defuse Fabrice's infatuation as well. The final scene shows the four women, Mamie, Zora, Noemie, and Helene at Noemie's estate, staring out to sea, their faces the picture of serenity and triumph.

As could be expected, while focusing on the film's feminism, critics found the film to be competent as a thriller. Leslie Camhi in the *Village Voice* calls it a "witty black comedy . . . [that] springs from the dark night of the French bourgeois imagination" and notes that the "beauty, cunning, and ferocious vitality [of Noemie's character] are captivating." Stephen Holden in the *New York Times* calls the film "gripping" and describes it as possessing "a savage comic edge." "The film's contempt for the male ego and sex drive is so unrelenting," writes Holden, "that *Chaos* should leave many men feeling momentarily ashamed of their gender and many women fired up for domestic battle."

—*Vivek Adarkar*

CREDITS

Helene: Catherine Frot
Paul: Vincent Lindon
Noemie/Malika: Rachida Brakni
Mamie: Line Renaud
Pali: Wojciech Pszoniak
Fabrice: Aurelien Wilk

Origin: France
Language: French
Released: 2001
Production: Alain Sarde; France 2 Cinema, Eniloc; released by New Yorker Films
Directed by: Coline Serreau
Written by: Coline Serreau
Cinematography by: Jean-Francois Robin
Music by: Ludovic Navarre
Sound: Pierre Lorrain
Editing: Catherine Renault
Art Direction: Michele Abbe
Costumes: Karen Serreau
MPAA rating: Unrated
Running time: 109 minutes

REVIEWS

Boxoffice. October, 2002, p. 55.
New York Times Online. February 21, 2003.
San Francisco Chronicle. April 4, 2003, p. D5.
Variety Online. October 19, 2001.
Village Voice Online. January 29, 2003.
Washington Post. May 23, 2003, p. WE41.

Charlie's Angels: Full Throttle

This summer the Angels are back.
—Movie tagline

Box Office: $93.1 million

During outtakes in the closing credits, the three crime-fighting, kick-boxing sexpots who are Charlie's Angels break out in laughter. Giggles and guffaws abound. Clearly, Cameron Diaz, Lucy Liu, Drew Barrymore, and the others involved in this movie were having a good time. Too bad audiences won't.

Charlie's Angels: Full Throttle has to be loads of fun, or it doesn't work. Unfortunately, despite the somewhat histrionic efforts of its director McG, there is not enough fun or action in this latest installment of a franchise that is rapidly losing energy. Instead, there are a lot of cloying, silly, and inconsequential sequences that fill the gaps between the cartoonish, poorly made spectacle scenes involving fighting, outrageous outfits, and deliberately corny lines. At points the movie gets just campy enough to work . . . and then it topples under its own weightlessness and lack of inspiration.

Charlie's Angels: Full Throttle is not really a movie; it's a series of music videos strung together by McG, a veteran director in that genre, and interspersed with really bad television scenes. Of course, this whole exercise in silliness started with bad television—a popular show from the 1970s that even then may have been spoofing its own formula. The TV version of *Charlie's Angels* was something of a tongue-in-cheek homage to a rapidly dying version of pumped-up ultra-femininity combined with ridiculous action heroics. It was like Barbie dolls crossed with Barbarella. But by now we've seen so many hot chicks with brains and weapons—sexy women in heroic, butt-kicking roles—that such characters no longer raise eyebrows or automatically entertain with their novelty. It's hard to make a movie that makes fun of the stuff in which it is, itself, wallowing knee-deep at the same time.

The first movie version of the franchise, starring this same trio, started explosively and promisingly as high camp but soon petered out into low buffoonery. This sequel doesn't even start with that ridiculously over-the-top energy, and then it veers incoherently between bizarre dialogue and utter brainlessness and only provides intermittent action. Even the most promising action scenes are robbed of their vitality by cheap-looking production values. A dirt bike race that might have been arousing and entertaining instead looks too obviously like it was shot on a studio set and then composed and placed on a background with computers. It's almost as if McG and company wanted to create an entire movie that looked fake. Although it's fun to be silly, there's no reason to make everything look ridiculous—not with this kind of budget and box-office potential.

Certainly, there was no need for pretense that any *Charlie's Angels* sequence would be anything more than silly to begin with, but there's a way to spoof a genre without making a film that looks like it was made on a low-end laptop. Never has so much slow-motion action been so fruitlessly used, and never have characters looked so garishly bright and loud against such drab backgrounds. It's like these women and their enemies are paste-on dolls. Most music videos are shot much more expertly than this film.

Among the trio of supposedly kick-ass stars, Cameron Diaz is the only one who gets it. In fact, Diaz may be the only one involved in the movie's entire production who understands what it should be aiming at, and that is an all-out spoof of sexpot fantasy women as action figures. Diaz lasciviously overplays all her scenes, caricaturing man-trap femininity with the abandon of a truly crazed comedienne. It starts during the first scene, in which the Angels are trying to rescue a U.S. Marshal being held in some version of a Mongolian biker bar. It's not important how he got there or why. Diaz, who plays Natalie, enters wearing a Nordic version of a stripper's costume, with a white fur coat and hat, high-heeled boots, and white fishnets, and speaks in a hilarious Scandinavian kittenish accent. She then hops accommodatingly and mindlessly onto a yak-like "bull" and rides it furiously; the idea is that she's supposed to provide a distraction while her partners rescue the marshal, but instead she easily steals the scene—and every other one in which she appears.

After an escape that involves the Angels taking on fifty armed men (such a mismatch in the Angels' favor that it "hardly seems fair," laughs a tongue-in-cheek Lucy Liu as Alex), things get more ridiculous in a hurry. As their armored vehicle is being destroyed by grenades, the Angels plunge off a bridge and fall impossibly onto a waiting jet copter, whose blades don't seem to pose any threat at all. After this breathless start (a beginning that looks like it would have worked better as a climax) the movie pauses, takes a breath, and introduces its setup—for those few moviegoers who might be new to all this. The Angels, of course, work for Charlie, a disembodied voice that gives

orders from a speaker box, while being helped along by their assistant, Bosley (this time played lamely by TV sitcom star Bernie Mac), who is their inept comic foil. A slapdash backgrounder shows how each of the Angels turned from a precocious kid to an overachieving adult. Alex was a gymnast who turned into a chess prodigy. Natalie is shown as a braces-wearing cheerleader who later becomes a crack veterinarian, or animal midwife, delivering a calf while splattering an onlooker with blood. Dylan (Drew Barrymore), the trailer-trash tramp of the trio, is a wrestler who grows up to be a monster truck driver. Then there are random shots of the Angels skating in a roller derby, and these end with a slow-motion shot of Alex tossing her long hair in the breeze—that was the trademark shot of the first film. If the movie had continued in this fast-paced, over-the-top fashion, it would have been tolerable.

Instead, the film lapses into its dreary plot. It involves two platinum rings that contain the names of all the people placed in the federal witness protection program—but only when the rings are placed together. They are known by the acronym HALO, which stands for something preposterous and forgettable. The Angels are trying to retrieve the rings from a series of malevolent characters, foremost among them Seamus, "Black Irish" mobster who looks like the devil incarnate and was once the boyfriend of Dylan. It turns out Dylan really isn't Dylan, but Helen Zaas, who was put into the witness protection program after seeing Seamus kill someone. (It's a measure of the inanity of this movie that after Dylan's real identity is revealed, the characters sit around making remarks about the name Helen Zaas—"You must have been the butt of every joke.")

But the real villain turns out to be a former Angel played by a famously revamped Demi Moore. This movie spawned more pre-packaged magazine stories than anything in recent memory; it seemed that every cover touted one or another of the angels as well as Moore's comeback. The best that can be said about Moore's return is that this sequel was such a flop, few will remember that Moore was revealed to be the overrated actress she has been all along. She isn't so much acting here as she is posing, showing off how fit and sculpted she is in her early 40s. She manages to make her character unappealing but not in the least bit singular or memorable.

As for the other Angels, Liu is freckle-faced, no-nonsense, and cold, while Barrymore is, regrettably, once again the center of the plot. Those who dressed and made up Barrymore decided to present her as a bit of white trash, a wise decision since she has long since ceased to be classy or sexy. Diaz's sexy spoofing is more appealing than either of her partners' sincere attempts to be sizzling. Their costumes are a hoot, but not enough to carry the movie through many dead spots.

Several peripheral characters come along for the ride for no apparent purpose. These include Alex's father, who is aghast to discover his daughter is not a physician; Alex's beau, a movie actor being given a romantic "time out" for reasons undisclosed; Natalie's live-in beau, a very square, preppie type who spawns great and ridiculous anxiety among the other Angels over a possible marriage; and a 15-year-old orphan also booted out of the witness protection program. The kid seems to have no plot purpose, so it's safe to assume he's there to provide an alter ego for all the 15-year-old boys who obviously make up the target audience for a film like this.

Then there's Mac, who doesn't do anything that's funny and looks confused throughout the film. He's probably why the kind of comedy he executes on the small screen isn't of much use here. He ranges from mediocre to embarrassingly bad, at his worst moments hearkening back to stereotypical images of pre-civil-rights-movement, bug-eyed black entertainers.

Since *Charlie's Angels: Full Throttle* can't really be taken seriously, and obviously doesn't want to be, it has to be judged as pure comedy. Unfortunately its humor is either non-existent or grating, like fingernails on a blackboard. As a series of music videos strung together, however, it's not bad; the music includes a thumping mix of songs from the last 40 years, from Beach Boys to Donna Summer to contemporary madness like the Electric Six's "Danger: High Voltage," and the music keeps things pumping even when the action goes limp. The songs, the costumes, and Diaz's petulant poses and wacky, over-the-top satire of Angel-style femininity are all that's happening here; if there is a next time, McG would do well to spare the expense of a writer and forget a script and plot altogether. They're instantly forgettable anyway.

—*Michael Betzold*

CREDITS

Dylan Sanders: Drew Barrymore
Natalie Cook: Cameron Diaz
Alex Munday: Lucy Alexis Liu
Jimmy Bosley: Bernie Mac
Madison Lee: Demi Moore
Pete: Luke Wilson
Jason: Matt LeBlanc
Thin Man: Crispin Glover
Ray Carter: Robert Patrick
Mr. Munday: John Cleese
Max: Shia LaBeouf
Kelly Garrett: Jaclyn Smith
Seamus O'Grady: Justin Theroux
Randy Emmers: Rodrigo Santoro
Momma Bosley: Ja'net DuBois
Roger Wilson: Robert Forster
Alan Caufield: Eric Bogosian
Mother Superior: Carrie Fisher

Coal Bowl Starter: Pink (Cameo)
Future Angel: Ashley (Fuller) Olsen (Cameo)
Future Angel: Mary-Kate Olsen (Cameo)
Charlie: John Forsythe (Voice)

Origin: USA
Released: 2003
Production: Leonard Goldberg, Drew Barrymore, Nancy Juvonen; Flower Films, Tall Trees, Wonderland Sound and Vision; released by Columbia Pictures
Directed by: McG
Written by: John August, Marianne S. Wibberley, Cormac Wibberley
Cinematography by: Russell Carpenter
Music by: Ed Shearmur
Sound: Willie Burton
Music Supervisor: John Houlihan
Editing: Wayne Wahrman
Art Direction: David Klassen
Costumes: Cheryl Beasley Blackwell
Production Design: J. Michael Riva
MPAA rating: PG-13
Running time: 105 minutes

REVIEWS

Chicago Sun-Times Online. June 27, 2003.
Los Angeles Times Online. June 27, 2003.
New York Times Online. June 27, 2003.
People. July 7, 2003, p. 37.
USA Today Online. June 27, 2003.
Variety Online. June 22, 2003.
Washington Post. June 27, 2003, p. WE34.

QUOTES

Madison (Demi Moore): "I don't take my orders from a speaker box anymore. I work for myself now." Natalie (Cameron Diaz): "Well, your boss sucks."

AWARDS AND NOMINATIONS

Golden Raspberries 2003: Worst Support. Actress (Moore)
Nomination:
Golden Raspberries 2003: Worst Picture, Worst Remake/Sequel, Worst Actress (Barrymore, Diaz), Worst Screenplay.

Chasing Papi

Three women. Three cities. Three times the trouble.
—Movie tagline

 Box Office: $6.1 million

The thing that makes *Chasing Papi* special is that it was to be a breakthrough American hit featuring Latinas. The film does a disservice to Latinas, though, by implying that they could be in no better movie that this silly fluff.

The movie is like one of those frothy romantic movies from the late 1950's/early 1960's with the wacky titles, the zany music and convoluted plot involving romance, some foreign intrigue and lots of good looking people. The "Papi" of the title is Tomas Fuentes (Eduardo Verastegui, a popular Mexican soap opera star and former member of the music group Kairo), a man who is so desirable that he could make a nun blush. We know this because, as she walks through an airport, a young nun gasps and whispers to her sister, "Is it too late to change my mind?"

Tomas travels a lot for his job and he has ended up finding girlfriends in three different cities. In New York, he loves Patricia (Jaci Velasquez, a popular Christian pop star), a spoiled rich girl who carries around her lap dog at all times. Patricia's mother (Maria Conchita Alonzo) wants nothing more than to marry her daughter off to a wealthy man. Patricia seems to have no other personality trait than wearing blue contact lenses. It's to show that she's not comfortable with her Latin heritage.

In Chicago, Tomas dates Lorena (Roselyn Sanchez). Lorena is a lawyer who defends the downtrodden. She is supposed to be uptight and buttoned-up, but even her glasses and pulled-back hair can't disguise the fact that she is gorgeous. In Miami, Tomas spends time with Cici (soap regular Sofia Vergara), a gaudily sexy Charo lookalike. Although she's a cocktail waitress, she dreams of being a dancer. Tomas isn't trying to trick the women; he has simply fallen in love with all three. "How can you choose between the colors of nature's beautiful flowers?" he wonders.

Fate decides to make him choose when all three women watch the same TV astrologer (Walter Mercado, a real life TV astrologer) and decide that they should show up at Tomas' Los Angeles house for a surprise visit. This is where the film enters *Three's Company* territory. The three each go into his house at roughly the same time, but all end up in different rooms so they don't see each other. Then, at exactly the same time, they all emerge from their rooms into a central hall wearing identical lingerie (gifts from Tomas). If this seems funny to you, then *Chasing Papi* is going to be a big treat for you. For those who don't get the humor, wacky music courtesy of Emilio Estefan Jr. (husband of singer Gloria Estefan), kicks in to each scene to heighten the zaniness quotient.

And there is a lot of music, because there is a lot of zaniness. After discovering that Tomas is three-timing them, the women agree that they will leave and not see him again. But, they all cheat and show up—again at roughly the same time—on Tomas' doorstep. The poor chap is overwhelmed with trying to keep the three apart and ends up overdosing on liquor and his anxiety medication. Thus, Tomas is out of commission for pretty much the rest of the movie. It's strange. As charismatic as Tomas is supposed to be, he's about as interesting passed out as he is when he's awake. He's certainly a more believable actor.

More silly things ensue. The women take Tomas to a posh hotel where Lorena is mistaken for the Miss Puerto Rico entrant for a Miss Latin America beauty contest. She goes along with it and relishes the chance to be appreciated for her beauty instead of her brains. In the meantime, there is some sort of cockamamie plot development involving Cici, a car delivery, a bag of money and some hapless crooks. There is also a team of FBI agents, led by Carmen (Lisa Vidal), chasing the crooks.

The movie turns into a Latina episode of *Charlie's Angels*. The three women are forced to do stuff like dress up as beauty queens or rip their clothing to masquerade as dancers at a big Latino festival. While all of this happens, the women each stay in their rigid stereotypical roles. Whenever something happens, writers Laura Angelica Simon, Steven Antin, Alison Balian and Elizabeth Sarnoff have the characters say a line that just reinforces their particular stereotype.

For example, rich girl Patricia is big on saying, "My mother's going to kill me." When they all fall asleep on Papi one night, each of them has a dream about winning Papi over that is geared to their particular one-note character. It's as though the writers didn't realize that anyone in the audience could figure out the character in about five seconds and wouldn't need constant review. It's easy to see why Tomas would not be content with any one of these women. Each of them is so one-dimensional, they would become boring after an hour.

Somewhere in the mix of goofy happenings, the women stop being enemies and start finding their own power. This is supposed to be the feminist part. Patricia realizes that she can live without her family's money. Cici realizes that she is ambitious as well as sexy. And Lorena realizes that she can be a lawyer and a hottie, too. Power to the women?

For a movie that's supposed to be a female power comedy, it's neither that woman-friendly or comedic. The empowerment that the women experience at the end of the movie seems more driven by plot necessity than a natural occurrence. And it's interesting that they have to find themselves all while wearing sexy clothing and being perfectly coifed. And the humor is just not there. It tends toward slapstick and madcap adventures that just aren't smart (or stupid) enough to play well.

The actors are appropriately glossy and good-looking, but they don't hint at any depth and that's probably because there wasn't any written for their characters. The only actress that makes an attempt is Vergara. Her lighthearted, over-the-top Cici has a hit of sadness behind her gaudy facade.

Critics didn't find the movie to be particularly good. Paul West of the *Seattle Post-Intelligencer* gave the film a C grade and wrote, "Most of *Chasing Papi* is a loud, frantic mess, a movie that wants to be a screwball farce but is simply farcical and screwy." Kevin Thomas of the *Los Angeles Times* wrote, "Not every Latina is going to go along with this message movie disguised as a comedy and may in fact find it patronizing. (Director Linda) Mendoza does keep everything light and swift, and the cast is undeniably easy on the eyes." And Dave Kehr of the *New York Times* wrote, "All of this self-actualization is accompanied by some of the most tiresome slapstick to be seen since the premature retirement of Pauly Shore. The spectator soon comes to envy Papi, who . . . spends most of the movie unconscious."

—*Jill Hamilton*

CREDITS

Tomas: Eduardo Verastegui
Lorena: Roselyn Sanchez
Cici: Sofia Vergara
Patricia: Jaci Velasquez
Carmen: Lisa Vidal
Victor: Freddy Rodriguez
Rodrigo: D.L. Hughley
Mary: Maria Conchita Alonso
Dr. Chu: Ian Gomez

Origin: USA
Released: 2003
Production: Tracey Trench, Forest Whitaker, Laura Angelica Simon; Spirit Dance Entertainment; released by Fox 2000 Pictures
Directed by: Linda Mendoza
Written by: Steve Antin, Laura Angelica Simon, Alison Balian, Elizabeth Sarnoff
Cinematography by: Xavier Perez Grobet
Music by: Emilio Estefan Jr.
Sound: Felipe Borrero
Music Supervisor: Frankie Pine
Editing: Maysie Hoy
Art Direction: Anthony Rivero Stabley

Costumes: Salvador Perez
Production Design: Candi Guterres
MPAA rating: PG-13
Running time: 92 minutes

REVIEWS

Chicago Sun-Times Online. April 16, 2003.
Los Angeles Times Online. April 16, 2003.
New York Times Online. April 16, 2003.
USA Today Online. April 16, 2003.
Variety Online. April 15, 2003.
Washington Post. April 16, 2003, p. C16.

QUOTES

Tomas (Eduardo Verastegui) says of his three girlfriends: "How can you choose between the colors of nature's beautiful flowers?"

Cheaper by the Dozen

The More . . . The Scarier!
—Movie tagline

 Box Office: $135.5 million

*C*heaper by the Dozen is a remake of the 1950 movie starring Clifton Webb and Myrna Loy as a two-career couple raising a brood of twelve kids. That film was based on the 1948 book by Frank Bunker Gilbreth, Jr., and sister Ernestine Gilbreth Carey detailing life in a family of twelve, helmed by parents who were internationally known efficiency experts. The father so believed in his science, which he called motion study, that he applied its techniques to raising his children. Every chore, from cleaning the house to taking a bath was done in a prescribed manner for the maximum time savings.

It's an interesting concept—the attempt to run a family like a business—but 2003's *Cheaper by the Dozen* writers Craig Titley, Joel Cohen, Sam Harper and Alec Sokolow, apparently didn't think so, because they dropped that whole angle. In fact, there are only two things in the latest film that are from the book—the title and the fact that there are twelve kids. Judging by the film, it's difficult to believe that they even glanced at the book or the earlier movie. If they did, they seemed to take the tack that if anything was witty, clever or entertaining in the first film, they should wipe it out and replace it with someone falling down, or perhaps something breaking.

Cheaper by the Dozen is as generic and witless as they come. It's as though the movie was created for some sort of demographic marketing program. The kids include Piper Perabo (of *Coyote Ugly*), Hillary Duff (of all things preteen), Tom Welling (*Smallville*). As one critic remarked, it's difficult to imagine that such kids could come from these parents (Steve Martin and Bonnie Hunt). To fill out the roster, there's a nerdy kid, a fat kid, a tomboyish girl, two sets of twins and, some other kids that aren't so noticeable. Actually, beyond their one set trait, none of the kids have any sort of recognizable personality.

Everything in the film has been wiped clean of any personality. Even the names of the parents, Frank and Lillian Gilbreth have changed to the blander Tom and Kate Baker. The kids' names have all been changed too. Instead of an Anne, there's a Nora.

This is a film in which one of the most memorable characters is a frog named Beans. His mother, naturally, was named Pork. This is a film that is constantly popping upbeat music into the proceedings, just to make darned sure the audience knows that it is having fun. This is a film that has the most obvious and obnoxious product placement of perhaps any film ever made. If at any point the movie becomes too boring, it's possible to still stay entertained by playing a sort of "Where's Waldo?" game with Crate and Barrel items. Truly, there are Crate and Barrel boxes in nearly every scene. The family uses the C and B boxes as some sort of decor. In the kitchen, there are several displayed artfully on their shelves; likewise in the bathrooms and the bedrooms.

When they are not arranging their Crate and Barrel boxes, the family lives in a sort of mildly controlled chaos in small Midland, Illinois. Tom is the coach of the local football team and Kate has given up her job as a journalist to raise this pack of kids. When Tom is offered his dream job coaching at his alma mater, Lincoln University, he moves the family to Evanston. The kids don't want to move, and complain ceaselessly. This is one of the conflicts in the movie.

Another conflict is that Kate, who has somehow found time to write a book about raising her kids, is in need of some time away from the family to promote her book. As Roger Ebert of the Chicago Sun-Times pointed out, her book is accepted, published and becomes a number one best seller in the course of about a week.

Mom and Dad are both trying to take advantage of these lucky breaks in their careers, but can't seem to balance that with their home life. When Kate leaves for her book tour, Dad can't manage to watch the kids for two weeks. Daughter Lorraine (Duff) says, "Call me crazy, Pops, but things are getting pretty crazy around here." When Dad decides that he needs to get some help, the soundtrack, with its usual obnoxious lack of subtlety, launches into the Beatles

"Help!" Tom calls in oldest daughter Nora (Perabo) who no longer lives with the family. She tries to help out, but the kids take an instant dislike to her stuck-up actor boyfriend, Hank (Ashton Kutcher). They let him know this by doing stuff like putting his underwear in meat so that dogs will chase him.

The film is not really about career and family conflicts though, it's about kids running amok. The movie shows the kids literally hanging from a chandelier. (That the chandelier is constantly coming down is one of the weak recurring jokes in the film.) There is running, falling, and a frog jumping into a plate of scrambled eggs. There is a scene in which the grand finale is a fat kid throwing up. The idea of twelve kids living in one house isn't used for anything more interesting than having a lot of kids running around yelling all of the time.

And there is a strange undercurrent in the film. This film seems to be portraying itself as aggressively normal and in the process gives out some subtle and not so subtle messages. From watching *Cheaper by the Dozen,* we might surmise that being a vegetarian is bad, following career dreams is a mistake, women should stay at home and one should never move. And if one is forced to move, there is no use trying to find the good in the new place. And perhaps the biggest message of all, if you're assigned to write a script based on a book and film, don't bother to look at either of them, just read the title and wing it from there.

The requisite outtake reel shown over the closing credits is the perfect capper for this lackluster film. One of the outtakes shows a set of the twins being forced to do another line reading. The little boys want to go out and play, but the director insists that they do it again. Not even the outtakes are funny.

Critics did not care for the film—at all. Roger Ebert of the *Chicago Sun-Times,* who was one of the kinder critics, wrote, "Hey, I liked *Cheaper by the Dozen.* These actors are skilled at being nice. It's just that the movie settles when it ought to push." Stephen Holden was less flattering in the *New York Times:* "*Cheaper by the Dozen* is a bubbling crockpot of farcical mush to warm the tummies of anyone who really and truly misses *The Brady Bunch,* and I mean really and truly." The *New York Post*'s Megan Lehmann concluded that "all you need to know about the slapdash, bogus kiddie flick *Cheaper by the Dozen* can be summed up by the fact that Ashton Kutcher, making a glorified cameo as a narcissistic model-slash-actor, is the best thing in it." Geoff Pevere of the *Toronto Star* warned, "Consumer beware: *Cheaper by the Dozen,* a movie about a brood of 12 country brats who move to the city and make life unspeakable for their less reproductively profligate neighbours, is a horror movie trying to pass as family values, feel-good holiday fare." Wesley Morris of the *Boston Globe* called the film "stultifying" and added, "Most of Tom and Kate Baker's kids seem to have been flown in from a casting office in

Burbank. They have the voices of fruit drink pitch persons and the unquenchable energy of in-the-flesh Rugrats. One likes fashion and beauty, one likes his skateboard, two like to wrestle, one loves his science equipment, and several sport lots of athletic wear. These aren't kids, they're aisles at Target."

—*Jill Hamilton*

CREDITS

Tom Baker: Steve Martin
Kate Baker: Bonnie Hunt
Nora Baker: Piper Perabo
Charlie Baker: Tom Welling
Lorraine Baker: Hilary Duff
Hank: Ashton Kutcher
Kevin Baker: Kevin J. Edelman
Sarah Baker: Alyson Stoner
Jake Baker: Jacob Smith
Jessica Baker: Liliana Mumy
Tina Shenk: Paula Marshall
Bill Shenk: Alan Ruck
Shake: Richard Jenkins
Nick Gerhard: Holmes Osborne
Diana Philips: Vanessa Bell Calloway
Coach Brinker: Rex Linn
Miss Hozzie: Amy Hill
Kim Baker: Morgan York
Mark Baker: Forrest Landis
Mike Baker: Blake Woodruff
Nigel Baker: Brent Kinsman
Kyle Baker: Shane Kinsman
Dylan Shenk: Steven Anthony Lawrence
Himself: Regis Philbin (Cameo)
Herself: Kelly Ripa (Cameo)

Origin: USA
Released: 2003
Production: Robert Simonds, Michael Barnathan, Ben Myron; released by 20th Century-Fox
Directed by: Shawn Levy
Written by: Sam Harper, Joel Cohen, Alec Sokolow
Cinematography by: Jonathan Brown
Music by: Christophe Beck
Sound: David Obermeyer
Music Supervisor: Dave Jordan
Editing: George Folsey Jr.
Art Direction: Scott A. Meehan
Costumes: Sanja Milkovic Hays
Production Design: Nina Ruscio
MPAA rating: PG
Running time: 98 minutes

REVIEWS

Chicago Sun-Times Online. December 24, 2003.
Entertainment Weekly. January 9, 2004, p. 59.
Los Angeles Times Online. December 24, 2003.
New York Times Online. December 25, 2003.
USA Today Online. December 24, 2003.
Variety Online. November 20, 2003.
Washington Post. December 26, 2003, p. WE39.

QUOTES

Tom (Steve Martin): "You were checking me out, weren't you?" Kate (Bonnie Hunt): "You got a problem with that?" Tom: "Twelve kids later and we still got the heat."

AWARDS AND NOMINATIONS

Nomination:
Golden Raspberries 2003: Worst Actor (Kutcher).

City of Ghosts

Where you go when you can't turn back.
—Movie tagline

Matt Dillon is hardly the first actor anyone would think capable of directing and co-writing an arty film about American exiles in Asia, but with *City of Ghosts,* he has made an admirable, often engrossing first film. Although *City of Ghosts* is not as accomplished and powerful as Philip Noyce's similar *The Quiet American* (2002), it is still an indelible portrait of Western guilt and responsibility abroad.

Co-written by Barry Gifford, who wrote David Lynch's *Lost Highway* (1997) and whose novel is the basis of Lynch's *Wild at Heart* (1990), *City of Ghosts* is an unusual treatment of a young man's coming of age because it is a very belated change and arrives only after considerable anguish. Jimmy Cremmins (Dillon) is a con man trained by his mentor, Marvin (James Caan), to pull scams and move on without thinking about the consequences. As the film opens in New York, Jimmy watches in horror television news accounts of hurricane damage on the East Coast, horrified because his and Marvin's fake insurance company has sold worthless policies to the innocent victims of the destruction. Artfully sidestepping FBI investigators, Jimmy flees first to Thailand and then to Cambodia, looking both for Marvin and a way to assuage his guilt.

City of Ghosts is notable for never telegraphing exactly where it is going. Jimmy has no definite plan but will think of something by the time he finds the elusive Marvin. Jimmy is perhaps not smart enough to have anticipated the havoc his cons could wreak on people's lives, and he is not certain how and if he can make recompense in some way, how he can save his soul. The film's seemingly aimless drifting is in keeping with the protagonist's unsettled state of mind. There is nothing predictable or mechanical about Dillon and Gifford's storytelling. If the situation is not easy for Jimmy, why should it be for the viewer?

With the help of Marvin's colleague Kaspar (Stellan Skarsgard), Jimmy makes his way to Phnom Penh and a hotel owned by Emile (Gerard Depardieu). Emile's bar is the center of expatriate activity, full of down-on-their-luck Americans and Europeans in motionless flight from the chaos of their previous lives. Jimmy's restlessness contrasts with their terminal stasis.

After finally connecting with Marvin, who is living in the former governor's mansion, Jimmy, instead of expiating his guilt, becomes caught up in another of his mentor's schemes. In league with an ex-general Sideth (Chalee Sankhavesa), Marvin plans an elaborate Las Vegas-style casino/hotel complex. Jimmy, ever the bewildered innocent, seeing poverty all around him, wonders who the customers will be. Jimmy, Marvin, Kaspar, Sideth, and the Russian mafia eventually converge in a violent resolution.

At first, Kaspar seems to be on Jimmy's side but proves to be untrustworthy, even treacherous. Jimmy finds new cohorts in the fearless Emile, Sophie (Natascha McElhone), a Brit working on preserving a local shrine, and Sok (Sereyvuth Kem), a cyclo driver and guide. The deceptively clever Sok, a former soldier hoping for a better life for his family, becomes Jimmy's confidante and the film's moral center.

The Jimmy-Sok relationship parallels that of the British reporter and his Vietnamese assistant in *The Quiet American,* though Dillon and Gifford's characters lack the ironic complexity of the protagonists in Noyce's film and Graham Greene's 1955 novel. As most of the reviewers of *City of Ghosts* observed, the film owes a debt to Greene, Joseph Conrad, and other writers who have depicted Western exiles adrift in Asia and Africa, searching for redemption. It is easy to find similarities between the film and Conrad's *An Outcast of the Islands* (1896), *Lord Jim* (1900), and, especially, *Victory* (1915), Paul Theroux's *Saint Jack* (1973), John le Carre's *The Honourable Schoolboy* (1977), and several works by Greene, most obviously *The Quiet American.*

The literary work and film that *City of Ghosts* most closely resembles, however, is not set in an exotic locale. Jimmy is a somewhat soiled version of Holly Martins, the wide-eyed American innocent abroad in post-World War II Vienna in Greene's novel and Carol Reed's film, *The Third Man* (both 1949). (In interviews, Dillon cites Reed's 1951 film of *An Outcast of the Islands* as an influence.) Just as Martins is shocked to discover the evil of his best friend, Harry Lime, Jimmy finds new truths about Marvin. Dillon and Gifford are to be commended, however, in striving to make Jimmy and Marvin less black-and-white than Greene's characters. Marvin is a ruthless criminal, but he has hidden depths.

The film also recalls the conflicting emotions and moral dilemmas seen in John Ford's greatest films, most notably *The Searchers* (1956), which has arguably had more influence on other filmmakers than any other film. The final scenes of *City of Ghosts* exhibit more than a touch of Ford's infamous sentimentality as Jimmy finds means of making up for his sins. While *The Third Man* ends profoundly and sadly with the heroine walking away from the hero, Dillon's film ends more optimistically with Jimmy walking toward the waiting arms of Sophie.

The latter loses some impact, however, because Sophie is underwritten and McElhone brings little to the role beyond her wide-eyed smile. The alarmingly expanding Depardieu brings considerable presence to another sketchily conceived part. The great French actor shines when Emile breaks up a fight while holding his child in his arms, and when his monkey steals Jimmy's sunglasses and he blankly denies knowing anything about any monkey. The amateur Kem, a cyclo driver in real life, demonstrates relaxed charm. Skarsgard, a veritable chameleon, creates several memorable moments, especially when the unstable Kaspar allows his racism to surface. Skarsgard is masterful at gradually revealing Kaspar's weaknesses. (Kaspar is the kind of role on which the late Denholm Elliott once held a patent.)

Easily the best performance is given by Caan. He is even better as an aging character actor than he was as a star during the 1970s, having toned down his mannerisms, and easily conveying complex emotions merely by raising an eyebrow. Caan is also to be commended for the courage to work with first-time directors such as Wes Anderson (*Bottle Rocket,* 1996), Christopher McQuarrie (*The Way of the Gun,* 2000), and now Dillon. Caan's best moment comes when Marvin takes a karaoke microphone to sing a banal pop song in Cambodian. This very strange scene, recalling Dean Stockwell in *Blue Velvet* (1986), must be Gifford's nod of acknowledgment to the influence of David Lynch on the film's style.

Dillon, a good actor perhaps handicapped by his looks to a degree, specializes in brooding, inarticulate characters. Despite such notable films as *Rumble Fish* (1983), *The Flamingo Kid* (1984), *Drugstore Cowboy* (1989)—his best performance—and *There's Something About Mary* (1998), his career has been rather spotty. While he doesn't do much new as an actor in *City of Ghosts,* he at least has had the opportunity to create a character suitable for his acting skills. While most other directors seem to be satisfied only with silent poses from the star, Dillon's Jimmy is more active and vocal than his usual characters.

In an interview with Charlie Rose, Dillon, whose only previous directorial experience was an episode of *Oz* and some music videos, said he gave early drafts of the screenplay to Cameron Crowe, Gus Van Sant, and Francis Ford Coppola for their comments. (He also consulted with Stanley Tucci about making the transition from actor to director.) Dillon said Coppola provided "interesting notes." Both Dillon and Caan are Coppola protégés, and there are similarities between Hyman Roth in *The Godfather, Part II* (1974) and Marvin. Likewise, the film's moral aimlessness/moral quest dynamic recalls Coppola's *Apocalypse Now* (1979), inspired by Conrad's *The Heart of Darkness* (1902).

The most obvious stylistic influence among the directors with whom he has worked, however, is Van Sant, who directed Dillon in *Drugstore Cowboy* and *To Die For* (1995). Like Van Sant at his best, Dillon's visual style and pacing are deceptively artless, recalling the languid pacing of European films, especially French and Italian films of the 1970s. (Dillon told the *Sydney Sunday Telegraph* that he attempted to emulate "any 1970s director who likes dream sequences.") As a result, *City of Ghosts* is one of those subtle films, a dreamy mood piece, that, despite its flaws, lingers in the memory.

—*Michael Adams*

CREDITS

Jimmy Cremmins: Matt Dillon
Marvin: James Caan
Sophie: Natascha (Natasha) McElhone
Emile: Gerard Depardieu
Sok: Sereyvuth Kem
Sideth: Chalee Sankhavesa
Kaspar: Stellan Skarsgard
Sabrina: Rose Byrne
Larry Luckman: Christopher Curry
Robbie: Shawn Andrews

Origin: USA
Released: 2003
Production: Willi Baer, Michael Cerenzie, Deepak Nayor; United Artists, Kintop Pictures, Mainline Productions, Banyan Tree; released by MGM
Directed by: Matt Dillon
Written by: Matt Dillon, Barry Gifford
Cinematography by: Jim Denault
Music by: Tyler Bates
Sound: Marc Fishman, Joe Barnett
Music Supervisor: Dondi Bastone
Editing: Howard E. Smith

Art Direction: Lek Chaiyan
Costumes: Moji Sangi
Production Design: David Brisbin
MPAA rating: R
Running time: 117 minutes

REVIEWS

Boston Globe. May 9, 2003, p. C6.
Boxoffice. February, 2003, p. 32.
Boxoffice. April, 2003, p. 86.
Chicago Sun-Times. May 9, 2003, p. 31.
Entertainment Weekly. May 9, 2003, p. 56.
Los Angeles Times. April 25, 2003, p. AR12.
New York. April 28, 2003, p. 84.
New York Daily News. April 25, 2003, p. 45.
New York Times Online. September 9, 2001.
New York Times. April 25, 2003, p. E25.
People. May 5, 2003, p. 37.
San Francisco Chronicle. May 9, 2003, p. D5.
Variety. August 26, 2002.
Variety Online. September 12, 2002.
Washington Post. May 9, 2003, p. C5.

QUOTES

Jimmy (Matt Dillon) to Marvin (James Caan): "I've got enough bad karma to last me six lifetimes."

City of God (Cidade de Deus)

Fight and you'll never survive. Run and you'll never escape.
—Movie tagline
15 miles from paradise . . . one man will do anything to tell the world everything.
—Movie tagline

 Box Office: $6.6 million

Fernando Meirelles's *City of God* brings to the screen a highly energetic film about gangs in Rio de Janeiro. It is with this film that the world is introduced to Meirelles and what an introduction it is! His film has been compared to *Goodfellas,* which isn't an altogether inaccurate comparison. There are many similarities, but make no mistake, *City of God* is in no way a rip off of *Goodfellas*—just similar in ferocity.

The story centers around gangs in Rio who live in slums separated entirely from the rest of the population in the city center. These slums are filled with music, life, color and fun in a dangerous and dark way. The opening scene shows one gang having a picnic that erupts in chaos when a chicken runs free. Rocket (Alexandre Rodrigues), who is the narrator of the film, chases down the chicken and ends up caught between two rivals: the gang on one side, the cops on the other.

Rocket flashes from his current situation back to a time when he was a small boy playing soccer in his housing development. It is the beginning of his story of the gang, the Tenger Trio. Rocket is a photographer who is close enough to the gangs to give an accurate and believable portrayal of their activities and lives, but not close enough to be horribly affected by it. His telling of the story is fascinating and not completely linear; he jumps in periodically with minor details about people or events. This sort of straying from the general path is one of the things that sets this film apart from many movies out there today.

The technique of the flashback, the shift in colors from the slum to the soccer field made it abundantly clear that this director had some fresh ideas to bring to the screen. I was enthralled by the techniques employed by Meirelles from start to finish. Cinematographer Cesar Charlone used quick cutting and a hand held camera in *City of God* and it fit the mood perfectly. I am not always sold on this look, but, with this film, it just seemed the natural choice.

One of the more disturbing aspects of the film is how young the gang members are. They are children as are their victims. I couldn't shake the images of these kids engaging in such violent acts all for the sake of survival.

The film clearly and succinctly points out how poverty has undermined the entire social fabric of the area. We know from other films in this genre that gangs provide much more than financial gain; they provide a type of family structure. There have been a number of such films, but what makes *City of God* stand apart is the age of the gang members. Even the leaders are shockingly young. The film makes the deaths of these young people viscerally moving in a way that other movies do not.

This movie is based on a novel by Paulo Lins, who used real events that took place in his home of Rio de Janeiro in the '70s as the basis of his story. Not only did screenwriter Braulio Mantovani adapt the book in a wonderfully visually expressive way, he and the director used the grittiness of the city to their advantage. They didn't shy away from or exaggerate the harsh reality of the setting, but rather embraced it and treated it like a brother. This added the element of reality and made this story seem like a piece of oral history. That is what true filmmaking from the heart is all about.

—*Laura Abraham*

CREDITS

Buscape/Rocket: Alexandre Rodriques
Ze Pequeno/Little Ze: Leandro Firmino da Hora
Bene/Benny: Phelipe Haagensen
Sandro Cenoura/Carrot: Matheus Nachtergaele
Manu Galinha/Knockout Ned: Seu Jorge
Cabeleira/Shaggy: Johnathan Haagensen

Origin: Brazil
Language: Portuguese
Released: 2002
Production: Andrea Barata Ribeiro, Mauricio Andrade Ramos; O2 Filmes, VideoFilmes; released by Miramax Films
Directed by: Fernando Meirelles, Katia Lund
Written by: Braulio Mantovani
Cinematography by: Cesar Charlone
Music by: Antonio Pinto, Ed Cortes
Sound: Guilherme Ayrosa, Paulo Ricardo Nunes
Editing: Daniel Rezende
Art Direction: Tule Peake
Costumes: Bia Salgado, Ines Salgado
MPAA rating: R
Running time: 130 minutes

REVIEWS

Boxoffice. January, 2003, p. 54.
Chicago Sun-Times Online. January 24, 2003.
Entertainment Weekly. January 24, 2003, p. 76.
Los Angeles Times Online. January 17, 2003.
New York Times Online. January 12, 2003.
New York Times Online. January 17, 2003.
Premiere. February, 2003, p. 43.
Sight and Sound. January, 2003, p. 28.
USA Today Online. January 17, 2003.
Variety Online. May 19, 2002.
Washington Post. January 24, 2003, p. WE39.

AWARDS AND NOMINATIONS

N.Y. Film Critics 2003: Foreign Film
Nomination:
Oscars 2003: Adapt. Screenplay, Cinematog., Director (Meirelles), Film Editing

Golden Globes 2003: Foreign Film
Ind. Spirit 2004: Foreign Film.

Civil Brand

*Never underestimate the power of a woman . . .
behind bars.*
—Movie tagline
Who ever heard of women taking over a prison . . .
—Movie tagline

In the 1960s and 1970s, the exploitative women's prison drama had its own little heyday. It wasn't really a creative heyday—these films weren't exactly what anyone would call good—but more of a prolific period. B-movie filmmakers like Roger Corman filled screens with such dramas *The Big Doll House* and *Caged Heat*. These exploitation films shared many of the same elements—scantily clad women, lesbian scenes, and strip searches. As in most prison dramas—regardless of the prisoners' genders—there would also usually be a good character forced into solitary confinement, a mean guard and/or warden and a climactic prison break.

Because *Civil Brand* is a women's prison drama, it automatically gets associated with those that came before. Director Neema Barnette, who comes from a background of theater, experimental film and TV (she was the first African-American woman to direct a sitcom), knows the conven[-fj]tions and tries to avoid them. Instead she strives to create a movie that has a broader social point. She is only partially successful.

Barnette does fine on the social issues point, specifically the issue of prison labor for profit. As one character explains, "We were high-priced stock down on Wall Street. We were sewing ski coats for $1.50 a day for some woman in France who would be paying like $1,000 for it next month."

The Whitehead Correctional Institute is a run-down old structure headed by a warden (Reed R. McCants) who is also a suave businessman; he has discovered the profitability of using his captives to do piecework for American corporations. While he schmoozes on golf courses with company bigwigs, he leaves the dirty work of the day-to-day doings of the prison to Captain Deese (Clifton Powell). The warden is likely well-aware that Deese is abusive and cruel to the female inmates, but as long as the prison keeps making money, the warden turns a blind eye to Deese's behavior. Among Deese's charming traits are forcing himself on women and insisting upon sexual favors.

When Frances Shepard (LisaRaye) arrives at prison, she's greeted with a "Welcome to the plantation, Sister Frances." Writers Preston A. Whitmore II and Joyce Renee Lewis portray today's prisons as modern day plantations. There's the captive (and mostly black) workforce headed by a dictator-like figure who cares little for working conditions.

Frances is the innocent of the film. She's a devoted mother who ended up in jail because she accidentally killed her abusive husband. But the writers are smart enough not to make this a film about women who are wrongly imprisoned. The other women prisoners have done bad things and they admit it. The film is not saying that they shouldn't be in prison; the film is saying that while they are serving their time, they need to be treated humanely.

In prison, Frances meets Little Momma (Lark Voorheis), a young, pregnant woman who takes on the role of cell block preacher. The other inmates include Wet (Monica Calhoun), who is adamant that the women get their justice, and Nikki (N'Bushe Wright), a strong, beautiful woman who retains her great dignity despite her circumstances. Sabrina (rapper DaBrat), a tough younger prisoner with a jaunty attitude, narrates the film.

Michael Meadows (rapper/actor Mos Def) is a law student who uses family connections to get a summer job at the prison. Michael is a gentle, fair-minded guy who is horrified by Captain Deese's loutish behavior. "What did the blind man say when he passed the fish market?" brays Deese. "'Morning, ladies!'" The distaste is mutual. Deese dismissively calls Michael "College Boy" and thinks that he is too soft to be much good for anything. As Michael learns more about the prison system and researches prison labor practices online, he starts sympathizing with the women prisoners and finds himself torn between performing his job and trying to be a humane person. In previous films, Mos Def has shown himself to be a subtle, charismatic actor and here he is just as good. He has a strong screen presence but he knows how to adjust it to help better highlight the characters around him. His quietly horrified reactions to Deese's boorishness serve to better show just how offensive the man is.

Barnette also tries to break free of the usual prison film conventions by arting up her film. Narrator Sabrina interrupts the film frequently to address the viewer directly. It adds an immediacy to the film and gives the story more weight. After all, if the events that Sabrina is talking about have gelled into an official story, then surely they will be interesting. Barnette also adds visual interest by using black-and-white footage and odd camera angles.

But the storytelling tricks can't hide the fact that there are only so many things that can happen in a prison. Perhaps it was inevitable that *Civil Brand* would fall into some of the usual prison film clichés. The most egregious of these examples is a scene in which Frances and Nikki are both sent to solitary confinement (in this movie it's called "the hole"). As they writhe around on the floor it becomes obvious that both of them are wearing attractive underwear.

From there, things fall into a predictable pattern. Because it is easier to tell a victorious story about fighting one bad guy than fighting an entrenched economic system, the movie eventually turns into a film about the women getting their well-deserved revenge on Deese. Despite its lofty aims, the movie ends up with a lot of the same old stuff. Still, clichés don't have to be bad. After all, they become clichés because they've proven themselves to be successful story elements. We've seen this stuff before, but it's still entertaining. The acting is solid, the story is compelling and Barnette wraps it all up in a pleasing package. (It's hard to believe the film was shot in a mere 15 days.)

The majority of critics disliked *Civil Brand,* although there were reviewers who thought the film provided a fresh take on the genre. Among those was Kevin Thomas of the *Los Angeles Times,* who declared, "As entertaining as it is pertinent, the well-paced *Civil Brand* is a potent calling card for the gifted, committed and versatile Neema Barnette." Sheri Linden of the *Hollywood Reporter* wrote, "Although the film loses its way in the late going with a preponderance of melodramatic elements that dilute the more compelling social message, for much of its running time it packs a visual punch, thanks in large part to a strong cast." Blake French of *Filmcritic.com* wrote, "*Civil Brand* might think that it carries an inspiring message about courage, hope, and sacrifice, but it's really nothing more than pieces of other movies' messages pasted together." And Peter Debruge of *Premiere.com* wrote that the film "loses its way among the movie's many political messages, defaulting to yet another tired retread."

—Jill Hamilton

CREDITS

Frances Shepard: (Lisa Ray MacCoy) LisaRaye
Michael Meadows: Dante "Mos Def" Beze
Nikki Barnes: N'Bushe Wright
Wet: Monica Calhoun
Sabrina: Da Brat
Sargent Cervantes: M.C. Lyte
Captain Deese: Clifton Powell
Little Momma: Lark Voorhies
Aisha: Tichina Arnold
Warden Nelson: Reed McCants

Origin: USA
Released: 2002
Production: Neema Barnette, Steve Lockett, Jeff Clanagan; released by Lions Gate Films
Directed by: M. Neema Barnette
Written by: Joyce Renee Lewis, Preston A. Whitmore II
Cinematography by: Yuri Neyman

Music by: Mandrill
Editing: David Beatty
Production Design: Cyndi Williams
MPAA rating: R
Running time: 95 minutes

REVIEWS

New York Times Online. October 10, 2003.
Variety Online. July 25, 2002.
Village Voice Online. October 8, 2003.

Cold Creek Manor

The perfect house hides the perfect crime.
—Movie tagline

 Box Office: $21.3 million

Documentary filmmaker Cooper Tilson (Dennis Quaid) and his wife Lea (Sharon Stone) lead a frantic, urban life. She has to fly off to business meetings with a boss who propositions her while dangling a vice presidency in front of her, he hustles through hectic mornings getting the kids ready for school and driving them there in the frenzied city traffic. But when their son, Jesse (Ryan Wilson), is hit by a car on the busy street in front of his own school, Cooper laments, "We've got to get out of the city."

And so Cooper, Lea, Jesse and their daughter Kristen (Kristen Stewart) drive out into the country looking for a new home. They end up in the small town of Bellingham and at the chained front gate of a bank-foreclosed country estate, Cold Creek Manor. Since the chain's lock isn't secured, the family wanders down the overgrown path to the stately but neglected home. The grass is brown, stagnant water is in the pool, rusted trucks lurk in the trees, and leaves and vines claim everything else. Finding the basement door also unlocked, they continue their exploration into the house itself. Although the inside is dusty and disheveled, it is completely furnished and looks as if the previous tenants had just left in a hurry. Books and papers overflow shelves, photos and toys hint that highly personal effects have been left behind, clothes are left hanging in closets, and the beds look to have been occupied recently. This is the house that Jesse says is "way cool" and should become the new Tilson home. With that the Tilsons walk out of their metropolitan frenzy of a life . . . and into someone else's.

The renovation process begins with an "out with the old" sale of much of the house's furniture to an antique appraiser. This seeming disregard for the house's previous owners' possessions rub some in the small community the wrong way, especially Ruby (Juliette Lewis) who works at Pinski's gas station, used car lot, restaurant, mini-mart, bar and local hang out. The reason for Ruby's anger is that she's the girlfriend of Dale Massie (Stephen Dorff) the house's previous owner who lost it after he went to prison for three years for killing a man in an accident that, according to Dale, wasn't his fault.

Imagine the Tilson's surprise, then, when they find Dale wandering about their new home. Fearing that this scruffy man might be out to make a scene about their buying his home or worse . . . out to harm them, they warily allow him to invite himself to dinner. To their relief, he sums up his apparent philosophical attitude to the whole thing with, "I screwed up, the bank took everything, you bought it."

Dale then asks the Tilsons if they would hire him to help them restore the house. Reluctantly, they agree to give him a one-week trial period in which he says he can get their swimming pool up and running. After all, who knows the house better than Dale, whose family has lived there for generations? Why, he can even identify the strange farm implements exhibited in a display case: they're hammers for killing sheep . . . but one is missing.

Soon more sinister clues begin to pop up around the house. The kids find a sign half buried in leaves out in the woods that has the word "evil" written on it. The sheriff (Dana Eskelson) turns out to be Ruby's sister and seems almost uninterested in protecting the Tilsons from the locals. Cooper finds compromising photos of Dale's wife. And Dale's family is missing. Well, his father is still around (an unrecognizable Christopher Plummer) but he is stashed in a nursing home where he sleeps, rambles, rants, eats chocolate cherries and in general is a real mean old man. (It's hard to believe the stately mansion of Cold Creek Manor belongs to such a seemingly inbred group of people.)

Then one morning the Tilsons wake up to a house full of snakes. They're crawling in their beds, slithering in the ceiling, creeping about under furniture. The family escapes to the roof where they are conveniently rescued by Dale and his work crew. While Cooper thinks Dale put the snakes in the house, he can't prove it. He does, however, terminate Dale's employment.

Now the war between Cooper and Dale heats up at the same time that Cooper is getting suspicious as to what happened to Dale's wife and two kids. What's incredible is that no one else in the town ever seems to have had the same questions. Director/writer Mike Figgis has painted the townies as seeming accomplices in any dirty deeds just by showing them as forming a solid front against outsiders. If we're supposed to wonder who the Tilsons can count on

when things turn ugly, the only ones who seem to care are the Pinskis, another transplanted family.

The problem is, this by-the-numbers mystery leaves us not really caring about the Tilsons. Oh, they're likeable enough in a cookie cutter kind of way, but they keep doing such stupid and predictable things. Who'd buy a house that looks as if the inhabitants had only just left without checking into what happened to them? Who could possibly think his sophisticated, good-looking wife would be romantically interested in an unkempt, uncouth felon like Dale? Not to mention stupid enough to hire him as a handyman in the first place. Who would run up stairs when escaping a killer only to be trapped on a roof, in a raging storm, no less? Who would stand at the edge of a deep, dark, deadly well practically inviting the murderer to push them in? Who, after arriving home to find the killer has set their car afire in the driveway, would go into the home and lock the door, never once thinking, "he got here first, he's probably inside the house already!"?

Director Mike Figgis is known for his off-beat films (*Leaving Las Vegas*, amd *Time Code*, for example) and *Cold Creek Manor* benefits from his skillful vision, but suffers badly not only from a profusion of cliches, but also from an almost deadly slow pace for the first half of the movie. The film sports a good cast (this is Sharon Stone's first film since her aneurysm) but they're wasted on lame characters and a hackneyed plot. 🎞

—*Beverley Bare Buehrer*

CREDITS

Cooper Tilson: Dennis Quaid
Leah Tilson: Sharon Stone
Dale Massie: Stephen Dorff
Ruby: Juliette Lewis
Kristen Tilson: Kristen Stewart
Mr. Massie: Christopher Plummer
Jesse Tilson: Ryan Wilson
Sheriff Ferguson: Dana Eskelson

Origin: USA
Released: 2003
Production: Mike Figgis, Annie Stewart; Red Mullet Productions; released by Touchstone Pictures
Directed by: Mike Figgis
Written by: Richard Jefferies
Cinematography by: Declan Quinn
Music by: Mike Figgis
Sound: Pawel Wdowsczak
Editing: Dylan Tichenor
Art Direction: Nancy Pankiw
Costumes: Marie-Sylvie Deveau

Production Design: Les(lie) Dilley
MPAA rating: R
Running time: 118 minutes

REVIEWS

Chicago Sun-Times Online. September 19, 2003.
Entertainment Weekly. September 26, 2003, p. 75.
Los Angeles Times Online. September 19, 2003.
New York Times Online. September 19, 2003.
Variety Online. September 18, 2003.

QUOTES

Dale (Stephen Dorff) after finding a snake in the pool: "If you folks are gonna live out in the country you can't be afraid of God's creatures."

Cold Mountain

Find the strength. Find the courage. No matter what it takes . . . find your way home.
—Movie tagline

Box Office: $91.3 million

Charles Frazier's *Cold Mountain* (1997) is an unusual novel in many ways. First novels by middle-aged writers rarely receive the attention and acclaim it did. The Civil War novel received almost unanimous critical praise, won the National Book Award for fiction, and spent over thirty weeks on *The New York Times* bestseller list. Unlike most bestsellers, it is a highly literary work: exceptionally well written, with strong, distinctive characters and a demanding narrative structure. It achieved the almost instant status of a literary classic, appealing equally to both male and female readers.

While Frazier's *Cold Mountain* is a masterful blend of romance and action, Anthony Minghella's mostly admirable film adaptation fails to achieve the same emotional impact. While the cliché that pulp fiction like Mario Puzo's *The Godfather* (1969) make great films while great novels do not is generally true, there is no reason great novels cannot become good films. *Cold Mountain* is good but nevertheless not good enough.

The film has a modified flashback structure with its hero, Inman (Jude Law), abandoning the Confederate army after sustaining a serious neck wound at the horrendous battle of Petersburg in Virginia. While Inman tries to make his way home on foot to Black Cove, North Carolina, the film shows some events from his pre-war life, primarily his meeting the lovely Ada Monroe (Nicole Kidman). Most of *Cold Mountain* cuts back and forth between Inman's perilous journey and Ada's efforts to survive on her farm after the sudden death of her minister father (Donald Sutherland).

Ada is aided in this endeavor by the third protagonist, Ruby Thewes (Renee Zellweger), a spunky young woman who shows up out of nowhere to teach Ada how to run a farm. Raised as a genteel lady in Charleston, South Carolina, Ada, like most of her kind, knows how to paint and play the piano but little else. As she tells Ruby, she knows how to arrange cut flowers but not how to grow them.

Ada's romance with Inman was just beginning when he left for the war three years earlier. In addition to pining for him and mourning her father, Ada's troubles include Teague (Ray Winstone), self-appointed leader of the local home guard, who tries to convince her that Inman will never return and that he is the man for her. Teague and his thugs are dastardly villains, running roughshod over the local populace while tracking down deserters. One of the most harrowing of several violent acts has Teague's goons killing Ada's nearest neighbor (James Gammon) and torturing his wife (Kathy Baker) for harboring their deserter sons.

Inman's adventures on the road include preventing the Reverend Vesey (Philip Seymour Hoffman) from killing the slave he has impregnated. Inman and Vesey meet up again later and decide to travel together. After they help Junior (Giovanni Ribisi) remove a dead bull from a stream, he repays their kindness by turning them over to the home guards. After escaping, Inman is cared for by the philosophical goat keeper Maddy (Eileen Atkins). Then he rescues a young widow (Natalie Portman) from being raped by Union soldiers. Many of these incidents have parallels to Homer's *The Odyssey*, in which the hero makes a difficult journey back to his beloved. Inman and Vesey are tempted by Junior's lewd wife and her sisters, just as the Sirens tempted Odysseus.

Indirectly connecting the two halves of the story is the unexpected appearance of Ruby's once abusive and neglectful father, Stobrod (Brendan Gleeson). Now a deserter, Stobrod claims to be a different person, having been transformed by the magic of music. With his fellow deserters Pangle (Ethan Suplee) and Georgia (Jack White) on banjo and mandolin, Gleeson plays traditional mountain folk tunes on his violin.

Music is an important motif for writer-director Minghella, a musician before he became a filmmaker. The title character in *The English Patient* (1996) knows the lyrics of hundreds of pop songs, and his nurse plays classical piano.

In *The Talented Mr. Ripley* (1999), the title character also plays classical piano, and his victim, played by Jude Law, was a saxophonist. Ada first tries to woo Inman by playing, as he plows a field, her piano from atop a traveling wagon. One of the film's best moments comes when the despicable Teague finally tracks down Stobrod, asks him and Pangle to play a tune before dying, and begins singing along with them. Music can touch even this most inhumane of villains.

Inman deserts because he has seen enough of war, of pointless deaths. Minghella makes this decision plausible by staging the Petersburg battle, in which 5,000 died, as truly horrifying. While the Confederate troops rest peacefully in their trenches, the ground suddenly erupts, the result of an explosion from a tunnel dug beneath them. But the Union strategy backfires when the Yankees become trapped in the crater left by the blast and are mowed down by the Rebels firing down upon them. Inman becomes truly disgusted by the glee of his fellow soldiers in shooting the helpless enemy.

Cold Mountain is a very violent novel, but there is a big difference between reading about violence and seeing it. Minghella's violence is relentless, giving the film most of its emotional content. The young widow's shooting of a relatively innocent Yankee is jolting.

This violence may have contributed to the film's lukewarm reception by some reviewers and its lackluster box office. While Frazier balances love and war, Minghella downplays the romance. Except for being the most attractive people in North Carolina, it is never quite clear why Ada and Inman become obsessed with each other, and there are few sparks between Kidman and Law.

On *Charlie Rose*, Minghella mentioned that his first edit of the film ran five hours and six minutes. Perhaps in cutting it down to a more manageable length, something important was lost. Ada and Inman seem almost as if they are merely playing host to a group of more colorful characters. One of the best parts of the novel is Ruby's teaching Ada how to do all the things she needs to know. In the film, all this is handled very quickly. Inman's Cherokee friend Swimmer (Jay Tavare) appears only briefly. As with many adaptations of novels with detailed plots, the director feels compelled to cover all the important story points at the expense of the essence of the work.

In *The Talented Mr. Ripley*, Matt Damon and Cate Blanchett attend a production of Tchaikovsky's opera *Eugene Onegin* (1881). The duel in the snow with one friend killing another has emotional impact because it reminds the haunted Ripley of his guilt. Minghella and cinematographer John Seale shot the scene from above, with the victim's blood spreading slowly in the snow. In *Cold Mountain*, they repeat this shot without the same emotional payoff. In all three of Minghella's big films, characters hold dead loved ones in their arms, but the scene in *Cold Mountain* is the least affecting.

To keep the cost of the production down, most of *Cold Mountain* was shot in Romania. While Minghella, Seale, and production designer Dante Ferretti do their best to make Central Europe look like North Carolina, the landscape is a bit too dark and forbidding. It looks too much like the Transylvania of Werner Herzog's *Nosferatu: The Vampyre* (1979).

It is interesting that Law, Winstone, Atkins, and Charlie Hunnam (as Teague's nastiest henchman) are British, Kidman is Australian, Gleeson is Irish, and Sutherland is Canadian, yet all do reasonably effective Southern accents. Law even sounds eerily like Frazier. Minghella told *The Los Angeles Times* that the actor studied Frazier's reading of the audio version of his novel. The only phony-sounding accent comes from the Texas-born Zellweger, who comes close to camping it up too much as the film's most colorful character. Yet with her squinty eyes and plump cheeks, she seems born to play Ruby.

Law had considerable charisma as the object of several characters' affection in *The Talented Mr. Ripley*, but he imbues Inman with little depth. Inman is a tormented soul, but Law seems merely annoyed. Likewise, Kidman gives Ada little weight, though both actors may be the victims of the necessary editing process. In her small role, Portman gives her best performance since *The Professional* (1994), conveying the widow's pain at losing her husband, her worries about her and her baby's survival, and her need for companionship all at once. In a world gone mad, she rages for order amid the chaos.

The film's best performance comes with Winstone's chilling portrayal of Teague. The character could easily have been a moustache-twirling melodramatic villain, but Winstone underplays the part, offering brief glimpses of his humanity. Best known to American audiences for being tormented by Ben Kingsley's devilish Don Logan in *Sexy Beast* (2001), Winstone's subtle evildoer is at the other extreme from Kingsley's.

Several reviewers, even some with misgivings, called *Cold Mountain* the best film ever about the War Between the States. With *The Birth of a Nation* (1915), D. W. Griffith virtually invented the language of the cinema, but the film—and not just because of its racism—is hard going for modern viewers, obviously important to the history of film but not engaging. *Gone With the Wind* (1939), despite many wonderful moments, is primarily hokum: big, colorful, sentimental, and aesthetically empty. John Huston's *The Red Badge of Courage* (1951) seems underdeveloped at only sixty-nine minutes. More recent efforts like Edward Zwick's *Glory* (1989) and Ang Lee's *Ride with the Devil* (1999) have their moments but finally disappoint. The reviewers who praise *Cold Mountain* are, however, forgetting *The General* (1927). Not only is it the best Civil War film but is one of the greatest films ever made. Co-directors Buster Keaton and Clyde Bruckman not only balance action and romance, but do so while creating highly original slapstick. *Cold Mountain* succeeds with individual scenes and performances but never coalesces as a whole.

—*Michael Adams*

New York Times Online. December 17, 2003.
New York Times Online. December 25, 2003.
People. December 22, 2003, p. 27.
USA Today Online. December 24, 2003.
Variety Online. December 7, 2003.
Washington Post. December 25, 2003, p. C1.

CREDITS

Inman: Jude Law
Ada Monroe: Nicole Kidman
Ruby Thewes: Renee Zellweger
Rev. Monroe: Donald Sutherland
Maddy: Eileen Atkins
Stobrod Thewes: Brendan Gleeson
Rev. Vessey: Philip Seymour Hoffman
Sara: Natalie Portman
Junior: Giovanni Ribisi
Teague: Ray Winstone
Sally Swanger: Kathy Baker
Esco Swanger: James Gammon
Bosie: Charlie Hunnam
Georgia: Jack White
Pangle: Ethan Suplee
Ferry girl: Jena Malone
Lila: Melora Walters
Oakley: Lucas Black
Shyla: Taryn Manning
Blind man: Tom Aldredge
Doctor: James Rebhorn

Origin: Great Britain, Romania, Italy
Released: 2003
Production: Sydney Pollack, William Horberg, Albert Berger, Ron Yerxa; Mirage Enterprises, Bona Fide; released by Miramax Films
Directed by: Anthony Minghella
Written by: Anthony Minghella
Cinematography by: John Seale
Music by: Gabriel Yared
Sound: Ivan Sharrock
Editing: Walter Murch
Art Direction: Robert Guerra
Costumes: Ann Roth
Production Design: Dante Ferretti
MPAA rating: R
Running time: 155 minutes

REVIEWS

Chicago Sun-Times Online. December 24, 2003.
Entertainment Weekly. January 9, 2004, p. 56.
Los Angeles Times Online. December 24, 2003.

QUOTES

Ada (Nicole Kidman): "What we have lost can never be returned to us."

AWARDS AND NOMINATIONS

Oscars 2003: Support. Actress (Zellweger)
Golden Globes 2004: Support. Actress (Zellweger)
Screen Actors Guild 2003: Support. Actress (Zellweger)
Nomination:
Oscars 2003: Actor (Law), Cinematog., Film Editing, Song ("Scarlet Tide"), Orig. Score
Golden Globes 2004: Actor—Drama (Law), Actress—Drama (Kidman), Director (Minghella), Film—Drama, Screenplay, Song ("You Will Be My Ain True Love"), Orig. Score
Writers Guild 2003: Adapt. Screenplay.

Confidence

It's not about the money. It's about the money.
—Movie tagline

 Box Office: $12.2 million

James Foley, who also helmed David Mamet's *Glengarry Glen Ross,* here summons the spirit of Mamet while directing this polished con flick that smacks of a lesser *House of Games.* Well made, with slick cutting, deft editing, and a stylish use of glowing colors, the weakness in *Confidence* lies with Doug Jung's too slick script in which numerous and somewhat pretentious twists and turns threaten to alienate viewers as well as the film's smarmy protagonist, Jake Vig. Vig, portrayed by Edward Burns, narrates the film in flashback while he's at gunpoint, and despite the studied trickiness of the plot, one can glean by his know-it-all attitude that neither he, nor the audience, will be very surprised when he triumphs in the end.

Jake Vig is a grifter, a con man who, along with a crack crew of specialists, craftily separates people from their money by setting up phony murders which serve to "convince" people to forget about the money they are owed and run for their lives. During the normal course of business, a deal goes a little differently than planned and Vig's crew inadvertently steals $150,000 from an evil crime lord with a bad reputation. Showing extreme displeasure with this turn of events, Winston King (Dustin Hoffman) swiftly brings his brand of justice down upon one of the members of Vig's crew. An outraged Vig heads to King's strip club—used to launder money for the Mob—to negotiate a deal with the crime kingpin. Vig convinces King to lend him another $200,000 in order to finance a scam that will supposedly bring in $5 million and is aimed at King's nemesis, Morgan Price (Robert Forster), a Mafia-controlled banker.

Jake sets about assembling a crew to pull off the job, including pretty pickpocket Lily (Rachel Weisz) and usuals Gordo (Paul Giamatti) and Miles (Brian Van Holt), along with two corrupt cops (Donal Logue and Luis Guzman). To make sure things go as planned, King also dispatches his henchman, Lupus (Franky G), to accompany Vig's gang. Naturally, this con is not the only one in the works, with King and Vig playing a complicated game of con within a con. Other forces are at play as well; Andy Garcia portrays mysterious federal agent Gunther Butan, who has been chasing Jake for some time but who seems to harbor some secrets of his own. Besides Butan, Vig also has to contend with the cops and Price's own henchman while planning this complicated con. Even members of Vig's own team come under suspicion, and from this point on, it isn't clear if anyone can be trusted.

By far the most interesting character onscreen, Hoffman's King is almost nerdish: bearded and bespectacled, he also suffers from Attention Deficit Disorder or ADD, a new tool in the typical gangster arsenal that also surfaced in Nicholas Cage's con man in *Matchstick Men*. His twitching hyperactivity provides some comic relief for the character of King, whose almost friendly demeanor can turn on a dime into fearsome anger. King further shows a unique multidimensional quality when he auditions a pair of strippers, who are also sisters, and suggests they keep their lesbian-themed act "tasteful." Though by far the most ruthless and depraved, Hoffman's character is also the only one we get a real sense of, and, at times, he's actually likeable.

Burns has the handsome good looks, charisma, and confidence to pull off the part of the leading man but lacks the intricacies and depth necessary to play a con man such as Jake Vig. It is all the more apparent when placed alongside Hoffman, who can always keep you guessing about what is really going on inside his head. While King flirtatiously compliments Vig on his firm gluteus at their initial meeting, you can't help but wonder what he's really doing. Such details are lost on Burns, who finds the broad strokes but misses the fine lines. Aside from looking fetching and acting uber-cool, Weisz has little to do with a character that was merely written as a love interest for Vig. Similarly, Vig's gang of usual suspects merely supports his more fully written character. Garcia is capable in an underwritten role.

Ironically, the real star of *Confidence* is its glossy noir-ish style. Ironic, because early in the film King warns Vig about the dangers of style, which "can get you killed." Here, style subs for substance in a film that ultimately fails to convince the audience this is a fresh original take on the timeworn con.

—Hilary White

REVIEWS

Boxoffice. April, 2003, p. 104.
Chicago Sun-Times Online. April 25, 2003.

Entertainment Weekly. May 2, 2003, p. 49.
Los Angeles Times Online. April 25, 2003.
New York Times Online. April 25, 2003.
Variety. May 13, 2002, p. 63.
Variety Online. April 27, 2003.
Washington Post. April 25, 2003, p. WE49.

Confusion of Genders (La Confusion des Genres)

The French film *Confusion of Genders* opens with Alain (Pascal Greggory of *Those Who Love Me Can Take the Train*) lying in bed with a lover. The two are breaking up. There is nudity. There are sighed lines like "I don't feel anything." As Alain talks, director Ilan Duran Cohen cuts in different actors of different genders speaking the lines of the lover. The scene has artiness, nudity, and a nihilism philosophy. In a way, there's no need for the movie to continue because this scene has it all. The rest of the movie is really just more of the same: more naked people in bed, more lovers' angst. Here is a sample line of dialogue. Man: "What are you doing today?" Woman: "I don't know—questioning myself, I guess."

There is nothing better than a movie with a lot of dialogue, affairs, naked people and French scenery, but somehow *Confusion of Genders* never quite works. It has many promising elements but screenwriter Cohen and Philippe Lasry can't tie them together with a compelling enough story. A large part of the problem is the character of Alain. Greggory is properly handsome and intense-looking, but his Alain's lack of conviction about anything doesn't make for an interesting character. If he doesn't seem to care very much with whom he ends up, why should the audience?

The gender confusion referred to in the title is Alain's confusion over his choice of lovers. He is reluctantly getting engaged to Laurence (Nathalie Richard), his boss at the law firm where they work. Laurence and Alain spend a lot of time together but don't have much of a sexual relationship. They also don't seem to have a particularly good time together. When they see each other, Laurence spends most of the time bemoaning her choice in men who don't love her. Alain stands there listening; but can't do much to console her since everything she says is true: he doesn't love her, and he doesn't desire her physically. It's a mystery why the two are getting married. It seems that they can muster neither the will nor the energy to do something else.

In the meantime, Christophe (Cyrille Thouvenin), the puppy-like younger brother of one of Alain's ex-conquests is in hot pursuit of Alain. He offers his love and his body to Alain and adds the extra incentive that the older man could be free to pursue anyone else he wants to. Alain puts up a fight, but ends up falling into bed with the young man. This sets the stage for their love affair. Christophe pursues, Alain is distant but succumbs, and the two end up in a passionate embrace. Alain shows what little passion he seems to have when Christophe is groping him, but for some reason he can't settle into this relationship. It doesn't seem to be a question of accepting his sexuality—he's open enough about that—and it's hard to understand why he can't be happy with his arrangement with Christophe.

Maybe it's that two lovers aren't enough for Alain. When Laurence sends him to work on a case defending Marc (Vincent Martinez), Alain botches the case and the attractive young man ends up in jail. Alain visits the handsome convict frequently, just to give himself the erotic charge. Marc knows about Alain's lust and uses it to get him to transmit messages to Babette (Julie Gayet). Marc is desperately in love with Babette and wants only for her to visit him in jail. Even though Marc is more like a stalker than a spurned boyfriend, Alain keeps delivering Marc's messages to Babette. When Alain finally balks at trying to get Babette to agree to a meeting with Marc, Marc offers to have sex with him if he does it. Alain agrees.

Alain, excited by the sexual intrigue involved, begins falling for Babette. She is an arty hairdresser who says wistful things like "I'm not complicated, everything else is." The characters barely seem to be talking to each other. They just sort of remark upon their listlessness and boredom, and look miserable. This sort of dialogue passes for courtship in this film.

Is Babette the person that Alain's been looking for? No. Alain seemingly cares for her, in the same way he tolerates Christophe and Laurence. Alain carelessly drifts in and out of his various affairs. Perhaps audiences have been too trained by goal-oriented Hollywood plots, but it's hard to stay interested in Alain's pursuits if they don't serve a larger purpose. This is a film about passion, but it exhibits strangely little. It seems that Cohen wanted to make a comedic sexual romp, but while *Confusion of Genders* is certainly sexual, it is hard to figure out what the comedy is. Perhaps it's the kind of thing that gets lost in the translation.

Even when Laurence gets pregnant after a strained and not especially enjoyable sexual encounter with Alain, the characters can't get roused from their ennui. The pregnancy makes Alain and Laurence plan more seriously for their wedding, but both just seem to be going through the motions.

The film does some things well. It's a pleasant change to see a film in which sexual orientation is not the focus of the film and can be a fluid thing. And the casual nudity in the film is so different from the charged nudity in American films. People just happen to be naked in scenes, like they would be in normal life. But the biggest difference is that the naked people aren't just 20 year-old busty young women, but also 40 year-old men and women who appear to have unenhanced bust lines.

Confusion of Genders had a limited release, and the critics who did see the film, didn't find it to be very involving. Stephen Holden of the *New York Times* said of the film: "If not much else, Ilan Duran Cohen's sexual comedy, *Confusion of Genders,* offers the pleasure of watching attractive bodies in various states of undress entangling and disentangling in a tormented erotic roundelay. But although its opening nude tableaus hint that it might venture into X-rated territory, *Confusion of Genders* quickly turns into an earnest talkfest (spiced with flashes of nudity and sexually explicit dialogue) that feels stiffly programmatic and ultimately false." Kevin Thomas of the *Los Angeles Times* described *Confusion of Genders* as "certainly sexy, entertaining and provocative—in several senses of the word—but it's also tiresome as only a French film can be when everyone in it has only sex and amour on his or her mind and is deadly serious about both." The *New York Post*'s Megan Lehmann claimed that, "the central character in the cynical French sex farce *Confusion of Genders* is such an odious piece of work—weak, indecisive and shallow—that it's hard to follow his carnal misadventures with anything approaching interest." And Jami Bernard of the *New York Daily News* summed up: "The sheets are mighty rumpled, but it turns out that Alain's lack of passion or direction is catching. Despite a plethora of 'naughty bits,' it's a yawn."

—*Jill Hamilton*

CREDITS

Alain: Pascal Greggory
Laurence: Nathalie Richard
Babette: Julie Gayet
Marc: Vincent Martinez
Christophe: Cyrille Thouvenin
Etienne: Alain Bashung

Origin: France
Language: French
Released: 2000
Production: Didier Boujard; Haut et Court, Alta Loma Films, Fugitive Productions; released by Picture This! Entertainment
Directed by: Ilan Duran Cohen
Written by: Ilan Duran Cohen, Philippe Lasry
Cinematography by: Jeanne Lapoirie
Music by: Jay-Jay Johanson
Editing: Fabrice Rouaud
Art Direction: Francoise Dupertuis
Costumes: Barbara Kraft
MPAA rating: Unrated
Running time: 94 minutes

REVIEWS

Los Angeles Times Online. August 15, 2003.
New York Times Online. March 28, 2001.
Variety Online. December 4, 2000.
Village Voice Online. July 9, 2003.

The Cooler

Love . . . you have to play to win.
—Movie tagline

Box Office: $7.6 million

Wayne Kramer's *The Cooler* is set in Las Vegas—not just the literal city but an almost metaphorical idea of a place where Lady Luck plays a major role in determining the fates of the characters. The conception of Kramer and co-screenwriter Frank Hannah is unique among Vegas films, situated somewhere between the grim city of lost souls of *Leaving Las Vegas* and the lighthearted, romantic playground of *Honeymoon in Vegas.* An adult fairytale, *The Cooler* manages to be both brutal and warmhearted, indulging both the harsh reality of Vegas's seamier side and the romantic optimism of lovable losers grasping at life's second chances. It also offers a unique insider's view by contrasting old-school casino operations with the family-oriented hotels that have sprung up on the strip in the past few years.

Bernie Lootz (William H. Macy) is a cooler at the Shangri La. His job is to turn winners into losers, not by some trick or underhanded scheme, he proudly tells a new friend, but "by being myself." By his very nature, he is a kind of bad luck charm; whenever a player is on a lucky streak, all Bernie has to do is stand alongside him to break his good fortune. This is the rare film with realistic characters and often gritty situations that nonetheless believes in an almost supernatural power of luck.

Bernie works for the ruthless director of operations, Shelly Kaplow (Alec Baldwin), with whom he has a long and complicated relationship. Long ago Bernie had a gambling problem and ran up such a debt that he was forced to work for Shelly to pay it off (Shelly once busted his knee to teach him a lesson, but Bernie harbors no ill will despite the limp he still has). With roughly a week left of his six years of servitude, the sad sack has made plans to leave Vegas for good.

Meanwhile, Shelly is having problems. To compete with the amusement park-like casinos and the family-friendly atmosphere of the new Vegas, his bosses have brought in a young business expert named Larry Sokolov (Ron Livingston) to modernize the operation. Shelly is the epitome of old-school Vegas and recoils at the thought of trying to be like the new boys in town, who, he says, have ruined the city by catering to the "stroller crowd." Even the practice of hiring coolers, rather than using subtle, subliminal ways to get people to lose, is considered old-fashioned. Shelly is a tough, shrewd, even sleazy operator, but there is also something tragic about the plight of a man whose sense of nostalgia blinds him to the realities of business. Because he has made a home for himself and is a king of sorts over his little dominion, seeing his palace invaded by some college boy spouting a new corporate line riles him up and frightens him.

Bernie's life begins changing for the better when he strikes up a friendship with a cocktail waitress named Natalie (Maria Bello), who, surprisingly enough, begins to take a liking to him. When she hints at having sex, he immediately thinks that she is a hooker, so amazed is he at his good fortune. She is not offended, however, and their sexual encounter back in his little motel room is sweet, hot, and awkward at the same time, propelled by his utter amazement that this woman is really interested in him. Macy and Bello make an oddly endearing couple and share some of the steamiest moments of the year. In one gleeful scene, they just scream and rock the bed so the neighbors, who are always keeping Bernie up with their lovemaking, will hear them.

One of the screenplay's big triumphs is the way it deftly balances the wistful longing of Bernie and Natalie and their playful romance with the brutality always threatening to burst out of nowhere. One such incident involves Bernie's grown son, Mikey (Shawn Hatosy), who comes to town with his pregnant wife, Charlene (Estella Warren), to shake his dad down for some cash. After Bernie gives him almost $3,000 and Mikey is caught cheating at the crap table, Shelly demonstrates how things are taken care of old-school style, which means administering a severe beating. Bernie intervenes to save his son's life by promising to make good on the $150,000 Mikey tried to steal and sticks to his promise even when Shelly punches Charlene in the stomach, revealing that her pregnancy is actually a pillow under her blouse.

Macy has played his share of losers, but he brings to Bernie the unique blend of a nervous schoolboy who is in love for the first time and a middle-aged man whose future is in doubt. But Natalie's love for him changes everything, not only giving him permission to see himself in a fresh way but also turning him into a good luck totem as people start winning whenever he goes to the casino, putting Shelly in an increasingly tenuous position.

It turns out that Bernie was not far from the truth when he thought Natalie was a hooker. Shelly paid her to be Bernie's companion, to keep him happy, and hopefully make him stay in Vegas, but he did not expect her to fall in love with the poor schlub. The part of Natalie could easily have devolved into the hooker-with-a-heart-of-gold cliché; she is even saddled with the hard-luck story of coming to Vegas to be a showgirl ten years ago and then seeing the dream fade away. But Bello transcends the type, never playing her as a floozy or begging for our sympathy. Natalie is savvy about her position in the casino but not so jaded that she cannot open up to the one guy who appreciates and loves her.

Baldwin also shines in a complex performance that engenders a surprising amount of sympathy for Shelly despite the horrible things he does. He is a second-rate hood who strong-arms anyone who threatens the niche he has carved for himself. He even gets Natalie to break up with Bernie so patrons will lose, but, when she returns to Bernie and his luck reverses yet again, Shelly gets so violent with her that she ends up crashing against a mirror and cutting her face. And yet Baldwin makes us understand that Shelly has an awareness of his precarious position as well as a sentimental soft spot for the city he loves. On some level, Shelly's brutality feels like a desperate way to hold on to not only the power that is slipping through his fingers but also to some pure, even strangely noble, belief in a Vegas that is also disappearing—one with old-time lounge singers, coolers, and high-rolling gamblers. He also has a unique rapport with Bernie, and Baldwin lets us see, under Shelly's hard exterior and selfishness, his genuine affection.

Natalie's confession to Bernie of the circumstances under which they met does not deter his love. Not many films could make a wild swing from graphic violence to the determined romanticism of Bernie, who says to Natalie, when she cannot bear to look at her bruised face in the mirror, "Look in my eyes. I'm the only mirror you're ever gonna need." The line even has a kind of poetry to it, which is a wonderful counterpoint to the decidedly unpoetic circumstances in which the characters find themselves.

After Bernie stands up to Shelly, contrasting the love he has found with Natalie with Shelly's friendless, empty existence, he goes to the crap table with $3,000 Natalie has given him (it was her payment for befriending Bernie) and gets on a winning streak, that Shelly refuses to stop despite Larry's protests. In the end, Bernie and Natalie leave Las Vegas with a small fortune. Dying as he lived, Shelly takes a bullet to the head for letting his old friend get away, and Natalie and Bernie narrowly escape death themselves. A highway patrolman, who is really an agent of the casino, stops them on their way out of the city, but, just as he is about to shoot them, he is mowed down by a speeding drunk driver. It seems that Lady Luck really is on their side.

The Cooler entertains on several levels, first as an offbeat, even charming fairytale. It ends happily for Bernie and Natalie, who are basking in the feeling that love can conquer all and turn bad luck to good. This may be a cliché, but Macy and Bello are such a winning couple that they make it work anyway. Moreover, Shelly's decision to help Bernie at the end, allowing him to have a shot at a new life, at the very cost of his own, gives the film an added poignancy. Shelly would have hated being forced out, which is clearly where he was headed, so at least he went out helping his old friend to flee the life that had imprisoned him. In the end, the footage of old casinos being exploded and toppling to the ground makes it clear that *The Cooler* is just as much a bittersweet homage to the spirit of the old Vegas as it is to the transforming power of love and second chances.

—*Peter N. Chumo II*

CREDITS

Bernie Lootz: William H. Macy
Shelly Kaplow: Alec Baldwin
Natalie Belisario: Maria Bello
Mikey: Shawn Hatosy
Larry Sokolov: Ron Livingston
Buddy Stafford: Paul Sorvino
Charlene: Estella Warren
Nicky "Fingers" Bonnatto: Arthur J. Nascarelli
Highway Cop: M.C. Gainey
Doris: Ellen Greene
Johnny Capella: Joey Fatone
Tony: Tony Longo

Origin: USA
Released: 2003
Production: Sean Furst, Michael Pierce; ContentFilm, Gryphon Films, Pierce-Williams, Furst Films, Dog Pond Films; released by Lions Gate Films
Directed by: Wayne Kramer
Written by: Wayne Kramer, Frank Hannah
Cinematography by: James Whitaker
Music by: Mark Isham
Sound: Stephen Halbert
Editing: Arthur Coburn
Costumes: Kristen M. Burke
Production Design: Toby Corbett
MPAA rating: R
Running time: 101 minutes

REVIEWS

Entertainment Weekly. December 5, 2003, p. 68.
Los Angeles Times Online. June 5, 2003.
Los Angeles Times Online. November 26, 2003.
New York Times Online. November 26, 2003.
People. December 8, 2003, p. 37.
Rolling Stone. December 11, 2003, p. 213.
USA Today Online. November 26, 2003.
Variety Online. January 21, 2003.

AWARDS AND NOMINATIONS

Natl. Bd. of Review 2003: Support. Actor (Baldwin)
Nomination:
Oscars 2003: Support. Actor (Baldwin)
Golden Globes 2004: Support. Actor (Baldwin), Support. Actress (Bello)
Screen Actors Guild 2003: Support. Actor (Baldwin), Support. Actress (Bello).

The Core

Earth has a deadline.
—Movie tagline
The only way out is in.
—Movie tagline

Box Office: $31.1 million

Suddenly pulled out of his classroom at the University of Chicago, Geophysics professor Josh Keyes (Aaron Eckhart) is escorted by government agents to Washington, D.C. There he runs into an old friend of his, Dr. Sergei Leveque (Tcheky Karyo), an expert in high energy weapons and electro-magnetics. The two men are led into a large room in which there are dozens of sheet-draped corpses. They are told by General Thomas Purcell (Richard Jenkins) nothing more than the fact that all of these people dropped dead at exactly the same time and within a 10 block radius. Quickly Josh deduces, from his and Sergei's areas of expertise, that there must have been a geological electro-magnetic pulse that disrupted these people's pacemakers and killed them. The General seems only interested in one question: was it caused by an unknown weapon? When Josh and Sergei indicate that it is unlikely, he dismisses them and seems unconcerned about what actually caused it.

Soon, there are more odd happenings. The pigeons in Trafalgar Square seem to be unable to navigate, crash into windows and cause traffic accidents. And then there's the troubled landing of the space shuttle, which suddenly undergoes a navigational glitch that throws it off course and causes it to land in the Los Angeles River. This event, of course, needs a scapegoat, and it's Major Rebecca Childs (Hilary Swank), the youngest person in space and co-pilot to Commander Robert Iverson (Bruce Greenwood) the pilot on the mission.

As Becca, as Rebecca is called, faces a military inquest into the events of the troubled shuttle landing her future very much in doubt, Josh is back in his lab with his assistants running tons of data on all the electro-magnetic anomalies that have transpired in the last few months. "Be wrong. Be wrong," Josh mutters as it slowly dawns on him what has caused those pacemaker deaths—something has happened to the Earth's core that is effecting its protective electro-magnetic field.

Josh gathers up his research and data and takes it to one of America's pre-eminent scientists, Dr. Conrad Zimsky (Stanley Tucci). Someone has to do something, but is this prima donna of a scientist the one to do it? Zimsky does take the information and is dismayed by what he sees. Together with Josh they brief General Purcell and other military/government representatives and tell them the bleak results: something has caused the Earth's core to slow down, our EM (electro-magnetic) field is crumbling, and when it goes we will all be cooked by solar winds.

The General, of course, wants to know what can be done about it and refuses to take "nothing" as an answer. But as Josh points out to him, "Even if we came up with a plan to fix the core, we just can't get there." Then quietly comes Dr. Zimsky's voice, "Yes, but what if we could?"

Zimsky takes Josh and the General to Salt Flats, Utah to meet a one-time colleague of his, Dr. Ed "Braz" Brazzelton (Delroy Lindo). Braz, however, has no love for Zimsky who he claims stole his research. Only reluctantly does he share with them the results of his work of the last 20 years. Braz has invented a sonic drill that neatly cuts away and vaporizes mountainsides and has also developed a new heat and pressure resistant element with a name consisting of 37 syllables which he has nicknamed inobtanium. Suddenly the core seems obtainable, but only if they can get there in time and Braz's inventions are only at the prototype stage.

There's also another problem. Imagine the panic when word gets out about the end of the world being nigh. To prevent this, the General brings on board a young computer hacker named Rat (D.J. Qualls) who is given unlimited resources and a neverending supply of Hot Pockets to control the flow of information on the internet.

With a huge influx of money and manpower from the government, Braz's invention quickly takes the shape of a giant worm that will tunnel its way to the core using a souped up cat scan to steer through the earth. On board the worm, which has been named Virgil after the Roman poet who led Dante through hell in *The Divine Comedy*, will be a crew of six terranauts: project leader Josh, pilot Iverson and co-pilot Becca, explosives expert Sergei, science advisor Zimsky and Braz in charge of Virgil itself. Mission control will be headed by the same woman who headed Iverson and Becca's shuttle mission (Alfre Woodard) and Rat will watch over it all at his master computer. Their goal: to get to the core, set off an explosive charge that will restart its spinning and save life as we know it.

Jon Amiel is a director who can't be pinned down. He has done musicals (*The Singing Detective* for British television), quirky romances (*Queen of Hearts,* his first feature), cat-and-mouse mysteries (*Entrapment*), historical mystery/romances (*Somersby*), serial-killer dramas (*Copycat*), and espionage thrillers (*The Man Who Knew Too Little*). *The Core,* is his first attempt at science fiction, but perhaps this incredibly adaptable director should have tried comedies instead, because this disaster film is almost inadvertently exactly that.

There is a decidedly old-fashioned feel about *The Core* starting with the acting. The film boasts a top-notch cast, but their blatantly earnest performances leads one to believe they think they're in the cerebral *2001: A Space Odyssey* as opposed to the campy *Journey to the Center of the Earth.* Aaron Eckhart plays Josh with perpetually bad hair and just a touch of humor, and that's helpful, as is Turkish-born Tcheky Karyo playing a weapons specialist as a charming family man (which is nice because Karyo can play very convincing heavies.) Of course the fact that his character is French and dies, in light of current events, subliminally may play well to American audiences.

Greenwood and Swank are suitably resolute and solemn as befitting commanders, and thank the cinema gods that there's no annoying romance between Josh and Becca. But looking as if he's in a totally different movie than the rest of the cast is Stanley Tucci, who chews the scenery in the best mad-scientist tradition and acting a lot like the preening Dr. Zachary Smith on television's *Lost in Space.*

In this kind of movie we know for sure several things will happen: there will be conflicts between the heroes, there will be snafus in the plan, eventually the problem will be fixed, and since not all the heroes will come back they will probably die nobly and in reverse order of their billing importance. With this kind of cookie-cutter story, what's to take seriously?

Well, nowadays in science fiction movies one takes the special effects very seriously. *The Core* does have some fun moments, but one of its best is also its most haunting. Similar to what happened to several movies i.e. *Spider-Man* after the September 11 attacks and *Phone Booth* after the D.C. sniper shootings, *The Core*'s filmmakers worried that maybe they should edit out the spectacular crash landing of the shuttle that begins the film after a real shuttle, the Challenger, crashed February 1, 2003. Trailers featuring the shuttle were quickly pulled from theaters, but in the end the scenes were left in the movie.

On the other hand, the explosion of the coliseum and Rome burning seem a bit cheesy by today's standards, and the Golden Gate Bridge collapsing may cause the ghosts of terrorism to lurk in the back of viewer's minds and take away from its spectacle. And while one does have to admit that Virgil's design seems practical and innovative (the press kit indicates that it came from combining the ideas of a rocket, a submarine, and an earthworm) but why on earth (in earth?) does it have a window?

This minor oversight is another problem that plagues *The Core*: the science is not all that trustworthy and that undermines a viewer's ability to suspend disbelief. For starters, the Earth's core doesn't really spin, it just moves a little faster than the mantle. But that's a minor quibble. The incredible coincidence that Braz's invention is ready just in time to save the Earth is another stretch—and who has been financing his expensive work over the 20 years he was working on it? But the gaffe that may cause the most laughs happens when Virgil gets stuck on the crystals of a giant geode and the crew dons space suits to go outside where we have been constantly warned about the intense heat and pressure. Those must be some suits!

The Core is just the latest in Paramount Studios' long contribution to end-of-the-world cinema. From *When World's Collide* (1951) and *War of the Worlds* (1953) through a few *Star Trek* movies and the more recent *Deep Impact* (1998), Paramount should be given the Irwin Allen award for combining science fiction and humans in peril in an attempt to make boxoffice gold.

But perhaps this is too harsh an analysis of *The Core*. Sure, it's based on an absurd idea, sure its colorful characters are right out of central casting, sure its special effects aren't always that special, and sure it seems dumb and old-fashioned, but it does have humor, it is fairly fast-paced and when it comes right down to it, it's not a bad movie to watch on a Saturday afternoon . . . when it's raining outside . . . and you don't have to pay full price . . . and you're 13 years old. It is possible to view *The Core* as goofy good fun, and at least it's more scientifically accurate than 1959's silly *Journey to the Center of the Earth*.

—*Beverley Bare Buehrer*

CREDITS

Dr. Josh Keyes: Aaron Eckhart
Major Rebecca "Beck" Childs: Hilary Swank
Dr. Ed "Braz" Brazzelton: Delroy Lindo
Dr. Conrad Zimsky: Stanley Tucci
Rat: DJ Qualls
General Purcell: Richard Jenkins
Dr. Serge Levesque: Tcheky Karyo
Commander Richard Iverson: Bruce Greenwood
Stickley: Alfre Woodard

Origin: USA
Released: 2003
Production: David Foster, Cooper Layne, Sean Bailey; released by Paramount Pictures
Directed by: Jon Amiel

Written by: John Rogers, Cooper Layne
Cinematography by: John Lindley
Music by: Christopher Young
Sound: Darren Brisker
Editing: Terry Rawlings
Art Direction: Sandra Tanaka
Costumes: Dan Lester
Production Design: Philip Harrison
MPAA rating: PG-13
Running time: 135 minutes

REVIEWS

Chicago Sun-Times Online. March 28, 2003.
Entertainment Weekly. April 4, 2003, p. 78.
Los Angeles Times Online. March 28, 2003.
New York Times Online. March 28, 2003.
People. April 7, 2003, p. 33.
Variety Online. March 22, 2003.
Washington Post. March 28, 2003, p. WE46.

QUOTES

Dr. Josh Keyes (Aaron Eckhart): "We did this to ourselves. We killed the planet."

Cradle 2 the Grave

Born 2 the life. True 2 the code. Bad 2 the bone.
—Movie tagline

 Box Office: $34.6 million

The title should be warning enough. *Cradle 2 the Grave* sounds like it could be a horror movie (and, for some people, it will be). Or it could be what it actually is—one of those newish rap- and martial arts-filled action movies that couple an African-American guy and an Asian guy teaming up to fight the bad guys or save the world or whatnot.

Roger Ebert of the *Chicago Sun-Times*, while not actually liking the movie, did see it as part of a cultural trend. He wrote, "*Cradle 2 the Grave* . . . demonstrates that a savvy producer like (Joel) Silver now believes a white star is completely unnecessary in a mega-budget action picture. At one point, there were only white stars. Then they got to have black buddies. Then they got to have Asian buddies. Then

Rush Hour proved that black and Asian buddies could haul in the mass audience. Long ago a movie like this used a black character for comic relief. Then an Asian character. Now the white character is the comic relief. May the circle be unbroken." Right. It's nice to fight the power and all that, but one would wish for a more auspicious way for films to be colorblind.

Producer Silver is teamed with director Andrzej Barkowiak, who also worked with him on *Romeo Must Die* and the wretched Steven Seagal mess *Exit Wounds. Cradle 2 the Grave* is not strictly a sequel but it does mark a reunion for Silver, Barkowiak and stars DMX and Jet Li (and co-star Anthony Anderson). They all worked together on the tonally similar *Romeo Must Die.*

It seems like maybe the team is trying to develop something similar to the Jackie Chan and Chris Tucker *Rush Hour* franchise. In modeling after the duo, this team has one big difference. Chan and Tucker are both capable of doing comedy, and sometimes even doing it well. Li and DMX, at least here, are glowering sour pusses. Their oddball match-up never produces the crackling tension of Chan and Tucker, instead it's like a blind date that never quite works out. Li is not yet very skilled at speaking English so out of necessity, he stays pretty quiet. (Even Li's curse words sound painfully phonetic.) DMX's character is too cool to waste his time chitchatting when it's not necessary. So instead we have them grimly driving together during the car chases, the fights and the explosions. This movie could really use a chatty Owen Wilson breaking the tension with one-liners.

DMX is Fait, which is pronounced "fate." Perhaps this is supposed to be meaningful, but this is not the type of movie where you should bother figuring that out. He leads a gang of thugs like girlfriend Daria (Gabrielle Union of *Deliver Us from Eva*) and rotund Tommy (Anthony Anderson). It's hard to imagine a gang that includes Union and Anderson being tough and/or effective, but that's the magic of Hollywood. The team breaks into a vault to get a bunch of jewels. They are interrupted when Su (Li) calls the cops on them. They escape, but have to leave everything except a bag of black diamonds.

After some action things happen like a guy gets killed and stuck into his own fish aquarium, writers John O'Brien and Channing Gibson throw us some more plot. It seems that the black diamonds are really some super advanced form of plutonium. Bad guys would need only activate the diamonds and they would have a bomb more powerful than any seen before. Bad guy Ling (Mark Dacascos of *Brotherhood of the Wolf*) and his group of baddies, including the sexy Sona (Kelly Hu of *X2: X-Men United*) want to get the jewels so that they can sell them to international arms dealers.

Su wants to get the jewels to return them to Taiwan, where they were first developed, so they can be destroyed. (Nitpicky questions: If Taiwan developed these stones, why do they want to now destroy them? And, Taiwan is a big

enough place. Did they not have any other agents available for such a big project? Saving the world from nuclear destruction doesn't exactly seem like a one-man task.) Somewhere in there is also Archie (Tom Arnold), a hyper black market trader. Sometimes the rest of *Cradle* is so dreary that it's a high point when Arnold has a scene. This is not a good thing.

Fait is perfectly willing to give the jewels to Ling, he just wants to be paid for them. Ling refuses and kidnaps Fait's beloved young daughter, Vanessa (Paige Hurd). We know Fait is devoted to his daughter because the filmmakers show us one scene of him tucking her in bed. She is cold to him until he presents her with a diamond necklace. Then she gives him a big hug. How touching.

Anyway, now things are personal and, inevitably, Fait and Su must team up to get Vanessa back and find the now-missing diamonds. "So I'm stuck with you—get it?" says Fait to new partner Su. Let the action commence. We see Fait and Daria doing jobs while wearing clingy tank tops. We see Fait doing jumps from rooftop to rooftop on an all-terrain vehicle. We see lots of slow mo running, motorcycle jumping and glass breaking. There are so many kicks and punches to groins that it's impossible to keep count. Su fights at an amateur fighting club and he's forced to fight many people at the same time. As is traditional in action flicks, the villains politely come at him one or two at a time instead of all running in at once. At one particularly low moment in tastefulness, Su fights off the aggressors using a little person as a weapon. Classy!

This movie tries to ramp up the action by blasting a soundtrack of LL Cool J, 50 Cent and DMX. It also caters to the ADD-afflicted film audience doing quick style cuts during the fight sequences. Often the director doesn't seem to have enough faith that audiences will find the sight of one fight entertaining enough so he'll have two or even three going on at the same time. The climax features Fait fighting a guy who has his daughter, Su fighting Ling—in a ring of fire, no less—and Daria and Sona in a girl fight. Surprisingly the girl fight does not take place in a rain storm. Idea for *Cradle 2 the Grave 2*?

What little dialogue there is is pretty bad. When Ling is meeting with the world's greatest arms dealers, he actually says to them, "You're the world's most foremost arms dealers." He sounds like he's on a infomercial. The meager dialogue also helps to cobble the plot together. In one scene, Fait decides that bad guy Ling has hidden the diamonds at his night club. How does he know this? "I know. I can just feel it," he says.

Cradle 2 the Grave hits all the right buttons. It has all the car chases, the hand to hand combat and the imminent world destruction, but it all seems a little tired. When are we going to get sick of seeing these same images repeated in action movies? Isn't part of being excited by a movie the element of surprise? If filmmakers keep trotting out these tired images out over and over, won't they eventually lose their power to arouse?

Critics didn't like the film, although it did have a few fans. Stephen Holden of the *New York Times* wrote that the movie "has the flailing momentum of a defective action toy run amok." Ebert, "The film itself is on autopilot and overdrive at the same time; It does nothing original, but does it very rapidly." And Cary Darling of Knight Ridder Newspapers wrote, "Fast-paced yet slowwitted and cobbled together like some kung-fu Frankenstein from remnants of every Hollywood and Hong Kong action movie of the past decade, *Cradle* boasts a couple of bravura fight and chase scenes, but they're stranded amid the predictable and the pedestrian." Scott Brown of *Entertainment Weekly* was more fond of the film: "By the time Li enters the obligatory 'ring of fire' to face his final opponent, you realize just how forthrightly rote and business-like *Cradle* is. And you don't mind. Because business, it turns out, is good."

—*Jill Hamilton*

CREDITS

Su: Jet Li
Tony Fait: DMX
Tommy: Anthony Anderson
Sona: Kelly Hu
Archie: Tom Arnold
Ling: Mark Dacascos
Daria: Gabrielle Union
Odion: Michael Jace
Chamber: Chi McBride
Christophe: Paolo Seganti
Miles: Drag-On
Vanessa: Paige Hurd

Origin: USA
Released: 2003
Production: Joel Silver; Silver Pictures; released by Warner Bros.
Directed by: Andrzej Bartkowiak
Written by: John O'Brien
Cinematography by: Daryn Okada
Music by: John (Gianni) Frizzell, Damon Blackman
Sound: Keith Wester
Music Supervisor: Tina Davis, Randy Acker
Editing: Derek G. Brechin
Art Direction: Richard F. Mays
Costumes: Ha Nguyen
Production Design: David Klassen
MPAA rating: R
Running time: 100 minutes

REVIEWS

Chicago Sun-Times Online. February 28, 2003.
Entertainment Weekly. March 7, 2003, p. 51.
Los Angeles Times Online. February 28, 2003.
New York Times Online. February 28, 2003.
People. March 10, 2003, p. 37.
USA Today Online. February 28, 2003.
Variety Online. February 27, 2003.
Washington Post. February 28, 2003, p. WE39.

TRIVIA

Director Andrzej Bartkowiak and actors Jet Li, DMX, and Anthony Anderson previously worked together on *Romeo Must Die.*

Criminal Lovers (Les Amants Criminels)

This flashback-heavy French fairytale about crime and passion begins with a blindfolded teenaged boy, Luc (Jeremie Renier), being sexually teased by his vixen-ish girlfriend, Alice (Natascha Regnier), in her bedroom. That Alice (Regnier resembles a sixties-era Catherine Deneuve) is a mistress of lying and manipulation will soon be all too clear. That pale, skinny Luc is a willing naïve patsy is also soon clear. From Alice's bedroom we switch to Said's (Salim Kechiouche); he's a handsome French-Algerian teen boasting about how he's going to get lucky since he's meeting a girl for sex in the boys locker room of their high school. Will it be any surprise that said female is Alice?

Alice and Luc go to the school gym and Alice makes her way into the locker room where she watches Said shower. They are soon fooling around on the bathroom floor as Luc watches—he opens a switchblade and, at a signal from Alice, suddenly stabs Said to death; the murderous twosome then use the shower to wash off the blood.

Luc is then seen at his home packing, taking a gun from his parents' bedroom as well as the family car. He goes back to the gym where Alice has been trying to wash all the splattered blood away, rather ineffectually, as she gazes triumphantly into the mirror. They wrap up Said's body and drag it to the car, where Alice asks if Luc loves her (a continuing theme), but he doesn't reply. They drive away without realizing that a man at the school has seen at least part of their escapade.

They drive into the country, stop in a small town to rob a jewelry store (Alice is particularly excited by their criminal activities), and to buy a shovel. They continue driving. The only time Alice shows any emotion besides impatience is when Luc accidentally runs over a rabbit and she insists they take the time to bury the poor creature. (Rabbits—dead and alive—are a big deal in this film.) They drive deeper into the forest. Eventually, they stop and then begin dragging their burden yet deeper into the trees. Alice proclaims her excitement over their adventure as they bury Said's body, but they don't realize that they are being watched.

Luc and Alice get lost trying to find their way back to the car and finally stumble across a boat moored by the bank of a slow-moving river. The two then drift with the current throughout the night into a misty morning. Luc is upset hearing Alice call Said's name in her sleep. They come to shore and Luc stalks off after arguing with Alice about what they should do. He comes across a rabbit caught in a trap and frees the creature. Luc continues to wander until he finds an old shack occupied by a hermit (played by director Miki Manojlovic). Luc rushes back to Alice, saying they can steal some food from the shack (where dead rabbits are hung from the walls), but they get caught and are forced into a rat-infested root cellar. Alice gets hysterical when she realizes that Said's body is also in the cellar.

The hermit reads Alice's diary, which details her fascination with Said. Another flashback shows Luc and Alice in school where Alice asks if Luc loves her. He says he does and she replies then he has to help her: "I've got to kill someone and you've got to help me." Luc thinks she's crazy. Later, in her bedroom, Alice says that Said's friends raped her while he took pictures. She wants Luc to help her kill Said in revenge: "Do it for me, Luc. For love." Alice tries to arouse Luc sexually but he can't respond.

The hermit lets Luc out of the cellar and makes Luc wash him. Since the cellar trapdoor opens a few inches, Alice can watch as the hermit reciprocates and bathes a humiliated Luc. The man then puts Luc on a makeshift leash and takes him into the woods to check his rabbit traps. They eat rabbit stew, although Luc has to turn away while his captor skins the creature, but the hermit refuses to feed Alice, saying he likes his girls skinny but his boys nice and plump. Luc fears the man is not only crazy but a cannibal. Later, the hermit takes Luc to bed and masturbates him as Alice watches.

Back at the high school, Luc, whom everyone seems to know is a virgin, covertly watches Said. He steals the boy's switchblade, which impresses Alice as it means their plan is going forward. Earlier, however, Luc is upset when he sees Alice kissing Said. Though he believes it's because she's setting Said up, Luc can't help but begin to cry.

Alice urges Luc to kill the hermit but he gets caught and is thrown back into the cellar. After another cold and dark night, Alice tells Luc that he must seduce the hermit, whom she refers to as the ogre, the way she seduced Said if they are to get what they want. Another flashback reprises the killing—only this time we learn that Alice has lied about the

rape. Alice's motives for wanting Said dead are never clear—is she just a thrill killer? Is she out for revenge because Said (unlike Luc) doesn't love her? Is this the ultimate test for Luc to prove his love? Luc is horrified by her lies, but, as Alice points out, it's too late to change their minds.

Luc is freed from the cellar but is once again leashed. The hermit then has sex with Luc. Alice hallucinates that she is wandering in the woods and sees the hermit choking Said to death after trying to seduce him. While the hermit sleeps, Luc manages to cut his leash, get the keys to the chained cellar door, and free Alice. She takes a knife to kill the hermit, but Luc stops her and they escape with the man's shotgun.

They run through the forest throughout the night. The next morning, a sunny day, they stumble across a rock pool and play at nature boy and girl, finally having sex (accompanied by lots of string music) as various forest animals watch in a kind of weird Disney-like porn moment. Then they hear dogs and see masked commandoes hunting them. As they run, Luc gets his foot caught in a trap and urges Alice to flee without him, giving her the gun. She comes to the river, but suddenly turns around and is killed in a hail of bullets (not quite Bonnie and Clyde but the visual is certainly there). The tracking dogs sniff at her bloody corpse (you think for a moment they're about to chow down).

A struggling Luc is thrown into the back of a police van. He sees the cops dragging the handcuffed hermit along the road; a cop throws the man to the ground as the anguished teen cries out that the man did nothing wrong. When the van drives away, Luc merely stares into the distance as the pictures fades into credits.

Director Francois Ozon partially based his script on the true story of a couple of teen killers and then went on to reference a variety of familiar sources from cinematic lovers-on-the-lam to a twisted version of Hansel and Gretel lost in the woods, with a wicked hermit substituting for a wicked witch. But the viewer is distanced from the characters and the action—even the sudden violence of Said's murder is somehow remote.

Maybe this is because the three protagonists are never clear: Alice is somewhere between a knowing Lolita and Lady MacBeth, while the insecure Luc is a blank page. Alice taunts Luc that he enjoyed being sexually initiated by the hermit and Luc's final cries to the uncaring cops when he sees the hermit being kicked seem out of place for a man who has kept him a prisoner and raped him. Did Luc in some fashion enjoy his subjugation? Why is he finally able to function sexually with Alice after their escape? And was the hermit going to eventually kill and eat them? Alice points out to Luc that part of Said's leg is missing and that the last meal Luc ate (after complaining that he didn't like rabbit) was probably not bunny. Yet, in some ways, this middle-aged man is very tender towards the boy—more so than

Alice much of the time. There are lots of symbols but maybe they really mean nothing—as pointless as the crime that starts our trip into the dark and forbidding woods.

—*Christine Tomassini*

CREDITS

Alice: Natacha Regnier
Luc: Jeremie Renier
Man in the woods: Miki (Predrag) Manojlovic
Said: Salim Kechiouche

Origin: France
Language: French
Released: 1999
Production: Olivier Delbosc, Marc Missonnier; Fidelite Productions; released by Strand Releasing
Directed by: Francois Ozon
Written by: Francois Ozon
Cinematography by: Pierre Stoeber
Music by: Philippe Rombi
Sound: Benoit Hillebrant, Francois Guillaume
Editing: Dominique Petrot
Art Direction: Arnaud de Moleron
Costumes: Pascaline Chavanne
MPAA rating: Unrated
Running time: 96 minutes

 ## REVIEWS

New York Times Online. July 21, 2000.
San Francisco Chronicle. September 1, 2000, p. C3.
Variety Online. August 23, 1999.

The Cuckoo (Kushka)

War makes strange bedfellows.
—Movie tagline

The Russian Federation production entitled *Kukushka*, or *The Cuckoo*, begins like a grim World War II film. The "cuckoo" of the title is an unwilling Finnish sniper named Veiko (Ville Haapasalo) who is pressed into service, dressed in a Nazi uniform, and chained, Prometheus-like, to

a rock on the top of a hill. Veiko is a student, and, as an intellectual, he is opposed to the war. The action is set in northern Finland in September of 1944, when the war is in its final stages. Gradually, however, the war fades into the background of the film, allowing space for humor and a brilliantly allegorical turn. The *New York Times* described *The Cuckoo* as an antiwar fable, which, given its larger message about human understanding and communication, seems an accurate label, but the film is difficult to classify.

In the first third of the film, which is essentially wordless and moves at a glacially slow pace, Veiko's ingenuity is tested as he ever so slowly works to release his chain from the rock to which it is secured. While he is working to free himself, he sees a Jeep on the road below strafed by two airplanes, and two of the three men in the Jeep are killed. The third, Ivan Psholty (Viktor Bychkov), is a disgraced Russian captain en route to his trial after being brought up on charges; he survives and is rescued by Anni (Anni-Kristiina Juuso), who drags Ivan back to her reindeer farm, where the young woman nurses him back to health. Anni is essentially a healer and a caregiver.

Meanwhile, after watching Ivan's rescue through the sniper's scope on his rifle, Veiko succeeds in extracting the spike that keeps him chained to the rock by removing gunpowder from his rifle shells and setting an explosion in the crevice of the rock where the spike was imbedded. Fortunately, a boulder is within easy reach, which enables him to pound the spike free.

Veiko strikes out for Anni's farm to procure the tools needed to break the manacle that remains around his ankle. Though Veiko can make himself understood to Anni, the situation quickly turns into a comedy of misunderstanding. Veiko does not speak Russian, and Ivan does not speak Finnish or Lapp, so he believes Veiko to be a German soldier and calls him "Fritz." Ivan becomes enamored of the angel who has saved his life, but Anni seems to prefer the younger Veiko, who she chooses to seduce, explaining that she has been four years without a man. The three characters often speak to one another at cross-purposes, which makes for decidedly comic dialogue.

Toward the end of the film, a low-flying biplane crashes in the woods, killing both the pilot and the co-pilot. The plane was sent out to release notes informing people that Finland is no longer at war. Ivan finds a loaded revolver in the cockpit, and, misunderstanding the plane's purpose and unable to grasp what Veiko is trying to tell him about the armistice, he shoots and nearly kills the young man. When Ivan finds one of the leaflets printed in Russian, he realizes what he has done and carries Veiko back to Anni's farm. She manages to nurse him back to health by using ritual magic in one of the most eerie dream sequences ever captured on film. We see Anni chanting over Veiko's body, beating a drum and blowing onto his face, then finally grasping his hand to lead him back into the realm of the living. This point of view alternates with the dream state of the wounded Veiko, who sees himself standing in the moonlight on a mountainside. An albino boy wearing a white robe gestures Veiko toward the spirit world, but Anni's magic keeps calling him back. After Veiko's recovery, he and Ivan part as friends and go their separate ways.

In an epilogue that concludes the film, Anni tells the story of Veiko and Ivan to the two sons she has borne them. Of course, she does not know what transpired between them in the woods and tells the boys a tale of the heroism of the two soldiers after "a bad man wounded one of them." Julian Graffy wrote in *Sight and Sound* that *The Cuckoo*, though comedic in what it suggests about the failure of the characters to communicate (Veiko is well read and wants to discuss Tolstoy, Dostoevsky, and Hemingway; Ivan and Anni are both uneducated), "is gradually revealed to be a sophisticated parable about nationality and gender, war and humanity, time and place, in which each protagonist provides a conventional representation of nation and character." Anni's later intrusion into the spirit world is anything but comic, except for viewers stupid enough to laugh at the "primitive" and ancient remedies.

Although he is not widely known in the West, St. Petersburg director Aleksandr Rogozhkin is regarded as one of contemporary Russia's most popular directors, known especially for his comedy *Peculiarities of the National Hunt* (1995) and for the more serious *Checkpoint* (1998). The *Sight and Sound* review also noted that *The Cuckoo* "has collected all the major recent Russian film prizes," including awards for best film from both the Nika and the newer Golden Eagle ceremonies. The film is warm, entertaining, spiritual, and worthwhile.

—*James M. Welsh*

CREDITS

Veiko: Willie Haapsalo
Anni: Anni-Kristina Usso
Ivan: Vikter Bychkov

Origin: Russia
Language: Finnish, Russian
Released: 2002
Production: Sergei Solyanov; CTB; released by Sony Pictures Classics
Directed by: Alexander Rogozhkin
Written by: Alexander Rogozhkin
Cinematography by: Andrei Zhegalov
Music by: Dmitri Pavlov
Sound: Anatoly Goudkovsky, Sergey Sokolov
Editing: Yulia Rumyatseva
Costumes: Marina Nikolaeva

Production Design: Vladimir Svetozarov
MPAA rating: PG-13
Running time: 104 minutes

REVIEWS

Entertainment Weekly. July 18, 2003, p. 88.
Los Angeles Times Online. July 11, 2003.
New York Times Online. July 11, 2003.
Variety Online. May 21, 2002.
Washington Post. September 12, 2003, p. WE39.

Daddy Day Care

Box Office: $104.2 million

Little hellions with potty mouths generally meet with stern disapproval, a time out, and sometimes even a well-placed swat. When they get a tad older though, these impudent live wires can sometimes find a more receptive audience, with hands clapping vigorously together instead of into their backsides.

Take Eddie Murphy for example, one of the more clever and successful young talents who burst onto the scene in the 1980's with comedy that was audacious, raunchy and even incendiary. Whether it was as a cast member of NBC's *Saturday Night Live,* in hit films like *48 Hrs.* (1982), *Trading Places* (1983) or *Beverly Hills Cop* (1984), or especially in concert, the air almost visibly sparked and crackled around him, an inspired, wickedly funny wild child. In recent years, however, the now forty-something father of four has steered his career onto a much different path, choosing roles with a greater accent on child than wild. Amongst some flops like *Metro* (1997), *Holy Man* (1998) and an embarrassing nadir entitled *The Adventures of Pluto Nash* (2002), Murphy has successfully detoured into more family friendly fare like the *Dr. Doolittle* films and *Shrek* (2001). In that tamer vein is the innocuous *Daddy Day Care,* in which the only thing popping in the air around this once dynamic performer is the repeated flatulence emanating from his pint-sized co-stars.

The film harks back to *Mr. Mom* (1983), with its theme of an out-of-work father staying at home and finding himself ill-prepared for the vagaries of child care. Here, Charlie Hinton (Murphy) and his entire division at an advertising agency lose their jobs after a disastrous focus group session in which a mob of kids make all too clear their lack of desire for a proposed healthful breakfast cereal made from broccoli and other vegetables. (The weasel boss explains after the dismissal that healthy food is just something the agency no longer wants any part of.) Also losing his job is Charlie's big burly buddy Phil (Jeff Garlin of HBO's *Curb Your Enthusiasm*).

With this sudden loss of income for both households, neither can afford to send their sons to pricey Chapman Academy, a scholastically-demanding establishment run by the forbidding and aptly-named taskmistress Gwyneth Harridan (Angelica Huston, playing a woman perhaps related to her character in 1990's *The Witches*). Chapman is one of those places that may push kids a tad too swiftly from diapers to diplomas. When Charlie and his lawyer wife Kim (Regina King) go tooling around in their Mercedes for a more affordable alternative to Chapman, we see some dreadful places similar in safety to the witch's house in Hansel and Gretel.

It is abundantly clear that neither Charlie nor Phil know much about meeting their own kids' needs: Charlie tells his little Ben (Khamani Griffin) that they are going to have fun and then they just stare at each other, and Phil lives in fear of changing his son's unusually malodorous diapers. Still, they decide to extend their lack of expertise to the children of others by starting Daddy Day Care.

Such a venture will make these suddenly-idle men feel useful again, but when Kim tells Charlie that the idea is crazy on ten different levels, it seems to us that there might even be a few more she had not even considered yet. However ridiculous, this decision must be made to set the stage for all the antics that will be so entertaining to the tots, who will undoubtedly enjoy seeing a horde of kids running roughshod over a couple of blundering and wholly outmaneuvered adults. Terms like "butthead" fill the air, along with plenty of high-pitched screaming and peals of raucous laughter, as the kids race around and break nearly everything except their dear little necks. The sugary foods the fathers foolishly feed the kids only serve to make matters worse. All sorts of disturbing things come out of various orifices. A girl kicks Phil in the groin. Charlie's shins get a similar treatment.

As if Charlie and Phil do not have enough trouble on their hands, they must now deal with the wrath of Harridan, who vows to quickly put an end to the steady draining away of students from Chapman to Daddy Day Care. (Why Daddy Day Care's enrollment continues to rise at the expense of a good if excessively ambitious school is a mystery, although it undoubtedly comes highly recommended by the children.) Miss Harridan tips off inspector Dan Kubitz (Jonathan Katz of Comedy Central's *Dr. Katz: Professional Therapist*) to check on their compliance with various regulations.

Things are actually looking up for the overwhelmed but determined fathers when they must hire childlike Marvin (affective Steve Zahn), who exhibits a genuine rapport with, and understanding of, the kids. (A Star Trek fanatic, he was shocked to learn that Spock's famous books on child

rearing were not written by the pointy-eared Vulcan.) Marvin's addition clearly benefits Daddy Day Care—both the endeavor and the film. Suddenly Daddy Day Care is making strides in helping the kids developmentally, starting now to stimulate them in much more productive ways than with massive sugar consumption. The kids are enthusiastic and enriched. The adults are enthusiastic and enriched. Now all they have to do is overcome a severe money shortage, a lack of required space, and continued hostilities from Harridan.

Then comes the inevitable lucrative job offer for Charlie and Phil to return to the agency, which forces them to ponder their priorities from their new perspective. Will the men find true happiness going back to work, which will fill up their wallets but not their souls? We know the answer and the eventual outcome long before they do. And when Charlie becomes distracted from crunching numbers by one of Ben's drawings in what appears to be his very first meeting back, we are hardly surprised. He and Phil quit, proudly proclaim that "Daddy Day Care is back in business," and rescue all the children who had returned to Chapman. The kids could have stayed there and gotten a serious but impressive, solid education, but where would the fun be in that? Apparently it was not enough for the filmmakers to have the founders of Daddy Day Care triumph over Miss Harridan, but they must also crush her like a bug, reducing her to being a crossing guard and (speaking of insects) having her be attacked by a swarm of angry bees.

Even though *Daddy Day Care,* produced on a $60 million budget, received mainly negative reviews, it still succeeded in grossing more than $100 million. It is primarily aimed at—and will unquestionably be enjoyed most by—those whose ages remain in the single digits, who are always in the mood for a good poop joke and find humor about passing gas more than passable. Like an afternoon in most day cares, the film will most likely keep the kids sufficiently occupied without doing them any harm. Parents will be pleased their kids are pleased, but will find the proceedings too bland and predictable.

Daddy Day Care comes to us as the feature film debut for screenwriter and former stay-at-home dad Geoff Rodkey, who, among other things, once wrote for *Beavis and Butthead.* His script is unspectacular, every bit as disposable as the kids' diapers. Speaking of the children, none is especially darling or memorable except Griffin, who is immensely appealing here. Amidst all the "Aww!," "Eww!," and "Oww!" moments, Murphy is flat but still sufficiently warm and winning, with the rest of the supporting cast merely adequate, all working hard to try and make the less-than-stellar material sparkle. At various points, the film strikes some serious, thoughtful notes about education and child care, fulfillment, working fathers who barely have/take time to get to know their kids, and the tugging at working mothers' heartstrings when the kids start to turn more to

Daddy for comfort even when she is there. *Daddy Day Care*, however, is not a film interested in dwelling on or delving into such issues, skipping along happily to the next poop joke. Its messages are hardly original but simple, and it generally passes by in a pleasant-enough fashion. Still, watching this uninspired film, one cannot help wishing that Eddie would go back to being a little more naughty and a little less nice.

—David L. Boxerbaum

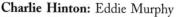

CREDITS

Charlie Hinton: Eddie Murphy
Marvin: Steve Zahn
Phil: Jeff Garlin
Kim Hinton: Regina King
Miss Gwyneth Harridan: Anjelica Huston
Jenny: Lacey Chabert
Beth-Anne: Sloane Momsen
Bruce: Kevin Nealon
Mr. Dan Kubitz: Jonathan Katz
Ben Hinton: Khamani Griffin

Origin: USA
Released: 2003
Production: John Davis, Matt Berenson, Wyck Godfrey; Revolution Studios, Columbia Pictures; released by Sony Pictures
Directed by: Steve Carr
Written by: Geoff Rodkey
Cinematography by: Steven Poster
Music by: David Newman
Sound: David MacMillan
Music Supervisor: Spring Aspers
Editing: Christopher Greenbury
Art Direction: Chris Cornwell
Costumes: Ruth Carter
Production Design: Gareth Stover
MPAA rating: PG
Running time: 92 minutes

REVIEWS

Chicago Sun-Times Online. May 9, 2003.
Entertainment Weekly. May 16, 2003, p. 52.
Los Angeles Times Online. May 9, 2003.
New York Times Online. May 9, 2003.
People. May 19, 2003, p. 37.
Rolling Stone. May 29, 2003, p. 71.
Variety Online. May 4, 2003.
Wall Street Journal. May 9, 2003, p. W1.
Washington Post. May 9, 2003, p. WE41.

QUOTES

Charlie (Eddie Murphy) about what to do with the kids: "We need some structure and some planned activities." Phil (Jeff Garlin) replies: "We need Ritalin and leashes."

The Dancer Upstairs

An honest man caught in a world of intrigue, power and passion.
—Movie tagline

Box Office: $2.3 million

John Malkovich has always demonstrated a full, adult command of film in his roles. He possesses a unique sense of detail regardless of the character and seems to exact the most perfect reactions. In his first film as director (he has directed stage productions), Malkovich does not stray from his path of perfect aesthetic detail and presents *The Dancer Upstairs* as the haunting yet beautiful story it is. Many thrillers rely on claustrophobic sets filled with choking darkness to draw the audience into the fear but in *The Dancer Upstairs* no such trickery is used, rather the audience is treated to a film which is part romance, part thriller, part political commentary.

The movie was filmed in Ecuador and stars Javier Bardem as Augustin, a man who left his law practice for the police force. I never fully understood this change in career, but the point seems to be that it's the result of the psychological war apparently being waged in Augustin's private life. His current position requires him to track down a terrorist named Ezequiel who recruits teenagers to be suicide bombers in order to assassinate officials. The terrorist, whose trademark is to leave dead dogs hanging in public view, has the police stumped and the population living in fear.

The movie is based on the novel by Nicholas Shakespeare. Shakespeare's book was inspired by the exploits of a terrorist group in Peru called The Shining Path. The book is really a fictionalized account of the pursuit and capture of Abiemal Guzman, the leader of The Shining Path. Having said that, this is not a docudrama about Peru, Guzman, or The Shining Path but rather a general, enlightening look at the ways terrorism takes its toll on a society as a whole

Augustin at first appears to be a quiet yet happy man. He dotes on his daughter and, although she is constantly obsessing about getting surgery on her nose, seems to love his wife. He is content, however, with long stints away from his family.

One might expect a movie directed by Malkovich to be contemplative and thoughtful, so it is not shocking that *The Dancer Upstairs* is just that. The romance that is sparked between Augustin and his daughter's ballet teacher is slow and reluctant. The characters realize their attraction to each other but choose not to act on their feelings.

I doubt that Malkovich ever intended to make a straight thriller with this film, as straightforward acting and, hence, direction is not his style. Augustin is a complex man stuck in a very confused life situation, and this really is the focus of the film. It is almost as if the social chaos is just a backdrop for the chaos in his mind. *The Dancer Upstairs* is deliberate in its pacing, as though Malkovich wants you to really chew on a few things here. He wants you to chew, swallow, and wait before you take the next bite, and for me this is a bit of refreshing filmmaking. What becomes clear toward the end of the film is that both Augustin and the society he is living in are functioning on the outside but are always on the verge of a great breakdown. The pacing of the film is what allows the audience to comprehend this.

John Malkovich has made a film that should serve as an example to the rest of Hollywood. It is a captivating story that, despite being difficult to watch, has all the elements of a good film.

—*Laura Abraham*

CREDITS

Agustin Rejas: Javier Bardem
Yolanda: Laura Morante
Sucre: Juan Diego Botto
Llosa: Elvira Minguez
General Merino: Oliver Cotton
Calderon: Luis Miguel Cintra
Ezequiel: Abel Folk
Sylvina: Alexandra Lencastre

Origin: USA, Spain
Released: 2002
Production: Andres Vicente Gomez, John Malkovich; Antena 3, Via Digital, Mr. Mudd; released by Fox Searchlight
Directed by: John Malkovich
Written by: Nicholas Shakespeare
Cinematography by: Jose Luis Alcaine
Music by: Alberto Iglesias
Sound: Antonio Bloch
Editing: Mario Battistel
Costumes: Bina Daigeler
Production Design: Pierre-Francois Limbosh

MPAA rating: R
Running time: 128 minutes

REVIEWS

Boxoffice. April, 2002, p. 173.
Boxoffice. February, 2003, p. 31.
Chicago Sun-Times Online. May 2, 2003.
Los Angeles Times Online. May 2, 2003.
New York Times Online. May 2, 2003.
Sight and Sound. December, 2002, p. 16.
Variety. January 21, 2002, p. 31.
Washington Post. May 9, 2003, p. WE48.

Daredevil

When justice is blind, it knows no fear.
—Movie tagline
When the streets have gone to Hell—have faith in the Devil.
—Movie tagline
Justice is blind. So is he.
—Movie tagline
Take the dare.
—Movie tagline

 Box Office: $102.5 million

An interesting trait that the more successful comic book-to-cinema adaptations share is the watchful eye of a strong, visionary director (or at least they prove to be such on that particular project). Take for example, Tim Burton and the gothic vistas he brought to both *Batman* and *Batman Returns*; or Sam Raimi's crowd-pleasing, post 9/11, heroic ode *Spider-Man*; or Bryan Singer's mega-successful alienation-obsessed *X-Men* films; there's also Richard Donner's near-perfect *Superman*; and even Ang Lee's *Hulk* offers a unique vision of the material. It's disheartening then, when a property such as Daredevil is given the short shrift in such a lifeless, artless, pointless film as this one. Granted, the aforementioned characters all have a bit more familiarity about them than Daredevil, and blame cannot be placed solely on the director when a film flounders. But, the fact of the matter is that *Daredevil* is a failure and it misses the mark on so many levels that it's hard not to think that if someone with a more definitive or personal vision of interpreting the character had held the reigns, then perhaps it might have fared better.

The film begins with a mortally wounded Daredevil (Ben Affleck) commenting that your life does flash before your eyes just before you die. For the next twenty minutes or so, the back-story and origins of the character are quickly addressed. Daredevil's alter ego is Matt Murdock, a Hell's Kitchen defense attorney who takes on cases for little or no money solely based on whether the client is innocent. But, at night, Matt dons a red leather jumpsuit and becomes Daredevil, or the "Man Without Fear." In this guise he dispenses the justice that the legal system has failed to impart (the impetus for Matt's penchant to fight for the little guy is his father's murder after refusing to throw a boxing match). Daredevil's super powers come from being blinded by radioactive waste while a boy. The loss of his sight heightened Matt's four-other sense to an uncanny level and afforded him radar-like sight.

Presently, Matt is languishing at a moral-crossroads and has begun questioning the validity of the vigilante tract he has chosen. The problem here is that Daredevil isn't sure if he's better than the criminals he punishes. That potentially rewarding narrative thread is quickly dropped when Elektra Natchios (Jennifer Garner) is introduced and the film spirals into a clumsy love story until Daredevil's nemesis, a crime-lord known as the Kingpin (Michael Clarke Duncan), dispatches the assassin Bullseye (Colin Farrell) to kill Elektra's father and Daredevil is implicated in the murder. A final showdown between Elektra, Bullseye, and Daredevil ensues. But, then again, this has all been seen before. There's nothing new, original, or creative about it. This is a cookie-cutter super hero movie of the worst kind—boring.

It's not that Daredevil isn't an interesting character. Since debuting during the "silver age" of comics in 1964, Daredevil has grown into a complex, brooding sack of repressed guilt (sort of a manic-depressive Batman). But, that just isn't explored in this film. It's alluded to but never really embraced. The closest the film comes to this kind of introspective self-analysis is Affleck pleading to a child that has just witnessed Daredevil's brutal beating of a mugger, "I'm not the bad guy kid." For what it's worth, it doesn't matter. No one cares. Other characters in the film are clichéd and the largely uninspired script allows them absolutely no chance for improvement (Farrell is the only actor that is able to salvage anything from his character). Ultimately, the film amounts to, as Owen Gleiberman noted in *Entertainment Weekly*, "little more than a hollow clone of Batman and Spider-Man." Gleiberman is referring to the characters here, but his conclusion easily applies to the films as well. In fact, *Daredevil* follows the *Spider-Man* template to a tee. Matt has an "accident" early on, uses his powers to punish some bullies who teased him in an earlier scene, loses his parent (Peter Parker also lost a parental figure), vows to fight injustice, falls in love, gets an arch-enemy, and has effects-laden climactic battle. The problem is that all the film wants to be is a copy of a blockbuster and never even approaches having its own identity.

This is no more evident than in the final confrontation between Daredevil and Bullseye. The two figures are seen flitting about atop the pipes of a mammoth church organ all the while trading punches, kicks, grunts, etc. This is less an allusion to *Crouching Tiger, Hidden Dragon* than a total rip-off with lifeless metal substituting for organic wistfulness. This, in essence is symptomatic of the major problem with *Daredevil*. It spends so much time aping other movies (*Spider-Man, Batman, The Matrix*, et al.) that it never develops its own voice and subsequently never amounts to anything of consequence. It just is. As Rick Groen wrote in the *Globe and Mail*, *Daredevil* is "not woeful, not wonderful, merely watchable." Director Mark Steven Johnson, is simply, as Elvis Mitchell alluded in the *New York Times,* "too worshipful of the idiom's conventions" to exhibit the creative flourish that the film needed to be anything more than ordinary. By not straying far from the successful formula of *Spider-Man*, Johnson's lazy script doesn't afford itself any leeway and, as Wesley Morris noted in the *Boston Globe,* "strains itself trying to catch up with Sam Raimi's web-slinging megasmash."

Daredevil has traditionally been Marvel Comic's answer to Batman. He was a super hero without any standard "super" powers. He wasn't from another planet, or the possessor of a fantastic power ring, and he wasn't bitten by a radioactive animal of any kind. But, in a post *X-Men* and *Spider-Man* world, the filmmakers apparently thought that Daredevil had to have the ability to bound from building to building like he was in fact Spider-Man (as well as be able to use martial arts, *Matrix* style). Again, this is yet another example of the film "borrowing" from another without thinking for itself. Part of the appeal of this character was always his conflicted vigilantism. That allure is wasted in this film and the character becomes just another super hero retread. As Kenneth Turan of the *Los Angeles Times* noted, that while Daredevil "seemed serious for a comic book, it is uninterestingly cartoonish for a movie."

—*Michael J. Tyrkus*

CREDITS

Matt Murdock/Daredevil: Ben Affleck
Elektra Natchios: Jennifer Garner
Kingpin/Fisk: Michael Clarke Duncan
Bullseye: Colin Farrell
Ulrich: Joe Pantoliano
Franklin Nelson: Jon Favreau
Jack Murdock: David Keith
Natchios: Erik Avari
Quesada: Paul Ben-Victor

Father Everett: Derrick O'Connor
Wesley: Leland Orser
Young Matt: Scott Terra
Jack Kirby (forensic lab tech): Kevin Smith

Origin: USA
Released: 2003
Production: Arnon Milchan, Gary Foster, Avi Arad;
Regency Enterprises, Marvel Enterprises, New Regency
Pictures, Horseshoe Bay; released by 20th Century-Fox
Directed by: Mark Steven Johnson
Written by: Mark Steven Johnson
Cinematography by: Ericson Core
Music by: Graeme Revell
Sound: Peter J. Devlin
Music Supervisor: Dave Jordan
Editing: Dennis Virkler, Armen Minasian
Art Direction: James E. Tocci
Costumes: James Acheson
Production Design: Barry Chusid
MPAA rating: PG-13
Running time: 114 minutes

REVIEWS

Boston Globe Online. February 14, 2003.
Chicago Sun-Times Online. February 14, 2003.
Detroit Free Press Online. February 14, 2003.
Detroit News. February 14, 2003, p. E1.
Entertainment Weekly. February 7, 2003, p. 21.
Entertainment Weekly. February 21, 2003, p. 125.
Globe and Mail Online. February 14, 2003.
Los Angeles Times Online. February 14, 2003.
New York Times Online. February 14, 2003.
People. February 24, 2003, p. 31.
Premiere. February, 2003, p. 46.
San Francisco Chronicle. February 14, 2003, p. D1.
TV Guide. February 8, 2003, p. 15.
USA Today Online. February 14, 2003.
Variety Online. February 14, 2003.
Washington Post. February 14, 2003, p. WE45.

QUOTES

The Kingpin (Michael Clarke Duncan) refers to Daredevil (Ben
Affleck): "How do you kill a man without fear?"

TRIVIA

Director Kevin Smith has a cameo as a forensic scientist.

AWARDS AND NOMINATIONS

Golden Raspberries 2003: Worst Actor (Affleck).

Dark Blue

Sworn to protect. Sworn to serve. Sworn to secrecy.
—Movie tagline

 Box Office: $9.2 million

Provocation is *Dark Blue*'s game—both the visual and cerebral kind. Working from a screenplay by David Ayer, director Ron Shelton throws a brutal world of corrupt cops and soulless thugs into your face, yet somehow manages to make a thought-provoking film. Shelton's career was built on sports movies (*Bull Durham, White Men Can't Jump, Cobb, Tin Cup*), but lately he seems more interested in the games cops and criminals play (*Play It to the Bone, Hollywood Homicide*). Throbbing with ugly violence and unsympathetic characters, *Dark Blue* is an unforgiving, politically incorrect, volatile, and boisterous exercise in cinematic rhetoric.

Dark Blue draws out at great lengths the motivations for the brutality and racism of its protagonist, an unscrupulous special investigations officer named Eldon Perry (Kurt Russell). And it showcases plenty of instances of egregious violence that almost—but not quite—support his worldview, which is that the streets need to be scrubbed clean of human vermin by whatever means necessary. Subversively, *Dark Blue* eventually suggests, however, that the system of corruption and vigilante law enforcement must collapse from its own contradictions, and that even the most brutal cops have moral limits.

It's a lot of emotional and philosophical weight for one plot to bear, but writer Ayer pulls it off skillfully, working from a novel by James Ellroy that was set during the time of the 1965 Watts riots. Updating it to 1991 Los Angeles, Shelton plays out the story's action against a backdrop of a jury pondering the fate of the four white policemen accused of beating black suspect Rodney King. Television reports of the jury deliberations play in the background of several scenes, as the L.A. police force and city remain on pins and needles awaiting the outcome. The backdrop of real events makes the story feel more authentic and compelling.

The film's no-holds-barred tale is an allegory for the fate of urban American police forces during this era, when their practices were being exposed and judged nationwide. It marks a cultural watershed of sorts. The story doesn't pull any punches by romanticizing either the cops or the street thugs. It's a constant battle in this film as to which character is the ugliest and most amoral, and Shelton doesn't allow the viewer to settle in comfortably with a preconceived notion of who's right and who's wrong. Even one of the victims turns out to be guilty.

Russell's Perry is an unapologetic, third-generation police cowboy, bent on administering justice single-handedly with his gun. Though his character is besotted with racism, his motives seem at least somewhat high-minded—he really does believe he's a good guy saving the lives of innocent victims by wiping out the bad guys.

As the film opens, Perry is training his new young partner, Bobby Keough (Scott Speedman), in his well-honed techniques for operating successfully as a tolerated outlaw within the ranks of the police force. Keough is in front of a police review board investigating whether his use of lethal force was "in policy" or out of line. A few important fabrications during his testimony and the assistance of a couple of key officers on the review board lead to his exoneration. Only later do we learn that Keough suffered qualms during the confrontation in question, and that Perry actually picked up his gun and shot the suspect.

Perry's shot so many bad guys he's lost count of them, and he does so without much hesitation. He later confides to Keough that the face of his first lethal shooting still haunts him—the guy was scum, but he had a wife and family, and the script allows Perry to display a smidgeon of guilt. Everything in the film depends on keeping the brutal Perry accessible and remotely sympathetic to the audience, and Russell, in one of his most gutsy, brilliant portrayals, pulls off this difficult task. Perry is a drunken, insensitive man. He doesn't hesitate to mace or pummel an innocent bystander to get information, and he's willing to blackmail officials and judges to get search warrants signed. But Russell allows us to see that these attributes have been burned into Perry through his family heritage and through years of working the streets and dealing with the worst that Los Angeles has to offer. He has somehow managed to retain just a shred of his humanity, even if he taps into it rarely.

Perry and Keough have become unwitting pawns in a power struggle for control of the police force. Perry works directly for the corrupt Jack Van Meter (Brendan Gleeson), who represents the racist white establishment within the force. Seeking to vault over him and become the city's first African-American police chief is Arthur Holland (Ving Rhames), but he needs dirt on Van Meter, his chief competitor, to bring him down.

Rhames portrays Holland as a tower of righteous strength, but it's one of the film's weaknesses that Holland does little or nothing on his own to accomplish his goals—his eventual victory will be handed to him on a silver platter. Sure, he's got his assistant, Sergeant Beth Williamson (Michael Michele), pulling files and fishing for dirt on Perry and Keough. It's only when she does so that Williamson discovers that the man she's been romancing for several weeks is Keough—they have disclosed to each other only that they both are on the force, but have refused to divulge their last names or their job postings. Van Meter, who keeps his empire in check through blackmail, among other means, also has dirt on Holland—old photos of when he and Williamson had a brief fling, and he uses them to drive a dagger through Holland's marriage.

Perry has marital problems of his own, stemming from his neglect of his wife Sally (Lolita Davidovich), a jail clerk, and his increasing obsession with his job. He's also neglectful of their son—but so is Shelton, introducing the boy only during the film's grandiose set-piece climax.

Early in the film, there's an excruciatingly brutal robbery of a party store, executed by a white and a black thug. They kill the store owner's wife and three customers and seriously injure a homeless man they run into during their escape. It turns out the pair are working undercover for Van Meter, who deftly puts Keough and Perry on the case. When the special-unit cops discover who the real suspects might be, Van Meter orders them to take down two substitute thugs instead—notorious criminals who are innocent of this particular crime. Keough objects, and Perry goes into a tirade, lecturing him on the importance of following orders. The events that unfold lead Keough eventually to turn to Holland's side, just at the same time that Van Meter figures out how to wrap up his affairs in a vicious manner that leaves the loyal Perry hanging out to dry.

The climax of the film is mesmerizing, as the characters come together violently just as the city explodes in anger over the Rodney King acquittals. As Perry makes his way through the carnival of looting, burning, and vengeance, Shelton concocts a Felliniesque street landscape that, as well as any film, captures the combination of glee, desperation, anger, and communal celebration that co-exist uncomfortably in a full-fledged urban riot.

Only the ending of the film slops over into melodrama: It's a full-fledged confessional scene in which Perry redeems himself and helps Holland bring down Van Meter. The film ends with the city burning and the whiff of change in the air within the police department. But even here, there is moral ambiguity. *Dark Blue* opts not for the easy refuge of political correctness nor the flip-side morass of justifying police anger. The city is a vicious, immoral quagmire, and there are no easy answers.

Russell's performance is outstanding, and Gleeson is also effective as his repulsively corrupt boss. The commanding and majestic Rhames has too little to do. Speedman is totally unbelievable as the young cop—he is too soap-opera handsome and squeamish, and he's never credible. Only a little better is his TV-star counterpart Michele. But the plot has little sustained interest in them, even though they represent the youthful hope for a more tolerant future on the force.

Shelton relies excessively on the use of close-ups, and the ultra-hip soundtrack is often jarring and overbearing (not so the great song in the closing credits, by Porno for Pyros). There's little subtlety to the film, and it doesn't have the nuanced thoughtfulness of a great cops movie like *Narc*. The plot gets a little heavy handed at times, and the dialogue strains a little too hard in spots to be streetwise and authentic. Yet *Dark Blue* succeeds very well in what it sets out to do. And rarely has Hollywood had the courage to look at an incendiary problem such as police violence in such a gritty, ambiguous, and complex way.

—*Michael Betzold*

CREDITS

Eldon Perry: Kurt Russell
Arthur Holland: Ving Rhames
Bobby Keough: Scott Speedman
Jack Van Meter: Brendan Gleeson
Beth Williamson: Michael Michele
Sally Perry: Lolita (David) Davidovich
Gary Sidwell: Dash Mihok
Darryl Orchard: Kurupt
Janelle Holland: Khandi Alexander
Maniac: Master P

Origin: USA
Released: 2003
Production: Caldecott Chubb, David Blocker, James Jacks, Sean Daniel; Alphaville, Im Film Produktion, Cosmic Pictures; released by United Artists
Directed by: Ron Shelton
Written by: David Ayer
Cinematography by: Barry Peterson
Music by: Terence Blanchard
Sound: Robert Eber
Editing: Paul Seydor
Art Direction: Tom Taylor
Costumes: Kathryn Morrison
Production Design: Dennis Washington
MPAA rating: R
Running time: 116 minutes

REVIEWS

Boxoffice. February, 2003, p. 58.
Chicago Sun-Times Online. February 21, 2003.
Entertainment Weekly. February 28, 2003, p. 54.
Los Angeles Times Online. February 21, 2003.
New York Times Online. February 21, 2003.
People. March 3, 2003, p. 31.
USA Today Online. February 21, 2003.
Variety Online. January 11, 2003.
Washington Post. February 21, 2003, p. WE33.

QUOTES

Eldon Perry (Kurt Russell): "At the end of the day the bullets are in the bad guys, not us."
Eldon Perry (Kurt Russell): "This city's here because I built it—with bullets!"

Darkness Falls

Evil Rises.
—Movie tagline

Box Office: $26.8 million

Just when we all thought we had discovered everything possible that there is to worry about, it turns out there's something more. The TOOTH FAIRY. Yes, horror movies have been so overdone that it is apparent that film writers have completely run out of new monsters. Thus, the scary baddie of *Darkness Falls* is the tooth fairy. (Next up: a rampaging Pillsbury Dough Boy?) Who is this movie for? The story requires an audience who both likes horror films and believes in the tooth fairy. Is this a previously untapped large contingent of moviegoers?

Perhaps writers (and with a film like this, you just know it's "writers" in the plural) John Fasano, James Vanderbilt and Joe Harris should get some sort of minute credit for managing to wring any scary moments whatsoever from such a ridiculous concept. That's not to say that *Darkness Falls* is all that scary. Most of its scary moments are immensely predictable. If first-time director Jonathan Liebesman is going to give audiences a jolt, he's prone to warn them ahead of time.

The best part of the film is the beginning in which we hear the legend of this scary tooth fairy. The eerie narration informs us that in the 1800s, a kindly old woman named Matilda Dixon used to give the local kids of Darkness Falls a gold piece in exchange for their baby teeth. One night, Dixon's house burns down and her face is terribly burned. She wears a porcelain mask to cover her hideous face (the movie is not exactly a boost to burn victim's self-esteem) and can only venture out in the night to avoid getting light on her sensitive face. The fickle townspeople decide that she is now completely unlikeable and, when two children disappear, she is blamed for it. Before she is put to death, the townspeople rip off her mask and she is so humiliated that she puts a curse on the town. The next day, the two boys show up unarmed. Ooops. It seems like the usual wisdom of an angry mob didn't hold true in this case.

The curse is sort of unclear, but it seems to involve kids being killed by this mean tooth fairy/Matilda/spirit thing when they lose their last tooth. The people in this town, besides being needlessly cruel to burn victims are also incredibly stupid. How else to explain why after countless kids have died after putting their last tooth under their pillow, subsequent kids would continue to do it? Is that quarter really worth it?

Kyle (Joshua Anderson) is one such dullard. His story is different though because he doesn't get killed, his mom does. Why the rules suddenly change and the mom dies instead of the tooth-loser is but one of this particular monster's inconsistencies. To reach her full potential as a truly scary monster, Matilda needs to hire some sort of secretarial service that can help her keep the tenets of her curse clear and organized.

After his mom's death, Kyle is sent off to a foster home and treated with various anti-psychotic medications. Despite the longtime evidence, the townspeople think that Kyle's tooth fairy story is crazy and that Kyle himself has killed his mother. When Kyle's in his early twenties, he (now played by Chaney Kley) returns home at the behest of his one-time girlfriend, Caitlin (Emma Caulfield of TV's *Buffy the Vampire Slayer*). It seems Caitlin's little brother, Michael (Lee Cormie) is suffering from night terrors and is worried about the tooth fairy.

Kyle is not exactly in the position to help anyone—he is a paranoid who carries around multiple flashlights to ward off the scary tooth fairy—but he is still hot for Caitlin, so he sticks around. Here, the movie settles into the groove that it remains in for the rest of its running time. There are attacks, they occur every few minutes or so and they increase in intensity. Of course this violates the course that Matilda has previously taken. Why, after following a strict formula of operation for 150 years, would Matilda start killing lots of people randomly in a wild killing spree?

Then there's also the question of Matilda and light. According to the legend, Matilda will be repelled by light. That's the reason that Kyle is always carrying around the flashlights. But, when the plot can't get around that, she seems fine with light. If the filmmakers were to follow their own rules, Matilda's killings would all be in total darkness. Of course, a completely black screen doesn't make for the most compelling viewing, so it's understandable why they bend the rule for this one.

But why doesn't lightning deter Matilda? And how come a single flashlight beam deters her in some scene, but in others, large patches of light don't seem to have an effect? And as Jonathan Foreman of the *New York Post* pointed out, "Too often you find yourself wondering why, if the light-fearing ghost can smash windows, drag people out of cars and cut off the electricity to a whole town, she can't just flip the switch on lamps or flashlights." Several other critics noticed that in a scene where the power to a hospital is cut off, the characters are able to board and ride an elevator with no problem.

The creature itself is not horribly creepy. It's a figure wearing a black dress that swoops into scenes like a big bird and snatches away its prey. Accompanying its entrance are some spooky sound effects that don't change throughout the whole movie. The things that can make a horror movie really scary are either A.) a very frightening concept or B.) some good startling moments. *Darkness Fall* certainly doesn't have B). And it doesn't have any good jolts. The director doesn't seem to understand that it's unexpectedness that makes the jolts, well, unexpected and scary. He gives us the scares with such mind-numbing regularity that it's never a surprise when the next attack comes. He could use a good refresher course in the concept of suspense.

The acting in the film is not good, but really, how could it be in such a film? Despite being a drug-popping, possessed guy, Kley's Kyle couldn't be more bland and boring. He doesn't seem nearly haunted enough as someone should be after fleeing such a terror for over 12 years. Caulfield's Caitlin is worried about her brother, but her concern seems as much a ruse to see her old boyfriend again.

Critics, who were generally too old to fall for this tooth fairy business, didn't care for the film. John Petrakis of the *Chicago Tribune* wrote, "Have you ever wondered why critics will sometimes give a film they heartily dislike as much as one star? It's so there is room left in the depths of the ratings netherworld for an abomination like *Darkness Falls,* a lame-brained attempt at horror that is just a derivative pastiche of ideas lifted from other bad films." Kevin Thomas of the *Los Angeles Times* wrote, "Liebesman and his large crew cram as much style and energy as they can into a hokey and morbid supernatural thriller plot. It's a downer to see so much effort expended on so much junk." And Stephen Holden of the *New York Times* called it "about as scary as a ride on a minor roller coaster."

—*Jill Hamilton*

CREDITS

Kyle Walsh: Chaney Kley
Caitlin: Emma Caulfield
Michael: Lee Cormie
Larry: Grant Piro
Matt: Sullivan Stapleton
Dr. Murphy: Steve Mouzakis
Dr. Travis: Peter Curtain

Origin: USA
Released: 2003
Production: John Hegeman, John Fasano, William Sherak, Jason Shuman; Revolution Studios, Distant Corners, Blue Star Pictures; released by Columbia Pictures
Directed by: Jonathan Liebesman
Written by: John Fasano, James Vanderbilt, Joe Harris
Cinematography by: Dan Laustsen
Music by: Brian Tyler
Sound: John Schiefelbein
Editing: Steve Mirkovich, Tim Alverson
Art Direction: Tom Nursey
Costumes: Anna Borghesi
Production Design: George Liddle
MPAA rating: PG-13
Running time: 85 minutes

REVIEWS

Los Angeles Times Online. January 24, 2003.
New York Times Online. January 24, 2003.
Variety Online. January 22, 2003.
Washington Post. January 24, 2003, p. WE40.

A Decade Under the Influence

The 70's films that changed everything.
—Movie tagline

The late 1960s comprised a crucial time in American cinema. As the old Hollywood studio system was breaking down and quickly losing credibility, a new generation of filmmakers was rising up to experiment with subject matter and methods. The documentary *A Decade Under the Influence,* directed by Richard LaGravenese and Ted Demme, who died shortly after filming began, traces the key forces and personalities of this fabled era. The filmmakers begin their story in 1967 with such seminal films as *The Graduate* and *Bonnie and Clyde,* bringing it to a close in 1977, when *Star Wars* ushered in the age of the blockbuster. *Decade* is an entertaining and informative account of a time when a group of young, idealistic filmmakers unleashed a new, creative spirit, and it is a good introduction for audiences with little knowledge of this period. But cineasts looking for sophisticated analysis will be disappointed; the

film lacks an original point of view beyond basking in the nostalgic glow of a bygone era and suffers by not taking any critical stance toward its subject.

Relying mainly on interviews with writers, directors, producers, and actors along with extensive film clips, *Decade* does a superb job of laying out the confluence of factors that made the period unique. Having grown increasingly out of touch with the public, especially a young audience politicized by the Vietnam War and the Watergate scandal and immersed in the drug culture, the studios turned control over to young filmmakers to reinvigorate a system that had been producing a stale product. Authority was being questioned everywhere, social movements were rising, and, as a result, audiences were looking for something new and authentic, which meant seeing their lives reflected on the big screen. Director Sydney Pollack, one of the most articulate of the film's interviewees, points out that the old ideal was to go to a movie whose story was quite distant from one's own experience (*Casablanca,* for example), whereas the new ideal was just the opposite—young people in the audience could look at *The Graduate's* Benjamin Braddock and vicariously see themselves drifting into an uncertain future.

For inspiration, this new generation of filmmakers looked to foreign directors, who had their own styles apart from classical Hollywood, as well as to old Hollywood auteurs, who worked within the system but were nonetheless able to leave a unique mark on their work. *Bonnie and Clyde,* for example, took the old gangster genre, imbued it with the sensibility of a foreign film like Truffaut's *Jules and Jim,* and even dealt with sexual behavior that would have been verboten just a few years earlier.

Decade maintains a light tone, taking us on a trip through classic cinematic highlights but eschewing controversy along the way. John Cassavetes's maverick spirit and his emphasis on inner emotions are cited as influences on other directors (the documentary title itself is a salute to one of Cassavetes's best works, *A Woman Under the Influence,* which starred his wife, Gena Rowlands, in an incredibly raw performance). But Cassavetes's loose, meandering style is not universally adored—it could even be labeled self-indulgent—and it is one of *Decade's* major shortcomings that no dissenting opinions are voiced about his work or, for that matter, anyone else's. Because LaGravenese and Demme obviously love this era, they maintain a worshipful tone, but it is an irony that a film celebrating rebellion and iconoclasm should adopt such a reverential point of view.

Likewise, every film discussed is treated as a classic when in fact many critics would argue that some of these films have not aged very well or were bad to begin with. Indeed, this period, like any before or since, produced plenty of awful movies. *Easy Rider* is a perfect example. From a sociological perspective, there is no doubt that Dennis Hopper's biker flick embodied the countercultural values of the time and launched a young Jack Nicholson into stardom.

But today it would be charitable to say merely that the film does not hold up; much of it is simply unwatchable.

However, from this documentary and especially Hopper's entertaining recollections on the filmmaking, one would assume that *Easy Rider* is on a par with another film from 1969—*Midnight Cowboy*, a gritty slice of New York life with galvanizing performances by Jon Voight and Dustin Hoffman. Actress Julie Christie, who is particularly astute in her interview clips, lavishes well-deserved praise on *Midnight Cowboy*. The film, despite assaulting traditional sensibilities with its tale of a male hustler and his crippled companion on the mean streets of New York, managed to win favor with the establishment as well as the Academy Award for Best Picture.

The most enlightening moments in the documentary are those in which the filmmakers give fans a new perspective on their films. Screenwriter Robert Towne discusses *The Last Detail*'s rough language, one of the new freedoms of the era, as an expression of the characters' impotence—not their power, as one might expect. Director William Friedkin touches on his use of the documentary style in *The French Connection*—particularly in the famous chase sequence—and the sense of realism he brought to the horror genre in *The Exorcist*, which was based on an actual case of demonic possession. He believed what was happening in the film and adopted an attitude of "we're not kidding, folks." Peter Bogdanovich talks about *The Last Picture Show*'s roots in his love of old Hollywood, with the added candor of clumsy teenage sex.

It is important to remember, though, that such freedom would have been impossible without the lifting of the repressive Production Code, which was instituted in 1934 and essentially censored specific subjects for more than three decades. No one interviewed mentions the abandonment of the Code, probably because acknowledging this important institutional change would weaken the documentary's portrait of individual filmmakers bucking the system and liberating American cinema in the process.

When the greats are given their due, however, they are discussed in ways that seem all too familiar. It is by now a cliché to call Robert Altman's *M*A*S*H** "deeply irreverent about war" or speak of the "subversion of genre" in the excellent, revisionist Western, *McCabe and Mrs. Miller*. But *Nashville*, arguably the filmmaker's most complex work and perhaps his most Altmanesque in its juggling of so many characters, its disinterest in traditional storytelling, and its kaleidoscopic view of American culture, is not mentioned. Francis Ford Coppola talks about his youth and Italian-American heritage helping him to snag the job directing *The Godfather*, which he saw as a Shakespearean tragedy dressed up in gangster garb. And Martin Scorsese ruminates on the dilemma of being an American filmmaker with a European sensibility. (We already know from Scorsese's documentary *My Voyage to Italy* how he was influenced by the Italian cinema of his youth.)

Social upheaval was just as significant as the rise of the visionary director in this era. Because women's roles were not very good at this time, Ellen Burstyn was thrilled to be offered *Alice Doesn't Live Here Anymore,* a movie about a single mother making her way in the world. It was a role that reflected the real experiences of many women as well as the burgeoning feminist movement. Other films reflected a climate of unease, from *All the President's Men* reinforcing a distrust in government to *Shampoo* satirizing the social, sexual, and political mores of the time and exploring, in screenwriter Towne's words, "all the hypocrisies great and small." It is not hard to see why Friedkin believes that "moral ambiguity" is the one phrase that best sums up the filmmaking of this time.

But there would soon be a cultural shift in favor of more positive, uplifting entertainment. The same year Hollywood released Martin Scorsese's *Taxi Driver,* a dark character study of a deranged yet oddly sympathetic loner bent on cleaning up a dirty New York City, and Sidney Lumet's *Network,* a scathing satire of the media, America also embraced *Rocky,* the optimistic tale of an underdog boxer who beats the odds. According to *Decade,* however, even more important than a change in the zeitgeist was the arrival of a new kind of movie—the blockbuster film—that is expensive to produce, plays in lots of theaters, and attracts audiences in huge numbers. Steven Spielberg's *Jaws* in 1975 followed by George Lucas's *Star Wars* two years later started this phenomenon, which is a major force to the present day. Since the typical blockbuster movie fit a certain mold and the unique sensibility of the filmmaker was not perceived as crucial to its creation, the studios regained the control they had ceded to the young upstarts years earlier.

Interestingly enough, Spielberg and Lucas declined to be interviewed for the documentary; perhaps they knew that their mass-audience appeal would frame them as the film's bad guys, the crowd pleasers who supposedly ended the independent spirit of the '70s. It is fascinating to see how other directors comment on their influence. "It's not the filmmakers' fault," Scorsese claims, instead blaming the studios for using Spielberg and Lucas as a gauge—a diplomatic way of criticizing the mentality they spawned rather than the filmmakers themselves. Bogdanovich, who has never had the widespread success or acclaim of Scorsese, is much stronger in his criticism, disparaging the whole phenomenon as "bread and circuses."

And yet while a case can be made that the rise of the blockbuster helped to end socially conscious, risky filmmaking, it is clearly a simplistic explanation and not the whole story. After all, the social and political climate could not remain in a rebellious mode forever, and changing times meant that different kinds of movies would be produced. More important, many of these giants simply lost their way.

After *Nashville* in 1975, Altman did not enjoy widespread critical success until *The Player* in 1992. Coppola got mired in his own Vietnam on the troubled *Apocalypse Now,* a film that still divides critics despite its sometimes brilliant passages. While it is not discussed in *Decade,* the overextended, over-budget shoot of *Apocalypse Now* could have provided a very different ending for this study by highlighting the egomania and self-indulgence of the quintessential '70s auteur, instead of pinning the decade's decline on Spielberg and Lucas.

Clearly LaGravenese and Demme did not wish to push any topics that would be less than flattering to their heroes. But if the artists interviewed had engaged in some measure of self-criticism, *Decade* would have been a much richer work instead of an often self-serving picture of a supposedly unblemished golden era. While celebrating the great work of this period, one should remember that every decade produces its classics, and directors today still make challenging, original films. They may not always be as overtly political or as widely embraced as they were in the years chronicled in this documentary, but they still flourish and await discerning audiences willing to seek them out.

—Peter N. Chumo II

CREDITS

Origin: USA
Released: 2002
Production: Richard LaGravenese, Ted Demme, Gini Reticker, Jerry Kupfer; Written in Stone, Constant Communications; released by IFC Films
Directed by: Richard LaGravenese, Ted (Edward) Demme
Cinematography by: Clyde Smith, Anthony Janelli
Music by: John Kimbrough
Sound: Andy Kris
Editing: Meg Reticker
MPAA rating: R
Running time: 180 minutes

REVIEWS

Boxoffice. April, 2003, p. 17.
Los Angeles Times Online. May 30, 2003.
Los Angeles Times Online. August 20, 2003.
New York Times Online. April 25, 2003.
Variety Online. January 24, 2003.

Deliver Us from Eva

Lead us into temptation but . . .
—Movie tagline

 Box Office: $17.3 million

Deliver Us From Eva was directed by Gary Hardwick, who also helmed the film *The Brothers.* Like that film, *Eva* is enjoyable to watch. It's full of good looking people wearing nice clothes, hanging out in attractively decorated apartments and saying mildly amusing things. And like that film, there's a mating dance that—and we don't think we're spoiling anything here—turns out well in the end. Even the problem with *Deliver Us From Eva* is the same one that *The Brothers* had. As pleasant as the film is to watch, it's the kind of thing that floats as quickly and easily from one's mind as painlessly as it came in. This is a pardonable flaw. *Deliver Us From Eva* isn't pretending to be any more than it is.

It's no mistake that the title makes a pun with Eva's name and "evil." To her sisters' men, Eva is an evil. Eva (Gabrielle Union) and her fellow Dandridge sisters, Kareenah (Essence Atkins), Bethany (Robinne Lee) and Jacqui (Megan Good), are the most desirable women in town. They are beautiful and ambitious. Their boyfriends or husbands would consider themselves the luckiest guys around except for the fact that Eva is way too involved with their lives.

When the girls were young, their parents died and Eva took on the role of authority figure for the girls. Now that the girls are women, they still turn to their big sister for guidance and advice. Eva relishes the role, perhaps too much. She is sharp-tongued and quick to criticize any real or perceived infraction by one of the men. Eva does such hideous things as making the guys give up watching a football game so that she and her sisters can have a book club. Lest we miss the message, Hardwick gives us such suggestive cuts as ending one of Eva's tirades on how bad men are with a shot of her roughly slicing a cucumber.

Actually, the Eva in this movie is pretty darn evil. She is a health inspector and delights in writing up restaurants, then berating the owners if they protest. Her life knowledge seems to come wholly from magazine articles she's read and she cites them with smug authority. She won't let Bethany live with boyfriend, Mike, saying that it's a bad idea. She interferes with the sex life of Jacqui and her postal carrier husband, Darrell. Kareenah won't have children with her husband Tim because Eva has counseled her to wait at least three years. Clearly, this lady has to go.

As anyone using sitcom logic would decide, Darrell (Dartanyan Edmonds), Tim (Mel Jackson) and Mike (Duane Martin) decide that the best way to rid themselves of the Eva problem is to enlist the help of the biggest player they know, Ray (rapper LL Cool J, who in this movie is billed by his given name, James Todd Smith). Their wacky idea is that they will pay Ray $5000 plus expenses to woo Eva, lure her out of town, then dump her. The fact that Ray takes this deal shows that he's not exactly fine date material, but in this movie, like in most romantic comedies, such large male lapses of morality are eminently excusable.

What gets Ray to accept the deal is seeing Eva yell at a hapless restaurant owner. "If I can get that woman, I'll go down in the Player Hall of Fame." It's an admirable goal indeed, so Ray gets to work. He woos Eva by the time honored technique of pretending to have a girlfriend. All of Eva's magazine reading is no help in this situation and she's soon interested. Ray's pretend girlfriend conveniently disappears from the scene and the two are free to date.

It doesn't seem like it would work. Eva is ruthlessly ambitious and organized and Ray is the kind of guy who drifts from job to job to keep from getting tied down. He picks up Eva for their date in the truck that he uses to deliver meat. But this is LL Cool J, after all, and those familiar with rap trivia will remember that the name stands for Ladies Love Cool James. No matter what happens on the date, Ray just keeps smiling his confident smile, as though he's having the best time in the world. It works, and soon the couple is having the kind of conversation that signify that movie couples are getting serious about each other. Yes, they talk about their feelings and encourage each other to follow their dreams.

Of course this is not the end of it. There is the obvious complication that Ray ends up falling for Eva. And of course Eva finds out about it and becomes angered. And there are some not so obvious complications, like the guys deciding it would be a good solution to their problems to fake Ray's death.

The commentary on the action is courtesy of the hairdressers at the local beauty parlor. The Dandridge sisters seem to spend an inordinate amount of time there while they discuss their love woes with the bawdy Ormandy (Kym Whitley) and sassy Telly (Royale Watkins). Ormandy and Telly are kind of one-hit wonders. Ormandy answers everything with some sort of comment about how she's going to get laid and the Telly schtick is that he's gay.

Eva's sisters and their significant others are true side characters. We get an idea of their relationship situations but nothing more than that. The wives are marginally more developed than the husbands/boyfriend. The guys are little more that a pack of defeated and pissed off men who follow behind the women grumbling among themselves. Union and Smith are good in their leads. Union doesn't hedge on showing the more unattractive qualities of Eva and her

Taming of the Screw-like melting is believable and well-paced. And Smith has an easy charisma that makes him a good romantic lead.

Many reviewers noted the similarities to *The Taming of the Shrew* and the sitcom quality of the story. Stephen Holden of the *New York Times* wrote, "If *Deliver Us From Eva* is amusing, it is not uproarious. Like all well-made sitcoms, it offers creaturely reassurance." Ty Burr of the *Boston Globe* wrote that the film "dawdles amiably and can't quite decide what it wants to be. It starts out as a boys-will-be-dawgs farce of bad behavior, downshifts into *The Taming of the Screw* territory, makes several stops in a local hair salon for some lesser *Barbershop* shenanigans, and then cruises into the home stretch as a likable but perilously thin buppie romance, complete with a final and dramatic declaration of love to send the dates home cuddling." Kevin Thomas of the *Los Angeles Times* wrote, "Smith and Union play off each other smartly—and steamily—and blend into an effective ensemble cast. *Deliver Us From Eva* flows smoothly, looks great and probably cost lots less than it looks."

—*Jill Hamilton*

CREDITS

Eva Dandridge: Gabrielle Union
Ray Adams: L.L. Cool J.
Mike: Duane Martin
Kareenah: Essence Atkins
Bethany: Robbine Lee
Jacqui: Meagan Good
Tim: Mel Jackson
Darrell: Dartanyan Edmonds
Ormandy: Kym E. Whitley
Telly: Royale Watkins
Oscar: Matt Winston
Rashaun: Ruben Paul
Lucius Johnson: Dorian Gregory

Origin: USA
Released: 2003
Production: Paddy Cullen, Len Amato; Spring Creek Productions, Baltimore Pictures; released by Focus Features
Directed by: Gary Hardwick
Written by: Gary Hardwick, James Iver Mattson, B.E. Brauner
Cinematography by: Alexander Grusynski
Music by: Marcus Miller
Sound: Russell Williams II
Music Supervisor: Alison Ball, David Lombard
Editing: Earl Watson

Art Direction: William Hiney
Costumes: Debrae Little
Production Design: Edward T. McAvoy
MPAA rating: R
Running time: 105 minutes

REVIEWS

Boxoffice. January, 2003, p. 27.
Chicago Sun-Times Online. February 7, 2003.
Entertainment Weekly. February 14, 2003, p. 54.
Los Angeles Times Online. February 7, 2003.
New York Times Online. February 7, 2003.
People. February 17, 2003, p. 34.
USA Today Online. February 7, 2003.
Variety Online. February 1, 2003.
Washington Post. February 7, 2003, p. WE48.

QUOTES

Ray (L.L. Cool J.) about Eva (Gabrielle Union): "If I can get that woman, I'll go down in the player hall of fame!"

Demonlover

There are films that seem destined to become cult films. Some of these are so quirky and unique that they will always find an audience. Others are just so darned weird that being a cult film is about the only way they have to go. Such is the case with *demonlover*, a film that is so strange it pushes the edges of being comprehensible. Many moviegoers complain that modern films are too predictable and formulaic; *demonlover* avoids those traps, but goes a little too far in the other direction. Creativity and lack of strict structure are generally good things, but some viewers might be put off by the lack of coherence here. Maybe some of us have become too accustomed to having our plots spelled out to us and just aren't smart enough to follow groundbreaking, newfangled storytelling. Maybe it's just that we expect movies to make some sense.

The film is the project of French filmmaker Olivier Assayas. In 1996, he made a similarly boundary-pushing film called *Irma Vep*. He followed this with some more traditional works like 2000's *Les Destinees*. But the writer/director is more interested in the art of the film than its ability to tell a straightforward story. Manohla Dargis of the

Los Angeles Times explains: "For Assayas, moviemaking isn't simply about beautiful images and novel stories; it's an epistemology—a way of understanding movies and, by extension, a way of understanding the world. The same goes for moviewatching. If that sounds like the makings of a dry intellectual exercise, the work itself is anything but academic. A former film critic, Assayas likes his visual pleasures. He may want to know why some images turn us on—why our skin tingles, our hearts pound—but he also enjoys making us swoon." Thus, it is possible to not at all understand *demonlover,* but to appreciate the images in it.

Most viewers will at least be able to stick with the story for the first part of the film because it's fairly conventional. It seems to be a straightforward corporate thriller. Karen (Dominique Reymond), an executive at VolfGroup, a French firm, is kidnapped by some bad guys, thrown into the trunk of the car and left. She eventually gets out, but her all-important briefcase has been stolen. While she is recuperating, her icy colleague Diane (Connie Nielsen) takes her place. Karen's assistant (Chloe Sevigny, who despite her name, had to learn the French for her role) has an instantly combative relationship with Diane. She also spars with her debonair coworker, Herve (Charles Berling), but their combative relationship also has a sexy undercurrent.

VolfGroup is trying to set up a deal with a Japanese company that is working on developing sexually explicit 3-D animation. As he is wont to do, Assayas lets his camera linger on whatever sexual and/or violent images his story comes upon. Here it's the 2-D sexually explicit material that the company is currently working on. We see something that looks like the anime of *Spirited Away,* but then the childlike girls in the film start doing some very non-childlike things with each other, with giant mutating creatures, with appliances that are lying around, etc. If anything sticks in your mind about the film, this probably would be it.

VolfGroup has some hesitations about working with the Japanese company, TokyoAnime, because it is suspected that they are involved with a secret online torture website called Hellfire Club. Again, Assayas enjoys showing the various torture situations on the site. It's hard to say which is more disturbing—this or the cartoon Pokemon-like girls having sex on the 2-D site.

There is also something in there about an American firm, demonlover, which is a direct competitor of the Japanese firm. This contingent is led by Elaine (Gina Gershon), a loud brash American. There is another competing firm called Magnatronics that is trying to spoil the deal. This is about the last coherent thing in the film. From here, there are plot twists that have good people turning out bad or vice versa. Diane might be a corporate spy. Things happen, or maybe they don't really. It's hard to say. It's hard to be upset about one character murdering another when it's not clear if it even happened. What is the point of showing a fight and murder that might not have even happened? Is it simply to show the violence? Assayas punctuates his startling visuals with an equally jarring soundtrack by Sonic Youth.

On the website *RottenTomatoes.com,* which compiles critical reviews, the reviewers were pretty evenly split on the merits of the film. Roger Ebert of the *Chicago Sun-Times* complained, "By the end of the movie, I frankly didn't give a damn. I think *demonlover* is so in love with its visuals and cockeyed plot that it forgets to think about its implications." Owen Gleiberman of *Entertainment Weekly* gave the film a B and commented, "No doubt about it: Assayas is a major talent. He also, unfortunately, has major pretensions. The movie morphs into a 'dream,' all right, but I confess that all I wanted to do was wake up from it and return to the slithery intrigue of corporate depravity." Dargis of the *Los Angeles Times* called it "an exasperating, irresistible, must-see mess of a movie about life in the modern world and so very good that even when its story finally crashes and burns the filmmaking remains unscathed." Ty Burr of the *Boston Globe* wrote, "'Everyone watches, but no one understands,' says Diane . . . She could be speaking for the characters and the audience, since this dark examination of the line between the real and the virtual ultimately disappears down its own digital rabbit hole."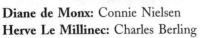

—*Jill Hamilton*

Diane de Monx: Connie Nielsen
Herve Le Millinec: Charles Berling
Elise Lipsky: Chloe Sevigny
Elaine Si Gibril: Gina Gershon
Karen: Dominique Reymond
Henri-Pierre Volf: Jean-Baptiste Malartre

Origin: France
Released: 2002
Production: Edouard Weil, Xavier Giannoli; TPS Cinema, Elizabeth Films, M6 Films; released by Palm Pictures
Directed by: Olivier Assayas
Written by: Olivier Assayas
Cinematography by: Denis Lenoir
Music by: Sonic Youth
Sound: Philippe Richard
Editing: Luc Barnier
Costumes: Anais Romand
Production Design: Francois-Renaud Lebarthe
MPAA rating: Unrated
Running time: 120 minutes

Boxoffice. July, 2002, p. 79.
Chicago Sun-Times Online. September 19, 2003.
Entertainment Weekly. October 10, 2003, p. 102.
Los Angeles Times Online. September 19, 2003.
New York Times Online. September 19, 2003.
Variety. June 3, 2002, p. 24.
Washington Post. September 19, 2003, p. WE41.

Dickie Roberts: Former Child Star

50 million people used to watch him on TV. Now he washes their cars.
—Movie tagline

Box Office: $22.7 million

It's not the most flattering thing for your movie career if critics repeatedly mention that another actor would have been better playing your role. This is especially true if said role is one that you wrote specifically for yourself. Such was the case with David Spade (known much more for TV roles on *Saturday Night Live* and *Just Shoot Me* than in movie roles like the title character of *Joe Dirt*) and his film *Dickie Roberts: Former Child Star.* He wrote the film with ex-*SNL* buddy Fred Wolf—the duo was also responsible for *Joe Dirt*—and presumably was trying to write a role that would be tailor-made for Spade's acting abilities. But Stephen Holden of the *New York Times* wrote of the film, "Should you choose to watch David Spade play the now grown up kiddie icon of a popular 1970's television sitcom in *Dickie Roberts: Former Child Star,* you may be nagged by the thought of how much funnier it might have been with Jim Carrey in the title role." Roger Ebert of the *Chicago Sun-Times* echoed the sentiment: "*Dickie Roberts: Former Child Star* has a premise that would be catnip for Steve Martin or Jim Carrey, but David Spade . . . casts a pall of smarmy sincerity over the material."

And a big part of the problem of *Dickie Roberts* does seem to be Spade. He's made his name playing a whiney, cranky guy who thinks he's an insider. In *Dickie Roberts,* he is required to be in some scenes that are sappy and sentimental. They are the kind of scenes that Spade's usual characters would dismiss with a pithy one-liner.

If the writers and director Sam Weisman (who helmed such fare as *George of the Jungle* and *What's the Worst That*

Could Happen?) had cut out the sap, *Dickie Roberts* might have been a much more enjoyable film. But the film was made by Adam Sandler's production company Happy Madison and like most of the films from that outfit tries the weird combo of comedy with one-dimensional sentimentality.

It all starts off well. The movie is set up like an episode of *E! True Hollywood Story*. It's telling the tale of adorable child actor Dickie Roberts, who was the breakout star of a 1970s sitcom. With his popular catchphrase, "This is nucking futs!" he was propelled to superstardom. But soon after, the show's ratings dropped, and the sitcom was abruptly canceled. His disinterested mother (she wore an "I'm with stupid" t-shirt with the arrow pointing to her belly when she was pregnant with Dickie) ditches Dickie when she moves "out of the area."

Now 35, Dickie (Spade) is an out-of-work actor who earns money as a valet parker at the Los Angeles eatery Morton's. In one of the more amusing parts of the film, Dickie shares a weekly poker game with other former child stars played by such real-life child stars as Danny Bonaduce, Leif Garrett, Corey Feldman, Dustin "Screech" Diamond and Barry "Greg Brady" Williams. The group bitterly complains about the current state of Hollywood: "George Clooney? What's that all about?" It's fun to imagine a weekly poker game of such folk and to see how they have weathered life since fame.

Even though it's been years since he was a star, Dickie still thinks he's on the verge of a comeback. He keeps searching for that one big break, even though his mean girlfriend, Cyndi (Alyssa Milano, a former child star herself), makes a big point of saying that's she quite doubtful that that's ever going to happen. His chance comes when Garrett mentions that Rob Reiner is casting a new film. Dickie knows that if he can get that part, he will become famous again, and all of his problems will be solved.

He asks his agent Sidney (Jon Lovitz) to get him a meeting with Reiner but Sidney says, "That's out of our league." In a lucky twist of fate, however, Dickie runs into Brendan Fraser (in a cameo) on the street, and despite insulting him, manages to convince Fraser to set up a meeting with Reiner. At the meeting, Reiner (also in a cameo) tells Dickie that he has the right look for the part, but won't get the role because he's "not a real person." Since Dickie never had a normal childhood, he doesn't know, and thus won't be able to play, the emotions required for the role.

A desperate Dickie decides that he needs to experience a normal childhood in the one month before Reiner starts casting his film. He takes $20,000 from a $30,000 advance he's gotten for a tell-all autobiography and hires a family to give him a normal childhood. This is the premise for the movie, and it is a bad one. Of course many movies require a certain suspension of disbelief, but this *Dickie Roberts* prem-

ise is just silly. Could anyone possibly believe that one month with a "regular" family could give a person the equivalent of a normal childhood? This is especially true of Dickie since he's the kind of showbiz-damaged person that wears gloves 24 hours a day.

To make matters worse, the writers show Dickie and his new family—career-obsessed absentee dad George Finney (Craig Bierko); "hot" mom Grace (Mary McCormack); and straight-arrow kids Sam (Scott Terra) and Sally (Jenna Boyd)—in the more stereotypical of suburban family situations. Grace and the kids, for example, stage a Christmas scene where Dickie gets a new red bike. In one scene, Grace pushes Dickie down the street in a baby stroller. In spite of the negligible funniness of this sight gag, what's the point? In another scene, Sam and Sally teach Dickie the joys of childhood by playing with a Slip 'n Slide. Dickie runs and dives before there's any water on it and gives himself a bad chest burn. Besides barely being funny, that particular scene also caused the producers of *Dickie Roberts* to be sued by the toy's makers for not showing the toy being used in a proper manner or by a person of appropriate age. There was nothing in the suit mentioning the toy being used in a scene lacking a proper level of humor.

As the movie progresses, things keep getting less funny and more sappy. Dickie starts thinking that the Finney kids are a-okay and helps them with the local bullies and the like. The family sees the good inner Dickie behind the would-be hipster. But perhaps most disturbing, Dickie starts falling for his "mommy." This relationship doesn't work on many levels. First, there's the whole mommy thing. And it isn't helped by the fact that the two actors have zero chemistry.

Unfortunately, the failure of the movie is aided by the acting of the kids portraying the two young Finneys. Terra, especially, doesn't seem to be able to form more than a couple of different expressions. He and Boyd play the "normal" kids like freakish Stepford children, and it doesn't seem like it's meant to be ironic.

The main thing this film has going for it is all the real child stars it contains. At the end of the film, there's a "We are the World"-style sing-along featuring a bleacher full of former child stars from shows like *What's Happening?*, *Eight is Enough*, and *Happy Days*. The idea of a movie that explores what it's like to be a former child star could have been quite good, but *Dickie Roberts* messes up the chance. Instead of following the interesting aspects of the concept, it goes with tired family sitcom-type jokes.

Critics didn't much like the film. Rob Blackwelder of *Spliced Wire* called it "another ill-conceived mish-mash of puerile humor and disingenuous sap from Adam Sandler's Happy Madison production company." Ebert wrote, "There are laughs, to be sure, and some gleeful supporting performances, but after a promising start, the movie sinks into a bog of sentiment." The *Washington Post*'s Ann

Hornaday said of the film, "*Dickie Roberts* is admittedly warmer and better-mannered than most of Sandler's lunkhead screeds—in other words, it's harmless—but it's never entirely likable." Of course, some disagreed. Kevin Thomas of the *Los Angeles Times* felt that the film was "full of sass and sentiment, managing to be both raunchy and sweet-natured."

—*Jill Hamilton*

CREDITS

Dickie Roberts: David Spade
Grace Finney: Mary McCormack
George Finney: Craig Bierko
Sidney: Jon Lovitz
Cyndi: Alyssa Milano
Peggy: Doris Roberts
Sally Finney: Jenna Boyd
Sam Finney: Scott Tessa
Neighbor: Edie McClurg
Himself: Rob Reiner (Cameo)
Himself: Leif Garrett (Cameo)
Himself: Brendan Fraser (Cameo)

Origin: USA
Released: 2003
Directed by: Sam Weisman
Written by: David Spade, Fred Wolf
Cinematography by: Thomas Ackerman
Music by: Christophe Beck, Waddy Wachtel
Sound: David M. Kelson
Music Supervisor: Michael Dilbeck
Editing: Roger Bondelli
Art Direction: Marc Dabe
Costumes: Lisa Jensen
Production Design: Dina Lipton
MPAA rating: PG-13
Running time: 99 minutes

REVIEWS

Chicago Sun-Times Online. September 5, 2003.
Entertainment Weekly. September 12, 2003, p. 130.
Los Angeles Times Online. September 5, 2003.
New York Times Online. September 5, 2003.
People. September 15, 2003, p. 39.
USA Today Online. September 5, 2003.
Variety Online. September 1, 2003.
Washington Post. September 5, 2003, p. WE41.

Die Mommie Die!

Hollywood . . . it's a dirty town but Someone *has to do it!*
—Movie tagline

When *Die Mommie Die!* opened for limited release in New York City and Los Angeles, large placards were placed outside of theater entrances saying that the theaters had a court-ordered mandate to say that the movie was based on the play *One Night Stand in a Lonely Hotel* by Charles Castillo. Castillo was waging a successful lawsuit against Charles Busch, who claims to have written the screenplay based on his own long-running stage play. A week or so later, the placards came down after a judge found insufficient similarities between *Die Mommie Die!* and Castillo's play.

The lawsuit was strange because *Die Mommie Die!* is so, well, unique. It's one thing that there would be, say, two similar action movies involving plots with one guy who saves the world from a new ultra-destructive weapon. It's quite another to discover that there are two involving dramatic drag queens playing 1960's-era murderous singing divas.

Busch has been a successful artist on the New York stage for years, as a drag performer and a writer (*The Tale of the Allergist's Wife*). *Die Mommie Die* is based on one of his plays which originated in Los Angeles in 1999. The film version first reached wider audiences as part of the Sundance Film series.

Busch's director, Mark Rucker, was a longtime theatrical director, but *Die Mommie Die!* was his first foray into film. The two decided that they wanted to make the film an homage to so-called "women's films" of the mid-part of the 20th century. They watched hundreds of hours of these kinds of films, with such stars as Joan Crawford and Bette Davis, and studied them intently to get a feel for the costumes, the lighting, the acting and the dialogue. The homework paid off. The biggest fun of *Die Mommie Die!* is seeing these recognizable elements playing out again. Costumer Thomas G. Marquez, for example, clothes heroine Angela Arden (Busch) in a mind-boggling array of stunning and over-the-top clothes. Even when doing something as simple as swimming, Arden is dressed to the nines, with a flowing, dramatic beach robe, fancy bathing cap, and the like. Busch has the kind of dignity that allows him to wear such over-the-top clothing and make it look like the kind of stuff that befits a grand dame. Director of photography, Kelly Evans, makes sure to use flattering camera filters and overly flattering lighting for her heroine. It's fun to notice all the artifice that goes into creating such a heroine. The film has a wonderful look and it's amazing to realize it was shot in only 18 days.

Angela is a songstress, once known as *America's Nightingale*, who's now retired and living in a failed marriage with her producer husband, Sol Sussman (Philip Baker Hall). When Sol isn't discussing his longtime constipation, he's barking out his motto, "Make it big, give it class, and leave them with a message." Daughter Edith (Natasha Lyonne) loves (or is in love with) her father and hates her mother for cheating on him. Gay son Lance (Stark Sands) has been suspended from school for engaging the entire math department in a sexual interlude.

Angela was once a part of a duo with her twin sister, Barbara, but Angela soon broke out on her own. Angela quickly became a singing sensation with her signature hit "Why Not Me?" (The "old" footage of her singing the song on stage is right on.) After Barbara's mysterious death, Angela abruptly quit the business. She occupies herself by tending her roses and having an affair with the handsome Tony Parker (Jason Priestly), a former actor and rumored gigolo.

When Sol finds out about the affair, he cuts Angela off financially, but demands she remain in the marriage. Angela can't think of any better solution to this new situation than to kill her husband. She does it by giving him a suppository that has been dipped in rat poison. Edith immediately suspects that her mother is behind the death and tries to enlist her brother's help in avenging her father's death. And the family's overly moralistic housekeeper, Bootsie Carp (Frances Conroy), may want to be in on the plan, too.

Although the plot has murder, orgies, surprise twists and even an evil twin, the real star of the film is the way it's all portrayed. The dialogue, for example, is perfect. Pills are called "dolls," people say things like "Amen, sister" and Angela is constantly saying such things as, "One feels the memory lingering, like smog over the canyon." When making a typically big exit, Angela spouts, "The only thing in this dump that doesn't make me puke is the door 'cause that's the way I'm getting out of here." After attending a show together, Sol tells Angela, "Shut up! The best performance of the night was you pretending to be a wife." And of course there is innuendo lurking everywhere. When Lance is told that "Sometimes you have to face things that are hard to swallow," his gaze immediately falls upon Tony's crotch.

Artifice is celebrated in this film. Whenever minor characters, such as a group of ambulance drivers, have a quick scene, they are invariably drop-dead gorgeous guys. The Sussman house is a Beverly Hills wonder, with period furniture and the requisite back yard pool. Even the film's opening credits are written in the kind of old-movie font that's instantly familiar.

But no matter how great the film looks, it's success rests on the performance of its lead actress/actor. Busch is up to the task. He's every inch the grand diva. Although the movie couldn't be sillier, Busch plays it straight. Angela is the type of woman who is always conscious that she's giving a performance, even if she's talking to her family. Busch has the haughtiness and sense of drama that's just right for Angela. He

easily carries the whole movie on his glamorously clothed shoulders.

Mostly, critics had a good time at the film. Kevin Thomas of the *Los Angeles Times* wrote, "*Die Mommie Die!* has great fun demolishing pretense and the facade of respectability while never hitting a false note." Wesley Morris of the *Boston Globe* observed, "Busch combines French absurdist theater and American performance art with a drag queen's flamboyant wit." And Stephen Holden of the *New York Times* stated, "*Die Mommie Die!* is really Mr. Busch's show. Within the cramped limitations of drag, he exudes a genuine screen charisma. That star quality as much [as] anything should earn the film a niche in camp heaven." Ruthe Stein of the *San Francisco Chronicle* wasn't a fan and complained, "*Die Mommie Die!* winds up neither hilarious nor a credible spoof of a genre intent on spoofing itself."

—*Jill Hamilton*

CREDITS

Angela Arden: Charles Busch
Edith Sussman: Natasha Lyonne
Tony Parker: Jason Priestley
Bootsie Carp: Frances Conroy
Sol Sussman: Philip Baker Hall
Lance Sussman: Stark Sands
Sam Fishbein: Victor Raider-Wexler
Shatzi Van Allen: Nora Dunn

Origin: USA
Released: 2003
Production: Dante Di Loreto, Anthony Edwards, Bill Kenwright; released by Sundance Films
Directed by: Mark Rucker
Written by: Charles Busch
Cinematography by: Kelly Evans
Music by: Dennis McCarthy
Sound: Jon Ailetcher
Editing: Philip Harrison
Costumes: Thomas G. Marquez, Michael Bottari, Ronald Case
Production Design: Joseph B. Tintfass
MPAA rating: R
Running time: 90 minutes

REVIEWS

Chicago Sun-Times Online. October 31, 2003.
Entertainment Weekly. November 7, 2003, p. 54.
Los Angeles Times Online. October 31, 2003.
New York Times Online. October 31, 2003.

Variety Online. January 21, 2003.
Washington Post. October 31, 2003, p. C5.

Dirty Pretty Things

Some things are too dangerous to keep secret.
—Movie tagline

Every dream has its price.
—Movie tagline

 Box Office: $8.1 million

"**W**ho are you?" asks a bag man, receiving illicit goods from three strangers in a London hotel parking garage, in an iconic scene in Stephen Frears's subtly intoxicating genre-smasher *Dirty Pretty Things.* "We are the people you do not see," answers Okwe (Chiwetel Ejiofor), the story's protagonist, an illegal alien and political exile from Liberia, standing with a Turkish and another African illegal. "We are the people who drive your cars, clean your rooms," and perform sexual services.

Far from being a film packed with such rhetorical flourishes, *Dirty Pretty Things* is straightforward, making this climactic declaration all the more effective. The illegal immigrants in this story must endure all manner of degradation, threats, and coercion before they achieve a gruesome and remarkable measure of vengeance and partial liberation. But Frears never comes close to romanticizing them or their plight, and he does not provide a satisfying, happy ending, only a hint of hope for a way out.

Dirty Pretty Things isn't a political statement about the oppression of undocumented foreigners in England—it's far too coy and clever and realistic to be waving any flags. It's also not just a character study, a love story, or a crime mystery—although it has elements of all three. The film is elusive, slippery, and not easy to pigeonhole. Just when you think it's settling down, it takes a surprising new turn. Yet it is also quiet, thoughtful, and not intended as just a crowd-pleaser.

At the center of the story is Okwe, who is both a larger- and smaller-than-life figure. Larger than life because he is kind, generous, and tireless; but smaller because he is beaten down and trapped, and because Frears refuses to make him into a heroic figure. Constantly on the go, he works two jobs—as a cab driver for a company that specializes in helping immigrants get from the airport and get set up somewhere in south London, and as a night clerk at a hotel where suspicious things are happening. He stays awake by getting some sort of herbal stimulant from some friends at a local store, and he almost naps on the couch at the apartment

of Senay (Audrey Tautou), a Turkish illegal who works as a maid at the same hotel.

But Okwe, for some reason, is afraid to fall asleep. It's not clear how long Okwe has been in London, but he seems to know a lot of people and have many contacts in the "underground" world of south London immigrants. One of them is a porter at the local hospital's morgue, a wise and wisecracking Asian man he constantly beats at chess and who is a source of help in getting medical supplies. Because it's become known to the person who runs the cab company that Okwe was actually a doctor in Nigeria, he fetches medicine to treat the boss and the workers there who have caught a sexually transmitted disease from a prostitute.

The film deftly illustrates how a great number of things happen in Okwe's world through bartering. Immigrants try to help each other as best they can—although some are out to exploit and take advantage of each other. There are petty bosses, like the man at the cab company, and more sinister higher-ups, like Okwe's boss at the hotel, the villain of the story. Even he was not so long ago an immigrant. The only "real" British person in the film is the fellow porter on Okwe's night shift at the hotel, and he is something of a light spoof on dissipated, amoral English manhood.

Frears is returning to his roots in gritty, working-class drama set among London's immigrant classes (as in *My Beautiful Laundrette*) after showing he could master Hollywood drama and comedy (*High Fidelity*). *Dirty Pretty Things,* surprisingly marks the screenwriting debut of Steve Knight, formerly known only as the co-creator of the hit TV game show *Who Wants to Be a Millionaire.* This is about as far from a game show as you can get. It's grim, unsparing, relentless, and beautifully human.

When a hooker named Juliette (Sophie Okonedo), the other African immigrant who appears in the confrontational closing scene, sends Okwe up to fix a clogged toilet in a room she's been using, he discovers a brutal secret that sets him off on the trail of discovering what his boss, Sneaky (Sergi Lopez), is really up to. He discovers a criminal underworld that preys viciously and heartlessly on the desires of immigrants to become legal citizens with papers and passports. But Okwe has grisly secrets of his own.

Ejiofor is on camera for almost the entire film, and he has one of the most open and likeable faces ever to grace a movie screen. His eyes are sincere, his grudging smiles are charming, and his humanity leaks out from behind his grim facade. To Senay, he is an emotional puzzle; she is intrigued by his hard facade, and occupied with trying to penetrate and soften it, because she knows he has a good heart.

Unlike almost any screen romance, the relationship between Senay and Ejiofor is as hidden and tentative as the furtive lives they each are forced to lead on the fringes of conventional society. The film doesn't give us background, it just plunks us down in Okwe's world, so it's not clear exactly how Okwe has come to share Senay's apartment, but their relationship is clearly not yet sexual, even if there are hints of attraction that blossom as the film proceeds. Tautou, who burst onto the global scene in the silly hit *Amelie,* here inhabits a different, tougher role, and she succeeds well enough, though her French accent is not believable in the character of a Turkish refugee.

The script tightens its grip on Senay's dilemma and forces her eventually to make impossible moral choices and to suffer degradation that only increases her desperation. Okwe wants to save her—he has the doctor's impulse to want to save everybody—but he, too, is shackled and hemmed in by his illegal status. It's only when he hatches an ingenious scheme that he is able to get her a ticket out of this misery.

Dirty Pretty Things isn't a grandstanding film; it is deliberate and low-key. It's effective, though, because of the way it immerses the audience in Okwe's world without condescending, sugarcoating, or moralizing. It's an observant movie and one that demands equanimity from its viewer. Yes, the villains are a bit too monstrous, but its central characters, especially Ejiofor's splendid Okwe, are inescapably realistic, and their plight is believable.

Frears gives the film an aching authenticity but never lets it bog down into a gritty character study. The film has a delirious zing to it, a kind of careening plot and unorthodox pace that makes it seem more complicated and more interesting than its spare, 94-minute screen time would seem to allow. It's a wonderful achievement, and by rights should propel Ejiofor into the ranks of the world's most sought-after actors. He makes Okwe memorable and, in spite of Frears's antihero treatment, palpably admirable, even when he indulges in the dirty, pretty things that the hotel specializes in. At bottom, this movie is a fearless testimony to the strength of even the most battered human spirit.

—*Michael Betzold*

CREDITS

Okwe: Chiwetel Ejiofor
Senay: Audrey Tautou
Sneaky (Juan): Sergi Lopez
Juliette: Sophie Okonedo
Ivan: Zlatko Buric
Guo Yi: Benedict Wong

Origin: Great Britain
Released: 2003
Production: Tracey Seaward, Robert Jones; BBC Films, Celador Films; released by Miramax
Directed by: Stephen Frears
Written by: Steven Knight
Cinematography by: Chris Menges
Music by: Nathan Larson

Sound: Peter Lindsay
Editing: Mick Audsley
Art Direction: Rebecca Holmes
Costumes: Odile Dicks-Mireaux
Production Design: Hugo Luczyc-Wyhowski
MPAA rating: R
Running time: 107 minutes

REVIEWS

Boxoffice. November, 2002, p. 123.
Chicago Sun-Times Online. August 1, 2003.
Entertainment Weekly. July 25, 2003, p. 53.
Los Angeles Times Online. July 18, 2003.
New York Times Online. July 18, 2003.
People. July 28, 2003, p. 30.
Sight and Sound. December, 2002, p. 32.
USA Today Online. July 18, 2003.
Variety Online. September 10, 2002.
Washington Post. August 1, 2003, p. WE37.

QUOTES

Guo Yi (Benedict Wong) to Okwe (Chiwetel Ejiofor): "There's nothing so dangerous as a virtuous man."
Guo Yi (Benedict Wong): "Good at chess usually means you suck at life."

AWARDS AND NOMINATIONS

Nomination:
Oscars 2003: Orig. Screenplay
Writers Guild 2003: Orig. Screenplay.

Divine Intervention: A Chronicle of Love and Pain (Yadon Ilaheyya)

Elia Suleiman's sophomore feature, *Divine Intervention,* lacks the boldness and originality of his debut, *Chronicle of a Disappearance,* but it is still a smart, funny, and intriguing work. Suleiman again tells tales, in vignette form, from the Middle East, mining the situation there for all its mordant tragedy and absurd comedy. We are witness to a hostile feud between Israeli and Palestinian neighbors, who throw their daily garbage bags on each other's property; a love story between a man living in Jerusalem and a woman living in Ramallah, who are only able to meet near the Israeli army checkpoint; and a showdown at the checkpoint between young Israeli soldiers and a Palestinian "Ninja" woman.

The last vignette, more a black-out sketch in the style of *Saturday Night Live,* is the weakest section of the film, partly because it jumps into the fantasy realm (a cardboard practice range target becomes the "Ninja" woman, fighting in levitated kung-fu fashion, a la *The Matrix* or *Charlies Angels*) and partly because it is so obvious a pop culture parody (bound to look very dated in the coming years). Here, especially, Suleiman disappoints those expecting more of his sensitive yet stinging satire from *Chronicle of a Disappearance,* which commented on the vanishing culture of Arabs in Occupied Territory.

Still, other parts of *Divine Intervention* show the director's skill at keeping an oblique distance from his subjects and creating a more nuanced critique. One such sequence features the director himself (playing the man from Jerusalem) waiting next to an Israeli man for a traffic light to change as his car radio blasts Screamin' Jay Hawkins's "I Put a Spell on You". In contrast to the silly "Ninja" climax, Suleiman's traffic light episode better expresses the rage of a resident in an occupied land (Suleiman remains silent and stone-faced during the encounter).

Speaking of stone-faced, Suleiman pays homage to Buster Keaton (as well as Jacques Tati and Sam Beckett) in the first sketch with its long-shot, long-take style (again, the lack of dialogue and absence of music makes the minimalist action more riveting). Likewise, in the opening sequence, which shows several Palestinian boys with stones chasing a man in a Santa Claus costume across a rocky landscape, Suleiman establishes a sinister, surreal atmosphere. The most moving portion of the film illustrates the dilemma of the Palestinian lovers living on opposite sides of the soldiers' checkpoint. Suleiman (looking like fellow actor Robert Downey, Jr.) and Manal Khader (in her debut) play the sad couple, and director Suleiman again uses silence effectively, this time to convey the pain of the tortured meetings.

However, not all critics have embraced Suleiman's tone or message. Manohla Dargis, of the *Los Angeles Times* wrote of the Santa opener, "Even after seeing the film twice, I am still trying to puzzle through if it's meant to depict internecine intolerance or if Suleiman just has a thing against Christmas." Jonathan Forman in the *New York Post* had an even harsher assessment: "This Franco-Palestinian coproduction veers uneasily and unsatisfyingly from kitschy, agitprop surrealism to a laconic spareness that is less profound than tedious." But Roger Ebert, in the *Chicago Sun-Times,*

saw a more humanitarian (and less polemical) message: "Suleiman's argument seems to be that the situation between Palestinians and Israelis has settled into an [sic] hopeless stalemate, in which everyday life incorporates elements of paranoia, resentment, and craziness."

In the end, perhaps no film about (or set in) the Middle East could possibly satisfy everyone. Moreover, as Dargis points out, "*Divine Intervention* is guaranteed to infuriate anyone with strongly partisan opinions about the region." As an example, one sequence features a red balloon bearing an image of Palestinian leader Yassir Arafat floating past the Israeli checkpoint and slyly evading the soldiers' bullets. No matter how lyrical or funny the sequence may be, anyone who dislikes Yassir Arafat will probably see the joke as an insult to Israelis.

For those who are able to see the bigger picture of irony and contradiction in this violent world, *Divine Intervention* should provide a tragicomic relief of sorts, but it does not measure up to the film one might have expected six years after the director's surprisingly wise and mature first effort.

—*Eric Monder*

CREDITS

E.S.: Elia Suleiman
The Father: Nayef Fahoum Daher
Auni: Amer Daher
Jamel: Jamel Daher
The Woman: Manal Khader
Santa Claus: George Ibrahim
Jerusalem Neighbor: George Khleifi
Trainer/Tax Collector: Ari Kleinberger

Origin: France, Germany
Language: Arabic, Hebrew
Released: 2002
Production: Humbert Balsan; Arte France Cinema, Lichtblick Filmproduktion, Ognon Pictures, Gimages Films, Soread 2M; released by Avatar Film Corporation
Directed by: Elia Suleiman
Written by: Elia Suleiman
Cinematography by: Marc Andre Batigne
Music Supervisor: Serge Guillerme
Editing: Veronique Lange
Art Direction: Miguel Markin, Denis Renault
MPAA rating: Unrated
Running time: 89 minutes

REVIEWS

Chicago Sun-Times Online. April 25, 2003.
Entertainment Weekly. February 21, 2003, p. 129.
Los Angeles Times Online. March 14, 2003.
New York Post Online. January 17, 2003.
New York Times Online. January 12, 2003.
Sight and Sound. January, 2003, p. 16.
Time. February 10, 2003, p. 78.
Variety Online. May 20, 2002.
Washington Post. January 31, 2003, p. WE39.

Dr. Seuss' The Cat in the Hat
(The Cat in the Hat)

Don't mess with the hat.
—Movie tagline
The Cat is Back!
—Movie tagline
The ultimate game of cat and house.
—Movie tagline

Box Office: $100.7 million

Given the box office success of 2000's *Dr. Seuss' How the Grinch Stole Christmas*, starring Jim Carrey, it surely surprised no one that Hollywood, always on the look-out for a formula promising an instant hit, promptly sought to imitate that success by making a movie version of "The Cat in the Hat." It must have seemed a simple formula: take another beloved Dr. Seuss story, expand the storyline to fill out the length requirements of a feature film, design an otherworldly, even childlike production inspired by the unique drawings in the book, and hire a popular comic actor to play the heavily costumed lead. *Grinch* producer Brian Grazer returned to bring the famous Cat to the big screen, this time teaming with first-time director Bo Welch (production designer for *Edward Scissorhands*, *Batman Returns*, and *Men in Black*) and star Mike Meyers, an actor whose comic style differs quite substantially from that of the rubber-faced, manic Carrey. Unfortunately, the formula for *The Cat in the Hat* left out some much-needed ingredients. Where *Grinch* made an effort to flesh out the children's story with a plot that explored its quirky characters (most notably the Grinch himself) and succeeded in staying faithful to the spirit of not only the book but the 1966 animated

version, *The Cat in the Hat* sorely lacks any "fleshing out" and strays inexplicably (and unnecessarily) from its source material. Ultimately the movie becomes little more than a showcase for Meyers in sketch-like bits and routines that almost seem to belong in some bizarre children's version of television's *Saturday Night Live*, the place where Meyers' fame began.

The basic plot of *The Cat in the Hat* resembles that of the book, but the fact that the children's book is only around 1000 words dictated that the movie had to expand the original story substantially—and the additions are definitely substantial. Like the book, this is a story about a boy and girl (Conrad and Sally, played by Spencer Breslin and Dakota Fanning) who find themselves bored and alone indoors on a rainy day. In the book, there are no other human characters except the children's mother, who makes a brief appearance at the end, but not surprisingly the movie introduces a slate of new characters. The mother, Joan Walden (Kelly Preston), works for a real estate agency run by Mr. Humberfloob (Sean Hayes), a germophobe who keeps himself and his employees well-stocked with hand sanitizer and who expects Joan's house to be the perfect model of order and cleanliness for an impending company reception she is hosting. Joan has reason to worry, though, because her son Conrad seems bent on making messes. He is so rambunctious and prone to destruction that Joan's boyfriend and neighbor Larry Quinn (Alec Baldwin) encourages Joan to send him off to Colonel Wilhelm's Military Academy for Troubled Youth. When Joan has to leave for work prior to the company party, she lays down the rules to the children—though Sally, a straight-laced, well-behaved girl who epitomizes orderliness, hardly needs any rules. "I wish I could trust you," Joan tells Conrad after he creates yet another mess. "Sometimes I wish I had a different Mom," he replies. Her quiet response seems a bit harsh for this story (and a bit cruel considering the nature of his "crimes"): "Sometimes I wish the same thing." For extra precaution, Joan hires a babysitter, Mrs. Kwan (Amy Hill), to watch the children while she's away at the office.

One of the movie's running gags is that Mrs. Kwan almost immediately falls asleep and does not wake up until the end of the movie. Initially there is some humor in the gag, but it soon gets old, and one may wonder why the character is present at all and whether she was created simply because it might seem like a dereliction of parental duty for Joan to leave her children at home unattended. Shortly after the babysitter arrives and falls asleep, it begins to rain (a plot point that almost seems random in the context of the movie but one that is an obligatory reference to the original story). What are two children to do while it's raining outside? Although it has already been established that Conrad normally finds plenty to do around the house and Sally usually has her whole day planned out on a To Do list and is rarely at a loss for ideas and advice, the children wind up sitting in front of a window staring sadly at the rain—another example of how the movie includes obligatory scenes from the book that don't necessarily mesh with the new material.

The boredom does not last long, however, for suddenly Conrad and Sally are visited by the six-foot-tall titular Cat (Mike Meyers), who has shown up to entertain them. He's not quite the Cat of Dr. Seuss' tale, who is a naïve character unaware of how much trouble his silly hijinks cause and who ultimately wears out his welcome. Meyers's Cat is akin to a verbal and physical comedian whose routine never ends, switching in and out of various character bits so often and throwing out so many jokes that it is difficult to ever really get a grasp on what his character is supposed to be. The children warm to him very quickly, and actually ask the Cat to stay and entertain them—a development that seems out-of-character for Sally, and is a significant departure from the original story. The Cat agrees to stay, but not until the children sign an enormous contract he suddenly produces out of thin air (along with a group of lawyers).

Fun and mayhem ensue, but real trouble starts when the Cat attempts to make muffins "from anything you want" and purple dough—or some such sticky concoction—winds up all over the house. Remembering their mother's edict about keeping the house tidy, the children demand that the Cat clean up the mess. In response, the Cat brings in a large red crate, from which appear Thing One and Thing Two, who are supposed to clean the house. However, instead of cleaning up, the two little creatures just "move" the mess and actually begin making a bigger mess. Well, of course the explanation for their behavior is that they do the opposite of what you tell them to do, but the children don't quite catch on to what they should tell the Things, so matters just worsen. Amid all the noise and confusion, Conrad opens the red crate—in defiance of the Cat's warning that it must not be opened—and lets loose a whirlwind of chaos. The Cat and the children manage to shut the crate temporarily by laying Mrs. Kwan's body on top of it, but the crate's padlock somehow finds its way to the family dog. The dog, in turn, escapes from the house, forcing the children and the Cat to go after him. Perhaps the filmmakers ran out of ideas for what could be done in the house, necessitating this venture out into the town. Every movie must have its villain, so scheming (and increasingly sleazy) neighbor Larry steps in to provide additional conflict as he spots the dog and sets to the chase, hoping to get Conrad into trouble so Mom will be persuaded to send him away to military school.

The next sequence of the film involves the children and the Cat finding the dog and then racing back home before their mother returns. Ultimately their quest seems a failure, as the house is literally torn to pieces, and the children finally tell the Cat to leave—"You don't know when it's enough!" they tell him. So he does leave, but then he returns shortly, driving a fantastic contraption that cleans up and puts the house back to normal. He then informs the children that

they've learned a lesson—how to have fun and how to know "when it's enough." The Phunometer now indicates that both Conrad and Sally are "Just Right."

Unfortunately, the same cannot be said for this movie. *The Cat in the Hat* aims to be a children's movie, as it should be, and many children may enjoy watching the constant antics and the fascinating production design, one of the movie's few strong points. At the same time, however, the nature of the comedy also attempts to appeal to adults, resulting in an odd and incongruous mix. Much of this may be due to Meyers, whose humor is often more appropriate for an older crowd ("Dirty hoe," he says to a garden tool that causes him pain in a very cartoonish way). Ironically, older audience members are not likely to find the story very interesting. Many of Meyers' character bits are humorous, but they rarely contribute to any kind of real storytelling. The movie is full of whirling action, but it is noticeably missing any real coherence or purpose, relying on joke after joke and routine after routine rather than a meaningful plot.

The Cat in the Hat even fails to deliver on the message it apparently attempts to convey, as slight as it is. Supposedly the children learn "when enough is enough," but only Conrad really needed to learn this lesson (one would think their experiences would reinforce Sally's initial attitudes). The lesson the children learned is hardly conveyed through the course of the movie. If anything, Sally and Conrad should have learned never to let six-foot-tall cats into their home, but the idea that they learned to have "a reasonable good time" does not flow logically from the story. Strangely, this "lesson" does not come from the book, either.

One of the many problems with the film is that it is based on a very short story, so it requires elaboration and detail that go far beyond the source. Turning it into a successful movie, on the other hand, would also require developing a coherent theme, a carefully planned plot, and fully realized characters that are consistent with the source. *The Cat in the Hat* falls short in all these areas, giving the impression that it sprang not from creativity and inspiration but from a whim to try to recapture the success of *The Grinch*. "What other famous Dr. Seuss story can we exploit?" is not the kind of origin a good movie needs, even if the movie is meant primarily for children.

—*David Flanagin*

CREDITS

The Cat: Mike Myers
Sally: Dakota Fanning
Conrad: Spencer Breslin
Mom: Kelly Preston
Quinn: Alec Baldwin

Mrs. Kwan: Amy Hill
Mr. Humberfloob/The Fish: Sean P. Hayes (also Voice)

Origin: USA
Released: 2003
Production: Brian Grazer; Imagine Entertainment, Universal Pictures, Dreamworks Pictures; released by Universal Pictures
Directed by: Bo Welch
Written by: Alec Berg, David Mandel, Jeff Schaffer
Cinematography by: Emmanuel Lubezki
Music by: David Newman
Sound: Pud Cusack
Editing: Don Zimmerman
Art Direction: Sean Haworth
Costumes: Rita Ryack
Production Design: Alex McDowell
MPAA rating: PG
Running time: 82 minutes

REVIEWS

Chicago Sun-Times Online. November 21, 2003.
Entertainment Weekly. November 28, 2003, p. 97.
Los Angeles Times Online. November 21, 2003.
New York Times Online. November 21, 2003.
People. December 1, 2003, p. 32.
USA Today Online. November 21, 2003.
Variety Online. November 21, 2003.
Washington Post. November 21, 2003, p. WE45.

AWARDS AND NOMINATIONS

Nomination:
Golden Raspberries 2003: Worst Picture, Worst Actor (Myers), Worst Support. Actor (Baldwin), Worst Support. Actress (Preston), Worst Director (Welch), Worst Screenplay.

Dopamine

Love. Real or just a chemical reaction?
—Movie tagline

One of the paranoid fears that media guru Marshall McLuhan foresaw in the late 1960s was that of people believing that they had been programmed, like computers. Mark Decena's quasi-romantic social comedy, *Dopamine,* is much too low-key and retrogressive in its ambitions to carry McLuhan's prediction to any dramatically, or even comically, satisfying end. Decena instead falls back on the safe bet of wringing tears out of the demise of the social institution of the nuclear family.

One of the first features in release from Sundance the distributor, *Dopamine* is preceded by a short in which Decena, as director and co-writer, outlines his motivation for tackling the film's subject matter: how the information age can paralyze us emotionally. Trouble is, Decena isn't able to dramatize his "obsession" as much as illustrate it. The film's formal cleverness in mixing computer-generated imagery with live action only points to the paucity of its filmmaker's imagination as a storyteller.

In the film's scheme of things, love is love whether it is from, for, or between parents, or between consenting adults aspiring to more than a one-night stand. Against this, runs the belief system of the film's central character, Rand (John Livingston), a twenty-something laid back software programmer in San Francisco, for whom love is an interaction between norepinephrine and dopamine, chemicals the human body produces, presumably to suit its own ends.

Rand's techno-project, on which he has been working for three years with the volatile Winston (Bruno Campos) and the devoted Johnson (Reuben Grundy), consists of producing a digital pet, a bird-like creature named Koy-Koy, who can be marketed as a companion for the lonely and the aged. The catalyst at the start of the film takes the form of a Japanese entrepreneur who would like to see Koy-Koy tested first on a group of kindergarten kids. Rand feels his creation is not yet ready, but he's outvoted.

Koy-Koy's testing coincides with the trials that Rand's own mindset is put through in relation to the concept of love. Coincidentally, what links these two plot lines is the strikingly attractive and intelligent Sarah (Sabrina Lloyd), whose path crosses that of Rand at a neighborhood watering hole, and who also turns out to be the teacher in charge of the tots on whom Koy-Koy has to work. So reserved is Rand at their first meeting that, in keeping with his beliefs, he is content only to sniff the fragrance of her hair, which in turn sets off a neurological charge inside his brain, which we come to know through a digital effect. However, it is the more forthright Winston who whisks Sarah off and even succeeds in taking her to bed that night, but on whom she chooses to walk out.

The next day when Rand sets up his equipment in her classroom. The project requires a two-way viewing mechanism: as the kids play with Koy-Koy, Rand will be watching them from his lab. Sarah, who remains opposed to the experiment, would have preferred a live rabbit. The test gets off to a shaky start as Koy-Koy freezes, which requires Rand to run over and make adjustments. Rand is able to smooth things over by getting Koy-Koy to sing a song. This also brings Rand and Sarah closer, but only to the extent that he can spout his theory of physical attraction. It does however inspire Rand to create a female mate for Koy-Koy.

As a subplot, we come to know Rand's frustration at not being able to communicate with his mother, who has been turned into a speechless zombie by Alzheimer's. While Rand's father, a scientist who has influenced Rand's thinking, still loves her, the situation only serves to reinforce Rand's belief in physiology as the dominating factor in "eternal love."

Sarah, as it happens, takes a liking to Rand and is even prepared to take the initiative in order to ease his shyness. When he drives her to his family's abandoned house in the country, they kiss but Rand admits to feeling no emotion. What works against the film by this point is that Rand seems actually to be feeling nothing, so that there is no chemistry between the two leads to hold audience interest.

That emotional lacuna is filled only in the film's final section when Rand stumbles upon the reason for Sarah's promiscuity: that she's trying to get over the loss of a daughter she was forced to give up for adoption. After the Japanese moneybags back out, and the Koy-Koy project falls through, Rand decides to chuck the software business and set off with Sarah to help her find her daughter, a resolve intended to end the film on a hopeful note.

Critics for the most part haven't forgiven the film's lackluster dramaturgy. As for the issues it raises, the *Boston Globe*'s Ty Burr finds Decena has "used them as talking points set to an indie-film guitar strum." Dave Kehr of the *New York Times* has a mixed reaction. He calls *Dopamine* "a wan, wistful Generation Y romance" embellished by "convincingly intimate, casual conversation," but whose story "begin[s] to feel somewhat undernourished, visually and dramatically."

—*Vivek Adarkar*

CREDITS

Rand: John Livingston
Sarah: Sabrina Lloyd
Winston: Bruno Campos
Johnson: Reuben Grundy
Tammy: Kathleen Antonia
Machiko: Nicole Wilder

Origin: USA
Released: 2003
Production: Tad Fettig, Debbie Brubaker; Kontent Films; released by Sundance Channel Pictures
Directed by: Mark Decena
Written by: Mark Decena, Timothy Breitbach
Cinematography by: Robert Humphreys
Music by: Eric Holland

Sound: Bob Gitzen
Music Supervisor: Jonathan McHugh
Editing: Jess Congdon
Art Direction: Joe Schlick
Costumes: Deidre Scully
Production Design: S. Quinn
MPAA rating: R
Running time: 79 minutes

REVIEWS

Boston Globe Online. October 10, 2003.
Boxoffice. December, 2003, p. 29.
Chicago Sun-Times Online. October 10, 2003.
Entertainment Weekly. October 17, 2003, p. 61.
Los Angeles Times Online. October 10, 2003.
New York Times Online. October 10, 2003.
Newsday Online. October 10, 2003.
Variety Online. February 2, 2003.
Washington Post. October 10, 2003, p. WE40.

Down With Love

The ultimate catch has met his match.
—Movie tagline

Box Office: $20.2 million

Two characters who are not what they pretend to be in a film that does not know what it wants to be: that is *Down with Love.* The film harks back to the popular Doris Day romantic comedies of the 1950's and 1960's in which suitors played by Clark Gable, Cary Grant, James Garner and, most memorably, Rock Hudson vied for the keys to her heart and her chastity belt. It was not that the characters Day played were uninterested in men, it was just that they knew darn well what most men were interested in—and what they would do to get it. Often an independent and capable career gal and always spunky, attractive, and of admirable moral fiber, she sported some of the most elegant, stylish outfits by the most sought-after designers, well turned out but in no hurry to put out. The number one draw at the box office at the dawn of the 1960's (the first woman to hold that position in years), Day's string of such films were made just before the sexual revolution came in and long before Hudson came out. They were generally fun and frothy and featured the pursuit of sex with Day, often including some form of deception as the men tried hard to get under her skin and then under the sheets. No wonder her guard was up.

For example, in 1959's *Pillow Talk*, Day plays an interior designer and Hudson a womanizer who initially only makes her heart race as she fumes over his tying up of the party line they share as he continuously warbles similar sweet nothings to an array of different woman. Neither character has actually seen the other and neither has any desire to do so, as she thinks he is a cad and he is sure she must be an unattractive, frustrated old maid. When he sees this supposed spinster taking a spin out on the dance floor, however, he wants her badly, and creates a fake persona in order to woo her. Of course his trickery is eventually revealed and she cuts him off cold, which is right around the time he realizes that his feelings for her are more than just lust. After further comedic complications, the dust settles and she ends up happily in the strong arms of her Prince Charming, presumably soon to be married.

While these films are tame by current standards, they featured risqué elements which titillated audiences of that time. The scripts were studded with clever double entendres that elicited knowing chuckles instead of shock and disapproval. The screenwriters knew, as did Day's characters, when to draw the line. For their part, the filmmakers had fun splitting the screen, as in *Pillow Talk*, to make it appear that Day and Hudson, conversing on the phone from their respective homes, were actually sharing a bathtub or bed. It was inoffensive, romantic, and sexy, with nothing base happening. The actors had palpable chemistry and audiences warmed up easily to the engaging characters as they warmed up to each other, caring about their eventual happiness after all the troubles were worked through on the way to the happy ending.

Now forty-odd years later comes the odd *Down with Love*, which is, like the characters Day played, rather difficult to pin down. First-time screenwriters Eve Ahlert and Dennis Drake and director Peyton Reed say that their goal was to replicate the magic of the old films, making the new film as if it were still the early 1960's. "Audiences will feel as if they're watching a movie made in the sixties," asserted Reed. "We don't show or say anything in *Down with Love* that wouldn't have worked in an early-sixties romantic comedy," insisted Ahlert. They are certainly successful in making it look like a film of that era, shooting it entirely on a back lot sound stage, splashing it with vibrant color, using period clothes and decor, and utilizing process shots so that what we see out car windows is stock footage from the early 1960's. (The film even begins with the old Cinemascope logo.) The fact is, however, that there is little that works well, and there are moments in the film that would have been neither attempted nor allowed in Day's day.

The film begins appropriately enough, all bouncy and sunny and color-saturated. We find ourselves in New York City in 1962, and new author Barbara Novak (Renee Zellweger) has come to the big city determined to sell the all-male board of Banner House Publishing on her manuscript entitled "Down with Love." Its incendiary advice to women is that they should be steadfastly independent while pushing onward to fulfill their goals in life, refusing to get sidetracked or, worse yet, derailed by falling in love. Women, like men, should indulge as they see fit in meaningless casual sex ("sex a la carte," as she calls it), devoid of the ties that bind. Live like a man, women, and what they have been able to achieve all these years can be yours, too!

Ultra-slick "ladies man, man's man, man about town" Catcher Block (Ewan McGregor), who writes for an Esquire-type magazine, is supposed to do a story on Barbara. Sure that she must be some spinster who could not capture a man's heart if she tried, he keeps calling her at the last minute with an excuse to postpone their meetings, usually with a giggling stewardess on his lap. (Shapely Jeri Ryan gets the most screen time.) After an appearance on the Ed Sullivan show, Barbara's book is a huge bestseller. "It is bigger than the Pill," cheers her editor Vikki Hiller (Sarah Paulson), but most men (and playboys like Catcher, in particular) find its message hard to swallow. He also chokes on her public assertion that he is a prime example of "the worst kind of man," to be avoided at all cost. Soon all his dates are calling him with cancellations, leaving him to angrily declare that he will bring down the author of "Down With Love." Catcher will catch her, making her fall in love with him and prove that she actually yearns for love and marriage like every other woman.

When Catcher just happens to bump into Barbara for the first time, he pretends to be a sweet, naive astronaut named Zip Martin who has never heard of her, and the two are soon painting the town together. She is in the mood for a little "a la carte," but that is (for once) not his goal. Both start to have some deeper feelings for each other, but are determined to stick to their stated goals. Eventually, she finds out who he really is, at which point he goes ahead and triumphantly announces that he got her to fall in love with him. The shaky wheels beneath the film now spin completely off. Barbara delivers a lengthy speech in which she trumps him by revealing that she is actually a former secretary of his named Nancy Brown who, not wanting to end up as just another pretty face, engineered everything that happened up to that point to snare him and make her the sole, standout woman he really loves and admires. Catcher's mouth falls open in disbelief, as do those of everyone in the audience. After some thoroughly unconvincing soul-searching and more strained, far-fetched manipulation and maneuvering on both sides, the two lovebirds end up heading off into the sunset together, ludicrously clinging to a rope ladder beneath a helicopter as it soars high over Manhattan. If they had lost their grip, it would certainly have added another meaning to the title.

Considering the undeniable talents of Zellweger and McGregor, not to mention the production team responsible for the Oscar-winning *American Beauty*, *Down with Love* seems especially disappointing. Also disappointing to those involved was the reception it received from many critics and the public, resulting in a less-than-hoped-for gross of just over $20 million. Business was down 28% during its third week in theaters, and 69% during the next. Older audience members who fondly remember the Day-Hudson films seem to have made up a sizeable percentage of audiences, and they generally found this film wanting. Some commented on being offended by the undeniable boost in bawdiness, including a split screen segment which made it look like Barbara and Catcher were enthusiastically engaging in multiple forms of sexual activity. What humor there is to be found is painfully overshadowed by the overplayed, exceedingly arch and gratingly cutesy performances of leads Zellweger and McGregor. It is difficult to care what eventually becomes of characters you could not stomach in the first place. There is little of the Day/Hudson chemistry between Zellweger and McGregor, and the latter is a poor choice as a stand in for the beefy and charismatic Hudson. More enjoyable is the subplot between Vikki and Peter MacMannus, Catcher's twitchy, neurotic boss, played quite well by David Hyde Pierce in a characterization not so far removed from his role on *Frasier*. Such a role was usually played in the old films by Tony Randall, who appears here as publishing tycoon Theodore Banner. The laughs any of these actors generate come more and more infrequently as the film grinds on—and increasingly grinds on our nerves, as well. Be it a celebration of, or homage to, the old enjoyable films, *Down with Love* pretty much misses the mark entirely, failing both as an homage to, and as a re-creation of, the old favorites. It plays more like a mocking parody, which can only serve to make audiences unfamiliar with the Day films laugh at the originals. "We decided to combine all the sex comedies of that era and throw them in a blender," says Reed. Unfortunately, the resulting concoction is sickeningly sweet and unpalatable, making *Down with Love* go down only with great effort.

—*David L. Boxerbaum*

CREDITS

Barbara Novak: Renee Zellweger
Catcher Block: Ewan McGregor
Peter McMannus: David Hyde Pierce
Vicki Hiller: Sarah Paulson
Theodore Banner: Tony Randall
Maurice: Jack Plotnick
Gladys: Rachel Dratch
E.G.: John Aylward
Gwendolyn: Jeri Ryan
Elkie: Melissa George
Dry cleaner's wife: Florence Stanley
Receptionist: Laura Kightlinger

Origin: USA
Released: 2003
Production: Bruce Cohen, Dan Jinks; Fox 2000 Pictures, Regency Enterprises, Mediastream Film; released by 20th Century-Fox
Directed by: Peyton Reed
Written by: Dennis Drake, Eve Ahlert
Cinematography by: Jeff Cronenweth
Music by: Marc Shaiman
Sound: John Pritchett
Music Supervisor: Chris Douridas, Laura Z. Wasserman
Editing: Larry Bock
Art Direction: Martin Whist
Costumes: Daniel Orlandi
Production Design: Andrew Laws
MPAA rating: PG-13
Running time: 94 minutes

REVIEWS

Chicago Sun-Times Online. May 16, 2003.
Entertainment Weekly. May 16, 2003, p. 49.
Los Angeles Times Online. May 16, 2003.
New York Times. May 9, 2003, p. E1.
New Yorker. May 26, 2003, p. 102.
People. May 26, 2003, p. 36.
Rolling Stone. June 12, 2003, p. 102.
Variety. May 12, 2003, p. 29.
Wall Street Journal. May 16, 2003, p. W1.
Washington Post. May 16, 2003, p. WE47.

QUOTES

Peter (David Hyde Pierce): "I think Vicki was only talking about marriage so I'd wanna have sex with her. And then I did, and now she never talks to me, except to come back for more. I feel so used!"

Dreamcatcher

Evil Slips Through.
—Movie tagline
Four friends hung a dreamcatcher in their cabin. It's about to catch something it cannot stop.
—Movie tagline
A circle of friends. A web of mystery. A pattern of fear.
—Movie tagline

Box Office: $33.7 million

Psychiatrist Henry Devlin (Thomas Jane) has more than the usual amount of insight into his patients' minds because he really does know what they're thinking. In his frustration he almost taunts them with his knowledge of the reasons for their wrecked lives, and this is driving him to the brink of his own destruction.

Car salesman Pete Moore (Timothy Olyphant) has a fondness for alcohol and no way with women. His best pick-up "line" seems to be an uncanny ability to find lost items, which makes him seem more scary than helpful, driving the ladies away and Pete deeper into the bottle.

History professor Jonesy (Damian Lewis) has a soft spot for scholarship students even when they cheat, and tooth-pick chomping Beaver (Jason Lee) is a ne'r-do-well with flashes into the future that are more fuzzy than useful. Nonetheless, when Beaver gets one of those unclear images that involves Jonesy, he doesn't hesitate to pick up the phone to warn him. But warn him about what? Perhaps it is to warn him not to run out into traffic because that's exactly what Jonesy does, leaving him a twisted human ruin in the middle of the road.

Beaver, Jonesy, Pete and Henry are all childhood friends. They share, however, more than a common past. They also share a kind of psychic connection, the result of knowing a fifth friend, Douglas Clavel, better known as Duddits (Donnie Wahlberg). In their pre-teen years, the foursome stumbled upon Duddits, a mentally challenged young boy, being tormented by several older boys. They step in and "save" the distraught Duddits whom Beaver calms by singing "Blue Bayou." They take him home and accept him into their circle of friendship.

Now, some 20 years later, the adult foursome rarely sees the housebound Duddits, but they do all get together every winter to spend time bonding, reminiscing and hunting in the woods of Maine. Although Duddits can't join them, he is there in spirit represented by the dreamcatcher he made for them many years ago that is hanging from the cabin's rafters. Dreamcatchers are a Native American symbol that are supposed to trap nightmares and give one a peaceful night's sleep. It's too bad Duddits' dreamcatcher can't stop the nightmare that is about to walk through their cabin door.

Amazingly, Jonesy has survived but is limping badly when, six months after the accident, the foursome again meet at the cabin. While Beaver and Jonesy sit in their hunting blinds watching the snow fall, Pete and Henry have gone off to Gosselin's Market for supplies. As the snow falls steadily and more heavily, Jonesy is about to give up when he spots a dazed and distressed hunter. Jonesy takes the half frozen man back to the cabin, warms him up and offers him some hot food, but the hunter seems to have a severe gastric disorder as he can't stop emitting gasses from his various orifices. As the hunter's condition worsens, Jonesy and the recently returned Beaver put him to bed and await Pete and Henry's return with their only car.

Meanwhile, Pete and Henry have run into trouble of their own. While driving in the storm, they almost run over another hunter sitting crossed-legged in the middle of the road. To avoid her they have run off the road and crashed the car. Although the woman seems frozen in place, Henry and Pete soon discover she is alive but virtually comatose . . . although that doesn't keep her from belching and farting. So while Pete waits with the woman, Henry sets off to walk back to the cabin for help.

Back at the cabin, however, something even odder is happening. Out the cabin window Jonesy and Beaver notice a procession of animals of all kinds (rabbits, wolves, deer, bear) all moving en masse away from something and all bearing odd red markings. When the men return back into the cabin to check on their hunter, he is no longer in bed but has worked his way to their bathroom . . . leaving a trail of blood. When the boys break into the blood-soaked bathroom they find the hunter keeled over dead, and some kind of snakey lethal-looking alien creature in their toilet. In an attempt to keep the creature from attacking them, Beaver traps it by sitting on the toilet lid while Jonesy goes out to the shed to find some duct tape to seal it into the bowl. (See, Tom Ridge was right, we do need to be prepared with duct tape!) This, unfortunately, gives rise to one of the film's most tense and silliest scenes.

Interestingly enough, the boys are not alone in the backwoods of Maine. Hovering overhead in a helicopter is Army Col. Abraham Curtis (Morgan Freeman) and his second in command Captain Owen Underhill (Tom Sizemore), and they've seen all this before. Curtis has been hunting these aliens for 25 years since this is not the first time they have landed here, spreading their red fungus that grows into aliens—which Curtis has dubbed The Ripley after the lead character in the *Alien* movies—in human beings, exiting through their backsides and further spreading the fungus.

So far Curtis' main way of dealing with the alien landings and human outbreaks is to quarantine the area and wipe out all traces of the infestation alien and human. In Curtis' own words, his policy is simply, "If The Ripley gets out of this pine tree paradise . . . well we just can't allow that to happen." As he tells Owen, "go in fast and hard and come out clean and smiling."

But Jonesy is about to break the quarantine. Possessed by the alien—who for some reason is called Mr. Grey and speaks with a British accent—Jonesy has snowmobiled, hitchhiked and carjacked his way out of the woods and is heading for a water supply that he will use to spread the alien infection. He is being pursued by Owen and Henry who have now called in their own type of reinforcements, Duddits, who is dying of lymphocytic leukemia but who seems to know all about these aliens.

Dreamcatcher was the first novel that the master of macabre, Stephen King, wrote after his near-fatal accident in 1999. (One can't help but wonder if Jonesy's similar pedestrian/automobile accident at the beginning of the film isn't an autobiographical scene.) As a 600 page book it is lavish in plot and character and details, but when translated to the screen, even at just over two hours, it may be too much. The movie has a feeling of overkill, and I don't mean alien body counts.

Each of the two main stories could have been a movie in themselves and each movie would have been a totally different breed of animal. The boyhood friends story is typical of King's more gentle (if that's a word one can use describing Stephen King stories) tales of humanity, humor, friendship and pop culture like *Stand By Me.* The alien story is strictly for scares and gore even though some people think aliens coming out of human backsides can pass for humor. The result of blending these two different stories is a confusion of styles and feelings and they don't convincingly go together. We are by turns made to feel scared and amused, nostalgic and heartless, agreeable and wary.

Even the characters are typical of this extreme spectrum story. Curtis is Ahab, obsessed by his white whale. (Note: originally Colonel Curtis was called Colonel Kurtz as in Marlon Brando's obsessed, over-the-edge character in *Apocalypse Now* and the same character in Joseph Conrad's *Heart of Darkness,* but it was changed so audiences wouldn't get hung up on it.) At the other end is the loving and likable Duddits. One character we distrust and come to dislike, the other we like but maybe don't understand, especially his role in the end of the movie.

This split-personality of a film is odd given the quality of the behind-the-scenes talent. Director/co-writer/producer Lawrence Kasdan has given us such great films as *Body Heat, The Big Chill,* and *Grand Canyon* and although he has co-written science fiction (*The Empire Strikes Back* and *Return of the Jedi*), this is his first try at directing it. Similarly in the A-list talent category is co-writer William Goldman (*All the President's Men, Butch Cassidy and the Sundance Kid*) who has also adapted two previous Stephen King stories (*Misery* and *Hearts in Atlantis*). Unfortunately, together these two talents couldn't seem to create a cohesive movie from a rich and long novel.

If the story is confusing, however, the movie looks great thanks to cinematographer John Seale (*The English Patient*), the visual effects team headed by Stefen Fangmeier (*The Perfect Storm, Twister*), and production designer Jon Hutman (*The West Wing*) whose cleverly designed "memory warehouse" is quite entertaining. There always seems to be some arresting image to watch when the story gets silly or baffling. Of special note is the special-effects scene of the animals fleeing and the repetition of the dreamcatcher image in unexpected places, i.e. the quarantine net map in Curtis' office, on the manhole cover that is the entrance to the water supply.

Dreamcatcher is not so much a modern horror story as it is typical of the classic sci-fi films from the 1950's. Back then aliens were often pretty transparent substitutes for our paranoia about being invaded by Communists. In light of our current apprehension over terrorism, one could assume that a revival of the alien genre is appropriate. Interestingly, the ill hunter who is not quite himself and is invited into the cabin and who ends up destroying them, is named McCarthy. This could be seen as an homage to Kevin McCarthy who starred in the classic '50's sci-fi film *Invasion of the Body Snatchers,* but who's to say it couldn't also reinforce the paranoia angle by standing for that Red Baiter Joe McCarthy?

In the end, *Dreamcatcher* is a great looking film with poorly developed characters, a confusing plot, and a bulging-to-overflowing story that carries perhaps too many of King's hallmarks: humanity, humor, horror, pop-culture, and gore. Sometimes simpler is better.

—*Beverley Bare Buehrer*

CREDITS

Col. Abraham Curtis: Morgan Freeman
Dr. Henry Devlin: Thomas Jane
Joe "Beaver" Clarendon: Jason Lee
Gary "Jonesy" Jones: Damian Lewis
Pete Moore: Timothy Olyphant
Owen Underhill: Tom Sizemore
Douglas "Duddits" Cavell: Donnie Wahlberg
General Mathison: Michael O'Neill
Roberta Cavell: Rosemary Dunsmore
Young Henry: Mike Holekamp
Young Beaver: Reece Thompson
Young Jonesy: Giacomo Baessato
Young Pete: Joel Palmer
Young Duddits: Andrew Robb

Origin: USA
Released: 2003
Production: Lawrence Kasdan, Charles Okun; Castle Rock Entertainment, Village Roadshow Pictures, NPV Entertainment; released by Warner Bros.
Directed by: Lawrence Kasdan
Written by: Lawrence Kasdan, William Goldman
Cinematography by: John Seale
Music by: James Newton Howard
Sound: Eric J. Batut
Editing: Carol Littleton, Raul Davalos

Art Direction: Helen Jarvis, Kendelle Elliot
Costumes: Molly Maginnis
Production Design: Jon Hutman
MPAA rating: R
Running time: 134 minutes

 REVIEWS

Chicago Sun-Times Online. March 21, 2003.
Detroit Free Press. March 16, 2003, p. E1.
Entertainment Weekly. March 28, 2003, p. 48.
Los Angeles Times Online. March 21, 2003.
New York Times Online. March 21, 2003.
People. March 31, 2003, p. 29.
USA Today Online. March 21, 2003.
Variety Online. March 16, 2003.
Washington Post. March 21, 2003, p. WE37.

Dumb and Dumberer: When Harry Met Lloyd

The Evolution of Dumb.
—Movie tagline

Before the first movie, there was high school. They missed the bus.
—Movie tagline

 Box Office: $26.1 million

In 1994, brothers Peter and Bobby Farrelly began their careers as a writing/directing duo with *Dumb and Dumber*, a tale of two bumbling idiots that reveled in crude and irreverent humor (much of it literally of the bathroom variety) and that seemed intent on exploring the boundaries of bad taste. The popularity of the film served not only to solidify Jim Carrey's status as a star, but also to lead the way for a series of Farrelly movies marked by a similar brand of humor (*Kingpin, There's Something About Mary, Shallow Hal*). *Dumb and Dumber*'s appeal also lay in the goofy yet endearing characters of Lloyd Christmas (Carrey) and Harry Dunne (Jeff Daniels), a pair of "lovable fools" that has been seen in many manifestations throughout the history of cinema. Given the success of the movie, it was almost guaranteed that someone would propose the idea of a sequel. However, the principal talent could not be brought back. Neither the Farrelly brothers nor Carrey and Daniels

could be persuaded (with a script or with enough money) to return for a second film. But that didn't stop the powers-that-be from deciding it was worthwhile to return to the well even if it meant going to a different one. Why not recast the leads (with relatively unknown actors) and make a prequel instead? Thus was the genesis of *Dumb and Dumberer: When Harry Met Lloyd*. Divorced from the creative personalities who had made the original watchable (and for many, a guilty pleasure), *Dumb and Dumberer* was a concept that never really had an audience. The film barely registered a presence at the box office and swiftly vanished from a theatrical run, ultimately ending up on many "Worst Films of 2003" lists. The movie is not without some funny moments and was probably not the worst film of the year, but it is a simplistic imitation of the original, an obvious attempt to cash in on what made *Dumb and Dumber* enjoyable (to some). While the lead actors do a good job of mimicking the mannerisms and behavior of Carrey and Daniels, the story itself is juvenile and pointless, and even the humor lacks originality, based mostly in pale retreads of gags pulled from the first movie.

The story takes us back to 1986, though the movie is filled with careless anachronisms in the form of comments, phrases, and even a few fashion styles that belong to a later time period. Lloyd Christmas (Eric Christian Olsen) actually lives in the high school he attends because his father is the janitor—the first sign that no one should take any of this seriously. Lloyd is a fun-loving goofball who runs out of the school building and down the street every morning to catch the school bus that will bring him back to where he started. Harry Dunne (Derek Richardson), a mild-mannered, self-conscious teenager who still plays with imaginary friends, has been home-schooled all his life but is now starting public school. In fact, he is on his way to school for the first time and Lloyd is on his way to catch the bus when the two of them meet, literally running into each other as they round a street corner. Their encounter leaves part of Lloyd's tooth in Harry's forehead, explaining why Lloyd has a broken tooth in *Dumb and Dumber*. After introducing themselves ("Harry . . . why is that name not familiar to me?" "We've never met." "No, that's not it."), the boys became fast friends and an inseparable duo at school.

Like the first movie, this one has a villain, but in place of gun-toting extortionists and kidnappers, the bad guy this time is a greedy high school principal, Mr. Collins (Eugene Levy), who's having an affair with a school lunch lady, Ms. Heller (Cheri Oteri). Hoping to buy a condominium for the two of them in Waikiki, Collins hatches a scheme to steal grant money by creating a faux "special needs" class. Evidently, Collins is either not very bright or else foolishly arrogant, as he records everything he says in his office and keeps the tapes in a large trunk (this makes things a lot easier for the good guys later on, of course). When he sees Harry and Lloyd hanging from the flagpole outside, courtesy of a bullying classmate, Collins realizes he's found the perfect students for the class. Harry and Lloyd are at once game to the idea, misunderstanding the term "special." Ms. Heller, their "teacher" for the class, gives them an important first assignment: to find new recruits for the class.

Touting the fact that their special needs class will basically be an easy ride, Harry and Lloyd persuade a group of kids to join them, including a guy on crutches and the bully who put them on the flagpole. The "students" are glad to be in the class and don't mind that they meet in the maintenance shed since it means they don't have to go to a real class where there would have to do actually work. There is one person who finds all of this suspicious, however, and that is Jessica (Rachel Nichols), an attractive girl who works for the school paper and smells a story when she hears about the special needs class. She has suspected Principal Collins of wrongdoing for some time, and now she thinks she's found her chance to expose him. When Ms. Heller takes the class on a field trip to a museum, Jessica follows and a car chase ensues. Heller manages to lose Jessica, and when she and the kids arrive at the museum, she pays the tour guide to keep the class busy while she leaves them for a couple hours. While they are at the museum, Harry and Lloyd (but especially Harry) become fond of a polar bear on display.

Later, Jessica encounters Harry and invites him to her house, an invitation he mistakes for signs of romantic interest. This sets up a sequence that is intentionally reminiscent of one of the more infamously memorable scenes in *Dumb and Dumber*. Prior to going to Jessica's house, Harry puts a large Hershey bar in his back pocket and obviously forgets about it. In Jessica's room, he stands too close to a furnace and discovers the chocolate has melted. Frantic, he goes to the bathroom, where in a panic he spreads the chocolate all over the walls, trying to clean himself. Having ruined his clothes, he sneaks into the bedroom of Jessica's parents, where he finds a suit to change into. Unfortunately, it's a woman's suit and it's too small for him, but still he puts it on and heads downstairs for dinner. It is not until Harry's departure that Jessica's father (Bob Saget) discovers the messy bathroom.

Embarrassed by the disaster at Jessica's, Harry becomes jealous when Jessica then seems to show interest in Lloyd. She asks Lloyd to take her to the principal's office at night (which, conveniently, Lloyd can do since he lives at the school). Lloyd thinks he's going to "get lucky," but of course Jessica just wants to find incriminating evidence against Principal Collins. After a very brief search, she doesn't find anything, though, and soon leaves Lloyd behind. Lloyd, on the other hand, finds Collins' secret trunk and believes it to be a "hidden treasure chest." He takes the trunk and gives it to Harry, along with the polar bear from the museum, as a way to mend their relationship.

Of course Collins is horrified to discover that his trunk is missing, but he assumes the culprit was Jessica, so he kidnaps her and demands to know what she did with his property. This sequence actually goes nowhere, even though Harry and Lloyd spot Collins and Jessica together and follow them, because ultimately the principal lets the girl go.

Meanwhile, the special needs class has been working on a float for the Thanksgiving Day parade. The subject of their float is George Washington, but Lloyd and Harry come up with the idea of turning George into Collins as a way of "honoring him." Simultaneously the other kids discover a tape in Collin's trunk that reveals his evil plot, and they all find a way to expose the principal by broadcasting the tape while the float is moving down the street.

As a summary of the movie demonstrates, the narrative structure doesn't hold up well. Granted, in a comedy such as this, the priority is to get to the next gag, but the gags rarely have any real connection to the overall plot. Worse, though, is the fact that most of the gags are imitations of the original movie. It may sound like a scary thought, but *Dumb and Dumber*, despite its simplistic plot and crudity, was far more complex and original than *Dumb and Dumberer*.

There are some humorous moments in the movie, but again, they pale in comparison to the laughs generated by Jim Carrey and Jeff Daniels. Watching Harry and Lloyd drinking slushies quickly to get a "brain freeze," playing tag in a convenience store, or washing a car with gasoline simply lacks the loveable goofiness and often truly bizarre humor found in *Dumb and Dumber*. Olsen does a great job of mimicking Jim Carrey, and that is perhaps the most enjoyable aspect of the film, but it certainly does not make it worthwhile. Oddly enough, whereas Harry was the "smarter" of the two in the original movie, Richardson's Harry is seemingly devoid of any sense or knowledge and actually needs Lloyd to "educate" him. This is an inconsistency that is symptomatic of the overall laziness with which this movie appears to have been made. Ultimately, one is drawn to the conclusion that the movie's title might just as well be a description of the genesis of this film. The filmmakers seem unaware that even a movie about two bumbling idiots should be intelligent in its design and execution.

—*David Flanagin*

CREDITS

Harry Dunne: Derek Richardson
Lloyd Christmas: Eric Christian Olsen
Principal Collins: Eugene Levy
Ray: Luis Guzman
Mrs. Heller: Cheri Oteri
Jessica: Rachel Nichols
Turk: Elden (Ratliff) Henson

Carl: William Lee Scott
Mrs. Dunne: Mimi Rogers
Lewis: Shia LaBeouf
Margie: Lin Shaye
Terri: Teal Redmann
Toby: Josh Braaten
Ching Chong: Michelle Krusiec
Jessica's mom: Julia Duffy

Origin: USA
Released: 2003
Production: Oren Koules, Charles B. Wessler, Brad Krevoy, Steve Stabler, Troy Miller; Dakota Pictures; released by New Line Cinema
Directed by: Troy Miller
Written by: Troy Miller, Robert Brener
Cinematography by: Anthony B. Richmond
Music by: Eban Schletter
Sound: Stacy Hill
Editing: Lawrence Jordan
Costumes: Susanna Puisto
Production Design: Paul Higgins
MPAA rating: PG-13
Running time: 82 minutes

REVIEWS

Entertainment Weekly. June 20, 2003, p. 53.
Los Angeles Times Online. June 13, 2003.
New York Times Online. June 13, 2003.
People. June 23, 2003, p. 35.
USA Today Online. June 13, 2003.
Variety Online. June 12, 2003.
Washington Post. June 13, 2003, p. WE34.

AWARDS AND NOMINATIONS

Nomination:
Golden Raspberries 2003: Worst Remake/Sequel, Worst Screenplay.

Dummy

Some People Can Say A Lot Without Moving Their Lips.
—Movie tagline

A comedy about finding your voice before you lose your mind.
—Movie tagline

Dummy is a small film with Adrien Brody, who won an Academy Award for his role in *The Pianist.* Given the attention Brody has received, audiences at first may find it difficult to focus on *Dummy,* which was made several months before *The Pianist.* That will only be a problem during the first few minutes, however, because this film has its own quirky life, worthy of praise. It is every bit as good as *The Pianist,* although it is at the opposite end of the emotional spectrum.

Brody stars as Steven, an office worker who still lives at home with his parents. He is nearing 30, living with a highly dysfunctional family, yet still hanging on to his dream of becoming a ventriloquist. He purchases a ventriloquist's dummy, immediately ensuring ridicule from those around him. The dummy eventually allows Steven to overcome his shyness by using humor to pull himself out of his shell. As he practices more and more, spending almost all his time with the unnamed dummy, he begins to understand his own faults and life choices. The dummy teaches him that he should embrace his life and live it rather than let it go to waste.

The supporting cast of *Dummy* is terrific. Milla Jovovich offers up a generally wonderful performance as Steven's best friend and neighbor, Fangora, a punk girl with a tough exterior. In her attempt to push Steven out of his inactive, passive existence, Fangora doles out pretty bad advice. Unfortunately, this backfires and lands Steven in some sticky situations.

Then there's Steven's sister (Illeana Douglas), a wedding planner who really wants to to be a singer. She is also living at home with the crazy family as she recently ended her engagement. Steven's mom and dad (Jessica Walter and Ron Leibman) had me laughing the hardest with their passive-aggressive, crazy parent stunts. Some of the behaviors were mildly stereotypical but hilarious all the same. Lorina (Vera Farmiga) is Steve's love interest who works at the employment office

Dummy is a small, quirky film about keeping your head in the clouds and focusing on your dreams. I like a film that makes the audience think about their own lives, their own choices, and has them probably feeling good about those choices. It is ultimately a film about offbeat people with a warm center. There is just a good feeling that comes from these comedic and almost surreal characters.

I was wonderfully surprised by this film. The fact that the ending was too much like a sitcom did not alter my general feeling of happiness after having watched this. Greg Pritikin is a great new director with much promise and a fresh voice. I look forward to his next creation.

—*Laura Abraham*

CREDITS

Steven: Adrien Brody
Fangora: Milla Jovovich
Heidi: Illeana Douglas
Lorena: Vera Farmiga
Fern: Jessica Walter
Lou: Ron Leibman
Michael: Jared Harris

Origin: USA
Released: 2002
Production: Richard Temtchine, Bob Fagan; Quadrant Entertainment; released by Artisan Entertainment
Directed by: Greg Pritkin
Written by: Greg Pritkin
Cinematography by: Horacio Marquinez
Music by: Paul Wallfisch
Sound: Theresa Radka
Editing: Bill Henry
Art Direction: Amanda Carroll
Costumes: Marie Abma
Production Design: Charlotte Bourke
MPAA rating: R
Running time: 90 minutes

REVIEWS

Boxoffice. October, 2003, p. 29.
Entertainment Weekly. September 19, 2003, p. 66.
Los Angeles Times Online. September 12, 2003.
New York Times Online. September 12, 2003.
People. September 22, 2003, p. 40.
Variety Online. March 26, 2003.

Duplex

Comedy has a new home.
—Movie tagline
Dream home. Nightmare neighbor!
—Movie tagline

 Box Office: $9.6 million

Director Danny DeVito, who first came to prominence as an actor playing the misanthropic Louie DePalma on TV's *Taxi*, probably knows he is never going to be tapped by Hallmark to make one of their heartwarming TV specials. His movies are pretty much the exact opposite of a Hallmark special. In his films, people don't discover their own goodness, they don't rise up to meet a lofty goal, and lessons are not learned. DeVito's oeuvre, *Throw Momma From the Train*, *Death to Smoochy*, and *The War of the Roses*, among them, are not exactly paeans to human goodwill. Eric Harrison of the *Houston Chronicle* called DeVito's earlier efforts "deliciously nasty." Eleanor Ringle Gillespie of the *Atlanta Journal-Constitution* stuck with the "nasty" theme and called DeVito "a nasty little sucker." Peter Howell of the *Toronto Star* wrote that "DeVito's filmmaking resume reads like a rap sheet for a homicidal maniac."

A DeVito film usually shows bad people doing bad things. Or sometimes they show people who seem to be good find out that they are really quite bad. *Duplex* is in the latter category. At first we think that Alex Rose (Ben Stiller) and Nancy Kendricks (Drew Barrymore) are, as their vivacious real estate agent, Kenneth (Harvey Fierstein), describes them, "a lovely young couple." Alex is an author working on his second book and Nancy has a job at a magazine. The couple has been priced out of Manhattan and is lured across the river to Brooklyn by what appears to be a fabulous brownstone. It's affordable, gorgeous and it's even near a little playground. Alex and Nancy can already imagine their picture-perfect life in the house—playing with their future child in the park, snuggling by one of the three fireplaces, Alex writing in a wood-paneled nook. And the house really is wonderful. It's full of beautiful wood wainscoting, original glass, and boasts lots of square footage. So beautiful is the house that Alex and Nancy are able to overlook the one catch—the fact that an elderly neighbor, Mrs. Connelly (Eileen Essell) still lives upstairs. Due to rent control, Mrs. Connelly is allowed to rent the upstairs apartment (for about $80 a month) until she passes on.

When Alex and Nancy look at the house, they try to visit the upstairs apartment, but Mrs. Connelly is too sick to let them in. In the first flash of what might be the unpleasant side of themselves, Alex and Nancy note that Mrs. Connelly's poor health might mean an imminent death and thus, the whole house for themselves. They are not displeased with this realization.

When the couple meets Mrs. Connelly again, they see that she is, alas, in fine health. The hearty Irish woman has more than enough energy to set about making life a big pain for Alex and Nancy. At first the annoyances are small. Mrs. Connelly blares her TV all night, filling Alex and Nancy's house with noise and keeping them awake. Their resulting sleep deprivation makes them quicker to get annoyed with Mrs. Connelly's other quirks. She interrupts Alex's writing time each day to have him complete tasks. He takes out her garbage (which erupts onto him) and takes her shopping (where she slowly counts each blueberry).

The rest of the film is pretty much the same thing, with everything amped up. Mrs. Connelly invites her brass band over in the morning to practice. The couple suffers. Mrs. Connelly witnesses Alex and Nancy having sex. The couple feels stupid. Mrs. Connelly chokes and Alex is forced to give her mouth-to-mouth resuscitation. The couple is grossed out.

No matter how the young couple try to handle the situation, it keeps getting worse. Soon, in typical DeVito fashion, they decide that the best solution to their problem would be to kill old Mrs. Connelly. You can imagine that this will not go as planned.

The movie, written by Larry Doyle (who wrote *Beavis and Butt-head* and worked on *The Simpsons*) raises the comedy level of the movie higher than it might have been. When DeVito is allowed to follow his instincts unchecked, he ends up with movies that are more mean-spirited than funny. As *Death to Smoochy* clearly showed, people doing mean things is not inherently funny. A mean act becomes funny because of the reasons behind it. The couple's meanness is funny because it is out of character. They are the type of people who, even though they are actively trying to kill Mrs. Connelly, still reflexively try to save her when she's choking.

Stiller's very presence helps the film a lot. As *Meet the Parents* and *There's Something About Mary* proved, it's funny to see Ben Stiller suffer. In one of the funniest running jokes, Alex does a slow burn as Officer Dan (Robert Wisdom) keeps misinterpreting his actions and accuses him of being first an elder abuser and then a wife beater. Stiller is so good at suffering humiliation that he can turn a not-so funny idea into a funny scene. He has the ability to even make a vomiting scene play well. *Duplex* is full of gross-out comedy, but somehow Stiller knows how to work it so that it seems somehow more dignified. When he is confronted with other people's gross smells, garbage, or bodily emissions, it's not just funny because of the shock value, but because of Stiller's horrified reactions. Stiller's skill is playing a character that strives for dignity but, due to outrageous circumstances, can never quite seem to get there.

Barrymore is a good physical comic, and also has the acting chops to show Nancy as a kind person who discovers that she is willing to do practically anything to pursue her yuppie dream lifestyle. Also good is octogenarian actress Essell who gracefully suffers through such indignities as having to call her pet parrot Little Dick.

Critics' opinions of the film seemed to hinge on their opinions of DeVito. Howell of the *Toronto Star* concluded, "We must fervently hope, pray even, that some tough-minded psychologist, social worker or parole warden gets to Danny DeVito and persuades him that cruelty isn't funny." Gillespie of the *Journal-Constitution* observed, "As can be true of DeVito's movies, *Duplex* is a bit over the top, but anyone with a strong stomach and a dark sense of humor will

enjoy it." And A. O. Scott of the *New York Times* called it "a refreshingly mean-spirited gothic real estate comedy."

—*Jill Hamilton*

CREDITS

Nancy: Drew Barrymore
Alex: Ben Stiller
Mrs. Connelly: Eileen Essell
Kenneth: Harvey Fierstein
Coop: Justin Theroux
Officer Dan: Robert Wisdom
Celine: Amber Valletta
Chick: James Remar
Tara: Maya Rudolph
Jean: Swoosie Kurtz
Herman: Wallace Shawn

Origin: USA
Released: 2003
Production: Ben Stiller, Nancy Juvonen, Drew Barrymore, Stuart Cornfeld, Jeremy Kramer; Red Hour, Flower Films; released by Miramax Films
Directed by: Danny DeVito
Written by: Larry Doyle
Cinematography by: Anastas Michos
Music by: David Newman
Sound: David M. Kelson
Editing: Lynzee Klingman
Art Direction: Mario R. Ventenilla
Costumes: Joseph G. Aulisi
Production Design: Robin Standefer
MPAA rating: PG-13
Running time: 88 minutes

REVIEWS

Chicago Sun-Times Online. September 26, 2003.
Entertainment Weekly. October 3, 2003.
Los Angeles Times Online. September 26, 2003.
New York Times Online. September 26, 2003.
USA Today Online. September 26, 2003.
Variety Online. September 21, 2003.
Washington Post. September 26, 2003, p. WE49.

AWARDS AND NOMINATIONS

Nomination:
Golden Raspberries 2003: Worst Actress (Barrymore).

Elephant

An ordinary high school day. Except that it's not.
—Movie tagline

 Box Office: $1.2 million

Gus Van Sant's much celebrated and unassuming thriller, *Elephant*, comes to American audiences after winning art-house cinema's most prestigious award, the Palme d'Or, at the Cannes Film Festival. Loosely based on the horrendous Columbine massacre, the film's weakest aspects remain its resemblance to that real-life tragedy.

For example, as writer-director, Van Sant keeps to the facts of two male gunmen, both in an upscale public high school. In so doing, his film says nothing about the possible role of prescribed and non-prescribed medications in making the two behave the way they do. Similarly, the film shows the young men ordering their assault rifles via the Internet from a mail-order business, a process that could never be as simple. By withholding all but the barest details serving to differentiate the two, and also filmically eschewing the blood and gore associated with their actions, Van Sant risks losing the audience that most needs to be shaken up by his film: the demographic group conditioned by the verisimilitude of, say, this year's chart-topping remake of *The Texas Chainsaw Massacre*.

But Van Sant can be forgiven his near-minimalist austerity as a storyteller if one is prepared to accept his film as an allegory on the foreclosed aspects of youth. On this profound level, its two monsters can be seen to represent not just their potential counterparts in other American high schools, but also the relatively recent global phenomenon of teens armed to the teeth, whose youthful fervor is made to serve political ends. Behind the film's nondescript Alex and Eric, lurk the ghosts of the Viet Cong, the Khmer Rouge and the Palestinian suicide bombers.

Van Sant admitted to the press, from the podium of the New York Film Festival, where *Elephant* was showcased, that he had started with the idea of the Columbine Two, then found a different way of telling his story, which would demand "the thought process" of the film's audience. His film, according to Van Sant, is intended to work as a "thought machine." No answers are provided to the harrowing problem of high school violence, because "there are as many answers as there are viewers." As for the film's title, Van Sant explained, "The entire school system, its size and the way it operates, is an elephant."

In filmic style, *Elephant* points in an ideological direction all its own. The film grammar that Van Sant uses to spin his eighty-odd minute tale emerges as a kind of manifesto to overturn the narrative codes that have fossilized since the inception of cinema. There are no scenes as such that move the story along. Instead, what becomes reinforced is the spatial continuum within which the horror will eventually take place. A scene, in such a scheme, is merely action that takes place within a continuity of space. This allows Van Sant to repeat its scenes, as certain bits of action, from a different perspective each time. Taken as a whole, these uneventful, non-dramatic scenes form a kind of circumference around a throbbing core that will eventually explode. This foregrounding of the spatial continuum of hallways, classrooms, washrooms, and the like allows Van Sant to adopt prolonged tracking shots, as the paths of the characters, most of whom will become victims of the massacre, appear to keep crisscrossing in a kind of existential matrix from which there is no escape.

Also, in terms of form, what emerges is a kind of "cinema of detail," for want of a better term, in which elements of setting, no matter how insignificant, become grist for the "thought machine" Van Sant intends his film to be. For example, the schizoid nature of the high school itself becomes evident in a huge mural that depicts an interracial mix when, in actuality, the students are predominantly white, with not even a handful of blacks. Similarly, a sign on the wall of the administrative office reads: "A man's mind stretched by a new idea cannot go back to its original dimension." This becomes an ironic comment on what possesses the two youths to eventually run amok.

Elephant can be divided into three distinct parts. In the first, we are introduced to those who, with two exceptions, will become the victims; in the second, we see the two young men at home, so to speak, and in the third, we see the carnage they wreak. The film opens with the blond-haired John McFarland (John Robinson) being driven to school down a suburban street by his drunken Dad (Timothy Bottoms in a cameo). Realizing his father's lack of control, John forces him out of the driver's seat and takes over. The next scene shows the camera buff, Elias (Elias McConnell) getting a punk couple to pose for him in the park while they're on their way to class. The scene ends with the film's first long take, a contemplative look at Elias walking away from the camera. John, it so happens, gets into trouble with the deputy principal, Mr. Luce (Matt Malloy), who orders him to report for detention.

We then move to the playing field, where the curly-haired, spectacled, plain-looking Michelle (Kristen Hicks) stops in the middle of her run to look up at the sky. The action is underscored by a flash forward on the soundtrack to Alex playing Beethoven's "Fur Elise" on the piano. The camera then follows, in the first of its many prolonged tracks, the handsome Nathan (Nathan Tyson) as he walks from the playing field toward the school building, then into the building, down a corridor, out of the building and into another building. The camera stops only when Nathan stops to greet his girlfriend, the young, attractive Carrie (Carrie Finklea), whom he kisses. Meanwhile, as he walks past them, we are introduced to three girls who look at him enviously: Brittany (Brittany Mountain), Jordan (Jordan Taylor) and Nicole (Nicole George). When this action is later repeated, the camera will remain with these girls and allow Nathan to walk out of frame.

When John, feeling sorry for himself, presumably because of his dysfunctional home life, retreats to a vacant lounge to cry in private, Acadia (Alicia Miles) walks up to comfort him and kisses him lightly on the cheek. We then see her enter a Gay Alliance meeting, where the topic under discussion is what constitutes a homosexual identity in terms of appearance.

Then, like a flash of lightning, we are introduced to the two young gunmen, the dark-haired Alex (Alex Frost) and the blond Eric (Eric Deulen). They are about to enter the school building, their guns concealed in backpacks and duffel bags. Their path crosses that of John and they warn him to keep away. When this action is repeated again before the film's climax, the camera stays with John as he, for his part, warns passersby not to enter the building.

After the small talk shared by Brittany, Jordan, and Nicole and a scene of Alex being humiliated in class by his fellow students, who throw food at him behind the instructor's back, we move to the second section of the film. Inside a plush, suburban home, we see Alex practicing on the piano. A circular track around his room shows the accoutrements of an upper-middle-class lifestyle: a boombox, sophisticated sound system, a set of weights, and a TV. Eric, his closest friend, one used to spending his nights in Alex's room, barges in and starts playing violent video games on Eric's laptop. The two also check on their Internet order from an outfit that calls itself "Guns USA."

The next morning, we hardly get to see Alex's parents, as he and Eric have breakfast. In their spare time, the two boys look at video clips of the Third Reich. When their assault rifles arrive in the mail, they cannot wait to test them out in a specially constructed work shed. On the morning of the climactic event, Eric joins Alex in the shower and briefly kisses him, their first kiss ever. They then cold-bloodedly chart their actions against a map of the school before getting into their car. Hanging from the mirror above the dashboard is what looks like a charm of Lucifer.

The third section of the film then begins. Michelle, who is stacking books in the library, is the first one we see being shot. Right there is Elias, who prepares to shoot Alex with his camera. Curiously, we don't see Elias getting shot. Brittany, Jordan, and Nicole, who happen to be in the washroom, are the next ones to get it. In the midst of it all, outside the building, John meets up with his worried Dad. The camera then follows Benny (Bennie Dixon), the only black among the victims, who first helps Acadia escape

through a window before walking boldly down the hallway. Eric shoots him dead. Eric then gives Mr. Luce a chance to run for his life, before shooting him in the back. Eric reunites with Alex in the blood-splattered cafeteria, where he reports that he shot the principal and everyone else in the office. Then, he too is shot dead, the bullet mysteriously striking him at the back of his neck.

In the film's final scene, Alex enters the cafeteria meat locker, where Nathan and Carrie are hiding. As Alex slowly starts reciting "eeny, meeny, miney, mo," and they plead for their lives, Van Sant's camera slowly pulls back, leaving the action suspended. The closing titles follow.

American critics, by and large, seem to have taken to Van Sant's observer stance. Manohla Dargis of the *Los Angeles Times* finds it in sharp contrast to what she calls Michael Moore's "self-serving" *Bowling for Columbine* (2002). In a similar vein, *Newsday's* Gene Seymour balances his praise for *Elephant* "as a masterwork" by noting that "something [is] being withheld by the movie, an emotional tether kept out of reach by Van Sant's vaguely chilly aesthetics." Elvis Mitchell in the *New York Times* seems to find this very quality providing a perspective "that whips the ordinary with the terrifying, an unforgettable mix."

—*Vivek Adarkar*

CREDITS

Alex: Alex Frost
Eric: Eric Deulen
John: John Robinson
Elias: Elias McConnell
Nathan: Nathan Tyson
Carrie: Carrie Finklea
Michelle: Kristen Hicks
Jordan: Jordan Taylor
Nicole: Nicole George
Brittany: Brittany Mountain
Mr. McFarland: Timothy Bottoms
Mr. Luce: Matt Malloy

Origin: USA
Released: 2003
Production: Dany Wolf; Meno Films, Blue Relief Inc.; released by HBO Films, Fine Line Features
Directed by: Gus Van Sant
Written by: Gus Van Sant
Cinematography by: Harris Savides
Sound: Felix Andrew
Editing: Gus Van Sant
Art Direction: Benjamin Hayden
MPAA rating: R
Running time: 81 minutes

REVIEWS

Boxoffice. November, 2003, p. 86.
Entertainment Weekly. October 31, 2003, p. 54.
Los Angeles Times Online. October 24, 2003.
New York Times Online. October 10, 2003.
Rolling Stone. November 13, 2003, p. 105.
Time. June 9, 2003, p. 74.
Vanity Fair. November, 2003, p. 128.
Variety Online. May 18, 2003.

AWARDS AND NOMINATIONS

Cannes 2003: Director (Van Sant), Film
Nomination:
Ind. Spirit 2004: Cinematog., Director (Van Sant).

Elf

This holiday, discover your inner elf.
—Movie tagline

Box Office: $173.3 million

In the Christmas comedy *Elf,* the title character is determined to travel on foot all the way from the North Pole to the Big Apple, sailing on an ice flow, marching through a snowy candy cane forest, traversing imposing mountains, and finally braving New York City traffic—whatever it takes to reach his goal. Will Ferrell, in the title role, is much the same way, going to whatever lengths necessary to win over his audience. The former *Saturday Night Live* cast member has shown himself to be a fearless comedic performer, someone who will do virtually anything for a laugh. He can go boisterously and wholeheartedly over the top, more than willing to let himself look utterly absurd or even repulsive. Anyone who has seen some of his more outrageous *SNL* skits or witnessed him unabashedly strutting his un-Adonis-like physique in this year's *Old School* can certainly attest to that. Sometimes it all works, and sometimes it really, really does not. When it was announced that Ferrell would be starring as a chipper six-foot-tall elf come Christmastime, many thought that it sounded like another ridiculous *SNL* sketch unwisely stretched into a painfully bad feature film. It is, however, supposed to be a time of miracles, and, lo and behold, many rejoiced upon seeing the surprisingly enjoyable *Elf.* The film is a silly, sweet holiday treat suitable for the entire family, and it works thanks in large part to Ferrell's appealing portrayal of the naive, sweet-natured, XXL-sized elf.

Actually, Ferrell's character is not really an elf at all, but a human raised by elves. As a baby in an orphanage, he crawled undetected into Santa's bag of gifts and was transported to the North Pole. Once there, he was given the name Buddy (because he wears Little Buddy-brand diapers) and was adopted by an older male elf who had somehow never gotten around to settling down and fathering children of his own due to his resolute commitment to making toys. Neither Papa Elf (wonderfully played by comic legend Bob Newhart) nor any of the other elves ever enlightened Buddy about the basic difference between himself and all the wee workers around him, and he has amazingly remained in the dark for thirty years. Perhaps not as bright as he is cheerful (and boy, is he ever cheerful), the lovable, childlike Buddy should have had a whole host of questions for Papa Elf by now, especially since he is of significantly greater proportions than everyone and everything around him. Buddy is also frustratingly all-thumbs when it comes to handcrafting toys. The other elves try to make him feel better, but sometimes he cannot help but feel like a cotton-headed "ninnymuggins."

One day, shortly before Christmas, Buddy finally overhears the stunning truth, and Papa Elf clues him in on his true, taller lineage. It is hilarious to watch poor Papa Elf's discomfiture as Buddy sits upon his lap for a heart-to-heart talk. It seems that while Buddy's mother is deceased, his father is alive and working for a book publisher in the Empire State Building. Although he is further informed by Santa (gruff but agreeable Ed Asner of *Mary Tyler Moore Show* fame) that his dad is on the dreaded naughty list, Buddy still would love to meet him and is sure that the man would feel the same. So Buddy says goodbye to Papa Elf, Santa, Leon the Talking Snowman (voiced by singer/musician Leon Redbone), and some cute animal buddies and jauntily makes his way to New York City.

Except for being mauled by a raccoon who would rather not be hugged, Buddy arrives safely and is awed by all he sees. While it is certainly possible to encounter more than a few peculiar people on the streets of Manhattan, few rank up there with a grinning six-foot three-inch man in an elf outfit replete with tiny hat, yellow tights, and shoes which curl up at the toe. It is clear from the reactions of passersby that they are not at all sure what to make of him. (For these scenes, spontaneous encounters between Ferrell and the unsuspecting public were filmed.) Buddy, oblivious, guileless, and sunny as ever, finds everything thrilling and magical. He sees a sign in a diner window promoting the "world's best cup of coffee" and bursts in to congratulate them. He giddily runs through a revolving door, stops to vomit, and then enthusiastically has another go-round. He is delighted to find gum stuck to the bottom of a subway railing, and (even though Santa warned him not to) pops it into his mouth. He (warily) masters an escalator but has more fun on an elevator, pushing all the floor buttons to make them light up in a glorious display. Oh sure, he also gets hit by a cab, but nothing can dampen his spirits.

Buddy's exceedingly joyful outlook and demeanor are a far cry from that of his prickly, workaholic father, Walter Hobbs (tough-guy James Caan of *Godfather* fame), who seems to pay much more attention to the proverbial bottom line than he does to his family. When Buddy arrives at Walter's office and ends up declaring his love in song in front of his father's coworkers, Walter looks baffled, wary, embarrassed, and irritated. Rejected and thrown out by security, Buddy soon finds himself at Gimbel's Department Store (actually no longer in existence), and not surprisingly is mistaken for one of their costumed holiday workers. There he meets the formidable store manager (Faizon Love of 2000's *The Replacements*), who is a little wary of Buddy's grinning ebullience; he also takes a shine to a dour but fetching worker named Jovie (Zooey Deschanel of 2002's *The Good Girl*), who is in serious need of some of Buddy's brand of Christmas cheer. Things also fail to go smoothly for Buddy here, as he naively follows the beautiful sound of Jovie's husky voice into the women's employee lounge, and then causes a tumultuous to-do by loudly proclaiming with authority that the store Santa is not the real deal: "You sit on a throne of lies!" Buddy shouts indignantly. The latter incident lands Buddy in the slammer. We see him sitting ludicrously in lockup, surrounded by some exceedingly tough-looking characters. Walter is called to bail Buddy out, and he is none too pleased about the uncomfortable position in which he finds himself. "Who the hell are you, and what is your problem?" he demands, clearly exasperated. Walter trots Buddy off for a DNA test, and is chagrined to learn that a long-ago relationship spawned this daffy man who insists he is one of Santa's elves. It is quite humorous to see how much Will Ferrell's character gives Walter the willies. Buddy is eager to hug and snuggle and tickle, but Walter looks like he is being tortured (when Buddy tries to grab his father's hand, Walter quickly bats it away).

At least for the time being, Walter takes Buddy home to stay with his family, including warm and amazingly accepting wife Emily (Mary Steenburgen of 2001's *Life as a House*) and ten-year-old son Michael (Daniel Tay, also in this year's *American Splendor*). Buddy has better luck bonding with both Emily and Michael, the latter especially appreciating him for fending off bullies with 90-mile-per-hour snowballs. Emily is just happy to see Michael happy, as he has been so sullen due to his father's lack of attentiveness. Watching Buddy's peculiar behavior around the house and when Walter takes him to work is amusing, including when he inadvertently angers a dwarf prospective author by greeting him warmly as a fellow elf. When we learn of Buddy's love for nauseatingly sugar-laden meals, it perhaps helps to explain some of his wired behavior.

Of course we know that, by the conclusion of *Elf*, Buddy will have shown everyone the way to a better, happier life. That is the way this type of film always ends, but sometimes the genre can get a little too gooey for many to

stomach. To its credit, *Elf* avoids this, only veering a tad in that direction at the very end. Walter is finally able to embrace both his sons, and Jovie is uplifted through time spent on the town with Buddy, but there is a final, somewhat less successful scene in which Santa's sleigh loses power over New York City due to a lack of Christmas spirit below. He crash-lands in Central Park and is being pursued by an ominous police unit, but Santa is able to take off once again thanks to the infectious good cheer spread by Buddy to his new—and newly merry—family and friends. In an epilogue, we see that all has ended well for everyone, and we witness Buddy and Jovie showing off their firstborn to a proud Papa Elf at the North Pole.

Enjoyably goofy and heartwarming, *Elf*, which was made on a budget of $33 million, far exceeded expectations by grossing more than $164 million. It was admirably directed by Jon Favreau (2001's *Made*) with an affectionate nod to other holiday classics such as *It's a Wonderful Life* (1946) and TV favorites like *Rudolph, the Red-Nosed Reindeer*. Kudos go to Rusty Smith for his creation of forced perspective sets and overall production design. While casting choices were sometimes surprising, all work surprisingly well. It is Ferrell who, like Buddy, provides the bulk of good cheer. "I'm good at that!" the character gushes. Yes, this *Elf* is quite good at that, indeed.

—*David L. Boxerbaum*

CREDITS

Buddy: Will Ferrell
Walter Hobbs: James Caan
Papa Elf: Bob Newhart
Santa: Ed Asner
Emily: Mary Steenburgen
Jovie: Zooey Deschanel
Gimbals Manager: Faizon Love
Michael: Daniel Tay
Miles Finch: Peter Dinklage
Deb: Amy Sedaris
Fulton: Michael Lerner
Morris: Andy Richter
Doctor: Jon Favreau

Origin: USA
Released: 2003
Production: Jon Berg, Todd Komarnicki, Shauna Robertson; Guy Walks Into a Bar; released by New Line Cinema
Directed by: Jon Favreau
Written by: David Barenbaum
Cinematography by: Greg Gardiner
Music by: John Debney
Sound: David Husby

Editing: Dan Lebental
Art Direction: Kevin Humenny
Costumes: Laura Jean Shannon
Production Design: Rusty Smith
MPAA rating: PG
Running time: 95 minutes

REVIEWS

Boxoffice. October, 2003, p. 14.
Chicago Sun-Times Online. November 7, 2003.
Entertainment Weekly. November 14, 2003, p. 94.
Los Angeles Times Online. November 7, 2003.
New York Times Online. November 7, 2003.
People. November 17, 2003, p. 32.
USA Today Online. November 7, 2003.
Variety Online. October 23, 2003.
Washington Post. November 7, 2003.

QUOTES

Buddy (Will Ferrell): "An elf's four major food groups are candy canes, candy corn, candy, and syrup."

The Embalmer (L'Imbalsamatore)

Two men are watching a vulture at the zoo. One is Peppino, a charming man of about 50, balding and under five feet tall. The other man is Valerio, about 20, handsome and over six feet tall. They watch the vulture with deep interest and try to recall how they know each other. During this discussion the point of view switches from the men to the vulture, with sound and visual distortion. Peppino explains he is a taxidermist and that animals are his passion.

Matteo Garrones's *The Emblamer,* is a study of two people, with a third acting as catalyst. Peppino is a man with a happy smile and a strong personality who likes to get his hands on young men by using his money to woe them. Valerio, who is not very bright, takes the bait and is told he is like a god. Peppino starts taking Valerio to clubs and getting hookers for the two of them. The men bed the hookers together, but Valerio doesn't understand that Peppino is less interested in the girls than he is in Valerio. The girls are just a means to an end for Peppino.

Peppino (Ernest Mahieux) is a man of extreme confidence and electric energy on the surface, but underneath there lurks something dark waiting to pounce. He finds Valerio (Valerio Foglia Manzillo) at his job and offers him more money to come work as a trainee taxidermist. Of course, Valerio takes the job and the money and soon is on his way to becoming a taxidermist himself.

Eventually, Peppino asks Valerio to move in with him, in order to save rent. Of course, by this point it is clear that his motivations are not that altruistic. Manuela (Marcella Granito) is Valerio's girlfriend and she is opposed to this move saying she has heard Peppino is connected to the mafia. She leaves Valerio, but very quickly he begins seeing Deborah (Elisabetta Rocchetti), who comes from a rich family and is immediately smitten with Valerio.

This film is great at hiding its true nature and revealing things only when it is ready. It is never clear whether Valerio really knows Peppino's intentions. It is hard to believe Valerio could be so completely naïve as to not see the truth. And if he knows, does he prefer Peppino to Deborah or does he just "go with the flow?" Is he one of those people who focuses on the person in front of them, forgetting what they may have with someone else?

We never know whether Peppino and Valerio ever have sex and are left scratching our head about this after one scene. Peppino gets in bed with Valerio after he sends their hookers home and we just never know for sure what happens, although Deborah screams at Valerio that she thinks something did, during a particularly rough moment between the two of them. This is not a comedy, but a serious look at two people who go after what they want with a vengeance. It is set on the Italian beach but in the gray season so the entire film seems cheerless and dead.

I thought Elisabetta Rocchetti was wonderful as Deborah, because she has such believable sexuality and handled this character with ease. Ernesto Mahieux as Peppino was one of the better casting decisions I have seen in a long time. This is an actor who despite his short stature holds each scene as his own. He is a man who knows how to get what he wants and the character is completely believable. Due in part to the wonderful acting of Ernesto Mahieux the plot of a balding midget with the incredible ability to take away a straight man from someone like Elisabetta Ricchetti seems plausible and almost likely.

—Laura Abraham

CREDITS

Peppino: Ernesto Mahieux
Valerio: Valerio Foglia Manzillo
Deborah: Elisabetta Rocchetti
Deborah's father: Pietro Biondi
Deborah's mother: David Ryall
Boss: Bernardino Terracciano

Manuela: Marcella Granito

Origin: Italy
Language: Italian
Released: 2003
Production: Domenico Procacci; Fandango; released by First Run
Directed by: Matteo Garrone
Written by: Matteo Garrone, Ugo Chiti, Massimo Gaudioso
Cinematography by: Marco Onorato
Music by: Banda Osiris
Sound: Maricetta Lombardo
Editing: Marco Spoletini
Art Direction: Paulo Bonfini
Costumes: Francesca Leondoff
MPAA rating: Unrated
Running time: 104 minutes

 REVIEWS

Box Office Magazine. Sept. 2003, p. 122.
Chicago Sun-Times Online. Nov. 14, 2003.
Detroit Free Press. Aug. 10, 2003, p. 3E.
L.A. Times Online. Oct. 3, 2003.
Variety Online. May 20, 2002.

Fellini: I'm a Born Liar (Fellini: Je suis un grand menteur) (Federico Fellini: Sono un gran bugiardo) (Fellini: Sono un gran bugiardo)

A good documentary can make anyone watching feel like an expert on its subject. Probably most folks watching the successful 2003 documentary *Spellbound*, for example, had a passing familiarity with the film's subject—spelling bees. At the end of *Spellbound,* however, a viewer would be aware of the attention surrounding the national bee, the kind of mighty ambition the young spellers have, and even various highly precise strategies for winning.

Fellini: I'm a Born Liar is not that kind of documentary, and perhaps it is not trying to be. Someone wanting to learn more about the great Italian director would probably be better off watching some of his most famous films, including *8¹/₂, Casanova,* or *La Dolce Vita.* Fellini was so great a filmmaker that critics easily refer to him as a "master" and was so renowned that his name was often tacked onto the front of his films' titles, as in *Fellini Satyricon.*

Fellini: I'm a Born Liar is less like a regular documentary and more like, say, the extra tracks that come with a boxed set of music. They're not the first examples a novice should experience, but rabid fans and completists will be sure to enjoy them. Director Damian Pettigrew seems to assume that his viewers are as knowledgeable about Fellini as he is. Sometimes, this makes the film more difficult to understand than it needs to be, and this is a drawback. For example, Pettigrew returns to the exact places where some of Fellini's most famous shots were taken, but doesn't bother to identify what they are or which film they are from.

The film's nascence was in the 1980s when Pettigrew was interviewing the writer Italo Calvino. Calvino invited Pettigrew for a homemade spaghetti dinner with Fellini. For years after this meeting, Pettigrew hounded Fellini to grant him an interview. Finally, the director agreed to talk with Pettigrew in 1993, just a few months before his death. Fellini commented about the interview, which ran ten hours, that it was "the longest and most detailed conversation ever recorded of my personal vision."

The film contains generous samplings from this interview as well as interviews with actors Donald Sutherland, Roberto Benigni, and Terence Stamp, plus collaborators like screenwriter Tullio Pinelli, cinematographer Giuseppe Rotunno, producer Daniel Toscan du Plantier, and Calvino. In but one of the overly obtuse things about the film, Pettigrew does not bother to identify the interviewees until the end of the film. It is a rare person that could recognize all of these people by sight, and it certainly doesn't seem like it would be a dumbing down of the movie to slap a few lines of text on the screen to identify the various speakers.

Curiously, there are no interviews with Fellini's wife and frequent star, Giulietta Masina, or actor/alter ego Marcello Mastroianni. Masina shows up very briefly on some old footage taken on the set; of her, Fellini comments, "I married the right woman for a man like me." Mastroianni does show up frequently in old footage, some of it never before seen, including the eight-millimeter, black-and-white footage of the shockingly young-looking duo working on *La Dolce Vita.* But we never hear what Mastroianni thought of his long working relationship with the director. We do get the interesting observation that the actor "would turn up tired in the morning, sleep between takes, and do whatever Fellini told him to do without complaining." Roger Ebert of the *Chicago Sun-Times* wrote, "That this approach created the two best performances in Fellini's work (in *La Dolce Vita* and *8¹/₂*) argues that Mastroianni may have been onto something."

That "something" may have been self-preservation. In his interview, Fellini talks of how he loves actors and always got along famously with them. The interviews with Stamp and Sutherland tell a different story. Sutherland, in particular, is bitter about his experience working on 1976's *Casanova*. He recalls that time as "hell on earth" and remembers Fellini as "a martinet, a tyrant, a dictator."

Part of the problems between actors and the director came from the fact that Fellini already knew exactly how he wanted his movies to look. It was frustrating for him when the actors did not just inherently know how to recreate what he was seeing in his head, thus Fellini micromanaged the achievement of that vision. He knew exactly how he wanted a swatch of fabric to look, exactly how the light should play on a character's face. (In one instance, inspired by a drive in the country in which he saw plastic spread over fields, he decided that he wanted to copy that look for the ocean. His set decorators had to rig up a machine with a series of wheels that caused a sheet of plastic to undulate from below. The idea was that the ocean should look "fake but believable.") To make sure that his actors were doing what he wanted, Fellini would stand right by the camera barking out instructions on every minute detail of the performance. (To make this possible he filmed the sequences without sound and dubbed in dialogue later.) In one scene, we see the director filming an orgy sequence for *Satyricon*. Fellini stands to the side, commanding every little move: "Now you lean up and kiss her. Then reach down her back. Turn your head and lean back." The director was filming his dreams and fantasies, and only he knew how they should properly play.

The old, discovered footage is fun to see, but the real heart of the film is the interview with Fellini. It's a pleasure to hear an artist ruminate on art and life. He talks about feeling somehow possessed when he makes movies, as though he is just the conduit for a stronger force. "It's someone else, not me, with whom I coexist, someone I don't know or know only by hearsay," he says. He discusses the vagaries of memory, and film's role in shaping memories. For instance, he relates how his filmed versions of his boyhood town of Rimini have become more real to him than the actual place. He tries to define his role as a director and artist and ends up making several conclusions. At one point he calls himself a magician, at another, a liar. He also describes himself as "an impostor, a clown, general, and chief of police" as well as a kind of godlike figure. Fellini admits that he made his films to get the money—to him, total artistic freedom is bad for an artist—but also says that when

he is away from his sets, he feels "exiled, a bit empty. I can't cope with what is called normal existence."

Usually films evoke a broad spectrum of critical opinion, but the reviews for *Fellini: I'm a Born Liar* sounded markedly similar. The consensus: serious fans will like it and others will not. According to A. O. Scott of the *New York Times*, "Mr. Pettigrew's affection for Fellini and his films animates this documentary and limits its appeal. Aficionados will be enthralled by the master's ramblings and ruminations, thrilled at behind-the-scenes glimpses of his working methods, and delighted to sample snippets of his movies, ones famous and obscure. But for skeptics and novices, the experience will be less satisfying: familiarity with Fellini's life and his oeuvre is assumed." William Arnold of the *Seattle Post-Intelligencer* gave the film a B– and concluded, "Unfortunately, the film assumes viewers have such a vast knowledge of Fellini's life and films that it's likely to play best to graduate film students. It also doesn't give the uninitiated any sense of the contours of Fellini's brilliant career or try to pin down exactly what his unique contribution to the cinema was—why, for instance, the word 'Felliniesque' is in the dictionary." Kenneth Turan of the *Los Angeles Times* wrote that the film is "made with an ambition the maestro himself would have appreciated and approved. For the rest of us, that is largely, but not entirely, a good thing," adding that "*Born Liar* is both completely fascinating and intermittently frustrating; however, as with Fellini's own films, the downside is far outweighed by the pluses." The *Chicago Tribune*'s Michael Wilmington gave the film 2¹/₂ (out of 4) stars and declared the documentary "a must for film scholars and Fellini lovers. But other viewers (including those who want to learn about a director once central to world film culture and now lesser known to younger audiences) may be frustrated by Pettigrew's neglect of crucial biographical information and the films made before *8¹/₂*." ⬛

—*Jill Hamilton*

CREDITS

Himself: Federico Fellini
Himself: Donald Sutherland
Himself: Terence Stamp
Himself: Giuseppe Rotunno
Himself: Roberto Benigni

Origin: Germany
Released: 2003
Production: released by First Look Pictures
Directed by: Damian Pettigrew
Written by: Damian Pettigrew, Olivier Gal
Cinematography by: Paco Wiser
Editing: Florence Ricard

MPAA rating: Unrated
Running time: 89 minutes

REVIEWS

Chicago Sun-Times Online. May 2, 2003.
New York Times Online. Dec. 11, 2003.

The Fighting Temptations

Don't fight the feeling.
—Movie tagline

Box Office: $29.8 million

A movie musical lives or dies on how it sounds. There are certainly ones that take the trouble to provide an engaging plot, like *The Sound of Music,* but a musical with a bad, or even embarrassingly bad plot, like *Purple Rain,* can be fine enough, too. Based on the music alone, *The Fighting Temptations* is a winner.

In a way, there's no chance it couldn't have been a success. Veteran producers Jimmy Jam and Terry Lewis oversaw the music and wrote some of the songs, too. Several members of the original O'Jays sing, as do Beyonce Knowles (formerly of Destiny's Child and currently in every tabloid modeling her latest premiere dress), MC Lyte, T-Bone, Lil' Zane, Melba More and the Reverend Shirley Caesar. Also to the music's credit is that the Blind Boys of Alabama and Angie Stone sing and Cuba Gooding Jr. does not.

The bad news for the movie is that writers Elizabeth Hunter and Saladin K. Patterson aren't exactly gifted in stringing together the many show-stopping musical numbers with a compelling plot to create a lovely tapestry of words and song. It's more like they were hard-pressed to come up with something, so they watched a few of Gooding's old movies then tossed this one together.

It doesn't help the film that the star is Gooding, a man whose hammy overacting can make even the best of material seem like, well, a Cuba Gooding Jr. movie. Even though he won rave reviews and an Oscar for his role in Cameron Crowes's *Jerry Maguire,* Gooding is not beloved by critics. His roles in films like *Snow Dogs* and *Boat Trip* have made critics dread the prospect of any new Gooding film. Their increasing annoyance at the actor's skills are not at all veiled in their reviews for *The Fighting Temptations.* Glenn Whipp of the *Los Angeles Daily News* wrote that the film "features wall-to-wall mugging from Cuba Gooding Jr., who strains

so hard to please every moment he's on screen that you may well find yourself rooting against his character in the vain hope that maybe the good Lord will call him home and put an end to our misery." Ty Burr of the *Boston Globe* wrote, "There's nothing here to match the horror that is the trailer for the upcoming *Radio,* in which Gooding plays a mentally challenged mascot for a white football team, but the shamelessness of the performance can still make you flinch." And A. O. Scott of the *New York Times* wrote, "Mr. Gooding can be so irrepressibly bouncy that you want to swat him with a tennis racket." For the sake of Gooding's mental health and personal confidence level, we shall hope that he is one of those actors who doesn't read their reviews.

As happened in both *Boat Trip* and *Snow Dogs,* Gooding again finds himself a fish out of water. And exactly as in *Snow Dogs,* he is once again spurred to live in a new place due to the wishes of a newly dead relative. And again, as in *Snow Dogs,* he will shun his materialistic ways and find true happiness. It's hard to see why anyone would ever bother to rip off *Snow Dogs.* To be fair, there is a major difference between *Snow Dogs* and *The Fighting Temptations.* In *Snow Dogs,* Gooding's character went from the south to the north; in *The Fighting Temptations,* he goes north to south.

Darrin Hill (Gooding) is a mid-level exec at a big Manhattan ad agency. He's starting to rise at the agency, but he's hiding a secret. He's not a Yalie who was raised in Monte Carlo, but rather a high school drop out from Montecarlo, Georgia. His mother (Ann Nesby) was kicked out of the local church and its choir when it was discovered that she was moonlighting as a nightclub singer. That would be singing the devil's music, according to Paulina Pritchard (LaTanya Richardson), the highly uptight and domineering sister of the meekly pliable Reverend Lewis (Wendell Pierce).

When Darrin's false background is discovered, he is quickly fired from the ad agency. At the same time, he's received word that his beloved yet neglected Aunt Sally has died. Darrin returns to his old hometown of Montecarlo and learns that his Aunt will leave him $150,000—if he takes over the duties of running the church choir and scores them a win in the big annual Gospel Explosion. Darrin is wholly unqualified and uninterested, but he's being hounded by creditors and needs to earn some fast cash. Also, he meets the lovely Lilly (Knowles), a sultry nightclub singer who has a similar backstory to dear old mom's.

Darrin starts with the business of getting his choir up and running. This is a problem since there are few members and no new prospective members. Also providing a possibly insurmountable obstacle for Darrin is Paulina, who is mad that he has taken over the choir job. It's hard to imagine that, in a movie like this one, such a closed-minded character would eventually triumph over all the other "good" characters with all their spunk and whatnot, but the screenwriters dutifully throw her in there anyway.

The town is populated with supporting actors who divert some of the spotlight away from Gooding. Steve Harvey is a drunken radio announcer and Mike Epps plays the kind of fast-talking, skirt-chasing guy that he always plays. Rue McLanahan of the *Golden Girls* is one of the choir members, but inexplicably she barely has any lines. Knowles has good presence onscreen, especially during the musical numbers. She plays the usual girl role in a big Hollywood movie—the one who gets lied to repeatedly by her would-be beau, but decides to take him back after he gives her that one big heartfelt apology.

Critics were split about 50/50 on the merits of the film. Roger Ebert of the *Chicago Sun-Times* observed, "*The Fighting Temptations* follows a formula in a kind of easygoing way, and you know it, but it generates so much good will and so many laughs that you don't really care." Steven Rea of the *Philadelphia Inquirer* called it a "woefully thin and pointless musical comedy boasting the no-chemistry couple of [Gooding and Knowles]." Scott Brown of *Entertainment Weekly* gave it a B + and called it "full-throated and good-hearted, yet tart and sharp in all the right places." Whipp of the *Daily News* summed up, "When anyone opens their mouth to sing, it's good; when anyone opens their mouth to talk, it's bad."

—Jill Hamilton

CREDITS

Darrin Fox: Cuba Gooding Jr.
Lilly: Beyonce Knowles
Lucius: Mike Epps
Paulina Pritchett: LaTanya Richardson
Miles Smoke: Steve Harvey
Bessie Cooley: Melba Moore

Origin: USA
Released: 2003
Production: David Gale, Loretha Jones, Jeff Pollack; MTV Films, Handprint Entertainment; released by Paramount Pictures
Directed by: Jonathan Lynn
Written by: Elizabeth Hunter, Saladin Patterson
Cinematography by: Alfonso Beato
Music by: Jimmy Jam, Terry Lewis, James "Big Jim" Wright
Sound: Michael Hilkene
Music Supervisor: Spring Aspers
Editing: Paul Hirsch
Art Direction: Cathrye Bangs
Costumes: Mary Jane Fort, Tracey A. White
Production Design: Victoria Paul
MPAA rating: PG-13
Running time: 123 minutes

REVIEWS

Chicago Sun-Times Online. September 19, 2003.
Entertainment Weekly. September 26, 2003, p. 74.
Los Angeles Times Online. September 19, 2003.
New York Times Online. September 19, 2003.
People. September 29, 2003, p. 33.
USA Today Online. September 19, 2003.
Variety Online. September 11, 2003.
Washington Post. September 19, 2003, p. WE43.

AWARDS AND NOMINATIONS

Nomination:
Golden Raspberries 2003: Worst Actor (Gooding).

Final Destination 2

Death may be closer than it appears.
—Movie tagline
You can't cheat death twice.
—Movie tagline

Box Office: $46.4 million

On the first anniversary of the crash of flight 180 bound for Paris, Kimberly Corman (A. J. Cook) has a premonition of a terrible, cascading, multi-car accident on the highway she and three friends are about to take on a brief vacation to warmer climes. In shock at the vividness of the accident that takes the lives of so many people, including herself, Kimberly becomes frozen with fear on the on-ramp of that highway, backing up traffic behind her. She desperately tries to tell her friends and then a police officer, Thomas Burke (Michael Landes), about what she has experienced, but none of them believe her and the drivers of the other cars are getting very exasperated until, that is, the accident happens right in front of them.

This is interesting because a premonition is exactly what had saved the lives of a handful of students on that airplane one year ago. But as everyone knows, all those who survived the crash were eventually claimed by death one by one until there was only one left, Clear Rivers (Ali Larter). (Ali Larter's Clear Rivers is the only character to carry over from *Final Destination* to *FD2*—not counting yet another cameo by the spooky undertaker, Mr. Bludworth, played by Tony Todd who was supposed to have had a bigger part this time around but doesn't.)

This coincidence is not lost on Kimberly who now desperately tries to convince the survivors that they must be on the lookout for death who now feels cheated because she has upset its plan. The survivors, Officer Burke, recent lottery winner Evan Lewis (David Paetkau), Nora Carpenter (Lynda Boyd) and her son Tim (James Kirk), a coke-head named Rory (Jonathan Cherry), a workaholic woman named Kat (Keegan Connor Tracy) and a motorcycle riding Eugene (T. C. Carson) all refuse to believe her. And then Evan dies—in a most awful manner.

If death is out to get you because you put a crimp in its plan, what can one do? Foil the plan again? But how does one do that? To find out, Kimberly goes to the one last survivor of flight 180, Clear Rivers, to find out how she has managed to cheat death yet again after a whole year. Clear has done this by voluntarily having herself locked up in a padded room at a psychiatric institution. "Is she dangerous or something?" Kimberly asks of the ward nurse. "No, Honey, she suspects you are," the nurse replies indicating Clear's incredible paranoia.

So what advice does Clear have for Kim? "Watch out for the signs," she tells her. "Have you ever seen anything creepy or ominous—an in-your-face irony kind of thing? Recognizing the signs can mean the difference between life and death." Beyond that, however, Clear is totally unwilling to leave her cell and put herself back into death's gameplan.

Soon Kim is seeing signs everywhere: pigeons, shadows of a man with hooks, drowning in a white van. She tries to use these warnings to save people, but she is usually too late. However, Kim has managed to shame Clear into leaving her sanctuary. Together, Clear takes Kim and Officer Burke to see the one person who might be able to shed some light on how to survive, undertaker Mr. Bludworth. On the one hand Bludworth tells them "You can't cheat death; there are no escapes," but then turns around and tells them that "if the plan is flawed it can be beaten." How? By introducing a life that was not meant to be one can cause death to start his plan all over again.

Suddenly Kim remembers a pregnant woman who was in line behind her on the on ramp, Isabella Hudson (Justina Machado). Since Isabella would have died in the accident, so, too would her baby. So if they can ensure Isabella delivers her baby before death can cash in her chips then maybe they can all be saved. But no one knows where Isabella is and while they set out to find her, more of the survivors meet incredible deaths. It gets so bad that one survivor, Eugene, even takes Officer Burke's gun and tries to kill himself. He fires it six times, but even though it is fully loaded, it constantly misfires. The reason is obvious: it is not his turn to die.

The fiendishly nervous tension that Eugene suffers is shared by those who watch this movie and is one of the reasons the first *Final Destination* was so successful. And like its successful predecessors such as *Jaws* and *Scream*, it

realizes that this tension has to be accompanied by nervous laughter in order to be a truly successful and scary film. Both films work at creating a profound sense of menace, teasing the viewer with death scenes in which we absolutely know for sure that the character will die, but in which we are so toyed with that we can never be sure how. Never have the words Rube Goldberg been used as much as they have been in describing the death scenes in these two films. In them everything, even the most mundane objects, become lethal.

The movie sets us up for a most obvious method of death but if it's conspicuous it won't happen. The death scenes constantly build as we try to figure out what's a red herring and what will be the actual instrument of death, and we giggle as we guess wrong and wince when the coup de gras is finally delivered, usually out of left field. Oil spills on a stove, a plastic magnet falls into Chinese food which explodes in the microwave, a diamond ring falls into garbage disposal and a hand gets stuck. Which will get him? the disposal's blades or a fire or maybe an explosion? Answer: none of the above. Perhaps a fall from the window as he tries to escape? Nope. Then it's got to be the result of a faulty fire escape, right? Well, sort of. Once one accepts that these very gory scenes will be purposefully contrived just for the fun of it, then the more far-fetched the better.

Granted these devilishly devised death scenes were one of the great novelties of the first film—that and making death the actual villain in the plot—and this sequel just seems to cash in on the original's premise. However, while it may be a paler imitation, it's still fun for those who like this sort of grisly mayhem.

Similarly, although the original posed a few interesting "philosophical" questions about death, the sequel doesn't seem to want to bother that much about the big questions the plot rests on. One wishes one character or another might have asked, if it's death (fate? God? Satan?) who comes looking to even the score, then "who" is responsible for the sudden premonitions in people who have never had premonitions before? And is there some kind of supernatural connection to the number 180; the number of the airline flight in the first movie, the number that is flashing on the warning sign on Kim's on-ramp, and the number of the mile marker where Kim and crew crash after just missing Isabella in a van going in the opposite direction? Or maybe just a simple explanation about the weird order of the deaths in this one, something that was pretty straightforward the first time around.

Final Destination grossed half its profits in just its first weekend of release in 2000 even though it had no star attraction. It took three years to get this sequel into theaters—even though part of this film's plot is that it is the one-year anniversary of the crash of flight 180 in the first film. In reality, though, *FD2* isn't really a sequel as much as a film made to the template of the first film's plot with the two touching at just a few points (the characters of

Clear and Mr. Bludworth, the anniversary, and an interesting relationship between the survivors this time and survivors last time).

The second film may not be as thoughtful as the first as the survivors finally figure out why they're dying and in what order, and the two films are about equal in the inventive death sequences and spectacular action, but the second film may have the first beat in sheer gruesomeness.

—*Beverley Bare Buehrer*

Clear Rivers: Ali Larter
Kimberly Corman: A.J. Cook
Officer Thomas Burke: Michael Landes
Eugene Dix: Terrence "T.C." Carson
Nora Carpenter: Lynda Boyd
Rory: Jonathan Cherry
Kat: Keegan Connor Tracy
Shania: Sarah Carter
Mr. Bludworth: Tony Todd
Isabella Hudson: Justina Machado
Evan: David Paetkau
Tim Carpenter: James N. Kirk

Origin: USA
Released: 2003
Production: Warren Zide, Craig Perry; released by New Line Cinema
Directed by: David R. Ellis
Written by: J. Mackye Gruber, Eric Bress
Cinematography by: Gary Capo
Music by: Shirley Walker
Sound: Ralph Parker
Editing: Eric A. Sears
Art Direction: James Steuart
Costumes: Jori Woodman
Production Design: Michael Bolton
MPAA rating: R
Running time: 100 minutes

REVIEWS

Chicago Sun-Times Online. January 31, 2003.
Chicago Tribune Online. January 31, 2003.
Los Angeles Times Online. January 31, 2003.
New York Times Online. January 31, 2003.
People. February 10, 2003, p. 37.
USA Today Online. January 31, 2003.
Variety Online. January 29, 2003.
Washington Post. January 31, 2003, p. WE41.

Kimberly (A.J. Cook): "I have this really bad feeling it's not over yet."

Finding Nemo

You've never seen fish prepared like this.
—Movie tagline
Sea it.
—Movie tagline
Fish are just like people, only flakier.
—Movie tagline

 Box Office: $339.7 million

Considering the track record of success for Pixar Animation Studios, Walt Disney Pictures will almost certainly do anything necessary to maintain its partnership with Pixar. After four spectacular hits in a row with *Toy Story* (1995), *A Bug's Life* (1998), *Toy Story 2* (1999), and *Monsters, Inc.* (2001), one might easily wonder if the winning streak could continue, but the unveiling of Pixar's underwater adventure *Finding Nemo* confirms that the co-venture with Pixar was one of the wisest decisions Disney has ever made, both creatively and financially.

Finding Nemo opened to bigger box office numbers than its four predecessors, even while competing head-to-head with the likes of Jim Carrey (*Bruce Almighty*) and *Matrix: Reloaded,* and was immediately received with some of the most glowing reviews of the year to date. The critical accolades and the enthusiastic public response were well-deserved. Though it may be a cliché that is over-used with such animated fare, *Finding Nemo* is truly the kind of film that can be enjoyed by all ages. However, though the storyline and themes of the movie are in themselves enough to endear *Finding Nemo* to viewers of any age, the film also excels on every other crucial level, from the performances to the overall visual artistry—so much so that many critics proclaimed it the best Pixar movie yet.

At the center of *Finding Nemo* is the tale of a father and son. The father is Marlin (voiced by Albert Brooks), an overly worrisome clownfish who suffers the worst kind of tragedy in the surprisingly disturbing opening minutes of the film when his wife and all but one of their soon-to-be-hatched children are killed by a vicious undersea predator. The son is Nemo (voiced by Alexander Gould), the one child lucky enough to be spared from the horrible fate of his siblings. Marlin becomes the model of an over-protective parent, making the unrealistic (though understandable) promise that "nothing will ever happen" to his son.

His concern for Nemo is magnified all-the-more by the fact that Nemo's fins are unusually small, making it harder for him to swim quickly and efficiently. "One thing to remember about the ocean—it's not safe," Marlin warns. When Nemo is old enough to attend school, Marlin accompanies him and fears letting him out his sight, wondering aloud whether his son is truly ready or not. Not surprisingly, Nemo is eager to experience some independence and resents his father constantly watching over his shoulder. Only moments later, in an act of open defiance of his father, Nemo swims out into the open sea and is suddenly caught by a human diver. The diver turns out to be a dentist, and Nemo soon finds himself in an office aquarium watching patients getting their teeth cleaned.

Panic-stricken and heart-broken, Marlin sets out to find his lost son. His frenetic search soon leads him into the company of Dory (voiced by Ellen DeGeneres), a friendly blue tang who cannot retain short-term memories, a character trait that results in some of the genuinely funniest moments in the film. Initially Marlin teams up with Dory only because he believes she can help him find Nemo, but the relationship between the two fish rapidly develops into one of the most interesting, character-driven elements of the story as their journey becomes one of both deepening friendship and self-discovery. Shortly after meeting, Marlin and Dory are lucky enough to stumble upon the goggles of the diver who took Nemo. Fortunately for them, the diver's address (somewhere in Sydney, Australia) is written on the goggles—and Dory just happens to be able to read.

Over the course of their journey, Marlin and Dory encounter a number of eccentric creatures inhabiting the sea, the first of which is a shark named Bruce (an homage to the behind-the-scenes nickname of the title character of *Jaws*), voiced by Barry Humphries. Bruce and his pals belong to an organization of Fish-Eaters Anonymous, whose slogan is "Fish are our friends, not food." They drag Marlin and Dory along to one of their group meetings, but the session takes a dangerous turn when Bruce gets a whiff of blood and promptly regresses, overwhelmed by his instincts. A chase ensues, resulting in the goggles falling into a deep, pitch-black trench. The two little fish descend into the darkness, where they meet a dangerous resident of the deep. They don't recover the goggles, but they do find them and get close enough for Dory to memorize the address. Luckily, by repeating the address over and over to herself, Dory finds she is able to retain the memory—which is quite an accomplishment for her.

Meanwhile, in the dentist's office, Nemo makes friends with fellow saltwater aquarium captives led by a Moorish Idol fish named Gil (voiced by Willem Dafoe). The mysterious and cunning Gil has long been trying to find a way to

escape, and the arrival of little Nemo inspires him to devise a new plan dependent on Nemo's size and ability to swim quickly. However, after a first escape attempt turns into a close call that's almost fatal for Nemo, Gil backs off, feeling guilty for having put Nemo in danger, and essentially gives up on the idea of winning their freedom. This is one of many poignant moments in the film, packed with emotional and character-driven depth as the other fish realize their chances of escaping are practically nonexistent now that Gil has given up. Nemo, of course, feels that he failed them all despite assurances to the contrary.

Back in the depths of the ocean, Marlin and Dory come across a school of fish that know the way to Sydney. After becoming irritated with Marlin, the fish privately tell Dory the direction that they must swim, which will take them first through a deep trench. The fish warn Dory to swim through the trench, not over it. When Dory shares the information with Marlin and they arrive at the trench, she does not remember the warning but does feel an "instinct" that they should not swim over the trench. Marlin takes a look at the trench, sees countless skeletons, and concludes that Dory has no idea what she's talking about. Despite Dory's appeals for him to trust her, Marlin insists that it would be easier and safer for them to swim over the trench—and so they do. However, Marlin soon discovers he should have trusted Dory when they find themselves surrounded by deadly jellyfish. Dory's subsequent near-brush with death makes Marlin realize how much his new friend means to him, but he still has not learned to really trust her.

As their undersea journey continues, the two fish spend some time riding an ocean current with a group of carefree sea turtles and find themselves in the belly of a whale (who actually turns out to be a kind soul giving them a free ride to Sydney). The story of their journey begins to spread through the ocean from sea-creature to sea-creature, eventually reaching the "ears" of a pelican who knows the fish trapped in the dentist's aquarium. Before long the news reaches Nemo himself, and hearing of his father's quest emboldens him to attempt Gil's dangerous escape plan once again.

There is no great surprise in the ending, for of course Nemo and Marlin are reunited and Dory practically becomes a part of the family. However, as expected as the conclusion might be, it is nevertheless satisfying and uplifting, for the real triumph of the story is in the journey, not in the ending. What makes *Finding Nemo* more sophisticated and ultimately much more satisfying than many films, both animated and live-action, is that its tale succeeds on more than a superficial level. Many filmmakers certainly attempt to make their stories more complex by infusing them with layers of meaning, but unfortunately that goal is not always reached, nor is it often reached without some clumsiness. The theme of "finding" is central to the story of Nemo, yet only superficially does it deal with the literal quest for the son, though that is the obvious meaning. The three major characters—Marlin, Nemo, and Dory—all embark on a journey, and each one finds something that enables him or her to grow (in fact, this is even true of other characters in the movie, a consistency in theme which is rarely so seamlessly achieved).

Marlin's quest for his son leads to a discovery about Nemo and himself—but perhaps the latter more. He comes to realize what many over-protective parents may find difficult to embrace—that he can never ensure the complete protection and safety of anyone and therefore must accept that risk is part of life. He also learns the importance of trusting others—not only Nemo, but Dory as well. His relationship with Dory reveals that he is not simply an overly worried father who's afraid of granting his child some independence; he in fact is an individual who has little faith in anyone and prefers maintaining as much control as possible over his little world. The adventures with Dory teach him otherwise—that he must loosen up and have faith in others, even when that means taking big risks.

Little Nemo experiences his own self-discovery. First, he learns that his father truly does care for him and has his best interests at heart. Second, he experiences some independence but also learns that independence isn't just about doing what you want. On top of all this is the lesson that even with a physical disadvantage that some might label a disability (i.e., his small fins), one can rise to the occasion and be as successful as anyone else—a theme particularly useful for children. Finally, even silly, lovable Dory (who deals with her own kind of "disadvantage" in the form of her memory loss) achieves self-discovery, almost in contrast to Marlin, as she learns to have faith in herself.

In terms of performances, *Finding Nemo* boasts an all-around excellent cast. The voice talents behind the animated characters are all genuine and perfectly suited to the characters—from Albert Brooks' nervous, sometimes dry, and occasionally clumsy tone befitting Marlin to Ellen DeGeneres' sweet-natured but goofy and often hilarious turn as the voice of Dory. Other standouts in the voiceover department include Willem Defoe, Barry Humphries, and director Andrew Stanton (as the sea turtle Crush), but the entire cast performs superbly. It is clear, simply from the voice work, that the actors involved in this production not only had a good time but were truly serious about what they were doing behind the microphone. Fortunately, they had a clever and sophisticated script to work with.

The heart of *Finding Nemo* is its character-driven, touching story of family love and self-discovery. The metaphorical icing on the cake comes in the form of the visual presentation—the richness, depth, and beautiful realism of the undersea environment. Watching a movie like *Finding Nemo,* one is reminded that each frame of film, in the hands of an artist, is a canvas capable of inviting us on a journey of our own—surprising us, delighting us, and touching both our hearts and minds along the way. *Finding Nemo,* like any great film, is a treasure to be appreciated long after it is experienced, and it is one that should not only be experienced by children, for its themes can touch us all.

—*David Flanagin*

CREDITS

Marlin: Albert Brooks (Voice)
Dory: Ellen DeGeneres (Voice)
Gill: Willem Dafoe (Voice)
Nemo: Alexander Gould (Voice)
Bruce: Barry Humphries (Voice)
Crush: Andrew Stanton (Voice)
Bloat: Brad Garrett (Voice)
Peach: Allison Janney (Voice)
Gurgle: Austin Pendleton (Voice)
Bubbles: Stephen (Steve) Root (Voice)
Deb & Flo: Vicki Lewis (Voice)
Jacques: Joe Ranft (Voice)
Nigel: Geoffrey Rush (Voice)
Anchor: Eric Bana (Voice)
Chum: Bruce Spence (Voice)
Coral: Elizabeth Perkins (Voice)
Sheldon: Erik Per Sullivan (Voice)
Fish School: John Ratzenberger (Voice)
Dentist: Bill Hunter (Voice)
Darla: LuLu Ebeling (Voice)
Pearl: Erica Beck (Voice)
Mr. Ray: Bob Peterson (Voice)

Origin: USA
Released: 2003
Production: Graham Walters; Pixar; released by Walt Disney Pictures
Directed by: Andrew Stanton
Written by: Andrew Stanton, Bob Peterson, Dave Reynolds
Cinematography by: Sharon Calahan, Jeremy Lasky
Music by: Thomas Newman
Sound: Gary Rydstrom
Editing: David Ian Salter
Production Design: Ralph Eggleston
MPAA rating: G
Running time: 101 minutes

REVIEWS

Chicago Sun-Times Online. May 30, 2003.
Entertainment Weekly. June 6, 2003, p. 53.
Los Angeles Times. May 4, 2003, p. E22.
Los Angeles Times Online. May 30, 2003.

New York Times Online. May 30, 2003.
People. June 9, 2003, p. 33.
Rolling Stone. June 26, 2003, p. 88.
USA Today Online. May 29, 2003.
Variety Online. May 26, 2003.
Washington Post. May 30, 2003, p. WE57.

QUOTES

Marlin (Albert Brooks) catching a ride on sea turtle Crush: "Oooh, my stomach . . . " Crush (Andrew Stanton): "Hey, no hurling on the shell, dude, okay? Just waxed it."

Dory (Ellen DeGeneres) to Marlin: "Awww . . . what's the matter mister grumpy gills?"

Sharks (reciting): "I am a nice, friendly shark. Not a fish-eating monster. Fish are our friends, not food."

AWARDS AND NOMINATIONS

Oscars 2003: Animated Film
Nomination:
Oscars 2003: Orig. Screenplay, Sound FX Editing, Orig. Score
Golden Globes 2004: Film—Mus./Comedy.

Fleeing by Night (Ye Ben)

Over the past decade or so we have been lucky enough to experience the "opening up" of Chinese cinema with such films as *Farewell My Concubine* from 1993 as well as the inspired work of Stanley Kwan's more recent *Lan Yu.* Among the latest offerings is *Fleeing by Night,* the sorrowful tale of love in 1930s China directed by Li-Kong Hsu and Chi Yin. Li-Kong Hsu was the producer behind such now classic Chinese films as *Eat Drink Man Woman* and *The Wedding Banquet.*

Fleeing by Night or *Ye Ben* introduces us to Wei Ing'er (Rene Liu) and her fiancé, Hsu Shao-dung (Lei Huang). Ing'er, the daughter of a wealthy theater owner, has been corresponding with Shao-dung during his time studying music in America. The pair's relationship intensifies after Shoa-dung returns to China, much to the distress of Ing'er's extremely traditional mother, who feels they are spending too much time together. Under the watchful eye of conser-vative Chinese society, these two people attempt to propel their relationship and their love forward.

Initially, the film leads the audience to believe the love affair between Ing'er and Shao-dung is the crux of the film. When we are introduced to Lin Chung, star of the opera playing at the theater, we begin to see a more tragic and moving story unfold. Both Ing'er and Shao-dung fall in love with the mystery that is Lin Chung, who is an orphan with a shadowy and tragic past. The tale becomes even more complex with the added dimension of an older man's obsession with the actor. The eventual "relationship" formed between these two characters is both unsettling and sadly realistic.

The real beauty of *Fleeing by Night* is the slow pacing. The directors do not rush into the storylines, but rather rely on the interactions of the characters to speak for themselves. The wonderful unfolding of the story is what drives the story itself and anything else would have seemed forced. The pacing of the story's lengthy timespan also showcases the actors' immeasurable talent and range as it allows them to age on screen.

There are times when the story wears thin and others when it teeters on melodrama, but by this time you are so hooked and interested in these characters that all is forgiven. Also, the inevitable comparison to *Farewell My Concubine* was hard to shake. All in all, however, these negative points do not detract from *Fleeing by Night,* and ultimately the story moved me with its flawless and real performances.

—Laura Abraham

CREDITS

Wei Ing'er: Rene Liu
Hsu Shao-dung: Lei Huang
Lin Chung: Chao-te Yin
Huang Zilei: Li-jen Tai
Wei Ing'er's mother: Ah-Leh Gua

Origin: Taiwan
Language: Chinese
Released: 2000
Production: Li-Kong Hsu, Shi-hao Chang; China Film, Beijing Film Studio, Zoom Hunt International; released by Strand Releasing
Directed by: Li-Kong Hsu, Chi Yin
Written by: Hui-Ling Wang, Ming-xia Wang
Cinematography by: Cheng-hui Tsai
Music by: Chris Babida
Editing: Po-wen Chen
Art Direction: Jun Sung
Costumes: Jien-hua Tzou

MPAA rating: Unrated
Running time: 123 minutes

REVIEWS

Boxoffice. July, 2002, p. 91.
Los Angeles Times Online. May 3, 2002.
New York Times Online. May 3, 2002.
Variety Online. November 20, 2000.

QUOTES

Wei Ing-er's mother (Ah-leh Gua) about opera performers: "Actors thrive on adoration."

The Flower of Evil (La Fleur du Mal)

Master French filmmaker and veteran of the French New Wave, Claude Chabrol, lays himself open to attack by a new generation of film audiences with his quasi-nostalgic thriller, *The Flower of Evil*. That he manages to fend off detractors is no surprise. In so doing, he is also contributing new vigor to a more than forty-year idolization of the film director as an author wielding a "camera-fountain pen."

Chabrol, like Claude Lelouch in *And Now, Ladies and Gentlemen* (reviewed in this volume), may, in fact, appear to be paying tribute to himself. In *The Flower of Evil*, Chabrol evokes the triumphs of his heyday when his thrillers seemed near perfect. Like Lelouch, he is not seeking to remake his own creative past, but to jog the memory of those among his fans who have been unable to forget it. *Flower*, with its quiet and refined facade, harks back to the masterwork *La Femme Infidele* (*The Unfaithful Wife*; 1969), in which a middle-aged husband sets out to murder his wife's young lover. Pauline Kael, writing in the *New Yorker*, described that film's style as one in which every setup was "perfect."

The subplot of the film thrillers that Chabrol managed to create during the late 1960s and 1970s revolved around the way in which the most decent and respectable of folks can be inexorably driven to commit the heinous act of murder. What kept us riveted was the veneer of bourgeois convention that was eventually shattered by the singular crime. After nearly three decades, Chabrol returns to this template and thereby takes on the challenge, as an auteur, to match his earlier accomplish-

ments in the eyes of his fans. Given the recent works of Lelouch and Roman Polanski, it would seem that great filmmakers never retire; they merely retreat into their own past.

At this consummate stage in his career, Chabrol interweaves his repeated covert indictments of the bourgeoisie into the overt political content of his latest effort. His central character in *Flower* is in fact a politician, and a new breed of one at that. Anne (Nathalie Baye), by her birth as a Vasseur, if not by her actions, embodies the evil in the film's title. She is a congenial aristocrat of a housewife who decides to run for town council. As her running mate and campaign advisor, she has chosen the smart and handsome Matthieu (Thomas Chabrol). Anne's political stance, as she claims, is "non-ideological" and focuses on the particular day-to-day needs of her local electorate. Her dedication to politics has alienated her from Gerard (Bernard Le Coq), her lackluster, middle-aged husband, a pharmacist with his own reasons to oppose Anne's entry into public life.

We soon come to know that Anne's marriage to Gerard took place after their respective spouses died in the same car crash over thirty years ago. Another skeleton in the closet concerns Grandpa Vasseur's collaboration with the Nazis, an issue about which Gerard remains touchy to this day. As if this weren't enough, Aunt Line (Suzanne Flon), Gerard's wizened but indomitable mother, was tried for murdering her father, although she was acquitted. Chabrol's narrative builds toward the revelation of the secret Aunt Line has been keeping all along, a revelation that will turn Anne's political quest into a mere subplot.

Chabrol's narrative omniscience finds its correlative in the iconography of his camera. From the very start of the film, and embodying a motif that is repeated throughout, it is as if the camera is an outsider, excluded from the comfort of hearth and home, prowling like a stalker through trees and windows, until it locates the source of its obsession. Much like Orson Welles's camera in the classic *Citizen Kane* (1941), what is evoked is not a voyeur after the thrill of transgressive behavior, but a visual narrator that reveals what the characters we are watching are too close to the trees to perceive. While Welles's camera hones in on the microcosmic detail of the "Rosebud" sled at the end of *Kane*, the secret that no one in the film has been able to guess, Chabrol's camera heads in the opposite direction, eventually detaching itself, in a near-transcendent manner, so as to reveal a macrocosm. Spinning its own ideological web (the word "web" figures prominently in a Scrabble scene), Chabrol's camera ends up indicting all of French society, unforgiving in its relation to the trauma of the "perpetual present" that Aunt Line admits to being trapped in.

Chabrol's narrative stance asserts itself in a quixotic preface of sorts, in which he skips to the film's climax to show a man's lifeless bleeding body in one bedroom of a mansion and a young woman on her knees in an adjoining room. This functions as a kind of teaser trailer. Chabrol seems to be assuring an impatient generation of filmgoers of the deadly substratum underlying the genteel veneer of the goings-on to follow.

The film's narrative proper then begins with the subplot of Francois (Benoit Magimel), the handsome, twenty-something son of the Vasseur family, returning from the States after a three-year sojourn. He is met at the airport by Gerard, who fills him in on Anne's pursuits and the condition of Aunt Line's lamprey, to which Chabrol devotes a loving and extreme close-up.

Before Francois, Gerard's biological son, has even unpacked, he finds that his earlier, quasi-incestuous relationship with his "sister" becomes rekindled. The sprightly, dark-haired, and attractive Michele (Melanie Doutey), Anne's daughter from her first marriage, is now a graduate psych major. Her analysis of Gerard's time in the U.S. studying law is that it was an attempt to get away from her.

This family's aristocratic-cum-bucolic post-lunch harmony on that first day is disturbed when Matthieu brings news of a slanderous leaflet directed against Anne. Chabrol weaves this plot strand with that of the developing intimacy between Francois and Michele, as it becomes clear to them that they might not even be cousins, and are thus free to interact as lovers. To this end, they run off to Aunt Line's beach house, where Chabrol's camera again follows them like someone about to intrude into their privacy. On a night of a full moon, when Michele is unable to sleep despite the consummation of her feelings for Francois, she admits she's troubled by the hate in the leaflet. Francois feels that it has to be Gerard who wrote it. Aunt Line, who comes to visit, agrees. "Gerard is a tyrant!" according to her. Soon she's all ready to use her access to Gerard's office space to hunt through his waste paper in order to find the incriminating evidence. She does not, and the audience never gets to know who really was behind the hatemongering.

Anne, who doesn't allow the leaflet to affect her composure, goes about her afternoon visits to selected dwellers in low-rent housing. She promises an old couple she'll look into the matter of a boiler. When she leaves, the husband denounces her as a "Nazi-lover's granddaughter." A young housewife, who is looking after a swarm of kids, accepts Anne as a friend of the family. At another apartment, a brute of a husband, whose wife has complained to Anne that he beats her, abuses Anne and does not even open the door. Anne and Matthieu merely scamper away. Before a televised debate, Anne confronts an opponent representing the far right and accuses him of having written the leaflet. He of course denies any such strategy, claiming they're "both on the same side." Gerard, for his part, uses the gathering to chat up the sultry Dominique (Dominique Pivain), who promises to visit his pharmacy, leading Gerard to insert a slip of paper with his phone number into her décolletage. Though she does as promised, Gerard's attempt at an extramarital fling doesn't attain the critical mass of a subplot.

As would be expected, things come to a head on election night. The returns show Anne leading comfortably, but Gerard is not there with her at her campaign headquarters to celebrate. In fact, he doesn't even vote for her. Gerard, presumably spurred by his unrequited lust, seeks out his stepdaughter instead. Michele, who has been working alone on a paper in Gerard's study, finds that she can only defend herself from his physical advances by bludgeoning him with the heavy, metal lamp base, which kills him instantly. Aunt Line advises Michele to drag the body upstairs and promises to take the blame for the murder. She then confesses to killing her own father for betraying her brother, who had become a Resistance fighter during the Second World War.

As Anne's victory party takes over the house, Aunt Line is there to help with the champagne. Chabrol's camera retreats from the living room to stop at the bottom of the vacant stairway, which becomes the subject of the film's final shot. Clearly, for fans of this auteur, known as the "French Hitchcock," the perfect crime has once again found its match in perfect filmmaking with *The Flower of Evil*.

The film's detached stance apparently evoked a mixed reaction from critics. Elvis Mitchell, writing in the *New York Times*, finds Chabrol failing to "tighten throats," as he has in the past. While seeming to agree, the *Washington Post*'s Desson Howe does praise "the care and precision Chabrol takes in the interaction among his characters." At the opposite end of the spectrum, Kevin Thomas of the *Los Angeles Times* finds the master "in top form." Writes Thomas: "Chabrol ponders the unresolved guilt that can endanger a family from one generation to the next yet also marvels at the paradoxical nature of the possibilities for redemption."

—Vivek Adarkar

CREDITS

Anne: Nathalie Baye
Francois: Benoit Magimel
Aunt Line: Suzanne Flon
Gerard: Bernard Le Coq
Matthiew: Thomas Chabrol
Michele: Malanie Doutey

Origin: France
Language: French
Released: 2003
Production: Marin Karmitz; MK2, France 3 Cinema; released by Palm Pictures
Directed by: Claude Chabrol
Written by: Caroline Eliacheff, Louise Lambrichs
Cinematography by: Eduardo Serra
Music by: Matthieu Chabrol
Sound: Thierry Lebon, Pierre Lenoir

Editing: Monique Fardoulis
Costumes: Mic Cheminal
Production Design: Francoise Benoit-Fresco
MPAA rating: Unrated
Running time: 105 minutes

REVIEWS

Boxoffice. December, 2003, p. 31.
Chicago Sun-Times Online. November 7, 2003.
Entertainment Weekly. October 17, 2003, p. 60.
Los Angeles Times Online. October 17, 2003.
New York Times Online. October 8, 2003.
Variety Online. February 10, 2003.
Washington Post. October 24, 2003, p. WE35.

The Fog of War: Eleven Lessons from the Life of Robert S. McNamara

In his breakthrough documentary feature, *Fog of War: Eleven Lessons from the Life of Robert S. McNamara*, veteran documentarist Errol Morris finally casts off the shackles of the "talking heads" form. His subject, former Secretary of State Robert McNamara—reputedly the chief hawk behind the Vietnam War—doesn't speak to the camera, as much as think aloud in front of it.

McNamara's words are intercut with documentary footage, most of it rather commonplace, which is underscored by the foreboding music of Philip Glass. There are also repeated shots of reel-to-reel tape decks and teletype machines, as if to show how that war was filtered through the communications technologies of the time. None of the above embellishments are particularly striking, especially when they are repeated, an aspect that proves the film's only drawback. What remains unaffected, however, is the bulk of the film, which puts McNamara under its own brand of scrutiny.

From the podium at the New York Film Festival, where his film was presented as the festival centerpiece, Morris revealed his secret: through his invention, which he calls the "Interrotron," the camera becomes "the third person" in the room, the other two being the filmmaker and the subject being interviewed. As he explains it, this device is basically an interface between the technology of the teleprompter and that of closed-circuit video transmission. The result is what Morris calls "true first-person cinema," where the subject being interviewed is looking at only an image of the interviewer, along with other video images, and responding to them. Thus, Morris retains eye contact with his subject, which is important for dramatic value, and at the same time is allowed as a filmmaker to become "one with the camera."

What Morris did not elucidate, but which *Fog of War* makes clear, is that through this novel process, the film's audience achieves a god-like, transcendent ability to see into the heart and soul of the subject, hitherto the domain of the fiction film. Its political implication is that the way the media chooses to interpret collective traumas or even how our leaders explain such events to us can now be measured against the way they explain the actions to themselves. Here, it is McNamara and his role in the Vietnam War, and, by extension, the role of contemporary political leaders in the cataclysmic events of our time.

Morris also made clear that while this interaction between politics and war, which is the prime concern of his film, is explored in relation to what happened over forty years ago, it remains valid for events that may be "four days old." McNamara, for his part, mustering up the wisdom of his eighty-odd years, rises to the occasion that such a perspective would demand. At the start of the film, he stakes out his ideological terrain as he muses aloud: "Any military commander who is honest with himself . . . will admit that he has made mistakes in the application of military power. He's killed people, unnecessarily . . . through mistakes, through errors of judgment . . . maybe even hundreds of thousands." What follows then is McNamara applying this ideology to his own "mistakes" and supplying Morris with a subtitle for the film: *Eleven Lessons from the Life of Robert S. McNamara*.

While McNamara speaks in concrete terms, these lessons emerge as mere pegs, abstractions, some of them banal, by which Morris attempts to subdivide his film. Morris's scope is not just McNamara's role as an architect of the Vietnam War, but the entire military career that preceded it as well.

Even so, the structure of the film is far from chronological. For example, "Lesson No. 1: Empathize with Your Enemy" refers to the Cuban missile crisis, but from what McNamara later says, it could also refer to the American experience in Vietnam. In the Cuban context, apparently all that was needed was to provide Russian Premier Krushchev with a face-saving exit strategy. In recalling the showdown over Cuba, what McNamara says about the decision-making behind it is far more insightful than the dates and quotes he cites or the accompanying footage of newspaper headlines. It seems that General LeMay wanted to "totally destroy

Cuba." McNamara's take as to what transpired within the highest echelons of power, both at the White House and at the Kremlin is this: "Rational individuals came that close to the total destruction of their societies." Stated in such bald terms at the start of the film, this insight, which McNamara himself calls "most important," forms the ideological substratum for the interrelationship between rational thinking and the exercise of military power that underlies the rest of what we find McNamara thinking through.

The past that McNamara reveals, right from his earliest memory as a two year old at the end of the First World War, seems linked either to political wars or his own private war to assert himself in "ethnically-dominated" schools. For example, he couldn't afford to go to Stanford, so he had to settle for Berkeley. It was the Second World War that put an end to his career as an assistant professor at Harvard. Under LeMay, he became a fighter pilot on the new B-29, flying on missions that destroyed Japanese cities. "Lesson No. 5" is, in effect, that "proportionality should dictate the guidelines of war." McNamara was to realize this in the context of the amoral nature of the decisions made during the Second World War, that ending the War justified turning Japanese cities into rubble and killing hundreds of thousands of civilians. Thus, the only "immoral" thing at the time, it seemed to him, was losing.

With the hindsight that today's film audience possesses, it becomes interesting to speculate whether Vietnam would have proven such a humiliating experience for the United States had McNamara remained in office. Curiously, when Morris questions him about why he didn't speak out against the war in Vietnam after he resigned, McNamara refuses to answer the question.

Before we get to that phase of his life that was to turn him into a household word, McNamara recounts the years that led to his becoming the top dog at Ford. There he instituted changes such as padded panels and seat belts that were to save countless lives. However, such noble pursuits didn't seem to be a part of his destiny. After five weeks as the highest paid executive at Ford, he quit to join the Kennedy administration as Secretary of State for a meager $25,000 a year salary.

As McNamara saw it, Kennedy's intention was to pull out the 16,000 or so military advisers who were in Vietnam by 1965. What scuttled the plan was the military coup in South Vietnam that overthrew Diem, an event for which the U.S. felt responsible.

Under Johnson, according to McNamara, confusion reigned. He traces the very origin of this costly war to a state of affairs where no one at the helm in America knew what was going on. He cites the instance of torpedo attacks on U.S. ships that never took place. This fiction became bolstered by what McNamara calls a wrong mindset that led Johnson to authorize, through the Gulf of Tonkin resolution, the bombing of North Vietnam in the belief that the enemy attacks were part of "a conscious decision on the part of the North Vietnamese political and military leaders to escalate the conflict and an indication they would not stop short of winning." It was this, according to McNamara, that marked the beginning of a military action that was to "carry such heavy costs".

The above leads McNamara to conclude, "We see incorrectly or we see only half the story at times." When Morris adds, "We see what we want to believe," McNamara answers, "You're absolutely right," then adds his own aphorism, "Belief and seeing, they're both often wrong." America saw Vietnam as part of a global war, when, as McNamara discovered long after, in actuality it was a civil war, and the Vietnamese perceived American interference as an initiative to enslave them, as had the French, rather than a desire to free them. Repeatedly, in his inimitable fashion, Morris cuts to a close-up of dominoes falling as an illustration of the misguided domino theory.

Morris's filmic gimmicks here allow McNamara to get off the hook in relation to the dissent of the time. It seems McNamara was aware of the self-immolation that took place under his office window, but not of the Peter Brook play, *US*, produced by the Royal Shakespeare Company, which made clear that the Vietnamese and the Chinese had been enemies for hundreds of years. Yet McNamara states his belated discovery of this fact as if it had been some arcane secret.

All this serves to substantiate the title of the film, inspired by a phrase McNamara recalls: "What 'the fog of war' means is war is so complex it's beyond the ability of the human mind to comprehend all the variables." The complexity that Morris's film presents carries a contemporary sting as it winds to a close. Capping his congenial erudition, McNamara argues: "We are the strongest nation in the world today. I do not believe we should ever apply that economic, political, and military power unilaterally." He goes on to conclude, "If we can't persuade nations with comparable values of the merit of our cause, we'd better reexamine our reasoning."

McNamara's long stint as the head of the World Bank as well as his work in the underdeveloped parts of the world is relegated to a mere end title. We take leave of Morris's film flushed with the feeling that we have been in the company of a brilliant and articulate wielder of power.

Critics of the film, gauging from their response after its New York Film Festival screening, were dazzled by McNamara's revelations of top-level decision-making. *Newsday's* Jack Mathews finds "[t]he film's greatest strength is its inadvertent timeliness. Parallels between LBJ's Vietnam policy and George W. Bush's Iraq policy go off in your head like flares." Stephen Holden writes in the *New York Times*, "The cumulative message" that emerges from Morris's "sober, beautifully edited" effort is that "in wartime nobody in power knows anything." 🎞

—*Vivek Adarkar*

CREDITS

Origin: USA
Released: 2003
Production: Errol Morris, Michael Williams, Julie Bilson Ahlberg; SenArt Films; released by Sony Pictures Classics
Directed by: Errol Morris
Cinematography by: Peter Donahue, Robert Chappell
Music by: Philip Glass
Sound: Steve Bores
Editing: Karen Schmeer, Doug Abel
MPAA rating: PG-13
Running time: 106 minutes

REVIEWS

Boxoffice. November, 2003, p. 88.
Entertainment Weekly. December 19, 2003, p. 55.
New York Times Online. October 11, 2003.
Newsday Online. October 10, 2003.
Variety Online. May 22, 2003.

AWARDS AND NOMINATIONS

Oscars 2003: Feature Doc.
Ind. Spirit 2004: Feature Doc.
L.A. Film Critics 2003: Feature Doc.
Natl. Bd. of Review 2003: Feature Doc
Nomination:
Directors Guild 2003: Feature Doc. (Morris).

Freaky Friday

Every teenager's nightmare . . . turning into her mother.
—Movie tagline
Get Your Freak On.
—Movie tagline

Box Office: $110.2 million

The success of *Freaky Friday* shows just how far storytelling has disintegrated in films in the past several decades. When *Freaky Friday,* starring Jodie Foster and Barbara Harris, originally came out in 1976, the film—based on the 1965 book by Mary Rogers—was considered a B-level film.

It was an okay sort of film, certainly enjoyable, but nothing that great.

In 2003, a remake of *Freaky Friday* was considered one of the better films of the year. It's not that the recent version of the film was stunningly better than the earlier one, it's just that comparatively movies had gotten so much worse. When *Freaky Friday* is one of the best stories of the year, it doesn't seem like such a good sign.

It's not that this *Freaky Friday* isn't charming and well-written, it is. It's well acted, too. This is a good thing since it certainly could be argued that body-switching films have been played out. Besides the original *Freaky,* there has been no dearth of such films, including *Face/Off,* and a spate of body-switches from the 1980s, like *Big* and *Vice Versa.* There was even yet another version of *Freaky,* a 1995 TV movie starring Shelley Long and Gaby Hoffman.

The latest *Freaky* borrows the idea of mom and daughter switching bodies, but otherwise the story is brand new. Anna Coleman (Lindsay Lohan, who also starred in another Disney remake, *The Parent Trap*) is a kid who has been getting too many detentions in school, is tormenting her brother, and is constantly fighting with her mother, Tess (Jamie Lee Curtis). Tess, a successful psychologist and author, is trying to raise her daughter and young son, Harry (Ryan Malgarini), on her own after her husband's death. She is also engaged to nice guy Ryan (Mark Harmon), but Anna is horrified by the idea of her mother remarrying. Tess is sympathetic to her daughter, but Anna doesn't see it. To her, Tess is too busy with her cell phones, patients, pagers, and fiancé to care about her daughter. To Tess, Anna is an overly dramatic teen who plays music too loud and doesn't try hard enough in school.

The elements in this film are all pretty contemporary. Mom does yoga and is wired with the newest gadgets, while daughter wears the latest fashions and plays guitar in a rock band. That's why the way the two do the body switch seems like, well, it came from a movie from 1950. The family goes to a Chinese restaurant and Anna and Tess start fighting. The resident Chinese matriarch (poor Lucille Soong) overhears the two and gives them some sort of magic fortune cookies. To further the idea of the mystical Chinese person, every time she appears, a gong sounds.

Otherwise, the whole thing, written by Heather Hatch and Leslie Dixon and directed by Mark Waters (*The House of Yes*), is a fun way to kill an hour and a half. Originally the film was to star Annette Benning in the Curtis role and Tom Selleck in the Harmon role, a version that would have been quite nice, but a large part of the film's charm comes from Curtis. She has a whole lot of fun with the role, and is game to make fun of herself. When Anna first inhabits Tess's adult body, she looks in the mirror and screeches, horrified, "I look like the crypt keeper!"

That they have to be in each other's bodies is bad enough but it so happens that the Friday on which it happens is a big day for both of them. Tess has the rehearsal dinner for her wedding and Anna has a chance to play with her band at the House of Blues. With typical movie character logic, the two decide that they will live the other person's life in the morning, then meet for lunch at the Chinese restaurant to straighten things out.

Of course it is not that easy. When Tess goes to school in Anna's body, she realizes that Anna's English teacher really is out to get her. Things are further complicated when she meets the scruffy biker boy, Jake (Chad Michael Murray) that her daughter has a crush on. Things aren't going any better for Anna in her mother's body. After having some fun in the morning maxing out credit cards by getting her mom's hair styled, a trendy wardrobe, and a new piercing, she tries to deal with her mother's patients. She's none too happy to realize that Ryan has booked a surprise TV talk show appearance for her to discuss her book. And when Ryan tries to get a little frisky with her, she is grossed out. Things get a little strange (as if they weren't already) when Anna, in Tess's body, runs into Jake at a coffee shop. As the two chat about their favorite bands, Jake finds himself irresistibly drawn to the woman he perceives as Anna's mom.

What makes the proceedings work is the writers' and actors' sense of fun about the whole thing. When Ryan and Anna in Tess's body are driving little Harry to school, Anna suggests that the boy can be dropped off miles from school. "You can walk," she smiles and secretly sticks her tongue out at him. Harry, naturally, is shocked to see his mother acting like this. Lohan is good when she's called upon to play Tess inhabiting Anna's body, at a rock concert. As Tess tries to "rock out" to help her daughter, it's funny to see what her ideas about looking cool in a band are. She rocks back and forth like a folkie from the 1960's and grins broadly, breaking several rules of rock star behavior. Woven gracefully into the silly story are some real, believable ideas about the relationship between this mother and daughter. Curtis, playing Anna inhabiting Tess's body, gives a speech at the rehearsal dinner. "It's great we're getting married—even though my husband died. How quickly I've been able to get over it."

Critics, who are not usually fans of such supernatural plot shenanigans, were willing to suspend their disbelief for this film and ended up having a good time. Lou Lumenick of the *New York Post* declared, "*Freaky Friday* is Disney's best comedy in years." Manohla Dargis of the *Los Angeles Times* assessed, "What makes *Freaky Friday* a charmer isn't how far-out things get for this mother and daughter, but how sweet and distinctly un-freaky a kid, her mom, and their love for each other can be." Roger Ebert of the *Chicago Sun-Times* praised the leads: "Lindsay Lohan . . . has that Jodie Foster sort of seriousness and intent focus beneath her teenage persona, and Jamie Lee Curtis has always had an undercurrent of playfulness; they're right for these roles not

only because of talent, but also because of their essential natures." A. O. Scott of the *New York Times* concluded, "Loud but never coarse, candid without being prurient, *Freaky Friday* . . . is a quick-witted, perfectly modulated family farce with a pair of beautifully matched performances from Ms. Lohan and especially Ms. Curtis, who does some of her best work ever."

—*Jill Hamilton*

CREDITS

Tess Coleman: Jamie Lee Curtis
Anna Coleman: Lindsay Lohan
Ryan: Mark Harmon
Grandpa: Harold Gould
Jake: Chad Michael Murray
Harry Coleman: Ryan Malgarini
Mr. Bates: Stephen Tobolowsky
Maddie: Christina Vidal
Pei-Pei: Rosalind Chao
Evan: Willie Garson

Origin: USA
Released: 2003
Production: Andrew Gunn; GUNNFilms; released by Walt Disney Pictures
Directed by: Mark S. Waters
Written by: Leslie Dixon, Heather Hach
Cinematography by: Oliver Wood
Music by: Rolfe Kent
Sound: Paul Ledford
Music Supervisor: Lisa Brown
Editing: Bruce Green
Art Direction: Maria Baker
Costumes: Genevieve Tyrrell
Production Design: Cary White
MPAA rating: PG
Running time: 93 minutes

REVIEWS

Chicago Sun-Times Online. August 6, 2003.
Entertainment Weekly. August 8, 2003, p. 50.
Los Angeles Times Online. August 6, 2003.
New York Times Online. August 6, 2003.
People. August 11, 2003.
USA Today Online. August 6, 2003.
Variety Online. July 20, 2003.
Washington Post. August 8, 2003, p. WE43.

AWARDS AND NOMINATIONS

Nomination:
Golden Globes 2004: Actress—Mus./Comedy (Curtis).

Freddy vs. Jason

Winner Kills All.
—Movie tagline

 Box Office: $82.2 million

This highly anticipated cinematic showdown between Freddy Krueger (Robert Englund) of *Nightmare on Elm Street* fame, and Jason Vorhees (Ken Kirzinger), the unstoppable killing machine from the *Friday the 13th* films begins with the clever premise that Freddy is dying due to neglect. It seems that the children of Elm Street have forgotten about him and if Freddy cannot inhabit their dreams to wreak havoc he will cease to exist. Krueger then gets it into his head to "scare" the real world into remembering and summons Jason from whatever hell he has been languishing in and encourages him to go on a "real world" killing spree. The only problem is that once Jason "frightens" the townspeople into remembering Freddy, he threatens to take center stage from Freddy. This is when the "versus" in the title is delivered.

Horror fans have been anticipating the Freddy/Jason face-off since it was teased at the end of *Jason Goes to Hell: The Final Friday* in 1992. At the time, New Line had just purchased the *Friday the 13th* rights and had hopes of combining the two franchises. Unfortunately, the project languished in the development abyss until scriptwriters Damian Shannon and Mark Swift came up with the Freddy summoning Jason angle. That, however, is where their inventiveness abandoned them.

While Ronny Yu's frenetic direction sets a suitable pace for the film, the story languishes as little more than an antiquated "slasher" film until the climactic battle following the prelude. However, the last third of the film proves more lively and entertaining than anything from the *Nightmare* canon since the third installment (*Dream Warriors*) and is far more thrilling and enjoyable than anything from the *Friday the 13th* saga. It is in this sequence that Yu's direction serves the film best. As Elvis Mitchell described in the *New York Times*, "the frenzied B-picture magic realism [Yu] brought to his 1993 action dreamscape, *The Bride With White Hair*, with bodies hurtling across the wide screen, brings . . . insane liveliness to the movie." Yu's Hong-Kong action style fits the otherworldly fight that ping-pongs from Freddy's dream world to Jason's Camp Crystal Lake. The over-the-top action never seems out of place in a fight between two supernatural killers. This final set piece is where the movie really finds its legs. Sadly, when Jason and Freddy are not on screen together, the film is merely a dried-up, "slasher" film.

A forgettable cast of victims (Monica Keena, Jason Ritter, et al.) does an adequate job playing off of Englund's scene-devouring Freddy and being dispatched by Kirzinger's Jason. But, this film isn't about the plot device used to unite the two horror stalwarts, nor is it about reinventing a long defunct genre. It's more germane to say that this film is all about nostalgia, the opportunity for these characters to have one final send-off that shows how much fun they once were. Of course, someone will probably decide that yet another sequel is in order and completely ruin everything. As Andy Klein wrote in *Variety,* the film is "more marketing concept than aesthetic." But, at least for now, there is an appropriately fitting end to these two franchises.

—*Michael J. Tyrkus*

CREDITS

Freddy Krueger: Robert Englund
Jason Voorhees: Ken Kirzinger
Lori: Monica Keena
Will: Jason Ritter
Kia: Kelly Rowland
Gibb: Katharine Isabelle
Marqueete Mark: Brendan Fletcher
Dr. Campbell: Tom Butler
Deputy Stubbs: Lochlyn Munro
Tim: James Callahan

Origin: USA
Released: 2003
Production: Sean S. Cunningham; released by New Line Cinema
Directed by: Ronny Yu
Written by: Damian Shannon, Mark Swift
Cinematography by: Fred Murphy
Music by: Graeme Revell
Editing: Mark Stevens
Art Direction: Ross Dempster
Costumes: Gregory Mah
Production Design: John Willett
MPAA rating: R
Running time: 97 minutes

REVIEWS

Entertainment Weekly. August 15, 2003, p. 52.
Entertainment Weekly. August 22-29, 2003, p. 112.
Los Angeles Times Online. August 15, 2003.
New York Times Online. August 15, 2003.
People. August 25, 2003, p. 35.
USA Today Online. August 15, 2003.
Variety Online. August 10, 2003.
Washington Post. August 15, 2003, p. WE34.

QUOTES

Freddy Krueger (Robert Englund): "I can't come back if nobody remembers me."

Friday Night (Vendredi Soir)

Hitherto politically-conscious French filmmaker Claire Denis' *Friday Night*, beneath its plotless narrative, is an assault on the conditioning of film audiences to the erotic in cinema and to the erotic as cinema. Her feminine, as against feminist, salvo goes beyond the mere depiction of sex to come up with her own brand of excitement, one where the filmmaking itself becomes imbued with eroticism.

As deceptively simple as Denis' film appears to be, the theoretical issue it raises needs to be dissected before we can grasp the extent of her originality in tackling it. Sex in all story films, it has to be admitted, remains bound with the readymade pleasure we get in looking. Psychoanalytic theory assumes this pleasure to operate on a level well below our conscious mind, that is, we enjoy it without being aware of the psychological mechanism involved. Feminist thought goes further to postulate that this pleasure has largely been at the expense of the woman within the film. Simply put, it is she who has always been the object being "looked at", while it is the male who has always done the "looking." This has found its corollary on the narrative plane where it is the male who advances the story, and who thus remains "active" throughout, while the woman becomes the spectacle that brings the story, as such, to a standstill, and hence, is doomed to play a "passive" role. The sharpest illustration of this theory can be found in the classic Hollywood western. Which is not to say there haven't been exceptions, such as Joan Crawford in Nicholas Ray's *Johnny Guitar* (1954). But even here, the "active" female has to assume a male role, and take on masculine characteristics.

Denis overturns this equation, or reverses its terms, to be more precise. Laure (Valerie Lemercier), her attractive, dark-haired thirty-something heroine, is trapped within a Paris "brought to a standstill" by a metro strike. The eponymous night is also significant for Laure, because the following day she will be moving out of her apartment, and in with the unseen Francois. What becomes clear then, as regards the "active" Laure, is that she has taken her life into her own hands. Thus, the opening scene is of her methodically sealing, marking, and packing boxes. But even here it is her femininity that is emphasized, as well as the feminine in the very gaze of the camera capturing her.

Denis executes a slow, languorous pan around the darkened room, with its packing boxes piled on top of each other. Through the window, we see the first glimmerings of dawn, an ethereal red streak behind the Eiffel Tower. Denis keeps to extreme close-ups to show Laure trying on a slinky skirt. We hear her thinking aloud, "Should I keep it?" She then rolls on the bed, as if reveling in its silken feel. When she gets up, she decides to pack the skirt. This practical-minded heroine, we are led to believe, will not repress her sensual desires.

Once Laure gets into her car, this sensuality again asserts itself as she dries her hair in the heat from the dashboard. Denis allows Laure's dark curls to fill the screen as she shakes her head. A stranger knocks on the car window, but is refused a lift. Laure then makes a call from a public phone booth, leaving a message for Francois that the dinner planned for tomorrow won't be at "our place." She then repeats the words, "our place" to herself, thereby signifying the end of a phase of her life. We come to know that even her car has a 'For Sale' sign on it.

But the end isn't always followed by a new beginning, the film seems to say. With all loose ends tied, Laure finds herself in the midst of gridlock. Denis' camera provides a social dimension by showing other motorists, some depressed, some angry, but all stuck. The entire city has come to a halt because the subway workers have gone on strike. The reporter on the radio even puts a cheerful spin on it all by saying that this is a great time for Parisians to get to know each other by offering lifts to those stranded, adding "carpooling can be fun." Laure's immediate reaction is to offer a male stranger a lift, but it seems he would rather walk.

Cleverly, Denis extends the civic stasis resulting from the strike first, onto the stasis in Laure's life and secondly, onto the narrative thrust of the film itself. The Friday night in the film's title also seems to have come to a grinding halt. Denis thus prepares her audience for a quite different narrative axis, one geared towards revealing facets of erotic love, as experienced by women in general, and by Laure in particular. In the midst of this stasis, Denis will use non-events to propel her tale forward. Audiences not prepared to accept such a dramaturgy may find themselves left behind in the gridlock.

The gaze that breaks through the quagmire that Laure is caught in belongs to Jean (French matinee idol Vincent Lindon), a stranger of roughly the same age, who needs nothing more than a lift to wherever Laure can take him. Laure boldly looks back at him, and even opens the door when he knocks. Jean's easygoing manner seems to connect with Laure's state of mind. He remarks on the warmth inside the car, then relaxes with his head thrown back against the headrest of the front seat. In the silence that follows, Jean clears his throat repeatedly while Laure looks bored, and nods off into sleep.

This is clearly not a romantic start for any affair, no matter how brief; neither is the background against which it will play itself out particularly enticing. With a slow track, underscored by somber music, Denis shows stranded commuters at a bus stop. Her technique for surmounting this social realism is to frame her erotic action in (sometimes extreme) close-ups.

Laure is forced to make her move when Jean gets out and starts walking away. She gives chase and invites him to a friend's place where she's headed for dinner. He accepts with a smile. An amusing flash forward convinces Laure that that wouldn't be such a good idea. In the car, she invites Jean to dine with just her. Again, he accepts.

She then steps out to call her friends to tell them she won't be coming. When she returns, she gets a shock as she finds her car missing. As she is walking, shivering, Jean catches up with her. He chides her for abandoning her vehicle, then takes over the wheel himself. Now, as if in tune with his machismo, the car speeds along. The quick track of buildings as they whizz past scares Laure. When she says she wants to get out, Jean promptly stops, and it is he who gets out.

Laure then drives around by herself, until she spots Jean in a café, and decides to join him. When they step out, the erotic in their relationship becomes overt as they kiss passionately in the street. From here on in, various aspects of the erotic—especially the world of signs and objects around the "active" Laure—begin to figure prominently. Out in the empty street, the café sign behind them goes off, as if granting the two the privacy of darkness.

Initially, despite the passionate kissing, there is an expression of dissatisfaction on Laure's face as Jean takes the initiative. Laure is clearly only responding, even though the kissing becomes prolonged and begins to seem an erotic end in itself. We know that that is definitely not so when both look at a hotel sign and smile at each other.

As in a recent foray into such forbidden realms, also from France, Frederic Fonteyne's *An Affair of Love* (reviewed in the 2001 volume), what emerges is that the truly erotic in cinema is not located in the realm of no-holds-barred sex, but rather in an attempt to retrieve from it its

repressed element, what cannot be expressed through the sex proper. Fonteyne's two romantic leads, also complete strangers, decide on a chance affair, after the man swears not to reveal the fulfillment of the woman's secret fantasy, which the audience never comes to know. So, when Fonteyne finally shows his lovers in the throes of conventional sex, we can see that it cannot be the real thing, at least as far as the woman is concerned.

In Denis' film also, both Laure and Jean grasp their way to the overtly sexual, but it is what has preceded it that proves more telling. Denis provides extreme close-ups of the most insignificant actions, which speak volumes about Laure's desire. We see her hand reaching for Jean's, making clear her need for security. Laure notices the blister on the sole of Jean's foot, which in turn reveals the earthy aspect of their sexual relationship. As they are eating in a restaurant, Laure fantasizes about Jean making love to the woman at the next table. Denis even shows the magical aspect of the erotic when a lampshade Laure has discarded reappears by her hotel bedside, as if to imply a kind of second chance.

In the film's final scene, Laure is forced to leave the sleeping Jean and run through the dark streets so as not to be late, in all probability, for the movers. And for the first time, we see a look of liberation on her face.

Denis' feminine look at sex within the bounds of contemporary filmic realism seems to have left most American critics of her film trapped within her gridlock. Stephen Holden in *The New York Times* sees Denis' extreme close-ups during the sex scenes as a sign of her lack of confidence as a filmmaker. For Holden, Denis seems to be "seeking new ways of looking at the body, without much idea of what . . . (she's) after." Worse, according to Holden, is the film's gross miscasting. "If the Jeanne Moreau and Marcello Mastroianni of the late 1960's had played the same roles . . ." he writes, "the corners of the screen would be curling up in flame." 🎞

—Vivek Adarkar

CREDITS

Laure: Valerie Lemercier
Jean: Vincent Lindon

Origin: France
Language: French
Released: 2002
Production: Bruno Pesery; Arena Films, France 2 Cinema; released by Wellspring Media
Directed by: Claire Denis
Written by: Claire Denis, Emmanuele Bernheim
Cinematography by: Agnes Godard
Music by: Dickon Hinchliffe

Sound: Jean-Louis Ughetto
Editing: Nelly Quettier
Art Direction: Katia Wyszkop
Costumes: Judy Shrewsbury, Catherine Leterrier
MPAA rating: Unrated
Running time: 90 minutes

 REVIEWS

Boston Globe Online. August 1, 2003.
Boxoffice. April, 2003, p. 86.
Chicago Tribune Online. July 18, 2003.
Christian Science Monitor Online. June 20, 2003.
New York Times Online. October 11, 2002.
New York Times Online. June 29, 2003.
Sight and Sound. September, 2003, p. 8.
Sight and Sound. October, 2003, p. 68.
Variety Online. September 3, 2002.
Washington Post. May 23, 2003, p. WE41.

Garage Days

What if you finally got your big break and you just plain sucked?
—Movie tagline

Garage Days is the filmic equivalent of a pop song that doesn't quite make it. It has some catchy parts and is enjoyable enough, but doesn't have that something extra that's going to turn the song into a classic—or even a summertime hit.

The odd thing about *Garage Days* is that it's a movie about a band that is much more interesting to look at than to listen to. For a movie about music, music is a strangely absent character in it. It does have a great soundtrack featuring songs by the Jam, The Specials, Violent Femmes, and the Cure, but we barely hear the movie's band (which seems to be nameless) play. As Jeffrey M. Anderson of the *San Francisco Examiner* notes, the band is usually seen just finishing up a song or being interrupted before they play. Even the first time we're supposedly seeing them play, at the beginning of the film, they are actually only lip-synching to an AC/DC song. Singer Freddy (Kick Gurry) is just having a dream. (The it's-just-a-dream plot twist is about the level of creativity in this screenplay written by director Alex Proyas, Dave Warner, and Michael Udesky.) Several critics noticed that the band barely even talks about music or how they could improve their music.

Still, the visual oomph of the film is almost enough to make up for it. Director Proyas of *The Crow* and *Dark City,*

obviously had a lot of fun working on the look of the film. One of his favorite, and most effective techniques, is taking a moment and slowing it down so we can see the beauty in it. There are a lot of moments that are akin to the one with the plastic bag in *American Beauty.* When one of the characters is sitting in the rain, Proyas slows down the action, and we see the drops, computer-generated orbs falling languidly to the ground. It's a good way of pausing the forward momentum of the story and letting the viewer enjoy the art in an ordinary moment. In another scene, the mohawked and drug-popping drummer Lucious (Chris Sadrinna), throws one of his beloved pills into the air to land in his mouth. As the pill twists and floats up, then down, Lucy reflects upon his enjoyment of this moment of anticipation before the drug takes effect. (He later ranks each drug from one to ten.) Sometimes Proyas throws in a visual effect, not for any obvious reason, but just because he likes to do it. When an elderly neighbor unplugs a fuse from the band's garage and tosses it into the air, we see the fuse rising from the point of view of a bird's nest. Proyas also peppers his film with various cutesy titles like "Fun with drugs, part one."

Besides Freddy and Lucy, this Aussie garage band includes Freddy's girlfriend, pixyish bass player Tanya (Pia Miranda) and troubled guitar player, Joe (Brett Stiller). Joe is cheating on his steady girlfriend, Kate (Maya Stange) with a suicide-obsessed goth queen who may or may not be imaginary. Kate, feeling snubbed, shares a passionate kiss with Freddy. Things are further complicated when Kate discovers that she is pregnant with Freddy's baby. To add extra soap opera spice to the proceedings, Tanya is dating Freddy but has been feeling unsatisfied with him.

It's amazing that with all the activity in their love lives the band finds time to further things with their career. Freddy's main dream, besides dating Kate, is too realize his dreams of having his band become famous. This is somewhat of a problem since the band has never even gotten a gig. They try to convince the owner of a local hotel bar where they hang out to book the band for a show, but the owner is more interested in installing some slot machines. Their manager Bruno (Russell Dykstra) is an older guy who doesn't do much but hang around with the band and eat. The band's big break happens when Freddy finds the wallet of super-manager Shad Kern (Marton Csokas). Maybe if they can just get in good with him, he could be their ticket to stardom.

The plot isn't particularly interesting but there are enough lively moments to keep the movie fairly entertaining. Some of the best scenes involve Joe's father, Kevin (Andy Anderson), who was once something of a rock star himself. He still proudly sports his rock star mullet and has an array of animal print bikini underwear. There are some good drug jokes, too. When one of the characters has taken too many drugs, he acknowledges a friend's arrival with a relieved, "Oh #$%$ I thought you were Satan." There is another scene when Tanya invites her rich, conservative parents to dinner with the band to hit them up for money to fund a demo. Lucy unhelpfully spikes the band members' drinks with LSD and they start hallucinating during the dinner. The dinner drug scene has become a bit of a trite device, but Proyas's version has an extra something because of his visual prowess. Joe sees Tanya's hair start on fire, Freddy discovers he has extra fingers and Lucy scuttles on the ceiling like a bug. Tanya watches her parents mutate into monsters as they dirty dance to Rick James's "Super Freak." Less successful is a bit involving Joe's desire to stick with Kate and be a father to his baby. He tries to show his commitment by carrying around a melon, which he names Mellie, and tending to it like a baby. The setup seems like it could be funny, but somehow it just never works.

In a way, *Garage Days* doesn't seem particularly modern. The soundtrack music is largely from the 1980s and the characters' looks seem from that era, too. (Unless Lucy's mohawk is so out that's it's become newly fresh). In his youth, Proyas was in an Australian garage band and maybe that's what he was drawing on for this film. Unfortunately it erases a certain amount of cool from the film. The style and music references are right on for people of a certain age, but that age would be late 30s/early 40s—probably not the young, hip audience the film is aiming for.

The film had its fans but the majority of critics didn't care for it. Anderson of the *Examiner* wrote, "*Garage Days* is absolutely the wussiest rock 'n' roll movie since Rick Springfield's *Hard to Hold*. It even makes *Crossroads* look hardcore." Owen Gleiberman of *Entertainment Weekly* gave the film a harsh F and complained, "There's something uniquely embarrassing about a rock & roll fable that is no more authentic (and no less coy) than an episode of *The Monkees* yet insists on presenting itself as the epitome of rebel-yell cool." Lou Lumenick of the *New York Post* declared, "Proyas embellishes nearly every scene with wearying visual pyrotechnics—slow motion, manipulated stills, and elaborate special effects—that distract from the fresh performances and give the whole thing the musty feel of a second-rate, mid-'90s music video." Roger Ebert of the *Chicago Sun-Times* praised the film as "a whimsical and kind of lovable story."

—*Jill Hamilton*

CREDITS

Kate: Maya Stange
Bruno: Russell Dykstra
Kevin: Andy Anderson
Shad Kern: Marton Csokas
Freddy: Kick (Christopher) Gurry
Tanya: Pia Miranda
Joe: Brett Stiller
Lucy: Chris Sadrinna
Thommo: Tiriel Mora

Origin: Australia
Released: 2003
Production: Topher Dow, Alex Proyas; Australian Film Finance Corp., Fox Searchlight; released by 20th Century-Fox
Directed by: Alex Proyas
Written by: Alex Proyas, Dave Warner
Cinematography by: Simon Duggan
Music by: Antony Partos, David McCormack
Sound: Peter Grace
Editing: Richard Learoyd, Michael Philips
Costumes: Jackline Sassine
MPAA rating: R
Running time: 105 minutes

REVIEWS

Box Office Magazine. April, 2003, p. 73.
Chicago Sun-Times Online. July 18, 2003.
Entertainment Weekly. July 25, 2003, p. 53.
L.A. TimesOnline. July 18, 2003.
Variety Online. Oct. 2, 2002.

Gerry

Gerry is a film in which not much happens, yet we sit and watch it anyway. The movie stars Casey Affleck and Matt Damon as two friends named Gerry who end up taking a very, very long walk in the desert and get lost. It really is that simple. They walk and walk through the desert, talking once in a great while, and then they walk some more.

Despite a good deal of negative criticism, few could argue that it wasn't gutsy. Director Gus Van Sant absolutely did what he wanted with this film regardless of what others might think. He is obviously more interested in challenging mainstream audiences than in packing theaters with people. For this I think he deserves praise. Whether the idea works or not is irrelevant, the fact he did it at all is wonderful!

Sometimes the camera doesn't move at all, and there are long, long stretches during which literally nothing happens. This really does force the audience to pay close attention to any sound or movement, no matter how small, and this is the real purpose of this film. With *Gerry*, Van Sant seems to be trying to teach us to sit, wait, and contemplate.

The basic premise, as little as there is, focuses on two friends (played by co-writers Matt Damon and Casey Affleck) who become lost in a desert after a short search for what they refer to as "the thing." Their friendship is made clear from the beginning, as if they've known one another so long that they needn't babble on about nothing. They understand one another fully, completely, and in a way few men do.

Gerry is not all existentialism and soul searching, however, and the screenplay does have some comical aspects to it. There are discussions of *Jeopardy* and video games until the severity of their situation finally becomes apparent to the duo. Over the course of the next three nights and four days, their journey turns into a struggle for survival. They are not equipped for any type of trek, let alone one of this magnitude, as they have no water or equipment. Still they struggle on and on. I mean this really is all that happens.

At times Van Sant films scenes that are so hauntingly beautiful you can't help but get sucked into the vast landscape. At other times you are so incredibly bored you want to end it all right there! This is the beauty of *Gerry*, in my opinion. I felt an inability to let go of the picture in case something worthwhile happened. I couldn't stop watching it until Van Sant let me. When he showed the last scene I finally accepted the fact that nothing was going to happen, but not a second sooner.

—*Laura Abraham*

CREDITS

Gerry: Matt Damon
Gerry: Casey Affleck

Origin: USA
Released: 2002
Production: Dany Wolf; My Cactus; released by ThinkFilm
Directed by: Gus Van Sant
Written by: Matt Damon, Casey Affleck, Gus Van Sant
Cinematography by: Harris Savides
Music by: Arvo Part
Sound: Felix Andrew
Editing: Paul Zucker
MPAA rating: R
Running time: 103 minutes

REVIEWS

Boxoffice. April, 2002, p. 171.
Chicago Sun-Times Online. February 28, 2003.
Entertainment Weekly. February 21, 2003, p. 127.
Los Angeles Times Online. February 14, 2003.
New York Times Online. February 14, 2003.
People. February 24, 2003, p. 32.
Sight and Sound. October, 2003, p. 50.
Variety. January 21, 2002, p. 36.
Washington Post. February 28, 2003, p. WE37.

Gigli

Murder. Blackmail. Temptation. Redemption. It's been a busy week.
—Movie tagline

 Box Office: $6 million

Memorable only as the origin of the portmanteau word "Bennifer," a combination of the names of the film's two stars, Ben Affleck and Jennifer Lopez, who reportedly became romantically entangled on this set, *Gigli* combines the famous assets of J. Lo and Ben with much less success. With its odd title (pronounced "jee-lee"), shaky plot, corny dialogue, dubious acting, and cardboard characters, *Gigli* moves at glacial speed toward a thankful ending after 124 grueling, joyless minutes. Throw in some gratuitous yoga moves and booty shots aplenty of J. Lo—whose posterior must surely have its own agent by now and definitely should be listed in the cast of characters here—and this movie may mark a new low for writer-director Martin Brest (*Beverly Hills Cop, Midnight Run, Scent of a Woman*) whose most recent disaster was the thoroughly unlikable *Meet Joe Black.*

The only surprising thing about the film is that Christopher Walken and Al Pacino would agree to appear in such a lifeless dud of a picture, their brief appearances betraying the energy that is lacking throughout this narrative about low-level gangster Larry Gigli (Affleck). Driving an old Chevy and wearing vintage-style clothing, this rehashed dim-bulb thug is commissioned to kidnap the mentally challenged son of a federal prosecutor in order to get a crime boss off the hook. Brian (Justin Bartha) is endearing as the handicapped boy who, much like Dustin Hoffman's character in *Rain Man,* is addicted to watching *Baywatch,* sings along to hip-hop music, and goes off on humorous Tourette's-like rants. Gigli's boss Louis (Lenny Venito), not thinking him capable enough of babysitting this docile hostage, sends in the more competent Ricki, a crime-world contractor, to keep an eye on them both in Gigli's run-down L.A. apartment. Gigli's vintage wardrobe, cool car, and bad New York accent (although he is an L.A. native) are seemingly included to add dimension to this cookie-cutter Italian-American thug with promise, but ultimately they fail and the character is never truly fleshed out. Ricki, however, is painted as a sort of Renaissance mobster for hire: alternately tough, warm, wise, and funny, she is a yoga-enthusiast and Eastern philosopher also schooled in the art of obscure martial-arts torture, which she gets to describe in detail to some rowdy teens later in the pic.

Once the action moves to Gigli's apartment, the plot basically consists of the tough but goodhearted Gigli trying to bed a resistant Ricki, who happens to be a lesbian. The Brest-penned monologues that follow have both characters waxing rhapsodic about the superiority of vital parts of their own gender's anatomy over those of the opposite sex. Ricki wins the argument, perhaps due to the fact that she performs her monologue while doing a series of yoga poses that cause Gigli to fall head over heels for his flexible partner in crime. What follows is more lame repartee that is supposed to pass as clever banter between the two, who can at least agree that, unfortunately, they have bonded with their cute captive. Brian's handicap leads to some crude jokes and treatment from Gigli, who then uses sappy sentiment to smooth things over. This highly dubious and dysfunctional family unit is complete when, amazingly, Gigli is able to convince Ricki to "hop the fence" and mommy and daddy finally consummate their turbulent relationship, but not before some completely distasteful talk about turkeys as well as who is the cow and who is the bull. The fact that Ricki is on top in the ensuing sex scene may settle that question once and for all. Though not all the revelations about the sexes are quite as objectionable, any genuine observations fall to the wayside beside cardboard characterizations and an aimless plot.

While Affleck is miscast as the badly written title character and his performance is lackluster, Lopez fares somewhat better as the eye-candy with attitude. Both are, naturally, flatteringly filmed, with Affleck's shirtless chest competing with J. Lo's plethora of posterior shots. Attempting to support the crushing weight of this sinking ship of a movie is Al Pacino (he won an Oscar for his performance in Brest's *Scent of a Woman*), who shows up as the high-level mobster, Starkman. Walken plays a police officer investigating the kidnapping, while Lanie Kazan, as Gigli's mother, takes a shine to Ricki. Unfortunately, their performances are all uninspired, although each adds a genuine energy otherwise lacking in the film.

—*Hilary White*

CREDITS

Larry Gigli: Ben Affleck
Ricki: Jennifer Lopez
Brian: Justin Bartha
Det. Stanley Jacobellis: Christopher Walken
Starkman: Al Pacino
Mother Gigli: Lainie Kazan
Robin: Missy (Melissa) Crider
Louis: Lenny Venito

Origin: USA
Released: 2003
Production: Martin Brest, Casey Silver; City Lights Productions; released by Revolution Studios
Directed by: Martin Brest
Written by: Martin Brest
Cinematography by: Robert Elswit
Music by: John Powell
Sound: Jeff Wexler
Editing: Billy Weber, Julie Monroe
Art Direction: Sue Chan
Costumes: Michael Kaplan
Production Design: Gary Frutkoff
MPAA rating: R
Running time: 124 minutes

REVIEWS

Chicago Sun-Times Online. August 1, 2003.
Entertainment Weekly. August 8, 2003, p. 49.
Los Angeles Times Online. August 1, 2003.
New York Times Online. August 1, 2003.
People. August 11, 2003, p. 33.
San Francisco Chronicle. August 1, 2003, p. D5.
Seattle Post-Intelligencer Online. August 1, 2003.
USA Today Online. August 1, 2003.
Variety Online. July 31, 2003.
Washington Post. August 1, 2003, p. WE37.

QUOTES

Larry Gigli (Ben Affleck): "You don't tell me what to do!" Ricki (Jennifer Lopez): "How 'bout this?! I'll kill you."

AWARDS AND NOMINATIONS

Golden Raspberries 2003: Worst Picture, Worst Actor (Affleck), Worst Actress (Lopez), Worst Director (Brest), Worst Screenplay
Nomination:
Golden Raspberries 2003: Worst Support. Actor (Pacino), Worst Support. Actor (Walken), Worst Support. Actress (Kazan).

The Girl from Paris (One Swallow Brought Spring) (Une Hirondelle A Fait Le Printemps)

Simple but charming, *The Girl from Paris* scored a big hit in France but made little impression in the U.S. The lack of sex and violence must have been liabilities for American distribution. In fact, the only violence in the film—some animal slaughtering—got *The Girl from Paris* into trouble: animal-rights activists protested the film's opening in France. But the questionable ethics of killing animals for a film (assuming it was for the film) does not entirely detract from the riches offered.

In Paris, Sandrine (Mathilde Seigner) is bored as a web design instructor. Against her mother's wishes, she signs up for a government farm-training program, with the idea of changing careers and buying a farm in the country. Sandrine meets Adrien (Michel Serrault), a widower who has become too old to work his farm in the Rhone-Alpes region. But Adrien resists selling his land to a young woman, fearing she will not be able to handle the job. Nevertheless, he finally agrees to the deal, on the condition he gets to stay on at the property. Sandrine begins her new venture by gutting Adrien's old dairy barn and turning it into a bed-and-breakfast for hikers. Surprisingly, Sandrine starts receiving guests, and Adrien admits to Jean (Jean-Paul Roussillon), his only friend, that he is jealous of Sandrine's success. Her boyfriend from Paris, Gérard (Frédéric Pierrot), also reveals his envy, particularly when he fails to convince Sandrine to return to her old job.

But when winter arrives, Sandrine receives her first real test. In a nasty ploy to make her more dependent on him, Adrien damages her electricity and forces her to move into his farmhouse. There he finally tells her about the tragic incident some years earlier that changed him forever: the police burned his property and confiscated his animals following a "mad cow disease" diagnosis. Sandrine begins to question her own commitment to farming and the country life after hearing Adrien's tale. When he experiences a stroke, they become closer, but Sandrine continues to have doubts and eventually leaves the farm. Her return to Paris, her teaching job, and Gerard, however, prove short-lived. Another incident changes everything for Sandrine again.

Christian Carion and Eric Assous's story and screenplay for *The Girl from Paris* keeps one guessing about the fate of the characters, and rarely, if ever, does it fall back on clichés about city life versus country life or the expected sentimental outcome of the relationship between the jaded young Sandrine and the curmudgeonly old Adrien.

What makes *The Girl from Paris* extra special is the approach director Carion takes to tell the story. The former documentarian opens his film with stunning, inviting shots of the Rhones-Alps region, which is a tease because the sequence is immediately revealed to be part of city mouse Sandrine's imagination of what farm life might be like. Later, Carion shows real farm life for all its difficulty and even ugliness (this is where the pig and cow slaughtering are shown). Moreover, Sandrine's disillusionment with farm life results as much from Adrien's crotchety attitude as the harsh winter she lives through. When Sandrine leaves the farm for her former life and the city (represented by shots of the Seine at night) the country ways seems more wonderful than ever. Carion, thus, effectively illustrates that the grass is always greener and everything truly is relative.

Carion gets a deep, moving performance from Mathilde Seigner, who is the less physically beautiful but equally talented sister of Emmanuel Seigner. Veteran actor Michel Serrault (best remembered in the U.S. as the drag queen in *La Cage aux Folles*) gives one of his greatest performances, making Adrien a fully-dimensional senior, hardened by harsh events but still showing glimmers of vulnerability. Serrault beautifully underplays the scene in which Adrien finally tells Sandrine the reason he is so embittered. The actor uses subtle gestures and facial expressions, which is quite a contrast to his over-the-top performance in *La Cage aux Folles*.

Carion's production team also helps turn *The Girl from Paris* into an artful and resonant work. Antoine Heberle's smooth, elegant cinematography captures both the gorgeous scenery and the gritty realism with similar assurance. Jean-Michel Simonet's spare production design does justice to both the city and country scenes. Andrea Sedlackova's clean, unobtrusive editing never interferes with the languid story telling. Best of all, Philippe Rombi's lush theme music lends a wistfully hypnotic tone and could stand on its own as a majestic original composition.

American critics were generally kind to *The Girl from Paris*. Carrie Rickey in the *Philadelphia Inquirer* called it "a lovely, keenly observed film." Desson Howe in the *Washington Post* said the film " has a calming quality. The story moves slowly but, given the milieu and pace of life, this seems perfectly appropriate." Other reviewers were less enthusiastic. V. A. Musetto in the *New York Post* described *The Girl from Paris* as "a sweet but lightweight French export," and Daniel Eagan in *Film Journal International* was even more dismissive: "Unfortunately, the actual storyline is much less interesting, and the lessons the film teaches feel too predictable." So maybe some of the U.S. critics, who are just as jaded as Sandrine, didn't help *The Girl from Paris* get the exposure it deserved. Luckily, films this good usually gain an afterlife.

—*Eric Monder*

CREDITS

Adrien Rochas: Michel Serrault
Sandrine Dumez: Mathilde Seigner
Jean Farjon: Jean-Paul Roussillon
Gerard Chauvin: Frederic Pierrot
Stephane: Marc Berman
Sandrine's mother: Francoise Bette

Origin: France
Language: French
Released: 2002
Production: Christophe Rossignon; Nord-Ouest, Mars Film Productions, Rhone Alps Cinema, StudioCanal; released by Mars Films
Directed by: Christian Carion
Written by: Christian Carion, Eric Assous
Cinematography by: Antoine Heberle
Music by: Philippe Rombi
Sound: Thomas Gauder
Editing: Andrea Sedlackova
Art Direction: Jean-Michel Simonet
Costumes: Virginie Montel, Francoise Dubois
MPAA rating: Unrated
Running time: 103 minutes

REVIEWS

New York Times Online. March 3, 2003.
Sight & Sound. July 2002, p. 44.
Variety Online. Sept. 28, 2001.
Washington Post. April 18, 2003, p. WE40.

Girl with a Pearl Earring

Beauty inspires obsession.
—Movie tagline

Box Office: $8.8 million

Like the Mona Lisa, Johannes Vermeer's painting *The Girl With a Pearl Earring* has a mysterious and alluring quality and almost nothing is known about the model's identity. A young lady with porcelain skin, wearing a unique cloth over her head (thought to be a Turkish costume), looks directly at the viewer over her left shoulder, her moist lips parted and her pearl earring poetically catching the light. The girl is featured atypically against a stark black background, unusual for an artist who preferred detailed settings. Very little is known about the Dutch artist himself, whose 36 paintings of seventeenth century everyday life in his native Delft, Holland, are renowned for the qualities of light Vermeer captured in paint. Tracy Chevalier's novel, on which this movie is based, presents a possible identity for the girl and explores her relationship with the enigmatic artist.

Echoing the painting, director Peter Webber's film is a small, quiet gem that doesn't aim for earth-shattering drama or startling revelations but instead proffers quiet, tension-filled moments brimming with unfulfilled possibilities. An excellent Colin Firth heads the cast as the Dutch painter and with characteristic British restraint fills the bill of the quiet but intense artist to a tee. Scarlett Johansson, bearing a remarkable resemblance to the real "Girl," is believable as the innocent servant girl on the verge of womanhood.

Living with a blind father who can no longer afford to support her, the teenaged Griet (Johansson) is sent to work in the Vermeer household populated by the artist and his perpetually pregnant wife, Catharina (Essie Davis), along with a number of small children and run with an iron fist by Vermeer's mother-in-law, Maria Thins (Judy Parfitt). For the naturally curious, intelligent Griet the home is an inhospitable environment where nobody especially appreciates her presence, including the spoiled children, jealous wife, and suspicious mother-in-law. However, when dispatched to clean the painter's studio, Griet's attention to detail and interest in art grabs the attention of the master, who recognizes a kindred spirit in the pretty young girl. Entrenched in the emotionally repressed atmosphere of the household and far too busy trying to provide for his ever-growing family, the distracted artist is unable to do much about his interest in the young maid.

The artist and his muse do share privately intimate moments, however, as in the emotionally charged scene when he enthusiastically explains to Griet how a camera obscura works and it is clear her interest extends beyond the lesson at hand. During the well-directed and delicately-executed scene in which she finally sits for the painting referred to in the title, the pair engage in a kind of figurative intercourse as Vermeer, who must fit Griet with the iconic pearl earring, takes a hot needle and pierces both her ears, causing the girl to cry out. The sexual tension becomes so great during the sitting that afterward Griet runs to her butcher's apprentice boyfriend, Pieter (Cillian Murphy), for some relief. It is obvious that, although she likes Pieter, it is

Vermeer about whom she is passionate and for whom she has enormous respect and reverence as well.

While Vermeer's interest in Griet can only remain platonic, the same is not true of Vermeer's wealthy patron, van Ruijven (Tom Wilkinson), who immediately pounces on the innocent maid. It is he, in fact, who commissions the famous painting of the girl, much to the chagrin of Catharina, who accuses her husband of infidelity when she discovers the painting. Vermeer's wife is further incensed by the fact that the girl is wearing her own cherished pearl earrings. The business-minded Maria, however, makes it clear that Vermeer must keep his clients happy at any cost. While characters and relationships are satisfyingly fleshed out, a portrait of Vermeer as an important artist fails to emerge as the filmmakers concentrate solely on his creation of a single painting. Acting is uniformly good, with standout performances from leads Firth and Johansson as well as impressive characterizations from supporters Davis and Parfitt.

With as much care as Vermeer took in creating his paintings, director Webber and the crew of *Girl With a Pearl Earring* took in crafting a meticulously detailed film that is as visually artistic as possible. Production designer Bed van Os and cinematographer Eduardo Serra create a richly designed, warmly lit romantic picture matched by the opulent score from Alexandre Desplat.

—Hilary White

CREDITS

Vermeer: Colin Firth
Griet: Scarlett Johansson
Van Ruijven: Tom Wilkinson
Maria Thins: Judy Parfitt
Catharina: Essie Davis
Pieter: Cillian Murphy
Cornelia: Alakina Mann
Tanneke: Joanna Scanlan

Origin: Great Britain, Luxembourg
Released: 2003
Production: Andy Paterson, Anand Tucker; Pathe Pictures, U.K. Film Council; released by Lions Gate Films
Directed by: Peter Webber
Written by: Olivia Hetreed
Cinematography by: Eduardo Serra
Music by: Alexandre Desplat
Sound: Carlo Thoss
Editing: Kate Evans
Art Direction: Christina Schaffer
Costumes: Dien van Straalen
Production Design: Ben van Os

MPAA rating: PG-13
Running time: 95 minutes

REVIEWS

Boxoffice. November, 2003, p. 96.
Chicago Sun-Times Online. December 26, 2003.
Entertainment Weekly. December 12, 2003, p. 60.
Los Angeles Times Online. December 12, 2003.
New York Times Online. December 9, 2003.
New York Times Online. December 12, 2003.
USA Today Online. December 12, 2003.
Vanity Fair. December, 2003, p. 112.
Variety Online. September 1, 2003.
Washington Post. January 9, 2004, p. WE37.

AWARDS AND NOMINATIONS

L.A. Film Critics 2003: Cinematography
Nomination:
Oscars 2003: Art Dir./Set Dec., Cinematog., Costume Des.
Golden Globes 2004: Actress—Drama (Johansson), Orig. Score.

Gloomy Sunday (Ein Lied von Liebe und Tod)

Gloomy Sunday offers an old-fashioned movie-going experience. It has a big sweeping story, a lovely setting and a haunting score. There's also a menage-a-trois, the Holocaust, and a mysterious song that seems to induce bad luck. Like an old Hollywood film, there is plenty of melodrama and a surprising, satisfying ending in which some receive their comeuppance. In the film's nearly two-hour running time, it encompasses a wealth of different moods and experiences. It's a rumination on dread, a tale of lighthearted sexual freedom and an affecting period piece. It's the kind of film that lingers with the viewer.

The film, which is in German with English subtitles, is the work of German filmmaker Rolf Schubel. Schubel directed the film and co-wrote with Ruth Toma. According to Roger Ebert of the *Chicago Sun-Times,* in New Zealand the film ran for more than a year and became a local phenomenon in Auckland. It's based on the novel of the same name by Nick

Barkow which was inspired by the legend of the song "Gloomy Sunday." Popularized in the United States first by Billie Holliday and more recently by Elvis Costello and Bjork, the song was composed in 1935 by two Hungarians. Rezso Seress wrote the music and Laszlo Javor wrote the lyrics. According to legend, the song, which is a love song to a departed lover, inspired a rash of suicides across Europe. At one point, the BBC banned it for its "depressing effect."

With such back story, there's not much chance *Gloomy Sunday* is going to be very uplifting, and it's not. It begins in the present day, give or take a decade, in Szabo's, an upscale restaurant in Budapest. A successful German businessman, Hans Wieck (Rolf Becker), has brought his wife and family for a celebration of his 80th birthday. He's not been to the restaurant since World War II. He proclaims nothing to be different and requests "the song." As he takes a drink of champagne, he spies an old picture of a beautiful young woman. He instantly collapses and dies.

Flashback to Szabo's in the 1930s. The beautiful woman of the photograph is Ilona (Erika Marozsan), a waitress at the restaurant. She's the striking mistress of the restaurant owner, Laszlo Szabo (Joachim Krol). Besides her obvious beauty (and frequent toplessness), we know that she is to be considered lovely because the director insists on shooting her in the kinds of scenes where she is always carrying a huge bouquet of vibrant flowers fresh from the market.

Ilona and Laszlo share a deep friendship and fulfilling sex life. The older Laszlo is a smart businessman, a freethinker, and a kind man. So freethinking is he that, when he and Ilona hire a new piano player, Andras (Stefano Dionisi), Laszlo allows Ilona to begin an affair with the musician. Laszlo asks only that he can remain Ilona's other lover—after all, part of Ilona is better than no Ilona.

The three get along about as well as could be hoped, considering the circumstances. Laszlo even helps Andras get a record deal for the new tune he has composed for Ilona, "Gloomy Sunday." (It's hard to say if it would be a compliment to have inspired such a song.) The song gains attention for its beauty, but also because a rash of young people has been found dead, clutching the record in their hands. Of the song, people say things like, "It's a strange song—as if someone is telling you something you don't want to hear but you know is the truth." Cheery thoughts like this, a few new suicides, and the fact that the song plays countless times gives the film a palatable feeling of dread.

Young, blonde Hans (Ben Becker) comes into the restaurant frequently, partly to eat the famous Magyar Roulade, which he crudely refers to as "beef rolls," but mostly to moon after Ilona. One night after dinner, he awkwardly proposes to her, promising to start a successful import-export business just for her. Ilona is unmoved by the idea of an import-export business and gently declines his proposal. The despondent Hans throws himself into a river. He's saved by Laszlo, who nurses him back to (relative) mental health.

Years later, Hans returns to the restaurant. He is now married and an officer in Hitler's army. He's in charge of preparing Hungary for Nazi takeover. His job is to round up all the Jewish people and deport them to concentration camps. It is in his power to give dispensation to those who are considered crucial to the war effort. Hans is also willing to save some of the Jews if they are able to come up with the huge fee that he demands for this service. Laszlo, who is Jewish, can't seem to understand that he is a target. For him being Jewish is just a happenstance of birth. If his parents would have been Iroquois, he explains, he could just as well be an Iroquois.

The Holocaust is obviously a huge topic on its own, and while *Gloomy Sunday* isn't specifically about that tragic event, the film weaves it into the narrative in a graceful manner. The horror isn't graphically addressed, but we get subtle hints of it in such details as the stars that Jews are required to wear and the marks placed on the front of Jewish businesses.

The acting is mostly excellent. Best is Krol as Laszlo. It's rare that a film shows a mild character that is also strong. Krol's character is kind and passionate, but not weak. It's a quiet performance and quite satisfying. Marozsan is appropriately radiant as Ilona. She is beautiful but also conveys the impression that she is a loving, down-to-earth person. And Ben Becker is effective as the spurned Hans. Even before he becomes a Nazi, there's something that seems creepy about him. Dionisi as Andras is less good. He's supposed to be the tortured, passionate artist, however his quietness doesn't come across as mystery, but rather as a lack of personality.

Critics split on the film. Among those that felt it worthwhile was Kevin Thomas of the *Los Angeles Times* who wrote, "*Gloomy Sunday* is a beautiful period piece, set against one of the world's glorious cities, adding poignancy. Twists and turns heighten a gradually accruing effect, building to a risky moment of truth, a coupe de theater that is as daring as it is satisfying." Lauren King of the *Chicago Tribune* gave the film 3½ stars (out of 4) and called it "sumptuous," adding "not only do the lush visuals, shot on location in Hungary, whisk one back in time and place, but the film itself is a throwback to the sort of powerful, straightforward romantic dramas set in turbulent times—classics such as *Casablanca* and the recent German hit *Nowhere in Africa*—that are sadly lacking from Hollywood these days." Critics who didn't like the film included the *Washington Post*'s Desson Howe, who wrote, "It's a piquant story but unfortunately the movie creaks with European-style artifice. It tells its story in a rather cinematically stilted style, and some of the dramatic moments come perilously close to unintentional parody. But an audience in the right frame of mind might find it enjoyable." And Stephen Holden of the *New York Times* said of the film, "If *Gloomy Sunday* were better written and acted, it might have transcended its own pretensions and cast a clammy spell. But the emotional turbulence of the menage a trois is so underplayed that the characters' feelings never come into focus."

—*Jill Hamilton*

CREDITS

Laszlo: Joachim Krol
Eichbaum: Sebastian Koch
Schnefke: Laszlo I. Kish
Wieck as an old man: Rolf Becker

Origin: Germany, Hungary
Language: German
Released: 2002
Production: Kerstin Ramcke; Focus Film, Studio Hamburg, Polygram Filmproduktion, Dom Film; released by Arrow Releasing
Directed by: Rolf Schuebel
Written by: Rolf Schuebel, Ruth Thoma
Cinematography by: Edward Klosinski
Music by: Detlef Petersen, Rezso Seress
Sound: Wolfgang Schukrafft
Editing: Ursula Hoef
Art Direction: Csaba Stork, Volker Schaefer
Costumes: Andrea Flesch
MPAA rating: Unrated
Running time: 114 minutes

 REVIEWS

L.A. Times Online. Nov. 7, 2003.
Variety Online. Dec. 11, 2003.
Washington Post. Nov. 7, 2003, p. WE50.

Gods and Generals

The nation's heart was touched by Gods and Generals.
—Movie tagline

 Box Office: $12.9 million

In Ron Maxwell's bloated epic *Gods and Generals,* audiences learn about the Civil War from the South's point of view. The much-anticipated prequel to Maxwell's epic *Gettysburg* is a Civil War re-enactor's dream, but it's also a confusing, unfocused, and bizarrely biased mass of distortions, confusions, and half-truths. Produced by Ted Turner, whose TNT channel premiered *Gettysburg,* this movie is also based on Jeff Shaara's trilogy about the war. Maxwell is planning a final film covering the post-Gettysburg part of the war, which he says will balance the overall viewpoint.

In the meantime, though, audiences are stuck with *Gods and Generals* and its unapologetically slavish devotion to the Southern generals' worldview. This film covers the period from the outbreak of hostilities in the spring of 1861 through the months leading up to the Battle of Gettysburg in 1863. But despite the film's gargantuan length (225 minutes), it manages to cover only three battles in those two years: the first Bull Run, Fredericksburg, and Chancellorsville. It never gives a clear overview of the entire war's progress, and its narrative proceeds in fits and starts.

Though its budget approached $100 million, and though its depiction of the Battle of Fredericksburg is both thorough and compelling, the film too often looks like a television movie rather than a theatrical motion picture. Its script is wooden and heavy-handed, and it is full of set speeches by the generals and officers, written in the authentic stilted language of the era. Despite a few moments of splendid emotion and grandeur, it is either cold and distant or shamefully melodramatic and manipulative.

For most viewers, the shocker will be its unorthodox and nearly heretical view of the causes and motivations for the war, and its shameless whitewashing and glorification of the Confederacy and its leaders. That there is some truth to its viewpoint, and that standard histories tend to be biased toward the Union side, does not exclude the distortions and inadequacies of this picture's facile arguments and depictions.

The film opens with an emissary of Abraham Lincoln offering General Robert E. Lee (Robert Duvall, replacing Martin Sheen, who starred as Lee in *Gettysburg*) the post of commander of the Union Army. Lee says he owes his loyalty to his home state of Virginia, and the way the conversation is written implies that the war secretary is trying to deceive Lee by telling him Virginia might not opt to secede.

In the view of the protagonists of *Gods and Generals,* who are primarily the Southern generals, the federal government is the aggressor and Lincoln is a tyrant. Lincoln is raising an Army to invade the South, and that is the provocation for war—as if the secession of Southern states should have been allowed to stand unchallenged. The war is being fought for the benefit of the Northern banks and the war profiteers—that is, Northern business interests—and the defense of the South is the defense of homes, families, heritage, birthright, and freedom itself. The Southerners are depicted as the true inheritors and preservers of American ideals, and the Northerners are the new tyrants and usurpers of those rights.

Slavery isn't mentioned until one hour into the movie, and an attempt at a balanced view isn't achieved until more than another hour in, when Joshua Lawrence Chamberlain (Jeff Daniels), a rather pompous Maine college professor, lectures his brother Thomas (C. Thomas Howell) on the importance of fighting to free the slaves. Even then, it's pointed out that ending slavery was not the initial motivation for the war, and Thomas proposes the view that Lincoln's Emancipation Proclamation was nothing more than a wartime tactic designed to get Southern slaves to rise up in rebellion and help the Union win the war. Thomas Chamberlain points out that many members of the Union army aren't that keen on giving their lives to defend the "darkies," and his more enlightened brother lectures him on the propriety of using the word "Negroes" instead of "darkies."

By then, the film has already painted a distorted and highly selective picture of the role of blacks in the South. General Thomas "Stonewall" Jackson (Stephen Lang) has hired an apparently free black man, Jim Lewis (Frankie Faison), as his cook, and in several scenes black individuals are seen cheering on the Confederate soldiers. But there weren't any freed black people in the South at that time, of course; all were enslaved or escapees. A family in Fredericksburg has a black maid and her three children, and their relationship is depicted as warm and loving—though the maid does confess to the Union soldiers that she would like very much to be free. Lewis prays with Jackson to petition God to ask why good Christian men allow slavery in their midst, but the question is shunted aside with spiritual double-talk. Southerners are portrayed as protective and loving toward blacks, not as their cruel masters, and if they are not entirely enlightened, they are in this film painted as being less racist than the Northerners.

The film is worshipful of the Southern generals, especially Jackson and Lee, and disdainful of their Northern counterparts. The Southern leaders are smart, upstanding, heroic, and resourceful; the Northern generals are stupid, insensitive toadies afraid to buck instructions from Washington. And though seemingly everyone is praying constantly in this film—about half of the movie is devoted to some kind of religious invocation or another—it is clear that the Southern leaders, especially Jackson, are more pious and righteous than their Northern counterparts. God, it seems, must be on their side, because their cause is presented as just.

The movie focuses too much on Jackson, especially in the second half. He is the real protagonist, and Chamberlain doesn't have much to do. After endless time introducing characters and showing preparations for war, Maxwell delves into the battle at Bull Run. Faithful to the reality of the senseless combat, Maxwell shows line after line of men advancing to be massacred by enemy cannons. But Jackson and his brigade save the day with a ferocious charge, and his men start calling him by the nickname "Stonewall." In this battle Maxwell drives home the religious passion that is joined to the war fever in a scene where a Southern officer reports that his men have named four howitzers Matthew, Mark, Luke, and John.

An inordinate amount of time is spent with characters reading the Bible, quoting from the Bible, praying before battle, and praying at the break of day. Jackson is an especially religious man. As played by Lang, however, he is not very compelling—stiff and unvarying in tone. The last half of the movie almost abandons the war entirely to dwell on the tragedies that befall Jackson. And it glosses over the general's legendary faults—he was, by most historical reports, an insensitive autocrat and a mentally troubled hypochondriac.

The highlight of this lengthy, curiously uninvolving film is the protracted Battle of Fredericksburg, in which the Union generals dully send their regiments across an open killing field surrounded by Confederate guns. One by one, the regiments cross the river, march through the town, reach the open field, and walk bravely to their slaughter. Absolutely nothing is accomplished by the battle, as the Union eventually retreats, and the film takes the opportunity to introduce a hypocritically congratulatory letter from Lincoln, which is greeted with sarcasm by surviving members of Chamberlain's Maine brigade.

The senselessness of the slaughter is driven home when a Northern all-Irish regiment marches on a wall behind which are soldiers of a Southern all-Irish regiment. The countrymen shoot on each other reluctantly, as the film observes the killing without comment. At the end of the battle, in a particularly effective scene, Chamberlain and a few of his surviving men spend the night hiding under corpses of their comrades. Unfortunately, at this emotional peak of the movie, exhibitors have chosen to place an intermission. And it's all downhill after that.

Gods and Generals might have been an effective film about the horrors of the Civil War had it not spent so much time on speeches glorifying the Southern cause. Much time is also wasted with parlor room pleasantries, toasting the gallant Southern women, and there's even a troupe that entertains the Southern leaders with a nifty ditty honoring the Confederate flag. *Gods and Generals* presents the Northern argument for the war only once, in Chamberlain's rather stilted speech, but it revels in the Southern justification, in its gallantry, its romanticism, and above all, in its piety.

The point of all this is hard to fathom. Certainly, *Gods and Generals*, which used thousands of Civil War re-enactors in its grand battle scenes, will be a hit among those who uncritically are devoted to anything that features the Civil War. (Unfortunately, many of the scenes seem designed to display the regiments of re-enactors, who aren't completely credible as actors.)

But as far as setting the record straight or contributing to a new and more balanced understanding of the war, the film falls flat on its face. Its actors, even Duvall, are flat and lifeless, and no amount of scenes of the Southern leaders praying proves anything about the righteousness of their cause. In the end, Maxwell has spent nearly four hours recreating three battle scenes and ceaselessly demonstrating that the leaders of the South believed in their cause and were pious men. So what? The film doesn't contribute to history, and it doesn't involve the viewer in the plight of any of its characters, even Jackson. It is one of the most lifeless, condescending, and propagandistic war movies ever made.

—*Michael Betzold*

CREDITS

Lt. Col. Joshua Chamberlain: Jeff Daniels
Gen. Stonewall Jackson: Stephen Lang
Gen. Robert E. Lee: Robert Duvall
Sgt. Buster Kilrain: Kevin Conway
Sgt. Thomas Chamberlain: C. Thomas Howell
Gen. John Bell Hood: Patrick Gorman
Gen. Winfield Scott Hancock: Brian Mallon
Col. Adelbert Ames: Matt Letscher
Gen. A.P. Hill: William Sanderson
Fanny Chamberlain: Mira Sorvino
Jim Lewis: Frankie Faison
Alexander Pendleton: Jeremy London
Anna Morrison Jackson: Kali Rocha
Gen. James Longstreet: Bruce Boxleitner
Gen. George Pickett: Billy Campbell
Major Walter Taylor: Bo Brinkman
Jane Beale: Mia Dillon
Capt. James Power Smith: Stephen Spacek
Gen. James Kemper: Royce D. Applegate
Col. Tarewell Patton: Ted Turner (Cameo)

Origin: USA
Released: 2003
Production: Ronald F. Maxwell; Ted Turner Pictures, Antietam Filmworks; released by Warner Bros.
Directed by: Ronald F. Maxwell
Written by: Ronald F. Maxwell
Cinematography by: Kees Van Oostrum
Music by: John (Gianni) Frizzell, Randy Edelman
Sound: Stephen Halbert
Editing: Corky Ehlers
Art Direction: Gregory Bolton
Costumes: Richard LaMotte
Production Design: Michael Z. Hanan
MPAA rating: PG-13
Running time: 220 minutes

REVIEWS

Chicago Sun-Times Online. February 21, 2003.
Entertainment Weekly. February 28, 2003, p. 58.
Los Angeles Times Online. February 21, 2003.
New York Times Online. February 21, 2003.
Smithsonian. February, 2002, p. 23.
USA Today Online. February 21, 2003.
Variety Online. November 10, 2002.
Variety Online. February 16, 2003.
Washington Post. February 21, 2003, p. WE35.

QUOTES

Gen. Robert E. Lee (Robert Duvall): "Though I love the Union, I love Virginia more."

Good Boy!

Earth is going to the dogs.
—Movie tagline
Rover is about to take over.
—Movie tagline

Box Office: $37.6 million

There is a hierarchy to the movies that parents have to sit through while their kids get their early moviegoing experiences. One level would involve movies that feature a dog as a main character. Lower than that would be a movie in which said dog can talk. In *Good Boy!* the talking dog is from outer space. That's probably lower on the scale. Still, talking animals aren't necessarily the death knell for a film. Films like *Babe* worked well. It's not the talking animals that ultimately make *Good Boy!* a failure. Actually, it's hard to say just what went wrong with this film.

That actors are not the problem. For such a lame premise, *Good Boy!* has a surprisingly stellar cast. The winsome young dog owner in the film, 12 year-old Owen Baker is played by the sad-eyed Liam Aiken (*Road To Perdition*). His parents are played by *Saturday Night Live* alums Kevin Nealon and Molly Shannon. Various dogs in the movie are voiced by Matthew Broderick, Carl Reiner, Brittany Murphy, Delta Burke, Donald Faison, and even Vanessa Redgrave.

The premise isn't necessarily the problem either. It's a little farfetched, to be sure, but it's a kids' movie and farfetched is good. In *Good Boy!* a cute little border terrier,

Canid 3942 (Broderick) is sent to earth from the home planet Sirius, of course. (No pun is discarded for this film.) Dogs, we discover, are the superior race of the universe. Eons ago, some dogs came to Earth and Canid 3942 has been sent by the Greater Dane (Redgrave) to investigate how the Earth dogs are faring. He expects to see dogs ruling the planet and dominating humans.

When Canid lands, there is some sort of problem and a human boy, Owen, somehow ends up with the ability to hear what dogs are saying. It has to do with some sort of spaceship doohickey or something. Owen is the right guy to get this power because the kid is crazy for dogs. He wants his own dog but must prove to his parents that he's responsible enough, so he gets a job walking the neighborhood dogs. So serious is he about his job that he actually wears a uniform to do it. The uniform thing might have something to do with why he has no friends at school, but the movie blames it on the fact that Owen's parents make their living buying, fixing up, and then reselling houses. Owen moves around so much that he never has time to build friendships.

When Owen goes to the animal shelter to pick out a dog, he sees Canid there and adopts him. He renames him Hubble and tries to have a regular dog-and-boy relationship with him. Hubble has other things on his mind. He refuses to act as an inferior's pet and he is disgusted with the way Earth dogs are behaving. When the Greater Dane arrives, Hubble is going to have to report that the dogs have lost control of the planet. Surely the Greater Dane will issue a "global recall" in which all of Earth's dogs are recalled.

Thus we have the major issue in *Good Dog!* The Greater Dane is coming, and Hubble and Owen must whip the local dogs in shape so as to avoid global recall. Along the way, Hubble and Owen start bonding and the standoffish dog will learn about the joys of having a friendship with a boy. The intellectual dog even becomes obsessed with mastering the game of Fetch.

The story, based on a screenplay called *Dogs From Outer Space*, is kind of interesting and could have made for a lively kiddie flick, but somehow it doesn't quite work. Part of it is the pacing. *Good Boy!* is just too slow. It's not slow in a gentle, leisurely storytelling way, but slow in a this-is-boring way. Perhaps fault lies with former actor John Hoffman, who directed the film and wrote most of it. This is his first time as a director, and maybe he's not figured out the rhythm of film yet.

The other part is the humor, which isn't funny enough. Anita Gates of the *New York Times* listed some of the attempts: "the ridicule of pet lovers who talk baby talk to animals; dogs falling asleep while trying to learn meditation; the comparison of canned dog food to pate; that old standby flatulence; and breed-specific behavior." The movie is also rife with puns like the name for an important part of the communication system on Hubble's spaceship: a "woofer." When Hubble sees someone using a toilet for its usual purpose, he says incredulously, "Did you . . .? I drink out of that bowl!" The most successful humor in the film, at least for the kids in one screening, was the slapstick. Kids yukked it up when the neighborhood dogs chased some bullies away. Also a hit: a pie landing on a dog's head.

It's strange that Nealon and Shannon were hired for this movie because they play their roles totally straight. With them in the film, and especially them together, it seems like any minute they might start being funny, but it just never happens.

Overall, the acting seems fine enough. Aiken is good as the lonely, serious Owen. Broderick conveys Hubble's transformation from efficient space dog to loving Earth dog. The actors voicing the other dogs are trying hard enough—it's just that their lines are bad and their characters are one dimensional, at best. Murphy's dog is nervous and hyper; Burke's is vain and preening, Reiner's is grouchy and old, and so on.

Critics, who generally tend to be adults, weren't very big fans of the film, although some were mildly charmed. Paul West of the *Seattle Post-Intelligencer* observed, *Good Boy!* is fairly good-natured and not as awful as it sounds, but it lacks distinction. Megan Lehmann of the *New York Post* commented that the film seemed "slightly anachronistic." The director, she added, "leaves no canine cliché unturned in his pandering script." *Gates of the Times* wrote, "The film suffers from a singular lack of imagination. And energy." Roger Ebert of the *Chicago Sun-Times* explained, "I am willing to accept this premise if anything clever is done with it. Nothing is." Scott Brown of *Entertainment Weekly* felt more kindly toward the film and gave it a B. "Little is asked of talking-animal movies, save charm, heart, and at least one scene where said animal wears a lampshade. *Good Boy!* has all those things, plus a winning story line."

—*Jill Hamilton*

CREDITS

Owen Baker: Liam Aiken
Mrs. Baker: Molly Shannon
Mr. Baker: Kevin Nealon
Connie Fleming: Brittany Moldowan
Frankie: Hunter Elliot
Hubble: Matthew Broderick (Voice)
Barbara Ann: Delta Burke (Voice)
Wilson: Donald Adeosun Faison (Voice)
The Greater Dane: Vanessa Redgrave (Voice)
Henchman: Richard "Cheech" Marin (Voice)
Nelly: Brittany Murphy (Voice)
Shep: Carl Reiner (Voice)

Origin: USA

Released: 2003
Production: Lisa Henson, Kristine Belson; Jim Henson Productions; released by MGM
Directed by: John Hoffman
Written by: John Hoffman
Cinematography by: James Glennon
Music by: Mark Mothersbaugh
Sound: Claude Letessier
Editing: Craig P. Herring
Art Direction: John Marcynuk
Costumes: Antonia Bardon
Production Design: Jerry Wanek
MPAA rating: PG
Running time: 89 minutes

REVIEWS

Chicago Sun-Times Online. October 10, 2003.
Entertainment Weekly. October 17, 2003, p. 62.
Los Angeles Times Online. October 10, 2003.
New York Times Online. October 10, 2003.
People. October 20, 2003, p. 34.
USA Today Online. October 10, 2003.
Variety Online. October 5, 2003.
Washington Post. October 10, 2003, p. C5.

QUOTES

Shep (voiced by Carl Reiner): "It may look like people are in charge but face it, you don't see us picking up *their* poop."

The Good Thief

He doesn't want money. He wants what money can't buy.
—Movie tagline

Box Office: $3.5 million

Of all Jean-Pierre Melville's increasingly popular crime films, *Bob le Flambeur* (1955) is perhaps the most beloved by cineastes. This portrait of a down-on-his-luck gambler, his criminal consorts, the young girl both he and his protégé love, his ambiguous friendship with a police detective, and the colorful milieu of mid-1950's Montmartre make for an atmospheric slice of low life. Melville's film is about character, place, and mood and is infused with a romantic, off-kilter, world-weary tone.

With *The Good Thief*, Irish writer-director Neil Jordan offers a very loose adaptation of *Bob le Flambeur*, wisely steering away from a painstaking homage to Melville's distinctive existentialism. In interviews, Jordan has referred to *The Good Thief* as a light-hearted romp, but since the man who created such masterpieces as *Mona Lisa* (1986), *The Crying Game* (1992), and *The Butcher Boy* (1997) is incapable of fluff, his Riveria-set caper film has some dark moments.

American expatriate Bob Montagnet (Nick Nolte) is more than an unlucky gambler: He is a heroin addict. In addition to his protégé, Paulo (Said Taghmaoui), attentive but less hero-worshipping than in Melville's film, Bob also acquires a young woman hanger-on, Anne (Nutsa Kukhianidze), a 17-year-old addict, prostitute, and recent immigrant to Nice from somewhere to the east. Both Paulo and Anne see Bob as a protective uncle, albeit a seedy one. Seemingly without effort, Bob is at the center of a netherworld where almost everyone he comes into contact with is living on the edge.

When an old comrade, Raoul (Gerard Darmon), proposes robbing the casino in nearby Monte Carlo, Bob quickly agrees. What does he have to lose? He kicks his heroin habit by handcuffing himself to his bed as Anne and Paulo watch over him. This sequence is reasonably realistic but not depressingly so because Jordan wants to avoid darkening the film's mood too much. Bob's relatively easy cold turkey made be a nod toward the alcoholic Yves Montand's quick jump back on the wagon in Melville's *Le Cercle Rouge* (1970).

Jordan's caper is much more complicated than the one planned by Melville's gambler. The casino has acquired an extensive collection of paintings by such artists as Van Gogh, Cezanne, and Picasso, but the paintings on display to the customers are actually fakes. The real paintings are in a tightly guarded vault in a nearby building. Vladimir (Emir Kusturica), who installed the vault's security system, is happy to work with the thieves to bypass it. Bob will make sure that details of his plan to rob the casino are leaked so that the police will be distracted from his real goal. Much of the rest of the film involves a cat-and-mouse game between Bob and his longtime friend and antagonist, Roger (Tcheky Karyo), a police detective.

To help finance the operation, Bob sells his most prized possession, a painting he says Picasso gave him in 1969 after losing a bet on a bullfight. Tony Angel (Ralph Fiennes), a sleazy art dealer who expects the painting to be worth at least $2 million in the United States, provides Bob with a bankroll.

Before the heist is played out, numerous obstacles come into play. The darkest is the jealous Paulo's vicious shooting of a drug dealer, Said (Ouassini Embarek), he suspects of dallying with Anne. This violent act has a jarring effect on the film's tone. The most humorous obstacle is the fear of spiders by a member of Bob's gang, Philippa (Sarah Bridges), a transsexual weight lifter. Roger thinks he has everything figured out but, of course, does not.

The original title of *The Good Thief* was *Double Down*, a gambling term and fitting name for a film loaded with fakes and doubles. The latter includes Paulo being a junior version of Bob and Bob and Roger being alike but opposite in their attitudes toward the law. The most amusing doubles are the identical Cockney twins Albert (Mark Polish) and Bertram (Michael Polish) who work in security at the casino, though their employer does not realize there are two of them. This fact is central to the completion of Bob's plan.

The presence of Albert and Bertram indicates the jokey approach taken by Jordan since the Polish brothers have written and directed such films as *Twin Falls, Idaho* (1999) and *Northfork* (2003), the latter starring Nolte. And Kusturica is also a director, best known for *Underground* (1995). He is a rock guitarist as well and plays his instrument in most of his scenes. The presence of directors as actors is usually a sign that the filmmaker sees his project as a bit of a lark.

Jordan has said he was much inspired by Robert Altman's 1973 adaptation of Raymond Chandler's *The Long Goodbye*. Jordan's alternately tongue-in-cheek and violent tone is more in keeping with that of Altman's film than of Melville's. Altman's film also features an outstanding performance by a film director, Mark Rydell. Jordan's use (twice) of Leonard Cohen's "A Thousand Kisses Deep" may also be a nod to Altman since Cohen's music is central to the director's masterpiece, *McCabe and Mrs. Miller* (1971).

Jordan rejected Melville's setting because he feels Montmartre has become too touristy, and he tries not to make the Riviera glamorous. Nice is fitting because of its mixture of the gaudy and the run-down. When Bob picks up Anne walking along the shore, the locale looks almost industrial. There is only a fleeting glimpse of the roads made famous in Alfred Hitchcock's *To Catch a Thief* (1955).

That *The Good Thief* works as well as it does is due much to Nolte, who effortlessly dominates the film. His distinctively gravelly voice has never sounded so rough, and his face is less lived in than stomped on. With parts of his visage bloated and other sunken, Nolte is beginning to resemble Chet Baker in the middle stage of his famous decline.

Shortly after *The Good Thief* was shown at the Toronto Film Festival in September 2002, Nolte was arrested for driving under the influence, and his widely circulated arrest photo is probably the most unflattering picture ever taken of a celebrity, the emaciated Baker included. Nolte just doesn't resemble Bob: He is Bob.

Nolte's confessions of his many sins in the interviews promoting *The Good Thief* and his performance in the film have solidified his stance as the successor to Robert Mitchum—someone who has seen the abyss but remains cool. Like Mitchum, Nolte's performance seems effortless. He is at his best in displaying Bob's conflicting feelings about Roger and Anne. Bob likes the policeman and almost feels sorry for having to trick him, and he realizes he and Anne may be attracted to each other for the wrong reasons, may be bad for each other, but still need to protect each other.

Bob recalls Nolte's two best performances: *North Dallas Forty* (1979) and Martin Scorsese's "Life Lessons" segment of *New York Stories* (1989). Nolte is almost as good here, though Bob doesn't quite have as much texture as the characters in the earlier two films. One of the highlights of *Bob le Flambeur* is the childlike delight of the hero (played by Roger Duchesne) when his gambling luck unexpectedly changes. This is a wonderful moment of illuminating an already vibrant character. In Jordan's film, the same moment is merely a plot device, and Nolte underplays the scene.

Casting director Susie Figgis has worked on most of Jordan's films, as well as such notable endeavors as *Local Hero* (1983) and *The Full Monty* (1997). The cast she has assembled from many nations works very well as an ensemble, but the multitude of English accents occasionally leads to some bewilderment. The outstanding supporting performance is given by Fiennes, star of Jordan's *The End of the Affair* (1999). This is not a case of a star walking through a small role as a favor for a friend but a full-blown character performance. Fiennes perfectly captures the nasty violence lurking just beneath the art dealer's sophisticated surface.

Bob le Flambeur works only if the viewer is in tune with Melville's patented deliberate pacing, and it is easy not to get his style. On the Criterion DVD of the film, Daniel Cauchy (who plays Paulo) admits that he feels the film is overrated. *The Good Thief* is much easier to get but still an entertainment of some substance because of Jordan's use of doubles and fakes to add some luster to his bright, if tarnished, diversion.

—*Michael Adams*

CREDITS

Bob: Nick Nolte
Roger: Tcheky Karyo
Paulo: Said Taghmaoui
Raoul: Gerard Darmon
Anne: Nutsa Kukhianidze
Vladimir: Emir Kusturica
Remi: Marc Lavoine
Albert: Mark Polish
Betram: Michael Polish
Said: Ouassini Embarek
Philippa: Sarah Bridges
Tony Angel: Ralph Fiennes (Cameo)

Origin: France, Great Britain, Ireland
Released: 2003
Production: Stephen Woolley, John Wells, Seaton McLean; Alliance Atlantis; released by Fox Searchlight
Directed by: Neil Jordan
Written by: Neil Jordan
Cinematography by: Chris Menges
Music by: Elliot Goldenthal
Sound: David Stephenson
Editing: Tony Lawson
Art Direction: Anthony Pratt
Costumes: Penny Rose
MPAA rating: R
Running time: 109 minutes

REVIEWS

Boston Globe. April 11, 2003, p. C1.
Boxoffice. November, 2002, p. 123.
Christian Science Monitor. April 4, 2003, p. 15.
Entertainment Weekly. April 11, 2003, p. 54.
Film Comment. March/April, 2003, p. 77.
Los Angeles Times Calendar. April 2, 2003, p. 6.
Maclean's. April 14, 2003, p. 56.
New York. April 7, 2003, p. 154.
New York Times. April 2, 2003, p. E1.
New Yorker. April 7, 2003, p. 96.
Sight and Sound. March, 2003, p. 42.
USA Today. April 2, 2003, p. D3.
Variety Online. September 6, 2002.
Washington Post. April 11, 2003, p. C5.

QUOTES

Bob's (Nick Nolte) motto: "Always play the game to the limit—damn the consequences!"

Gothika

Because someone is dead doesn't mean they're gone.
—Movie tagline

 Box Office: $59.4 million

It is the proverbial dark and rainy night at the stereotypical gothic asylum that sits atop a hill surrounded by a dark and isolating forest. Inside, gunmetal blue-green cages line up against similarly cold-colored walls. Everything is grey in the psychiatric ward of Woodward Penitentiary, including the doctor: Miranda Grey (Halle Berry).

We first meet Miranda as she interviews inmate Chloe Sava (Penelope Cruz). Chloe, it seems, believes the devil visits her in her cell at night and beats her up and copulates with her. Of course this can't possibly be true, for not only does the devil not exist, this is a very secure facility. Perhaps these are nothing more than the delusions of a woman who has experienced severe sexual trauma. Miranda tries her best to get Chloe to make this connection, but the inmate refuses. She doesn't trust Miranda because, in her own words, "You can't trust anyone who thinks you're crazy." These are words that will come back to haunt Dr. Grey.

Until then, however, life goes on as usual for Miranda. She swims a few laps in the prison pool, drops in to say hi to her boss Doug (Charles S. Dutton) who also happens to be her beloved husband, and then sets out to drive home . . . on that dark and stormy night.

Unfortunately for Miranda, the storm has flooded the roads and, when she comes up to a blockade, her husband's best friend, Sheriff Ryan (John Carroll Lynch), informs her that she'll have to take a detour. This route change will also change her life. While crossing a bridge, Miranda suddenly sees a young girl standing in the pouring rain right in the middle of the road. Miranda slams on her brakes and gets out of the car to help the poor thing . . . only to have both women suddenly burst into flames. The screen goes black.

When Miranda comes to, she's in prison garb and in an observation cell in her own prison psychiatric ward. She's having a very difficult time trying to understand what is happening to her until another doctor, Peter Graham (Robert Downey Jr.), tells her the unthinkable: "Doug is dead. You killed him."

Miranda cannot believe what Pete is telling her. She couldn't have killed her husband; she loved her husband. She has no motive for and no memory of doing this unspeakable act. However, all the evidence points to her. Later, in the ward, she is greeted by Chloe, who says "Hello, Miranda, welcome. You're one of us now." Chloe then asks the former doctor, "are you scared?" Miranda replies that she's not to which Chloe chillingly tells her, "you should be."

It's only going to get worse for Miranda. As the ward's florescent lights constantly flicker, she finds the words "not alone" written in fog on her cell's glass wall. Then while "washing away her sins" in the shower, Miranda is attacked and cut 35 times with a scalpel. But there's no one there. And when she tears off the bandages later, the cuts on her arm again spell out "not alone." They were also written in her husband's blood on the walls of her home where he was murdered.

Realizing that she may have to solve this riddle herself, Miranda manages—most improbably—to escape her cell. While making her way through the prison she discovers several things. First of all, it turns out that the penitentiary director's teenage daughter, Rachel (Kathleen Mackey), died four years ago and had committed suicide, jumped off that same bridge where Miranda had seen the flaming young girl on that rainy night.

Secondly, when passing Chloe's cell, Miranda sees the back of a man actually attacking her as Chloe had recounted to her many times in their sessions together. Miranda can't make out who it is, but she does see his flamboyant tattoo of a woman in flames, the anima sola.

So many questions, and so little good plot to explain them. How could what started as a good idea turn so sour by the time it hits theaters?

Dark Castle Productions, the brainchild of producer Joel Silver and Robert Zemeckis, was created to bring horror films to theaters at Halloween to celebrate the legacy of Schlock 50s horror director William Castle. They began with remakes of Castle's films *House on Haunted Hill* and *Thirteen Ghosts*. These were followed last year by the original film *Ghost Ship* and now we have *Gothika*. The idea that there are filmmakers out there who actually want to make scary films for audiences at Halloween is a great one, unfortunately, with this latest entry, Dark Castle seems to have sacrificed any quality on the altar of the schedule . . . or at least close to schedule, since *Gothika* missed Halloween and was released in late November. This was probably due to the fact that production had to go on hiatus for a month after Halle Berry broke her arm while shooting.

It is said that screenwriter Sebastian Gutierrez pitched his idea for *Gothika* to Dark Castle with no script, but within six months there was an approved script and A-list actress Berry signed on to star. This fast tracking may have been the first source of problems with the movie, as Gutierrez's script seems to resort to mixing and matching cliches from different film genres that don't mix and certainly don't match. It's as if instead of coming up with an original plot to carry through on a basically promising premise he instead took two parts mystery, one part ghost story, one part women-in-prison, and a dash of serial-killer, mixed them all together and hoped no one would notice.

And even after resorting to this trick, Gutierrez wasn't careful enough to check for plot holes, inconsistencies, and just plain groan-inducing stupidity. For example, we're never sure about the ghost's relationship with Miranda. Is she out to punish her? It sure looks like it, but why? Is she out to use Miranda for her vengeance? That seems more likely, but then why keep pestering her once she's used her to that end? Is the ghost trying to make Miranda discover the truth of the ghost's own death and in the process save another life? Well, that one works, too, but then why treat her so badly? In other words, all explanations work, yet they also all conflict.

In the "sure, that's going to happen" category is the idea that assuming a murder case like this actually existed, do you think Miranda would really end up in her own institution?

Being treated by people who were her former colleagues and presumably are still her friends? Incarcerated alongside the patients she formerly treated and being investigated by her own husband's best friend? Doubtful.

This is not to say that there aren't a few redeemable points about *Gothika*. Cinematographer Matthew Libatique does a stylish job of creating an eerie atmosphere in the prison and showing the fog of uncertainty lifted in the daylight of the farmhouse where everything becomes clear to Miranda. This atmosphere is also helped by the haunting music of John Ottman and the incredible setting that has the now abandoned, turn-of-the-century St. Vincent-de-Paul maximum-security prison in Laval, Quebec doing a credible job standing in for Woodward Prison.

Unfortunately, the prison may do the best acting in the movie. *Gothika* is Halle Berry's first starring vehicle, and also her first project after receiving her Oscar for *Monster's Ball*. It was not a good choice. Her character lacks depth, and emotions take the form of histrionic expressions: confusion, fright, and shock among the most common. Berry may be a first-class actress, but she fails to make a very convincing psychiatrist. One flashes to Jennifer Lopez doing a similarly contrived stint in *The Cell*. Robert Downey Jr.—trying to rebuild his career after rehab—does a relatively restrained job in a relatively thankless role, however.

Fault also must lay with French director Mathieu Kassovitz, who relies too much on style as well as those obligatory false scares instead of sending the screenwriter back to his room to fix the script. As a result, *Gothika* is a poorly written and directed movie that assumes technique and atmosphere can distract a viewer from a story that cheats at several turns, asks audiences to accept an awful lot of inconsistencies and coincidences, and then not be insulted by the whole process. It is a ludicrous thriller that can't seem to decide on exactly what kind of movie it wants to be and consequently never gets the audience involved. At least it moves quickly and has a short run time.

—*Beverley Bare Buehrer*

CREDITS

Miranda Grey: Halle Berry
Pete Graham: Robert Downey Jr.
Douglas Grey: Charles S. Dutton
Chloe Sava: Penelope Cruz
Sherrif Ryan: John Carroll Lynch
Phil Parsons: Bernard Hill
Teddy Howard: Dorian Harewood
Irene: Bronwen Mantel
Rachel Parsons: Kathleen Mackey

Origin: USA

Released: 2003
Production: Joel Silver, Robert Zemeckis, Susan Levin; Dark Castle Entertainment, Warner Bros., Columbia Pictures; released by Warner Bros.
Directed by: Mathieu Kassovitz
Written by: Sebastian Gutierrez
Cinematography by: Matthew Libatique
Music by: John Ottman
Sound: Patrick Rousseau
Editing: Yannick Kergoat
Art Direction: Isabelle Guay
Costumes: Kym Barrett
Production Design: Graham Walker
MPAA rating: R
Running time: 95 minutes

REVIEWS

Chicago Sun-Times Online. November 21, 2003.
Entertainment Weekly. November 28, 2003, p. 98.
Los Angeles Times Online. November 21, 2003.
New York Times Online. November 21, 2003.
People. December 1, 2003, p. 30.
USA Today Online. November 21, 2003.
Variety Online. November 17, 2003.
Washington Post. November 21, 2003, p. WE46.

QUOTES

Miranda (Halle Berry): "You can't trust somebody when they think you're crazy."
Miranda (Halle Berry): "We all create our realities to some degree."

Grind

This summer the underdogs have their day.
—Movie tagline
Live Fast. Play Hard. Die Laughing.
—Movie tagline

 Box Office: $5.1 million

Unfortunately for *Grind,* this skateboarding comedy came out when the documentary *Dog Town and Z-Boys* was still fresh enough in critics' minds. The film, which detailed the lives of a group of skateboarders in Santa Mon-

ica in 1975, was an indie hit and gave people who didn't know a half-pipe from a deck the idea that they were skateboarding experts. Roger Ebert of the *Chicago Sun-Times* actually wrote the words, "I am no expert on the sport, but I have seen the 2002 documentary *Dog Town and Z-Boys*" before launching into his critique of the skateboarding stunts in the film.

The thing is, Ebert's and other critics' analysis of the moves in *Grind* are right on. While movies about skateboarding don't promise much in the way of plot or character development, it seems that the bare minimum a boarding film should provide is some cool tricks to watch. Expert Ebert wrote, "They seem to be repeating the same limited moves over and over again." And *Spliced Wire* critic Rob Blackwelder, who writes that he's been a boarder himself since the 1970s wrote that the characters "perform only one trick (at the very end) that's beyond the abilities of any dedicated junior high school punk with a modicum of talent."

Although the skating sequences were shot by Matt Goodman, skateboarder Tony Hawk's partner in the extreme sports media company 900 Film, they suffer from weak tricks and hard to follow visuals. Goodman is faced with the large problem that none of his leads seem to be competent on skateboards. Thus he is forced to shoot skating sequences using pro skaters. This means the camera jumps around incessantly so that no one can see it's not the real stars that are skating. This lessens the excitement of the tricks since it's difficult to follow what's going on. It also doesn't work. For one thing, his insistence on never showing the actors' faces while they perform starts to become obvious. It's like when pregnant TV actresses are constantly hiding their growing bellies behind large, strategically placed houseplants. And whoever chose the stunt doubles apparently gave no thought to choosing stuntmen who resembled the actors' body types. Thus when there is a skateboarding sequence, it doesn't seem like it's the characters who are skating, but rather just some other random guys who vaguely resemble the characters and have an odd style of skating in which they awkwardly duck their faces from the camera.

The plot of the film concerns wannabe skater Eric (Mike Vogel of *Grounded for Life*) and his desire to get sponsored on a skating tour. He figures that the best way to do this is to get a video of himself and his buddies skating into the hands of pro skater Jimmy Wilson (Jason London). Eric, a blandly good-looking blonde, decides he needs to follow Jimmy's tour around the country. Maybe if he hangs out, Jimmy will see him and immediately sign him up. Actually the plan is not as clear as that, but it does provide the chance for a road trip.

First, he recruits buddy Matt (Vince Vieluf of *Rat Race*), a goofy-looking class clown-type who says crude things to women, then wonders why they don't fall for him. The rubber-faced Vieluf is like some sort of modern version of Bert Lahr (aka the Cowardly Lion). He looks a lot like him, but his schtick is strictly X-rated.

Next up is Dustin (Adam Brody of *The O.C.*), an overly verbal guy who resembles a cross between Tom Hanks and Robert Downey, Jr. He is the one who funds the trip using the college money he's saved up as a cashier at the Chili 'N Such. Brody is a good actor—too good for a film like this, but nonetheless, it's good he's here. Brody has good comedic timing and it's fun to watch him sell lines that wouldn't otherwise work. Anyone who gets stuck watching this movie can still have an enjoyable time just watching Brody when he's in the background. Even when he's not the main focus of a scene, he's still intently there, working away.

Last up in the group is Sweet Lou (Joey Kern), a guy who's chosen because he has a van. Sweet Lou—it's never just Lou—is a guy who's already graduated from high school but still hangs around to chase high school girls. According to the script, Sweet Lou is irresistible to the ladies. He has a bevy of honeys for each day of the week and, if he ever needs more, he needs merely to sidle up to a new one and say "Wanna make-out?" Never since Henry Winkler played the lady-killing Fonzie has an actor's actual sexual desirability been so far away from his script-given desirability. Sweet Lou, who seems to be trying to be Matthew McConaughey but looks more like Tom Petty, is a mysterious fellow. Is it a joke that this guy, who thinks it is cool to crank up Poison and refers to himself in the third-person, is supposed to be so irresistible? It's possible. In between lots of puerile jokes about poop and such, writer Ralph Sall has stuck some sly humor in there.

The nominal plot is occasionally interrupted by meetings with actors who have made poor career moves by showing up in this film. A practically unrecognizable Dave Foley shows up as Wilson's tour manager. Also shaming themselves are Tom Green as a stoned skateboard repair man, Randy Quaid as Matt's clown father and Bob Goldthwait as a gross motel owner. When the guys come upon the hotel's pool filled with years of garbage and debris, Goldthwait's character comments, "My skimmer has been broken." There must have been some reason these guys got involved with this film. Perhaps an earlier version of the film was much funnier.

It's easy to believe that the film was once much better. Despite the plethora of embarrassingly tacky and offensive toilet jokes (i.e. a fat guy running desperately into a portable potty), there are some clever moments casually dropped in. The best of these happens when the four guys stop into a nightclub, then hear "Bust a Move." They break into a hilarious and quite good dance routine, complete with robot and break dancing moves. The dance sequence is far more accomplished and exciting than any of the skating sequences. Unfortunately lines of bad dialogue mostly smother the clever moments.

Critics gave the film low marks, including a C− from Lisa Schwarzbaum, who called *Grind* a "braying teen sports fantasy." Gary Dowell of the *Dallas Morning News* complained, "The movie is called *Grind* but *Drag* would have been a better choice. It's barely watchable and utterly disposable." Lou Lumenick of the *New York Post* described the film as "a yawnfest that's less exciting than watching the spin cycle at the laundromat." Liz Braun of the *Toronto Sun* called it "a mess, technically speaking" but allowed that it was "sweet and fairly amusing." And Wesley Morris of the *Boston Globe,* who generally liked the film, wrote that it "is what happens when an entire movie is composed of outtakes."

—Jill Hamilton

CREDITS

Matt Jensen: Vince Vieluf
Eric Rivers: Mike Vogel
Dustin Knight: Adam Brody
Sweet Lou: Joey Kern
Jamie: Jenny Morrison
Jimmy Wilson: Jason London
Mr. Jensen: Randy Quaid
Mr. Rivers: Christopher McDonald
Wynona: Summer Altice

Origin: USA
Released: 2003
Production: Bill Gerber, Hunt Lowry, Casey La Scala; Pandora Film, Gaylord Films, 900 Films; released by Warner Bros.
Directed by: Casey La Scala
Written by: Ralph Sall
Cinematography by: Richard Crudo
Music by: Ralph Sall
Sound: Lance Brown
Editing: Eric Strand
Costumes: Tangi Crawford
Production Design: Perry Andelin Blake
MPAA rating: PG-13
Running time: 100 minutes

REVIEWS

Chicago Sun-Times Online. August 15, 2003.
Entertainment Weekly. August 22-29, 2003, p. 114.
Los Angeles Times Online. August 15, 2003.
New York Times Online. August 15, 2003.
USA Today Online. August 15, 2003.
Variety Online. August 15, 2003.
Washington Post. August 15, 2003, p. WE35.

The Guru

When he talks, women listen.
—Movie tagline
Unleash the tiger within!
—Movie tagline

 Box Office: $3 million

When director Daisy von Scherler Mayer (1995's cult hit *Party Girl*) was working on her culture clash/romantic comedy film *The Guru,* the studio, Universal Pictures, tried to steer the movie toward the kind of broad comedy that would please the most people possible. Von Scherler Mayer attempted to do this, reporter Sorina Diaconescu wrote in an article in the *Los Angeles Times,* but according to the director, "it was very hard. Unfortunately, the substance just creeps in."

The substance of the movie has to do with poking fun at some cultural differences between East Indians and Westerners, particularly those religion-hopping Westerners who believe that Indian people are bastions of spirituality. The movie is so fun and light, though, that no one will feel like they are being preached to. As von Scherler Mayer put it, "If you can say something meaningful in a comedy context, it's much more powerful." Even if audience members get no message whatsoever from the film, it should still be an enjoyable experience. If nothing else, it's a movie that has plenty of bright colorful stuff to look at.

The film begins with a young Indian boy, Ramu, watching one of the typically over-the-top, dance-filled Bollywood musicals. Many Americans don't know it, but India's Bollywood film industry is bigger than Hollywood's. Bollywood puts out a tremendous amount of films, over 800 a year. Most of these are over three hours long, feature beautiful costumes and boast the kind of elaborate dance sequences that would put Busby Berkeley to shame. The films are not explicit—they contain nary a kiss—but can be romantic and are certainly melodramatic. As a boy, Ramu sneaks out of one such Bollywood movie and into a neighboring theater showing John Travolta and Olivia Newton-John in *Grease.* As he watches the two shimmying, he knows he has found his place.

Years later, Ramu (Jimi Mistry of *East is East* and *The Mystic Masseur*) still hasn't lost his love for American culture. His friend, Vijay (Emil Marwa), has moved to New York and reports in his letters that he's doing very well there. Ramu, who teaches dance to older women in saris, informs his class that he's moving to America to be a star. "You're going to drive a cab?" asks one of the women. In a country

where Apu, the owner of the Kwik-E-Mart on *The Simpsons* is the most well-known Indian star, the dream of becoming a famous star is pretty unrealistic. "That's why they call it a dream," says one of Ramu's friends, "Because it only happens when you're asleep."

Once in America, Ramu quickly learns that Vijay was lying. Instead of living in a penthouse and driving a Mercedes, Vijay shares a dumpy apartment with two other guys in Queens. Ramu reluctantly takes a job serving jerky customers in an Indian restaurant, but still pursues his dreams of becoming a star. He gets an audition with movie producer, Dwain (Michael McKean), but is too much of an innocent to realize that he's auditioning for a porn flick. When Dwain asks him to strip, Ramu takes it as an invitation to strip to his underwear and do the Tom Cruise dance from *Risky Business.*

When Ramu gets on the set, he finds himself unable to, er, perform. His costar, Sharrona (Heather Graham), lends a sympathetic ear and offers to tutor him in achieving the proper mind set. Meanwhile, in one of the many plot contrivances (which aren't too annoying since everything's done in such fun), Ramu ends up getting another surprise job. At a party he's catering for an uptight, society woman, Chantal (Christine Baranski), the guru that she's hired to entertain her flaky spirituality-seeking daughter, Lexi (Marisa Tomei), passes out from drinking too much. Ramu is tapped to impersonate a guru.

Devoid of any true spiritual wisdom, Ramu goes out to the crowd and tells them the same stuff that Sharrona has told him. "Your genitals are the windows to your soul," he says, to the receptive crowd. He breaks into the macarena and Lexi gleefully interprets it as being "one of those spiritual dervish things." The crowd breaks into a big flashy dance number and *The Guru* suddenly turns into a Bollywood film. It's a glorious thing to watch. The dancers have the moves down—the head cocks, the broad smiles and gleeful dance steps. The best scenes of *The Guru* are when the cast breaks out into dance. It's not corny, but exhilarating—the best that a musical can be.

Believing that he's really a guru, Lexi becomes Ramu's business and sexual partner. "There are a lot of unhappy people out there," says Lexi earnestly. "And I know most of them." Ramu's message of sexual liberation is popular with his clients, after all, having sex is a lot more fun that having to give up certain foods or spend time chanting. Ramu quickly becomes a Deepak Chopra-type of celebrity and gets the nickname "The Guru of Sex." He appears on talk shows and gets enough money to buy fine clothes, cars and automobiles for himself and his roommates.

Of course, Ramu needs to keep coming up with new material, and he has no where to get that but from Sharrona. In a *Three's Company* level plot device, he goes to Sharrona and pretends that he needs more help with his porn performance anxiety, but is really taking the information to pass on to his followers. Sharrona, a part-time teacher, is engaged to a boring fireman who believes she's a virgin. During Ramu and Sharrona's learning sessions they start falling for each other. In the typical offbeat fashion of this film, their most romantic scene involves them writhing sexually on the floor while singing the Billy Joel song, "Just the Way You Are."

The Guru knows it's following certain conventions and it has fun with that. Yes, Ramu and Sharrona predictably fall in love. Yes, the fish-out-of-water makes good, and yes, there is the big romantic climax that involves people showing up at Sharrona's wedding to break it up. But writer Tracey Jackson adds fun twists to the usual situations. The wedding scene is particularly rollicking.

And there is good humor throughout the film. The best lines are between Lexi and her brittle mother who is continually disappointed in her. "How's your mother?" asks one of Lexi's friends. "Practically lifelike," answers Lexi. In another scene, Chantal barks to Lexi, "I'll meet you in the kitchen." "Do you know where it is?" replies Lexi. And in a scene where Chantal is defending her character, she cites her own good deeds. "I feed the homeless—things I would feed myself, if I still ate carbs."

Baranski is particularly good as the society mom, though this is a role she has certainly honed elsewhere. Graham does a nice job as the good girl/porn star, but again, this is not new material for her. Mistry has the kind of silent star good looks that are right for this role, but his accent seems a little off. Perhaps it's because the star is not actually from India and his real speaking voice is more Manchester, England, than New Delhi. And Tomei is good as the rich American who is so eager to find a religion that will give her life purpose.

Critics were split on the film. Some thought the humor and dancing were great and others thought that the mix of Bollywood and Hollywood didn't work. Bob Strauss of the *Long Beach Press-Telegram* called it "a delightfully silly masala of Hollywood conventions, Bollywood fantasy and porn movie stupidity." Manohla Dargis of the *Los Angeles Times* called it "a gaudy, raucous romp." Daphne Gordon of the *Toronto Star* wrote, "A major-studio film starring actors with big box-office oomph, it feels like an upstart indie, thanks to its original script, endearing performances, colourful aesthetic, uplifting soundtrack, parodic undertones and the compelling theme of ethnic assimilation." And Lisa Schwarzbaum of *Entertainment Weekly* wrote, "Bright dialogue and finely embroidered performances adorn *The Guru* like festive beading on a pair of made-in-India bedroom slippers—unexpected and inordinately cheering in the drab dead of winter." Others weren't so charmed. Stephen Holden of the *New York Times* wrote, "The outcome of this nervy conceptual hybrid is a movie that plays stylistic hopscotch as it jumps from one square to the next, teetering perilously each time it lands on one quaking ankle."

—*Jill Hamilton*

CREDITS

Ramu Chandra Gupta: Jimi Mistry
Sharonna: Heather Graham
Lexi: Marisa Tomei
Dwain: Michael McKean
Chantal: Christine Baranski
Josh: Rob Morrow
Father Flanagan: Malachy McCourt
Rusty: Dash Mihok

Origin: USA, Great Britain, France
Released: 2002
Production: Tim Bevan, Eric Fellner, Michael London; Working Title Productions, StudioCanal; released by Universal Pictures
Directed by: Daisy von Scherler Mayer
Written by: Tracey Jackson
Cinematography by: John de Borman
Music by: David Carbonara
Sound: Robert Carr, Matthew Iadarola
Editing: Cara Silverman, Bruce Green
Costumes: Michael Clancy
Production Design: Robin Standefer, Sean Afshar
MPAA rating: R
Running time: 91 minutes

REVIEWS

Boxoffice. November, 2002, p. 136.
Entertainment Weekly. February 7, 2003, p. 53.
Los Angeles Times Online. January 31, 2003.
New York Times Online. January 31, 2003.
People. February 10, 2003, p. 37.
Sight and Sound. October, 2002, p. 40.
USA Today Online. January 31, 2003.
Variety Online. August 18, 2002.
Washington Post. February 14, 2003, p. WE45.

A Guy Thing

Boy meets girl. Boy meets girl's cousin.
—Movie tagline
He Finally Found The Perfect Girl(s).
—Movie tagline

Box Office: $15.4 million

The best part of *A Guy Thing* is probably the first few minutes. The credits for the film set up a mood of early 1960s films. There are wacky shapes and fun fonts that promise a lighthearted romantic romp. Then, in the first scene, a guy without a last name, Paul (Jason Lee), is having his bachelor party at an offbeat tiki bar. There is a cool retro band featuring a band member playing a stand-up bass. It seems like no matter what the movie brings, at least it will be done with a bit of style and flair. Perhaps the budget for the art director ran out after the first minutes of the film because the rest of the movie is run-of-the-mill stuff featuring such tired farcical scenes as a guy escaping from an upper window of a house by climbing into a tree.

The worst part of *A Guy Thing* is harder to peg. Could it be the part where a character says with a nudge, "I got waylaid (nudge, nudge), you know what I mean, WAY LAID"? Or perhaps it's the part where Paul gets crabs and goes to the drugstore to get some ointment, but guess who's there? His future mother-in-law! A large problem with *A Guy Thing* is that it relies way too heavily on coincidences to get its characters into the barely funny plot situations. The whole movie is based on the coincidence that Paul's one almost one-night stand, Becky (Julia Stiles), just happens to be his fiancé Karen's (Selma Blair) cousin. Can you picture writers Greg Glienna, Pete Schwaba, Matt Tarses and Bill Wrubel desperately pitching this story line to the studio? "And Becky is, get this, her COUSIN! Isn't that a RIOT?"

Paul's problems start at his bachelor party. He's not having a good time and starts getting drunk. The next morning he wakes up in bed with Becky, who was one of the Hawaiian-themed strippers from the party. Apparently they didn't do anything, whew! But, uh-oh, Karen is coming over right away. Paul hustles Becky out of his apartment just in time. Inexplicably, considering she had no reason to be naked, Becky leaves her underwear behind. (Do you think it will be found by Karen later?)

This is the part where more coincidences are shoved in to make the plot move forward. Otherwise, Karen would not know about the Becky incident and there would be no further problems. But no, the writers felt compelled to make Becky a wacky free-spirit. That means she is constantly trying out new jobs. So when Paul goes to a record store, there she is, working as a clerk. When he goes to a toll booth, there she is, despite the unlikeliness of his happening to get her particular booth on the one day she is working.

When Becky shows up at Paul and Karen's engagement party—she is a cousin after all—Paul reacts in a stupid, plot-forced manner. Instead of trusting that she will have some discretion, he decides the best way to handle the situation is to pretend to have hideous diarrhea so he can hide in the restroom all night. To add believability to his ruse, he makes sound effects by squirting out a squeeze bottle of lotion. So, which is the tackier scene—this one or the one in which he is suffering from crabs and frantically pawing at his groin? Hard to say.

Becky and Paul are further forced together by the existence of Karen's freakishly buff and jealous ex-boyfriend, Ray (Lochlyn Monroe). This forces Paul and Becky to break into his apartment to get, oh something, like incriminating photos or something. Why both of them need to go is a mystery. While the two are working together, Becky teaches Paul the joy of being a free spirit. She does this by driving really fast down hills in San Francisco. Paul teaches Becky, well, nothing. But she does seem to like him because he is not only nice, but straight.

As it must, it all comes down to a wedding scene that needs to be interrupted by another party. It would seem that some engaged couples could figure out that they're not right for each other before they drag all the relatives out in the formal attire, but alas it is not so. Before the big, exciting climax, there are some comedy set pieces that are only moderately charming. In one, a drugstore worker posing as a caterer (don't ask, it's one of those wacky coincidences again) serves drug-laced food to Paul's parents and in-laws. They all get high and act goofy! There are some nice characters actor here, including Julie Hagerty of *Airplane!* as his mother and James Brolin as the uptight father-in-law, but they never raise the humor level above that of a middling sitcom. In another, more successful sequence, Karen and Paul take dance lessons and Paul dances a loving tango with his strangely graceful instructor (Jay Brazeau).

Lee, who's been good as the sidekick in films like *Chasing Amy*, has an offbeat charisma that could make him a leading man, but here he's not right for this part. He has a sly quality and would do well in a film with lots of witty banter. Blair doesn't make much of an impression as the clueless fiancé. She looks nice but that's about it. And it's nice to see Stiles on-screen but, again, this is not the kind of material that helps anyone's career.

Several critics noted the fact that Glienna, one of the writers and the person who did the original stories, also wrote the successful film, *Meet the Parents*. Many noted the fact that *A Guy Thing* played like a weak version of that film. Desson Howe of the *Washington Post* wrote, "The rest of the plot includes situations that look ineptly borrowed from *Meet the Parents*. You have to wonder if *A Guy Thing* was one of Glienna's earlier scripts that, after *Parents* did well, he got to make." And Stephen Holden of the *New York Times* wrote, "Much of it plays like a confused, desperate rehash of that hit comedy (*Parents*)."

Owen Gleiberman of *Entertainment Weekly* really didn't like the film and wrote, "In *A Guy Thing* you can see the promise of stardom dribbling through Jason Lee's fingers.

To begin with, this former skate punk looks terrible in sweaters; they turn him into the kind of emasculated dork you don't want to spend 90 minutes watching find his courage." Thelma Adams of *Us* wrote for its attention-span challenged readers, "Snoozy in Seattle." And Ty Burr of the *Boston Globe* wrote, "Some of the gags are solid, but this sort of thing lives or dies on the strength of its cast and, unfortunately, the leads are playing against their own strengths."

—*Jill Hamilton*

CREDITS

Paul: Jason Lee
Becky: Julia Stiles
Karen: Selma Blair
Jim: Shawn Hatosy
Ken: James Brolin
Sandra: Diana Scarwid
Ray: Lochlyn Munro
Dorothy: Julie Hagerty
Aunt Budge: Jackie Burroughs
Buck: David Koechner
Pete: Thomas Lennon

Origin: USA
Released: 2003
Production: David Ladd, David Nicksay; released by MGM
Directed by: Chris Koch
Written by: Matt Tarses, Bill Wrubel, Greg Glienna, Pete Schwaba
Cinematography by: Robbie Greenberg
Music by: Mark Mothersbaugh
Sound: Larry Sutton
Music Supervisor: Maureen Crowe
Editing: David Moritz
Art Direction: Patrick Banister
Costumes: Pamela Ball Withers
Production Design: Dan Davis
MPAA rating: PG-13
Running time: 101 minutes

REVIEWS

Los Angeles Times Online. January 17, 2003.
New York Times Online. January 17, 2003.
People. January 27, 2003, p. 31.
USA Today Online. January 17, 2003.
Variety Online. January 15, 2003.
Washington Post. January 17, 2003, p. WE41.

The Hard Word

All it takes is a little persuasion.
—Movie tagline
In a word, they're gone.
—Movie tagline
They set out to pull off the perfect heist.
—Movie tagline

It's hard to know what to make of *The Hard Word*. Starting with the inscrutable title, this Australian caper film can't seem to settle on a satisfying tone. Writer Scott Roberts, making his directorial debut, has penned an inconsistent, unoriginal script that skimps on action and has a wan, strained wit. It's neither quirky enough nor dramatic enough to please audiences. And that's part of the reason why the American release date of this 2002 movie kept getting pushed back, and why it went straight to video in all but a few U.S. markets in 2003.

Roberts presumably was aiming for the kind of cool-crooks casualness that characterizes the genre that was reenergized by Quentin Tarantino's *Pulp Fiction*. But the plot is wholly unsatisfying. The protagonists are three brothers who are also partners in crime. They're a trio of goodhearted bank robbers who have never hurt a soul during their jobs, which is a facile way of trying to get audiences to root for them. Dale Twentyman (Guy Pearce) is the brains behind the outfit. Mal Twentyman (Damien Richardson) is a baby-faced, sweet-souled butcher; he looks a little like Jack Black. The third brother, Shane (Joel Edgerton), is not the brightest bulb, but he's always willing for an assignment.

As the movie begins, the brothers are in prison for bank robbery. Their crooked lawyer Frank Malone (Robert Taylor) has a deal for them. Frank seems to have contacts everywhere, and he and two corrupt police detectives have arranged a scam. The brothers can leave prison on day passes so that they can pull robberies and split the proceeds with Frank and his pals. If they do so, Frank promises that they will have their sentences shortened. The brothers are released and quickly pull off a nice little job on an armored car. Frank brings Dale's wife, Carol (Rachel Griffiths), to the warehouse where they are dividing up the money, and husband and wife ardently resume their acquaintance while Frank and his cohorts take the brothers' hard-earned cash.

But once they're all back in prison, Frank tells Dale that there's a problem: security tape has captured some of the brothers' faces. Dale thinks something is fishy, especially since he's beginning to suspect that Frank is having an affair with Carol. Frank eventually tells Dale that everything will be set straight—they'll get their release and their money—if the brothers help pull off an improbable robbery, sticking up the bookies that have collected bets on the Melbourne Cup,

Australia's premiere horse-racing event. The brothers don't have much of a choice, even though by this point they don't trust Frank.

They get their release to pull the job, but not until after the film wraps up a subplot. While in prison, Shane has fallen in love with a prison psychiatrist (Rhondda Findleton); their counseling sessions serve as a way to provide some backstory about the brothers' brutal upbringing. As with many of these interludes, the mood is light and slightly tongue-in-cheek. Shane falls ill from food poisoning after eating some of Mal's special blood sausages that he cooked up in prison for Shane's birthday. The psychiatrist then disappears from the movie, serving no purpose for the blundering plot.

Recovering from this romantic detour, *The Hard Word* lurches back toward its big heist scene. It's not a particularly clever or thoughtful caper as movie crimes go. As the horse race starts, the bookies all congregate in the same hotel ballroom, and, improbable as it may seem, they all obligingly bring big bundles of cash with them. Frank has an "inside man" who takes care of the hotel's security system, and the brothers—and a loose cannon that Frank has hired to work with them—pose as hotel employees. Once the bookies are all secured in the room, Frank announces it's a stickup, and they all get down on the floor. The scheme goes bad because the hothead who's working with the Twentymans (over their vociferous objections) starts shooting up the place.

The brothers manage to escape while lugging bulging duffel bags full of cash. Roberts's attempt at a chase scene is a little pathetic: The brothers run around Melbourne, grunting and groaning under their heavy loads, while they are pursued by Frank, driving a red station wagon. The brothers attract no attention leaving the hotel or running around the streets. Then they make an improbable escape by jumping off a bridge onto the top of a train. After that, no authorities pursue them even though the multi-million-dollar robbery is the biggest crime story of modern times in Australia, and all the bookies have seen their faces.

The rest of the movie seems uncertain where to go, so it peters out. As the brothers are on the lam, they commandeer a car driven by an agreeable young woman (Kate Atkinson), with whom Mal becomes immediately smitten. Dale decides to hide the loot in the posterior of a restaurant designed like a giant cow. Then there's not one, but two separate confrontations involving Frank and Carol, as the plot plods toward a rather hokey resolution. Locations jump from here to there without explanation. Frank keeps driving different vehicles, without explanation. And there's never any clue about what the title means.

Roberts has made a movie out of a half-baked idea that is further done in by a plot that seems cobbled together from snippets of other, better movies. There's so little action and tension in this film that it should have become more of a comedy. But the attempts at humor are also halfhearted.

The film looks good, at least. Roberts is a facile if uninventive director, and he tries to make the most out of his characters, but none of them are sufficiently developed. It's not clear why Frank bothers with the brothers, since he seems to have connections everywhere. It's not clear with whom Carol really sides, and why. And though the brothers banter a bit, there's not the kind of camaraderie that makes them a memorable crime family. There's some clever dialogue, in spots, but otherwise the film is limp.

Pearce is as good as he can be with a character that is paper thin. His talents are suited to bigger challenges, as he made plain in *Memento*. Griffiths, so endearing as the loving wife in the baseball film *The Rookie*, here looks a little ridiculous in a bad blonde dye job. Though she tries her best to make Carol a memorable femme fatale, she's also struggling with an underwritten character. Richardson is engaging as Mal, but Edgerton never gives his character much of an imprint. And for a villain, Taylor is rather bland and unconvincing.

It doesn't help that the Australian accents are a little tough to follow at times, and since the editing is jumpy and the plot full of holes, you're left in a muddle most of the time, trying to piece together what's happening and why, especially at the beginning of the film. As for the humor, it's just not sly enough to work. *The Hard Word* is hardly the worst caper movie ever made, but with little suspense and lame stabs at wit, it's more tedious than engaging.

— *Michael Betzold*

CREDITS

Dale Twentyman: Guy Pearce
Carol Twentyman: Rachel Griffiths
Frank Malone: Robert Taylor
Shane Twentyman: Joel Edgerton
Mal Twentyman: Damien Richardson
Jane Moore: Rhonda Findleton
Pamela: Kate Atikinson
Det. Mick Kelly: Vince Colosimo
Det. Jack O'Riordan: Paul Sonkkila
Paul: Kim Gyngell
Tarzan: Dorian Nkono

Origin: Australia, Great Britain
Released: 2002
Production: Al Clark; Australian Film Finance Corp., Alibi Films International, Wildheart; released by Lions Gate Films
Directed by: Scott Roberts
Written by: Scott Roberts
Cinematography by: Brian J. Breheny
Music by: David Thrussell

Sound: John Schiefelbein
Editing: Martin Connor
Art Direction: Jeff Thorp
Costumes: Terry Ryan
Production Design: Paddy Reardon
MPAA rating: R
Running time: 102 minutes

REVIEWS

Boxoffice. July, 2003, p. 43.
Chicago Sun-Times Online. June 27, 2003.
Entertainment Weekly. June 20, 2003, p. 56.
Los Angeles Times Online. June 20, 2003.
New York Times Online. June 13, 2003.
Variety. June 3, 2002, p. 21.
Washington Post. June 16, 2003, p. WE36.

QUOTES

Carol (Rachel Griffiths): "I thought you liked me being a tart."
Dale (Guy Pearce): "I like you being my tart."

The Haunted Mansion

Check your pulse at the door . . . If you have one.
—Movie tagline

 Box Office: $74.4

Once upon a time there was a masked ball in a great Southern mansion. At this ball there is a man and woman who are madly in love with each other. Unfortunately someone interferes in their love, causing the woman to drink poisoned wine. In his grief over her death, the man hangs himself. A sad ending to a beautiful party.

Flash forward to the present day and the mansion sits cold, neglected, and silent behind locked gates. A young boy standing before the gates is suddenly spooked and the fliers he was delivering for Evers and Evers Real Estate end up drifting along the road. One of the Evers pictured on the flier is Jim Evers (Eddie Murphy), a real estate agent so driven to make a sale that he even misses his own wedding anniversary with the other Evers appearing on the flier, his wife Sara (Marsha Thomason). Jim has sold an impressive seven houses this month but in the process has missed not

only his anniversary but barbecues, sporting events, and many other family happenings.

This coming weekend, however, will be special because Jim and Sara and their two children, Megan (Aree Davis) and Michael (Marc John Jefferies), are heading out in their car to spend a few days together at the lake. Megan is your typical thirteen-year-old, jaded, perpetually bored and more inclined to listen to her music on isolating headphones than listen to her parents. Ten-year old Michael is afraid of spiders (which will inevitably become important at a critical point in the story), but his father gives him the typical macho advice, "Don't be afraid of anything. They'll use it against you."

Unfortunately for the Evers family, a phone call will cause their simple family vacation to be sidetracked by a tempting, money-making real estate opportunity. It seems that the owner of the fairytale mansion, the site of that masked ball, is now interested in selling. Although the phone offer was made specifically to Sara who would have no trouble passing it up for her family, it's just too good for workaholic Jim to pass up. He promises that they'll be making only a slight side trip on their outing.

At the mansion the family finds several unusual things: a locked gate that mysteriously opens, a cemetery in the back yard, and a very stiff butler by the name of Ramsley (Terence Stamp). Eventually the mansion's owner, Master Edward Gracey (Nathaniel Parker), arrives. The house is his birthright and inheritance, but an increase in "disturbances" lately has prompted him to sell it. Seems easy enough that the Evers family soon should be on their way, but then Ramsley announces that a storm has flooded the road and there will be no leaving the mansion. The family must spend the night in this spooky old building.

Ramsley is an odd duck and, like the mansion, a remnant from a bygone era. His code is "attend to details, understand priorities and know one's place." Master Gracey, too, seems to be from another time for he is all graciousness and attentiveness yet oddly distant and inordinately interested in Sara.

When Sara runs after the disappearing maid, Emma (Dina Waters), she runs into the solemn Gracey who begins to explain to her the history of his house. "These walls are filled with so many memories," he tells her. "Some of them painful." When pressed further about his sadness he tells her the story of Elizabeth, whose "story haunts these walls." Elizabeth was the woman at the ball who had killed herself by drinking poison. In despair Gracey's grandfather hanged himself, and his ghost haunts the house, waiting for her return. "If you listen carefully," he tells Sara, "you can still here the beating of his breaking heart."

While Gracey entertains Sara with his sad tale, Jim finds himself in the library where he accidentally leans against a bust and opens up a secret passage. With a realtor's curiosity, it's not surprising when Jim enters the passage and gets trapped there. Meanwhile, elsewhere in the house,

Megan and Michael find themselves following a glowing orb through the corridors and stumble upon a room where they find a crystal ball inhabited by Madame Leota (Jennifer Tilly), the voice to the spirits. Jim, too, makes his way to Madame Leota after finding an exit from the secret passages through a painting in the portrait gallery (where the paintings' eyes really do follow them).

Typical of disembodied voices from another world, Madame Leota gives Jim all sorts of cryptic messages such as "The key is the answer to all." These send Jim and his kids off in search of a way to set free all the ghosts trapped on the mansion's grounds and to save their mother as well. And what does their mother need to be saved from? When they stumble upon a portrait of Elizabeth, they are startled to discover that she looks exactly like Sara. Master Gracey is planning on wedding their mother for it was he and not his grandfather who had hanged himself at the loss of his love who will now be restored through Sara.

The Haunted Mansion begins with a disembodied voice that says, "Welcome, foolish mortals." We won't realize how prophetic that statement is until we leave the theater and realize that we foolishly spent perfectly good money to see this dull film. This is the third movie to be based on a ride at a Disney theme park. The first was the bomb *The Country Bears*, which was followed by the mega-hit *Pirates of the Caribbean*. With this pedigree, *The Haunted Mansion* seemed to have at least a fifty-fifty chance of success.

As a starting point, the Imagineers (what Disney calls it creators) who put the original Disney ride together also wrote a ten-page story about the house and Master Gracey. While that information does not appear in the ride, it did form the foundation for the movie. In fact, the character of Gracey was named for Yale Gracey, one of the original Imagineers, while Madame Leota was named for Imagineer Leota Toombs Thomas.

While the exterior of the house as presented in the movie does not match that of the Disneyland ride, the movie does try to pay homage to it. There are the ballroom dancers, the corridor of doors, the room that stretches, the ghostly hitchhikers, and characters from the cemetery make cameo appearances. There is also the four-part harmony of The Singing Bust with its multiple personalities. In one of the few amusing scenes in the film, the singing heads finish all of Jim's sentences with songs. (It is said that one face is that of Imagineer Paul Frees, another is Thurl Ravenscroft, who sang lead on the original "Grim Grinning Ghosts," and I swear one of them looks suspiciously like Walt Disney himself.) The Dapper Dans, the barbershop quartet that performs on Main Street USA at Disneyland, also make a cameo appearance.

Unfortunately director Rob Minkoff (*The Lion King* and the two *Stuart Little* films) seems unable to offer any interesting vision to this stale movie. And even screenwriter David Berenbaum, a graduate of Disney's own Writers in Residence Program who is also responsible for writing the entertaining 2003 Christmas season hit *Elf*, can't find anything truly creative to do with the material. The story is so thin and timeworn that there's little to pique our interest. "Ghost stories are about guilt and unresolved issues," says Berenbaum, but there's nothing here we haven't seen before. The script is lackluster and uninspired, so the actors have little with which to work.

Eddie Murphy looks as if he'd rather be anywhere than in this movie. When he's not looking bored, he's trying to cover his ennui with a steady stream of patter—which gets very annoying very quickly. Again playing a put-upon father, Eddie's motor-mouth Jim is no more funny than the mansion's ghosts are scary. He's not even likable because he always seems more concerned with selling the house than in saving his wife. Even his actions seem totally predictable. When he says, "I have everything under control" you just know he doesn't.

The rest of the Evers family fares no better. Poor Marsha Thomason is given little to do but look beautiful, react to Gracey's advances and gripe at Jim. The Evers kids seem to be there primarily as a marketing tool, offering pre-teen identification, as well as to show up their Dad.

About the only interesting characters in the film are Wallace Shawn's grumpy but obsequious servant; Jennifer Tilly's disembodied gypsy, Madame Leota, whose lines are among the best that the dialogue has to offer; and a gaunt-looking Terence Stamp, who turns in a campy performance worthy of anything Vincent Price did in all those Roger Corman pictures. Lovingly rolling his R's and delivering all his lines in deadpan fashion, Stamp steals the scenes he's in, even with a severe case of bed hair.

If there is a star to this picture it is the eponymous mansion. Production designer John Myhre (*X-Men* and *Elizabeth*) designed Master Gracey's home from the Grand Hall to the graveyard. The Oscar winner for *Chicago* provides one of the few fascinating "characters" in *The Haunted Mansion*. Myhre manages to give the estate personality by making it seem creepy and decayed yet luxurious and elegant at the same time.

Mona May's costume designs also help to make *The Haunted Mansion* at least look richly detailed. Perhaps her most innovative effort involved sewing onto the ghosts' costumes tiny spherical mirrors—the same as those used on highway signs—that reflect light back to the camera and produce an eerie glow. Special make-up effects were provided by Rick Baker, famous for his work on various ape movies as well as helping Eddie Murphy become the many Klump family members he portrays in *The Nutty Professor*. Here, Baker has done his usual skillful work creating ghosts and zombies and also creating the makeup for Edward Gracey and butler Ramsley.

But these paltry pluses can't begin to make up for the feeble storyline and slight characters. One eventually becomes so bored that belief is no longer suspended and one begins to look for problems: Megan has studied Latin for three years? That is certainly convenient. And where did all those pre-lit torches come from in the long-abandoned mausoleum?

In the press kit the filmmakers talk about "ghost logic," a set of rules that govern the appearance and physical attributes of the Gracey mansion's spirits—what they can and cannot do or look like. It's too bad this level of thought wasn't put into the script with a sort of "moviegoers logic"— what will and won't scare audiences or make them laugh. *The Haunted Mansion,* while trying to be a scary and funny movie, does neither. There are no scares, no laughs, no thrills, and no chills in this film. And whose bright idea was it to release this movie over the Christmas holiday season? After the success of *The Pirates of the Caribbean, The Haunted Mansion* offered promise, but this time the ride is much more fun than the movie. We're back in *The Country Bears* territory here.

—*Beverley Bare Buehrer*

REVIEWS

Chicago Sun-Times Online. November 26, 2003.
Entertainment Weekly. December 5, 2003, p. 64.
Los Angeles Times Online. November 26, 2003.
New York Times Online. November 26, 2003.
People. December 8, 2003, p. 34.
USA Today Online. November 26, 2003.
Variety Online. November 26, 2003.
Washington Post. November 26, 2003, p. C14.

QUOTES

Jim Evers (Eddie Murphy): "Honey! Ya know they have dead people in the backyard!"

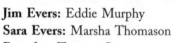

CREDITS

Jim Evers: Eddie Murphy
Sara Evers: Marsha Thomason
Ramsley: Terence Stamp
Ezra: Wallace Shawn
Madame Leota: Jennifer Tilly
Master Gracey: Nathaniel Parker
Michael: Marc John Jeffries
Megan: Aree Davis
Emma: Dina Waters

Origin: USA
Released: 2003
Production: Don Hahn, Andrew Gunn; Walt Disney Pictures; released by Buena Vista
Directed by: Rob Minkoff
Written by: David Barenbaum
Cinematography by: Remi Adefarasin
Music by: Mark Mancina
Sound: David Wyman
Editing: Priscilla Nedd Friendly
Art Direction: Beat Frutiger
Costumes: Mona May
Production Design: John Myhre
MPAA rating: PG
Running time: 99 minutes

He Loves Me. . . . He Loves Me Not (A la Folie. . . . Pas de Tout)

Discover the fine line between love and obsession.
—Movie tagline
Is she crazy in love, or just crazy?
—Movie tagline

 Box Office: $1 million

For American audiences, *He Loves Me. . . . He Loves Me Not* was worth a closer look because of its star, the French actress Audrey Tautou. Although Tautou is a familiar sight to French audiences, to Americans she was known for her starring role in the quirky, romantic arthouse hit, *Amelie.* The gamine star quickly became synonymous with all things sprightly and whimsical.

When *He Loves Me. . . . He Loves Me Not* begins, it looks like the audience will be in for more of the same. The fresh-faced Angelique (Tautou) is at a quaint French flower store ordering a single red rose. She says that she is getting it for her boyfriend to remind him of the first time they met. At first the proprietor doesn't want to waste his delivery boy on such a small order, but Angelique is so darn cute and smiley and it is rather romantic to order just one rose. Cut to next scene—the delivery boy is begrudgingly delivering the flower.

He takes it to Loic (Samuel Le Bihan), a prominent cardiologist who smiles quietly at getting the rose and tells others its from his wife. Angelique confides the details of the affair to her friends Heloise (Sophie Guillemin), a fellow waitress, and David (Clement Sibony), a medical student who obviously has a big crush on Angelique. When they worried about their friend, Angelique tells them that yes, it is unfortunate that Loic is married, but he promises that he will be leaving his wife very soon. Angelique is undeterred by the fact that his wife Rachel (Isabelle Carre) is very pregnant. Angelique is giddily in love. In an art class, she paints the nude model's body, but tops it with a perfect likeness of Loic's face.

Angelique is too in love to care that at a party that Loic attends, she must not speak with him because his wife is present. After he leaves, she steals out into the night after him. She paints a portrait of him and delivers it to his office, only saying that it's from "a friend." But soon things become too one-sided even for Angelique. Loic does not return her phone calls and worse, doesn't show up at the airport for a trip that the couple planned to take together.

Angelique starts becoming unhinged. At the nice home where she is housesitting, she lets things get filthy as she sinks into depression. Although she is a talented artist who has just been awarded a scholarship, she doesn't care about her future if it won't involve Loic. As she deteriorates, she starts destroying things in the house, even ripping down the family's pictures. And she concocts a plan to get a body part from David's medical practice to send as a hideous goodbye gift to Loic. When Loic is accused of accosting one of his female patients, Angelique is horrified. The next day, Angelique shows up at work with a wrecked scooter and a bloody arm. Perhaps not so coincidentally, Loic's accuser has been killed.

Here is the big twist of the film. First time filmmaker, Laetitia Colombani, a 25-year-old actress, spent four years writing the script and her attention to plot details shows. Right in the middle of the film it flashes backwards through the entire film and starts again at the beginning. But this time, the story is told from Loic's point of view. As seen through his eyes, Angelique's obsession with love is a lot more ominous. Some critics noted that the obsessive love in this film is the flip side of Amelie's somewhat obsessive love in that film. Loic, who is quite in love with Rachel, only knows her in passing as the girl who is housesitting for the neighbors' house next door.

During the second half of the film, there is a mild *Sixth Sense* enjoyment at seeing the events play out with a wholly different interpretation. When Loic hears the news that his wife is pregnant, for example, he buys her a big bouquet of flowers. As he carries them into the house, he spots Angelique and impulsively hands her one of the blooms. Loic's story makes it a lot more obvious why he never calls her or why he doesn't show up for their trips. He is wholly unaware of his involvement in Angelique's fantasy affair.

A few things don't work with this film. For one thing, the second half suffers from being from Loic's point of view. While Le Bihan is a talented enough actor, he doesn't have nearly the screen presence of Tautou and the movie misses her. Angelique's character is also a bit of a problem. Even when we believe her to be just an innocent girl stuck in a dead-end affair with a callous married man, she is not a very sympathetic character. She's so obviously fooling herself with her dreams of Loic leaving his wife that she seems more dense than pitiable. When the affair appears to be faltering and she starts wallowing in self-pity, self destructive acts and odd behavior, it's hard not to miss the perky lovestruck girl that the movie started with.

What does work is that *Sixth Sense* re-viewing of the events. The events in *He Loves Me* are never as clever as those, but it's still fun to see the same things play out in different ways. After Angelique sneaks off with Loic during the party scene, for example, she returns to the main room with a secret little smile. Her would-be boyfriend, David, quietly seethes with jealousy. When we see the scene a second time, however, it's much different. Loic simply goes to the restroom and Angelique follows him. The two exchange the polite small talk of strangers over the wash basin. The meeting is enough to fuel Angelique's affair fantasies and gives her the secret grin. It would be nice if the twists were just a tad more clever, but they're just interesting enough to keep the movie afloat.

Critics were about evenly split over the film. Stephen Holden of the *New York Times* wrote, "The notion of turning Ms. Tautou's waifish charms back on themselves to suggest a demonic witchery may be a dramatic conceit. But it never registers as more than a gimmick in a movie conceived as a sophisticated Gallic stunt." Kevin Thomas of the *Los Angeles Times* wrote, "*He Loves Me. . . . He Loves Me Not* is an impressively assured and confident first film and has been made with such attention to detail and mood that it's possible to regret not paying closer attention to its cleverly deceptive first part." And Mick LaSalle of the *San Francisco Chronicle* called it "an acerbic examination of erotic obsession" and wrote that it "represents about as assured a debut as they come."

—*Jill Hamilton*

CREDITS

Angelique: Audrey Tautou
Loic: Samuel Le Bihan
Rachel: Isabelle Carre
Heloise: Sophie Guillemin
David: Clement Sibony

Origin: France
Language: French
Released: 2002
Production: Charles Gassot; TF-1 Films, Telema, TPS Cinema, Cofimage 12; released by Samuel Goldwyn Films
Directed by: Laetitia Colombani
Written by: Laetitia Colombani, Caroline Thival
Cinematography by: Pierre Aim
Music by: Jerome Coullet
Sound: Marc-Antoine Beldent, Cyril Holtz
Editing: Veronique Parnet
Art Direction: Jean-Marc Kerdelhue
Costumes: Jacqueline Bouchard
MPAA rating: Unrated
Running time: 92 minutes

REVIEWS

Entertainment Weekly. February 21, 2003, p. 127.
Los Angeles Times Online. February 14, 2003.
New York Times Online. February 14, 2003.
USA Today Online. February 14, 2003.
Sight and Sound. December, 2002, p. 47.
Time. March 3, 2003, p. 70.
Variety. April 8, 2002, p. 30.

Head of State

The only thing white is the house.
—Movie tagline

 Box Office: $40 million

Woe to the Chris Rock fan who wants to see him in a good comedy. To fans, bad Chris Rock movies are an all too common occurrence. It's a cycle that's as predictable as bad puns on the local news. First, word hits the trades that Rock is working on a movie and this makes the fans happy. The setup for the film is announced, i.e. Rock as a black president, Rock as a CIA agent, Rock as a black guy in a white man's body. Fans may feel a bit dubious, but still have hope. Rock makes the rounds of the talk shows, declaring that this, finally, is the film he's wanted to make. Fans are still hopeful. The film comes out, and fans' hopes are dashed. *Head of State* may well be the film that makes

Rock's fans give it up for once and for all. There are only so many bad movies you can accept from someone before it just becomes too unrewarding.

The ironic thing is that Rock does know how to make a good comedy. It's just that all his good comedic movies have been him doing standup. Chris Rock doing only standup for a whole film is brilliant. He commands the stage, his observations are searing and brilliant and he manages to make lots of pointed commentary without seeming offensive. The man is one of the top, if not the top, standup comedian working today.

It's hard to imagine another performer who has been so outstanding in one field and so hideous in another. (Okay, Madonna, but one would have to accept that she is a brilliant singer.) Why can't Rock just accept that standup is his thing and give up on the movies?

Rock's movies have all kinds of things wrong with them. For one, Rock is not the best actor in the world. He's not horrible, and it wouldn't be much of a problem if his material were interesting enough to draw attention away from his acting. Second, and most importantly, Rock doesn't seem to have any idea what makes a movie funny. The jokes in *Head of State* are sparse and not that funny. It's odd that someone who has such a good sense of funny would be so inept at putting funny things in a film script. It's as though having to structure his comedy into the typical three act structure constricts the comedy-producing part of Rock's brain.

And third, the edge that is such a big part of Rock's standup is largely missing from *Head of State*. Yes, he gets a dig or two in at a malt liquor company that's marketing to kids, but the film is full of missed opportunities for Rock's famous biting humor. The man is running for president, after all. And, if anyone's noticed, the country is not in ideal shape. Surely there might be a few comments Rock would make about how he would run things. *Head of State* promises the prospect of a United States according to Rock, but instead it's a tepid, timid trifle. It's not like Rock had to compromise his vision. He produced, co-wrote (with Ali LeRoi) and directed the film himself.

Rock is Mays Gilliam, a D.C. alderman who takes his job seriously and tries to help his neighbors out. When the Democratic presidential and vice-presidential candidate are killed when their planes crash into each other, the party scrambles for a replacement candidate. Bill Arnot (James Rebhorn) knows that the election is going to be a losing one. They are running against a popular eight-year vice-president, Brian Lewis (Nick Searcy), who is a war hero and some sort of cousin of Sharon Stone. The Sharon Stone joke is mentioned repeatedly. Not only is it not funny, but such a celeb connection doesn't guarantee much. Anyone remember Olympia Dukakis and cousin Michael?

Arnot and his campaign advisors Martin Geller (Dylan Baker) and Debra Lassiter (Lynn Whitfield) decide since the candidate is going to lose anyway, they may as well score some points with the African-American voters by running a black guy. After they see Mays on TV rescuing an elderly woman from a burning building, they know they have their man. (Why they would go for a more known person closer to the party is but one of the things in the film that don't make a whole lot of sense.)

Head of State is not without its funny bits. A TV smear ad against Mays mentions ominously that Mays was not present at a rally to fight cancer. Obviously, the ad concludes, Mays is pro-cancer. It's also familiar smart Rock commentary that his opponent's popular catchphrase is "God bless America—and no place else." Mays gets to make some sharp points like, "What kind of drug policy makes crack cheaper than asthma medicine?" or "How many of you work at a hotel you can't afford to stay in?" "That ain't right," roars his audience. He makes good points, but they are arguably more depressing than gut-busters.

Rock's riff about how bad his neighborhood is is good. "I work in a neighborhood so bad that you can get shot while you're getting shot." Rock's absurd humor shows up a few—too few—times. When Mays imagines himself as president, he pictures himself standing on a lectern and getting out, "My fellow Americans . . ." before promptly being shot. And whenever a character hears news on the radio, it is followed by, "And we return you to the Jay-Z song already in progress."

But a lot of the humor falls into racial jokes that aren't that funny. When candidate Mays livens up a dull Washington fund-raiser by taking to the turntables (why would there be turntables set up conveniently in the house?), he shouts the song line, "The roof, the roof, the roof is on fire." The woefully unhip white oldsters, run out screaming, thinking the roof is really on fire. After choosing his bailbondsman brother, Mitch (an underused Bernie Mac), as his running mate, Rock paints his campaign bus to look like a rap group tour bus. The whites are shocked, simply shocked. Even the lamest Hollywood hack can write jokes about how white people are not cool and need to loosen up.

And Rock veers into heavily non-PC territory when he jokes about women. One of his running gags is that Kim (Robin Givens), the fiancee who spurned him when he was a nobody, starts stalking him after he becomes a candidate. He frequently calls out "Security!" when he sees her and she is violently whisked away. One of the perks Mays discovers when he becomes a candidate is Nikki (Stephanie March). "We got tired of getting caught up in sex scandals," explains Martin, "So we commissioned our own team of superwhores." The gorgeous Nikki is, of course, delighted to be of service. The "good" woman is Lisa (Tamala Jones), a hardworking waitress/gas station attendant. The scenes between the two are dull and have a palpable lack of romantic chemistry.

Critics were split on whether *Head of State* was a winner or not. Manohla Dargis of the *Los Angeles Times* wrote, "Rock can't set up a decent-looking shot, and he doesn't care about niceties such as character development and all that narrative

downtime between jokes. But he nonetheless wrings biting humor from serious issues with the sort of ferocity that made Richard Pryor and Lenny Bruce men of respect as well as comedy." A. O. Scott of the *New York Times* wrote that "the very confusion that has made him unpredictable and funny onstage makes this on-screen exploration of contemporary racial mythologies curiously tentative and unfocused." Rob Blackwelder of Spliced Wire wrote, "Smart, sharp political satire it's not. But Chris Rock's *Head of State* . . . mixes a few stinging zingers into its generally crowd-pleasing brand of snickers and knee-slappers."

—*Jill Hamilton*

CREDITS

Mays Gilliam: Chris Rock
Mitch Gilliam: Bernie Mac
Martin Geller: Dylan Baker
Brian Lewis: Nick Searcy
Debra Lassiter: Lynn Whitfield
Kim: Robin Givens
Lisa Clark: Tamala Jones
Nikki: Stephanie March
Senator Bill Arnot: James Rebhorn
Bernard Cooper: Keith David
Meat Man: Tracy Morgan
Adviser: Robert Stanton
Mr. Earl: Jude Ciccolella
Himself: Nate Dogg

Origin: USA
Released: 2003
Production: Ali LeRoi, Chris Rock, Michael Rotenberg; 3 Arts Productions; released by Dreamworks Pictures
Directed by: Chris Rock
Written by: Chris Rock, Ali LeRoi
Cinematography by: Donald E. Thorin
Music by: Marcus Miller, David "DJ Quik" Blake
Sound: Whit Norris, John Pritchett
Editing: Stephen A. Rotter
Art Direction: Ray Kluga
Costumes: Amanda Sanders
Production Design: Steven Jordan
MPAA rating: PG-13
Running time: 95 minutes

REVIEWS

Boston Globe Online. March 28, 2003.
Chicago Sun-Times Online. March 28, 2003.
Entertainment Weekly. April 4, 2003, p. 75.

Los Angeles Times Online. March 28, 2003.
New York Times Online. March 28, 2003.
USA Today Online. March 28, 2003.
Variety Online. March 22, 2003.
Washington Post. March 28, 2003, p. C1.

QUOTES

Presidential candidate Mays Gilliam (Chris Rock): "What kind of a drug policy makes crack cheaper than asthma medicine?"

Hero
(Ying Xiong)

How far would you go to become a Hero?
—Movie tagline

Hero is inevitably compared to *Crouching Tiger, Hidden Dragon,* Ang Lee's sword fighting film that was hugely successful with Western audiences. Both films are Mandarin; both Lee and the director of *Hero,* Zhang Yimou, are considered "independent, art house" filmmakers; and both have Zhang Ziyi in a major role. The general casts are the same too. This is really where the comparisons stop, however. Zhang Yimou has taken a very well known story and put a new spin on it, which is not an easy task. He reduced the story down to its basics: a King under threat of assassination.

Jet Li plays a warrior who presents himself to the King of Qin (Daoming Chen) with a tale of killing the king's worst enemies. These enemies are three assassins: Broken Sword, Flying Snow, and Sky. Clearly this act is designed as an attempt to gain access to the king's inner circle. The unnamed warrior, or Nameless as he is called in the film, is invited to sit near the King and recount his story of victory. As Nameless tells the tale, the holes in his story grow larger, and the King becomes skeptical of this man and his claims.

The majority of the movie involves the warrior's account of the assassins' defeat. The film uses a series of flashbacks to unfold the tale of Nameless as he describes how he first killed Sky and then used this death to divide and conquer the other two assassins.

While some critics may contend the story has been told better, with more intricate plotlines, few could argue that the production design and cinematography is anything less than beautiful. Christopher Doyle is the same man who brought us the wonderful visual treat *In the Mood for Love* in 2000. Doyle has an unusual eye for set design not seen in many Western films as well as a very distinct palette of colors. He uses rain

and rich colors in his films to produce a luxurious visual image. The flashback scenes all have their own color schemes, and the scope of the visuals are quite simply incredible.

Despite comparisons to *Crouching Tiger, Hidden Dragon,* the whirling hair and fabrics in *Hero,* along with the rich color schemes make me think more of the films of Kar Wai Wong, whose previous collaborations with Doyle likely influenced the cinematographer here. Some of the shots of a fight between Nameless and Broken Sword are filmed from under water as the battle skips across the surface above. Most of the fight scenes were just visually stunning.

The cast is rather stunted in this film although most of them have done wonderful work in other films. Overlooking this drawback is not difficult because the fight scenes are so engaging and the sets so lavish. Whether or not one is generally a fan of martial arts films, *Hero* is a must see. It's a rich visual treat not to be missed.

—*Laura Abraham*

CREDITS

Nameless: Jet Li
Flying Snow: Maggie Cheung
Sky: Donnie Yen
Moon: Zhang Ziyi
Broken Sword: Tony Leung Chiu-Wai
King of Qin: Daoming Chen

Origin: Hong Kong, China
Language: Mandarin
Released: 2003
Production: Zhang Yimou, Bill Kong; Beijing New Picture Film Company; released by Focus Features
Directed by: Zhang Yimou
Written by: Zhang Yimou, Li Feng, Wang Bin
Cinematography by: Christopher Doyle
Music by: Tan Dun
Sound: Tao Jing
Editing: Zhai Ru, Angie Lam
Costumes: Emi Wada
Production Design: Huo Tingxiao, Yi Zhenzhou
MPAA rating: PG-13
Running time: 98 minutes

REVIEWS

Box Office Magazine. Nov. 2003, p. 82.
Box Office Magazine. Dec. 2002, p. 33.
New York Times. Jan. 2, 2003, p. B1.
New York Times Online. April 11, 2003.
Variety Online. Jan. 9, 2003.

Holes

Some secrets are too big to keep hidden.
—Movie tagline

 Box Office: $62 million

Most adults probably don't have much idea who Armpit, X-Ray and Zero are, but there are lot of middle-school kids who would immediately recognize those names as being characters from the book *Holes*. The book, by Louis Sachar, has become hugely popular among the 'tween set. It's also been a favorite in the literary world and won many awards, including a Newberry Medal and a National Book Award.

When the time came to bring the book to the screen, young fans wondered if the movie would remain true to the book. And by almost all accounts, the movie succeeded. A large part of this is probably due to the fact that Sachar wrote the screenplay himself. He had never written a screenplay before, and perhaps that's why he was able to keep the film so fresh. Even though he studied film writing techniques like creating story arcs, unlike a lot of films, the film never seems like it's rotely following a prescribed pattern. It must have been a difficult task to condense the book into a coherent movie. After all, there are flashbacks to two different historical times. Sachar was also able to keep the particular offbeat tone of his book in the film.

The hero of the film is Stanley Yelnats IV (Shia LaBeouf of Disney's *Even Stevens*). In one big change from the book, the overweight Stanley has become a regular-weight nerdy guy. The palindromically named boy lives with his failed inventor father (Henry Winkler), his grandfather (director Andrew Davis' own grandfather Nathan Davis) and long-suffering mother (Siobhan Fallon Hogan), in a cramped city apartment. Stanley's father has been working for years on an invention to remove foot odor.

This is why, when a pair of shoes fall from the sky and hit Stanley on the head, he picks them up, smells them, then carries then home. But police intercept him on the way. It turns out that the shoes were stolen from a homeless shelter and had been donated by ballplayer Clyde "Sweetfeet" Livingston (Rick Fox of the Lakers.) A judge gives Stanley the choice between going to jail or attending Camp Green Lake for 18 months. Stanley opts for the camp.

Camp Green Lake turns out to be in the middle of a desert where there's no lake and nary a tree. The camp, run by the sunflower seed-chomping Mr. Sir (Jon Voight) has the philosophy that bad boys become good boys by digging holes. Each day the boys are given shovels and the instructions to dig a hole five feet wide by five feet deep. Mr. Sir is aided by psycho babble-spouting camp counselor Dr. Pendanski (Tim Blake Nelson).

Stanley is picked on by his fellow inmates and is lowest in the pecking order except for the tiny Zero (Khleo Thomas). Zero, who is the fastest digger around, is considered to be dumb because he never talks. Part of the story has to do with how Stanley gains acceptance with his peers, while managing not to betray Zero in the process. Another part has to do with the much-feared warden (Sigourney Weaver), a tough woman who paints her nails with rattlesnake venom. Is the Warden having the boys dig so many holes because she truly believes it builds character or is she looking for something buried beneath the ground?

Maybe it has something to do with the flashbacks in the story. Stanley's grandfather told him that there is a curse on the men in the Yelnats family. It all started in Latvia when Stanley's great-great-grandfather (Damien Luvara) broke a promise to a local fortune teller, Madame Zeroni (Eartha Kitt). Then there's a story about Kate Barlow, (Patricia Arquette) a frontier school teacher who falls in love with an onion seller, Sam (Dule Hill of *The West Wing*). The locals disapprove of the interracial pair and kill Sam. Kate gets revenge by becoming the Kissing Bandit, known for kissing her victims on the cheek after killing them. What does this have to do with Stanley and all those holes? The fun of the movie is watching it all unfold and tie together.

Director Davis (*The Fugitive*) has done a fine job of bringing the book to the screen. One of his most memorable shots is an overhead of the desert with hundreds of holes stretching for miles. It's eerie and beautiful. His Camp Green Lake is so dry and desolate that theaters must have noticed a big increase in soda sales during the showing.

There are a lot of different characters in the book, but Davis makes it easy to keep them straight. Davis also gets good acting from his actors. The young people playing the campers seem like real kids and lack the usual cute-kid-actor-with-a-bowl-cut mugging. Voight is over-the-top as the bowlegged grizzled old-timer who likes to say, "This ain't no Girl Scout camp" or "This ain't no kindergarten in the sandbox." Weaver is coolly menacing as the warden who can range from sweet to sinister, depending on how the digging is going. And LaBeouf plays a real-seeming kid who can be heroic, but can also feel a quiet flush of pride when his peers give him the nickname Caveman. Davis offsets the action with low-key music from Beck and the eels. And he leaves the scenes that are funny to kids, like a dinner scene where the food includes green beans, refried beans, garbanzo beans and banana jello.

Most critics were as enthusiastic about the film as young readers were about the book. A. O. Scott of the *New York Times* enthused, "*Holes* is one of the few recent movies I have seen that plunged me into that rare, giddy state of pleasurable confusion, of not knowing what would happen next, which I associate with the reading and moviegoing experiences of my own childhood." Lisa Schwarzbaum of

Entertainment Weekly wrote, "Like its much more famous cousins in best-sellerdom, the *Harry Potter* books, the story balances seriousness, silliness, and bravery, and what *Holes* lacks in *Potter* magical grandeur (and budget) on screen, it makes up for in intimacy and its affection for the look of sun-baked earth and dirty-faced kids." And Kenneth Turan of the *Los Angeles Times* wrote, "*Holes* is successful . . . for the most old-fashioned of reasons: It's got an involving, adventurous story to tell and the wherewithal to tell it correctly. And while young adults may think this is intended only for them, in truth it's their elders who are especially starved for this kind of entertainment."

—*Jill Hamilton*

CREDITS

The Warden: Sigourney Weaver
Mr. Sir: Jon Voight
Kissin' Kate Barlow: Patricia Arquette
Stanley Yelnats: Shia LaBeouf
Dr. Pendanski: Tim Blake Nelson
Sam: Dule Hill
Stanley's father: Henry Winkler
Stanley's grandfather: Nathan Davis
Zero: Khleo Thomas
Squid: Jake M. Smith
Armpit: Byron Cotton
X-Ray: Brendan Jefferson
Magnet: Miguel Castro
ZigZag: Max Kasch
Twitch: Noah Poletiek
Clyde "Sweet Feet" Livingston: Rick Fox
Trout Walker: Scott Plank
Carla Morengo: Roma Maffia
Madame Zeroni: Eartha Kitt
Stanley's mother: Siobhan Fallon

Origin: USA
Released: 2003
Production: Mike Medavoy, Andrew Davis, Teresa Tucker-Davies, Lowell Blank; Chicago Pacific Entertainment, Phoenix Pictures, Walden Media; released by Walt Disney Pictures
Directed by: Andrew Davis
Written by: Louis Sachar
Cinematography by: Stephen St. John
Music by: Joel McNeely
Sound: Steve Nelson
Music Supervisor: Karyn Rachtman
Editing: Tom Nordberg, Jeffrey Wolf
Art Direction: Andrew Max Cahn
Costumes: Aggie Guerard Rodgers

Production Design: Maher Ahmad
MPAA rating: PG
Running time: 111 minutes

REVIEWS

Chicago Sun-Times Online. April 18, 2003.
Los Angeles Times Online. April 18, 2003.
New York Times Online. April 18, 2003.
People. April 28, 2003, p. 33.
USA Today Online. April 18, 2003.
Variety Online. April 16, 2003.
Washington Post. April 18, 2003, p. WE34.

QUOTES

Mr. Sir (Jon Voight): "You take a bad boy, make him dig holes all day long in the hot sun, it makes him a good boy. That's our philosophy here at Camp Green Lake."

Hollywood Homicide

 Box Office: $30.9 million

The films of Ron Sheldon don't fall into any easy categories. His movies, like *White Men Can't Jump, Tin Cup* and *Play It to the Bone* are not so plot-driven, not so action-driven and not particularly driven by sexual conquest. While not focusing on any these, they all have those elements. They are also about men talking and men having relationships with each other. It might be a hard sell to get men to go see a movie about men's relationships, so Sheldon's movies also often have a big dose of sports in them. There aren't sports, except yoga, in *Hollywood Homicide,* so Sheldon breaks out another male movie staple, the cop drama. To make his film seem even more appealing to his demographic, he's included the usual mismatched cop buddy element.

Mismatched buddy number one is Joe Gavilan (Harrison Ford). He's a longtime LAPD detective who's been divorced three times and is looking to score big in real estate. He's not terribly dedicated to his job but happens to be good at it so he's sticking with it until he makes his big money. He's partnered with new guy K.C. Calden (Josh Hartnett). Like Gavilan, Calden is not particularly enthralled with detective work. He gets squeamish at the morgue and is a terrible shot. The only reason he seems to be a cop is to honor his father, who was killed on duty, possibly by a dirty cop. Calden teaches yoga and, since it is Los Angeles, wants to become an actor.

The central, and oft repeated, joke of *Hollywood Homicide* is that these two cops are as multitasking as the rest of America in the early 21st century. Thus we have many scenes of career conflict. When Gavilan is involved in a tense car chase, he's also on his cell phone trying desperately to broker a big real estate deal. When Calden is trying to get information about a murder from some people at a record company, he's also networking on behalf of his acting career. When Calden hijacks a family's van and proceeds to involve them in a scary car chase, the kid in the back screams, "We're going to die!" Calden, using his yoga teaching, answers, "Yes, we are all going to die." It's a fairly good joke but Sheldon relies on the two-careered men gag too many times.

The most ludicrous example is an interrogation scene in which Gavilan and Calden are being questioned in side-by-side rooms. In one room, Gavilan refuses to answer questions because he keeps being interrupted by his constantly ringing phone (Would police really allow this to happen during a questioning?) Gavilan's phone rings so much—with its annoying "My Girl" ring—that's it's one of the major characters in the film. In the next room, Calden averts his questioner by getting into yoga poses and insisting on "centering" himself. Not that this is a documentary, but again, would officers really allow someone they are questioning to stand on the table doing yoga poses?

In the film, Calden and Gavilan are trying to solve the murder of an up and coming rap group at a nightclub owned by Julius Armas (Master P). It seems as though the prime suspect might be the owner of their record company, the fancy-suited, P. Diddy-like Antoine Sartain (Isaiah Washington). While questioning Armas about the murder, Gavilan discovers that he is looking to spend $6 million on a mansion. Gavilan hands him a business card and spends the rest of the movie trying to solve the crime and broker a deal between Armas and an old time producer (Martin Landau) who is trying to sell his house. This is enough to deal with but writers Sheldon and LAPD veteran Robert Souza, throw some more uninvolving plot issues in the mix. There is the matter of figuring out if there was indeed a dirty cop who killed Calden's father. And Gavilan is trying not to be fired for co-mingling funds by his adversary on the force, Bennie Macko (Bruce Greenwood).

The movie is not without action. The initial murder in the club is shown and there is the requisite climatic car chase that involves spectacular elements—in this case, it's a helicopter and Robert Wagner. But there's not enough action here to satisfy fans of typical action flicks. Sheldon seems to put the action in the film because it's part of the convention. Even though he puts it in, he doesn't take his action sequences too seriously. In one chase scene, Calden is chasing someone he wants to question, K-Ro (Kurupt), through the canals of Venice. Calden is on foot and K-Ro rides a paddleboat and wades through the channels. It's a slow-moving, pretty funny chase and a nice change from the usual

tense and dramatic chase sequence. In the final big chase, there are a few little comedic touches. At one point, the only available vehicle for Gavilan is a girl's bike with a pink basket on the front. He rides it grimly. In another part of the chase, he hijacks a cab (driven by Smokey Robinson). As he gets to his destination, the driver demands $10. Gavilan pays, then waits for the receipt to print so that he can take it.

The movie is filled with cameos. Gladys Knight shows up, as do Eric Idle, Frank Sinatra Jr., and Lou Diamond Phillips as a cop in drag. Dwight Yoakam has a more fleshed out role as bad cop turned bad guy Leroy Wasley. Also showing up are Lolita Davidovich as Cleo, a madam who might have some good information for Gavilan, and Lena Olin as Ruby, a talk radio psychic and Gavilan's new girlfriend.

The thing that seemed to affect whether or not critics gave the thumbs up or down to *Hollywood Homicide* was how well they could accept Harrison Ford in a comedic role. Some thought his performance stiff and lifeless, even desperate. Others found the role a charming fit and along the lighter quality of characters like Indiana Jones and Han Solo. A.O. Scott of the *New York Times* was of the pro-Ford camp, writing, "He slips into the role as if it were a pair of well-worn loafers, the left inherited from Peter Falk, the right from Clint Eastwood, and then proceeds, with wry nonchalance, to tap-dance, shuffle and pirouette through his loosest, wittiest performance in years." Megan Lehmann of the *New York Post* felt differently and wrote, "You'll merely feel embarrassed for him when he sets out in hot pursuit on a pink child's bicycle or makes a pre-coital quip to Ruby: 'If I take my gingko, I can remember where I put the Viagra.'" Owen Gleiberman of *Entertainment Weekly* wrote, "Is it, you know, fun? There is a rote quality to the way this half-dumb, half-sly movie resolves itself into an intentional debauch, a pileup of villainy and heavy metal."

—*Jill Hamilton*

CREDITS

Joe Gavilian: Harrison Ford
K.C. Calden: Josh Hartnett
Ruby: Lena Olin
Julius Armas: Master P
Lt. Bernie Macko: Bruce Greenwood
Leon: Keith David
Antoine Sartain: Isaiah Washington IV
Cleo: Lolita (David) Davidovich
Jerry Duran: Martin Landau
Leroy Wasley: Dwight Yoakam
K-Ro: Kurupt
Wanda: Lou Diamond Phillips
Olivia Robidoux: Gladys Knight
I.A. Det. Jackson: Meredith Scott Lynn

Danny Broome: James MacDonald
Coroner Chung: Clyde Kusatsu
Marty Wheeler: Frank Sinatra Jr.
Cabby: Smokey Robinson
Himself: Robert Wagner
Celebrity: Eric Idle (Cameo)

Origin: USA
Released: 2003
Production: Ron Shelton, Lou Pitt; Revolution Studios; released by Columbia Pictures
Directed by: Ron Shelton
Written by: Ron Shelton, Robert Souza
Cinematography by: Barry Peterson
Music by: Alex Wurman
Sound: Kirk Francis
Editing: Paul Seydor
Art Direction: Christa Munro
Costumes: Bernie Pollack
Production Design: James Bissell
MPAA rating: PG-13
Running time: 111 minutes

REVIEWS

Boxoffice. April, 2003, p. 34.
Chicago Sun-Times Online. June 13, 2003.
Entertainment Weekly. June 20, 2003, p. 52.
Los Angeles Times Online. June 13, 2003.
New York Times Online. June 13, 2003.
People. June 23, 2003, p. 35.
USA Today Online. June 13, 2003.
Variety Online. June 8, 2003.
Washington Post. June 13, 2003, p. C5.

TRIVIA

The car driven by Ford and Hartnett in the film is the S281 model from boutique automaker Saleen.

Honey

Her dreams. Her terms.
—Movie tagline

Box Office: $30.2 million

In his review of the film, *Honey,* Roger Ebert of the *Chicago Sun-Times* sensed a level of predictability in the plot: "If I were to tell you (a) that Jessica Alba works as a dance instructor in a neighborhood center, (b) that she discovers Lil' Romeo and his friends break-dancing in the streets, (c) that city inspectors shut down the center because of leaks and unsafe construction, and (d) that there is an empty church nearby that could be borrowed for an evening, what would you say the chances are that Alba will hit on the notion of using the old church to put on a show with the kids, to raise money for the community center?"

As the Magic Eight Ball would put it, "Outlook good." Very good. Even though *Honey* is a new movie using sparkling fresh hip-hop stars, it's just a modern variation on a formula that's been around since movies began. Even the Little Rascals' *Our Gang* comedies used the let's-put-on-a-show idea. But just because an idea has been around for awhile, doesn't automatically mean it's a bad one. This theme has been so enduring because it's entertaining. No matter how movie audiences' taste changes through the years, they still like seeing choreographed groups of people dancing to songs.

Pretty much everything in *Honey* is as predictable as the idea of the characters putting on a show. The main theme in the film is that Honey Daniels (Jessica Alba of TV's *Dark Angel*) is someone who is going to go against the odds to follow their dream. The *Boston Globe*'s Wesley Morris calls such a film a "reach-for-the-stars-drama." The dream in Honey's case is to be a choreographer for hip-hop videos. At the beginning of the film, she's not very close to her dream. She toils at two jobs—one as a record store clerk and one as a bartender. Despite the encouragement of her sassy best friend (is there any other kind in moviedom?), Gina (Joy Bryant of *Antwoine Fisher*), the most dancing Honey ever does is at night clubs and as a dance instructor at a Bronx youth center.

She loves teaching the local kids, many of whom come from troubled homes, how to do the latest hip-hop moves (and she's not above borrowing steps from them), but thinks that her real future will begin when she gets into videos. Her mother (Lonette McKee) thinks Honey's future would be better realized by studying ballet, and she spends a lot of time pursing her lips disapprovingly. Despite mom's seriousness, it's pretty certain that by the end of the movie she will be won over—as will everyone else—by the power of hip-hop dancing.

One night Honey gets involved in a dance-off with her mean rival Katrina (Laurie Ann Gibson, who, in the most clever thing about the movie, is actually the real choreographer of the film.) Someone videotapes Honey dancing, and big time video director, Michael Ellis (David Moscow) ends up seeing the tape. The director, who is white, but enjoys speaking as though he is not, invites her to dance in a video with nary an audition. Her good (or perhaps we shall say ludicrous) luck improves further when, within minutes of her arrival, Michael sets her up as the choreographer for the whole video. Of course her rapid ascent might have something to do with the fact that Michael wants Honey in more than professional ways.

Honey is soon a popular choreographer and in demand by artists such as Ginuwine, Missy Elliot and Jadakiss. All the artists play themselves and the standout among them is Elliot. She's a straight-talking force of nature who walks around spouting off insults to everyone she encounters. When she sees the dance moves Katrina has come up with for her new video, Elliot tells her that she should return the stolen steps to MC Hammer. Elliot's good-natured don't-give-a-damn presence would be welcome in another, better film.

As Honey becomes more successful, she has to face a few mild dramas that give her something to do between the dancing scenes. She also gets a boyfriend, Chaz (Mekhi Phifer), who's a local barber and seems to represent the black man who has made it without resorting to crime. And . . . that's about it. Otherwise he's around to tell Honey that she "can do it" and the like. It's nice to see him onscreen, but his only reason for existence is to give Honey success in love as well as career. But Honey finds that having a successful career is an emptier experience than she was expecting and soon finds herself being pulled back to her work with the kids. She's especially drawn to Benny (Lil' Romeo, son of rap mogul Master P), a talented boy who's started down the wrong path working for the local drug dealer.

When the Center is closed down, Honey decides that she is going to use her own money to build a new dance studio for the kids. Her plans are thwarted, though, when she spurns some sexual advances from Michael, who turns out to be the jerk everyone guessed he would, and he immediately fires Honey and blackballs her. It's worse because Honey has promised the kids that they could work on this video and when she is fired, they are too. But with so much pluck, we just know that Honey will somehow be able to "reach for the stars" and get all these problems sorted out.

Alba seems to be trying her darnedest in *Honey*. She does her own work in the dance sequences, which are high energy and appear to be difficult. Alba is up to the task and does a good job. Director Bille Woodruff, himself a former video director, keeps the camera on Alba and makes it plain that Alba really can dance. Several critics suggested that her bellybutton had as much screen time as the rest of her. Where Alba is lacking is in street credibility. Few people have sounded more white than she does when she gives such lines as, "Their flava's hot." She's also sort of overly wholesome and bright-eyed, but perhaps that's appropriate for a character who has to deliver lines like, "I was counting on that money. Not for me—for the kids!"

Most critics were not fans of *Honey* though some liked it well enough. Ebert felt that "the warmth of Jessica Alba and likability of Mekhi Phifer were real enough—a consolation even when their characters were repeating all the old moves." He added, "*Honey* doesn't have a shred of originality (except for the high-energy choreography), but there's something fundamentally reassuring about a movie that respects ancient formulas; it's like a landmark preservation program." A. O. Scott of the *New York Times* considered the film noteworthy, claiming that "the ease with which Honey moves between the streets of the Bronx and the glittering whirl of the music industry reflects the current self-image of hip-hop itself, with its aggressive celebration of upward mobility and its simultaneous embrace of democratic, street-level authenticity. *Honey* brings out the wholesome, affirmative side of the hip-hop aesthetic without being overly preachy, and it offers a winningly utopian view of show-business success without real costs or compromises." Critics who were less entertained by the film included the *Boston Globe*'s Wesley Morris, who wrote, "Neither hot nor square, it's as simple and earnest as any after-school special and as cameo-laden as any rap video." And several critics noted the similarities between *Honey* and another dance film, *Breakin' 2: Electric Boogaloo*. Scott Brown of *Entertainment Weekly* gave the film a C, commenting, "A hoofer captivates the hip-hop world, but this is no *Electric Boogaloo*." And Robert K. Elder of the *Chicago Tribune* wrote, "Apparently the moviegoing public demanded a remake of *Breakin' 2: Electric Boogaloo*, and the producers of *Honey* have bravely answered the challenge."

—*Jill Hamilton*

CREDITS

Honey Daniels: Jessica Alba
Chaz: Mekhi Phifer
Gina: Joy Bryant
Benny: Lil' Romeo
Michael Ellis: David Moscow
Mrs. Daniels: Lonette McKee
Raymond: Zachary Isaiah Williams
Katrina: Laurie Ann Gibson
Mr. Daniels: Anthony Sherwood
Herself: Missy Elliott (Cameo)

Origin: USA
Released: 2003
Production: Marc Platt, Andre Harrell; NuAmerica; released by Universal Pictures
Directed by: Bille Woodruff
Written by: Alonzo Brown, Kim Watson
Cinematography by: John R. Leonetti

Music by: Mervyn Warren
Sound: Douglas Ganton
Editing: Mark Helfrich, Emma E. Hickox
Art Direction: Anastasia Masaro
Costumes: Susan Matheson
Production Design: Jasna Stefanovich
MPAA rating: PG-13
Running time: 94 minutes

 REVIEWS

Chicago Sun-Times Online. December 5, 2003.
Entertainment Weekly. December 12, 2003, p. 59.
Los Angeles Times Online. December 5, 2003.
New York Times Online. December 5, 2003.
USA Today Online. December 5, 2003.
Variety Online. December 5, 2003.
Washington Post. December 4, 2003, p. WE36.

QUOTES

Gina (Joy Bryant) warns Honey (Jessica Alba): "Every guy's a director when he wants some booty."

House of Fools (Dom Durakov)

House of Fools might seem like another quirky war "comedy" from Emir Kusturica, but in fact it comes from Andrei Konchalovsky, the old Russian master who once made a splash in Hollywood with *Runaway Train.* Though too cute at times, *House of Fools* shows grit and spirit.

Based on a true story, *House of Fools* is set in 1996, on the Chechen border, when mental ward workers fled the area, abandoning the hospital inmates. Somehow, the patients survived and persevered. One particular member of the ward, Janna (Julia Vysotsky), a charming young woman who calms the more violent patients with her accordion playing, falls in love with a Chechen soldier, Ahmed (Sultan Islamov). Janna fantasizes that Ahmed wants to marry her, and that she must choose between him and her long-standing fiance. Ahmed continues movements with his troops, telling Janna he never wanted to marry her. But a sudden setback in the war forces Ahmed back to the hospital, where Janna and her friends help hide him from the Russian enemy.

Independent films today seem to have a need to find their inner quirkiness. *House of Fools* starts out in an all-too-familiar way, with the mental patients looking like parodies of the gang in *One Flew Over the Cuckoo's Nest* or *King of Hearts.* In fact, the film seems to continue where Tom Tykwer's *Princess and the Warrior* left off, although in that story the heroine worked on the staff of the mental asylum. Nevertheless, the silly, crazy, pseudo-charming tone threatens to undermine what seems like a story worth telling. In fact, the earliest scenes involve Janna's dream of Canadian singer Bryan Adams (playing himself and singing his hit theme song, composed by Michael Kamen, from *Don Juan de Marco*).

But just before the precious bits of business by the supporting cast or Janna's elaborate fantasies set up *House of Fools* to be insultingly superior to the characters, writer-director Konchalovsky turns the film into the involving, even moving film one would have expected and hoped for. Konchalovsky achieves much of his aim by allowing his leading players to flesh out their roles. Julia Vysotsky is superb as Janna, particularly as the story progresses and the character's world falls apart. The scene where she finds her roommate shot to death by a soldier is spine tingling. And by this narrative point Konchalovsky integrates Janna's fantasies in more profound, less "adorable" ways. Konchalovsky's casting of Sultan Islamov as Ahmed took some courage, for he hardly fits the image of the heroic, handsome "Freedom Fighting" soldier.

Konchalovsky could be faulted in the casting of actual mental patients in some of the supporting roles. This was something director George Sidney was criticized for in *The Red Danube* (1949); the only difference here is that Konchalovsky doesn't even achieve the effect of heightening the realism, assuming that was his intention (if anything, the non-performers come across like bad actors). Ethically and artistically, this aspect of the film fails.

But much else about the film succeeds, particularly the way *House of Fools* exemplifies psychiatrist-writer Thomas Szazz's theory that "craziness" is a relative thing and, if anything, insane people seem quite normal next to the warmongers of the world. Aesthetically, too, *House of Fools* drives home its message effectively with a well-mounted, well-designed production. Konchalovsky deserves credit, but so do cinematographer Sergei Kozlov and production designer Lyubov Skorina.

—Eric Monder

CREDITS

Janna: Julia Vysotsky
Ahmed: Sultan Iskamov
Himself: Bryan Adams

Doctor: Vladas Bagdonas
Ali: Stanislav Varkki
Vika: Marina Politseimako

Origin: Russia, France
Language: Russian
Released: 2002
Production: Andrei Konchalovsky, Felix Kleiman; BAC Films Ltd., Hachette Premiere et Cie, Persona; released by Paramount Classics
Directed by: Andrei Konchalovsky
Written by: Andrei Konchalovsky
Cinematography by: Sergei Kozlov
Music by: Eduard Artemyev
Sound: Vladimir Orel, Eugeny Terehovsky
Editing: Olga Grinshpun
Costumes: Svetlana Volter
Production Design: Lubov Skorina
MPAA rating: R
Running time: 104 minutes

 REVIEWS

Chicago Sun-Times Online. May 16, 2003.
Los Angeles Times Online. April 25, 2003.
New York Times Online. April 25, 2003.
Variety Online. September 9, 2002.

House of 1,000 Corpses

The most shocking tale of carnage ever seen.
—Movie tagline

 Box Office: $12.5 million

House of 1,000 Corpses is a disjointed and thoroughly confusing homage to horror films akin to *The Texas Chainsaw Massacre* or *Last House on the Left*. First-time director Rob Zombie has an honest affection for the films he references and painstakingly recreates. Unfortunately, his movie is a hodge-podge of stories with no clear narrative direction. It's stylish and kitschy enough to find success as a cult film. But, it lacks enough tangible scares or actual dramatic tension to sustain any kind of historical importance. None of the film's episodes really fit together. It's a lark fueled by good intentions that ultimately fails.

After a promising preamble featuring the demented, yet firmly tongue-in-cheek character of Captain Spaulding (Sid Haig) the film plunges into a haphazard story about a group of college students looking for the final resting place of the notorious homicidal maniac Dr. Satan. Following the inevitable picking up of the hitchhiker they shouldn't pick up, the breaking down of the car in the rain, the arrival at the decrepit farmhouse, the poking around where they shouldn't, the film's plodding construction becomes evident. It is little more than a collection of recreated episodes from far superior films held together by nothing in particular and a faulty narrative connected in no discernibly comprehensible way.

The mood and story arc that was promised during the preamble is unfortunately discarded. Zombie then allows the film to decay into a series of increasingly bizarre, incoherent, and repulsive scenes that amount to little more than chances for him to indulge his wanton love of the gore genre. However, the film is less an homage to the films it was inspired by than an aping of scenes and motifs from them. As Wesley Morris pointed out in the *Boston Globe,* while "Zombie may understand how to appreciate horror, he has no clue how to write or film it." Zombie's inability to restrain himself ultimately dooms the film. Whereas if he had taken the time to organize and pace, to some extent, the frenetic randomness of the bare-bones story, there might have been some real horror here. In a film like this, there has to be something to polarize the audience, whether it is sympathy for the lead character or the simple shock value of the violence inflicted in the film. The main characters (that is, the ones who are not psychotic) are played by complete unknowns and will probably remain that way. This ironically seems to be exactly what Zombie intended since he seems most at home showcasing the freaks. Similarly, the violence portrayed in the film is brutal and graphic. There is no buildup of suspense or fear, just scene, followed by scene, followed by scene, of something getting mutilated or desecrated or worse. Zombie has forgotten what made films like The *Texas Chainsaw Massacre* successful, or as Wesley Morris writes, "how much scarier it can be to just watch an innocent person get hit with a hammer and dragged behind a shed without explanation." Instead, he is more concerned with eliciting a constant chorus of approving grunts and chuckles from his niche audience.

House of 1,000 Corpses is not as horrifying or clever as its predecessors (*The Texas Chainsaw Massacre, Last House on the Left,* et al.). In fact, it is essentially a re-imagining of *Massacre* with a forced ending that is clumsily foreshadowed in the preamble. Ultimately, everything is a foregone and disappointing conclusion. While the film is slick enough to be a cult success, it lacks the tension and shock value to make it a seminal horror film like the ones Zombie references time and again. It is a labor of love that ultimately fails. Reputation may predispose you to think this is a gorefest. It is not.

The most terrifying moment of all is the promise of a sequel at the film's conclusion.

—*Michael J. Tyrkus*

CREDITS

Captain Spaulding: Sid Haig
Otis: Bill Moseley
Mother Firefly: Karen Black
Baby: Sheri Moon
Jerry Goldsmith: Chris Hardwick
Denise Willis: Erin Daniels
Grampa Hugo: Dennis Fimple
Mary Knowles: Jennifer Jostyn
Steve Nash: Walton Goggins
George Wydell: Tom Towles
Stucky: Michael J. Pollard
Don Willis: Harrison Young

Origin: USA
Released: 2003
Production: Andy Gould; released by Lions Gate Films
Directed by: Rob Zombie
Written by: Rob Zombie
Cinematography by: Tom Richmond, Alex Poppas
Music by: Rob Zombie, Scott Humphrey
Sound: Buck Robinson
Editing: Robert K. Lambert, Sean Lambert, Kathryn Himoff
Art Direction: Michael Krantz
Costumes: Amanda Friedland
Production Design: Greg Gibbs
MPAA rating: R
Running time: 88 minutes

REVIEWS

Detroit Free Press. April 13, 2003, p. 7F.
Los Angeles Times Online. April 14, 2003.
New York Times Online. April 12, 2003.
Variety Online. April 13, 2003.

QUOTES

Otis (Bill Moseley): "Guess what? The Boogeyman is real, and you've found him."

House of Sand and Fog

Some dreams can't be shared.
—Movie tagline

Box Office: $12.3 million

House of Sand and Fog is a bad dream disguised as a movie. The thoughtful, dour miscalculation that was the novel written by Andre Dubus II has all its warts exposed in a faithful cinematic adaptation by Vadim Perelman, a Russian director making his feature-film debut. Ably assisted by two luminous actors in the lead roles—the magnificent Ben Kingsley and the riveting Jennifer Connelly—Perelman, who also wrote the screenplay, has done all he can with an unmanageable, deeply unsatisfying story that is nonsensical and remorseless.

There's nothing wrong with tragedy, but to be compelling, a tragedy needs sufficient motivation or explanation. Are the characters done in by cruel fate, deep character flaws, irresolvable conflict, or impossible goals? The trouble with *House of Sand and Fog* is that none of these tragic underpinnings are present. Yes, there's a conflict over who has the right to a house, but it's hardly a battle of epic proportions, and neither of the two principal characters battling for the abode does sufficiently immoral things to justify the arbitrary and capricious results that follow.

It's a slow, inconsequential story that doesn't bear the ponderous weight of the treatment it's given. Perelman tries to punch up the atmospherics with shots of fog and clouds and sunsets and ocean coasts in the San Francisco Bay area, where the film is set. But how many times can you see speeded-up racing clouds, a cliche to begin with, before the effect becomes enervating? Perelman constantly sets an ominous tone with brooding close-ups and gloomy music. Whenever Connelly's character smokes a cigarette, the gloom gathers, as if the act of smoking is inspiring evil thoughts.

The story's set-up is interesting enough; it's the tortuous resolution that is off-putting. Connelly plays Kathy Nicolo, a down-and-out woman whose spirit has been crushed. Her husband left her months ago, because, at least according to her, he didn't want to have kids and she did. So now she's alone in the beachfront house that her father spent 30 years working to pay off. Her beloved dad is dead, her husband is gone, and she is childless. She cleans houses for a living, and is trying to maintain a hard-won sobriety—she's gone three years without a drink, but it's implied she was addicted to harder drugs.

When her mother calls from back East, Kathy can't bring herself to tell her the truth about her husband—she's too ashamed and embarrassed. As she hangs up from her mother's 6 a.m. call, there's a knock at the door. It's suddenly broad daylight, and a group of officials (who must have reported to work *very* early) arrive to summarily announce she's being evicted for nonpayment of business taxes. It's a mistake, because she's never been in business, but she hasn't been opening the mail containing the eviction warnings, so she's taken aback. A sheriff's officer, Lester Burdon (Ron Eldard) offers to help her pack and move—he seems inordinately interested in her. The next day, he cruises by the storage facility where she has put her belongings, and she happens to be there, poring over her childhood photos. "I just wanted to come by and see how you were doing," he says—as if the storage facility were her home address! Well, it's that kind of moviemaking—don't bother with small instances of illogic, there are grander themes to grind out.

Kathy goes to a legal aid office run by Connie Walsh (Frances Fisher), who promises to get the situation straightened out by contacting the county and unraveling the mistake. But it's too late—the house has immediately been auctioned for sale (rather quick work by the local bureaucracy), and the Behrani family has moved in.

Kingsley plays Colonel Massoud Amir Behrani, a former high-ranking military officer in Iran, who once enjoyed a sumptuous lifestyle with his family in Tehran, but has been driven out for political reasons. This doesn't track unless the year is about 1980, and it doesn't appear to be; but no matter, he and his family are somehow in southern California and are downwardly mobile. Behrani's wife Nadi (Shohreh Aghdashloo) is used to a comfortable lifestyle, and she is holed up with their son Esmail (Jonathan Ahdout) in a cellar suite at a local hotel. Every day, Behrani leaves home wearing his suit and tie, changes in the hotel bathroom, and goes to work on a road construction crew; he also works nights at a convenience store. But he hides his degrading employment from his family. Why the colonel can't get a better job is unclear; they have legally immigrated and are American citizens.

Behrani buys Kathy's house for a quarter of what it's worth, and immediately the family moves in. Behrani plans to live there with his family for just a few months; his goal is to turn a profit and he immediately puts the house up for sale. So confident is he that he quits his construction job. Only then does he receive a notice from Walsh and discover how the house was put up for auction. Walsh tells him the county is willing to refund him the purchase price. But Behrani is unsympathetic. His attitude is that he did nothing illegal, so why should be penalized? But Kathy also has done nothing wrong, and her house has been taken away. And therein lies the conflict.

It's a neat little conundrum, made more interesting by the culture clash between the antagonists. To Behrani, who is a devout Muslim, the house is God's blessing to his family, and it would be almost sacrilegious to throw away the opportunity. His wife erupts in angry tirades on two occasions over her husband's imperious rule, but she is immediately silenced; he makes all the important decisions on his own. Their son is a quiet, kind, respectful teen who is trying to heed his father's wishes and stay loyal to his culture and religion while making his way as an American. One problem with the plot is that the son, a peripheral character, suddenly becomes central late in the story.

Kingsley is a marvelous performer who manages to be sympathetic despite his character's patriarchal, unyielding ways. Of British, East Indian, and African descent, Kingsley is expert at adapting to characters of different cultures. He is passable as a Middle Easterner, relying on his customary blend of stern visage and admirable principals and heart. The role is another triumph for the man who won an Oscar for playing the Indian political activist in the 1982 film *Gandhi*.

The Behranis' solid family values, religiosity, and traditionalism make a compelling contrast with Connelly's character's drifting, aimless, amoral qualities. Her Kathy is not a bad person, but she is weak and whiny and angry and volatile, seemingly capable of exacting revenge. Connelly plays this difficult part with admirable restraint, keeping Kathy sympathetic despite her less-than-heroic demeanor and actions. Smoldering with repressed passion, she is a seductive target for Lester's heat-seeking desire—clearly there has never been a more attractive homeless person. Connelly wrestles to break loose of the director's insistence on heightening her malevolent potential at every turn. The suggestion is that Kathy is about to explode, especially once she starts drinking, but the problem is that she crumples into a suicidal character, and her role as a protagonist is abandoned in the horrible climax of the film.

As thoroughly as Nadi is controlled by Colonel Behrani, so Kathy comes to be a pawn in the clumsy games played by Lester. Although the actions of Kathy and Behrani can be justified by their plight and circumstances, Lester's actions cannot. He uses the cover of his badge to threaten and harass the Behranis, and he uses Kathy as an excuse to walk away from his wife and two children. Eldard plays him so flatly that the audience response to the character is indifference, even though Perelman slaps us in the face with his turpitude.

Perelman's decision to remain extremely faithful to the novel means that the film suffers from the novelist's rather bizarre resolution. The book, written alternately in the first person of both Behrani and Kathy, emphasized the dual perspective. Perelman fails to make the cultural gap sufficiently relevant to explain the events that unfold. Instead of daring to do something more appealing with the story's horrible ending, Perelman expends most of his artistic energy in hammering home a melancholy mood. A few of his atmospheric scenes are majestic, but most are terribly trite.

There is something deeply amiss with a plot in which secondary characters take on key roles at the climax, while the principal antagonists are left essentially on the sidelines. The last half-hour of this film is unsatisfying and almost abhorrent on many levels, and it leaves the entire story cloaked in an aura of senselessness. What's the point of all this tragedy? It's not as if the conflict over the house is symbolic of deep cultural differences that must be resolved in a violent way—the story's bones aren't strong enough to hold up this structure. The dispute over the house isn't monumental enough to bear the weight of the casualties it engenders. In the end, despite the brilliant performances of Kingsley and Connelly, you're left wondering why the movie was made in the first place.

—*Michael Betzold*

CREDITS

Kathy Nicolo: Jennifer Connelly
Massoud Amir Behrani: Ben Kingsley
Lester Burdon: Ron Eldard
Nadi Behrani: Shohreh Aghdashloo
Connie Walsh: Frances Fisher
Carol Burdon: Kim Dickens
Esmail Behrani: Jonathan Ahdout
Soraya Behrani: Navi Rawat
Lt. Alvarez: Carlos Gomez

Origin: USA
Released: 2003
Production: Michael London, Vadim Perelman; Cobalt Media Group; released by Dreamworks Pictures
Directed by: Vadim Perelman
Written by: Vadim Perelman, Shawn Otto
Cinematography by: Roger Deakins
Music by: James Horner
Sound: William B. Kaplan
Editing: Lisa Zeno Churgin
Art Direction: Drew Boughton
Costumes: Hala Bahmet
Production Design: Maia Javan
MPAA rating: R
Running time: 126 minutes

REVIEWS

Boxoffice. January, 2004, p. 24.
Chicago Sun-Times Online. December 26, 2003.
Entertainment Weekly. December 19, 2003, p. 52.
Los Angeles Times Online. December 19, 2003.
New York Times Online. December 19, 2003.

People. December 22, 2003, p. 28.
USA Today Online. December 14, 2003.
Vanity Fair. December, 2003, p. 40.
Variety Online. November 10, 2003.
Washington Post. December 26, 2003, p. WE43.

AWARDS AND NOMINATIONS

Ind. Spirit 2004: Support. Actress (Aghdashloo)
L.A. Film Critics 2003: Support. Actress (Aghdashloo)
N.Y. Film Critics 2003: Support. Actress (Aghdashloo)
Nomination:
Oscars 2003: Actor (Kingsley), Support. Actress (Aghdashloo), Orig. Score
Golden Globes 2004: Actor—Drama (Kingsley)
Ind. Spirit 2004: Actor (Kingsley), First Feature
Screen Actors Guild 2003: Actor (Kingsley).

Housekeeper (Une Femme de Menage)

A love story that's about to get messy.
—Movie tagline

In the context of contemporary filmic realism, Claude Berri's minor French masterpiece, *Housekeeper,* points to the honesty of a veteran filmmaker. Not only does Jacques (Jean-Pierre Bacri), the film's dejected, middle-aged central character, resemble Berri, right down to the balding pate, both protagonist and filmmaker seem to embody a similar case of repression.

We are never quite sure of just what is troubling Jacques or preventing him from enjoying his life. While Berri's honesty can be seen to hold an aesthetic value, it makes for poor dramatic involvement. This drawback cripples an otherwise consummate work of artistry during the third of the film that precedes the last scene. The film's final moments, however, pack a transcendental wallop, for want of a better term. With the sure touch of a master, Berri rises above the forward thrust of his narrative to strike a profoundly existential note.

This self-reflexivity extends to Jacques's profession which, like Berri's, has become subject to the complexities of modern technology. Jacques is a Parisian sound engineer-cum-record producer of classical CDs. As with all such professionals, tedium has set in as the logical outgrowth of a successful career. That his modicum of prosperity has not brought Jacques love—read romance—is one of the mid-life enigmas that he cannot seem to grasp. He has, as he no doubt sees it, a mature charm. Yet he inexplicably manages to strike out whenever he approaches a woman he finds desirable. Like him, we too are at a loss to understand why.

In the film's opening scene, when we first see Jacques in his messy, but obviously opulent, one-bedroom apartment, he looks a scruffy, unshaven, grim-faced lout. Berri's camera executes a circular pan during the film's opening titles to reveal the disarray and frustration of his lifestyle. Jacques has allowed everything, including his appearance, to go to seed. When he ambles down to get his daily bread and morning newspaper, he finds a notice on a bulletin board from a young woman seeking work as a housekeeper.

Laura (Emilie Duquenne), the soft, open-faced, pretty young thing who takes on the title role, manages to shake Jacques out of his lethargic domestic doldrums by her very presence. Before she has even cleared the first piece of trash, she seems to represent what Jacques has been repressing in his life. When he meets her in a neighborhood café, she is wearing a low-cut dress that makes her look elegant. However, he notices a splotch of dirt on her left cheek, which seems to bely a sexy lack of concern. As she wipes it off, she says it's from her work with plants. Jacques, for his part, immediately employs her to clean his apartment once a week. The fact that Laura's duties will involve doing away with Jacques's dirt, as it were, means she will have access to an intimate plane of his life, a fact that Jacques represses by focusing only on the functional aspect of their relationship. After their first meeting, they part with a handshake and a smile.

We then see Jacques with Claire (Brigitte Catillon), his mature lady friend of many years who, like him, also looks strained and withdrawn. Through her, we learn that Jacques's wife has left him, just as Claire's husband has left her. Jacques remarks that the workaday week prevents him from feeling lonely; it's just that "the weekends are long." She too admits to "feeling like a dog." The scene makes it clear that, whatever Claire's value as a confidant, she cannot fill the vacuum in Jacques's life.

But at this stage, neither can his super-efficient new housekeeper. When Jacques returns from work, he finds his apartment spic and span. As if to make a clean start, he tears up photos of his wife, the dark-haired Constance (director Catherine Breillat in a cameo), who, we later learn, is behind the crank calls he has been receiving. On this particular evening, we see Jacques take out the garbage, then have dinner by himself in the kitchen. Clearly, this is a man too mature to be swayed by any momentary impulse. Berri shows him getting into bed, then turning the lights out, after which there's a cut to an aerial shot of the neighborhood, as if to signify Jacques's normalcy.

That said, Berri also makes clear, in very stark terms, that Jacques is not afraid to let his depression show in public. We see him on the metro, looking positively despondent as he lifts his gaze to take in a woman, who in turn looks equally sad. At work, however, with the power of the massive control board at his fingertips, Jacques is far from distracted. When he takes time out to call his housekeeper, it is to compliment her, albeit underhandedly.

Berri then goes on to hint at the difference in tastes that separate his two leads and, in so doing, reveals the first symptom of his own repression as a filmmaker. We see Laura sweeping Jacques's floor, her boombox turned way up, blasting French hip hop. For Berri, the music holds no cultural radicalism, much less does it signify an alien assault upon the French sensibility. Its violent iconoclasm is merely a musical novelty that is energizing the nubile Laura by the fact of its freshness. Conversely, when Berri shows Jacques alone at a crowded table in a jazz club, keeping time to the beat, it makes sense that Jacques is not truly liberated by the feel of the music, since it later becomes clear to us that he is there in a professional capacity, that is, to listen to the ensemble he will be recording. Given a choice, Jacques would rather be home by himself.

Having presented what would appear to keep his two leads confined to their respective worlds, Berri then charts the developing intimacy between his odd couple. Rather than have Laura come in only on Monday, when he is away at work, Jacques has her come in on a Friday as well, at a time when he plans to be at home. Not that this move is allowed to spill over into anything beyond mere congeniality, or so it would seem at the start. Jacques serves Laura coffee during her break, and the two of them sit across from one another in the living room, silently sipping from their cups and making small talk. Subtly, however, Laura is encroaching upon Jacques's middle-aged detachment. As she sits on the arm of a sofa and crosses her legs, she is sexy without knowing it, like Nabokov's Lolita. However, the camaraderie between them is quickly squelched when friction arises. As Laura performs her chores in the kitchen to the beat of rhythm and blues in English, Jacques tries reading his newspaper. When the music proves too loud, he retreats to the bedroom and puts on a classical CD. When that doesn't help, he turns up the volume. What results is a blend that, owing to the postmodern eclectic nature of contemporary pop, doesn't sound too bad. It also foreshadows the merging that will take place, however temporarily, of their two parallel lives.

The next stage of intimacy is reached when Laura confides her problems to Jacques. It seems it's over between her and the boyfriend with whom she has been living and now she needs a place to stay. Jacques promptly rules out having her move in, but then agrees, if only for a few days. As she and Jacques are riding the metro to her place to retrieve her things, she asks him his first name. When they return, they spread a clean, white sheet on the bed, again, as if signifying a fresh start.

However, the irony and maturity in Berri's approach to life and love rules out any such possibility. For one, Jacques's roving eye leads him to keep approaching women in the street, who keep rejecting him before he has even had a chance to speak to them. Secondly, Constance keeps harassing him with her anonymous calls, which seem to come at the oddest moments. Her motive becomes clear when she finally decides to make an appearance and convince him, and us, that he still loves her, though of course he will never admit it.

This is where the film hits rock bottom in terms of involving its audience in Jacques's plight. When he makes love to Laura, he feels no sense of release or liberation. For her, however, it is the real thing, or so it would seem. But we cannot identify with the joy on Laura's face. Berri's dramaturgy has seen to that; his film remains firmly oriented around Jacques, and therein lies its weakness and, as we realize in its final moments, its strength.

Surmounting an amusing, minor subplot—having to do with Ralph (Jacques Frantz), Jacques's beefy longtime friend with a house in the country, where he raises, paints, and eats chickens—Berri's film reaches its crescendo on a crowded beach in Brittany. Soon after Jacques discovers that Constance has been seeing Ralph behind his back, he becomes convinced he has also lost Laura to some nondescript youth. He then decides to allow the youth's dark and seductive mother, Helene (Axelle Abbadie), to lead him out into the water. When he's up to his neck, he is seized by a cramp. As he thrashes around, he is thrown into a panic. When Helene and a lifeguard finally lead him onto the beach, he collapses on the sand, and looks out at the sea. From a close-up, the fear on his face becomes evident, as if what he is really gazing out at is the prospect of eternity.

Critics by and large seem to have been smitten by the film's uniquely easygoing Gallic charm, coming as it does from "the last free country in the movies," according to Desson Howe in the *Washington Post*. Stephen Holden of the *New York Times*, however, while calling the film "a miniature but tasty French soufflé," is less forgiving of its lighter aspects. "The movie's biggest weakness is Laura," he concludes. For Holden, her character is "such a blank" that the movie "take(s) on a creepy, psychotic undertone . . . that leaves you with a sense of incompletion."

—*Vivek Adarkar*

Origin: France
Language: French
Released: 2002
Production: Claude Berri; TF-1 Films, Pathe; released by Palm Pictures
Directed by: Claude Berri
Written by: Claude Berri
Cinematography by: Eric Gautier
Music by: Frederic Botton
Sound: Gerard Lamps
Editing: Francois Gedigier
Art Direction: At Hoang Than
Costumes: Corinne Jorry
MPAA rating: R
Running time: 86 minutes

REVIEWS

Boston Globe Online. July 25, 2003.
Chicago Sun-Times Online. August 1, 2003.
Entertainment Weekly. August 22, 2003, p. 112.
Los Angeles Times Online. July 11, 2003.
New York Times Online. July 11, 2003.
St. Louis Post-Dispatch Online. August 15, 2003.
Variety. June 24, 2002, p. 29.
Washington Post Online. August 1, 2003.

How I Killed My Father (Comment J'ai Tue Mon Pere)

One man who thought he had it all, will find that his past is the one thing missing.
—Movie Tagline

How I Killed My Father is not literally about murder, as I initially thought. It is, instead, a film about a man who has been so emotionally damaged by his father that he feel the urge to kill him. This is really a pretty straightforward movie about healing and taking responsibility for one's life.

Jean-Luc (Charles Berling) is a bitter man whose father chose a life of freedom on a continent far from his children. When Jean-Luc was ten years old, his father, Maurice (Michel Bouquet), left him to move to Africa. Unable to let go of the pain of this rejection, Jean-Luc has been incapable of living a functional life. He has spent his adult life denying himself love and family and as a result has, himself, ensured

CREDITS

Jacques: Jean-Pierre Bacri
Laura: Emilie Dequenne
Claire: Brigitte Catillon
Ralph: Jacques Frantz
Constance: Catherine Breillat
Helene: Axelle Abbadie

his unhappiness. At the heart of this very interesting and harrowing tale is the idea that each of us is accountable for our own happiness and making our dreams a reality.

It is now thirty years later and Jean-Luc lives with his trophy wife, who is also a perfect hostess. They don't have children because he decided it would be too dangerous. He works as a doctor, running a clinic that promises to combat the process of aging. He also finds himself the caretaker of his younger brother, Patrick (Stephane Guillon), a loser eventually hired as Jean-Luc's driver and assistant.

One day Maurice shows up, able to push buttons and irritate with his mere presence. He does not need to say a word to rustle the feathers of Jean-Luc. Patrick doesn't remember his father, so he's not as affected by Maurice's desertion. It is Jean-Luc who has been a father figure for him. Patrick likes Maurice well enough based on how little he knows the man, but Jean-Luc will not allow himself to be hurt again and is resentful and bitter toward his father. What is funny and so realistic is that strangers seem to like Maurice more than his own children do.

Although the audience waits expectantly for a violent outburst, it never comes. Violence isn't absent from the film altogether, it is just understated. Fontaine decides that following the old adage "less is more" is absolutely the way to go. I, for one, was thrilled with the underlying tension throughout the movie; it had me sitting on the edge of my seat.

This story made me feel sorry for almost the entire cast of characters. Each of them has been dealt a cruel blow in their lives. Even Jean-Luc's wife and brother, who seem to be relatively unscathed, have to live without his love or kindness, though both benefit from the financial security he provides. *How I Killed My Father* is ultimately not a story of lost childhood or family but a moral tale that advises us to live our lives and accept the inevitable mistakes. Whether the motives of others are good or bad, in the end only we can change our circumstances.

—*Laura Abraham*

CREDITS

Maurice: Michel Bouquet
Jean-Luc: Charles Berling
Isa: Natacha Regnier
Myriem: Amira Casar
Jean-Toussaint: Hubert Kounde
Patrick: Stephane Guillon

Origin: France, Spain
Language: French
Released: 2003

Production: Philippe Carcassonne; Cine B, France 2 Cinema; released by New Yorker Films
Directed by: Anne Fontaine
Written by: Anne Fontaine, Jacques Fieschi
Cinematography by: Jean-Marc Fabre
Music by: Jocelyn Pook
Sound: Jean-Claude Laureux
Editing: Guy Lecorne
Art Direction: Sylvain Chauvelot
Costumes: Corinne Jorry
MPAA rating: Unrated
Running time: 100 minutes

REVIEWS

Entertainment Weekly. Sept. 6, 2002, p. 58.
New York Times Online. Aug. 23, 2002.
Sight & Sound. June 2002, p. 56.
Variety Online. Dec. 11, 2003.

How to Deal

A lesson in love for non-believers.
—Movie tagline
Rule #1: There are no rules.
—Movie tagline

Box Office: $14.1 million

With only a couple of films under her belt, there is already sort of a Mandy Moore-type of film. Such films have lots of melodrama and angst. Her first film, *A Walk to Remember,* livened up the usual teen girl film proceedings with a fatal case of cancer. This one doesn't have a deadly disease, but it does have a car crash, a sudden death, a divorce, and a teen pregnancy. It's the kind of film that makes one jumpy. If a character goes, say, swimming, it's difficult not to feel a near-drowning is inevitable.

Despite the many traumas, *How to Deal* is a far more palatable film than *A Walk To Remember. How to Deal* is way less preachy and a lot more realistic. In this film, Moore's character acts more like a regular teen than the smug advertisement for a particular brand of Christianity that she was in the previous one.

The film, written by Neena Beber, was adapted from Sarah Dessen's popular young adult books, *Someone Like You* and *That Summer.* Moore, who first became known as a blonde, squeaky-clean pop singer, plays Halley Martin.

Halley is a teen who is skeptical about love. And it would seem that she has good reason to be. Her parents, Lydia (Allison Janney) and Len (Peter Gallagher), are just finalizing their divorce. Len has also just announced that he is going to marry the young traffic reporter (Laura Catalano) from the soft rock FM station where he's a well-known DJ. Gallagher's character, by the way, is a joy to behold. He's the kind of over-the-hill FM DJ who tries to keep living what he perceives as the rock and roll lifestyle. He says things, in all seriousness, like "I'm the big dog of soft rock!" Halley's older sister, Ashley (Mary Catherine Garrison), chooses the day that the divorce becomes final to rush into the Martin kitchen to joyfully announce that she's going to marry her fiancé, Lewis (Mackenzie Astin). This does nothing to change Halley's view of love since Lewis seems like an uptight rich boy who's still controlled by his parents. Halley walks around pondering pseudo-deep musings on love like, "How can you promise you're going to feel the same way forever?" To most grown-ups, these kinds of teen ponderings aren't terribly interesting or compelling, but perhaps to the teen girls who watch such films, it is. (At an opening weekend showing at a Southern California theater, there was exactly one guy in the audience. He was with a date.)

Halley is further grossed out on love when she walks in on her best friend, Scarlett Smith (Alexandra Holden) making out with boyfriend, Ronnie (Enis Esmer). Scarlett is all giddy and is at the stage of love where everything relates to her beloved ("Wouldn't that shirt look great on Ronnie?"). Halley is shocked that Scarlett hadn't told her that she and her boyfriend were going "all the way." Scarlett, who perhaps had seen *A Walk to Remember*, thought Halley wouldn't understand the whole premarital sex thing.

The more Halley goes around saying stuff like "The quickest way to ruin a relationship is to get in a relationship," the more we know that she's going to be a goner. When she meets school bad boy Macon Forrester (Trent Ford) in the guidance counselor's office, we can guess that he's the one. Some in the audience would hope not since he's the type of guy who thinks it is cool to quote *Star Wars* to woo a girl, but in the context of this film, that apparently is a suave thing to do. He also wears dorky vests, but again, in this film, that seems to be more proof of his depth and outsider status. Actually director Clare Kilner is never very kind when she picks men for her female characters. Halley's mother's new suitor (Dylan Baker) is a Civil War re-enactor. This is not exactly the stuff of romance novels. (The fact that one of Baker's previous roles what playing a creepy child molester in Todd Solondz's film *Happiness* doesn't help much either.)

To live up to its title, *How to Deal* needs to give Halley some things to deal with and it gives her plenty. Just as Scarlett and Ronnie are beginning to enjoy their love, Ronnie collapses and dies. But this is apparently not enough suffering for Scarlett. After Ronnie dies, she finds out that she is pregnant. Maybe the film should have been about how

Scarlett deals. Her problems make Halley's look laughable. Kilner tries to balance out the drama with light moments that aren't terribly funny. One recurring joke concerns Halley's grandmother (Nina Foch), who takes medical marijuana on a regular basis. Kilner spends lots of time on Granny being high and doing things like getting the munchies.

The best part of the movie is the performances. Janney is predictably good as Halley's mom. She's bitter about her divorce, but tries to keep a sense of humor and tries to dissuade the girls from hating their father. "You're father's a good man," she tells them, as much to convince herself. Moore is her usual fresh-faced self. She has the kind of impossibly flawless face that's interesting to watch even when she's saying icky things like "Some people fall in love—I had to crash into it." Ford has enough personal charisma to make even his frequent Jedi references a forgivable flaw. And Holden is good as a regular teen girl trying desperately to stay a regular teen girl despite the upheavals in her life.

Critics weren't huge fans of the film, though many recognized the film's attempt at thoughtfulness. A. O. Scott of the *New York Times* wrote, "*How to Deal* is an awkwardly directed, unevenly acted, sloppily written, movie. But adolescence is a sloppy, ungainly, awkward time, and after awhile, the bad lighting, graceless editing, sluggish dialogue and self-conscious performances begin to seem like marks of authenticity, as if the movie had been made not just for and about teenagers, but by them." Carla Meyer of the *San Francisco Chronicle* considered the film "a thoughtful but uneven teen picture" that "also has too much going on." Owen Gleiberman of *Entertainment Weekly* gave the film a B, and commented," Moore makes Halley's awakening organic and touching. In an age when most teenagers are up to their eyeballs in postmodern consumer glitz, her movies seem radical not just in their retro squareness but in their unfashionable embrace of faith over ironic flippancy." Wesley Morris of the *Boston Globe* assessed, "This movie is the worst episode of *Gilmore Girls* ever."

—*Jill Hamilton*

CREDITS

Halley Martin: Mandy Moore
Lydia Martin: Allison Janney
Len Martin: Peter Gallagher
Macon Forrester: Trent Ford
Scarlett Smith: Alexandra Holden
Steve Beckwith: Dylan Baker
Lewis Warsher: MacKenzie Astin
Marion Smith: Connie Ray
Grandma Halley: Nina Foch

Carol Warsher: Sonja Smits
Ashley Martin: Mary Catherine Garrison

Origin: USA
Released: 2003
Production: William Teitler, Erica Huggins; Radar Pictures, Golden Mean; released by New Line Cinema
Directed by: Clare Kilner
Written by: Neena Beber
Cinematography by: Eric Alan Edwards
Music by: David Kitay
Sound: Henry Embry
Music Supervisor: Jon Leshay
Editing: Janice Hampton, Shawna Callahan
Art Direction: Andrew M. Stern
Costumes: Alexandra Welker
Production Design: Dan Davis
MPAA rating: PG-13
Running time: 101 minutes

REVIEWS

Chicago Sun-Times Online. July 18, 2003.
Entertainment Weekly. July 25, 2003, p. 50.
Los Angeles Times Online. July 18, 2003.
New York Times Online. July 18, 2003.
People. July 28, 2003, p. 29.
USA Today Online. July 18, 2003.
Variety Online. July 13, 2003.
Washington Post. July 18, 2003, p. C1.

How to Lose a Guy in 10 Days

One of them is lying. So is the other.
—Movie tagline

Box Office: $101 million

A double deception is this vapid but glossy romantic comedy's "unique" twist, and one that threatens the would-be happiness of a sassy magazine columnist and an arrogant advertising executive. Though thoroughly a paint-by-numbers project, Hollywood progeny Kate Hudson lends a gracefulness and dingy wit to her role as a women's magazine writer who longs to prove herself as a serious journalist but is, alas, relegated to penning "Ten Tips to

Please Your Mate" columns. Donald Petrie, director of such films as *Mystic Pizza* and *Miss Congeniality,* has honed his style as a consummate purveyor of inoffensive fluff, of which *Lose* may be the pinnacle.

Hudson is Andie Anderson, a young go-getter living in Manhattan and working for *Composure* magazine. However, the blond and good-looking Andie is unhappy with her present beat, which consists of writing inane how-to columns for frustrated housewives, and yearns to cover more serious topics like world politics. Her no-nonsense boss, Lana (Bebe Neuwirth), has little sympathy for Andie's dreams and denies her constant requests for a crack at real writing. Looking to fill her column, Andie finds inspiration in a sad sack coworker (Kathryn Hahn) whose failed romance seems to be the result of the classic mistakes women make in relationships. Andie decides to illustrate personally the dangers of neediness and dependence by finding a suitable man to fall for her, then deliberately driving him away.

Enter the mark: ambitious advertising exec Ben Barry (the equally blond and good-looking Matthew Mc-Conaughey). Even as Andie hones in on her unwitting victim, it never occurs to her that Ben might have a hidden agenda of his own. Ben has to convince his boss (Robert Klein) he's capable of taking over a diamond jewelry account from an all-female creative team, so the ad man wagers that he can make an eligible woman fall in love with him in ten days, thereby proving he can sell anything to women. With the amusing, high concept plot now thoroughly in place, the lovers at cross-purposes engage. He's determined to get her while she's equally determined to drive him away; the comedic possibilities seem ripe.

What ensues, however, is predictable middle-brow humor and mediocre gags made more palatable by the charming Hudson and talented but miscast McConaughey. What the two stars lack in chemistry, they make up for with comic proficiency, although the comedy itself is uninspired. Andie initially shows her true nature as the down-to-earth, laid-back kind of girlfriend that can be sexy and still enjoys sports. Thrilled, Ben thinks he can coast for the next nine days, assured that the willing Andie has already fallen for him.

Meanwhile, Andie is preparing for phase two of the plan that gives the movie its title. During the exciting final moments of a Knicks play-off game, Andie suddenly turns pouty and demands that Ben immediately go and buy her a soft drink. When Andie goes from delightfully bad to deliciously worse, it seems that Ben will have his work cut out for him. Andie's well-designed plan to drive away even the most hardcore suitor includes: leaving piles of teddy bears in his bachelor pad; obnoxiously breaking up his poker game with the boys, then dissolving into tears; toting around an annoying little dog that urinates on his pool table; and, most objectionable, giving a very feminine nickname to a very masculine part of his anatomy. Hudson undertakes all these screwy antics with unabashed glee. Her comedic talent has never been more apparent than it is in this role, which gives her a chance to be delightfully wacky with a touch of the usual leading-lady seriousness.

Although Andie has effectively turned into some sort of estrogen-fueled monster—she and her miniature dog dressed in matching outfits, plying him with baby talk—an exasperated but resolute Ben keeps coming back for more. We realize that that is as much because of his desire to win the bet as his growing affection for the Andie that he knows is somewhere underneath all the pink, frilly, gushy, mushy goo. Andie also realizes she's falling for the charming ad man and reverts back to her down-to-earth ways when he takes her to visit his good-natured family on Staten Island. When the jig is finally up and the pair realizes they've each been subjected to a ruse, whatever charm the movie has had up to that point shrivels up and dies. Both overreact to the rather harmless news, wind up singing an unimaginably horrific duet of "You're So Vain," engage in a chase to the airport, and wind up lip-locking on the Manhattan Bridge. So much for modern love.

Underused in their supporting roles, Klein and Neuwirth make one wish a reasonable subplot could've been developed just for them. In sum, *How to Lose a Guy in 10 Days* is technically sound, the pacing is acceptable and the editing adroit, and it has lovely, well-lit shots of New York.

—Hilary White

CREDITS

Andie: Kate Hudson
Benjamin: Matthew McConaughey
Tony: Adam Goldberg
Spears: Michael Michele
Green: Shalom Harlow
Lana Jong: Bebe Neuwirth
Phillip Warren: Robert Klein
Michelle: Kathryn Hahn
Thayer: Thomas Lennon
Jeannie: Annie Parisse

Origin: USA
Released: 2003
Production: Lynda Obst, Robert Evans, Christine Peters; released by Paramount Pictures
Directed by: Donald Petrie
Written by: Kristen Buckley, Brian Regan, Burr Steers
Cinematography by: John Bailey
Music by: David Newman
Sound: Tod A. Maitland, Douglas Ganton
Music Supervisor: Dana Millman-DuFine

Editing: Debra Neil-Fisher
Art Direction: Brandt Gordon, James Feng
Costumes: Karen Patch
Production Design: Therese DePrez
MPAA rating: PG-13
Running time: 112 minutes

REVIEWS

Chicago Sun-Times Online. February 7, 2003.
Entertainment Weekly. February 14, 2003, p. 53.
Los Angeles Times Online. February 7, 2003.
New York Times Online. February 7, 2003.
People. February 17, 2003, p. 33.
USA Today Online. February 7, 2003.
Variety Online. January 26, 2003.
Washington Post. February 7, 2003, p. WE48.

QUOTES

Andie (Kate Hudson): "Our love fern! You let it die!" Benjamin (Matthew McConaughey): "No, honey, it's just sleeping."

Hulk

The inner beast will be released.
—Movie tagline
Rage. Power. Freedom.
—Movie tagline
Unleash the hero within.
—Movie tagline

 Box Office: $132.1 million

Although comic book heroes have been brought to the silver screen on a regular basis for decades, whether in the form of old B-movie serials or the kind of more "serious" films following in the footsteps of Richard Donner's *Superman* (1978), the decade surrounding the turn of the century has seen a proliferation of comic book heroes making their way from the page to the screen in hopes of becoming the next blockbuster or, better still, the launching pad for a new cash-generating franchise. The early 1980s belonged to Superman and the early 1990s belonged to Batman, but even though *Spider-Man* (2002) rapidly surpassed both the Man of Steel and the Dark Knight on the list of all-time box office champions, the web-spinning hero has not been the virtual "Lone Ranger" that the former two were. *X-Men* (2000), for example, was successful enough to spawn a sequel (with at least one more in the works), which did even better business than the first film. It had to be inevitable, then, that the Hulk (a Marvel comics hero created by Stan Lee, just like Spider-Man and the X-Men) would make his way to the big screen. When he finally showed his green face, though, many viewers were surprised, puzzled, or disappointed due to director Ang Lee's unconventional approach to the film. While most super hero movies concentrate on straightforward action-filled stories, Ang Lee (*Sense and Sensibility* and *Crouching Tiger, Hidden Dragon*) took a different approach with *Hulk,* daring to focus more on the characters' psychological demons and interpersonal relationships than on action sequences. Lee also risked alienating viewers with a unique and kinetic visual style that is partially inspired by comics themselves. Ultimately, *Hulk* is a creative and interesting (one might even go so far as to say "experimental") film that resembles nothing else in the genre to which it belongs; ironically, that is the source of both the movie's strengths and its failures. The darker, psychologically-driven storyline and the unusual editing style, combined with the fact that the Hulk himself generally looks cartoonish, did not resonate very well with audiences who were expecting something a bit more familiar. Despite a big opening weekend, *Hulk* disappeared from the top ten grossing movies after just four weeks.

The dark nature of *Hulk* is appropriate for the story, as the character of the Hulk is a man tortured by his special powers. The Hulk is not a hero who sets out to use his power for the betterment of society. He has no control over that power; it controls him. Dr. Bruce Banner (Eric Bana) becomes enraged, transforms into the Hulk, and turns his anger on those who would threaten him. It is like an affliction that haunts him, one which he cannot escape. Tragically, as the opening sequences of the film explain, this affliction was inherited from his father, David Banner (Nick Nolte). The elder Banner, a scientist working at a military base, experimented on himself, altering his DNA in an attempt to develop a "super immune system" as part of an overall goal to achieve human regeneration, but in an unforeseen chain of events, the genetic alteration was passed on to his son. David's selfish nature and amoral tendencies are solidified when he becomes fascinated rather than horrified by the legacy that he has bestowed on his child. Eventually he does feel some measure of guilt, leading him to try to find a cure, but his research is cut short by General Ross (Sam Elliott), who does not trust him. The beginning of the film does not reveal exactly what happens next, but a tragic accident and an explosion on the base leave little Bruce without parents.

The story leaps forward to the present, revealing that Bruce has become a bright young scientist working alongside Betty Ross (Jennifer Connelly), the daughter of the general who was Bruce's father's nemesis. It's soon clear that Bruce and Betty love each other, but an attempted relationship had ended because Bruce is "emotionally distant." Those words accurately describe Bruce, for Bana plays him somber throughout the movie. Bruce often seems detached, trapped in his own haunted world. Yet there is a strong bond between Bruce and Betty, clearly portrayed in both performances, giving the story an undercurrent of regretful pathos as it becomes clear that the two will never really get together.

Bruce and Betty are working on a way to enhance the immune system, but their lives are interrupted by a sequence of events that will change them forever. A lab accident involving gamma radiation alters and mutates Bruce's genetic code even further, literally bringing out the beast from within as he finds himself transforming into a green "monster" when he gets angry. The film's most clear-cut villain, Talbot (Josh Lucas), is a businessman who shows up with a plan to turn Bruce's research into a method of creating super-strong, self-repairing soldiers. When the Hulk appears and is identified as Bruce, Talbot sets out to capture him to extract the secrets of his powers. To compound the conflict, Bruce's father also appears out of the blue. Despite his initial expressions of concern about Bruce, it becomes clear that he has not changed over the years. His interest in Bruce revolves solely around the green creature that he becomes. At first shocked, he then becomes fascinated with the Hulk, seemingly genuinely concerned about him—more than he is concerned about Bruce. "He's unique," David Banner says. "The world will not tolerate his existence." At one point, the father even claims that the Hulk is his son, not Bruce.

On an outward level, the rest of the plot is propelled by the conflict between Bruce/the Hulk and those who pursue him. Talbot succeeds in capturing the creature and attempts to uncover the genetic means of his transformation, but the Hulk escapes, tearing up an underground military facility in the process. Predictably, the military then goes after the Hulk, led by General Ross, in an attempt to recapture him—for the protection of society, not for research—or to kill him. Instead of rushing to defend Bruce or proclaim her love for him, Betty tries to remain as rational as she can in order to truly help him. She persuades her father to let her reach out to him and calm him. Indeed, she does just that, for she is the only one capable of reaching the man within.

Meanwhile, David Banner visits the lab where Bruce and Betty did their research, determined to recreate the events that led to Bruce's transformation. However, the results are not what he expected. David's body is transformed so that he can assimilate and in effect become whatever he touches. Not unexpectedly, the final confrontation in the story occurs between Bruce and his father, who maniacally believes that he has evolved beyond humanity to achieve some kind of godhood. The titan-like battle between father and son, which takes them to several locations, seems to be a draw, if not a likely victory for David, so Ross finally resorts to a nuclear blast to stop the powerful entity that David has become. The father is destroyed in the process and it appears that the Hulk was destroyed as well. However, the end of the film, jumping forward a year, reveals that Bruce is very much alive and living in the jungles of South America, where he works as a doctor.

Although the story is filled with the kinds of conventional conflicts one would expect in a comic book movie—or monster movie, for that matter—the more interesting and the more complex levels of conflict in *Hulk* are the psychological ones. The inner struggle Bruce must endure sets him off as a tragic hero. He is a man haunted by distant fragments of memories from a painful past and cursed with powers he does not want. Yet at the same time, the story acknowledges the reality of human nature, the fact that there is a bit of darkness in even the best individuals. "What scares me the most," Bruce says, "is that when it comes over me and I totally lose control, I like it." The psychological conflict with his father, tied inextricably to his own inner struggle, is yet another layer to the drama that goes beyond conventional good-versus-evil plotting. While Talbot and Ross are antagonists in the story, the real villain is David, whose character is a Dr. Frankenstein type, a man who meddles with nature for his own glory and then refuses to truly take responsibility for his actions. The difference between *Hulk* and many other super hero movies is that it probes more deeply into issues of the soul, and it does so effectively.

An unusual dichotomy exists in the visual effectiveness of *Hulk*. On one hand, Lee employs many creative and unusual editing techniques to mimic the look of comic books. For example, in many instances he uses split screen effects, multiple angles of the same subject simultaneously, and unusual tracking shots to give the film a kinetic, lively atmosphere that truly does seem like a comic book in motion. The various techniques are initially jarring because they are so uncommon in films, but they are skillfully integrated into the story. On the other hand, one of the weakest elements of the movie is the presentation of the Hulk himself. The Hulk is a completely CGI character, and unfortunately that fact is painfully obvious throughout the movie. Actually, it is somewhat surprising that with the amazing advances in CGI technology in recent years (witnessed in the *Star Wars* prequels and especially in the *Lord of the Rings* trilogy), such an obviously artificial character would be put on screen, especially considering the budget of a film like this. In some close-up shots the Hulk is more convincing, but even then his movements and expressions lack all the nuances and textures that are needed to be realistic. Ironically, the artificiality of the Hulk makes the movie seem more real when he is not on screen, which is obviously not what the filmmakers intended. Rather than use such a cartoonish creation, the filmmakers would have been better off with a human actor, even though it would

have complicated many of the Hulk's physical feats in the story. As it is, the unrealistic nature of the character tends to distance the viewer from the story and comes close to undermining some of the film's most powerful, and most realistic, moments.

—David Flanagin

CREDITS

Bruce Banner: Eric Bana
Betty Ross: Jennifer Connelly
Glenn Talbot: Josh(ua) Lucas
General "Thunderbolt" Ross: Sam Elliott
David Banner: Nick Nolte
Young David Banner: Paul Kersey
Edith Banner: Cara Buono
Teenaged Bruce: Mike Erwin
Mrs. Krensler: Celia Weston
Security Guard: Lou Ferrigno (Cameo)
Security Guard: Stan Lee (Cameo)

Origin: USA
Released: 2003
Production: Gale Anne Hurd, Avi Arad, James Schamus, Larry J. Franco; Marvel Enterprises, Valhalla Motion Pictures, Good Machine; released by Universal Pictures
Directed by: Ang Lee
Written by: James Schamus, Michael France, John Turman
Cinematography by: Frederick Elmes
Music by: Danny Elfman
Sound: Drew Kunin
Editing: Tim Squyres
Art Direction: John Dexter
Costumes: Marit Allen
Production Design: Rick Heinrichs
MPAA rating: PG-13
Running time: 138 minutes

REVIEWS

Chicago Sun-Times Online. June 20, 2003.
Entertainment Weekly. June 6, 2003, p. 30.
Entertainment Weekly. June 27, 2003, p. 111.
Los Angeles Times Online. May 4, 2003.
Los Angeles Times Online. June 20, 2003.
New York Times Online. May 11, 2003.
New York Times Online. June 20, 2003.
People. June 30, 2003, p. 33.
Rolling Stone. July 10, 2003, p. 76.
TV Guide. June 21, 2003, p. 22.

USA Today Online. June 20, 2003.
Variety Online. June 12, 2003.
Washington Post. June 20, 2003, p. WE37.

QUOTES

Bruce Banner (Eric Bana) to a bad guy: "You're making me angry. You wouldn't like me when I'm angry."

The Human Stain

How far would you go to escape the past?
—Movie tagline

 Box Office: $5.3 million

Adapting Philip Roth's *The Human Stain*, a sprawling novel of racial identity set against Clinton-era scandal and hypocrisy, screenwriter Nicholas Meyer and director Robert Benton were faced with some tough choices. There was no way that this ungainly, hefty novel, with its lengthy character digressions and shifts back and forth in time, could be adapted to the screen intact. Whole episodes would have to be deleted, and various characters streamlined. The main challenge, however, and one that the filmmakers could not meet, was finding a suitable dramatic structure that could turn Roth's highly intellectual, discursive musings into a satisfying story. Despite some very accomplished individual scenes and fine performances, the movie does not overcome a tedious, plodding quality when it should instead have the gravity of a modern-day Greek tragedy.

Coleman Silk, played by Anthony Hopkins in the film, is an esteemed professor of classics at Athena College in Massachusetts. One day he is excoriated by the college for allegedly uttering the racial slur "spooks" in class, even though it is clear from the context that he used the term to mean "ghost" or "specter." Two students who had never shown up for his class infuriated him so much that he asked in exasperation, "Do these people exist, or are they spooks?" He did not know that they were black (he had never seen them), but the students lodged a complaint, leading Coleman to resign in a fury. When his wife, Iris, dies from an embolism that very day, he claims that the school killed her.

In the wake of his disgrace, he becomes friends with Nathan Zuckerman (Gary Sinise), a writer who has retreated to the woods after undergoing two divorces and prostate cancer. Nathan is not only Coleman's confidant but

also the narrator of the story and thus our window into this world.

The once distinguished professor becomes involved with Faunia Farley (Nicole Kidman), who is on the custodial staff at the college and also works at the post office and local dairy farm. A survivor of a sexually abusive stepfather and a violent, delusional ex-husband, Lester (Ed Harris), she is roughly half Coleman's age when they embark on an intensely physical affair, one with which she wants no complications. "I don't do sympathy," she warns him, and Kidman makes us understand how, on some primal level, this woman, constantly battered by life, uses sex to push away intimacy rather than to embrace it. Kidman took heat from critics for being too beautiful and elegant to play a lower-class cleaning woman, but Faunia was not always poor, and the traces of her once privileged life are still detectable in Kidman's wary, almost aloof demeanor, which is coarse yet sensual. It is a tricky combination that this gifted actress makes quite persuasive.

But far more compelling than Coleman's rejuvenation at the hands of Faunia is the maturation of young Coleman (Wentworth Miller) in East Orange, New Jersey, in the 1940s and how he came to construct a lie around his very being. It is during these flashbacks that we learn his secret: he is actually the product of a middle-class, black household but so light skinned that he is able to pass for white. He exhibits great promise as a boxer, and his coach believes that a scholarship could be in his future if he does not mention his race; since his coach is Jewish, people will think Coleman is as well. Thus is planted the seed of a lifetime of deception.

His first great love is a Danish-Icelandic girl by way of Minnesota, Steena Paulsson (Jacinda Barrett), from whom he withholds his secret until a visit to his mother's home reveals his background. When Steena rejects him, tearfully confessing, "I can't do this, Coleman," it becomes the turning point in his life, the moment when his self-loathing reaches its apex. In his next boxing match, he knocks out his opponent in the first round, even though he had been asked to carry the guy for a while to give the crowd a good show. The opponent is black, and, in pummeling him, Coleman is clearly pummeling himself, venting all the rage he feels at his own blackness and rejecting identity politics to fashion a new self. He enters the Navy as a white man and later goes on to marry Iris, a white woman, and he keeps his racial background a secret throughout his distinguished career.

Roth's novel takes the temperature of our recent past, which he sees as full of sanctimony over a president's sexual transgressions and the scourge of political correctness run amok in academia, represented principally through a feminist colleague of Coleman's, Delphine Roux, who becomes his antagonist. She barely appears in the film, which focuses more on the revitalized Coleman, whose Viagra-powered affair with Faunia takes center stage. (Even in the novel, one gets the sense that Roth sees the character, at least in part, as an often lyrical tribute to the restorative powers of the little blue pill.) The unfortunate result, however, is that the larger social issues and sardonic take on campus politics elude the filmmakers, and the failure to place Coleman's story in a larger context diminishes its wider relevance.

Also downplayed considerably from the novel is Lester Farley's painful attempt to find closure for the horrors he experienced in Vietnam, and Ed Harris's solid performance is not enough to make us care about this wounded man. While Lester's back story could not be effectively translated to the screen without turning the film into a mini epic, its absence reduces the character to a mere device—the method by which Coleman pays for his reckless behavior and lifelong deceit. Because we know from the film's opening minutes that Coleman and Faunia will meet their end being run off a snowy road by Lester's red truck, the narrative lacks suspense; the first time Lester confronts Coleman and Faunia in a violent rage, we know exactly where we are headed.

But the biggest problem with this adaptation is inherent in the very construction of Roth's work. It is more a novel of grand ideas than a traditional plot that builds a cumulative power over a succession of events, and Meyer's script does not find a way to make this work on the screen. Coleman's story should unfold like the grand tragedies he teaches, evoking the pity we would have for a tragic hero's fall from grace; after all, his trajectory fits the grand American myth of shedding an old identity to create a new one (in this sense, Coleman is Jay Gatsby to Nathan's Nick Carraway). However, we never feel fully invested in what Coleman is going through or the enormous cost he had to pay to live a lie. There is great irony, of course, in his being falsely accused of racism in the "spooks" incident when he is in fact a racist in a deeper way—a man who turned his back on his race to pose as white. But while this conceit works on a cerebral level, it fails to strike an emotional chord.

Hopkins's casting was roundly criticized, with reviewers pointing out that he does not look either Jewish or black, but this, of course, is the central point of his character. What is worse, Hopkins has not shed his clipped English accent (a passing reference to Coleman teaching in England does not solve this problem). But more important, without the novel's copious description that cuts to the heart of Coleman's masquerade, we are left watching a pathetic old man having a disastrous final fling, an ill-fated May-December romance, not a great man undone by his duplicity. Hopkins's performance, which is actually decent if not great, cannot overcome the thin characterization in the script itself.

The most painful scene in the novel is young Coleman's rejection of his family and specifically his mother. When he informs his mother (Anna Deavere Smith) of his plan to tell Iris that both of his parents are dead and his mother realizes that she will never know his family, we see the sting. "You're white as snow, and you think like a slave," she tells him, but his stunning betrayal, which, in the film, has been moved near the end, does not carry the emotional weight of a climax despite Smith's heartbreaking performance.

Even Coleman's death does not stir our feelings. It just seems that he slept with the wrong woman and her jealous ex-husband got revenge. Moreover, Faunia's story feels disconnected from Coleman's, which is not a problem in a novel that encompasses so many disparate threads but is a major weakness in a movie. While they do share a bond when he tells her his secret, something he could not do with anyone else, this does not link them in a larger sense. Nonetheless, Nathan makes a clumsy attempt to connect the two characters in a voiceover, suggesting that Coleman ran away from race the way Faunia ran away from privilege. But the parallel is disingenuous and forced; he made a calculated choice to live a falsehood, whereas she fled a life of sexual abuse and, in the process, lost her class privileges.

Despite all of the talent involved (including an Oscar-winning director and two Oscar-winning actors), *The Human Stain* is a tepid collection of scenes that do not coalesce into a coherent drama or even an illuminating character study. Perhaps the greatest disappointment is that the rich, controversial issues it raises about race and political correctness are deserving of a thoughtful treatment that brings out their nuances. *The Human Stain* does not come close to being that movie, and, while it is not a disaster, it feels like a missed opportunity.

—*Peter N. Chumo II*

CREDITS

Coleman Silk: Anthony Hopkins
Faunia Farely: Nicole Kidman
Lester Farely: Ed Harris
Nathan Zuckerman: Gary Sinise
Young Coleman: Wentworth Miller
Mr. Silk: Harry J. Lennix
Mrs. Silk: Anna Deavere Smith
Steena Paulsson: Jacinda Barrett
Iris Silk: Phyllis Newman
Ellie: Kerry Washington
Psychologist: Margo Martindale
Herb Keble: Ron Canada
Young Iris: Mili Avital
Professor Delphine Roux: Mimi Kuzyk

Origin: USA
Released: 2003
Production: Tom Rosenberg, Gary Lucchesi, Scott Steindorff; Lakeshore Entertainment, Stone Village, Cinereta-Cineepsilon; released by Miramax Films
Directed by: Robert Benton
Written by: Nicholas Meyer

Cinematography by: Jean-Yves Escoffier
Music by: Rachel Portman
Sound: Claude La Haye
Music Supervisor: Dondi Bastone
Editing: Christopher Tellefsen
Art Direction: Zoe Sakellaropoulo
Costumes: Rita Ryack
Production Design: David Gropman
MPAA rating: R
Running time: 106 minutes

 REVIEWS

Boxoffice. November, 2003, p. 97.
Chicago Sun-Times Online. October 31, 2003.
Entertainment Weekly. November 7, 2003, p. 47.
Los Angeles Times Online. September 7, 2003.
Los Angeles Times Online. October 31, 2003.
New York Times Online. October 31, 2003.
People. November 10, 2003, p. 37.
Rolling Stone. October 16, 2003, p. 95.
Time. October 27, 2003, p. 78.
USA Today Online. October 31, 2003.
Variety Online. September 2, 2003.
Washington Post. October 31, 2003, p. WE43.

QUOTES

Coleman (Anthony Hopkins) about Faunia (Nicole Kidman): "Granted, she is not my great love, but she sure as hell is my last love. And that deserves some respect."

The Hunted

Some Men Must Be Found.
—Movie tagline
In this game of hide and seek, if you're it . . . you're dead.
—Movie tagline

 Box Office: $34.2 million

A prologue defines the plot's backstory: in 1999 in war-torn Kosovo an Army-trained Special Forces killer named Aaron Hallam (Benecio Del Toro) worked as an expert assassin, sent into former Yugoslavia, for example, in order to take out a brutal Serbian officer responsible for the mass killings of Albanians. It's obvious that Hallam is a professional killer because he makes his own knives, smears his face with charcoal, and has no remorse for his homicidal actions. Somebody even calls him, believe it or not, "a killing machine." Years later, Hallam, who is good at his work, has been employed by the Feds as an undercover assassin; but when he goes berserk, he has to be hunted down. It seems he's now trying to protect wildlife by butchering hunters in the wild (is one a sort of reparation for the other?). Why? He is offended that they use military telescopes and high-powered rifles that give them an unfair advantage. The man best suited to hunt down and stop this renegade assassin is L.T. Bonham (Tommy Lee Jones), who trained Hallam in the art of killing years before. Since this is not the first time Jones has been assigned such a role, the casting involves certain expectations, so Jones plays him, as Todd McCarthy noted in *Variety,* as a "cranky loner with an unusual gait" who probably prefers animals to human beings.

Regardless, L.T. Bonham is a peaceful guy, really, except he, too, is an obsessed environmentalist. He lives in the north woods and he wants to protect wildlife. Viewers can believe that because they have seen him tracking an injured wolf in British Columbia. When L.T. finds the trapper whose trap injured the wolf, he "cracks his skull," demonstrating for *Washington Post* reviewer Rita Kempley that L.T. and Aaron clearly "are on the same wavelength when it comes to wildlife conservation." But L.T. never killed anybody, he insists—no, he just trained others to do so (which presumably exonerates him; the paint-by-numbers script by David Griffiths, Peter Griffiths, and Art Monterastelli is not exactly a model of moral clarity). First he tells the FBI "I don't do that kind of work any more" when asked to help track down his protégé who has gone 'round the bend, but eventually he agrees to hone his tracking and fighting skills and go after his former pupil. Of course, he wants to work alone, but FBI agent Durrell (Connie Nielsen) in charge of the investigation also wants to be involved. This provides a bit of dramatic conflict, but does a woman belong in a movie like this one? Reviewer Lisa Schwarzbaum dismissed her merely as an "inconvenience," since in this movie "it's clear that real men fight the biblical way, with their hands."

As if we didn't already know, this whole mentor-protégé thing is tantamount to a father facing the prospect of killing his son. Enter the sepulchral voice of Johnny Cash to emphasize the obvious by intoning lyrics from Bob Dylan's "Highway 61 Revisited" ("Oh, God said to Abraham, 'Kill me a son'"). Superficially, this seems apt enough, but when one thinks about it, the parallel breaks down: There's no God-figure around, and Hallam lacks the innocence of Isaac. As for L.T., he doesn't seem too put out about dispatching Hallam. No big message here, really, just atmospheric music. But that didn't keep *Entertainment Weekly* from waxing philosophical: "Are L.T. and Aaron a variation on father and son, their bond sealed by shared guilt about the terrible things one has taught the other to do?" Lisa Schwarzbaum remembered other William Friedkin films, like *The Exorcist* (1973) and *The French Connection* (1971) that might be considered moral allegories. Then she came to her senses. "I would feel more inclined to ponder the deeper psychological themes that the director and writers propose if the movie weren't so obviously turned on by the fetishism of the story: This is a parable of Thou Shalt Not Kill that's boyishly aroused by the ingenious ways a person can kill—and the more special-ops the method, the more excited the filmmaker."

Since this is, after all, a William Friedkin movie, what follows is a series of loosely-connected chase sequences, in which Hallam returns to the home of his girl friend and daughter (for no apparent reason, other than to lead the Feds to them), escapes the Feds, then wrecks dozens of cars during a high-speed chase (actually, it's more of a bumper-car affair), climbs a high bridge tower only to plunge into the cataract below, and fights a climactic battle with L.T. in the north woods. Never mind that the continuity here is virtually nonexistent (one minute the characters are here, the next minute they're there, for example), we are at least treated to not only car crashes but also a crash course in woodcraft. Both Hallam and L.T. scorn Wal-Mart weaponry; they'd rather fashion their own axes and blades (no doubt anyone could forge an iron blade from an ordinary campfire). And they leave behind conveniently visible bent twigs, blood spills, and footprints for each other to follow. Some may enjoy the lesson in woodlore from Hallam to his little girl, as he demonstrates how to track critters in the front yard.

This is a man's movie, for guys who like knives rather than a film about family values. The credits reveal the film's priorities, listing not one but two "knife-fight choreographers" as well as a "tracker technical adviser." *Variety* reviewer Todd McCarthy praised director William Friedkin for pulling off "a couple of intense, in-tight-and-personal knife fights" between Jones and Del Toro, but otherwise found the film to be a "routine, superficial manhunt," likely "to score a decent opening based on star power and the lure of macho action," but also likely to "tail-off in short order," which was pretty much what happened after the film's release. The chemistry between Jones and Del Toro was agreeable enough for *Post* reviewer Rita Kempley, who considered the teamwork "essential," because the film was a "two-man show," involving "a tango between father and son." Lisa Schwarzbaum's *Entertainment Weekly* review concluded by protesting that the film "stalks the masculine psyche with sharp knives, but it tracks its audience too noisily to bag us."

In truth, *The Hunted* was not a very good movie. It's too obviously patterned after another whacked-out movie survivalist, John Rambo and another Tommy Lee Jones movie, *The Fugitive* (1993), but in this one the characters remain blank slates lacking a convincing backstory motivated by

psychological complexities. Only with difficulty could anyone manage to summon up sympathy for poor Tommy Lee Jones, who has to huff and puff his way through the role (unless one considers the obvious: that Jones may be getting too old for such roles). But we do have Caleb Deschanel's superb photography in Oregon's Cascade Mountains, and, for the target audience of lustful teenagers, a foxy FBI agent in tight, government-issue jeans, and that nicely-executed bumper-car street chase. This is the stuff of adolescent male fantasy, pinned together with knives and murderous action. Probably not exactly the perfect date movie.

Cash and his song return at the end. More about Abraham and God and "words written down" and Biblical injunctions, and all that. At the end of her *Washington Post* review headlined "A Stalk on the Wild Side," Rita Kempley assured readers that "No hunters were harmed in the making of this movie." Though not with a whole lot of enthusiasm, *Variety* called it a "Gritty Suspenser [that] Goes for Jugular," adding significant qualifiers, however, to the initial capsule summary: "an unpleasant action suspenser more dedicated to hurtling relentlessly forward than to vesting audience interest"; whereas *Entertainment Weekly* simply thought it was "Way Off Track." This was not a movie for discriminating viewers.

—James M. Welsh and John C. Tibbetts

CREDITS

L.T. Bonham: Tommy Lee Jones
Aaron Hallam: Benicio Del Toro
Abby Durrell: Connie Nielsen
Irene: Leslie Stefanson
Ted Chenoweth: John Finn
Moret: Jose Zuniga
Van Zandt: Ron Canada
Dale Hewitt: Mark Pellegrino
Zander: Lonny (Lonnie) Chapman
Powell: Rex Linn
Richards: Eddie Velez

Origin: USA
Released: 2003
Production: Ricardo Mestres, James Jacks; Lakeshore Entertainment, Alphaville; released by Paramount Pictures
Directed by: William Friedkin
Written by: David Griffiths, Peter Griffiths, Art Montersatelli
Cinematography by: Caleb Deschanel
Music by: Brian Tyler
Sound: Edward Tise, Kirk Francis
Editing: Augie Hess

Art Direction: Beatriz Kerti
Costumes: Gloria Gresham
Production Design: William Cruse
MPAA rating: R
Running time: 94 minutes

REVIEWS

Chicago Sun-Times Online. March 14, 2003.
Entertainment Weekly. March 21, 2003, p. 81.
Los Angeles Times Online. March 14, 2003.
New York Times Online. March 14, 2003.
USA Today Online. March 14, 2003.
Variety. March 17, 2003, p. 40.
Washington Post. March 14, 2003, p. C1.

QUOTES

L.T. (Tommy Lee Jones) explains about Aaron (Benicio Del Toro): "I trained him to survive, I trained him to kill."

I Capture the Castle

I love, I have loved, I will love.
—Movie tagline
You can't chose who you fall in love with.
—Movie tagline
In the shadows of a great castle, two sisters must choose between the men who love them and the men they love.
—Movie tagline

 Box Office: $1.1 million

Novelist Dodie Smith, best known for the children's book-cum-Disney-classic, *The Hundred and One Dalmatians,* penned the first few chapters of *I Capture the Castle* in 1943 and immediately garnered attention from another big Hollywood movie studio, MGM. Smith declined the studio's offer to have the novel rushed into production by dictation to a studio secretary, instead preferring to finish the novel at her leisure some years later in 1948. More cozily (read: smaller budget) produced in Britain, director Tim Fywell filmed for his first feature this story of a quirky English novelist and his family on the Isle of Man.

Rooting the story is the talented Romola Garai as 17-year-old Cassandra, a diarist who narrates the tale of her eccentric family that lives in a once stately but now run-down little castle in 1930s Suffolk, England. Cassandra's father is the famous novelist James Mortmain, who, after a very successful and well-regarded first novel, has had nothing but long years of writer's block. This has led to the dilapidated state of the castle as well as their family, which includes Cassandra's older and more obviously pretty sister Rose (Rose Byrne), her Harry Potter look-alike brother Thomas (Joe Sowerbutts), and her bohemian stepmother Topaz (Tara Fitzgerald). While Topaz, a former artists' model and perpetual muse, gracefully takes to this life of poverty (in an effort to bring some color to their lives she dyes green the family's increasingly sorry garments), Rose proves not as well suited to barely scraping by and declares desperately, in one humorous scene, that she will sell herself on the city streets to earn some money just to leave behind the leaking, rat-infested castle. Rounding out the dysfunctional domestic scene is handsome local teenager, Stephen (Henry Cavill), who helps out the family and is secretly in love with Cassandra, who, unlike her romance-starved sister, is determined to never fall in love.

Just as the royalties from James' twenty-year old novel, *Jacob Wrestling*—and the Mortmain's only source of income—finally dry up completely, a letter arrives stating that their generous landlord Sir William Cotton has died and that two years arrears rent is now due. Suddenly, Cotton's appealing young heirs, Simon (Henry Thomas) and Neil (Marc Blucas), along with their strong-willed mother Elspeth (Sinead Cusack), arrive in Suffolk and soon meet the fetching but unusual Mortmain sisters. For Rose, who is at the end of her rope, their arrival is the answer to a prayer or, more precisely, a deal with the devil, as she had just sworn an oath on one of the castle's gargoyles that she would do anything to escape her impoverished condition. After an awkward initial meeting, the brothers are quickly invited to the humble castle where an over-eager Rose makes a bad first impression with her poor piano playing and singing skills. Cassandra, who thus far has no interest in either brother, is incensed when she overhears the boys making fun of her family and Rose's impromptu concert. Invited to the Cotton's more plush estate for dinner, however, a slightly wounded Rose manages nonetheless to garner attention from both brothers who display their growing affection for her in different ways. Simon is quite obvious, while Neil prefers to pretend to abhor her (and she him). Setting her sights on Simon, the elder, more reserved, and more affluent brother, Rose admits to Cassandra that she would marry him even if she didn't love him just to flee their poverty. Further romantic embroilments occur during dinner when a saucy-tongued Mrs. Cotton makes a very favorable impression on James—causing Topaz to fear she will be replaced as muse—while architect Aubrey Fox-Cotton

(James Faulkner), a guest who recognized Topaz from her modeling days, becomes her eager suitor. Even Stephen, though pining for the indifferent Cassandra, finds a wealthy, older patroness in Aubrey's wife, Leda Fox-Cotton (Sarah Woodward), who turns the chiseled local into a model, lover, and, later, movie actor.

From this point on, the tone of the movies changes from fanciful to more dramatic. Cassandra finds she is falling for her sister's fiancé, Simon; ironically she helped her sister to ensnare the elder brother by leading Neil away for a swim in the moat in order to give Simon a chance to propose. To model her into a proper bride-to-be for a Cotton, Rose is whisked away to the city for a suitable makeover. Sporting a new bobbed hairdo, Rose thoroughly enjoys spending Simon's money and pretends to be happy. Still locked up in the castle without prospects of her own, however, Cassandra innocently experiments with the smitten Stephen in the woods one day only to discover she really loves Simon. She is given an opportunity to find out if he shares her feelings when the rest of the Mortmain family leaves for London to prepare for the upcoming nuptials and Simon is sent to Suffolk alone. During an intimate evening, a blasé Simon kisses the shocked Cassandra who has very different interpretations of what it all means. When Simon leaves without a word the next day, Cassandra also heads to London for a chat with Rose, who admits she isn't in love with Simon but still wants to go through with the marriage for the family's sake. Stephen shows up with a proposal for Cassandra, but she refuses, acknowledging the absurdity of the abundance of unrequited love: "It's like some hideous party game where nobody gets the prize they want."

With Topaz and her siblings still in London, Cassandra forlornly makes her way back to the castle, where she confronts her stubborn father about his writer's block and devises a clever, albeit somewhat harsh method of curing it. Railing against what he imagines as cruel treatment, father and daughter somehow manage to reconcile with each other and the events of the past, including a violent incident with James and his first wife, her subsequent death, and his brief imprisonment, all having left him bitter and blocked. With James busily writing once again, Topaz soon returns happily to her role as resident Mortmain muse.

Meanwhile, taking his cue from Cassandra, Stephen manages to break up the mismatched lovers when he approaches Neil with the truth about Rose's feelings for Simon. Rose disappears and a distraught Simon enlists the help of Cassandra to find her, which they quickly do, in a seaside hotel in the arms of Neil. Neil then marries his Rose and leaves for the States, leaving a broken Cassandra and Simon to each other. Simon pragmatically suggests they get together while the more romantic Cassandra is willing to wait for love—either his, eventually, or someone else's.

Garai and Nighy are the films' standouts, both giving totally real, touchingly emotional performances. Garai effortlessly radiates a budding femininity underneath a somewhat tomboyish attitude: denouncing love and tossing a tennis ball against the wall of a barn, Garai seamlessly flows into a hopeless romantic with a crush on Simon. Nighy as the Mortmain patriarch initially exudes confidence, exclaiming dramatically in the film's opening scene that he will produce masterpieces in their new castle. He then easily transitions into a self-doubting recluse with only glimpses of the former genius he once displayed, and then, after a heart-wrenching battle with himself, finds his writer's voice once again. The chemistry between Garai and Nighy is palpable, especially as the thoroughly fed-up Cassandra is forced to become the equivalent of a parental figure to her emotionally stilted father. When she is compelled to "ground" him by locking him up, he just as convincingly becomes the child figure, throwing an all-out temper tantrum. Byrne is also very appealing and gives Rose a perfect balance of gold digger and a heart of gold, while Fitzgerald steals most of her scenes with the gracefully restrained performance of her over-the-top character. Thomas and Blucas, however, seem hopelessly miscast and appear stiff and one-dimensional.

First time screenwriter Heidi Thomas's adaptation is appealing: initially light and comedic when introducing the eccentric but lovable Mortmains, then gently turning more dramatic as the sisters come of age, grappling with their respective romantic entanglements and the harsh realities of life. The picture also manages to stay true to the novel's un-Hollywood ending where romance triumphs although nothing is completely resolved and the heroine ends up alone. The picturesque English backdrop and period setting evoke a decidedly BBC feel (one of the film's producers), which is not especially surprising given that many in the cast are British television regulars and screenwriter Thomas and Fywell had previously collaborated on the award-winning British television project, *Madame Bovary*. Not only important for establishing a convincing period feel, the film's costumes are also vital in establishing the difference between the classes: the downwardly-mobile yet artistic country-living Mortmains and the well-off, citified Cottons. This is never more delineated than in the scene where Rose is shipped off to London for a respectable makeover, seated in a department store featuring sleek, geometric Art-Deco designs and bobbed-haired extras.

—*Hilary White*

CREDITS

Cassandra Mortmain: Romola Garai
Rose Mortmain: Rose Byrne
Simon Cotton: Henry Thomas
Neil Cotton: Marc Blucas
James Mortmain: Bill Nighy

Topaz Mortmain: Tara Fitzgerald
Elspeth Cotton: Sinead Cusack
Stephen Colley: Henry Cavill
Aubrey Fox-Cotton: James Faulkner
Leda Fox-Cotton: Sarah Woodward

Origin: Great Britain
Released: 2002
Production: Anant Singh, David Parfitt, David M. Thompson; BBC Films, Trademark Films; released by Samuel Goldwyn Films
Directed by: Tim Fywell
Written by: Heidi Thomas
Cinematography by: Richard Greatrex
Music by: Dario Marianelli
Editing: Roy Sharman
Art Direction: Leigh Walker, Mike Stallion
Costumes: Charlotte Walter
Production Design: John Paul Kelly
MPAA rating: R
Running time: 113 minutes

REVIEWS

Chicago Sun-Times Online. July 18, 2003.
Entertainment Weekly. July 25, 2003, p. 54.
The Guardian Online. May 9, 2003.
Los Angeles Times Online. July 11, 2003.
New York Times Online. July 11, 2003.
The Observer Online. May 11, 2003.
People. July 21, 2003, p. 38.
San Francisco Chronicle. July 18, 2003, p. D5.
Sight and Sound. May, 2003, p. 50.
Variety Online. January 15, 2003.
Washington Post. July 18, 2003, p. C5.

QUOTES

Cassandra (Romola Garai): "I'll never fall in love. Life is dangerous enough."

AWARDS AND NOMINATIONS

L.A. Film Critics 2003: Support. Actor (Nighy).

Identity

The secret lies within.
—Movie tagline

 Box Office: $52.1 million

In *Identity,* director-writer James Mangold has managed to marry the kind of shocking mayhem that might cause screams to erupt at drive-in movie theaters with a nifty though somewhat muddled pseudo-psychological framework that leads to surprising plot twists near the end. Though none of its plot devices are very original, *Identity* packs a wallop, and it's both scary, hokey and thought-provoking. You wonder, though, if it might have been even more successful without the hackneyed psychological baggage of a central character with multiple personality disorder.

Mangold's biggest prior hit was *Girl, Interrupted,* an intense psychological drama about a woman trying to recover from borderline psychological disorder. Obviously, Mangold has read his psychology textbooks. *Identity,* written by Mangold with Michael Clooney, also combines some of the police drama elements of Mangold's *Copland.* But Mangold has pumped up his storytelling with some crowd-pleasing shock elements, and he has shot this movie with cinematographer Phedon Papamichael in a jazzed-up, nightmare-quality fashion. It's also filled with a slew of pitch-perfect performances from a couple of stars and an ensemble of worthy character actors.

Identity has thrown together a veritable kitchen's sink of horror and murder movie standards so that by the end of this film there's hardly a cliche left standing. But somehow it all works. Ten strangers are compelled, seemingly by fate, to spend the night together at a seedy Nevada hotel in the middle of nowhere, and they start dying. Throughout the night, there's a pounding, drenching downpour from a relentless thunderstorm—surely breaking all meteorological records for rainfall in a desert region (it looks like there's more precipitation in one night than Nevada normally gets in a decade).

Mangold serves up not one, but two, people brutally assaulted by motor vehicles, one decapitated head in a laundromat, a tormented psychic who senses danger from a lost Indian burial ground, a monstrous-looking blond serial killer on the loose, a bad girl trying to go straight, an ex-cop trying to forget horrible memories, a mute and creepy-looking little boy, disappearing bodies, and room keys left in descending order (10-9-8-7) with the bodies of the victims (in case you're a dolt, one character blurts out early on: "It's like a countdown!").

Mangold offers an intriguing prelude during the opening credits that efficiently tells the story of a tortured multiple murderer revealing his demons to a psychiatrist (Alfred Molina)—at the age of nine, he was abandoned in a motel by his mother, a prostitute, while she turned tricks; later, he killed six people in a motel. And then we learn that, on the night before his scheduled execution, the killer's defense team has turned up the man's diary, prompting a late-night judicial review to see if key evidence has been withheld by the state.

It's a neatly handled prologue, dense and effective, and Mangold follows it up with a jolting, nerve-wracking half-hour or so that details how all the characters end up at the motel. During this part of the movie, Mangold places some scenes out of chronological order, and in doing so quite artfully builds up a mood of disorientation. Ed (John Cusack), driving a limousine for a snooty, over-the-hill actress (played in wonderfully campy fashion by the delightful Rebecca DeMornay), is trying to retrieve something in the car for her when he slams into Alice (Leila Kenzle), who is standing next to her car placing her hands on the window against the hands of her son Timothy (Bret Loehr)—and this brutal scene alone makes *Identity* well worthy of its R rating. Alice's husband and Timothy's stepfather George (John C. McGinley) is changing a flat tire caused by a puncture from a high-heel shoe that is on the road because a sinister gust of wind has blown a bag of belongings out of the car of Paris (Amanda Peet), a hooker leaving Las Vegas to return to the Florida orange groves of her childhood (which are set against a backdrop of mountains—obviously Mangold has never been to Florida).

The storm also strands a couple of newlyweds, Ginny (Clea DuVall) and Lou (William Lee Scott), at the hotel. Ginny is an emotional wreck spooked by a brochure about the Indian burial ground, and she's something of a psychic who seems to sense trouble when it arrives; she also confesses to her new husband that she has faked being pregnant in order to get him to marry her. The trouble she senses pulls up in a police vehicle bearing Detective Rhodes (Ray Liotta), who is transporting a serial killer, a menacing animal played by Jake Busey. All the guests are given an incredulous, nervous reception by the hotel manager, Larry (John Hawkes), who has his own secrets.

Cusack's Ed emerges as the central character. He heroically stitches together the neck wound of Alice, the woman he has run down, and, when the first murder occurs, reveals he's an ex-cop and begins to team up with Liotta's Rhodes to try to track down the killer. As the bodies begin to mount, the terror becomes more intense, and Ed tries to hold everyone together. Cusack and Liotta—two splendid actors—give the sometimes-breathless movie some needed solidity. Cusack is his usual lost soul, with an extra measure of heroic effort, and Liotta is his patented, one-screw-loose, teetering-on-the-edge control freak. Peet is fascinating and earnest, and DuVall makes hysteria watchable. Many of the rest of the actors are forced to play characters who are little more than cliches, but they all perform admirably.

Mangold doesn't shy from using the standard shock techniques, with the score providing the usual auditory clues as to when something is about to occur, and there are the requisite assortments of creaking gates, slamming doors, silhouettes of the murderer, and visual and aural fits and starts—not to mention gruesome murders, sudden revelations of characters' secrets, and the expected loss of electricity, flooded roads, phones that don't work (even cell phones), and a dead body falling out of a freezer. The movie goes gleefully over the top, around the bend, and back home again—no holds barred and proud of it. The cinematography, editing, acting, and technical deftness pull it above the swirling waters of a plot that threatens to drown everything in its recycled stew of stock shock devices.

Then, about two-thirds of the way through, *Identity* pulls its biggest surprise, and everything is revealed in the new light cast by the bizarre psychological diagnosis of the murderer who is about to be executed. As certain protagonists are revealed to be not who they are, some of the tension that's been built up is dissipated. The downside of what happens with the plot is that it's hard to care about the remaining, still-surviving characters as much as we ought to. The upside is that the movie becomes more challenging intellectually and more complicated. And it all works as a setup for the boffo ending, which will leave audiences jacked up.

Something of a tour de force for pushing emotional buttons, *Identity* is a psychological mish-mash, and after you puzzle out the plot in light of the new revelations of the latter part of the movie, some things make sense and other things don't seem to add up. But the overall effect is a pleasant mental and emotional buzz. Sometimes even the most jaded moviegoer doesn't mind being manipulated, if it's done with enough expertise and vigor. And *Identity* doesn't lack for nervy confidence. It jolts along like an express train to hell.

—*Michael Betzold*

CREDITS

Ed: John Cusack
Caroline Suzanne: Rebecca DeMornay
Rhodes: Ray Liotta
Robert Maine: Jake Busey
Paris: Amanda Peet
Ginny: Clea DuVall
Lou: William Lee Scott
George York: John C. McGinley
Alice York: Leila Kenzle
Timmy York: Bret Loehr
Larry: John Hawkes

Malcolm Rivers: Pruitt Taylor Vince
Doctor: Alfred Molina
Asst. District Attorney: Matt Letscher
Defense Lawyer: Carmen Argenziano
District Attorney: Marshall Bell
Judge: Holmes Osborne
Detective Varole: Frederick Coffin

Origin: USA
Released: 2003
Production: Cathy Konrad; Konrad Pictures; released by Columbia Pictures
Directed by: James Mangold
Written by: Michael Cooney
Cinematography by: Phedon Papamichael
Music by: Alan Silvestri
Sound: Jim Stuebe
Editing: David Brenner
Art Direction: Jess Gonchor
Costumes: Arianne Phillips
Production Design: Mark Friedberg
MPAA rating: R
Running time: 90 minutes

REVIEWS

Chicago Sun-Times Online. April 25, 2003.
Entertainment Weekly. May 2, 2003, p. 48.
Los Angeles Times Online. April 25, 2003.
New York Times Online. April 25, 2003.
People. May 5, 2003, p. 37.
Variety Online. April 19, 2003.
Washington Post. April 25, 2003, p. WE49.

In America

Box Office: $13.5 million

Autobiographical filmmaking is tricky turf, especially when it involves painful family memories. Brilliant Irish filmmaker Jim Sheridan navigates the territory astoundingly well in the wondrous, heartfelt, unfortunately named drama *In America*. Though it is a story about an immigrant family's first year in New York City, it is more about making one's way on unfamiliar emotional ground than it is about the strangeness of a new land.

Sheridan wrote the film with his daughters, Kirsten and Naomi, thinly fictionalizing the family's own tragic experi-

ence with the loss of a child, Frankie. In the film, the death occurs a year before the family, in the early 1980s, sneaks into the United States, telling customs officials they're only taking a vacation. The unspoken assumption is that the radical change of geography has as much to do with attempting to erase the memories of the dead child—who fell down the stairs at age two and then succumbed after a three-year battle to a brain tumor caused by the fall—as it does with father Johnny's efforts to land an acting job on a Manhattan stage. It's not clear, however, why the family is entering the country from Canada and driving a station wagon.

What is abundantly clear early on is that the family is full of a somewhat reckless love that is trying to contain an ocean of deep, unceasing pain. But they're also game to be wacky and up for new adventures. Their entrance into Manhattan is awash in childish awe. Mother Sarah (Samantha Morton), a pixie whose emotions are barely contained by a bitter adult outlook, rolls down the windows as they drive into central Manhattan and waves her arms at ordinary people on the sidewalk. Ten-year-old Christy (Sarah Bolger) speaks little but records everything on her primitive red Camcorder. Four-year-old Ariel (Emma Bolger) beams like an angel and asks precocious questions. Even troubled Johnny (Paddy Considine) manages a grin.

It's the whimsical entrance of a group of mystical dreamers into a land they hope will be enchanted. To them, even the worst New York has to offer is a godsend. Unable to find a decent place to live, they are grateful to land in a graffiti-covered, ratty walkup in a building full of junkies, prostitutes, and transvestites; pigeons are nesting in their top-floor tenement apartment. "Can we keep the pigeons?" Ariel asks. Johnny says no, but they keep the ambience—a tub in the middle of the floor, painted posts in the room—even as they dress up the place with their own eccentric, hard-won furnishings.

Early on, there's a scene involving Johnny's battle for an air conditioner—he drags a scavenged unit down a busy street and hauls it up the stairs to save his family from 100-degree heat. It's a Herculean effort that demonstrates his determination to care for his family. Unfortunately, such resolve cannot help him break through to an acting job, so he eventually drives a taxi at night while Sarah scoops cones in a nearby ice cream parlor.

These parents are so desperate to make their children happy—and help them forget the tragedy—that when Ariel complains Johnny doesn't play with her like he used to and mourns the alien creature in *E.T.* after they go see the movie to escape the heat, Johnny and Sarah risk all their rent money trying to win an E.T. doll at a street carnival. It's an astonishing moment that helps audiences see the emotional desperation of this family—the extremes to which they will go to maintain their precious, against-all-odds love. Johnny in particular has been so devastated by his son's death that he cannot regain his old exuberance and charm, and everything he does seems forced and false. So these shows of bravado are all he can manage to keep his children happy and forgetful. But none of it works; no one has forgotten Frankie.

In America is awash in gritty sentimentality. Unlike his uncompromising earlier masterpieces about Irish history and politics (*In the Name of the Father, My Left Foot*), this film is Sheridan's bouquet to life's possibilities. It's unabashedly emotional but stops short of being mawkish because the material is tinged with tragedy, the performances are so marvelous, and the moviemaking is first-rate. Sheridan doesn't flinch from the toughest moments, and his artistry allows us to see the situation from multiple perspectives—Johnny's, Sara's, and each of the children's, especially Christy's, whose "home movies" provide yet another distancing and focusing device. Astonishingly, in a child's eyes, the forces of nature—as shown in the passing seasons, summer storms, a gleefully anarchic blizzard—frame the story despite the gritty urban setting. The movie is lyrical and magical.

As a drenching summer thunderstorm breaks the unbearable heat wave, Sarah sends the children to the ice cream parlor under the care of a co-worker. As they sit at a picture window eating bowls of ice cream and watching the deluge outside, their parents make ardent love amid the cracking of the lightning and the rumbling thunder, while in the apartment below, an artist uses his own blood to make a painting. Afterward, Sarah lies still, her emotional defenses broken, and talks about their lost son. The film is about the family's halting efforts to close this gaping wound, and it's full of resounding, aching, beautiful moments like these scenes.

Sheridan can be forgiven for making the artist neighbor, Mateo (Djimon Hounsou), into a falsely frightful figure. He's a towering, deeply black African, with a bare head and chest and an earring, and he looks more than a little dangerous. But such is this family's bravery—or naivete, or trust, it's hard to tell which—that the parents allow their trick-or-treating children to enter his lair on Halloween, despite his scrawled message on the door to keep away. Mateo turns out to be a gentle giant, in touch with the magic of his ancestors, and—we soon learn in dramatic fashion—dying of AIDS. Hounsou's thoughtful, understated acting transforms what could have been an overly simplistic, romanticized figure into a touching, commanding, unforgettable character.

Sheridan makes the most out of this intimate, sometimes scanty, and precariously sentimental material, so that it doesn't come off as contrived. Its basis in reality—as a version of the filmmaker's own family story—keeps it grounded, and its willingness to take flights of fancy makes it appealingly cinematic. As always, Sheridan is daring in his use of a musical score, which ranges from pop classics like the Lovin' Spoonful's "Do You Believe in Magic?" and the Byrds' "Turn, Turn, Turn" to insistent, unlikely Latin rhythms. And he's equally daring in framing the action with bizarre twists, and in visiting the scene through the eyes of the children, who are wonderfully portrayed by the en-

chanting Bolger sisters, acting neophytes who charmed the pants off the moviemakers. Best of all is Morton, whose maternal stoicism masks her depthless sea of pain and loss, and whose wistful, silent expressions are full of mysterious longing and muted eroticism.

To say that *In America* is enchanting in spite of its limitations is to flatter it insufficiently. It is a rare combination of brilliantly daring filmmaking and powerful human emotion. It is one of the best stories about a family ever filmed, for it gives its characters equal measures of dignity, respect, human flaws, and aching fear. It's a film that precariously balances between melodrama and anarchy, between crowd-pleasing moments and off-putting moments, between pain and the delicacy of revelation. There are awkward moments when the script gets needlessly transparent (Sarah telling Johnny that his inability to feel emotion is ruining his chances at landing an acting job, Christy telling Johnny that it is she that has been holding the family together) but these are errors that are due to an excess of caring and daring. For Sheridan, making this movie must have been cathartic, and for audiences in the right frame of mind the film is powerfully liberating too. Substitute your own family traumas and you will be right there with Sheridan and his stand-in family—in the company of a brave and inventive filmmaker who is willing to risk baring his soul and expanding his career.

In America has the faults associated with trying too hard and risking too much, but these are also the faults of the family in the film, and presumably Sheridan's family's as well, and there is nothing shameful about sentiment rooted in pain and love. Despite settings which to some may seem false (how could a family live in such squalor?) there is an undeniable authenticity to this film, and it is as unique as any family's story ought to be. For those who can stand some enchantment without the sugar-coating, Sheridan shows us a magical way home from tragedy and turmoil to joy and peace. And, mercifully, there's not a drunken, brawling Irishman in sight.

—*Michael Betzold*

CREDITS

Johnny: Paddy Considine
Sarah: Samantha Morton
Christy: Sarah Bolger
Ariel: Emma Bolger
Mateo: Djimon Hounsou

Origin: Ireland, Great Britain
Released: 2002
Production: Jim Sheridan, Arthur Lappin; Hell's Kitchen; released by Fox Searchlight

Directed by: Jim Sheridan
Written by: Jim Sheridan, Naomi Sheridan, Kirsten Sheridan
Cinematography by: Declan Quinn
Music by: Gavin Friday, Maurice Seezer
Sound: Daniel Birch
Editing: Naomi Geraghty
Art Direction: Susan Cullen
Costumes: Eimer Ni Mhaoldomhnaigh
Production Design: Mark Geraghty
MPAA rating: PG-13
Running time: 103 minutes

REVIEWS

Boxoffice. December, 2002, p. 55.
Chicago Sun-Times Online. November 26, 2003.
Entertainment Weekly. December 5, 2003, p. 70.
Los Angeles Times Online. November 26, 2003.
New York Times Online. September 7, 2003.
New York Times Online. November 26, 2003.
People. December 8, 2003, p. 34.
Rolling Stone. December 11, 2003, p. 214.
USA Today Online. November 26, 2003.
Variety Online. September 17, 2002.
Washington Post. November 26, 2003, p. C12.

QUOTES

Mateo (Djimon Hounsou): "I love anything that lives."

TRIVIA

The film is dedicated to Jim Sheridan's brother, Frankie, who died at the age of 10.

AWARDS AND NOMINATIONS

Ind. Spirit 2004: Cinematog., Support. Actor (Hounsou)
Nomination:
Oscars: Support. Actor (Hounsou)
Oscars 2003: Orig. Screenplay, Support. Actress (Morton)
Golden Globes 2004: Screenplay, Song ("Time Enough for Tears")
Ind. Spirit 2004: Actress (Morton), Director (Sheridan), Film, Support. Actress (Bolger)
Screen Actors Guild 2003: Cast
Writers Guild 2003: Orig. Screenplay.

The In-Laws

The cake is going to hit the fan.
—Movie tagline

Box Office: $20.4 million

"I was laughing so hard at *The In-Laws* that after a while I was crying," raved the *New York Times,* calling it an "altogether sidesplitting movie." The *New Yorker* called it "inspired." *Time* insisted it delivered "more whopping laughs than any other film this year." Unfortunately for Albert Brooks and Michael Douglas, the above quotes are from 1979 and pertain to the memorable, distinctive, truly zany little gem that starred Alan Arkin and Peter Falk and not the actors' remake. In a film that has since become a cult favorite, Arkin played mild-mannered and highly-controlled dentist Sheldon Kornpett, whose daughter's impending marriage will link him to Vince Ricardo (Falk). Ricardo, who may work for the CIA or may just as likely be certifiable, sets Kornpett's head spinning as the perplexed doctor is drawn into a madcap adventure leading down to a Central American country run by a deranged general who converses with his hand a la Senor Wences.

As proof of his true identity as an agent, Ricardo shows Kornpett an autographed photo of President Kennedy from after the Bay of Pigs with the succinct inscription "At least we tried." Ricardo has many strange tales to tell about the unusual and exotic locations to which his job has taken him, including one where immense tsetse flies swoop down and carry away unsuspecting children. Is Ricardo serious, or just seriously ill? An overwhelmed Kornpett does not know what to think, and looks like he would welcome one of those tsetses to take him away from his plight.

The film's screwball script, written by Andrew Bergman (who previously worked with Mel Brooks on 1974's *Blazing Saddles*) is uneven but a hoot, including numerous lines that fans continue to quote from, like Ricardo's repeated injunctions to "Serpentine!" while Kornpett fretfully takes zigzagging evasive action. Both Arkin and Falk are hilarious and make all this ridiculousness work. Far less hilarious and memorable is the new film, a middling comedy, which was sometimes described by its makers as a remake and sometimes as a totally different work that merely uses the original's basic premise as a jumping-off point. Judging the new *In-Laws* as a remake, it cannot be recommended. However, in an attempt to be completely fair and judge the film on its own merits, it still cannot to be recommended.

Part of the fun of the original is that the audience keeps wondering along with the dismayed dentist whether his curious travel companion is really a CIA agent or only suffers from delusions of grandeur (and possibly other kinds, as well). In the new version, we know exactly what to make of him from the beginning (even if the doctor, once again, does not), which takes an important ingredient out of the film. Here, he is Steve Tobias (Douglas, fresh off a disappointment at the box office entitled *It Runs In the Family*), a cross between a cooly-efficient James Bondian character and a glad-handing, ultra-slick salesman. His devotion to his job as a deep cover agent has strained his relationship with his son Marc (Ryan Reynolds) and led his wife Judy (always fun Candice Bergen) to divorce him and seek the comforts of an ashram to recover.

As the film begins, we see Steve involved in risky business with shadowy Russian figures, narrowly escaping with some expert moves and leaving behind bullet-riddled bodies, exploding planes, and angry authorities. It is clear that this man is supremely confident and in charge, pumped full of adrenaline and enjoying every drop of it. The film immediately draws a stark contrast between Steve and Jerry Peyser (Brooks), who lives the much more prosaic life of a Chicago podiatrist, urging the proper powder or ointment on his patients to keep fungi and other such evils at bay.

Jerry is more of a vaguely queasy passenger than a cocksure driver in life, with nails dug into the dashboard for security. While Steve thrives on pressure, Jerry needs everything under control and is plagued by panic attacks and a gnawing sense of doom. His dyspepsia increases as he endeavors to plan the perfect wedding for his only daughter Melissa (Lindsay Sloane), continuously searching for just the right caterer and inflating what she had hoped would be an intimate ceremony into something almost as intricately planned and grandiose as one of Steve's covert operations.

Jerry's concern grows upon meeting Steve for the first time. The exuberant man breezes in so late that the meal Jerry carefully prepared has shriveled into nothingness, then surreptitiously snatches Jerry's watch as an "ice breaker," and finally, taking charge, herds everyone out for oriental food at a restaurant of his choosing. (Marc urges his father to "take it down a notch.") During dinner, Jerry finds Steve huddled in a men's room stall with a woman, and then violence erupts from a triggerman at the urinal, all of which make Jerry flee the establishment with his wife and daughter in tow, badly shaken and utterly perplexed by what he has seen. "You fix this!" Marc demands of his father.

Any hope of poor Jerry keeping his ordered life from the Tobias treatment is lost when Steve's visit to apologize also involves planting a vial of fissile nuclear waste from a Russian sub on the unsuspecting doctor. This leads to Jerry being put through the ringer, first by the FBI and then by Steve and his voluptuous but volatile sidekick Angela (Robin Tunney). He gets smashed in the face, and is repeatedly ridiculed for his omnipresent fanny pack filled with things like a sanitary collapsible drinking cup, Lorna Doones to ward off dips in

blood sugar, and a blaring personal alarm device. After a drug is slipped into his drink, Jerry is horrified to find himself on a plane heading for France, which Steve has "borrowed" from Barbra Streisand. Jerry is hysterical yet again, but once again the film is not.

Once in France, Jerry is instructed by Steve to pose as brutal crime boss Fat Cobra, a lewd moniker which arouses the amorous intentions of maniacal arms dealer Jean-Pierre Thibodoux (David Suchet). While Steve is at work accessing information from Thibodoux's computer files, Jerry must don a bright red thong and keep Thibodoux occupied in a hot tub that threatens to get way too hot for Jerry's liking. All the while the perplexed podiatrist grapples to comprehend what is happening to him, what lively livelihood Steve is actually in, and whether the man is villainous or virtuous.

The two fathers are able to get back just in time for the rehearsal dinner, where everyone laughs off Jerry's frantic pleas to be rescued from Steve's clutches. He is literally in the agent's grasp when the two parachute off the John Hancock Building to escape from Agent Will Hutchins (Russell Andrews) and a swarm of FBI men. Their descent signals the film's unfortunate degeneration into a rather sappy tale of Steve's redemption. Jerry turns to chastising him for a lack of involvement in Marc's life (instead of complaining about an excessive involvement in Jerry's own), then Marc's frat brothers say they never even knew he existed. Steve gets all thoughtful, moody and contrite.

Since Marc and Melissa's song is "Get Down Tonight" by K.C. and the Sunshine Band, Steve hires the group to perform it at the rehearsal dinner. When it looks like Melissa is bolting the wedding ceremony (it is actually Angela, a turncoat in disguise who is working with Thibodoux, which comes as little surprise), Steve gets down on one knee and begs her to go through with her marriage to his son. He urges Hutchins to let him see his son's wedding before they cart him off for questioning.

In the end, Steve makes up with everyone, even having a nice moment with his ex. Even Hutchins, now realizing that the man is, indeed, with the CIA, somehow performs the ceremony. Finally, Steve and Jerry unite in ridiculously defeating Thibodoux's attempted torpedoing of the festivities from the huge Russian submarine somehow positioned just off shore in Lake Michigan. (So much for recent expenditures on homeland security.) The tidal wave that results from the sub's explosion makes the guests as soggy as the script has become. The film ends on an all-too-easy joke about the joys of prison life that await the captured homosexual arms dealer.

More frantic than funny, purposefully kinetic more than comedic, *The In-Laws* failed to impress many critics. Made on a budget of $30 million, it grossed just over $20 million. The film's screenplay was written by Nat Mauldin (1998's *Dr. Doolittle*) and Ed Solomon (1997's *Men In Black*) from Bergman's original idea, and directed by Andrew Fleming (1999's

Dick). While the filmmakers used a special effects budget to generate explosions and such, they fail throughout to generate enough laughter, even though the leads, in particular, are trying hard. Douglas certainly plays his role with relish, and Brooks is his usual neurotic self, delivering most of the film's more humorous lines. (One involves Jerry's attempt to avoid Thibodoux's hot tub, asserting that he is not waterproof due to a rare congenital birth defect.) Best advice: serpentine to the video store and rent the original *In-Laws.*

—*David L. Boxerbaum*

CREDITS

Steve Tobias: Michael Douglas
Jerry Peyser: Albert Brooks
Judy: Candice Bergen
Angela Harris: Robin Tunney
Mark Tobias: Ryan Reynolds
Melissa Peyser: Lindsay Sloane
Jean-Pierre Thibodoux: David Suchet
Katherine Peyser: Maria Ricossa
Agent Will Hutchins: Russell Andrews

Origin: USA
Released: 2003
Production: Bill Gerber, Elie Samaha, Joel Simon, Bill Todman Jr.; Franchise Pictures, Further Films, Gerber Pictures, MHF Erste Academy Film & Co. Produktions; released by Warner Bros.
Directed by: Andrew Fleming
Written by: Nat Mauldin, Edward Solomon
Cinematography by: Alexander Grusynski
Music by: Jocelyn Pook
Sound: Bruce Carwardine
Editing: Mia Goldman
Art Direction: Dennis Davenport
Costumes: Deborah Everton
Production Design: Andrew McAlpine
MPAA rating: PG-13
Running time: 98 minutes

REVIEWS

Chicago Sun-Times Online. May 23, 2003.
Entertainment Weekly. May 30, 2003, p. 92.
Los Angeles Times Online. May 23, 2003.
New York Times. May 23, 2003, p. E18.
People. June 2, 2003, p. 34.
Rolling Stone. June 12, 2003, p. 102.
Variety. May 12, 2003, p. 26.
Washington Post. May 23, 2003, p. WE36.

In the Cut

Everything you know about desire is dead wrong.
—Movie tagline

 Box Office: $3.9 million

Nothing in Meg Ryan's career could have prepared anyone for her taut, challenging role in Jane Campion's erotic thriller, *In the Cut.* Gone is the perky, sweet, lighthearted girl-next-door, and in her place is a brainy, daring, disturbed, cynical woman-in-the-next-apartment. Ryan has always played well as a frothy delight; Campion transforms her into a dark, urban contra-feminist, a college English teacher in Manhattan whose spirit is beaten down by the constant dangers and challenges of big-city life.

In the Cut, perhaps the most harrowing and sexually explicit mainstream movie since *Last Tango in Paris,* is an interesting step outside of stereotype for Ryan, who has found that with slight aging, roles for chipper all-American girls dwindle rapidly. The film is no surprise at all coming from Campion, who specializes in provocative movies about odd, steamy relationships between damaged men and women. Campion, who was born in New Zealand and now makes her home in Australia, rose to international prominence with *The Piano,* a raw tale about a rugged man who awakens the illicit passion of a downtrodden, deaf-mute woman. Despite an Academy Award for her screenplay and a nomination for best director, along with Holly Hunter's Oscar for best actress, Campion has made precious few movies since then, her last being *Holy Smoke,* featuring Kate Winslet as a cult member and Harvey Keitel as the deprogrammer her family hires to save her, but who ends up seducing her.

Sex as a sort of fiery crucible is the common denominator of those two films and this one as well. If a man were writing and directing films like these, in which a woman's better judgment is often overcome by her consuming sexual passion, some critics might accuse him of being a chauvinist. In Campion's daring treatment, however, the stories are transformed with her heroines' frank and seasoned perspectives, along with their assertiveness and intelligence, even when in the thrall of overwhelming desire. Think of how Adrian Lyne might have handled the scene in which Ryan's character handcuffs her hard-bitten police detective lover to a pipe and then sexually uses him, and compare it with the way in which Campion directs the scene. In Lyne's version, the woman probably would have been the one to get handcuffed, and it would have been simply exploitative. In

Campion's hands, however, such scenes are still unsettling yet compelling as well.

Women-in-peril movies have been a staple of filmmaking since the days of the silents. But Campion's achievement is to make that peril so palpable that it is part of the fabric of her protagonist's daily existence. Not since *Taxi Driver* has Manhattan looked quite this cheesy and dangerous. Every day Ryan's Franny Thorstin dodges dangerous traffic and walks a landscape scarred with graffiti and peopled by hookers, drug pushers, menacing thugs, and lurking strangers. She has somehow adapted herself, like millions of other women in this world, to an existence in which a mugging or rape might be just around the corner. And—even scarier—as an older, single woman interested in men, she has to come to grips with a world where the sunny promise of courtship might suddenly flip into mayhem.

Sure, this is not the first movie to attempt to fashion a courageous love story amid the ruins of an inhuman landscape, which in Franny's case is a harrowing neighborhood where a vicious murderer is dismembering women's bodies. This is, however, one of the few films to make such a situation inescapably palpable. Campion is a hothouse director; her every scene and camera angle is artfully planned to add to the mood she wants to create. It's a nightmarish world of dark places and harsh sunlight, of harsh realities and twisted fantasies, and cinematographer Dion Beebe captures the daily struggle of living and working in Manhattan with deft touches. Campion shows it as a place of constant danger for women by, for instance, including a random, unexplained shot of a woman running down the street.

But Franny, despite her fears, is driven to explore the dark corners of her world by an untamed curiosity and a longing for escape from her own isolation and numbing routine. Inexplicably, she meets one of her students, Cornelius (Sharrieff Pugh), in a sleazy bar rather than a coffeeshop, and it raises the question of whether she is leading him on or she is interested in more than just her ostensible linguistic project about street slang. In the bar, she goes down the basement to the rest room and stares in fascination at a man and a woman engaging in a sex act whose significance will only later become apparent. Franny is a voyeur, but perhaps also a cat ready to spring. With men, she has been a failure. She is trying to avoid her most recent mistake, a sad sack named John Graham (played brilliantly against form by Kevin Bacon), who is obviously emotionally unstable and desperate.

Nothing about Franny's life seems solid, except her interest in literature. She rides the subways and finds inspiration in quotes posted aboard the trains; these serve as a sort of Greek chorus for the plot, highlighting moods and lessons. Franny has her students reading Virginia Woolf's *To the Lighthouse,* even though they complain it's irrelevant. How can one dying lady in Edwardian England raise an eyebrow in a violent milieu where so many people are suffering every day?

Even Franny's most important relationship—the one with her stepsister, Pauline (Jennifer Jason Leigh)—seems at times edgy and even precarious. They talk frankly of sex; the way the women look to each other for solace verges at times on the erotic as they cuddle and touch in their shared refuge. Pauline is a shameless libertine who keeps urging Franny to make the transition from her fantasy world to actual engagement, while she, herself, unable to make progress in any part of her life, lives above a strip club and longs for a meaningful romance.

Campion constantly toys with the juxtaposition of romance and brutality. A man on a subway platform carries a huge heart-shaped wreath; later Franny sees a bride and her bridesmaids on the platform and then on the train. She flashes back repeatedly to a hyper-romanticized scene of her parents' courtship on an ice-skating rink. Taken by her mother's charms, her father spurned his fiancee for a sudden, love-at-first-sight romance. The romance ultimately shatters and the father leaves the family; Pauline is his bastard child. And when the worst kind of tragedy strikes, Franny's memory turns into horror.

How is romance possible in Franny's awful, graffiti-covered, and gang-scarred world? What is left of the remains of heterosexual love? That's the tough territory *In the Cut* attempts to negotiate. Franny connects viscerally with Detective James Malloy (Mark Ruffalo), a crude, profane cop on the trail of the murderer who is dismembering women's bodies. But it seems a dangerous path to follow: at times, the evidence appears to point to Malloy, himself, as the murderer. And Malloy is not exactly a sweet romancer. His idea of a date is to take Franny to a local bar, then size up other women with his partner, Detective Rodriguez (Nick Damici), and make lewd comments. He seems interested mainly in rough talk and even rougher sex, but she finds herself pulled into his orbit, because she has a penchant for edgy liaisons herself.

Their sex scenes—and even more audacious sex talk—test what taboos remain in mainstream movies. But they don't do so in the gauzy, dreamlike style of an Adrian Lyne film. This is not a sanitized Hollywood version of the forbidden extremes of male-female encounters, not with the career-risking exposure of Ryan's body, changing her from good girl to bad girl. This is tawdry, authentic, and merciless filmmaking. And when the violence escalates and moves closer to home, the film becomes absolutely harrowing. Clearly, *In the Cut* is not everyone's cup of tea. Some critics and audiences found it repulsive, others found the genre conventions a bit formulaic.

While Campion's film is not for the faint of heart, it can arguably be viewed as a slightly flawed masterpiece. Ryan refuses to make her character sympathetic or smooth-edged; she is as raw and unpolished as many men are allowed to be, and in this sense this is a groundbreaking role not just for her, but for women in general. Ruffalo's performance is fantastic; the transformation from his shy, riveting character in the acclaimed *You Can Count on Me,* to this semi-malevolent, piggish, yet, perhaps, valiant and heroic, or evil and villainous cop is simply astounding. Franny flees and embraces Malloy by turns; Ruffalo makes Malloy's spell-binding web-weaving believable, and his true nature opaque. Just in the cracks of his hard-boiled surface are the inklings of a gentle soul, quickly snuffed out; just as Franny's softer side is largely hidden beneath the cynical facade she has built for survival.

Campion has made an undeniably artsy film, fabulously rich in palette and texture, masterfully staged and directed, intricately nuanced and structured. Her opening scene is beautiful and breathtaking, and even if the film bogs down later in some of the tawdriest of the female-in-peril conventions, it never sinks. Campion is always capturing Ryan's vulnerability, heightening contrasts and contradictions, plunging audiences into heavy emotional territory, and challenging them. Once again, her latest film questions the conventional views of female sexuality and explodes the cultural cliches of female sensuality; she focuses on a damaged woman as her protagonist and refuses to apologize for it. *In the Cut* is far braver, more shocking, and more beautiful than *The Piano,* but it will not get nearly the recognition because it is too bold and brutal, too risky and unconventional, too tawdry and bloody, too plainspoken and profane. Ryan is to be saluted for taking on this difficult part, and at least some will be astonished at her newly revealed depths.

Campion has done a dirty, daring deed, taking a perky American sweetheart, the protagonist of so many frothy, phony "date movies," and plunging her into a cauldron of dangerous realism, throwing all that coy romance back in the faces of Ryan's fans. Perhaps Campion has gone too far and is rubbing our faces in her oppositional version of the Meg Ryan persona. Hers is confrontational moviemaking, to be sure, but it is also high art, masterfully executed and deadly effective. *In the Cut* is dark, dangerous, devilish, despicable—and astounding.

—*Michael Betzold*

CREDITS

Frannie Avery: Meg Ryan
Detective Malloy: Mark Ruffalo
Pauline: Jennifer Jason Leigh
John: Kevin Bacon
Detective Rodriguez: Nick Damici
Cornelius Webb: Sharrieff Pugh

Origin: USA, Australia

Released: 2003
Production: Laurie Parker, Nicole Kidman; Pathe Productions; released by Screen Gems
Directed by: Jane Campion
Written by: Jane Campion, Susanna Moore
Cinematography by: Dion Beebe
Music by: Hilmar Orn Hilmarsson
Sound: Ken Ishii
Music Supervisor: Laurie Parker
Editing: Alexandre De Francheschi
Art Direction: David Stein
Costumes: Beatrix Aruna Pasztor
Production Design: David Brisbin
MPAA rating: R
Running time: 113 minutes

REVIEWS

Boxoffice. November, 2003, p. 97.
Chicago Sun-Times Online. October 31, 2003.
Entertainment Weekly. October 31, 2003, p. 51.
Los Angeles Times Online. October 22, 2003.
New York Times Online. October 22, 2003.
People. November 10, 2003, p. 40.
Rolling Stone. November 13, 2003, p. 106.
Sight and Sound. November, 2003, p. 16.
Variety Online. September 9, 2003.
Washington Post. October 31, 2003, p. WE43.

QUOTES

Malloy (Mark Ruffalo) to Frannie (Meg Ryan): "Tell me what you want me to be."

In the Mirror of Maya Deren (Im Spiegel Der Maya Deren)

For Maya Deren's legacy, *In the Mirror of Maya Deren* could turn out to be as much a blessing as a curse. The legendary "underground" filmmaker grappled so eloquently with issues of identity in her films, one wonders if the late Ms. Deren would totally approve a film that tries (in mostly conventional terms) to declare who she was. On the other hand, exposure for any artist is crucial and this documentary, made more than 40 years after Deren's death, could attract a whole new audience for the filmmaker.

Certainly, few could accuse director Martina Kudlacek of trying to exploit her subject, despite including some intimate personal history. Rather, Kudlacek is highly respectful, even reverential at times. Moreover, the film quickly establishes its intention to show what made Maya Deren a special person as well as artist. That doesn't mean, however, *In the Mirror of Maya Deren* completely avoids the pitfalls inherent in such a project.

As indicated, Kudlacek takes a conventional documentary approach—using "talking head" interviews with former Deren colleagues and associates, and interspersing them with archival photos and footage. The interviews are sometimes revealing, occasionally informative, but also a bit dull and self-serving. The footage chosen from Deren's work presents its own set of problems.

We learn the basic facts of Deren's life through people like Alexander "Sasha" Hammid (Deren's collaborator and second husband), editor Miriam Arsham, critic Amos Vogel, filmmaker Stan Brakhage, dancer-choreographer Katherine Dunham, and (best of all) the voice of Deren herself. Deren was born Eleanora Derenkowsky in Kiev, Ukraine in 1917, but was raised in Syracuse, New York. She was a political activist in her youth in the 1930s and had already been divorced when she met and married Hammid, a Czech filmmaker, with whom she made the seminal, dreamlike experimental *Meshes of the Afternoon* in 1943. She took the name Maya because she and Hammid liked its mythological associations. Deren applied for and won the first Guggenheim Award ever given to a filmmaker (thanks in part to the backing of Joseph Campbell, Margaret Mead, and Gregory Bateson). She used her award money to travel to Haiti, where she studied and recorded voodoo trance rituals and later wrote a book about her experience called *Divine Horsemen: The Living Gods of Haiti*. Deren divorced Hammid and married composer Teiji Ito in the 1950s. Filmmaking was becoming increasingly expensive, so she completed only a few more films, while starting Cinema 16, the first independent American film movement (the New American Cinema filmmakers included Brakhage and Bruce Conner, but few women). She died in poverty from a cerebral hemorrhage in 1961 at the age of 44.

From the interviews, one gets the sense that Maya Deren was as avant-garde a person as she was a filmmaker: she wore her hair in long, curly "hippie" styles decades before it was fashionable; she traveled around the world to better understand other cultures and absorb them into her work; and she preferred to be destitute rather than compromise her artistic vision.

Yet, with all this information, the documentary's protective veneer allows only a glimpse into Deren's darker side.

For example, she had a passionate temper and her use of "speed" may have hastened her death. Other issues get skimmed over, too: her Russian-Jewish heritage, her political beliefs, even her feminism. Not surprisingly, her colleagues are hardly interrogated by director Kudlacek: yes, Deren divorced Hammid in the late 1940s, but according to those interviewed here, he was something of a saint—so one might wonder, why the split? It would also be interesting to know what Hammid (still spry in his 90s) thought when Deren and Teiji Ito in 1952 added tantalizing Eastern-themed music to the hitherto silent Deren-Hammid classic, *Meshes of the Afternoon*. Actually, we do know what Hammid thinks (without his saying a word) because Kudlacek never uses the Ito score whenever she runs the excerpts (she could have at least shown it both ways, since the film is much better known today with the music). Thus, it seems the filmmaker has either acquiesced to a demand by one of her interview subjects or made a faulty aesthetic decision. Ironically, in the process—and either way—Kudlacek compromises her main subject's vision. (We also wonder what Ito thinks of the matter, but we only see him playing instruments in archival footage.)

As expected, Kudlacek offers Deren's work in fragments: after all, how could she show each entire Deren film (along with the biographical portions) and still maintain a reasonable running time? But truth be told, *In the Mirror of Maya Deren* would benefit greatly from having much more of Deren's early masterpieces, *Meshes* and *At Land* (1944), and much less of her dance-inspired later work: *A Study in Choreography for Camera* (1945), *Ritual in Transfigured Time* (1946), and *Meditation on Violence* (1948). Despite the on-screen protests from her friends, the earlier films are better—both artistically and thematically. It was in her first two films, for example, that Deren toyed self-reflexively with temporal and spatial tropes, which inspired an entire generation of avant-garde filmmakers (and, in turn, many mainstream artists of today). The later films, on the other hand, seem more like ethnographic records of exotic dances, offering little in terms of cinematic technique.

Deren's last completed film, *The Very Eye of Night* (1954) combines lively modern dancing with engaging special effects, but even it gets overshadowed by the on-the-set footage of Deren directing the dancers. The outtakes and scenes from unfinished Deren projects (also included) don't add much to the oeuvre, despite independent film maven Jonas Mekas's claim that they represent a cinematic "holy grail."

Intermittently, in the newly-shot portions, *In the Mirror of Maya Deren* forges a kind of Deren-like cine-poetry. Kudlacek films a woman at a steambeck, opening cassette tapes, et al., presumably with the hope of evoking Deren's spirit, but the result is something more akin to a re-enactment from a lurid cable-TV series about dead celebrities. In other bits, Kudlacek inserts shots of cool blue running water, a repetitive and all-too-obvious reference to

Deren's own fascination with the element. These "poetic" touches are saved only by John Zorn's rich, melancholic musical score. Clearly, though, Deren created true poetry, while the well-meaning Kudlacek can only conjure warmed-over prose.

At least those who never heard of Maya Deren will now have a documentary resource, however flawed, and Deren followers will probably settle for this tribute until something more fitting comes along.

—*Eric Monder*

CREDITS

Origin: Austria, Germany, Switzerland
Released: 2002
Production: Johannes Rosenberger, Constantin Wulff; Navigator Film, Dschoint Ventschr, TAG/TRAUM Filmproduktion; released by Zeitgeist Films
Directed by: Martina Kudiacek
Written by: Martina Kudiacek
Cinematography by: Wolfgang Lehner
Music by: John Sorn
Sound: Jan McLaughlin, Carl Fuermann
Editing: Henry Hills
MPAA rating: Unrated
Running time: 103 minutes

REVIEWS

Christian Science Monitor Online. January 24, 2003.
New York Post Online. January 24, 2003.
New York Times Online. January 24, 2003.
San Francisco Examiner Online. May 16, 2003.
Variety Online. June 18, 2002.

In This World (MII875II)

The journey to freedom has no borders.
—Movie tagline

In This World is a strange creature—a documentary that's not really a documentary. It sure does a great impression of one, though. It details the efforts of a young boy and his older cousin to smuggle themselves from an Afghan refugee camp in Pakistan to England. What's the point of making a staged story play like an unstaged one? In the case of *In This World*, it's to provide a reality and urgency that make the story seem all the more compelling. The details of the cousins' journey seem as harrowing as if it really did happen. Indeed, so realistic is *In This World* that it's possible to watch the film and not realize that it is fiction

In This World was part of the Sundance Film Series. The series released four different films to theaters; their only commonality was that they were deemed worthy of a wider audience by the Sundance powers-that-be. A clip of one of the filmmakers explaining what they were trying to do with the film introduced each of the offerings. In addition to Sundance, *In This World* was also a hit at other festivals and won the Golden Bear at Berlin.

The director of *In This World*, British filmmaker Michael Winterbottom, has made an eclectic roster of films. He was behind such diverse fare as *Welcome to Sarajevo, 24 Hour Party People, Wonderland,* and the Thomas Hardy adaptation, *Jude.* In the introduction to this latest film, he explained that he filmed much of it on the fly, without telling some of the people in the scenes that they were being filmed. Other things that helped the film get its natural look was that it was shot on a small handheld digital camera. They used natural light and many natural sounds. Instead of following a specific script, the actors were given general guidelines for their scenes. Tony Grisoni, who wrote the script, based the scenes on interviews he'd had with others who had made the perilous journey. The film was shot on the real, arduous route that smugglers take. Producer Anita Overland was a couple days ahead of the production and would set up scenes in advance.

Sixteen year old Jamal (Jamal Udin Torabi) and his older cousin, Enayat (Enayatullah) are played by nonprofessional Afghanis from refugee camps. The film introduces them at the Shamshatoo refugee camp in Pakistan. The people in the camp are there due to the 2001 U.S. bombing and the 1979 Soviet invasion. It is a place with little more than tents on dirt.

Enayat's family decides that he should go to London, England, to seek a better life. His young, bright-eyed cousin Jamal is sent along because he can speak English. The only way they can get to England is illegally. The two rustle up a big stack of money and give it to a middleman who will in turn pay the various helpers on the way when the two arrive in London.

According to the film, nearly one million people a year try to smuggle themselves from one place to another, but the process is by no means streamlined. The route from Afghanistan to London involves a motley series of dusty rooms, trucks, rail cars and boats. Much of the time, Jamal and Enayat, are waiting around trying to figure out what to do next. They are supposed to meet various people along the way who may or may not be there. They're not sure who to trust and, at more than one point on their journey, they're forced to come up with even more money for payment and/or bribery.

Winterbottom contrasts the scenes of tense danger with the off time between legs of their journey. At nearly every stop, no matter what country they're in, it's easy to find a group of boys willing to kick a soccer ball around. It's especially poignant to see these refugees finding refuge in a simple ball game.

There's not a lot of dialogue in the film. Enayat is quiet much of the time. He is old enough to realize the seriousness of their trek. Jamal is a more lighthearted boy. As the two lay awake at night in yet another unfamiliar bed, Jamal tries to amuse his cousin by telling silly stories.

The danger in the film seems very real. The cousins have to hide themselves on a series of trucks, including a fruit truck and a sheep truck. On one day, the two have to travel by hiding themselves under the body of a train. In another scene, the duo travels over a mountain range at night. The scene is filmed at night and lit only minimally. As the guys run over the range, the camera bumps and jostles behind them. The dim lighting, the nervous camera and the presence of nearby Turkish police toting guns make it seem all too real. Later, Jamal and Enayat make it to a bus only to be signaled out for being Afghans by authorities.

The most unsettling of these scenes is one in which they have to travel in a storage compartment of a ship. Their co-riders include a couple with an infant. The air starts running out and they start banging on their compartments and yelling for help. The trip is so harsh that some of the travelers will not make it out alive. *In This World* makes for fascinating, unsettling viewing.

A. O. Scott of the *New York Times* liked the film and pointed out that Winterbottom, "uses the raw immediacy of digital video and the open, dignified faces of his nonprofessional cast to emphasize what should be obvious but somehow never is: that each of these uprooted people is a distinct and precious human individual." Kenneth Turan of the *Los Angeles Times* observed, "The story *In This World* . . . finally wins us over because it is too disturbing and well told not to. When things go wrong for the travelers, we feel for them in the pit of the stomach every bit as much as if what happened was real." The *Chicago Tribune*'s Allison Benedikt gave the film 4 out of 4 stars and called it "breathtaking" and "amazing," adding that "the filmmakers' passion and urgency informs every inch."

—*Jill Hamilton*

CREDITS

Jamal: Jamal Udin Torabi
Enayat: Enayatullah
Travel agent: Imran Paracha
Enayat's brother: Hiddayatullah
Enayat's father: Jamau
Enayat's uncle: Wakeel Khan
Enayat's uncle: Lal Zarin
Jamal's older brother: Mirwais Torabi
Jamal's younger brother: Amanullah Torabi

Origin: Great Britain
Language: English, Farsi, Pashtu
Released: 2003
Production: Andrew Eaton, Anita Overland; BBC Films, Revolution Films, Film Consortium; released by Sundance Channel Pictures
Directed by: Michael Winterbottom
Cinematography by: Marcel Zyskind
Editing: Peter Christelis
MPAA rating: R
Running time: 88 minutes

REVIEWS

Box Office Magazine. Nov. 2003, p. 82.
Chicago Sun-Times Online. Sept. 19, 2003.
Entertainment Weekly. Oct. 10, 2003.
L.A. Times Online. Sept. 19, 2003.
New York Times Online. Sept. 19, 2003.
Variety Online. Dec. 11, 2003.
Washington Post. Sept. 19, 2003, p. WE41.

Intacto

All Bets Are On.
—Movie tagline

The Spanish film *Intacto*, like the recent Sundance entry *The Cooler*, asserts that luck is a commodity that can be given and received, won or lost, or traded away. Most people have ordinary luck, some have unusually good or bad luck, and then there are those like Tomas (Leonardo Sbaraglia), who is the only survivor of an airplane crash, beating the odds of 237 million to 1. He obviously has a gift very few possess, and that makes him a commodity.

The movie revolves around a man named Sam (Max von Sydow), who survived the Holocaust and now operates a remote casino at which rich people bet against his luck, usually unsuccessfully. So unshakable is his confidence that he will remove one bullet from a six-chamber gun, then bet that he will not die. (Interestingly, in *The Seventh Seal* Von Sydow played a game of chess with Death.) Sam believes that he will lose his luck if the wrong person looks at his face at the wrong time, or takes his photograph. To guard himself, he must often sit in a closed room with a hood over his face. One wonders if he thinks this is a high price to pay for good fortune. Sam has a young man named Federico (Eusebio Poncela) as his confederate; Federico also has good luck, and he searches for others who have this gift. When Sam and Federico have a falling out, Sam steals his luck, leaving Federico with little else to do but go searching for a protégé of his own. In his search he finds Tomas.

The themes of luck and gambling are also present in the similar film *The Cooler*. William H. Macy plays a man whose luck is so bad that he is employed by a casino to merely rub up against someone having a winning streak; then his luck changes. The narrative in *The Cooler*, though it is relatively straightforward, involves an element of fantasy. By comparison, *Intacto*, directed by the talented, young Juan Carlos Fresnadillo, is visually more wild. Using a fractured camera style, which can be effective at times, here seems to betray a lack of confidence in the story. *Intacto* does have another more human element that centers on Sara (Monica Lopez), a cop who is chasing Tomas while grieving from a tragic loss of her own.

More than I liked *Intacto*, I admired the film for its ingenious construction and the way it keeps a certain chilly distance between its story and the dangers of popular entertainment. It's a Hollywood premise, rotated into the world of the art film through mannerism and oblique storytelling.

There's a fashion right now among new writers and directors to create stories of labyrinthine complexity, so that watching them is like solving a puzzle. With *Intacto*, I knew as I walked out of the theater that I would need to see it again. I liked the film the second time, having gained a different perspective. I liked it the first time, too, but through instinct, not understanding.

When you solve the puzzle that is this film, have you learned anything you wouldn't have learned through a straight narrative, or have you simply had to pay some dues to arrive at the same place? Depends. *Pulp Fiction*, which jump-started the trend, depends crucially on its structure for its effect. *Intacto*, which is not as complex, may have an added layer of style, just for fun. That is permitted, but somewhere within that style there may be a hell of a thriller winking at us.

—*Laura Abraham*

CREDITS

Samuel Berg: Max von Sydow
Tomas: Leonardo Sbaraglia
Federico: Eusebio Poncela
Sara: Monica Lopez
Alejandro: Antonio Dechent
Ana: Paz Gomez

Origin: Spain
Language: English, Spanish
Released: 2001
Production: Fernando Bovaira, Enrique Lopez Lavigne; Sogecine, Telecino; released by Lions Gate Films
Directed by: Juan Carlos Fresnadillo
Written by: Juan Carlos Fresnadillo, Andres M. Koppel
Cinematography by: Xavier Jimenez
Music by: Lucio Godoy
Sound: Aitor Berenguer
Editing: Nacho Ruiz Capillas
Art Direction: Cesar Macarron
MPAA rating: R
Running time: 108 minutes

REVIEWS

Chicago Sun-Times Online. February 21, 2003.
Entertainment Weekly. January 10, 2003, p. 50.
New York Times. December 13, 2002, p. B28.
Variety Online. December 12, 2001.
Washington Post. January 24, 2003, p. WE41.

Intolerable Cruelty

A romantic comedy with bite.
—Movie tagline
Engage the enemy.
—Movie tagline

 Box Office: $35.1 million

For the first time, the sardonic satirists Joel and Ethan Coen have made a film that did not originate with them. They were hired by producer Brian Glazer to work on an existing script that was to be directed by Ron Howard, Glazer's usual partner. Somewhere along the line, Howard dropped out, and the Coens decided to make *Intolerable Cruelty* themselves. As their previous films have shown, the Coens are fans of classic American cinema, and they say they were drawn to this project because of its similarities to screwball comedies. Despite some occasionally amusing moments, the result, alas, is disappointing.

Miles Massy (George Clooney) is the most prominent divorce attorney in Beverly Hills. Marylin Rexroth (Catherine Zeta-Jones) hires private investigator Gus Petch (Cedric the Entertainer) to follow her philandering, very rich, much older husband, Rex (Edward Herrmann). After Rex is caught in a motel with a scantily clad blonde, Marylin files for divorce, and Rex seeks Miles's help.

Miles finds a surprise witness, Heinz, the Baron Krauss von Espy (Jonathan Hadary), who presents evidence that Marylin is a serial golddigger, thereby saving Rex's fortune. Marylin's developing revenge plot is aided by Miles's obvious infatuation with her luscious charms.

Marylin surprisingly arrives at Miles's office with her new fiancé, oil heir Howard D. Doyle (Billy Bob Thornton), to arrange for Miles's famous ironclad prenuptial agreement designed to protect Howard's wealth from scheming Marylin. (Harvard Law School offers a course on Miles's prenup.) Miles is torn between wanting to prevent Marylin's possible mischief and his distress that she is unavailable to him. His suspicions are confirmed when Howard tears up the prenup during the wedding ceremony and Marylin dumps her new husband shortly afterward.

In Las Vegas to address a divorce-attorney conference, Miles meets Marylin again, and before he knows what is happening, they are at a cheesy wedding chapel. A changed man because of his love for Marylin, Miles decides to abandon the divorce business and devote his legal energies to more worthy pursuits. But many more surprises are in store for the protagonists before they can find the inevitable true love.

Joel and Ethan Coen have cowritten three very good films that have also been directed by Joel: *Blood Simple* (1984), *Raising Arizona* (1987), and *The Man Who Wasn't There* (2002). These films exhibit an offbeat humor, a lucid visual style—greatly aided by Barry Sonnenfeld's ever-restless cinematography in the first two—unexpected plot developments, and excellent performances. The Coens are often criticized for being cold, cynical, heartless, and even cruel, traits that began to come to the fore with *Miller's Crossing* (1990) and *Barton Fink* (1991). Their most highly praised and most popular film, *Fargo* (1996), shows the Coens at their best and worst: highly original characters and situations and wonderful dialogue yet condescension toward the characters and jolting shifts in tone.

Intolerable Cruelty is intended to be Coen "light," but it seems too inconsequential and too ragged. The classic screwball comedies, such as *The Awful Truth* (1937), *Bringing Up Baby* (1938), *His Girl Friday* (1940), and *The Lady Eve* (1941), are extremely well made, with few elements not contributing to the overall effect. They celebrate the silliness of romantic love and lead logically to happy endings. Except for occasional sneering at the hoi-polloi, especially in *The Awful Truth*, they are never cruel and even praise, especially with Preston Sturges's films, eccentricities.

The influence of Sturges, the greatest writer-director of romantic comedies before Woody Allen, can be seen in the femme-fatale-seeking-revenge-against-besotted-male plot borrowed from *The Lady Eve*. Rex Rexroth's obsession with trains recalls the dining-car high jinks in Sturges's *The Palm Beach Story* (1942), and Miles's constant shifting from suavity to farcical confusion and back resembles Rex Harrison's jealous symphony conductor in *Unfaithfully Yours* (1948). Having a camp character with a name like Heinz, the Baron Krauss von Espy is also typical of Sturges's humor.

Despite these echoes, however, the style and tone of *Intolerable Cruelty* is more similar to the strained, often crude romantic comedies of the 1950s and 1960s, such as Frank Tashlin's *The Girl Can't Help It* (1956) and *Will Success Spoil Rock Hunter?* (1957), and the Doris Day-Rock Hudson sexless sex romps. Like the latter, *Intolerable Cruelty* has ugly cinematography, especially in the scenes in Miles's office, and, like them, it exudes a smug if superficial sophistication. As such, it is inferior to the more obvious Rock-and-Doris parody, *Down with Love* (2003), which at least has fun with the conventions of the genre.

Intolerable Cruelty has the edge on *Down with Love* only by having more charismatic stars. The immensely likable Clooney has said in interviews that Miles is a descendent of his singing hillbilly from the Coens' *O Brother, Where Art Thou?* (2000), whose title is borrowed from Sturges's *Sullivan's Travels* (1941). While both characters lurch from one mishap to another with bug-eyed bemusement, Clooney provides some variation with a few deadpan responses to the turmoil surrounding him. Other than the sleek suits and an obsession with his toothy smile, Miles is merely a sketch of a character, but Clooney makes him charming nonetheless.

Stars such as Humphrey Bogart, Cary Grant, Audrey Hepburn, Robert Mitchum, and Robert Redford are not performers who flaunt their acting skills the way people such as Marlon Brando and Meryl Streep do, and their efforts may seem to the unsophisticated eye not to be acting at all. These actors, however, recognize the value of underplaying their parts, trusting the camera to catch their subtleties. The camera loves Zeta-Jones, and she fleshes out the underwritten Marylin with her charisma. Even more than in the showier *Chicago* (2002), she gives a true movie-star performance, dominating every scene in which she appears.

Thornton offered an appropriately minimal performance as the blank-faced existential protagonist of *The Man Who Wasn't There*. Here, he is anything but minimal as the swaggering millionaire, imbuing Howard's apparent joy in Marylin with considerable gusto. The revelation late in the film that "Howard" is merely a soap-opera actor hired by Marylin to trick Miles makes Thornton's line readings even funnier in retrospect. Howard has a script and is determined to deliver all his lines, regardless of any interruptions or unforeseen developments.

At the beginning of the film, a television producer (Geoffrey Rush) drives home while singing along to Simon and Garfunkel's "The Boxer." The Marylin-Howard wedding opens with the priest walking toward the couple, playing a guitar, and singing "April Come She Will." During the

Marylin-Miles wedding, "Bridge Over Troubled Water" is played on bagpipes. The latter two are amusing, but the Simon and Garfunkel reference is inexplicable. Typical of the Coens' worst tendencies, a moronic hit man (Irwin Keyes) kills himself by accident and his death is supposed to be hilarious. Even worse, *Intolerable Cruelty* ends with a spoof of reality/hidden-camera/game-show television productions. Don't the Coens realize that one of the many reasons people have for going to theaters and watching DVDs is to avoid such depressing mindless trash? Intolerable cruelty, indeed.

—*Michael Adams*

Boston Globe. October 10, 2003, p. C1.
Chicago Sun-Times Online. October 10, 2003.
Entertainment Weekly. October 17, 2003, p. 58.
Los Angeles Times Online. October 10, 2003.
Maclean's. October 20, 2003, p. 57.
New York Times. October 10, 2003, p. E1.
People. October 20, 2003, p. 31.
Rolling Stone. October 30, 2003, p. 100.
San Francisco Chronicle. October 10, 2003, p. D1.
Sight and Sound. November, 2003, p. 30.
Time. October 20, 2003, p. 76.
USA Today. October 10, 2003, p. E5.
Variety Online. September 3, 2003.
Wall Street Journal. October 10, 2003, p. W1.
Washington Post. October 10, 2003, p. C1.

CREDITS

Miles Massey: George Clooney
Marylin Rexroth: Catherine Zeta-Jones
Donovan Donaly: Geoffrey Rush
Gus Petch: Cedric the Entertainer
Rex Rexroth: Edward Herrmann
Freddy Bender: Richard Jenkins
Howard Doyle: Billy Bob Thornton
Wrigley: Paul Adelstein
Wheezy Joe: Irwin Keyes
Sarah Sorkin: Julia Duffy
Herb Myerson: Tom Aldredge
Heinz, Baron Krauss von Espy: Jonathan Hadary
Bonnie Donaly: Stacey Travis
Mr. Gutman: Royce D. Applegate

Origin: USA
Released: 2003
Production: Ethan Coen, Brian Grazer; Imagine Entertainment, Alphaville; released by Universal Pictures
Directed by: Joel Coen
Written by: Joel Coen, Ethan Coen, Robert Ramsey, Matthew Stone
Cinematography by: Roger Deakins
Music by: Carter Burwell
Sound: Peter Kurland
Editing: Roderick Jaynes
Art Direction: Tony Fanning
Costumes: Mary Zophres
Production Design: Leslie McDonald
MPAA rating: PG-13
Running time: 100 minutes

REVIEWS

Atlanta Journal and Constitution. October 10, 2003, p. D1.
Baltimore Sun. October 10, 2003, p. E1.

QUOTES

Miles (George Clooney) ordering Marylin a steak: "I presume you're a carnivore?" Marylin (Catherine Zeta-Jones) replies: "Oh, Mr. Massey, you have no idea."
Rex (Edward Herrmann): "My wife has left me between a rock and a hard place." Miles (George Clooney): "That's her job. You should respect that."

TRIVIA

Bruce Campbell, who worked with the Coens' in *The Hudsucker Poxy*, cameos as a soap-opera actor.

Irreversible

Time destroys everything.
—Movie tagline

Iconoclastic French firebrand Gaspar Noe, in his electrifying, quasi-pornographic melodrama, *Irreversible,* explodes not just the tenets of linear film narratives, but the sterility of form that sustains them as well. In his first feature, *I Stand Alone* (1998), which was a New York Film Festival selection, and one that found distribution in the U.S. only belatedly, Noe interrupted the flow of his film to give the audience thirty seconds to leave the hall before its final half hour. In the case of *Irreversible,* the squeamish would be well advised to stay away altogether.

To do it justice, Noe's latest achievement has to be viewed outside the context of arthouse cinema. In his elemental vitality, as writer-director, Noe questions the very practice of turning films into aesthetic, "good" objects, despite the medium's origins in, and its proven propensity for, spectacle, sensation and vulgarity. Thus, regrettably,

Irreversible will not be seen by the very audience who are in a position to respond to its earthy realism, owing to the fact of the film being released only in a subtitled version.

Noe, while no means unique in his aspiration to turn linear film storytelling on its head, uses his license to do so by mixing in shocks and jolts that are bound to make the most jaded arthouse regular want to look away from the screen. *Irreversible* thus deserves to be described as much in terms of its sensationalistic aspects as by its dramatic quotient. What makes its sensationalism appear as pure spectacle is that we can make no narrative sense of it, while it assaults us. Eventually, of course, the scenes all hang together. What is remarkable, however, is that this antinomy in the film's narrative content is reflected in the film's form as well. The topsy-turvy, vertiginous camerawork, conveniently used for transitions, becomes difficult to watch, for sure. Ironically, however, the one prolonged shot lasting many minutes, where Noe's camera simply holds motionless, proves the most painful to endure.

Noe makes his narrative and formal intent known when he reverses the customary flow of credits to open his film with what is generally the tail end of the end credits: the union logos and copyright information. As the credits roll backwards, they begin to look jumbled as well. The action proper then begins with a handheld camera appearing to rotate around the brick façade of a seedy looking building. Shorn of all bearings to a physical reality, the viewer becomes dislocated, as in an avant-garde short. As bold as Kubrick in the final section of *2001: A Space Odyssey* (1968), Noe makes us feel we are watching an experimental film rather than one intended to tell us a story.

When he finally does cut to a scene, we get the feeling that the action is taking place in a kind of limbo. Two middle-aged male degenerates, one of them nude, appear lost in detumescent contemplation. "Time destroys all things," says the portly nude man. He then goes on to say how he was imprisoned for having slept with his daughter, but that she was all he had. The other man comforts him by saying that there are no bad deeds as such, "just deeds." This conversation on amorality by characters we will never see again prepares us ideologically for the harrowing action to follow. First, all we hear are the sirens.

We then find our bearings in front of the entrance to a sex club for homosexuals called "The Rectum." A body, that of Marcus (Vincent Cassel), is brought out on a stretcher. Then follows the battered body of Tenia (Jo Prestia). Last out of the building is Pierre (Albert Dupontel) in police custody. Inside the ambulance, Pierre looks after Marcus.

Noe then cuts to Marcus and Pierre entering that very club earlier that evening. Marcus looks muscular, large and outgoing, while Pierre looks just the opposite. They have come hunting for Tenia. In the process, they have to brush aside lewd proposals in a phantasmagoric world of "anything goes," rendered in red monochrome. When Marcus does

manage to locate his quarry, Tenia tries to sodomize him. Pierre then lifts a fire extinguisher and bludgeons Tenia repeatedly.

Noe then takes up the action in the police van as Pierre is questioned, then released. We then see Marcus, Pierre and two thugs as they are combing a side street for clues as to who raped Marcus's beautiful girlfriend, Alex (Monica Bellucci). A she-male prostitute tells them about Tenia and his hangout. Pierre tries to talk sense into Marcus, but the latter is consumed by a madness for revenge.

The scene that follows has Pierre and Marcus, carefree and jaunty, earlier that night, as they step out of a building, and into a commotion in the street. With a shock, Marcus sees that all the excitement is around the rape of Alex, whose body on a stretcher, her face battered beyond recognition, is wheeled past him. Pierre pleads with Marcus to follow the ambulance to the hospital, but Marcus can think of only revenge. Two thugs, who claim to know the turf, promise to find the rapist for a fee, so that Marcus can have his way, instead of the animal merely serving time in prison.

All the frenetic action we have been witnessing thus far now leads to the centerpiece of the film's narrative axis. Calm and cool, in a backless halter held up by strings around her neck, Alex steps out into the urban night. We see her only from the back. After being unable to hail a cab, and also unable to cross the busy thoroughfare, she decides to use an underpass. In the deserted passageway, she sees Tenia and a woman approaching. Tenia violently threatens the woman he's with before turning to Alex. He first gets Alex to lie face down on the ground. It becomes clear that his anger against her is class-oriented. Repeatedly, through this one-shot sequence, he curses her for being a rich woman, no doubt belonging to an economic strata from which he has been excluded. He then gets down himself and mounts her from the back, untying the strings of her "classy" dress.

Way in the background, as if to make plausible what would otherwise strain our credulity, a stranger enters the underpass, then walks away. Tenia stifles his victim's screams with one hand, as he sodomizes her, fully clothed, while ordering her to call him "Daddy." "Tell Daddy it's good!" he keeps repeating. When he has relieved himself, he falls on his back and sniffs from a tiny bottle. As Alex slowly gets to her knees, he stands up and kicks her in the face, intending to disfigure her beauty. When she falls helplessly, he kicks her in the head. He then smashes her face repeatedly on the concrete, abusing her verbally all the while. This is where Noe's camera at last moves to take in Tenia from a low angle, its very movement appearing a relief.

After what must surely be the most brutal depiction of hostility towards a woman in cinema, Noe returns to his handheld swirls of indecipherable physical reality. This time he settles on Pierre and Marcus at a party, where the two are snorting lines of white powder in the bathroom. Alex, in the very dress she was raped in, is dancing with two females.

What will slowly become clear is that Alex was Pierre's ex. We now see Marcus coming up from behind and embracing her lovingly. Alex however is quick to spot signs of illicit drug use from his face. "Your eyes look strange," she says to him, "and your jaw is flapping!" In protest, she decides to walk out of the party on her own, and into the start of the previous scene.

From this point on, Noe piles on the lyricism, at times extracting it from the most banal of scenes. A conversation on sexuality between Marcus, Pierre and Alex inside a subway on their way to the party never transcends the level of a TV sitcom, except for the bandying of four-letter words. Pierre says to Marcus, "What is it that you do that I couldn't do?" Alex interjects to argue that a woman's pleasure issues from the pleasure a man feels, that it is ineffable because it is the man's "body talking."

There then follows a sequence of Marcus and Alex in bed, at the start of the evening. Their sexual frolicking, despite the male frontal nudity, appears tame in relation to what Noe has bombarded us with. When Marcus steps out to get liquor before Pierre arrives, Alex gives herself a pregnancy test and is pleasantly surprised to find it is positive.

Noe then cuts to a shot of a pregnant Alex in bed, as she's feeling her abdomen. His camera then takes in the walls of the apartment with its poster of the "Star Child" from Kubrick's *2001*. However, it is not so much the latter that Noe seems to be paying tribute to as much as to the ending of another visionary masterwork, John Boorman's *Zardoz* (1974). In a manner identical to Boorman, Noe uses Beethoven's "Symphony No. 7" for his coda.

The film's final scene shows Alex reading a philosophical text, while on an idyllic picnic on the grass. Nearby, kids are playing near a rotating water hose. In a tribute to the philosophical exuberance of silent cinema, Noe ends his film with a title in a bold heading that reads: "Time destroys all things."

Critics have been unable to forgive the film's sensationalistic aspects or find anything redeeming in its depiction of depraved sexuality. At one end of the spectrum, Lou Lumenick in the *New York Post* calls Noe "a blatant opportunist exploiting violence and hatred to manufacture controversy." On a more generous scale, Elvis Mitchell in the *New York Times* finds "ambition and drive" in Noe's "prodigious filmmaking technique" which, according to Mitchell, results in *Irreversible* emerging as a "punk-operatic meditation on life, love, anger and—most important—guilt."

—*Vivek Adarkar*

CREDITS

Alex: Monica Bellucci
Marcus: Vincent Cassel

Pierre: Albert Dupontel
Le Tenia: Jo Prestia
Philippe: Philippe Nahon

Origin: France
Language: French
Released: 2002
Production: Richard Grandpierre, Christophe Rossignon; Nord-Ouest; released by Lions Gate Films
Directed by: Gasper Noe
Written by: Gasper Noe
Cinematography by: Gasper Noe
Music by: Thomas Bangalter
Sound: Jean-Luc Audy
Editing: Gasper Noe
Art Direction: Alain Juteau
MPAA rating: Unrated
Running time: 99 minutes

REVIEWS

Boxoffice. August, 2002, p. 55.
Chicago Sun-Times Online. March 14, 2003.
Entertainment Weekly. March 14, 2003, p. 45.
Los Angeles Times Online. March 7, 2003.
New York Times Online. March 2, 2003.
New York Times Online. March 7, 2003.
People. March 17, 2003, p. 36.
Rolling Stone. March 20, 2003, p. 74.
Sight and Sound. February, 2003, p. 20.
Sight and Sound. March, 2003, p. 46.
Variety. June 3, 2002, p. 22.
Washington Post. April 11, 2003, p. WE44.

It Runs in the Family

Some families can survive everything. As long as they have each other.
—Movie tagline

Box Office: $7.4 million

It Runs in the Family arrived in theaters with a big selling point. It had three generations of the Douglas family sharing the screen. The film looked like it might resemble the real-life-intersecting-with-drama dynamic that Jane and Henry Fonda had in *On Golden Pond*. In *It Runs in the Family*, the Douglas clan are too cool, or too timid, to let any real hurts and heartaches creep into the picture. Their characters collide, fight and resent each other but it never has the kind of unflattering desperation and misunderstanding that Jane Fonda's best scenes with Henry Fonda had. The Douglas' play at showing reality but it never seems more than play. Still, there's something to be said for the fun of figuring out the real-life from fictionalized aspects of the story.

Some of the dramas in the script, penned by Jesse Wigutow, seem to be drawn from the Douglas' real lives, or at least their real lives as viewed from the distance of tabloid reports. Alex Gromberg (Michael Douglas), for example, gets involved in extramarital activities and son Asher (Cameron Douglas) faces drug problems. The patriarch, Mitchell (Kirk Douglas), is a feisty old man who is aging and dealing with the slurred speech from his stroke.

What *It Runs in the Family* does best is offer a look at every age. The problems of youngest son, Eli (Rory Culkin), are given as much attention as the problems of Mitchell. Movies often stick with one age range, usually the demographically desirable 14-32 and offer the other ages as comic relief or inconsequential. The film is particularly good at offering an unflinching look at old age. Mitchell's speech impediment is treated, not as something tragic or to be heroically overcome, but just as something that is to be lived with.

The film shows the old man jogging, albeit very slowly, through the park and bumped aside by uncaring young people in a hurry. It's not there to show "look at the poor old man" but more to show what it's like to try to maintain dignity in a world that doesn't see you as quite human anymore. Stephanie Zacharek of *Salon* wrote, "the elderly characters in *It Runs in the Family* are the most vital ones, maybe because the movie doesn't condescend to them. It doesn't make them the butt of cutesy *Grumpy Old Men*-type jokes. Nor does it look like an AARP brochure loaded with pictures of cheerful, vigorous seniors leading active and productive lives (the reality is that some are simply not able.)"

The film doesn't follow one big plot line, but has several things going on at once. At the beginning of the film, the family all meet for a Seder dinner. Evelyn (Diana Douglas, Kirk's first wife and Michael's mother) tries to soothe the hurt that Mitchell's harsh remarks make. Alex is a successful lawyer at the firm that his father founded, but he wishes for some sort of approval from his father. His wife, Rebecca (Bernadette Peters) is a successful psychologist and she takes the Evelyn junior role, soothing the tension between the men. Asher is a slacker kid who likes to get high and has started dealing drugs. Eli is an overly controlled kid who presents his parents with a spread sheet detailing his expenses when he wants a raise in his allowance.

Many of the Douglas, er, Gromberg men are having female troubles. Eli is a good boy who is nursing a crush on a bad girl with a nose ring (Irene Gorovaia). Asher is starting to pursue a relationship with a go-getter fellow student, Peg

Maloney (Michelle Monaghan). And Alex, who volunteers in a soup kitchen, gets involved in some heavy foreplay with another worker, Suzie (Sarita Choudhury). Even though the two don't have "sexual relations," the Gromberg's marriage starts to fall apart when Rebecca discovers women's panties in her husband's pocket. It's interesting that in this possibly-biographical film, the marital troubles don't involve real infidelity but only semi-cheating. Even during his clench with Suzie, Alex is basically attacked by the lusty coworker and therefore someone relieved of any misdoings. (Odd that in several Michael Douglas films, he has been the victim of female sexual aggressiveness.)

Things happen. There are two deaths. Asher gets busted from growing pot in his room. Asher catches a big fish. But the events are secondary to the way the characters react to each other about these events. Director Fred Schepisi (*Roxanne* and *Last Orders*) keeps the disparate plot points in a coherent order.

The performances are fun to watch, if not for their technical perfection, for the voyeuristic thrill of watching a family act together. Best is Kirk, whose warts and all performance is liberating, fun and poignant at the same time. Diana, who has been amicably divorced from Kirk for over 50 years, is strong and loving, as the mother who knows just how to hold the family together, as mothers seem to be able to do. Michael is blander that usual as the son wanting approval from his dad, while at the same time neglecting his own sons. There is the sense that he is unable to be as open playing himself (or a version of himself) than he is playing a completely made-up character. Cameron is suitably directionless as the confused pothead son. The non-Douglas members give good performances. It's nice to see Peters on the screen as the wife whose world is shattered by her husband's indiscretion. And Culkin (yet another member of his own acting family) is appropriately inscrutable as the 11-year-old that his parents can't figure out.

Critics had mixed reactions to the film. Roger Ebert of the *Chicago Sun-Times* wrote, "The movie is simply not clear about where it wants to go and what it wants to do. It is heavy on episode and light on insight, and although it takes courage to bring up touchy topics it would have taken more to treat them frankly." Stephen Holden of the *New York Times* was not immune to the celebrity-gawking aspect of the film and wrote, "Fiction and reality are so seamlessly blended in *It Runs in the Family*, a surprisingly complex and subtle portrait of the Grombergs, a high-powered clan of New York lawyers, that the temptation to assume its characters are modeled after the actors playing them is almost irresistible." Stephanie Zacharek lauded Kirk's performance and wrote, "Kirk Douglas, at 86, isn't just playing old; he is old. That fact hasn't escaped him for a minute, and he puts it in front of the camera, baldly, without vanity." Rita Kempley of the *Washington Post* also noted Kirk's acting. "Michael, not at the top of his game here, is upstaged by his 86-year-old dad. The old guy still has a twinkle in his eye, scene-stealing savvy and most of all, the courage to fail."

—*Jill Hamilton*

CREDITS

Alex Gromberg: Michael Douglas
Mitchell Gromberg: Kirk Douglas
Evelyn Gromberg: Diana Douglas
Asher Gromberg: Cameron Douglas
Eli Gromberg: Rory Culkin
Rebecca Gromberg: Bernadette Peters
Peg Maloney: Michelle Monaghan
Malik: Geoffrey Arend
Suzie: Sarita Choudhury
Deb: Annie Golden
Abby Staley: Irene Gorovaia
Stephen Gromberg: Mark Hammer
Sarah Langley: Audra McDonald

Origin: USA
Released: 2003
Production: Michael Douglas; Further Films, Metro-Goldwyn-Mayer, Buena Vista; released by MGM
Directed by: Fred Schepisi
Written by: Jesse Wigutow
Cinematography by: Ian Baker
Music by: Paul Grabowsky
Sound: Michael Barosky
Music Supervisor: Sue Jacobs
Editing: Kate Williams
Art Direction: George Allison
Costumes: Marit Allen
Production Design: Patrizia Von Brandenstein
MPAA rating: PG-13
Running time: 101 minutes

REVIEWS

Chicago Sun-Times Online. April 25, 2003.
Entertainment Weekly. May 2, 2003, p. 51.
Los Angeles Times Online. April 25, 2003.
New York Times Online. April 25, 2003.
People. May 5, 2003, p. 38.
Variety Online. April 20, 2003.
Washington Post. April 25, 2003, p. WE50.

QUOTES

Alex (Michael Douglas) in response to a crisis: "We're a family. We'll figure it out."

The Italian Job

Get in. Get out. Get even.
—Movie tagline

 Box Office: $106.1 million

There is a scene early on in *The Italian Job* in which Edward Norton's character unleashes a startlingly savage assault on his comrades, blasting round after round in a relentless, ruthless onslaught. It is a highly effective, jolting moment, a chilling display by a fiercely determined, merciless monster. If one wonders how the actor got into the proper frame of mind to make such an ugly spectacle believable, perhaps he might have been thinking about the executives at Paramount Pictures who forced him into making the film against his will. It seems the studio finally lost patience with Norton after he had continuously rejected projects in recent years which would have completed the three picture deal he signed back in the 1990's. Norton had no interest whatsoever in making *The Italian Job*, and was livid about being compelled to join the cast. If his anger fueled the ferocity of his performance (which harks back to his role in 2001's *The Score*), it served him well.

The production Norton was required to be a part of is a satisfactorily involving heist film featuring high speed car, boat and helicopter chases, it is also a remake of the 1969 film which failed to find an audience in the U.S. but remains a particular favorite in England and Italy. That film featured one of the most bizarrely diverse casts in film history, including Michael Caine, Noel Coward, Benny Hill, and Rossano Brazzi. It was a caper comedy about Charlie Crocker (Caine) and a motley crew who steal $4 million in gold in Turin and then escape the massive traffic jam they cause by dashing off in sporty little MINI Coopers. The remake puts a greater emphasis on action and suspense than laughs, although there are some to be had here. Director F. Gary Gray referred to his film as an homage to, or "reinventing" of, the original. While basic elements, such as the MINIs (recently reintroduced by BMW), the heist, the traffic jam, and the car chases have been kept, the rest has undergone an extensive overhaul.

For the film to succeed, the filmmakers must get the audience to like, and root for the success of, a bunch of thieves. Besides fostering our sneaking admiration for their startling talents and precision teamwork, there is a successful effort from the beginning to make them affable and to humanize them, particularly with the character of John Bridger (Donald Sutherland, who previously had a most memorable cinematic trip to Venice in 1973's *Don't Look Now*). The film opens with John, an old hand at safe-cracking, having a warm telephone conversation with his daughter Stella (Charlize Theron). Half a world away on what he assures her will be his "last job," John clearly misses her and tries to make up for yet another absence from her life by sending his love in the form of "something sparkly." Stella obviously worries about the danger inherent in his chosen field and wants him out of it for good, no doubt preferring his actual presence to any compensatory bauble. Stella asks if his immensely capable protege Charlie (Mark Wahlberg, much better here than in his last remake outing, *The Truth About Charlie*) is there, and the fact that he is the master-mind of "the Italian Job" seems to reassure her, but only to a certain degree. Although this scene seems to foreshadow something ominous on the horizon for John and creates a sense of foreboding, when we meet the expert crew assembled to pull off this verboten Venetian venture there appears to be little reason for concern. There is inside man Steve (Norton), computer whiz Lyle (Seth Green), explosives expert Left-Ear (Mos Def) and getaway driver/lothario Handsome Rob (Jason Statham). The heist itself is an ingenious, brazen, and meticulously planned scheme to extricate $35 million dollars (inflation, you know) in gold bricks from a safe guarded within an Italian palazzo. Instead of trying to make their way in with guns blazing, they opt to have the gold come to them by exploding away the floor beneath the safe and having it drop down into the canal below where they lay in wait. The execution of this plan is not only successful, it's undeniably impressive and exciting, featuring boats careening at fierce speeds through the city's historic, beloved, and carefully preserved canal system. (Gray had to get special permission to film these sequences, which were strictly regulated by local government officials.) While the realism of these scenes may be questionable, they certainly grab attention. Dramatic, urgent music is used to good effect to further intensify the action throughout

After the job is done, the camera sweeps high up into the sky, and when it comes back down to Earth we are deposited amongst the remote, forbidding but beautiful scenery of the Italian Alps, where all are gathered to toast their success. Here, while various members of the group dream of the glorious things their take might bring them, John talks wistfully about what his pursuit of ill-gotten gains has cost him, especially missed time with Stella. He offers sage advice to Charlie about taking the time to find a girl and true happiness, which once again hints broadly that John is not long for this world. Sure enough, Steve soon whips out his gun for the aforementioned chilling moment amongst the

frigid scenery, killing John and trying to slaughter the rest, as well. The stunning bursts of gunfire, as well as the eerie silences between as Steve scans the water for confirmation of his former comrades' demise, have a great and unsettling impact. There is also some admirable camera work from under the water's surface. The survivors, particularly Charlie, are rocked by the fact that one of their own has committed a double-cross and killed the group's venerable father figure. It will now be a supreme test of their abilities for the remaining thieves to catch the one that got away with all the loot. There is, it appears, honor amongst thieves, and the ferocity and cold-bloodedness of Steve's abhorrent attack has served to put us squarely in their corner.

The setting then shifts to Philadelphia one year later, and we see that Stella is as practiced as her father at opening safes, only she does it legally when an owner requests assistance. Charlie arrives to tell her that Steve and his stash have been located in Los Angeles, and she at first wants no part of any plan, not at all eager to rip open emotional wounds that are still very much in evidence. Still, she ends up agreeing to lend her expertise so Steve will get his comeuppance. There are exciting hitches, such as when Stella, having posed as a cable repairwoman in order to scope out Steve's lavish abode, accidentally blows her cover. Learning that the gang's all there and after him, Steve puts his own plan into action to transport the bullion south of the border. A determined battle is on between the two sides to outwit each other, and once again the action is sufficiently fast paced and riveting to successfully detour past questions of plausibility. While Steve fumes overhead in a helicopter, the truck with gold is stalled in traffic and the pavement below it falls away thanks to Left-Ear's well-placed explosives. In getting away with the bullion, Charlie and company thread MINI Coopers through all the standing vehicles, jolt down the stairs and into the subway, and whiz through storm drains with the bad guys gaining on them all the while. The suspense of these scenes is greatly enhanced by expert cutting and effective use of dynamic music. When Steve finally gets what is coming to him, and his former partners in crime are seen celebrating and getting satisfaction out of what their efforts have brought them, we are satisfied, as well.

Hearing Wahlberg say that even thinking about *The Italian Job* makes him queasy sounds uncomplimentary to the finished product until you learn that his nausea results from recalling all the lightning-fast, stomach churning car maneuvers practiced by the actors at California's Willow Springs Raceway before production began. Gray made a conscious decision not to rely on computer generated imagery to make his action scenes eye-catching, preferring real vehicles, driven as much as possible by the actors themselves. While Theron especially relished all the twisting, turning, and up-shifting, Wahlberg was busy upchucking. He exhibits more command over his role than his lunch, however, anchoring the film with a solid, amiable (if somewhat bland) performance. Wahlberg worked previously with Gray on music videos back when the actor was rapping under the moniker Marky Mark. Next to Norton, perhaps the most memorable performance is that of Green, who adds levity as the cranky computer genius who insists that the idea for Napster was stolen from him by his college roommate while he took a nap. (Napster founder Shawn Fanning has a cameo.) It is interesting to note that Gray had his cast pull off a heist of items including computers, old movie posters, and even daily rushes from the *How To Lose a Guy in 10 Days* set on the Paramount lot, which understandably caused considerable outrage at the studio (even though all of the items were later returned). Made on a budget of $75 million, *The Italian Job* grossed over $103 million. The majority of reviews were favorable. It roared into theaters during a year which featured plenty of automotive excitement in *2 Fast, 2 Furious*, *Charlie's Angels: Full Throttle*, and *The Matrix: Reloaded*, among numerous others. *The Italian Job* compares favorably as slick and enjoyable summer fare.

—*David L. Boxerbaum*

CREDITS

Charlie Croker: Mark Wahlberg
Steve: Edward Norton
Stella Bridger: Charlize Theron
Left Ear: Dante "Mos Def" Beze
Lyle: Seth Green
Handsome Rob: Jason Statham
John Bridger: Donald Sutherland
Christina Griego: Christina Cabot
Wrench: Franky G.
Mashkov: Olek Krupa

Origin: USA
Released: 2003
Production: Donald De Line; released by Paramount Pictures
Directed by: F. Gary Gray
Written by: Wayne Powers, Donna Powers
Cinematography by: Wally Pfister
Music by: John Powell
Sound: Douglas B. Arnold
Music Supervisor: Kathy Nelson, Julianne Jordan
Editing: Richard Francis-Bruce, Christopher Rouse
Art Direction: Doug Meerdink, Mark Zuelzke
Costumes: Mark Bridges
Production Design: Charles Wood
MPAA rating: PG-13
Running time: 111 minutes

REVIEWS

Chicago Sun-Times Online. May 30, 2003.
Entertainment Weekly. June 6, 2003, p. 55.
Los Angeles Times Online. May 4, 2003.
Los Angeles Times. May 30, 2003, p. E8.
New York Times. May 30, 2003, p. E13.
People. June 9, 2003, p. 34.
Rolling Stone. June 26, 2003, p. 87.
Variety. June 2, 2003, p. 42.
Wall Street Journal. May 30, 2003, p. W9.
Washington Post. May 30, 2003, p. C1.

QUOTES

Charlie (Mark Wahlberg): "You know what "fine" means? Freaked out, irrational, neurotic, and emotional."

TRIVIA

BMW, which bought Rover, the Mini Cooper's original manufacturer, in 1994, reintroduced the car to the U.S. market in 2002.

Jeepers Creepers 2

He can taste your fear.
—Movie tagline

Box Office: $35.6 million

*J*eepers Creepers 2 is the sequel to the 2001's *Jeepers Creepers*. In that film, a brother and sister driving through the middle of nowhere (mental note: to avoid crazed and/or supernatural killing beings, avoid trips through the middle of nowhere, especially in questionable vehicles) stumbled upon a cave full of corpses artfully arranged on the walls and ceilings. The cave was the handiwork, the hobby, if you will, of one freaky killing monster referred to as The Creeper (Jonathan Breck). In that movie we learned that the Creeper eats various people. Like humans and their food pyramid, the Creeper makes his choices according to his nutritional needs. If he needs new eyes, for example, he picks someone with superior eyesight, as the hero of the first film learned in the particularly memorable ending. We also learned the important fact that anyone who is going to die hears the song "Jeepers Creepers." It was a strange choice of song, but that was part of the first movie's semi-charm. For some reason, even though the film received its name from this particular characteristic, *Jeepers Creepers 2* never once mentions the song.

This Creeper also eats every 23 years for 23 days, then goes into some sort of hibernation. At the time of the second movie, there are only a couple of days left in the Creeper's feeding cycle. At the beginning of the film, the audience sees the words: "Every 23rd spring . . . for 23 days . . . it gets to eat." That short sentence is spread out over three different screens for those who are not the quickest of readers (and we are not, by any means, suggesting that the viewers of *Jeepers Creepers 2* are anything but the most literate of folks.) Still, some of the movie's first dialogue is this: Dad: "Billy!" Billy: "Help!" "Billy!" "Help!" "Billy!" "Help!" (keep repeating).

It's odd that the makers of *Jeepers Creepers 2* backed themselves into such a corner with this timing thing. Will future sequels have to take place 23 years in the future? Or will they wait 23 years to make the next one? Most likely, we can expect sequels to detail the Creepers various killings on, perhaps, days 10 through 12.

You'd think that a mysterious winged creature swooping down out of the sky and snatching up kids for dinner would rate a mention on the news and thus some sort of police action. At the very least, you'd think that people might want to avoid the area, but horror movies often require human stupidity, and here that is in full supply.

A bus carrying a high school basketball team, the Bannon High Bantams, is driving on a lightly used road as the team celebrates their recent victory at the state championships. (Why are the victims of horrible creatures never, say, plump middle-aged suburbanites?) The team is accompanied by various adult chaperones and the cheerleaders. One obnoxious guy, Scott Braddock (Eric Nenniger) is complaining to his girlfriend that he doesn't get played enough because the coach favors the black players. To add to his charm, he also likes to make fun of the guy he suspects of being gay. Later in the film, you can bet that he will be the one urging the group to split up.

As the kids are merrily rolling along, the bus suddenly lurches. It seems the bus's tire has been a victim of some sort of throwing disk made of claws. For extra decoration, the person who made the disk added a human tooth sitting jauntily in the middle. While they wait for help to come, the riders stand around mystified and do things like making fun of each other and peeing in a nearby field. This is the chance for writer-director Victor Salva, who also helmed the first film, to flesh out the characters. Since the characters don't have any depth, this doesn't take too long, although it sure seems like it. When it becomes apparent that no help is coming, the driver decides to limp the bus along. But soon another claw-Frisbee thing hits another tire. This one is decorated with what looks an awful lot like a human belly button.

This time the bus isn't going anywhere. The driver tries vainly to radio for help and the coaches try to keep their rowdy crew in line. Soon all the grown-ups are offed. One minute they are standing there, then in the next, they are picked up by some sort of flying creature and whooshed away. The kids are alone, trapped in a bus and they are being stalked by the monster. The confined quarters might provide for some sort of psychological drama with the characters, but instead it just makes the whole movie confined. The lack of variety makes it seem like it was developed from some sort of really bad stage play.

To fill time, the characters split up, leave the bus, get back on the bus and do it all again. Along the way, many of them are eaten in a variety of yucky ways. There are a lot of shots of the kids stuck in the bus, cramming their faces against the windows to get a good look at just what the heck that is outside. This quickly grows tedious.

Jeepers Creepers offers little in the way of surprise except, breaking horror movie convention, the white guys go first and the black guys get to live longer. And there is a cool sequence in which Minxie Hayes (Nicki Aycox) has psychic insights into the killer. In the scene, she sees characters from the first film frantically waving to her and the bus riders to turn back. It's nicely eerie.

If any critics had anything to say that was positive about the film, it usually had something to do with the direction of Francis Ford Coppola protégé Salva. Even when he's filming schlock, he makes it look nice. The cornfields are nicely lit and the shots are well composed. The odd thing is that he wrote such wretched stuff for himself to film.

Otherwise, critics weren't enthralled. Dave Kehr of the *New York Times* wrote, "Salva will have to make his creature something more than a slithering, slobbering, wholly malignant presence if he wants his franchise to succeed. Even monsters need more than one dimension to make it in the movies." Scott Brown of *Entertainment Weekly* gave the film a C– and wrote, "Salva squanders all of his original movie's not-entirely-awfulness and bumbles into the realm of unintentional comedy. (Two words: Headless break dancing.)" Ellen Fox of the *Chicago Tribune* gave the film 1 1/2 stars out of 4 and wrote, "Horror movies don't have to make sense in the real world, but when you have to help their internal logic along this much, it's pretty much a cue for heckling—or checking your watch." Roger Ebert of the *Chicago Sun-Times* wrote, "*Jeepers Creepers 2* supplies us with a first-class creature, a fourth-rate story, and dialogue possibly created by feeding the screenplay into a pasta maker."

—*Jill Hamilton*

CREDITS

Jack Taggart: Ray Wise
The Creeper: Jonathan Breck
Garikayi Mutambirwa: Deaundre "Double D" Davis

Scott Braddock: Eric Nenninger
Minxie Hayes: Nicki Aycox
Izzy Bohen: Travis Schiffner
Chelsea Farmer: Lena Cardwell
Bucky: Billy Aaron Brown
Johnny: Drew Tyler Bell
Rhonda Truitt: Marieh Delfino

Origin: USA
Released: 2003
Production: Tom Luse; United Artists, American Zoetrope, Myriad Pictures; released by MGM
Directed by: Victor Salva
Written by: Victor Salva
Cinematography by: Don E. Fauntleroy
Music by: Bennett Salvay
Sound: Steve Aaron
Editing: Ed Marx
Art Direction: Nanci B. Roberts
Costumes: Jana Stern
Production Design: Peter Jamison
MPAA rating: R
Running time: 103 minutes

 REVIEWS

Chicago Sun-Times Online. August 29, 2003.
Entertainment Weekly. September 12, 2003, p. 132.
Los Angeles Times Online. August 29, 2003.
New York Times Online. August 29, 2003.
USA Today Online. August 29, 2003.
Variety Online. August 28, 2003.
Washington Post. August 28, 2003, p. WE35.

Jet Lag (Decalage Horaire)

The battle of the sexes just got sexier.
—Movie tagline

Jet Lag opens with a wistful voiceover by the beautiful Rose (Juliette Binoche), in which she marvels at all the seemingly impossible dreams that get fulfilled in American movies and wishes for a day when her life could resemble such a fantasy. It is not hard to guess that her hope will soon be fulfilled. Stranded in Charles de Gaulle Airport, Rose meets a man named Félix (Jean Reno), who at first appears to be totally wrong for her but may understand her better than anyone. That they will fall in love is a given in a film

that relies on the old formula that opposites attract, no matter how many personality conflicts they need to overcome. While *Jet Lag* may not break new ground cinematically or do anything boldly original, it consistently pleases on the strength of its two leads and its sweetly old-fashioned belief in romance and the surprise of love in the most unexpected of places.

Binoche and Reno are not generally known for light comedy and may seem an unlikely couple, but somehow the odd combination of her radiance and his glumness works perfectly. Even when the characters are making unbelievably wide swings from casual acquaintances to friends to enemies to possible lovers in the matter of just a few hours together, we believe in them. Apart from a bit of frank sex talk and reliance on the cell phone as a prop bringing the lovers together, *Jet Lag* could be a 1930s Hollywood romantic comedy, an *It Happened One Night* in which the mismatched couple do not hit the road but rather stay in one place to discover their affection for each other.

The screenplay, written by director Danièle Thompson along with her son, Christopher Thompson, conspires, through a series of delays (a strike, computer failure, bad weather), to keep its would-be lovers grounded, constantly missing flights so they can explore a developing attraction neither would have anticipated. The setup may be familiar, and the thin plot might not have been very compelling with any other actors. But Binoche's winning combination of sex appeal and smarts is charming, and Reno complements her nicely in his rumpled, perpetually panic-stricken state.

Félix and Rose are not only stranded physically but emotionally and romantically as well. He is trying to get to Munich so he can get back in touch with an old girlfriend who does not want anything to do with him, while Rose is trying to flee a 12-year-long, dead-end relationship and get a fresh start in Acapulco. Through a series of comic mishaps, beginning with Rose's need to borrow Félix's cell phone after she flushes hers down a toilet, they get acquainted, and, when her jealous, abusive boyfriend, Sergio (Sergi Lopez), shows up, Félix gives her the encouragement to walk away.

Feeling sorry that she has to sleep in the airport waiting area, Félix offers to share his hotel room, and, almost immediately, silly little differences suggest their incompatibility. Félix is hot and opens the window; Rose later closes it. Her perfume is too strong for him, and her liberal use of hairspray will probably make matters worse. She has a sentimental streak, crying when she hears "La Marseillaise" on TV because it is a reminder of her Communist upbringing, whereas he keeps his emotions tightly guarded.

Engaging in the witty, biting banter that is a hallmark of the best romantic comedies, each is able to point out the other's foibles, especially the barriers that prevent them from having healthy relationships. Félix is a former chef who now lives a workaholic existence running a successful frozen foods company. The transition he has made in life is telling;

he has forsaken the sensual art of cooking for the cold world of commerce. To strengthen the metaphor, his foods are frozen, just as he is romantically. At one point, Rose tells him that he needs to thaw out and compares him to a duck in orange sauce frozen in a plastic bag. Her life may be chaotic, but at least she engages in sensual pleasures—something she implies that he is unable to do. He is always moving from country to country and doing business on the Web, the most sterile of environments. There are no smells on the Web, she points out, and she personally loves all kinds of smells. His allergies and anxieties, it seems, represent a deeper problem, an allergy to people and the exciting messiness of life.

But if he needs to take life a little easier and open himself up emotionally, maybe Rose needs to let the world see her natural beauty. She is a beautician whose fondness for cosmetics and lots of hairspray makes her seem superficial, and Félix is not afraid to comment that she wears too much makeup. To her, it is like clothing, she cheerfully declares, but maybe it is a kind of façade that she puts up, separating her from others and possibly preventing the real Rose from emerging.

Only when she removes her makeup, in fact, does Félix see a woman he could love. If she has been hiding, however, so has he, having given up his true talent in the kitchen for the business world. But in his effort to impress Rose by renting the hotel kitchen and cooking her a sumptuous, late-night meal, he rediscovers himself in the process. Despite Rose's initial shallowness and concern with surfaces, Binoche never plays her as someone to be made fun of. On the contrary, Rose's passion becomes infectious, and reminding the dour Félix that he can embrace life as she does may be her greatest gift to him.

That night he tells Rose about the defining moment of his youth when, at 17, he cooked a special dish for his father, who would not recognize its greatness. Félix left home the next day and has not returned since. This big revelation is the film's only major misstep—how could a longstanding feud between a father and son erupt over a single meal? It is a ludicrous story that serves merely as a setup for a reconciliation, as if we needed more proof beyond his love for Rose that Félix is becoming a better man.

Jet Lag may rely on one plot contrivance too many to keep the lovers apart only to have them later reunite. But the innate appeal of the leads keeps us interested. Just as it seems Félix has backed out on seeing Rose before her flight finally takes off, he arrives but is too late. He calls the airport in Acapulco so that he can get a message to her, declaring his love and asking her to fly back and meet him at the airport in Paris. (Conveniently enough, she is still carrying his cell phone.) Devising this last-minute scheme to win her back, Félix demonstrates that he has truly fallen for Rose. After all, he is forced to make a spontaneous gesture of devotion,

something he is not used to doing in his well-ordered life. The conclusion may be a bit cumbersome and not as sweepingly romantic as the final clinch we may have been hoping for, but seeing Rose's smile at the end is enough to send the audience out smiling as well.

—*Peter N. Chumo II*

CREDITS

Rose: Juliette Binoche
Felix: Jean Reno
Sergio: Sergi Lopez

Origin: France, Great Britain
Language: French
Released: 2002
Production: Alain Sarde; TF-1 Films, Pathe; released by Miramax Films
Directed by: Daniele Thompson
Written by: Daniele Thompson, Christopher Thompson
Cinematography by: Patrick Blossier
Music by: Eric Serra
Sound: Pierre Gamet
Editing: Sylvie Landra
Art Direction: Michele Abbe
Costumes: Elisabeth Tavernier
MPAA rating: R
Running time: 81 minutes

REVIEWS

Boxoffice. November, 2002, p. 130.
Entertainment Weekly. June 20, 2003, p. 55.
Chicago Sun-Times Online. June 27, 2003.
Los Angeles Times Online. June 13, 2003.
New York Times Online. June 13, 2003.
Variety Online. October 2, 2002.
Washington Post. June 27, 2003, p. WE34.

Johnny English

He knows no Fear. He knows no Danger. He knows Nothing.
—Movie tagline
He isn't the best they have . . . he's the only one left.
—Movie tagline

Box Office: $28 million

Some people are fans of Rowan Atkinson's mostly-silent and hapless Mr. Bean. Some people are fans of Rowan Atkinson's malevolently funny Black Adder. But even the biggest fans of the undisputed comic genius of Rowan Atkinson—of whom this writer is one—are going to find *Johnny English* may not be worth the price of admission. Its story is incredibly predictable, the gags groanable, the characters time-worn, and there's nary a laugh in sight.

The movie begins with the suave secret agent Johnny English (Rowan Atkinson) sneaking into a manor house, diverting vicious guard dogs with squeaky toys, easily doing away with machine-gun toting guards, and seducing a sexy villainess all without a drop of perspiration breaking out on his brow. Immediately one knows this has to be a dream or a daydream just because of what one knows about Rowan Atkinson. And so it is.

Johnny English is not a secret agent, he's just another drone working in British intelligence and wanting nothing more than to be James Bond. When all of Britain's secret agents are killed at a funeral—how probably is this?—the only possible person to fill the ranks is the inept, pompous Johnny English. His first mission, to guard the crown jewels, which are going on exhibit again at the Tower of London after being restored by a corporate sponsor, Sauvage Industries . . . a French company.

The head of this company is Pascal Sauvage (John Malkovich) who is very bitter because 200 years ago his family should have inherited the throne of Britain but was cast aside. Pascal wants to be king of England. To accomplish this he must do the following: get the Queen to abdicate, which he accomplishes by putting a gun to her corgi's head; put a crony in the position of archbishop of Canterbury who will perform the coronation; and steal the crown jewels in order to have a crown to put on his head.

This last necessity puts Sauvage in contact with English. It also puts English in contact with lovely Interpol agent Lorna Campbell (Aussie pop star Natalie Imbruglia in her first feature film). It doesn't take a set of tarot cards to predict that Johnny will unsuccessfully try to seduce Lorna while insulting host Sauvage whom he mistakes as a waiter. Then, during the unveiling, the lights go out, the jewels are stolen and Johnny, of course, hits the head of British security over the head. To distract from his faux pas—something he does a lot—English stages a fake fight with a fake assailant whom he describes to a police sketch artist using a bowl of fruit as his inspiration.

Following the tunnel below the stolen jewels, English and his trusty sidekick Bough, which is pronounced "Boff" (Ben Miller), arrive just in time to see them being loaded into a casket and a hearse. A slapstick chase follows and you don't need a Ouija board to know they will end up following the wrong hearse and seriously interrupting a real funeral trying to expose the jewels. The rest of the movie is spent with Johnny knowing Sauvage is up to something evil but being unable to prove it to his boss and botching every opportunity to do so.

Johnny English has been a huge hit throughout Britain. It has opened in the number one position in at least 30 countries and has remained in a top 10 position for six weeks in every country where it has played . . . except America. Perhaps this is due to the fact that American audiences haven't been primed for the Johnny English character the way Britain and other countries have been. For, you see, Johnny English began his career in television commercials. From 1992 to 1997 Rowan Atkinson appeared in a series of 17 award-winning and hugely popular ads for a British credit card (Barclaycard) as an accident-prone spy. But a 60-second bit of fun may not translate well to a ninety minute movie.

Rowan Atkinson is an inspired comic who is capable of creating laughter through physical silliness and glib verbal banter. He can be funny with nothing more than a look that passes across his rubbery face. If one isn't familiar with him from his innocent Mr. Bean or his time-hopping Black Adder incarnations, then one might remember him as the befuddled vicar in *Four Weddings and a Funeral* or the narcoleptic Italian in *Rat Race* or the threatening but silly theme-park owner in *Scooby-Doo*. Of course these were relatively small parts, and after the not-so-enthusiastic reception of his only other staring feature film, *Bean—The Ultimate Disaster Movie*, *Johnny English* is yet another disappointment for Atkinson's fans.

In this film, Johnny English is hopelessly inept and pretentious but is also almost alarmingly self-confident and eager. He is enthusiastically clueless, which makes him incredibly prone to mistakes that are dealt with using lies, denials or his sidekick Bough to save his neck. As Lorna describes him, he is "a pompous, known-nothing asshole." He is Inspector Clouseau without the innocence or the great gags.

This last problem is the big downside of the movie and whether one wants to place the blame at the feet of director Peter Howitt or the film's writers William Davies and duo Neal Purvis and Robert Wade is almost irrelevant. Virtually anyone could figure out the plot after just a few minutes and every joke is so corny and so tired that we see it coming well in advance of the punchline. There are no surprises here, and considering the fact that writers Purvis and Wade also wrote two Bond films (*The World Is Not Enough* and *Die Another Day*) this is even more astounding.

Want proof? See if you find any of the following funny or surprising. Every time English handles his gun it falls apart or doesn't fire. When he says "The mysteries of the Orient are no mysteries to me," in a sushi bar he won't be able to figure out the chopsticks. When he has to parachute onto Sauvage's headquarters, which is a building identical to the city hospital next door, which one do you think he'll land on but treat as if it were the headquarters? Given a ring with devices for injecting two potions, one a muscle relaxant and the other truth serum, do you think he'll get them mixed up? And could he possibly end up injecting himself with one of them?

When he sees the fake Archbishop of Canterbury has a tattoo on his bum, what are the odds he'll end up publicly exposing the bum of the real archbishop? When Johnny and Lorna have to gain access to Pascal's chateau in northern France do you think he'll climb up a pipe that turns out to have a direct connection to the castle's lavatory? And do you think there will be an easily accessible ladder right next to it he could have taken? When there are two DVDs in the story, one a secret surveillance tape showing English lip-synching to ABBA's "Does Your Mother Know?" in the privacy of his bathroom and one with Pascal laying out his entire plot to take over England and turn it into a giant penal colony, guess which one he steals to show to the world? And finally, do you think his leading lady will, despite all that's logical, fall in love with him? And do you think while smooching in his James Bond equipped car he'll hit the seat ejection button by accident?

We've been watching spy/crime dramas for decades and we've even watched more than our share of James Bond spoofs from Dean Martin's *Matt Helm* through James Coburn's *Flint* movies and the *Austin Powers* series, not to mention the truly funny *Spy Hard*, the less-than-funny Jackie Chan *Tuxedo*, and the pubescent *Agent Cody Banks*, as well as TV's *Get Smart*. The point here is that we've see it all before and *Johnny English* offers nothing new.

Where Mr. Bean is an imaginative luckless spastic, and that blackguard Black Adder is wickedly cruel, Johnny English is just plain stupid. Atkinson deserves a smarter script and another chance to win American audiences.

—*Beverley Bare Buehrer*

CREDITS

Johnny English: Rowan Atkinson
Pascal Sauvage: John Malkovich
Lorna Campbell: Natalie Imbruglia
Bough: Ben Miller
Prime Minister: Kevin McNally
Pegasus: Tim Pigott-Smith
Klaus Vendetta: Douglas McFerran
Agent One: Greg Wise
Archbishop of Canterbury: Oliver Ford Davies

Origin: Great Britain, USA

Released: 2003
Production: Tim Bevan, Eric Fellner, Mark Huffam; Universal Pictures, Working Title Productions, StudioCanal; released by Universal Pictures
Directed by: Peter Howitt
Written by: Neal Purvis, Robert Wade, William Davies
Cinematography by: Remi Adefarasin
Music by: Ed Shearmur
Sound: Peter Lindsay
Music Supervisor: Nick Angel
Editing: Robin Sales
Art Direction: Chris Seagers, John Frankish
Costumes: Jill Taylor
MPAA rating: PG
Running time: 86 minutes

REVIEWS

Chicago Sun-Times Online. July 18, 2003.
Entertainment Weekly. July 25, 2003, p. 51.
Los Angeles Times Online. July 13, 2003.
Los Angeles Times Online. July 18, 2003.
New York Times Online. July 18, 2003.
People. July 28, 2003, p. 31.
Sight and Sound. May, 2003, p. 52.
USA Today Online. July 18, 2003.
Variety Online. April 7, 2003.
Washington Post. July 18, 2003, p. WE32.

QUOTES

Lorna (Natalie Imbruglia) to Johnny English (Rowan Atkinson): "Get out there and save your country!"

TRIVIA

Rowan Atkinson actually appeared in a James Bond film, *Never Say Never Again*, with Sean Connery.

The Jungle Book 2

Feel the jungle heat.
—Movie tagline

Box Office: $45.5 million

Ever since Disney began taking its animation division down the well-worn path of sequel production, attempting to cash in on the popularity of a successful animated feature, the majority of such sequels have been direct-to-video releases. Generally, that venue has been appropriate for these features, as they are usually characterized by more simplistic plots and lower production values, more akin to standard TV cartoon fare. It was somewhat unusual, then, that Disney decided on a theatrical run for *The Jungle Book 2*, a sequel to the classic 1967 feature that was inspired by, yet bore very little resemblance to, Rudyard Kipling's book of the same name. Evidently the studio had bigger hopes (and plans) for this latest sequel, utilizing the voice talents of more recognizable actors such as John Goodman, Haley Joel Osment, Phil Collins, and John Rhys-Davies. However, the film does not quite fit into the same class as its predecessor or even more recent big-screen animated features (including 2002's *Lilo & Stitch* and *Treasure Planet*). On the other hand, it has more of a "big screen" quality than direct-to-video releases such as *Cinderella II* or *The Little Mermaid II*.

The original *Jungle Book* told the story of Mowgli, a boy raised by wolves in the jungles of India. When Mowgli was 10 years old, the wolves decided he must leave the jungle because the fearsome tiger Shere Khan had returned to their part of the jungle and had sworn to kill the boy. A friendly panther named Bagheera volunteered to take Mowgli to the nearest man-village, a journey that formed the plot of the movie (and one which Mowgli was opposed to making). Along the way, Mowgli befriended a music-loving, carefree bear named Baloo and found himself in several adventures with animals of the jungle until he was finally lured into the man-village by the sight of a cute little girl on the banks of a river.

The Jungle Book 2 picks up where the original movie left off. Mowgli (voiced by Haley Joel Osment) has been "adopted" by a kind man (voiced by John Rhys-Davies) and woman who warn him not to cross the river into the dangerous jungle. His two pals are the little boy Ranjan (voiced by Connor Funk) and Shanti (voiced by Mae Whitman), the girl Mowgli saw at the end of the first film. The movie opens with Mowgli using puppets to tell the story of his adventure in the jungle (a convenient way to remind the audience of the events from the first picture), a story that excites and inspires young Ranjan but does not really seem to impress Shanti, who is more straight-laced and wary of the dangers beyond the village. Mowgli, in fact, encourages Ranjan's fascination with the jungle, leading to friction between him and Shanti. When she does not know Mowgli is listening, Shanti does admit to Ranjan that she likes Mowgli, but she is afraid the boy's attachment to the jungle will lead to trouble.

Soon thereafter, Mowgli leads Ranjan and other village children in a rousing, catchy song called "Jungle Rhythm" and then proceeds to lead them all out of the village toward the river. They are stopped, however, by his adopted father, who scolds Mowgli and sends the children back home. He does, however, understand Mowgli's feelings, observing that "You can take the boy out of the jungle, but you can't take the jungle out of the boy." Not surprisingly, Mowgli echoes the same sentiments when he returns home and softly, sadly sings to himself one of the lines from "Jungle Rhythm:" "You can high-tail it out of the jungle but it never leaves your heart."

Meanwhile, back in the jungle, Baloo the bear (voiced by John Goodman) laments to Bagheera the panther (voiced by Bob Joles) that he misses Mowgli, but it soon becomes clear that Baloo not only misses the boy but seems obsessed with bringing him back to the jungle. Bagheera reminds him that Mowgli really belongs in the man-village and that Shere Khan will undoubtedly seek vengeance on the boy. Not persuaded, Baloo sets out for the man-village in an attempt to meet Mowgli. Bagheera and a herd of elephants led by Colonel Hathi (voiced by Jim Cummings), returning from the original movie, do their best to stop Baloo, but the bear manages to slip by them.

Elsewhere in the jungle, Shere Khan (voiced by Tony Jay) makes his first appearance in a scene in which he is teased by a vulture named Lucky (voiced by Phil Collins), friend of the four hippie vultures seen in the original *Jungle Book*. "Ask me if I can whoop that tiger," he tells the four, and when they ask him, he responds, "I *Shere Khan*." The tiger is not amused, of course, but he does manage to trick Lucky into revealing that Baloo is on his way to the man-village to find Mowgli. Delighted by the opportunity to finally catch the boy, Shere Khan heads for the village behind Baloo.

When Baloo sneaks into the village and meets Mowgli, the boy is delighted to see him, of course, but they are soon spotted by Shanti, who assumes that Baloo is hostile and begins yelling for help. When Baloo takes Mowgli out of the village, Shanti thinks the boy has been taken against his will and follows them. In the meantime, Shere Khan shows up in the village and is seen just as Shanti begins yelling for help; the men of the village assume the girl is screaming because of the tiger and chase Shere Khan away with fire.

While Baloo and Mowgli are off playing in the jungle, Shanti finds herself lost in the frightening wild and almost winds up as lunch for the snake Kaa (also voiced by Cummings), but she is saved by little Ranjan, who—fortunately for Shanti—followed her out of the village. From this point the story follows three subplots—Mowgli and Baloo, Shanti and Ranjan, and the solitary Shere Khan—and does not really take any surprising turns along the way. Mowgli and Baloo discover that men from the village are searching for the boy and then later encounter Shanti and Ranjan. Predictably, Mowgli begins to realize he does in fact miss the village and finds himself torn between two worlds. The big climax occurs when Shere Khan finally catches up with

Mowgli and chases him into an ancient man-city now occupied by monkeys. Baloo and Shanti team up to save Mowgli, and in the end the tiger winds up falling into a pit where he is trapped under the large stone head of a broken statue.

The film concludes with a resolution that is probably intended to be "happier" than that of the original *Jungle Book*. Baloo very reluctantly encourages Mowgli to return to the village, but when the boy arrives back home, he meets unexpected sympathy from his adopted "Pop," who tells him, "I'm sorry—I should have understood the jungle is part of who you are." The final scene reveals that "Pop" and other adults have relaxed the rules about not crossing the river into the jungle. Mowgli, Shanti, and Ranjan are allowed to venture into the jungle to visit their animal friends.

The Jungle Book 2 is an enjoyable movie, probably more so for the young children to whom it is targeted, but overall it suffers in comparison to its predecessor. The production values are relatively strong. The animation, though not innovative in any way, is of the quality that audiences have come to expect from a Disney big-screen feature. In fact, color, depth, and detail actually surpass that of the original film. The musical score, which is generally lively and upbeat in comparison to the more subdued sound of the first film, is first-rate, and the two original songs ("Jungle Rhythm" and "WILD") are memorable and fun even though they lack the distinctive style of the original movie's songs (including "The Bear Necessities," which Mowgli and Baloo sing at least twice in this new film).

Vocal performances, too, are first-rate. Haley Joel Osment brings Mowgli to life and gives him a personality that is likeable, believable, and multi-layered. John Goodman voices Baloo with gusto, supplying the character with color and a bombastic charisma reminiscent if not duplicative of the late Phil Harris' memorable performance in the original movie. The same is the case across-the-board, as all the performances handle the material with top-notch quality.

The material, however, is the weak element of *Jungle Book 2*. As mentioned before, the story is straightforward and predictable, following the kind of plot one might expect in a direct-to-video release. The story does not take any unexpected turns and lacks much of anything that could be called original. Mowgli misses the jungle; Mowgli returns to the jungle; Mowgli realizes he misses humans, too; his human friends realize the jungle is not as scary as they thought it was. It is not the kind of plot one would expect in a big-screen production. In fact, the plot suffers the worst kind of "sequel-itis," in that everything about it hinges on the idea of revisiting places and characters from the original, not for the sake of the plot but for the sake of seeing them again.

For example, almost every character from 1967's original makes an appearance—Baloo and Bagheera, of course, but also Kaa the snake, Shere Khan, the "hippie" vultures, the jazz-loving monkeys (though their leader King Louie is sadly absent), and Colonel Hathi along with his elephant regime. Unfortunately, however, most of these characters (except Baloo) do not really serve to advance the plot (what plot there is) in any meaningful way. It seems as if they have been included simply for their nostalgic value, too obviously meant to prompt a sort of "Look, there's Colonel Hathi!" response. Oddly, this is even true of the story's villain, Shere Khan, who makes an appearance in the beginning and then is glimpsed only in brief segments before his confrontation with Mowgli at the end. Actually, the tiger also seems inserted just for the sake of including him, because he is not really important in terms of the story's main plot. The story chiefly concerns itself with Mowgli's attachment to the jungle and his need for his human friends. The Shere Khan subplot does very little to drive the plot, not even its true conflict, and as such it comes across as merely an obligatory inclusion.

Even though the plot is quite slim and simplistic, a few unusual developments might puzzle viewers who are familiar with the first movie. Baloo, for instance, seems obsessed with rejoining Mowgli and bringing the boy back to the jungle. In *The Jungle Book* Baloo certainly developed a close friendship with the boy, but by the end of the movie he seemed to fully understand that the boy needed to grow up among humans; in fact, he angered Mowgli by telling him that he was going to have to leave the jungle. The Baloo seen in the sequel seems to have lost that understanding and appears to have become fixated on the boy. Ironically, in the new film, Mowgli realizes his need for the humans before Baloo recognizes it and admits it.

Ultimately, then, *The Jungle Book 2* suffers from a general lack of consistency. It is not a bad movie, and certainly may be fun for children, but it is far less sophisticated than most animated features Disney releases theatrically. The movie looks good, sounds good, and includes a few good laughs along the way, but in the long run its story is one that probably should have taken it straight to video.

—David Flanagin

CREDITS

Baloo: John Goodman (Voice)
Mowgli: Haley Joel Osment (Voice)
Shanti: Mae Whitman (Voice)
Shere Khan: Tony Jay (Voice)
Ranjan: Connor Funk (Voice)
Bagheera: Bob Joles (Voice)
Ranjan's father: John Rhys-Davies (Voice)
Lucky: Phil Collins (Voice)

Origin: USA
Released: 2003

Production: Christopher Chase, Mary Thorne;
DisneyToon Studios; released by Walt Disney Pictures
Directed by: Steve Trenbirth
Written by: Karl Guers
Music by: Joel McNeely
Editing: Peter N. Lonsdale, Christopher Gee
Art Direction: Michael Peraza
MPAA rating: G
Running time: 72 minutes

 REVIEWS

Chicago Sun-Times Online. February 14, 2003.
Entertainment Weekly. February 21, 2003, p. 129.
Los Angeles Times Online. February 14, 2003.
New York Times Online. February 14, 2003.
People. February 24, 2003, p. 32.
USA Today Online. February 14, 2003.
Variety Online. February 7, 2003.
Washington Post. February 14, 2003, p. WE46.

QUOTES

Baloo (John Goodman) to Mowgli (Haley Joel Osment): "In case you haven't noticed kid, I'm no wild animal except at parties."

Just Married

It was the perfect honeymoon. . . . Until it began.
—Movie tagline

 Box Office: $56.1 million

Right before *Just Married* arrived in theaters, its costars, Brittany Murphy and Ashton Kutcher made a big public coming out as a couple. The randy pair, who could barely seem to keep their hands off each other (and often didn't) showed up on radio shows, TV entertainment shows and the must-stop for attracting the teen girl audience, MTV's *TRL*. (On one such show, Kutcher earnestly went on about how his girl had taught him the most he'd ever learned from any costar. Murphy lovingly replied, "Ditto." Sigh.) Either the couple was just giddy (momentarily) with love and anxious to share it with the whole darn world, or they knew that *Just Married* was going to need a little push in the publicity department. If the latter was true, the duo also

wisely realized that the best selling point of their movie was the two stars' own friskiness. *Just Married* is not really a good movie, but it is saved from being unwatchable by the charisma of the two leads. The two are so gosh-darned cute, and they look so good in their clothes, and they have such a perky puppy dog chemistry, that it's fun to just watch them. And there's a fun voyeurism in watching the couple for signs of their budding relationship in real life. That is, if you're a 14-year-old. Or, like some of us, just retain the immaturity of a 14-year-old.

As a few critics pointed out, *Just Married* is a typical "January movie," as A.O. Scott of the *New York Times* put it. December is filled with prestige projects, epic dramas and the kind of serious, important fare that garners Academy Award nominations. By January, the studios think that movie-goers are ready for the usual lightweight fluff, and the lighter, the better. *Just Married* is the perfect January movie. There is no symbolism, no pesky subtitles and nothing that requires the mind to do much more than sit and watch. Look at the pretty lady. See the handsome man.

Director Shawn Levy (*Big Fat Liar*) knows this and gives us plenty to look at. There are many scenes in which Kutcher, for no apparent reason, is wearing only boxer shorts. (This is not a complaint. Kutcher's frequent half-naked appearances are much less objectionable than the many scenes in say, *The Hot Chick,* when Rob Schneider, for no apparent reason, dons underwear.) There are scenes of big fancy houses, well-dressed relatives and fine furnishings. The less sexually- or materialistically-inclined can enjoy many lovely shots of scenery around Europe, including snowcapped mountains, canals in Venice, and the French countryside.

From there, though, things go downhill because we start getting into the territory of the plot. The film starts off promisingly. Tom Leezak (Kutcher) and Sarah McNerney (Murphy) have arrived in LAX after a disastrous honeymoon. Their main goals seem to be to make each other the most furious. Sarah tosses gum in Tom's hair and Tom causes a stranger to spill coffee on Sarah. It's doesn't sound particularly funny on paper, but the two are so zealous about making the other miserable that there's a wild energy to the scene.

Tom, who works the graveyard shift doing traffic reports on a local radio station, soon gives us the flashback to how these two got to such a point. He morosely remembers the good times starting with their cute meeting. While playing football on the beach, he had tossed a football right into Sarah's head. This was a big foreshadowing of the rest of their relationship (and for the audience, alas, it's a big foreshadowing of the much forthcoming unfunny slapstick) but the two don't seem to pick up on it.

The two come from different backgrounds—Tom's a community college graduate who's just getting by and Sarah's a Wellesley graduate from a very well-off family—

but they are wild about each other and are sure that their love will conquer all. Sarah's family, especially Dad (David Rasche) thinks that his little girl could do a lot better. When the two announce that they are getting married, Mr. Mc-Nerney does not shy away from continuing to lobby for the more economically suitable beau, Peter Prentiss (Christian Kane).

In the last minutes before the wedding, Tom's boorish sidekick Kyle (David Moscow), continually warns Tom that he will never be able to sleep with anyone else again. "You are, like, the worst best man ever." We bring this up because it is one of the few line readings that Kutcher gives that sounds realistic.

Once on their honeymoon, the pair embarks on a series of wacky adventures. They try to have sex in the airplane restroom, but Tom gets his foot stuck in the toilet. They try to have sex in their room at their fancy French hotel but Tom gets a sex toy stuck in the incompatible European outlet. The couple are chronically accident-prone. They try to consummate their marriage in a Venetian hotel room and end up crashing their bed through the wall. Pretty much the whole joke in the film is that the two want to have sex, but instead have slapstick.

More troubling for those who are really monitoring the viability of this relationship will be the fact that the two seem to have little in common but wanting to jump on each other and being supremely accident-prone. Sarah is cultured and wants to communicate with the locals and see the historical sights. Tom is a boorish American who wants the French hotel to be like Howard Johnson's and wants to spend his time in Venice watching a ball game on TV.

Of course, many in the audience won't be thinking that hard. On a date night showing in an Orange County, California theater, the young audience was yukking it up over such sight gags as Tom getting a cockroach stuck on his neck and Tom ramming a gate with his car.

It would be interesting to see the actors in something with a better script because they have an appealing chemistry. Murphy, especially, has been a bright spot in everything she's been in. Usually, she plays a character that's kind of crazy or over-the-top or both, and it's interesting to see her playing someone reasonably normal. And Kutcher is not a fabulous actor, but he has a genial big lug kind of screen presence.

Critics did not exactly fall in love with the film. Ty Burr of the *Boston Globe* wrote, "*Just Married* is reasonably painless if you've never seen a comedy about the travails of newlyweds, but considering that the film industry has been cranking them out since 1915's *Over Night*—which quite possibly featured some of the same jokes—the natural audience for this one has to be 20-year-olds and younger. Everyone else may safely consider other engagements." Kevin Thomas of the Los Angeles Times wrote, "*Just Married* is unrelenting in its tediousness, and its ending is totally pre-

dictable. It's like a bright and shiny package tied up neatly with a ribbon, but there's nothing inside it." Owen Gleiberman of *Entertainment Weekly* wrote, "*Just Married* collapses into the most generic sort of teen movie-ville, just at the moment it's convinced you that its lightly appealing stars are capable of better."

—*Jill Hamilton*

CREDITS

Tom: Ashton Kutcher
Sarah: Brittany Murphy
Peter Prentiss: Christian Kane
Kyle: David Moscow
Lauren: Monet Mazur
Mr. McNerney: David Rasche
Mrs. McNerney: Veronica Cartwright
Mr. Leezak: Raymond J. Barry
Willie McNerney: Thad Luckinbill
Paul McNerney: David Agranov
Dickie McNerney: Taram Killam

Origin: USA
Released: 2003
Production: Robert Simonds; Mediastream Film; released by 20th Century-Fox
Directed by: Shawn Levy
Written by: Sam Harper
Cinematography by: Jonathan Brown
Music by: Christophe Beck
Sound: Marc Weingarten
Editing: Don Zimmerman, Scott Hill
Art Direction: Troy Sizemore
Costumes: Debra McGuire
Production Design: Nina Ruscio
MPAA rating: PG-13
Running time: 94 minutes

 ## REVIEWS

Chicago Sun-Times Online. January 10, 2003.
Entertainment Weekly. January 17, 2003, p. 54.
Los Angeles Times Online. January 10, 2003.
New York Times Online. January 10, 2003.
People. January 27, 2003, p. 32.
USA Today Online. January 10, 2003.
Variety Online. January 1, 2003.
Washington Post. January 10, 2003, p. WE42.

Nomination:
Golden Raspberries 2003: Worst Actor (Kutcher), Worst Support. Actress (Murphy).

Kangaroo Jack

He stole the money . . . and he's not giving it back.
—Movie tagline

 Box Office: $67 million

In more ways than one, *Kangaroo Jack* looked to be a nobrainer. It was going to be dumb. And no one was going to be so dumb that they would actually want to see it. The ads for the movie showed two guys, who let us say, were probably not in the accelerated reading group in grade school, who lose $50,000 by putting it in a jacket on a kangaroo. With this premise, how could such a film be funny? Even if the most witty minds on the planet worked on the film, they would still have to show the dreariness of two dopes chasing a kangaroo around the outback.

It was pretty surprising then when *Kangaroo Jack* came out and promptly took the number one spot at the boxoffice. That means that not only did someone go see the movie, but lots of people did—the most people of any movie. How could this be? As it turns out, ads for *Kangaroo Jack* had been running consistently during kids' TV programs. The sheer repetition (always a winner with kids) and the fact that the ad showed a talking kangaroo made the movie a must-see for families with kids. (Sometimes the idea of "the wisdom of a child" is not that accurate.)

Such an inane movie actually found itself the center of a bit of a controversy when the parents gave into the ceaseless begging, took their kids to the movie and found themselves watching some pretty racy stuff. It wasn't *Deep Throat*, but there were some jokes about a male reproductive part and some cleavage grabbing. There was also a bit of violence. These were not the sorts of the things that parents were expecting in a PG-rated film. Perhaps even more upsetting was that the kangaroo, which talked in the commercials, only talks once during the film. Apparently, the type of people who want to see a talking kangaroo get pretty surly when they don't get their talking kangaroo fix.

How did such fare finds its way into a kiddie movie? Well, *Kangaroo Jack* wasn't always a kiddie film. As entertainment columnist Patrick Goldstein noted in the *Los Angeles Times, Kangaroo Jack* started out as a mob action flick.

It's genesis was a meal that producer Steve Bing (best known for fathering Elizabeth Hurley's child) and screenwriter Scott Rosenberg took. Bing related an urban legend about some guys who had their money stolen by a kangaroo. The two men thought the story would make for a perfect movie. Such an idea, which most of us might have had, then discarded for being a bad idea, is the reason that these two make the big bucks.

They got action movie guy Jerry Bruckheimer (*Pearl Harbor, Gone in 60 Seconds,* and *Bad Boys II*) to produce the film and David McNally (*Coyote Ugly*) to direct it. They made their action-oriented mob film. But in screenings, the film did very poorly. The marketing folks noticed that little kids liked the part with the kangaroo. Because the guys making the film were not exactly the types to talk about such stuff as "artistic integrity" or their original vision, they readily agreed to changing the whole focus of the film and making it a lighthearted romp for kids. They filmed a few more scenes and they had themselves a new movie. Thus we have a movie with scenes like the one in which Estella Warren walks around in a wet T-shirt followed by scenes of a computer-animated kangaroo rapping in an Australian accent to the Sugar Hill Gang's "Rapper's Delight."

It all starts when Charlie Carbone (Jerry O'Connell) gets talked into another crazy scheme by his rotund buddy Louis Booker (Anthony Anderson). Why is Charlie so agreeable to Louis's wacky plans? In a flashback, we learn that as children, Louis saved Charlie from drowning in the ocean. Years later, Louis is still milking that incident for all it's worth and using it to make Charlie do his bidding. This time Louis gets Charlie to help him deliver some contraband for some bad people. This, in turn, somehow lands them in trouble with Charlie's stepfather, weird mob boss Sal Maggio (Christopher Walken). To redeem themselves, Sal sends Louis and Charlie on a mission to deliver $50,000 to a guy in Australia. What Sal doesn't mention is that they are delivering payment to a hit man who is supposed to kill them.

Once in Australia, Charlie hits a kangaroo with his car and after some dutiful mourning, they decide that they will take funny pictures of themselves with the kangaroo. And better yet, the kangaroo will be wearing Louis's lucky jacket. Then—this must be the part that said "movie material" to the writers—the dead kangaroo, who is not actually dead, leaps up and hops away in the jacket. Tediously, the jacket contains the money so the guys must chase the thing all over Australia. Even more worrisome is the amount of times the Men at Work chestnut "Land Down Under" is played.

To do this, they involve an expert on Australian wildlife, Jessie (Warren), who, for unknown reasons, happens to be American. They also have to yell "Aaaaaah!" a lot. This phrase comes in handy when they are doing things like jumping over something in a car, falling out of something, etc. The script must have had many pages where the action was described and the actors' lines were simply, "Aaaaaaah!" Imagine them working out the lines beforehand at home: "Hon, do you think I should say it as 'AH!' or more of an 'Aaaaaah'?"

The whole thing is pretty much one long "Road Runner" cartoon with the wily kangaroo escaping the bad guys, repeat, repeat, repeat. But to liven up the formula, there's also some lame and/or gross jokes thrown in. There's a scene in an airplane bathroom that's on the level of *Three's Company* writing in which the guys are talking about the bag of money, but due to a wacky misunderstanding, the other passengers think they're talking about poop. There are also some camels suffering from flatulence and did we mention the rapping kangaroo?

To make sure the movie is truly, truly bad, the writers also included the usual bad guy who ruins his chance of killing the heroes by explaining how he going to kill him plus a needlessly sappy ending. As their adventures come to a close, Louis and Charlie have a heart-to-heart talk about friendship. Charlie actually says, "You save my life everyday, Louis."

It's not a big surprise that critics didn't much care for the film. Jan Stuart of *Newsday* wrote that it was "88 minutes of desperate gyrations intended to simulate humor." Lisa Schwarzbaum of *Entertainment Weekly* called it "a junky kids' comedy" and a "charmless, expense-deductable business trip to Australia." A.O. Scott of the *New York Times* wrote, "There is something crass and ugly about the way *Kangaroo Jack* develops its hackneyed, potentially amusing premise." And Carla Meyer of the *San Francisco Chronicle* wrote, "O'Connell and Anderson appear to have come not from Brooklyn but from a Hollywood sitcom factory that churns out genial, unthreatening actors devoid of regional traits."

—*Jill Hamilton*

CREDITS

Charlie Carbone: Jerry O'Connell
Louis Booker: Anthony Anderson
Jessie: Estella Warren
Frankie: Michael Shannon
Sal Maggio: Christopher Walken
Blue: Bill Hunter
Mr. Smith: Marton Csokas
Mr. Jimmy: David Ngoombujarra

Origin: USA
Released: 2002
Production: Jerry Bruckheimer; released by Castle Rock Entertainment
Directed by: David McNally

Written by: Steve Bing, Scott Rosenberg
Cinematography by: Peter Menzies Jr.
Sound: Gary Wilkins
Editing: John Murray, William Goldenberg
Art Direction: Brian Edmonds
Costumes: Eliza Goodman, Jon Boyden
Production Design: George Liddle
MPAA rating: PG
Running time: 88 minutes

REVIEWS

Entertainment Weekly. January 24, 2003, p. 77.
Los Angeles Times Online. January 17, 2003.
New York Times Online. January 17, 2003.
People. January 27, 2003, p. 32.
USA Today Online. January 17, 2003.
Variety Online. January 11, 2003.
Washington Post. January 17, 2003, p. WE42.

AWARDS AND NOMINATIONS

Nomination:
Golden Raspberries 2003: Worst Support. Actor (Walken), Worst Support. Actor (Anderson).

Kill Bill: Vol. 1

Here Comes The Bride.
—Movie tagline
A Roaring Rampage of Revenge.
—Movie tagline

 Box Office: $69.8 million

Quentin Tarantino, the writer-director of two of the most acclaimed films of the 1990s, *Reservoir Dogs* (1992) and *Pulp Fiction* (1994), has not made a film since 1997's *Jackie Brown*—a decidedly low-key effort compared to the narrative and visual embellishments of his earlier films. *Kill Bill: Vol. 1* finds Tarantino returning to his more flamboyant form. Like his first two films, *Kill Bill: Vol. 1* is action packed and stylish. Even more than before, Tarantino, the biggest film geek ever to become a director, piles on references to his favorite films and directors (the more obscure the better). While the result has generated considerable controversy because of its violence, *Kill Bill: Vol. 1* is clearly the work of an inspired, original talent.

Even more than with *Pulp Fiction,* Tarantino plays with the timeline of the narrative. The entire film is a series of flashbacks, presenting its two major sequences out of chronological order and interspersing glimpses of events that led to the protagonist's quest for revenge. The unnamed main character, known simply as the Bride (Uma Thurman), is shot, during her El Paso wedding ceremony, by her former colleagues in the Deadly Viper Assassination Squad (DiVAS). Everyone at the wedding is killed except the pregnant Bride. Her mentor and lover, Bill (David Carradine), shoots her in the head and leaves her for dead. Four years later, she awakes from a coma and sets out to track down Bill and the DiVAS.

The film has a frustrating habit of presenting more questions than answers to various plot points. For example, just as Bill shoots the Bride, she reveals that she is carrying his child. What ended their relationship? Who is the groom? What happened to the baby? Why did Bill want the Bride killed? How did she become an assassin in the first place? Why do the assassins have snake code names? All these questions will hopefully be answered in *Kill Bill: Vol. 2.*

The rest of *Kill Bill: Vol. 1* presents the Bride's prolonged effort to escape from the hospital where she has spent four years, her journey to Okinawa where she convinces retired sword master Hattori Hanzo (Sonny Chiba) to create the ultimate sword for her, her confrontations with two of the DiVAS, and assorted flashbacks of earlier events.

The Bride's knife fight with Vernita Green (Vivica A. Fox) in the latter's Los Angeles home is relatively brief. Her Tokyo battle with O-Ren Ishii (Lucy Liu) is another matter altogether. Since O-Ren left Bill's employment, she has become the ruler of Tokyo's underworld and has a small army of sword-wielding thugs. To kill O-Ren, the Bride must fight her way through nearly one-hundred bodyguards (a scene that took eight weeks to shoot). As several observers have pointed out, all this would be much simpler if guns were involved, but then there would be no story. Entering the Tarantino universe precludes certain logic.

The showdown with O-Ren is the most controversial aspect of *Kill Bill: Vol. 1* because so many limbs are severed and entrails eviscerated (although there is no lack of violence elsewhere in the film). Not only does blood spurt all over the place, but Tarantino and his technicians have created several new sound effect variations to intensify the gore. The sound of violence is actually much more disturbing than the look of it.

This twenty-minute sequence has led many critics to label *Kill Bill: Vol. 1* the most violent American film ever made. In a *USA Today* editorial, Michael Medved said it "represents a new low in its jeering, pseudo-sophisticated celebration of meaningless brutality." *The San Francisco Chronicle* attacked the director for encouraging children to see the film. That newspaper's critic, Mick LaSalle, called the film indefensible pornography.

Tarantino and his supporters point out that his violence is tame compared to that in the Asian films he is emulating, but few in the mainstream American film audiences are familiar with these films. Clearly, Tarantino's violence is justifiably disturbing to some, but it is unrealistic, stylized, even cartoonish, and essential to what he wants to achieve. The Bride's threats to O-Ren henchwoman Sofie Fatale (Julie Dreyfus) have more emotional impact than what she actually does to Sofie.

Some reviewers have complained, with some justification, about the film's lack of emotional content, that it is expertly choreographed action and little else. There is considerable depth, however, in the animated account of how O-Ren became an assassin. This presentation of a young girl's witness of her parents' murders and subsequent revenge, was praised by many as the best part of the film and makes O-Ren more rounded than the other characters. This ten-minute sequence, which took forty Production I.G. animators a year to complete, is, ironically, the most graphically violent part of *Kill Bill: Vol. 1.* It also seems to feature what is no doubt the first instance of child-adult sex in a mainstream American film (the villain is a pedophile). Making O-Ren have the same motivation as the Bride gives the film some psychological complexity, as does Vernita's four-year-old daughter's seeing her mother's death at the hands of the Bride. The child is the same age the Bride's would be.

Another major complaint leveled on the film is the decision by Tarantino and Miramax's Harvey Weinstein to divide the film into two parts (some have accused this decision of being based solely on greed). The Bride's tracking of five perpetrators is going to take some time, and few would be willing to sit through three-plus hours of almost non-stop action. Some of the Asian films serving as Tarantino's models have also appeared in multi volumes. As it is, *Kill Bill: Vol. 1* is more than aesthetically, if not emotionally, exhausting than most other films.

In a charming, sympathetic portrait of Tarantino by Larissa MacFarquhar in *The New Yorker,* the writer-director's film geekdom is analyzed at some length. He doesn't just have boundless enthusiasm for obscure, often trashy films that few others could take seriously; he seems to find something to like about almost every film he's ever seen. *Kill Bill: Vol. 1* is a virtual catalog of his passions and influences.

Because the most obvious influence is Asian martial-arts films, the opening credits include the logo of Hong Kong's Shaw Bros., once the dominant force in the genre. O-Ren is named for Teruo Ishii, maker of 1960s yakuza epics, and Tasashi Ishii, who made a series of female revenge films.

In *True Romance* (1993), the Tony Scott film written by Tarantino, the protagonists meet at a triple feature of Japanese action films starring Sonny Chiba, so Chiba appears in *Kill Bill: Vol. 1* as the master swordsman. O-Ren's gang wears masks like Kato (played by martial-arts star, Bruce Lee, in the 1960s television series *The Green Hornet*; a snippet of the program's theme music is heard during their battle). The yellow outfit worn by the Bride in Tokyo recalls Lee's in *Game of Death* (1978). David Carradine is best known as the star of the martial-arts series *Kung Fu*, and he replaced the late Lee as the star of *Circle of Iron* (1979). Vernita is living as Jeannie Bell, the name of the Playboy playmate who appears in several 1970s blaxploitation films, a genre beloved by Tarantino. Another influence cited by Tarantino is *Cleopatra Wong* (1978), a Singapore variation on blaxploitation. Bell also appears in Martin Scorsese's *Mean Streets* (1973) in which Carradine has a cameo as a character assassinated for revenge.

Tarantino also likes the biker films of the 1960s and 1970s, which often feature revenge plots, so there is a cameo by Larry Bishop, who appears in several of these films. Tarantino uses Nancy Sinatra's rendition of "Bang Bang (My Baby Shot Me Down)" rather than the Sonny and Cher original because Sinatra stars in the best-known biker film, Roger Corman's *The Wild Angels* (1966).

Assassin Elle Driver (Daryl Hannah) sneaks into the Bride's hospital and steals a nurse's outfit, a nod to the nightmare ending of *Dressed to Kill* (1980) by Brian De Palma, once Tarantino's favorite director. Elle's eye patch is a tribute to the Swedish thriller *They Call Her One Eye* (1974).

The soundtrack samples scores from several films, including the great Bernard Herrmann's *Twisted Nerve* (1969), a film Tarantino has shown at his personal film festival. The most significant sampling is from Ennio Morricone's *Death Rides a Horse* (1967). Echoes of the Morricone style are heard throughout the film, especially with a Zamfir pan flute piece at the end. The major influence on *Kill Bill: Vol. 1* are spaghetti Westerns, particularly those directed by Sergio Leone and scored by Morricone. There is very little dialogue, much like Leone's *Man with No Name* trilogy, and the revenge plot is heavily influenced by Leone's masterpiece, *Once Upon a Time in the West* (1968). (The closing credits acknowledge the passing of that film's star, Charles Bronson.) Tarantino has said that the showdown between the Bride and O-Ren is his tribute to the ending of Leone's *The Good, the Bad, and the Ugly* (1966). All these allusions are Tarantino's playful winks at his audience, acknowledging that they are co-conspirators in delighting in the same genres. There are even self-references: such as the DiVAS resemblance to the fictional television series Fox Force Five described by Thurman's character in *Pulp Fiction*.

It is ridiculous to criticize *Kill Bill: Vol. 1* as yet another example of style over substance. Where is the substance in twenty-first-century American popular arts? In an era when marketing rules all, where is any distinctive style? Great art,

whether the music of Beethoven, the paintings of Rembrandt, the fiction of William Faulkner, or the films of Ingmar Bergman, is great because of its style. If there is any substance, that's all the better. Tarantino may be a geek, but he has style and a strong personal vision. He knows how to make films better than almost anyone else. For this, he should be celebrated.

—*Michael Adams*

CREDITS

The Bride/Black Mamba: Uma Thurman
O-Ren Ishii/Cottonmouth: Lucy Alexis Liu
Vernita Green/Copperhead: Vivica A. Fox
Budd/Sidewinder: Michael Madsen
Elle Driver/California Mountain Snake: Daryl Hannah
Johnny Mo: Gordon Liu
Hattori Hanzo: Sonny Chiba
Sheriff Earl McGraw: Michael Parks
Go-Go Yubari: Chiaki Kuriyama
Boss Tanaka: Jun Kunimura
Sophie Fatale: Julie Dreyfus
Larry: Larry Bishop
Buck: Michael Bowen
Bill: David Carradine (Voice)

Origin: USA
Released: 2003
Production: Lawrence Bender, Quentin Tarantino; A Band Apart; released by Miramax
Directed by: Quentin Tarantino
Written by: Quentin Tarantino
Cinematography by: Robert Richardson
Music by: The RZA
Sound: Mark Ulano
Editing: Sally Menke
Art Direction: Daniel Bradford
Costumes: Catherine Thomas, Kumiko Ogawa
Production Design: David Wasco, Yohei Taneda
MPAA rating: R
Running time: 110 minutes

REVIEWS

Atlanta Journal and Constitution. October 10, 2003, p. D1.
Baltimore Sun. October 10, 2003, p. E1.
Boston Globe. October 10, 2003, p. C1.
Chicago Sun-Times Online. October 10, 2003.
Entertainment Weekly. October 17, 2003, p. 57.
Los Angeles Times Online. October 10, 2003.
Maclean's. October 13, 2003, p. 1.
New York Times Online. September 5, 2002.

New York Times Online. July 16, 2003.
New York Times. October 10, 2003, p. E1.
New Yorker. October 13, 2003, p. 112.
People. October 20, 2003, p. 32.
Rolling Stone. October 20, 2003, p. 99.
San Francisco Chronicle. October 10, 2003, p. D1.
Sight and Sound. October, 2003, p. 12.
Time. October 20, 2003, p. 70.
USA Today. October 10, 2003, p. E1.
Variety Online. September 28, 2003.
Washington Post. October 10, 2003, p. C1.

QUOTES

Budd (Michael Madsen) about The Bride: "That woman deserves her revenge and we deserve to die."

AWARDS AND NOMINATIONS

Nomination:
Golden Globes 2004: Actress—Drama (Thurman).

Lara Croft Tomb Raider: The Cradle of Life

 Box Office: $65.6 million

Lara Croft Tomb Raider: The Cradle of Life is a rarity in Hollywood—a sequel that's far better than the original. Of course, that's not saying all that much since the first movie, *Lara Croft Tomb Raider*, in 2001 was an incomprehensible mess. The script made little sense and involved something about somebody trying to control time. There was little to no sense of pacing, and director Simon West accomplished the amazing feat of making Angelina Jolie seem uninteresting to watch.

According to Manohla Dargis of the *Los Angeles Times,* before the second film came out, the filmmakers promised to do a better job this time, but they didn't hold up their end of the bargain: "Plugging the movie, the filmmakers recently vowed in *Entertainment Weekly* that this time there would be a script for Lara to follow and some emotional texture, but the thin concept of Dean Georgaris' screenplay proves this was a bold and empty boast." Still, it helps a lot that director Jan De Bont, who did *Speed* and *Twister* and was Paul Verhoeven's cinematographer for more than 20 years, has

replaced the inept West. De Bont does a far better job of conveying the story. He paces the action well and, perhaps best of all, gives Lara more of an identifiable character. This is a challenging task since the "real" Lara is a video game action heroine. It doesn't seem like an action movie would be terribly dependent on fleshing out characters, but it can make a big difference in how engaging the movie is.

Here Lara (Jolie) is one tough chick. In one scene, she rides her horse sidesaddle through her ample estate. While she gallops wildly through her forest, she shoots her gun at targets she's strung up in the trees (hitting every time, naturally.) This scene doesn't have much to do with the story, but it does set forth a few ideas about Lara. She's rich, she's well bred, she's very talented and she's a wild thrill-seeker. As much as Lara's character has evolved from the first film, it still has a long way to go to become a classic movie character. Jolie seems to be trying her darnedest, but somehow the character isn't as full as it could be. Despite being best known for this film series and her abrupt marriage to and divorce from Billy Bob Thornton, Jolie is actually a very talented actress. With her natural cool, surreally good looks, and dangerous edge (much to the chagrin of her insurers, Jolie insisted on doing most of her stunts herself), Jolie could easily become the action movie hero of the 21st century. But in this film, it hasn't quite gelled. As Andrew O'Hehir wrote in his review in *Salon.com,* "Jolie hasn't yet found the vehicle for her extraordinary, unclassifiable talent."

When Jolie arrives on the screen in *Lara Croft,* she's riding a jet ski—fast, of course. There's an earthquake, an underwater fight and a search for the lost Lunar Temple of Alexander the Great. At one point, Lara saves herself from drowning by slicing her arm and letting the blood attract a shark. When the shark comes calling, she rides it to the surface. It's just a regular old day for Jolie.

In all this, there's some sort of business about Pandora's Box. As often happens in this film, another character helpfully explains this particular plot issue with "Oh, Pandora's Box? You mean the ancient Greek myth where . . . ,"then proceeds to spell it out for the audience. Later in the film, when Lara's romantic interest/partner in crime Terry Sheridan (Gerard Butler) is introduced, a secondary character wordily comments, "Terry Sheridan—the former commander with the Royal Marines turned mercenary and traitor." Anyway, it seems that this Pandora's Box has a bad disease in it or forbidden knowledge or something like that. Dr. Jonathan Reiss (Ciaran Hinds), the requisite action movie Euro bad guy, is a mean man who likes to sell biological weapons to errant dictators around the world.

To find the box, Lara and the doctor must first get their hands on a mysterious orb that doubles as a map. The doctor and Lara engage in various shenanigans to steal the orb from one another. There is a fight in a Shanghai neighborhood that involves Lara swinging from neon signs, there is a shoot out in a mall and some leaping off a skyscraper while wearing wings. The fights take place in picturesque locales, including Cambodia and East Africa, which provides a nice travelogue aspect to the film.

During her quest she springs ex-boyfriend, Terry, from jail so that he can help her find a mysterious Asian gang in possession of the orb. The two still are attracted to each other, but Terry's about as wily and untrustworthy as Lara. He makes a good strong match for Lara, which is a bonus for the film.

In the course of doing her business, archeologist Lara doesn't seem to show much respect for ancient rarities. As Dave Kehr pointed out in his review in the *New York Times:* "Lara Croft's record on preserving important historical sites ranks with that of the Taliban; the new film finds her destroying both a long-lost Greek Temple and a Chinese emperor's tomb in her quest."

Helping her in her quest to save the world and wreck plenty of artifacts along the way are her at home support staff, Bryce (Noah Taylor) and Hillary (Christopher Barrie). When Lara arrives in Africa to find the box, a helpful tribesman, Kosa (Djimon Hounsou, *Gladiator*), decides that she seems sincere and, ignoring ancient tribal wisdom, leads her straight to the hidden box.

Kehr of the *New York Times* declared, "*Lara Croft* lopes from one action set-piece to the next without developing any real rhythm or drive. Too many of the stunts are too obviously digitally enhanced to carry much sense of danger." Roger Ebert of the *Chicago Sun-Times* observed, "This is a better movie than the first one, more assured, more entertaining. Jan de Bont demands a certain logic from his screenwriters, so that although the story is completely preposterous, of course, it is consistent within its own terms." O'Hehir of *Salon.com* enthused, "This is a highly enjoyable summer thrill ride with an action heroine who likes to be on top, literally and figuratively. Girls as well as boys can look up to her, and admire." Thelma Adams of *Us* giddily wrote, "This Cradle rocks with the babelicious Jolie!" And in an especially bad pun, Tom Gliatto of *People* magazine quipped, "Bottom Line: Better Crofted."

—*Jill Hamilton*

Origin: USA
Released: 2003
Production: Lawrence Gordon, Lloyd Levin; Mutual Film Corporation, BBC (British Broadcasting Corporation), Tele Munchen Productions, Toho-Towa, Eidos Interactive; released by Paramount Pictures
Directed by: Jan De Bont
Written by: Dean Georgaris
Cinematography by: David Tattersall
Music by: Alan Silvestri
Sound: Simon Kaye, Chris Munro
Music Supervisor: Peter Afterman
Editing: Michael Kahn
Art Direction: John Fenner
Costumes: Lindy Hemming
Production Design: Kirk M. Petruccelli
MPAA rating: PG-13
Running time: 116 minutes

REVIEWS

Chicago Sun-Times Online. July 25, 2003.
Entertainment Weekly. August 1, 2003, p. 60.
Los Angeles Times Online. July 25, 2003.
New York Times Online. July 25, 2003.
People. August 4, 2003, p. 32.
USA Today Online. July 25, 2003.
Variety Online. July 25, 2003.
Washington Post. July 25, 2003, p. WE34.

QUOTES

Terry (Gerard Butler) to Lara (Angelina Jolie): "You can break my wrist—but I'm still gonna kiss you."

AWARDS AND NOMINATIONS

Nomination:
Golden Raspberries 2003: Worst Actress (Jolie).

CREDITS

Lara Croft: Angelina Jolie
Terry Sheridan: Gerard Butler
Jonathan Reiss: Ciaran Hinds
Sean: Til Schweiger
Kosa: Djimon Hounsou
Bryce: Noah Taylor
Hillary: Chris (Christopher) Barrie
Chen Lo: Simon Yam

The Last Samurai

 Box Office: $110.1

It is 1876, America's centennial year, and in San Francisco a Winchester firearms sideshow salesman is hyping the achievements of their pitchman, the most decorated soldier from the famed 7th Cavalry and Medal of Honor winner, Nathan Algren (Tom Cruise). But the drunken Algren misses his cue. When he finally does stumble out from behind the stage he slurs out the story of the Indian wars using a diorama and a most cynical manner. Winchester Rifles will not require his services much longer.

Zebulon Gant (Billy Connolly) is in the crowd that day with a job offer for Algren under whom Gant served as a sergeant. Japan wants to be considered a "civilized" country and will pay him $400 a month to train its imperial army and suppress rebel samurai leaders. The cocky and soused Algren demands $500 a month not only for himself but also for Gant and another $500 when they're finished. This upsets Colonel Bagley (Tony Goldwyn) who has set up the meeting and with whom Algren has an unpleasant, but at this point unknown, history. But the Japanese, represented by Mr. Omura (Masato Harada), are impressed with Algren's record and hire him.

Algren seems so haunted by something in his past that he now has no scruples about who he trains or who he kills, and Bagley is obviously a source of this torment. "For $500 a month I'll kill anyone you want," Algren tells Bagley, "but keep this in mind—I'd happily kill you for free." But Bagley excuses whatever it is they have between them with an "I did what I had to do."

Algren and Gant soon find themselves disembarking a ship in Yokahama Harbor, where they are met by Simon Graham (Timothy Spall), a British expatriate photographer who will act as their translator and connection to the court of the Meiji emperor (Shichinosuke Nakamura). The emperor is a quiet young man who seems ruled by a progressive council, which is led by Omura. The council is committed to Westernizing Japan as fast—and as profitably for them—as possible. However, the traditional Japanese samurai class feels that the change is happening much too quickly. Consequently the samurai, who consider themselves loyal to the emperor but distrustful of his council, have started to rebel against any attempts at modernization. This is the case with the samurai leader Katsumoto (Ken Watanabe).

Algren sets out to learn all he can about the samurai, not out of any sense of respect but out of a desire to know his enemy. In the meantime, while Captain Algren and his drill sergeant Gant attempt to train an imperial army made up of peasant conscripts, Katsumoto is destroying rail lines and refuses even to dishonor himself by resorting to firearms. Algren is ordered to take his raw recruits into battle to put down the rebellion. Though Algren realizes his soldiers are nowhere near ready for battle, Bagley refuses to accept the idea that a modern, gun-toting soldier, no matter how ill-prepared, could possibly be beaten by backward, sword-wielding samurai, and they are ordered out.

In a mist-shrouded forest, Algren's troops quickly show their inability to fight. They are terrified of the legendary samurai, they fire too early to be effective and are routed. Algren plunges into the battle, but he is soon badly wounded and surrounded by samurai. He fends them off only with the help of a pole on whose end is a banner featuring a white tiger . . . a symbol that had appeared to Katsumoto while meditating. When one of Katsumoto's warriors attempts to behead Algren, the American uses his last strength to kill him instead. The unexpected spirit and death-be-damned attitude of the soldier—as well as the sudden connection with the white tiger—piques Katsumoto's interest and Algren is taken back to the samurai's village to recuperate and to wait out the winter.

Algren is put under the care of Katsumoto's sister, Taka (Koyuki), whose husband was the samurai Algren had killed. But Taka has to nurse more than Algren's battle wounds for he also goes through alcohol withdrawal. At first he demands and is given sake as it becomes apparent he is drinking to suppress the memory of the slaughter of innocent Native American women and children—a slaughter ordered by Bagley. But as he mends, Algren begins to wander about the samurai village, always escorted by a silent guard who Algren calls Bob. Eventually he is called to meet with Katsumoto. When Algren asks him why he wasn't killed and what the samurai wants with him, Katsumoto replies, "To know my enemy." It is the start of a common bond between the two men because they are, in Katsumoto's words, "both students of war."

Slowly Algren earns the villagers' and samurai's begrudging respect . . . or is it sympathy? At the same time Algren comes to understand and appreciate the samurai: their sense of honor, their desire for perfection, their devotion to discipline, their loyalty in service to the emperor and what they feel is best for Japan. Algren even comes to study the soon-to-be-archaic samurai sword fighting and martial arts. As a result, for the first time in many years, Algren has his first untroubled sleep and no longer desires alcohol to kill his memories.

It should come as no surprise, then, that when Omura sends a troop of ninja warriors to kill Katsumoto in a sneak attack on the samurai, Algren finds himself fighting alongside his former enemy. Katsumoto, who survives the attack, is given safe passage to Tokyo to meet with the Emperor and his counci, but he discovers how intolerant of the samurai tradition the government has become. Katsumoto's son, Nobutada (Shin Koyamada), is assaulted in the street by government agents, his sword is confiscated, and he is insulted by having his topknot cut off. There is no honor here nor in the emperor's council chamber, nor with the silent emperor himself who seems cowed by the council that is getting rich off of Japan's modernization. Katsumoto is greatly saddened when he tells Algren that "the emperor could not hear my words," to which Algren replies, "Together we will make the emperor hear you." But it will take a slaughter of the samurai before the Emperor hears.

The Last Samurai has been compared to many other films: Lawrence of Arabia (the Westerner adopting foreign ways), Dances with Wolves (the wounded soldier seeking escape and finding healing in a "foreign" culture), Braveheart (futile last stands of noble inferior forces against ignoble superior ones) and The Charge of the Light Brigade (suicidal battle tactics). But this should not dismiss what the film does have going for it, especially its handsome cinematography and stunning battle sequences. Cinematographer John Toll, who received his first Oscar filming director Zwick's Legends of the Fall, not only manages to capture the majestic scenery—although it seems one just can't go wrong filming in gorgeous New Zealand—and the reverence for nature inherent in Japanese culture but also to portray blood-thirsty warriors in all their exalted reverence.

Another reason The Last Samurai looks so good is the attention to detail. Production designer Lilly Kilvert, who also worked with Zwick on Legends of the Fall, here recreated 1870's Tokyo in, of all places, the "New York Street" on Warner's back lot. She created Katsumoto's village from scratch in New Zealand like a seasoned city planner and built Katsumoto's Tokyo house on Warner's backlot "Walton's Pond" where the television shows The Waltons and Gilligan's Island were filmed. Another interesting detail is that more than 150 portable cherry trees were built for the film, complete with wooden trunks and removable branches that could be changed to reflect the seasons ... and Katsumoto's poetry. Similarly costume designer Ngila Dickson (The Lord of the Rings trilogy) created authentic samurai armor and period kimonos from scratch.

Going back to cinematographer Toll, it is also to his credit that the battle scenes look as good as they do because short changing them on film would have been a crime considering the effort that went into them. Even the small one-on-one battles required considerable expertise, and Tom Cruise trained hard under the direction of "sword master" Nick Powell who also trained Russell Crowe for Gladiator and Mel Gibson for Braveheart. But it is the dazzling choreography of the larger battles and how they are extraordinarily depicted on the screen that makes The Last Samurai worth the price of admission. Sure, the final battle makes no sense tactically; it is so futile that it is virtually incomprehensible (even the suicidal Battle of Thermopalyae, which is mentioned in the film, had a purpose: to buy time for the Greek navy during the Persian Wars). But somehow it all seems so noble when seen on such a grand scale.

Hundreds of extras and only a minimum of CGI effects (the thick shower of arrows would have put too many at risk as would the fireballs, so they were added later) were used to bring these amazing battles to the screen. Ultimately, when the jaw-dropping spectacle has worn off a bit, one begins to rethink all those senseless deaths. Several of the filmmakers give credit and pay homage to famed Japanese director the late Akira Kurosawa as their inspiration for these sequences. They should probably have paid more attention to his later film Kagemusha than his earlier film The Seven Samurai, however. By that time Kurosawa had stopped presenting battles as noble but as brutal. The true horror of the battle in Kagemusha shows through the relative silence with which it is filmed. There is nothing virtuous about all the meaningless killing, nothing heroic about suicidal sacrifice.

Director Edward Zwick (Legends of the Fall, Courage Under Fire) has fused history with dramatic narrative before with Glory. Stories in which bravery in war and courageous last stands seem inevitable are told by him with an incisive and brisk style, even if the stories themselves sometimes feel as if they are being manipulated to serve this purpose. (The Last Samurai was written by John Logan who himself is no stranger to fusing history and drama as he did in Gladiator.)

Within the film's casting there are also pluses and minuses. On the good side are some immensely watchable small parts, such as the wry humor of Billy Connolly, the earnestness of Timothy Spall, and the villainy of Tony Goldwyn, all from the Western members of the cast. Strong performances from Eastern castmembers include the quiet strength of Hiroyuki Sanada (a major star in Japan with more than 50 films to his credit, including the popular Ring thrillers), the tentativeness of Shichinosuke Nakamura (who comes from a family of Kabuki performers), the beauty and fortitude of Koyuki (a popular Japanese model turned actress), the skill of Shun Sugata (the jujitsu master who recently appeared in Quentin Tarantino's Kill Bill), and the opportunistic greed of Masato Harada (a famed Japanese director making his film debut as an actor).

By far the best performance in The Last Samurai is given by Ken Watanabe. His dignified presence and the sheer power of his demeanor make it hard to believe that he once was the skinny, ramen-noodle eating sidekick in 1986's epicurean classic Tampopo. Now bald and beefed up—from eating all those ramen noodles?—Watanabe radiates both sides of a samurai's seemingly paradoxical nature: power and compassion. At the same time he seems to exude a wisdom that goes beyond knowledge, but one finds oneself wondering, where did he learn such impeccable English?

The weakest link in the acting of The Last Samurai, unfortunately, is Tom Cruise. There is no doubt that he put a lot of time and effort and energy into the movie, but he seems to be one of those actors who can't transcend their own star status. In fact one of film's biggest blunders may be its ending. Watching a battered Cruise do a star turn by showing up in the Meiji Emperor's palace with Katsumoto's sword when everyone else on the battlefield has died, totally undermines the entire film's believability. Cruise's last attempt at historical fiction was 1992's laughable Far and Away, and he fares little better here. Cruise always seems to be Tom Cruise no matter what part or what risks he takes. He doesn't seem able to overcome his boyish good looks and disarming smile. Perhaps he is just too contemporary for historical films.

In the end, though, *The Last Samurai* is a bit of romantic fabrication which perpetuates some questionable history. The filmmakers are so busy extolling the heroic values of the samurai that they fail to mention such things as how most of Japan's population were kept in a serf-like status, serving the needs of the samurai for centuries. Their desire to stop modernization was not necessarily a choice of good values over bad, but one that was based in their unwillingness to give up their special status.

Similarly, Japan's path to modernization is presented in the movie as a result of the desire for profit of a few entrepreneurs, much to the detriment of the country in general, when in reality it was far more complicated than that. From the time Commodore Perry used gunboat diplomacy to force open Japan to Western trade, the country recognized that modernization was necessary for their survival. Otherwise Japan would become just another bone, like China and much of Africa, for imperial Westerners to fight over. To the country's credit, just 30 years after the time period of this film Japan would beat a Western power in the Ruso-Japanese war in 1905. It was the quick studies in Asia that survived.

And one last nitpicky point: When Japan did deliberately choose to go down the path of modernization she wisely shopped around and chose the best the West had to offer. To build her navy, she went to the ultimate naval power, Britain. When she wanted an army and modern armaments, she went to Germany—specifically Prussia—Europe's ultimate military state. Speaking of the German-Japanese connection, *The Last Samurai* provides a sympathetic portrayal of the samurai as the final link to a civilization that was honorable and ethical, yet it was that same samurai "ethic" that made it so easy to create a military state that would side with Germany during World War II.

—*Beverley Bare Buehrer*

CREDITS

Captain Nathan Algren: Tom Cruise
Katsumoto: Ken(saku) Watanabe
Simon Graham: Timothy Spall
Zebulon Gant: Billy Connolly
Col. Bagley: Tony Goldwyn
Omura: Masato Harada
Ujio: Hiroyuki Sanada
Taka: Koyuki
Winchester Rep: William Atherton
Ambassador Swanbeck: Scott Wilson

General Hasegawa: Togo Igawa
Nakao: Shun Sugata
Nobutada: Shin Koyamada
Emperor Meiji: Shichinosuke Nakamura

Origin: USA
Released: 2003
Production: Edward Zwick, Marshall Herskovitz, Tom Cruise, Paula Wagner, Scott Kroopf; Radar Pictures, Bedford Falls, Cruise-Wagner Productions; released by Warner Bros.
Directed by: Edward Zwick
Written by: Edward Zwick, John Logan, Marshall Herskovitz
Cinematography by: John Toll
Music by: Hans Zimmer
Sound: Jeff Wexler
Editing: Steven Rosenblum, Victor du Bois
Art Direction: Kim Sinclair
Costumes: Ngila Dickson
Production Design: Lily Kilvert
MPAA rating: R
Running time: 150 minutes

REVIEWS

Boxoffice. November, 2003, p. 28.
Chicago Sun-Times Online. December 5, 2003.
Entertainment Weekly. December 5, 2003, p. 63.
Los Angeles Times Online. December 5, 2003.
New York Times Online. December 5, 2003.
People. December 15, 2003, p. 30.
USA Today Online. December 5, 2003.
Variety Online. November 30, 2003.
Washington Post. December 5, 2003, p. C1.

QUOTES

Katsumoto (Ken Watanabe): "Do you believe a man can change his destiny?" Algren (Tom Cruise): "I believe a man does what he can until his destiny is revealed."

AWARDS AND NOMINATIONS

Nomination:
Oscars 2003: Art Dir./Set Dec., Costume Des., Sound, Support. Actor (Watanabe)
Golden Globes 2004: Actor—Drama (Cruise), Support. Actor (Watanabe), Orig. Score
Screen Actors Guild 2003: Support. Actress (Watanabe).

L'Auberge Espagnole (The Spanish Apartment) (Euro Pudding)

They came from Paris, Rome, London, and Berlin to . . . L'Auberge Espagnole . . . where a year can change a lifetime.
—Movie tagline

 Box Office: $3.8 million

Cedric Klapisch's *L'Auberge Espagnole* is a scintillating filmic sitcom from France, a refreshing look at the new mores, sexual and otherwise, spawned by Europe's new transcultural lifestyle. The film's box-office success, both in France and here, can only leave its fans hoping that it will give rise to a new subgenre: the erotic Euro-comedy.

What raises Klapisch's romp above the level of a sitcom is its timeliness. The film's handsome but lachrymose, twenty-something protagonist, Xavier (Romain Duris), hails from the macrocosmic cultural diversity of today's Paris. His work, however, leads him to discover his European identity within a microcosmic niche in Barcelona, as diverse as the Europe it is meant to represent. In the final analysis, *L'Auberge Espagnole,* also known as *Euro Pudding,* is really about making the most, especially sexually, out of the least, in this case, living space.

The modality within which Klapisch's characters, foreigners in Barcelona, find their new identity remains sexual, thereby turning the film into an unabashedly erotic soufflé. But on one level, *L'Auberge Espagnole* can be seen as propaganda for the benefits of the euro. We swallow the film's socio-political agenda because Klapisch puts it across in such a breezy manner. For the duration of the film, we forget how the globalism spawned by the euro is crippling the Continent's less privileged workers, as in Fernando Leon de Aranoa's *Mondays in the Sun* (reviewed in this volume).

Klapisch's ideological backing of the New Europe requires him to be as objective as possible. This objectivity then gets extended to Xavier's perspective, which is expressed through voiceover. The film's very first shot functions like a crystallization of Xavier's plight; we see him sitting stark nude in front of his personal computer. Xavier comments not only on his own situation, but also on the state of civilization. Klapisch uses cyberspace to imaginative, dazzling effect in order to grab his audience at the very start of the film. The opening titles themselves are superimposed over stills from scenes to come. The visual collage also includes flags from various European countries. Xavier starts telling us his story, then backtracks, and starts again, reveling in the fluidity that only cyberspace can grant.

Through pixillated movement, we see Xavier being led through the corridors of a hi-tech office environment until he reaches a cubicle where a friend of his father's is waiting to receive him. This is Xavier's situation: There is a need for an economist who knows about the Spanish market; Xavier would have to spend a year in Catalonia, in northeast Spain, in order to study the field; and all Xavier knows is a little Spanish, not the Catalan that is spoken in that region. What will see Xavier through is the Erasmus Exchange Program, intended to encourage young scholars to venture beyond their national boundaries. First, however, Xavier has to tangle with the Program's bureaucracy. As a female official recites a litany of forms he must complete, her speech goes into fast forward, and we see the screen filling up with the actual forms. The dizzying pace at which Xavier is required to function has him wondering to himself, "Why is the world such a mess?"

To add to it, he has to take leave of his girlfriend, the pretty Martine (Audrey Tautou), who is pained to see him go for a year. In a very emotional farewell, she turns away from him at the airport, while he says goodbye to his mother. As Xavier walks to the plane, we see him crying, but they cannot; his tears continue even after he is seated. While he's collecting his bags from the luggage carousel in Barcelona, a neurologist, Jean Michel (Xavier De Guillebon), and his beautiful wife, Anne-Sophie (Judith Godreche), latch onto him; the pair, Xavier's voiceover tells us, are just the kind of people he hates.

When he hits Barcelona proper, the city appears, again through special effects, as a cyber-reality before his eyes. "Any city is just a mass of secrets," he muses. In a flash, he actually sees himself as he would look once he has gotten to know the place.

Xavier's main problem, at this point, is finding accommodations. The first arrangement—staying with a Chilean friend of his mother's—doesn't quite work. The presence of her indomitable grandfather has Xavier moving out the next day, and he arranges to sleep, for the time being, on the sofa in the cheery apartment of the neurologist. He finds that he and Anne-Sophie have one thing in common: they both know little Spanish. He feels even more at home when Jean Michel tells him that he would like Xavier to take Anne-Sophie sightseeing.

Xavier's relationship with Anne-Sophie continues to provide a counterpoint of stability as his life is overturned by the European pastiche of which he's to become a part. After he replies to an ad, Xavier is interviewed by five of his future roommates. His congenial disposition endears him right away to the German Tobias (Barnaby Metschurat), the British Wendy (Kelly Reilly), the Italian Alessandro (Federico D'Anna), the Danish Lars (Christian Pagh) and the

Catalan Soledad (Christina Brondo). They promptly invite him to share their sexy, cramped lifestyle. For Xavier, it spells a new freedom, despite his mere cubbyhole of privacy and the overflowing fridge, in which shelf space is separated by nametags. Xavier's Belgian friend from the university, Isabelle (Cecile De France), will later join the group.

Klapisch's objective stance in sketching the background to Xavier's story now becomes extended to the film's more immediate erotic concerns. In this, what Klapisch shows is that the eroticism, as experienced by the viewer, remains, in a sense, distinct from the erotic urges of his characters within a particular scene. For example, when Xavier takes Anne-Sophie to a scenic spot, Klapisch photographs them from the back, in medium shot, so as to emphasize Anne-Sophie's ample figure. This, at a time when Xavier feels far too inhibited to think of her in anything but platonic terms. Similarly, Klapisch keeps to a medium shot to show Lars, Alessandro, Tobias and Xavier seated on a sofa, bored, watching TV at night. Isabelle enters and throws herself on Xavier's side of the sofa, forcing him to move over. What is curious is that Xavier knows Isabelle to be an incurable lesbian; consequently, he's not aroused. The viewer, however, cannot help but be struck by the erotic charge in Isabelle's behavior, especially as Klapisch captures it.

If this very entertaining mix can be deemed to have a drawback, it is that in comparison to its bold eroticism, its narrative progression keeps, for the most part, to the humble and the familiar, that is, to situations that would transpire in any realistic sitcom. An exception is when Xavier has a hallucination that the figure of Erasmus (Jacques Royer) appears to him in the flesh. Jean Michel gives him a CAT scan and assures him it's just stress. In the process, however, Jean Michel "sees into" Xavier's brain in a surreal fantasy and learns of his wife's adultery.

Wisely, Klapisch confines the thrust of what could have been a sprawling narrative to scenes that lead Xavier to bond with his roommates. From the start Xavier becomes, as it were, their conscience. It is he who negotiates with the irate landlord. When he reminds Wendy that her affair with the American hulk, Bruce (Olivier Raynal), is improper in light of the fact she has a boyfriend in England, she retorts, "It's just sex!" When Alistair (Iddo Goldberg), the boyfriend in question, pays a surprise visit, it allows Klapisch to execute a tour-de-force, as in his celebrated social comedy *When The Cat's Away* (1977), in which a number of characters scurry about a district of Paris looking for a cat. As Xavier and the others, via their cell phones, learn of Alistair's arrival, they do their damnedest to warn Wendy, who is at that moment in bed with Bruce. It is Xavier who gets to the scene first and is able to stall the boyfriend in the stairwell. But it is Wendy's brother William (Kevin Bishop), a houseguest, who saves the day when he climbs the outside of the building onto the balcony, gets Wendy to hide as he leaps into bed with Bruce, and pretends to be his lover just as Alistair opens the door.

Klapisch's episodic tale shows Xavier breaking all ties in his life by the time he returns to Paris; Martine, he discovers at the end, has also fallen out of love with him. Worse, even in Paris he feels a "foreigner amongst foreigners." He does manage to pass his exams, and armed with the respectable office position his training has secured him, Xavier is now ready to take off, as it were.

The film's closing moments show him gathering himself together in front of his PC as he sets down his experiences with the "Euro pudding," of which he still feels a part. A childhood photograph comes alive to remind Xavier that he always wanted to write books. "I'm French, but I'm Spanish and Danish as well!" he tells himself, then adds, "Like Europe, I'm a real mess!"

Most critics here seem to have taken to Klapisch's hang loose treatment of a timely subject. Kevin Thomas, writing in the *Los Angeles Times,* even calls the film an "exhilarating comedy . . . rich in details both comic and poignant that come only from personal experience." For Thomas, the film exudes a "warm, embracing spirit [that] is refreshing in these divisive times." In a similar vein, A. O. Scott points out in the *New York Times* that what the mix of Europeans in the film really stands for is "the transformation of Europe from a battleground to a consumerist, hedonist playground."

—Vivek Adarkar

CREDITS

Xavier: Romain Duris
Martine: Audrey Tautou
Anne-Sophie: Judith Godreche
Isabelle: Cecile de France
Wendy: Kelly Reilly
William: Kevin Bishop
Jean-Michel: Xavier De Guillebon

Origin: France, Spain
Language: English, French, Spanish
Released: 2002
Production: Bruno Levy; BAC Films Ltd., France 2 Cinema, StudioCanal, Mate Productions; released by Fox Searchlight
Directed by: Cedric Klapisch
Written by: Cedric Klapisch
Cinematography by: Dominique Colin
Sound: Cyril Moisson
Editing: Francine Sandberg
Art Direction: Francois Emmanuelli
Costumes: Anne Schotte
MPAA rating: R
Running time: 117 minutes

REVIEWS

Boston Globe Online. May 23, 2003.
Boxoffice. July, 2003, p. 46.
Chicago Sun-Times Online. May 23, 2003.
Chicago Tribune Online. May 23, 2003.
Entertainment Weekly Online. May 23, 2003.
Houston Chronicle Online. June 6, 2003.
Los Angeles Times Online. May 16, 2003.
New York Times Online. May 16, 2003.
USA Today Online. May 16, 2003.
Variety Online. May 19, 2003.
Washington Post. May 23, 2003, p. WE35.

QUOTES

Lesbian Isabelle (Cecile de France): "I wish you were a woman."
Xavier (Romain Duris): "The world is badly made."

Laurel Canyon

On the road to the perfect life, Sam and Alex took a little detour.
—Movie tagline

 Box Office: $3.6 million

Frances McDormand got a lot of critical attention for her role in *Laurel Canyon* as Jane, a pot-smoking, booze-guzzling, promiscuous, latter-day-hippie pop record producer. But although McDormand is good, the best acting in this unsatisfying, episodic picture is by Christian Bale as her son Sam, a young man trying desperately to carve out his own identity as the straight-laced, serious polar opposite of his mother. Bale's Sam is a cauldron of seething resentment, a formidable mind trying to stifle dangerous emotions, and a lost soul unable to find his way past a thicket of adolescent remorse into the sunlight of adulthood.

In the very last scene of the film, Sam sinks down into the pool of his mother's Laurel Canyon house, and, although his future isn't spelled out, you're supposed to get the impression that this is a moment of awakening and acceptance. His mother has just apologized to him for screwing up her parenting duties, and Sam has learned that his fiance Alex (Kate Beckinsale) really wants him. It's a standard Hollywood happy ending, but it's by no means clear how Sam's head is going to be any straighter after the bizarre events of the film.

Sam, the only significant male character, is, ironically enough, the most well-drawn and interesting of the quintet of major players in this too-predictable film by writer-director Lisa Cholodenko. Not in the running is Ian (Alessandro Nivola), a young singer-songwriter who is Jane's latest client and sex partner. He's a thinly drawn put-on artist, a shallow cad with a rude though somehow endearing cockiness. That Jane is smitten with him—they have a push-and-pull, dominant-and-submissive liaison—is one measure of how pathetic she is. Jane is a mature woman only in chronological years who's gone through plenty of men and now is dallying with one half her age, while continuing to act half her age. That Alex also becomes attracted to Ian is much harder to swallow.

Alex's fall from grace into the clutches of what is portrayed as Jane's netherworld of sex, drugs, and rock and roll would be laughably corny were it not played so seriously. Cholodenko sets up the plot like a paint-by-numbers, and Beckinsale's character gets the most constraining lines. She is an uptight, Ivy League graduate student who is working on her dissertation on human genomics, specifically, the genetic imprint of fruit fly reproduction (or something like that—the subject matter allows one of Ian's bandmates to get in a dig about insect sex). Before she departs with Sam for Los Angeles, her father gives Sam a lecture about his chosen field of psychiatry, telling him he should consider a more respectable branch of medicine—a snooty comment indeed.

The plot is a clunkily contrived setup. Sam has chosen to do his residency at a psychiatric hospital in Los Angeles because, he explains, it has the best program in his chosen specialty. But it's a return to the domain of his mother, who inhabits a world he professes to hate. Jane, a record producer who has had her share of success but has never grown up, is an embarrassment to him, and he even tries to portray her defects to Alex as some form of mental illness.

They are supposed to stay temporarily in his mother's Laurel Canyon home because she has told him she is living at her beach house. But when they arrive, they find out that she has broken up with her last boyfriend and he has taken the beach house, and Ian's band is making a record at the Laurel Canyon home in a recording studio on the property. So Alex and Sam have to stay there for at least a few days. Sam is concerned that her mother's wild, loud lifestyle will make it impossible for Alex to stay at home and work on her dissertation as Sam spends his days at his job in a nearby hospital.

The plot is telegraphed in clumsy fashion as Ian leers and ogles Alex, and his band members and Jane work to break down her icy demeanor. Eventually, as Alex returns from a jogging grocery trip (she at first refuses to even share food with the disgusting rock-and-rollers), Ian happens by on a motorcycle and insists he give her a ride back. Meanwhile, on his way to work on the very first morning, Sam almost collides on a canyon road with Sara (Natascha Mc-Elhone). When he gets to work, he finds Sara is a fellow resident, showing Cholodenko, for all the arthouse pretensions of her previous film, *High Art,* prefers the plotting devices of TV soap operas. It's painfully obvious that both Alex and Sam will be tempted to abandon their straight-laced propriety. And it's equally obvious what the outcome will be, because, for all its dabbling with naughtiness, this is plainly a movie with conventional mores.

The next step is that Alex must descend from her lofty "ivory tower" into the raunchy temptations offered by the music and loose morals of Ian and Jane. That she would do so is inexplicable, and so poor Beckinsale must undergo the obvious transformations that signal the moral undoing of a straight-laced intellectual—first her hair comes down, then her glasses go off, her clothes become a little more risque, and one day she simply gives up her dissertation and goes down to smoke some weed with Jane and the band. Later, she suddenly jumps into the pool with Ian and Jane and starts kissing each of them. In its characterization of Alex, *Laurel Canyon* follows the plot devices of pornography. It poses a ridiculous dichotomy between intellectualism and eroticism, between scientific brainpower and musical hipness, creating a character that is unbelievably uptight and then unraveling her with a few glances from a randy man.

For all the effort and authenticity contributed by Mc-Dormand, the character of Jane is almost as one-dimensional and stereotypical as Alex. Though McDormand gives Jane an appealing backbone and an unpredictable sassiness, she is scripted as a never-grown hippie who somehow manages to get her records produced despite smoking an enormous amount of marijuana and consuming alcohol in huge quantities. Jane is pathetic in that she believes in her own current relationships no matter how ridiculous they are. She could have been made a much stronger character without losing any of her edge. But Cholodenko makes her into a cliche, and McDormand fails to bust out of that cliche completely.

McElhone's character Sara serves mainly as an empty placeholder in the drama. She is competent, open, and depthless, and she comes after Sam without much reservation. Wide-eyed and speaking with a heavy European accent, McElhone's Sara is nothing more or less but a temptress, posing a difficult moral dilemma for Sam. Sam, you see, doesn't want to do anything that would indicate he has some of the same human weaknesses as his mother; he wants to be her opposite in every way.

Sam is one of those movie shrinks who himself needs therapy. Bale brings a complexity to the role that supercedes the script, which keeps thrusting him into impossible emotional situations. He is angry and put off when Alex falls into the clutches of his mother, and he is conflicted about Sara, but decides to continue to pretend he is an automaton.

Cholodenko doesn't tell this story very smoothly. The movie is chock full of abrupt scene endings and blunt cuts, with moods trimmed short and emotional scenes truncated. The film has all the subtlety of a sledgehammer, despite its occasionally artsy shots. The pop soundtrack also is used as a blatant mood signpost, thwarting any possible ambiguity. Various subplots involving Sam's work go nowhere; and every scene is pointed toward the film's big lesson—which is the struggle to accept oneself and others as they are. It's trite, and it's flat.

As a comedy drama, *Laurel Canyon* has very little comedy and not nearly enough drama. There are few surprises in the proceedings, as the inevitable conflicts unfold like clockwork, and the ending also eschews adventuresomeness for a sort of squishy, feel-good ambiguity.

For the way it opposes Jane's scene and Alex's sensibilities, Los Angeles moral slovenliness and East Coast intellectual uptightness, *Laurel Canyon* is awash in false dichotomies. And for all its emphasis on the temptations of a free-and-easy sexual lifestyle, the film is markedly unerotic. In fact, the most erotic scene is one in which Sara and Sam sit in a car and talk about what they want to do to each other sexually; this dialogue is daring. But everything else is perfunctory, and McDormand isn't convincing as a mature sexpot; she and Nivola have absolutely no chemistry, as he is merely annoying. And the idea that Alex and Jane have some sexual energy comes out of left field. Too many scenes are embarrassingly like soft pornography, and too many others are simply lifeless and predictable.

Credit Cholodenko for seeing McDormand's potential, and credit McDormand with jumping at a part that allows her to show a much different side of her than her famous *Fargo* role. But the hard-working, under-appreciated Bale is the real revelation here. He is the only character who makes his emotional conflict transcend the hackneyed and predictable bounds of the script.

—Michael Betzold

CREDITS

Jane: Frances McDormand
Sam: Christian Bale
Alex: Kate Beckinsale
Ian: Alessandro Nivola
Sara: Natascha (Natasha) McElhone

Origin: USA
Released: 2002
Production: Susan A. Stover, Jeff Levy-Hinte; Good Machine, Tucker Tooley; released by Sony Pictures Classics
Directed by: Lisa Cholodenko

Written by: Lisa Cholodenko
Cinematography by: Wally Pfister
Music by: Craig (Shudder to Think) Wedren
Music Supervisor: Karyn Rachtman
Editing: Amy Duddleston
Art Direction: Stephanie Gilliam
Costumes: Cindy Evans
Production Design: Catherine Hardwicke
MPAA rating: R
Running time: 101 minutes

REVIEWS

Boxoffice. November, 2002, p. 126.
Entertainment Weekly. March 14, 2003, p. 45.
Los Angeles Times Online. March 7, 2003.
New York Times Online. March 7, 2003.
People. March 17, 2003, p. 38.
Vanity Fair. March, 2003, p. 130.
Variety. May 27, 2002, p. 29.

AWARDS AND NOMINATIONS

Nomination:
Ind. Spirit 2004: Support. Actor (Nivola), Support.
Actress (McDormand).

Lawless Heart

Is the life you have the life you want?
—Movie tagline
We think we live in a rational world . . . then we screw it up.
—Movie tagline

Consider this British drama "A funeral and three crises." The funeral is that of Stuart (David Coffey, whom you only see in home movies), who has drowned in a boating accident in the small Essex seaside town of Maldon where he grew up. His funeral is the jumping-off point for three interlocking stories of characters whom the viewer sees at Stuart's wake and whom we gradually learn about as they deal with the aftermath of Stuart's death.

The first crisis is that of Dan (Bill Nighy), who turns out to be Stuart's brother-in-law. A generally morose farmer, Dan seems to be catapulted into the throes of a mid-life crisis by Stuart's passing. At the wake, Dan strikes up a conversation with Frenchwoman Corinne (Celarie), the local florist who's supplied the funeral flowers. Corinne's an attractive woman of a certain age with a generally worldly outlook on life. She asks Dan if he's depressed and he replies that he doesn't know—he also doesn't know if he's happy or feeling much of anything at all. Life has become narrow and Corinne tells Dan that it's not easy to change—change needs a crisis and the courage to follow through.

Judy (Ellie Haddington), Stuart's older sister, is going over his financial papers. He didn't make a will and died intestate, thus making her his heir. But the gay Stuart had a partner, Nick (Tom Hollander), with whom he shared a house and a local restaurant and Judy thinks it's only fair that Nick get Stuart's money. Dan objects because they have a family and can use the inheritance themselves. He figures the younger Nick will be able to take care of himself and will go back to London (where he and Stuart met) to start over.

Later, Dan is doing the shopping at the supermarket and runs into Corinne. During their casual, if awkward, chat, she invites him for dinner. It's an odd situation: does she know Dan is married and is she hinting at having an affair with him (she's already told him about a married lover who couldn't make a decision about his life) or is it simply a friendly gesture because he seems so lost? In a quandary, Dan tells Judy he's going to pop into a party at Nick's house and then spends his time in a pub. (The viewer sees that it's not dinner a deux; Corinne has invited several friends, although Dan doesn't know this.) Nick walks into the pub and they have a drink and a very stilted conversation about fidelity. Nick thinks Dan is questioning his commitment to Stuart while Dan is wondering if he could have an affair.

It all comes to naught when Dan, who is sitting in his car outside Nick's house, is mistaken for a mini-cab driver by the inebriated Michelle (Sally Hurst) and he winds up driving her home—and getting paid with oral sex. An upset Judy later tells Dan that she thinks Nick has already found someone else, a girl named Charlie (Smith) who is waitressing at the restaurant where Judy has a very uncomfortable birthday celebration with her family.

A return to Stuart's funeral leads to the second crisis, which is Nick's. Neo-hippie n'er-do-well Tim (Douglas Henshall), Stuart's cousin, returns in time for the wake after being away for eight years. Estranged from his parents, Tim is seeking a bed and Nick offers. He moves in as Judy and Nick are clearing out Stuart's belongings and Nick talks about going back to London. Tim throws a party at the house and Nick finds a naked, passed-out young woman in his bed. This turns out to be the socially graceless but good-hearted Charlie, who's been abandoned by her lout of a boyfriend.

When Nick gives her money for a cab the next morning, she promises to pay him back. They meet again in the supermarket where Charlie works as a cashier and she is suddenly showing up on Nick's doorstep like a friendly stray that Nick is too soft to shoo away. When she visits, Judy is upset to see Charlie so apparently at home and abruptly tells

Nick that she and Dan have decided they need Stuart's money after all.

Meanwhile, Nick has decided to re-open the restaurant, although he is having employee trouble; he's touched when Charlie decides to help him out part-time. Nick is also desperately missing Stuart and has some bad nights, which aren't helped by Tim's drunken thoughtlessness. He finally kicks Tim out. The next day, Nick and Charlie go walking by the marshes and Charlie impulsively breaks into an empty beach hut—abruptly the two have sex. As they drive back into town, they pass a forlorn Tim walking by the roadside.

And now it's time for the third crisis—that of Tim. At Stuart's wake, he mooches a place to stay off Nick and re-establishes his friendship with his adoptive brother David (Stuart Laing), who works for Dan on the farm. Tim also learns that David has gotten divorced, apparently because he had an affair. Within days of being home, Tim's trying to pick up local dress shop owner Leah (Josephine Butler), whom he invites to his party. She comes, but abruptly sneaks off after seeing David. It's easy to connect the dots and realize that it's Leah that David was seeing during his marriage. She sees Tim again and tells him she's willing to have a casual relationship and Tim eventually learns about her and David's shared past.

A friend of Tim's shows up and offers him a partnership in a London bar if he can raise his share of the cash. His latest drunken episode leads to Nick chucking Tim out and he is forced to ask if he can stay at his parents' (who refuse to loan him any money). He and David clean out his old room and store the junk in the family beach hut. David and Tim get into a fight over Leah, whom Tim is suddenly serious about, but he finally realizes that Leah is still hung up on David and advises David not to blow his second chance. Having managed to talk Nick into letting him stay again, the two—both miserable—have a drink and a heart-to-heart.

A sort of coda ties up many of the loose ends: Nick and Charlie have a talk and she realizes that what happened was a one-time experience, but they can remain friends. Nick visits Judy and Dan to tell them he has decided to move back to London. He explains to Judy about Charlie; Judy has also had a change of heart and tells Nick that she'll give him Stuart's money. Nick then offers Tim a loan for his bar project and they all gather to watch some home movies of a happy Stuart as the credits come on.

It takes a bit of doing to fill in the gaps between the three stories although writer/directors Neil Hunter and Tom Hunsinger don't go out of their way to withhold information—even minor incidents such as birthday scarf and a bouquet of flowers are all eventually accounted for. Although, since the viewer is only seeing a certain moment in time in the lives of these people, you never learn too much about their pasts. While Dan seems to be having a standard long-married, middle-aged man cri de coeur, what's Corinne's story? She's an exotic bloom among a field

of daisies and it's a credit to the brief moments of screen time that actress Celarie has that you're interested in knowing more about her.

You also don't know how long Stuart and Nick were together or why they moved from London to Stuart's obviously backwater hometown. Hollander's Nick is a passive reactor stunned by grief. His befriending the hapless Charlie gives him someone else to concentrate on and you can even understand their sudden sexual encounter—and Nick's devastating loneliness for its happening at all.

Tim is a longtime wanderer of uncertain talents (except for freeloading) and, while his pursuit of the attractive Leah is reasonable, his sudden seriousness about their possible relationship and his willingness to settle down seems out of character. Has Stuart's sudden death caused Tim to exam the fecklessness of his own life? While actor Henshall has a certain shaggy appeal, Tim is not a particularly interesting character.

The secondary characters of Judy, Charlie, Leah, and David—and the actors who portray them—fill in their roles nicely and the marshy coastal scenes are an attractive change from the more common London settings of any number of British pictures. Hearts might rule heads in this melancholy drama but, as it turns out, that organ is very intelligent indeed.

—*Christine Tomassini*

CREDITS

Nick: Tom Hollander
Tim: Douglas Henshall
Dan: Bill Nighy
Corinne: Clementine Celarie
Leah: Josephine Butler
Judy: Ellie Haddington
David: Stuart Laing
Charlie: Sukie Smith
Stuart: David Coffey
Darren: Dominic Hall
Mrs. Marsh: June Barrie
Mr. Marsh: Peter Symonds

Origin: Great Britain
Released: 2001
Production: Martin Pope; released by First Look Pictures
Directed by: Neil Hunter, Tom Hunsinger
Written by: Neil Hunter, Tom Hunsinger
Cinematography by: Sean Bobbitt
Music by: Adrian Johnston
Sound: John Pearson
Editing: Scott Thomas

Art Direction: Cristina Casali
Costumes: Linda Alderson
Production Design: Lynne Whiteread
MPAA rating: R
Running time: 99 minutes

REVIEWS

Boxoffice. April, 2002, p. 189.
New York Times Online. February 16, 2003.
New York Times Online. February 21, 2003.
Sight and Sound. July, 2002, p. 47.
Variety. August 20, 2001, p. 26.
Village Voice Online. February 19, 2003.
Washington Post. May 9, 2003, p. WE48.

QUOTES

Dan (Bill Nighy): "I once faked a broken heart, but I ran out of energy."
Dan (Bill Nighy): "I supposed I have emotions, but I don't make a meal of them."

TRIVIA

The farmhouse that serves as Dan and Judy's home is where director Neil Hunter grew up.

AWARDS AND NOMINATIONS

L.A. Film Critics 2003: Support. Actor (Nighy).

Le Cercle Rouge (The Red Circle)

Jean-Pierre Melville is one of the most distinctive of French film directors. From the exoticism of the (implied) brother-sister incest of *Les Enfants Terribles* (1949), to his evocative treatment of the Paris criminal underworld in *Bob le Flambeur* (1955), to his masterful blending of Zen and existential cool in *Le Samourai* (1967), Melville's famously slow-paced films display a highly original blending of American influences (particularly the Warner Brothers gangster films of the 1930s) and French

sensibility. He has influenced filmmakers from Robert Bresson, Francois Truffaut, and Jean-Luc Godard—appearing in the latter's *A Bout de Souffle* (*Breathless;* 1960)—to John Woo and Quentin Tarantino. The exotic strangeness of Woo's early films is at least partially due to Melville, and the studied artlessness of Tarantino's *Jackie Brown* (1997) is almost an homage to the director. The six no-frills, increasingly abstract, crime thrillers Melville made from *Le Doulos* (1962) to *Un Flic* (1972) are French film noir at its best.

Le Cercle Rouge, the twelfth of Melville's thirteen films, was first released, barely, in the United States in a dubbed, truncated version with forty minutes removed and the director's distinctive style destroyed. American viewers can now see for the first time the entire film, which was restored by Rialto Pictures, with new subtitles by Lenny Borger, and which is "presented" by Woo. *Le Cercle Rouge* is central to Melville's world where both criminals and their pursuers are bound by codes of honor.

The enigmatic convict Corey (Alain Delon) is about to be released from prison in Marseille when a guard (Pierre Collet) talks him into organizing and carrying out a robbery. Meanwhile, the solemn policeman Mattei (Andre Bourvil) is escorting the criminal Vogel (Gian-Maria Volonte) to prison by train. Melville cuts between these two stories for the first quarter of *Le Cercle Rouge* until they converge. This is inevitable in a Melville film because his world is governed by fate. It is also typical of the director's understated approach that we never know exactly what crimes the two protagonists have committed, although Vogel is obviously the more dangerous. Too much information would detract from Melville's tough-guy romanticism.

Melville takes this approach even further in his next and final film, *Un Flic,* in which the protagonists played by Delon (the cop of the title) and Richard Crenna are acquaintances, perhaps friends, and both are in love with Catherine Deneuve, who seems to love both. How these three got together is never explained; what matters is the dynamics of the triangle.

A similar situation is at the heart of *Le Cercle Rouge.* The first place Corey goes after his release from prison is the apartment of Rico (Andre Ekyan), the crime boss for whom he once worked. Their reunion is tense for several reasons, among them the fact that Corey's former lover (Anna Douking) is now Rico's girlfriend. Rico clearly sees Corey as a threat to the stability of both his personal and private lives. What their relationship was before Corey went to jail is not explained; neither is it made clear whether the woman took up with Rico after Corey's imprisonment or betrayed him beforehand. What is clear is Corey's smoldering resentment toward them both. Interestingly, except for customers and performers in a nightclub, this woman is the only female in the film, and she has no lines. For the most part, Melville's women stand by and watch helplessly as their men destroy each other and themselves.

Vogel escapes from Mattei by picking the lock on his handcuffs and jumping feet first out the window of their train compartment. While Mattei organizes a massive manhunt—more proof of Vogel's dangerous status—the fugitive makes his way to a diner's parking lot and hides in the trunk of Corey's car. Such a coincidence might be laughable in another context but works wonderfully in Melville's fate-ruled universe. Later, Mattei arrests a student on trumped up charges of selling drugs in order to persuade his father, nightclub-owner Santi (Francois Perier), to betray the thieves.

The audience does not know that Corey has seen Vogel enter the trunk until the car is stopped at a police roadblock and Corey cleverly avoids having the trunk inspected by claiming that the car dealership where he just bought the vehicle failed to give him the necessary key. When Rico's thugs track down Corey, Vogel returns the favor by emerging from the trunk with gun blazing. The mixture of unexpected humor and stylized violence in this tremendous scene is typical of the styles of both American and European films of the period. See, for example, other such films starring Volonte as Sergio Leone's *Per un Pugno di Dollari* (*A Fistful of Dollars*; 1964) and Elio Petri's *Indagine su un Cittadino al di Sopra di Ogni* (*Investigation of a Citizen Above Suspicion*; 1970).

The pair make their way to Paris and begin planning their crime. It is also typical of Melville's style that the audience learns what they are up to only a bit at a time. This element is especially important when Corey recruits ex-policeman Jansen (Yves Montand) as the third member of the gang. Jansen is a skilled marksman, but how this ability will come into play is never clear—until it happens, again, in a clever, sudden burst of action.

Jansen is anything but a cool trigger man when first seen in the throes of delirium tremens with a multitude of insects and rodents crawling over him. This fantastic touch, atypical of Melville, is unsettling, but the director's aim is always both to keep well ahead of his viewers and to keep them off balance. Jansen's transformation from grubby, sweaty alcoholic into well-dressed professional is just as startling.

Le Cercle Rouge appeared during a period when the great Montand was at the pinnacle of his powers, most notably with his performances in Costa Gavras's *Z* (1969), *L'Aveu* (*The Confession*; 1970), and *Etat de Seige* (*State of Seige*; 1973). That he would even undertake a small character part at this time is notable, but Montand fleshes out his character with small gestures that break through Jansen's world weariness to suggest he wants to assert his individuality. Jansen is the most existential character in his overt attempt to define himself through his actions, while also perhaps getting back at those in power who have wronged or neglected him. When he and Mattei confront each other during the violent conclusion and the good cop exclaims, "You!" that one word speaks volumes about Jansen's spotted history.

Bourvil also gives a solid performance as the no-nonsense policeman, whose polished professionalism resembles that of Corey and Jansen. Melville greatly admires those who know how to do things well and are proud of their work—on both sides of the law. He makes Mattei just as distinctive as the criminals by showing he is resented by his bosses, who pay his concierge to spy on him, and by showing glimpses of his private life. There is a photograph of a woman in Mattei's apartment with no explanation of who or where she is. He becomes a different person as soon as he arrives at home, enthusiastically and affectionately greeting and feeding his three cats. (This entrance is shown twice to emphasize how Mattei is obsessed by routine.) Why he keeps the door to the kitchen closed is yet another mystery.

The female Siamese who refuses to budge from her comfortable chair is the pet Melville was often photographed with, and the other cats are also the director's. By including them, is the director calling attention to similarities between himself and Mattei: mostly objective with undercurrents of passion yet always in control? Bourvil inhabits the detective so well in part because of his bland everyman looks. It is hard to believe that he was once a beloved music-hall comedian. The actor died after making one more film.

Delon, star of three of Melville's final four films, embodies the essence of Melville cool. The actor's rather blank prettiness is quite fitting for a Melville hero because all his protagonists are wearing masks. Corey seems to display no emotions because he knows his enemies will capitalize on any signs of weakness, as Rico has apparently done regarding the woman.

The centerpiece of *Le Cercle Rouge* is the robbery of the swank jewelry shop in which Jansen's expertise is used to foil the alarm system. Even in the age of high-tech caper films like *Entrapment* (1999), Melville's decidedly low-tech approach is still thrilling. The robbery is seemingly carried out in real time with the director lingering lovingly over all the details, especially the circuitous route Corey and Vogel take to enter the building. (The robbery in *Un Flic* is even more deliberately paced.) While such a heist would be the main point of many films, for Melville, it is almost window dressing to his study of masculine behavior. The film gains additional texture from the cinematography of Henri Decae, who began his long career with Melville. Decae's muted colors almost approximate black and white at times.

It is Melville's attention to detail, his calculated pace, that obviously bewildered the film's original American distributor. No one at that time could have gotten away with a 140-minute thriller. In his final films, Melville seems to be striving for greater and greater simplicity and achieving it through a lack of speed bound to infuriate almost any viewer other that devout cineastes. *Le Cercle Rouge* is not as wonderful as *Les Enfants Terribles*, *Bob le Flambeur*, or *Le Samourai*, but it is still an exhilarating experience. The film can be better appreciated now than in the 1970s because its distinctively cool style stands out from the crowd more than ever.

—*Michael Adams*

CREDITS

Corey: Alain Delon
Vogel: Gian Marie Volonte
Jansen: Yves Montand
Mattei: Andre Bourvil
Santi: Francois Perier

Origin: France
Language: French
Released: 1970
Production: Robert Dorfman; Films Corona, Selenia; released by Rialto Pictures
Directed by: Jean-Pierre Melville
Written by: Jean-Pierre Melville
Cinematography by: Henri Decae
Music by: Eric De Marsen
Sound: Jean Neny, Jacques Carrere
Editing: Marie-Sophie Dubus
Costumes: Theo Meurisse
MPAA rating: Unrated
Running time: 140 minutes

REVIEWS

Chicago Sun-Times Online. May 23, 2003.
Entertainment Weekly. March 7, 2003, p. 52.
Los Angeles Times Online. March 14, 2003.
New York Times Online. January 5, 2003.
New York Times Online. January 10, 2003.
Washington Post. April 11, 2003, p. WE45.

QUOTES

Mattei (Andre Bourvil): "All men are guilty. They're born innocent, but it doesn't last."

Le Divorce

Everything Sounds Sexier In French.
—Movie tagline

For two American sisters in Paris, loving again is the best revenge.
—Movie tagline

 Box Office: $9 million

Merchant-Ivory adaptation based on Diane Johnson's best-selling 1997 novel, *Le Divorce* is a comedy of manners that explores the complex nature of American-French relations. Kate Hudson stars as Isabel Walker, a young Californian (and recent USC dropout) from Santa Barbara who flies to Paris to visit her expatriate sister, Roxy (Naomi Watts). An acclaimed poet who is pregnant with her second child, Roxy finds her personal life falling apart when her Parisian husband Charles-Henri (Melvil Poupaud) leaves her for a Russian woman named Magda.

While Isabel attempts to help her sister during this difficult time, she also finds herself carrying on an affair with Edgar (Thierry Lhermitte), an older, married French diplomat who also happens to be Roxy's brother-in-law. As the mistress to worldly Uncle Edgar, Isabel is given an education in haute cuisine and haute couture. Edgar's penchant for bestowing gifts on his lovers is well known, and when he presents Isabel with an incredibly expensive, red Hermès Kelly handbag (named after Grace Kelly) that she carries with her everywhere, all of Paris knows she is a kept woman. With every tryst, Isabel's transformation from casual Californian to chic, sophisticated Frenchwoman becomes more evident.

Meanwhile, the heartbroken Roxy nobly suffers as her caddish husband presses for "le divorce," which she refuses to grant him. The kinship between Roxy and her husband's family turns sour when Charles-Henri decides he's entitled to half of a valuable Georges de La Tour painting that has been in his wife's family for years. Suzanne de Persand, the snobbish matriarch (Leslie Caron) of Charles-Henri's family, would like to see her clan acquire part ownership of the painting too. Suzanne is also Edgar's sister, and she quickly learns about his dalliance with Isabel, as does his wife, which, naturally, further provokes familial discord.

Relations between the American and French families become even more complicated when Roxy's and Isabel's cheerful parents (played by Sam Waterston and Stockard Channing) show up in Paris to lend their support to Roxy and put an end to the tussle over the painting. Viewers get a quick lesson in art values when experts from both the Louvre and Christie's have opposing opinions on the authenticity of the painting. The scenes involving Channing and Waterston are mildly amusing and add warmth to the film. However, it's Thomas Lennon as Roger, the brother of Isabel and Roxy, who generates the most laughs. Although his character doesn't get much screen time, Lennon has the best lines in *Le Divorce*, and he plays them for all they're worth.

This comedy of clashing cultures, which primarily focuses on romance in the glamorous City of Light, takes a bizarre turn when Magda's jealous husband (Matthew Modine) goes ballistic in a strange scene atop the Eiffel Tower. The action won't be revealed here, but the odd turn of events is highly contrived and doesn't conform to the rest of the movie.

In addition to Modine's enraged husband, several other supporting characters show up throughout the film. Glenn Close is memorable as Olivia Pace, a wise expatriate author and one of Edgar's many ex-lovers, who serves as a mentor to Isabel. Bebe Neuwirth and Stephen Fry make appearances as art experts, and Jean-Marc Barr plays an attractive divorce attorney.

Unfortunately, *Le Divorce* is so busy and crammed with characters and relationships that it's impossible to engage the audience with one specific story. Infidelity, pregnancy, attempted suicide, murder, and the struggle for custody of a painting are just a few of the situations stuffed into this movie. Both Watts (an Oscar nominee for this year's *21 Grams*) and Hudson (acclaimed for her performance in 2000's *Almost Famous*) get shortchanged here. There's just too much going on in *Le Divorce* and not enough emphasis placed on character development and plot.

Critical reaction to the film was decidedly lukewarm. Most critics thought *Le Divorce* was dull and missed its intended mark. Its detractors cited a hectic story and too many characters as the film's weak points. Although the cast is full of fine actors, they're not given a chance to shine in this trifle that never achieves the witty tone or speed of farce.

It's interesting to note that *Le Divorce* is the twenty-fifth literary adaptation from the Merchant-Ivory team. Although producer Ismail Merchant, director James Ivory, and screenwriter Ruth Prawer Jhabvala were trying for a light touch with this urbane comedy of manners, their languid take on the continental divide never sizzles.

—*Beth Fhaner*

CREDITS

Isabel Walker: Kate Hudson
Roxeanne de Persand: Naomi Watts
Edgar Cosset: Thierry Lhermitte
Charles-Henri de Persand: Melvil Poupaud
Suzanne de Persand: Leslie Caron
Olivia Pace: Glenn Close
Margreeve Walker: Stockard Channing
Chester Walker: Sam Waterston
Roger Walker: Thomas Lennon
Tellman: Matthew Modine

Magda: Rona Hartner
Maitre Bertram: Jean-Marc Barr
Piers Janely: Stephen Fry
Julia Manchevering: Bebe Neuwirth
Antoine de Persand: Samuel Labarthe
Charlotte de Persand: Nathalie Richard
Yves: Romain Duris
Louvre Expert: Daniel Mesguich

Origin: USA
Released: 2003
Production: Ismail Merchant, Michael Schiffer; Merchant-Ivory Productions, Radar Pictures; released by Fox Searchlight
Directed by: James Ivory
Written by: Ruth Prawer Jhabvala
Cinematography by: Pierre Lhomme
Music by: Richard Robbins
Sound: Ludovic Henault
Editing: John David Allen
Costumes: Carol Ramsey
Production Design: Frederic Benard
MPAA rating: PG-13
Running time: 115 minutes

REVIEWS

Chicago Sun-Times Online. August 8, 2003.
Entertainment Weekly. August 15, 2003, p. 51.
Los Angeles Times. May 4, 2003, p. E31.
Los Angeles Times Online. August 5, 2003.
Los Angeles Times Online. August 8, 2003.
New York Times Online. August 8, 2003.
People. August 18, 2003, p. 36.
San Francisco Chronicle. August 8, 2003, p. D1.
USA Today Online. August 8, 2003.
Vanity Fair. August, 2003, p. 64.
Variety Online. July 24, 2003.
Washington Post. August 8, 2003, p. WE41.

The League of Extraordinary Gentlemen

Prepare for the Extraordinary.
—Movie tagline

The power of seven becomes a league of one.
—Movie tagline

A Rogue. A Scientist. A Spy. A Hunter. A Vampire. A Beast. An Immortal.
—Movie tagline

 Box Office: $66.4 million

As the Bobbies make their nightly rounds in 1899 London, a rumbling suddenly starts to shake the streets. Tiles fall from roofs and dogs scramble away in terror as a tank breaks through a wall. A tank? Yep, an honest to goodness, armor-plated, military-action, artillery-toting tank. Hey wait a minute, isn't this 1899? OK, let's give the filmmakers a break . . . at least for now. The tank smashes into the Bank of England, but its seemingly German crew is not after money. They want the antique Leonardo da Vinci plans for the city of Venice that are stored there.

A month later it seems that it's the turn of British soldiers to break into a Berlin dirigible factory and blow it up. Is this retaliation for the Bank of England caper? But then we notice that there is a mysterious masked man orchestrating it all. His name is The Fantom and when one of the zeppelin scientists asks him what he wants, his reply is "The world. I want the world." What the Fantom really wants is to start a world war that will engulf Europe into an arms race from which he, with superior weapons, will profit enormously.

But a war in Europe is sure to overflow into America and Asia and Africa too, so an agent of the British government, Sanderson Reed (Tom Goodman-Hill) has been sent to Kenya to enlist the help of the legendary hunter Allan Quatermain (Sean Connery). The retired Quatermain, however, has no interest in coming to the aid of the Empire. Not, that is, until men dressed in body armor and firing automatic weapons shoot his friend Nigel (David Hemmings) and blow up his club. "The war has arrived," Sanderson tells him. "Very well, Reed, I'm in," replies Quatermain.

At a meeting in London not long afterward, Allan meets the man who has brought him there, the mysterious "M" (Richard Roxburgh). M explains that several times in history men with extraordinary abilities have been called upon to save the Empire, and this is one of those times. The Fantom plans on blowing up Venice in order to prevent a peace meeting from taking place that would stop the war from which he is planning to profit. Quatermain and the others M has called upon must stop him.

Quatermain now meets three of the other extraordinary people M has brought in for the mission: famed Indian pirate and techno-whiz Captain Nemo (Nasseruddin Shah) whose massive submarine, the Nautilus, will transport them to Venice in just four days; the elusive and now totally invisible gentleman thief Rodney Skinner (Tony Curran); and the beautiful Mina Harker (Peta Wilson). The last's special talent, the fact that she's a vampire, will be revealed when the quartet go to the house of another whose talents they want to enlist, Dorian Gray (Stuart Townsend).

The jaded, handsome and young Gray initially has no interest in joining Quatermain's team, but when he sees his old flame, Mina, he changes his mind. Gray's talent? He is actually very old and has lots of experience and he seems to be indestructible . . . as long as he never looks at the painting of himself, which ages so he won't. We know he's indestructible because those men in armor are back and shooting up his living quarters, trying to kill the league before it's even formed.

During the shootout Quatermain suddenly realizes there is another in the room who is on their side, a young American secret service agent and sharpshooter named Thomas Sawyer (Shane West), and together the six manage to win the battle. Now they set off to Paris to pick up the seventh and last member of their league, Dr. Jekyll (Jason Flemying) who, at the time they arrive, is racing across rooftops as the humongous and hostile Mr. Hyde. This member they can't enlist with logic or even feminine wiles. This guy will need ropes and chains and a pardon that will allow him to return to Britain after the mission.

So this is the League of Extraordinary Gentlemen, although "gentlemen" may be quite a stretch, and one of them is a woman. Each, does, however, bring something special to the group: Hyde has his superhuman strength, Gray's age has given him experience, Mina has become a scientist, Quatermain is the great hunter, Skinner's invisibility gives him stealth, and Nemo has undreamed of technology. As for Sawyer, well, maybe he's the comic relief? The rest of the plot to *The League of Extraordinary Gentlemen,* or *LXG* as 20th Century Fox refers to it, involves saving Venice, preventing the war, and bringing down The Fantom. Along the way we will discover traitors, heroes, hidden identities, phony missions and deceptive practices.

The idea of creating a fin-de-siecle version of the X-Men by creatively using familiar literary characters is a most appealing one. The movie began its life in 1998 as a six-part comic book/graphic novel written by Alan Moore and illustrated by Kevin O'Neil. Moore realized that the copyrights to most 19th-century literature had expired and he was free to expropriate and expand on the now-familiar characters they contained. (One exception is the *Invisible Man,* whose original character was named Hawley Griffin, but who has been replaced with a character named Rodney Skinner because H. G. Well's estate still controls his works.)

Among other changes, the movie has added a character not in the comic: Thomas Sawyer. It's never really explained if this is a grown up version of Mark Twain's Tom Sawyer, but one would be forgiven if they assumed so. So why was he added? To make the League less exclusively British, to appeal to the younger viewer, and to act as a surrogate son for Connery's Quatermain and make him seem less hostile and cantankerous. Not good enough reasons to add a character who seems to do nothing but be a distracting, snarling cowboy. (Dorian Gray was not in the original comic but does join the League in the next book.) The movie also drops one character which, considering the casting of Sean Connery, might have been much more interesting. Campion Bond is the overweight ancestor of 007 . . . but James Bond is an MGM character and this is a Fox movie.

Also in the original story the leader is not Allan Quatermain but Mina Harker. But this is Peta Wilson's first major film and one can imagine that nobody upstages Sean Connery. And finally in the original comic book each of the League members has a serious problem: H. Rider Haggard's African adventurer Quatermain is addicted to heroin, Hyde is insane, Nemo a megalomaniac, and Mina a social outcast as much for believing in issues like obtaining the right to vote for women as for being a vampire. Now their weaknesses are just the all-to-human traits of distrust, paranoia, bitterness.

Another intriguing side of *League* is its cross referencing of other Victorian references such as when Quatermain complains that he didn't make as good a travel time as did Phileas Fogg, or when Nemo's first mate (Terry O'Neill) says, "Call me Ishmael," or when Mr. Hyde is discovered creating havoc in the Rue Morgue in Paris. One wishes the filmmakers had done more with this idea, but perhaps all these literary references are just too obscure for many of the kids trapped in sub-par education systems. Or maybe the filmmakers don't trust the intelligence of their audience in the same way the comic book writer trusted his. It's a shame that the film traded much of the comic's intelligence and wit for explosions and chases and lumbering fights and not-so-special effects.

While the costumes and sets of *League* are interesting, in the end they have a cheap quality to them, and that is especially true for the film's special effects. The first hint that someone cut corners in this area is when Quatermain's club explodes in Kenya. There seems to be no structural damage to the building and flames are superimposed over the building's image as if the effect had been created in the 1960s for television. And speaking of silliness and destruction, there's a car chase in Venice where there are no roads but canals and where the car does as much property destruction as The Fantom's bombs. (And where jittery cameras cheaply substitute for the shaking ground created by bombs going off.) Not to mention just the common sense notion that watching Venice crumble into itself when we know that it is still there harmed only by rising sea water and not bombs, stretches our sense of disbelief beyond what will help the film.

In fact, this type of literary-inspired story didn't need to strain our sense of disbelief at all for it to be engaging and fun. Dr. Jekyll and Mr. Hyde would have been enough just for their character differences but why did Mr. Hyde have to end up looking like The Hulk? And how did Quatermain's

crew know exactly where to set up the nets to capture him as he runs over Paris rooftops? The Fantom's flame-throwing robots also push the groaning factor in this film as does its total disregard for literary "truths." (How can vampire Mina have no trouble at all standing about in the noonday sun?) And tell me no one notices that behemoth of a ship, the Nautilus, rising at the docks in London or travelling down the Seine—one assumes—to Paris, or hiding in the canals of Venice?

Adding to the confusion of the story is the Fantom's fortress/factory in Mongolia. Is it old or new? It's churning out the latest in weapons yet there are fallen columns and statues all over the place. He has supposedly built it where he has because of the inaccessibility created by Mongolia's frozen lakes, but then how did he get everything there himself?

One explanation for how the imaginative comic *The League of Extraordinary Gentlemen* became the movie-as-videogame may be that director Stephen Norrington, whose only mainstream movie before this was the Wesley Snipes-starrer *Blade*, got his start in films designing special effects. Consequently one imagines he just took the comic and went with his strengths and dumped those of the original graphic novel. As an aside, Sean Connery, who supposedly took this job because he had turned down both *The Lord of the Rings* and *The Matrix* on the grounds he didn't understand them and didn't want to let another big film get past him, reportedly had such a difficult time on the set with director Norrington that it's said the two won't even speak to each other now. And each probably blames the other for the film's failure at the box office.

Maybe *League* was doomed from the start. In early August 2002, as the film was in production in Prague, Czech Republic, the city was hit with the worst flood in more than 130 years. The waters rose 20 feet inside the warehouse that held the film's sets and did $7 million worth of damage. It destroyed virtually everything inside the building, including Nemo's submarine, and delayed filming by five weeks. Connery even made a televised plea for assistance on behalf of the beleaguered city.

It's too bad he couldn't have made a televised plea on behalf of the beleaguered comic book on which his film is based for *League* is a lost opportunity. The story is muddled and the dialogue wooden. It sacrifices cleverness on the altar of special effects. It substitutes corny anachronisms for truly material-inspired insight. It takes itself too seriously instead of being subversively satirical. It takes characters who could have been fascinating to expand upon and turned them into cardboard entities. It takes the seeds of a literate and clever graphic novel and replaces them with a sloppy and heavy-handed story. As the *Los Angeles Times'* reviewer Manohla Dargis so aptly noted, "These guys have dumbed down a comic book." 🎞

—*Beverley Bare Buehrer*

CREDITS

Allan Quartermain: Sean Connery
Dorian Gray: Stuart Townsend
Mina Harker: Peta Wilson
Tom Sawyer: Shane West
Rodney Skinner: Tony Curran
M/James Moriarty: Richard Roxburgh
Henry Jekyll/Edward Hyde: Jason Flemyng
Captain Nemo: Naseeruddin Shah
Nigel: David Hemmings
Ishmael: Terry O'Neill
Dante: Max Ryan
Sanderson Reed: Tom Goodman-Hill

Origin: USA
Released: 2003
Production: Don Murphy, Trevor Albert; Mediastream Film; released by 20th Century-Fox
Directed by: Stephen Norrington
Written by: James Robinson
Cinematography by: Dan Laustsen
Music by: Trevor Jones
Sound: Mark Holding
Editing: Paul Rubell
Art Direction: James McAteer, James F. Truesdale, Elinor Rose Galbraith, Jindrich Koci
Costumes: Jacqueline West
Production Design: Carol Spier
MPAA rating: PG-13
Running time: 110 minutes

REVIEWS

Chicago Sun-Times Online. July 11, 2003.
Entertainment Weekly. July 18, 2003, p. 88.
Los Angeles Times Online. July 11, 2003.
New York Times Online. July 11, 2003.
New York Times Online. July 13, 2003.
People. July 21, 2003, p. 37.
USA Today Online. July 11, 2003.
Variety Online. July 9, 2003.
Washington Post. July 11, 2003, p. WE37.

QUOTES

Allan Quatermain (Sean Connery): "I'm not the man I once was."

Legally Blonde 2: Red, White & Blonde

This summer . . . justice is blonde.
—Movie tagline
Join the party!
—Movie tagline
Bigger. Bolder. Blonder.
—Movie tagline

Box Office: $89.9 million

So determined were the makers of *Legally Blonde 2: Red, White & Blonde* to let audiences know that the film is about a blonde (meaning: funny blonde jokes!), that they put the word in the title two times. For a seven-word title, that's a lot of mentions. The title could serve as sort of a microcosm for the whole movie because the film suffers from the same sort of desperation. It's as though the filmmakers don't think you'll get the joke so they keep repeating it. And we use the phrase "the joke" advisedly because *Legally Blonde 2* is pretty much about one joke. That joke would be that Elle Woods (Reese Witherspoon reprising her role) is a perky, blonde, Bel-Air sorority sister who happens actually to be smart. This joke is told countless ways in the film's 95-minute (though it felt like more) running time. Who knows, making a movie based solely on one joke could possibly work, but the chances for "Legally Blonde 2" to be funny go down considerably since the first "Legally Blonde" was based on that same joke. And maybe the clunky humor could work better if it was handled especially well, but it's not. Charles Taylor of *Salon.com* wrote, "If you're an adult watching *Legally Blonde 2* you're liable to feel like someone is talking to you as if you were a 5-year-old. [Director Charles] Herman-Wurmfeld apparently doesn't trust us to get any of the jokes. Nearly every one is followed by a reaction shot reminding us that what's just happened is really funny! And each time he uses the device, he kills the laughs."

Of course there could be more to all this than meets the eye. The *Toronto Star*'s Daphne Gordon raved about the film. She conceded that "straight, male audiences probably won't find this interesting or funny," but added that "for women it could be an important, inspiring, and empowering pop cultural experience. It has the potential to change the way women see themselves, the way they act in the workplace, and the way they relate to each other." Gordon goes on to say, "This film is really a deeply feminist criticism of gender politics in the 21st century that far surpasses its predecessor—which was a cute but formulaic romantic comedy—in depth, importance, and fashion." If it's still unclear just how intellectual *Legally Blonde 2* is, Gordon further explains: "The story and characters are fun, campy, and over the top, but don't take them literally. They're just exaggerated metaphors for what it's like to be a woman in a male-dominated workplace, what it's like to feel the pressure to conform to male standards of dress, language, values, and ideals, what it's like to repress one's femininity in favour of being taken seriously by people who are threatened by a woman who is too powerful because she's sexy and smart." It's hard to imagine a film that prominently features a tiny, yippy dog wearing tiny clothing being some sort of touchstone for feminism, but perhaps we need to give it some more scholarly study.

Others who take the film at face value will find a silly picture that seems desperate to recapture whatever it was about the first film that made it a surprise hit and big moneymaker. No one involved with the film seems to be that clear on what, exactly, that might have been, so they take the position that they will just do a lot more of the same stuff that was in the first film.

This time, the plucky Elle is working at a big Boston law firm and is about to get a promotion. She's also planning her wedding to Emmett Richmond (Luke Wilson), the nice guy Harvard Law professor cutie that Elle snagged in the first film. In planning the wedding, she decides that she needs to find the birth mother of her beloved dog, Bruiser (played by the dog actor Moondoggie). She hires a detective who informs her that Bruiser's mommy is alive and still in Boston. Elle goes to the address that the detective gives her and is thrilled that the building is marked Versace. But her excitement cools when she realizes that it is actually V.E.R.S.A.C.E., which stands for something having to do with testing animals for cosmetics. She must do something about it. As she says in one of her many speeches in the film, "In this case, the cost of beauty is too high—I can't believe I said that, but it's true."

Elle discovers that her firm represents one of the players in the field of cosmetic animal testing and asks that the firm put the pressure on to stop the testing. For this, Elle is promptly fired. Undaunted, as usual, Elle heads to Washington. She gets a job with fellow sorority sister, Representative Rudd (Sally Field). Rudd is pushing through a bill to stop animal testing and Elle will be her new legislative aide. In a scene cited by many critics as a favorite, Elle shows up for her first day dressed in a pink Jackie Kennedy-type suit, complete with a pillbox hat. Several people direct her to the interns' room.

Elle's perkiness is met with disdain by the rest of Rudd's staff, especially the surly Grace Rossiter (Regina King of *Jerry Maguire* and *Boyz N the Hood*). Grace believes that Elle is a fool and that she will need to learn to do things "the Washington way." Elle disagrees and says that she will do

things "the Elle way." The Elle way involves being really spunky and schmoozing with various powers that be. She wins over the tough representative from Texas (Dana Ivey) by showing up at her hairdresser's and doing the secret sorority handshake. She gets the support of another toughie, a Southern conservative (Bruce McGill), when they discover that each of their dogs is gay, and that the two pooches love each other. Elle develops a bill to end animal testing called "Bruiser's Bill." In another example of the main joke of the film being milked yet again, Elle presents the bill in a pink scented binding.

Elle is also helped out by a team of sorority sisters, who make contacts via their emergency phone tree and by Paulette Parcelle (Jennifer Coolidge of *A Mighty Wind*), the beautician from the first film. Paulette is so weird and ditzy that she makes Elle seem like a hardheaded straight shooter. When Elle shows her a snow globe, she holds it up to her ear and says, "I can hear the ocean!" Emmett helps out by showing up a couple of times and telling Elle that she can do it. It's kind of funny to see a man playing the supportive spouse role that women usual play, but funny in an interesting way, not funny in a humorous way. Elle's biggest help comes from Sid Post (an ill-used Bob Newhart), a doorman who knows all the inside Washington doings. At one particularly embarrassing point in the film, Newhart is forced to speak a line in Snoop Dogg's "izzle" language.

The film is filled with jokes that don't fly and moments that can be truly cringe-worthy: "Emmett and Elle: they're like Romeo and Juliet—without the dying," is a typical oneliner. Or this one from Elle: "I haven't been this excited since Gucci went public," and "Is bill-writing fun or what?!" The most desperate moment of the film comes when Elle gathers the interns together to do a cheerleading routine in the capitol. They chant "Go, Bruiser's Bill, Go!" while grinding to George Clinton's "Atomic Dog." The movie tries to be funny and inspiring at the same time and usually ends up being neither. In one supposedly rousing speech, Elle says, "Speak up, America. Speak up for the home of the brave. Speak up for the land of the free . . . gift with purchase." Pause, wait for laugh.

According to *RottenTomatoes.com*, a web site that compiles critical reviews, about two-thirds of critics gave the film a negative rating. Charles Taylor of *Salon.com* was in that group: "*Legally Blonde* wasn't a good movie, but it was funny and painless. The new sequel, *Legally Blonde 2: Red, White & Blonde*, calcifies everything that was enjoyable about the first movie. *Legally Blonde* was content to tickle you. The new one is something akin to a band that has a surprisingly successful debut deciding to rerecord all their originals and release a *Greatest Hits* collection for their second CD. It's both familiar and off." Elvis Mitchell of the *New York Times* wrote that the film "is a movie for people who somehow managed to miss the point of the first picture." The *Globe and Mail*'s Rick Groen concluded: "As with most movies whose title is followed by a low number, *Legally Blonde 2* is both more and less of the same—more of that hot-pink couture, a whole lot more of that diminutive doggie, less reason to laugh even if you're a tank-topped 16-year-old."

—*Jill Hamilton*

CREDITS

Elle Woods: Reese Witherspoon
Congresswoman Victoria Rudd: Sally Field
Sid Post: Bob Newhart
Emmett Richmond: Luke Wilson
Paulette Parcell: Jennifer Coolidge
Grace Rossiter: Regina King
Stanford Marks: Bruce McGill
Libby Hauser: Dana Ivey
Reena Gulani: Mary Lynn Rajskuls
Margot: Jessica Cauffiel
Serena: Alanna Ubach
Timothy McGinn: J Barton

Origin: USA
Released: 2003
Production: Marc Platt, David Nicksay; Type A Films; released by MGM
Directed by: Charles Herman-Wurmfeld
Written by: Kate Kondell
Cinematography by: Elliot Davis
Music by: Rolfe Kent
Sound: Kim Harris Ornitz
Music Supervisor: Anita Camarata
Editing: Peter Teschner
Art Direction: Mark Worthington
Costumes: Sophie de Rakoff Carbonell
Production Design: Missy Stewart
MPAA rating: PG-13
Running time: 95 minutes

REVIEWS

Chicago Sun-Times Online. July 2, 2003.
Los Angeles Times Online. July 2, 2003.
New York Times Online. July 2, 2003.
People. July 14, 2003, p. 33.
USA Today Online. July 2, 2003.
Variety Online. June 30, 2003.
Washington Post. July 2, 2003, p. C1.

QUOTES

Elle Woods (Reese Witherspoon) to Congresswoman Rudd (Sally Field): "Is bill-writing superfun or what?"

Levity

With its enormously deceptive title, writer-director Ed Solomon (*Bill and Ted's Excellent Adventure*) tells the tale of one man's search for redemption. Solomon, however, seems to be overcompensating for his most famous screenwriting effort with this dreary, melancholic offering that virtually smells of hopelessness. Though graced with a touching story, top-notch cast, and above par cinematography, *Levity* ultimately flounders amid its fatal plot flaws and relentlessly despondent tone.

With his vaguely religious sounding name (Emmanuel, the river Jordan) and long, stringy Christ-like hair, Manuel Jordan (Billy Bob Thornton) has just been released from prison after serving a 22-year sentence for murder. It seems the young Manuel was involved in the robbery of a convenience store and fatally shot the seventeen-year-old clerk Abner Easely. Though a killer, the sensitive, soft-spoken Manuel kept the picture of Abner from the newspaper reporting his death taped to his cell wall for all those long years, pondering the nature of forgiveness and redemption.

Much is made of, and indeed the plot entirely revolves around, the topic of redemption and whether it is possible. Manuel explains why he thinks his odds of being forgiven are virtually nil: "I read a book that was written in the eleventh century. A man said that there was five steps toward making amends. The first involved acknowledging what you did. The second involved remorse. The third involved making right with your neighbor. Like if you stole his chicken, you'd have to go and bring him another. Only then were you able to go to step four, which was making it right with God. But it wasn't until step five that you could really get redeemed. It had to do with being at the same place and the same situation. That as it goes, you'd go and do something different. Only I can't bring Abner Easely back like he was some stolen chicken. Certainly made sure of that 23 years ago. And I don't believe in some God that's gonna open His arms to me even if I did. So there goes steps three and four. And as for step five, time makes sure we're never in the same place twice, no matter how much we wish it. Which is why, for me, I know I'll never be redeemed." The fact that he thinks redemption will forever elude him makes his subsequent, half-hearted tries pointless and just plain hard to watch.

Manuel does, nonetheless, try to atone to some degree. Upon his release, he wanders back to the area nearby the site of the murder and meets friendly preacher Miles Evans (Morgan Freeman), who offers the aimless drifter a room in his center for troubled youth in exchange for housework. It is there that Manuel meets the pretty but troubled Sofia Mellinger (Kirsten Dunst) who takes drugs and frequents a nightclub conveniently situated across from Reverend Evans's center. Manuel also encounters Abner Easely's sister, Adele (Holly Hunter), who is now a mother with a young son named for her late brother. The two strike up a friendship and become more and more attracted to each other, but Manuel is afraid to reveal his true identity.

In the meantime, however, young Abner (Geoffrey Wigdor) has become somewhat of a troubled soul himself and has been hanging around a bad group of kids. Manuel can see the danger Abner faces and, as he attempts to help Sofia straighten out her life, he similarly tries to help his victim's nephew, hoping to prevent the youth from sharing his own fate. Abner's criminal antics escalate, however, until real trouble looms in a climactic scene that takes place in an alley, where Manuel finds himself, much as his book described, in "the same place and the same situation."

Thornton does the best with what's required of him, which is to wander around like a ghost haunting his hometown, spiritually bankrupt and fearing his ultimate ruin yet still managing to find a purpose in life. The rest of the performances are uniformly good—especially Dunst's, whose character injects some life into the proceedings—and most are able to rise above the melancholy script. Moody and dark, Solomon claims he worked on the script for his feature directing debut for some 20 years after getting the initial idea for the film while tutoring teenagers in a maximum security juvenile prison when he was in college. Filmed in Montreal, Canada, cinematographer Roger Deakins, who worked with Thornton in the Coen brothers' black and white *The Man Who Wasn't There*, perfectly captures the stark mood.

—*Hilary White*

CREDITS

Manuel Jordan: Billy Bob Thornton
Miles Evans: Morgan Freeman
Adele Easely: Holly Hunter
Sofia Mellinger: Kirsten Dunst
Mackie Whittaker: Dorian Harewood
Abner Easely: Geoff Wigdor
Claire Mellinger: Catherine Colvey
Senor Aguilar: Manuel Aranguiz
Young Abner Easely: Luke Robertson
Don: Billoah Greene

Origin: USA

Released: 2003
Production: Richard N. Gladstein, Adam Merims, Ed Solomon; Entitled Entertainment, Revelations Entertainment, FilmColony, Echo Lake Productions; released by Sony Pictures Classics
Directed by: Edward Solomon
Written by: Edward Solomon
Cinematography by: Roger Deakins
Music by: Mark Oliver Everett
Sound: Claude La Haye
Music Supervisor: Liza Richardson
Editing: Pietro Scalia
Art Direction: Pierre Perrault
Costumes: Marie-Sylvie Deveau
Production Design: Francois Seguin
MPAA rating: R
Running time: 100 minutes

REVIEWS

Boxoffice. April, 2003, p. 74.
Chicago Sun-Times Online. April 25, 2003.
Entertainment Weekly. April 18, 2003, p. 48.
Los Angeles Times Online. April 4, 2003.
New York Times Online. April 4, 2003.
Variety Online. January 19, 2003.
Washington Post. April 25, 2003, p. WE51.

TRIVIA

Filmed on location in Montreal, Quebec, Canada.

The Life of David Gale

The crime is clear. The truth is not.
—Movie tagline

Box Office: $19.6 million

Many viewers will probably leave this thriller-cum-social protest film scratching their heads, trying to sort out the reversals that come thick and fast at the end. One can hardly blame them, although, in retrospect this picture basically plays fair with viewers. What is amazing, however, is the fact that such an overheated and impassioned protest over the ruthlessly efficient capital punishment system in the state of Texas could have been sanctioned by the Texas Film Commission. It is difficult to imagine how the picture slipped in under Texas's radar, since it's wearing its agenda right out there on its sleeve. And how are Texans portrayed? In the words of one outraged reviewer, "as spittle-spewing trolls with hair up their noses."

Director Alan Parker is a firebrand whose earlier and better films have been critical of American values, most notably his civil rights picture *Mississippi Burning* (1988), followed by *Come See the Paradise* (1989), an expose of how Japanese-Americans were treated during World War II. This time Parker sets out to compete with the Robert Wise classic *I Want to Live!* (1958), which won an Academy Award for Susan Hayward, and the more recent *Dead Man Walking* (1995), which also earned an Academy Award for Susan Sarandon and Academy Award nominations for Sean Penn as Best Actor and Tim Robbins as Best Director.

The film begins with a long shot. Level horizon. A car enters the frame, coming to a stop. A woman emerges and runs frantically out of the frame. We don't know who she is and what is happening until the penultimate scenes, when we realize she is an investigative reporter desperately trying to stop an impending execution. This is then followed by a flashback. Four days before his scheduled execution, accused rapist and murderer David Gale (Kevin Spacey) summons a reporter named "Bitsy" (believe it or not, played by Kate Winslet) to his cell. Gale, a former Rhodes Scholar who has published two books, who has served as head of the Philosophy Department at Austin University and who is a dedicated opponent of the death penalty, has agreed, for an exorbitant fee, to tell his life story.

Hard-bitten New York magazine veteran reporter Bitsy Bloom arrives, an intern named Zack in tow (played by Gabriel Mann). What transpires are three extended flashbacks-within-flashbacks as Gale's backstory swims into focus (replete with a silly series of camera-twisting flashframes of words like "lust," "murder," "rape," etc.). Withholding until the last day the facts of the murder accusation, brief vignettes depict Gale's participation with "Deathwatch," a death penalty abolitionist group; a class lecture on Lacanian philosophy (no doubt intended as a key to the film's denouement); his attendance at a party where he's seduced by a student (Rhona Mitra); his subsequent arrest for rape; his decline into drink and unemployment (even though the charges are dropped); and his later arrest and incarceration on charges of the murder of Constance Harraway (Laura Linney), the leader of an Austin Deathwatch group. It's only near the end that we learn that Constance was the alleged murder victim.

All the while, Gale protests his innocence to Bitsy, even though, curiously, he stood by silently while his defense attorney seems to have botched the case. Bitsy, in the meantime, becomes emotionally involved, even though the evidence against Gale is overwhelming—his semen was found

in the victim's body, his fingerprints are on the plastic bag covering her head, etc. Further confirming evidence appears when a video tape mysteriously shows up in her motel room, revealing the final death throes of the victim (her head encased in a sack, her hands handcuffed behind her). But Bitsy's closer look at the tape reveals troubling details. She deduces that Constance wasn't a murder victim at all, but a suicide. This is confirmed when Bitsy and her intern invade the house of Constance's accomplice and find a more extended videotape revealing Constance arranging her own death. She speeds to the prison but when her car breaks down she arrives too late to save Gale.

In the final scene, Bitsy receives a package at work. Inside is Gale's son's stuffed toy. And inside the toy is another videotape. This time, the tape is the complete record of the suicide. And in it, appearing beside Constance's dead body, is Gale himself. The implication is that Gale and Constance both conspired to unmask the flaws of the death penalty system: Gale will ultimately be revealed as innocent, and the state of Texas will be culpable for having killed an innocent man. But there are too many diversions in the screenplay by Charles Randolph, such as the complicated plot apparatus involving a mysterious man in a truck who is stalking Bitsy and her intern. This proves to be a rather outrageous red herring, as he turns out to be an accomplice of Constance and the lawyer. It is he who delivers the money collected from Bitsy's magazine to Gale's wife and child in Barcelona. Why Barcelona? Because Gale's father had once served as ambassador to Spain.

There is a grisly, perverse voyeurism at work behind this film, almost equal to the machinations of Constance and Gale, since the film offers repeated views of the videotape of Constance's nude body in its death throes; and Bitsy's replication of the death scene, even to tying a plastic bag over her head. *Washington Post* reviewer Rita Kempley was really offended by the "smutty, misogynistic tape" and saw no "justifiable reason" for repeating it. Her colleague Desson Howe agreed: "The only difference between this film and snuff porn is a matter of dramatic emphasis," he wrote.

The reviews were not very positive. Rita Kempley, who titled her *Washington Post* review "Death by Haranguing," took exception to what she considered a preachy message movie from Alan Parker, "that self-impressed Brit who loves nothing better than to come over here and lecture us on our ethical standards." Stanley Kauffmann of the *New Republic* was critical of what he considered a thematic flaw. The film intends to show that innocent men and women can be executed, but "this is really a critique of police and legal work, not of capital punishment." For him the "highest moral argument" is not that "such mistakes can be made," as should be obvious, but that "whether or not the prisoner is guilty, capital punishment degrades the society that uses it."

On one point, the reviewers were in agreement. Rita Kempley called Laura Linney's portrayal of Constance Hallaway "the movie's only worthy performance," and other reviewers agreed. But one other reviewer was puzzled throughout by the disparity between the voluptuous body type of the victim as seen in the videotape and the emaciated figure we have seen of Constance, who suffers from leukemia throughout the film. In his *New Republic* review, Stanley Kauffmann also found merit in Kevin Spacey, "a good actor, reaching down into himself to find a source of verity for this plot-constructed character." In other words, the fault can be traced to the screenplay, not the actor. Likewise with Kate Winslet, who is "a gifted actress walking through some gross motions of a part while waiting for the script to arrive."

The Life of David Gale was Charles Randolph's first produced screenplay. A 39-year-old import from academia, the son of missionaries expelled from Jordan for trying to convert Muslims, Randolph was a graduate of the Yale Divinity School who apparently has taught philosophy abroad. "Every character represents a different philosophy," Randolph told the *New York Times*. "David Gale is the Socratic figure. The cowboy [played by Matt Craven] it the classical Stoic figure. And Constance is a second-wave feminist." Keen on film theory and fond of discussing "paratextuality," Randolph seemed pleased with his ability to add an "extra twist" to the plot. Director Alan Parker called him "a genuine intellectual," but added, "some people are too clever for their own good." *Entertainment Weekly*'s Owen Gleiberman refused to discuss the plot so as not to "give away the big twists, which grow more ludicrous by the minute," but went on to criticize the film as "a self-righteous mishmash that can't decide whether to be a tribute to the fanatical leftist passion that thrives in college towns, an indictment of that very same fanaticism, or a ghoulishly didactic snuff-video thriller." He concluded that "there ought to be a law against a message movie this contrived."

The screenplay, then, is something of a puzzler. Viewers might wonder, for example, why the videotape was placed in Bitsy's motel room. Was it intended that Bitsy would divine the truth behind Constance's death? If not, why is the tape there? And was it further intended that Bitsy would arrive at the prison in time to stop the execution? The rented car breaks down from overheating. *Variety* reviewer David Stratton wanted to know why they didn't get a replacement car but answers his own question by pointing up a flaw in the screenplay: "They don't, of course, because the overheating auto will play a key role later in the movie." Was Gale intending all along to find himself exonerated at the last minute? And was the car failure that delayed Bitsy an unforeseen tragic detail that thwarted that plan? Or did Gale intend to die all along, a martyr to his cause? The critical consensus was that the film was muddled, but the ambiguity could also be defended as adding an interesting texture to the film, as the clock counts down the final minutes to Gale's execution.

—*James M. Welsh and John C. Tibbetts*

CREDITS

David Gale: Kevin Spacey
Bitsey Bloom: Kate Winslet
Constance Harraway: Laura Linney
Zack Stemmons: Gabriel Mann
Dusty Wright: Matt Craven
Berlin: Rhona Mitra
Braxton Belyeu: Leon Rippy
Duke Glover: Jim Beaver

Origin: USA
Released: 2003
Production: Alan Parker, Nicolas Cage; Saturn Films, Dirty Hands; released by Universal Pictures
Directed by: Alan Parker
Written by: Charles Randolph
Cinematography by: Michael Seresin
Music by: Alex Parker, Jake Parker
Sound: David MacMillan
Editing: Gerry Hambling
Costumes: Renee Ehrlich Kalfus
Production Design: Geoffrey Kirkland
MPAA rating: R
Running time: 130 minutes

REVIEWS

Boxoffice. April, 2003, p. 11.
Chicago Sun-Times Online. February 21, 2003.
Entertainment Weekly. February 28, 2003, p. 57.
Los Angeles Times Online. February 21, 2003.
New Republic. March 17, 2003, p. 24.
New York Times. February 23, 2003, p. 42.
New Yorker. March 13, 2003, p. 94.
People. March 3, 2003, p. 31.
USA Today Online. February 21, 2003.
Variety. February 17, 2003, p. 43.
Washington Post. February 21, 2003, p. C5.
Washington Post Weekend. February 21, 2003, p. 34.

The Lizzie McGuire Movie

The Only Risk In Taking An Adventure Is Not Taking It At All.
—Movie tagline

She's going places.
—Movie tagline

Box Office: $40 million

Lizzie McGuire, a TV show on the Disney Channel, is the number one program on basic cable for girls 6 to 14. Disney, not a company to pass on financial rewards, was quick to cash in further on such a phenomenon and *The Lizzie McGuire Movie* is the result. The film is so perfectly aimed toward its particular demographic, it's as though it was created in a laboratory using real 12-year-old girls' brains as subjects. The 'tweens are crazy for this stuff.

With such precision appeal to that group, there's a lot of people (i.e. grandparents, parents, aunts and uncles, unlucky older siblings, etc.) who aren't going to be as enamored of the film's charms. After all, some girls at an early showing of the film in Long Beach, CA, spent their time before the film yelling out, "We must, we must, we must increase our bust!" then bursting into giggles. When there was a momentous, though highly chaste, kiss at the end of the film, girls in the audience shrieked with excitement. It's hard to know for sure, but it didn't seem like any of the parents in the audience were reacting the same way to the lip lock.

The Lizzie McGuire Movie is a fantasy for the 'tweens. The plot is pretty much what a 'tween would say if you asked them what the best weekend of their life would be like. It involves new clothes, pop stardom and, of course, a cute boy.

Lizzie (Hilary Duff, of the TV show and also *Agent Cody Banks*) is supposed to be a gawky 8th grader who's plagued by klutziness and lack of popularity. At her 8th grade graduation, her former friend and now rival, Kate (Ashlie Brillault), calls her an "outfit repeater." Horrors. Then, to make matters worse, at the ceremony, she makes a fool of herself by giving a bad speech, then tripping and causing the stage to fall apart. This gets picked up by the national news story as a light human interest story and gets played all over the country. Her parents (Robert Carradine and Hallie Todd) are of little help to her. Her dad is so clueless that he delights in painting garden gnomes.

After the graduation fiasco, Lizzie looks to her class trip to Rome as a way to reinvent herself. Snobby Kate is going on the trip, but so is her best buddy, Gordo (Adam Lamberg) a nerdy nice guy who seems to be nursing a big crush on Lizzie. The group is headed by drill sergeant-like Ms. Ungermeyer (Alex Borstein of *Mad TV*) who grouchily refers to her charges as "mouth breathers."

While the group is looking at Trevi fountain, Lizzie tosses a Euro in, makes a wish and suddenly makes eye contact with cute boy Paolo (Yani Gellman). Paolo is staring so intently at her because he is shocked at her remarkable resemblance to his singing partner, Isabella (also played by Duff). It seems that Paolo is a famous Italian pop star and he needs Lizzie to take Isabella's place in a big music awards show coming up in the Roman Colosseum. He tells Lizzie that Isabella, who was once his girlfriend, has run off and refuses to perform.

Lizzie starts sneaking away from her group to work on her singing and dancing and to ride around with Paolo on his scooter. Paolo only has a few days to make Lizzie passable as Isabella. This is when we have the requisite trying-on-clothes sequence. Even though Lizzie looks just like Isabella, it seems odd that no one would notice that she now seems to speak only English. But, hey, if people are buying that a tourist in Italy can turn into a pop star in days, a language shift is not that much more to swallow.

The climax (or low point, depending) of the film is a sequence in which Lizzie hawks, er, performs a song. To further the consumer messages of the film, the song is indeed available for purchase by moviegoers. A line of Lizzie McGuire clothing is also on its way.

Like Ally McBeal, poor Lizzie suffers from overabundant fantasy sequences. Lizzie has an animated version of herself that occasionally offers commentary on the action. These moments don't add anything to the movie except lame jokes. When Paolo calls Lizzie "magnifico," cartoon Lizzie swoons, "I don't know Italian, but I know what that means!" When someone mentions jewelry, the cartoon Lizzie says, "Jewelry! Now that's a word every girl understands!" And, no, this film, written by Susan Estelle Jansen, Ed Decter and John J. Strauss, wasn't written in 1952.

It was filmed in Rome but director Jim Fall, doesn't make good use of it. There are some scenic montages of the city but they could have saved some money and just used stock footage for as much as they take advantage of it. There is some nice scenery though. Roger Ebert of the *Chicago Sun-Times* pointed out that the class checks into a hotel that looks like it cost about $500 a night. That is a lot of bake sales and car washes.

Also, as Gene Seymour of *Newsday* points out, it's difficult to believe that Duff, who's probably in the top 1% of attractiveness, is a gawky loser. She "looks like the kind of junior-high heartbreaker who'd be inflicting embarrassment rather than absorbing it," he wrote. Aside from an overabundance of tripping episodes, she seems to be free of the usual awkward years appearance problems that plague girls at this age.

Few critics would admit to liking this film. The most that they could usually muster was that the film was good for the audience it was intended. Megan Lehmann of the *New York Post* wrote that it "plays like a feature-length shampoo commercial—benign, aspiration and sudsy." William Arnold of the *Seattle Post-Intelligencer* wrote, "Disney's big-screen spinoff of its hit cable series *Lizzie McGuire* is so fluffy and sitcom shallow that it makes *Gidget Goes to Rome* and it's other many predecessors in the young-American-girl-goes-to-Italy-and-falls-in-love genre look like high art." David Kronke of the *Los Angeles Daily News* wrote that the film was "for fans only. Everyone else will be torn between whether they should claw out their eyes or puncture their eardrums." But Dave Kehr of the *New York Times* felt more kindly toward the movie and wrote, "The picture unfolds as a light romantic comedy that adults will probably find familiar but tolerable, while their age-appropriate offspring will be transported to new heights of cinematic enchantment."

—Jill Hamilton

CREDITS

Lizzie McGuire/Isabella: Hilary Duff
Sam McGuire: Robert Carradine
Jo McGuire: Hallie Todd
Matt McGuire: Jake Thomas
Paolo: Yani Gellman
Gordo: Adam Lamberg
Sergei: Brendan Kelly
Kate: Ashlie Brillault
Ethan: Clayton Snyder
Miss Ungermeyer: Alex Borstein
Melina: Carly Schroeder

Origin: USA
Released: 2003
Production: Stan Rogow; released by Walt Disney Pictures
Directed by: Jim Fall
Written by: Edward Decter, John J. Strauss, Susan Estelle Jansen
Cinematography by: Jerzy Zielinski
Music by: Cliff Eidelman
Sound: Darren Brisker
Music Supervisor: Elliot Lurie
Editing: Margaret Goodspeed
Art Direction: Patrick Banister
Costumes: Monique Prudhomme, David C. Robinson
Production Design: Doug Higgins
MPAA rating: PG
Running time: 90 minutes

REVIEWS

Chicago Sun-Times Online. May 2, 2003.
Los Angeles Times Online. May 2, 2003.
New York Times Online. May 2, 2003.
People. May 12, 2003, p. 39.
San Francisco Chronicle. May 2, 2003, p. D5.
USA Today Online. May 2, 2003.
Variety Online. May 1, 2003.
Washington Post. May 2, 2003, p. WE52.

QUOTES

Lizzie (Hilary Duff) about Paolo's Vespa: "Are you sure you know how to drive this thing?" Paolo (Yani Gellman): "This is Rome. Nobody knows how to drive."

Looney Tunes: Back in Action

Real life has never been so animated.
—Movie tagline
How do they solve a mysery when they don't have a clue?
—Movie tagline

 Box Office: $20.9 million

A clever, intelligent blending of live action and animation, *Looney Tunes: Back in Action* is a faithful, giddy salute to the spirit of the old Warner Bros. cartoons. Its main conceit is to have fun with the rivalry between Bugs Bunny and Daffy Duck, which was central to many of the old-time shorts. But director Joe Dante, who has exhibited a fondness for animation (as well as a fan's zeal for science fiction and fantasy) in his other films, and screenwriter Larry Doyle take the rivalry a step further—placing it in the context of Hollywood moviemaking. *Looney Tunes: Back in Action* is a self-reflexive film (much like *Who Framed Roger Rabbit*) in which cartoons and humans coexist on the Warner Bros. studio back lot. There is plenty of anarchic action, including wild chase scenes and explosions, that will appeal to children as well as adults who are kids at heart. But audiences who appreciate spotting references to old movies and genre settings along with satiric jabs at Hollywood's corporate thinking will especially appreciate the sophisticated humor.

The film opens as a classic Warner Bros. short: Elmer Fudd is hunting, and Bugs tries to convince him that it is duck season, while Daffy insists that it is rabbit season. The sequence ends with Daffy getting his head blown off several times, and then suddenly we are in a studio boardroom where Daffy the actor, tired of getting blasted all the time and playing second fiddle to Bugs, is protesting his onscreen treatment. Kate (Jenna Elfman), the high-strung vice president in charge of comedy, fires Daffy, explaining that Bugs has a broad fan base while Daffy appeals to "angry fat guys in basements." She is meant to satirize studio executives who look to the bottom line to make their decisions and talk in advertising speak, spouting off meaningless but important-sounding jargon like "reposition your brand" and "leverage your synergy."

Brendan Fraser plays DJ, a Warner Bros. security guard who wants to be a stuntman fulltime but cannot seem to get a break. While he could trade on the fact that his father, Damian Drake (Timothy Dalton, spoofing his brief stint as James Bond), is a big-time action hero for the studio, DJ would rather try to succeed on his own. DJ is ordered to escort Daffy off the lot, whereupon the mischievous duck leads him on a raucous chase that ends with a huge water tower falling on Kate's car, which results in DJ himself being fired and stripped of his security guard uniform. At home, he receives a video message from his father telling him to go off in search of a mysterious artifact known as the Blue Monkey diamond. Damian appears to be in trouble, and it turns out that he is not just an actor who plays a secret agent but an actual spy. For help, DJ must find Dusty Tails (Heather Locklear), a singer in a Las Vegas show. As DJ and Daffy head to Vegas, the Warner brothers watch dailies of the new film and realize that it simply does not work without Daffy as a foil to Bugs, so Kate must go out and bring Daffy back in order to save her own job.

The true pleasure of *Looney Tunes: Back in Action* is the offhanded jokes that round out the self-reflexive world of the film: Porky Pig and Speedy Gonzalez complaining that political correctness has made work difficult for them; Kate explaining to Bugs that they need to find him a hot female love interest because when he does the part in drag it is now more disturbing than funny; and DJ boasting to Daffy that he did the stunt work for Brendan Fraser in *The Mummy* movies. The best self-reflexive moment occurs when Kate stumbles upon Bugs in the shower, and he imitates the famous scene from *Psycho* (sans knife) in a virtual shot-for-shot, black-and-white re-creation. The extra touch is that we see a can of Hershey's chocolate syrup poured down the drain to simulate blood, which pays homage to Hitchcock's method while also mocking gratuitous product placement prevalent in movies today.

The movie also makes pointed jabs at corporate culture, not just in the jokes at the expense of Warner Bros. but also in the nefarious scheme of the evil Acme Corporation. Mr. Chairman (Steve Martin), the head of Acme Corporation, is holding Damian Drake prisoner and covets the Blue Monkey diamond because of its supernatural powers. The diamond will turn human beings into monkeys, a cheap form of labor, and then turn the monkeys back into humans, who will in turn be good consumers of the shoddy goods that Acme produces. The quest for the Blue Monkey is the thinnest of plots, really amounting to a loose framework for a series of frenetic gags and the pretext for madcap globe-trotting.

In a Las Vegas casino run by Yosemite Sam, DJ meets up with songstress Dusty Tails, who also happens to be a spy working with Damian and who gives DJ a Queen of Diamonds playing card (overtones of *The Manchurian Candidate*) to help him in his quest to track down the Blue Monkey. Pursued by Sam, who is working for Acme, and his henchmen, DJ and Daffy career through the streets of Las Vegas, ultimately meeting up with Kate and Bugs, and their souped-up spy car enables them to escape the bad guys.

They reach the desert and see a Wal-Mart; "Is it a mirage or just product placement?" Bugs muses, but Kate deadpans, "The audience expects it," thus having fun with our own complicity in Hollywood's marketing machine. The big set piece in the desert is a compound run by the government—not the fabled Area 51, as we might think, but Area 52, which is overseen by Mother (Joan Cusack). Area 52 plays as an homage to 1950s science fiction. *Forbidden Planet's* Robbie the Robot is there, as is Kevin McCarthy from *Invasion of the Body Snatchers*, who walks through holding a giant pod and carrying on like a madman. Mother is a gadget person like Q in the Bond movies, and she tells DJ to look behind the Queen's smile (the face of the Queen is the Mona Lisa). After doing battle with aliens and monsters led amok by Marvin the Martian, another Acme agent, the heroes go to the Louvre in Paris to see the real Mona Lisa.

Despite its real-world setting, the film enjoys the freedom of a cartoon, letting its heroes magically transport themselves half a world away in an instant. At the Louvre, they use the playing card as an X-ray device to see through the painting and get their next clue—to go to Africa for the Blue Monkey. Before they can get to Africa, though, Elmer Fudd, yet another Acme operative, tries to thwart them. In the film's most creative sequence, Bugs and Daffy lead him on a surreal chase through the paintings of the museum, with the characters taking on the appearance and style suggested by the artwork. When they run through the melted timepieces of Dali's *Persistence of Memory*, their speech is slurred, Elmer's rifle melts, and their movements are sluggish. As they travel through Munch's *The Scream*, Elmer looks like the dreaded screamer. At Seurat's *A Sunday Afternoon on the Island of La Grande Jatte*, high art meets pop culture as Bugs defines pointillism for the audience and then turns Elmer into a pile of dots.

No sooner do the heroes find the Blue Monkey in a jungle adventure modeled after the opening sequence of *Raiders of the Lost Ark* than Mr. Chairman seizes it, and they are beamed back to Acme headquarters for a big climax fought on several fronts. Marvin the Martian is sent to the Acme satellite to plant the diamond, while Damian Drake, surrounded by TNT, is tied to a train track with an anvil dangling over him. DJ saves his dad, and Daffy, in his Duck Dodgers persona, defeats Marvin and foils Acme; in the end, Mr. Chairman is the only human turned into a monkey.

Daffy is thrilled to be the hero of the story, but everything we have seen, it turns out, has been a movie, so Daffy in essence was tricked into being part of Bugs's feature film. Bugs promises that they will now be equal partners, but he is promptly whisked away in a limousine, while poor Daffy is flattened by the Warner Bros. logo. Some things, it seems, will never change.

In a world dominated by the likes of Bugs and Daffy, the humans are bound to get short shrift, but Fraser and Elfman are likable counterpoints to the frenzy whirling around them. Fraser is especially adept at acting opposite cartoons as if he really shared the space with them when they were filming. Martin, with his lisping voice and herky-jerky body movements, comes the closest to actually simulating a cartoon himself, which is just right since he plays most of his scenes opposite a fawning board of directors who are anything but animated.

In films like *Gremlins* and his segment of *Twilight Zone—The Movie*, Dante has had a knack for reworking the genres he loves in fresh ways, at once embracing popular entertainment and casting a skeptical eye on its power. In *Looney Tunes: Back in Action*, Dante entertains with broad slapstick and wild action while gently poking fun at the studio machinations and corporate politics behind the scenes. Such good-natured irreverence is the best tribute a director could pay to the Looney Tunes tradition.

—*Peter N. Chumo II*

CREDITS

DJ Drake/Himself: Brendan Fraser
Kate: Jenna Elfman
Mr. Chairman: Steve Martin
Damien Drake: Timothy Dalton
Dusty Tails: Heather Locklear
Mother: Joan Cusack
Mr. Smith: Bill Goldberg
Bugs Bunny, Daffy Duck, Beaky Buzzard, Sylvester, Mama Bear: Joe Alaskey (Voice)
Elmer Fudd, Peter Lorre: Billy West (Voice)
Yosemite Sam, Foghorn Leghorn, Nasty Canasta: Jeff Glenn Bennett (Voice)
Tweety Bird, Speedy Gonzalez, Marvin the Martian: Eric Goldberg (Voice)

Origin: USA
Released: 2003
Production: Paula Weinstein, Bernie Goldman; Baltimore Pictures, Spring Creek Productions; released by Warner Bros.
Directed by: Joe Dante
Written by: Larry Doyle
Cinematography by: Dean Cundey
Music by: Jerry Goldsmith

Sound: Ken King
Editing: Marshall Harvey, Rick W. Finney
Art Direction: Paul Sonski
Production Design: Bill Brzeski
MPAA rating: PG
Running time: 91 minutes

 REVIEWS

Chicago Sun-Times Online. November 14, 2003.
Entertainment Weekly. November 21, 2003, p. 62.
Los Angeles Times Online. November 14, 2003.
New York Times Online. November 14, 2003.
People. November 24, 2003, p. 29.
USA Today Online. November 14, 2003.
Variety Online. November 10, 2003.
Washington Post. November 14, 2003, p. WE47.

The Lord of the Rings 3: The Return of the King

 Box Office: $361.9 million

The third installment of Peter Jackson's adaptation of J.R.R. Tolkien's *The Lord of the Rings* trilogy, *The Return of the King*, is easily the best film of the series. "As good as each individual movie is," attests Claudia Puig in *USA Today*, "the third film vaults the work into the stratosphere of classic movies." Indeed, the critical and commercial success of not only the third installment of the trilogy but of all three films has solidified a place in film history as quite possibly the greatest trilogy ever made.

As with the second installment of the trilogy, it would probably be of benefit, to not only the uninitiated and the devout fan, to take a look at the previous chapters of the trilogy prior to experiencing *The Return of King*. As I wrote in last year's review of *The Two Towers*, this "is by no means meant to imply that if you haven't seen the earlier films that you won't find [*Return of the King*] entertaining, it's just that you may find yourself a bit bewildered by the complexity of the proceedings." Like *The Two Towers*, Jackson chooses to not start the film with the standard "the story so far" recap. Instead, he offers up a short vignette that gives a glimpse of Gollum's back story. Specifically, how he came into possession of the One Ring while he was still the fisherman Smeagol and how the power of the Ring corrupted and deformed him into the tragic Gollum.

The Return of the King (which foretells the ascension of Aragorn (Viggo Mortensen) to the throne of Gondor) begins, like its predecessor, almost precisely where the previous installment left off. Although victories were had at Helm's Deep and Isengard, the fate of Middle-earth still resides solely in the hands of the hobbits Frodo (Elijah Wood) and his ever-faithful companion Sam (Sean Astin) as they make their way to Mordor to destroy the One Ring. They are still being led by the increasingly conflicted Gollum who plans on betraying them and reclaiming the Ring as his own.

Meanwhile, Gandalf (Ian McKellen) and Peregrin Took (Billy Boyd) travel to Minas Tirith with warnings of an impending attack by Sauron's forces. The slightly mad Denethor (John Noble), in machismo defiance refuses to accept aid from the kingdom of Rohan (although Gandalf sends for assistance anyway). Back in Rohan, Eowyn (Miranda Otto), Merry (Dominic Monaghan), and King Theoden (Bernard Hill) gather forces in preparation for the massive battle against the forces of Sauron at Minas Tirith. Similarly, Aragorn, along with Gimli (John Rhys-Davies) and Legolas (Orlando Bloom), is assembling allies to fight the dark forces as well. These stories move effortlessly until the final battle between men and Orcs at the gates of Mordor; and between Frodo, Sauron, and the power of the Ring. Following what may be one of the more moving denouements ever filmed, Jackson ties up all of the trilogy's loose ends with a series of wrap-ups that succinctly and satisfyingly conclude the saga.

As with *The Fellowship of the Ring* and *The Two Towers*, Jackson has again endowed the world of Middle-earth with enough breadth and scope that it is impossible to discern where the reality ends and the illusion begins. In fact, the production seems far grander for this episode than the previous two. The Battle of Pelennor Fields could arguably be the greatest battle sequence ever committed to film. The use of CGI and other effects is absolutely flawless. There isn't a frame in this film that isn't breathtaking. The scene where the signal fires of Gondor are lit and the beacons across Middle-earth are illuminated is a microcosm of the emotional resonance present throughout the entire film. While *Return of the King* is the longest of the three films, it hardly plays as a plodding epic. That is not to say that the film is non-stop action. While the action is plentiful, there are far more reflective and emotional episodes than before (after all, everything needs to be wrapped up before the film is over). This is largely due to the fact that the script is far more intricate than in *Fellowship* or *Towers*. For, as Desson Thomson pointed out in the *Washington Post*: "What makes this enormous undertaking work so well is the interweaving of the small- and large-scale plots." The Academy-Award winning script by Jackson, Fran Walsh, Philippa Boyens, and Stephen Sinclair deftly combines the myriad story arcs and manages to tie them all up by the end of the film without any eccentricities while maintaining an emotional consistency that wasn't as prevalent in the previous films. (The fate of Saruman (Christopher Lee), however, is strangely absent from *Return of the King*. Apparently his "final" scene was held out of *The Two Towers* and ultimately cut from the final version of the third film. Although it will more than likely appear on the Extended Edition DVD.) As was the writing for *Return of the King*, the superb production work was also rewarded with Oscars for practically every non-acting category (art direction, costume design, editing, makeup, music [including best song], sound mixing, and visual effects). This speaks to the vision of the people involved in the project from its genesis. The entire trilogy, as Tom Long wrote in the *Detroit News*, "reflects a willingness to take chances and work large scale beyond the typical Hollywood star system, a belief in the scope and power and potential of cinema, and a faith in audiences to recognize greatness."

The Return of the King does a wonderful job of completing every character's story arc (the Saruman example notwithstanding). Again, the most complex and interesting character is Gollum. Gandalf is allowed a bit more heroism than he had before but it is still Gollum that succeeds in delivering the greatest emotional impact. Interestingly, female characters are also afforded a bit more independence in this film. Previously, as Roger Ebert alleges in the *Chicago Sun-Times*, "the series has never known what to do with its female characters. J.R.R. Tolkien was not much interested in them, certainly not at a psychological level." Eowyn however, is given the chance to become an action hero of sorts when she rides into battle alongside the army of Rohan. Similarly, Arwen (Liv Tyler) asserts her independence and take charge of her own life. At the heart of all of this however, is the simple cautionary warning that temptation is always present and while heroes ultimately prevail, evil does have the ability to corrupt. Although free will is desired, it must be tempered with some amount of social responsibility.

In addition to the numerous Academy Awards the production crew received for the work done on *Return of the King*, director Jackson garnered the Best Director and Best Picture awards as well. (These 11 awards tied the film with *Ben Hur* and *Titanic* for the most Oscars won.) The critical and commercial success that Jackson has been showered with now suggests that he has created possibly the greatest trilogy in the history of film. While that may seem a bold statement given the films that would be left in the wake of *The Lord of the Rings* (*The Godfather* as well as the *Star Wars* films for example), it is important to ruminate on the fact that both of those series had episodes that weren't up to par with their counterparts. Jackson's trilogy however, got better each time out and suffered not one miss. *The Lord of the Rings* is, as Christopher Tookey asserts in the *Daily Mail*, "a major cultural landmark, a masterpiece that will inspire future generations of filmmakers, and it will be watched with admiration for as long as cinema exists." 🎞

—*Michael J. Tyrkus*

CREDITS

Frodo: Elijah Wood
Sam: Sean Astin
Aragorn: Viggo Mortensen
Legolas: Orlando Bloom
Gimli: John Rhys-Davies
Gandalf: Ian McKellen
Pippin: Billy Boyd
Merry: Dominic Monaghan
Arwen: Liv Tyler
Theoden: Bernard Hill
Eowyn: Miranda Otto
Faramir: David Wenham
Eomer: Karl Urban
Elrond: Hugo Weaving
Gollum: Andy Serkis
Galadriel: Cate Blanchett
Denethor: John Noble
Bilbo: Ian Holm
Boromir: Sean Bean
Witchking/Gothmog: Lawrence Makoare
Celeborn: Marton Csokas

Origin: USA
Released: 2003
Production: Barrie M. Osborne, Fran Walsh, Peter Jackson; Wingnut Films; released by New Line Cinema
Directed by: Peter Jackson
Written by: Peter Jackson, Fran Walsh, Philippa Boyens
Cinematography by: Andrew Lesnie
Music by: Howard Shore
Sound: Hammond Peek
Editing: Jamie Selkirk, Annie Collins
Art Direction: (Peter) Joe Bleakley, Phil Ivey, Simon Bright
Costumes: Ngila Dickson, Richard Taylor
Production Design: Grant Major
MPAA rating: PG-13
Running time: 200 minutes

REVIEWS

Chicago Sun-Times Online. December 17, 2003.
Entertainment Weekly. December 19, 2003, p. 51.
Los Angeles Times Online. December 16, 2003.
New York Times Online. December 14, 2003.
New York Times Online. December 16, 2003.
People. December 22, 2003, p. 27.
San Francisco Chronicle. December 16, 2003, p. D1.
USA Today Online. December 16, 2003.
Variety Online. December 5, 2003.
VLife. October, 2003, p. 48.
Washington Post Online. December 16, 2003.

QUOTES

Gimli (John Rhys-Davies): "Certainty of death. Small chance of success. What are we waiting for?"

AWARDS AND NOMINATIONS

Oscars 2003: Adapt. Screenplay, Art Dir./Set Dec., Costume Des., Director (Jackson), Film, Film Editing, Makeup, Song ("Into the West"), Sound, Visual FX, Orig. Score
Directors Guild 2003: Director (Jackson)
Golden Globes 2004: Director (Jackson), Film—Drama, Song ("Into the West"), Orig. Score
L.A. Film Critics 2003: Director (Jackson)
N.Y. Film Critics 2003: Film
Screen Actors Guild 2003: Cast
Nomination:
Writers Guild 2003: Adapt. Screenplay.

Lost in La Mancha

Lost in La Mancha delights in its own irony as it documents the real-life Don Quixote saga of director Terry Gilliam's ill-fated attempt to helm a modern version of Cervantes's tale about that dreamy knight. Out of the chaos of the Gilliam production emerges this moving yet informative film. Directors Keith Fulton and Louis Pepe were assigned to create a short "making-of" cinema verite documentary of Terry Gilliam's epic, *The Man Who Killed Don Quixote,* but they ended up with their own feature-length saga about the demise of the Gilliam film.

Lost in La Mancha begins with Gilliam's dream to make a new movie based on Miguel De Cervantes's novel, *The Adventures of Don Quixote,* acknowledging that Orson Welles once also tried to make a film based on the same material but never completed it. Gilliam's maverick status has been established by his past choices of odd but intriguing subject matters, including *Time Bandits* (1981), *Brazil* (1985), and *The Fisher King* (1991). Only *The Adventures of Baron Munchausen* (1989) failed both at the box-office and with critics, yet it takes Gilliam several years, beginning in 1996, to find financing for *The Man Who Killed Don Quixote,* finally securing a $40,000,000 budget purely through European backers. Despite the director's track record and the star presence of Johnny Depp (who is cast as Don Quixote's sidekick, Sancho Panza), the Hollywood studios refuse to contribute to a co-production.

Pre-production includes many meetings between Gilliam and his crew about the kind of look he wants to achieve. The designers study Gilliam's storyboards and begin work on the elaborate sets and costumes. Locations are scouted in Madrid, Spain, where the production is scheduled to start in September of 2000. Gilliam's first choice to play Don Quixote, legendary French actor Jean Rochefort, not only agrees to play the lead, he learns English for the part!

But just as the filming begins, trouble intercedes. The backers insist on cuts in the budget and Gilliam reluctantly scales it back to $32,000,000. F-16s flying overhead interrupt the shooting on several occasions. A hailstorm halts production temporarily. Finally, when Jean Rochefort suffers a back injury (from mounting a horse in his knight costume), he is sent away to a hospital to recover. Meanwhile, Gilliam and the rest of the cast and the crew try to shoot around Rochefort, but after weeks without a lead, production halts altogether. The backers get increasingly nervous as Gilliam tries to decide whether to recast his leading actor, continue to wait for his return, or shut down the film. As Gilliam makes the painful choice to stop filming, and the cast and crew disperse, the director still hopes someday to revive his project.

Obviously, *Lost in La Mancha* makes great hay out of the parallels between Gilliam and the character of Don Quixote. The film's greatest irony is that its creator is "an impossible dreamer" who "tilts at windmills." This is not the first documentary about the making of a film to show a director as a visionary battling the forces that be (see Les Blank's *Burden of Dreams* [1982] about Werner Herzog's production of *Fitzcarraldo* [1979]). But *Lost in La Mancha* contains the sad yet amusing spectacle of a director living out the very story he wants to tell (unlike some directors in films-about-films, the strange but charismatic Gilliam also makes an interesting protagonist for such a drama). Another small irony is the title Gilliam used for his version of the tale, but just who is the man who killed this Don Quixote? Is it some reluctant (never interviewed) financier or Rochefort, whose injury does indeed kill the project, or perhaps Gilliam, himself, with his all-too ambitious aspirations?

The documentarians Fulton and Pepe miss an opportunity to trace the history of putting Don Quixote on film (there are no mentions of G. W. Pabst's 1933 version or any of the other 20-plus movie and television adaptations). Brief clips are included from Orson Welles' aborted version (started in 1955), but few of the telling parallels are made: that both films were started by maverick directors; both were forced to depend on European money; both were postmodern variations, interpolating modern-day elements into the story; both were shot in Europe with a mostly European cast and crew; and, of course, both films were never finished. Fulton and Pepe also miss an opportunity to make larger points (through voiceover narrator Jeff Bridges, the star of Gilliam's *Fisher King*) about the cultural and artistic significance of lost and unfinished films, what they have in common with each other, and how films that get made avoid the traps and pitfalls that imperiled *The Man Who Killed Don Quixote.*

Yet there is much to like about *Lost in La Mancha.* One especially amazing thing is how much access Fulton and Pepe were given to the cast and crew, particularly after the problems start. The way Fulton and Pepe capture the most significant moments in the offices and on the set during filming seems almost too perfect. But there is no evidence (at the time of this writing) that anything was staged or restaged for their benefit (a la "reality" TV shows). Gilliam's direction of Johnny Depp's fight with a fish marks a highlight of *Lost in La Mancha.* Johnny Depp fans may be disappointed by how little the actor appears in other scenes being filmed or as the production comes apart, but true aficionados at least can now purchase the DVD featuring "extras" that include an interview with Depp and more deleted sequences. The dearth of interviews with the money people comprises the only real loss in the coverage.

But Fulton and Pepe are thorough in illustrating the trials and tribulations of a film production. In fact, the most everlasting aspect to *Lost in La Mancha* is the methodical way it depicts the process of pre-production and location shooting (of course, there is no post-production to show). So aspiring filmmakers and other industry members could actually learn from this effort. Others less interested in the nut-and-bolts should at least be touched by the personal story provided by Gilliam and company.

—*Eric Monder*

CREDITS

Narrator: Jeff Bridges

Origin: Great Britain
Released: 2003
Production: Lucy Darwin; Quixote Films, Low Key Pictures, Eastcroft Productions; released by IFC Films
Directed by: Keith Fulton, Louis Pepe
Written by: Keith Fulton, Louis Pepe
Cinematography by: Louis Pepe
Music by: Miriam Cutler
Sound: Michael Kowalski
Editing: Jacob Bricca
MPAA rating: R
Running time: 93 minutes

REVIEWS

Boxoffice. January, 2003, p. 26.
Chicago Sun-Times Online. February 14, 2003.
Entertainment Weekly. February 14, 2003, p. 54.
Los Angeles Times Online. January 31, 2003.
New York Times Online. January 31, 2003.
People. February 17, 2003, p. 34.
Time. February 17, 2003, p. 72.
Variety Online. February 28, 2002.
Washington Post. February 21, 2003, p. WE33.

Lost in Translation

Everyone wants to be found.
—Movie tagline

Box Office: $27.3 million

When Sofia Coppola made her first film, *The Virgin Suicides,* she was most known for her ill-fated appearance in dad Francis Ford Coppola's *The Godfather 3. The Virgin Suicides* was, to many, a surprisingly accomplished film. Some attributed the film's success to help from the elder Coppola or from her husband at the time, Spike Jonze (*Being John Malkovich* and *Adaptation*). With the near universal acclaim for *Lost in Translation,* however, Coppola proves that she has her own strong, distinct directorial style.

The title of the film has to do not only with misinterpreted language, but also with the sense of dislocation felt in an unfamiliar setting as well as the dislocation between people. Bob Harris (Bill Murray) is an American movie star who is in Tokyo to film a Japanese liquor commercial. Since it is a rare person who makes liquor commercials for fun, it's a pretty sure bet that Bob is at a point in his career where he's doing things just for the money. The Suntory whiskey people have put him up at the swank Park Hyatt Hotel in Tokyo. When he's not filming the commercials, Bob has a lot of time to kill and being unable to sleep adds to the problem. He spends much of his free time in the hotel's penthouse bar, listening to the American singer cover bad songs.

In *The Virgin Suicides,* Coppola was a stickler for the tiny details. The furniture, fabrics and even the knickknacks of the 1970s-era homes were dead on. Here she shows the same knack for capturing the feeling of being an American in Japan. She based much of the detail on her own experiences doing promotions in Japan. Coppola easily manages to convey the particular Japanese juxtaposition of frenzy and calm: the pachinko parlors are filled with noise and garishly lit with flashing colorful lights, but a flower arranging class populated by older Japanese women is exquisitely peaceful and calm.

Some of the funniest scenes in *Lost in Translation* have to do with Bob trying to get along in a world where he doesn't speak the language. In one, the Suntory people have sent what seems to be a prostitute to Bob's room. Bob just wants her to leave, but the middle-aged woman refuses to go, urgently insisting that he do something to her stocking. He's not exactly sure what she wants him to do, and as he struggles to understand, Bob's sadness and loneliness are evident, despite the humor of the situation.

Bob also has some difficulties on the set of the whiskey commercial. The director shouts passionate, lengthy direction to Bob, but the translator interprets these seemingly descriptive directives into such clipped statements as, "He says, 'Look intense.'" When a confused Bob tries to give the director what he wants, however, he only succeeds in eliciting a further torrent of direction. The way Coppola thought scenes through is apparent. In the *New York Times,* she said that she deliberately gave the director in the scene "lame directions" so that he would appear somewhat inept. She also didn't let her American actors in on what the Japanese words were so that they would be as confused as their characters.

Murray is masterful as Bob, especially when Coppola allows the funnyman to improvise. He perfectly conveys the isolated actor's depression but keeps the character from becoming maudlin by injecting his portrayal with humor. Bob has a job he's not excited by, in a country that is strange to him, and he's separated from his wife by both geography and emotions. He is constantly receiving faxes from his wife, who is obsessing over such trivial details as what color the carpet in the den should be, but who seems unwilling to discuss the details of their relationship. Under Bob's caustic exterior, however, there is also a warm, burning humanity. That Murray can play all these traits so well and have them coexist in one character is a delight.

Murray has long since transcended his earlier slick persona from *Saturday Night Live* and *Ghostbusters,* but it seems like many have been slow to give him credit. His work in films like *Groundhog Day* and, especially, *Rushmore,* has been terrific. With *Lost in Translation,* it seems certain that his fine acting ability will finally get its due. As an example of how far Murray has come is a scene in which Bob gets up to sing a karaoke song. Elvis Mitchell of the *New York Times* observed, "Certainly we anticipate Mr. Murray's trashy sarcasm when he steps in front of a microphone, but we cringe slightly; if he whips Bryan Ferry's doomed narcissism around his throat like a scarf, the kind of thing he did when he invented this routine in the late 1970's on *Saturday Night Live,* he'll get his laugh and demolish the movie. Instead he renders the song with a goofy delicacy; his workingman's suavity and generosity carry the day."

Perhaps part of what makes Murray so successful in the film is the fact that the role was written expressly for him. Reportedly Coppola wasn't going to make the film without him, but getting him to star in the picture was an arduous task. Coppola set out on a campaign to get him to do it. She explained in the *Los Angeles Times:* "Bill has an 800 number and I left messages. This went on for five months. Stalking Bill became my life's work."

Murray's costar and the person who brings out Bob's humanity is Charlotte (Scarlett Johansson of *Ghost World*). Johansson, who plays the wife of young, hotshot photographer, John (Giovanni Ribisi), is a formidable enough actress to match Murray scene for scene. Charlotte can't quite figure out what her place in the world is going to be, but she covers her character's confusion and near-panic with a calm exterior. She's also unsettled by her husband's attention to bubbly, airheaded starlet, Kelly (Anna Faris of *Scary Movie*). John leaves her at the hotel while's he off on shoots and she finds herself wandering around Tokyo in search of . . . something. Because she, too, is unable to sleep, she spends a lot of time in the Hyatt bar and quickly ends up running into Bob.

Combined, their mutual loneliness, confusion, and lack of direction become just the opposite. The two are an odd couple but form a strong connection: not exactly lovers, nor father and daughter figures, but rather very intimate friends. When Charlotte introduces Bob to a bunch of Tokyo club kids, the group goes out to experience the Tokyo nightlife, and both Bob and Charlotte realize that they are having fun and might actually feel alive.

Critics ate it up. Kenneth Turan of the *Los Angeles Times* enthused, "Statistics are hard to come by, but citizens hungering for meatier roles for Bill Murray could be the largest unorganized group of moviegoers in the country. For all those people—and you know who you are—consider this official notification: *Lost in Translation* is what you've been waiting for." Mitchell of the *New York Times* lauded the obvious rapport between Coppola and Murray, declaring that the film is "one of the purest and simplest examples ever of a director falling in love with her star's gifts. And never has a director found a figure more deserving of her admiration than Bill Murray." *Us* magazine's Thelma Adams pointed out that "this romance from up-and-coming director Sofia Coppola . . . has 2003's most tender but chaste love scene. It's dead sexy in a less-is-more way." *Entertainment Weekly*'s Lisa Schwarzbaum gave the film an A and concluded, "Much of what's astonishing about Sofia Coppola's enthralling new movie is the precision, maturity, and originality with which the confident young writer-director communicates so clearly in a cinematic language all her own."

—*Jill Hamilton*

CREDITS

Bob Harris: Bill Murray
Charlotte: Scarlett Johansson
John: Giovanni Ribisi
Kelly: Anna Faris
Commercial Director: Yutaka Tadokoro
Jazz Singer: Catherine Lambert
Charlie: Fumihiro Hayashi

Origin: USA
Released: 2003
Production: Ross Katz, Sofia Coppola; American Zoetrope, Elemental Films Productions; released by Focus Features
Directed by: Sofia Coppola
Written by: Sofia Coppola
Cinematography by: Lance Acord
Sound: Drew Kunin
Music Supervisor: Brian Reitzell
Editing: Sarah Flack
Art Direction: Mayumi Tomita
Costumes: Nancy Steiner
Production Design: K.K. Barrett, Anne Ross
MPAA rating: R
Running time: 105 minutes

REVIEWS

Chicago Sun-Times Online. September 12, 2003.
Entertainment Weekly. September 19, 2003, p. 65.
Los Angeles Times Online. September 12, 2003.
New York Times Online. September 12, 2003.
People. September 22, 2003, p. 37.
Rolling Stone. October 2, 2003, p. 124.
USA Today Online. September 12, 2003.
Vanity Fair. September, 2003, p. 178.
Variety Online. August 31, 2003.
Washington Post. September 12, 2003, p. WE39.

AWARDS AND NOMINATIONS

Oscars 2003: Orig. Screenplay (Coppola)
Golden Globes 2004: Actor—Mus./Comedy (Murray), Film—Mus./Comedy, Screenplay (Coppola)
Ind. Spirit 2004: Actor (Murray), Director (Coppola), Film, Screenplay
L.A. Film Critics 2003: Actor (Murray)
N.Y. Film Critics 2003: Actor (Murray), Director (Coppola)
Natl. Soc. Film Critics 2003: Actor (Murray)
Writers Guild 2003: Orig. Screenplay (Coppola)

Nomination:
Oscars 2003: Actor (Murray), Director (Coppola), Film
Directors Guild 2003: Director (Coppola)
Golden Globes 2004: Actress—Mus./Comedy
(Johansson), Director (Coppola)
Screen Actors Guild 2003: Actor (Murray).

Love Actually

The ultimate romantic comedy.
—Movie tagline

 Box Office: $59.3 million

Love Actually feels like one of those puzzle pictures that asks you how many tables you can find in this picture. I've tried counting the love stories in it and I can come up with anything from six to 16, that's how intertwined they are and how many of them have love stories within the love stories. Counting the love stories might actually become a party game.

Set in London in the weeks before Christmas, the movie features the following basic set-ups. First is the story of aging rocker Billy Mack (Bill Nighy) who has done a remake of the Trogg's song "Love Is All Around" but now it's a Christmas song . . . a bad Christmas song. Much to his long-suffering manager's (Gregor Fisher) dismay, Billy constantly makes fun of his song while doing the publicity tour and even jokingly offers to sing it naked on Christmas Eve, should it improbably reach number one status.

The second story involves Daniel (Liam Neeson) whose wife has just died and left him with her son, his stepson, Sam (Thomas Sangster). They, of course, are devastated by this death and bound together by a love for each other, but the "real" love story of this plot line actually revolves around Sam's unspoken infatuation for beautiful and talented classmate Joanna who is about to return to America without his ever telling her of his feelings.

A third story begins with the wedding ceremony of Peter (Chiwetel Ejiofor) and Juliet (Keira Knightley) with special surprises provided by the best man Mark (Andrew Lincoln) such as a hidden church choir singing "All You Need Is Love" accompanied by musicians hidden amongst the guests. Juliet doesn't think Mark likes her very much because he seems to treat her so coldly, but later she will discover that he is positively smitten with her.

Writer Jamie (Colin Firth) comes home from Peter and Juliet's wedding only to find his wife in bed with his brother. Consequently he runs off to the south of France to work on

his latest mystery novel . . . only to fall in love with his non-English speaking, Portuguese housekeeper Aurelia (Lucia Moniz).

The next story centers on Karen (Emma Thompson) and Harry (Alan Rickman) who have been married for many years. Unfortunately for Karen, Harry's eye is about to be caught by his sexy, young secretary Mia (Heike Makatsch) who wants him very much. Also in Harry's office is a young woman named Sarah (Laura Linney) whose life revolves around her brother, who has been confined to a mental hospital and who calls her on the phone constantly. Sarah, however, is desperately in love with the office's chief designer, Karl (Rodrigo Santoro).

There's still the story of Colin (Kris Marshall), a young man who has had so little success with women that he has decided to sell everything and buy a ticket to America, where he's sure all the women will swoon after hearing his British accent. What happens to Colin in Wisconsin should have every young British man immediately booking a flight to the Midwest.

In one of the higher-profile plots, the newly-elected British Prime Minister (Hugh Grant) has been so busy with his political career that he never married . . . and then falls for his Rubenesque catering manager Natalie (Martine McCutcheon) only to see her become sexually compromised by the President of the United States (Billy Bob Thornton) and fired.

This abundance of affection springs from the mind of first-time director Richard Curtis, who is best known as a screenwriter for television on *Mr. Bean* and *Blackadder* and for such feature films as *Four Weddings and a Funeral* and *Notting Hill*. With this latest opus, Curtis undeniably sets himself apart as a filmmaker who can make intelligent, funny, touching and masterful romantic comedies that are profitable. (He is the first British screenwriter to have his films earn more than $1 billion worldwide.)

There is no doubt that Curtis is a dyed-in-the-wool optimist—which may be too treacly for some—but he uses everyday, common social events to deftly explore all forms of positive human relationships, especially love. Since the norm in today's films seems to be car-chases, explosions, murder and mayhem, sex and violence, Curtis' vision of the world is a nice change. It feels good to have a movie make you laugh—and not at someone's expense—and care about characters at the same time.

Of course a lot of that caring comes compliments of some superior acting. At the top of the list is Curtis' long-time movie stand-in, Hugh Grant. Shy, self-deprecating, handsome and incredibly funny, Grant seems constantly surprised at his own appeal, to moviegoers and the other characters. Many have indicated that in the realm of romantic comedies Hugh Grant is the next Cary Grant, but it's a bit difficult to imagine Cary dancing in No. 10 Downing Street to the Pointer Sister's "Jump".

Love Actually abounds in talent and everybody has a chance to shine. Witness the hurt in Emma Thompson's eyes when she realizes the beautiful necklace her husband bought was not for her, Keira Knightley's radiant face as she watches the wedding video the smitten best man has prepared, only to realize all frames are of her face in closeup and what that means, Alan Rickman as the confident but confused middle-aged man being seduced by his secretary, Liam Neeson's touching relationship with his stepson as he doles out love advice while suffering a loss of love himself, Colin Firth nursing love wounds and writing his novel as he slowly falls for his housemaid, Laura Linney in one of the few unrequited love segments sacrificing her love for Carl for the love of her ill brother, the agonizingly slow process of Rowan Atkinson's salesclerk wrapping and wrapping and wrapping Harry's clandestine gift before his wife gets back and discovers his cheating ways, and especially Bill Nighy (further developing his character from *Still Crazy*) playing the aging rocker not as arrogant and self-absorbed but as straightforward and good-natured. There's not a clinker performance in the batch.

Curtis has delivered yet another clever and well-crafted script about a likeable topic and featuring A-list talent. He gives his actors intelligent dialogue and appealing characters to play. The film moves quickly, thanks to some gifted editing by Nick Moore, and tells an incredibly complicated, many-threaded story without ever being confusing.

While occasionally Curtis may dip into the well of predictability (When Daniel jokes that he'd leave Sam flat if Claudia Shiffer ever showed up and she does, or when Colin comes home from Wisconsin bringing along his trophy girlfriends: Shannon Elizabeth and Denise Richards), he still shows a knack for making feeling good a good thing.

Curtis has said that this movie was inspired in part by all the messages sent by the victims of 9/11. They were facing their own demises and they had a chance to communicate a final message. And what did they send? Messages of love.

That's why Curtis chose to begin and end his film at an airport. As he explains in the film's press kit, "We were shooting a film in Los Angeles and I had to stand at the airport for about an hour waiting for a package. It was an extraordinary sight to see—these really ordinary faces of people looking bored while they waited suddenly exploding with all of this love and affection. You could see the complexity of their relationships right there in their faces, and that's the kind of truth I'm trying to show."

And that's why Hugh Grant's voice can be heard commenting over the scenes of the many airport reunions, "general opinion's starting to make out that we live in a world of hatred and greed. But I don't see that. Seems to me that love is everywhere. Often it's not particularly dignified or newsworthy—but it's always there—fathers and sons, mothers and daughters, husbands and wives, friends and strangers. If you look for it, I've got a sneaking suspicion that love actually is all around." If you just know where to look for it, that is, and Curtis seems to know. If that's too sappy for some jaded folks, well, that's just their loss.

—*Beverley Bare Buehrer*

CREDITS

Prime Minister: Hugh Grant
Natalie: Martine McCutcheon
Billy Mack: Bill Nighy
Karen: Emma Thompson
Harry: Alan Rickman
Mia: Heike Makatsch
Juliet: Keira Knightley
Peter: Chiwetel Ejiofor
Mark: Andrew Lincoln
Sarah: Laura Linney
Karl: Rodrigo Santoro
Sam: Thomas Sangster
Daniel: Liam Neeson
Colin: Kris Marshall
Jamie: Colin Firth
Aurelia: Lucia Moniz
Judy: Joanna Page
John: Martin Freeman
U.S. President: Billy Bob Thornton
Rufus: Rowan Atkinson
Carol: Claudia Schiffer
Harriet: Shannon Elizabeth
Carla: Denise Richards
Jamie's girlfriend: Sienna Guillory
Joe: Gregor Fisher

Origin: Great Britain
Released: 2003
Production: Duncan Kenworthy, Tim Bevan, Eric Fellner; Working Title Productions, DNA Films Ltd., StudioCanal, Universal Studios; released by Universal Pictures
Directed by: Richard Curtis
Written by: Richard Curtis
Cinematography by: Michael Coulter
Music by: Craig Armstrong
Sound: David Stephenson
Music Supervisor: Nick Angel
Editing: Nick Moore
Art Direction: Rod McLean, Justin Warburton-Brown
Costumes: Joanna Johnston
Production Design: Jim Clay
MPAA rating: R
Running time: 129 minutes

REVIEWS

Chicago Sun-Times Online. November 7, 2003.
Entertainment Weekly. November 14, 2003, p. 93.
Los Angeles Times Online. November 7, 2003.
New York Times Online. November 7, 2003.
People. November 17, 2003, p. 31.
Rolling Stone. November 27, 2003, p. 103.
USA Today Online. November 7, 2003.
Variety Online. October 24, 2003.
Washington Post. November 7, 2003, p. WE45.

QUOTES

Billy Mack (Bill Nighy): "When I was young, I was greedy and foolish, and now I'm left alone with no one. Wrinkled and alone."

AWARDS AND NOMINATIONS

L.A. Film Critics 2003: Support. Actor (Nighy)
Nomination:
Golden Globes 2004: Film—Mus./Comedy, Screenplay.

Love Don't Cost a Thing

Love Don't Cost a Thing but it pays to be yourself.
—Movie tagline

 Box Office: $21.8 million

Love Don't Cost a Thing is a remake of the 1987 teen film *Can't Buy Me Love*. The film, which starred Patrick Dempsey, was shown quite a bit on cable and perhaps, due to all the repetition, found some fans. *Love Don't Cost a Thing*, is pretty much the same thing, but this time the main characters are African-American. And in the remake, instead of donning some Ray Bans to turn cool, the main character puts on Sean John clothing. Director Troy Beyer rewrote the script with Michael Swerdlick, who wrote the original. (Talk about found money for Swerdlick. He needed only to comb over the original references, replace them with words like "bling" and wait to cash his check.)

This story takes place in an upper-middle-class Long Beach, California, neighborhood. Alvin Johnson (Nick Cannon, who brought charm to *Drumline*) is a nerdy high school student who works as a pool boy. He's been working to save money to buy a cam shaft for a car that he is going to enter in a big science competition. By cleaning the pools of his wealthier neighbors, he's earned the $1500 he needs to get the part. Winning the contest could assure him a successful future. When not discussing engine parts, Alvin and his group of nerdy friends (Kal Penn, Kenan Thompson and Kevin Cristy) discuss their unhappiness with their woefully intact virginities. Alvin focuses his sexual fantasies on a girl at his school, Paris Morgan (Christina Milian). Paris is wealthy, popular, and dates an NBA player. She represents everything that Alvin hopes to achieve, except perhaps the NBA player part.

Alvin gets his big chance when Paris's mother goes out of town and Paris, out clubbing with friends, accidentally wrecks her mom's luxury SUV. Paris brings the auto into the shop where Alvin works. He sees her crying over the $3000 price that his boss quotes her. Alvin offers to do the repair work on the car for free and to give Paris his $1500 savings. Well, perhaps, give isn't the right word. Paris can have the money if she agrees to pretend that Alvin is her boyfriend for two weeks. Sex will not be part of the agreement. This is not prostitution because, well, because the movie says it is not. Paris takes the deal because she's desperate to get the car fixed. Also, she is feeling unsettled since she saw her boyfriend being interviewed on an ESPN show in which he claimed to be a free agent in dating.

Paris's approval opens up a new world for Alvin. His school is one in which there are certain hallways and bleachers that are the domain of popular kids. He is thrilled when he gets to go down the popular kids' hall for the first time. Paris's friends are mystified as to why she would have befriended this social pariah, so she decides to give him the usual movie makeover.

Paris gets Alvin involved in some previously untried grooming techniques, which is a good thing since he sports a huge afro and an almost equally huge unibrow. The odd couple goes shopping and Paris buys Alvin a lot of new clothing, almost all of it Sean John, as the movie is careful to tell us over and over again. Scott Brown of *Entertainment Weekly* termed it "monstrous product placement," adding, "Oh, yeah, and remember kids, appearances don't matter."

As the two spend more time together, they start having the kind of semi-deep conversations that in movies always leads to l-o-v-e. Paris shares her dream of leaving behind her life of privilege and becoming a singer/songwriter. Alvin listens and encourages her. Paris starts falling for her little nerd. But Alvin starts behaving like quite a jerk. He actually becomes popular and starts acting rude to his old friends. To make himself look like more of a player, he puts down Paris in front of the whole school. He cares about clothes, ignores his schoolwork and puts on a fake tough guy act. His sister, Aretha, comments, with disgust, "Urkel has gone gangsta."

Alvin's mother (Vanessa Bell Calloway) doesn't care for these changes in her son, but his dad (Steve Harvey) is secretly delighted. The dad fancies himself somewhat of a player himself and is thrilled that his son is going to follow in his footsteps. In several scenes that were funny to some critics and disgusting to others, dad tutored his son in the use of condoms. It is funny to see Harvey showing the boy how to lustfully rip open a condom. But when Harvey starts demonstrating his sensuous hip movements, a line is crossed and we're all about as uncomfortable as poor Alvin.

One of the problems with the film is that director Beyer, who has herself acted in films, including *B*A*P*S* and *John Q,* doesn't make good use of lead actor Cannon. When he is nerdy, he is so nerdy that it is difficult to see the diamond in the rough. He looks really, really bad and his personality is as dull as his wardrobe. Cannon has a lot of natural charisma but here it is totally obscured. After he becomes "cool," he is such a fake character that again, it's difficult to like the guy. The scenes in which we're supposed to see the real Alvin are short and don't exactly hammer in the point. So mostly, Alvin is either a nerd or a fake cool guy. What's lacking is the charming Alvin that we know Cannon could easily play in his sleep.

Still, the movie has some nice touches. When Alvin sits in his living room, his legs stick to the plastic covering that's on all the upholstered furniture. And Harvey has some good moments. It's funny to see him dancing to old soul hits and imagining his good old days as a ladies' man. After Alvin's transformation, his nerdy trio of friends come to the door. Dad answers and says, "Alvin's got a date. He don't need to be hanging out with your scientific-looking &%#$ no more."

Critics didn't seem to care much for the film, though none seemed to be overly riled up by it. Dave Kehr of the *New York Times* gave the film this faint praise: "The cast is uniformly high spirited and attractive, and Ms. Beyer's direction, apart from a few over weighted Wellesian camera angles, is functional." Wesley Morris of the *Boston Globe* wrote, "(Beyer's) movie is flat and witless and moves at the speed of a mid-tempo ballad." Roger Ebert of the *Chicago Sun-Times* said of the film: "For its running time *Love Don't Cost a Thing* does its job, and a little more. It has better values than the original, a little more poignancy, some sweetness. And Cannon and Milian have a natural appeal that liberates their characters, a little, from the limitations of the plot." Carla Meyer of the *San Francisco Chronicle* wrote, "The mildly entertaining 1987 teen comedy *Can't Buy Me Love* has been remade into the mildly entertaining new teen comedy *Love Don't Cost a Thing,* and no one will be the better or worse for it."

—*Jill Hamilton*

CREDITS

Alvin Johnson: Nick Cannon
Paris Morgan: Christina Milian
Walter Colley: Kenan Thompson
Kenneth Warman: Kal Penn
Clarence Johnson: Steve Harvey
Mrs. Johnson: Vanessa Bell Calloway
Big Ted: Al Thompson

Origin: USA
Released: 2003
Production: Andrew A. Kosove, Broderick Johnson, Mark Burg, Reuben Cannon; Alcon Entertainment; released by Warner Bros.
Directed by: Troy Beyer
Written by: Troy Beyer, Michael Swerdlick
Cinematography by: Chuck Cohen
Music by: Richard Gibbs
Sound: Stephen A. Tibbo
Music Supervisor: Michael McQuarn
Editing: David Codron
Art Direction: David Ellis
Costumes: Jennifer Mallini
Production Design: Cabot McMullen
MPAA rating: PG-13
Running time: 101 minutes

REVIEWS

Chicago Sun-Times Online. December 12, 2003.
Entertainment Weekly. December 19, 2003, p. 56.
Los Angeles Times Online. December 12, 2003.
New York Times Online. December 12, 2003.
USA Today Online. December 12, 2003.
Variety Online. December 11, 2003.

Love Liza

A Comic Tragedy.
—Movie tagline

Love Liza, which won an award for best screenplay at the 2002 Sundance Film Festival, is more of a rumination upon a state of mind than a plot-driven film. In the script by Gordy Hoffman, brother of lead Philip Seymour Hoffman, things happen, but characters don't change, learn things or grow. The state of mind that the film focuses on is grief. It's not the cheeriest subject matter, and *Love Liza* is not a cheery movie, but strangely the movie is kind of funny—in a dark and uncomfortable way.

Wilson Joel (Philip Seymour Hoffman) is a successful Web designer whose wife Liza has just committed suicide by inhaling gas fumes. Wilson is trying to go on with his life but just can't seem to get the hang of it. At work, after one of his coworkers tells a joke in the break room, everyone laughs. But after the laughter has stopped, Wilson keeps laughing. And laughing. And laughing. His laughter is a kind of misdirection of crying. The scene is sort of funny, but it's also terribly horrible and sad.

Liza is also survived by her mother, Mary Ann Bankhead (Kathy Bates). Mary Ann is paralyzed by grief but she tries to help Wilson. She tries to get him to sleep in a bed instead of his usual spot on the floor, but her meddling doesn't help Wilson and just makes him feel more isolated. His well-meaning mousy coworker, Maura Haas (Sarah Koskoff) also tries to help Wilson, but she just alienates him by telling him she's attracted to him.

Wilson starts dealing with his grief by inhaling gasoline. He might have chosen it to, in some way, be closer to his exhaust-inhaling wife. When he's sniffing the gas, the world becomes blurry and strange, and thus easier to deal with. When Maura comes to his house for a surprise visit, she smells the gas and asks him about it. He concocts a lie about being a big fan of remote control airplanes. Maura happens to have a brother Denny (Jack Kehler) who is very interested in remote control, or r.c. as the crowd calls it. She sends Denny over to visit Wilson and Wilson is forced to rush out and buy a plane.

Because he doesn't seem to know what else to do and because it provides a cover for his addiction, Wilson takes r.c. on as a hobby. He impulsively goes on a road trip to attend a big r.c. boat race. While there, he meets Denny and helps him with his big race. As Denny's boat races, Wilson cheers wildly. Too wildly. It's as though he hoping that if he acts enthusiastically enough about r.c., he will soon start caring about it. While at the meet, Wilson shows how disjointed he is by going in for a swim in the lake where the boats are racing. "It's okay," explains Denny to the angered racers. "His wife just killed herself."

Wilson finds a suicide note from Liza in his bed and this throws him into another tailspin. Wilson can't bring himself to open it, but his mother-in-law is desperate for him to read it. In her grief, she thinks that her dead daughter's words will provide her with some sort of answers. She starts hounding Wilson, partly to comfort him and partly to figure out if he's read the letter yet. Their relationship continues to deteriorate when Mary Ann refuses to give Wilson any pictures of her daughter. Wilson's life gets worse still when he returns home to find that his house has been burglarized. The robbers have taken everything, and his house is even barer than it was before.

And, as it goes in this bleak film, things aren't going very well at work either. Wilson is asked to take a break so that he can get his head together. He signs up to do some freelance work for Tom Bailey (Steven Tobolowsky) and Tom sends him some work to do at home. Wilson handles his duties by ignoring them and never opens up the boxes containing computers from Tom. When Tom arrives at his house to check on him, Wilson is sitting on the unopened boxes, doing some gas sniffing with two local teens.

The film gives Wilson some chances for an upturn. Denny is a weird guy, but perhaps his strange friendship can help Wilson reenter the world. Or maybe he and Mary Ann could connect in their grief and perhaps find healing together. The job for Tom looks like it could help Wilson find his way back into the work force. But none of these can quite do it, and Wilson founders.

As the film ends, Wilson is no better off than he was at the beginning. In fact, he might even be worse. Eventually, he does read the note. It's pleasant enough but it doesn't really answer any questions. At least when the note was unopened, it had potential for healing. After he opens it, he lights it on fire. This quickly catches Wilson's apartment on fire, and his clothes, too. As the film ends, Wilson is stripped to his underwear, walking dazedly down the middle of a street. It's not clear if he's ever going to get better.

In his other films, Hoffman has mostly been a side character. He's good at playing strange people outside of normal social conventions. Here, though Hoffman's the star, he's still playing a man on the outside. He's not afraid of looking weird or creepy or pitiful. Even though his character's life is mostly internal, Hoffman is able to take, and even thrive under, such intense scrutiny from the camera.

Critics split on the small, strange film. Lou Lumineck of the *New York Post* wrote, "Quirkily directed by actor Todd Luiso—best known for playing a music nut in *High Fidelity*—*Love Liza* is an oddly endearing little chamber piece that provides a terrific showcase for Hoffman, surely the best actor who has never been nominated for an Oscar." Sean Axmaker of the *Seattle Post-Intelligencer* wrote, "Hoffman brings discomforting emotions to vivid life on the screen in his uncompromising performance. But while each moment of this broken character study is rich in emotional texture, the journey doesn't really go anywhere." Carrie Rickey of the *Philadelphia Inquirer* wrote, "It's . . . a showcase for an actor's actor rather than . . . a drama that engages our hearts." And A.O. Scott of the *New York Times* wrote, "At its best the film has some of the unadorned, incisive strangeness of the minimalist American fiction of the 1980's, but it also shows the limitations of minimalism, and feels, even in its relative brevity, about half an hour too long."

—*Jill Hamilton*

CREDITS

Wilson Joel: Philip Seymour Hoffman
Mary Ann Bankhead: Kathy Bates
Denny: Jack Kehler
Tom Bailey: Stephen Tobolowsky
Maura Haas: Sarah Koskoff
Brenda: Erika Alexander

Released: 2002
Production: Ruth Charny, Chris Hanley, Fernando Sulichin, Jeff Roda; Black List Films, Kinowelt Filmproduktion, Wild Bunch, Studio Canal Plus, MUSE Productions; released by Sony Pictures Classics
Directed by: Todd Louiso
Written by: Gordy Hoffman
Cinematography by: Lisa Rinzler
Music by: Jim O'Rourke
Sound: Skip Gordon
Editing: Ann Stein
Art Direction: Tim Cohn
Costumes: Jill Newell
Production Design: Stephen Beatrice
MPAA rating: R
Running time: 90 minutes

REVIEWS

Boxoffice. April, 2002, p. 175.
Chicago Sun-Times Online. February 7, 2003.
New York Times Online. December 30, 2002.
Sight and Sound. February, 2003, p. 51.
Variety. January 28, 2002, p. 32.
Washington Post. February 7, 2003, p. WE44.

AWARDS AND NOMINATIONS

Sundance 2002: Screenplay.

Love the Hard Way

When two worlds collide.
—Movie tagline

In this so-called "romance-crime-comedy-drama" the romance is pretty sleazy and not very convincing, while the comedy is nearly non-existent. Jack (Adrien Brody) seems little more than a scheming ne'er-do-well who runs a confi-dence game with his partner, Charlie (Jon Seda). In cahoots with a crooked hotel desk clerk and two hookers, they scam unsuspecting Manhattan tourists by setting them up with the hookers, then pretending to be vice cops, raiding their rooms, but allowing themselves to be bribed before making arrests. But, viewers are asked to believe, Jack also has a sensitive side and turns out to be a budding novelist who is secretly working on a pulp fiction novel, that seems to be mainly autobiographical.

Maybe that explains why Claire (Charlotte Ayanna), a graduate student seriously interested in cell biology (and who ought to be smart enough to know better) is strangely attracted to Jack, a rude and swaggering hood, by all appearances, so of course she is hooked. When Jack and Charlie encounter her on campus the next day, their rude and ignorant behavior should mark them as undesirable riff-raff, but bold Jack, in the presence of Claire's boyfriend, tells her that he will be waiting for her the next afternoon at 5 p.m. at the terminal for the Staten Island ferry, and, sure enough, she's there to keep the date. He takes her to a fine restaurant, one that looks way too classy for him. Maybe she wants to live dangerously?

It turns out that Jack is being investigated by police detective Linda Fox (Pam Grier), who is wise to his game. Hence trouble looms on the horizon. The film is unconvincingly driven by the star power of Grier and Brody, which is not strong enough to overcome problems with the implausible script, although Grier seems more at home than Brody in the noir-ish setting.

Jack and Claire shack up the night of their first date, but Claire, still a "good" girl, needs to hit the books before a morning exam. Jack ignores her then for two weeks until she can't stand it any more and calls him up. One line Jack had used to seduce Claire was to tell her that he had slept with 200 women. She has the wit (let's call it) to inform him that Wilt Chamberlain had slept with 20,000 women, which makes Jack look like a punk, an assessment that is pretty much on target. Later on sensitive Jack writes down that exchange in his cheesy novel manuscript. Call it "inspiration."

The plot builds absurdly on Claire's foolishness. After Claire calls, Jack insults her by setting up a date and then sending his sidekick Charlie out to service her, but she forces Charlie to lead her to Jack. While Jack and Charlie's next scam is being set up, Detective Fox turns up with four uniformed officers and arrests the hookers, leaving their tourist scam without bait. Charlie suggests that they use Clair to bait their trap. Will Jack be tempted? Is he such a cad?

Claire leaves town, but when she comes back she catches Jack in the sack with one of his entrepreneurial hookers. So what's going on here? Is Jack trying to drive Claire away in order to save her? If so, it doesn't work, since before long Claire is turning tricks for the German hotel clerk, who serves as her pimp. When Jack and Charlie break into the hotel room and find Claire on top of their mark, Jack freaks out and beats up the john. But Claire has now chosen to degrade herself. Charlie's observation is that Claire is "out of control." No doubt about that, but, then, by this time the whole movie seems to be out of control.

Jack starts to stalk Claire as she turns tricks at night, as if punishing himself for what she has become. In fact, Jack is out of control, as demonstrated when a black pimp offers to drive him home one night, and then Jack steals his Cadillac. Both Jack and Claire seem to be headed for some kind of physical breakdown. After they have a brief "romantic" reconciliation (in truth, this film is too cynical for true romance), Jack and Charlie get busted on their next hotel extortion scam and are arrested by Detective Fox and her vice squad. After the arrest, her vice squad finds Claire collapsed at Jack's apartment, apparently a victim of attempted suicide.

The action then cuts to "Two Years Later," when Jack and Charlie are serving hard time in prison. Jack gets stabbed in a kitchen brawl, and when Detective Fox visits him in the hospital (for whatever reason), she tells him about Claire. When Jack is released from prison, he gets his notebook, intending to finish his novel. Jack calls Claire at the research laboratory where she now works and tells her to meet him at the storage cubicle where he wrote his novel. When she gets there, she finds his manuscript on the desk and reads it. Afterwards, she seems to forgive him and the two of them seem reconciled and ready to return to a more "normal" relationship, unlikely though that may be.

In describing the action, the *New York Times* noted that Charlotte Ayanna's "sweet young biology major " somehow found "something attractive about her new boyfriend's dangerous world," while, at the same time, he felt "drawn to the honest, aboveboard life." Well, yes, serving hard time in prison might have that effect on even the most stupidly reckless of criminals. But the great flaw in the screenplay is the utter lack of motivation it provides for Claire's spiral descent into degradation and shame, and her apparent rapid recovery after Jack has been imprisoned.

It's baffling that an actor as gifted as Adrien Brody, who won the best actor Academy Award in 2002 for his lead role in Roman Polanski's *The Pianist,* should be playing such a low-life con man in *Love the Hard Way,* a film so stupidly conceived that it almost immediately disappeared from sight and went quickly to video. This film, directed by Peter Sehr in 2001, might have been shelved and forgotten had it not been for Brody's later astonishing success. It's nothing the actor should be especially proud of.

—*James M. Welsh*

CREDITS

Jack Grace: Adrien Brody
Claire Harrison: Charlotte Ayanna
Charlie: Jon Seda
Linda Fox: Pam Grier
Jeff: August Diehl

Origin: USA
Released: 2001
Production: Wolfram Tichy; released by Kino International
Directed by: Peter Sehr
Written by: Peter Sehr, Marie Noelle
Cinematography by: Guy Dufaux
Music by: Darien Dahoud
Sound: Michael Barosky
Music Supervisor: Sue Jacobs
Editing: Christian Nauheimer
Art Direction: Peter Yasair
Costumes: Kathryn Nixon
Production Design: Debbie DeVilla
MPAA rating: Unrated
Running time: 104 minutes

REVIEWS

Boxoffice. April, 2002, p. 184.
Entertainment Weekly. June 13, 2003, p. 75.
Los Angeles Times Online. June 13, 2003.
Rolling Stone. June 26, 2003, p. 88.
Variety Online. September 7, 2001.

Lucia, Lucia
(La Hija del Canibal)
(The Cannibal's Daughter)

She's on an adventure that could change her life . . . if she doesn't turn back.
—**Movie tagline**

The best part of *Lucia, Lucia* is that its title character is a liar. This is something that Lucia (Cecilia Roth of Pedro Almodovar's *All About My Mother*) readily admits. "This is a story. This is a lie," she warns before telling parts of her tale. This provides for some creative touches from Mexican director Antonio Serrano (whose first film *Sex, Shame and*

Tears was a hit in Mexico but nowhere else). In the midst of telling some of her story, Lucia will interrupt and explain that things weren't like that at all. In one scene, she says that her apartment wasn't as nice as she has been telling. Instantly, the apartment in the film changes into a more modest one. Several times throughout the film, she changes hair colors and even style of dress. In one part of the film, she is a prim, drab housewife; in another, she appears more glamorous and sexually free. Unfortunately, the way Lucia tells her story ends up being more interesting than the story itself. Plus, the script, written by Serrano and based on the novel *La Hija del Canibal* (*The Daughter of the Cannibal*) by Rosa Montero, is already mighty confusing. Lucia's coyness with truth just makes it all the more so.

It all begins when Lucia and her longtime husband, Ramon (Jose Elias Moreno) are at the Mexico City airport, ready to go on a vacation in Rio de Janeiro to celebrate New Year's Eve. Ramon, who's been a low-level government bureaucrat for 12 years, goes to the restroom but doesn't come back. Lucia waits, and their plane finally leaves without them. Alarmed, Lucia finally goes into the men's room, bangs open every stall door and finds them all empty.

Lucia rushes to the police, led by Inspector Garcia (Javier Diaz Duenas), but ends up defending herself against invasive questions like, "Was he having an affair?" and "Were you having an affair?" Having little faith that the police have the competence, or even the desire, to locate her husband, Lucia heads home to her apartment. She starts spending time with her neighbor, Felix (Carlos Alvarez-Novoa), a kind-eyed old man who once lived an adventurous, dangerous life fighting in the Spanish Civil War. The duo is joined by Adrian (Kuno Becker), a handsome young musician who likes to cite ancient philosophers. Improbably, the three all start living together in Lucia's apartment and become an ersatz sort of family.

The three have good talks, eat nice food, and drink fine wine. Although the purpose of the three all being together is ostensibly to solve the mystery of Ramon's disappearance, Lucia starts to realize that the life she was leading before was somewhat dull. "To mature," she muses, "It means 'beginning to rot.'" Is she really all that anxious to find Ramon and step seamlessly back into her former life?

Then there's the matter of Adrian. He obviously adores her and says that he finds the wrinkles around her eyes charming. Lucia says she's much too old for him, but still, the guy's pretty cute. She finds herself drawn into a fling with him. She shares a different kind of love with the older Felix. Perhaps a more interesting movie could have been made with Lucia falling in love with the more complex Felix, but love stories featuring an old man are not considered to be sexy cinema.

The circumstances involving Ramon's disappearance become more confusing and jumbled. It turns out that Ramon had squirreled away a pretty large fortune. Did he embezzle it from work? Did he steal it from a radical group? What kind of secret life was he living? Is it possible that he disappeared on purpose? Ramon's supposed kidnappers contact Lucia and ask for the money as a ransom.

All of this provides much fodder for the three to have various adventures. They doubt each other, betray each other and have an exciting motorcycle chase. There are several attempts to deliver the ransom money, but none of them work. Plus, things may or may not be as they seem. Besides Lucia's lying, which colors the whole story, there are questions about Adrian's loyalty. Could he be working for someone else? And are the police somehow involved with all this?

In the end, there are too many questions, and by this time it just seems too tedious and uninteresting to find out what all the answers are. As a whodunit, *Lucia, Lucia* is a bust. All that is left are the relationships and the story of a woman coming into her own. On that level alone, the film works. The trio is an odd set of friends, but the movie makes it believable. Alvarez-Novoa brings an understated power and a vague sense of yearning to the role of the gentle Felix. Becker is also good as the puppy-like Adrian. He is thrilled with the idea of love and finds the older Lucia to be an exotic treat.

But the toughest acting job falls on Roth. Roth has the difficult task of playing a character that gradually comes into her own power. A lot of this is slow and internal so it's not the kind of thing to show with a few quick gestures. And, since her character so often misrepresents herself, she has to play Lucia in different ways. In some of the scenes, her Lucia is timid and mousy and in others, she is bold and alluring. Roth makes all of them seem real and does something even more difficult—lets them all seem to be part of the same person.

Critics didn't give the import a warm reception. Carla Meyer of the *San Francisco Chronicle* wrote, "Serrano applies the fantasy device so haphazardly as to render it irritating instead of surprising. He fills the movie with anticlimaxes: People revealed to be crooks are revealed to be crooks again, and flagging story lines stretch forever. The tone is also random, shifting from farce to telenovela camp to serious thriller." Kevin Thomas of the *Los Angeles Times* felt *Lucia, Lucia* was "a charming romantic fable that could have been even more so were it not so long-winded." *Entertainment Weekly*'s Owen Gleiberman gave the film a C and complained, "Anxiety is a fair response to a midlife crisis, but that hardly means that we want to see the heroine of a movie spend scene after scene trapped in a nervous dither of indecision." And Elvis Mitchell of the *New York Times* commented, "*Lucia* . . . has such a vortex of plot that the film begins to suck everything around it into a kind of black hole." 🎞️

—*Jill Hamilton*

CREDITS

Lucia: Cecilia (Celia) Roth
Felix: Carlos Alvarez-Novoa
Adrian: Kuno Becker
Ramon: Jose Elias Moreno
Lucia's mother: Margarita Isabel
Inspector Garcia: Javier Diaz Duenas
Lucia's father (The Cannibal): Hector Ortega

Origin: Mexico, Spain
Language: Spanish
Released: 2003
Production: Epigmenio Ibarra, Carlos Payan, Inna Payan, Christian Valdelievre, Matthias Ehrenberg; Titan Productions, Lola Films, Argos Communications, Total Films; released by Fox Searchlight
Directed by: Antonio Serrano
Written by: Antonio Serrano
Cinematography by: Xavier Perez Grobet
Music by: Nacho Mastretta
Sound: Evelia Cruz
Editing: Jorge Garcia
Art Direction: Brigitte Broch
Costumes: Mariestela Fernandez
MPAA rating: R
Running time: 113 minutes

REVIEWS

Boxoffice. September, 2003, p. 120.
Chicago Sun-Times Online. July 25, 2003.
Entertainment Weekly. August 8, 2003, p. 54.
Los Angeles Times Online. July 25, 2003.
New York Times Online. July 25, 2003.
Variety Online. July 15, 2003.

Luther

Rebel. Genius. Liberator.
—Movie tagline

Box Office: $5.7 million

The opening sequence shows a man running through the dark, avoiding bolts of lightening. Finally he falls to his knees screaming that he will become a monk and devote his life to the church if he is saved. Immediately we are introduced to Martin Luther (Joseph Fiennes) and his psyche with this dramatic opening.

The film begins in the year 1505 when Luther decides to drop his law studies and enter an Augustinian monastery the day after the bolts of lightening scare. Historical dramas often take liberty with the facts and add elements to make a more believable or interesting film. Some films, however, stick directly to the facts and add nothing. Luther is defiantly a film of the latter type, never straying for a moment from the bounds of Martin Luther.

The story then follows him on his pilgrimage to Rome in the year 1510. He immediately stumbles upon what he believes is a corruption of the church—the selling of indulgences. The church, at this point does not view this as corruption in their pursuit of spiritual guidance, while Luther sees this practice as completely corrupt. It becomes his mission to move through the hierarchy of the church to keep it pure in spirit. He sees this particular practice as greedy, as it makes the church wealthy while ignoring the many needs of the poor.

Obviously, a man going against the grain of the status quo will not be embraced by many in the hierarchy. We see Luther being rejected by many including Father Johann von Staupitz (Bruno Ganz) and the Pope Leo XII (Uwe Ochsenknect). This film shows the life of Luther, an outlaw who struggles with his faith as more and more people turn against him. We see him in exile in the tower of the Wartburg Castle and wrestling with spiritual angst. As Luther struggles, the masses are beginning to be awakened by his talk and they start to follow him. We really do see how this German monk was a true leader of the church as well as society in his day.

Ralph Fiennes does a wonderful job of taking a difficult and lengthy historical drama and making it seem real and relevant to today. He has the ability to show this character as more than a rebel, but as a legitimate person with shyness, charisma, and leadership qualities. He made this character his own and helped us understand a very complicated and fascinating man and a moment in history within the church.

Peter Ustinov is Friedrich the Wise, a prince who was one of the first to believe in and ultimately support this rebel and his ideas. Ustinov gives this oftentimes bloody and overly intense drama the comic relief it needs. Through Luther's sermons Friedrich gains courage to support these unconventional ideas about the church and defend Luther.

Obviously, this film is an educational look into the life of a very important part of the church, but it is also designed to inspire people already religiously inclined. For those people with less religious leanings, the film may be a bit bland and controlled, bordering on mundane.

—*Laura Abraham*

CREDITS

Martin Luther: Joseph Fiennes
John Tetzel: Alfred Molina
Girolamo Aleander: Jonathan Firth
Katerina von Bora: Claire Cox
Prince Frederick the Wise: Peter Ustinov
Father Johann von Staupitz: Bruno Ganz
Pope Leo XII: Uwe Ochsenknecht
Cardinal Cajetan: Matthieu Carriere
Professor Caristadt: Jochen Horst

Origin: Germany
Released: 2003
Production: Dennis Clauss, Kurt Rittig, Gabriela Pfander, J. Daniel Nichols; Neue Filmproduktion Teleart; released by RS Entertainment
Directed by: Eric Till
Written by: Camille Thomasson, Bart Gavigan
Cinematography by: Robert Fraisse
Music by: Richard Harvey
Sound: Ed Cantu
Music Supervisor: Sandy McLelland
Editing: Clive Barrett
Art Direction: Christian Schafer, Ralf Schreck
Costumes: Ulla Gothe
Production Design: Rolf Zehetbauer
MPAA rating: PG-13
Running time: 112 minutes

REVIEWS

Boxoffice. November, 2003, p. 106.
Chicago Sun-Times Online. September 26, 2003.
Entertainment Weekly. October 10, 2003, p. 101.
Los Angeles Times Online. September 26, 2003.
New York Times Online. September 26, 2003.
Variety Online. September 25, 2003.
Washington Post. Septmber 26, 2003, p. WE50.

Madame Sata

The revolutionary fervor often buried under the rubric of Third World Cinema is brought dazzlingly to life in Karim Ainouz's debut feature from Brazil, *Madam Sata.* While set in the Rio of the early 1930's and confining itself to the subculture of the downtrodden, depraved, and sexually transgressive, the film strikes a politically universal chord.

The central character, Joao Francisco (Lazaro Ramos), who is based on a real-life individual, searches for his identity, allowing the violent urges within him to tear at his insides and at his squalid world. As a young, hotheaded black, he embodies Frantz Fanon's assertion in the book *The Wretched of the Earth* that the only way a colonialized man can become human is through violence. Joao is thus one uprising removed from the lumpen proletariat depicted in Gillo Pontecorvo's *The Battle of Algiers* (1965), part of the amorphous class of street drifters deployed to fight colonialist oppression. The fact that Joao discovers his true self by venting the violence within him makes for the film's revolutionary impact.

Joao makes his existence bearable through poetry and music; in this, he's no different from those closest to him. There's the attractive Laurita (Marcelia Cartaxo), the woman he's looking after, and Taboo (Flavio Bauraqui), his lookalike "brother-in-poverty." Ainouz lights up their faces against the dark, gritty backgrounds of their dwellings and juxtaposes their dead end lives with Rio's two most redeeming features: the sea and the spirit of the Carnival.

The film's first shot confronts us with an unwavering mid-close up of a battered Joao while an authoritative voice-over intones the charges against him. This is not just a female impersonator, but a depraved one at that, a pederast living out of the gutter with no regular source of income. His life has been steeped in degradation as a male prostitute. All this has led him to attack a police officer and commit first degree murder. This slide is supposed to have begun in Rio in 1932.

During the opening titles, the audience is introduced to the long flashback that comprises most of the film. Inside a dowdy nightclub in Lapa, the bohemian district of Rio, Vitoria dos Anjos (Renata Sorrah) is performing a fan dance to a ballad about Scheherazade. Her dresser, Joao, watches enviously from the wings, mouthing the words she is singing. After a brief trolley ride, Joao hits his own hangout, an illicit gambling den in the red light district, where he's greeted by Laurita, who works there as prostitute. This is the point at which the film slams us headlong into Joao's transgressive behavior. Joao follows Renatinho (Felipe Marques), a scruffy but good-looking white male, into the toilet down below, while reciting a paean to Satan. He then grabs the stash Renatinho is snorting and goes on to lick and bite at his neck. It is clearly an act of lust mixed with an assertion of street power. Then, while Joao is dancing with Laurita, a lout pulls her away and out into the street. When Joao gives chase and the drunk takes out a gun, Joao, unfazed, kicks the gun out of his hand, then picks it up and lightly runs it over the man's face before deciding to keep it.

In the harsh light of morning, we see the grungy, open courtyard with its grimy, peeling walls that Joao shares with Taboo, Laurita, and her baby. We can see that Taboo, who is dressed in female undergarments, is a less self-empowered version of Joao, someone who looks so much like him and longs to be dominant, but is too kind to ever become so. Joao, no doubt realizing this, treats him like a servant. This "domestic" scene reveals Joao's tender side as well as his desire to break out of his degradation.

The scenes that follow play upon the antinomy of Joao's talent and aspirations set off against his lust and his propensity for violence. Through it all, Ainouz repeatedly shows Joao staring at himself in the mirror, sometimes while singing, as if trying to convince himself that he is better than the reflection looking back at him.

In her dressing room backstage, Vitoria also stares at herself in the mirror, lamenting the fact that she has been singing the same song for two years and that the public wants something new. When the proprietor, Gregorio (Floriano Peixoto I), enters, Joao demands his pay but is told to wait until the next day. As a mere servant, Joao can only watch as Vitoria goes off with Gregorio.

That night, outside his own hangout, Joao is accosted by Renatinho, who wants Joao to teach him how to fight. At first Joao refuses, calling him an "Indian Prince," someone too pure for the ways of the street. But once inside Joao's room, the two men kiss passionately in the film's first flagrant homosexual love scene. In this, as in other such scenes, Ainouz's camera becomes like a third partner, so that what is transmitted is not any erotic aspect, for viewers who might find it so, but a transgressive vitality. It could be argued that an objective camera would have resulted in a desire to shock the audience, as in Hong Kong director Wong Kar-Wai's *Happy Together*, which captures its two young male protagonists thrashing around in bed. What further surmounts the sex is Joao's awakening to romance as he sings to Renatinho the song whose refrain will be repeated throughout the film: He sings about how the moon feels pity for him because his lover is lying asleep in the moonlight. After a farewell kiss, Joao tells Renatinho to "fly away . . . from this stinking, depraved world."

The encounter also awakens Joao's artistic aspirations. Alone, inside the dressing room at the club, he puts on Vitoria's costume and pretends to be her pretending to be Scheherazade. When she catches him at it, she thinks he's making fun of her and shouts at him to remove the getup. Joao, no doubt reacting to a feeling of inferiority, tears the clothes off, then smashes everything in the room and almost strangles her. When Gregorio storms in, Joao tells him he wants to quit and demands his pay. When Gregorio spits out his refusal, the two break into a violent fight that marks a turning point in Joao's life. As he himself puts it, he is no more the artiste, but is reborn as an outlaw.

On the street, Joao and Taboo target the white Alvaro (Guilherme Piva) as a mark. Joao takes Alvaro to his room and loosens his inhibitions by pretending to be pimping for his sister, Josefa. He then places the panting Alvaro's hand on his thigh and kisses him. Here, Joao's actions serve to highlight his male homosexual cravings as sheer depravity. Taboo meanwhile sneaks in, takes the money out of Alvaro's trousers and screams that the police are raiding the place. As Alvaro runs off, Joao and Taboo laugh in triumph.

From this point on, Joao's life becomes a series of reversals. In his sex with Renatinho, Joao allows himself to be mounted, playing the female. The scene sheds a curious light on Joao's talent for female impersonation, which will later come to dominate his life. Here, it can be seen as the liberation of the psychological female inside him. For the moment, however, the repression of his talent results in unwarranted outbursts of rage. When refused admission into a club, he kicks the doormen, knocking one of them unconscious. That night, as Laurita tries to talk sense into him, Joao defends himself by claiming that the doorman unjustly called him a bum despite the stylish way he was dressed. According to Joao, he was like anybody else. "But you're not like anybody else!" Laurita argues. Joao then turns on her for being frank, but he does admit that he wants to straighten out. He adds that he doesn't know what is eating him. "It's an anger without end!" he says.

Joao's story takes on a political tinge when he becomes the victim of a false charge filed by Gregorio. Again, Joao lashes out at those who have come to arrest him, and even manages to run away, but only for a while. As he's hosed in the prison yard, we see him in full frontal nudity for the first time. The film skips over his incarceration. Upon his release, Joao learns from Laurita that Renatinho had been gunned down.

A new chapter then opens for Joao as he puts his grief behind him and pursues a career as a bouncer-cum-female impersonator at the Blue Danube Club, which is owned by the kindly, middle-aged Amador (Emiliano Queiroz). Joao draws his inspiration from watching Josephine Baker at the movies. His act, which proves a huge success, is an iconoclastic transmogrification of folk myths. It all caves in when a racial bigot spews the usual epithets at him as he's helping Amador close up for the night. Joao tracks the man down and, with the gun we saw him acquire, shoots him dead.

The film then returns to the mid-close shot with which it opened. Joao's own voiceover rises above that of the voice of authority. We learn that after serving his ten-year sentence, Joao goes on to win many contests as a female impersonator, bursting upon Rio's Carnival scene in the guise of the title character from the 1930 Cecil B. Demille film, *Madam Satan*. "Madame Sata," we are informed, died in 1976 at the age of 76.

Critics seem to have accepted the spirit animating Ainouz's bio of his nonconformist hero. In the *San Francisco Chronicle*, Edward Guthmann calls the film "a thrilling feature debut . . . [that] doesn't glorify dos Santos but examines the hot, reckless fever of his life in all its thorny complexity." Stephen Holden's rave in the *New York Times* calls *Madame Sata* a "voluptuous, hot-blooded portrait of a social outcast

... who, in acting out his gaudiest Hollywood dreams, transcendentally reinvented himself." Holden lauds Lazaro Ramos in the title role, saying his "incendiary performance burns like a fuse, lighted from deep inside his skin, that explodes with devastating emotional fireworks."

—*Vivek Adarkar*

CREDITS

Joao Francisco dos Santos: Lazaro Ramos
Laurita: Marcella Cartaxo
Taboo: Flavio Bauraqui
Renatinho: Felippe Marques

Origin: Brazil, France
Language: Portuguese
Released: 2002
Production: Isabel Diegues, Mauricio Andrade Ramos, Donald Ranvaud, Marc Beauchamps, Walter Salles; VideoFilmes, Wild Bunch, Lumiere, Dominant 7; released by Wellspring Media
Directed by: Karim Ainouz
Written by: Karim Ainouz
Cinematography by: Walter Carvalho
Music by: Marcos Suzano, Sacha Ambak
Sound: ALoysio Compasso
Editing: Isabela Monteiro de Castro
Costumes: Rita Murtinho
Production Design: Marcos Pedroso
MPAA rating: Unrated
Running time: 105 minutes

REVIEWS

Boxoffice. September, 2003, p. 121.
Chicago Sun-Times Online. August 22, 2003.
Los Angeles Times Online. August 17, 2003.
Los Angeles Times Online. August 22, 2003.
New York Times Online. July 9, 2003.
San Francisco Chronicle Online. July 11, 2003.
Variety Online. May 20, 2002.

QUOTES

Joao (Lazaro Ramos): "I choose to be a queen but that doesn't make me less of a man."

The Magdalene Sisters

In a place that defied belief their only hope was each other.
—Movie tagline
The triumphant story of three women who found the courage to defy a century of injustice.
—Movie tagline

 Box Office: $4.6 million

Silence covered by ritual, things unsaid, taboos made into fetishes, blame and guilt parcelled out by the privileged—this is the stuff of repressive religious authoritarianism, and Peter Mullan nails the whole thing cold in the brilliant opening scene (and all the subsequent scenes) of *The Magdalene Sisters*. In this frighteningly powerful portrayal of the iron grip of conservative patriarchal Catholicism in twentieth century Ireland that manages to make both a scathing indictment of mainstream Irish Catholicism—not so far removed from the present—and also an achingly humanistic and redemptive film, Mullan accomplishes what all great movies achieve—univeralism that springs out of specificity. Mullan's tale of wayward young women assigned to brutal virtual prisons run by sadistic nuns is an unsparingly authentic portrait of the uniquely Irish brand of religious repression, but it achieves universal significance as an exquisitely powerful shorthand for all the variants of those potent moral systems that oppress women because of the sexual dangers, real and imagined, they pose to a repressive society.

Mullan sweeps us into this closed world in a powerful opening scene at a wedding reception near Dublin in 1964. It begins with a priest playing a traditional Irish drum, and wailing a traditional song. The priest is sweating profusely and playing passionately, suggesting that his musical performance is a physical outlet for his own restrained sexual desire—or perhaps a shorthand for it. In short order, Margaret (Anne-Marie Duff), who is at the wedding, is taken upstairs and raped by her cousin, who seems little more than a callous, unthinking teenager. The lad and then his prey are seen sneakily coming down a set of stairs and re-entering the reception. As the band plays a jig, we literally see the story of what has happened spread—the dialogue drowned out by the music—when Margaret speaks to a female, who tells another, who tells a couple of men, who grab the priest and go behind closed doors, then emerge to point out Margaret, and take her rapist away by the shoulder. In a few minutes, Margaret's fate has been sealed, and Mullan's method of conveying the judgment on the parties involved is as brutally economic as the way the matter has been decided. In this society, as in many where truths are suppressed and important matters left unspoken, expression itself—questioning, discussing, deciding—is forbidden. Everything is circumscribed, but especially language, the vehicle of independent thought, because that is the most dangerous thing of all.

In the very next scene, Margaret is shown being roused from the bedroom she shares with her siblings by her father, and shoved into a car driven by a priest. While her brother asks what is happening, her mother watches silently from a window, knowing she is helpless to interfere. Margaret is being sent off to a Magdalene convent because her rape has made her unfit for society; the unspoken, unquestionable assumption is that she is to blame for her violation just for being female.

The fate of Bernadette (Nora-Jane Noone) is equally unjust. She is a beautiful, saucy-looking orphaned teenager. When boys from a neighborhood school come to flirt with the orphanage girls one day, she lingers too long at the fence, though she is denying the boys' requests for a kiss. Mullan shows the backs of two heads—a nun's and a priest's—looking out a window at Bernadette standing near the fence. In the next scene, she is also being hustled off to the same convent. When she later dares to ask why she has been sent there, swearing that she has done nothing sinful (which is certainly true), the convent head, Sister Bridget (Geraldine McEwan), explains: "All men are sinners, therefore all men are prone to temptation, so we must remove the source of their temptation." Bernadette is being removed from society simply because she is too beautiful.

The third woman to be introduced is Rose (Dorothy Duffy), who we meet in a hospital bed with her newborn baby, an illegitimate child. She tries unsuccessfully to get her mother, who is sitting stonefaced next to the bed, to look on the child. In the hallway, her father stands expressionless as a priest tells Rose the child will live a horrible life as a bastard and so she must sign him away for adoption. Confused, she does so, and then screams as the priest takes her baby immediately away, and pounds on her impassive father's chest as she tries to reverse her decision.

Margaret, Rose, and Bernadette are next shown arriving together at the Magdalene convent. There is something wondrously eerie about the scene in which they are escorted to the corridor outside Sister Bridget's office. Muted golden lights shine through tall windows at the end of the hall, and the three girls are in deep shadows. Cinematographer Nigel Willoughby shoots the film in grainy, sometimes near-sepia tones which emphasize the mustiness and gloom of the convent's interior, and at times, as in this corridor scene, the techniques verge on the primitive and remind one of the strangest, most evocative scenes in silent classics. Mullan wants to give the film an almost documentary feel, and he usually succeeds, with few exceptions, failing to succumb to the many temptations to sensationalize the story for entertainment purposes or to give it a modern glossy look.

The bulk of the movie is an engrossing, if often difficult to watch, depiction of the conditions inside the convent, and the trio of characters' halting efforts to cope with it, rebel against it, or escape from it. The women are virtual slaves to the nuns who run the convent, working long hours in the laundry as a way to "cleanse" their souls, purify their bodies and banish their evil thoughts. They sleep in two rows in a cabin-like dormitory, are roused early each day for breakfast by a nun who claps her hands and turns on the bright lights, and one of them is assigned to read prayers or Scripture each morning as they eat oatmeal and scraps of bread. Meanwhile the nuns sit on an elevated table behind a wooden screen and eat hearty breakfasts of bacon, toast, eggs, and orange juice. Silence is required at all times, but Mullan delightfully shows how the workers circumvent this rule by exchanging snippets of conversation while prayers are being recited in unison, or as they meet in the middle of a task of jointly folding sheets.

Mullan, who is Scottish, wrote the script as well as directed, and the film was shot in Scotland, though it was a joint Scottish-Irish production. In the hands of a less facile storyteller, *The Magdalene Sisters* could easily have descended into dreariness or melodrama, but Mullan keeps the plot cooking while managing to convey the drudgery and the brutality of convent life. The absolute authority of the regime is unveiled at every turn, and it surpasses that of most prisons, where the inmates at least have nominal rights and some humanity. Sister Bridget even has the power to change the inmates' names, thus Rose becomes Patricia since they "already have a Rose." The nun also symbolically takes away the power and femininity of an attempted escapee by shaving her head (this rebellious woman is eventually so subdued she decides to join the religious order and become one of the nuns from whom she tried to escape). Two of the other nuns delight in lining up their charges after a shower, making them jog in place in the nude, and comparing their breasts, buttocks, and pubic hair. All the charges wear the same long, drab brown dresses and change modestly into their pajamas by putting them over the uniform first, and then wriggling out of the dress.

The Vatican's quick condemnation of this film as an affront to the Catholic Church is revealing: If the church no longer endorses the brutal repression of women as depicted in this movie, then why would it be threatened? Anyone who was raised Catholic during this era, whether in Ireland or not, will recognize many of the motifs in this movie, though perhaps not in such an extreme form. Of course, the figure of the ruler-wielding, authoritarian nun has been repeatedly lampooned in everything from *The Blues Brothers* to Broadway musicals like *Nunsense*, but there is nothing funny about McEwan's Sister Bridget. There is something familiar about her though—the combination of cool authority, smug superiority, and brutal rage; the way she lampoons those who question her as "simpletons;" and her delight in whipping and beating those who defy her. In essence, she is a petty dictator. Yet McEwan depicts her as very human, not a monster, thus making her all the more frightening and realistic.

There is one scene in the film which is worthy of the best of Orson Welles or Luis Bunuel or the masters of early cinema. When Bernadette is caught trying to escape after a desperate but fairly ingenious scheme in which she tries to bribe a visiting laundry deliverer to take her away by giving him a glimpse up her dress, Sister Bridget and the other nuns fly into a rage, chopping off her hair with a scissors as she struggles against them. Willoughby then mounts an incredible, unforgettable shot: the entire screen is filled with one of Bernadette's eyes, its rims and lashes caked with dried blood, and in the pupil is reflected the image of a cajoling Sister Bridget, leaning into her face to lecture her about her depravity and guilt and the penance she must face. It is absolutely chilling, effective, and unique—an iconic piece of moviemaking.

Much of the plot, as it unfolds, involves a fourth woman, dubbed Crispina (brilliantly played by Eileen Walsh) by the nuns. Crispina, another mother of an illegitimate child who is also a bit simple-minded, gets occasional visits from her sister and her young son, who appear at the gate and wave to her while she hangs out the laundry. Crispina wears a St. Christopher's medal, just like the one given to her son before they parted, and she believes it is her way of communicating with her lost child, like a telephone. She becomes distraught and suicidal when the medal is stolen by Bernadette.

The film is expert in depicting how the residents of this institution internalize their own oppression and turn against one another, while sometimes forming temporary alliances for selfish gain. Why don't they all rebel? Because there is no place for them in society, because many of them have been brainwashed to believe they are sinful and shameful and guilty and need to do penance, and because the fear of the ubiquitous power of the Church is deeply ingrained. So powerful is the Church in this society, in fact, that even the men who benefit from its order are afraid of it. And it is the brief portraits of the men in this film that are most frightening. They are crude, silent, raging, fearful—both powerful and protected yet impotent in the face of the larger authority of the unseen religious rulers.

Mullan's only misstep in this masterful piece of filmmaking may be his use of a piece of visual humiliation in a subplot involving the partial unmasking of an abusive priest. But it is so important to the credibility of the film to establish the hypocrisy at the root of this system that it's also a powerful piece of narrative. He is not guilty so much of exaggeration but of giving in—in only this one instance— to the temptation to "Hollywoodize" the story.

In its entirety, however, *The Magdalene Sisters* is a testament to the triumph of the human spirit, and the final

scenes give some measured, if mixed, hope for light at the end of the tunnel. But viewers may gasp at the close to discover that this is not a story that could only take place long ago and in another time—the last Magdalene convent wasn't closed until 1996, and, in all, 30,000 Irish women were subjected to this brutality and humiliation. While great strides have been made in Ireland to free women—and men—from the power of this system, the struggle is far from finished there, and it is hardly begun in many other places in the world where religious doctrine grinds down human beings and their freedoms.

Mullan has made an important, sobering, and brilliant film that is far more entertaining than it has any right to be. Much of that is due not only to his well-paced and often astounding direction, but also to the fine performances from the entire ensemble. Rose, Bernadette, Margaret, and Crispina depict a variety of female predicaments, temperaments, and responses to oppression, and it is to Mullan's credit that he does not romanticize or glamorize any of them. Instead he merely shows what can happen to the human spirit when it is crushed, and how sometimes it can still flower and survive. *The Magdalene Sisters* does not flinch from showing the damage of intolerance, but neither does it bow down and succumb.

—*Michael Betzold*

CREDITS

Sister Bridget: Geraldine McEwan
Margaret: Anne-Marie Duff
Bernadette: Nora-Jane Noone
Rose/Patricia: Dorothy Duffy
Crispina: Eileen Walsh
Una: Mary Murray
Katy: Britta Smith
Sister Jude: Frances Healy
Sister Clementine: Eithne McGuinness
Father Fitzroy: Daniel Costello

Origin: Great Britain, Ireland
Released: 2002
Production: Frances Higson; Scottish Screen, Irish Film Board, Momentum Pictures, PFP Films, Temple Films; released by Miramax Films
Directed by: Peter Mullan
Written by: Peter Mullan
Cinematography by: Nigel Willoughby
Music by: Craig Armstrong
Sound: Colin Nicholson
Editing: Colin Monie
Art Direction: Jean Kerr, Caroline Grebbell
Costumes: Trisha Biggar

Production Design: Mark Leese
MPAA rating: R
Running time: 119 minutes

REVIEWS

Boxoffice. November, 2002, p. 123.
Chicago Sun-Times Online. August 15, 2003.
Entertainment Weekly. August 8, 2003, p. 51.
New York Times Online. September 28, 2002.
New York Times Online. July 27, 2003.
Premiere. July/August, 2003, p. 23.
Sight and Sound. March, 2003, p. 50.
USA Today Online. August 1, 2003.
Variety Online. August 30, 2002.
Washington Post. August 15, 2003, p. WE34.

QUOTES

Bernadette (Nora-Jane Noone) on the Magdalene asylums: "All the mortal sins in the world wouldn't justify this place."

AWARDS AND NOMINATIONS

Venice Film Fest. 2002: Film
Nomination:
British Acad. 2003: Film, Screenplay
Ind. Spirit 2004: Foreign Film.

Malibu's Most Wanted

Ever feel like you don't belong?
—Movie tagline
Don't be hatin'
—Movie tagline

Box Office: $34.3 million

Malibu's Most Wanted plays like a *Saturday Night Live* skit stretched to the big screen. It has a sharp, accessible, funny character, but one that can live more comfortably in the short space of a skit. In a movie, with the requisite lame and silly plot grafted awkwardly on, it just doesn't pack the same punch. The skit-turned-movie feel probably comes from the fact that *Malibu's Most Wanted* is

from a skit. Jamie Kennedy created the character of Brad Gluckman on his WB show, *JKX: The Jamie Kennedy Experience.* Brad is an upper-class white kid from Malibu who thinks he's black.

Brad calls himself B-Rad and has a dream of becoming a famous rapper and rapping about life in the treacherous hills of the 'Bu, as he calls Malibu. "Everyone's strapped with a nine," he says, meaning a nine iron. He wears a lime green velour jumpsuit with a visor turned sideways and leads a little posse, including Middle Easterner, Hadji (Kal Penn). Poor Hadji never escapes from stereotypes. When the gang tries to gather some weapons, Hadji gets a grenade launcher from Uncle Ahmed. The group complains about the life in their hood (like when "the public be up on your private beach") and terrorize people like the little old lady who works in the scented candle shop to get their parking validated.

Kennedy got the idea for the character from a real person. "I used to see this kid in a West Hollywood coffee shop order vanilla lattes and be like, 'I want some soy milk, bitch. Don't you know I'm lactose intolerant?'" Kennedy said in an interview with *US* magazine. "He always talked about his problems. He drove a Mercedes."

Brad has no idea that he comes across as such a poser. To him, speaking like a gangsta is how he really is. Even when he tries, he's unable to drop the slang. "I'm the shiznit," he says in his best Snoop Dogg style. "I ams who I say I ams." As he was growing up, his parents, politician Bill Gluckman (Ryan O'Neal, looking less puffy than he has of late) and wife (Bo Derek) ignored the boy and he coped by listening to rap music.

The biggest obstacle Brad has to becoming a rapper is that he is horrible. "Livin' in the 'Bu/Life's a beach and then you die/I could tell you stories, make your caterer cry," he raps in all seriousness. His other problem comes from his dad. Bill Gluckman is running for governor and Brad's shenanigans are threatening his campaign. His ruthless campaign manager (Blair Underwood) suggests that they get some African-American guys to scare Brad straight. The manager hires two classically trained actors, PJ (Anthony Anderson in about his 500th movie of the year) and Sean (Taye Diggs) to impersonate gangstas. The two are to take Brad to South Central and "scare the black out of him." The only thing is, PJ and Sean are middle-class guys who know nothing about gangsta ways. One of the more funny ideas in the film is how PJ and Sean approach the gig as a serious acting challenge. The adopt gangsta names, Tre and Bloodbath, and study the slang as though learning Shakespeare. "Dis," reads Sean, quizzically. The two try out angry poses and test out various outfits, then critique each others' performances. "Was I indicating too much?" they ask each other fretfully.

The duo's only hood connection is PJ's cousin Shondra (Regina Hall). At first she's too sensible to go along with their plans of using her house as a base for their plan, but she's lured in by the money. She wanted to open her own beauty salon and the money would go a long way in helping her achieve that goal.

This plot is what takes down the movie. Several ridiculous things happen. The most ridiculous is that Shondra starts falling for Brad, even though he's quite an unlikable character. PJ and Sean try to scare Brad but he overhears them talking and realizes the scam. He decides that since it's all faked, he will take advantage of the situation. So, when Shondra's real gangsta ex-boyfriend, Tec (Damien Dante Wayans), shows up brandishing firearms, Brad takes advantage of the situation. He grabs a pair of big guns, stands on top of a car and starts shooting wildly, believing the guns to be fake. His crazy performance earns him the respect of the guys in the hood, who invite him into their gang.

Things reach their silliest in a scene where Brad's dad ends up crashing through Tec's wall with his oversized luxury vehicle. The movie loses whatever bite it had in the final scenes, where Brad's dad realizes that (sniff) he needs to pay attention to his son and accept him for who he is. And oh yes, Brad's "cool" behavior earns him the respect of the folks in the hood who help vote Mr. Gluckman into office.

No one can complain that Kennedy's impression isn't right on. He's got the moves and slang of a gangsta down cold. The man must have studied hours of videos and rap records to be this on. But being accurate and being interesting or likable isn't the same thing. We get the point that Brad sounds just like a real rapper; it's just not enough to sustain a whole film. Brad doesn't change or grow more likable. All he does is become more tiresome.

Anderson and Diggs are entertaining as the Julliard and Pasadena Playhouse alums trying to get into their roles, but the joke never progresses from there. Diggs especially is charismatic, and it's a shame to see him in such a lame movie. Underwood is nicely crisp as the tightly wound campaign manager and Snoop Dogg shows up as the voice of a mouse who gives Brad some advice. Poor Hall is stuck with an impossible role. How could she find herself drawn to a guy who's such a clueless loser that during a rap contest, he wears his pants so low that he moons the audience?

Most reviewers seemed to take the point of view that the movie was taking on a provocative concept which was ripe with humor, but it ended up failing in the execution. Daphne Gordon of the *Toronto Star* wrote, "The concept makes for a potentially funny parody of Eminem's recent hit about a white kid who makes good in the hood, *8 Mile*, but fails in that . . . it's not funny." Owen Gleiberman of *Entertainment Weekly* wrote, "*Malibu's Most Wanted* is a send-up of rap personality in which no one actually has a personality. The joke, alas, is on the movie." Stephen Holden of the *New York Times* wrote, "Before it chokes on its own formula, the hip-hop comedy *Malibu's Most Wanted* tosses around enough zany notions about race, pop culture

attitudes and stereotypes to prove that it has at least half a brain in its head. That's considerably more gray matter than can be found in most teenage-slanted comedies these days." Charles Taylor of *Salon* wrote, "Watching Jamie Kennedy hoax people on his WB show *The Jamie Kennedy Experiment*, or watching his extended wigga routine in *Malibu's Most Wanted*, you're convinced that sooner or later, every kid you knew in school who ate paste is going to get his own three-picture deal."

—*Jill Hamilton*

CREDITS

Brad "B-Rad" Gluckman: Jamie Kennedy
Sean: Taye Diggs
PJ: Anthony Anderson
Tom Gibbons: Blair Underwood
Shondra: Regina Hall
Bill Gluckman: Ryan O'Neal
Bess Gluckman: Bo Derek
Tec: Damien Dante Wayans
Dr. Feldman: Jeffrey Tambor
Ronnie Rizzat: Snoop Dogg (Voice)

Origin: USA
Released: 2003
Production: Mike Karz, Fax Bahr, Adam Small; released by Warner Bros.
Directed by: John Whitesell
Written by: Jamie Kennedy, Fax Bahr, Adam Small, Nick Swardson
Cinematography by: Mark Irwin
Music by: John Van Tongeren, Damon Elliott
Sound: Geoffrey Patterson
Editing: Cara Silverman
Art Direction: Daniel A. Lomino
Costumes: Debrae Little
Production Design: William A. "Bill" Elliott
MPAA rating: PG-13
Running time: 86 minutes

REVIEWS

Chicago Sun-Times Online. April 18, 2003.
Los Angeles Times Online. April 18, 2003.
New York Times Online. April 18, 2003.
People. April 18, 2003, p. 34.
USA Today Online. April 18, 2003.
Variety Online. April 13, 2003.
Washington Post. April 18, 2003, p. WE40.

Mambo Italiano

It's not a democracy, it's a family.
—Movie tagline
Times change. Family doesn't.
—Movie tagline

 Box Office: $6.2 million

It was difficult to find a review for *Mambo Italiano* that didn't contain a reference to *My Big Fat Greek Wedding.* Some of the comments: "This year's entry in the *My Big Fat Greek Wedding* sweepstakes"; "*Big Fat Greek* wannabe"; and "we can refer to [it] for convenience as *My Big Fat Gay Wedding.*" It's easy to see why filmmakers would want to follow in the footsteps of *My Big Fat Greek Wedding.* That movie went from tiny indie to box office powerhouse and famously made piles of money. This movie uses the same basic formula: youngish travel agent runs into problems with love and ethnic family. But *Mambo Italiano* changed the ethnic group from Greek to Italian and the sexual orientation from straight to gay. Voila! It's like *Big Fat,* but new! The only thing left to do would be to sit back and wait for the money to roll in.

Unfortunately for the filmmakers, it will be a pretty long wait because if humor could be rated scientifically, *Mambo Italiano* would come up several humor units less than *Big Fat.* The film was adapted by French-Canadian director Emile Gaudreault and Steve Galluccio from Galluccio's play, and the two seem to think that more stereotypes equals more humor. They can't seem to get beyond the idea that all Italian parents are yelling, overly dramatic folks who never really left the old country. It's as if their characterizations were formed solely on the basis of watching TV portrayals of Italians. The duo is also fond of the one liner. Sometimes they work, sometimes they don't. For example: A priest asks, "Is your son gravely ill?" The woman in the confessional answers, "No, he's gravely gay!"

The story takes place in the Little Italy section of Montreal, Canada. It's a charming neighborhood where everyone knows everyone else (and everyone else's business.) Angelo Barberini (Luke Kirby) is in his late 20s and still lives with his parents. His mother Maria (Ginette Reno) and father Gino (Paul Sorvino) are straight out of Italian central casting. The mom is large and likes to fret and swat her children when they displease her—even when they're adults. Dad is blustery, likes to yell and wave his fists around. Angelo would like nothing more than to move out of his parents' home, but according to the film, in Italian families, there are only two ways to move out of your parents' home—you get

married or you die. That's not much comfort to Angelo, since he seems pretty healthy and he's not going to be getting married anytime soon, at least not to a woman.

Poor Angelo is gay and terrified of telling his parents. The two are so old-fashioned that it seems entirely plausible that wouldn't even know what gay means. "There is no fate worse than being gay and Italian," Angelo mourns. The only family member who knows is his sister, Anna (Claudia Ferri), who has her own issues with her parents. When Angelo asks for her advice on whether he should break the news to their parents, Anna answers, "This is going to kill them." Pause, wait for beat. "Tell them!" The film is chock-full of such humor. The trouble is, it's not really that funny. It's okay, as in sitcom level okay. Watching it at home for free would be fine. Paying money to see it in a theater is not fine.

Angelo does move out and moves in with Marco Paventi (Peter Miller). Marco, we learn, was Angelo's best friend in childhood. The two did everything together until Marco ditched Angelo for a more popular crowd. Now Marco is a macho, closeted cop. Despite Marco's betrayal, Angelo is delighted to have him back.

Life for Angelo and Marco goes smoothly enough. Angelo spends his days at the travel agency and toils on his own trying to become a TV writer, although he seems to have little talent for it. The big problem comes when Angelo decides he wants to come out of the closet. Marco is happy with his secret life and is against any change. But Angelo eventually prevails if for no other reason than to move the plot along. After all, the main reason for the existence of this movie is so that, at some point, Angelo can tell his parents and we can watch these traditionalists take it poorly.

Of course they do. There is screaming, tears and Angelo is kicked out of the family. Marco is horrified to learn that Angelo's parents have told his equally traditional mother (Mary Walsh). Mrs. Paventi can't accept that her strapping son could possibly be gay—he just hasn't met the right woman. There is more screaming, tears and the like. Marco can't accept being a gay man and forces himself to start dating the requisite Italian woman, Pina Lunetti (Sophie Lorain).

Part of the lack of success with the film is the casting of Angelo. Kirby is not a very interesting actor. He's kind of nerdy but not in a cool way. And certainly a less bland actor could make the one-liners sound a lot snappier. The rest of the acting in the film is difficult to rate since it is pretty over-the-top. If a character is not realistic, is it possible to give a realistic performance? Such questions didn't bother Paul Sorvino. In an interview with the *Minneapolis Star Tribune,* he said that, for his part, he was delighted with his role. "So often, what you get back is not what you intended," he told writer Jeff Strickler. "This is the first time in years I've seen the performance I gave end up on the screen."

Critics weren't especially fond of the film, though most found it tolerable enough. Sean Axmaker of the *Seattle Post-Intelligencer* gave the film a C– and added, "There's likely an interesting kernel of identity crisis buried somewhere in this script but director Emile Gaudreault . . . has chucked it for one liners." *Entertainment Weekly*'s Scott Brown, who gave the film a B, concluded, "This is feel-good filmmaking, to be sure, but the culture clash here is more than a meaningless vehicle for fizzy wish fulfillment. The not-unpleasant result is hearty Italian fare with the half-life of Chinese takeout." Dave Kehr of the *New York Times* summed up, "As Angelo, Mr. Kirby has a boyish charm, which is probably the best that can be said for this film as well."

—*Jill Hamilton*

CREDITS

Angelo Barberini: Luke Kirby
Maria Barberini: Ginette Reno
Gino Barberini: Paul Sorvino
Anna Barberini: Claudia Ferri
Nino Paventi: Peter Miller
Lina Paventi: Mary Walsh
Pina Lunetti: Sophie Lorain
Peter: Tim Post

Origin: Canada
Released: 2003
Production: Denise Robert, Daniel Louis; Cinemaginaire Inc.; released by Samuel Goldwyn Films
Directed by: Emile Gaudreault
Written by: Emile Gaudreault, Steve Galluccio
Cinematography by: Serge Ladouceur
Sound: Claude La Haye
Editing: Richard Comeau
Costumes: Francesca Chamberland
Production Design: Patricia Christie
MPAA rating: R
Running time: 99 minutes

REVIEWS

Chicago Sun-Times Online. October 17, 2003.
Entertainment Weekly. September 26, 2003, p. 75.
Globe and Mail. September 6, 2003, p. R8.
Los Angeles Times Online. September 19, 2003.
New York Times Online. September 19, 2003.
Variety Online. June 6, 2003.

QUOTES

Angelo (Luke Kirby) on living with his Italian immigrant family: "We leave the house only two ways: married or dead."

A Man Apart

Love changes a man. Revenge tears him apart.
—Movie tagline

Box Office: $26.2 million

The pretensions of *A Man Apart* are right there in the title. A . . . Man . . . Apart. Sounds like it's going to be about a guy who has to break out of the system to do what he must do. His task will be hard. And he will have to do most of it alone since he is . . . A Man Apart. And all that, sadly, is pretty much what the film is all about.

Not content to be yet another shoot 'em up action film "A Man Apart" tries to set itself Apart by attempting to also be about a man shooting stuff up for a deep reason. Sean Vetter (Vin Diesel) kills a bunch of people and generally acts like a violent, out-of-control jerk, but he's not doing it because he's a bad guy; he's doing it because he has loved so much. The movie's philosophy basically is: what better way to celebrate love than by going on a vengeful killing spree? The film is full of such interesting philosophies. The characters fighting the drug war blame the fact that America's the number one drug consuming nation, not because it has the most drug users, but because other countries are sending their drugs here. It's painful to say so, but the film should have just stuck with the action and not tried to be something more meaningful.

As the film opens, DEA agent Vetter and his faithful partner, Demetrius Hicks (Larenz Tate), are finally busting a drug kingpin they've been trailing for seven years. As the kingpin, Memo Lucero (Geno Silva), is led away he threatens Vetter ominously, "You have no idea what kind of mistake you're making." Vetter may have no idea, but it becomes pretty clear in the next scenes, which show him and his candle-making wife, Stacy (Jacqueline Obradors), smooching a lot. After a party they have to celebrate the bust, the happy couple dance in the moonlight on the beach in front of their gorgeous house. How a DEA agent can afford a beachfront home while his partner has a run-down bungalow isn't explained. Perhaps Stacy's candle-making business is incredibly lucrative. Anyway, the couple is much too happy, which makes it all the more obvious that Stacy's not going to be around long. With tedious predictability, a masked gunman heads over to the Vetter house, a shoot-out ensues, and Stacy ends up dead.

Vetter broods a lot, but Stacy's death does give him the opportunity to start acting like a one-man army to avenge his wife's death. Because, you see, if he kills a bunch of people, that will help him in his grieving process. Or something like that. Look it up, it should be in Elisabeth Kubler-Ross' *On Death and Dying*. In case Vetter's having any ethical doubts about his behavior, a friend advises him, "To defeat a monster, you must become a monster." In other words, two wrongs (or more) do indeed make a right.

With Lucero in jail, the drug cartel's in an upheaval. A mysterious drug lord named Diablo (the original and arguably preferable title) has been staking a claim by killing a bunch of low-level guys. This allows audience members the delightful reward of seeing such scenes as a bunch of newly dead guys in a crack house with their eyeballs poked out. Periodically, Vetter loses his cool and starts shooting people. After a guy says he killed Stacy, Vetter beats him to death with his fists. (Not to be a nit-picker but does anyone else remember how after September 11, the studios solemnly vowed to stop making violent films?) But Vetter's thirst for vengeance is not slaked. There must be more scenes of killing. After a drug buy setup turns into yet another shoot-out, Vetter's boss decides that maybe the agent could use a little time out to grieve. Tediously, Vetter turns in his badge as many renegade movie cops have done before and decides to fight the drug cartel alone. Yes, another renegade cop. Vetter is the man for the job. After all, when he's chasing someone in a cab, he actually catches up to his prey on foot.

The violence is strangely unengaging. The shoot-outs are plentiful, but director F. Gary Gray (*Set It Off, Friday*) films the scenes in such a way that it's difficult to tell who's shooting who. Barely any of the "good guy" characters are established other than Vetter and Hicks, so when someone gets shot, it's hard to know if it is a DEA agent or drug gangster.

So we are left with the prospect of Diesel trying to expand his acting range. It doesn't work. The scenes that try to establish Vetter as a nice guy don't ring true. Stacy watches as Vetter pals around with Hicks' little girl. "I love to see you with her," coos Stacy, her maternal instinct clicking in. It's just . . . ewww. Vin Diesel is not a good softie. When he goes on his killing spree, it's difficult to be rooting for his maverick ways. Yes, the man has been deeply hurt and yes, he's responding to his hurt with violence, but geez, does he have to be so violent? When his boss kicks him off the force, the boss seems like he's making a wise decision instead of being The Man trying to stifle Vetter's unorthodox ways.

Critics were pretty united in not liking the film. Andrew Johnston of *US* magazine wrote, "The film takes itself way too seriously, and Vetter's tortured angst doesn't really play to Diesel's strengths. For a movie loaded with bloody shoot-outs and fiery moments, *Man* is inexcusably dull." Kenneth Turan of the *Los Angeles Times* wrote, "Now that there's a real war going on, the euphemistic war on drugs that has taken up so much screen time seems more and more meaningless, and movies about it, like the current *A Man Apart*, feel increasingly anachronistic." And Roger Ebert of the *Chicago Sun-Times* wrote, "*A Man Apart* sets chunks of nonsense floating down in a river of action. The elements are all here—the growling macho dialogue, the gunplay, the drugs, the cops, the revenge—but what do they add up to? Some sequences make no sense at all, except as kinetic energy."

—*Jill Hamilton*

CREDITS

Sean Vetter: Vin Diesel
Demetrius Hicks: Larenz Tate
Hollywood Jack: Timothy Olyphant
Memo Lucero: Geno Silva
Stacy Vetter: Jacqueline Obradors
Ty Frost: Steve Eastin
Mateo Santos: Juan Fernandez
Pomona Joe: Jeff Kober
Big Sexy: George Shaperson

Origin: USA
Released: 2003
Production: Tucker Tooley, Vincent Newman, Joseph Nittolo, Vin Diesel; released by New Line Cinema
Directed by: F. Gary Gray
Written by: Christian Gudegast, Paul Scheuring
Cinematography by: Jack N. Green
Music by: Anne Dudley
Sound: Walt Martin
Music Supervisor: Dana Sano
Editing: William Hoy, Robert Brown
Art Direction: Tom Reta
Costumes: Shawn Barton
Production Design: Ida Random
MPAA rating: R
Running time: 114 minutes

REVIEWS

Chicago Sun-Times Online. April 4, 2003.
Entertainment Weekly. April 11, 2003, p. 57.
Los Angeles Times Online. April 4, 2003.
New York Times Online. April 4, 2003.
People. April 14, 2003, p. 38.
Variety Online. March 31, 2003.
Washington Post. April 4, 2003, p. WE45.

The Man on the Train (L'Homme du Train)

A poet. A thief. Two strangers with nothing in common are about to trade their lives for a chance to cheat their destinies.
—Movie tagline

 Box Office: $2.5 million

The very productive French director Patrice Leconte is known for turning out almost a film a year, each of them dealing with different periods, genres, and subjects. Leconte, in fact, is often criticized in France for failing to have a personal style. *The Man on the Train* finds Leconte working on a smaller scale than usual. He and screenwriter Claude Klotz have created a gentle, subtle, compassionate film—with a dollop of violence—about aging and the path not chosen.

Even though the film is set in present-day France, it is, in many ways, a tribute to the spaghetti Westerns of the 1960s and 1970s. It opens with Milan (Johnny Hallyday), whose name suggests an Italian connection, arriving in a sleepy provincial town on the train, much as Charles Bronson does at the beginning of Sergio Leone's *Once Upon a Time in the West* (1968), by far the greatest of the Italian Westerns. Hallyday even bears a strong resemblance to Bronson.

Suffering from a headache, Milan wanders into a pharmacy for a cure and meets Manesquier (Jean Rochefort), a retired teacher. Because the village's only hotel is closed for the winter, Manesquier offers to let Milan stay at his small, decaying chateau. Milan's response upon entering the house helps establish the film's theme. The schoolmaster apologizes for the clutter accumulated by his mother. Even though she has been dead fifteen years, Manesquier has not changed anything because he is too passive, too accepting of the status quo. The house's furnishings and knickknacks seem from another era but are charming to Milan because the house looks so lived in, so permanent—unlike his peripatetic existence.

The protagonists envy each other, much to the surprise of each, neither of whom see anything enviable about their lives. Manesquier feels he has wasted his life by remaining in his native village, by teaching rather than doing something more adventuresome, and by not marrying. He is attracted to the roughhewn Milan, whom he sees as his exact opposite—a man who takes chances. While Milan is out, Manesquier puts on his guest's slightly ridiculous fringed leather jacket and poses in front of a mirror, spouting clichés, in English, from American Westerns.

Manesquier romanticizes that Milan is in town to rob the local bank and turns out to be right. The fiftyish Milan has grown weary of the criminal life, however, and longs for the kind of peace and quiet the teacher disdains. Just as Manesquier dresses in Milan's jacket, the visitor tries his host's pipe and slippers.

While an American film dealing with the same subject would have the characters literally switch roles, Leconte and Klotz try for a softer effect. A creature of habit, Manesquier has had lunch in the same café for years. Milan joins him, and when they are disturbed by the rowdy behavior of two young men, the criminal encourages the schoolmaster to confront them. Manesquier does, and is surprised to be greeted with an enthusiastic poetry recitation from a former student. Though Manesquier is retired, he still tutors an occasional pupil. When a student arrives while he is out, Milan tries his hand at explaining a Balzac work he has not read. In both instances, the men realize the absurdity of their trying to change.

The final minutes of *The Man on the Train* cut back and forth between the two friends as Milan joins his gang to rob the bank and Manesquier goes to a hospital for bypass surgery. While Leconte's style has been conservative to this point, he tries some trickery with his ending that will seem fitting to some and confusing to others. It is obvious from early on that the fates of the two men will be intertwined, but Leconte and Klotz make this come about in a somewhat surprising but appropriately poetic way.

The Man on the Train is Leconte's twenty-second feature film. His best known earlier films are the psychological thriller *Monsieur Hire* (1989), the romantic comedy *The Hairdresser's Husband* (1990), the costume comedy of manners *Ridicule* (1996), the fantasy *The Girl on the Bridge* (1999), and the period melodrama *The Widow of Saint-Pierre* (2000). Because of his work in several genres and his lack of a distinctive style, Leconte is often called a throwback to the Hollywood studio directors of the 1930s and 1940s, a comparison the director takes as a compliment.

French critics have given little support to Leconte's work. The animosity between the filmmaker and the press reached its apex following attacks on *The Girl on the Bridge* when Leconte wrote a private letter to the Society of Auteurs, Directors, and Producers, railing against the "sadism, arrogance, and treachery" of critics. A group of filmmakers took up Leconte's cause, demanding that films not be reviewed until the week after their release so that audiences could encounter them unencumbered by preconceptions. The controversy, which raged for several weeks, did not bring about this change, though *The Widow of Saint-Pierre* was treated less harshly than is usual for

Leconte. Ironically, the director's wife is on the staff of *Cahiers du Cinema*, the best-known French film journal.

Some interpreted the casting of pop-star Hallyday as a thumbing of his nose by Leconte at his critics, but the singer-actor initiated *The Man on the Train* by telling the director he wanted to work with him. Leconte approached Klotz, who had written *The Hairdresser's Husband*, with an idea about two aging men of different backgrounds, and Klotz wrote the script in three weeks.

The Man on the Train is a small, subtle, fragile film that cannot withstand too high expectations. Like Manesquier's life, the film is a collection of quiet moments. Anthony Lane of the *New Yorker* said that it thrives on lowlights. The best bits include Manesquier's discovery of a photograph of the young Milan apparently in the American West and Milan's subsequent confession that the photo was staged. The host gets his hair cut to look more like Milan, only for the criminal to remove his beard to be more like the mustachioed Manesquier. Then there is Sadko (Pascal Parmentier), a member of Milan's gang who utters only one enigmatic sentence, like clockwork, every twenty-four hours. The only false step is an unnecessarily awkward meeting between Milan and Manesquier's off-and-on girlfriend (Isabelle Petit-Jacques).

When Leconte was a struggling young director of short films and Rochefort the star of films directed by the likes of Luis Bunuel and Bertrand Tavernier, the actor agreed to star in Leconte's first feature, *Les Veces etaient fermes de l'interieur* (1975), and the two have worked together several times since, most notably on *The Hairdresser's Husband*. Rochefort's deft style is perfect for Manesquier. Rochefort conveys the character through brief gestures, especially the twinkle that enters his eye over Milan's company.

Hallyday is often called the French Elvis. He has been a pop singer since he was fifteen and became his country's first rock star with his version of Chubby Checker's "Let's Twist Again" in 1961. Despite selling over 100 million records in France, Hallyday's popularity has never carried over to the English-speaking world, and the British, in particular, have always sneered at his efforts. In Neil Jordan's *The Good Thief* (2003), Nick Nolte's character refers to Hallyday's "Black Is Black" as proof that the French do not get rock and roll.

Ironically, Hallyday, born Jean-Philippe Smet, was an actor before he was a singer, appearing as a schoolboy in Henri-Georges Clouzot's classic thriller *Les Diaboliques* (1955). He began singing only to pay for his acting lessons. Hallyday's films, like Elvis Presley's, were mostly lightweight musicals until Jean-Luc Godard cast him in *Detective* (1985). The surprising depth of his Milan has been the highlight of his spotty career, winning him the Prix Jean Gabin.

In the great tradition of Charles Bronson and Clint Eastwood, Hallyday has little to say in *The Man on the Train*. The strength of the performance comes from the actor's ability to reveal layers of melancholy and loneliness through the force of his powerful visage, almost as ravaged as Keith Richards's is.

Although the character is called Milan in the film's credits, no name is actually attached to the stranger, making him like Eastwood's Man with No Name in Leone's Westerns. Manesquier plays the piano, and when he asks Milan if he is musical, the tough guy replies that he once had a harmonica. Not only is this a joking nod to Hallyday's other career but a reference to Bronson, whose loner plays a forlorn tune on his harmonica before shooting the bad guys in *Once Upon a Time in the West*. Pascal Esteve also provides Milan with signature guitar twangs reminiscent of Ennio Morricone's distinctive scores for Leone.

Despite his rugged looks and criminal past, Milan proves to be as delicate in feelings as his host seems to be. Manesquier, on the other hand, proves to be tougher than he initially appears. A lovely contemplation on an unusual friendship, *The Man on the Train* is not as great a film about aging as Vittorio de Sica's *Umberto D* (1952), Akira Kurosawa's *Ikiru* (1952), or Ingmar Bergman's *Wild Strawberries* (1957), but it is an eloquent, surprisingly unsentimental treatment of the subject.

—*Michael Adams*

CREDITS

Manesquier: Jean Rochefort
Milan: Johnny Hallyday
Luigi: Jean-Francois Stevenin
Max: Charlie Nelson
Viviane: Isabelle Petit-Jacques
Manesquier's sister: Edith Scob
Sadko: Pascal Parmentier

Origin: France
Language: French
Released: 2002
Production: Philippe Carcassonne; Cine B, Rhone Alps Cinema, Pandora Film, Zoulou Films, Tubedale Films; released by Paramount Classics
Directed by: Patrice Leconte
Written by: Claude Klotz
Cinematography by: Jean-Marie Drejou
Music by: Pascal Esteve
Sound: Paul Laine
Editing: Joelle Hache
Costumes: Anne Perier
Production Design: Ivan Maussion
MPAA rating: R
Running time: 90 minutes

REVIEWS

Entertainment Weekly. May 16, 2003, p. 54.
Los Angeles Times Online. May 9, 2003.
New Republic. May 19, 2003, p. 26.
New York Times. May 9, 20033, p. E15.
Sight and Sound. April, 2003, p. 39.
Time. May 12, 2003, p. 78.
Variety Online. September 3, 2002.
Washington Post. May 16, 2003, p. WE49.

QUOTES

Manesquier (Jean Rochefort): "I always wanted to be a silent brooder."

AWARDS AND NOMINATIONS

L.A. Film Critics 2003: Foreign Film.

Manic

You can't escape yourself.
—Movie tagline

i am human
—Movie tagline

Mental institution dramas are a staple of Hollywood. Maybe it's for the gawking factor—it's oddly interesting to watch the quirks of others. Or maybe it's because they provide such an excellent forum for actors. In films like *One Flew Over the Cuckoo's Nest* or *Girl, Interrupted* actors like Jack Nicholson and Angelina Jolie got some of their first acclaim by playing over-the-top characters. In these films, the characters rage against the bad, and it's easy to tell what the bad is—the structured, soul-deadening world of the institution.

In *Manic,* it's not so clear cut. The patients of the private California mental institution of the film can and do rage against their circumstances, but it's not certain that that's such a great idea. After all, the institution might be their only hope for ever being able to reenter the *regular* world. And the lead character, Lyle Jensen (Joseph Gordon-Levitt from the TV sitcom *3rd Rock from the Sun*), is full of rage and passion but his anger is much more subtle than Nicholson's wacky acting up.

Rage is the reason that Lyle arrives at the institution. His mother has him committed after he nearly beats a peer

to death with a baseball bat. Lyle's estranged father also had an anger management problem and this is not the first time that Lyle has had a violent outburst. Though Lyle resented his father's violence and the fact that it was often directed against him, he thinks that he doesn't have a problem. In his mind, the people that he beats up have all "deserved" it.

He thinks he is nothing like all the weird people he's forced to live with. His roommate, Kenny (Cody Lightning), is a young man who was abused by his parents. Sara (Sara Rivas) is a pierced goth who wasn't accepted by her peers at home. Chad (Michael Bacall, who co-wrote the film with Blayne Weaver) is a rich trust fund kid who suffers from bipolar disorder. Chad has little interest in taking his medicine. "I'd rather feel like God half the time and $%$# half the time, then just feel ok all the time. %$%$ mediocrity," he explains. Tracy (Zooey Deschanel) is a girl with extremely low self esteem who wakes up screaming from nightmares. Lyle's main nemesis is Michael (Elden Henson), a beefed-up white guy who seems to think he is a cool black homie. Michael enjoys fighting and makes it his mission to provoke Lyle.

Gordon-Levitt could have played his character as a Michael—a dumb lunkhead who tries to pick fights with everyone. But the best part about this film is that Gordon-Levitt takes an opposite tack. His handsome Lyle is closed off and seemingly calm. He sits back and watches the action and appears to a quiet, thoughtful kid. When he bursts into violence, like when he beats Michael senseless in a bathroom, it's as disturbing for him as it is for the audience. For Lyle, violence is a release and an uncontrollable behavior. His outbursts are like a bender for an alcoholic.

Gordon-Levitt has grown up a lot since *3rd Rock* and he's picked a role that's far away from his character on that show. Most reviewers, regardless of how they felt about the film, signaled out Gordon-Levitt's acting for praise. Philip Wuntch of the *Dallas Morning News* wrote that he "does a splendid job as Lyle, the closest thing this movie has to a protagonist. Mr. Gordon-Levitt's kind, at times serene, face heightens the shock of Lyle's violent tendencies, and he locates the often conflicting layers of Lyle's personality." Manohla Dargis of the *Los Angeles Times* wrote, "It's a measure of just how persuasively he inhabits the character that it may take you awhile to recognize the youngest cast member of *3rd Rock from the Sun.* The performance and Lyle, a hard character to cozy up to, couldn't be further from the charms of that sitcom, which is precisely why the actor and (director Jordan) Melamed are two to keep an eye on."

Also excellent is Don Cheadle as David, the counselor for the kids. David, who has had a substance abuse problem in the past, wonders daily whether he's helping the kids. He's good at talking to them and making them feel safe, but they don't get fabulous insights that suddenly make them understand their problems. In a Hollywood movie, that's what we'd expect, and it seems like that's what David's hoping for too. But *Manic* is more like real life. The kids seem to be improving then might start a riot or regress into cutting themselves. A lot of bad things happen on David's watch. They aren't really his responsibility, but still.

The epiphanies in *Manic* are small and ephemeral. A kid thinks they might try treatment a little longer, another finds a friend. But a lot of the kids' problems don't seem to be solvable. David can be as understanding and insightful as possible, and it's not going to help some of these patients. In fact, many of them are just going to get worse. This is not uplifting stuff and *Manic* can be a depressing movie. The movie's theory is that life is bad and that you just have to keep plugging along. It's not exactly fodder for an enjoyable matinee.

Director Melamed is good at getting strong performances out of his actors. The former commodities trader lets the actors act, but doesn't let them overact. The patients seem like real kids, even though their characters don't stretch much beyond their individual mental quirks. Melamed is also the downfall of *Manic*. He shot the film on digital video and is overly fond of shaky, jittery camera work. Perhaps he is going for a tense, you-are-there feel, but his nervous camera is distracting and annoying.

Manic first premiered at Sundance in 2001, but didn't make it to theaters until a year and a half later. The general consensus among critics seemed to be: performances good, direction bad. Lisa Schwarzbaum of *Entertainment Weekly* was one of the critics who found fault with Melamed's camera work. She wrote, "There's something already exhausted, however, in the intrusively gauzy, wobbly, blurry, zoomy digital video look of the piece. I'm guessing the art photography is meant to signify a fragile state; instead, it suggests an attention disorder to which camcorder-wielding filmmakers are dismayingly susceptible." Dave Kehr of the *New York Times* wrote, "The camera work is so self-conscious and so intrusive that it consistently overrides our interest in the characters and their individual dramas. The film finally seems to be about an invisible, camcorder-wielding presence that has come to haunt a mental institution, as if there were an extra character in every scene that none of the other performers can see." And Lou Lumineck of the *New York Post* wrote, "Excellent performances redeem Jordan Melamed's gritty teenage version of *One Flew Over the Cuckoo's Nest*."

—*Jill Hamilton*

CREDITS

Lyle: Joseph Gordon-Levitt
Dr. David Monroe: Don Cheadle
Tracy: Zooey Deschanel
Kenney: Cody Lightning
Sara: Sara Rivas
Chad: Michael Bacall
Diego: William Richert
Mike: Elden (Ratliff) Henson
Charlie: Blayne Weaver

Origin: USA
Released: 2001
Production: Kirk Hassig, Trudi Callon; released by IFC Films
Directed by: Jordan Melamed
Written by: Michael Bacall, Blayne Weaver
Cinematography by: Nick Hay
Music Supervisor: Dierdre O'Hara
Editing: Madeleine Gavin, Gloria Rosa Vela
Art Direction: David Broer
Costumes: Dahlia Foroutan
Production Design: Carol Strober
MPAA rating: R
Running time: 100 minutes

REVIEWS

Entertainment Weekly. May 16, 2003, p. 53.
Los Angeles Times Online. May 9, 2003.
New York Times Online. April 25, 2003.
Variety. February 19, 2001, p. 44.
Village Voice Online. April 23, 2003.

Manito

M*anito* is a small film with big themes—tragedy, family betrayal, new love, poverty and chances for redemption. The film has followed the typical indie path. It screened at several festivals and racked up many awards, including a special grand jury prize at the Sundance Film Festival. It got an extra publicity push when its star, Franky G., garnered good attention for his roles in *Confidence* and *The Italian Job. Manito* was actually his first film; it just took a little longer to make it into theaters.

Manito was in fact a first time project for many of the people involved. It's the debut of director and writer Eric Eason. And many of the actors in the film were nonprofessionals. One, Jessica Morales, is a medical assistant by day. Sometimes in small films like these, the lack of professional skill is bad for the film. There can be awkward acting, unpolished camera work or just overwrought plotting. In this case, though, the inexperience lends a freshness to the proceedings. Instead of seeming like aspiring film actors practicing their craft, the actors seem like real people having a real life. The naturalistic style of Eason and cinematographer Didier Gertsch's camera work makes the film almost look like a documentary and lends a sense of realism to it all. (The film was shot on digital video and transferred to film.) Sometimes the lighting is bad and the film looks like an amateur home movie, but that's part of its charm. Maybe a scene showing a graduation party should look like a home movie. It just serves to drive home the point that we are watching something that really happened.

For all the casual acting and natural camera work, the plot is actually quite intense. It's just hard to realize that until it's all over. The film begins with peeks into each of the characters' lives. Manual Moreno (Leo Minaya), the Manito of the title, is hanging out with a bunch of buddies, preparing for graduation. Many of the kids in this Washington Heights neighborhood don't have plans beyond high school, and Eason captures this odd, nerve-wracking time accurately. Manito is different from his friends. He's the salutatorian of his class and has a full scholarship to college. He's a nice, quiet guy and simply by going to college, he's become the hope of his family.

His older brother, Junior (Franky G.), who is serving as a father figure to Manito, is hoping that the boy's success will herald a new direction for the family. Junior himself is an ex-con and is trying to go straight with his painting business. At first it seems clear what kind of guy Junior is. He's a violent guy who cheats often on his wife and is not above going into a rage over a missing bottle of whiteout. But Junior's jail time had less to do with him than his father, Oscar (Manuel Jesus Cabral). Oscar was a crack dealer and let Junior take the fall for him. During Junior's long prison term, Oscar never once visited him.

At first Junior's animosity toward his father seems inexplicable. Oscar sends over a giant-sized sub sandwich to the big party that Junior is throwing for Manito. When Junior discovers the sandwich, he flies into a rage. Only after we understand the dynamics of their relationship do we understand why Junior would be so unwilling to accept his father's gesture.

In this film, Franky G. shows that he has the acting ability to back up the charisma he showed in his other films. He manages to make his character both hateful and sympathetic. A. O. Scott of the *New York Times* observed, "His acting may be rough and unmodulated at times, but he shows the complexity of Junior's temperament with a furious economy. Junior's flaws are entangled with his virtues: he is both a family man and a compulsive philanderer, at once dishonest and dependable. His angry masculine bravado seems edged with panic, just as his brutal impatience is a reflection of his tenderness."

Most of the charm of *Manito* doesn't come from the big dramatic moments of the plot, however, but rather from the offhand stuff that comes between them. *Manito* is a nice

peek into a culture. Eason seems to realize that a lot of people will be seeing the film as somewhat of a travelogue and he lets his camera linger on street scenes and everyday life. We see the small shops on the street, the vendors hawking their wares and the food offered up. The characters, mostly Dominican, speak to each other in a mixture of English and Spanish (subtitles are added as necessary).

Eason takes his time taking the film where he wants it to go. The graduation party scene is quite long, giving it more of a you-are-there feel. We see many of Manito's friends and family members take the microphone to sing the boy's praises. Instead of being tedious or overindulgent, this helps show Manito's place in the family and the neighborhood. It's actually quite sweet. One of Manito's teachers presents him with an envelope of money that the other teachers have collected for him. Some people give good speeches, some give bad ones, just like a real party.

There's not a weak spot in this ensemble cast. It's hard to say if Eason is just gifted at garnering strong performances from his actors or if the casting director was just remarkably skilled at discovering unknown talent. Each of these actors plays their part in a way that makes the ensemble seem like a real family. Manito's old world grandfather, Abuelo (Hector Gonzalez) is a dapper gentleman who sells lingerie to brothels. Miriam (Julissa Lopez) is Junior's wife. She's quite aware of his philandering and hates it, but knows that she is going to be there for him. Marisol (Jessica Morales) is the tough street kid who Manito shyly asks to his graduation party. Their first-date awkwardness is sweet and right on. Several reviewers noted newcomer Morales's striking acting skill.

Critics rightly liked the film. Kevin Thomas of the *Los Angeles Times* praised Eason and Gertsch's work: "Their grasp of the expressive power of movie-making is at the heart of the success of this raw, edgy film. Eason also elicits an array of riveting portrayals from actors who in some instances are inexperienced but not awkward or self-conscious, so often the curse of such low-budget productions." Scott of the *New York Times* observed that the film was "made with very little money, a fair amount of skill and a great deal of heart" and added that the film "has the lilt and momentum—the swing—of a musical performance." And John Anderson of *Newsday* summed up, "Eason has made a film about family tragedy that sings along on an electrical pulse of energetic editing, convincing naturalism, and a confident sense of turf." 🎬

—*Jill Hamilton*

CREDITS

Junior Moreno: Franky G
Manuel Moreno: Leo Minaya

Oscar Moreno: Manuel Cabral
Abuelo: Hector Gonzalez
Miriam: Julissa Lopez
Marisol: Jessica Morales

Origin: USA
Released: 2003
Production: Allen Bain, Jesse Scolaro; 7th Floor,
Smashing Entertainment; released by Film Movement
Series
Directed by: Eric Eason
Written by: Eric Eason
Cinematography by: Didier Gertsch
Music by: Saundi Wilson
Sound: Lanre Olibisi
Editing: Kyle Henry
Art Direction: Melissa Imossi
Production Design: Christine Darch
MPAA rating: Unrated
Running time: 77 minutes

 REVIEWS

Chicago Sun-Times Online. June 13, 2003.
Los Angeles Times Online. June 13, 2003.
New York Times Online. June 13, 2003.
Variety. January 21, 2002, p. 34.

Marci X

Hip-Hop meets shop til you drop.
—Movie tagline
Uptown gets down.
—Movie tagline

 Box Office: $1.7 million

There are so many things wrong with *Marci X* that it's
difficult to know just where to begin. Distaste for the
film was nearly universal. Audiences ignored it and critics watched it only because they were paid to do so. At
RottenTomatoes.com, a website that compiles critical reviews,
Marci X scored a mere 8% of positive reviews. Critics rarely
agree on anything, but they were united by their dislike of
Marci X. The studio that released the film, Paramount
Pictures, obviously knew what kind of film they had on their
hands; they did not pre-screen the film for reviewers. They

must have known that no manner of creative cutting and
pasting could make the brutal reviews ("*Marci X* gives *Gigli* a
run for its money as the summer's worst movie," observed
the *New York Post*'s Lou Lumenick) sound positive enough
for use in print ads.

That the film is so bad is kind of a surprise because there
were some talented folks involved with it. There was director
Richard Benjamin (*My Favorite Year*), screenwriter Paul
Rudnick, (*In and Out*), producer Scott Rudin (*The Hours*)
and songwriter Marc Shaiman (*Hairspray*). There's also
some strong comedic talent from Lisa Kudrow (*Friends*),
Daman Wayans, and Christine Baranski.

Kudrow is a fine actress, but perhaps she was miscast
here. Actually, it seems likely that the whole character was
just misconceived. Marci Feld (Kudrow) is a rich Manhattan
socialite and the daughter of businessman, Ben Feld (director Benjamin). She lives in her protected world and spends
her time shopping and raising money for odd charities. One,
for example, is for kids who have no feeling in their arms.
This is supposed to be funny. Marci is supposedly in her 30s
(but Kudrow looks somewhat older) but acts more like a
teenager than a woman. Relentlessly perky and dressed in
pink suit sets, Marci seems like a character developed by
someone whose entire knowledge of women was based on
Clueless and *Legally Blonde*.

Marci's safe world is rocked when an uptight, ultra-
right wing senator, Mary Ellen Spinkle (a tight-faced
Baranski), launches an attack on the latest CD by rap artist
Dr. S (Wayans). She takes exception to songs like "The
Power's in My Pants" and "Shoot the Teacher." Senator
Spinkle calls for a boycott of all products from Ben Feld
companies since one of his holdings is Felony Assault Records, Dr. S's label. Feld's stock immediately takes a plunge
and this is so upsetting to Ben Feld that he immediately
suffers a heart attack.

With her dad out of commission, Marci decides that
she will fix everything and make it all right again. Astute
(and still awake) viewers will note that Mr. Feld could
simply drop Dr. S from his label and be done with it, but
that would leave no more room for the movie to try to wring
yuks from its audience. So, Marci goes to a Dr. S concert and
asks him to apologize for his lyrics. Dr. S, naturally, is
insulted and brings Marci onstage to show how "real" she is
and perform a spontaneous rap for the audience. After a few
false starts, Marci comes up with "The Power in My Purse."
It turns into a big production number and involves her
naming off various designers in lyrics like, "I'm white, I'm
blonde, I'm Jewish/Can it get any worse?/But I've got the
power in my purse." The black audience, who seems to have
all simultaneously lost any ability to judge talent, cheer
Marci and her lame rap on.

Dr. S inexplicably does some of the things that Marci
asks of him, including public service announcements, but the
Senator continues her attack on the rapper and Feld. This

forces Marci and the Doctor to spend some time together battling evil. Naturally they start to fall for each other. Unfortunately, the pair doesn't seem to have much in the way of chemistry. Kudrow and Wayans simply do not make a believable couple and since their pairing is the big focus of the movie, this is a problem.

Marci X is a disaster on every level. The characters are given little or no personality, the story is ridiculous, and the romance is tepid at best. To top that off, Rudnick adds plenty of jokes that just aren't funny. Most of these involve white people trying to act black. Some society ladies, for example, say of Dr. S, "We're his bitches." There are also some jokes about the guys in boy bands being gay. Again, not the freshest of material. The moralistic Senator Spinkle privately listens to a Dr. S CD and is so captured by the beat that soon she's gyrating around her study like an exotic dancer. An uptight moralist covering up repressed sexuality might have been a good twist had Dana Carvey's Church Lady not done the same thing over a decade ago.

As stated, the critics were not kind. "To watch it is to feel sorry for the actors," wrote Mick LaSalle of the *San Francisco Chronicle*. Stephen Holden of the *New York Times* wrote, "This is the kind of comedy in which the characters are construction-paper cutouts whose abrupt changes of heart are dictated entirely by the preposterous plot and not by psychological or social reality." Liz Braun of the *Toronto Sun* was the rare voice who spoke in favor of the movie. "If 'Written by Paul Rudnick' means anything to you, you won't want to miss *Marci X,* a deeply subversive comedy that makes fun of almost everybody."

—*Jill Hamilton*

CREDITS

Marci Feld: Lisa Kudrow
Dr. S: Damon Wayans
Ben Feld: Richard Benjamin
Sen. Mary Ellen Spinkle: Christine Baranski
Yolanda Quinones: Paula Garces
Lauren: Jane Krakowski
Caitlin: Veanne Cox

Origin: USA
Released: 2003
Production: Scott Rudin; released by Paramount Pictures
Directed by: Richard Benjamin
Written by: Paul Rudnick
Cinematography by: Robbie Greenberg
Music by: Mervyn Warren
Sound: Danny Michael
Editing: Jacqueline Cambas
Art Direction: Nicholas Lundy

Costumes: David C. Robinson
Production Design: Therese DePrez
MPAA rating: R
Running time: 97 minutes

REVIEWS

Entertainment Weekly. September 15, 2003, p. 57.
Los Angeles Times Online. August 25, 2003.
New York Times Online. August 23, 2003.
People. September 8, 2003, p. 40.
Variety Online. August 22, 2003.

Marooned in Iraq (The Songs of My Homeland) (Avazhaye Sarzamine Madariyam)

Marooned in Iraq garnered terrific critical notices in 2003, but this overrated indie, filmed in Iran, contributes little to one's understanding about the war-torn region of the world. The film was released in the U.S. by Wellspring in the midst of the 2003 U.S. war against Iraq, but the story here takes place after the Iran-Iraq war and around the time of the first U.S. war against Iraq (circa 1989–91). Did Wellspring or the writer-director Bahman Ghobadi want to reveal information that would help viewers understand these wars, or was the timing of *Marooned*'s release a gambit to commercially capitalize on world events? We'll never know, but Iraq wasn't even mentioned in the film's original 2002 title (i.e. *Songs Of My Motherland*). In any case, *Marooned in Iraq* wouldn't be the first film to exploit a tragedy.

In Bhobadi's story, Mirza (Shahab Ebrahimi), an elderly Kurdish musician finds himself in an Iranian refugee camp after Saddam Hussein's bombings force the Iraqi Kurds to flee their homes. Mirza enlists the aid of his two grown sons, Barat (Faegh Mohammadi) and Audeh (Allah-Morad Rashtian), also musicians, to help him find his former wife, Hanareh, after he receives word she is singing for the refugees on the Iran-Iraq border and needs his help.

Barat and Audeh are reluctant to search for Hanareh because they are busy with their work and have multiple wives and children to support, but Mirza convinces them to help by telling them he was never really divorced from Hanareh, thus removing a mark against the family name.

The father and sons embark on a journey that takes them to towns and villages along the Iran-Iraq border. They meet up with a variety of characters, most of whom are not very helpful in finding Hanareh: a thug who forces a woman to marry him and the men who sing at the wedding party; a singer who wants to join the brothers on the road, but is forbidden because of her gender; a matchmaker who double-crosses the brothers; a teacher who wants the brothers to adopt some orphans; and, again, the lady singer, who finally leads Mirza to Hanareh, and the very sad reason she called for him to come.

On several levels, *Marooned in Iraq* fails to live up to the hype surrounding the film at the time of its release. Most disturbingly, Bahman Ghobadi stays completely clear of criticizing or even weighing U.S. policy against Iraq. The humanistic focus on the story's characters makes the first Persian Gulf War merely a colorful backdrop (not unlike the way *Cold Mountain* turns the Civil War into a romantic setting for two star-crossed lovers).

Almost as unfortunate is the way Ghobadi portrays these characters. The Kurds deserve to have their story told, and perhaps we should be grateful for *any* kind of portrait on screen, but the writer-director turns most of his characters into buffoons or objects of pity. In a way Ghobadi takes the worst excesses of Emir Kustirica (who applied a Marx Brothers approach to the Balkan war in *Underground* [1995]), and tries, at the same time, to make the Kurds "his special project." As he demonstrated in his first feature, *A Time for Drunken Horses* (2000), about child smuggling, Ghobadi demonstrates he is a humanist manque (remember the sappier original title of the film, *Songs Of My Motherland*).

Of course, critics went wild over *Marooned in Iraq* for the simple reason that it would be politically incorrect to dislike an Iranian or Iraqi movie by a native filmmaker that centers on the plight of the Kurds. Some reviewers even attempted to read into the film an anti-American attitude, as a way to substantiate their kudos. Others loved the film while acknowledging the way it implicitly supported the gung-ho efforts of both Bush administrations to go to war. Bob Strauss of the *Lost Angeles Daily News* wrote: "Filmed in Iran, *Marooned* devastatingly presents the case for Saddam's ouster, regardless of how much a threat he may or may not have been to anyone beyond his borders." *Newsday*'s John Anderson also admitted: "Some may tend to think the timing of Bahman Ghobadi's film (his feature follow-up to

the powerful *A Time for Drunken Horses*) was an out-and-out endorsement of recent U.S. foreign policy, and it well may be taken that way."

Meanwhile, Jonathan Curiel in the *San Francisco Chronicle* defended the attempt at laughs: "Bahman Ghobadi infuses his movie with a humor that can almost be called Seinfeldian, and it's this mix of laughter with tears that gives *Marooned in Iraq* its big impact."

Technically, *Marooned in Iraq* appears proficiently made, with smooth, even elegant cinematography by Sa'ed Nikzat and Shahriar Asadi and Ghobadi's vivid art direction, but there are also drawbacks, particularly an irritating overuse of Arsalan Komkar's musical score. Just as the critics fell in rapture to *Marooned in Iraq,* so did the film festivals. But all the awards (from the Cannes Film Festival, the Chicago International Film Festival, the Human Rights Film Festival, among others) don't make *Marooned* a better or more important film than it is. If anything, they reveal the hollowness.

—*Eric Monder*

CREDITS

Mirza: Shahab Ebrahimi
Barat: Fa-eq Mohammadi
Audeh: Alahmorad Rashtiani
Hanareh: Iran Ghobadi

Released: 2002
Production: Bahman Ghobadi; released by Wellspring Media
Directed by: Bahman Ghobadi
Written by: Bahman Ghobadi
Cinematography by: Saed Nikzat, Shahriar Asadi
Music by: Arsalan Komkar
Editing: Hayedeh Safi-Yari
Art Direction: Bahman Ghobadi
MPAA rating: Unrated
Running time: 97 minutes

REVIEWS

Los Angeles Times Online. May 23, 2003.
New York Times Online. April 25, 2003.
San Francisco Chronicle. June 6, 2003, p. D5.
Variety Online. May 23, 2002.

Masked and Anonymous

Would you reach out your hand to save a drowning man if you thought he might pull you in?
—Movie tagline

The title of *Masked and Anonymous* is a lot like the movie. At first, it seems interesting and memorable, but when it comes down to it, it's not. The film certainly has a lot of promise. For one, it's the first film from Bob Dylan since 1987's *Hearts of Fire.* (He also appeared in and directed 1978's *Renaldo and Clara.*) Dylan may be unpredictable and, at times, unintelligible, but the man is not boring.

Masked and Anonymous marks the feature debut of director Larry Charles, who is generally considered to be something of a sitcom master, having worked on *Seinfeld* and *Mad About You,* among others. Charles has lined up one heck of a cast for this film; besides Dylan, there's Jeff Bridges, Penelope Cruz, John Goodman, Jessica Lange, and Luke Wilson. And those are just the major roles. There are scores of cameos by folks like Cheech Marin, Angela Bassett, Bruce Dern, Val Kilmer, Christian Slater, Chris Penn, Giovanni Ribisi, Ed Harris, and an unrecognizable Mickey Rourke.

Maybe it's a too-many-cooks-spoil-the-broth thing, but what all these talented folks end up with is a mess. Rene Fontaine and Sergei Petrov supposedly wrote the movie, but it was actually penned by Dylan and Charles. Maybe that's the problem right there—sitcom guy and enigmatic rock legend aren't exactly the most natural combination. And what they come up with has neither the Dylan mystique or the Charles personality and humor. It's like they canceled out each other's strong points and brought out each other's worse trait. *Masked and Anonymous* is long, windy, and tedious. It's like a really bad version of *Slackers,* but with famous people instead of strange Austin, Texas, denizens.

It's hard to say what, exactly, the film is about, but a few things can be gleaned from it. It appears to be set in some sort of parallel America-like country, or America of the future. It's a multiethnic country plagued by poverty and presided over by a dying dictator/president (Richard Sarafian). A power-hungry successor (Rourke) is poised to take over and shape the country to his ideals. The desolate country has a lot of fighting and infighting between the government, the rebels, and the counter-rebels. Ribisi's character explains the confusion of not knowing for whom to fight since all the factions seem to be corrupt. His musing on incomprehensibility is one of the few understandable moments in the film.

The big and blustery promoter Uncle Sweetheart (Goodman) is in charge of recruiting talent for a benefit concert to raise money for, oh, the government? Or maybe it's the rebels? Despite the fierce warnings from his high-strung TV producer boss, Nina Veronica (Jessica Lange), Sweetheart is unable to come up with any big-name talent. (There is also some sort of subplot involving some bad guys to whom Sweetheart owes money.) He lines up some circus performers, like a Gandhi impersonator, and scores a headliner in Jack Fate (Dylan). Fate, who's in jail, was at one time a big-named legend who is now largely forgotten. It is typical of the tired symbolism in the film that his name would be fate.

Somewhere in there, there's a weary reporter, Tom Friend (Bridges) who's trying to uncover some sort of dirt on the concert, and his strange, religious girlfriend, Pagan Lace (Cruz, whose sole take on her character involves twisting a tendril of her hair nervously). Bobby Cupid (Wilson) is Fate's protector and friend. Other than bringing Fate Blind Lemon Jefferson's old guitar, his main purpose seems to be standing around. And it turns out that Fate is actually the dictator's son. (Imagine the ego blow of being asked to play Dylan's father.)

Most of the so-called action in the film is the conversations that Fate has as he travels to the gig and once he gets there. There is nothing wrong with deep musings in a film, but the particular musings in this particular film are intolerable. "Who created man?" wonders Kilmer in one scene. Fate says lots of stuff like "All of us in some sense are trying to kill time, but time ends up killing us." A. O. Scott of the *New York Times* found this perplexing Dylanism in the film, "It's in the grass. Cows can digest it. But you can't, and neither can I."

A little of this could be okay, perhaps charmingly enigmatic, but this is the whole film. "What's bugging you?" asks Pagan Lace. "The absurdity of a lifetime of menial labor," replies Friend. Later he tells a story: "Once I was walking by a cathedral. A white dove was carrying a branch and dropped it at my feet." Don't these people ever make small talk?

There is one funny moment in the film, but it's probably not supposed to be so. In one scene, Fate beats up the much larger reporter. There is no amount of special effects that could make the stiff, frail Dylan look like he's beating up anyone twice his size. Dylan barely appears to have the energy to lift his leg to give a knee in the groin. Dylan attacks with an awkward, weak hit to Bridges and Bridges falls to the ground, writhing in pain. The whole thing is kind of embarrassing.

The one strong point of the film is the music. Dylan and his band give several good performances and the soundtrack is made up of various odd covers of Dylan tunes, like the Magakoro Brothers' Japanese version of "My Back Pages." The best one is done by a young girl, Tinashe Kachingwe, who comes up to Fate and performs a fresh, a cappella version of "Times They Are A-Changin."

Critics were angry with the film for taking up one hour and 47 minutes of their lives and let their ire show in their reviews. Jeffrey M. Anderson of the *San Francisco Examiner* railed, "It's a huge mess of a movie, an ugly digital video blob packed full of incomprehensible dialogue and strange characters." (Anderson also was not a fan of Dylan's acting, commenting that he "walks around as if the camera were causing him physical pain, like a magnifying glass trying to set him on fire.") Kevin Thomas of the *Los Angeles Times* observed, "The look of the film is great, the soundtrack glorious, but more often than not the dialogue is atrocious, featuring a lot of long-winded gobbledygook." *Entertainment Weekly*'s Lisa Schwarzbaum, who gave the film a C, concluded, "Looking for meaning in *Masked and Anonymous* is the kind of limiting, linear activity that can drive a person mad." Scott of the *New York Times* described the film as "an unholy, incoherent mess," and added that only a Dylan fan "could walk away from this film feeling nourished. And some, undoubtedly, will. You may encounter people who tell you it's a stone masterpiece. The thing to do is nod politely. They mean no harm. For all I know, they may be right."

—*Jill Hamilton*

CREDITS

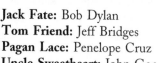

Jack Fate: Bob Dylan
Tom Friend: Jeff Bridges
Pagan Lace: Penelope Cruz
Uncle Sweetheart: John Goodman
Nina Veronica: Jessica Lange
Bobby Cupid: Luke Wilson
Mistress: Angela Bassett
Editor: Bruce Dern
Oscar Vogel: Ed Harris

Origin: USA, Great Britain
Released: 2003
Production: Nigel Sinclair, Jeff Rosen; BBC Films, Marching Band Productions, Spitfire Pictures, Grey Water Park; released by Sony Pictures Classics
Directed by: Larry Charles
Written by: Rene Fontaine, Sergei Perov
Cinematography by: Rogier Stoffers
Music by: Bob Dylan
Sound: Susumu Tokunow
Editing: Pietro Scalia
Art Direction: Kristan Andrews
Costumes: Abigail Murray
Production Design: Bob Ziembicki
MPAA rating: PG-13
Running time: 113 minutes

REVIEWS

Boxoffice. April, 2003, p. 77.
Chicago Sun-Times Online. August 15, 2003.
Entertainment Weekly. August 8, 2003, p. 53.
Los Angeles Times Online. July 25, 2003.
New York Times Online. July 24, 2003.
Variety Online. February 3, 2003.
Washington Post. September 5, 2003, p. WE42.

Master and Commander: The Far Side of the World

Box Office: $92.2 million

The twenty seafaring adventure novels by Australian Patrick O'Brian (1914-2000) surprised many by finding a large international readership during an age—the 1980s and 1990s—expected to perceive such books as old-fashioned. With their Napoleonic War setting and loose plots, O'Brian's tales offer an unusually detailed view of a time and place in the distant past. *Master and Commander: The Far Side of the World*, drawing upon the first and tenth novels and using both titles, follows O'Brian's characters on a voyage from the coast of Brazil, around Cape Horn, to the Pacific, a new battleground for the French in their war with Great Britain. Writer-director Peter Weir's adaptation is faithful to its source, perhaps the most exciting seagoing film since *The Crimson Pirate* (1952), a return to form for a filmmaker who had been in a prolonged slump, and yet another triumph for superstar Russell Crowe.

Some reviewers complained that *Master and Commander* has no plot. While the entire film involves chasing and being chased by a French frigate, Weir, following O'Brian's lead, focuses primarily on the daily life aboard ship. O'Brian's novels, even more than C.S. Forester's Horatio Hornblower tales, aim less at exciting readers with rousing adventures than at transporting them to another highly credible world. While most adventure films have interludes devoted to the details of time, place, and character, the interludes of *Master and Commander* are the battles. What is most important are atmosphere and getting to know the protagonists. As a mood piece, *Master and Commander* is surprisingly similar to Weir's first great film, the hauntingly mysterious *Picnic at Hanging Rock* (1975).

Master and Commander takes place in 1805 as Napoleon Bonaparte tries to conquer Europe. Captain Jack Aubrey (Russell Crowe), known affectionately as "Lucky Jack," rules the HMS *Surprise* as a benevolent commander, trying to balance his tasks in the Royal Navy with concern for the welfare of his men. Weir and co-screenwriter John Collee alternate between Aubrey and his officers, Tom Pullings (James D'Arcy) and William Mowett (Edward Woodall), and scenes involving the midshipmen and crew members such as the steward, Preserved Killick (David Threlfall), and the oldest seaman, Joe Plaice (George Innes). The most significant character after Aubrey is the ship's surgeon, Dr. Stephen Maturin (Paul Bettany). One of Maturin's most memorable scenes comes after a battle, when he is removing a ball from Plaice's skull in full view of the crew, pointing out the patient's brain to the onlookers. Two subplots deal with Blakeney (Max Pirkis), the youngest midshipman, whose badly wounded arm is amputated, and Hollom (Lee Ingleby), the eldest midshipman, whose lack of respect from the crew has tragic consequences.

Aubrey and Maturin are best friends and spend their infrequent leisure time in the captain's cabin unwinding by playing the violin and viola. There is no explanation of how they came to be friends and no background information about any of the characters. Weir essentially tosses the viewers into the middle of an ongoing situation and lets them find their way by observing life aboard ship. Aubrey's and Maturin's characters are unveiled a layer at a time, growing in each scene. Aubrey's concern for the welfare of his men extends especially to Maturin, whom he sees as an equal and who is, of course, invaluable as the surgeon. Higgins (Richard McCabe), the surgeon's mate, seems uncertain of himself and is a bit of a bumbler.

The film's centerpiece comes when Howard (Chris Larkin), captain of the Royal Marines, while trying to kill an albatross, accidentally shoots Maturin in the abdomen. Because Higgins is uncertain about how to proceed, Maturin removes the bullet himself. Aubrey ignores his charge to engage the enemy, deciding his friend's recovery is more important. This sequence takes place in the Galapagos Islands, where Maturin regains strength. An amateur naturalist, he explores the terrain looking for previously undiscovered species.

This expedition is typical of Weir's narrative approach. On the surface, it seems to have little to do with the rest of the film. Yet it develops Maturin's character by emphasizing his intellectual curiosity, it expands Aubrey's character by highlighting his decision to extend his friend's convalescence and allow two crew members to accompany the doctor in gathering specimens, and it also underscores the irony of war by finding peace and beauty amid death. An additional layer of irony occurs when Maturin stumbles across the French fleet and must leave most of his finds behind to return to camp and warn Aubrey.

The Galapagos scenes are beautifully photographed by Russell Boyd, who shot all of Weir's films from *Picnic at Hanging Rock* through *The Year of Living Dangerously* (1982) but no others until *Master and Commander*. Boyd excels at outdoor cinematography and helps make the battle scenes especially realistic. His greatest moment comes with the terrifying first shot of the soon-to-be-omnipresent French frigate as it emerges slowly from a thick fog.

Weir has always been an expert director of actors, and he obtains excellent performances from the entire cast. The most notable supporting performances are by Robert Pugh, as Allen, the avuncular ship's master, and Innes as the somewhat world-weary Plaice. Each of the crewmembers displays different skills as well as shortcomings that Aubrey and the others must help them overcome. Pugh and Innes create miniature portraits of memorable seamen who probably could not cope with life ashore. Both veteran English character actors previously worked together in the miniseries *Danger UXB* (1979), which similarly looks at the camaraderie of ordinary men during wartime.

Bettany made his first significant impression on American audiences as Russell Crowe's imaginary friend in *A Beautiful Mind* (2001). While his English student at Princeton is effectively creepy, given that he is the creation of a tortured mind, Bettany's Maturin is at the other extreme: brave, resourceful, and witty. Some fans of O'Brian's saga feel that the doctor is the more appealing character, and Bettany captures this essence. Maturin's kindly, calm resolve is necessary to balance the film's more extreme elements. It is a bit jarring during the final battle when Maturin abandons his usual post to charge onto the French frigate, guns blazing. Weir and Collee have not prepared the audience for such an abrupt departure from the doctor's routine.

After showing considerable promise early in his career, especially with *Proof* (1991), Crowe demonstrated with *L.A. Confidential* (1997) that he had the makings of a major star. He went on to become exactly that while showing amazing range with his performances in *The Insider* (1999), *Gladiator* (2000), and *A Beautiful Mind*. *Master and Commander* only adds to his stature because these five great performances come with such different characters in both epic and intimate films. Aubrey is essentially a genial host to the diverse personalities under his charge, and Crowe underplays the part. Yet his unique blend of strength, sensitivity, and humor enhance the character considerably. Crowe is a throwback both to such masculine Hollywood leading men as Kirk Douglas, Burt Lancaster, and Robert Mitchum and such tormented, sometimes overly sensitive souls as Marlon Brando, Montgomery Clift, and James Dean. His screen presence and depth make him unlike any other contemporary actor. It is hard to imagine anyone else embodying Lucky Jack.

Weir established himself as a major director with such films as *Picnic at Hanging Rock*, *The Last Wave* (1977), *Gallipoli* (1981), *The Year of Living Dangerously*, and *Witness*

(1985). These films focus on ordinary people caught up in unusual circumstances, often in settings new (and dangerous) to them. Since *Witness*, however, Weir's films have been more conventional, as with the solemn *Dead Poets Society* (1989), the lightweight *Green Card* (1990), and the pretentious *The Truman Show* (1998). Despite occasional flashes of brilliance, these films have been generally disappointing.

Master and Commander is a return to Weir's earlier form, a near-perfect blending of the small personal drama and the large-scale adventure. The stirring shots of the ships in full sail, the scenes of the seamen at odds with the elements, the battles during which it is always easy to determine who is doing what to whom, and the many quieter moments, especially Aubrey's and Maturin's musical evenings together, display the director's range. Weir subtly depicts how music helps the protagonists deal with the harshness of everyday life. He shows the same masterly control as his hero.

—*Michael Adams*

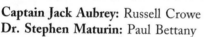

CREDITS

Captain Jack Aubrey: Russell Crowe
Dr. Stephen Maturin: Paul Bettany
Barrett Bonden: Billy Boyd
Lord Blakeney: Max Pirkis
1st Lt. Thomas Pullings: James D'Arcy
Mr. Hogg: Mark Lewis Jones
Captain Howard, Royal Marines: Chris Larkin
Mr. Higgins: Richard McCabe
Mr. Allen: Robert Pugh
Hollom: Lee Ingleby
Joe Plaice: George Innes
Killick: David Threlfall
2nd Lt. William Mowett: Edward Woodall
Mr. Hollar: Ian Mercer
Peter Calamy: Max Benitz

Origin: USA
Released: 2003
Production: Peter Weir, Duncan Henderson, Samuel Goldwyn Jr.; Samuel Goldwyn Films, 20th Century-Fox, Miramax Films, Universal Pictures; released by 20th Century-Fox
Directed by: Peter Weir
Written by: Peter Weir, John Collee
Cinematography by: Russell Boyd
Music by: Christopher Gordon, Iva Davies, Richard Tognetti
Sound: Art Rochester
Editing: Lee Smith
Art Direction: Hector Romero

Costumes: Wendy Stites
Production Design: William Sandell
MPAA rating: PG-13
Running time: 139 minutes

REVIEWS

Chicago Sun-Times Online. November 14, 2003.
Entertainment Weekly. November 21, 2003, p. 56.
Los Angeles Times Online. November 14, 2003.
New York Times Online. November 14, 2003.
People. November 24, 2003, p. 29.
Rolling Stone. November 27, 2003, p. 102.
USA Today Online. November 14, 2003.
Variety Online. November 3, 2003.
Washington Post. November 14, 2003, p. WE45.

QUOTES

Jack Aubrey (Russell Crowe) to his crew: "Quick's the word and sharp's the action."

AWARDS AND NOMINATIONS

Oscars 2003: Cinematog., Sound FX Editing
Natl. Soc. Film Critics 2003: Cinematog.
Nomination:
Oscars 2003: Art Dir./Set Dec., Cinematog., Costume Des., Director (Weir), Film, Film Editing, Makeup, Sound, Sound FX Editing, Visual FX
Directors Guild 2003: Director (Weir)
Golden Globes 2004: Actor—Drama (Crowe), Director (Weir), Film—Drama.

Matchstick Men

Lie. Cheat. Steal. Rinse. Repeat.
—Movie tagline

  Box Office: $36 million

Matchstick Men, a film about con artists, is itself a stylish, cleverly-conceived con which ends badly. For most of its 120-minute running time, it breezily goes about hoodwinking us with a fair amount of success, but then the film bungles things just when it is about to make a pretty clean getaway. Still, at least until getting to this unfortunate finale, most viewers of the film will enjoy being taken for a ride.

At the core of *Matchstick Men* is the character study of Roy Waller (Nicolas Cage of last year's *Adaptation*, yet again in quirky mode), a gifted L.A. grifter or "matchstick man." His life centers around pulling off small-time jobs which successfully separate unsuspecting people from their hard-earned money. While smoothly carrying out these cons with his partner/protégé, Frank Mercer (Sam Rockwell of 2002's *Confessions of a Dangerous Mind*), he manipulates his quarry with immense skill. His success can be chalked up in part to careful planning and deft execution. However, another factor is the medication Roy takes to keep his formidable emotional problems at bay. When not on the meds, he is thrown way off his game, reduced to a sweaty, tortured mass of twitches and tics, his obsessive-compulsive disorder and agoraphobia make it excruciatingly difficult to function, let alone flimflam anyone. His home is kept inordinately orderly, and while it is so immaculately clean that you could eat off the floor, such a thing would make this neat freak come unhinged. He could single-handedly keep the makers of Lysol and Mr. Clean in business with his overwhelming drive to wash and vacuum and disinfect. Roy becomes apoplectic if shoes are worn while walking on his pristine, light-colored carpet. Even a tiny stain or bit of lint is cause for alarm. Roy's diet consists mainly of tuna eaten right out of the can to avoid dealing with dirty dishes and utensils. When finished, he wears gloves while carefully rinsing out the can, sealing it in a plastic bag before disposing of it. When going through a door, he first cracks it open three times, counting aloud as he does so. Once outside, Roy's senses are apt to overload. He finds sunlight in his eyes particularly unnerving, which can be crippling to someone living in Southern California. God forbid a single leaf should fall into his swimming pool.

Soon after we meet Roy, he accidentally drops his medicine down the drain, and so all that torments him makes a ferocious return. Frank suggests that a psychiatrist named Dr. Klein (Bruce Altman of last year's *Changing Lanes*) might be of assistance, and so Roy, at a loss, agrees to go. At first he is guarded with the doctor (claiming, for example, to be in the antiques business), but soon a torrent of words starkly reveal his inner anguish. It seems that Roy may have a teenage daughter out there whom he has never met, the product of an unhappy marriage long since ended, and he feels a gnawing sense of guilt about never being a part of the girl's life. Klein suggests that they contact Roy's ex, and, as Roy is too nervous to do so himself, the doctor does it for him. Shortly thereafter, Roy learns that he does, indeed, have a 14-year-old daughter named Angela (Alison Lohman, memorable in last year's *White Oleander*), and that she would like to meet him.

While watching Roy and Frank in action is certainly intriguing, what is most compelling in *Matchstick Men* is the relationship which develops between Roy and Angela. It is quite affecting to see him approach her for the first time with a clear mix of tender sincerity and obvious uncertainty. Telling shots of Roy plainly reveal the feelings that lie beneath the surface. We feel for him as his problems start to intrude on this important and meaningful moment. It is a lot for Roy to take in, especially since, outside of his business partnership with Frank, the man's only other interpersonal relationship consists of always having his cans of tuna rung up by the same pretty cashier at the grocery store. What really throws Roy, however, is when Angela shows up on his doorstep after a fight with her mom and asks if she can temporarily take refuge with dear old dad. He dutifully takes her in, albeit reluctantly, realizing with obvious trepidation what her presence might mean to his carefully controlled life, not to mention his well-ordered, antiseptic abode.

Angela is a sparkplug of a girl, a beguiling mix of vivacity and vulnerability. She satisfies her curiosity about her father by asking questions of him, as well as snooping through his things when he is not around, things that hint at a profession quite removed from antiques. A typical teenager, she likes to scarf down pizza, tries some alcohol, stays out later than she should, and is fairly unacquainted with fastidiousness. We chuckle as Roy struggles to rise to the demands of his new job as father ("I'm not good at being a dad," he laments. "I barely get by being me."). Things get even more complicated when Angela extracts from him exactly what he does for a living. She excitedly begs him to teach her some tricks of his trade, and Roy does so with exceeding reluctance. He fears he is corrupting her, even though Angela cheerfully divulges that she is not exactly an unsullied innocent. His uneasiness intensifies when she picks up on her first larcenous lesson with amazing ease, successfully scamming a woman out of $300 with a bogus winning lottery ticket. There is also, however, evidence of delight and pride at the skill she appears to have inherited from him. When Roy makes her give the cash back, saying that he would not be a responsible parent if he let her keep the money from the con he just taught her, we have to chuckle at his curious reasoning. Still, no one can deny that illegal activity has brought this father and daughter closer together, and Roy now seems so much more relaxed and contented.

Soon it comes time for Roy and Frank's first big score, something for which the latter had especially yearned. Unfortunately, when Frank alerts his partner that the opportune moment has arrived, Roy is out bonding with Angela and he has no choice but to bring the thrilled teen along. While it initially seems that she has helped them pull off their con of equally shady, boorish businessman Chuck Frechette (Bruce McGill of 2002's *The Sum of All Fears*), it is soon revealed that she may have seriously endangered both the operation and her two partners in crime. Some potent ups and downs, a bitter rift, and a touching reconciliation between Roy and Angela follow. The film makes a jolting shift to a much darker tone when things go terribly wrong at Roy's home, and Roy and Frank are left wounded, while the vengeful Frechette is shot to death by Angela. After Frank spirits Angela away and her father chivalrously takes the blame for the homicide, Roy is sent reeling when he learns that all his money is gone, and that everything leading up to that point has been an extraordinary, masterful con pulled by Frank, Klein, and Angela, who is not really Roy's daughter. Some in the audience will have figured all this out earlier or at least suspected as much, but all viewers will be struck by the look on Roy's face as the enormity of what has happened sinks in. He had lost sight of the very first rule he taught Angela: "Make sure that the person you are conning isn't conning you."

Matchstick Men then skips ahead a year, and we see Roy working as a salesman in a carpet store. A customer comes in with a girlfriend in tow, and it turns out to be Angela. She and Roy have a curiously restrained reunion, and it is clear that, amazingly, there is still some caring between them. While some viewers, especially those familiar with the much bleaker ending of the Eric Garcia novel upon which this film is based, may have a problem with such a scene, many more will balk at the believability of the film's final image, which shows Roy enjoying domestic bliss with the grocery store cashier, who is radiantly pregnant with his child. It is an uplifting but unconvincing conclusion, an abrupt jump to a warm-and-fuzzy situation that feels false.

Depending on which source you believe, *Matchstick Men* was made on a budget somewhere between $29 and $80 million. It grossed a disappointing $36.8 million at the box office. Critical reaction was generally positive. The film was directed by Ridley Scott, who was eager to paint on a smaller canvas after massive, exhausting projects like *Gladiator* (2000) and *Black Hawk Down* (2001). *Matchstick Men* is a generally enjoyable but not exactly distinguished effort, with echoes of the far more memorable *Paper Moon* (1973). Unquestionably, the best things that *Matchstick Men* has going for it are Cage and Lohman. Cage, who has been accused of overacting more than once in his career, keeps a fairly good grip on his portrayal of a man in danger of losing his. He makes us see and, more importantly, care about what is underneath all the quirks. Lohman, a decade older than her character, is remarkably believable, clearly headed for a fine career. Although Rockwell is also good, the chemistry between Cage and Lohman is the chief reason the modestly successful *Matchstick Men* catches fire.

—*David L. Boxerbaum*

CREDITS

Roy Waller: Nicolas Cage
Angela: Alison Lohman
Frank Mercer: Sam Rockwell
Dr. Harris Klein: Bruce Altman
Chuck Frechette: Bruce McGill
Kathy: Sheila Kelley
Laundry Lady: Beth Grant
Husband: Steve Eastin

Origin: USA
Released: 2003
Production: Ridley Scott, Steve Starkey, Sean Bailey, Jack Rapke, Ted Griffin; Scott Free, LivePlanet, Imagemovers, Rickshaw Productions; released by Warner Bros.
Directed by: Ridley Scott
Written by: Ted Griffin, Nicholas Griffin
Cinematography by: John Mathieson
Music by: Hans Zimmer
Sound: Lee Orloff
Editing: Dody Dorn
Art Direction: Michael Manson
Costumes: Michael Kaplan
Production Design: Tom Foden
MPAA rating: PG-13
Running time: 120 minutes

REVIEWS

Chicago Sun-Times Online. September 12, 2003.
Entertainment Weekly. September 19, 2003, p. 62.
Los Angeles Times Online. September 12, 2003.
New York Times Online. September 12, 2003.
People. September 22, 2003, p. 39.
Rolling Stone. October 2, 2003, p. 129.
USA Today Online. September 12, 2003.
Vanity Fair. September, 2003, p. 102.
Variety Online. September 2, 2003.
Washington Post. September 12, 2003, p. WE41.

QUOTES

Roy (Nicolas Cage): "I'm not very good at being a dad. I barely get by being me."

The Matrix Reloaded

Free your mind.
—Movie tagline

 Box Office: $281.5 million

The Matrix Reloaded picks up the story of *The Matrix* (1999) six months after the events that ended the first film. More people have been awakened and unplugged from the Matrix that sapped them for energy. In fact, more people have been freed in the past six months than were freed in the previous six years. Consequently, a war is looming between those who were enslaved by the Matrix and those who enslaved them. Now a machine army is drilling closer and closer to the human underground haven of Zion. At the rate of 100 meters an hour, the machines and 250,000 sentinels, a fighting machine for every man, woman and child in the city, should reach Zion in 72 hours.

The Council of Zion is debating battle plans, but a split is developing between those such as Commander Lock (Harry Lennix) who want to follow a preemptive strategy and attack the diggers before they get to Zion and those such as Morpheus (Laurence Fishburne) who are willing to make the leap of faith and trust the Oracle's (Gloria Foster) prediction that a young computer hacker, Thomas Anderson, now known as Neo (Keanu Reeves), is "The One" who will save humanity. This is a division that is made even more heated for the two men due to the fact that Commander Lock's current girlfriend is Captain Niobe (Jada Pinkett Smith) who was once Morpheus' girlfriend.

Unfortunately in the past six months, the Oracle has not contacted Neo and as he laments to his comrade in arms— both military and romantic arms—Trinity (Carrie-Anne Moss), "I just wish I knew what I'm supposed to do." However, Neo has not been idle. In the past few months he has learned to better control his avatar in the Matrix. His fighting skills are greater as is his ability to decode Matrix entities and his ability to move about in it. In fact he can now fly, or "do his superman thing," as his contact on their ship, the Nebuchadnezzar, Link (Harold Perrineau) calls it.

In Zion, Neo is worshipped. To many, he is their savior. A lot of this is due to the proselytizing of Morpheus who unwaveringly says things like, "There's only one way to save our city: Neo." But as Commander Lock tells him, "Not everyone believes what you believe." To which Morpheus' John the Baptist character replies, "My beliefs do not require that they do."

Of course Neo is not the only one to evolve in the world of the Matrix. "Hmmm, upgrades," Neo comments in his first fight with Matrix agents. But of all the agents to vex Neo, the worst was Agent Smith (Hugo Weaving). At the end of the first movie, audiences assumed Agent Smith was destroyed, but one should never assume in a movie created by the writing/directing team of the Wachowski Brothers. Agent Smith is back and he's badder than ever. In fact, he now has the ability to reach into any Matrix "being" and change its programming into another Agent Smith. Even worse for Zion, Agent Smith can "reach" into one of their representatives while they're in the Matrix, infect them, and travel with them back to their ship where he makes that person a fifth columnist and traitor.

Furthermore, Agent Smith now has a bigger ego— when Neo sees him for the first time he automatically groans, "Oh God," to which Agent Smith replies, "Smith will suffice." Seems he's also developed a sense of humor . . . and his desire for revenge against Neo is razor sharp. Agent Smith, however, is no longer an agent of the Matrix. He is a rogue program who seems to exist only to have his revenge on Neo. The system has called for his deletion, but he has become a program driven for vengeance.

Agent Smith is not the only rogue program lurking in the Matrix. For example, there is the decadent Merovingian (Lambert Wilson) and his wife the sensuous Persephone (Monica Bellucci) who manipulate and feed off the emotions of the "beings" in the Matrix. Surrounded by goons like the lethal and ghostly twins (Neil and Adrian Rayment), they are powerful, rich, urbane and unscrupulous.

But what is their purpose in the Matrix? Maybe they don't have one. "Every story you've heard about vampires, werewolves or aliens is the system assimilating some program that's doing something [it's] not supposed to be doing," the Oracle tells Neo. And when a program goes wrong what happens to it? It can chose exile, or remain in the Matrix or return to the mainframe. And how does the Oracle know all this? Because when Neo finally does get the call from her he discovers that she is not human, she's another program, a part of the system, a part of the control. This revelation really complicates things. Is The Oracle here to help humans or not? Will following her instructions save Zion or doom it?

According to The Oracle, Neo can only save Zion if he reaches The Source, and to do that he will need The Keymaker (Randall Duk Kim) who just happens to be a captive of the Merovingian. While the Merovingian plans on keeping the Keymaker, his wife Persephone will give him up . . . in exchange for a passionate kiss from Neo. It is a price Neo only reluctantly pays, but soon the Keymaker is theirs with the Merovingian and his goons in hot pursuit.

Now Trinity, the Keymaker, and Morpheus must evade razor-wielding thugs, car-crushing Matrix agents, and the many car accidents all this causes to the oblivious "humans" commuting on the freeway, while Neo is stuck in the Merovingian's chateau miles and miles away. Will he be able to do his Superman thing and save the day? And even if he does how will the Keymaker get him to The Source. And just what exactly will The Source tell him?

As a clue, the Merovingian cryptically tells Neo, "I have survived your predecessors and I will survive you." Neo has had predecessors? Someone has tried all this before? Who? When? And why doesn't anyone know about it? Ah, just more questions for The Source.

The first installment in what will eventually become a *Matrix* trilogy was an unexpected hit. Audiences found it not only entertaining but overflowing with innovative special effects, stylish heroes and thoughtful and surprising story-telling. The first film returned moviegoers to the days when science fiction movies had brains as well as brawn and special effects. As a result it grossed nearly half a billion dollars in worldwide theatrical release and won four Academy Awards.

The Matrix was a good, solid, stand-alone movie, but the same cannot be said of part two. Filmed back to back with part three (*The Matrix Revolutions*, set to debut in November of 2003) and costing more than $300 million, the last two parts have taken more than four years to make it into theaters. They've been a long time coming, but the feeling after watching *Reloaded* is, "where's the rest of the movie?" *Reloaded* ends quite abruptly, with a lot of characters and ideas left hanging, and an annoying "to be concluded" mocking us on the screen.

This is not to say that *Reloaded* doesn't have a lot going for it. For one thing it shows a more satisfyingly romantic relationship between Neo and Trinity. Oh, they still kick butts and watch each other's backs, but the steamy love scenes work to reinforce one of the plot's motives that will become very important at the end of the film and probably to part three, too.

Secondly, the "real" world (and one has to use this word judiciously in a Wachowski Brothers movie) is given much more substance and detail in *Reloaded,* especially the human haven, Zion. Depicted as an underground cathedral, it is a temple of stalactites and stalagmites and industrial pipes with halls of earth and steel and stone populated by beautiful, multi-ethnic citizens dressed in found items and organic cloth.

There are two things, however, that anyone going to a *Matrix* movie expects in spades and they are action and thought, and here *Reloaded* does not disappoint. There are several action sequences that are destined to make the movie hall of fame. One the filmmakers have dubbed "the burly brawl." Like all the fight sequences in the *Matrix* movies, this, too, was choreographed by *Crouching Tiger, Hidden Dragon*'s Yuen Wo-ping. Intricately planned out and astonishing in their complexity—but sometimes a bit repetitive—these fights are intense and breathtaking. The "burly brawl" has Neo fighting not one, not two, but 100 Agent Smiths. A combination of Hugo Weaving, stunt men and computer technology, it is a surreal exercise in Matrix physics.

The second truly memorable action sequence is the freeway chase. It took seven weeks to film this amazing 14-minute chase. Obviously the filmmakers couldn't tie up a real (there's that word again) freeway for that long so they built a mile-and-a-half long, closed-loop freeway complete with a 19-foot high wall and two overpasses on a runway at the Alameda Naval Base. Interestingly, it was built out of lumber and plywood, then plastered to look like concrete. Even more interesting, after filming was finished, the freeway was torn apart and the lumber sent to Mexico to be used in the construction of 100 low-income family homes.

Using the futuristic looking Cadillac CTS and the EXT and a Ducati motorcycle, Trinity must try to escape with The Keymaker while bullets and crashes and gravity-defying agents dodge and weave after them. The filmmakers used computer generated "Pre-visualization" to map out the complex shots and deliver up what amounts to "an impossible event captured at impossible camera angles."

When one's eyes aren't popping from the special effects, though, the *Matrix* movies also give one's brains something to think about, because, right from the start, *the Matrix* has been a thinking person's action film. The first installment was heavy on epistemology and ontology: what is reality and how can we know what is real and unreal? While this element is not forgotten (in fact at the end of the film, two characters are in comas. Are they experiencing yet another level of reality?), it takes a back seat to the philosophical examination of the concept of free will in the second installment.

"What is control?" Councillor Hamann (Anthony Zerbe) asks, because in the west we believe that the more control we have the freer we are. Thus begins the audience's fall into the philosophical rabbit hole of free will vs. determinism. "We're all here to do what we're here to do," the Oracle tells Neo, falling into the determinists' camp. Programs control everything; we're all doing what we're supposed to do and the programs' strings are invisible. There is no free will, our choices are already made. The only thing to do is to understand why we made the choice, because that would be the start to seeing the invisible strings of the program. "Whatever happens happens for a reason," says Agent Smith, also siding with the determinists. "We're not here because we're free, we're here because we're not free," he continues. The program has dictated the future and all they can do is be puppets in The Source's play.

Even the Merovingian believes that no action is truly free, no choice freely chosen. That every action has a preceding action that has caused it. It is inevitable. "You were told to come here and you obeyed," he says to Neo indicating the inescapable causality of his own actions. We are slaves to causality and our only hope is to understand why we have to chose the choices we chose. That is as close as we can ever get to freedom and power.

Aren't there any indeterminists in the Matrix? "We do only what we're meant to do," says the Keymaker. How about among the humans? "There are no accidents. I do not believe in chance, providence and purpose. It is our fate to be here. It is our destiny," says Morpheus. Hey, where are the Heisenberg chaos theory champions in this reality? Is freedom, choice, control nothing more than an illusion? And is this true in just the Matrix reality or does it include the "real" reality of Zion too?

Well, this is just another level of the many one passes through as one falls down the Wachowski Brothers' rabbit hole. Add a touch of Christian messianism—do we really need to go over the symbolism of Neo as savior?—a bit of Greek myth, and an iota of Gnosticism, a dash of French history, etc. and the result is a pop-philosophy that should give people something to actually talk about after the movie is over. Although one often wished all this wasn't presented in as ponderous a style as it was. Sometimes the dialogue just stopped the story in its tracks.

Undoubtedly, one thing people will be talking about is how many hanging pieces there are to *Reloaded*. Everything from what happened to Tank (Marcus Chong), the human born outside the Matrix who saved them all in the first movie (Hint: salary dispute) to what will happen to the Oracle in *Revolutions* since the actress who plays her, Gloria Foster, died September 29, 2001 of diabetes. She had finished shooting *Reloaded* but had not begun filming *Revolutions*. Some characters (Seraph and Niobe in particular) and things (that spoon given to Neo) seem important but aren't. Perhaps they'll turn up again in part three and all will be clear. And tell me why the Wachowski Brothers did nothing with Commander LOCK and the KEYMASTER. Was it just too obvious?

This is part of the problem with *Reloaded:* one feels as if they've been left hanging. Mysteries are unresolved, but instead of leaving one wanting more it makes one feel cheated. Similarly it doesn't have the same initial inventive excitement of the original, nor does it generate the same satisfying sense of wonder. Consequently, unlike the first film, *Reloaded* has a hard time standing alone. It is really the first part of a much longer film—as is attested to by that "to be concluded" that abruptly appears at the end of the movie. Perhaps this movie will fare better when it can be hooked up to the third and final installment. In the meantime, *Matrix* still has its devoted fans. Part two grossed a whopping $93.3 million its opening weekend, but, relatively speaking, dropped rather quickly after that. *Bruce Almighty* seemed easily to knock it out of its #1 slot the next weekend.

Perhaps not as many people want to sit through this hanging story of technological alienation, the cost of ignorance, and the price of knowledge. Or maybe it's the case that just not as many fans want to sit through it again and again and again. But for all the analysis and examinations of the *Matrix* phenomenon and philosophy, I just wish someone would tell me why people who live in caves underground find it necessary to wear sunglasses there. Perhaps that's

another mystery that will be answered in part three, which I now have no choice but to see.

—*Beverley Bare Buehrer*

CREDITS

Neo: Keanu Reeves
Trinity: Carrie-Anne Moss
Morpheus: Laurence "Larry" Fishburne
Agent Smith: Hugo Weaving
Niobe: Jada Pinkett Smith
Persephone: Monica Bellucci
The Oracle: Gloria Foster
Zee: Nona Gaye
Keymaker: Randall Duk Kim
Merovingian: Lambert Wilson
Link: Harold Perrineau Jr.
Commander Lock: Harry J. Lennix
The Architect: Helmut Bakaitis
Councillor Hamann: Anthony Zerbe
Twin #1: Neil Rayment
Twin #2: Adrian Rayment
Agent Thompson: Matt McColm
Agent Johnson: Daniel Bernhardt
Cas: Gina Torres
Seraph: Sing Ngai
Bane: Ian Bliss
Councillor Dillard: Robyn Nevin
Maggie: Essie Davis

Origin: USA
Released: 2003
Production: Joel Silver; Village Roadshow Pictures, NPV Entertainment; released by Warner Bros.
Directed by: Andy Wachowski, Larry Wachowski
Written by: Andy Wachowski, Larry Wachowski
Cinematography by: Bill Pope
Music by: Don Davis
Sound: David Lee
Editing: Zach Staenberg
Art Direction: Hugh Bateup
Costumes: Kym Barrett
Production Design: Owen Paterson
MPAA rating: R
Running time: 138 minutes

REVIEWS

Chicago Sun-Times Online. May 14, 2003.
Chicago Tribune Online. May 14, 2003.
Entertainment Weekly. April 18, 2003, p. 26.

Entertainment Weekly. May 16, 2003, p. 24.
Los Angeles Times Online. January 19, 2003.
Los Angeles Times Online. May 14, 2003.
New York Times Online. May 11, 2003.
New York Times Online. May 14, 2003.
Newsweek. December 30, 2002, p. 80.
People. May 26, 2003, p. 35.
Premiere. May, 2003, p. 44.
Rolling Stone Online. May 14, 2003.
San Francisco Chronicle. May 15, 2003, p. E1.
Time. May 12, 2003.
USA Today Online. May 14, 2003.
Variety Online. May 7, 2003.
Village Voice Online. May 14, 2003.
Washington Post Online. May 14, 2003.

QUOTES

Neo (Keanu Reeves): "What happens if I fail?" The Oracle (Gloria Foster): "Then Zion will fall."

AWARDS AND NOMINATIONS

Nomination:
Golden Raspberries 2003: Worst Director (Wachowski), Worst Director (Wachowski).

The Matrix Revolutions

Everything that has a beginning has an end.
—Movie tagline

 Box Office: $139.2 million

When we last left our hero Neo (Keanu Reeves) he was lying unconscious aboard a hovercraft next to Bane (Ian Bliss). That accounts for Neo's body, but now we find that his mind is caught in a sterile, white subway station called Mobil (which one can easily unscramble to realize that Neo's mind is in limbo). This station is somewhere between the Matrix and the real world and the only way out is through safe passage via the Trainman (Bruce Spence). The Trainman, however, is controlled by the Merovingian (Lambert Wilson) who, as was discovered in *The Matrix Reloaded,* is not overly fond of Neo.

All this is revealed to Morpheus (Laurence Fishburne) and Trinity (Carrie-Anne Moss) when they visit the Oracle (Mary Alice). "Your friend is in trouble," she tells them,

"and he needs your help. He needs all our help." Trinity, Morpheus, and the Oracle's guard Seraph (Colin Chou) then set out to confront the Merovingian. It is no easy task getting in to see the Merovingian, but after a gravity-defying gun battle in the cloakroom the three end up in a Mexican standoff with every major character having a gun pointed at his or her head. Eventually, of course, a deal is worked out and Neo is released.

Back in the Matrix, Neo again goes to the Oracle for guidance, but what she tells him is as obtuse as ever. And after *The Matrix Reloaded* we're not even sure she should be trusted. After all, wasn't it revealed in part two that her prophecy about "The One" may be nothing more than another control program instituted by the Architect (Helmut Bakaitis) and whose purpose may be nothing more than to ensure the continuation of the cycle? Couldn't all her predictions and proddings be just another predestined action to push Neo in the direction the Architect wishes?

What we do know is that Neo's powers have increased and he is now able to move between the real world and the Matrix with his powers intact. We also know that Agent Smith (Hugo Weaving) has been busy taking over the bodies of "people" in the Matrix and endlessly replicating himself. He, too, has learned how to cross from the Matrix into the real world because he has "infected" one of the hovercraft crewmen—Bane. This increased human contact has made Agent Smith more and more unstable. He's feeling anger and jealousy and his ego is running wild as he continues to replicate himself. However, Smith's constant cloning will soon gain him enough power to destroy the world. (But no one explains why he would want to do that.)

Smith is one side of an equation for which the other side is Neo. It is the Architect's purpose to balance the equation, but Smith's multitude of duplicates are throwing the equation off. Not to mention the fact that it also appears that the Oracle's purpose is also to unbalance the equation.

Meanwhile, as the Oracle (symbol of choice) takes on the Architect (the symbol of causal determinism), the machines are attacking the underground refuge of Zion. In a last-ditch attempt to work out a truce, Neo and Trinity travel to the machine city where Neo tells them that Smith poses just as big a threat to them as the machines pose to the humans. Eventually convinced, the machines jack Neo into the Matrix where he takes on Smith in an epic battle. At the same time, the humans of Zion are voraciously defending themselves from their own Armageddon.

When the first *Matrix* hit screens in 1999, audiences loved its combination of philosophical conundrums and eye-popping action. It also contained characters we cared about. We could identify with Neo. He was someone who questioned his reality and was astounded by the answers being revealed to him. By the time *The Matrix Revolutions* shows up, although Neo's still confused about things—as are audiences after *The Matrix Reloaded*—he seems so wooden in the pursuit of answers that we just don't care about him that much anymore ... except in a purely intellectual way to know how this triptych of a story will end. By *Revolutions,* Neo seems as mechanical as the programs and machines he's fighting. And he's not the only one. Most of the characters seem as robotic as the machines and unfortunately they even spew robotic dialogue. Most ridiculous of all is the way love is treated. Neo and Trinity's love scenes are inept and rigid and are marred by laughably lumbering dialogue.

The only one who looks like she's having any fun in this stiff finale is the pumped-up Jada Pinkett Smith as Niobe. There is one other prankster having a bit of fun in *Revolutions,* the mysterious Oracle. Unfortunately the original Oracle, Gloria Foster, died in late 2001 before she could start work on *The Matrix Revolutions.* Consequently she has been replaced by actress Mary Alice (who coincidentally once starred opposite Foster in the 1995 Broadway play "Having Our Say"). Those with less than pristine memories or those who haven't seen the previous *Matrix* films more than once, may not notice the change in actresses, so seamlessly is it done.

Just as the acting seemed to get stiffer with each movie, so too has the story become less challenging and more concerned with special effects. *The Matrix Revolutions* only hints at the depths of ideas that so caught our imaginations in the first film. In *The Matrix* we were faced with the possibility that reality is an illusion and the problem of trying to figure out how can we prove or know for sure what reality actually is. In *The Matrix Reloaded* we find the idea that our lives could either be predetermined by factors beyond our control or they are entirely in our own hands and subject to choices we freely make. By the time we get to *The Matrix Revolutions,* however, all ideas take a back seat to action.

Not counting the battle for Zion, there are two big special effects fight scenes in *The Matrix Revolutions.* The first takes place in the Merovingian's Club Hell coat check area when Trinity, Morpheus, and Seraph try to reclaim Neo from limbo. It features startling gun fights on walls and ceilings, but it feels as if most of the gunmen have terrible aim no matter which way is up. While there's another fight aboard the hovercraft between Neo and Smith, it is claustrophobic and instead of worrying about who will win we instead wonder if the hovercraft will ever move again after all the firepower damage. The Super Burly Brawl, as the filmmakers call the final showdown between Smith and Neo in the Matrix, should be the battle that ends all battles, but it is so overdone and artificial and the two sides are so evenly matched that it is totally uninvolving.

The battle for Zion which cost $40 million (two-thirds of the original *Matrix*'s entire budget), seems interminable. Thousands upon thousands of rounds of ammunition are spent in an attempt to kill the invading sentinels but it's like trying to stop a swarm of bees with a shotgun ... and looks just as silly. There's also the added hypocrisy of the human hubris of trying to stop machines with machines. Surely

there could have been a more innovative, more "human" way to stop the sentinels invasion of Zion. Maybe one that didn't even involve Neo, but that would deny the filmmakers their messianic ending in which Neo becomes the sacrificial lamb for humanity.

Unfortunately, although action will be the hallmark of *Revolutions,* it is cliched. There is barely a hackneyed plot device that isn't used here. And by the time we reach the final battle, the movie actually looks more like a computer game than a story about actual people. And that is yet another huge distancing factor for the last of the *Matrix* movies. The first *Matrix* was innovative and energizing. We were kept off balance and gradually saw the light while we were also treated to creative special effects and a visual world unlike any we'd seen before. After that we were hungry for part two. In *The Matrix Reloaded* we hoped for more eye-popping effects, more explanations of the original story and more originality in that explanation. We got the visuals but the story was confusing and the explanations terminated so abruptly many worried that they wouldn't remember the intricacies well enough to understand what was dished up in the finale. Now we have *Revolutions* and the story is concluded, but just as the effects seem either a little stale or a little overdone, the story seems to end on a flat note that relies too much on a "War of the Worlds" battle than the intelligent wrapping up of the original, mind-bending plot.

—*Beverley Bare Buehrer*

CREDITS

Neo: Keanu Reeves
Morpheus: Laurence "Larry" Fishburne
Trinity: Carrie-Anne Moss
Agent Smith: Hugo Weaving
Oracle: Mary Alice
Persephone: Monica Bellucci
Niobe: Jada Pinkett Smith
Link: Harold Perrineau Jr.
Zee: Nona Gaye
Councillor Hamann: Anthony Zerbe
Merovingian (The Frenchman): Lambert Wilson
Lock: Harry J. Lennix
Seraph: Sing Ngai
Bane: Ian Bliss
Trainman: Bruce Spence
Cas: Gina Torres
The Architect: Helmut Bakaitis
Sparks: Lachy Hulme
Councillor Dillard: Robyn Nevin
Maggie: Essie Davis
Ghost: Anthony Wong
Deus Ex Machina: Kevin M. Richardson

Origin: USA
Released: 2003
Production: Joel Silver; Village Roadshow Pictures, NPV
Entertainment, Silver Pictures; released by Warner Bros.
Directed by: Andy Wachowski, Larry Wachowski
Written by: Andy Wachowski, Larry Wachowski
Cinematography by: Bill Pope
Music by: Don Davis
Sound: David Lee
Editing: Zach Staenberg
Art Direction: Hugh Bateup
Costumes: Kym Barrett
Production Design: Owen Paterson
MPAA rating: R
Running time: 130 minutes

REVIEWS

Chicago Sun-Times Online. November 5, 2003.
Chicago Tribune Online. November 5, 2003.
Entertainment Weekly. November 14, 2003.
Los Angeles Times Online. November 5, 2003.
New York Times Online. November 5, 2003.
People. November 17, 2003, p. 32.
Rolling Stone Online. November 3, 2003.
San Francisco Chronicle. November 5, 2003, p. D1.
USA Today Online. November 5, 2003.
Variety Online. Novmember 2, 2003.
Village Voice Online. Novmeber 5, 2003.
Washington Post. November 5, 2003, p. C1.

QUOTES

The Oracle (Mary Alice): "Nothing ever works out the way you
want it to."
Agent Smith (Hugo Weaving): "You're a symbol for all your kind,
Mr. Anderson. Helpless, pathetic, wanting to be put out of your
misery."

TRIVIA

The film opened simultaneously on 18,000 screens worldwide in an
attempt to thwart piracy efforts.

AWARDS AND NOMINATIONS

Nomination:
Golden Raspberries 2003: Worst Director (Wachowski),
Worst Director (Wachowski).

The Medallion
(Highbinders)

Box Office: $22 million

It's obvious that Hong Kong police inspector Eddie Yang
(Jackie Chan) has a soft heart for the underdogs and the
helpless in this world. Why he'll even give his dinner to a
homeless dog. This kindness, however, does not seem to
extend to the local Interpol representatives, especially leader
Arthur Watson (Lee Evans). Arthur is officious, insensitive,
bumbling and just plain stupid.

All this becomes increasingly apparent as Arthur forces
Eddie to sit on the sidelines as he and his Interpol team
ineptly chase after a ruthless international crime lord,
Snakehead (Julian Sands), inside a Chinese temple. But as
Eddie stews at his exclusion he notices a bright light coming
from a nearby manhole cover. Eddie follows this light into
the sewers below the temple and eventually into the temple
itself. There he finds Snakehead confronting a small, meditative boy, Jai (Alexander Bao). Jai, it seems, holds the secret
to a powerful medallion. Only he can combine the two
halves of the medallion to create one, but it will give the
person possessing it immortality and superhuman powers.
And Snakehead will do anything to get it.

When Eddie prevents Snakehead from procuring the
boy and the medallion, Snakehead sets the area around Jai
on fire and Eddie is forced to chose between saving the boy
from burning alive or collaring Snakehead himself. Much to
Arthur's anger, Eddie chooses Jai, but at least someone
finally knows what Snakehead looks like.

Two weeks latter, Eddie has tracked Snakehead's thugs
to Hong Kong harbor and discovers they have kidnapped Jai
and are bound for Dublin, Ireland. Because he knows what
Snakehead looks like, Eddie is sent to the Interpol office in
Dublin, which is also near Snakehead's headquarters. There
Eddie meets an old flame, Nicole (Claire Forlani) and a not-
so-old nemesis, Arthur Watson.

Interpol team meets the ship containing the kidnapped
boy at the Dublin docks and Eddie finds himself battling
Snakehead's gang and suddenly locked into a container with
Jai. When the container is knocked into the water, Eddie
uses his last breaths to protect the boy. Jai is saved, but Eddie
drowns. Just before this happens, though, Jai slips the coveted medallion into Eddie's hands.

Later in the morgue, Watson is saying goodbye over
Eddie's corpse only to suddenly find Eddie alive and standing beside him. The medallion has saved Eddie's life and

given him superhuman powers. This later development Eddie discovers to his amazement as he again tries to protect Jai from Snakehead's goons. After several kidnapping attempts, Snakehead is finally successful, and Eddie must save Jai and defeat Snakehead.

The Medallion is the creation of multi-talented producer Alfred Cheung, who is best known for his roles as writer, director and star of several insightful social comedies to come out of the Hong Kong film industry. The story is based on the mythology of the Chinese Highbinder knights. In fact, the working title of the film was *Highbinders*.

A story based on warrior knights and good vs. evil should be filled with action and adventure. And when it comes to action, very few can do it better than Jackie Chan. Unfortunately, lately Chan's action has been tempered by digital effects, and possibly his advancing years—he'll be 50 soon—much to the detriment of what makes Chan's films so special. A perfect example was this year's earlier Chan release *The Tuxedo* a disastrous combination of bad special effects, silly story, and less-than-impressive acting.

Unfortunately, *The Medallion* repeats all of *The Tuxedo*'s mistakes. When Jackie is doing his own stunts, he is a marvel to behold, but when the movie switches to CGI effects or fancy wire work, one feels cheated. It is also unfortunate that many of the action sequences are filmed with such tight framing. Half the time it's impossible to tell who's doing what to whom.

One exception to the troubling action/fight sequences is the final showdown between Snakehead and Eddie. While it's still shot too closely, the fight on the Escheresque staircases is very interesting . . . and too fleeting. At least audiences can always count on Jackie Chan's immense likeability as an actor. We can forgive him almost anything as he smiles self-deprecatingly at his own actions.

The same cannot be said about Lee Evans. Normally a talented comedian, here he's just not funny at all. In fact, he's positively annoying. His Arthur Watson is all bluster, bumble, anger and incompetence. He is Jerry Lewis playing Johnny English! (As an aside, Rowan Atkinson who played that title character a few months earlier, was in the running to play Arthur Watson. I don't think it would have helped.) When Nicole says, "We need Watson for this investigation," we're left dumbfounded and wondering why. It's a question that's never answered.

The Medallion is a big disappointment for most Chan fans and will probably not win him any new ones. Despite the fact he provides the few good things in the movie, they are not enough to overcome yet another silly story based on a muddled mythology and featuring few moments of good acting.

—*Beverley Bare Buehrer*

CREDITS

Eddie Yang: Jackie Chan
Nicole James: Claire Forlani
Snakehead: Julian Sands
Arthur Watson: Lee Evans
Commander Hammerstock-Smythe: John Rhys-Davies
Lester: Anthony Wong
Charlotte Watson: Christy Chung
Giscard: Johann Myers

Origin: USA, Hong Kong
Released: 2003
Production: Alfred Cheung; Golden Port Productions Ltd.; released by TriStar Pictures
Directed by: Gordon Chan
Written by: Gordon Chan, Bey Logan
Cinematography by: Arthur Wong
Music by: Adrian Lee
Sound: Paula Farifield
Editing: Chan Ki Hop
Art Direction: Oliver Wong
Costumes: Grania Preston
Production Design: Joseph C. Nemec III
MPAA rating: PG-13
Running time: 90 minutes

REVIEWS

Chicago Sun-Times Online. August 22, 2003.
Entertainment Weekly. September 5, 2003, p. 57.
Los Angeles Times Online. August 22, 2003.
New York Times Online. August 22, 2003.
People. September 8, 2003, p. 40.
USA Today Online. August 22, 2003.
Variety Online. August 22, 2003.
Washington Post. August 22, 2003, p. WE34.

A Mighty Wind

Back together for the first time, again.
—Movie tagline

 Box Office: $17.4 million

My initial reaction to the news that Christopher Guest and his cohort of usual suspects were going to make a satirical mockumentary about early folk music was disbelief. Folk music of the 1950s and 1960s? It sounded like a ho-hum object of derision. And it turns out it is. Guest, reunited with band mates Harry Schearer and Michael McKean from their pioneering *This Is Spinal Tap*, has produced something truly underwhelming. *A Mighty Wind* tries to hit a target that's paper thin and a mile wide, and it somehow manages to miss more often than it scores.

This smug and nearly lifeless comedy uses the same make-it-up-on-the-spot, hit-and-miss technique that was a success nearly 20 years earlier in *Spinal Tap*, a film that concocted a mock band of rock-and-rollers and followed them on a concert tour. In more recent years, Guest has used a similar technique for small-town theatrical groups in *Waiting for Guffman* and to satirize dog shows in *Best of Show*. Both of these films were much acclaimed by those who enjoyed Guest and company's particular brand of deadpan winking at inane middle-brow entertainment.

But there's a mean-spiritedness underneath the silly lightheartedness that characterizes all three of these recent Guest spoofs. Satire is a terrific way to make fun of people, institutions, and cultural icons that are self-important, take themselves too seriously, are manipulative, or prey on the hapless masses. Thus, *This Is Spinal Tap* was funny because it punctured the pretentiousness of rock stars just at the time when rock music had clearly lost its authenticity and had become pompous, repetitive, predictable, and commercialized. The objects of derision in that film were musicians short on brains and talent who had adopted the poses and practices of commercially successful bands, capitalizing on the stupidity of musical consumers who didn't know the difference between originality and fakery.

But when Guest turned that same focus on a theater troupe in small-town middle America, and then on dog breeders and fanciers, and now on folk musicians, the target of satire shifted from smug impostors deserving of ridicule to people sincerely enjoying an amusement that might seem pedestrian to others but isn't awash in hypocrisy or pretension. It's easy to make fun of small-town, no-talent theater people, or to mock those obsessed with dogs. And it's easy to make folk musicians and their outdated outfits and concepts look ridiculous 40 and 50 years later.

But was there much insincerity about the American folk music scene that grew out of Greenwich Village and the coffeehouse circuit of the late 1950s and early 1960s? Was there too much self-importance? Is there anything, really, to make fun of? *A Mighty Wind* certainly gives it a game try, but the choice of subject matter dooms the film to poking fun at trivial, forgotten, and inconsequential things. It steers clear of any big issues, not daring to satirize the attitudes and values of the folkies, but merely making fun of the way they dressed and the songs they did. And while a few of the songs

are pleasant takes on folk music styles, and a couple are funny satires of stilted folk lyrics, there aren't nearly enough of those.

Instead, most of the movie consists of put-on documentary interviews. Guest, employing his stock players, once again dares to proceed without a script, allowing his actors to concoct their own dialogue, with the kind of uneven results you would expect from such an approach. But even the movie's own style is inconsistent. Some scenes are played as mock interviews, but a lot of others are not, as if the filmmaker didn't even care enough to keep his own internal concept alive.

The thin plot, such as it is, involves the son of a legendary folk music producer (Bob Balaban) staging a reunion concert in a New York concert hall in memory of his father, who has just died. (His father seems more interesting than any of the characters that are actually in the film.) The three acts that will appear at the concert, which ends up being aired on public television, are a trio called the Folksmen (Guest, Schearer, and McKean), modeled loosely after the Kingston Trio; the New Main Street Singers, modeled obviously after the New Christy Minstrels, and Mitch and Mickey, probably modeled after the somewhat obscure Canadian folk duo Ian and Sylvia.

One of the funnier bits in the film comes as we are introduced to the Folksmen, who explain how they were downgraded by their record company to a small label that was so low-budget that the records were produced without any holes in them; consumers had to punch their own to play the albums. We later see the Folksmen struggling through a few rehearsal sessions, and there is a minor bit of tugging and pulling among them, but not too much that is laugh-provoking. Schearer plays a bald-headed baritone (though his baldness is obviously faked; you can see gray stubble all over his head) who is a little slow on the uptake; Guest is the alto who is even more lost, and McKean is the only member of the group who seems to have his head above water. But none of these characters is as funny or iconic as any of the band members of Spinal Tap; they are, in fact, lame and bland.

By contrast, Eugene Levy, who plays Mitch, is annoying and idiotic as a folk singer who fought bitterly with his former partner Mickey (Catherine O'Hara) and then descended into a lifetime of repressed anger and emotional problems. Levy, who has done better work in other movies, sports a pair of straight, thick, blackened eyebrows that look like a poor imitation of Groucho Marx, and he speaks in a halting, pinched monotone that is one of the worst attempts at expressing mental instability that I've ever seen in a movie. Levy is not merely never funny, he is constantly off-putting. It's one of the worst performances ever. That's too bad, because O'Hara gives perhaps the best performance in the film. She looks and acts the part of a woman who was once smitten with her partner and has never quite gotten over the loss of their romance, and her angst provides the film's only impact, though it's considerably deadened by the fact that she's playing opposite an automaton.

A little funnier is the duo at the heart of the New Main Street Singers, a group of younger singers who are reviving the style of their predecessors, the Main Street Singers. The group is a bunch of squeaky-clean musicians; the men wear identical blue sweater-vests and the women sit on stools and wear perky yellow-and-blue outfits, and they sing upbeat covers of other groups' material. The talented Parker Posey plays the daughter of one of the group's original members, but she is given little to do. Jane Lynch and John Michael Higgins get most of the interview time as Laurie and Terry Bohner. Lynch has a funny bit when, with her toothy smile and perky fake showbiz manner, she breezily describes a career trajectory that included a stop as a porn actress. Later, we see the husband-and-wife duo explaining their personal philosophy, which involves colors as the essence of life, and engaging in a few strange New Age-type rituals. These are amusing although they don't fit at all with the image of the band or the rest of the movie.

The early album covers and the restaged early concert clips are expertly done, and Guest and his fellow songwriters are adept at recapturing some of the more pointless folk material of the era. But when the concert is finally staged, there are only six songs performed, which would make for about a 20-minute show. By then, however, you're glad that the movie ends fairly abruptly. The funniest sequence is in the epilogue, where the New Main Street Singers manager (Fred Willard) explains the idea for a TV show called "The Supreme Folk" in which the nine band members are U.S. Supreme Court justices by day and folksingers by night. Willard does his usual wacky run-off-at-the-mouth routines, and he looks sillier than ever in big Hawaiian shirts and spiky white hair (inconsistently colored from scene to scene).

Willard is the most effective of many lesser characters in the film who provide filler to obscure the insufficiency of material to support the core concept. Others include a corporate sponsorship duo that includes Jennifer Coolidge playing an imbecile, and Ed Begley Jr. playing a Swedish TV producer who tries to court Balaban's character's favor by using a lot of Yiddish idioms. Levy, Willard, O'Hara, Balaban, and Posey were all in *Waiting for Guffman;* and they joined Coolidge, Higgins, Lynch, Begley and others in *Best of Show.* These are not untalented people, but they need more direction and focus. The dearth of material becomes painfully obvious when Guest even uses a running gag about an overactive couple in the room adjoining Mitch's motel room—not once, but twice.

A Mighty Wind has a few funny lines, and people old enough to remember the heyday of the folkies might get a kick out of seeing the groups gently spoofed. But there is no substance to the satire, and it completely lacks bite. Worst of all, it's hardly ever more than merely amusing, and it's often dreadfully unfunny. One shudders to think whom Guest and his cohorts might go after next in their quest to spoof things that don't need spoofing: Bubblegum music? Craft shows? Quilting bees?

—Michael Betzold

CREDITS

Jonathan Steinbloom: Bob Balaban
Alan Barrows: Christopher Guest
Terry Bohner: John Michael Higgins
Laurie Bohner: Jane Lynch
Mitch Cohen: Eugene Levy
Mickey Devlin Crabbe: Catherine O'Hara
Jerry Palter: Michael McKean
Sissy Knox: Parker Posey
Mark Shubb: Harry Shearer
Mike LaFontaine: Fred Willard
Lars Olfen: Ed Begley Jr.
Wally Fenton: Larry Miller
Amber Cole: Jennifer Coolidge
Lawrence F. Turpin: Michael Hitchcock

Origin: USA
Released: 2003
Production: Karen Murphy; Castle Rock Entertainment; released by Warner Bros.
Directed by: Christopher Guest
Written by: Christopher Guest, Eugene Levy
Cinematography by: Arlene Donnelly Nelson
Music by: John Michael Higgins, Eugene Levy, Catherine O'Hara, Michael McKean, Harry Shearer, Annette O'Toole, C.J. Vanston
Sound: Marc Weingarten
Editing: Robert Leighton
Art Direction: Pat Tagliaferro
Costumes: Durinda Wood
Production Design: Joseph T. Garrity
MPAA rating: PG-13
Running time: 92 minutes

REVIEWS

Chicago Sun-Times Online. April 16, 2003.
Los Angeles Times Online. April 16, 2003.
New York Times Online. March 19, 2003.
New York Times Online. April 13, 2003.
New York Times Online. April 16, 2003.
People. April 28, 2003, p. 33.
Rolling Stone. May 7, 2003, p. 63.
USA Today Online. April 16, 2003.

Vanity Fair. April, 2003, p. 162.
Variety Online. April 13, 2003.
Washington Post. April 18, 2003, p. WE34.

AWARDS AND NOMINATIONS

N.Y. Film Critics 2003: Support. Actor (Levy)
Nomination:
Oscars 2003: Song ("A Kiss at the End of the Rainbow")
Ind. Spirit 2004: Screenplay.

The Missing

How far would you go, how much would you sacrifice to get back what you have lost?
—Movie tagline

 Box Office: $26.9 million

Set in 1885 New Mexico, Ron Howard's *The Missing* unfolds in a harsh, violent world, a frontier that is dangerous and scary, and tinged with the supernatural menace of witchcraft that threatens an already fractured family. Cate Blanchett gives a fierce performance as Maggie Gilkeson, a woman trying to put her family back together after Indians kidnap her older daughter. *The Missing* is a solid if familiar piece of Western entertainment, generating the needed suspense in the rescue plot and giving us heroes to root for and a villain to fear. But the central conflict between Maggie and her estranged father, Jones (Tommy Lee Jones), does not take on the complexity that it does in Thomas Eidson's *The Last Ride* (the novel upon which the film is based), thus stripping the film of a potentially powerful subtext. The oddest and most crippling change from novel to screenplay, credited to Ken Kaufman, is the tendency to modernize the characters and their dilemmas, as if they were our contemporaries, not 19th century frontier people.

Maggie is a healer with two daughters and a ranch hand boyfriend named Brake (Aaron Eckhart). Her older daughter, Lilly (Evan Rachel Wood), is feminine and forward-looking. Defiantly wearing fancy clothes to do farm work, she would rather visit the city to get a glimpse of the future at the fair than work on the ranch. Little Dot (Jenna Boyd), on the other hand, is a spunky girl who seems at home with ranch life.

Into this household one day rides Jones, who has come back to reconnect with his daughter and try to make amends for deserting her as a little girl to live with the Indians. Blaming him for her mother's death, Maggie wants nothing to do with this man with long, braided hair and beads around his neck. His efforts at reconciliation fall on deaf ears until Lilly is kidnapped and Brake is killed by renegade Apaches. We see only the aftermath of the deserted crime scene, with Brake's body hanging in a bag made of animal skins and Dot running around frantically. Punctuated by Maggie's look of abject terror and piercing scream, it is a horrifying scene precisely because it leaves to the imagination the specifics of what happened.

Because the local sheriff and the U.S. Army are unable to help, Maggie must turn to Jones to find Lilly before the Apaches sell her, along with other female captives, into prostitution in Mexico. As many critics noted, *The Missing* strongly evokes the plot of *The Searchers,* but Howard and Kaufman's simplification of the characters leaves their film standing in the shadow of John Ford's masterpiece, whose conflicted, often unsympathetic hero is one of the genre's most memorable creations.

Kaufman's screenplay is faithful to the broad outlines of Eidson's story while departing from it in key ways, beginning with the essential family structure. In the novel, Maggie and Brake are married with two daughters and a son. They are an intact family. But in the film, Maggie and Brake are not married, sharing a bed on the sly when the girls will not notice. Maggie's past is also sketchy in the film. She was married to Dot's father but barely knew Lilly's. Maggie, then, becomes a completely contemporary character—the single mother who has had several men in her life, none of whom stayed very long (a pattern begun by her father). Perhaps the filmmakers thought that an audience could better identify with a woman whose life seems very modern, or maybe they thought they were giving Maggie a more heroic posture by turning her into a single mother raising a family on her own. But whatever the reason, the result feels awkward since her behavior would not be accepted in the 19th century. If she is going to be a feminist rebel living life on her own terms, then at least her unconventionality should be acknowledged and worked into the story.

On a visceral level, Howard expertly creates a sense of danger and menace with an especially brutal bunch of villains, led by a creature called Pesh-Chidin (Eric Schweig), a witch or *brujo,* who uses supernatural powers to kill his enemies. At its core, however, *The Missing* is a fairly conventional chase movie, with the pursuers trying to close in on the kidnappers and the audience wondering what will happen when the two parties finally meet.

Indeed, while the adventure yarn has some exciting moments, it is not especially rousing, and Kaufman's streamlining of the novel's conflicts robs the story of its richness and believability. The film makes only a bare reference to the tension in the novel between Maggie's deeply held Christian beliefs and Jones's pagan rituals. For the most part, the beliefs of father and daughter seem to be fairly compatible. In the aftermath of a failed ambush, Maggie loses a hairbrush that is retrieved by Pesh-Chidin, who uses it to put a curse on her. She grows very ill, and a combination of her father performing an Indian ritual and her daughter reading out of the Bible saves Maggie. She also wears a cross around her neck that she gives to her father before the climactic battle, as if acknowledging that their belief systems can coexist relatively comfortably. In a 19th-century context, a frontier woman accommodating such a syncretic approach to religion feels like an anachronism.

But if the film has simplified much of the conflict between Maggie and her father, Jones and Blanchett supply the subtext—we see the regret for the years that have gone by in faces that are hardened and sad. Whereas Jones maintains a laconic stance for much of the film, Blanchett expresses a swirl of emotions all shot through an unflagging determination to find her missing girl. Blanchett's unconventional beauty, somehow both hard and soft at the same time, is perfect for the role. She is the rare actress today who seems completely at home on the frontier, creating a Western heroine of enormous fortitude and resilience in the face of crisis.

Howard does not shy away from sequences that are unflinching in their violence, especially an ill-conceived attempt to buy Lilly from her captors. Jones happens to come upon an old friend, Kayitah (Jay Tavare), whose son's fiancée has also been kidnapped, and together they try to get the girls back. But the rescue effort fails, resulting in Kayitah's death and a severe beating for Jones. The next attempt, however, proves successful; Maggie and Jones free all the captives and then, pursued by the Apaches, make their way to a mountain to await a final confrontation.

In a brief respite, Maggie tries to find closure for the questions she has, but the screenplay once again departs from the richness of the novel and leaves her desire unfulfilled. Indeed, the most infuriating change from novel to film is Jones's back-story. In the novel, he reveals heartwrenching and surprising reasons for deserting his white family to be with an Apache wife. He had been this woman's husband before he knew Maggie's mother and returned to his former life because the Apaches were in trouble and needed him. The novel develops an intricate and touching web of family relationships, a beautiful vision of the ties that bind together two families. In the film, however, all Jones has to offer Maggie is that "There's always the next something" to keep a man wandering, a lame explanation that lacks the moral ambiguity of a man whose sense of duty to two families tugged at his conscience. Father and daughter may come to a mutual understanding, but it is not grounded in the novel's epiphany; he just seems like a restless guy who

shirked responsibility most of his life to find his own way in the world—yet another very modern approach to living.

In the final battle, Jones gives his life to protect his daughter when he attacks Pesh-Chidin and they both fall off the mountain together to their deaths, leaving Maggie and the girls to make the journey home. Interestingly enough, despite the film's attempt to build up Maggie's heroic stance as a single mother, it offers a more conservative view in the end, suggesting that it takes a man to protect her family and put it back together.

The Missing is an entertaining if predictable adventure elevated by the actors, particularly Blanchett, who brings many emotional shadings to her role, an especially impressive achievement given the thin script. But as well made and beautiful as the film is (thanks to the cinematography of Salvatore Totino), it could have been much more if the filmmakers had trusted the original material and not modernized the characters and their situations. If the film were a revisionist Western, this approach may have been odd yet effective. But *The Missing* is a traditional Western in every other way, thus making the changes feel like anachronisms and a concession to modern audiences unable to understand an era different from their own.

—*Peter N. Chumo II*

CREDITS

Samuel Jones: Tommy Lee Jones
Maggie Gilkeson: Cate Blanchett
Pesh-Childin: Eric Schweig
Dot Gilkeson: Jenna Boyd
Lilly Gilkeson: Evan Rachel Wood
Two Stone: Steve Reevis
Russell J. Wittick: Ray McKinnon
Lt. Jim Ducharme: Val Kilmer
Brake Baldwin: Aaron Eckhart
Honesco: Simon Baker
Kayitah: Jay Tavare
Emiliano: Sergio Calderon
Sheriff Purdy: Clint Howard
Anne: Elissabeth (Elisabeth, Elizabeth, Liz) Moss
Isaac Edgerly: Max Perlich

Origin: USA
Released: 2003
Production: Brian Grazer, Ron Howard, Daniel Ostroff; Revolution Studios, Imagine Entertainment; released by Columbia Pictures
Directed by: Ron Howard
Written by: Ken Kaufman
Cinematography by: Salvatore Totino
Music by: James Horner

Sound: Bayard Carey
Editing: Dan Hanley, Mike Hill
Art Direction: Guy Barnes
Costumes: Julie Weiss
MPAA rating: R
Running time: 135 minutes

 REVIEWS

Chicago Sun-Times Online. November 26, 2003.
Entertainment Weekly. November 28, 2003, p. 100.
Los Angeles Times Online. November 26, 2003.
New York Times Online. November 26, 2003.
People. December 8, 2003, p. 33.
USA Today Online. November 26, 2003.
Variety Online. November 17, 2003.
Washington Post. November 26, 2003, p. C1.

Mona Lisa Smile

 Box Office: $63.6 million

Katherine Watson (Julia Roberts) is a first year teacher who has graduated from Oakland State University in California and has now realized her dream of teaching at Wellesley College in New England, one of the most conservative colleges in America. While Katherine may not seem like the traditional sort of candidate who usually is accepted for employment in the prestigious women's college, she obviously makes up in brains what she lacks in credentials. It is the start of the fall term of 1953 and Katherine's more subversive frame of mind becomes evident when she says, "I didn't come to Wellesley to fit in but to make a difference." The college administration, the alumni association, and her students, however, will make this very difficult.

Katherine takes up residence in a chintz-bedecked home owned by Nancy Abbey (Marcia Gay Harden) the school's elocution and poise instructor. Also in residence is the school's more liberal-minded nurse, Amanda Armstrong (Juliet Stevenson), who warns Katherine on her first day of class, "Be careful, they can smell fear."

Katherine has reason to be fearful when she steps into her History of Art 100 class. Using the department head's syllabus, she quickly learns that her students know everything about the slides she shows them. From cave drawings through Egyptian and Minoan art they know all the names, places and dates of each work. A class that probably should have lasted an hour is over in minutes as the women indicate

that they have all read the text from cover to cover and memorized all the information. It is every teacher's dream ... as well as their nightmare. "A long way from Oakland State," they throw at their new teacher before they scornfully dismiss themselves from class leaving Katherine bewildered and more than a little mortified. It is about to get worse.

Katherine learns from the college president (Marian Seldes) that not only wasn't she the school's first choice for her position, she was their last resort. The original candidate went to Brown at the last minute and there was no one else left to fill the spot. It's almost as if she can't be humiliated any more, so why not go for broke.

And that's what she does the next day in class. Totally jettisoning the syllabus, she projects the image of a 1925 painting called "Carcass." The girls nervously shuffle through their textbooks looking for it so they'll know what to say and think, but it's not there. Katherine then asks them a question they are totally unprepared for, "Is it any good?" These women are not used to generating opinions of their own; they are experts at echoing the thoughts of others but not at thinking for themselves. The question does begin to engender a degree of tentative discussion, though, and Katherine informs her students that their new syllabus will now reflect basic questions: What is art? What makes it good or bad, and who decides?

Soon the girls' personalities begin to show. There's ultra-conservative, know-it-all Betty Warren (Kirsten Dunst), the daughter of the powerful head of the alumni association, whose acid tongue often does more harm than good. She's scheduled to be married in November and will become the bane of Katherine's more liberal ways. Joan Brandwyn (Julia Stiles) is also a traditionalist who wants to marry and have children, but she is intrigued by Katherine's new ideas. Katherine discovers her secret interest in attending law school, and her whole pre-ordained future is up for grabs when she applies to Yale and is accepted.

Giselle Levy (Maggie Gyllenhaal) is probably the most progressive and sexually active of the girls. When she reveals that Nurse Armstrong has given her an illegal diaphragm, Betty writes a scathing article about the scandal in the school newspaper causing Amanda to be fired after 20 years of working at Wellesley. Finally there is Connie Baker (Ginnifer Goodwin); a bit unsure of herself and terrified that she'll never have a boyfriend or get married, she's captivated by Katherine and her way of thinking as well as the possibilities these new ideas might open up in her life.

When Betty temporarily leaves school for her wedding and honeymoon with the prestigious Spenser Jones (Jordan Bridges)—about whose family the phrase "keeping up with the Joneses" was coined—the three remaining girls bond together behind Katherine's progressive teachings, including a viewing of a revolutionary Jackson Pollock painting. With Betty's return, however, Katherine once again feels the pressure to leave tradition undisturbed.

Wedded bliss for Betty, though, leaves something to be desired. Her husband has been made a junior partner in his firm and is often away from home. Betty suspects the trips are for more than just business, but she refuses to admit this to anyone.

In the meantime, Katherine is having romance troubles of her own. She has left her boyfriend Paul Moore (John Slattery) back in California and, in his absence, finds herself attracted to the school's Italian language teacher Bill Dunbar (Dominic West). The situation becomes especially complicated when Paul surprises her with a Christmas visit and an engagement ring she doesn't want, and when she learns that not only was Bill having an affair with her student Giselle, but he has lied to her about his background.

At the end of the spring semester Katherine's term of employment is up for review, and she and the school are faced with a quandary. For the school it is the fact that this rebel has shaken up their complacency and many want her gone, yet her classes for the coming fall semester have the highest enrollment figures in the history of the school. Katherine struggles with choosing to stay at the school of her dreams—though those dreams may be rather different from those she had initially—at the same time adhering closely to the college's rules. She begins to think of Wellesley as "a finishing school disguised as a college." "By demanding excellence I would challenge the roles you were born to fill," Katherine tells her students. Though she was beginning to believe she was making a difference in her student's lives, she soon realizes that tradition is not so easily overcome. In her frustration she lashes out, "I thought I'd be educating future leaders, not their wives." Katherine must face the question: Is it worth it?

The title *Mona Lisa Smile* stems from a scene in the film where it is indicated that the facial expression of Da Vinci's famous subject may not really reveal what is going on in her mind. "But is she really happy?" The same is being asked about these women. Could the external smiles of these tradition-bound women hide souls desperate to achieve something else in life.

Writers Lawrence Konner and Mark Rosenthal (*The Jewel of the Nile* and *Star Trek VI*) interviewed not only Wellesley alumnae who had gone on to fulfill the expected role of wife and mother but also those who had managed to achieve successful careers. Considering some of Wellesley's alumnae (Madeleine Albright, Diane Sawyer, Ali McGraw, Cokie Roberts, Madame Chiang Kai-shek, and the authors' personal inspiration, Hilary Clinton), it would seem that watching feminism bloom on this campus in particular should be quite interesting. However, a film like this also takes a risk by putting very modern young actresses into the confining roles of the 1950s. The actresses were aided in their portrayals by etiquette expert Lily Lodge, who taught them how to walk, talk, sit and act; American Ballroom Theater instructor Yvonne Marceau, who taught them to

tango, waltz, swing and rumba; and the clothing of costume designer Michael Dennison, who cinched them up in period foundation garments that made their posture appear as rigid as their minds.

Obviously it is the liberated character of Katherine that allows the actress in the role the most flexibility, and Julia Roberts does bring a high degree of intelligence and animation to this nonconformist teacher. It does, however, make one wonder about three things. Could Katherine have wooed and won the girls if she hadn't been so pretty and perky? Could even the best teacher have won converts so easily if she had been homely and boring? Secondly, it's hard to believe the intelligent Katherine wouldn't have realized how conservative a school as traditional as Wellesley would be. Is it possible that no one at Wellesley had ever challenged the status quo before California Katherine got there? Was California really so much more progressive than the East Coast that just by being born and raised there Katherine becomes endowed with her feminist outlook? Something hints that there is more to Katherine's story than is imparted in the script. Finally, the film would seem to indicate Katherine has one really cushy job because she's only shown teaching one group of students. Can she really have a class load consisting of that one class? How odd.

Thankfully star Roberts does not overshadow the splendid young actresses who support her. Kirsten Dunst's Betty is wonderfully bitchy and narrow-minded, and even though she seems to spend most of the film wanting everyone to be trapped in her same hell, redemption does seem within the realm of possibility for her. Julia Stiles does a pitch perfect upper-class voice and convincingly plays a woman of the period who, although she might be tempted by alternatives, makes marriage a valid choice because it is just that—a choice.

Of special interest, though, is Marcia Gay Harden's Nancy Abbey. She may seem like nothing more than a peripheral character, but if one really examines her role, it is the perfect example of what can happen to Wellesley girls when the dreams don't turn out as the fairytales—and their mothers—tell them. Her dream of being wedded happily ever after has been trashed and now she leads a shell of a life that revolves around her favorite television programs. If they look closely, the girls of Wellesley may have more to learn from Nancy than table settings and what dinners to serve their husbands' bosses.

The lush sets, especially that of the college campus itself, become another important "character" in the film. Wellesley College looks like a picture postcard for everyone's dream of what a college campus should be, and the school was wisely very welcoming to the filmmakers. They opened up their campus and their archives in an attempt not only to give the movie authenticity but also to help show that the Wellesley of yesterday is not exactly the Wellesley of today.

A perfect example of this is the hoop rolling race recreated in the film. It used to be said that the winner of this race would be the first girl to marry. In the 1980s it was changed to indicate who would become the first CEO of a major corporation. Today it is simply supposed to show who will be the first to realize her dreams.

Director Mike Newell has proved himself to be not only a versatile director (*Donnie Brasco* to *Enchanted April*), but one who can easily handle ensemble casts performing in intelligently crafted stories (*Four Weddings and a Funeral*). He brings these sensitivities to bear on *Mona Lisa Smile* and helps to raise it above the bland but sanctimonious piece of historical fiction it could have been.

Mona Lisa Smile does belong in the "inspiring teacher" film genre that includes such movies as *Dead Poets' Society*, *The Prime of Miss Jean Brody*, and even *Dangerous Minds*. The formula seems to be that teachers challenge tradition, get into trouble with the establishment in some way, but have their students rally behind them in the end, so, in that respect, *Mona Lisa Smile* is a bit predictable. Just as Katherine undertakes a paint-by-numbers version of Van Gogh's *Sunflowers* and asks, "Is it art?" so, too, have the filmmakers undertaken a paint-by-numbers story that, while not high art, is entertaining nonetheless.

—*Beverley Bare Buehrer*

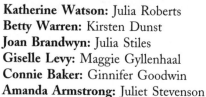

CREDITS

Katherine Watson: Julia Roberts
Betty Warren: Kirsten Dunst
Joan Brandwyn: Julia Stiles
Giselle Levy: Maggie Gyllenhaal
Connie Baker: Ginnifer Goodwin
Amanda Armstrong: Juliet Stevenson
Bill Dunbar: Dominic West
Tommy Donegal: Topher Grace
Paul Moore: John Slattery
Nancy Abbey: Marcia Gay Harden
Spencer Jones: Jordan Bridges
President Jocelyn Carr: Marian Seldes
Mrs. Rigby: Donna Mitchell
Dr. Edward Staunton: Terence Rigby

Origin: USA
Released: 2003
Production: Elaine Goldsmith-Thomas, Deborah Schindler, Paul Schiff; Revolution Studios, Red Om Films; released by Columbia Pictures
Directed by: Mike Newell
Written by: Larry Konner, Mark Rosenthal
Cinematography by: Anastas Michos
Music by: Rachel Portman

Sound: T.J. O'Mara
Music Supervisor: Randall Poster
Editing: Mick Audsley
Art Direction: Patricia Woodbridge
Costumes: Michael Dennison
Production Design: Jane Musky
MPAA rating: PG-13
Running time: 117 minutes

REVIEWS

Chicago Sun-Times Online. December 19, 2003.
Entertainment Weekly. December 19, 2003, p. 53.
Los Angeles Times Online. December 19, 2003.
New York Times Online. December 19, 2003.
People. December 22, 2003, p. 28.
USA Today Online. December 19, 2003.
Variety Online. December 10, 2003.
Washington Post. December 19, 2003, p. C1.

QUOTES

Katherine (Julia Roberts): "It's brilliant really, when you think about it, a finishing school disguised as a college."

AWARDS AND NOMINATIONS

Nomination:
Golden Globes 2004: Song ("The Heart of Every Girl").

Mondays in the Sun (Los Lunes al Sol)

This film is not based on a real story. It is based on thousands.
—Movie tagline

Fernando Leon de Aranoa's unassuming comedy-drama from Spain, *Mondays in the Sun*, packs a revolutionary wallop beneath its flow-of-life exterior. While it sides with the underprivileged, it admits they are no match for the faceless corporate elite who are pulling the strings. Corporate villainy, in the film's non-Marxist scheme of things, can only be opposed by the power of one.

That one is Santa (Javier Bardem), whose thin beard and rugged physique are deployed to mask the humiliation of his plight at having been recently laid off. In his first scene, he walks onto the deck of a ferry boat with no ticket, as if it were his God-given right. He greets the middle-aged, stocky Lino (Jose Angel Egido), who is on his way to one more hopeless job interview. Also providing Lino moral support is the equally thin-bearded Jose (Luis Tosar) who, unlike Santa, is thin, and lacking the laid-back sensibility of his cohorts.

The opening credits continue over a vista of the ferry boat in the light of early morning, with an unidentified town on a hill in the background. A tuneful, lyrical harmonica subsumes any dreariness we could have imagined in the life of our protagonists.

After a brief shot of Lino waiting within an office hall, the film cuts to its true center of gravity, a small bar known as "The Shipyard," which is a hangout for unemployed and partially employed former shipyard workers. Here we see that Santa, Jose and Lino are like dinosaurs, relics of a bygone age, put out to pasture by the company that would rather close down its yard and open one in Korea than meet their demands. The lackluster bar itself is owned and run by Rico (Joaquin Climent), a kindly soul, who has set it up with his severance pay. His congenial teenage daughter, Nata (Aida Folch) works there part-time as a waitress while nursing a crush on Santa. Other regulars include Reina (Enrique Villen) who has found work as a security guard at a sports stadium, Amador (Celso Bugallo), a neurasthenic alcoholic, and the out-of-place Sergei (Serge Riaboukine), who was in training in the Soviet cosmonaut program.

What strikes us about this lot is the blow that they are suffering, not to their standard of living so much, as to their male pride. Santa demonstrates that unemployment, meted out by corporate giants, doesn't have to dampen male machismo. He thus functions as the morale booster of the group. Enjoying the sunlight, on a Monday morning, sprawled at the tip of a pier, Santa tries to make Lino see the possibility of starting life afresh in the boonies of Australia, with free land and a dream. Thanks to Rico, the drinks go on account, while Reina gets them into the soccer matches for free, even if it is from the stadium roof, with only a partial view.

As a counterpoint to this carefree male romping, the film shows us Ana (Nieve de Medina), Jose's attractive but overworked wife, who sometimes has to take on a double shift, packing cans of tuna on an assembly line. She returns home to spray her body free of the smell of fish; Jose, however, lovingly embraces her, calling her a mermaid. Similarly, being out of work doesn't prevent Santa from having a sexual fling with Monica (Monica Garcia), a young mother, whom we see only once.

What upsets this equilibrium is the legal notice Santa receives. At the hearing, we learn that Santa has been fined 8,000 pesetas for breaking a streetlight during the labor demonstration we see as part of the film's prologue. His lawyer (Andres Lima) accepts the penalty. In the hallway outside the courtroom, Santa barks at him, "How can I pay? I'm laid off!" The Lawyer tells him he has no choice. For Santa, it is a double whammy. The streetlight is owned by the company that has laid him off, and manufactured by another large company, which has chosen to determine its worth. "For me, it's like having to pay 100 million," he says, then adds, "morally speaking."

As it happens, Santa swallows his pride, along with his conscience, and sets about earning the amount. The film shows us only flashes of these instances, leaving it to us to assume a deeper truth. What is preventing Santa from making something out of his life is not a lack of intelligence or diligence, but his indignation at the injustice that surrounds him. Nata comes to his rescue when she lets him have her babysitting assignment, after taking her commission. The next thing we see is Santa, Lino, Jose and Sergei having drinks on the patio of a house owned by a shoe manufacturer, while his little boy is watching TV inside. In an amusing scene, Santa reads the bedtime story "The Ant and the Grasshopper" to the kid. He then curses the moral, which is that the Ant worked hard and the Grasshopper didn't. "Some are born grasshoppers!" he rants at the kid.

A subplot shows Santa's rebellious stance towards authority infecting Jose. The latter steals a pair of dress shoes for Ana from the shoe magnate's house. The next morning, when he accompanies Ana to a bank in order to secure a loan, he overreacts to being made to feel useless because he's temporarily unemployed. Though the loan is taken up for consideration, he rips the application from out of the "Out" tray and storms out. On the street, Ana can only lament that, though she loves him, she has nothing, "no house, no kids".

Aranoa, as writer-director, makes us feel how difficult it is for these Mediterranean males to sacrifice their dignity for the sake of finding work. Lino, for example, sheepishly buys a hair dye for women, then applies it in the bathroom before an interview; not that that helps. In comparison, Santa has confidence to spare. At the end of a night at the bar, he helps Amador home and tucks him into bed. That is when he discovers that his friend has been living without running water, and that his kitchen is a filthy mess. Santa opens the fridge to find it empty. Similarly, Jose, by himself at home, looks at photographs of himself and Ana taken in happier times. He then looks out the window to see Ana being dropped home from work, and notices how her male colleague squeezes her hand. When Ana herself keeps this a secret from him, it causes Jose no end of consternation.

After stints of distributing fliers, Santa is able to collect only half the amount needed to pay the fine. At the bar, he decides he will face prison rather than pay. Reina then offers to pay the other half. Before the occasion, Santa gathers himself in front of a bathroom mirror. Then, in a close-up, we see eight large currency notes handed over. His lawyer then gives him a lift in his car. "These things make you more mature," the lawyer says. Santa asks him to stop, then gets down, and picks up a small rock. After making sure no one is looking, he hurls it like a missile at a streetlight, splintering it into fragments, as the Lawyer looks on, shocked.

At the bar that night, Santa voices his working class anger against the system. "The Koreans build ships cheaper than us!" he begins. "They're going to tear down the ship-yards and build luxury apartments. Let the Koreans come and live there!" Santa's real grouse is how the bosses drive a wedge between workers by laying off some and getting others to sign a contract. "That's how we got screwed!" Santa curses. "You signed away your kids!" Santa rails at Lino and Reina. They in turn accuse him of doing nothing.

Even so, Santa isn't just the moral center of his group; he is their therapist as well, a position he takes on with responsibility. When Jose comes to him with his suspicions about Ana, Santa tells him it's natural for a woman who's "a looker" to attract overtures from men. Jose's real fear is that Ana might leave him. Santa thus provides him moral support to confront her. It is precisely this side of Santa's character that receives a shattering jolt when he discovers that Amador has committed suicide by jumping off his balcony. Santa looks up at the lifeless body over the building entrance in the dead of night, and his face contorts with grief.

The others are forced to get on with their lives, but a change overcomes them. As Lino sits waiting for yet another interview, his name is called out repeatedly, but this time he doesn't get up, scoring his own private victory of sorts. But it is left to Santa to strike back in a spectacular way. He takes his cohorts onto the ferry in the middle of the night. After breaking a lock, he makes his way to the bridge. He then hotwires the engine as they pull anchor. Silently, the boat sets sail with the nightscape of the city as a backdrop. Santa wants to scatter Amador's ashes over the water, but no one knows what has happened to the urn. Instead of feeling sad, they all laugh.

Then, in the early morning light, we see a crowd of commuters stuck on the pier, while the ferry boat is stock-still in the middle of its route. As Jose stirs awake on deck, Santa says to him, "What day is it?" Before Jose can answer, the film abruptly cuts to the end credits.

If A. O. Scott's review in *The New York Times* is any indication, critics cannot but feel the impact of Bardem's performance. While reviewing the film at the time of its being showcased as part of the Museum of Modern Art's annual *New Directors New Films*, Scott calls Bardem's screen presence "galvanic." "With his heavy brow and dented nose," Scott notes, "he moves with a heavy, taurine grace that recalls Anthony Quinn in his prime." While finding the

film "meandering and anecdotal", and even "slow" at times, Scott admits "that (it) examines, with pessimism and compassion, the present condition of the continent's working class."

—Vivek Adarkar

CREDITS

Santa: Javier Bardem
Jose: Luis Tosar
Lino: Jose Angel Egido
Rico: Joaquin Climent
Ana: Nieve De Medina
Reina: Enrique Villen
Amador: Celso Bugallo

Origin: Spain
Language: Spanish
Released: 2002
Production: Elias Querejeta; MediaPro; released by Lions Gate Films
Directed by: Fernando Leon de Aranoa
Written by: Fernando Leon de Aranoa, Ignacio del Moral
Cinematography by: Alfredo Mayo
Music by: Lucio Godoy
Sound: Pierre Lorrain
Editing: Nacho Ruiz Capillas
Art Direction: Julio Esteban
MPAA rating: R
Running time: 113 minutes

REVIEWS

Boxoffice. April, 2003, p. 80.
Chicago Sun-Times Online. August 8, 2003.
Entertainment Weekly. August 15, 2003, p. 54.
Los Angeles Times Online. July 25, 2003.
New York Times Online. March 27, 2003.
Variety Online. October 1, 2002.
Washington Post. August 15, 2003, p. WE34.

AWARDS AND NOMINATIONS

Nomination:
Oscars 2002: Foreign Film.

Monsieur Ibrahim (Monsieur Ibrahim and the Flowers of the Koran) (Monsieur Ibrahim et les Fleurs du Coran)

Francois Dupeyron's quasi-religious nostalgic coming-of-age story from France, *Monsieur Ibrahim*, does not suffer for its lofty ideological aspirations. Set in an ethnic neighborhood of Paris, presumably in the late '70's, the film's antinomy revolves around the nondescript Jewish teenage Momo (Pierre Boulanger), who lives with his Father (Gilbert Melki), a weary bureaucrat-cum-book collector, above a street ruled by streetwalkers and other lowlife, whom Momo admires for their worldliness. In the musty world of his apartment, Momo cannot even let in the sunlight for fear that it might damage the bindings of the books. Just across the street is the grocery run by the eponymous Ibrahim (Omar Sharif), "the neighborhood Arab", which is generic for any Middle Easterner who keeps his store open from 8 am to midnight, even on Sundays.

Given such interesting plot elements, one would expect Dupeyron to spin a fable revealing the quirky universality of characters living under such heterogeneous pressures. Instead, his film seems to revel in its slice-of-life ordinariness, dabbing its sentimentality with American pop standards on the soundtrack. Within this mosaic of the commonplace, Omar Sharif's extraordinary, though abbreviated, performance provides the sole redeeming narrative element.

Cesare Zavattini, one of the architects of Italian neorealism in the early 50s, argued that if story films could only shed their contrivance, they might be able to bring to light the social problems besetting any human society. Zavattini's ideal film, which he never got to make, was ninety minutes in the life of a man during which "nothing happens." Dupeyron is nowhere as bold to attempt such a task; Sharif's performance, on the other hand, seems up to the challenge. While Dupeyron remains content to tag on banal lyrics set to a reggae beat ("Why can't we all get along?") in order to drive home the point of his tale, Sharif, through his non-verbal responses during those few moments when "nothing happens," makes that point far better, with the result that the events that do "happen" in the film appear far too trite to hold our attention.

What makes Ibrahim's words and actions memorable is that they embody an antinomy of their own: he is an orthodox Muslim ("Everything I know, I know through the Koran!") and at the same time, a Sufi mystic ("No book can reveal what God can!") As Momo comes under his sway, their relationship resembles that in Gus Van Sant's *Finding Forrester* and Michael Cuesta's *L. I. E.* Whereas the former tried to span boundaries dictated by race and cultural upbringing and the latter took the side of overthrowing libidinal norms, what Ibrahim has to teach Momo is mostly religious. In fact, the film's French subtitle reads *The Fruits of the Koran*. Interestingly, what Momo shares in common with his transatlantic cousins in the two films cited is the fact that the elderly male who takes the youth under his tutelage becomes a substitute father. When Momo looks up Sufism in the dictionary, he finds it defined as a revolt against legalism. After realizing how his father embodies the latter, Momo opts for the former.

It is through his home-cum-street life that we're introduced to Momo. After enviously watching the streetwalkers ply their trade, his hormones racing, Momo breaks open his piggy bank and decides to leap into the fray himself. After being turned down repeatedly for being too young, even though he is 16, Momo eventually finds the prettiest of the lot, the voluptuous blonde Sylvie (Anne Suarez), taking him on. If there's a lesson in that, Momo is too excited to grasp it. Sylvie on her part does all she can to make what he says is his first time memorable. Momo is also drawn to the perky Myriam (Lola Naynmark), who is his own age, and who lives on the floor below. She is always practicing popular dance steps, which also excites Momo. The only time that Momo's father has for him he uses to bark at Momo for lapses in his shopping, cooking and keeping of accounts.

It is against this background that Momo comes to know Ibrahim who, in his late middle-age, resigned and unshaven the first time we see him, looks no different from any irate immigrant shopkeeper. For Momo, Ibrahim's store serves as his one-stop shop. What's not made clear is what Ibrahim sees in Momo, which leads the circumspect Muslim to shed his archetypal mask and reveal the individual within.

We soon learn Ibrahim is not an Arab at all but a Turk, and a lonely widower. Not only does he read the Koran in each spare moment, but he also practices the generosity prescribed therein. When Momo shoplifts, Ibrahim piles on more goodies so that Momo can keep his father happy. However, it is the nuggets of wisdom related to daily living ("Slowness is the key to happiness!") that prove his real gift. When Momo feels heartbroken over Myriam, it is Ibrahim who sees him through this rite of passage by reminding him that she can only reject his love, "not destroy it." Ibrahim goes on, "What we give remains ours; what we keep is lost forever!"

What shakes Momo, and the film, out of its doldrums is when Momo's father gets fired. Soon after, he vanishes, leaving behind some money and a note. Momo then is free to get himself adopted by Ibrahim. Their relationship, however, doesn't change in any dramatic way. When Momo learns that his father has committed suicide by jumping in front of a train in Marseilles, he is despondent, but only for a day. When his mother (Isabelle Renauld), who has never seen him as a boy, comes calling, Momo says he's someone else.

The film's final section binds Ibrahim and Momo together in a father-son relationship that now becomes more symbiotic than ever. Ibrahim decides to buy a car even though he doesn't know how to drive. At the showroom, the two choose a flashy red convertible. When the question of a driving license comes up, Ibrahim shows the salesman a letter written in Arabic. At first, Ibrahim is told he cannot pay for the car in cash and that delivery will take two weeks. "I will be dead in two weeks!" he roars. The salesman agrees to have the vehicle delivered the next day. Outside the store, Ibrahim lets Momo in on his secret: the letter he showed was a fake. The two chuckle in complicity.

Momo, however, still has to teach Ibrahim how to drive, a feat accomplished with the aid of a book. "It makes my brain shrink!" Ibrahim complains. With Momo's help, rendered through a code of coughs, Ibrahim tackles the driving test, which he passes, in the words of the examiner, "just about." With all the red tape behind them, the real reason for Ibrahim's lavish purchase becomes clear. He wants to drive Momo to his hometown in Turkey.

Motoring through Switzerland, Ibrahim points out that the one indication of a rich country is "more rubbish." Albania, with its poverty, proves just the opposite. When the two get to Istanbul, it is as if they have reached the most sacred spot on earth. We first see a vista of the city from the deck of a ferry, after which Ibrahim leads Momo, blindfolded, into an Orthodox Christian shrine, so that he can smell the incense more acutely and behold the grandeur that rises above religious barriers. The two then visit a mosque, where Ibrahim kneels down to pray in the traditional manner.

It is only when they enter a Sufi monastery that the underpinnings of religion take on a practicality. As they watch the dervishes, dressed in immaculate white, spinning while they dance, Ibrahim points out: "They spin so as to be released from the burden of balance!" We can see from Ibrahim's envious expression that it is a level of spirituality he feels he will never be able to attain.

The next day, before they get to his village on the other side of a hill, Ibrahim tells Momo to wait by the road. He will need to proceed alone in order to get his bearings, since so much will have changed since he saw the place last. Alone, Momo befriends an urchin. Inspired by Ibrahim's generosity, Momo gives him his camera. Soon a man on a motorcycle comes to fetch Momo. On their way to Ibrahim's house, they whizz past the overturned red convertible burn-

ing by the side of the road. The motorcyclist stops in front of a modest single-story dwelling in the village. Momo rushes in to find Ibrahim lying prostrate on a mattress. "The journey ends here!" he says to Momo. "I have arrived. All rivers flow into the same sea." With that, a crying Momo watches Ibrahim breathe his last.

In the next scene, Ibrahim's will is read out to Momo, who learns that he has been left all the deceased's "material possessions." There is also a letter, which ends with the admonition: "All there is to know is in the Koran."

In a brief epilogue of sorts, we see Momo as he looks today, a content, mature thirty-something, now himself "the neighborhood Arab."

Critics here have lavished praise on Sharif's performance and noted the film's timely message. A.O. Scott in *The New York Times* calls the story "a parable of tolerance and understanding." Kevin Thomas in *Los Angeles Times* describes Dupeyron's effort as "heartfelt" and its idealism as "fervent but not preachy spirituality." For Thomas, the film expresses "an ecumenical spirit in a most understated way at a time when such a sentiment could scarcely be more welcome." 🎞

—Vivek Adarkar

CREDITS

Ibrahim: Omar Sharif
Momo: Pierre Boulanger
Momo's father: Gilbert Melki
Myriam: Lola Naymark
Sylvie: Anne Suarez
Momo's mother: Isabelle Renauld
The Star: Isabelle Adjani

Origin: France
Language: French
Released: 2003
Production: Laurent Petin; ARP, France 3 Cinema, Canal Plus; released by Sony Pictures Classics
Directed by: Francois Dupeyron
Written by: Francois Dupeyron
Cinematography by: Remy Chevrin
Sound: Francois Maurel
Editing: Dominique Faysse
Costumes: Catherine Bouchard
Production Design: Katia Wyszkop
MPAA rating: R
Running time: 94 minutes

REVIEWS

Box Office Magazine. Nov. 2003, p. 96.
Entertainment Weekly. Dec. 12, 2003, p. 58.
L.A. Times Online. Dec. 5, 2003.
New York Times Online. Dec. 5, 2003.
USA Today. Feb. 13, 2004, p. 17D.
Variety Online. Sept. 3, 2003.

Monster

Charlize Theron's performance in *Monster* goes so far beyond what is normally considered superb acting that it seems to defy categorization. It is one of the rare instances in cinema in which actor and role meld into a third thing, an entity unto itself that is greater than either. Theron received nearly unanimous praise for her uncanny transformation into real-life prostitute and serial killer Aileen Wuornos, who was executed by the state of Florida in 2002 after 12 years on Death Row. Part of the widespread acclaim is attributable to the sheer unexpectedness of her utter transformation: one of the most stunningly gorgeous actresses today gaining 30 pounds, wearing false teeth, and donning makeup that renders her totally unlike her normally beautiful self. Moreover, while Theron has been in a number of successful films, she has played ancillary roles like the supportive girlfriend or wife. Very few people would have expected the former model from South Africa to turn in a fully realized performance—a ferocious, go-for-broke portrayal that will forever change the way she is perceived. But then again, maybe that is because she had never been given such an opportunity until first-time writer-director Patty Jenkins chose her to play Aileen.

Aileen Wuornos lived a horrific childhood. Raped at the age of eight, giving up a child for adoption at 13, and hooking as a teenager, she reveals herself, in her opening voiceover, as a girl who once had big dreams of being discovered for the movies. As an adult, she keeps dreaming of a better life, a hope constantly at odds with her reality as a roadside prostitute who risks her life every time she hops into a stranger's car.

At an especially low point, her life changes for the better when she enters a gay bar for a drink and meets a woman named Selby (Christina Ricci), who is hungering for companionship. Although Aileen says she is not a lesbian, the women take an instant liking to each other, and Selby lets her new friend spend the night. Selby is living with family friends because she kissed a girl back home, and her parents think that time away will cure her lesbian tendencies. Aileen is smitten with Selby because she is an oasis in a very troubled life. After all, here is a woman who takes a genuine interest in her as a person, not a commodity. In the film's one moment of unmitigated happiness, the pair go roller skating together and fall for each other as Journey's "Don't Stop Believin'" plays in the background. Aileen loves the song, which could be her personal anthem since it expresses the unflagging optimism to which this poor, abused, uneducated castoff tries to cling.

An act of self-defense triggers Aileen's killing spree when she is tied up and brutally beaten, raped, and tortured by one of her johns (Lee Tergesen). Finally freeing herself, she repeatedly shoots her assailant and lets out a scream that is chilling, as if she has been liberated and were purging all of her pent-up rage in one definitive act.

Motivated by her love for Selby, Aileen persuades her new friend to run away with her by promising good times she has no way of delivering. It is Aileen's defining characteristic that, no matter how awful her life, she tries to believe in herself and stay optimistic. The two live a day-to-day existence on the road, never seriously considering what kind of future they could possibly have together.

Aileen also believes in love, perhaps naïvely so, since Selby is hardly worth the effort. She is petulant, needy, and demanding, and expects her new girlfriend to support them, even if it means telling her to go back to hooking when a brief foray into the straight world fails miserably. (Despite wanting for a legitimate job, Aileen has no clue how to present herself in an interview and, even if she did, has no real work experience.) Selby is a user, but, since Aileen is used to abuse rather than affection, she sees only the positive in this girl who seems to love her.

Ricci's performance poses a dilemma: it is very flat and one-dimensional, and she employs a limited repertoire of reactions in scene after scene. But this may be just the note Ricci was aiming for to show that Selby is shallow, selfish, and confused, and Aileen, who is thankful to have someone who wants her, is willing to kill her johns and steal from them to keep the relationship going. The paradox is that, while Selby appears to be the more stable of the two, she is actually void of humanity, while Aileen, who grows more unhinged as the body count grows, never loses her vitality and passion.

The script does not offer pat explanations for Aileen's transformation into a serial killer, although the rape and her ultimate devotion to Selby certainly play a big part in bending her mind to murder. Given Aileen's upbringing and the kind of life she has led, however, it is more shocking that she made it as long as she did before she cracked. And yet Aileen still surprises us. Stunned to meet a timid, stuttering fellow (Pruitt Taylor Vince) who has never had sex before and does not want to get rough with her, Aileen is taken aback, sparing his life and demonstrating her humanity, which, it seems, can emerge even in the most sordid of encounters.

Theron's performance is not the result of amazing makeup, incredible as that may be (thanks to Toni G), but is rather a complete portrayal that nails every physical and emotional detail. Even the way she ravenously stuffs a sandwich into her mouth, for example, is evocative of a woman living an animal-like existence for survival. From the way Aileen walks with a forced bravado—her gait is somehow ungainly and yet swaggering at the same time—to the way she flicks a cigarette lighter in a grand gesture to impress Selby, she is always trying to pump herself up emotionally. A simple act like brushing her hair with great care (as if she were going to a lavish party) and then staring at her reflection and telling herself how good she looks suggests this damaged woman is desperately holding on to some shred of dignity.

And no character in recent memory goes through such an array of emotions. From rage to fear to hope, Aileen is a mass of conflicted impulses, and Theron is a marvel showing all of them, sometimes in the blink of an eye. In one mesmerizing speech, an increasingly deranged Aileen justifies the killings to Selby, who is in denial about what is happening. "People kill each other every day," Aileen exclaims, her eyes bulging as if the need to explain the horrors of the world were suffocating her. But an instant later, seeing that her hold on Selby is slipping, a forlorn Aileen is pleading with her to stay and trying to convince both of them that a better future is still possible.

While the portrait of Aileen is very sympathetic, the film does not shy away from the damage she inflicted. Her last victim (Scott Wilson) only wants to help her—he does not even want sex—but the murders have gone on for so long that she cannot let a witness live. This final killing reminds us that her victims had families and that no matter how much empathy we may develop for Aileen and how scummy most of her johns are, the choices she made had far-reaching consequences.

Before law enforcement's net closes in on Aileen, her only true friend, a damaged veteran, Tom (Bruce Dern), senses that the police are near—he has seen the news reports of the killings on TV—and he offers her a chance to run off with him. Only moments after she turns him down, she is arrested, and Selby testifies against her in court, which sends Aileen into a rage before the film's final fadeout. To be betrayed by the one person she truly loved is finally too much for her. Selby, Aileen finally sees, is no better than everyone else who took advantage of her.

The film's title most obviously refers to Aileen's public image as an inhuman killer demonized by the media, but, because she is so human, the title could also be taken ironically. If she is a monster, the question becomes who created her, and the answer lies in her pitiless environment that offered nothing but degradation from an early age. Like Frankenstein's monster, she has been abandoned in her childhood and only wants someone to love. But the screenplay directly addresses the title in yet another way. In one of her voiceovers, Aileen tells a story from her childhood about a Ferris wheel called the Monster, which she looked forward to with great anticipation but which made her nauseous when she finally rode it. The title, then, could be a metaphor for her life—at first full of hope and expectation but ultimately making her sick—rather than a description of the woman herself.

It is a tribute to Aileen's spirit that right until the end, she never gives up hope. There is a sense of optimism behind everything she does, which is finally what makes her life all the more tragic. If she were a nihilist who killed for kicks, we would only be repulsed, but she has faith too long in platitudes like "All you need is love and to believe in yourself" only to discover that they are not enough. They are the essence of the American Dream, but, for a dreamer without resources, talent, or someone to love, they are ultimately meaningless.

—Peter N. Chumo II

CREDITS

Aileen Wuornos: Charlize Theron
Selby Wall: Christina Ricci
Thomas: Bruce Dern
Horton: Scott Wilson
Gene: Pruitt Taylor Vince
Vincent Corey: Lee Tergesen
Donna Tentler: Annie Corley

Origin: USA
Released: 2003
Production: Mark Damon, Clark Peterson, Donald Kushner, Brad Wyman, Charlize Theron; Media 8 Entertainment, DEJ Productions, K/W Productions, Denver & Delilah Films; released by Newmarket Films
Directed by: Patty Jenkins
Written by: Patty Jenkins
Cinematography by: Steven Bernstein
Music by: BT (Brian Transeau)
Sound: Peter J. Devlin
Music Supervisor: Howard Paar
Editing: Arthur Coburn, Jane Kurson
Art Direction: Orvis Rigsby
Costumes: Rhona Meyers
Production Design: Edward T. McAvoy
MPAA rating: R
Running time: 111 minutes

REVIEWS

Chicago Sun-Times Online. January 9, 2004.
Entertainment Weekly. January 9, 2004, p. 62.

Los Angeles Times Online. December 26, 2003.
New York Times Online. December 24, 2003.
People. January 19, 2004, p. 29.
Variety Online. November 17, 2003.
Washington Post. January 9, 2004, p. WE37.

AWARDS AND NOMINATIONS

Oscars 2003: Actress (Theron)
Golden Globes 2004: Actress—Drama (Theron)
Ind. Spirit 2004: Actress (Theron), First Feature
Natl. Soc. Film Critics 2003: Actress (Theron)
Screen Actors Guild 2003: Actress (Theron)
Nomination:
Oscars 2003: Actress (Theron)
Ind. Spirit 2004: First Screenplay.

My Boss's Daughter

He's in love. She's off limits.
—Movie tagline
There are some things you just don't do.
—Movie tagline

 Box Office: $15.5 million

About forty years ago, the tremendously able British actor Terence Stamp earned an Oscar nomination for his screen debut in *Billy Bud* (1962), followed soon after by his acclaimed and riveting performance in *The Collector* (1965). Flash forward to today, when we find him in the negligible misfire entitled *My Boss's Daughter,* suffering the indignity of bending over and having his bare behind scrutinized by a roomful of people for evidence of rump rash. The obnoxious, unfunny scene brings a question immediately to mind: Could this be, in more ways than one, the end of Terence Stamp? His career certainly seems to have hit rock bottom with a role in which he initially shines, then disappears for about a half hour, reappearing in time to flatline along with everything else around him thanks to increasingly weak material. In the forefront of this supposed romantic comedy which features few laughs and little sexual chemistry is Ashton Kutcher, best known for his goofy but lovable character on Fox TV's *That 70's Show* until he received even greater recognition for squiring around actress Demi Moore, sixteen years his senior. Here he plays Tom Stansfield, who is employed as a lowly researcher at a big Chicago publishing firm and who wonders if his full creative potential will ever be recognized by his intimidating boss, Jack Taylor (Stamp). Tom asserts in an initial voiceover that he feels wonderful things are about to happen, but most of what soon transpires is pleasing to neither Tom nor the audience. On the way to work, after finding a lost briefcase on the subway, Tom is mortified when it falls open revealing a stash of gay porn just as he dares to go and sit next to his boss's fetching daughter Lisa (limited actress Tara Reid of the *American Pie* films). Once at the office, he is summoned to Jack's office for what he anxiously hopes will be his big break, only to find that his boss is perplexed and perturbed by some information about the young man passed along by a just-fired fellow employee (Dave Foley, formerly of NBC's *NewsRadio*). After Tom tastes the revolting coffee made by Jack's secretary, Audrey (Molly Shannon, former cast member of NBC's *Saturday Night Live*), Jack cruelly inquires whether her ineptitude stems from some form of retardation and fires her, asserting that a squirming Tom had endorsed his decision. This scene elicits some chuckles thanks to Stamp's scowling intensity as he delivers his lines, but Kutcher and Shannon are barely perceptible presences.

Soon Tom is asked to the Taylor family mansion by the lovely Lisa. He thinks he is invited to a party, but it turns out he is to house-sit while she cavorts elsewhere with her boyfriend. When Tom arrives at the home, blissfully unaware and full of anticipation, he is quickly deflated by Jack, who takes the unwitting house sitter on a tour of an abode that is kept obsessively immaculate. Jack even makes Tom don sterile surgical booties before proceeding to show off all sorts of things which will make suitably loud crashing, crunching, and ripping noises when they are destroyed later on. Then there is Jack's cherished pet owl O. J., bizarrely pampered with its own room and in need of two pills a day—one orally and one rectally. With an ominous threat to guard everything with his life, Jack walks out, thus setting the stage for mayhem. He stipulates that there are to be no guests whatsoever, but where would the comedy be in that? First to show up is black sheep son, Red (Andy Richter, former sidekick on NBC's *Late Night with Conan O'Brien*), who immediately involves an unsuspecting Tom in drug trafficking shenanigans. Soon an unhappy Audrey arrives hoping to get her job back, spitting an unwanted licorice into an antique bowl before making herself at home in the kitchen. She brings her violent, foulmouthed, belching, beer-swilling, Jew-hating boor of a boyfriend, to boot. (Speaking of boots, need we add that the ones he is wearing leave big black footprints all over Jack's pristine carpets?) A dangerous, shady figure named T. J. (Michael Madsen of 2002's *Die Another Day*) arrives for the drugs. A group of Audrey's peculiar friends appear out of thin air, one of which is played (and we mean that in the loosest way possible) by voluptuous Carmen Electra (2000's *Scary Movie*). To no one's surprise, her T-shirt is soon made all clingy and see-through by a tumble into a fountain in a lingering shot perhaps best described as "udderly" gratuitous.

By this time, a lot of complications have been added to the mix, but it is a lot of effort with virtually no comedic payoff. O. J. eventually flies the coup (full of cocaine, no less), and who can blame him for wanting to escape it all? Throughout all the commotion, Kutcher reacts to everything going to pieces (both figuratively and literally) by looking aghast, wriggling suggestively when O. J.'s dinner mice get loose and crawl into his pants, careening to and fro, and periodically taking a dive over various objects. This physical comedy might have worked if it were part of proceedings that were truly humorous. (When Tom asks "Could I make a bigger ass out of myself?" we have to bite our tongues.) Just to torture him some more, Lisa arrives home fresh from a fight with Hans (Kenan Thompson of 2002's *The Master of Disguise*) and proceeds to do a sort of striptease in front of him because she thinks he is gay and therefore harmless. She is absolutely horrified to learn that she just acted suggestively in front of a heterosexual male, and says that she thought he was gay because her father told her so. It is a head-scratching moment, since we remember the earlier scene in which it is she who gets the wrong idea about Tom thanks to the "reading" material in the briefcase he was carrying. Perhaps even the filmmakers could not bear to go back and see what had gone before.

While it might seem impossible for a film that never really takes off to take a nosedive, *My Boss's Daughter* does so anyway with an increasing reliance on unfunny attempts at the exceedingly broad, gross, and offensive. A distraught Hans arrives and proceeds to hang himself. A shriveled old codger with his young, voluptuous, dumb-blond wife exhibits the equally shriveled part of Evander Holyfield's ear chewed off by Mike Tyson. Then there is the bandaged young girl with the seeping head wound and the exceedingly bitter blind quadriplegic whose wheelchair is kicked with derision. There are the retarded jokes, the O. J. Simpson jokes, and a line about examining breasts for cancer that falls with a thud. O. J. returns, urinates endlessly on Jack's precious furnishings, gets killed and buried in the yard, comes to life again, and gets killed again. One of Audrey's companions gets into the peeing party, and even Tom takes out what he refers to as his "gun," but only in self defense. (Don't ask.) There is a "joke" about feeling special if you are singled out to be raped. Then there are the jokes about horrific folliculitis of the behind, which Tom thinks Jack has, but it turns out that the ointment for the fiery skin condition actually belongs to the aptly-nicknamed Red. When Jack comes back, everything predictably and ludicrously falls into place for all. First, though, the cold, tyrannical father gets a disgusting comeuppance, falling out of a tree and getting a mouthful of gutter sludge that is followed by a mouse chaser. He is subsequently able to show warmth toward non-feathered members of his family, gives Hans a

job, and praises Tom for his great book ideas (which actually were jotted down by one of Audrey's quirky cohorts). Before we see Tom and Lisa snuggling together into the sunset, there is a little more urinating, as well as some vomiting. In a final voiceover, Tom asserts that everything must happen for a reason, but it is hard to fathom the reason why *My Boss's Daughter* ever came about.

The film was shelved for some time before finally being released, no doubt to capitalize on all the Kutcher-Moore hoopla. Understandably, Dimension Films did not make the movie available to critics before its release, hoping to take in as much money as possible before the public got wind of this stinker. Reviews were decidedly negative and dismissive, and the film, made on a budget of $14 million, succeeded in grossing only a fraction of that. It was poorly written by David Dorfman (also responsible for this year's *Anger Management*), who apparently was aiming for the Farrelly brothers but missed. It was directed by David Zucker, whose work here comes in well below the zany, farcical fun he achieved in the past with such films as *Airplane!* (1980), *Ruthless People* (1986), or the *Naked Gun* series. The tagline for *My Boss's Daughter* was "There are some things you just don't do." Too bad Mr. Stamp and the filmmakers failed to heed that warning.

—*David L. Boxerbaum*

CREDITS

Tom Stansfield: Ashton Kutcher
Lisa Taylor: Tara Reid
Jack Taylor: Terence Stamp
Ken: Jeffrey Tambor
Red Taylor: Andy Richter
T.J.: Michael Madsen
Paul: Jon Abrahams
Speed: David Koechner
Tina: Carmen Electra
Audrey Bennett: Molly Shannon
Hans: Kenan Thompson

Origin: USA
Released: 2003
Production: Gil Netter, John Jacobs; released by Dimension Films
Directed by: David Zucker
Written by: David Dorfman
Cinematography by: Martin McGrath
Music by: Teddy Castellucci
Sound: Eric J. Batut
Music Supervisor: Madonna Wade-Reed, Jennifer Pyken
Editing: Patrick Lussier, Sam Craven
Art Direction: Kevin Humenny

Costumes: Daniel Orlandi
Production Design: Andrew Laws
MPAA rating: PG-13
Running time: 84 minutes

REVIEWS

Entertainment Weekly. September 5, 2003, p. 55.
Los Angeles Times Online. August 25, 2003.
New York Times. August 23, 2005, p. B14.
People. September 8, 2003, p. 39.
Variety. September 1, 2003, p. 49.
Wall Street Journal. August 29, 2003, p. W5.

AWARDS AND NOMINATIONS

Nomination:
Golden Raspberries 2003: Worst Actor (Kutcher), Worst Support. Actress (Reid).

My Life Without Me

In *My Life Without Me*, Sarah Polley gives a luminous performance as Ann, a woman who tries to make the most of her final months of life after being diagnosed with terminal cancer. Her performance is so heartbreaking that it goes a long way toward covering up the film's troublesome premise that impending death gives one license to act in ways that are not as loving as they might at first appear. *My Life Without Me* wants to be a tough, realistic look at dying and the way one woman tries to cope, but Ann's choices too often strain believability. Moreover, while the film truthfully depicts everyday working-class struggles, ultimately it presents too pretty a picture of death that ends up undercutting the film's realism.

Ann has not had many breaks in life. She got pregnant at 17 and married the only man she had ever been with. Another child followed, and now she and her family live in a trailer behind her mother's house. Working nights as a janitor in the university she could never hope to attend, Ann, at the young age of 23, seems, surprisingly enough, to have a fairly content life. She is very accepting of a husband, Don (Scott Speedman), who works only sporadically, and she does not seem to resent the fact that her life has been a constant struggle, with little or no respite, to barely make ends meet (she and Don have never even had a vacation).

Ann has an innate toughness, and when her doctor (Julian Richings) delivers the fateful news, she accepts her death sentence with surprising equanimity. She even chides the shy doctor for lacking the courage to look her in the eye as he tells her the news, but over time he develops a better bedside manner under her influence.

My Life Without Me is based on a short story by Nanci Kincaid called "Pretending the Bed Is a Raft" (from a collection of the same name), and the biggest change made by writer-director Isabel Coixet is that the protagonist of the film does not tell her family about her condition—she claims that she has anemia—thus making her final months a solitary odyssey. It is a strange choice, made less plausible by the fact that Ann has a happy home. Indeed, some of the film's warmest moments capture the rhythm of Ann's everyday life: playing with her daughters as she puts them to bed; tenderly singing "God Only Knows" to her husband because he likes it so much; and recalling with Don how they met at Nirvana's last concert when Don gave her a T-shirt to wipe away her tears. Yet Ann believes that she is doing the generous thing by not putting her family through the trauma of watching her die, and only her stalwart conviction and Polley's sweet demeanor disguise how simplistic and even selfish this choice really is.

Learning that she will soon be gone forces Ann to focus her life, and she makes a list of things to do before she dies. The list includes such everyday activities as telling her two daughters that she loves them and getting a new hairstyle as well as more ambitious yet morally dubious projects like sleeping with other men just to see what that would be like and making someone fall in love with her.

Ann is surrounded by quirky oddballs who make her approach to life seem clearheaded and down-to-earth, and these characters inject some humor into what could have become a somber movie. Her friend at work, Laurie (Amanda Plummer), is obsessed with diet and her weight even though she is clearly not fat. The hairdresser (Maria de Medeiros) Ann meets is fascinated by disgraced pop duo Milli Vanilli and thinks braids would look good on Ann, mainly, it seems, because she likes braids on herself. Ann's mother (Deborah Harry) is a bitter woman who works a hard job and has settled into a weary acceptance that her life did not turn out better. Watching *Mildred Pierce* on TV and then relaying the plot to her granddaughters as if it were a fairytale, Ann's mother may not be the best babysitter, but she has a good heart underneath her tough exterior.

One night in the Laundromat, Ann meets Lee (Mark Ruffalo), a young man who is instantly smitten with her, and, in one of the film's weak plot turns, Ann is soon sneaking out to meet him and having an affair. There is no reason for her to cheat on Don, a decent fellow who really loves her, apart from the fact that it takes care of some items on her list; this makes Ann more of a writer's conceit than a realistic character with authentic motivations. It is understandable that Ann would find Lee attractive: he has lived abroad (something Ann could only dream of) and has an intellectual side that Ann herself possesses but is unable to express in her circumscribed life. Still, her fundamental dishonesty makes us question whether Ann is a sympathetic character and, perhaps more important, whether she is believable. If she was conflicted about what she is doing or struggling with her choices, then perhaps we could understand the complexity of this woman, but instead we see someone betraying the family she loves out of some half-baked notion that she needs to experience more of life before it is too late.

Ruffalo is sympathetic as the lover whose last girlfriend cleaned out his apartment, leaving him with hardly anything. His devotion to Ann is touching, and she seems to have genuine affection for him as well, but we know that their relationship cannot go anywhere, so we are left with the nagging sense that Ann is using him.

However, many of Ann's decisions are truly emotionally wrenching, as when she sits in the car alone with a small recorder and tapes a series of future birthday messages for her daughters that will carry them through high school. The scene by its very nature is quite moving, but behind it is something deeper—an imaginative way for Ann to stay connected to her girls because she knows they will probably end up having only the vaguest memories of her. Without making the scene maudlin, Polley very beautifully lets us see Ann's yearning to be a part of their lives, but at the same time we are left wondering why Ann is spending so much time with Lee instead of the children she loves so much. In another poignant scene, Ann visits the incarcerated father (an unbilled Alfred Molina) she barely knows. Around them hovers all the things that cannot be said, all the frustration for lives that did not go the way everyone would have hoped.

Mixed with such subtle, understated moments, however, is a contrived subplot. Ann hopes to find Don a new wife, and a neighbor (Leonor Watling) conveniently appears next door, a nurse who loves children and just happens to share Ann's first name. Soon Ann is having her girls visit this woman and is inviting her over for dinner in the hope that Don will like her as well. Ann has such a sense of peace about her impending death that she is more concerned about how life will carry on without her than with how sick she will become. It may be refreshing to see a character who does not go through the usual anguish about dying young, but it is more than odd that a woman might not want her husband to wait a little while before remarrying. In the short story, Ann's replacement is a former childhood friend of her husband, so at least it is more probable he could fall in love with her.

When we are submerged in Ann's consciousness, the film takes on a lyrical quality that reveals her depths. She has so readily accepted the reality of her demise that her haunting internal monologues are spoken in the second person, as if she has separated herself from her body and can take an objective approach to her condition: "Now you feel like you want to take all the drugs in the world, but all the drugs in the world aren't going to change the feeling that your whole life's been a dream and it's only now that you're waking up." While Ann seems able to disassociate herself from her body, her voiceovers also have the effect of drawing us in (she is, after all, addressing us as well as herself) so that we are dying with her. The film also takes us into Ann's fantasy life as she pictures people in a grocery store suddenly dancing; despite the labels that tell us how many chemicals are in our food, Ann concludes, "No one ever thinks about death in a supermarket." The observation demonstrates Ann's keen intelligence and unique outlook, and the scene's surreal beauty makes us wish the film experimented more with such fantasy interludes.

From the cramped room of the family's trailer to the heroine's less-than-perfect teeth, the movie presents a milieu grounded in lower-class reality where dreams more often than not go unfulfilled. And yet the screenplay advances an idealized view of death in which the heroine never grows visibly weaker and gets everything she wants after she is gone. Indeed, Ann's life without her appears to play out exactly as she planned in the tape-recorded messages she left behind for her loved ones: her mother is out on a date and enjoying herself for the first time in years; Don and neighbor Ann are a happy family with the two girls; and Lee is sprucing up his apartment so he might have better luck attracting women. It is as happy an ending as this story could deliver, yet for a film predicated on the unyielding disappointments of a hard life, that the protagonist's death should have such a profound, restorative effect on everyone in her life is farfetched.

Nevertheless, Sarah Polley accomplishes something quite extraordinary in *My Life Without Me*. She plays a character whose actions are questionable at best and selfish at worst, and yet Polley makes her sympathetic and likable. Here is a woman dying of an inoperable tumor who does not share the bad news with her devoted husband and adoring daughters and has an affair with a virtual stranger, but her duplicity is never an issue. It is merely a given, as if a death sentence explained away or excused such choices. While the screenplay seems to avoid building a coherent protagonist we can understand, the gifted Polley plays her with such a fierce resolve and inner grace that we believe in her anyway.

—*Peter N. Chumo II*

CREDITS

Ann: Sarah Polley
Don: Scott Speedman
Lee: Mark Ruffalo
Ann's mother: Deborah Harry
Ann's father: Alfred Molina

Ann: Leonor Watling
Laurie: Amanda Plummer
Dr. Thompson: Julian Richings
Hairdresser: Maria De Medeiros

Origin: Canada, Spain
Released: 2003
Production: Esther Garcia, Gordon McLennan; El Deseo, Milestone Productions; released by Sony Pictures Classics
Directed by: Isabel Coixet
Written by: Isabel Coixet
Cinematography by: Jean-Claude Larrieu
Music by: Alfonso de Villalonga
Sound: Sebastian Salm
Editing: Lisa Robinson
Costumes: Katia Sano
Production Design: Carol Lavalle
MPAA rating: R
Running time: 106 minutes

REVIEWS

Boxoffice. September, 2003, p. 116.
Chicago Sun-Times Online. October 17, 2003.
Entertainment Weekly. October 3, 2003, p. 50.
Los Angeles Times Online. September 26, 2003.
New York Times Online. September 26, 2003.
Variety Online. February 11, 2003.
Washington Post. October 17, 2003, p. WE48.

Mystic River

We bury our sins, we wash them clean.
—Movie tagline

 Box Office: $80.1 million

Mystic River is a beautiful and tragic odd duck. Directed by old cowboy Clint Eastwood, it has more crying and emotionally wrecked men than a John Cassavetes movie. It packs a tremendous number of wrenching emotional punches interspersed with an equally amazing amount of lifeless police investigation scenes. It is lifted up by the strength of its remarkable actors—in particular, the great Sean Penn and an intriguing Tim Robbins, playing against type—and dragged down by a sometimes brilliant but often lame script and a plot that sinks under its own mythic burdens and leaden climax. It's an exhilarating, depressing, fantastic, but ultimately unsatisfying film.

Eastwood saddles the story with a bloated, majestic score he composed, punctuating significant scenes with soaring, fateful flourishes. Instead of the minimalism that might have best suited an adaptation of the fascinating book written by Dennis Lehane, Eastwood strains repeatedly for the grandiose, zooming in on Boston neighborhood locations with aerial shots, panning to wide, white heavens to invoke the divine, seeking to make the ordinary majestic, and suggesting that human tragedy is profound even as it is tawdry. The result is mixed.

At its best points, Eastwood's confident, gripping style suggests a male version of *The Hours,* a swirling, seething portrait of the hearts of three men whose lives were all marked, to a greater or lesser degree, by a harrowing childhood incident. As Eastwood cuts back and forth between grieving father Jimmy Markum (Penn), disturbed father Dave Boyle (Robbins), and abandoned father Sean Devine (Kevin Bacon), all caught in a tangled, intense emotional web, he captures moments of universal human truth. But then he repeatedly loses his way, tripped up by the baldly written script (by Brian Helgeland) and by his own pretentiousness.

The conceit of *Mystic River* is that our life choices are constrained by inexplicable fate expressed in chance occurrences. Its characters are not able to escape the scars left by growing up in a neighborhood where everyone knows everyone's business. But while the old, Irish, working-class neighborhood of East Boston is the star and protagonist of the novel, it fades in Eastwood's rendering into a barely defined background. So much detail is missing that it's not even clear it's an Irish area. Eastwood shoots this film like it was a western, taking every opportunity to exploit the vastness of sky and river, and in doing so he misses the point entirely. Lehane's tragedy is not about endless horizons, but about thwarted opportunities, about not being able to escape the peculiar limits of the urban human condition.

The entire story is pinned on what happens one day when the three 11-year-old versions of the main characters are playing street hockey. Jimmy talks Sean and Dave into writing their names in newly poured cement on a sidewalk, and a man pretending to be a policeman collars them, picks up Dave, and takes him away. The man and his fellow molester hold the boy captive for four days before he escapes. Eastwood presents this sequence with breathless, bold abandon, and then plunges headlong into a terrific half-hour that introduces us to Jimmy's tragedy—the murder of his beloved 19-year-old daughter Katie (Emmy Rossum).

Brilliantly paced, edited, and acted, the sequences about the murder, its discovery, and its effect on Jimmy are among the most emotionally gripping in movie history. But Eastwood is cheating here, as he does throughout the movie: He's stacking the deck for maximum emotional effect. The audience knows Katie has been murdered long before Jimmy does, and so we watch a sense of vague disturbance wash over Penn as he helps out at the grocery store he owns and witnesses a younger daughter's First Communion. Eastwood is rubbing our face in his grief.

Fortunately Penn transcends the material. Moments usually spared a movie viewer are detailed in all their agony: Jimmy discovers that police have cordoned off an area containing his daughter's car; Sean tells Jimmy that his daughter is missing; Jimmy breaks through police lines to get close enough to the murder scene to learn the truth. And there is a magnificent shot from above, of a writhing Jimmy in the arms of policemen trying to restrain him. Quieter but no less intense scenes follow: Jimmy identifying the body at the morgue; Jimmy and wife Annabeth (Laura Linney) talking to the detectives (Bacon's Sean and his partner, Whitey Powers, played by Laurence Fishburne), Jimmy getting through an impromptu wake that originated as a first communion party, and more intense grieving. Penn is riveting, outrageous, broken, and determined, a man trying to regain direction.

The police detective's investigation parallels one launched by Jimmy, an ex-con who has a couple of associates start digging for information. In another set-up, the plot fingers Dave as the killer from the start. Dave comes home the night Katie is murdered with a bloody hand and a sliced stomach, and tells his wife, Celeste (Marcia Gay Harden), who is Annabeth's sister, that he may have killed a mugger. Celeste is suspicious, and her suspicions grow as Dave seems to be losing more and more of his mind.

The character of Dave is the most problematic in the film. Robbins almost disappears into the role of an abused man-child still trying to make sense of his life. Robbins plays Dave as lethargic, haunted, and prone to fits of crazed rage that seem to surprise his wife. He gives himself a speech and another to his wife about vampires and wolves, talking about his childhood abuse incident. It's a stretch to believe he would talk in such elegant metaphors, and more of a stretch to think this kind of craziness would lie dormant for so many years. And there's altogether too many references by Sean and Jimmy to what happened to Dave earlier. The point that he was abused and is still suffering from it is hammered home, and at times, despite Robbins's valiant efforts, Dave comes close to being a caricature, a kind of philosophical straw man for Lehane's arguments.

It doesn't help that the movie plods along as Sean and Powers conduct their investigation into the obvious. There's not much suspense because the deck is stacked. Dave behaves so suspiciously that there are only two alternatives: either the plot is hopelessly transparent, or all the evidence that points to Dave is a red herring. Either way, the film loses its energy rapidly and wastes its time trying to shoehorn into the movie minor aspects of the novel. What's going on, for instance, with Sean's estranged wife, who calls him from

time to time but doesn't speak? We never find out why she is speechless and what has come between them. It's a distracting little enigma that should have been discarded or explained, rather than skimmed over.

When we find out who the real killers are, it doesn't wrap up the plot into a neat package, it unravels it. The killers and their motives are insubstantial, cheap, and insignificant, and so the ground of the tragedy shifts and expands. The meaning that Jimmy seeks in tracking down the killer and avenging his daughter's death slips through his hands, and he is the cause of another meaningless tragedy.

In an epilogue scene, Annabeth tells him he's a big-hearted, strong king who is the one counted on to take care of the whole neighborhood. This scene is evocative but makes little sense, partly because the film has neglected the theme of the neighborhood and partly because Jimmy hasn't acted regally at any point in the story. You are left with a new sense of raging injustice and an inability to do anything about it.

Certainly there's nothing wrong with an unsettling ending, but it's also unsatisfying that none of the characters comes off as heroic. The film stacks the deck in favor of sympathy or antagonism toward certain characters, then reshuffles the deck to turn heroes into contemptible villains and the weak and villainous into martyrs. It's a depressing story, and Eastwood's attempts to make it grand and universally meaningful only serve to spotlight its inherent weaknesses. It's as if Eastwood, the great Hollywood hero, is searching somewhere, anywhere, for a hero—and so is the audience.

Without a doubt, *Mystic River* is loaded with fine acting, elegant directorial flourishes, and an admirable willingness to take risks with difficult material. It aspires to a greatness, however, that this tale cannot provide, at least in this form. All the high-powered star talent in the world—and it's hard to think of a film with a better acting pedigree than the six stars at the top of its credits—can't make this a likeable, sensible movie-going experience.

—*Michael Betzold*

CREDITS

Jimmy Markum: Sean Penn
Dave Boyle: Tim Robbins
Sean Devine: Kevin Bacon
Whitey Powers: Laurence "Larry" Fishburne
Celeste Boyle: Marcia Gay Harden
Annabeth Markum: Laura Linney
Brendan Harris: Tom Guiry
Val Savage: Kevin Chapman
Katie Markum: Emmy Rossum
Silent Ray Harris: Spencer (Treat) Clark

Nick Savage: Adam Nelson
Esther Harris: Jenny O'Hara
John O'Shea: Andrew Mackin
Kevin Savage: Robert Wahlberg

Origin: USA
Released: 2003
Production: Clint Eastwood, Robert Lorenz, Judie G. Hoyt; Village Roadshow Pictures, NPV Entertainment, Malpaso Productions; released by Warner Bros.
Directed by: Clint Eastwood
Written by: Brian Helgeland
Cinematography by: Tom Stern
Music by: Clint Eastwood
Sound: Walt Martin
Editing: Joel Cox
Art Direction: Jack G. Taylor Jr.
Costumes: Deborah Hopper
Production Design: Henry Bumstead
MPAA rating: R
Running time: 137 minutes

 REVIEWS

Boxoffice. November, 2003, p. 83.
Chicago Sun-Times Online. October 8, 2003.
Entertainment Weekly. October 10, 2003, p. 97.
Los Angeles Times Online. October 8, 2003.
New York Times Online. October 3, 2003.
People. October 13, 2003, p. 29.
Rolling Stone. October 16, 2003, p. 94.
Sight and Sound. November, 2003, p. 12.
USA Today Online. October 3, 2003.
Variety Online. May 23, 2003.
Washington Post. October 10, 2003, p. WE39.

AWARDS AND NOMINATIONS

Oscars 2003: Actor (Penn), Support. Actor (Robbins)
Golden Globes 2004: Actor—Drama (Penn), Support. Actor (Robbins)
Natl. Bd. of Review 2003: Actor (Penn), Film
Natl. Soc. Film Critics 2003: Director (Eastwood)
Screen Actors Guild 2003: Support. Actor (Robbins)
Nomination:
Oscars 2003: Adapt. Screenplay, Director (Eastwood), Film, Support. Actress (Harden)
Directors Guild 2003: Director (Eastwood)
Golden Globes 2004: Director (Eastwood), Film—Drama, Screenplay
Screen Actors Guild 2003: Actor (Penn), Cast
Writers Guild 2003: Adapt. Screenplay.

National Security

He only looks like a cop.
—Movie tagline

 Box Office: $35.8 million

No one going to see the Martin Lawrence/Steve Zahn action comedy *National Security* should be very surprised about what they're getting. It's the latest edition of a longtime trend in black guy/white guy, buddy/action comedies. The two partners are usually forced together, they're usually mismatched guys who hate each other at first, but grow to depend on each other. Between their witty banter, lots of stuff blows up and they solve some sort of crime or something. See also, *48 Hours,* et al. In recent years, the genre has shifted to also include Asians, particularly Asians who know some sort of martial art, in films like *Shaghai Knights.*

Here it's same old, same old. All that stuff happens except the witty banter isn't nearly as witty as we'd hope. The one thing that we know to expect from such comedies is that one of the guys, usually the African-American one, will be a fast-talking, funny hustler type. Lawrence dutifully tries to do these things, but he's just not wild enough here. It's a surprise since Lawrence is playing exactly the same sort of character that he has played since he first reached the popular consciousness. Instead of saying anything truly funny, he resorts to spouting catch phrases. His favorite is "What the problem is?" So funny do he and the writers find this line that they have Lawrence say it many times.

The other comedy crutch that writers Jay Scherick and David Ronn rely on is racial humor, although perhaps humor is too strong a word. Lawrence is constantly spouting off about the imagined racism that he finds himself subjected to. This joke was funny when Chris Rock did it years ago as Nat X on *Saturday Night Live* ("Why do the white chessmen get to move first?"), but here it falls flat. The only thing it does seem to do is mock people who suffer from real, legitimate racial discrimination. Making someone's true concerns into comedy fodder, and lame comedy fodder at that, seems crass.

There is the usual "action," which means things blowing up, things moving fast, and, oddly things moving really slowly. The latter would be something like a car leaping over a chasm as the occupants yell. And can one thing blowing up be more thrilling than another? Here, the explosions seem pretty uninspired. As Rob Blackwelder of *Spliced Wire* put it, *National Security* is "the kind of movie in which there are flammable 55-gallon drums everywhere—on a police training course, at an abandoned military fort—so they can explode in slow-motion during the action scenes that are played completely straight, as if they were part of a Steven Seagal movie, not a Martin Lawrence comedy."

But perhaps the writers make up for the tepid comedy and tired action with clever pacing and sparkling plot twists? Unfortunately not. Earl Montgomery (Lawrence) is a tightly-wound goofball who is rejected from the police academy after hitting some of those aforementioned exploding drums while on a police drivers' training course. Straight-arrow LAPD officer Hank Rafferty (Zahn) is mourning the recent death of his partner who was killed by some bad guys. The two meet when Hank discovers Earl trying to get into a locked car in Echo Park. A bee flies by and Earl starts screaming in terror about how he's very allergic to bee stings. Hank starts swatting at Earl, trying to get the bee away from him. A nearby Latino fellow with a video camera starts filming the scene which looks an awful lot like Hank is beating Earl. This scene is the single most clever thing about the film, although again, one would question the propriety of joking about a very real racial issue.

Earl claims that the swelling from the bee sting is due to Hank's beatings and the incident gets Hank kicked off the force. The two meet up again, as the script dictates that they must, at the National Security Company (hence the genesis of the generic movie title) where they are looking for jobs. For unknown reasons, they decide to team up to solve the mystery of Hank's partner's killing.

The bad guys are led by Nash (Eric Roberts), who dresses well and sports a blonde coif. He's smuggling some sort of space age alloy in the form of beer kegs. In the race to find him, we are subjected to scenes like the one in which there is a shoot-out in a Coke factory. Here, there are prominently displayed bottles of Coke products. It's difficult to gauge whether Coke got a good deal by purchasing this particular product placement. Does seeing barrels of Coke products being shot by machine guns make consumers wish to purchase extra soft drinks?

The only thing that's even remotely surprising in this film is Zahn, who's playing against type. Usually he's played the sort of slow-witted stoner type in such films as *Happy, Texas* and *Riding in Cars With Boys*. Here he is a very by-the-book, straight-laced police officer. His character is given a modicum of depth by the fact that his wife is African-American. But this is not nearly enough to make a movie.

Also on board are Detective Frank McDuff (Colm Feore) and Lieutenant Washington (Bill Duke). One of these guys is there to play the good cop that's secretly crooked. The other is there so that he can say stuff like, "Hank, you're too close to this case to get involved!" and "You know that's against protocol!"

Perhaps no one should have expected very much from this film, considering the resumes of those involved behind the scenes. Director Dennis Dugan was responsible for

Beverly Hills Ninja and *Saving Silverman*. Writers Scherick and Ronn did *Serving Sara*

Critics didn't like the film all that much, although it had its fans. One of those was Kevin Thomas of the *Los Angeles Times* who wrote, "*National Security*, a funny, raucous action comedy, effectively teams Martin Lawrence and Steven Zahn in a film that's both laugh out loud funny and surprisingly subtle." And *Chicago Tribune* critic Michael Wilmington commented that Lawrence and Zahn "generate enough comic tension and mayhem to jump-start this mass of action-comedy clichés into a fairly amusing show." Ann Hornaday of the *Washington Post* felt otherwise and stated, "Lawrence's appeal is still incomprehensible—to call him a poor man's Richard Pryor libels not just Pryor but also the 33 million Americans currently living under the poverty line." A. O. Scott of the *New York Times* summed up, "The problems of *National Security* are extensive enough to defy summary in the available space."

—*Jill Hamilton*

CREDITS

Earl Montgomery: Martin Lawrence
Hank Rafferty: Steve Zahn
Nash: Eric Roberts
Lt. Washington: Bill Duke
Det. Frank McDuff: Colm Feore
Charlie Reed: Timothy Busfield
Denise: Robbine Lee
Robert Barton: Matt McCoy
Heston: Brett Cullen
Billy Narthax: Stephen Tobolowsky
Owen Fergus: Joe Flaherty

Origin: USA
Released: 2003
Production: Robert Newmyer, Jeffrey Silver, Michael Green; Outlaw Productions, Intermedia Films, Firm Films; released by Columbia Pictures
Directed by: Dennis Dugan
Written by: Jay Scherick, David Ronn
Cinematography by: Oliver Wood
Music by: Randy Edelman
Sound: Joseph Geisinger
Music Supervisor: Michelle Kuznetsky, Mary Ramos
Editing: Debra Neil-Fisher
Art Direction: Christa Munro
Costumes: April Ferry
Production Design: Larry Fulton
MPAA rating: PG-13
Running time: 90 minutes

Northfork

Box Office: $1.4 million

This eccentric and peculiar story apparently takes place on two levels, the terrestrial and the celestial, though the latter is implied rather than seen. Angels appear and debate a possible rescue mission, but none of the human characters can see them. Ostensibly, *Northfork* is a story of the evacuation from a region to be flooded following the building of a dam in 1955 Montana, "The Treasure State," if one can believe the license plate motto; but another evacuation of a divine nature turns out to be the dominant motif. On this level, it is the story of a "lost" angel, represented as a young orphan boy named Irwin (Duel Farnes) whose wings have been clipped (and who therefore looks like a normal boy). Irwin, who is ailing and has no parents to look after him, desperately wants to be rescued by a motley crew of four skeptical senior angels that are living in an abandoned house on the flood plain. The two worlds overlap interestingly but mysteriously.

Normal plot logic does not seem to apply here, even in the earthly surface story. In the banal world of 1950s "progress" and dam-building, two-man crews of government agents are sent out in black Fords and fedoras two days before the region is to be flooded to warn people who need to be evacuated. These agents are supposed to go door-to-door, offering cash settlements, but some of the residents will not be moved. The photography is utterly realistic, but the characters seem to exist in a dreamy world of magic realism. One fellow sits on his porch, armed with a shotgun to keep the agents at bay. Another, apparently a Mormon, lives with his two wives in an ark he has constructed, like Noah, awaiting the flood. Only the women can be persuaded to leave.

Existing on the edge of this story and situation is the boy Irwin, whose foster parents return him to Father Harlan, played by Nick Nolte. This minister of God works to save the boy's life (and soul?), but ultimately to no avail. Aside from showing concern for the boy, Nolte has little to do in this picture, but he does it extremely well. The film takes viewers into Irwin's consciousness as he auditions before his angelic panel of judges, whose job it is to determine whether or not to embrace and save him. The boy goes in spirit to an abandoned place, described by one reviewer as a "halfway house between heaven and earth." Oddly (or conveniently) enough, one of the government agents (James Woods) who visits the same apparently abandoned "halfway" house has in the trunk of his Ford a suitcase that contains the boy's severed wings. This provides the "evidence" needed to authenticate the "lost" angel, who is then transported (in spirit) to heaven in a World War II bomber, piloted by an angelic crew led by Anthony Edwards. As the boy's spirit is transported, his body is left behind, meanwhile, to be tended to by the grieving minister. Despite the implausible plot, the lamentation is genuinely moving.

Two of the government agents, Walter (James Woods) and Willis (Mark Polish, who co-authored the screenplay with his twin brother, Michael), are father and son. The two of them have to decide whether or not to dig up Walter's late wife for burial on higher ground, or to let her rest in peace beneath the reservoir. This dilemma is prefigured early in the film when a coffin is seen rising to the surface of the lake that will eventually form. In order to fit this detail into the plot, coherence has to be overridden. But the opening image of the rising coffin is haunting, and lingers in the mind.

The Polish brothers, Mark and Michael (who also directed), made their feature filmmaking debut at the Sundance Film Festival in 1999 with *Twin Falls Idaho*, in which they also played dying conjoined twins. Another strange and dreamy picture, it was hailed as a "sublime, if mildly flawed masterpiece." Born in 1972 and trained at the California Institute of the Arts, Michael Polish initially directed an award-winning short film, *Bajo del Perro* (1996) and that same year appeared with his brother Mark as twins in *Hellraiser: Bloodline. Northfork* is the third part of what is proposed as the American heartland trilogy, starting with *Twin Fall Idaho* and the following film, *Jackpot* (2001). All three film titles are names of actual places: Twin Fall, Idaho; Jackpot, Nevada; and Northfork, Montana.

Reviewers were hard pressed to explain the strangeness of *Northfork. Washington Post* reviewer Desson Howe, for example, complained that the movie was "just too lost in its own presumed self-enchantment," and claimed, reasonably enough, that the film was "daunting to understand—assuming that there's a method to the muddiness in the first place." Well, clearly the "method" is there. It's just that the human characters are beyond explication, since their motivation is not clearly explained. Instead viewers are provided inexplicable nuggets of folk wisdom, such as: "The world is divided into two types of people: Ford people and Chevy people." The government agents must be "Ford people," but knowing that gives no further insight into their characters.

The angelic characters are even more ambiguous. Reviewers were at a loss to find analogues, from Frank Capra's sentimental Clarence to the guardian angels of Wim Wenders's *Wings of Desire* (1987). But neither analogue works for *Northfork*, which is nothing, if not strikingly original. One of the Polish angels, looking like a young Dennis Hopper wearing a Stetson, communicates only by writing cryptic letters, while another, a nearsighted angel named Happy, appears to translate with some enthusiasm. The apparent leader, an older somewhat fey fellow given to making tea, wears a ratty looking feathered boa. Daryl Hannah plays the fourth angel, who argues the case for the Irwin who needs to be rescued. One reviewer described her as an "oversized Raggedy Ann angel" who manages to "poke through the screenplay's proverbial platitudes."

Reviewers had to scramble for adjectives and analogues to describe this film: "Brooding, funny, stylish, pretentious, profound and often confoundingly hermetic," in the words of *Washington Post* reviewer Ann Hornaday, who urged viewers to think of Ethan and Joel Coen "at their most deadpan and self-consciously mannered." But that is debatable. The Coen brothers are not nearly so eccentric or spiritual as the Polish brothers. Moreover, the Coens also tend to be more nasty, even murderous, and smug. The work here is decidedly eccentric, but not in the manner of the Coens or of David Lynch or Tim Burton, for that matter. Their work is unique, however, and deserves to be praised, in the words of Ann Hornaday, as a "strange hymn to desolation" that possesses "an undeniable, haunting grandeur."

Cinematographer M. David Mullen gets the credit for visualizing that "haunting grandeur." In his *Film Comment* review, Michael Koresky praised Mullen's "faded panoramic tableaux of the majestic Montana Plains [that] become snapshots of paradise." The film's pictorial excellence is obvious, but *Premiere* reviewer Glenn Kenny compared it to "the work of a couple of ardent art students" who appear to be "very keen on pleasing their teacher." Mullen's beautiful images did not seem to Kenny "to be the product of a genuine vision but rather of some idealization of what a genuine vision 'should' be." Koresky described *Northfork* as resembling Elia Kazan's *Wild River* (1960) "as reimagined by Wim Wenders, a precarious balance of New Age mysticism, cryptic satire, and devout regionalism." At least this description puts the Polish brothers in good company, while carving out "a niche for themselves in indie cinema," though revealing a "wide-eyed optimism eschewed by other, more skilled, storytellers such as the Coens or [Jim] Jarmusch."

Michael Koresky aptly described the state-funded Evacuation Committee (which included Peter Coyote, along with James Woods and Mark Polish) as "Angels of Mercy masquerading as Angels of Death in their trenchcoats and fedoras." But it is surely worth mentioning that this Evacuation Committee is balanced out by the angelic "Evacuation Committee" intent upon rescuing Irwin. This film can be criticized for being frustratingly tangled up in its own metaphysical artifice but it cannot be faulted for its vision: "When what passes for religious inquiry in American film is *Bruce Almighty*," Koresky wrote in defense of the film, "the frustrating work of the Polish Brothers becomes nearly indispensable," even if the film may hover "in an airless space between piety and whimsy." In conclusion, then, as Hollywood films become increasingly witless, noisy, and pointless, the films of the Polish Brothers deserve to be watched, and even cherished. *Northfork* was not destined to become a box-office champ, but it could eventually achieve cult status, and it should play very well to European audiences.

—*James M. Welsh*

CREDITS

Walter O'Brien: James Woods
Father Harlan: Nick Nolte
Mrs. Hadfield: Claire Forlani
Irwin: Duel Farnes
Willis O'Brien: Mark Polish
Flower Hercules: Daryl Hannah
Cod: Ben Foster
Happy: Anthony Edwards
Cup of Tea: Robin Sachs
Marvin: Graham Beckel
Eddie: Peter Coyote
Arnold: Jon(athan) Gries
Mr. Stalling: Marshall Bell
Mr. Hope: Kyle MacLachlan
Mrs. Hope: Michele Hicks
Matt: Josh Barker

Origin: USA
Released: 2003
Production: Mark Polish, Michael Polish; Romano/Shane Productions, Departure Entertainment; released by Paramount Classics
Directed by: Michael Polish
Written by: Mark Polish, Michael Polish
Cinematography by: M. David Mullen
Music by: Stuart Matthewman
Sound: Matthew Nicolay
Editing: Leo Trombetta
Art Direction: David Storm

Costumes: Daniel Glicker
Production Design: Ichelle Spitzig, Del Polish
MPAA rating: PG-13
Running time: 103 minutes

REVIEWS

Boxoffice. April, 2003, p. 73.
Chicago Sun-Times Online. July 11, 2003.
Entertainment Weekly. July 18, 2003, p. 88.
Los Angeles Times Online. July 11, 2003.
New York Times Online. July 11, 2003.
Premiere. July/August, 2003, p. 23.
USA Today Online. July 11, 2003.
Variety Online. January 27, 2003.
Washington Post. July 18, 2003, p. C5.

QUOTES

Father Harlan (Nick Nolte): "We are all angels. It is what we do with our wings that separates us."

AWARDS AND NOMINATIONS

Nomination:
Ind. Spirit 2004: Cinematog.

Nowhere in Africa (Nirgendwo in Afrika)

1938. One family's story of a homeland lost and new one found.
—Movie tagline

 Box Office: $6.1 million

At first glance, director Caroline Link's most recent film seems to be merely the tired story of a German Jewish family moving to escape the Holocaust. Within minutes, however, it becomes clear that *Nowhere in Africa* is going to be so much more than that. It moves beyond my initial expectations of a sugary, uplifting, predictable film about a family's move to Kenya in order to escape the Nazis to a decidedly deep and intricate tale of family commitment.

The opening sequence cuts back and forth between Kenya and a desperately ill Walter Redlich, and Germany, where his wife, Jettel, is making plans to meet him in Africa with their 5-year-old daughter. This allows us to experience the difference in lifestyles, cultures, and personalities very early on in the film. It is clear from the beginning that Jettel will have a difficult time adjusting to the harsh reality of Kenya, where her husband is committed to helping his family escape what is happening in Germany.

After the family is reunited in Kenya, the length of their stay is an inevitable and persistent question. Daughter Regina takes to Kenya immediately, making friends with the African children and loving the vast expanses of land. The cultured Jettel, however, is not as lucky and is painfully unhappy in her new surroundings. At first, the change for Walter, as he moves into the unfamiliar yet acceptable role of farmer, is not very difficult. Navigating through the middle of nowhere and grappling with different cultures and problems in different ways and at different paces are the issues that move this film in the proper direction.

The relationship of young Regina with the family's dignified, African cook, Owuor, was wonderful to watch. Owuor is a character trying to balance his cultural ideas with those of his employer, at first finding it quite difficult. After building a bond with the child, he learns that sacrifice is sometimes well worth it.

Films with a resounding ring of truth to them are often based on a real life story. Not surprisingly then, *Nowhere in Africa* is rooted in the autobiographical novel by Stefanie Zweig about her childhood in Kenya after her family fled their homeland of Germany. The book was a highly successful bestseller in her country before being made into this poignant and intelligent look at an innocent family forced to make life-altering decisions. Director Caroline Link took special care to lace the story with conflict and compassion and avoid the sticky sweet path of overdone sentiment. Link previously directed the 1998 Academy Award nominated film *Beyond Silence*.

The film was moved along by the brilliant performances of the main characters, especially Juliane Köhler as Jettel Redlich. Many films involving family dynamics allow only very specific characteristics for each role, never allowing the characters to sway in their convictions or main ideals. The actors are not confined in this way here. Köhler moves the multidimensional character of Jettel through anger to coping, to love, to despair with ease. There is a feeling of empathy for the character as a result of this deft performance.

The cinematography of *Nowhere in Africa* allows us to breathe in the beauty of the continent without fake scenery or overdone graphics. As the film unfolds, Kenya comes alive for us in all it's intimidating beauty.

It really did not come as a shock to me that *Nowhere in Africa* walked away with five German Film Awards, including best feature, best director, and best cinematography. After this amazing victory, the film went on to win a 2003 Academy Award for best foreign language film.

The relationship between Jettel and Walter changes and shifts throughout the film, though their commitment to each other is never questioned. Their lives and their relationship oftentimes seem fragile, which could be disconcerting for the audience, yet the success of *Nowhere in Africa* lies in the genuineness of the characters. The complexities of a family in chaos are what make this film so watchable.

—*Laura Abraham*

CREDITS

Jettel Redlich: Juliane Kohler
Walter Redlich: Merab Redlich
Regina (teen): Karoline Eckertz
Regina (child): Lea Kurka
Susskind: Matthias Habich
Owuor: Sidede Onyulo

Origin: Germany
Language: German
Released: 2002
Production: Peter Herrmann; Constantin Film, MTM Medien & Television, Bavaria Films, MC-One; released by Zeitgeist Films
Directed by: Caroline Link
Written by: Caroline Link
Cinematography by: Gernot Roll
Music by: Niki Reiser
Sound: Andreas Wolki
Editing: Patricia Rommel
Costumes: Barbara Grupp
Production Design: Susann Bieling, Uwe Szielasko
MPAA rating: R
Running time: 141 minutes

REVIEWS

Boston Globe. March 28, 2003, p. D1.
Boxoffice. April, 2003, p. 105.
Chicago Sun-Times Online. March 21, 2003.
Entertainment Weekly. March 14, 2003, p. 45.
Los Angeles Times Online. March 14, 2003.
New York Times Online. February 23, 2003.
New York Times Online. March 7, 2003.
Sight and Sound. April, 2003, p. 45.
Variety Online. March 1, 2002.
Washington Post. March 28, 2003, p. C5.

Oscars 2002: Foreign Film.

Old School

All the fun of college. None of the education.
—Movie tagline

 Box Office: $73 million

Mitch Martin (Luke Wilson) is a very ordinary, subdued, and cautious man. He also seems to be a man for whom nothing goes right. He is troubled when the seat belt in his taxi doesn't work, and leave it to Mitch to set off the metal detector at the airport time after time after time. So it should come as no surprise that when he returns home early from a business trip he finds his girlfriend Heidi (Juliette Lewis) in bed, watching hardcore porn, and with a naked, blindfolded couple emerging from his bathroom.

With Heidi now history, Mitch moves out and into a new house located on the campus of the local university. This is perfect as far as his pal Beanie (Vince Vaughn) is concerned. The very married Beanie, who is always toting around a kid or two, plans on using Mitch's house to recapture his own college days starting with one hell of a party, the Mitch-a-palooza.

All this questionable activity soon has the guys running afoul of university authorities in the form of Dean Pritchard (Jeremy Piven), someone the guys knew and taunted when younger. Evidently Pritchard really knows how to hold a grudge because he has the house rezoned for campus use only. But does that stop Beanie? Heck no! He just turns the house into a fraternity.

The pledges attracted to this "civilian" fraternity are an odd lot: there's a few college boys, all losers (you know, the ugly, the pimple faced, the overweight); but there's also more thirty-somethings like Beanie and Mitch's good friend, the newly married Frank (Will Ferrell), and a few other adult men trying to recapture their youth; and one really old man, Blue (Patrick Cranshaw), who will quickly die of shock—or ecstasy—during the frat's first K-Y Jelly, topless wrestling match.

The popularity of the fraternity soon earns Mitch the title of "The Godfather" and the vengeance of Dean Pritchard, who now sets out to destroy the fraternity. He will make them take unpassable tests and then drive them out of existence. Of course failing these tests and disbanding the fraternity is nothing to the men in it, but to the college students it means expulsion. Consequently the frat "boys" band together to pass the Dean's tests and, as one can easily predict, end up succeeding after lots of impossible things happen: i.e. the really fat member doing highly coordinated and gravity-defying gymnastics and Frank going into a "coma" to debate James Carville and winning.

Beyond a doubt, this is a guys' film. (What's the opposite of a chick flick? A macho movie?) This is a middle-aged man's fantasy, and they and adolescent boys may be the only ones able to say with any degree of sincerity that this is a funny, good movie. True, it does try to get a few laughs and some comedic mileage out of men's foibles, for example, a mechanically-inept and newly-married Frank working on a Trans Am in his driveway, drinking beer and listening to very loud music, but the jokes may cause more wincing than laughing in anyone with an IQ higher than beer's alcohol content.

In fact, many of the scenes in *Old School* seem to have no purpose other than to set up a joke: Beanie's son's birthday party doesn't move the plot forward one bit but does allow for a cameo by Seann William Scott, an animal tranquilizer joke, and a running gag about a breadmaker. With lame jokes about adults acting like juveniles and avoiding responsibility and a boilerplate minimal plot, what else can go wrong? How about a few groaning implausibilities? Forget James Carville, what are the odds Snoop Dogg would actually deign to play at a white frat boys' backyard party?

Then there's the amateurish editing and camerawork that is so jittery in some scenes that audiences could be at risk for sea sickness. Oh, and how about the nonsensical non-sequiturs. For example the Mitch-a-palooza is held on Thursday night and at the party Frank talks about his shopping plans for "tomorrow," Saturday. Not to mention the fact that the day after this party of house-destroying magnitude, Mitch comes home to find an organized and clean home. And no one comments on this?

Worst of all, though, may be the questionable virtues this movie touts as being cool: driving recklessly, cheating on tests, casual sex, sleeping with underage girls, binge drinking, public nudity, trashing marriages. One doesn't have to be a prude to believe sometimes humor can just be too lowbrow to be funny anymore.

This is the second teaming of director/writer Todd Phillips and co-writer Scot Armstrong who also worked together on 2000's *Road Trip*. But what's interesting is that this movie's executive producer is Ivan Reitman who also produced *Animal House*, another and far superior lampoon of fraternities, to which many will compare *Old School*. Also of interest is that Phillips won the Sundance 1998 Grand Jury Prize for a documentary called *Frat House*, which may have been the inspiration for this movie, but which HBO refused to air because of claims that the film had committed the ultimate documentary sin: staging scenes.

The main actors in *Old School* are likeable enough. Luke Wilson as Mitch is a genial everyman, but he is also a smart actor who deserves better. Vince Vaughn plays a character very similar to his slightly seedy *Swingers* self. His all-bark-no-bite talk about sleeping with young co-eds while being truly faithful to his wife could have been poignant but instead is treated just as one more toss away joke. While Will Ferrell's character, with it's descending dignity, does offer inspired if not organic moments of humor, I'm afraid his naked bum just isn't that funny. In the end Frank is more tragic than outrageous and we feel guilty at laughing at someone so pathetic.

Of course, as expected in a guy's film, the women in *Old School* are nothing but props like beer cans. They are the stereotypical assortment: the teenage seductress, the controlling wife, the innocent love interest, the unfaithful girlfriend, etc.

Perhaps if the filmmakers had kept *Old School* entirely in the realm of the "old," if they'd actually put some thought into the real humor behind a bunch of aging guys dodging and wrestling adult responsibilities in a "fraternity" setting there might have been a truly funny film here. Instead the writers went for the easy laughs. There's no wit here. It's a lazy writer's movie.

One reviewer has intimated that *Old School* is *National Lampoon's Animal House* meets *Jackass*. That summary isn't far wrong. And it's a sad commentary on the state of the American sense of humor that so many people may find this *Jackass* of a movie to be uproariously funny instead of the sophomoric cinema it really is.

—*Beverley Bare Buehrer*

CREDITS

Mitch: Luke Wilson
Frank: Will Ferrell
Beanie: Vince Vaughn
Nicole: Ellen Pompeo
Heidi: Juliette Lewis
Lara: Leah Remini
Marissa: Perrey Reeves
Darcie: Elisha Cuthbert
Dean Gordon Pritchard: Jeremy Piven
Spanish: Rick Gonzalez
Goldberg: Terry O'Quinn
Booker: Artie Lange
Hatch: Matthew Carey
Mr. Springbrook: Harve Presnell
Animal caretaker: Seann William Scott
Mark: Craig Kilborn
Gary: Andy Dick (Cameo)
Himself: Snoop Dogg (Cameo)

Origin: USA
Released: 2003
Production: Daniel Goldberg, Joe Medjuck, Todd Phillips; Montecito Picture Co.; released by Dreamworks Pictures
Directed by: Todd Phillips
Written by: Todd Phillips, Scot Armstrong
Cinematography by: Mark Irwin
Music by: Theodore Shapiro
Sound: Petur Hliddal
Music Supervisor: Randall Poster
Editing: Michael Jablow
Art Direction: Max Briscoe
Costumes: Nancy Fisher
Production Design: Clark Hunter
MPAA rating: R
Running time: 90 minutes

 REVIEWS

Chicago Sun-Times Online. February 21, 2003.
Entertainment Weekly. February 28, 2003, p. 59.
Los Angeles Times Online. February 21, 2003.
New York Times Online. February 21, 2003.
People. March 3, 2003, p. 32.
USA Today Online. February 21, 2003.
Variety Online. February 12, 2003.

On Guard! (Le Bossu) (En Garde)

Si tu ne viens pas a Lagardere, Lagardere ira a toi!
—Movie tagline

Beautifully lensed, old-fashioned swashbuckler, *On Guard* paved the way for 2003's surprise hit, *Pirates of the Caribbean: The Curse of the Black Pearl,* although it has the dubious distinction of being slightly less silly. *On Guard* was actually produced in 1997 and it took all these years for it to cross the ocean from France, where it was called *Le Bossu* (*The Hunchback*). Obviously, that title wasn't very effective, even in France, because it was alternately titled *Il Cavaliere di Lagardére* and finally, in the U.S., *On Guard,* a symbolically simplistic title.

The conventional story by Philippe de Broca and Jean Cosmos, from the 1857 novel by Paul Feval, is set in France in the early 1700s, toward the end of Louis XIV's reign. When the wicked but poor Gonzague (Fabrice Luchini) discovers that his wealthy playboy cousin, the Duc de Nevers (Vincent Perez), seeks to marry the mother of the illegitimate child he has fathered, Gonzague schemes to kill the unwelcome heirs. Gonzague tracks Nevers through the countryside, where Nevers plans to wed Blanche (Claire Nebout), the mother of Aurore. Nevers faces danger on the trip, but is saved by Lagardere (Daniel Auteuil), a mere proletariat next to Nevers but a fencing master with grace and skill.

Despite Lagardere's protective presence, Gonzague and his minions finally murder Nevers, along with several guests, during the country wedding. Meanwhile, Blanche vanishes as Lagardere escapes with little Aurore. Largardere finds refuge for himself and the infant by joining a traveling theatre troupe. Through the years, Lagardere becomes an integral member in the acting company and he alone raises Aurore (Marie Gillain) into a stunning young woman.

Lagardere is reluctant to tell Aurore of her background until they find themselves in Paris and he sees Blanche living as a recluse under the watchful eye of Gonzague. Lagardere and Aurore plot to save Blanche by dispatching the villainous Gonzague. Pretending to be a hunchbacked accountant, Lagardere infiltrates Gonzague's inner circle. When the time is right, Lagardere challenges his boss to a duel, which Lagardere wins. Aurore then helps Blanche out of her solitary life, reveals she is her daughter, and declares her love for her guardian, Lagardere.

It was the ending to the film that caught a few critics off-guard (if one pardons the pun). Some reviewers, like Edward Guthmann of the *San Francisco Chronicle,* compared Aurore's love for Lagardere to the Woody Allen-Soon-Yi Previn scandal, which had transpired shortly before the making of *On Guard.* Having a young woman end up with her father-figure, or the man who has raised her, may upset some tastes in the U.S., although the near-incest plot device is not really new to romance novels, swashbucklers, or even Hollywood movies in general (Does anyone remember *That Hagen Girl* (1947), in which Shirley Temple's character ends up romantically paired with her caretaker—played by Ronald Reagan?)

Romance movie fans might be more bothered by the fact that the handsome would-be hero of the piece (played by Vincent Perez) dies early in the story. Unlike Sabatini's protagonist, Scaramouche, Nevers does not become a more compassionate person through Lagardere—he is killed off too soon for that. But there are precedents for this plotting as well. In fact, there is nothing especially original about the narrative (some critics compared it to a Victor Hugo saga and Hugo was a contemporary of novelist Paul Feval). Though Hollywood never tackled this particular Feval novel, France had already filmed the same story four other times, the first in 1924.

If one likes the swashbucklers of "the Golden Age," one should enjoy *On Guard.* Director de Broca (best known for 1967's *King of Hearts*) makes maximum use of the wide-screen frame to showcase the lavish sets and costumes and, of course, the swordfights. No sequence compares to the graceful Errol Flynn set pieces or the athleticism of Douglas Fairbanks's best work, but *On Guard* is better than some more recent attempts at reviving the genre (e.g. *The Count of Monte Christo*). Jean-François Robin's cinematography also neatly captures the gorgeous mountain scenery, although the best-looking parts are the very stylized theatre scenes, which evoke both Marcel Carne's *Children of Paradise* (1945) and George Sidney's underrated second Hollywood version of *Scaramouche* (1952). Though de Broca may lack the cinematic gifts of either Carne or Sidney (one might have expected de Broca to show more of his irreverence), at least *On Guard* pays respectful homage with a classy production. It would be just too much to expect true revisionism or attempts at postmodernism. Beyond a few gauche sex jokes, it's an old-hat movie. Come to think of it, the sex jokes are pretty old-hat, too.

—*Eric Monder*

CREDITS

Lagarere/Le Bossu: Daniel Auteuil
Gonague: Fabrice Luchini
Nevers: Vincent Perez
Aurore: Marie Gillain
Cocardasse: Jean-Francois Stevenin
Passepoil: Didier Pain
Blanche: Claire Nebout
Philippe d'Orleans: Philippe Noiret
Peyrolles: Yann Collette

Origin: France, Italy, Germany
Language: French
Released: 2003
Production: Patrick Godeau; Gemini Film Productions, D.A. Films, TF-1 Films, Alicelio; released by Empire Pictures
Directed by: Philippe de Broca
Written by: Philippe de Broca, Jean Cosmos, Jerome Tonnerre
Cinematography by: Jean-Francois Robin
Music by: Philippe Sarde
Sound: William Flageollet
Music Supervisor: Valerie Lindon
Editing: Henri Lanoe
Art Direction: Bernard Vezat

Costumes: Christian Gasc
MPAA rating: Unrated
Running time: 128 minutes

REVIEWS

Box Office Magazine. Jan. 1999, p. 49.
Hollywood Reporter. April 28-May 4, 1998.
Sight & Sound Magazine. Sept., 1998, p. 39-40.
Variety. Jan. 5, 1998, p. 79.

Once Upon a Time in Mexico

The time has come.
—Movie tagline

 Box Office: $55.8 million

R obert Rodriguez apparently does everything with remarkable verve or not at all, and there seems to be little he does not do. Often photographed with a big smile and an even bigger cowboy hat, Rodriguez actually wears a number of other hats as well, being a virtual one-man-band of filmmaking. For his latest effort entitled *Once Upon a Time in Mexico*, which was shot in just seven weeks, he serves as writer, director, producer, director of photography, editor, production designer, and composer. Holed up on a sixty-acre ranch outside of Austin, Texas, and surrounded by family and all the technical wizardry he could need, Rodriguez contentedly works long hours (often through the night) putting together his productions. He is evidently a firm believer in the old saying that too many cooks spoil the broth, choosing to formulate the recipe, carefully select the ingredients, and indefatigably cook it all together into the concoction he envisions. His crews are small and so are his budgets, the latter fact allowing him to go about his business with relatively little studio interference. His hard work has paid off handsomely for all concerned in recent times, particularly with the highly successful *Spy Kids* trilogy (over $500 million worldwide) which wrapped up this year. It is clear that there is more than just mileage which separates Rodriguez from much of the moviemaking going on in Hollywood.

Once Upon a Time in Mexico is the epic culmination of the Mexican-American director's other trilogy which began in 1993 with the bargain basement-budgeted but Sundance Film Festival-heralded *El Mariachi*. It told the violent tale of a guitarist who must defend himself against a drug lord and assorted goons when mistaken for a killer. Rodriguez said he had hoped his little film, in Spanish with subtitles, would garner at least some interest amongst the Mexican-American community, but was surprised and delighted when it turned out to have broader appeal. As a result there was *Desperado* in 1995, an English language sequel/remake with a slightly larger budget which also succeeded in making a profit. That film featured a higher body count, a better-known actor in the lead role (Antonio Banderas) and virtual unknown Salma Hayek as love interest Carolina. Now comes *Once Upon a Time in Mexico,* which winds up the story of El Mariachi with the accent definitely on wind, as it is an often confusing, convoluted story zigzagging in time which features characters whose allegiances shift this way and that like snakes slithering through the arid Mexican countryside.

Despite the film's excessive piling on of violence and the storyline which will make even the most attentive beg more than once for clarification, there are some beautifully filmed, undeniably gripping, and weirdly-humorous sequences. The latter are thanks to a memorably loopy performance by Johnny Depp, who steals the film away from lead Banderas. Throughout all the mayhem and destruction, you can tell that Rodriguez is having a blast. The often over-the-top violence is so choreographed and cartoonish that it is hard to take it very seriously, and the director helps set this playful tone from the start with credits which read "a Robert Rodriguez flick" and "shot, chopped and scored by Robert Rodriguez."

The film begins by introducing Depp as Sands, an amoral rogue CIA operative and one of the strangest birds ever to grace the silver screen. It seems that the new President of Mexico (Pedro Armendariz) is coming down hard on drug lords like Barillo (a curiously-cast Willem Dafoe), and so Barillo is funding a coup spearheaded by brutal General Marquez (Gerardo Vigil). Sands finds out from talkative, one-eyed Belini (Cheech Marin), and we find out through flashbacks, that Marquez was responsible for the slaughtering of El Mariachi's beloved Carolina and their child. (Hayek only appears in these intermittent and relatively brief flashback sequences.) Sands wants to find someone to kill Marquez before he can actually come to power, the unbalanced operative coolly insisting such an act would restore balance. As El Mariachi has, of late, been alone with his despair and incommunicado, Sands enlists the menacing Cucuy (Danny Trejo) to try and find him, spurring this savage-looking brute on to be a "Mexi-can" and not a "Mexi-can't." When El Mariachi is brought in to meet with Sands face to face, the agent calmly relays the complex and baffling reasoning behind his plans, successfully stoking the mariachi's suppressed desires for revenge. Sands (something

of an epicurean) then heads back through the kitchen to shoot the cook for making his meal too delicious.

While El Mariachi enlists the help of loyal fellow mariachis Lorenzo (singer Enrique Iglesias in his feature film debut) and alcoholic Fideo (Marco Leonardi), Sands is popping up in all sorts of places with all sorts of people to try to make them do all sorts of things. It seems to become clear (or at least as clear as anything is in this film) that Sands is hoping to personally (i.e. monetarily) benefit from all he is engineering. Sands also plays upon the thirst for retribution within retired FBI agent Jorge (Ruben Blades), who has been shadowing Barillo since the kingpin tortured and killed his partner. Then we see Sands meeting at a bullfight with the president's devoted aid (Julio Oscar Mechoso), who turns out to be not so devoted after all. When meeting again with Belini, Sands reveals a gun-toting real arm beneath a fake one and shoots the man, plumbing various orifices for whatever it is he is looking for before throwing the corpse in a river. We also witness the peculiar carnal relationship Sands has with shady Mexican agent Ajedrez (Eva Mendes), who he finds even more stimulating when she is shooting at him.

As the film progresses, allegiances change nearly as often as lives are snuffed out. By the time Billy, Barillo's Chihuahua-toting henchman (Mickey Rourke), and numerous other characters have switched sides or revealed their true colors, it will be hard for many viewers to discern what is really going on. It is even harder for Sands to take it all in once Barillo has reduced him to stumbling around town with eyes ground to nothingness by a fierce-looking drill. Amidst the carnage and chaos of the coup attempt, El Mariachi and his comrades fare much better, mowing down Marquez and heroically saving the president so that Mexico can pick up the pieces and proceed down a free and honorable path, although there are certainly going to be an awful lot of pieces to pick up. The nation saved and the troublemakers dispatched in various spectacular and satisfying ways, El Mariachi kisses the Mexican flag he wears as a sash and marches off once and for all, perhaps thinking he is getting too old for such stuff.

Rodriguez's biggest influence is obviously 1968's *Once Upon a Time in the West* and the other "spaghetti westerns" of director Sergio Leone. It was director Quentin Tarantino who suggested the title and it is certainly apt, as Rodriguez's film contains many elements reminiscent of Leone's legendary work. For example, the lead character here is a strong, quiet man referred to simply as El Mariachi or El, similar to the "Man With No Name" played by Clint Eastwood in the trilogy that began in 1964 with *A Fistful of Dollars*. Both are mythic, larger-than-life characters. As in Leone's work, there is a great emphasis here on style. Like *Once Upon a Time in the West,* Rodriguez's homage is painted on an epic canvas, and effectively captures the gold tones of the dry, sun-drenched town and terrain. Both directors use carefully choreographed and stylized scenes of potent violence which are as beautiful as they are bloody and brutal. Rodriguez often uses his camera similarly to Leone, such as the utilization of close-ups to capture the intensity of combatants' faces. There is also a purposeful use of music to set a tone here, though not nearly as memorably as in Leone's Westerns.

Made on the relatively lean budget of $29 million, *Once Upon a Time in Mexico* grossed almost $56 million domestically before heading overseas to a receptive European market. While it is not, on the whole, as compelling as the works which inspired it, the film has enough wild and witty moments to recommend a look. There is the flashback scene in which El Mariachi and Carolina, handcuffed together and under siege, rappel down the side of a hotel, jump onto a passing bus and then leap to safety before it collides with a tanker and explodes into a massive fireball. There is another in which a shootout takes place in a church, first with silencers and then with thunderous eruptions of gunfire, pausing respectfully to let an old woman take her leave before resuming. There is also a scene in which Sands, blood oozing down his face from behind dark sunglasses, has the last laugh on two bad guys guffawing at his predicament. There has been talk of bringing back Depp's vivid, sightless character, reprehensible and yet in the end startlingly sympathetic, in a future Rodriguez film. It could be a success, too, for even though Sands has little idea where he is headed, the same cannot be said for the man who created him.

—*David L. Boxerbaum*

CREDITS

El Mariachi: Antonio Banderas
Sands: Johnny Depp
Barillo: Willem Dafoe
Carolina: Salma Hayek
Billy Chambers: Mickey Rourke
Ajedrez: Eva Mendes
Cucuy: Danny Trejo
Lorenzo: Enrique Inglesias
Fideo: Marco Leonardi
Belini: Richard "Cheech" Marin
Jorge: Ruben Blades
President: Pedro Armendariz Jr.
Marquez: Gerardo Vigil

Origin: USA
Released: 2003
Production: Elizabeth Avellan, Carlos Gallardo, Robert Rodriguez; Troublemaker Studios; released by Columbia Pictures
Directed by: Robert Rodriguez

Written by: Robert Rodriguez
Cinematography by: Robert Rodriguez
Music by: Robert Rodriguez
Sound: Edward Novick
Editing: Robert Rodriguez
Art Direction: Meno Hinjosa
Costumes: Graciela Mazon
Production Design: Robert Rodriguez
MPAA rating: R
Running time: 101 minutes

REVIEWS

Chicago Sun-Times Online. September 12, 2003.
Entertainment Weekly. September 12, 2003, p. 128.
Los Angeles Times Online. September 12, 2003.
New York Times Online. September 12, 2003.
People. September 22, 2003, p. 40.
Rolling Stone. October 2, 2003, p. 124.
USA Today Online. September 12, 2003.
Variety Online. August 28, 2003.
Washington Post. September 12, 2003, p. WE41.

Once Upon a Time in the Midlands

A tinned spaghetti western.
—Movie tagline

After working with mostly non-professionals in his first two films, writer-director Shane Meadows uses a cast of well-known English and Scottish character actors in *Once Upon a Time in the Midlands*. This blending of working-class drama, romantic comedy, crime film, and Western parody is only fitfully engaging.

Jimmy (Robert Carlyle), a small-time Glasgow criminal, awakes on his sofa to see his ex-girlfriend Shirley (Shirley Henderson) on a television talk show. He watches in horror as Shirley's current beau, Dek (Rhys Ifans), proposes to her, only to be relieved when she rejects him. After escaping with the loot following a robbery bungled by his gang, Jimmy makes his way to Nottingham to try to win Shirley back. (Oddly, the only reference to the film's location is a comment about a Robin Hood theme park.)

Observing the tug of war for Shirley's affections are Marlene (Finn Atkins), her twelve-year-old daughter by Jimmy; Shirley's best friend, Carol (Kathy Burke), who is also Jimmy's foster sister; and Charlie (Ricky Tomlinson), Carol's estranged husband. Charlie, a bar owner who fancies himself a country-music singer, lives alone but spends much of his time at Carol's with her and their kids.

Much of the humor in *Once Upon a Time in the Midlands* comes from the eccentricities of Charlie and Dek. The latter runs a garage, and the joy of his life, after Shirley, of course, is his car, which he calls "Baby." The rising conflicts between the protagonists result in the two-time vandalizing of Baby, although neither occasion is as funny as Meadows and co-writer Paul Fraser seem to think. Jimmy tries to woo Shirley by winning Marlene over, and while the girl is willing to give him a chance, she clearly loves Dek, the only father figure she has ever known. All this leads to a series of showdowns between Dek and Jimmy.

While Meadows's *Twentyfourseven* (1997) and *A Room for Romeo Brass* (2000) had some labeling the director as a potentially great British filmmaker, these gritty yet sentimental urban dramas have uneven performances and underdeveloped ideas. Likewise, *Once Upon a Time in the Midlands* meanders a bit. It starts off with Jimmy as a sympathetic anti-hero. The opening scenes seem to imply he is worthy of Shirley's affection. And when the robbery goes wrong, he does not leave his cohorts out of malice but because there is no way he can wait for them without also being caught by the approaching police. He feels genuine remorse for being stuck with the proceeds. Yet almost immediately upon arriving in Nottingham, he becomes a crude, vulgar thug and sinks even lower as the film progresses.

When Jimmy's colleagues arrive, Dek takes them to Charlie's, where Jimmy has been staying, and the would-be singing star is beaten. This is the worst of several tonal offenses in what is essentially a light-hearted comedy. Meadows and Fraser are striving for a naturalistic, almost improvisatorial style and are obviously not interested in adhering to any pre-fab formula, but the resulting sudden shifts in tone are disruptive, irritating, and often badly staged, as with Carol's taking a crowbar to Baby after learning Dek is responsible for Charlie's beating.

Meadows has often been compared to such directors as Ken Loach, Bill Forsyth, and Mike Leigh. His working-class subjects resemble Loach's, but his treatment of these themes is less realistic and political than those in *Kes* (1969), *Riff-Raff* (1990), and *My Name Is Joe* (1998). Meadows's film lacks the whimsy of such Forsyth films as *Local Hero* (1983), though having Jimmy's gang rob a carload of clowns without ever explaining why the victims are dressed this way recalls the offbeat humor of the criminals in Forsyth's *Comfort and Joy* (1984).

Once Upon a Time in the Midlands is, however, almost an homage to Leigh's kitchen-sink grumpiness. As is often the case with Leigh, there is a thin line between treating the working class realistically and being condescending toward their bad taste. Except for Shirley and Jimmy, who wears only jeans, a t-shirt, and a leather jacket, everyone dresses badly, and all the furnishings are tacky. (They are also the only thin people in the Midlands.) When Shirley and Carol's families gather, all they do is lie about watching telly.

Because of the increasingly negative way Jimmy is presented, the initial dramatic tension about which suitor Shirley might choose is quickly dissipated. The element of the film that works best is the Western parody suggested by its title. At first, Jimmy resembles the mysterious Charles Bronson character in Sergio Leone's *Once Upon a Time in the West* (1968), seeking revenge for a wrong done years earlier, yet he gradually assumes the very villainous persona portrayed by Henry Fonda in that great film. John Lunn's score often recalls the use of electric guitar by Ennio Morricone in Leone's film.

Dek is a variation on the Western cliché of the unheroic farmer or shopkeeper forced to reach deep inside himself to find the courage to face down the gunfighter or outlaw. Of the numerous films presenting such circumstances, one of the most famous is George Stevens's *Shane* (1953), in which farmer Van Heflin finds the courage to confront bad-guy Jack Palance and win back the respect of his wife and son. The parallels between this film and *Once Upon a Time in the Midlands* are appropriate since Meadows was named for the Alan Ladd character in *Shane*.

Jimmy is also a blending of Carlyle's two most famous characters: the psychopath in *Trainspotting* (1996) and the working-class man who hopes to win back his wife in *The Full Monty* (1997). An excellent actor, who gives one of the greatest television performances ever as a frustrated man who becomes a skinhead racist in a 1994 episode of *Cracker*, Carlyle has little to do here but look menacing. He also uses a thick Glaswegian accent that makes a good portion of his dialogue impenetrable.

Ironically, Ifans's character is more like Carlyle's in *The Full Monty*. Much heavier than he is in *Notting Hill* (1999), his most famous role, Ifans gives Dek some offbeat charm, but the character, as written by Meadows and Fraser, is a bit creepier than he needs to be. What Shirley has ever seen in him is not that clear.

Marlene likes Dek because he is more immature than she is, and Atkins does an excellent job of suggesting depths of feelings in the budding adolescent. With her thin face and slightly pointed nose, she even looks like she could be Henderson's daughter. Henderson, Carlyle's co-star in the 1990s television series *Hamish Macbeth*, is unconventionally attractive, clearly from a working-class background, but as Shirley, she has considerable star charisma. She employs a distinctive Midlands accent, drawing out certain words, especially Jimmy. Most memorable to American audiences as one of the singers in Leigh's *Topsy-Turvy* (1999) and as Moaning Myrtle in *Harry Potter and the Chamber of Secrets* (2002), Henderson, unlike much of the rest of the cast, does not strain for effect. Very subtly, she makes clear why Dek and Jimmy are fighting over Shirley. 🎞

—Michael Adams

CREDITS

Jimmy: Robert Carlyle
Dek: Rhys Ifans
Shirley: Shirley Henderson
Carol: Kathy Burke
Charlie: Ricky Tomlinson
Marlene: Finn Atkins

Origin: Great Britain
Released: 2002
Production: Andrea Calderwood; FilmFour, Senator Film Entertainment, Slate Films, Big Arty; released by Sony Pictures Classics
Directed by: Shane Meadows
Written by: Shane Meadows, Paul Fraser
Cinematography by: Brian Tufano
Music by: John Lunn
Sound: Colin Nicolson, Paul Hamblin
Music Supervisor: Liz Gallacher
Editing: Trevor Waite, Peter Beston
Art Direction: Anthea Nelson
Costumes: Robin Fraser-Paye
Production Design: Crispian Sallis
MPAA rating: R
Running time: 104 minutes

 REVIEWS

Boston Globe. September 5, 2003, p. E6.
Boxoffice. November, 2002, p. 137.
Chicago Sun-Times Online. September 19, 2003.
Entertainment Weekly. September 5, 2003, p. 58.
Los Angeles Times Online. August 29, 2003.
New York. August 25, 2003, p. 181.
New York Times. August 29, 2003, p. E1.
Sight and Sound. September, 2002, p. 68.
Variety. May 27, 2002, p. 26.
Washington Post. September 26, 2003, p. WE50.

Only the Strong Survive

A celebration of soul.
—Movie tagline

Right at the beginning of *Only the Strong Survive* we learn that, "Memphis has two kings: Elvis Presley and Rufus Thomas." For those who don't know Rufus Thomas, this movie aims to set that straight. But the directors, longtime documentarians Chris Hegedus (*Startup.com*) and her husband, D. A. Pennebaker (*Don't Look Back*), plus inter-

viewer and entertainment journalist, Roger Friedman, don't teach us about soul in a straightforward manner. Soul is something that the filmmakers leave for the audience to feel for themselves.

The film largely features Memphis soul artists, particularly those who recorded at Stax Records, a less famous relation to Detroit's Motown. (A similarly-themed film focusing on Motown, *Standing in the Shadows of Motown*, came out the previous year.) *Only the Strong Survive* focuses on the kind of passionate soul music that thrilled in the late 1960s and early 1970s, until disco came along and took over the radio airwaves. There are performances by Sam Moore of Sam and Dave, Rufus Thomas and daughter Carla Thomas, Isaac Hayes, Wilson Pickett, Mary Wilson, the Chi-Lites, Ann Peebles and Jerry Butler. Before each performance, Friedman peppers the performers with a few lightweight questions. While Friedman does come across as overeager, he is shown to be the soul fan that he is. Unfortunately Friedman has no instinct for following a line of questioning. While he's driving around town with Moore, Moore points out a street and mentions that he spent a stint of time selling heroin and cocaine there. Friedman asks a couple of questions, but he doesn't get at the reasons why Moore turned to dealing drugs. Though his questions seem to be lacking, he's so obviously in awe of these soul legends that he is able to put them at ease. All the performers seem happy to be interviewed by this guy and are glad to talk with him.

The film doesn't seem to have a solid story structure. While the film mostly focuses on Stax artists, Chicago's Chi-Lites and Motown's Mary Wilson are also covered. There are the performances, but they aren't all at the same event. There is some backstory, but we never learn that much about the performers' lives or even why they were/are famous. For example, Friedman spends one of the longer bits of time with Carla Thomas. He takes her to the vacant lot that once housed Stax, and she relates a couple of anecdotes. She performs a version of "B-A-B-Y," which was a hit for her, not that you'd know for sure from the movie. The only way to tell that the song must have been significant somehow is to look at the faces of the other people listening.

Oftentimes, performers are not well identified. There might be a person talking and the audience will have to glean who they are from other clues, like hearing someone else in the scene refer to them by name or seeing them break into a famous soul standard. It's as though Pennebaker and Hegedus didn't bother to shape the raw footage for the film in post-production. The argument could be made that a documentary is more "real" with this sort of fly-on-the-wall, minimal editing approach, but the watchability suffers. The cohesiveness of the film might have been helped considerably by a brief history of each performer before that performer's segment or even some more informative, strategically placed voiceovers.

That said, the subjects of *Only the Strong Survive* are such powerful characters that the movie is good viewing. Everything that the filmmakers don't tell the viewers explicitly is there in each of these performers very presence. For example, the movie doesn't focus on the way that soul artists were not rewarded financially for their work, but Moore mentions that he is seeking money for past performance rights. He and his wife are also hoping that he has one more "Soul Man" in him. In another part of the film, Moore describes soul music as "a feeling. You put the emphasis on what you're saying—that's soul." He shows this better than he could ever explain it when he sings an impassioned version of "When Something is Wrong With My Baby." He puts so much life into the song that even those who aren't particularly fans of this type of music will be enthralled.

The quality of the performances vary but when they are good, they are amazingly good. A disappointment is Wilson, who takes over the lead vocals on old Supreme songs. Her voice is strong enough, but all her performances prove is that Diana Ross was indeed the one with the distinctive voice that made those song hits. Two of the better numbers come from Carla Thomas. Her father, Rufus, was a soul star and Carla became a star herself when she was a teenager. Now a middle-aged woman and missing a tooth or two, she still has a high, clear voice and sounds every bit a teen again when she sings, "Gee Whiz (Look at His Eyes)." For those who watched singers like Frank Sinatra and Mick Jagger suffer from deteriorating voices as they aged, Thomas's voice is something of a medical marvel.

Also entertaining is Wilson Pickett doing "In the Midnight Hour." To emphasize some of the song's more suggestive lyrics, the aging Pickett thrusts his hips and says "That's what I'm gonna do." He gets carried away with the song and invites a very large older woman from the audience to dance with him. After some demurring and shy looks down, she is hoisted up on the stage by a few burly men, then starts dancing with Pickett. The woman then starts suggestively bumping and grinding with the receptive Pickett like the two are alone. It's a priceless moment.

The Chi-Lites are still in fine voice and can still hit the high notes in "Have You Seen Her?" They reminisce about some wonderful costumes that they once wore. So magnificent were these outfits that the audience couldn't stop cheering when the performers came out. The film cuts to a picture of said outfits—over-the-top 1970s jumpsuits with huge flair pants. And Isaac Hayes's performance is good for the sole fact that the man is still so cool. The voice behind *South Park*'s Chef and the singer of the theme from *Shaft*, Hayes is one of the few still successful people in the film. It's a kick to see the ultra-smooth Hayes admitting that the reason he started wearing his trademark dark glasses was to give him a "security blanket" to deal with his shyness.

Most critics liked the film. The *Boston Globe*'s Wesley Morris commented on the spiritual nature of the subject: "I'm not sure where you go to church, but you're unlikely to experience anything as holy as Jerry Butler doing a live version of his soul classic 'For Your Precious Love.'" Stephen Holden of the *New York Times* wrote, "The classic soul that pumps, struts, growls, and cries through 'Only the Strong Survive' is so adrenalized that a young audience encountering the music for the first time could easily find themselves converted into old fogies, longing for the good old days before the ascendance of cooler pop sounds that ride on digital beats." *Entertainment Weekly*'s Owen Gleiberman gave the film a B+, concluding, "*Only the Strong Survive* doesn't have a lot of structural unity, yet when you're listening to some like Moore, or to Memphis 'king' Rufus Thomas doing 'Walking the Dog' with a bawdy wink that belies his 82 years, it's one of the happiest movies around."

—*Jill Hamilton*

CREDITS

Origin: USA
Released: 2003
Production: Frazer Pennebaker, Roger Friedman; released by Miramax Films
Directed by: Chris Hegedus, D.A. Pennebaker
Cinematography by: Chris Hegedus, D.A. Pennebaker, James Desmond, Nick Doob, Jehane Noujaim
Editing: Chris Hegedus, D.A. Pennebaker, Erez Laufer
MPAA rating: PG-13
Running time: 95 minutes

REVIEWS

Detroit News. May 9, 2003, p. 2E.
Entertainment Weekly. May 16, 2003, p. 53.
Los Angeles Times Online. May 9, 2003.
New York Times Online. May 9, 2003.
People. May 19, 2003, p. 40.
USA Today Online. May 9, 2003.
Variety Online. January 25, 2003.
Washington Post. May 9, 2003, p. WE48.

TRIVIA

Rufus Thomas died in December, 2001, as the film was being completed.

Open Range

No place to run. No reason to hide.
—Movie tagline

Box Office: $58.3 million

After a considerable slump, Kevin Costner returns to form as an actor and makes his best film as a director with *Open Range.* He takes a simple story that can be seen as both clichéd and archetypal and invests it with the leisurely yet visually striking style of such masters of the Western as John Ford and Howard Hawks.

Boss Spearman (Robert Duvall) and Charley Waite (Kevin Costner), partners for ten years, are "freegrazers," using any available rangeland for their herd of cattle. Their only helpers are the large, good-natured Mose (Abraham Benrubi), and Button (Diego Luna), a young Mexican that Boss has rescued from a squalid homelessness. Their relatively idyllic existence begins to unravel when Mose is sent for supplies to the nearby town of Harmonville and lands in jail, having been provoked into a fight by thugs in the hire of Denton Baxter (Michael Gambon), owner of the area's largest ranch and much of the town.

Boss and Charley take the badly beaten Mose to the local doctor (Dean McDermott), and Charley experiences an immediate affinity with Sue Barlow (Annette Bening), whom he takes to be Doc Barlow's wife. Later, they leave Mose and Button alone with the herd to go track down the men who attacked Mose. When they return, however, Mose is dead and Button badly wounded.

Open Range is clearly a tribute to the classic Westerns of the 1940s and 1950s, and the shootings of Mose and Button recall the killing of one of the young Earp brothers in John Ford's *My Darling Clementine* (1946). In Ford's great film, this murder leads Henry Fonda's Wyatt Earp to become a lawman to clean up the local corruption. Costner has visited this story before as the star of Lawrence Kasdan's rather inept *Wyatt Earp* (1994). Unlike Fonda's Earp, Boss and Charley are not interested in restoring the law but in revenge against Baxter and his men. The ostensible moral point about the cowboys' right to grazing is not dwelled upon, though Baxter's obvious legal authority is ignored in the interest of celebrating a certain type of rugged American freedom.

Much of *Open Range* consists of the slow buildup to the confrontation with Baxter and the eventual shootout. Along the way, the two outsiders endear themselves to the local citizens through such acts as Charley's rescue of a puppy from a flooded street. (The bad guys have also killed Char-

ley's beloved dog.) At first, the situation resembles Fred Zinnemann's somewhat overrated *High Noon* (1952), in which a community of shopkeepers is too cowardly to back up lawman Gary Cooper. Costner's citizens are afraid of Baxter but gradually come around entirely to the cowboys' side, with the way led by scrawny little Percy (Michael Jeter), who runs the stable. A parallel slow development is the romance between Charley and Sue after he learns she is the doctor's sister.

Once the inevitable gunfight begins, it proves well worth the wait. It is almost as if the shootout is Costner's rationale for making the film. While it is often difficult to tell what is happening to whom during the O. K. Corral scene in *Wyatt Earp,* Costner seems determined to get it right this time. Not only is Costner's staging expert, but editors Michael J. Duthie and Miklos Wright cut the lengthy sequence so that the audience always knows where the heroes are in relation to the villains and the townspeople. Production designer Gae S. Buckley's job is not just to design an authentic 1882 Western town but to arrange the buildings to facilitate the effectiveness of the showdown.

The gunfight goes on for some considerable time, with first Percy and then other citizens joining in. Even Button rises from his sickbed to add a gun. This battle is realistic—up to a point. Unlike Sam Peckinpah and his admirers, Costner is not interested in gore or stylized violence but in prolonging the dramatic situation. As a result, some may quibble about the realism of the dozens of missed shots. Baxter, for example, has to be shot at least five times with another fifty or so bullets missing him. While Costner's gunfight lacks the poetic imagery of Ford's in *My Darling Clementine,* still the best such scene ever, he matches its emotional intensity.

Some may also complain that *Open Range* is too leisurely, and it is unusually slow compared to other action films of the past decade. However, Costner and screenwriter Craig Stoper, adapting a novel by Lauran Paine, are primarily interested in mood and character. Among the many effective small touches is a wonderful scene in which Boss and Charley, knowing they may be dead soon, visit the general store to buy treats for themselves. Boss asks for the store's most expensive chocolate and, when he learns the shopkeeper has never dared try it, gives the man a piece. Charley gets so caught up in preparing for the battle that he lets his precious candy melt. Other highlights come when the two longtime friends finally reveal their complete names and when, eager to make a good impression, Charley picks up the clumps of mud his boots have left on Sue's carpet.

With the exception of his performance in *Bull Durham* (1988), still the best film with which he has been associated, Costner has not been given much credit by reviewers for his acting. As with many of his characters, Charley is an aging adolescent, and Costner presents the cowboy with subtle touches. Charley tries to hide behind a manly façade, yet

Costner gives viewers glimpses of what lies beneath the hard exterior: Charley's body language as he approaches his dead dog, his surprised expression when he learns Sue is not married, his embarrassment when he tells Boss his full name.

Duvall has been a treasure of a film actor for almost forty years and gives one of his best performances here. In an earlier era, Duvall might have specialized in Westerns, but his most notable accomplishment in this genre has been playing the villain opposite John Wayne in *True Grit* (1969). While Boss has superficial similarities to Duvall's character in the television miniseries *Lonesome Dove* (1989), Boss lacks that cowboy's eccentric flamboyance. Duvall creates a larger-than-life character much more subtly, perfectly capturing the tension within a man who both realizes his time has passed and refuses to admit to himself or anyone else that he is old. Life is to be lived, as Boss demonstrates in the general store scene, and Duvall gives a lovely look of pity at the storekeeper's timidity. This is his best performance since *True Confessions* (1981).

Bening has less material to work with, and for much of the film it is not clear why someone of her stature has taken such a relatively thankless role. Yet Sue demonstrates near the end of *Open Range* that she is equal to, if not superior to, the cowboys in strength of character. Gambon, one of the world's greatest actors, also has little to do until the gunfight but then, with his villainous sneer, makes Baxter both frightening and amusing. The heir to a long line of stage actors that includes Laurence Olivier, John Gielgud, Ralph Richardson, and Alec Guinness, he gets to do something none of them ever did—play cowboy.

Costner's much-overrated directorial debut, *Dances with Wolves* (1990), has its moments, especially with the performances of the Native American actors, but it is essentially a lightweight variation on earlier filmmakers' treatment of the white man discovering the nobility of the red man, as in the much better films *Broken Arrow* (1950), directed by Delmer Daves, and *Little Big Man* (1970), which was helmed by Arthur Penn. Costner's second effort, *The Postman* (1997), was justifiably reviled by reviewers as a boring embarrassment. *Open Range* is notable as a major comeback. As an actor, he has not been this likable since *Tin Cup* (1996). As a director, he displays considerable skills in handling his actors, dealing equally effectively with quiet domestic scenes and action sequences, in pacing the film, and in composing shots.

Costner frames the actors against the landscape to call attention to the way they are both a part of the natural world and apart from it. The beauty of the landscape—the film was shot in Alberta, Canada—as well as the relatively claustrophobic doctor's quarters are captured well by James Munro, a longtime camera operator making his debut as cinematographer. Munro worked previously with Costner on *Field of Dreams* (1989), *Dances with Wolves,* and *JFK* (1991), and his other impressive credits include *L.A. Confi-dential* (1997), *Titanic* (1997), and *The Insider* (1999). Costner and Munro also devise one unusual shot, at least in the pan-and-scan era, with a profile of the head and shoulders of Boss and Charley in each corner of the frame and an enormous space between them, emphasizing the gulf that separates even the best of friends.

Costner and screenwriter Craig Stoper, adapting a novel by Lauran Paine, are well aware of the conventions of the genre. There is even a nod to the homoerotic overtones of sidekicks when Boss observes that he and Charley are like an old married couple. *Open Range* has flaws, such as dialogue that occasionally strains for lyricism and spells out matters too obviously. Combined with long, continuous shots and a lack of flashy editing, however, the result is a throwback to the Westerns of earlier eras. *Washington Post* reviewer Stephen Hunter called Costner the best director of 1957. *Open Range* is a wonderful example of a film having simplicity and scope at the same time.

—Michael Adams

CREDITS

Boss Spearman: Robert Duvall
Charley Waite: Kevin Costner
Sue Barlow: Annette Bening
Denton Baxter: Michael Gambon
Percy: Michael Jeter
Button: Diego Luna
Sheriff Poole: James Russo
Mose: Abraham Benrubi
Doc Barlow: Dean McDermott
Butler: Kim Coates

Origin: USA
Released: 2003
Production: David Valdes, Kevin Costner, Jake Eberts; TIG Productions, Cobalt Media Group; released by Touchstone Pictures
Directed by: Kevin Costner
Written by: Craig Storper
Cinematography by: James Muro
Music by: Michael Kamen
Sound: Glen Gauthier
Editing: Michael J. Duthie, Miklos Wright
Art Direction: Gary Myers
Costumes: John Bloomfield
Production Design: Gae Buckley
MPAA rating: R
Running time: 135 minutes

REVIEWS

Atlanta Journal Constitution. August 15, 2003, p. E1.
Boston Globe. August 15, 2003, p. C1.
Boxoffice. August, 2003, p. 14.
Chicago Sun-Times Online. August 15, 2003.
Christian Science Monitor. August 15, 2003, p. 16.
Entertainment Weekly. August 23, 2003, p. 113.
Los Angeles Times Online. August 15, 2003.
New York Times. August 15, 2003, p. E1.
New Yorker. September 1, 2003, p. 130.
People. August 25, 2003, p. 33.
San Francisco Chronicle. August 15, 2003, p. D1.
USA Today. August 15, 2003, p. E4.
Variety Online. August 10, 2003.
Washington Post. August 15, 2003, p. C1.

QUOTES

Boss Spearman (Robert Duvall): "Cows is one thing, but one man telling another man where he can go in this country is something else."
Charley (Kevin Costner): "There's some things gnaw on a man more than dying."

TRIVIA

Charley's dog is named Tig, which is the name of Kevin Costner's production company.

The Order (Sin Eater)

Behind the disguise of good hides the soul of evil.
—Movie tagline
Every soul has its price.
—Movie tagline

Box Office: $7.6 million

When *A Knight's Tale* was released in 2001, it became a popular hit with audiences. Its high-energy combination of historical comedy and rock and roll music made the inherent anachronisms a thing of fun, not ridicule. It just didn't take itself very seriously, and everyone—actors and audiences alike—had a good time.

So one can imagine the high expectations that accompanied the re-uniting of the main cast and the director from *A Knight's Tale* for *The Order*. One can also imagine Fox's publicity department churning out the "together again" promos for the film. Unfortunately, expectations went unmet and Fox had so little faith in the movie that although they did promote it . . . slightly, they refused to let critics view the customary early screening in order to produce timely reviews. This is virtually a kiss of death for any film.

Brian Helgeland, the director of *A Knight's Tale* and screenwriter of *L.A. Confidential*, had wanted to do a movie based on the concept of a sin eater for more than three years. Originally he wanted Paul Bettany (who played Chaucer in *A Knight's Tale*) to be cast in the lead role of Priest Alex with Antonio Banderas playing the sin eater. Eventually, Bettany was dropped because it was felt he didn't have a name strong enough to carry the film and Banderas was replaced with Vincent Cassel (*Brotherhood of the Wolf*) who dropped out after only one day's filming. Already things were not looking good for *The Order*.

The plot of this ill-fated film begins in Rome with Brother Dominic (Francesco Carnelutti), who is an outsider in the Catholic hierarchy. We know this because he lives in a Gothic tower with no electricity but lots of books and with two silent and scowling children permanently camped outside his door. When Dominic is found dead, the Catholic Church decides it was a suicide caused by the despair he lived with due to his ex-communication. They notify Dominic's only two students from earlier in his life, Alex (Heath Ledger) and Thomas (Mark Addy), who, upon examining Dominic's body, believe he is the victim of a ritual murder.

After stealing their mentor's body and secretly burying it in hallowed ground, Alex begins to investigate the mysterious marks on Dominic's body and the cryptic Aramaic writing found written in the dust of his home: "blood in, blood out."

Alex and Thomas are all that are left of an ancient Catholic order called the Carolingians. They are an arcane order (hence the movie's title) who specialize in all the mysticism of Catholicism: stigmatas, exorcisms, saints, and demons. They are learned in these esoteric ways of the church, which luckily gives Alex and Thomas a leg up on the mystery. In fact, the Carolingians are supposed to "surpass the Jesuits in their search for knowledge." It is even said that Dominic "would have sold his soul for knowledge." Is that what he has done?

Eventually they come to discover that Dominic has died as a result of a sin eater. Sin eaters are men who free other men's souls of sin but in the process damn their own. They provide redemption for the unrepentant which the church dislikes because they offer salvation by doing an end-run around the church's authority. In fact, sin eaters actually can nullify the church's most potent tool, excommunication.

This is why the excommunicated and therefore damned Dominic has called in a sin eater. But sin eaters will only take on another man's sins for a price. What did the impoverished Dominic have to offer him?

Eventually Thomas and Alex follow leads through an underground Roman S-M club where knowledge is gained from the mouths of dying men hanged just for this purpose by a mysterious, hooded figure who presides over it all. From this source they are told, "The Other will find you. He will bring you the keys to the kingdom." The Other does find Alex. He is William Eden (Bruno Furmann), a seemingly cosmopolitan, educated, and unthreatening young man. He tells Alex how he became a sin eater in the 1500s when St. Peter's was being built. Alex's brother was the main builder and he died when scaffolding collapsed. His brother, however, also died under excommunication (he gave holy water to a thirsty Arab during the crusades), but his soul was saved when a sin eater was brought in just as he took his last breath. In exchange for his services, the sin eater takes young Eden under his wing and teaches him the trade. Now, 500 years later, Eden is tired and wants out, but before he can die he must find someone to assume all his sins and become the next sin eater.

For some totally inexplicable reason, Alex has brought with him to Rome a woman named Mara (Shannyn Sossamen). Her veiled background indicates that Alex once performed an exorcism on her brother; she is also a talented artist, gets terrible headaches and hears nightingales, she once tried to kill Alex, and was sentenced to a mental institution . . . from which she has just escaped. Nice travelling companion. Of course, in this type of movie one just knows that she's also there to test Alex's commitment to his vow of celibacy. "She sees things differently, she feels things differently, and I wish I'd never seen her face," says the conflicted priest.

As it turns out, Mara's real role in the story is one that has been set for her by Eden, one guaranteed to set into motion events that will force Alex to become the next sin eater.

The Order belongs to a sub-genre of horror films that are noted for having one foot in traditional religion (usually Catholicism) and one foot in the supernatural. (Think *The Omen* and *The Exorcist*.) Unfortunately *The Order* has little in it that is scary and even less that actually makes sense in the realm of the Catholic Church. Even if one were to accept the fictitious order to which Dominic, Alex and Thomas belong, the Carolingians, wouldn't the church want to keep a tight control over an order like theirs? (And by the way, the term Carolingian is usually used in connection with the reign of Charlemagne, but that's a totally excluded reference in the film and distracting in its omission.)

The Order actually had its release date postponed more than once, and one of the reasons was that Fox decided the original special effects of the "sin" leaving a person's body, which were done by Mill Film (*A Knight's Tale*, *Lara Croft Tomb Raider*), weren't scary but instead were unintentionally funny. Word had it that the effects looked like calamari, so Asylum VFX (*Moulin Rouge*) was called in to fix the problem. However, the "sin" now looks like a giant squid. Not much of an improvement.

While original concerns were that Paul Bettany was too unknown to headline this film, one could also make the case that Heath Ledger is too light-weight to carry so dark a film. He spends most of the movie with a tormented expression on his permanently 5-o'clock shadowed face. Similarly, Sossamon's Mara is supposed to be a talented but tortured artist, but she comes across as lethargic and colorless. Only Mark Addy as Eden seems to be having even the dimmest spark of fun with the movie. And while he doesn't go about with any kind of tortured look on his face, his character is actually the only one tortured.

The most interesting character is that of the sin eater William Eden. Is he evil or a force of good that the church wants silenced? Are we supposed to hate and fear Eden or not? He performs a divine function, but at what price? His intentions may be (are?) noble, but sometimes his tactics are immoral. Answers to questions like these surrounding Eden's mythology would have helped clarify the storyline of the movie and maybe save it from its worst sin: It is a truly unique story that is badly carried out. Its story is murky and muddled and is mired in artificial seriousness. The whole movie is heavy-handed with self-conscious if not outright ludicrous dialogue. It lacks any shocks or tension and no one looks like they're having any fun.

The Order may not be a good film, but it's not a total disaster either. It didn't deserve the premature burial given it by Fox Studios. However, it's also nothing like *A Knight's Tale* and is bound to be a disappointment to those expecting the re-teaming of that film's talent to produce a similarly entertaining film.

—*Beverley Bare Buehrer*

CREDITS

Alex: Heath Ledger
Mara: Shannyn Sossamon
Eden: Benno Furmann
Thomas: Mark Addy
Driscoll: Peter Weller
Dominic: Francesco Carnelutti

Origin: USA
Released: 2003
Production: Craig Baumgarten, Brian Helgeland; released by 20th Century-Fox
Directed by: Brian Helgeland

Written by: Brian Helgeland
Cinematography by: Nicola Pecorini
Music by: David Torn
Sound: Bernard Bats
Editing: Kevin Stitt
Art Direction: Branimir Babic, Domenico Sica
Costumes: Caroline Harris
Production Design: Miljen Kreka Kljakovic
MPAA rating: R
Running time: 102 minutes

REVIEWS

Entertainment Weekly. September 19, 2003, p. 64.
Los Angeles Times Online. September 8, 2003.
New York Times Online. September 6, 2003.
Sight and Sound. November, 2003, p. 62.
Variety Online. September 5, 2003.

QUOTES

Eden (Benno Furmann): "The problem with the truth is that sometimes you find it."
Eden (Benno Furmann): "God exists, He just doesn't give a damn."

TRIVIA

The scenes at the Vatican were actually recreated at Caserta's Royal Palace and on Cinecitta Studio's soundstages.

Out of Time

How do you solve a murder when all the evidence points to you?
—Movie tagline

Box Office: $41 million

A script can keep an audience engaged and unsettled by utilizing twists and turns, but if those moves are too numerous or too jarring the audience can disengage, their suspension of disbelief transforming into an awareness of being jerked this way and that by the screenwriter's pen. Once the spell is broken, we cannot quite get all worked up about how it all turns out. This is particularly true after what

seems like the hundredth time a film's central character manages to duck and dodge—just in the nick of time— what appeared to be certain, inescapable danger. The thriller *Out of Time* is just such a film, relatively unspectacular yet spectacularly contrived, but somehow it still works to a sufficient degree, primarily due to Denzel Washington's solid and charismatic screen presence. With a lesser and less likeable actor in his role, we might have merely rolled our eyes as he—and the script—strove to overcome the repercussions of what might be called inadvisable choices. With Washington, however, we keep caring about the character, and find ourselves still rooting for him each time he manages to skirt trouble, even when his circumvention becomes implausible.

There have been other, more notable films in which a character, like Washington here, endeavors to prove his own innocence even as all the evidence appears to point directly to his guilt. *The Big Clock* (1948), its remake *No Way Out* (1987), and Alfred Hitchcock's *To Catch a Thief* (1955) are some highlights of the genre. *Out of Time* never rises to the level of these highly memorable films, nor is its hero as completely innocent.

Washington (last year's *John Q*) plays Matt Whitlock, the handsome chief of police of a relatively sleepy backwater town in Florida. An easygoing charm and magnetism seem to shimmer off Matt like the equally potent heat rising from the streets of his Banyan Key. Things are nearly as steamy inside as out, as Matt is summoned by lover Anne Merai Harrison (Sanaa Lathan of last year's *Brown Sugar*) to play an intensely thorough investigator to her damsel in distress in some lusty role playing. They have known each other for years and are married to other people, but neither union is going well. Matt's marriage to Alex (Eva Mendes, who previously worked with Washington in 2001's *Training Day*) is stumbling toward divorce, even though there is still fondness beneath all the friction. She has left town to become a big city homicide detective. For no apparent reason, Anne Merai is sticking with her volatile husband Chris (Dean Cain from TV's *Lois and Clark*), a menacing jock whose dreams of a lengthy and illustrious football career have crumbled into a job in a hospital's morgue. Chris is suspicious and jealous of Matt (apparently with good reason), making ominous, thinly veiled threats against him. A tense scene in a bar in which their mutual animosity simmers just below the surface is particularly effective.

It is during one of Matt's on-duty dalliances with Chris's wife that she is called to a hospital and informed that her cancer has spread and is now terminal. Matt has accompanied her (pretending to be her brother) and is clearly stunned by the news, but he tries to comfort her and pumps the doctor for information on any last-ditch, experimental treatments that might save her. We get a close-up of Matt's face, one of many in the film which serve to get us to connect with him and his struggles. Unfortunately, any such treatments would cost more money than Anne Merai has at her disposal, but then Matt remembers the large sum of cash, seized during a newsworthy drug bust, that is sitting in his office safe, where it must remain until a lengthy appeals process is over. He offers it to her, and she accepts. Of course it is an extremely bad idea, but we want to give Denzel the benefit of the doubt, believe that he is a good but flawed man doing something wrong but with the best of intentions, making him more noble than numbskull. Her announcement that she is changing the beneficiary on her insurance policy from Chris to Matt as a way of paying him back makes us even more certain that nothing good can come of all this.

Sure enough, Matt almost immediately gets a lot of grief for his attempted gallantry. "My intent," said first-time screenwriter Dave Collard, "was to get the audience to like the character, then sort of throw him in a blender for the second half of the movie, hit blend, and watch him try to stay away from the blades." In actuality, Collard not only gleefully hits blend but also chop, puree, and a couple of other buttons for good measure as his script throws a continuous chain of nerve-racking revelations and complications Whitlock's way. First there is a suspicious fire at the home of Anne Merai and Chris that leaves a pair of charred corpses; it appears that the money Matt has given her has also gone up in smoke. Matt is obviously shaken and further troubled by the fact that a neighbor's visiting mother had caught a glimpse of him in the dark outside Anne Merai's that evening. When they learn about the illicit affair and that he was just named as the beneficiary of her insurance policy, Matt figures the authorities will think he set the blaze. To add to his discomfiture, Matt's highly capable and fiercely determined estranged wife is called to the scene to investigate the double homicide. Then, the Drug Enforcement Agency suddenly and inexplicably demands that Matt immediately turn over the confiscated cash, forcing him to do some quick thinking and slick stalling when the no-nonsense agents come knocking. On top of that, Matt is sent reeling when he learns that Anne Merai never had cancer, and the doctor from the other day was no doctor at all. Matt realizes he has been set up and must now conduct his own frantic investigation in order to prove his innocence, while staying at least one, clever, fleet-footed step ahead of Alex's official one.

Time and again, Matt is able to do just that, so many times that our ability to accept everything that is happening onscreen is sorely tested. It starts to seem like maybe Matt may have tapped into some of Cain's old Superman abilities. When the witness states that the person she saw looked an awful lot like Matt, he flashes a broad, charming, and disarming smile and everyone ends up having a good laugh at the poor, misguided old woman's fingering of the chief of police, of all people. Matt is able to snatch a fax with Anne Merai's phone records and alter it with lightning speed before Alex gets hold of it. Separate cell phone records also

threaten to reveal his closeness to Anne Merai, but Matt also finds a way around that one with mere moments to spare. There are numerous other quick saves, including the most dramatic, amounting to a visual representation of all the close calls in *Out of Time:* during a visit Matt makes to a hotel to confront the phony doctor, actually Chris's fellow morgue attendant, the two men struggle as a balcony railing gives way and Matt is just able to hang on and climb back inside, while his adversary is not nearly as lucky. Even when it seems highly improbable, Matt somehow miraculously succeeds, just like the film itself in its ability to maintain its grip on us when, perhaps, by all rights, that hold should have been broken. We may have reservations about the foolhardy things he has done but we are willing to overlook them, just as we end up making allowances for the script's incredible and implausible machinations.

Alex's realization that she has been hunting her hubby comes at about the same time that he catches up with the very much alive Harrisons. Anne Merai tells Matt all the details of Chris's scheme, including her unwilling participation, just before shooting her husband and revealing that she was the real mastermind behind it all. We see this coming but Matt is shocked, and we are incredulous at his incredulity. In the end, Alex not only saves Matt from being finished off by Anne Merai, but also from any revelation that he was intimately involved in the whole mess rather than merely investigating it. The long-past-impatient Feds finally get their money, and, in an ending that seems a little too quick and sunny, Alex and Matt harmoniously glide back into cohabitation. It is as if the script is now too exhausted from all its twisting and turning to avoid such an easy, predictable, run-of-the-mill conclusion.

Made on a budget of $50 million, *Out of Time* managed a less-than-hoped-for gross of just over $40 million. It was generally well received by most major critics, although many noted that their ability to suspend disbelief got quite a workout. *Out of Time* is the latest offering from actor-turned-director Carl Franklin, who previously worked with Washington in *Devil in a Blue Dress* (1995). He keeps things moving along at a nice pace here, although the film does not really start to catch fire until the Harrison's house does. All the actors do sufficiently good work, perhaps the most enjoyable a scene-stealing John Billingsley (last year's *High Crimes*) as Chae, the town's scruffy, mirthful medical examiner and sidekick to Matt. While Washington is good and brings the aforementioned indispensable presence to the character, this role is not nearly as memorable nor does it provide as potent a performance as his Oscar-winning portrayal of the cop in *Training Day*. Still, without Washington's magnetism at its core to overcome questions of plausibility, *Out of Time* would have been out of luck.

—*David L. Boxerbaum*

CREDITS

Matt Lee Whitlock: Denzel Washington
Alex Diaz Whitlock: Eva Mendes
Ann Merai Harrison: Sanaa Lathan
Chris Harrison: Dean Cain
Tony Dalton: Robert Baker
Cabot: Alex Carter
Chae: John Billingsley

Origin: USA
Released: 2003
Production: Neal H. Moritz, Jesse B'Franklin; Original Film, Monarch Pictures; released by MGM
Directed by: Carl Franklin
Written by: Dave Collard
Cinematography by: Theo van de Sande
Music by: Graeme Revell
Sound: Walter Anderson
Editing: Carole Kravetz
Art Direction: Gary Kosko
Costumes: Sharen Davis
Production Design: Paul Peters
MPAA rating: PG-13
Running time: 114 minutes

REVIEWS

Boston Globe. October 3, 2003, p. D5.
Chicago Sun-Times Online. October 3, 2003.
Entertainment Weekly. October 10, 2003, p. 98.
Los Angeles Times Online. October 3, 2003.
New York Times. October 3, 2003, p. E13.
People. October 13, 2003, p. 31.
Rolling Stone. October 30, 2003, p. 100.
USA Today Online. October 3, 2003.
Variety. September 15, 2003, p. 26.

Owning Mahowny

Whatever it takes to win.
—Movie tagline

When we first meet Dan Mahowny (Philip Seymour Hoffman) in the Canadian film *Owning Mahowny*, he's introduced as a model citizen. At the bank where he works, he's just been promoted to assistant manager, the youngest in company history, and his superior cites his "impeccable record and excellent judgment."

But filmmaker Richard Kwietniowski (*Love and Death on Long Island*) doesn't let this false image settle long in the viewer's mind. Suddenly a couple of sleazy gamblers show up in Mahowny's office, and bookie Frank Perlin (Maury Chaykin), who's been advancing Mahowny money to play the ponies, demands payment. Mahowny glibly lies to his assistant about who his visitors are, and we see that he's quite capable of oily duplicity.

There's an easy way for Mahowny to solve his immediate financial problem, and the camera lingers over his anguish as he signs off on a form that allows him to get cash on a loan account for a fictitious person. Once he's crossed this moral line, there's no turning back. Instead of paying off his debt, Mahowny uses his embezzled money to hop a flight to Atlantic City, where he quickly gambles his way deeper in the hole.

Clearly, Mahowny is a compulsive gambler who can't help himself, and Hoffman makes the character extremely credible. Here's an actor who's specialized in portraying anti-charismatic people sunk in a cycle of shame, remorse, and rebellion; after all, he first made his mark playing a compulsive masturbator in Todd Solondz's *Happiness*. Compared to Mahowny, though, Hoffman's previous roles look glib and glamorous. Hoffman has nailed down the anguish of being in the throes of addictive behavior; he's all sweaty and appears to be in a trance. When the croupier announces it's 6:30 a.m. and the gaming tables are closed for a couple of hours, Hoffman looks as if he's been awakened from a dream.

But as successful and determined as Hoffman is not to flinch from the unappealing grip of his character's compulsion, his monochromatic performance leads to a couple of unsettling questions. First, if Mahowny is this addicted, how come he hasn't run off the rails long ago? And secondly, where is the joy he is getting from the gambling? There are no "highs" that register on Hoffman's demeanor, only lows.

It's true that addicts are adept at hiding their behavior and papering over their tracks and that their compulsion worsens as their behavior gets riskier and the rewarding adrenaline rush they gain by indulging their addiction gets harder to achieve. But Hoffman never displays *any* signs of enjoying what he's doing. And there is no back-story about Mahowny to explain what character flaws or traumatic experiences might have led him to sink this deep into anti-social, blinkered compulsion. One thing that's unsatisfying about this film is that Mahowny arrives and exits the plot as something of a lackluster stereotype; he's a full-blown nut case who just slides further down. Mahowny is not in the slightest way an interesting guy: he's not witty or endearing, and not even particularly clever at covering up his behavior, although he's sometimes lucky at avoiding being discovered. And Hoffman's characterization, while completely credible, utterly lacks an emotional hook for the audience. He doesn't do anything that's not completely predictable. Instead of following a character arc, seeing Mahowny is like watching a man with a terminal disease waste away.

Inexplicably, Mahowny has a live-in girlfriend, Belinda (Minnie Driver), who, also inexplicably, loves him and sticks by him. Driver tries to look like she's a loser, with a dreadful mane of long dyed blonde hair that clashes with her black eyebrows, and with oversized glasses and nightmarish makeup that looks like it was done by Kmart beauticians. The script also is bereft of any back-story or even current story for Belinda, whose character is so underwritten she might as well be a paper doll. Driver, who is as talented as Hoffman, tries gamely to milk some emotion out of the few scenes where she's allowed a voice. But Kwietniowski, struggling with a bland script he penned along with Maurice Chauvet and based on a novel by Gary Ross, doesn't provide us with Belinda's perspective to make us understand why even a character so empty would be in love with a man with so many unredeeming qualities as Mahowny.

The filmmakers do admirably well in stripping down the proceedings of any extraneous humanity and highlighting the isolation of Mahowny in his own cruel, detached world. A clever, jazzy score and some spare, knowing photography by cinematographer Oliver Curtis give the film an appropriately diminished quality. We get Mahowny captured on video cameras, scrutinized by the casino owner (John Hurt) who is courting him as his latest easy mark. We get scenes of his late-model car parked in the same airport parking lot, and his returning to it dejected. And we get lots of closeups of Mahowny sweating or displaying a blank countenance or downcast eyes as he acts out his shameful compulsion. All this suits the mood just fine, and gives the film enough power to overcome its lethargic script. It might have been wise to go one step further and exaggerate the resemblance to 1930s German expressionism, though, because at too many points Owning Mahowny comes dangerously close to looking like one of those educational films from the 1950s about the dangers of vice.

To be fair, there doesn't seem to be much to work with here. Mahowny's no inventive, handsome shyster like Leonardo DiCaprio's Frank Abagnale in Catch Me If You Can; he's not an amusingly quirky con man like Nicolas Cage's Roy Waller in Matchstick Men; he's not even a glib-talking minor crook from any caper film by David Mamet. He's more like a zombie. Hoffman pushes any traces of dignity and personality so deeply down into Mahowny's addiction that it's hard to care about his character's fate.

Another problem is that what passes for a plot in the film is unnecessarily murky. Basically all that happens is that Mahowny keeps embezzling more money from the bank and keeps gambling his way deeper into debt, but the script introduces a lot of needless confusion about what he's doing. There's a hope raised that he might be doing something that's actually clever or surprising, but that fails to materialize. Even the prospect of an appealing cops-closing-in scenario fizzles; nothing intriguing transpires among the chasers until one day, all of a sudden, the authorities just close in.

Mahowny's compulsion becomes more and more detached from logic; he spontaneously places baseball bets on all the home teams in the National League and all the visiting teams in the American League, for instance. He is so single minded he spurns the casino's free gift of a glamorous hooker. He has no appetites, no desires, no quirks other than his gambling, and no reasons he can articulate for doing that.

All this is not far-fetched; many addicts get little joy out of their "highs" as the highs get harder to reach. But there is at least some adrenaline rush, and Hoffman acts just as downtrodden and monosyllabic when he wins, as when he loses; he's a man simply going through the motions until he is caught. Amazingly, because of the many admirable stylistic touches of the filmmakers, the thin story and these unremarkable characters manage to hold one's attention until about halfway through. But by the time the 104 minutes are up, it seems as if 70 would have served quite adequately.

Based on real events that occurred in Toronto between 1980 and 1982, Owning Mahowny could have used some embellishing of the truth to make it into a more appealing and exciting story. We've had more than our share of films about gamblers in recent years, and it's hard to figure what the point of this one might be. Absent a juiced-up story line, the only refuge for Owning Mahowny is to make it a character study, but a character study about a non-entity, even one as cleverly filmed and expertly acted as this one, can't turn out a winner. The odds are too long.

—Michael Betzold

CREDITS

Dan Mahowny: Philip Seymour Hoffman
Belinda: Minnie Driver
Frank Perlin: Maury Chaykin
Victor Foss: John Hurt
Dana Selkirk: Sonja Smits
Detective Ben Lock: Ian Tracey
Bill Gooden: Roger Dunn
Dave Quinson: Jason Blicker
Bernie: Chris Collins

Origin: Canada, Great Britain
Released: 2003
Production: Andras Hamori, Seaton McLean, Alessandro Camon; Alliance Atlantis, Natural Nylon Entertainment; released by Sony Pictures Classics
Directed by: Richard Kwietniowski
Written by: Richard Kwietniowski, Maurice Chauvet
Cinematography by: Oliver Curtis

Music by: Richard Grassby-Lewis
Sound: Bill McMillan
Editing: Michael Munn
Art Direction: Diana Magnus
Costumes: Gersha Phillips
Production Design: Taavo Soodor
MPAA rating: R
Running time: 107 minutes

REVIEWS

Chicago Sun-Times Online. May 16, 2003.
Los Angeles Times Online. May 2, 2003.
New York Times Online. May 2, 2003.
Variety Online. January 26, 2003.
Washington Post. June 6, 2003, p. WE37.

QUOTES

Casino boss Victor (John Hurt) about Dan (Philip Seymour Hoffman): "You know why he wants to win? So he has the money to keep losing."

TRIVIA

Richard Kwietniowski previously worked with John Hurt on 1997's *Love and Death on Long Island.*

Party Monster

good. evil. fun.
—Movie tagline

Till Death Do They Party.
—Movie tagline

Filmmakers Fenton Bailey and Randy Barbato have made somewhat of a niche for themselves covering such gay-friendly subjects as club culture, music for TV specials, and Tammy Faye Bakker in the fine documentary *The Eyes of Tammy Faye.* In 1998, they made a documentary called *Party Monster* based on the killing of suspected drug dealer Angel Melendez by noted club kid Michael Alig. The 2003 *Party Monster* is, in effect, a remake of their own movie, only this time it's a drama "based on a true story."

The most notable thing about *Party Monster* though is that it marks Macaulay Culkin's first movie appearance since 1994's *Richie Rich.* The former child star made his name

(and boatloads of money) with his stint in the first *Home Alone* movies. (Sadly, the *Home Alone* franchise continues to limp alone without Caulkin over a decade later.) Perhaps spurred by his brother Kieran Culkin's successful appearance in the arty *Igby Goes Down,* the elder Culkin chose quite an edgy vehicle to make his comeback. The sight of the former *Home Alone* kid wearing full make-up and short shorts that expose his skinny white legs is enough to make anyone realize that this is not a little boy any more. And full credit has to be given to Culkin for taking on such an outrageous and unexpected role.

Michael Alig (Culkin) arrives in New York fresh from South Bend, Indiana. He meets the self-proclaimed "original club kid" James St. James (Seth Green, best known as Dr. Evil's son in the *Austin Powers* films) and persuades him to teach him the elements of fabulousness. In a seedy diner, James gives Michael an amusing primer on such important lessons as how to work the room at a party and get one's picture in the media.

James, who uses his trust fund to pay for his increasingly outrageous outfits and large drug habit, considers himself to be the alpha male in the relationship, but the cunning Michael soon starts co-opting James's ideas and mannerisms. Somehow Michael convinces Peter Gatien (Dylan McDermott), the owner of failing club Limelight, to let him promote some parties. At first the parties are utter failures. James and cross-dresser Christina (Marilyn Manson) are the only people to show up to the first one. The unflaggingly upbeat Michael just takes this as a sign that Peter needs to give him more money to throw better parties. Michael, inspired by the recent death of Andy Warhol, decides that he too will create some superstars.

Michael enlists the aid of handsome baggage handler, Keoki (Wilmer Valderrama), making him his boyfriend and "superstar DJ." He allows his wannabe hanger-on, Angel Melendez (Wilson Cruz), to join the group as the drug dealer. Michael considers his blessing to be so fabulous that he doesn't feel the need to pay for the drugs. His acceptance of Angel is payment enough.

Somehow Michael's chutzpah pays off. His efforts at Limelight made the club one of the most popular for late 1980s club kids. He also throws impromptu bashes in places like the back of a truck and a fast food restaurant. Wild costumes and rampant drug use characterized the parties. The drug of choice was Special K, an animal tranquilizer, but Michael and James were quite happy to dabble in heroin, crack, and just about anything else that they could get their hands on.

Michael is good at creating fabulousness, possibly because he's an utter failure at everything else. He is the most superficial of people and can't seem to have a relationship without screwing over the other person. He gets his supportive mom (Diana Scarwid) addicted to ecstasy and mocks his mentor James on a TV talk show (hosted by John Stamos).

At one point, he serves urine to James and claims it's Champagne.

But Michael's lack of feeling for others goes deeper than just being a bad son or friend. He's also an unrepentant killer. In the opening scene of the film, we witness a murder. In the next scene, Michael and James are in bed about to do some drugs, and Michael casually mentions that he has killed Angel. To him, it's not worth being horrified over.

The film is done in an overly self-conscious style. It starts with narrator James saying provocatively "Come with me on the last night of my life—the night of my overdose." James passes out and Michael takes over the narration duties, claiming that the film's really about him. Throughout the film, the two argue over the story and how it should be told. "Don't turn this into an Afterschool Special," warns James at one point. There is also some storytelling by a rat that lives in the apartment of Michael and his crew. The gimmicky techniques aren't really clever enough to merit their appearance, but they're not offensive either.

The best part of watching *Party Monster* is the sheer spectacle of it. The parade of costumes is unbelievable. The club kids' costumes include medical gear festooned with fake blood, lederhosen and a Hitler mustache, a flower costume, and a bird. It crosses the line from glamour to silly. On a par is watching Culkin and Green ham it up. It's hard to say whether Culkin is really, really bad or really, really good in his role. He says his lines with an overt theatricality that makes him seem like he's doing a reading for acting class. This would normally be bad—quite bad—but in the case of Michael it might be appropriate. His character is all about artifice and creating a persona rather that just reacting as a human being. When Keiko demands his records back, Michael says, "Your records? Ha!" Culkin actually says, "Ha!" as though he's in a play. He says all his lines with the same effeminate lilt and follows them with a stilted giggle. It might be the worst acting of the year or not, but it's sure fun to watch.

Green does about the same thing, but somehow his performance seems slightly less stagey. His eyes suggest a bit more depth than Culkin's do, but again Culkin's character is not supposed to have much to him. Chloe Sevigny shows up as Michael's new girlfriend Gitsie and gives the film a better pedigree. And an unrecognizable Natasha Lyonne plays an overweight and dredlocked fan from Dallas. McDermott is not especially believable as the club owner, but that might be because his character is not particularly believable. It's hard to see why he would continue to give in to Michael's increasingly outrageous demands even as it becomes obvious that Michael is losing control of his life.

Critics didn't give *Party Monster* high marks, though the film found some fans. Kevin Thomas of the *Los Angeles Times* wrote, "*Party Monster* is a time capsule for its era and locale. For all its decadence, it moves effectively from outrageous camp humor to stark pathos and in the process manages to be oddly touching. As for Culkin, he succeeds as an adult actor in completely unexpected ways." Jami Bernard of the *New York Daily News* was more harsh, saying of Culkin, "His performance in *Party Monster* is so embarrassing one doesn't know where to look." And Mark Caro of the *Chicago Tribune* felt that the film "comes on with the uninhibited glee of boys dressing up in their mothers' clothes to play house, and it boasts a similar level of sophistication."

—*Jill Hamilton*

CREDITS

Michael Alig: Macaulay Culkin
James St. James: Seth Green
Gitsie: Chloe Sevigny
Brooke: Natasha Lyonne
Angel: Wilson Cruz
Keoki: Wilmer Valderrama
Peter Gatien: Dylan McDermott
Freeze: Justin Hagan
Michael's Mom: Diana Scarwid
Christina: Marilyn Manson

Origin: USA
Released: 2003
Production: Christine Vachon, Fenton Bailey, Randy Barbato, Jon Marcus, Bradford Simpson; Killer Films, World of Wonder; released by Strand Releasing
Directed by: Fenton Bailey, Randy Barbato
Written by: Fenton Bailey, Randy Barbato
Cinematography by: Teodoro Maniaci
Music by: Jimmy Harry
Sound: Frank Gaeta
Music Supervisor: Howard Parr
Editing: Jeremy Simmons
Art Direction: Laura Ballinger
Costumes: Michael Wilkinson
Production Design: Andrea Stanley
MPAA rating: R
Running time: 98 minutes

REVIEWS

Boxoffice. April, 2003, p. 84.
Chicago Sun-Times Online. September 5, 2003.
Entertainment Weekly. September 12, 2003, p. 131.
Los Angeles Times Online. September 5, 2003.
New York Times Online. September 5, 2003.
Variety Online. January 20, 2003.

Paycheck

Remember the future.
—Movie tagline
The future depends on a past he was paid to forget.
—Movie tagline

 Box Office: $53.4 million

Paycheck is based on a short story published in 1953 by science fiction writer Philip K. Dick, whose work has inspired several other movies, among them *Total Recall* and *Blade Runner*. The original story ran only 29 pages; the movie version runs 119 minutes. That means that there's a lot of filler in there. Director John Woo, infamous for his action-packed movies, adds various car chases, shoot-outs, and the like to fill the void.

Dick is known for his stories about alienation, humans' relationships to technology, and defining reality and the self. But that stuff is kind of hard to get on film, at least it seems so in *Paycheck*. Why bother debating philosophical issues when there are cans of gasoline sitting around waiting to be blown up? Screenwriter Dean Georgaris obliges by filling the script with various and assorted mayhem.

It's a pity because there are some interesting ideas in *Paycheck*. Michael Jennings (Ben Affleck) is a highly-paid expert on reverse engineering. What he does is get his hands on a competitor's product, then figures out how to copy it. He makes a couple of changes in order to avoid patent violations and makes a new version for the company that hired him. At the opening of the film, Jennings is working on copying a computer that has a 3-D monitor. Jennings gets a machine, then copies the design, with the added touch of eliminating the monitor entirely. His boss and old chum, Rethrick (Aaron Eckhart), the CEO of Allcom, is thrilled with the results and hands Jennings a fat check.

The thing that sets Jennings's job apart from those of any other corporate drone is that after he completes his work, his memory of the weeks it took to do the job are erased. This is done by his friend, Shorty (Paul Giamatti of *American Splendor*), in a process that involves heating the brain enough to erase memory but not enough to cook it. (One shudders to imagine how they must have perfected this technique.)

For Jennings, losing his memory is an okay deal. He's a slick guy who has a fancy apartment and likes to dress well. He thinks of memory as just a collection of highlighted moments. "What did you do the last two months?" he asks by way of an explanation. He is happy to trade some of his memory in for the chance at a big paycheck. When Rethrick offers Jennings a job that will erase three years of his life, Jennings is willing to think it over. Because this is an action movie, the mulling over of this dilemma takes about two minutes, if that. Jennings decides he will do it.

Three years later, Jennings completes the job and has the memory erasure. He heads to the bank to collect his $92 million paycheck, but discovers that he has signed away rights to it. Instead, he has apparently sent himself an envelope full of seemingly worthless objects. There's a bus pass, a fortune cookie, a crossword puzzle, some hair spray, and the like.

As Jennings puzzles over this perplexing development, he notices that some of the objects have come in mighty handy just at the moment he needs them. Extrapolating quickly—he is a genius after all—he somehow figures out that the project he was working on at Allcom must have been a machine to predict the future. Jennings figures that before he left the company, he must have seen the future, not cared for it, and sent these items to help guide his future self.

It's a cool idea, but the objects don't come into play nearly as ingeniously as they could have. For example, when Jennings is being chased in a bus station, he pulls out . . . a bus ticket. It's not the most exciting use of an object. Better is when he finds a microscopic image hidden in the eye of a picture of Einstein on a postage stamp.

Jennings also discovers that he seems to have fallen in love with his co-worker, Rachel Porter (Uma Thurman), a botanist at Allcom. She is devastated to realize that he doesn't remember any of their time together. She does look just like Uma Thurman, however, and Jennings is willing to hang out with her until he figures out how he does feel about her. Meanwhile, Rethrick and the guys at Allcom are after Jennings because, well, it's kind of hard to remember, but the point is that they want to get him. The FBI is also after him because he seems to have killed someone during his time of memory loss and the FBI doesn't care for such behavior.

For his part, Jennings wants to get back to the machine he's built and destroy it. He discovers by looking into the machine that world leaders will use it for no good. These leaders will look into the machine, see that a country is arming itself, and launch a preemptive attack against said country. Such tactics will lead to nuclear war and that mushroom cloud that no one wants to see. That would be bad, decides Jennings. Besides, he says, in one of his deeper moments, "If you take away the mystery, you take away hope."

So, based on such fascinating concepts as the value of memory and the problems with seeing into the future, we end up with . . . some chasin' and fightin'. The best sequence takes place in Rachel's greenhouse lab. When Jennings is battling all those faceless movie-bad-guys-with-the-short-life-spans, Rachel grabs a sort of electronic claw, and uses it to snatch a gun from a baddie and hand it to Jennings.

Most critics found this work to be derivative of Woo's own work. It's hard to say whether this was because Woo was in some sort of a rut or because his work has been so copied that it seems like cliché. Elvis Mitchell of the *New York Times* mentioned the Woo staple of the police inquisitor who shows his displeasure by crossing his arms and lifting a single eyebrow. The *Boston Globe*'s Wesley Morris noted "the usual Woo-vian visual and formal tics," including "shattered glass that falls like rain, large pistols at the end of fully extended arms, slow-motion shoot-outs and smackdowns and, that John Woo favorite, the salvation-signifying dove."

The movie is also filled with plenty of age-old action film conventions. When the diabolical plans are discussed, the number two man at Allcom always chuckles evilly. If he had a mustache, he surely would have twirled it. When Jennings puts a makeshift bomb in a tube, he uses tubes numbered 1 through 6. The tubes will fire in numeric order. He doesn't just put the bomb in tube 3 for quicker, more guaranteed results, he puts it in tube 6 so that the bad guys have ample time to catch up and so that Woo can cut back to the tubes in moments of tension. And of course, the final confrontation over the future of civilization comes down to a face-to-face fight between Jennings and Eckhart.

According to the *Toronto Star*'s Peter Howell, "Jennings is far too complex a character for Affleck, whose 15 minutes of fame must surely soon be up, and Woo seems content to coast on his reputation as a director of slo-mo action and chop-socky flips." Lisa Schwarzbaum gave the film a C + in *Entertainment Weekly* and said, "As for Affleck and Eckhart, rarely have two cleft chins faced off with such thrust—or absence of consequence." Roger Ebert of the *Chicago Sun-Times* wrote, "There was a basic level at which I enjoyed the movie, just for the scope of the production and the way that Affleck doggedly puzzled his way through that manila envelope. But at the end, we get the sense that Woo is operating with a clipboard and a checklist, making sure everyone is killed in the right order. There's simply not enough urgency involved." Colin Covert summed up in the *Minneapolis Star Tribune*: "Not only did they title this lame thriller, *Paycheck*, that's obviously how everyone connected thought of it. Every scene screams, 'I'm only doing this for the money.'"

—*Jill Hamilton*

CREDITS

Michael Jennings: Ben Affleck
Rethrick: Aaron Eckhart
Rachel Porter: Uma Thurman
Shorty: Paul Giamatti
Wolfe: Colm Feore
Agent Dodge: Joe Morton
Agent Klein: Michael C. Hall

Origin: USA
Released: 2003
Production: John Woo, Terence Chang, Jon Davis, Michael Hackett; Davis Entertainment Company, Lion Rock; released by Paramount Pictures
Directed by: John Woo
Written by: Dean Georgaris
Cinematography by: Jeffrey L. Kimball
Music by: John Powell
Sound: Eric J. Batut
Editing: Christopher Rouse, Kevin Sitt
Art Direction: Sandy Cochrane
Costumes: Erica Edell Phillips
Production Design: William Sandell
MPAA rating: R
Running time: 110 minutes

REVIEWS

Chicago Sun-Times Online. December 24, 2003.
Entertainment Weekly. Janaury 9, 2004, p. 57.
Los Angeles Times Online. December 24, 2003.
New York Times Online. December 25, 2003.
Variety Online. December 22, 2003.
Washington Post. December 26, 2003, p. WE41.

AWARDS AND NOMINATIONS

Golden Raspberries 2003: Worst Actor (Affleck).

People I Know

He thought he's seen it all, until the night he saw too much.
—Movie tagline

People I Know is supposed to take place over a period of 24 hours and it seems to drag on so long that it is as though the movie takes place in real time. Al Pacino pops pills, rages, cavorts with models, and deals with celebrities (or semi-celebrities, at least) and somehow it's all just a big drag.

Pacino, doing his darnedest to do some acting with a capital A, is Eli Wurman, a longtime New York publicist. Several decades ago, he was a major power broker. He was close to Martin Luther King, Jr. and Robert Kennedy. Now he is down to one client, Cary Launer (Ryan O'Neal), a handsome older actor who has political ambitions. Now Eli finds himself becoming increasingly irrelevant. "I had Monty Cliff! I had Mama Cass!" he yells, not realizing how much this dates him. "A lot of good you did them," replies another character, unimpressed. (Reportedly Eli is based on old-style publicist Bobby Zarem).

Now Eli spends most of his time playing baby-sitter to Cary. Eli gets a call late one night from Cary, asking him to bail his starlet girlfriend, Jilli Hopper (Tea Leoni), out from jail, then put her back on a plane for Los Angeles. Eli is depressed that his job has evolved into this, but he knows Cary is his last connection to any kind of power, and he has to do whatever the demanding star asks.

Once he bails Jilli out, he finds himself getting into trouble. Jilli takes him to a secret drug den that operates out of a high rise on Wall Street. While there, he sees that this is a hangout for Elliot Sharansky (Richard Schiff) one of the richest liberal and most prominent Jewish powerbrokers in New York. Jilli is in search of her "toy," which is later revealed to be a tiny secret camcorder.

Eli downs a lot more drugs, then ends up in a hotel room with Jilli. He lies in the bathtub and semi-coherently calls his doctor, Sandy Napier (Robert Klein), to moan about his health. As he's passing out in the bathtub, someone comes in the room and murders Jilli. Eli sort of saw it, but isn't really sure about what he saw since he's so out of it.

This seems like story enough, but New York playwright Jon Robin Baitz, puts in more stuff. While all of this is going on, Eli is trying to finish plans for a big benefit for some Nigerian men who are being wrongly deported. He doesn't have the big stars that he needs and, throughout the night, he is placing desperate phone calls to people like Regis Philbin. He is also trying to bring together Jews and African-Americans by having Sharansky and a black activist, Lyle Blunt (Bill Nunn), appear together at the benefit.

Eli's life has become sordid and frantic. His only hope for redemption seems to be his brother's widow, Victoria Gray (Kim Basinger). Whereas the city and his clients (or lack thereof) give him only grief and stress, Victoria offers love and a life of peace back in the South. Eli likes to play up his Southern roots and is constantly saying things like, "Maybe I'm just a cracker from down South . . ." but New York seems to be what fuels him.

Pacino certainly looks hangdog enough for the role. Eli's half out of it from lack of sleep and the many substances that he's taking, but is still driven by a manic energy and desire to succeed. Pacino looks tired and haggard and seems to be plugging away only through sheer will. He makes up for the more unsavory aspects of his job by sticking with his 1960's idealism. In his mind, a successful benefit for the Nigerians will somewhat negate the humiliation of having to clean up Cary's messes. What doesn't work about Pacino's performance is his accent. He interprets a Georgia accent to mean sounding a lot like Dustin Hoffman's character in

Tootsie. Actually, maybe if she were in this film, she could talk some sense into Eli. Pacino's acting is intrusive. If you're noticing it, it's not good, and in *People I Know,* Pacino is noticeably "acting."

People I Know is filled with the cynicism of the New York publicity scene. When the film opens, Eli is attending a play that he's supported. It is horrible, but he smiles and pretends it is great. Cary is a drug addict and womanizer, but feels that he is a good candidate for political office. He's well known and good-looking enough that his goal is perfectly reasonably. Even Eli's trusted doctor turns out to be an evil guy who dispenses drugs to the rich and famous. Everyone seems tired and beaten down by life in this movie. As Jilli says wearily, "Everybody is looking for an out clause." It's all pretty heavy.

The only characters who aren't so defeated are the ones that don't really belong in this world. Victoria is just visiting to save Eli. And Eli's young assistant (Mark Webber) isn't going to be able to make it in the world. He sees Eli's life and realizes the smallness of it.

People I Know was made in early 2001 but wasn't released until 2003. Reportedly because there were some prominent shots of the World Trade Center. Lou Lumenick of the *New York Post* wrote that there had been a deleted sequence in which "an inebriated Eli sees the World Trade Center towers lying on their sides." Jami Bernard of the *New York Daily News* wrote, "It was filmed in and around the World Trade Center, and the subsequent cuts, reshoots and sleights of hand designed to obscure that fact prove devastating."

Perhaps because of their close proximity to publicists, many critics liked the film. Geoff Pevere of the *Toronto Star* wrote, "As much as is left to doubt in Dan Algrant's watchable but dramatically scattered *People I Know,* there is no doubt that Al Pacino is having a great time." Liz Braun of the *Toronto Sun* wrote, "*People I Know* has an amazing script and a stellar cast, which is why the thing works. . . . The film plays like a brilliant piece of theater." Stephen Holden of the *New York Times* felt differently and wrote, "When not facetiously dropping names, the movie lumbers between a cliched bleeding-heart fable of lost 60's dreams and a half-baked thriller in which nasty people in high places try to cover up a murder. Any one of those concepts might have worked on its own, but forced together, they don't allow one another to breathe."

—Jill Hamilton

CREDITS

Eli Wurman: Al Pacino
Victoria Gray: Kim Basinger
Cary Launer: Ryan O'Neal

Jill Hopper: Tea Leoni
Elliot Sharansky: Richard Schiff
Rev. Lyle Blunt: Bill Nunn
Sandy Napier: Robert Klein
Ross: Mark Webber

Origin: USA
Released: 2002
Production: Michael Nozik, Leslie Urdang, Karen Tenkhoff; Myriad Pictures, South Fork Pictures; released by Miramax Films
Directed by: Dan Algrant
Written by: Jon Robin Baitz
Cinematography by: Peter Deming
Music by: Terence Blanchard
Sound: Michael Barosky
Editing: Suzy Elmiger
Art Direction: Charles E. McCarry
Costumes: David C. Robinson
Production Design: Michael Shaw
MPAA rating: R
Running time: 95 minutes

REVIEWS

Boxoffice. April, 2003, p. 104.
Entertainment Weekly. May 2, 2003, p. 51.
Los Angeles Times Online. April 25, 2003.
New York Times Online. April 25, 2003.
People. May 5, 2003, p. 38.
Variety Online. October 8, 2002.

QUOTES

Eli (Al Pacino): "This is not my life. I can't live like this."

Peter Pan

Let the fight begin.
—Movie tagline

The timeless story as you've never seen it before.
—Movie tagline

The legend you thought you knew becomes the adventure you never imagined.
—Movie tagline

 Box Office: $47.6 million

*P*eter Pan is a rare kind of film. The story has been dramatized many times before, on film and on stage, yet this new adaptation is both truer to the original source material and more complex than the versions that have come before it. Previous adaptations of J. M. Barrie's tale of the boy who refused to grow up have glossed over or ignored altogether some of the more "grownup" themes of the story. Director P. J. Hogan's *Peter Pan*, on the other hand, does not shy away from the more bittersweet (and even dark) elements of this coming-of-age tale, and the result is a refreshingly unique and multi-layered film that is both an imaginative fairy tale (in the best sense of the word) and a reflection on the transition from youth to maturity. The movie is full of visual wonders, not because of spectacular special effects but because of wonderfully crafted settings that seem to be lifted straight from a storybook. And for the most part, the actors deliver strong performances that bring the characters to life and allow the audience to empathize with them. Even the nasty Captain Hook elicits a few moments of sympathy, even though he is the most authentically dangerous Hook ever seen on screen.

The character truly at the heart of *Peter Pan* is Wendy Darling (Rachel Hurd-Wood, in her first movie role), an imaginative thirteen-year-old girl who entertains her brothers and parents with lively, romantic stories of adventure. While her mother (Olivia Williams) and father (Jason Isaacs) enjoy the stories, her aunt Millicent (Lynn Redgrave) cautions her that "novelists are not easy to marry" and admonishes that it is time for her to start growing up. She's not quite ready to grow up, but when the sprightly, elf-like boy Peter Pan shows up in her room, trying to catch his runaway shadow, Wendy is obviously ready to acknowledge her developing interest in the opposite sex. She is immediately drawn to Peter, and Peter is likewise drawn to her, although he seems completely naïve about the underlying reason he finds her so fascinating. On a superficial level, Peter is interested in her stories—he wants to know the ending to her telling of Cinderella—but there is clearly more in the way he looks at her and interacts with her; however, he doesn't understand what it is. As Wendy will sadly discover later, Peter has shut himself off from "feeling" because it could lead to his growing up. When Wendy says that she would like to give Peter a kiss, he has no idea what a kiss is. Losing her courage, Wendy gives him a thimble instead. Though Peter appears to be oblivious to the source of his interest in Wendy, the attraction between the two is not lost on the little fairy Tinkerbell, who immediately fumes with jealousy. "Come away to Neverland!" Peter urges Wendy. When she resists the idea of leaving home and her parents behind, Peter tries to appeal to her brothers

Michael (Freddie Popplewell) and John (Harry Newell) by telling them that they will get to see "mermaids, Indians, and pirates!" Peter's allure turns out to be irresistible, for Wendy, Michael, and John soon find themselves soaring through the stars toward the magical realm that Peter has made his home.

Neverland is a fascinating realm, a world that is inextricably linked to Peter. The weather, for example, is determined by Peter's presence and his mood. When he is away, the world is dark and cold—Captain Hook's ship is first seen stuck in the ice—but when he returns to Neverland, it is like the coming of spring—the ice melts, the flowers bloom, and the world returns to life. The clouds, where Peter and the children stop to spy down on Captain Hook's crew, look something like pink marshmallows. In fact, the look of the entire realm has a storybook quality to it, and purposefully so. The world is like a colorful product of the imagination, both realistic in some ways and artistically artificial in others. Neverland is not meant to appear as a real place, for it is a land that exists somewhere between the worlds of reality and make-believe, just like Peter himself.

Peter introduces Wendy to his friends, the Lost Boys, a group of children who have no memories of their families but who are evidently desperate to find some parents. They ask Wendy if she will be their "Mommy," and she does in fact play that role alongside Peter, who plays the role of "Daddy." Oddly enough, both Wendy and Peter play "grownup" when they act out the roles of parents, but only Wendy sees the significance of that. Actually, the dynamics between the Lost Boys and Wendy and Peter are both interesting and complex. The boys have been away from home so long that they cannot remember where they came from, like Peter, yet they yearn for a mother, indicating an innate need that they acknowledge but which Peter has apparently shed—or buried deep within himself. The subtext of the "make-believe" marriage between Peter and Wendy is hardly subtle, bringing to the surface what is already obvious—to Wendy and to the viewer, at least—but Peter still seems clueless as to the meaning of his attraction to Wendy.

The infamous Captain Hook complicates the plot by capturing Michael and John and taking them to his Black Castle, forcing Peter to rescue them (though Wendy has to first remind Peter who the two boys are, as he repeatedly forgets them). The children gain their freedom after the arrival of Hook's dreaded foe, the giant crocodile that robbed Hook of his hand. However, the wicked pirate soon discovers there is a better way to defeat Peter.

Hook enters into the relationship between Wendy and Peter when he sees the two dancing in the air among the treetops (having been inspired by a pair of dancing fairies). The scene is unexpectedly one of the most memorable—and one of the most touching—moments in the movie, for when Hook realizes that Wendy and Peter are attracted to each

other, and that he therefore could "lose" Peter to the girl, he suddenly becomes forlorn and envious, reflecting that he is "lonely." In this scene Hook is joined by Tinkerbell, who also experiences jealousy. The pairing of the two is an interesting twist, as normally they would be considered enemies, but in this moment they share the same feelings. The dance among the treetops ends, however, when Wendy mentions love to Peter and he quickly becomes upset, not wanting to hear talk of love. They part, both angry.

Captain Hook cunningly uses Wendy's disappointment to his advantage. His men kidnap Wendy and take her to his ship, where he persuades her to become a pirate whose duty would be to "tell stories." Wendy had often imagined herself as a pirate, and Hook uses his charm to appeal to her, telling her that Peter can never love because he has no feelings. A handful of critics have gone so far as to say there is a disturbing subtext in the interest Hook shows in Wendy and her "attraction" to him in turn, but such a Freudian analysis is not supported by the story. Hook's only interest in Wendy lies in how he may use her to get to Peter—and to make sure he keeps them apart because he wants Peter to be as lonely as he is. Wendy, on the other hand, does see in Hook something to admire, but it is the quality that seems to be missing in Peter. Upon returning to the lair of the Lost Boys, Wendy tells Peter that "I feel Captain Hook to be a man of feeling," and obviously she says this in order to wound Peter. At this point, it becomes clear that Wendy has reached the realization that to some extent she is ready to grow up. She tells the boys it is time to go home, and she invites all the Lost Boys to go with her (and Michael and John) back to London.

Hook and his crew wind up capturing Wendy and all the boys, leading to the rousing climax of the film, in which Peter shows up to save the day. Hook knows all too well Peter's weakness, though, and soon gains an advantage over him. He taunts Peter, telling him that Wendy is leaving and that she wants to grow up. She no longer wants to be with him, he says, and one day she will find a husband. This is worse than any physical assault, for it sends Peter into a painful despondency, and he gives up completely, dropping to the deck of the ship. Wendy then comes to his rescue by leaning over him, telling him "This will always be yours," and giving him a kiss. Peter smiles, awakens from his despair, and returns to his swordfight with Hook. As anyone familiar with the story knows, Hook ultimately meets his end in the jaws of the giant crocodile.

The end of *Peter Pan* is actually very bittersweet. Wendy and the children return to London, where her parents actually adopt the Lost Boys, who are overjoyed that they finally have parents. Peter, however, cannot allow himself to go with them. He appears once again on Wendy's windowsill, and although she clearly cares for him—and vice versa—she almost seems resigned to the fact that they cannot be together. "Will you come back?" she asks. "To hear a story," Peter replies. "About me." He flies away, returning to

Neverland, and the film ends on a note that is as sad as it is happy. Peter's inability to grow up is not exactly a triumph, since he appears doomed to loneliness.

With its many layers of meaning, its psychological depth, and its willingness to tackle some of the more complex themes arising from Barrie's original story, *Peter Pan* improves on its predecessors. Bolstered by superb cast performances and visual artistry, the film tells a story that does more than extol the virtues of imagination, make-believe, and childhood. *Peter Pan* also explores the sometimes painful process of maturing and clarifies that the process is a necessary one. As even Aunt Millicent comes to realize, though, growing up does not mean tossing imagination and all the spontaneities of childhood aside.

—David Flanagin

CREDITS

Mr. Darling/Captain Hook: Jason Isaacs
Peter Pan: Jeremy Sumpter
Wendy Darling: Rachel Hurd-Wood
Mrs. Darling: Olivia Williams
Tinker Bell: Ludivine Sagnier
Smee: Richard Briers
Aunt Millicent: Lynn Redgrave
Sir Edward Quiller Couch: Geoffrey Palmer
John Darling: Harry Newell
Michael Darling: Freddie Popplewell
Narrator: Saffron Burrows

Origin: USA
Released: 2003
Production: Douglas Wick, Lucy Fisher, Patrick McCormick; Revolution Studios; released by Universal Pictures
Directed by: P.J. Hogan
Written by: P.J. Hogan, Michael Goldenberg
Cinematography by: Donald McAlpine
Music by: James Newton Howard
Sound: Ben Osmo
Editing: Garth Craven, Michael Kahn
Art Direction: Richard Hobbs
Costumes: Janet Patterson
Production Design: Roger Ford
MPAA rating: PG
Running time: 113 minutes

REVIEWS

Chicago Sun-Times Online. December 24, 2003.
Entertainment Weekly. January 9, 2004, p. 58.
Los Angeles Times Online. December 24, 2003.
New York Times Online. December 25, 2003.
People. January 12, 2004, p. 33.
USA Today Online. December 24, 2003.
Variety Online. December 14, 2003.
Washington Post. December 25, 2003, p. C1.

QUOTES

Peter (Jeremy Sumpter): "Come away to Neverland where you'll never, never have to deal with grown up things again." Wendy (Rachel Hurd-Ward): "Never is an awfully long time."

Phone Booth

Your life is on the line.
—Movie tagline

Box Office: $46.5 million

Long delayed for political reasons, *Phone Booth* quickly turns into a tense cat-and-mouse game between the Caller (the Cat, played by Kiefer Sutherland) and the Victim (Stu, the Mouse, played by Colin Farrell). Motive seems something of a mystery, but otherwise the gimmicky plot works to create a tense thriller, confined to the "phone booth" of the title, someplace on 8th Avenue in the Borough of Manhattan (though actually shot in Los Angeles). It's the last old-fashioned phone booth in the city, an anachronism becoming ever more so during the months the release of the Joel Schumacher film was delayed, first because of terrorists threats, then because of the crime spree of the so-called Washington snipers, who in fact killed most of their innocent victims in the state of Virginia and in Maryland.

Stu Shepard (Farrell) is a fast-talking, self-centered jerk, a married man who is courting a mistress, Pam (Katie Holmes), an innocent new to the City, and an easy mark for a lying philanderer. He uses a pay phone to call the girl so that his wife, Kelly (Radha Mitchell), cannot trace his calls; but, oddly enough, Stu feels guilty. When he enters the phone booth he takes off his wedding ring.

What is most creepy but improbable about the plot is that the Caller seems to have taken an unusual interest in Stu, who is nothing if not shallow. He knows that Stu uses that particular telephone booth with some frequency, and he has fully researched Stu's hollow affairs. Knowing that he intends to hold Stu hostage in that phone booth, he arranges to have a pizza delivered just after Stu enters the booth. Stu, of course, is rude to the delivery man. The Caller knows far more about Stu and his habits than anyone should want to, enough that his voice passes for Stu's conscience. The question is, why would he bother? Why Stu, who is truly a nobody and a phony? The Caller needs to get a life, rather than taking one.

The claim is that screenwriter Larry Cohen dreamed up this story 30 years ago, then had to make major adjustments to make it happen in the present age of cell phones where everybody, included Stu, is wired. Stu lives by his tongue, by his glibness, by his lies, and by his telephone. The phone booth becomes his fortress; first, after being trapped there (if he hangs up, the Caller threatens to shoot him), he has to protect his turf against a trio of hookers (Paula Jai Parker, Arian Ash and Tia Texada) who demand that they be able to take over the booth. Then against their pimp (John Enos III), who is armed with a baseball bat, until the Caller picks him off. This brings an army of police, and accusations from the hookers that Stu was the shooter. The Caller will not allow Stu to clear himself of these accusations. Suddenly, a dozen police snipers have him in their sights. Before long wife Kelly is at the scene, and mistress Pamela turns up a little later, providing two more targets the Caller can use to torment Stu.

Forest Whitaker, an actor far too talented for this small role, takes charge on the street as police Captain Ramey, who has to figure out the situation after it becomes apparent that Stu will not leave his phone booth upon police orders. The Caller has three targets to keep him there. Stu can't simply reach for his cell phone, because the police will think it is a weapon and fire upon him. The telephone booth is wired, so the Caller hears everything. The Caller intimidates Stu and then humiliates him by making him confess what a miserable human being he is, with the television cameras rolling, which is only to state the obvious. The whole exercise is pointless and insane, but that is probably the point.

The film was directed by Joel Schumacher, who understands the rhythms and pressures of urban life, and how it can drive people crazy. He also directed Michael Douglas in another urban paranoid nightmare, *Falling Down* (1993). The film begins and ends in space, as the telephone signal bounces off a satellite for transmission down to Manhattan. Schumacher uses the same kind of split-screen images that Mike Figgis has used in *Time Code* (2000). Everyone Stu talks to is seen on split screen images, except, significantly, the Caller, whose voice is always in the audience's head.

The critical response to this film was split. *Washington Post Weekend* reviewer Michael O'Sullivan called it "gripping," though he found the "idea of an omniscient, moralistic, avenging angel" with a compulsive "need to punish liars" more than a "little silly." First-string *Washington Post* reviewer Stephen Hunter noted that the film was "82 New York minutes long, all of them exciting." Although it may be more of "a gimmick than a movie," he added, "it hammers you flat the whole way through," and that seems a fair and accurate account. Hunter explained that the film was "famously delayed during the tragic events" of the Washington, D.C., sniper shootings, "although at no point does its bravura decadence connect with the squalor of the reality." That, too, was well said.

For *Baltimore Sun* reviewer Michael Sragow, on the other hand, the movie was simply a "Bad Connection" and "a mess from the word hello." It was also a "Bad Connection" for Owen Gleiberman of *Entertainment Weekly*, even though he gave the film a "grade" of B-minus. *Variety*'s Todd McCarthy thought the film might have worked better in a "half-hour TV slot," but the usually canny McCarthy was wrong about this one. The delay of the film's release actually might have helped its initial reception. Star Colin Farrell had quickly become a "hot" property as a result of his performances in *Tigerland* (his breakthrough film for Schumacher in 2000), *Minority Report* (for Spielberg, and holding his own against Tom Cruise, 2002), *The Recruit* (for Roger Donaldson in 2002), quickly followed by his high-profile role as the villainous Bullseye in 2003's *Daredevil*. No doubt about it, Colin Farrell is a rising star.

It's difficult to slight the work of Colin Farrell, whose Irishness is erased into a reasonably convincing Bronx Italian accent. As Stu Farrell is about as nasty a piece of sleaze as Tony Curtis's Sidney Falco in *The Sweet Smell of Success* (1957), as multiple reviewers reminded readers. Mike Clark of *USA Today*, who thought the film "rings a little too hollow" and couldn't resist a cute phrase, wrote the weakest and crummiest lead sentence: "With two lackluster *Batman* movies already on his resume, director Joel Schumacher now ventures into Superman territory." "Phone Booth," get it? But lame jokes could not stay the momentum of this film. As Tom Shales noted in the *Washington Post*, this "low-budget, high-tension thriller grossed $15 million and took over first place at the box office" on its opening weekend, eclipsing Vin Diesel's *A Man Apart*.

Writer Larry Cohen told *New York Times* reporter Dave Kehr that he had once suggested to Alfred Hitchcock, "How about a movie that all happens in a telephone booth?" Although Hitchcock did not spring for the bait, the idea is Hitchcockian: put a victim in a menacing box with no exit, and see what happens, but something interesting needs to happen, and a conclusion must be reached. The script took 10 days to write, 12 days to shoot, but over 30 years to produce, according to Cohen.

Phone Booth premiered at the Toronto Film Festival in September of 2002, but its general release was delayed by another six months because of the much-publicized Washington snipers. "I've made 18 films," Joel Schumacher told Dave Kehr of the *New York Times*. "I think that, even including the first one, this was the most frightening I've ever done." Ninety minutes in a phone booth Schumacher considered "insane," but Colin Farrell made it happen. Once again, the actor and director achieved a winning combination, creating a nifty but modest thriller. The trick ending is a little too tricky for its own good, creepy, to be sure, but improbable. No one is going to believe that the pizza guy did it, but how did the Caller keep the pizza guy at hand during the ordeal? Extricated from the fatal phone booth, Stu is put in an ambulance and medicated. As the drugs start to take effect, the Caller comes calling again, this time in person (though this could be a hallucination). Schumacher leaves the impression that the Caller will live to see another ordeal, which might be a real inducement for Stu to behave himself in future. If so, that might be for the best, since Farrell actually makes the audience believe that Stu might be worth saving. And that's no easy trick.

—James M. Welsh

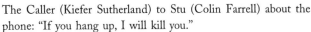

CREDITS

Stu Shepard: Colin Farrell
Captain Ramey: Forest Whitaker
Pamela McFadden: Katie Holmes
Kelly Shepard: Radha Mitchell
The Caller: Kiefer Sutherland
Sergeant Cole: Richard T. Jones
Adam: Keith Nobbs
Pimp: John Enos
Negotiator: James MacDonald
Mario: Josh Pais
Felicia: Paula Jai Parker
Asia: Tia Texada

Origin: USA
Released: 2002
Production: Gil Netter, David Zucker; Fox 2000 Pictures; released by 20th Century-Fox
Directed by: Joel Schumacher
Written by: Larry Cohen
Cinematography by: Matthew Libatique
Music by: Harry Gregson-Williams
Sound: Jay Meager
Editing: Mark Stevens
Art Direction: Martin Whist
Costumes: Daniel Orlandi
Production Design: Andrew Laws
MPAA rating: R
Running time: 81 minutes

REVIEWS

American Cinematographer. November, 2002, p. 60.
Boxoffice. November, 2002, p. 127.

Chicago Sun-Times Online. April 4, 2003.
Entertainment Weekly. April 11, 2003, p. 52.
Los Angeles Times Online. April 4, 2003.
New York Times. March 30, 2003, p. 28.
New York Times. April 4, 2003, p. E1.
People. April 14, 2003, p. 37.
Sight and Sound. April, 2003, p. 48.
USA Today. April 4, 2003, p. E6.
Variety. September 16, 2002, p. 32.
Washington Post. April 4, 2003, p. C1.
Washington Post. April 9, 2003, p. C1.
Washington Post Weekend. April 4, 2003, p. 45.
Washington Times. April 4, 2003, p. B5.

QUOTES

The Caller (Kiefer Sutherland) to Stu (Colin Farrell) about the phone: "If you hang up, I will kill you."

Pieces of April

She's the one in every family.
—Movie tagline

 Box Office: $2.5 million

April Burns (Katie Holmes) is the black sheep of her family. She lives a bohemian kind of existence in a Lower East Side tenement building, sports a thrift store style of fashion (including black nail polish, a tattooed neck, and magenta pigtails), and has not had contact with her loved ones for some time. But she has invited her family for Thanksgiving dinner, determined to reconnect with them on this day that, perhaps more than any other holiday, is reserved for family. Because her mother, Joy (Patricia Clarkson), is dying of cancer, this may be the last time they are together; making the trek is a chore for her, punctuated by bouts of nausea. Joy is accompanied by her supportive husband, Jim (Oliver Platt), their other two children, Timmy (John Gallagher, Jr.) and Beth (Alison Pill), as well as Joy's mother, Dottie (Alice Drummond).

Pieces of April, written and directed by Peter Hedges and inspired in part by his own mother's battle with cancer (the film is dedicated to her), takes place over a single Thanksgiving Day and follows a very simple yet moving story. April prepares the meal encountering plenty of pitfalls along the way, while her family makes a road trip from the suburbs to get to her apartment. Cutting between these two main plots, Hedges expertly juggles a tart, wry outlook on family relationships with a generous understanding of the bonds, often tenuous, that keep a family together. Shot on digital video on a shoestring budget, *Pieces of April* often has a dull, washed-out look, especially in outdoor scenes, but overall it looks better than many films shot in this format and is an impressive directorial debut for Hedges.

April has done very little cooking for herself, let alone preparing a grand meal for a large group, and her struggle just stuffing the turkey and sewing it up shows that she is out of her element. But disaster strikes when she discovers that her oven does not work and she must scramble through her apartment building to find a neighbor to help her. It is, of course, the irony that her misfortune allows her to meet neighbors whom she would not otherwise get to know, and they form a kind of cross-section of the American family. A black woman, Evette (Lillias White), at first scoffs at what a privileged, white girl might need, but very soon she is crying over April's sad family story, and she and her husband, Eugene (Isiah Whitlock, Jr.), become April's allies. Eugene is a kind of Thanksgiving purist, turning up his nose at store-bought stuffing and cranberry sauce from a can, and he teaches April how to cook from scratch. They allow her to use their oven for a while, but then she must find someone else to finish the job.

April meets one man with so many cats that she balks at using his facilities, and a vegan objects to April cooking an animal. April's best prospect appears to be Wayne (Sean Hayes), a fastidious twit who is very proud of all the features on his brand-new oven. He seems to like April but is socially awkward, and, when he sees that he is getting nothing in return for his generosity, he turns surly, and for a while poor April is left with her turkey essentially held hostage in his apartment.

April's escapades are funny, but there are touching moments that hint at her ambivalence toward the whole endeavor, and Holmes, eschewing her usual radiance and natural charm, taps into a darker current that demonstrates her range. April obviously wants to show her family that she is capable of throwing a dinner party but, at the same time, has difficulty letting go of old hostility. When her boyfriend, Bobby (Derek Luke), puts up some decorations, she snaps that her family is not worth the trouble. Later, she is making place cards for the table and writes "Mom" on one, then discards it and starts over with "Joy," obviously not feeling that she is very close to her mother.

Even more revealing about the family history are the dynamics on the road. Jim is obviously the glue in the family, trying to keep everyone happy and upbeat, even as he deals with his wife's debilitating illness. Beth is the goody-two-shoes daughter, who resents even having to make the trip and considers April's invitation selfish because it forces their sick mother to travel. Timmy keeps quiet most of the time,

helping his mother when she needs him and taking pictures to document the journey. Grandma seems to be going senile but is able to inject a barbed comment at Joy when she is rude to Beth.

The most compelling character is the imperious Joy, whose sardonic point of view relieves the tension of the journey. When they stop at a Krispy Kreme, she recommends ordering extra doughnuts because April is cooking. At another point, she seems prepared to give a poignant speech about what to do after she is gone, but instead she gives mock instructions on how to dispose of April's food without really eating it.

Clarkson, who has given a string of great supporting performances in the last few years, makes this movie her own. She keeps in balance Joy's mordant sense of humor, which is probably her only defense against impending death, and a deep-seated vulnerability, the feeling that she could snap and break down at any moment. In one scary scene, after being unable to recall even one endearing memory of April's childhood, Joy practically flees from the family station wagon to hitchhike a ride back home. Only Jim's calming influence and his assurance that they will be creating a good memory (whether or not he believes it himself is debatable) can get her back in the car. In this one confrontation, Clarkson and Platt let us understand a couple who have spent many years together, have been through a lot, and are facing yet one more crisis in what has probably been a whole series of crises.

The story also periodically cuts to Bobby and his big errand for the day, getting some nice clothes for the special occasion, which means seeing his friend at the Salvation Army. Bobby obviously wants to do his best to make a good impression on April's family, and he probably knows that being black is one extra hurdle he may have to overcome in winning them over, but his scenes tend to feel like filler and are not nearly as much fun as April's travails in the kitchen or as emotional as her family's road trip. His day ends badly when April's ex-boyfriend, Tyrone (Armando Riesco)—a white punk who tries to act black—and his friends surround Bobby for a fight. Bobby ends up beaten up, and, when he happens to meet up with April's family just as they are pulling up in front of her apartment, they panic and flee before April has a chance to greet them. The fight is an incongruous element, coming out of nowhere and feeling like a plot contrivance so that a bruised Bobby will scare the family away.

April is left in tears, while her family goes on to a restaurant. Beth, of course, is convinced that they did the right thing, but Joy has a change of heart when she witnesses a mother lashing out at her little daughter. Staring at this crestfallen little girl, Joy probably sees herself in the angry mother and is reminded of her own shortcomings. It is a tribute to Clarkson's performance that this brief, subtle moment speaks volumes about Joy's troubled relationship with April.

Back at the apartment, Bobby and April are having dinner with a Chinese immigrant family (they saved the day by finishing the cooking of the turkey) when Joy and Timmy, having hitched a ride with some motorcyclists, arrive at April's door. April and her mother embrace, and the moment freezes as a snapshot. Then the rest of the family appears, and everyone enjoys dinner together—April and her family as well as her neighbors, who have become like a second family to her. Even April and Beth seem to let go of their differences and hug each other. The final sequence unfolds without dialogue. Instead of showing us what April and her family might say to each other, with all the awkward pauses and fumbling for the right words, Hedges captures the holiday in its essence—people sharing each other's company in precious moments. Perhaps the emotions run so deep that words could not do them justice, and to include dialogue would risk turning a heartfelt moment and perfect ending into a clichéd family reunion.

When she encounters her Chinese neighbors early in the day, April tries to explain the meaning of Thanksgiving, eschewing a historical account for a more philosophical explanation: "Once there was this one day where everybody seemed to know they needed each other. This one day when they knew for certain that they couldn't do it alone." Clearly, April is expressing her own hopes for an ideal Thanksgiving experience, one devoid of old grudges and built on everyone's mutual acceptance of each other, and the film's final, beautiful moments become the visual fulfillment of her longing.

—Peter N. Chumo II

CREDITS

April Burns: Katie Holmes
Joy Burns: Patricia Clarkson
Jim Burns: Oliver Platt
Bobby: Derek Luke
Beth Burns: Alison Pill
Grandma Dottie: Alice Drummond
Wayne: Sean P. Hayes
Timmy Burns: John Gallagher Jr.
Latrell: Sisqo
Eugene: Isiah Whitlock Jr.
Evette: Lillias White

Origin: USA
Released: 2003
Production: John Lyons, Gary Winick, Alexis Alexanian; InDigEnt, Kalkaska Productions; released by United Artists

Directed by: Peter Hedges
Written by: Peter Hedges
Cinematography by: Tami Reiker
Music by: Stephen Merritt
Sound: Aaron Rudelson
Editing: Mark Livolsi
Costumes: Laura Bauer
Production Design: Richard Butler
MPAA rating: PG-13
Running time: 81 minutes

REVIEWS

Boxoffice. April, 2003, p. 80.
Chicago Sun-Times Online. October 24, 2003.
Entertainment Weekly. October 24, 2003, p. 85.
Los Angeles Times Online. October 17, 2003.
New York Times Online. October 17, 2003.
People. October 27, 2003, p. 29.
Rolling Stone. October 30, 2003, p. 100.
Vanity Fair. September, 2003, p. 178.
Variety Online. January 20, 2003.
Washington Post. October 24, 2003, p. WE33.

QUOTES

April (Katie Holmes) trying to explain Thanksgiving: "Once there was this one day where everyone seemed to know they needed each other. This one day when they knew for certain they couldn't do it alone."

AWARDS AND NOMINATIONS

Natl. Bd. of Review 2003: Support. Actress (Clarkson)
Natl. Soc. Film Critics 2003: Support. Actress (Clarkson)
Nomination:
Oscars 2003: Support. Actress (Clarkson)
Golden Globes 2004: Support. Actress (Clarkson)
Ind. Spirit 2004: First Feature, Screenplay, Support. Actress (Clarkson)
Screen Actors Guild 2003: Support. Actress (Clarkson).

Piglet's Big Movie

A tale you'll never forget.
—Movie tagline

 Box Office: $23.1 million

Piglet's Big Movie is only the second full-length feature about the Winnie the Pooh gang. The first was *The Tigger Movie*, which came out three years previous. It's difficult to believe that it took this long for someone to make a long form movie from A. A. Milne's popular stories from the late 1920's. (A Pooh short, *Winnie the Pooh and the Blustery Day* won an Oscar in 1968, and Pooh TV programs have been a TV staple.) Pooh has been such a kid favorite that there are two versions of the bear, the Disney version and more Milne-like "classic" Pooh. That way two giant corporations can make money from the silly old bear.

Piglet's Big Movie is actually more like "Piglet's Three Smaller Movies." It's adapted from *Winnie-the-Pooh* and *The House at Pooh Corner*. The three tales it takes from are "In Which Kanga and Baby Roo Come to the Forest and Piglet Has a Bath," "In Which Christopher Robin Leads an Expedition to the North Pole" and "In Which a House Is Built at Pooh Corner for Eeyore." The three stories are connected by the theme that even though Piglet is small, he can still do big things. It's not the most surprising and brilliant message, but it's better than the message of a lot of kids' movies which often boils down to "farting is funny."

Piglet's Big Movie is a slow and gentle film that will be well appreciated by parents and kids looking for a respite from the fast and furious tone of many kid flicks. Piglet is voiced by 77-year-old John Fiedler, who has been giving voice to the little guy since 1968. None of the other voice actors return but most of the new folks do a good job. Jim Cummings does Winnie the Pooh and Tigger and is right on in his characterizations. His Pooh is befuddled, kindhearted and usually looking for something good for his tummy. And his Tigger is bouncingly boisterous. Ken Sansom's Rabbit is uptight and quick to judge and Kath Soucie's Kanga is all motherly kindness and wisdom. Andre Stojka's Owl is an old windbag and Nikita Hopkins' Roo is full of energy. The only voice that seems a little off is Peter Cullen's hapless Eeyore. His Eeyore is certainly depressive enough, but he doesn't sound like the more familiar Eeyore from previous adventures.

In this film, Piglet and his gang in the Hundred Acre Wood are set to gather some honey, but his friends decide that he is too little to do the job. A storm whips up and suddenly Piglet's friends realize that their little buddy has

disappeared. The gang discovers Piglet's book of memories, his scrapbook of drawings about their adventures, and with Milne-esque logic they decide that Piglet's book of memories will surely be able to remember where Piglet is.

Each page takes them to a new destination where they remember a particular incident from their past. In one story, Rabbit leads a hate campaign against new neighbor Kanga and her baby, Roo. He wants to drive her out of town and concocts a plan in which they'll kidnap Roo and have Piglet take his place. Kanga is on to the ruse so she subjects the bathphobic Piglet to a good scrubbing. She then gives him a big dose of motherly love, including a nice cookie and a Carly Simon song, "Mother's Intuition." It all turns out well, the animals realize Kanga is nice and Rabbit and Roo bond. Pouring over the scrapbook, Piglet's friends realize what a big part their little friend played in making the happy ending.

In the North Pole story, Christopher Robin makes an appearance as the leader of an expedition to find the North Pole. He's not exactly sure what they're looking for, but confident that he will recognize it when they find it. In the story, Roo falls in a rushing river (it's not rushing fast enough to frighten any tots). The bigger guys try to save Roo, but keep messing up. Finally it is our Piglet who grabs a nearby pole and gets the wet Roo. The pole is dubbed the North Pole, and again Piglet is the unsung hero.

In the other story, the critters decide that Eeyore needs a new house. They surprise him by building one (inadvertently tearing down his old one down for the lumber.) The house falls down and they resign themselves to the fact that Eeyore will be homeless. But tenacious Piglet sneaks back and secretly rebuilds Eeyore's house. Everyone's happy, but Piglet is not properly credited and indeed suffers the additional indignity of having Pooh name Eeyore's lot Pooh Corner.

As the guys retell the stories, they realize how underappreciated Piglet has been. In one of the more touching scenes in the film, they all draw their own pictures of their favorite memories with Piglet and paste them all over the walls of his house. The film is mostly filled with sweet moments like this that seem true to Milne's vision, but the Disney folks can't resist throwing a little cliffhanging (literally) razzle-dazzle for the big finish. In a needless bit of extra excitement, Pooh ends up hanging for his life over a rushing waterfall. His friends link hands and make a chain to save him but come up just a little short. If only they had someone just about the size of, say, Piglet. Right in the nick of time, Piglet shows up and saves the day again. That message again: he may be small, but he's just the right size. Or as Piglet puts it, "I may be small, but in the biggest, helpfullest way."

A new touch that works with the Pooh stories is the addition of eight songs from Carly Simon. She wrote some of the tunes, including "Sing Ho for the Life of the Bear," which she adapted from Milne's writing, and does some of the classic Sherman Brothers songs, including the Winnie the Pooh theme, which she sings with her son Ben Taylor.

During the closing credits, the live-action Simon shows up strumming her guitar in a field. It's hard to not think of it being an ad for Carly Simon, but these days, one obvious product placement in a film isn't so bad.

Most critics liked the film. Stephen Holden of the *New York Times* wrote, "The movie . . . tells its story plainly, with a minimum of gimmickry and hyperkinetic action. The spare, lightly textured illustration is true to the spirit of the E. H. Shepard drawings for the Milne books. In the knockabout world of animated movies, *Piglet's Big Movie* is an oasis of gentleness and wit." Megan Lehmann of the *New York Post* wrote, "When the world gets too big and scary, the Hundred Acre Wood remains a clearly delineated comfort zone." And Kevin Thomas of the *Los Angeles Times* wrote, "Parents may find their attention wandering, but the simple tale contains valuable life lessons for their youngest offspring, who will likely be enchanted."

—Jill Hamilton

CREDITS

Piglet: John Fiedler (Voice)
Winnie the Pooh/Tigger: Jim (Jonah) Cummings (Voice)
Kanga: Kath Soucie (Voice)
Roo: Nikita Hopkins (Voice)
Owl: Andre Stoja (Voice)
Christopher Robin: Thomas Wheatley (Voice)
Eeyore: Peter Cullen (Voice)
Rabbit: Ken Sansom (Voice)

Origin: USA
Released: 2003
Production: Michelle Pappalardo-Robinson; Walt Disney Pictures; released by Buena Vista
Directed by: Francis Glebas
Written by: Brian Hohlfield
Music by: Carly Simon, Carl Johnson
Lyrics by: Carly Simon
Sound: Donald J. Malouf
Editing: Ivan Bilancio
Art Direction: Fred Warter
MPAA rating: G
Running time: 75 minutes

REVIEWS

Los Angeles Times Online. March 21, 2003.
New York Times Online. March 21, 2003.
Variety Online. March 20, 2003.
Washington Post. March 21, 2003, p. WE39.

Pirates of the Caribbean: The Curse of the Black Pearl

Prepare to be blown out of the water.
—Movie tagline

 Box Office: $275 million

Young Elizabeth Swan is sailing to Port Royal where her father, Weatherby Swann (Jonathan Pryce), is to be Governor. Suddenly Elizabeth is awakened from her reveries of a pirate's life on the high seas by the sight of a burning ship, and floating amongst the flotsam and jetsam is a young lad, Will Turner. Will is unconscious but wears a gold medallion around his neck that bears a pirate skull. Fearing he'll be mistaken for a pirate and arrested by the ship's imperious Captain Norrington (Jack Davenport), Elizabeth takes the necklace and hides it.

Years later the grown Will (Orlando Bloom) has been apprenticed to a drunken blacksmith but has managed to become a master swordmaker. As he delivers one of his masterpieces to the Governor—who will present it to Norrington as he is made a commodore—it becomes apparent that Will is smitten with the now grown Elizabeth (Keira Knightly). Although she may have feelings for Will, too, the obvious gulf in their social standings make a relationship between the two virtually impossible. In any event, her father has already set his eye on the soon-to-be Commodore Norrington to be his son-in-law. He has even brought Elizabeth the latest fashion from London to wear to the ceremony, including a stifling corset, to help the relationship between the two move along, but at the last minute she also dons Will's medallion.

Meanwhile, down at the harbor, a ship is simultaneously drifting into port and sinking. It reaches the dock with only its crow's nest above water and a blithe Captain Jack Sparrow (Johnny Depp) jauntily stepping ashore from the perch. As it turns out, Jack used to be the captain of the fabled Black Pearl, a pirate ship now "crewed by the damned and captained by a man so evil that hell itself spit him out." The Black Pearl's new captain is a man named Barbossa (Geoffrey Rush), who led a mutiny against Sparrow and left him to die on a desert island. Now Jack's all-consuming goal is to get his ship back. But his path is about to cross that of Elizabeth, Norrington and eventually Will.

The dress must have done the job, because after the ceremony Norrington takes Elizabeth out to the fort's ramparts and proposes to her. Unfortunately for him, her corset has also done its job and has caused her to faint and fall from the high wall, plunging her into the waters below . . . close to Jack Sparrow who jumps in to save her. When they are both plucked from the water, however, the ingrate Norrington has no thanks for Jack whom he exposes as a pirate and has arrested and carted off to jail.

But more has been set in motion by Elizabeth's fall, for when her medallion touched the water it sent a signal throughout the seas and now, under cover of night, the Black Pearl is gliding into port searching for the medallion and its owner. After sending volley after volley of cannon fire into the port and causing chaos, the Black Pearl's crew set out into the city looking for the medallion. The gold calls to them and leads them to the governor's palace and Elizabeth. No retiring English rose, she puts up quite a fight but is eventually captured and taken to Barbossa where she tells him her name is Turner and is a maid.

This is just what Barbossa was hoping for. There is a curse on him and his crew. Because they stole and spent a cache of Aztec gold they have been turned into the undead, something that becomes apparent only when the men appear under the moonlight and become a real skeleton crew. To lift the curse they must return all the gold along with a blood payment from each person who spent it. They have only one coin left and only one person from whom they need the blood . . . the descendent of a crewman named "Bootstrap" Bill Turner, Will's father.

Well, to make an even longer story as brief as possible, since she's not really a Turner, Elizabeth's blood obviously won't lift the curse; Jack and Will join forces and steal a British ship in order to rescue Elizabeth and reclaim the Black Pearl; Commodore Norrington and Governor Swann pursue Jack and Will and Elizabeth and Barbossa; and Barbossa is after the real Turner in order to shed his blood and become human again.

Is it really surprising that few people held out a lot of hope for Pirates of the Caribbean? I mean, pirate movies haven't had a particularly good track record since Errol Flynn was Captain Blood. Think 1980's The Island with Michael Caine, or 1986's Roman Polanski helmed Pirates, or for a real shudder remember 1995's Geena Davis disaster Cutthroat Island, directed by her then husband Renny Harlin.

But there was another reason to wonder what on earth the filmmakers must have been thinking when they came up with this film idea. Action/adventure movies usually inspire amusement park rides, not the other way around. And, to make matters worse, this gimmick was tried last year (not with a lot of success) with another Disney amusement part attraction, The Country Bears.

So one couldn't really be blamed for not expecting too much from Pirates of the Caribbean: The Curse of the Black Pearl, and one can't really help but be pleasantly surprised that this movie is as good as it is. It is fast-paced, suspenseful, colorful, and just plain fun. It never takes itself too seriously and walks just the right line between comedy and action and even throws in just a dash of romance.

A large part of the credit for this success belongs to the film's co-writers Ted Elliott and Terry Rossio, who were also the writing talent behind the hit animated movie Shrek. Right from the start they establish the dual personality of the movie. There is the serious beginning—the young Elizabeth witnessing the burning ship from which Will is plucked—in which the ominous, nightmarish part of the pirate world is established; and a comic beginning—Captain Jack "sailing" into harbor in his crow's nest—to let us know that the movie has its tongue firmly planted in its cheek.

Pirates is a witty tribute to everything a pirate story should be, including lifting scenes directly from the Disney ride: jailed pirates trying to coax a dog to bring them the keys, drunken pirates yo-ho-hoing it up in a tavern with some lusty serving wenches. There's flamboyant clothing, battles at sea, black-hearted deeds and even a parrot perched on one pirate's shoulder . . . although he is a mute and the parrot functioned as his voice. As with the parrot, having fun with the conventions brings an extra layer of fun to this movie. For example, usually treasures are discovered, then carried away, but here the pirates spend the entire film putting the treasure back. And in one action-packed sea battle humor comes when the cannons are loaded with anything available, including silverware, which leaves a very funny visual image when sticking out of the wood of the other ship, not to mention sticking out of the ill-fitting substitute eye of one of the pirates.

If the writers of the film were having fun, then so, too, was its primary star, Johnny Depp. Depp has claimed that as inspiration for his role as Captain Jack Sparrow he turned to the cartoon character Pepe Le Pew, the Rolling Stone's Keith Richards, and threw in a little Rastafarian. It paid off. His Captain has the slightly slurred speech of too much rum and the addled presence of someone who is crazy like a fox. He is a con artist with the heart of gold . . . sort of. He is the embodiment of sashaying feyness and one might doubt his sexual orientation except that women keep slapping him for past transgressions. With gold-capped teeth and twittering hand gestures, Depp is sheer fun as the comic relief and yet also the heart of the film.

Also having fun with his role is the over-the-top amusing villainy of Geoffrey Rush's Barbossa and his crew that by turns are either Nazi storm troopers or the Keystone cops. (Fans of BBC America's The Office will be amused with Mackenzie Crook's shift from officious business drone to the pirate with the "wandering" eye.)

At the solid core of the film, though, are two actors who are not allowed to have as much fun, but, by doing so, provide an anchor around which all the antics can take place. Orlando Bloom's Will Turner evolves nicely from the bashful, love-struck, under-appreciated background character to the sword-wielding, honest and valiant hero. Known for his previous appearance as the elf Legolas in *The Lord of the Rings* movies, Bloom could easily become the latest movie heartthrob. Similarly Keira Knightley's (*Bend It Like Beckham*) Elizabeth is not the typical cowering damsel in distress. She can give as good as she gets and gives voice to all women everywhere who have been victimized by fashion. She is a good straight man for both Depp's and Rush's characters and a convincing love interest for Bloom's.

Responsible for putting all these factors together into an effective package is director Gore Verbinski. Known mostly for the comedy *Mouse Hunt* and the Japanese inspired *The Ring*—not to mention the Budweiser frog commercials—Verbinski is known for his striking visuals which help create atmospheres that can suck a viewer into a story. From costumes to sets to music to special effects, Verbinski pulls them all together to create a convincing world. This is perhaps one of the film's strongest points, although one can also blame the director for one of the film's few weak points. It could use a bit of editing. Some of the swordfights, especially, overstay their welcome. After all, you can't kill the undead, so where's the suspense.

But even with a running time that's a bit too long, *Pirates of the Caribbean* is an entertaining and colorful romp highlighted by colorful characters and tongue-in-cheek scenes. Its engaging cast, astounding special effects and lush look are suitable for summer entertainment and give one hope that maybe a movie created from a Walt Disney ride can be worth watching. Let's hope so because next up is a movie based on The Haunted Mansion.

—*Beverley Bare Buehrer*

CREDITS

Jack Sparrow: Johnny Depp
Barbossa: Geoffrey Rush
Will Turner: Orlando Bloom
Elizabeth Swann: Keira Knightley
Governor Weatherby Swann: Jonathan Pryce
Norrington: Jack Davenport
Joshamee Gibbs: Kevin McNally
Anamaria: Zoe Saldana
Kohler: Treva Etienne
Pintel: Lee Arenberg
Grapple: Trevor Goddard
Cotton: David Bailie
Ragetti: Mackenzie Crook

Bosun: Isaac C. Singleton Jr.
Mallot: Brye Cooper

Origin: USA
Released: 2003
Production: Jerry Bruckheimer; released by Walt Disney Pictures
Directed by: Gore Verbinski
Written by: Ted Elliott, Terry Rossio
Cinematography by: Darius Wolski
Music by: Klaus Badelt
Sound: Lee Orloff
Music Supervisor: Bob Badami
Editing: Craig Wood, Stephen E. Rivkin, Arthur P. Schmidt
Art Direction: Derek R. Hill
Costumes: Penny Rose
Production Design: Brian Morris
MPAA rating: PG-13
Running time: 134 minutes

REVIEWS

Chicago Sun-Times Online. July 9, 2003.
Chicago Tribune Online. July 9, 2003.
Entertainment Weekly. July 18, 2003, p. 53.
Los Angeles Times Online. May 4, 2003.
Los Angeles Times Online. June 20, 2003.
Los Angeles Times Online. July 9, 2003.
New York Times Online. July 9, 2003.
People. July 21, 2003, p. 36.
USA Today Online. July 9, 2003.
Variety Online. July 6, 2003.
Washington Post. July 9, 2003, p. C1.

QUOTES

Jack Sparrow (Johnny Depp): "You look familiar, have I threatened you before?" Will Turner (Orlando Bloom): "I make it a point to avoid familiarity with pirates."

Norrington (Jack Davenport): "You are without a doubt the worst pirate I've ever heard of." Jack Sparrow (Johnny Deep): "Ah, but you have heard of me."

TRIVIA

This is the first PG-13 rated film from Walt Disney Pictures. The rating is for action/adventure violence.

Screen Actors Guild 2003: Actor (Depp)
Nomination:
Oscars 2003: Actor (Depp), Makeup, Sound, Visual FX
Golden Globes 2004: Actor (Depp).

Platform (Zhantai)

latform, or *Zhantai,* covers a tumultuous time in Chinese history and spotlights the dramatic events in the lives of several characters, yet Zhang Ke Jia's sophomore effort is devoid of conventional dramatic presentation. The unusually detached approach will undoubtedly divide viewers as much as it has the critics. The film itself has had its own tumultuous history, from the difficulty the director experienced producing a film that is critical of the Chinese government in that same country, to the film's auspicious debut on the festival circuit in 2000, to its much-bowdlerized official release in 2003.

The story of *Platform* involves a group of theatrical players starting out in 1979 in the rural northern province of Fenyang, who perform Maoist propaganda set pieces for the local villagers. Soon, China undergoes major changes that affect the traveling actors. The rise of Deng Xiaoping after the fall of Mao Zedong creates an opening for Western influences, including rock music and American-style clothing. The troupe's socialist style thus gives way to a colorful pop look. The younger performers generally welcome the changes, but a sadness underlies their entry into this more modern world. Cui Minliang (Wang Hong-wei) hesitantly and awkwardly courts Ruijuan (Zhao Tao), while Zhong Pin (Yank Tiang-yi) gets an abortion following her impassioned affair with Zhang Jun (Liang Jing-dong). Later, both women find the troupe confining and quit, new members replace them, and life goes on. But for all the social upheaval, poverty still exists, affecting where and how the troupe performs.

The difference of opinion about *Platform* kept the film from being an arthouse favorite in 2003: The *Village Voice's* J. Hoberman called it "one of the richest films of the past decade," but Andrew Howe at filmwritten.org wrote, "It's a featureless, tedious exercise in impenetrability." Some reviewers even found themselves divided as did the *New York Times's* A. O. Scott, who said the film was "an intellectually engaging movie" but also wrote that "the characters in

Platform live through a lot of history, but the history—and the film itself—never really come alive."

The reason the history and the film "never really come alive" for Scott is obvious: Ke Jia's approach is deliberately distanced. We never get to know the characters very well (some disappear without explanation), the pacing is slow, and nearly all of the action takes place in medium and long shot tableaux. Ke Jia eschews any trace of Hollywood high style, even in the theatrical/musical pieces, which are intentionally amateurish. Of course, such naturalism works against the film's entertainment value, which explains the disappointment of some viewers (A. O. Scott compares the film unfavorably to *Boogie Nights,* a very different chronicle of an entertainment industry in flux). Perhaps one should be grateful Ke Jia cut the film down from 195 to 155 minutes for the U.S. release. On the other hand, choosing to present history on the screen in this unusual way highlights the social and political points without getting lost in the usual melodrama.

The real problem with *Platform* is that its socio-political statement seems blunted not by melodrama, but by obscurity. For example, the only mention of Tiannamen Square or the government quelling of the burgeoning democracy movement of the late 1980s comes—toward the end of the film—in a bit of dialogue that is *not* translated in the English subtitles! We still get the idea, however, that the more things change, the more they stay the same, and neither Eastern nor Western culture has done right by the working people.

What stands out artistically and thematically about *Platform* are certain indelible moments: a troupe member introducing a boom-box radio to his comrades; Zhong Pin giving Ruijuan make-up tips; Zhong Pin feeling forced—by the men in the troupe—to get the abortion. Like the Neorealist films of the 1940s and '50s, Ke Jia uses nonprofessional actors, all of whom are exquisitely at ease in front of the camera. Produced without the Chinese government's okay, *Platform* also reconstructs, with seeming authenticity, pre-Westernized cities and destitute provinces (the director was born in the town of Fenyang in the Shanxi province).

Platform, which takes its title from a rock song, is best compared to *Bye Bye Brazil* (1979), another film (set in a very different place) about the tough life of modern-day troubadours. Although *Platform* lacks some of the charm—and more pointed criticism—of that older film, it also finds a haunting resonance in the same subject matter.

—*Eric Monder*

Minliang: Hong-wei Wang
Ruijuan: Tao Zhao

Chang Jun: Jing-dong Liang
Zhong Pin: Tian-yi Yang

Origin: Hong Kong, Japan, France
Language: Chinese
Released: 2000
Production: Kit-ming Li, Shozo Ichiyama; Hu-Tong
Communication, T-Mark, Artcam International; released
by Open City Films
Directed by: Zhang-ke Jia
Written by: Zhang-ke Jia
Cinematography by: Lik-wai Yu
Music by: Yoshihiro Hanno
Sound: Yang Zhang
Editing: Jing-lei Kong
Art Direction: Qiu Sheng
Costumes: Lei Qi, Xiafei Zhao
MPAA rating: Unrated
Running time: 155 minutes

 REVIEWS

New York Post Online. March 14, 2003.
New York Times Online. October 7, 2000.
Variety Online. September 13, 2000.
Village Voice Online. March 12, 2003.

Poolhall Junkies

Sometimes you get a second shot . . . make it.
—Movie tagline

Being hooked on the game could cost you your life.
—Movie tagline

It's your shot. Take it.
—Movie tagline

Poolhall Junkies is the first major film to be made by Mars Callahan. It's safe to say that you haven't seen his first feature, *Zigs*, made under the name Gregory "Mars" Martin. *Poolhall Junkies* is another indie film, but it got a pretty wide release. Callahan is all over this film; besides writing and directing, he also stars as Johnny. When leads write themselves into a movie, often the roles end up being self-serving and sort of pitiful; other characters tell them how great they are, and even unattractive and undesirable actors will prove irresistible to the ladies. But Callahan has enough charisma to make Johnny believable.

Poolhall Junkies is (another) movie about following your dreams, but the best part of it is watching the tiny con games that pepper the movie. In one scene, a guy bets another that he can down two big glasses of beer in the time that it takes him to drink two shots. The rules are that neither can touch the other's glass. The con guy says that, to make it fair, he should first be able to drink his glass of beer. He does so and puts it upside-down over one of the shot glasses. Yes, the con was recycled from Steve Buscemi's indie *Trees Lounge,* but it's always enjoyable to watch a good scam played out.

The other good thing about *Poolhall Junkies* is the cast that Callahan was able to wrangle for this film. The older folks include Rod Steiger (in one of his last roles), Chazz Palminteri, and Christopher Walken. The younger folks are less illustrious—Rick Schroder and Michael Rosenbaum (*Smallville*)—but they hold their own in a less showy way.

Johnny is a great pool player who was recruited by the pros when he was a young teen. His parents had abandoned him and he was taken in by Joe (Palminteri), but Joe threw away the invitation from the pros and didn't tell Johnny. He wanted to keep Johnny with him so that they could hustle together.

Johnny had always dreamed of becoming a pro and after thinking that they never wanted him, resigns himself to being a smalltime pool hustler. But too many years of Joe's abuse turn Johnny against him. Disgusted, Johnny quits pool and tries to get a regular job. This pleases his girlfriend, Tara (Alison Eastwood, Clint's daughter), an aspiring attorney who doesn't like Johnny's pool playing ways. Johnny proves himself to be an unsuccessful carpenter and mobile home salesman.

At a party with Alison's coworkers, Johnny meets the similarly-coiffed Mike (Walken), a very rich man who, unbeknownst to Johnny, happens to be Alison's uncle. The two end up playing pool with Alison's boss. Things escalate until Johnny is betting that the boss will give Alison a job once she takes the bar exam. As he always does, Johnny wins. His girlfriend, not knowing about the bet, is mad that Johnny spent most of the party playing pool and breaks up with him.

Things don't improve much for Johnny. Joe breaks his hand, preventing him from playing well. Johnny's little brother, Danny (Rosenbaum) ends up in jail after being hustled by a pool pro, Brad (Schroder). And Johnny is realizing that selling mobile homes is not quite as interesting as being a great pool player. As in all sports movies, however, Johnny will be able to solve all his problems conveniently by playing that one big game. He will get the girl, save his brother, put Joe out of business, and, for all we know, finally get that junk drawer organized by winning the game.

To Callahan's credit, that one big game is entertaining. Johnny's in jeopardy but not as much as Joe, since Johnny has the backing of Mike. As Mike puts it, "I'm a millionaire. If I lose $80,000, I'll just get another $80,000." The big match is solved in a quite satisfying way, and appropriately, involves a bit of a con game.

All of this has been covered before in films like *The Hustler* and *The Color of Money,* and *Poolhall Junkies* doesn't add anything new to the genre. Still, it's an entertaining story, with colorful characters. The film is less successful when it tackles humor. In one scene, Danny's nervous friend is saying, "There is no way we can possibly have a party at my parent's house tomorrow night." Cut to next scene, and there's the party. Later, the guy screeched, "In a million years, you can never get me to pawn my car." Can anyone guess what the next scene will be? Callahan also has his characters telling lame jokes. One says, "Do you know what you call a field full of lawyers buried up to their necks in sand? Not enough sand." It's not exactly your A-level material.

With the exception of Eastwood, who seems to be reciting lines rather than acting, the acting in the film is good. Palminteri is doing the bad guy routine he's done countless times before, but he's good at that. As for Schroder, it's nice to see the former, cute child star playing a bitter pool hustler. Walken is typically good as the suave rich uncle who bets on Johnny. Steiger is stuck playing the grizzled old pool hall owner who has to say grizzled old pool hall owner words of wisdom like, "Boy, you go around thinking you're a loser and you'll become a loser." Callahan holds up surprisingly well against all this talent. He has a strong, quiet screen presence that works well here.

Critics didn't much care for the film. Manohla Dargis of the *Los Angeles Times* observed, "Like Ed Burns and Vin Diesel, both of whom have starred in features they've directed, Callahan has an attractive self-confidence that helps smooth over the roughness, but like them, he might best apply his talent in front of the camera." *Newsday*'s Jan Stuart really didn't like the film, giving it one star out of four. "*Poolhall Junkies*," she concluded, "is one of those unstoppably wrongheaded pictures that makes you feel giddy from the accumulation of purple dialogue, campy zoom shots and high-testosterone vulgarity." Lou Lumineck of the *New York Post* wrote, "This film coulda been a contender if Callahan hadn't worn so many hats—but it has moments that make it worth waiting for on video." And A.O. Scott of the *New York Times* added, "If Mr. Callahan had not been so determined to prove his own coolness, he might have made a better movie."

—*Jill Hamilton*

CREDITS

Johnny Doyle: Mars Callahan
Danny Doyle: Michael Rosenbaum
Joe: Chazz Palminteri
Nick: Rod Steiger
Mike: Christopher Walken
Brad: Rick Schroder
Tara: Alison Eastwood
Chico: Glenn Plummer
Tang: Ernie Reyes Jr.
Philip: Peter Mark Richman
Chris: Anson Mount

Origin: USA
Released: 2002
Production: Vincent Newman, Karen Beninati, Catherine Bailey; released by Gold Circle Films
Directed by: Mars Callahan
Written by: Mars Callahan, Chris Corso
Cinematography by: Robert Morris
Music by: Richard Glasser
Sound: Peter Geoco
Editing: James Tooley
Art Direction: Newt Lee
Costumes: Kristin Petersen
Production Design: Robert Laliberte
MPAA rating: R
Running time: 94 minutes

REVIEWS

Boxoffice. April, 2003, p. 99.
Chicago Sun-Times Online. February 28, 2003.
Los Angeles Times Online. February 28, 2003.
New York Times Online. February 28, 2003.
Variety. July 1, 2002, p. 28.

QUOTES

Mike (Christopher Walken): "I'm gonna step outside and get some smog."
Nick (Rod Steiger) to Johnny (Mars Callahan): "You have the ability to be the best. If you think you're a loser, you will be a loser."

Prey for Rock and Roll

It's difficult to make a good movie about rock and roll. There's no doubt that it's an appealing subject. It's sexy, there's good music, and the kids like the stuff. But somehow, the very effort of making a movie about rock and roll takes the rock and roll out of it. Playing in a band and saying, "When I play, I feel safe," is cool. When a character in a movie says the same thing in a film, some sort of lameness quotient is added. It's elusive but it's there.

The same problem plagues *Prey for Rock and Roll*. The characters and their rock and roll lifestyle don't come across as cool as the filmmakers seem to think. Part of this may be bias since the film was written by a rocker. The film is based on an autobiographical play by failed 1980s rocker Cheri Lovedog (she collaborated on the screenplay with Robin Whitehouse.) The film was director by Alex Steyermark, a film music supervisor making his directorial debut here.

Not surprisingly, based on its source, the film concerns a female rocker who doesn't seem to be making it. Jacki (Gina Gershon) is nearing 40 and has been plugging away in various bands for almost 20 years. Jacki may be close to 40, but she's certainly wearing it well. As lovestruck critic Mick LaSalle of the *San Francisco Chronicle* wrote, "Anyone in any doubt that 40 is the new 30 needs to take a look at Gina Gershon in *Prey for Rock and Roll.* Joan Crawford in *Mildred Pierce* never looked like this: With her tight stomach muscles, tattoos, three-toned hair and enough attitude for two 20-year-olds, Gershon has to be one of the coolest women on the planet." Jacki certainly does have the proper swagger. She is the rare woman that can wear leather pants, calls everyone "dude," and look cool covered with 35 tattoos. (The tattoo-free Gershon had to spend time in make-up each filming day to reapply the tattoos.) The best part of *Prey for Rock and Roll* is just seeing Gershon play a character with this much attitude.

Jacki's current band, Clamdaddy, is taking her no closer to the rock and roll success she's dreamed of since she first heard Tina Turner and X. She loves playing, but is getting mighty tired of lugging around her own gear, playing dingy clubs, and having no health insurance. At one gig, she mentions casually that each of her band members will take home approximately $13.

To make enough money to cover rent, Jacki owns a tattoo parlor. Her bassist, Tracy (Drea de Matteo of *The Sopranos*) is living off her family's money and is suffering from a serious drug problem. Guitarist Faith (Lori Petty) is in her 40s and spends her days giving guitar lessons to bratty, talentless teens. Drummer Sally (Shelly Cole) is Faith's 23-year-old girlfriend, and an innocent who hides a dark family secret.

Although this is a girl-centered movie in which girls rule, girls date mostly girls, and girls call each other by a vulgar term for male genitalia, there are a few men around. The "good" one is Sally's brother, Animal (Marc Blucas of *Buffy the Vampire Slayer*), who's just been released from prison. Despite his name and former living quarters, Animal's a sweetie—a virgin, even—who has a crush on Jacki. Jacki finds him somewhat intriguing. The bad man is Tracy's boyfriend (Ivan Martin). He keeps pestering her to try "the fantasy." His beloved fantasy turns out to be a scene in which he beats and rapes her. A rape does occur, although Tracy is not the victim, and here the movie takes another turn.

The film starts by questioning whether one should keep following a youthful dream as one gets older. It's also about the day-to-day business of being in a band. But the writers don't seem to think that this is adequate drama for a feature film, so the rape is added. At that point, the movie turns into more of a melodrama. More than one critic compared the film to something that might appear on the Lifetime Network, albeit with more tattoos. The melodrama is kind of a cop-out, as is giving the tough, bisexual Jacki such a milquetoast love interest. The writers thought that there was enough of an interest factor in rock and roll to make a movie about it, but then didn't have enough faith that it alone could sustain a movie.

It's difficult to gauge whether or not Clamdaddy is supposed to be a good band or not. The songs were all written by Lovedog and have a 1980s feel. Presumably, she was trying to write good songs, but they sound dated and generically grungy. Gershon, who started out in musical theater and recently appeared in a revival of *Cabaret,* has a husky rock and roll voice that serves the songs well. She can shout out her lyrics with the kind of punk commitment that they need.

Critical opinion formed an almost perfect bell curve. Some sort of liked it, some sort of hated it, few felt excessively committed one way or the other. Bob Strauss of the *Los Angeles Daily News* wrote, "The film, shot appropriately on grime-emphasizing digital video, also boasts terrific performances, lots of obviously lived-through-this insight . . . and terrific, hard-driving songs. The tattoos are pretty awesome as well." Lou Lumenick of the *New York Post* felt that "it becomes almost laughably melodramatic and wields just about every rock movie cliché in the book, [but] Gershon's latest (which she also produced) holds interest, thanks to her fiercely committed and sexy performance as a scowling bisexual singer." Elizabeth Weitzman of the *New York News* wrote, "Powered by an unsteady blend of Hollywood clichés and indie-inspired grrl power, Alex Steyermark's rocker chick is oddly, almost unrelentingly, grim. Thanks to several strong performances, however, it does hit its share of high notes." Stephen Holden of the *New York Times* assessed, "[I]f the movie is terrific on ambiance and street language (the women call one another Dude), much of its melodramatic story involving a rape and payback feels forced."

—*Jill Hamilton*

CREDITS

Jacki: Gina Gershon
Tracy: Drea De Matteo
Faith: Lori Petty
Sally: Shelly Cole
Animal: Marc Blucas
Nick: Ivan Martin

Origin: USA
Released: 2003
Production: Gina Resnick, Donovan Mannato, Gina Gershon; released by Mac Releasing
Directed by: Alex Steyermark
Written by: Cheri Lovedog, Robin Whitehouse
Cinematography by: Antonio Calvache
Sound: Steve Weiss, Tim O'Heir
Music Supervisor: Linda Cohen
Editing: Allyson C. Johnson
Costumes: Vanessa Vogel
Production Design: John Chichester
MPAA rating: R
Running time: 104 minutes

REVIEWS

Boxoffice. September, 2003, p. 116.
Entertainment Weekly. October 31, 2003, p. 56.
Los Angeles Times Online. September 26, 2003.
New York Times Online. October 17, 2003.
Variety Online. June 9, 2003.

Radio

His courage made them champions.
—Movie tagline

Box Office: $43.5 million

When a movie like *Radio* comes around, you pretty much know what to expect. It's all standard stuff in what might be called the mentally-challenged genre. There's said mentally-challenged person, obstacles to overcome, and lots of goodness all around. Portraying the mentally-challenged person is a good career move and sometimes it can even be the ticket to an Oscar. Tom Hanks in *Forrest Gump* and Dustin Hoffman in *Rain Man* discovered that such roles are a good way to show people that you can act.

Cuba Gooding Jr. already has his Oscar (for *Jerry Maguire*), but after a string of movies that were not exactly Academy Award material, including *Snow Dogs* and *Boat Trip,* he needed a vehicle to remind people that he is actually a good actor. The short route to credibility? Play the mentally-challenged person.

Actually, *Radio* could have been a train wreck of a movie. Gooding is not the most subtle actor, and one can easily imagine him playing a disabled person in the most over-the-top way. The story, about goodhearted townsfolk taking in a local oddball, could have been packed with overly tender moments and amped up emotional moments. It could have been overly self-congratulatory. Of course lessons are learned in *Radio,* but at least director Mike Tollin (*Summer Catch*) doesn't cram them down our throats with a sweeping orchestral score. Actually, *Radio* isn't nearly as bad as it looked like it would be.

Radio is based on a true story, which was covered in the 1996 *Sports Illustrated* article, "Someone to Lean On," by Gary Smith. It takes place in the small town of Anderson, South Carolina, where James Robert "Radio" Kennedy grew up. Radio (Gooding, sporting some really bad teeth) has something wrong with him, but his mother, Maggie (S. Epatha Merkerson), is not sure quite what. Maggie tells the coach that the doctor said Radio was the same as everyone else "just a little slower than most." Radio spends his days wandering around town, pushing a shopping cart and listening to a radio. Everyone in town pretty much ignores him because, well, no one has tried to talk to him and the guy does seem pretty strange. What the movie never delves into is that Radio is black and the townsfolk (or at least much of them) are white. But the town seems to be a model of colorblindness. Indeed, the high school administrator, Principal Daniels (Alfre Woodward) is not only black, but a woman.

When the coach of the high school football team, Harold Jones (Ed Harris) comes upon some of his team torturing Radio, Jones decides to take action. He makes the boys run laps (a coach's all-purpose solution to most issues) and takes Radio under his wing. He starts inviting him to the practices and buys him meals at the local diner. (The two also do many plugs for Burger King. The Coach often is noticeably eating Burger King and at one point even comments upon how they are the best burgers around.)

To add some drama to all of this, writer Mike Rich (*Finding Forester*) dutifully puts in some conflict. Since the coach is spending so much time treating Radio like his long lost son, he doesn't spend enough time with his wife, Linda (Debra Winger) and daughter, Mary Helen (Sarah Drew). And there are some townspeople that aren't too happy about Radio hanging around the school. Local banker, Frank Clay (Chris Mulkey) has a son, Johnny (Riley Smith), on the team and views Radio as a distraction. When the townsmen all meet in the local barbershop after the games, Frank is the one who tries to organize discontent against the Coach and his new buddy. Johnny does his part at the high school level by tricking Radio into walking into the girls' locker room to get the guy into trouble. By the last reel, you can be sure that Johnny will have changed his ways so much that he will be wholeheartedly agreeing with the Coach's words, "We haven't been teaching Radio; he's the one who has been teaching us." The third obstacle is a local school board reviewer who keeps coming by the school and trying to get Principal Daniels to get rid of Radio.

All of these conflicts are set up, but only one of them, the one with the banker, is really resolved. The other two just sort of disappear. The coach's wife and daughter resent the attention that their man is giving Radio, but they get over it easily because they understand that this is something that the Coach just has to do. Problem solved!

Probably the best thing about the film is Harris's performance. He is one of those kinds of hard-looking, muscled guys that just look like they should be a coach. As Roger Ebert of the *Chicago Sun-Times* put it, Harris "brings along confident masculine authority without even having to think about it." Harris has a certain grace about him that allows him to say things like, "I just figured it was the right thing to do," without sounding like a show-off. Winger is also quite good. Her part is just barely there—one critic noted that the female characters in *Radio* are "criminally underused"—but through sheer force of acting will, she manages to give her barely written character some fierce heart and personality. It's actually quite amazing to watch her wring out what she can from so little. Gooding is surprisingly understated in his role. He plays Radio as a gentle soul who's both frightened by people but intrigued by belonging to a group.

Critics had pretty strong reactions one way or another to the film. Wesley Morris of the *Boston Globe* claimed, "*Radio* is a tall glass of hogwash that's terrified to declare itself the racial-healing melodrama that it is." Stephen Holden commented that "Gooding creates a convincing portrait of a persecuted innocent" but went on to add that the film "is a synthetic mush of molasses-soaked pablum." Ebert of the *Sun-Times* observed, "For families, for those who find most movies too cynical, for those who want to feel good in a warm and uncomplicated way, *Radio* is a treasure. Others may find it too slow and sunny or innocent. You know who you are." And Peter Howell of the *Toronto Star* concluded, "Rarely have good intentions been wrapped in such a sticky package as they are in *Radio*, a contender for the year's most cloying film."

—*Jill Hamilton*

CREDITS

Radio: Cuba Gooding Jr.
Coach Jones: Ed Harris
Principal Daniels: Alfre Woodard
Maggie: S. Epatha Merkerson
Frank: Chris Mulkey
Mary Helen Jones: Sarah Drew
Johnny: Riley Smith
Tucker: Patrick Breen
Honeycutt: Brent Sexton
Linda Jones: Debra Winger

Origin: USA
Released: 2003
Production: Mike Tollin, Brian Robbins, Herbert W. Gains; Revolution Studios, Tollin/Robbins Productions; released by Columbia Pictures
Directed by: Mike Tollin
Written by: Mike Rich
Cinematography by: Don Burgess
Music by: James Horner
Sound: Jeffree Bloomer
Music Supervisor: Laura Z. Wasserman
Editing: Chris Lebenzon, Harvey Rosenstock
Art Direction: Thomas Minton
Costumes: Denise Wingate
Production Design: Clay A. Griffith
MPAA rating: PG
Running time: 109 minutes

REVIEWS

Chicago Sun-Times Online. October 24, 2003.
Entertainment Weekly. October 31, 2003, p. 52.
Los Angeles Times Online. October 24, 2003.
New York Times Online. October 24, 2003.
People. November 3, 2003, p. 36.
USA Today Online. October 24, 2003.
Variety Online. October 13, 2003.
Washington Post. October 24, 2003, p. WE34.

AWARDS AND NOMINATIONS

Nomination:
Golden Raspberries 2003: Worst Actor (Gooding).

Raising Victor Vargas (Long Way Home)

 Box Office: $1.65 million

In his startling debut feature, *Raising Victor Vargas*, Peter Sollett steers clear of the major pitfalls that have hampered other gritty efforts in the subgenre of the adolescent drama. Vargas has none of the sensationalism of Larry Clark's *Kids* (1995) or the adult-oriented lyricism of the

French classic, *The 400 Blows* (1959) by Francois Truffaut. Vargas's closest cousin would be Patricia Cardozo's *Real Women Have Curves* (reviewed in the 2003 volume), which is also about the Hispanic neo-immigrant adolescent experience, but unlike Cardozo, Sollett resists the temptation to expand his focus from what is of everyday concern to his teen protagonists.

Thus, on one level, *Vargas* emerges as nothing more than a teenage love story, but one which is rare in the annals of contemporary filmic realism: a film that can be enjoyed by the demographic group that comprises its subjects, instead of only by art cinema's adult cognoscenti. No surprise then that the film's universal appeal led to its being selected to open the Museum of Modern Art's prestigious "New Directors New Films" Showcase of 2003.

What appears even more remarkable, in the above context, is Sollett's self-effacingly objective stance. A New York University film school graduate, Sollett wisely keeps his costs down by shooting mostly in extreme close-ups. However, the emotional performances he extracts from his untrained lead actors keep the viewer's attention riveted. What works in Sollett's favor is that his technique of isolating his action functions as a formal correlative of the nature of the contemporary adolescent experience he is depicting. Like his leads, Sollett too shuts out the world and bestows the utmost significance upon the most trivial of pursuits.

At the same time, owing to his uncompromising stance, *Vargas* emerges as a grand tribute to the Italian neorealist master, Vittorio De Sica, who believed that anyone from the street could play a leading role in a film, provided what the actor was portraying was close to that individual's daily experience. Wisely, the film's storyline confines itself to a narrative of daily life amongst a dysfunctional family hailing from the Dominican Republic and living on New York City's Lower East Side.

Without as much as a Main Title, the film opens with a medium shot of the dark, skinny Victor (Victor Rasuk) in a white vest and sporting an out-of-style afro, standing against a yellow wall. Victor begins by making his lips more desirable by licking them. He then starts to take off his vest, and we realize that he has been preparing himself for sex with the plump Donna (Donna Maldonado), also a Hispanic teen, on the one condition that she tell no one. This plan blows up in his face when his sister, Vicki (Krystal Rodriguez), fat and bedraggled, blows his cover in the presence of Harold (Kevin Rivera), who is taller and spectacled, and Victor's closest buddy. He calls out from the street below just as Victor is about to leap into action with Donna.

When Victor rushes home, he snatches the phone out of Vicki's hands and throws it out the window before she can call anyone and tell them that Victor has been sleeping with the "fat and ugly" Donna. But Victor's gesture proves too late. At the public swimming pool that afternoon, we see the news has spread quicker than a brushfire. As Victor

prepares to make his move on his pretty heartthrob, the fair-skinned Judy (Judy Marte), whom he has been admiring from afar, she is gossiping with her friend, the spectacled, plain-looking Melonie (Melonie Diaz), who is pointing out Victor as the one who is sleeping with Donna. In his customary open and disarming manner, Victor approaches Judy, with Harold in tow. Melonie promptly tells Victor that Judy "has a boyfriend." Judy herself then tells him rudely that she "has a man." Victor wisely retreats to plan his next move.

We then see Judy and Melonie bonding in the confines of Judy's room. "Guys are dorks," Judy says, "we don't need them." In actual fact, she needs Victor as much as Melonie needs Harold. Judy needs Victor as an armor against being hassled by the macho boys on the block; Melonie needs Harold because he reveals to her an aspect of herself that was hiding behind her bookish appearance.

Meanwhile, Victor's Grandma (Altagracia Guzman), thin but indomitable, returns home and becomes enraged by the broken phone. As punishment, she puts a lock on the device, so that no one except her will be able to use it. Her favorite in the family is Victor's younger brother, Nino (Silvestre Rasuk), who seems to have adopted Victor as his role model in appearance. Nino, unlike Victor, is musically talented, to the point of being able to play the melodic line of Bach's "Concerto for Piano in F Minor," one note at a time. The lyrical grace of his playing repeatedly soothes Grandma after her verbal lashings at Victor.

To advance his crush on Judy, Victor gets into a deal with Carlos (Wilfree Vasquez), Judy's flabby kid brother, who in turn uses Victor to further his own crush on Vicki. Carlos formally introduces Victor to Judy just as she's coming down the street, burdened by groceries. Victor uses the occasion to apologize for having approached her at the pool and shakes her thumb, by reaching under a bag she's carrying.

This time, Victor's good-natured humility wins him a walk with Judy, which ends with him bringing her home, while everyone is away at mass. He gets her a beer, but she prefers a glass of water. As Victor takes her through a tour of the family photo gallery, we learn that Vicki is Victor's half-sister and that Victor hates her father. Victor's favorite amongst his forebears is his dashing Grandfather, now a mere sepia-tinted presence. As Victor draws Judy into the room he shares with Vicki and Nino, he points out the canopy he has built over his bed for privacy. Judy is suitably impressed, and says as much, calling him her "new man." Victor needs to go no further. When he's with his buddies, he's leaping in joy and tells them why.

In the subplots, Carlos makes little headway with Vicki, while Harold scores a home run with Melonie. The latter's intimacy with Harold leads her to tell him of a pact she had made with Judy not to let anyone intrude on their relationship. This subplot then intersects with the main plot when Harold tells Victor of the pact. The latter then confronts Judy, who defends herself by accusing Victor of using her in the same manner "to cover up for Donna." When Judy storms off, Victor kicks his first garbage can in frustration.

A more important subplot starts brewing as Victor instructs Nino on how to score with girls, a conversation overheard by Grandma, who then rails at Victor, "You're training him to be a gigolo!" As if that weren't enough, Grandma's ire against Victor grows exponentially. In the kitchen, she finds the glass with Judy's lipstick stain, but keeps the secret to herself. Then, when she stumbles upon what she suspects as Nino playing with himself in the bathroom, she takes it out on Victor for having taught him, and that becomes the last straw. We then see Grandma and the kids in Family Court, where she tries to leave Victor in the hands of the state.

A kindly, black female social worker (Gladys Austin) then has to explain to Grandma that unless Victor breaks the law, he is entitled to the refuge of his home. The noble soul that he is, Victor even packs to leave, until Nino begs him to stay. After Victor apologizes to Grandma, matters are ironed out. Under the good graces of the Church, Grandma and the kids decide to make "a new beginning."

That new start includes having Judy over for a dinner specially prepared by Grandma. It is just plain burgers, but Grandma's specialty. Judy graces the occasion by wearing a chic, low-cut dress. All goes well until Grandma confronts Judy with two glasses, both bearing identical lipstick marks. The fact that she was lied to by Victor makes the old lady livid. Judy quickly walks out, but before Victor can follow her, Grandma threatens to throw him out of the house. She repeats her favorite line: "The only thing you have in the world is me!" This time, Victor shoots back, from across the generational chasm, "No, Grandma, the only thing you have in the world is us!"

Strangely, the event brings Victor and Judy closer to each other. Judy at last admits that she lied about there being a man in her life, and that her relationship with Victor is the closest she has been with a boy. She then feels his face, embraces him, and kisses him lovingly. When she leads him to her bed, he lies down behind her, and the screen bleaches out.

As Nino plays the Bach Concerto on the piano, there is a montage that shows Victor bringing Grandma a toasted sandwich, then Victor raising Judy out of her bed, and finally, Victor and Judy embracing at the entrance of her building. Then, Judy smiles and disappears inside. As part of this denouement, we see Victor, alone, with a serious expression, instead of his earlier euphoric infatuation. As he crosses the street, the camera captures him from behind, the burden of adulthood already upon his scrawny shoulders.

Critical reception to the film has emphasized the impact of its naturalistic performances. There has been further praise for the film's storyline. Elvis Mitchell in the *New York Times* notes that Sollett "doesn't cheapen" his narrative "by splashing it with overbearing melodrama . . ." Mitchell's rave concludes by calling the film "a true find, a picture with a vital daffiness that's all its own, rather than a film that lives on the leavings of other movies."

—*Vivek Adarkar*

CREDITS

Victor Vargas: Victor Rasuk
Judy Ramirez: Judy Marte
Melonie: Melonie Diaz
Grandma: Altagracia Guzman
Nino Vargas: Silvestre Rasuk
Vicki Vargas: Krystal Rodriguez
Harold: Kevin Rivera

Origin: USA
Released: 2003
Production: Robin O'Hara, Scott Macaulay, Alain de la Mata, Peter Sollett; Forensic Films; released by Samuel Goldwyn Films, Fireworks Pictures
Directed by: Peter Sollett
Written by: Peter Sollett
Cinematography by: Tim Orr
Music by: Roy Nathanson
Sound: Steve Borne
Editing: Myron Kerstein
Costumes: Jill Newell
Production Design: Judy Becker
MPAA rating: R
Running time: 87 minutes

REVIEWS

Boxoffice. March, 2003, p. 42.
New York Times Online. March 23, 2003.
New York Times Online. March 26, 2003.
People. April 7, 2003, p. 36.
Variety Online. May 29, 2002.

AWARDS AND NOMINATIONS

Nomination:
Ind. Spirit 2004: Director (Sollett), Film, Debut Perf. (Rasuk, Marte), First Screenplay.

The Recruit

Trust. Betrayal. Deception. In the C.I.A. nothing is what it seems.
—Movie tagline

 Box Office: $52 million

The Recruit was made under the working title "The Farm," as the facility where CIA recruits are trained is known, but for obvious reasons, that title would have been confusing and misleading. The film concerns the initiation of a young man, James Clayton (Colin Farrell), into the CIA. He is a computer genius recruited by CIA professional Walter Burke (Al Pacino), who is not quite what he seems to be, but that is a continuing theme throughout the film: nothing is what it seems to be. For some reviewers it seemed to be one spy film too many, but, despite an over-the-top performance by Al Pacino, the film was effectively directed by the dependable but not always inspired Roger Donaldson, who has a sort of track record for action vehicles. The focus seems misplaced, however, since the film should belong to Farrell, but instead it belongs to Al Pacino's shadowy master manipulator.

Although perhaps contorted with too many double-crosses, the story, concocted by Kurt Wimmer, Mitch Glazer, and Roger Towne, seems to hold together well enough, if one doesn't worry too much about the villain's motives—after figuring out who the villain is. Clayton is recruited away from a well-paying computer job to serve his country by training for the CIA. The recruiter seems to have known Clayton's father, who was killed in a plane crash in Peru when Clayton was a boy of twelve; Clayton therefore wants to know more about his father, who might have been a secret agent. He is sent to the "Farm," located in Virginia, where, apparently, recruits are put through a process resembling boot camp in the military. The skeptical *New Yorker* critic David Denby couldn't shake the "unfortunate impression that the recruits are training less for intelligence work than for action movies."

Once there, Clayton meets a young lovely named Layla Moore (Bridget Moynahan), and sparks begin to fly. But just as their "chemistry" pulls them together, circumstances pull them apart. It appears that Clayton washes out of training after allowing himself to get "captured" by the "enemy" in what turns out to be an exercise "op."

But, no, all is not lost, Walter tells him. He held up under torture longer than any other recruit had done, Walter explains, and he seems to be back in the game as a secret operative. Clayton believes this, since he has no reason to

doubt Walter, and since he tends to view Walter as a father figure. (Walter encourages the son to think his father died in Peru while working for the CIA, but this is impossible to confirm.) Walter then sells Clayton a phony bill of goods, telling him that Layla is not who she appears to be but a mole, a counterspy purposefully planted in the Agency. Clayton is assigned to watch and follow her. She seems to be stealing computer files for the "ICE-9" program, which an enemy could use to shut down the government's computer system. Clayton, who loves Layla by this time, is conflicted. He follows Layla. She passes a note to another agent, who turns out to be Zack (Gabriel Macht), their classmate at the Farm. Clayton had reason to believe that he killed Zack in a trackside scuffle in Washington's Union Station (supposing that all is what it appears to be).

Walter gives Clayton what appears to be a loaded pistol, and the assignment, apparently, to kill Layla, after retrieving her laptop. He chases her down and stops her, but he cannot assassinate her, and lets her go, as he heads for the expected showdown in the final reel with Walter (who may not be what he appears to be). The film is about trust and betrayal and good intentions gone awry, but it's not exactly a spy movie, since, as the worn-out mantra goes, things are not what they appear to be. *Washington Post* critic Stephen Hunter yearned for a movie made along "everything-is-exactly-what-it-seems-lines."

What can be said of Pacino's acting? That there's madness in his Method? He shouts, he chants, he raves, he rants. His talent is at the heart of the picture. It's fascinating, but it's also fascinatingly overdone. A. O. Scott of the *New York Times* invented a genre for *The Recruit:* "the Al Pacino crazy mentor picture." Other films in this genre would be *Donnie Brasco* (1997), *Scent of a Woman* (1992), *Devil's Advocate* (1997), and *Any Given Sunday* (1999). Scott found everything done by Pacino in *The Recruit* "tiresomely predictable." The *New Yorker*'s David Denby found Pacino in his "domineering-satanic mode, complete with glittering eyes and an opera-house Mephistopheles goatee." One suspects that Pacino is coasting here. Glenn Kenny suggested that Pacino was "just phoning in the world-weary gruffness that's become his default acting mode in recent years." The film therefore loses its focus because the studio pretends that it is a Pacino vehicle. It would take a far better writer, David Mamet, for example, to give Pacino a noticeable edge here. The closest he comes is when he tells Clayton, "You want answers. I only have secrets." The voice is there, still a magnificent instrument, but there is no conviction driving it. According to Denby, "Burke is not a man; he's a melodramatic device."

Denby thought the "only deeply felt emotion" in the film was "paranoia," which, he suspects, "shows up so often in thrillers because it's the dominant emotion of people in the movie colony." Why? Because of their fear of failure, which persuades them to make "bankable but unadventurous movies like this one, which, ironically, fail anyway." Gary Arnold of the *Washington Times* was more direct when he dismissed the film simply as a "shamelessly arbitrary thriller." *Premiere* magazine reported last February that the film went through something like fifteen different rewrites. Perhaps that explains why there are three credited writers assisted by lord knows how many script-doctors on the writing team. Glenn Kenny told *Premiere* readers that there might be "a nifty little spy thriller secreted somewhere in this bloated picture." But he couldn't find it.

Washington Post reviewer Stephen Hunter complained that once the actors are off the "Farm," the action "becomes weaker and weaker," as director Roger Donaldson "really earns his money staging hubbub and nonsense." What's wrong with this picture? "It's not bad, but it's not good, either," Hunter complained. "It's nothing but style and noise, threadbare of content, empty of ideas." But the best that was said of *The Recruit* was that it wasn't half bad. "By contemporary standards," Michael Sragow wrote in the *Baltimore Sun*, "*The Recruit* is a halfway decent spy melodrama—at least to the halfway point." So, it's halfway decent, halfway through? That's no way to sell tickets.

The *New Yorker* critic David Denby found the film "quick and tense" and even fun at times, but his major complaint was that he could not "believe a single thing in it, and the over-all effect of the movie is to make one depressed that the Christmas 'art' season is over." Though the film is, assuredly, a "well-made product," Denby rightly concludes, "Essentially, you've seen it before." One benchmark for evaluating spook movies about the CIA is whether they can compare favorably to the well made weekly CBS television series, *The Agency*. *The Recruit* fails that comparison. Unfortunately, though understandably, these are not powerful endorsements.

—James M. Welsh

CREDITS

Walter Burke: Al Pacino
James Clayton: Colin Farrell
Layla Moore: Bridget Moynahan
Zack: Gabriel Macht
Dennis Slayne: Karl Pruner
Husky Man: Eugene Lipinski

Origin: USA
Released: 2003
Production: Roger Birnbaum, Jeff Apple, Gary Barber; Spyglass Entertainment; released by Touchstone Pictures
Directed by: Roger Donaldson
Written by: Roger Towne, Mitch Glazer, Kurt Wimmer
Cinematography by: Stuart Dryburgh

Music by: Klaus Badelt
Sound: Douglas Ganton
Editing: David Rosenbloom
Art Direction: Dennis Davenport
Costumes: Beatrix Aruna Pasztor
Production Design: Andrew McAlpine
MPAA rating: PG-13
Running time: 105 minutes

REVIEWS

Chicago Sun-Times Online. January 31, 2003.
Entertainment Wekly. January 24, 2003, p. 74.
Los Angeles Times Online. January 31, 2003.
New York Times Online. January 31, 2003.
People. February 10, 2003, p. 37.
USA Today Online. January 31, 2003.
Variety Online. January 20, 2003.
Washington Post. January 31, 2003, p. WE41.

QUOTES

Walter Burke (Al Pacino): "You want answers, you're in the wrong job. I only have secrets."

Respiro (I Breathe) (Respiro: Grazia's Island)

As unique as the paradise she lived in.
—Movie tagline

 Box Office: $1 million

Emanuele Crialese's visionary neorealist fable from Italy, *Respiro*, foregrounds a philosophical side of the most influential movement in film history, a side often masked by that movement's air of social protest. When Italian neorealism ran into trouble with the state because its view of the country was hurting the tourist trade, Vittorio De Sica and Cesare Zavattini, its founders, shot back in 1951 with the classic, *Miracle in Milan*. This fairy tale of poverty showed how there are experiences of beauty, which are a part of day-to-day life, that only the poor have access to; society's privileged being trapped in their closed urban worlds.

Crialese picks up this visionary gauntlet like no other recent Italian filmmaker exposed to audiences here. Unlike, say, Gianni Amelio, whose celebrated *The Way We Laughed* (reviewed in the 2002 volume) used the tenets of neorealism to affirm a peculiarly Italian identity in the context of today's globalization, Crialese could be said to be illustrating super-latively, and in a timely manner, the relationship that De Sica envisioned between poverty and the experience of beauty.

Crialese's milieu is the starkly beautiful seaside terrain on the island of Lampedusa near western Sicily. His is a self-enclosed world comprising a small town on a hill, its craggy promontories with breathtaking views of the silent dark green ocean way down below. Satellite technology seems to have left the place to itself. There's hardly much of a beach to speak of and, consequently, there are no tourists. Thus, the natural beauty that evokes the sublime becomes part of the everyday; subsistence for the fisherfolk, and a terrain for teen gangs to rumble.

The film opens with the stalwart Pasquale (Francesco Casisa), in his early teens, getting the better of a rival gang who are there to hunt birds. Before we see who has won, the film cuts to an idyllic courtyard in Pasquale's house, where the beautiful young Grazia (Valeria Golina) is singing along to a tuneful pop song, with Filippo (Filippo Pucillo), Pasquale's little but feisty kid brother by her side. Grazia, as we begin to discover, is a dysfunctional mother. Estranged from her fisherman-husband, Pietro (Elio Germano), she has left the running of the house mostly to Nonna (Emma Loffredo), the Grandmother. Despite this, Grazia commands the warmest affection from her two sons and her grown-up daughter, the plump Marinella (Veronica D'Agostino).

Given the backbreaking exertion of everyday life, Grazia appears removed from it all. When Pasquale goes to wake her up in the morning, she gets him to shut the windows, so that she can remain in bed, inside a dark room, while the sun is shining outside. Curiously, Pasquale, and even Filippo, don't just love their mother, they also understand her, and so, they turn custom on its head by function-ing as adults in relation to the childish and neurotic in Grazia's personality.

While Pietro is the only one who goes out to sea, everyone else in the family makes a quick buck, or tries to, off the fishing industry. Filippo and his friends clean the boats, while Pasquale helps in preparing the ice. Even Grazia and Marinella work on an assembly line cleaning fish. This source of income allows the boys to stroll down the Via Roma in the evenings and whistle at girls, and Grazia to own her own scooter, which she drives to the beach.

A typical everyday scene, as the film would have us believe, shows Grazia overloading her scooter with Pasquale and Filippo and driving them for a swim, after dropping off food for the pariah dogs awaiting execution. By the water, Grazia boldly strips down to her panties and em-braces the ocean. Again, as an inversion of custom, it is the boys who are concerned with her safety, rather than the other way around. They scream at their mother to return to the shore. Grazia instead calls them in. They are eventually swayed by her hedonism, and the mother and her two sons horse around in the pristine water, until a fishing boat, drawn by the sight of the bare Grazia, passes too close for comfort.

All is well until the family's dinner is interrupted by the father of one of Pasquale's friends, who claims that Pasquale bruised his son's eye, which has now been bandaged. Pietro feels it is fair for the son, the injured Vito, to flog Pasquale. Vito's Father feels Pietro should punish his son himself. Pietro acquiesces, then allows Vito to inflict his share of pain on Pasquale. He then invites Vito's Father in for coffee. When Pietro calls out to Grazia to serve them, she literally goes ballistic, smashing crockery, until Pietro has to physi-cally restrain her and inject her with a sedative.

In the next scene, we see Pietro and Nonna consulting the town pharmacist, whose brother-in-law works in a men-tal hospital in Milan. They see Grazia as someone with sharp mood swings, who can be both aggressive and affec-tionate "without any reason". For all their kind intentions, this makes things worse in the close-knit world of the small town. As the gossip spreads that Grazia is going to be sent away, it comes back to her in the assembly line. Here again, she cannot control her rage, and storms out.

We then see her walking barefoot to a precipice over the ocean. She stands contemplating the vastness below her, then jumps straight down. The camera follows her underwa-ter, with electronic music on the soundtrack functioning as a correlative to the crystalline purity of nature. As she floats in her dress, her arms and legs spread out, her eyes are closed in serene triumph.

Crialese peppers Grazia's story with digressions that capture the simplicity of life on the island. After Pasquale collects sea urchins from the ocean floor, the rival gang whom he had attacked at the start of the film get their revenge. Pasquale, whose genitals are left hurting, is then made to lie down at home and be treated with sliced cucum-bers placed on his back. Similarly, when a young cop in the town develops a crush on Marinella—after stopping her repeatedly for taking more than one person on her scooter—she leads him to a secret spot overlooking the sea. Then, from inside a cave, she pulls out the discarded front seat of a car, which she places on the edge of the rocks. As she and the young cop sit there admiring the view, they recall De Sica's shanty dwellers in *Miracle in Milan*, who pay a lira to sit on a chair and admire the sunset.

The focus returns to Grazia after Pietro takes away her dog. In the middle of the night, Pasquale is ordered to tie the

---

mongrel to the wagon attached to Pietro's scooter. Pietro then drives off, but we don't know where he goes. The next morning, Grazia calls for her dog, but Pasquale keeps the secret to himself. On the pier, Grazia finds two Frenchmen who invite her onto their boat. Here again, it is the boys who become the adults. They plead with her to come off the boat. Filippo then tries to pull her off, but cannot, and so decides to stay with her as her guardian. As the boat is about to cast off, Pietro dives in and clambers aboard to pull Grazia off by her hair. On the pier, she slaps him for killing her dog. Pietro is prevented from hitting her by rival fishermen, and a fight breaks out between the men.

We then see Grazia throw open the doors of the dog pound by the beach. This results in the pack of stray dogs running wild through the town. The men bring out their rifles and shoot them from rooftops. When the last yelping has ceased, the women wash the blood off the street. At Pietro's house, a decision is reached at a morose family gathering. Nonna tells Grazia that she will be sent away to Milan, to which Grazia retorts: "I'll kill myself first!"

This sets the stage for the climax that extends beyond Grazia's family to take in the townsfolk, so that the resolution of the domestic crisis takes on a social, and even philosophical, dimension. When Grazia runs away, it is Pasquale who catches up with her on the road. He takes her to his secret hiding place, a cavernous grotto from where all one can see is the ocean. As Pietro hunts for Grazia, he finds her dress, and soon gives her up for dead. Pietro even goes to the extent of placing a statue of the Virgin Mary on the ocean floor in Grazia's honor, thereby turning her into a saint.

Then, at the annual San Bartolo's Feast on the beach, as towers made out of junk, to which the whole town contributes, are burnt at night, Pietro spots Grazia in the water. He swims to her amidst golden sheaths, reflecting the fires on the beach. The townsfolk dive in after him.

We then see Pietro embracing Grazia underwater. As they surface, a huddle grows around the woman everyone now sees as a saint. The camera, however, remains underwater to show only their legs thrashing from below, thereby making the film's final image appear a revelation: all the divisiveness that humans have been prey to on land has been surmounted in their original home.

Critics can be expected to be regaled by the film's vision of lives lived close to nature, as demonstrated by Stephen Holden's review in *The New York Times* when the film was showcased as part of the Museum of Modern Art's "New Directors New Films." Holden calls the film a "pungent portrait of a fishing community" that "bursts with such pulsing vitality and sensual appreciation of nature that you can almost taste the salty air and feel the sun beating down on your shoulders."

—*Vivek Adarkar*

CREDITS

Grazia: Valeria Golino
Pietro: Vincenzo Amato
Pasquale: Francesco Casisa
Marinella: Veronica D'Agostino
Filippo: Filippo Pucillo
Grandmother: Muzzi Loffredo
Pier Luigi: Elio Germano

Origin: Italy, France
Language: Italian
Released: 2002
Production: Domenico Procacci; Fandango, Roissy, Medusa Film, Les Films de Tournedos, Telepiu; released by Sony Pictures Classics
Directed by: Emanuele Crialese
Written by: Emanuele Crialese
Cinematography by: Fabio Zamarion
Music by: John Surman
Sound: Pierre-Yves Lavoue
Editing: Didier Ranz
Art Direction: Beatrice Scarpato
Costumes: Eva Coen
MPAA rating: PG-13
Running time: 95 minutes

REVIEWS

Boxoffice. April, 2003, p. 95.
Chicago Sun-Times Online. June 13, 2003.
Los Angeles Times Online. May 23, 2003.
New York Times Online. March 28, 2003.
Sight and Sound. September, 2003, p. 60.
Vanity Fair. May, 2003, p. 94.
Variety Online. May 19, 2002.

Revolution #9

A man's paranoia finally overtakes him in *Revolution #9*, a fair but flawed low-budget drama. Feature films don't get much more personal than this. Tim McCann not only wrote, directed, and co-produced *Revolution #9*, he also photographed and co-edited the film. McCann's story centers around James Jackson (Michael Risley), a seemingly normal New Yorker who reviews websites for a living. After a year and a half of going together, James asks Kim (Adrienne Shelly), his girlfriend, to marry him. But soon after she agrees to the engagement, James becomes unglued: he is certain someone has been rearranging the things on his desk and he accuses friends and co-workers of sending him strange email messages. James goes totally over-the-edge when he receives a mysterious e-mail containing a short, strange film called *Rev 9*. Although Kim also sees the film, she dismisses it as an ad campaign for a new fragrance. Indeed, Revolution #9 is the name of a cosmetics company, but James still believes the film represents an evil message and that the company is trying to "infect" his mind.

Kim takes charge by finding James a psychiatrist and attempting temporarily to place him in an institution. In the meantime, James researches the Revolution #9 ad and company, and when he finds the number for the campaign director, Scooter McCrae (Spalding Gray), he sets out to harass then confront the man. James poses as a journalist and gets an interview with McCrae. During the interview, James attacks McCrae, then flees. James is hurt in the street during his escape, but Kim finds him in time to help him and take him for treatment at a mental hospital. Although James resists being admitted, he ends up placed for a few weeks of recovery. After he is let out, James proceeds to commit the ultimate act of self-destruction.

Revolution #9 is hardly the first film to document someone's descent into "madness." The pedigree for this film subgenre (of disease/cure melodramas) is generally pretty good; after all, there is Polanski's landmark *Repulsion* (1965). More recently, the independent film scene has exploded with many of these types of films, all denying the "cure" component: *Clean, Shaven* (1995), *Pi* (1998), and *Buddy Boy* (2000) are examples. Each of these small movies demonstrates slightly different approaches to similar material: *Clean, Shaven* contains the most sustained subjective point-of-view of the disturbed protagonist; *Pi* incorporates the most extreme tone of paranoia; and *Buddy Boy* features the most dark humor and strange plotting. Then of course there is Hollywood's upbeat, Oscar-winning take on the subject, *A Beautiful Mind* (2001). *Revolution #9* distinguishes itself by actually sending a message about the failures of the current U.S. healthcare system and pervasive lack of understanding of the mentally ill. By including Kim's story as much as James (co-star Adrienne Shelly co-produced the film), *Revolution #9* shies away somewhat from having the audience identify with the protagonist's warped inner world. Therefore, there are fewer stylistically tricky effects than in the previous films of this type. Digitally manipulated photography, distorted sound, and other cinematic techniques stand out when they are employed, but they are clearly setting James apart from everyone else and are used sparingly.

The filmmakers obviously want to make a point through dramatic, even suspenseful storytelling, though that point might have been more forceful without overemphasizing the villainy or ineptitude of the doctors and healthcare workers portrayed. The lack of humor also hurts because

such a story cries out for ironic contrasts between the "normal" outside world and James's condition, but Tim McCann and company must truly feel that there is an ideal of normal to aspire to because James is as much isolated and ostracized by the other characters, including in some ways Kim, as the filmmakers. The lead performers (Michael Risely and Adrienne Shelley) make the most of the material, but even they seem caught up in TV disease-of-the-week fare in the subpar hospital scenes.

The Spalding Gray sequences at least contain the most potential for dark, knowing comedy. Gray plays the pompous, pretentious commercial director just right, but the writing and direction in these scenes feature little satire of the ad industry or anything else. Moreover, since Spalding Gray's apparent suicide, his performance in these scenes take on an unintentionally sad, ominous tone. The extra-textual irony of *Revolution #9* is that Spalding Gray was reportedly a depressed individual—though here he plays the nemesis of the disturbed protagonist.

Some critics were impressed by the independent film, including A. O. Scott of the *New York Times*, who called it an "unadorned, unsparing chronicle of a young man's descent into a nightmare of delusion, paranoia, and self-destructive behavior." In the *Los Angeles Times* Kevin Thomas said the film is "a taut, intelligent psychological drama." Occasionally, *Revolution #9* involves the audience and lives up to Scott's and Thomas's praise, but more often, particularly in the last third, the lapses (and lack of originality) outweigh the virtues.

—*Eric Monder*

CREDITS

James Jackson: Michael Risley
Kim Kelly: Adrienne Shelly
Scooter McCrae: Spalding Gray
Stephanie: Callie (Calliope) Thorne
Dr. Ray: Sakina Jaffrey
Joe Kelly: Michael Rodrick

Origin: USA
Released: 2001
Production: Tim McCann, Shannon Goldman, Michael Risley; Rockville Pictures; released by Exile Productions
Directed by: Tim McCann
Written by: Tim McCann
Cinematography by: Tim McCann
Music by: Douglas J. Cuomo
Sound: Stephen Rajkumar
Editing: Tim McCann, Shannon Goldman
Costumes: Nives Spaleta
Production Design: Elise Bennett

MPAA rating: Unrated
Running time: 91 minutes

REVIEWS

Boxoffice. March, 2002, p. 57.
Eye Weekly Online. September 6, 2001.
Los Angeles Times Online. December 13, 2002.
New York Times Online. November 15, 2002.
Variety. April 30, 2001, p. 32.
Village Voice Online. November 13, 2002.

Rugrats Go Wild!

The family vacation just went overboard.
—Movie tagline

Spike Speaks.
—Movie tagline

Box Office: $39.4 million

In his review of *Rugrats Go Wild, New York Times* writer Dave Kehr observed, "When studios start cross-breeding their franchises, it's usually a good sign that the properties involved are slowing down. It was true when Abbott and Costello met Frankenstein in 1948, and it is true today." And such films are generally not very good. The same is true of *Rugrats Go Wild.* (The film was originally called *The Rugrats Meet The Wild Thornberrys,* but reportedly the powers-that-be at Nickelodeon decided to go with the name of the more popular—and more marketable—series.) The things that make each of these series fun on TV don't get enough time in a combo film to do them justice. Plus, there are just too many characters for 82 minutes of film and none of them gets fully realized. Marianne Thornberry (voiced by Jodie Carlisle) is onscreen just enough to show herself as competent and resourceful. Debbie Thornberry (Danielle Harris) is just as Valley Girl-ish as ever, but the script doesn't have any fun with her, unlike in *The Wild Thornberrys Movie.* Patriarch Nigel Thornberry (Tim Curry) can be a funny, fusty Brit, but here his schtick just falls flat. Some scenes in which Nigel thinks he is a baby have the potential to be pretty funny but writer Kate Boutilier doesn't push the concept into anything inspired.

So how do the two clans meet? The Rugrats group is set to go on a luxury cruise but end up missing the boat. To cheer everyone up, Stu (Jack Riley) charters a small boat. Here we see a reference to *Titanic,* just one of the many films

that *Rugrats* references. Astute viewers, or bored grown-ups looking to pass the time, might note references to *The Poseidon Adventure, The Perfect Storm, Cast Away,* and even *Tea and Sympathy.*

The ship sinks and the crew ends up marooned on a deserted island. Only the island is not so deserted. On the other side, Nigel Thornberry and his family are camped out while they film one of the their nature documentaries. Besides the parents, Debbie is big sister to gawky, Eliza (Lacey Chabert, *Party of Five*), who has the ability to talk to the animals, and finally there is wild child little brother, Donnie (grunted by Flea of the Red Hot Chili Peppers).

When the Rugrat group hits the island, they separate and set off on different adventures. While the grown-ups do some sort of grown-up thing, Tommy (E. B. Daily), who is a big fan of Nigel Thornberry, leads the pack of babies to find him so that they can be rescued. Bratty Angelica (Cheryl Chase) tries to get the babies to worship her as a god, but after that doesn't work, she stumbles upon equally bratty Debbie Thornberry. After watching Debbie bully Eliza's monkey into serving her a drink, Angelica realizes that she has met the master, and decides to hang around to pick up some pointers. Kids get lost, Donnie steals clothes and Nigel and the babies end up in a submarine that's running out of oxygen. A lot of stuff happens but nothing shapes itself into a serviceable plot.

Everyone experiences various troubles and adventures. Thanks to Eliza's ability to talk to the animals, we get to hear Spike, the Pickles' dog, speak for the first time. Pickles (voiced by Bruce Willis), gets to sing, of course. His performance in this film shows that his singing in the 1980s wine cooler commercials was actually his finest moment in song. Much better is his partner in song, Chrissie Hynde of the Pretenders who plays jungle cat Siri. Actually, the music in the film is not so bad. Credit that to Mark Mothersbaugh (of the band Devo) who scored the film and peppers it with songs from the Clash and Iggy Pop.

Like the characters, the humor is fleeting and sketchy. There are poop jokes galore. "I can't even sniff my own butt, and God knows I've tried," complains Spike. Babies need diapers changed, babies eat bugs and boogers, and wedgies are given. The babies say things in a cute way, which actually isn't all that cute. The rainforest is the "drainforest" and instead of being lost, the kids are "losted." The babies are still wise beyond their years. "You're just a backyard baby with a diaper full of dreams," says Angelica to Tommy.

Perhaps aware of the lame project on their hands, Nickelodeon offered an additional enticement to potential viewers. Kids could pick up Odorama scratch 'n sniff cards at a particular fast food outfit to use during appropriate scenes in the film. (John Waters, who used this concept in 1981's *Polyester,* was reportedly considering taking legal action.) During certain scenes, a number would pop up on the screen, directing viewers which scent they should sniff. The scents included stinky feet, root beer, tuna fish, and peanut butter.

Critics didn't really care for the movie, though they did acknowledge that kids like it. Liz Braun of the *Toronto Sun* declared, "The film is a bit flat. A lot of the material seems stale, and as if to offset that, the animated action is hyper. Still, if your kids love the Rugrats and the Wild Thornberrys, then *Rugrats Go Wild* is a sage family bet for you." Louise Kennedy of the *Boston Globe* concluded, "Slapstick and potty humor for the kids, sly allusions and famous voices for the adults and a light coating of aren't-we-lucky-to-have-each-other schmaltz at the very end—yep, Nickelodeon has the family-flick formula pretty much down. And, like most formulas, it won't kill you, but it will leave you longing for tastier fare." Roger Ebert of the *Chicago Sun-Times* wrote, "Certainly this is not a film an adult would want to attend without a child; unlike *Finding Nemo*, for example, it doesn't play on two levels, but just one: shrill nonstop action." Kehr of the *Times* didn't seem to see the high level of action that Ebert saw and suggested that instead of the current title, the film should have been called "Rugrats Quietly Go About Their Business As Usual."

—Jill Hamilton

CREDITS

Tommy Pickles: Elizabeth (E.G. Dailey) Daily (Voice)
Chas Finster/Drew Pickles: Michael Bell (Voice)
Marianne Thornberry: Jodi Carlisle (Voice)
Chuckie Finster: Nancy Cartwright (Voice)
Eliza Thornberry: Lacey Chabert (Voice)
Didi Pickles: Melanie Chartoff (Voice)
Sir Nigel Thornberry: Tim Curry (Voice)
Angelica Pickles: Cheryl Chase (Voice)
Donnie Thornberry: Flea (Voice)
Debbie Thornberry: Danielle Harris (Voice)
Darwin: Tom Kane (Voice)
Spike the Dog: Bruce Willis (Voice)
Siri the Leopard: Chrissie Hynde (Voice)
Dil Pickles: Tara Strong (Voice)
Stu Pickles: Jack Riley (Voice)
Betty, Phil, Lil DeVille: Kath Soucie (Voice)
Charlotte Pickles: Tress MacNeille (Voice)
Susie Carmichael: Cree Summer (Voice)
Kimi: Dionne Quan (Voice)
Piki: L.L. Cool J. (Voice)

Origin: USA
Released: 2003
Production: Arlene Klasky, Gabor Csupo; Nickelodeon; released by Paramount Pictures

Directed by: Norton Virgien, John Eng
Written by: Kate Boutilier
Music by: Mark Mothersbaugh
Sound: Beth Sterner
Editing: John Bryant, Kimberly Rettberg
Production Design: Dima Malanitchev
MPAA rating: PG
Running time: 81 minutes

REVIEWS

Chicago Sun-Times Online. June 13, 2003.
Entertainment Weekly. June 20, 2003.
Los Angeles Times Online. June 13, 2003.
New York Times Online. June 13, 2003.
USA Today Online. June 13, 2003.
Variety Online. June 9, 2003.
Washington Post. June 12, 2003, p. WE35.

QUOTES

Spike the Dog (Bruce Willis): "Woof! Yes, I said woof!"

Runaway Jury

Trials are too important to be decided by juries.
—Movie tagline

Box Office: $48.4 million

Throughout much of the 1990s, when John Grisham's legal thrillers regularly topped the bestseller lists, securing the movie rights to one of his novels seemed to be the first step in an almost surefire formula for creating a successful film. The first group of movies based on Grisham's books—Sydney Pollack's *The Firm* (1993), Alan J. Pakula's *The Pelican Brief* (1993), and Joel Schumacher's *The Client* (1994) and *A Time to Kill* (1996)—were all box office hits and generally well received by critics as well. However, even though Grisham's novels continue to be bestsellers, more recent film adaptations—*The Chamber* (1996), *The Gingerbread Man* (1998), and *The Rainmaker* (1997)—failed to attract large audiences (*The Gingerbread Man* hardly experienced anything resembling a theatrical release). Critically, of those last three, only Francis Ford Coppola's *The Rainmaker* received generally favorable reviews, but the significant drop in audience numbers raised the question of whether Grisham-inspired films had simply run their course. The dismal performance of the last three pictures, coupled with a five-year delay in the production of any big-screen features based on Grisham's stories, very likely lessened expectations regarding the 2003 release of *Runaway Jury* because it seemed a movie could no longer be considered a "sure thing" simply because it had Grisham's name attached in some way. Indeed, the eventual release of *Runaway Jury* suggested that general audiences may have lost interest in Grisham movies or perhaps that too much time had lapsed between the release of the book and the release of the movie. Despite good reviews, strong performances from the cast, an entertaining and tightly woven plot structure, and an emotionally resonating story, *Runaway Jury* drew no more business than *The Rainmaker*.

The legal/political issue fueling the plot of Grisham's novel *The Runaway Jury* is a conflict with the tobacco industry, but the makers of the movie, apparently believing the controversy was less interesting or too outdated due to recent real-life developments in the tobacco conflict, decided to center the movie's story around gun control. The issue comes to the fore in the opening scenes, a tragic sequence in which a young broker (Dylan McDermott), almost immediately established as a loving husband and father, is gunned down at the office by a disgruntled (and sociopathic) former coworker. The story then flashes forward several months; the victim's wife is now going to court against gun manufacturers, claiming they are partially liable for her husband's death because of the ease with which deadly semi-automatic weapons can be obtained. She is represented by Wendell Rohr (Dustin Hoffman), a successful and decent New Orleans attorney who idealistically believes in the legal system and who is motivated by a genuine desire to see that justice is served rather than a desire to win a case at any cost. The gun manufacturers are represented by attorney Durwood Cable (Bruce Davison), but the shots are being called behind the scenes by the ruthless Rankin Fitch (Gene Hackman), a powerhouse jury consultant who has a special knack for "reading" people and whose strategic ingenuity almost guarantees verdicts in favor of his clients. Fitch and his technologically savvy minions gather information on potential jurors and pore over the data to identify people who would most likely be sympathetic to their side and play right into their hands. "Trials are too important to be left up to juries," Fitch proclaims.

One of those potential jurors is Nick Easter (John Cusack), a likeable young man who gives the impression that he wants to get out of jury duty. Fitch determines that the young man is a risk because he's an entertainer who "wants to make everyone happy." However, Nick's complaints about missing a video game contest lead the judge to give him a lecture on civic duty, and consequently both Cable and Rohr feel pressured to select him as a juror.

It turns out that Nick's behavior was a ploy to ensure his position on the jury, because in reality he is in league with a female friend, Marlee (Rachel Weisz), in an elaborately planned scheme to cash in by selling the jury, and hence the verdict, to the high bidder. Shortly after the jury is selected, both sides in the case receive plain envelopes with a simple message inside: "Jury for Sale." Marlee then calls Rohr and Fitch and names the price: $10 million.

Rohr's reaction is that of slight concern and disgust, but he remains convinced that the jury will ultimately be guided by its conscience. Fitch is unconvinced there is any real threat from "amateurs," though he does want to learn the identity of the culprits. However, the seriousness of the threat gradually becomes clearer as Nick's influence on the jury begins to show itself. Nick cleverly maneuvers the jurors into selecting a blind man as their foreman, while Fitch had been counting on the selection of an ex-Marine; Nick manages to convince the judge to treat the jury to lunch (the first sign to Fitch that Nick could be one of the troublemakers); and after Marlee calls Fitch again to say, " I hope you're feeling patriotic," the jury surprises everyone in the courtroom by standing up and reciting the Pledge of Allegiance. Finally, Fitch becomes nervous enough that he sends one of his minions to Nick's apartment to search for evidence of Nick's involvement in the scheme, but Nick discovers the intruder and chases him away. Fitch's anger and bewilderment accelerate as he sees more and more evidence that Marlee and Nick really do have the power to influence the jury. "Find her!" he barks to his underlings, insisting that they discover the identity of the woman who has been calling. "You're losing my jury!"

The conflict turns especially dirty when Fitch's people go after other jurors, uncovering their personal demons, targeting their weaknesses, and making their lives miserable (they nearly drive one woman to suicide and manage to get another woman's husband arrested). Another trip to Nick's apartment leaves the place in shambles and uncovers an MP3 drive containing encrypted data. When he realizes how ugly and dangerous things have become, to the point that people are getting hurt, Nick considers abandoning the scheme, but Marlee encourages him to strive forward with the plan. Once again the two of them outwit Fitch when they send the judge a video of Nick's ransacked apartment, which results in the sequestering of the jury.

Meanwhile, Rohr finds himself struggling with his own morality as he realizes that, indeed, the system seems to be failing him and his client. He confronts Fitch and condemns his unethical manipulations, but Fitch dismisses him. "You're a moral man living in a world of moral relativity," he says. Rohr does not play as big a role in the story as Nick or Fitch, but one of the film's most interesting and humanly realistic subplots deals with the principled attorney wrestling with hhis moral dilemma, knowing that his client may very well lose unjustly. Rohr briefly considers paying the $10 million, and for a moment it seems he has lost all hope when he goes to his firm and asks for access to the emergency reserves. "Gentlemen, I've lost my footing in this case," he says somberly. But it is a momentary lapse into despair, for he soon latches onto his ideals once again.

The tension between Fitch and the duo of Nick and Marlee escalates until Fitch agrees to pay the $10 million; however, instead of paying, he authorizes an attack on Marlee. The tables turn again, though, when Marlee kills her attacker and then calls Fitch with the news that the price just went up to $15 million. As the trial moves forward to final jury deliberations, Fitch ultimately capitulates and agrees to pay, while Rohr refuses.

As the story rushes toward a conclusion, true motivations are uncovered and Fitch realizes, too late, that he has been set up. Fitch pays the $15 million, but Nick actually encourages the jury to listen to everything that's been said in court, to truly deliberate, and to reach a decision that is just. In the meantime, Marlee calls the police and reports Fitch's illegal tampering, leading to a raid on his high-tech operation. When the jury reaches a verdict, it decides in favor of the plaintiff, to the tune of $110 million. It turns out that Nick and Marlee had a vendetta against Fitch (he had worked a case years before in which Marlee's sister had been killed in a school shooting) and have actually been scheming to make sure that Fitch's behind-the-scenes maneuvering failed. "I didn't sway anybody," Nick tells Fitch. "I just stopped you from stealing them."

The best elements of *Runaway Jury* are the performances and the proficiently paced editing that propels the plot. Cusack handles the role of Nick with subtlety and affability that encourages the viewer to sense the character's innate goodness even when his motives appear self-serving and his actions amoral (apparently willing to sell the verdict to either side, regardless of what is "right"). Hackman, no stranger to playing gritty antagonists in Grisham movies, imbues Fitch with an intelligent, arrogant nastiness and a believability that dominate every scene he's in. As for his character, the power that Fitch wields, and the success he finds in using it, leads one to wonder about the extent to which similar (though hopefully less dramatic) behind-the-scenes manipulation may influence major courtroom battles. Hoffman is just as convincing in the role of Rohr, and his few scenes with Hackman stand out as some of the most well-played, intense scenes in the movie. Surprisingly, though, his character is often in the background and seemingly unaware of all that is really going on, to the point that he often comes across as a minor player. In fact that is not far from the truth, since his idealism and his belief in the justness of the legal system prevent him from getting too involved in the conflict.

Runaway Jury, like the best of Grisham's stories, offers a large dose of suspense. The plot threads are woven together seamlessly, constantly leaving the viewer to wonder what will happen next. Much of the story moves like a fast-paced competition, a series of moves and counter-moves that has no obviously predictable resolution. What also makes the story more challenging and thought-provoking is the relative ambiguity that complicates everything. It is not a clear-cut competition between "right" and "wrong," for even though Fitch is established as a villain early on, Nick and Marlee are uncertain elements. What they are doing at first seems as "wrong" as what Fitch does for a living, yet the audience is moved to root for them, a feeling that is only validated when the surprise ending reveals that they are actually seeking justice. Even Rohr, the decent, faithful idealist, experiences moments of moral uncertainty. The story could have been much more simplistic, but it would have been far less interesting and far more predictable.

The film is not without its plot holes—how Nick manages to ensure that he will be summoned for jury duty is not explained, for example—and some elements of the courtroom battle and deliberation process are thinly treated. The overall story of the controversy surrounding gun control could have been further developed if more of the actual testimony and more of the jury's discussion had been fleshed out. This lack of attention to the gun control issue itself could lead many viewers (especially those already inclined to oppose gun control legislation) to mistakenly assume that the film is simply an attack on "the right to bear arms" or that its chief purpose is to be propaganda for the proponents of more restrictive gun control. While it is true that the gun manufacturers themselves are portrayed rather unsympathetically, the differing opinions of average citizens are expressed by members of the jury, and ultimately the movie does clarify that the true issue is the easy availability of weapons designed solely for killing large numbers of people, versus weapons for hunting or defense.

The real story here is the conflict between Nick (and Marlee) and Fitch—the struggle between the disillusioned, one-time idealist and the selfish, moral relativist who has no problem manipulating the justice system for his own profit. The story is about having faith in the legal system and believing that justice will ultimately prevail—the gun control issue is actually just the backdrop. The question raised is whether justice, in the face of amoral, greedy scheming, can in fact prevail without some kind of intervention. And, as with any thought-provoking, challenging story, the answers are not clear, nor are they simple. The important thing is that the question is asked and discussed.

—*David Flanagin*

CREDITS

Nick Easter: John Cusack
Rankin Fitch: Gene Hackman

Wendall Rohr: Dustin Hoffman
Marlee: Rachel Weisz
Durwood Cable: Bruce Davison
Judge Harkin: Bruce McGill
Lawrence Green: Jeremy Piven
Doyle: Nick Searcy
Garland Jankle: Stanley Anderson
Frank Herrera: Clifford Curtis
Janovich: Nestor Serrano
Lamb: Leland Orser
Vanessa Lembeck: Jennifer Beals
Herman Grimes: Gerry Bamman
Celeste Wood: Joanna Going
Lonnie Shaver: Bill Nunn
Loreen Duke: Juanita Jennings
Amanda Monroe: Marguerite Moreau
Stella Jullic: Nora Dunn
Eddie Weese: Guy Torry
Millie Dupree: Rusty Schwimmer

Origin: USA
Released: 2003
Production: Arnon Milchan, Christopher Mankeiwicz, Gary Fleder; Regency Enterprises, New Regency Pictures; released by 20th Century-Fox
Directed by: Gary Fleder
Written by: Brian Koppelman, David Levien, Rick Cleveland, Matthew Chapman
Cinematography by: Robert Elswit
Music by: Christopher Young
Sound: Jay Meager
Music Supervisor: Peter Afterman
Editing: William Steinkamp
Art Direction: Scott Plauche
Costumes: Abigail Murray
Production Design: Nelson Coates
MPAA rating: PG-13
Running time: 127 minutes

REVIEWS

Chicago Sun-Times Online. October 17, 2003.
Entertainment Weekly. October 24, 2003, p. 81.
Los Angeles Times Online. October 17, 2003.
New York Times Online. October 17, 2003.
People. October 27, 2003, p. 29.
Rolling Stone. November 13, 2003, p. 105.
USA Today Online. October 17, 2003.
Variety Online. October 11, 2003.
Washington Post. October 17, 2003, p. WE52.

The Rundown

cut to the chase
—Movie tagline

 Box Office: $47.6 million

Just before all hell breaks loose for the first time in the surprisingly enjoyable *The Rundown*, Dwayne "the Rock" Johnson just happens to walk by another action film star by the name of Schwarzenegger. "Have fun," says the performer-turned-Governor of California, their meeting being a sort of symbolic passing of the torch from one of the most successful members of the genre's old guard to one of its most promising up-and-comers. Following The Rock's small part in 2001's *The Mummy Returns* which led to his successful spin-off/prequel *The Scorpion King* (2002), the former wrestling superstar attempted to cement his star status outside the ring with *The Rundown*. He might be a limited performer, sinking like, well, a rock in anything outside this type of film, but the bulk of this bulky actor's fan base is not expected to be clamoring for anything like a Shakespearean turn. There is certainly enough in *The Rundown* to satisfy their thirst for loud, raw, impressive, and exciting spectacle (World Wrestling Federation honcho Vince McMahon is an executive producer), but there is more here than merely a lot of motion and commotion. What makes it fun is the film's injection of humor and, most significantly, the Rock's formidable but appealing presence. It is an engaging turn, playing a somewhat different sort of hero, one who could easily get you to come around to his way of thinking with explosively-violent subjugation—but would rather not.

For his job as a Los Angeles-based "retrieval expert" (or bounty hunter, to most of us), Beck (The Rock) always gives his quarry two choices: "Option A," which means cooperating peacefully, is always politely offered and sincerely preferred by Beck to having to resort to the much less pleasant "Option B," which he is more than capable of exacting. Of course there would not be much interest in a film in which everyone chooses Option A and marches off arm-in-arm and chatting happily with The Rock. Therefore, not surprisingly, we see a lot of Option B. Still, the character does have an aversion to the use of guns and would rather employ the power of his own massive arms than any firearms. Furthermore, he would like to chuck it all and start his own restaurant, preferring porcini mushrooms to punches. So The Rock comes off as a refreshingly reluctant hero, not just another all-powerful, brutal behemoth but instead a man who struggles to overcome his share of problems and exasperations along the way. He is a character to be taken seriously, played by an actor willing to let us laugh at his travails.

Beck's problems begin early, when he is sent by his shady boss, Walker (William Lucking of 2002's *Red Dragon*), to see a pro football quarterback about some unpaid gambling debts and calmly offers his ubiquitous pair of options. The cocky jock first tries to brush Beck off, then throws a drink in his face. Instead of going berserk, the retrieval expert walks with admirable composure into a nearby restroom to phone his boss. Beck inquires whether he should really hurt the quarterback and his hovering posse of mean-looking offensive linesmen because, after all, he would not want to do anything that would hurt the team's chances of another championship. Another attempt to reason with the players does not fly, and so bodies and furniture do instead as Beck successfully takes care of business. It once again makes him wish that he was in the restaurant business instead, and so he asks his boss for his release. Beck is told that one final job will wipe the slate clean between them and get him his eatery: finding Walker's handful-and-a-half of a son somewhere down in the Amazonian jungles of Brazil. We immediately (and, it turns out, correctly) conclude that retrieving wiseass Travis will not be as easy as pie when we see that he is played by Seann William Scott, zany Stifler of the *American Pie* films.

A plane held together by duct tape and flown by a nearly incomprehensible pilot (Ewen Bremner of 2001's *Black Hawk Down*) deposits Beck, eyes wide with alarm, in the isolated village of El Dorado. He finds Travis with amazing ease in a bar run by smart and sensuous Mariana (Rosario Dawson of 2002's *Men In Black II*), a woman as deserving of the adjective sultry as the steamy atmosphere that envelopes the densely-forested region. Travis cares less about going back to his father than his father actually cares about him; instead, he would rather continue to hunt for a fabled gold artifact called El Gato Diablo. Naturally, Travis ignores Option A and the fighting begins. Entering the melee is ominous oddball Hatcher (Christopher Walken, Oscar-nominated for last year's *Catch Me If You Can*), who would like Travis to find the treasure so he can then snatch it for himself. The always welcome Walken is his usual quirky, edgy self, his oft-imitated delivery capable of making even the simplest of lines sound weird and hysterically funny. His Hatcher basically controls El Dorado and everyone in it, enslaving the locals and getting rich while they toil for unconscionably cheap wages in his gold mining operation. In the face of fists, whips, and guns, Beck acrobatically (and highly successfully) escapes with the unwilling Travis in tow.

The Rock and Scott have a pleasing, antagonistic, bantering chemistry which works throughout the film. It is humorous to watch Beck attempt to keep his cool while trying to escort his squirrelly and sassy charge back to the airstrip, like some mammoth creature being constantly annoyed by a pesky and tenacious mosquito. First the two take a ridiculously long tumble down an embankment. Then a handcuffed, whining Travis urges a repulsed Beck to give him a hand (literally) so he can urinate. Then the two are hoisted into the forest canopy by some unseen snares, left to hang upside down and shout recriminations at each other. They are temporarily (but acutely) distracted from their mutual enmity by some monkeys whose interest in the men is, shall we say, aroused in more ways than one. Rescued from this predicament by Mariana, who turns out to be a rebel leader when not pouring drinks, the three agree to go on a quest to locate the gold Gato. She altruistically wants it because its value will get her impoverished people out from under evil Hatcher's thumb, while Travis is interested in making a name for himself.

Their intriguing journey is ultimately successful, but not without some amazingly brutal fisticuffs with the natives (expertly choreographed by Jackie Chan stuntman Andy Cheng) prior to the actual suspenseful retrieval of the artifact from its cavernous lair. Beck and Travis must also deal with the unpleasant (but hilarious) hallucinogenic effects brought on by the unusual fruit a mistrustful Mariana uses to temporarily disable the men and get the Gato safely into her own hands. When Beck learns that Hatcher has relieved her of the treasure and is torturing her, the chivalrous, honorable man cannot just take off with Travis. His back to the wall, Beck is forced to set aside his aversion to artillery, and the result is a roaring, highly explosive, and lethal (for Hatcher, anyway) showdown. Magnanimously leaving the precious piece for Mariana and the other townspeople, Beck travels with Travis back to California. There, Beck not only gains his own freedom from Travis's brutal father but, showing his heart is as big as the rest of him, uses some of Mariana's hallucinogenic produce to rescue Travis, as well.

The Rundown was directed by actor-turned-director Peter Berg, whose *Very Bad Things* (1998) was a very bad thing, indeed. This film, originally titled *Helldorado* and envisioned almost a decade ago as a vehicle for Patrick Swayze, certainly shows more promise. While Beck's time in the Amazonian jungle was certainly eventful and fraught with danger, so was the real-life trip taken by Berg and various producers in June of 2002. While scouting locations in remote parts of Brazil, they were robbed at gunpoint of cash and equipment by a group of roving bandits. After this harrowing experience, they took The Rock's initial suggestion that the film be shot instead in beautiful, lush, and infinitely safer Hawaii. This striking scenery is one of the film's greatest strengths. While critical reaction to this amiable adventure was generally positive, *The Rundown*, made on a budget of $85 million, only grossed just over $47 million. With some echoes of the much more memorable *Romancing the Stone* (1984), the resulting film has a mix of action and humor which should have pleased those previously unacquainted with The Rock, as well made fans from his wrestling days "smackdown" more of their cash.

—David L. Boxerbaum

REVIEWS

Chicago Sun-Times Online. September 26, 2003.
Entertainment Weekly. October 3, 2003, p. 48.
Los Angeles Times. September 26, 2003, p. E1.
New York Times Online. September 26, 2003.
People. October 6, 2003, p. 34.
USA Today Online. September 26, 2003.
Variety. September 22, 2003, p. 22.
Wall Street Journal. September 26, 2003, p. W1.
Washington Post. September 16, 2003, p. WE48.

Sade

Give in to your desires.
—Movie tagline
Follow your instinct.
—Movie tagline

Sade follows on the footsteps of the highly successful film *Quills*. Both were made in 2000 and both are portrayals of the Marquis de Sade, so it is near impossible to discuss the former without a mention of the latter. In *Quills*, Geoffrey Rush gives a pulsating performance as the Marquis de Sade, making him come alive on screen. Daniel Auteuil, in *Sade*, gives as good a performance as Rush but in a much different environment. While Rush was given the more difficult Sade, showing an emotional range from agony to self-importance, Auteuil's Sade seems to be a bit oblivious to his surroundings. *Sade* is a study of culture more than anything, while *Quills* was a study of human interactions. This is the main difference in the films and one of the reasons Rush's performance was given so much attention.

Sade is based on the book, *La Terreur dans le boudoir*, thus the language is rich and the anecdotes sharp tongued. The characters in this film spend their time cheating and lying to each other for the entire breath of the film. One character who captivated me was Sensible (Marianne Denicourt), due in part to her ability to show her character as multi-dimensional. It is necessary for Sensible to be both passive and strong in order to survive the times. It is not enough to be passive, but sometimes her strength must give way to the social confines of the day, as well. Her scenes with Sade are peppered with flirtation and wisdom. I thought their scenes together not only displayed the social situation of the time between men and women, but on a more intimate scale between two people swimming in a pool of uncertainty.

Islid Le Besco does a solid job of playing a young teenager, Emilie, who gives in to Sade. It is never clear whether she has a real sense of what she is doing or why, however. The film never explored the idea of social confinement and claustrophobia as reasons for her behavior, and just left it to the emotionality of adolescence.

Sade was lacking in raciness, which would have brought the audience closer to what they would expect in a movie about the Marques de Sade. This coupled with the "foreignness" of the film, with its subtitles and unknown actors, and we are left with a film not seen or embraced by many Americans.

I believe with the two most recent films about the writer, Marques de Sade, we have extremes on both ends. In Philip Kaufman's *Quills* it's as if they went overboard in showing the uninhibited passions of the writer in his later years. On the other hand, with Benoit Jacquot's *Sade* there seems to be nothing more to the character than a somber, misunderstood man. Surely as with all things, the truth of this fascinating writer lives somewhere in the middle.

Sade focuses on a short period in history during the French Revolution when the writer was imprisoned, not for the first time, in Picpus. He is surrounded by aristocrats who have been placed in exile in Picpus as well. Sade recruits the people in this dark and desolate place with him to "act" in his bizarre stage shows. Sensible is his saving grace by hooking up with a Robespierre sympathizer to keep him safe in his confines.

Sade is a well thought out and executed costume drama showing the brutality of this particular historical era. If you are looking for some kinky sex, as I assume many people looking at a film about the Marquis de Sade would be, you will be sorely disappointed.

This film ultimately does little to enlighten us to the sexual practices or perversity one thinks of with the Marquis de Sade, thus making for less than a titillating film. The long scenes in various places where Sade spews his thoughts on freedom and living life to it's fullest get a bit boring and drag on in places. As a historical drama *Sade* is a fine example of what can be done, however as a character study of a man who rocked polite society, it falls short.

—*Lauara Abraham*

CREDITS

Sade: Daniel Auteuil
Sensible: Marianne (Cuau) Denicourt
Fournier: Gregoire Colin
Emilie: Islid Le Besco
Madame Santero: Jeanne Balibar
Le Vicomte de Lancris: Jean-Pierre Cassel
Augustin: Jalil Lespert

Origin: France
Language: French
Released: 2000
Production: Patrick Godeau; TF-1 Films, Alicelio, Cofimage 11; released by Empire Pictures
Directed by: Benoit Jacquot
Written by: Jacques Fieschi, Bernard Minoret
Cinematography by: Benoit Delhomme
Sound: Dominique Gaborieau, Michel Vionnet

Editing: Luc Barnier
Art Direction: Sylvain Chauvelot
Costumes: Christian Gasc
MPAA rating: Unrated
Running time: 100 minutes

 REVIEWS

Boxoffice. November, 2000, p. 168.
New York Times Online. April 21, 2002.
New York Times Online. April 26, 2002.
Variety. August 28, 2000, p. 26.
Washington Post. June 7, 2002, p. C5.

Scary Movie 3

Great trilogies come in threes.
—Movie tagline

Box Office: $110 million

Scary Movie 3 was an early Christmas present for Dimension Films. It's hard to believe that the studio had very big expectations for the movie. It was a film that already looked played out even before it hit theaters. Everything about it seemed tired. The first *Scary Movie* was a Wayans brothers' project and was a welcome satire on popular teen horror films. By *Scary Movie 2,* the Wayans seemed to be running out of smart ideas and, instead, filled their movie with gross-out gags and boundary-pushing sexual humor. For *3,* Dimension Films replaced the Wayans with David Zucker, one of the guys behind *Airplane!* and the *Naked Gun* movies. Zucker is a genius of parody films, but it seemed as though his hit-making days might be behind him. After all, part of the humor of his earlier movies came from how outrageously different they were. Once you've been doing that kind of thing for several decades, the outrageousness loses a lot of its punch.

So *Scary Movie 3* surprised everyone when it came out, took a top spot on the box office charts and stayed there. It even got some good reviews. Director Zucker, working off a script by Craig Mazin and Pat Proft, proved that there's still an audience for his fast and furious brand of movie spoofs, visual gags, and non-sequiturs. He follows his usual film-making philosophy—if you don't like this joke, wait a couple seconds and there will be another one. The laugh per joke ratio might not be that high, but the sheer volume of gags means the laughs per hour should get bumped up.

This film starts out on a typically Zuckerian low (or high, depending on your point of view) note. Katie (Jenny McCarthy) and Becca (Pamela Anderson), who are clad, naturally, in push-up bras, are watching TV when they see a scary image reminiscent of *The Ring*. They start having a fun pillow fight which escalates into hitting each other with lamps, chairs, and the like. Jenny's character, Katie, is hit too hard. Becca, seeing her friend turning blue, shakes her and asks, "Katie, are you okay?" Katie's head falls off and Becca asks, again, "Katie, you okay?" It's absurd, has cameos, and makes fun of a movie cliché. Typical Zucker; in one of his movies, anything can happen. When one character comments to another that the dogs have been acting strange, the camera pans over to some dogs driving a chariot and others smoking something out of a hookah. Part of the wild ride is the uncertainty of never knowing which way the plot's going to twist.

Because the plot has to accommodate so much ridiculousness, it has to be pretty fluid. The fact that the screenwriters are also trying to tie together *8 Mile, Signs,* and *The Ring,* among other movies, doesn't help matters. There is a farmer, Tom (Zucker regular Charlie Sheen), his late wife (real life wife Denise Richards) and brother, George (Simon Rex). The brothers are terrified by the mysterious crop circles that have appeared in their cornfield. "What could it mean?" wonders Tom. The camera zooms back and we see that it forms the shape of an arrow pointing at his house with the words, "Attack here."

George is a wannabe rapper who lacks talent. This story line provides a chance for some *8 Mile* parodies, which are the weakest in the film. George raps very poorly, there's a joke about a hooded sweatshirt that looks like a KKK hood, and Simon Cowell of *American Idol* shows up as a rap contest judge. Anthony Anderson is George's best buddy Mahalik.

In the meantime, there's a creepy videotape that's come to the attention of local TV news reporter, Cindy Campbell (Anna Faris from the first two installments). Anyone who watches this video, which shows creepy images of a scary little girl, soon gets a phone call in which a creepy voice tells them that they will die in seven days. When Cindy gets the call, she is confused. "Is that seven business days? Are you counting Monday as a holiday?"

Cindy has custody of her nephew, Cody (Drew Mikuska), a kid who has a *Sixth Sense* kind of ability to see into the future. He walks around tossing off his psychic insights to whomever he sees. "Smile all you want," he tells one person, "You're going to get hit by a bus." To another happy pair at a party he says to one of them, "You're going to get lucky tonight." To the other he says, "He doesn't know you're a guy."

The stories are linked together when Cindy heads to the farmhouse to investigate the crop circles. It seems that the crop circles have something to do with the scary videotape

and something to do with some aliens that are going to land on Earth. It's pretty hard to figure out, actually.

The film is filled with visual gags. When a character goes on the Internet to do some research, we wait while her screen slowly fills up with about 30 pop-up ads. When the TV station airs some footage that has "terrifying shots" of the aliens on Earth, it's like a D-level horror movie. Poorly costumed aliens run through benign settings like backyard barbecues. Tasteless humor abounds. When a body is thrown around and eventually ripped apart at a funeral— don't ask—a piece of it flies off and a boy catches it. "I got something! I got something!" he cries happily.

Also showing up are George Carlin as the sex-starved Architect, Regina Hall as Cindy's best friend and Camryn Manheim as a state trooper. Queen Latifah is the Oracle who annoys her husband, Orpheus (Eddie Griffin), by constantly announcing the results of basketball games before they start. *Saturday Night Live*'s Darrell Hammond is Father Muldoon who, naturally, really enjoys babysitting young Cody.

Most critics accepted that they weren't watching *Masterpiece Theater* and liked the film. Kevin Thomas of the *Los Angeles Times* said of the film: "*Scary Movie 3* is sharp and smart-looking and Dimension's willingness to play freely with the series' format to keep it funny may well keep the franchise alive." Stephen Holden of the *New York Times* wrote, "Mr. Zucker almost makes a virtue of the non sequitur. The barrage of jokes and references flies by so thick and so fast that there is usually no time to react to one gag before two more have passed." *Newsday*'s Gene Seymour summed up, "Crass, crude and sledgehammer-subtle. Yet you can't help giggling yourself stupid, even at the more obvious sight gags." ✪

—*Jill Hamilton*

CREDITS

Cindy: Anna Faris
Mahalik: Anthony Anderson
President Harris: Leslie Nielsen
Trooper Champlin: Camryn Manheim
George: Simon Rex
The Architect: George Carlin
The Oracle: Queen Latifah
Orpheus: Eddie Griffin
Annie: Denise Richards
Brenda Meeks: Regina Hall
Tom: Charlie Sheen
Becca: Pamela Anderson (Cameo)
Katie: Jenny McCarthy (Cameo)
Ross Giggins: Jeremy Piven (Cameo)
John Wilson: D.L. Hughley (Cameo)

Ja Rule (Cameo)
Master P (Cameo)
Macy Gray (Cameo)
Redman (Cameo)
Raekwon (Cameo)
The RZA (Cameo)

Origin: USA
Released: 2003
Production: Robert K. Weiss; Brad Grey Pictures;
released by Dimension Films
Directed by: Jerry Zucker
Written by: Craig Mazin, Pat Proft
Cinematography by: Mark Irwin
Music by: James L. Venable
Sound: Michael J. Benavente
Music Supervisor: Randy Spendlove, Rachel Levy
Editing: Malcolm Campbell, Jon Poll
Art Direction: Willie Heslup
Costumes: Carol Ramsey
Production Design: William Elliot
MPAA rating: PG-13
Running time: 90 minutes

REVIEWS

Chicago Sun-Times Online. October 24, 2003.
Los Angeles Times Online. October 24, 2003.
New York Times Online. October 24, 2003.
USA Today Online. October 24, 2003.
Variety Online. October 24, 2003.
Washington Post. October 24, 2003, p. WE34.

School of Rock

Take notes.
—Movie tagline
He just landed the gig of his life: 5th grade.
—Movie tagline

 Box Office: $81.2 million

In Stephen Frears's wonderful *High Fidelity,* Jack Black played John Cusack's fellow record store employee, Barry. Barry was a musical snob you loved to watch berate customers who didn't have sufficiently cool taste in tunes. Black, who had already recorded one solo record album in a

nascent musical career, went on to create his self-proclaimed "greatest rock band in the history of the world," Tenacious D. With Black's all-out wild-man on-stage antics and lunatic ability to spoof the excesses of rock posers, Tenacious D enjoyed a cult success among fans of tongue-in-cheek mockrocking.

Black completes his journey as a satiric rock icon as the centerpiece of director Richard Linklater's surprising and hilariously entertaining film *School of Rock.* Linklater was widely criticized for being too gloomy, introspective, and unstructured in the wildly innovative 2001 film *Waking Life,* which combined armchair philosophy with groundbreaking animation. Also that year, Linklater released *Tape,* a talky three-character play set and shot entirely in a motel room. His latest film is very different than these, as well as his earlier efforts, which were deep, thoughtful character and societal studies. This is pure entertainment, stylistically his most conventional film. It has all the earmarks of potential commercial success—except a big star. But Black does better than any mega-celebrity. In fact, only Black could succeed in a role that has many potential comic pitfalls.

In this film, Linklater "disappears" as a director and allows the audience to enjoy the antics of Black, the clever screenwriting of Mike White, a great soundtrack of rock music, some brilliant acting by Joan Cusack, the virtuoso charm of a group of appealing young musician/actors, and a wacky, offbeat, and just-short-of-heartwarming fantasy story that will appeal to ages 10 and up. Baby-boomer and Gen X adults will get even more of the jokes and cultural references.

Forget *Mr. Holland's Opus* and all those other films about music and arts teachers who find gems hidden among the student body. No one's more inspired than Black's rockcrazed Dewey Finn, an overgrown prepubescent boy who thinks he's just one great performance away from rock stardom. As the film opens, Finn is the front man for a goingnowhere hard rock group, but the other members feel his 20-minute guitar solos and head-first, bare-chested dives into the crowds are an embarrassment. He's also become something of a headache for his friend Ned Schneebly (Mike White, the film's author), or, more specifically, his no-nonsense girlfriend Patty (Sarah Silverman), who, now that she's moved into their shared apartment, keeps urging Ned to get up the gumption to demand that Dewey pay his long-overdue rent or get out. Dewey reacts to the suggestion with amazement: after all, can't everyone see his mission in life is to "change the world" with great rock and roll? Why should he be harassed by working stiffs who don't understand that Led Zeppelin is what life's all about?

Ned has a job as a substitute teacher, and when Dewey gets a phone call from a private school principal who is desperate for a long-term sub, he has a brainstorm. Patty and Ned have been bugging him to get money, so why not horn in on Ned's work? Pretending to be Ned, he shows up at

Horace Green Preparatory School in an appropriately tweedy outfit, complete with bowtie and scarf. After a short talk with Principal Mullins (Cusack), he walks into a classroom and introduces himself as "Mr. S," because he can't spell Schneebly's name on the blackboard. Once Mullins leaves, he asks who has food and announces that the kids can now slack off and do nothing for the rest of the day, and the rest of his time with them. While a few students greet his new no-grades, no-work policy with glee, others, including the "class factotum" and grade-grubbing high achiever, Summer (Miranda Cosgrove) are upset. She points out that her parents are paying $15,000 a year for an education and she demands to learn something. Her plea at first falls on deaf ears.

After Mr. S listens in on the students' orchestra practice one day, he discovers that several are excellent musicians, and he gets the idea that he can form them into a band. Ever since he was kicked out of his own band, he has wanted to form another to win the local "Battle of the Bands." But first he must shape his young, stuffed-shirt preppies into kick-ass rock-and-rollers.

That's the setup for the film; which subsequently spends a long, hilarious time detailing Black's educational techniques. He assigns all the students a role: Summer is band manager; the class goof-off, Frankie (Angelo Massagli), is the drummer; and there are roadies and groupies as well. One of the girls assigned to be a groupie returns the next day to complain that she looked up "groupie" on the Internet and found out they were "sluts"; Mr. S. assures her that's not the case, that they're more like "cheerleaders." It takes him awhile to school their musical tastes as well; when he asks the students what their "influences" are, he gets responses naming Christina Aguilera, Puff Daddy, and Liza Minnelli. Black winces and contorts his face in agony, and he embarks on a long education about Yes, AC/DC, the Who, and others in his hard-rocking musical pantheon.

All this is more than a little far-fetched, but it's a pleasingly wacky fantasy. The idea that a latter-day rock "true believer," who still thinks that the music ought to be all about "sticking it to the man," is embarking on instructing the sons and daughters of Yuppies in how to be cool and rock out, may sound a little strained, but it is irresistible in the hands of Black, a lunatic with a natural gift for the role. It's virtually written for him, because who else could believably launch into an impromptu song about math when the principal makes a surprise room visit. And though Black's character stops just short of absurd in his worshipful parody of rock-and-roll's supposedly transformative attributes, Black brings such sincerity to his rants about the power of rock that he overcomes cynicism and is simply delightful.

The youthful we-can-change-the-world naivete that informed rock music during the counter-cultural period of the 1960s and early 1970s may now seem silly in retrospect, but it was sincere at the time. It's a fascinating concept that a latter-day true believer, an adolescent at heart who still delights in the rebellion that has been crushed by the music business, is the one who can teach today's uptight, square kids how to act more like kids.

The movie has surprising resonance despite the hackneyed concept (how many times have teen music movies hinged on a "battle of the bands"?). It helps immensely that Linklater gets nuanced, amusing performances from the entire cast. Cusack thoroughly inhabits her role as a mousy, spirit-crushed headmistress who spreads gloom and soaks up resentment. It doesn't add a whole lot to the plot, but it does make for plenty of strange enjoyment, when Mr. S takes her to a bar and loosens her up with a Stevie Nicks song on the jukebox, and Cusack melts into the music and her stuffy facade drunkenly unravels.

Though White's plotting at times gets a little convoluted and hard to believe (Why are enraged parents who come to parent-teacher night still all there the next day? Why is the Battle of the Bands during the day? How is it possible the rock band's practice isn't heard throughout the school?), it doesn't interfere with the fantasy. And the dialogue is full of great riffs on rock and roll craziness. When Mr. S asks the two groupies to think of names for the bands, they come up with the "Koala Bears," and when he says that's too cute, they suggest "Pig Rectum." *School of Rock* comes with a PG-13 rating, but only because the language borders on the adult, and it never gets too crude.

Making the whole thing work splendidly is Black's task, and he's more than up to it. You'd think the "teaching" he does, which takes up most of the film, might get dull and repetitive, but it doesn't, mostly because Black's unique, rubber-faced, rock-poser-mocking acting is wildly entertaining. And the children in the film are mostly marvelous. Though some veer close to being too precocious and cutesy, they're a diverse, enjoyable gang of believable kids who possess uncanny talent. The script and Linklater do a good job of giving each kid his or her due without delving too much into distracting subplots.

There's a semi-triumphant ending, of course, and a wonderful closing-credits song that is a highlight of the movie. It's fun to watch these kids morph from shy, conservative junior academics to wild-haired, costumed rockers, and it's clear that they are responding onscreen to Black, who's like a pied piper of rock 'n' roll. There's a lot of chemistry on camera, even if the story is hokey and really just a rock twist on the usual unorthodox-teacher-opens-students'-eyes saga. When Black asks the students what irks them, and turns their petty annoyances into an impromptu rock song, he's getting at the raw essence of rock rebellion — the annoyance at everyday convention which fueled the music in the first place but has, indeed, gotten lost beneath the blanket of commercialism, as Dewey never tires of pointing out. Though Black's character clearly is satirizing a certain sensibility, there's an undeniable appeal in his message of rebellion, even if today it can only be told in this kind of mock-fantasy setting.

The film's music is terrific, and Linklater handles the concert and other scenes deftly. He's proven once again he's masterful at many genres, and *School of Rock* is a rare comic gem. It's one of the funniest and most entertaining and most musically appealing movies of any year, and it also succeeds as a showcase for Black, giving him a chance to rise farther than he has. Certainly no one else could have made this central character into such a rollicking, rocking success.

—*Michael Betzold*

CREDITS

Dewey Finn: Jack Black
Rosalie Mullins: Joan Cusack
Ned Schneebly: Mike White
Patty Di Marco: Sarah Silverman
Zack: Joey Gaydos
Summer Hathaway: Miranda Cosgrove
Freddy: Kevin Alexander Clark
Katie: Rebecca Julia Brown
Lawrence: Robert Tsai
Tomika: Maryam Hassan
Marta: Caitlin Hale
Alicia: Aleisha Allen
Billy: Brian Falduto
Gordon: Zachary Infante
Marco: James Hosey
Frankie: Angelo Massagli
Leonard: Cole Hawkins
Eleni: Nicole Afflerbach
Michelle: Jordan-Claire Green
Theo: Adam Pascal
Doug: Chris Stack
Zack's dad: Tim Hopper
Razor: Nicky Katt

Origin: USA
Released: 2003
Production: Scott Rudin; New Century, Munich Film Partners, SOR Productions; released by Paramount Pictures
Directed by: Richard Linklater
Written by: Mike White
Cinematography by: Rogier Stoffers
Music by: Craig (Shudder to Think) Wedren
Sound: Jeffrey Stern
Music Supervisor: Randall Poster
Editing: Sandra Adair
Art Direction: Adam Matthew Scher

Costumes: Karen Patch
Production Design: Jeremy Conway
MPAA rating: PG-13
Running time: 108 minutes

REVIEWS

Boxoffice. November, 2003, p. 106.
Chicago Sun-Times Online. October 3, 2003.
Entertainment Weekly. October 3, 2003, p. 47.
Los Angeles Times Online. September 7, 2003.
Los Angeles Times Online. October 3, 2003.
New York Times Online. October 3, 2003.
People. October 13, 2003, p. 30.
Rolling Stone. October 30, 2003, p. 100.
USA Today Online. October 3, 2003.
Variety Online. September 9, 2003.
Washington Post. October 3, 2003, p. WE40.

QUOTES

Dewey Finn (Jack Black): "One rock concert can change the world!"

AWARDS AND NOMINATIONS

Nomination:
Golden Globes 2004: Actor—Mus./Comedy (Black).

Seabiscuit

You're never too far behind to come back.
—Movie tagline
A long shot becomes a legend.
—Movie tagline

 Box Office: $120.1 million

Near the end of the Great Depression, Americans went crazy for a misshapen thoroughbred racehorse named Seabiscuit. Rising from the obscurity of the fledgling California racing circuit, Seabiscuit captured the imagination of a nation of people who, like him, had been through hard times and hadn't quit. His rapid rise to fame came just as a drop in prices made radio sets affordable for most

Americans. Seabiscuit's races were the first sporting events to galvanize and unite the nation, paving the way for a sports mania that has gripped the country ever since. His race against War Admiral on November 1, 1938, was the most famous sporting event of the first half of the twentieth century; per-capita, it was tuned into by more people than have ever watched a Super Bowl or World Series—and that on a weekday afternoon.

Every American who lived through that era knew the story of Seabiscuit. In 1949 Hollywood made a laughably lame Shirley Temple movie about the horse, after which the legend gradually faded into obscurity. The story of a beloved racehorse seemed a cultural artifact that could hardly compete against the excitement of modern sporting spectacles. Then, in 1998, a Hollywood studio optioned the rights to a novel in progress, at the time titled *Four Good Legs*. The novel, written by an unknown freelance writer named Laura Hillenbrand, was retitled *Seabiscuit: An American Legend*. Its author, like her three central characters, overcame great setbacks: Hillenbrand wrote the book while suffering from a severe case of the mysterious disease known as Chronic Fatigue Syndrome. Unable to travel and often unable even to sit for long periods of time, she researched the story using the Internet and conducted interviews with key eyewitnesses by phone.

The book ultimately became a bestseller by word-of-mouth. Hillenbrand knew that the obvious part of the Seabiscuit legend had been laid out in newspapers, but her love of fiction made her dig for telling details and juicy anecdotes that made her characters come back to life. Rather than the mere story of a horse that bucked the odds and captured the hearts of a nation, Hillenbrand's book was by turns a dark, prickly, heartwarming, and rich tale about the intertwining lives of three men—the horse's owner, trainer, and jockey—as well as the morbid and breathtaking sacrifices jockeys make for the thrill of the ride. It was also an unvarnished and thoughtful portrait of America at a time when the will to triumph over long odds was literally keeping millions of people alive.

A movie based on Hillenbrand's book seemed to be a natural winner, with great characters and a compelling story full of tragedy and triumph. And Gary Ross's film has all the ingredients of a champion—breathtaking photography, beautiful performances, and not one, but two, climactic races designed to bring audiences to their feet cheering.

The casting of this film was crucial because the three male leads had to be both quirky and sympathetic, complicated yet accessible. As Red Pollard, a literature-quoting, yarn-spinning, injury-prone jockey, Tobey Maguire proves that he has become one of the great young actors; his homespun, boyish qualities and self-deprecating manner make him a perfect Pollard, an unforgettable character. Chris Cooper again shows his incredible ability to submerge himself physically and emotionally into a character as the

plainspoken trainer Tom Smith, a cowboy with thinning white hair and a gift for touching a horse's hidden heart. Jeff Bridges also shines as millionaire Charles Howard, a former bicycle repairman and car dealer whose life is dedicated to the American urban future, just as Smith's is iconic of the fading frontier past.

Introducing these three characters and giving their back stories is crucial, but it's just as difficult for Ross to do them justice as it is for Hillenbrand. Their lives are so rich and meaningful and their stories so bizarre that they suffer when overly condensed. Ross chooses to cut back and forth between them, gambling that the viewer will be intrigued and not puzzled by the rapidly moving snippets of their stories in the early part of the film. When he succeeds in this intertwining, it's almost like a male version of the opening scenes of *The Hours;* more often the effect is a little frustrating, as if you're viewing a Cliffs Notes version of bigger stories.

Howard morphs from New York City bicycle repairman to San Francisco auto dealer to the patriarch of a millionaire's estate in the blink of an eye; then tragedy strikes (his son dies while taking a car for an outing) and in the wake of their grief his wife leaves, he gets a divorce in Tijuana, and remarries. The scenes relating to his son's death are handled with masterful respect and reverence; one of him clutching his dead son's body on his front porch is wrenching and unforgettable. However, Ross and his writers have chosen to make this son the only Howard child, when in fact there were four—a bad sign considering the only purpose it serves is to milk a tragedy that is awful enough on its own. And that's emblematic of the only real problem with this movie: a tendency toward emotional manipulation and preachiness.

As Howard rapidly rises and then falls, Pollard is experiencing his own emotional purgatory. Growing up in Alberta (left out of the movie was the fact that Pollard's father founded the city of Edmonton), he shows an aptitude for riding horses and an appetite for classic literature. When his family is rendered destitute by the Depression, his parents send him away to be a groom for a horseman. While still a teenager, he becomes an itinerant prizefighter and jockey, taking hard knocks on the track and in the ring, including one that injures his eye. An early race on a dirt track in an unidentified cow town depicts "jockeying" in two different ways. Not only do the jockeys vie desperately for the lead by pulling, hitting, and knocking each other—jockeying for position—they also yell, scream, and insult each other, engaging in the equivalent of baseball's "bench jockeying." The sequence is scrappy and breathtaking and beautifully shot, showing the no-holds-barred nature of early, unregulated horse racing, another forgotten slice of Americana.

Tom Smith's character is less well developed, but that is also the case in the book. Smith is one of the last real cowboys, herding horses on the open range until, to his dismay, the automobiles take the road and cause the land to be fenced off. He ends up kicking around as a handler and farrier on a "Wild West" show and eventually becomes an unorthodox trainer. Smith is quiet and sensitive, and the only quibble with Cooper's wonderful performance is that he makes the gruff man a little too sweet.

The narrative arc takes all three men to Tijuana, the center of horse racing during Prohibition, a time when gambling on horses is forbidden in the United States. There, we are introduced to George "Iceman" Wolf (played by real jockey Gary Stevens), a playboy jockey with a fancy car, a way with women, and a big heart. He and Pollard strike up an unusual friendship. Unfortunately, the film makes short shrift of Wolf's character and doesn't sufficiently explain their friendship. Similarly, the movie quickly passes over some of the less savory aspects of the jockey regimen, including the trials riders go through to keep their weight down. More of Pollard's ordeals as a boxer and jockey—and a little less maudlin attention to his feelings about being abandoned by his parents—would have made the film grittier and more compelling.

It's not that Seabiscuit totally succumbs to easy sentiment, although the dialogue does shout out the meanings and lessons of the film in snippets of speech that seem forced. Ross and his scriptwriters should have counted on the great strengths of the story and the power of their characters to enable the messages to emerge. Audiences can draw their own conclusions; they don't need to be told this is a story about broken men and how they were repaired by a horse that itself was broken. This is obviously a story about overcoming mistreatment, bad luck, and tragedy, and about believing in life despite its imperfections. But the film wants to force its conclusions on us, and preach about what's happening.

The way the story is told is also problematic. A voice-over is employed in fits and starts to give us a feel of the Depression while Ross uses stills to give the movie its historical anchor. Some of this works nicely, but at other times it feels like an educational television special; at its worst moments, the script uses the events of the Depression to milk obvious points about what is happening to the characters. While Seabiscuit's tale was certainly emblematic of Depression values, not every twist and turn in it corresponded to a national mood or event.

Ross also veers dangerously into mistaking sentimentality for the deeply human experience of overcoming obstacles and being knocked down again. One of the most compelling things about the way Hillenbrand presents the story of this famous racehorse is her refusal to gloss over all the inconsistencies and messy sidetracks that the Seabiscuit story contains. For the sake of moving the film along, of course, the script has to truncate some of these hard-to-explain situations—like the manner in which Seabiscuit's famed showdown with War Admiral was postponed because of Seabiscuit's handlers' aversions to wet tracks and bad

odds. But the script does too much smoothing out and makes the story too cloying and digestible. It's fine for the movie to alter reality so that owner, trainer, and jockey come together in Saratoga, New York, rather than in Detroit—that makes narrative sense—and for the secret of Pollard's blindness to be revealed, but only to those in Seabiscuit's inner circle. Ross can even be excused for overplaying the haughty, patrician nature of War Admiral's owner, for that horse was indeed the scion of the Eastern establishment, and Seabiscuit, despite also coming from fine stock, did indeed represent the hopes of the unwashed populist masses. The movie is diminished, however, by making Smith into a gentle saint rather than a grizzled curmudgeon; by smoothing out the blowhard aspects of Howard's media-hungry personality and omitting his own manipulation of the press; and by turning Howard's second wife (Elizabeth Banks) into a cardboard figure of supportive, never-questioning femininity rather than the hard-bitten, dynamic woman she really was. Banks's character contributes so little she might as well not even be there. Inexplicably, the filmmakers also missed a great chance to add a little improbable romance to this very macho tale by omitting Pollard's marriage to the nurse who tends him during his recuperation from an injury.

The film's most potent scene is not any of the thrilling races but a gritty sequence in which Pollard is thrown from another horse and is dragged helplessly to his apparent doom. It is sickening and effective—and in the way it shows the dangers of the jockeys' lives, it plays on one of the strengths of the book. More such unflinching realism would have helped balance some of the many saccharine scenes.

Ten different horses—or more, by some accounts—shared in playing Seabiscuit, but there are moments when the switch in coloring and stature are too obvious. Seabiscuit doesn't look always like the same horse, and that contributes to something of a void at the heart of the film. Though this is rightly more a movie about the three men than about the horse, it still should be a film that leaves indelible images of this extraordinary animal, one that didn't look like a champion, and it fails in that respect.

The script can't be faulted for its major innovation: creating a character that didn't actually exist—Tick-Tock McGlaughlin—to represent the press, which played an important role in creating and sustaining Seabiscuit's popularity. William H. Macy provides some needed comic relief and perspective, creating a memorable minor character who embodies the hokum of all radio personalities of that era or since. The real strength of the film, however, lies in the performances of Cooper and Maguire and, to a lesser degree, Bridges, as well as in the marvelous cinematography, editing, and computer wizardry involved in the mesmerizing race scenes, which are top-notch.

Seabiscuit takes its audience into the fray of the jockey's world better than any movie ever made, throwing us smack dab into the chaos of the tight corners, the glances, the shouts and curses, and the frantic speed of the races. Instead of the hackneyed pounding hooves coming down the track, we get the jostling backs of the jockeys and horses and the jerking faces and bodies of the animals and their mounts. We get Pollard's ineffable humor and wild exhilaration, too, and Maguire's performance is exceptional. Jockeys are strange men whose boyish stature belies the toughness earned from the hard knocks of their profession; they are seen by spectators as little more than passengers on these incredible animals, but it is their split-second timing and intelligence that separate the champions from the also-rans, often by a nose. Maguire captures all the contradictions of his character—a learned man who is also a scrapper, a man with an odd mixture of pride and humility, a man with guts and heart whose face betrays both the fear and joy of racing—and it's a performance that is Oscar-quality.

As he did in his Oscar-winning role in *Adaptation*, Cooper disappears completely into his character, and what we see on screen is a wise, soft-spoken, hard-bitten but sensitive man, aging rapidly before our eyes and representing a passing age. Bridges is a little less successful as Howard; at times he seems simply to be reprising his role as an early-day futurist in *Tucker: The Man and his Dream*, though there is nothing flawed about his performance—it just lacks the genius of his co-stars.

In a summer of blockbusters that were tired and trite, *Seabiscuit* burst on the scene as a loveable underdog, full of the heart and compassion missing from so many cynical, rote action-thrillers. It's certainly a crowd-pleaser, and deservedly so. But Ross should have trusted this wonderful story to speak for itself instead of telling us, over and over, what to make of it.

—*Michael Betzold*

CREDITS

Red Pollard: Tobey Maguire
Charles Howard: Jeff Bridges
Tom Smith: Chris Cooper
Marcela Howard: Elizabeth Banks
"Tick-Tock" McGaughlin: William H. Macy
George Woolf: Gary Stevens
Samuel Riddle: Eddie Jones
Charles Strub: Ed Lauter
Mr. Pollard: Michael O'Neill
Dutch Doogan: Royce D. Applegate
Mrs. Pollard: Annie Corley
Annie Howard: Valerie Mahaffey
Narrator: David McCullough

Origin: USA
Released: 2003

Production: Kathleen Kennedy, Frank Marshall, Gary Ross, Jane Sindell; Universal Pictures, Dreamworks Pictures, Spyglass Entertainment, Larger Than Life; released by Universal Pictures
Directed by: Gary Ross
Written by: Gary Ross
Cinematography by: John Schwartzman
Music by: Randy Newman
Sound: Tod A. Maitland
Editing: William Goldenberg
Art Direction: Andrew Neskoromny
Costumes: Judianna Makovsky
Production Design: Jeannine Oppewall
MPAA rating: PG-13
Running time: 140 minutes

REVIEWS

Chicago Sun-Times Online. July 25, 2003.
Entertainment Weekly. August 1, 2003, p. 58.
Los Angeles Times Online. January 19, 2003.
Los Angeles Times Online. July 25, 2003.
New York Times Online. July 25, 2003.
People. August 4, 2003, p. 31.
Rolling Stone. August 21, 2003, p. 81.
USA Today Online. July 25, 2003.
USA Weekend. July 18, 2003, p. 14.
Variety Online. July 15, 2003.
Washington Post. July 25, 2003, p. WE34.

QUOTES

Announcer "Tick-Tock" McGlaughlin (William H. Macy) about racing prize money: "$100,000? Makes me wanna walk on all fours and put a saddle on my back."

AWARDS AND NOMINATIONS

Nomination:
Oscars 2003: Adapt. Screenplay, Art Dir./Set Dec., Cinematog., Costume Des., Film, Film Editing, Sound
Directors Guild 2003: Director (Ross)
Golden Globes 2004: Film, Support. Actor (Macy)
Screen Actors Guild 2003: Support. Actor (Cooper), Cast
Writers Guild 2003: Adapt. Screenplay.

Secondhand Lions

The McCann brothers have finally met their match.
—Movie tagline

 Box Office: $41.5 million

Tim McCanlies's *Secondhand Lions* is a sweet throwback to the old family films that Disney used to produce with regularity. These were movies that could appeal to adults and children alike and combined memorable characters with a sense of whimsy and a belief in the essential decency of humanity. Set in the early 1960s, *Secondhand Lions* proudly advances the old-fashioned notion that the older generation has valuable lessons to teach the younger, that male role models are crucial in a young man's development, and that serious ideas can be communicated through exciting storytelling.

McCanlies weaves a heartfelt coming-of-age story around one boy's memorable experience living with two eccentric uncles. Dumped off in the middle of Texas by his irresponsible mother, Mae (Kyra Sedgwick), 14-year-old Walter (Haley Joel Osment) is forced to spend the summer with his great-uncles, Garth (Michael Caine) and Hub McCann (Robert Duvall). They mysteriously resurfaced after being away for 40 years and are rumored to be worth millions of dollars, so Mae suggests that, if Walter works his way in to their good graces, they might remember him in their will. Mae is the kind of woman who bounces from one bad relationship to another and is unable to provide a stable life for her son. Claiming to be going off to court reporting school in Fort Worth, she ends up in Las Vegas instead.

Old bachelors Hub and Garth are set in their ways and do not like having a child disturb their lives. Their idea of entertainment is to sit on their porch and shoot their rifles at the traveling salesmen that have the temerity to drive up their road. A sense of mystery shrouds the brothers—one local rumor says that they were hit men for Al Capone—and they speak nonchalantly of old age and impending death, making Walter afraid to be staying there. This is an ideal transition for Osment, making the move from child actor to teenager by playing a character that grows up in the course of the film.

Walter is puzzled by his new environment but finds a sympathetic ear in Garth, the more sensitive, fatherly of the brothers. He tries to do his best by Walter and knows how to persuade him to return to the farm when the frightened boy runs away. Depressed about being old and feeling that he has outlived his usefulness, Hub is rougher around the edges and

takes some time to warm up to Walter. Caine and Duvall work well together as brothers, giving the casual feeling of two men who have known each other so long that a mere glance can communicate more than words.

Walter begins to have a salutary effect on his uncles. He gets them to begin enjoying life and spend some of their money, first on a skeet machine, then on some crop seeds because gardening, according to Garth, is what retired people do. In a cute scene, it slowly dawns on them that the seed salesman cheated them: all of their crops are corn, not the variety they thought they had purchased. The McCanns may begin to soften up a bit, but they do not lose their lovably eccentric edge. They purchase a lion because they think it would be fun to hunt it and hang up the trophy over the fireplace (they do not have a fireplace, but Hub is confident they can buy one). The lion, however, turns out to be old and lethargic, "defective," as Garth puts it, so they let Walter keep it as a pet.

Interspersed with everyday life on the farm are Garth's swashbuckling yarns, revealed in flashbacks, of his and Hub's wild youth, which capture Walter's imagination and suggest that Hub's frustration with old age is rooted in memories of the dashing young man he once was. According to Garth, he and Hub were shanghaied into the French Foreign Legion and had exotic adventures in Africa. Garth's flashbacks have a feisty, comical, Indiana Jones quality, full of narrow escapes, tongue-in-cheek humor, and a love story involving Hub and the beautiful Princess Jasmine (Emmanuelle Vaugier), who is rescued by Hub from a powerful sheik. Hub and Jasmine spent several happy years together, but the sheik remained Hub's enemy, placing a bounty on his head. The McCanns finally cooked up a scheme to outsmart their rival: Garth, in disguise, turned his brother in for a huge reward and the resourceful Hub broke through his chains and escaped. Defeating the sheik in a final sword fight, Hub spared his foe's life, and in return the sheik never again pursued him, either out of fear or respect.

Back on the farm, Hub still yearns to be the hero doing good in the world. In one of the film's most entertaining scenes, he gets the chance to educate some punk teenagers who harass him. Cocky and tough, these junior hoodlums take on Hub, who fights and defeats the whole gang single-handedly. McCanlies, however, does not end with the hilarious, albeit improbable, sight of an old man easily beating up some young toughs but rather suggests that there is something deeper at stake. After the brawl, Hub and Garth bring the boys home and feed them dinner, and Hub gives them his famed lecture on what a boy needs to know to become a man, in essence leading them down the right path in life.

But Walter soon grows worried about Hub's mental state. Instead of being energized by the fight, he seems depressed by it, as if that were his last hurrah before dying. Walter confronts Hub and asks him what happened to Jasmine (Garth insists that Walter hear the end of the story from Hub himself), only to learn that Jasmine died in child-birth along with their baby. A grief-stricken Hub returned to the Foreign Legion, then finally made the trip to Texas to live out his remaining days with his brother.

Walter is so moved by the story that he needs to know if it is really true and not just a tall tale. Hub tells him that it does not matter and goes on to deliver the film's core philosophical statement. "Sometimes the things that may or may not be true are the things that a man needs to believe in the most," Hub tells Walter. These things include the goodness of people; the importance of honor, courage, and virtue; the insignificance of power and money; the triumph of good over evil; and the endurance of true love. The lesson may be simple and obvious, even a tad corny, but it comes from a well of experience, and Duvall lends the words a kind of poetry and a genuine sense that wisdom is being handed down through the generations. But Walter does something for Hub in return by begging him to stick around to be his uncle and telling him how much he needs him. When they embrace, it is a touching moment because it comes out of a true need each has for the other in his life.

The new bond between Hub and Walter is the emotional high point of the movie. The rest of the film ties up the key plot threads. Walter follows Garth into the barn one night and discovers where his uncles keep their fortune. They have piles and piles of cash, and, since the money looks like it may have been stolen, Walter seems suspicious and even conflicted. Then Mae returns with a new boyfriend, a lowlife named Stan (Nicky Katt), who pretends to be a detective in pursuit of the McCanns and claims they were bank robbers in the 1920s and '30s. It is clear that Stan is a phony who just wants their money, but Walter at first is not sure what to believe. Finally, however, he takes a stand by declaring his faith in the stories his uncles told him. When Stan tries to rough up Walter, his lion, which has been named Jasmine, comes to his aid and attacks Stan. In all of the commotion, Jasmine dies when her heart gives out defending Walter.

Saying good-bye to his uncles is hard for Walter, but he is devastated when he discovers that his mom is planning to nurse Stan back to health and marry him. A determined Walter pleads with her to let him make his own choice and return to the farm to live with his uncles. This poignant conclusion even redeems Mae, whose selfishness gives way so that her son can have a chance at a better life.

The film ends in the present day as the grownup Walter (Josh Lucas) is summoned to the farm and learns that his uncles were killed in an airplane accident. Trying to fly upside down into their barn and crashing instead, Hub and Garth died heroically, living their final moments with the gusto that exemplified their youth. The best part of the ending is the surprise landing of a helicopter, out of which appears the sheik's grandson. He has come to pay his respects to the only men ever to outwit his grandfather, not

only confirming once and for all the veracity of the old tales but also reinforcing the film's theme of stories being passed down from generation to generation, even half a world away.

Eschewing the irony and hipness that often feel obligatory in family films today (so that anyone over twelve can feel such movies are not just for children), *Secondhand Lions* hearkens back to a purity that may make it seem as stuck in the past as its bachelor brothers recalling the good old days. But for audiences seeking upbeat, playful family entertainment peppered with homespun life lessons along the way, this easygoing story of a boy's world opening up is a welcome treat.

—*Peter N. Chumo II*

CREDITS

Garth: Michael Caine
Hub: Robert Duvall
Walter: Haley Joel Osment
Stan: Nicky Katt
Mae: Kyra Sedgwick
Princess Jasmine: Emmanuelle Vaugier
Young Hub: Christian Kane
Young Garth: Kevin Michael Haberer
Adult Walter: Josh(ua) Lucas
Skeet machine salesman: Adrian Pasdar

Origin: USA
Released: 2003
Production: David Kirschner, Corey Sienega, Scott Ross; Digital Domain, Avery Pix; released by New Line Cinema
Directed by: Tim McCanlies
Written by: Tim McCanlies
Cinematography by: Jack N. Green
Music by: Patrick Doyle
Sound: Scott Wolf
Editing: David Moritz
Art Direction: John R. Jensen
Costumes: Gary Jones
Production Design: David J. Bomba
MPAA rating: PG
Running time: 107 minutes

 REVIEWS

Chicago Sun-Times Online. September 19, 2003.
Entertainment Weekly. September 26, 2003, p. 74.
Los Angeles Times Online. September 19, 2003.
New York Times Online. September 19, 2003.
People. September 29, 2003, p. 34.

USA Today Online. September 19, 2003.
Variety Online. September 11, 2003.
Washington Post. September 19, 2003, p. WE47.

QUOTES

Hub (Robert Duvall) about caring for their teen great-nephew: "We're old, damn it, leave us alone. We don't know nothing about kids."

The Secret Lives of Dentists

 Box Office: $3.5 million

D irector Alan Rudolph started out as an apprentice to Robert Altman and seems to be trying to rise to Altman's preeminence, with decidedly mixed results. *The Secret Lives of Dentists,* despite its awkward title and internal irritations, is one of Rudolph's more successful adaptations and is recognized as one of the director's best films. Surveying Rudolph's career in his book, *Alan Rudolph: Romance and a Crazed World* (1996), Richard Ness claimed that by the mid-1990s, Rudolph had not "made a film which [had] been unanimously praised or condemned." If so, *The Secret Lives of Dentist* might prove an exception to that rule. It demonstrates a tendency that Ness discerned in an earlier Rudolph film, *Mrs. Parker and the Vicious Circle* (1994), notably a "new realism in the director's work, particularly in the attention to detail in capturing its period and characters." With one possible exception, the characters in Rudolph's latest film are carefully observed and realistically presented.

After working with Altman on *The Long Goodbye* (1973), in 1975 Rudolph was assigned to be assistant director to Altman on *Nashville,* one of Altman's biggest breakaway hits. By the following year Rudolph worked as co-writer with Altman on *Buffalo Bill and the Indians,* but by the end of 1976 he had also directed *Welcome to L.A.* solo.

Rudolph then went on to become one of the very first successful independent directors, long before Spike Lee, Quentin Tarantino, and Kevin Smith became popular or even thought about directing. Over the years Rudolph has developed a reputation as an actor's director, and, as was also the case with his mentor, actors have sought Rudolph out for the privilege of working with him. In fact, the actor Campbell Scott first recommended the Craig Lucas screenplay for

The Secret Lives of Dentists to Rudolph and eventually the actor himself ended up with co-producing credit for the film. Campbell Scott had worked with Rudolph in 1994 when he played Robert Benchley in *Mrs. Parker and the Vicious Circle.*

With *Breakfast of Champions* (1999) Rudolph had bravely attempted to adapt Kurt Vonnegut's surreal novel to the screen, with disastrous results at the box office. Vonnegut's novel was simply too strange to be mainstreamed, but at least Rudolph was willing to try. With *The Secret Lives of Dentists* Rudolph turned his talents to the fiction of Jane Smiley, with far better results, perhaps because *The Age of Grief,* Smiley's source novella, told a more conventional story that was less grotesque and involved only one truly irritating character. In this instance, moreover, the novella had already been reshaped and adapted by Craig Lucas, whereas Rudolph had attempted to adapt Vonnegut's novel himself. Lucas had done journeyman service for the later film, and Rudolph apparently trusted his work. "I stuck with the whole script," Rudolph remarked in the *New York Times.* "It's 90 percent as it was written, if not more."

Not much really happens in the film's plot, since the conflict is far more internal than external. As Stanley Kauffmann wrote in his *New Republic* review, "It has almost no story: its claim on our interest is in the texture of family life, which is really what fills the screen." Such as it is, the story involves a married couple, David and Dana Hurst, blessed with three children (Gianna Beleno, Cassidy Hinkle, and Lydia Jordan). Both of the parents (Campbell Scott and Hope Davis, both equally praised for their "great, confidently modest performances") are dentists, sharing an office for their combined practices; but their "secrets" are more personal than professional.

Dana looks forward to performing in the chorus with a local opera company. While attempting to visit her backstage to wish her luck before the performance, David sees her apparently being intimate with another man. Dana is unaware of David's backstage visit and the fact that she has been observed. David therefore believes his wife is having an affair, but he lacks the will to confront her directly about her infidelity. He does not want to wreck the family, which he values.

At this point the plot takes a surreal turn, as David's anxiety over his suspicions takes the form of an imaginary friend, or, more accurately, the decidedly antagonistic voice of his conscience. This "friend" is first introduced as an irritating malcontent of a patient named Slater (Denis Leary), who first comes to David's office to complain about a botched filling. Even though David offers to replace the filling, Slater later threatens to wreck David's reputation by confronting him in public in the crowded auditorium the same night Dana is performing.

Slater appears more and more frequently, until he appears to be David's constant companion, "a nightmarish, comedic monster from his unconscious," in the words of one critic, though, of course, no one else in the family sees him. Slater therefore becomes a symbolic embodiment of the male ego, a self-absorbed bachelor whose wife has left him, and whose misogyny threatens to lead David astray. But David will not be led to the dark side. One critic speculated that perhaps David's saintly patience, his "steely will at resisting" Slater's baiting him, may explain why "Dana is so bored with him." Critic Andrew Sarris aptly described the film's central conflict as the "titanic moral contest between the eternal husband and the eternal bachelor in every man." *Film Comment* praised the Lucas screenplay for its "Buñuelian ease at blending the stuff of daydreams with waking life."

In his *Premiere* review, Glenn Kenny praised the film as being "intelligently written and beautifully acted throughout." Believing that other reviewers had undervalued the film, Andrew Sarris claimed in the *New York Observer* that *The Secret Lives of Dentists* was "the most passionate defense of monogamy and marriage from a male perspective" that he had ever seen in an American movie. The issue of fidelity is central to any domestic melodrama, but arguably Rudolph probes the issue more successfully than even Stanley Kubrick did in *Eyes Wide Shut* (1999). At least the viewer is better able to view the dynamic of this threatened marriage from the inside out, even though Dana's adulterous partner is never seen clearly. The audience senses that Dana is somehow alienated from her daughter Leah (Cassidy Hinkle), which, perhaps, suggests something about her commitment to the marriage. On the other hand, Dana is never demonized for her presumed indiscretion. The family is pulled together by something as mundane as a bout of intestinal flu. A small climax and turning point is achieved when Leah finally allows herself to be hugged and comforted by her mother.

Andrew Sarris, who established his critical credentials by evaluating and ranking American directors, considered *The Secret Lives of Dentists* the "most coherent and most convincing achievement" of Rudolph's 30-year career, concluding that the film had already earned a place on his ten-best list for the year. Even in his early work, Rudolph showed a talent for constructing elaborate fantasies, a talent that is successfully harnessed in *The Secret Lives of Dentists*. In the past, Rudolph had critical support for several projects, but not often or as extensively as for this remarkable adaptation.

In his *New Republic* review, Stanley Kauffmann approached the film "cautiously," realizing that Rudolph's "past work has been spotty." But, Kauffmann added, Rudolph's "stress here on familial sovereignty is moving, as is his direction of the three children." This is a very knowing film that embraces the wisdom Rudolph had accumulated over 20 years of married life with photographer Joyce Rudolph. The substance of the film is about what Jane Smiley has called the "ironic middle." In his *New York Times* review

Elvis Mitchell observed that "families in flux, nuclear and otherwise, are consistently at the heart of Mr. Rudolph's pictures."

Rudolph commented in the *Washington Post* that, "whether they work out or not," marriages are difficult and perhaps even unnatural. He added, "To put two people together intentionally for life, for truth, for real is . . . probably the highest-risk [endeavor] of anything in society, and yet, of course, so commonplace." The film celebrates the victory of the commonplace over the exotic and of the rational over the irrational. It constitutes an original and perhaps even unique accomplishment that deserves high marks for its basic decency. It also deserves a wider audience than the film enjoyed.

—*James M. Welsh*

CREDITS

David Hurst: Campbell Scott
Dana Hurst: Hope Davis
Slater: Denis Leary
Laura: Robin Tunney
Dr. Danny: Kevin Carroll

Origin: USA
Released: 2002
Production: Campbell Scott, George Van Buskirk; Holedigger Films, Ready Made Film; released by Manhattan Pictures International
Directed by: Alan Rudolph
Written by: Craig Lucas
Cinematography by: Florian Ballhaus
Music by: Gary DeMichele
Sound: William Sarokin
Music Supervisor: Jonathan McHugh
Editing: Andy Keir
Art Direction: Anna Louizos
Costumes: Amy Westcott
Production Design: Ted Glass
MPAA rating: R
Running time: 104 minutes

REVIEWS

Boxoffice. November, 2002, p. 129.
Chicago Sun-Times Online. August 1, 2003.
Entertainment Weekly. August 8, 2003, p. 54.
Los Angeles Times Online. August 1, 2003.
New York Times Online. August 1, 2003.
People. August 18, 2003, p. 37.
Premiere. July/August, 2003, p. 24.
USA Today Online. August 1, 2003.

Variety Online. September 17, 2002.
Washington Post. August 15, 2003, p. WE33.

QUOTES

David (Campbell Scott) about wife Dana (Hope Davis): "I wish she would look at me with desire instead of regret."

AWARDS AND NOMINATIONS

Ind. Spirit 2004: Support. Actress (Davis)
N.Y. Film Critics 2003: Actress (Davis).

Shanghai Knights

A Royal Kick In The Arse.
—Movie tagline

Box Office: $60.4 million

Something's afoot in the Forbidden City in Peking, China in 1887. Someone has designs on the Imperial Seal which is guarded by Chon Lin's (Singapore pop star Fann Wong) father and to get it, the villain is more than willing to commit murder. As a result, despite Chon Lin's valiant martial arts efforts, her father is murdered and the seal stolen.

Meanwhile, in Carson City, Nevada, sheriff Chon Wang (Jackie Chan) has been so successful taming the wild west that he actually uses a stamp that says "Arrested" to mark the status of the many wanted posters in town. But then one day he gets a letter from his sister Lin. She tells him of their father's death and how she has tracked the murderer and the seal to London. Chon will quickly do his filial duty and come to his sister's aid.

First, however, he must go to New York City to get some travelling cash from his friend Roy O'Bannon, who has been busy investing their money. Unfortunately for Chon, Roy has misspent most of the money publishing pulp novels like "Roy O'Bannon and the Mummy" in which he is the hero and Chon his trusty sidekick. And while the books sell well, he doesn't seem to be making money from them for now he is nothing more than a waiter in the Ritz Hotel, although he does do quite a side business in womanizing . . . especially the mayor's daughters. This last miscalculation

quickly has Roy escaping New York City and accompanying Chon to London.

In England we quickly realize that the seal stealer and murderer is none other than an aristocrat of the realm, Lord Rathbone (Aidan Gillen of BBC's "Queer as Folk"), tenth in line to the throne and a favorite cousin of Queen Victoria. So what on Earth does he want with the Chinese Imperial Seal? Well, it's a part of a deal he has made with Wu Chan (Donnie Yen) an exiled member of the Chinese royal family. Wu will help Rathbone become King of England by arranging for the assassination of the nine family members in line in front of him, including the Queen, and Rathbone will give him the seal which will make Wu the new Emperor of China.

Consequently, not only do Chon and Lin have to avenge their father's death and retrieve the seal, they now have to uncover and foil the plot against the royal family. To do this they have a little help not only from Roy, who quickly falls in love with Lin, but also from a Dickensian street urchin named Charlie (Aaron Johnson) and a seemingly bumbling Scotland Yard Detective named Artie Doyle (Thomas Fisher) who, in reality, has highly polished deductive skills.

The route to the film's finale has a number of stops along the way. One stop is the Jubilee Ball for the queen at Rathbone's country estate where Roy takes his name from a nearby clock—Sherlock Holmes—and Chon becomes an Indian Raja from the Nevada Province. There is a careening car ride that ends with a crash into Stonehenge. Stops also include the Puss 'N' Boots Boarding House in Whitechapel—the haunt of Jack the Ripper; Madam Toussaud's Wax Museum; and eventually up the heights of Big Ben. (And while revelations about Charlie and Doyle are almost groaner surprises, finally finding out what "really" happened to Jack the Ripper was a hoot.)

As anyone who has ever seen a good Jackie Chan movie knows, the plot is really nothing more than a framework on which to hang his incredible action sequences. These bloodless ballets that pass themselves off as to-the-death fights are really highly inventive dances choreographed to include anything and everything that is lying around the set. A revolving door through which Chon must exit immediately becomes a wheel of mischief in which characters actually exchange clothing. In Jackie Chan's mind a seemingly sedate library becomes a swashbuckler's paradise what with its sliding ladders and secret entrances. Everything from globes to vases to books becomes a weapon of one kind or another. And wouldn't Gene Kelly have loved that Jackie Chan does as an homage to "Singin' in the Rain" in a Covent Garden-like setting that involves using the food stall's canvass roofs as trampolines and includes the obvious umbrellas?

But these creative "fight" scenes are just one ingredient in a successful Jackie Chan movie. Another is sight gags.

One of the best involves Roy and Chon running down a White Chapel street streaming feathers behind them because they've just been involved in a pillow fight with a few ladies of the evening (see, even the sex is funny in his movies). Another has Roy, bound and dangling upside down in the background, being dipped in and out of water as Chon fights in the turnstile that control's Roy's altitude and fate.

But what sends Chan's best movies over the top is the way all the physical action is punctuated by comic banter and throwaway lines. This is where Owen Wilson comes in. His laid-back, surfer-dude persona is perfect for dispensing his lines in such a sly or goofy way that the delivery is often funnier than the dialogue.

Jackie Chan is a delightfully open actor whose appeal lies as much in his silly putty face as it does in his kick-ass martial arts ability. He is graceful and silly, a powerful cream puff. He is capable of communicating an almost innocent belief in Boy Scout virtues like honesty and dependability and loyalty. These are all virtues Wilson's Roy can easily live without but at the same time, in Wilson's capably comic hands, Roy is never craven or unlikable. We may pity him a little, but we never despise him.

Because of this, Chan and Wilson have an effortless chemistry together. These guys are obviously having fun and are an inspired team to watch in action—far superior to that of Chan and the shrieking Chris Tucker in the *Rush Hour* movies. While a sequel to the original *Rush Hour* is basically inexplicable, a sequel to Wilson's and Chan's 2000 *Shanghai Noon* was on the drawing board before the first film was even released.

The result is a movie as good or maybe even better than the first . . . and certainly better than Chan's last film, the lame *The Tuxedo*. And while there are a few things one wishes the filmmakers had not done (such as the use of totally out of place music like The Who's "Magic Bus" and The Zombies' "Time of the Season"), viewers will probably be pleased that they have also set the stage for yet another sequel. This one set in Hollywood.

—*Beverley Bare Buehrer*

CREDITS

Chon Wang: Jackie Chan
Roy O'Bannon: Owen C. Wilson
Rathbone: Aidan Gillen
Chon Lin: Fann Wong
Wu Chan: Donnie Yen
Queen Victoria: Gemma Jones
Chon Wang's father: Kim Chan
Charlie: Aaron Johnson
Artie Doyle: Thomas Fisher
Jack the Ripper: Oliver Cotton

Origin: USA
Released: 2003
Production: Gary Barber, Roger Birnbaum, Jonathan Glickman; Spyglass Entertainment; released by Touchstone Pictures
Directed by: David Dobkin
Written by: Alfred Gough, Miles Millar
Cinematography by: Adrian Biddle
Music by: Randy Edelman
Sound: Ian Voigt
Editing: Malcolm Campbell
Art Direction: Giles Masters, Anthony Reading
Costumes: Anne Sheppard
Production Design: Allan Cameron
MPAA rating: PG-13
Running time: 107 minutes

REVIEWS

Chicago Sun-Times Online. February 7, 2003.
Chicago Tribune Online. February 7, 2003.
Entertainment Weekly. February 14, 2003, p. 51.
Los Angeles Times Online. February 7, 2003.
New York Times Online. February 7, 2003.
People. February 17, 2003, p. 34.
USA Today Online. February 7, 2003.
Variety Online. January 26, 2003.
Washington Post. February 7, 2003, p. C1.

QUOTES

Roy (Owen Wilson): "I'm a 30-year-old gigolo. Where's the future in that?"

TRIVIA

Filmed on location in the Czech Republic.

The Shape of Things

Seduction Is An Art.
—Movie tagline

Relationships between the sexes are full of deceit and manipulation in Neil LaBute's uncompromising films, and *The Shape of Things* is his boldest experiment since his controversial debut film, *In the Company of Men*. In that earlier film, LaBute followed the immoral exploits of two men who decided to seduce and abandon a mousy secretary at their firm, pumping up her ego in order to deflate her. In *Your Friends and Neighbors*, LaBute wove a web of sexual betrayal and intrigue among several couples. After detours into lighter but quirkier fare with *Nurse Betty* and *Possession*, LaBute returns to his original themes in *The Shape of Things*, but with the shoes on the other feet. This time it's a woman who's the chief manipulator.

The new film, like his earlier efforts, is all words and little action—basically a filmed stage play, with only four speaking parts. And the dialogue is more than a little contrived. But it's also terribly clever—all part of LaBute's no-holds-barred send-up of the way in which needy people manipulate themselves and others in the service of love.

The film opens in a museum, where fine arts graduate student Evelyn (Rachel Weisz) is taking pictures of a sculpture of a classical nude male figure. When she climbs over the rope around the statue, she catches the attention of museum guard Adam (Paul Rudd), a fellow student who is working part-time at the museum. Evelyn exudes defiance, but in a coy manner, wondering what will happen if she refuses to step back from the statue. Adam says he's not sure. Evelyn then produces a can of red spray paint. There's a fig leaf over the statue's genitals, and she says that offends her because it makes the art "untrue," and she implies she's going to deface it. Adam says his shift is over, and he leaves, but not before asking for Evelyn's phone number. Since neither of them has a pen, she spray-paints it on the inside of his scruffy sports coat.

In the next scene, Evelyn and Adam are talking on campus. At the museum, Evelyn told Adam he was cute but needed to do something with his scraggly hair. He's already trimmed it so it's neater, and Evelyn is flirting with him. Adam's a shy, nerdy guy, and he's not used to this kind of attention from such a provocative, sexy woman. She tries to get him to kiss and become passionate in public, and he balks. He wonders why she's attracted to him, and she stalks off, saying the only thing that's not attractive is that he has such self-doubts.

Evelyn is a challenging handful, but she's also a godsend to Adam, whose lack of self-confidence has prevented him from making much progress romantically. In particular, he's failed for three years to connect romantically with Jenny (Gretchen Mol), and now it's too late. Jenny has announced her wedding engagement to Phillip (Frederick Weller), who is Adam's former roommate from freshman year. The two couples go on a double date, and afterwards Phillip and Evelyn get into a huge fight when Evelyn insists that the defacement of the statue, which has been in the news, might have been an artistic statement, a "manifesto." Phillip, who's a cocky male chauvinist, sees the act as simply mindless vandalism. Asked by Evelyn for her opinion, Jenny

seems to lack the courage to say anything at all. Adam is mortified.

It's a first test for Adam. Evelyn challenges him on why a jerk like Phillip is his friend, and it's clear that it's another example of Adam's passive approach to life. Adam is overwhelmed by the pleasures of having a woman as smart and sexy as Evelyn as a girlfriend, and he's willing to go along with her radical ideas—like videotaping their lovemaking.

Evelyn's influence on Adam changes him rapidly. He loses the scraggly hair and scruffy clothes, replaces his glasses with contact lenses, and begins to see himself as an attractive person. Jenny notices the change too. Jenny calls Adam for a meeting in a park and she confesses to him her worries about Phillip—Phillip is suddenly acting so nice that Jenny is suspicious he's seeing another woman, because that was the case on the only other occasion when he acted this way. Jenny has doubts about Phillip, but now she's also overwhelmingly attracted to Adam. She's always liked him, but now that he has been remade by Evelyn's love, he is irresistible to her. And so they kiss—and then agree to go to the beach to "bury" their attraction, since each of them is already spoken for.

Jenny unwisely tells Phillip about the kiss—but LaBute implies there was more to disclose than just the lip-lock. Now Phillip and Adam fight. Phillip is unhappy about Jenny's dalliance, and he is outraged that Adam has finally gotten rid of his plaid "lumberjack" jacket that Phillip says cost them a lot of potential dates in freshmen year. The two friends are now enemies.

Evelyn wants Adam to get plastic surgery—a nose job to correct what she sees as a small defect—and she continues to slyly use her seductive powers to get him to comply. Adam is eager to please her despite his doubts. And when she asks him to make the ultimate sacrifice to repair the damage he has done by his dalliance with Jenny, he is eager to comply. LaBute sets up his surprise ending perfectly. We know that Evelyn is a shameless manipulator, but we have no idea until the elegant payoff just what she's really been up to.

This is not for the emotionally faint-hearted or conventional filmgoer. As with LaBute's earlier films, he is eager to raise challenging questions about ethical behavior in interpersonal relationships. He's interested in showing not only how willing Adam is to change his physical appearance, but how his need and desire for the love of Evelyn change his morals as well. As he grows more confident, he exchanges his former honesty for a more flexible ethical outfit. He's willing to lie and cover up, to deceive and betray his friends, in order to maintain the love that he feels he needs. And LaBute wants us to see that this behavior, which makes him more "normal," may in fact be reprehensible.

The Shape of Things is cleverly written. All four characters are gentle satires on partially formed young adults. Phillip is an uncaring egotist, but his air of superiority masks a deeper insecurity. Jenny, who appears to be a sweet and submissive type, actually is a cauldron of passionate emotions. Adam is a hollow vessel, allowing himself to be shaped into a cunning pawn. Evelyn is a parody of the radical performance artist, who is willing to do anything in the service of her art, but the real intrigue in the film is to what extent she is morally culpable or driven by her own unmet desires.

Adapted from his theatrical script—which had been performed on stage by the same four actors—LaBute has written some wonderfully funny and provocative dialogue, allowing us to see the perversities of what passes for normal conversation. He's like a teacher giddily presenting a lesson plan in ethics, but who makes the medicine go down easily. His ensemble cast helps immensely. Rudd is compelling as the object of Evelyn's attention, a barely grown boy-child eager to lap up his girlfriend's affections and to bend his fallow mind around her challenging ideas. A less believable, more cynical Adam would have ruined this picture; but Rudd makes us believe both in Adam's naivete and his eventual moral slipperiness; he is a totally sympathetic victim, but in LaBute's view that makes him even more open to critical examination.

Weller is hilarious as Adam's opposite—a smug jerk who doesn't seem to have many moral compunctions. He provides plenty of needed comic relief. Mol is terrifically understated as the compliant, slow-burning Jenny, but her character could have benefited from a little more complexity.

Weisz is the emotional and moral center of the film, and she carries the day with a complex performance that never crosses over into abject villainy. Her Evelyn is brave and heartless, unbending in her artistic quest, and believably cunning. Her seductiveness never lapses into parody, but always teeters on its edge. Only her militant feminist artistry seems a bit cliched.

LaBute knows what he is doing, but his film suffers from its usual static nature. The camera is observant of its characters but the film never provides any escape from its own, sometimes ponderous, moralism. With farces like *Nurse Betty,* LaBute proved he is capable of more cinematic directing, but *The Shape of Things* seems cramped and dry—more like a lecture in psychology than a movie.

In some ways, LaBute is reminiscent of the master surrealist Luis Bunuel in that he is capable of exposing the hypocrisies inherent in everyday human interaction—the lies and pretense that pass for normality. But LaBute completely shuns the fantasy and dream elements and the other artistic trappings of surrealism. In form his films are more like the moral medicine of an Ingmar Bergman, stark in their insistence on exposing the cruelty of human relationships.

The Shape of Things is a masterfully written and well-acted cinematic essay on human ethics, and it's clever enough to be watchable, but it lacks the kind of tension, drama, and memorable images that give film its vitality. LaBute has to find a way to do what David Mamet has done—make his stagey, talky dramas come alive on the screen. LaBute likes to explore the impact of the mundane, but the plot devices on which the film turns—a bandaged nose, a new jacket—are static and one-dimensional. The challenge for LaBute is to take the kind of delightful set-up he has concocted—an inventive form of emotional sadism—and illustrate it with a broader, more complex and more engaging cinematic story. Now that would be a movie—because there is virtually no one braver and more thoughtful than LaBute when it comes to delving into the dark side of love.

—*Michael Betzold*

CREDITS

Adam: Paul Rudd
Evelyn: Rachel Weisz
Jenny: Gretchen Mol
Philip: Frederick Weller

Origin: USA
Released: 2003
Production: Neil LaBute, Gail Mutrux, Philip Steuer, Rachel Weisz; Working Title Productions, StudioCanal, Pretty Pictures; released by Focus Features
Directed by: Neil LaBute
Written by: Neil LaBute
Cinematography by: James L. Carter
Music by: Elvis Costello
Sound: Richard E. Yawn
Editing: Joel Plotch
Art Direction: Christopher H. Lawrence
Costumes: Lynette Meyer
Production Design: Lynette Meyer
MPAA rating: R
Running time: 96 minutes

REVIEWS

Chicago Sun-Times Online. May 9, 2003.
Entertainment Weekly. May 16, 2003, p. 50.
Los Angeles Times Online. May 9, 2003.
New York Times Online. May 9, 2003.
People. May 19, 2003, p. 38.
USA Today Online. May 9, 2003.
Variety Online. January 20, 2003.
Washington Post. May 9, 2003, p. WE49.

Shattered Glass

Read between the lies.
—Movie tagline

He'd do anything to get a great story.
—Movie tagline

 Box Office: $1.9 million

From the time Stephen Glass joined Washington's venerable and prestigious magazine the *New Republic* in 1995, he wowed colleagues and readers alike with an uncanny knack for ferreting out especially fascinating people who said or did particularly fascinating things. His articles were cleverly written, rich with telling detail and studded with wonderful quotes, all of which made the pieces highly readable and often quite memorable. Glass got noticed, which led to freelance assignments from other high profile publications, including *Harper's, Rolling Stone,* and *George.* What those who marveled at the young writer's ability did not know until 1998 was that there was definitely a secret to his success in finding such great material: he made most of it up. At first he would invent material to jazz up or buttress a piece, and then he moved on to creating complete fabrications. He wrote vividly about people who did not exist and occurrences that never took place. Since a reporter's job is to dig up—not make up—his stories, Glass, once a rising star, ended up a disgrace to his profession by the time he was twenty-five. The highly involving *Shattered Glass* effectively tells the story of his journey from promise to pariah, from fabulous to fabulist.

There are two major questions most people will ask: why did Glass do it, and how did he get away with it for as long as he did at such notable periodicals? When writer and first-time director Billy Ray began work on *Shattered Glass* (which is based upon a 1998 *Vanity Fair* piece by Buzz Bissinger), he consulted Glass's editors and fellow writers in order to understand and accurately portray how such a thing happened. (Glass declined any involvement in the project, remaining mum until May of 2003 when he made an appearance on *60 Minutes* to plug his mediocre novel, which barely fictionalized these events.) Seeing here how Glass went about his deception sheds more than a little light on his peculiar reasoning, as well as on how things were able to get so out of hand.

As portrayed by Hayden Christensen (Anakin Skywalker in 2002's *Star Wars: Episode 2—Attack of the Clones*), Glass comes off as bright and boyish, nerdy and needy. He loves what he does and is good at it, but he still insecurely strives to gain the approval of others. To insure that he garners this much-needed approbation, he apparently engages in conscious, calculated manipulation of those around him, his motivation seeming more pathetic than sinister. Glass compliments and flatters. "That necklace is you!" he enthuses. "That lipstick is the bomb!" he gushes. (After making such comments, he then frets that someone will think he is gay.) Glass delights colleagues with his retention of personal bits of information mentioned long ago or in passing. He arranges assistance for two female coworkers who need to purchase shower gifts. He both asks for and offers guidance, assistance, and praise. While much of this ingratiation may come off as grating to the viewer, the staff (particularly the women) at the *New Republic* found his unctuousness rather sweet and endearing. Everyone seems to have wanted to go easy on immature, vulnerable Glass, the youngest member of a uniformly young *New Republic* "family," because he came off not as a pompous, know-it-all kisser-of-behinds but as a fragile psyche trying too hard. As fellow writer and staunch friend Caitlin Avey (Chloe Sevigny of 2000's *American Psycho*) tries to explain at one point, "We're all he has!" Over and over, we hear Glass's plaintive cries of "Did I do something wrong?" and "Are you mad at me?" In story conferences, he entertainingly pitches his ideas, clearly basking in the glow of his colleagues' admiration, and then tries to clinch their support by pitifully muttering things like "It's silly, I'll probably just kill it" or "I don't even know if I'm going to finish it." Yes, he is obviously working them, but one also clearly senses here a deep-seated need for reinforcement and stroking.

So in his continued neurotic strivings, Glass began to try to ensure that the applause not only continued but increased by allowing himself to embellish a little here and there. At first it was just a quote or bit of information that could turn a good piece into a jaw-dropping grand slam. Michael Kelly (Hank Azaria of 2001's *America's Sweethearts*), recently killed covering the war in Iraq but at the time the magazine's charismatic editor who was revered by Glass and the rest of the staff, gently questioned Glass when the first red flag was raised. We are shown how agile Glass's mind is, how he is able to lie his way out of trouble with masterful (not to mention disconcerting) ease. The film steadily gains momentum as things begin to unravel for Glass. He has written a particularly sensational piece entitled "Hack Heaven," in which he has given himself the green light to fabricate an entire piece from beginning to end. It is this thoroughly "cooked" story that cooks Glass's goose. When Adam Penenberg (Steve Zahn of 2001's *Joy Ride*), a reporter for web-based *Forbes Digital Tool,* is berated by his editor (Cas Anvar) for letting stodgy old *New Republic* get the scoop on the hacker story, Penenberg ends up uncovering an even bigger story when he discovers that absolutely nothing in Glass's article checks out. Penenberg contacts the *New Republic,* and the shattering of Glass begins.

Even though Glass created, in more than one sense of the word, his own predicament, you cannot help but feel some sympathy for him as he struggles to forestall the revelation which will ruin him. He crafts a fake website to try to prove a nonexistent company's existence. He prints business cards for someone he invented. He claims to have legitimate phone numbers and e-mail addresses for his fictitious contacts, although he cannot seem to find them all just now amongst his notes. He has his brother in California place a call and pose as one of these bogus sources. Glass then tries to wriggle his way out of things by claiming that he is the victim here, unwittingly duped by deceitful sources. There is an extremely potent, extended close-up of the *New Republic*'s new editor, Chuck Lane (excellent, versatile Peter Sarsgaard of last year's *K-19: The Widowmaker*), as the truth and the enormity of the situation finally sink in. There is also the powerful scene in which Lane orders Glass to accompany him to the place where the events chronicled in "Hack Heaven" supposedly occurred, and we uncomfortably anticipate the inevitable and painful moment for both men when Glass finally cracks.

As Glass finally falls to pieces, the film becomes more and more a story about Lane coming into his own. Since being elevated from writer to editor, he has had to deal with the resentment and jealousy of the other writers, who think him undeserving and who are still bemoaning the departure of the immensely popular Kelly. We watch as Lane, faced with the unexpected and highly significant problem Glass has created, slowly but surely rises to the occasion. He is warned that many at the magazine might resign in support of Glass. Lane emerges as a strong, fair, and forceful voice for an ethical adherence to truth. In another excellent sequence, Lane goes through back issues of the *New Republic* and scrutinizes all of Glass's articles with newly-opened eyes, and as the magazines stack up on the floor, so rises Lane's outrage and certitude. It is revealed that Glass fabricated all or part of twenty-seven of the forty-one pieces he wrote for the *New Republic*, not to mention those for other publications. When Lane fires Glass, a close-up of the sniffling writer reveals that he is, indeed, shattered: utterly devastated and at a complete loss for what to do next. He hints at thoughts of suicide, which might be sincere or might be a last-ditch effort at eliciting sympathy. Lane clearly thinks it is the latter: "Stop pitching, Steve," he says. "It's over." Once Glass's supporters on the staff realize the extent to which he lied, both in his work and to them, they rally around Lane.

Shattered Glass was originally to be made for HBO and then was turned down by almost two dozen independent film studios before arriving at Lions Gate. Made on a budget of $6 million, the film only grossed about a third of that in limited release. Critical reaction, however, was quite positive. Endeavoring to tell this true story about reporters at work in as engrossing a manner as possible, Ray viewed *All the President's Men* (1976) dozens of times. Although the source material here is not nearly as dramatic or consequential, Ray unquestionably succeeds in fashioning a clear, fair, accurate, and compelling account, having committed himself to "the cinematic equivalent of good reporting." Christensen creates a fascinating, complex, highly-believable characterization of the talented and troubled Glass; Sarsgaard's understated yet commanding performance is also laudable, and he deservedly received a Golden Globe nomination; and the rest of the cast is entirely effective. The message here about the importance of ethics and responsibility in journalism is of even greater interest now in light of Jayson Blair's recent troubles at the *New York Times*. It is an important cautionary tale, successfully illuminated through *Shattered Glass*.

—*David L. Boxerbaum*

CREDITS

Stephen Glass: Hayden Christensen
Chuck Lane: Peter Sarsgaard
Caitlin Avey: Chloe Sevigny
Andie Fox: Rosario Dawson
Amy Brand: Melanie Lynskey
Adam Penenberg: Steve Zahn
Michael Kelly: Hank Azaria
Rob Gruen: Luke Kirby
Kambiz Faroohar: Cas Anvar
Marty Peretz: Ted Kotcheff
Lewis Estridge: Mark Blum
Caterina Lane: Simone-Elise Girard
David Bach: Chad E. Donella

Origin: USA
Released: 2003
Production: Craig Baumgarten, Adam Merims, Gaye Hirsch, Tove Christensen; Cruise-Wagner Productions, Forest Park Pictures; released by Lions Gate Films
Directed by: Billy Ray
Written by: Billy Ray
Cinematography by: Mandy Walker
Music by: Mychael Danna
Sound: Pierre Blain
Editing: Jeffrey Ford
Art Direction: Pierre Perrault
Costumes: Renee April
Production Design: Francois Seguin
MPAA rating: PG-13
Running time: 99 minutes

REVIEWS

Boxoffice. November, 2003, p. 96.
Chicago Sun-Times Online. November 7, 2003.
Entertainment Weekly. November 7, 2003, p. 50.
Los Angeles Times Online. September 7, 2003.
Los Angeles Times Online. October 31, 2003.
New York Times Online. October 19, 2003.
New York Times Online. October 31, 2003.
People. November 10, 2003, p. 38.
Rolling Stone. November 13, 2003, p. 106.
USA Today Online. October 31, 2003.
Variety Online. September 3, 2003.
Washington Post. Novmeber 7, 2003, p. WE44.

QUOTES

Stephen Glass (Hayden Christensen): "Are you mad at me?"

AWARDS AND NOMINATIONS

Natl. Soc. Film Critics 2003: Support. Actor (Sarsgaard)
Nomination:
Golden Globes 2004: Support. Actor (Sarsgaard)
Ind. Spirit 2004: Cinematog., Film, Screenplay, Support. Actor (Sarsgaard).

Sinbad: Legend of the Seven Seas

 Box Office: $26.4 million

The "traditional" animated film is becoming more and more a rarity on the big screen, thanks to the enormous success of recent computer-animated films (*Monsters, Inc., Ice Age, Shrek, Finding Nemo*) and the relative failure of high-profile traditional animation (*Atlantis, Treasure Planet*). In fact, Disney closed its Florida-based animation studio following the disappointing performance of the films recently produced there, choosing to focus more on the kinds of blockbuster computer-animated films it has co-produced with Pixar Animation Studios (a partnership that will end in 2006). This is not to say that traditional animation for the big screen has been abandoned altogether, as Disney in particular has produced a few recent hits (*Lilo &*

Stitch, Brother Bear—though the latter was more of a moderate success). However, with each failure, studios have begun to reach the consensus that audiences have lost interest in old-style animation. Unfortunately, DreamWorks' *Sinbad: Legend of the Seven Seas* did not alter that perspective. Despite having voice talent from several big-name stars (and a marketing campaign that tried to use that talent as a box office draw), *Sinbad* was a huge box office disappointment. Though it performed poorly, the movie is actually quite entertaining. While it does not measure up to the best Disney films, *Sinbad* is a better-than-average film, richly animated, fast-paced, and infused with some thoughtful themes about friendship and sacrifice.

Of course there are number of tales about Sinbad the sailor, many of which have been told in previous movies, but in this version Sinbad (voiced by Brad Pitt) is a pirate and sailor living in a mythic (and often anachronistic) ancient world where the hub of human civilization is the city of Syracuse. Sinbad once lived in Syracuse, where he became good friends with Proteus (Joseph Fiennes), the son of King Dymas (Timothy West), but one day he left the city to set out on a life of sailing the seas. When the story begins, ten years have passed since Sinbad left Syracuse, and we first meet him as his ship bears down on a vessel under Proteus's command. Sinbad intends to steal the Book of Peace, a powerful and invaluable tome that Proteus is taking back to Syracuse (the film never explains where the Book had previously been located or why it is being moved now). When Sinbad and Proteus meet, Proteus tries to appeal to their past friendship to dissuade the pirate from stealing the Book, but Sinbad does not change his mind.

However, before Sinbad can take the Book and sail away, the two ships suddenly come under attack from a sea monster. The crews defeat the creature, but Sinbad is pulled from the ship and sinks into the sea, where he comes face to face with Eris (Michelle Pfeiffer), the Goddess of Chaos. The seductive goddess, who is the villain of the story, offers to spare Sinbad's life and make him a very wealthy and powerful man if he will bring her the Book of Peace. She tells Sinbad she likes him because he is, like her, ruthless and "doesn't have a heart." Sinbad says the deal sounds good, but only if Eris will keep her word.

After returning to his ship, Sinbad and his crew accompany Proteus back to Syracuse. There they are introduced to Marina (Catherine Zeta-Jones), Proteus's fiancé, who coyly asks Sinbad, "Which are you? A thief or a hero?" The question is obviously central to the story, and it is a question most savvy viewers know will predictably be answered by the end of the film. During this relatively quiet sequence of the movie, Proteus and Marina share a moment in which the differences in their personalities foreshadow their future together. Marina gazes out at the sea and wonders at its beauty, while Proteus stands in awe of the tower his father built to house the Book of Peace. The two care for each other deeply, but Proteus tells Marina he does not want her to marry him just because their marriage was arranged for them years before; he wants her to be with him if that is what she truly desires.

Meanwhile, Eris shows up to create trouble. Disguising herself as Sinbad, she enters the tower and steals the Book of Peace. Syracuse immediately feels the effects, as the city grows dark and loses its beauty. Everyone assumes Sinbad stole the Book (a logical assumption), so he is arrested and informed he will be put to death if he does not return it. When Sinbad protests that he is innocent, Proteus actually believes him and claims "the right of substitution," offering to take Sinbad's place while the pirate retrieves the stolen Book. The downside is that if Sinbad fails to return with the Book in ten days, Proteus will be executed in his stead.

When Sinbad sets sail, he tells the crew they're headed for Fiji, despite the protests of the first mate, Kale (Dennis Haysbert), who tries to remind Sinbad of his debt to Proteus. However, Sinbad soon discovers that Marina is on board the ship, intending to make sure he gets the Book. Sinbad refuses to take responsibility, saying that he didn't steal the Book and he didn't ask Proteus to intervene, but Marina persuades him to change his mind with several large diamonds. When Sinbad announces to the crew that they're going to sail for Tartarus, the realm of Eris, Kale suspects that Sinbad's acceptance of Marina's bribe was a cover-up to protect his ruthless reputation.

What follows is a series of adventures as they meet danger after danger on the way to Tartarus (some of the obstacles are sent by Eris herself). Though Marina and Sinbad start off as rivals who engage in constant verbal sparring, Marina soon endears herself to the crew when she saves them all from the mesmerizing, seductive wiles of a group of water Sirens in a treacherous passage called the Dragon's Teeth. After an encounter with a giant sea creature that initially appears to be an island and a confrontation with a monstrous snowbird, Sinbad and Marina acknowledge the inevitable—that they are attracted to each other. Sinbad even admits to Marina that the reason he left Syracuse ten years before was that he became jealous of Proteus when Marina first arrived by ship one day.

When Sinbad finally reaches Tartarus, a haunting realm just beyond the edge of the world where rolling sand dunes cover and then uncover ancient wrecked ships, armies turned to stone, and a ruined city, Eris taunts him and insists that he has a cold heart, that he would never do anything self- lessly. Marina protests that Eris is wrong, but the goddess is so sure of herself that she promises Sinbad she will return the Book of Peace if he will answer one question truthfully. "If you don't get the Book, will you go back to die?" she asks. Sinbad answers that he will, but the test of his truthfulness lies before him. He and Marina find themselves back on the ship, without the Book. Ironically, it is now almost as if the characters of Sinbad and Marina are reversed, for Sinbad

intends to return to Syracuse, but Marina urges him not to. "I can't watch you die," she says. "I love you."

The climactic scenes of the story are fairly predictable. Sinbad returns to Syracuse just in time to save Proteus. When he takes Proteus's place and rests his head on the chopping block, abruptly Eris arrives to intervene. Enraged that Sinbad has proven her wrong, the goddess is bound to her promise and returns the Book. The world subsequently returns to normal, King Dymas apologizes to Sinbad, and Syracuse celebrates. Proteus, ever the gentleman, tells Ma- rina that her heart lies with the sea (though unspoken, he also knows her heart belongs to Sinbad) and that she should follow her heart. She does just that, sailing away with Sinbad when he sets out on his next adventure.

One of the more interesting things to note about *Sinbad,* in terms of its characters, is that Proteus in many ways exemplifies the traits of a hero more so than Sinbad. Proteus is unfailingly kind, loyal, and selfless. His past friendship with Sinbad means more to him than it means to Sinbad (or so it seems), and he believes in Sinbad even when he probably shouldn't. He literally lays his life on the line to protect his old friend, trusting that Sinbad will find and retrieve the Book of Peace. He clearly loves Marina, but he displays no jealousy when he realizes she would rather be sailing the seas with his rival. In short, Proteus is a perfect example of the virtues of true love. Ironically, he is also not as interesting a character as Sinbad, probably because he is a static character who has nowhere to go—or grow. Still, his heroic sensibilities serve to provide an appropriate standard by which Sinbad's character can be judged.

Sinbad, in contrast, initially appears to be something of an anti-hero, one who claims only to be concerned about himself, even when he sees the self-sacrificial behavior of his old friend Proteus. However, even with Sinbad's protesta- tions that he "is not responsible," and even with Eris's claims that he has no heart, it is rather clear to the viewer (as it is to Kale and eventually to Marina) that he does have a con- science just waiting to be lured out into the open. Therefore, his development throughout the story holds no surprises. Still, the final test of his character does raise an ethical question that is worth pondering, and his decision to go back to Syracuse and face certain death is not simply a token gesture. The question is not a simple one, and certainly not one whose relevance is limited to an audience of children: "Would you lay down your life for a friend?"

Visually, the most exciting sequences in *Sinbad* are those involving the deadly encounters at sea. The sea crea- tures, the Dragon's Teeth and the Sirens, the snowbird, and the eerie landscape of Tartarus are all lively, colorful, dy- namic scenes, testaments to the power of animation. The city of Syracuse is a place of wonder, but compared to much of the rest of the film it seems oddly lacking in depth and detail, as do some of the minor characters, who seem to be less carefully drawn. The story, too, is not as rich or complex as those of the best animated films, but it is more sophisticated than most. In fact, there is a kind of sensual ambience throughout the film that is apt to be missed by younger audiences: Eris, for example, moves very seductively and openly admits her attraction to Sinbad. Even some of the humor is targeted more toward adult audiences: one scene offers a glimpse of Sinbad's buttock, while in another Sinbad tells large-chested Kale to "put a shirt on before you poke someone's eye out." Moments like these are genuinely humorous, if for no other reason than that they would probably never be seen or heard in a Disney film.

Overall, *Sinbad: Legend of the Seven Seas* is full of imagination, capable of taking the viewer on an enjoyable, energetic ride. Although it is not as memorable an experience as *Finding Nemo*, it is also not a movie that should be labeled as another "nail in the coffin" for the future of non-computer-animated films.

—*David Flanagin*

CREDITS

Sinbad: Brad Pitt (Voice)
Marina: Catherine Zeta-Jones (Voice)
Eris: Michelle Pfeiffer (Voice)
Proteus: Joseph Fiennes (Voice)
Kale: Dennis Haysbert (Voice)
Dymas: Timothy West (Voice)
Rat: Adriano Giannini (Voice)

Origin: USA
Released: 2003
Production: Mireille Soria, Jeffrey Katzenberg; released by Dreamworks Pictures
Directed by: Tim Johnson, Patrick Gilmore
Written by: John Logan
Music by: Harry Gregson-Williams
Sound: Andy Nelson, Anna Behlmer
Editing: Tom Finan
Production Design: Raymond Zbach
MPAA rating: PG
Running time: 86 minutes

REVIEWS

Boxoffice. June, 2003, p. 28.
Chicago Sun-Times Online. July 2, 2003.
Entertainment Weekly. July 11, 2003, p. 60.
Los Angeles Times Online. July 2, 2003.
New York Times Online. July 2, 2003.
People. July 14, 2003, p. 36.
USA Today Online. July 2, 2003.
Variety Online. June 30, 2003.

Washington Post. July 2, 2003, p. C1.

QUOTES

Eris (Michelle Pfeiffer): "Enough talking! Time for some screaming."

The Singing Detective

When it comes to murder, seduction and betrayal, he wrote the book. Now he's living it!
—Movie tagline

In 1986, British television aired Dennis Potter's six-part mini-series, *The Singing Detective*. The series was generally considered to be fine, perhaps even great television. Lisa Schwarzbaum called it a "masterpiece." A. O. Scott of the *New York Times* wrote that it was "the kind of television production that justifies the existence of the medium—a gloomy, episodic swirl of old pop music, film noir and psychological subtext that rewards repeated viewing."

How does one follow up such an unequivocal success? For Potter, the follow-up was to do pretty much the same thing. He wrote a screenplay for a film version of *The Singing Detective*. Two years later, in 1994, he died. Nearly ten years later that screenplay finally made it to the screen. It's difficult if not impossible to find a critic who thinks that the big-screen version of the story is an improvement over the original. Actually, it's odd that Potter was so eager to dabble in movies again because he'd already had bad luck in that medium. Another of his BBC miniseries, *Pennies From Heaven*, was made into an unsuccessful movie starring Steve Martin. Supposedly Potter hated the adaptation.

If nothing else, *The Singing Detective* offers a chance to see two handsome Hollywood leading men in an anti-vanity project. The film's protagonist, Dan Dark (Robert Downey Jr.) suffers from psoriatic arthropathy (a condition with which Potter also suffered). The disease makes moving the limbs difficult, if not impossible, and causes the patient to be covered with a mess of painful, ugly welts. As Dark describes it, he looks like "a human pizza." Director Keith Gordon (*Waking the Dead*, *A Midnight Clear*) doesn't shy away from pushing his camera right into Dark's face. Many scenes start or end with an extreme close-up of Dark's red, crusty, lumpy face. Suffice it say, he is not looking his usual dapper self.

Mel Gibson, one of the producers of the film (along with Bruce Davey and Steven Haft), isn't looking so great either. Hospital psychologist, Dr. Gibbon (Gibson), is a short, stocky man with a messy comb-over and the kind of glasses that make his eyes appear huge. It's quite a bit of fun to watch Gibson reveling in being so owlish and nerdy. He's actually quite a good actor and, if he weren't busy being one of the world's top leading men, he could have had a successful career as a character actor.

But the biggest acting kudos belong to Downey. Most critics, even if they hated the film, had a kind word for the actor. Bob Campbell of the *Newark Star-Ledger* commended Downey's "virtuoso work." Jonathan Foreman of the *New York Post* wrote, "It is worth catching *The Singing Detective* to see the brilliant Robert Downey Jr. in another extraordinary performance." Kevin Thomas of the *Los Angeles Times* called it "a boldly theatrical portrayal that represents a personal career high watermark." And *Entertainment Weekly*'s Schwarzbaum wrote that the actor "is great in a role no one less magnetically reckless would dare approach." Even covered in welts, Downey is a fascinating and appealing presence. He's witty, verbal, angry and bitter. When attractive Nurse Mills (Katie Holmes) needs to put ointment onto a very personal body part, Dark recites a list of unsexy thoughts to keep the encounter non-embarrassing. "Denim accessories," he mutters in a staccato fashion. "Organic pizza crust."

Frustrated by his pain (both emotional and physical), Dark lashes out at everyone. When he's sent to see Dr. Gibbon, he chides the doctor for sitting on the edge of his desk, "Little men shouldn't sit where their feet don't touch the floor." He's even meaner to his ex-wife Nina (Robin Wright Penn). He imagines that she is having an affair and when she finally gets the courage to visit his hospital room, he screams at her.

Dark is a novelist who writes old time detective novels, the kind in which people are called things like gumshoes and dames. One of them, *The Singing Detective,* he plans to resell as a screenplay. Dark is refusing pain drugs for his condition and his agony causes him to lapse in and out of fantasy and paranoia. He gets the idea that Nina and her new lover have stolen his screenplay and plan to sell it themselves. He also lapses into fantasies in which he imagines scenes from his unmade film. These sequences star the people that populate his real life present and past. For example, the all-purpose bad guys in his imaginary film (Adrien Brody and Jon Polito) are some men that Dark encountered on a bus ride as a boy.

Without any warning, people in the film are apt to burst out into big musical numbers. While Dark is being examined by a group of hospital staff, including the chief of staff (Alfre Woodard) and skin specialist (Saul Rubinek), the lights fade and they suddenly burst out in song. In these fantasies, Dark also appears without his skin problem as a handsome confident crooner. (In the film version, the songs from the 1940s have been switched out for songs from the 1950s.) In all of this hubbub, there are also flashbacks to Dark's past to explain how he became this kind of man. We see the young Dark hiding in the barn behind his parents' rundown gas station in the middle of nowhere. While he's hiding, his mother (Carla Gugino) sneaks in with his father's partner (Jeremy Northam) and has sex with him.

There's a lot thrown up there on the screen. The result is that the film is intermittently entertaining but never quite works as a whole. The parts that work are the scenes between Gibson's folksy, yet oddly effective doctor and Downey's reluctant patient. Also good are Downey's harangues. "I'm a prisoner in my own skin," he rails. At one point he becomes so frustrated, he starts crying, only to find that his own tears burn his skin.

The film wasn't a big hit with critics, nor with audiences. Scott of the *New York Times* concluded, "A lot has been lost in translation. On its way to the big screen, Potter's intricate, fascinating story has shrunk. The ideas that lurked in the mini-series' shadows and alleyways are now placed squarely in the spotlight, where they look obvious and thin." Thomas of the *Los Angeles Times* observed, "Even though Downey and Gibson rise to their challenging roles and have solid support, this *Singing Detective* is too flat and academic to come alive." Ron Stringer of the *LA Weekly* felt that "Potter's script pares down to virtual nothing the very narrative threads that allowed us, in the full-length version, to identify with his prickly protagonist, and knocks us upside the head with a hyperkinetic, disorienting first act from which audiences—especially those approaching this material cold—are unlikely to recover."

—*Jill Hamilton*

CREDITS

Dan Dark: Robert Downey Jr.
Nicola/Nina/Blonde: Robin Wright Penn
Dr. Gibbon: Mel Gibson
Mark Binney: Jeremy Northam
Nurse Mills: Katie Holmes
First Hood: Adrien Brody
Second Hood: Jon Polito
Betty Dark/Hooker: Carla Gugino
Skin specialist: Saul Rubinek
Chief of staff: Alfre Woodard

Origin: USA
Released: 2003
Production: Mel Gibson, Steven Haft, Bruce Davey; Icon Productions, Haft Enterprises; released by Paramount Classics
Directed by: Keith Gordon
Written by: Dennis Potter
Cinematography by: Tom Richmond
Sound: John Nutt
Music Supervisor: Ken Weiss
Editing: Jeff Wishengrad
Costumes: Patricia Norris
Production Design: Patricia Norris

MPAA rating: R
Running time: 109 minutes

REVIEWS

Boxoffice. April, 2003, p. 73.
Entertainment Weekly. October 31, 2003, p. 55.
Los Angeles Times Online. October 24, 2003.
New York Times Online. October 24, 2003.
People. November 3, 2003, p. 36.
Variety Online. January 19, 2003.
Washington Post. November 7, 2003, p. WE51.

QUOTES

Dan Dark (Robert Downey Jr.): "Words make me want to hold my breath. Who knows what they're going to say. Who knows where they've been?"

Something's Gotta Give

After a lifetime of going from girl to girl, the ultimate bachelor is about to encounter something new.
—Movie tagline

Box Office: $121.9 million

In *Something's Gotta Give,* writer-director Nancy Meyers (*What Women Want*) brings Diane Keaton and Jack Nicholson together in one of the year's best romantic comedies. Keaton, who has enjoyed a lengthy and illustrious Hollywood career (*The Godfather, Annie Hall, The First Wives Club*), delivers another Oscar-worthy performance as long-divorced, Broadway playwright Erica Barry. As a middle-aged woman who is used to being self-sufficient, Erica finds her quiet life disrupted by matters of the heart when she discovers she has two very different men pursuing her romantically.

When Erica arrives at her vacation home in the Hamptons with the intention of getting some writing done, she's shocked to discover her beautiful daughter, Marin (Amanda Peet), there with a much older man. Harry Sanborn (Jack Nicholson) is a wealthy, record label executive and famous bachelor in his sixties who is known for dating women half his age. In fact, he prides himself on never having dated a woman older than thirty.

Although Erica isn't thrilled about her daughter dating this devilish playboy, she invites them to stay for dinner—a situation that soon turns uncomfortable for Harry when Erica and her feminist sister (Frances McDormand) grill him about his preference for younger women. Later that evening, Harry suffers a mild heart attack while he's fooling around with Marin, and he's rushed to the hospital where a young, handsome doctor (Keanu Reeves) attends to him. It turns out that Dr. Julian Mercer is a huge fan of Erica's plays and he's thrilled to meet her. Meanwhile, Harry shuffles around the hospital with his bare tush hanging out the back of his gown (much to the audience's amusement).

Upon Harry's release from the hospital, he's not healthy enough to travel and must recuperate at Erica's beach house, while Marin returns to her job as a Christie's auctioneer in the city. Of course, this arrangement conveniently allows for Harry and Erica to spend a lot of time together. Just as the two are getting to know each other better and realizing that they have much in common, Erica is surprised when Julian asks her out on a date. After suffering through a long dating drought, Erica suddenly finds herself rediscovering love with not one, but two potential suitors.

Ultimately, Erica has her heart broken by one of the guys, which inspires her to write a successful play called "A Woman to Love." It's a phrase she picked up from one of her suitors and a fitting title for her new play, which is clearly based on events that took place in the Hamptons and which allows her to get revenge on the man who let her go. Specific details won't be given away here, but the scene in which the heartbreaker sees the play and recognizes himself is downright hilarious. The movie then swings through Manhattan, the Caribbean, and Paris before Erica finally ends up with the right man.

Above all, *Something's Gotta Give* is blessed with a brilliant cast. The performances from the leads as well as the supporting actors in this movie are first-rate. Both Keaton and Nicholson bring so much experience and heartfelt nuance to their roles that they're convincing as these middle-aged characters who take a late chance on love. Although some critics carped that Nicholson was just playing himself, he excels as a randy, old skirt-chaser who conceals a more tender and serious side. However, the film clearly belongs to the delightful Keaton. Smart, funny, and vulnerable, Keaton steals every scene she's in and brings everyone around her up to her level. With wide critical acclaim, a Golden Globe Award, and an Oscar nomination, Keaton is at the top of her game with her portrayal of an independent-minded woman who finds that life can be full of surprises and joy—at any age.

The excellent supporting cast includes Frances McDormand in a humorous performance as Erica's no-nonsense sister and a professor of women's studies. It's too bad that her character doesn't get more screen time, because she has some of the wittiest lines in the film. Amanda Peet turns in a fine performance as Erica's daughter, and Keanu Reeves is solid (and gorgeous) in his role as the smitten doctor. Actor-director Jon Favreau also appears in a few entertaining scenes as Leo, Harry's long-suffering assistant.

Amusing and refreshing, *Something's Gotta Give* was a hit with both moviegoers and critics. Reviews were overwhelmingly positive with critics hailing the fine acting—especially Keaton's performance. However, the film had a few detractors who cited the long run time as a weak point. Overall though, that's a small quibble for a polished film that truly delivers as an adult romantic comedy. In his review for the *Chicago Sun-Times*, Roger Ebert wrote: "[Nicholson and Keaton] bring so much experience, knowledge, and humor to their characters that the film works in ways the screenplay might not have even hoped for." Tom Long of the *Detroit News* also gave the film high praise, stating that "*Something's Gotta Give* is a well-felt celebration of romantic, emotional, and physical maturity, filled with laughs and tears. It's also something of a revelation when it comes to Diane Keaton's range. This may be a career-topping performance, but it's also proof that the best may be yet to come."

Hollywood would be wise to note that moviegoers happily embraced a film featuring a mature romantic relationship. Perhaps *Something's Gotta Give* will be the start of a new trend. It wouldn't be such a bad thing—especially if it involves the impressive team of Jack and Diane.

—*Beth Fhaner*

CREDITS

Erica Barry: Diane Keaton
Harry Sanborn: Jack Nicholson
Dr. Julian Mercer: Keanu Reeves
Marin Barry: Amanda Peet
Zoe: Frances McDormand
Dr. Martinez: Rachel Ticotin
Dave: Paul Michael Glaser
Leo: Jon Favreau
Kristen: KaDee Strickland

Origin: USA
Released: 2003
Production: Bruce A. Block, Nancy Meyers; Columbia Pictures, Warner Bros., Waverly Films; released by Columbia Pictures
Directed by: Nancy Meyers
Written by: Nancy Meyers
Cinematography by: Michael Ballhaus
Music by: Hans Zimmer
Sound: Art Rochester
Music Supervisor: Bonnie Greenberg
Editing: Joe Hutshing

Art Direction: John Warnke
Costumes: Suzanne McCabe
Production Design: Jon Hutman
MPAA rating: PG-13
Running time: 124 minutes

REVIEWS

Chicago Sun-Times Online. December 12, 2003.
Detroit News. December 12, 2003, p. E1.
Entertainment Weekly. December 12, 2003, p. 56.
Los Angeles Times Online. December 12, 2003.
New York Times Online. December 12, 2003.
People. December 22, 2003, p. 27.
USA Today Online. December 12, 2003.
Variety Online. December 5, 2003.
Washington Post. December 12, 2003, p. C1.

QUOTES

Julian (Keanu Reeves): "You must beat them away with a stick." Erica (Diane Keaton): "No, no, men my age . . ." Julian: "Men your age may be really stupid. Did you ever think of that?"

TRIVIA

Nancy Meyers wrote the part of Harry specifically for Jack Nicholson.

AWARDS AND NOMINATIONS

Golden Globes 2004: Actress—Mus./Comedy (Keaton)
Natl. Bd. of Review 2003: Actress (Keaton)
Nomination:
Oscars 2003: Actress (Keaton)
Golden Globes 2004: Actor—Mus./Comedy (Nicholson)
Screen Actors Guild 2003: Actress (Keaton).

Spider

The only thing worse than losing your mind, is finding it again.
—Movie tagline

 Box Office: $1.6 million

David Cronenberg's bleak *Spider* has the studied, stifling air of a silent film. It might as well be silent, since its tortured protagonist, "Spider" Cleg (Ralph Fiennes), hardly ever speaks an intelligible word; instead, he mumbles gibberish or halting fragments of language. And Cronenberg's compositions are sparse, elemental, striking, and old-fashioned. In many shots, Cleg is in his bare room, scribbling in his journal. In one, he is standing by a low wall where it joins a slanted ceiling, and Cronenberg lights the shot so that Spider's shadow makes a 45-degree turn at the wall joint, evoking the ancient cinematic shorthand for a cramped or distorted personality. There are many moments like this, scenes and shots that employ classic cinematic visual language.

It's quite a departure for Cronenberg, who has always been a modernist and has usually delighted in filling the screen with astoundingly disturbing and barely palatable grotesques. Like many of Cronenberg's films, however, *Spider* is demanding and difficult to watch. Not that there are his customary gruesome visuals, but, perhaps even more disturbing than those, there is an emotional landscape of intense fear and despair, one from which the filmmaker offers audiences absolutely no respite.

The title character never gets any respite, either, from the horrors that haunt him. We first meet him getting off a train in London's South End, but only after Cronenberg's camera has wheeled through a bustling crowd of normal, functioning, and busy departing passengers. Cleg descends the steps of the train and picks his way across the platform, and then down city streets, with the gingerly, defensive mannerisms of a frightened visitor to a strange planet. He picks up bits of odd litter or cigarette butts along the way, and his hunched and wary posture bespeaks a human being totally lost and befuddled in his environment.

He is on his way from an asylum to a halfway house run by Mrs. Wilkinson (Lynn Redgrave), who is later described by one of the residents as the tyrant queen of an island where the inhabitants are protected from the world. But if her whims are defied, she has the power to send any resident back to the asylum. After he checks in, Cleg, at Mrs. Wilkinson's insistence, takes a bath in a tub of rusty water. There's a haunting shot of him curled up in a semi-fetal position in the tub, unmoving, terrified.

Cronenberg's direction and Fiennes's performance combine to create one of the most disturbing and powerful characterizations of crushed, confused humanity ever put on film. We become totally immersed in Spider's life-as-a-waking-nightmare. Fiennes shuns the kind of scenery-chewing grandstanding or exaggerated tics and quirks that mark most actors' portrayals of characters whose sanity is precarious. Instead, he folds his face, his body, his gestures, and his vocalizations in upon himself, creating a being who is totally defensive, so stifled by fear that to even contemplate having a personality is unthinkable. His every movement speaks totally of defeat, and he is unremittingly mournful and forlorn.

Cronenberg puts Spider in shadows, in corners, up against walls, under tunnels, and even when he is outside he seems to huddle against the landscape, his physical presence crushed and overwhelmed by the world. The soundtrack takes us subtly into Spider's world as well. A bit reminiscent of David Lynch's *Eraserhead* but less abrasive, the ambient sound contains hissing, whirring, and machine-like clattering. This can be explained by the presence of a gas works across the canal from the halfway house, but it evokes the kind of mental noise that presumably has never stopped washing through Spider's brain. And only the end of the film explains why that sort of noise would be ever present for him.

Based on a novel by Patrick McGrath, who adapted it for the screen himself, *Spider* is more successful as a character study than as a psychological puzzler. The protagonist's prize possession is a journal, which he hides carefully and writes in assiduously. It is filled with pages and pages of scribbles not identifiable as any language, but a hieroglyphic alphabet of his own invention. In between scenes of him writing in his journal, usually on his dresser in his cramped room or atop his suitcase as he is sitting on his bed, Spider revisits scenes from his childhood, in which he observes himself as a boy (played by Bradley Hall).

Cronenberg has Fiennes looking through windows, crouching in corners, or sitting at tables in pubs as the storyline plays out in his memory and in front of our faces. Some of these scenes could have been cloying or hackneyed—since this is a cinematic device that has been used many times before—but the combination of Fiennes's astoundingly disturbing demeanor and the director's brilliant composition makes most of these scenes compelling.

Playing in these mental tableaux are the boy's memories of crucial scenes with his mother (Miranda Richardson) and father (Gabriel Byrne). His parents' sexual relationship inexplicably is something that is of paramount importance to Spider. He is close to his mother, who feeds his fascination for webs. The boy constantly has a cat's cradle in his hands, and his bedroom is intricately strung with ropes and strings fashioned into weblike structures. Hall, whose face is round and shiny, his eyes wide open, and his attitude one of unspoiled vulnerability, is perfect in the role.

Spider's view of his mother is relayed in several scenes: Spider catches his mother modeling a new nightgown she has bought to please her husband; he spies out the window as his father begins pawing at her before they even leave the courtyard to go out together; and he converses with her as she puts on lipstick. Cronenberg gives us just enough of this material to make the Oedipal attraction obvious without overdoing it and making it laughable.

Another key scene has Spider sent to the local pub to fetch his father for dinner. There, a crude, witless tart (also played by Richardson) flashes her breasts at him, apparently traumatizing the boy, especially since he later uncovers—or imagines—his father's affair with the floozy. It is a measure of Cronenberg's mastery in presenting this simple yet difficult tale that the surprise twist to the boy's story—and the revelation of the source of his disease—comes as a genuine shock.

As psychology, however, the story is farfetched. It is a fantasy that demands a severe suspension of disbelief. But it is carried off so magnificently that it almost works. There is a beautiful spareness to the storyline and to the way it is filmed, but it is not enough to overcome questions about why this is all playing out at this time in Spider's life. Is this his constant preoccupation, to mull over and write about this material? Or, by writing this down, is he uncovering memories and "making progress," as his fellow resident asks? And, if so, why now? What is it about his present situation that is releasing him, or immersing him further, in his pain? Is this a voyage of self-discovery?

The film is murky on these points, and maybe it's by design. Perhaps more literal, conventional explanations would wring the thin plot dry. The decision to rob Spider of language, and the ability to convey in words the unfolding of his childhood trauma, is an intriguing one. If he were writing in real words in his journal, the audience might understand more. But then the film might end up being as pat as, say, *A Beautiful Mind*, which provides a satisfactory answer to each of the protagonist's mental quirks. *Spider* is all the more disturbing because it doesn't use language to explain the mental web in which its lead character is inextricably caught. At the same time, it's frustrating not to know or to understand more. In the end, the audience is trapped too.

In most storytelling, on film or not, revelations usually lead to explanations and then conclusions. There is the satisfaction of learning something salutary. Daringly, Cronenberg denies us all of that. He takes us into a bleak world and offers no relief—and even when the explanation for all that troubles Spider is fully revealed, it is seen to be utterly useless. There is no possibility of rehabilitation, let alone redemption.

This is probably why the high hopes for this film—it was originally to be released in 2002, in time for Oscar nominations—were doomed to be dashed. Fiennes's performance is brilliant, but because it offers us nothing to like or admire in the character, nor anything to redeem him, it probably won't get many accolades. The always-dependable Richardson deftly manages a rather remarkable triple portrayal. Only Byrne, who always seems too likeable to be a cad or a villain, seems a little out of step in this bewildering universe.

Whereas Cronenberg in the past often seemed to be riffing Luis Bunuel and other surrealists, here his bleak, unsparing efforts are worthy of Ingmar Bergman, but without the sermonizing in which the great Swedish director always seemed prone to indulge. *Spider* is a brave and often brilliant step back into classic, slow, excruciatingly intense cinema—the undaunted cinema of brutal character study and unrepentant tragedy. It offers us no way out.

—Michael Betzold

CREDITS

Dennis "Spider" Cleg: Ralph Fiennes
Yvonne/Mother/Mrs. Wilkinson: Miranda Richardson
Bill Cleg: Gabriel Byrne
Young Spider: Bradley Hall
Mrs. Wilkinson: Lynn Redgrave
Terrence: John Neville
Freddy: Gary Reineke
Gladys: Sara Stockbridge
John: Philip Craig

Origin: Canada, Great Britain
Released: 2002
Production: David Cronenberg, Samuel Hadida, Artists Independent Network; Capitol Films, Grosvenor Park, Andreas Klein; released by Sony Pictures Classics
Directed by: David Cronenberg
Written by: Patrick McGrath
Cinematography by: Peter Suschitzsky
Music by: Howard Shore
Sound: Glen Gauthier
Editing: Ronald Sanders
Art Direction: T. Arrinder Grewal
Costumes: Denise Cronenberg
Production Design: Andrew Sanders
MPAA rating: R
Running time: 98 minutes

REVIEWS

Boxoffice. August, 2002, p. 55.
Boxoffice. February, 2003, p. 29.
Chicago Sun-Times Online. March 14, 2003.
Entertainment Weekly. March 7, 2003, p. 49.
Globe and Mail. September 29, 2001, p. R8.
Los Angeles Times. December 8, 2002, p. E14.
Los Angeles Times Online. December 20, 2002.
New York Times Online. February 23, 2003.
New York Times Online. February 28, 2003.
People. March 10, 2003, p. 37.
Rolling Stone. March 20, 2003, p. 74.
Sight and Sound. January, 2003, p. 12.
USA Today Online. February 28, 2003.
Variety. May 27, 2002, p. 28.
Washington Post. March 14, 2003, p. WE41.

AWARDS AND NOMINATIONS

Genie 2002: Director (Cronenberg)
Nomination:
Genie 2002: Adapt. Screenplay, Art Dir./Set Dec., Costume Des., Sound.

Spirited Away (Miyazaki's Spirited Away) (Sen to Chihiro—No Kamikakushi)

 Box Office: $10 million

It is difficult to get film critics to agree on much of anything. What was fresh and charming to some critics about the French film *Amelie* was cloying and cutesy to others. Amazingly, though, the critics were nearly unanimous in their praise of *Spirited Away*. On *Rotten Tomatoes.com*, a web site dedicated to compiling movie reviews, 99 percent of the critics gave the film a positive review. That kind of agreement is a rare thing. Apparently Hollywood agreed as well: the film won an Oscar in 2003 for best animated feature. After the attention at the Academy Awards, *Spirited Away* was given wider release in American theaters in hopes of spreading the film to a larger audience. In Japan, where director Hayao Miyazaki is from, the film was the largest grossing film ever.

Prior to the relative success of *Spirited Away*, Miyazaki was largely unknown to the American public, except for fans of Japanese anime. His films like *My Neighbor Totoro*, *Kiki's Delivery Service*, and *Princess Monoke* garnered him cult success in America. Disney decided that it might be possible to cash in on his success and decided to distribute *Spirited Away* in America under the supervision of John Lasseter (*Toy Story*) and Kirk Wise (*Beauty and the Beast*). The company promoted the film as "Disney's *Spirited Away*" to the chagrin of some purists, who were also disappointed by the fact that in translating the film for American audiences, some of the characters overexplain their actions. Some of the explanations are necessary, however. When one character, for example, comes upon a building that has a sign that surely must say "Bathhouse," she says aloud, "It's a bathhouse." Perhaps it's not the smoothest moment in the film,

but for Americans who are unfamiliar with the look of a Japanese bathhouse, not to mention unable to read the sign, it's a big help.

Critics compared *Spirited Away* to Miyazaki's earlier films as well as to *The Phantom Toll Booth*, but the most frequent comparison was to *Alice in Wonderland*. Indeed, ten-year-old Chihiro (voiced by Daveigh Chase of *Lilo and Stitch*) does enter a world every bit as odd and off-kilter as Lewis Carroll's.

Chihiro is pouting in the back seat of the car as her parents (Michael Chiklis and Lauren Holly) drive her to their new home. She clutches some flowers that a friend gave her and complains that she liked her old school just fine. Her dad decides to take a shortcut and the family ends up by an old building with a mysterious tunnel. Chihiro is scared to go in the tunnel but her parents insist it will be an adventure.

On the other side, the family finds what they believe to be an old abandoned amusement park. There are beautiful buildings and a street full of empty attractions. Chihiro's portly father smells some good cooking odors drifting down the street and follows the smell until he gets to a counter full of food. Chihiro's mom surveys the food and says, "Looks delicious!" (This is one of those moments that doesn't translate exactly to American audiences since prominently displayed on one of the plates is a big fish head.) Although there is no one working at the counter, mom and dad dig in, insisting that they will pay the owner whenever she or he gets back. Ravenous, they gobble down the food.

While they are eating, Chihiro steals away to explore a bit. She meets a boy, Haku (Jason Marsden), who is a little older than she is and who tensely warns her to get back before the sun sets. Chihiro rushes back to her parents, but is shocked to find that they have been turned into large pigs. This would be the point where the story turns weird. She meets Haku again and he tells her that the only way she can rescue her parents is to ask for a job from Kamaji (David Ogden Stiers). Kamaji is a multi-armed creature who runs the boiler room and has turned little bits of soot into tiny creatures that can load coal into the fire. The coal critters are just the first of an array of strange beings in this place.

Chihiro discovers that she is in a bath house that is for spirits. It's run by Yubaba (Suzanne Pleshette), an old woman with a gigantic head. Her one love, besides money and power, is her gigantic baby. In a typically fanciful touch, her baby is so large that he lives in a warehouse-sized room with people-sized dolls as playthings. Reluctantly, Yubaba agrees to give Chihiro a job working in the bathhouse with Lin (Susan Lin). Yubaba makes Chihiro sign a contract stealing the girl's name and gives her the new name Sen. The frightened Chihiro cries herself to sleep.

As Chihiro plots how she is going to save her parents, she is put through various tests in this strange land. Her first bath client is a Stink Spirit, a creature so vile that the other workers flee to plug their noses. Using spunk, creativity, and bravery, Chihiro is able to survive and succeed in her task. In this strange world, Chihiro has to rely solely on her intuition because it's hard to tell who is good and who is evil. She is warned that Haku is a bad guy who's become Yubaba's henchman and has to figure out if she should trust him or not. A mysterious creature called No Face is similarly perplexing. It helps Chihiro with the Stink Spirit, but also goes on a eating rampage, angrily eating several bath house workers.

Half the fun of the film is seeing the various forms that these apparitions take. The Stink Spirit, for example, is a slow moving bubbling pot of what looks to be excrement. Yubaba's thugs are a set of three bouncing green heads. Some of the bathhouse guests include giant baby chicks and a creature resembling a sumo wrestler with two trunk-like appendages protruding from its head. The group is reminiscent of the crowd that populated the *Star Wars* cantina.

Another big part of the fun is the look of the film. Miyazaki uses a combination of hand drawn animation and computer-generated images. The result is an ever-shifting mix of surreally precise details with more impressionist, painterly images. The details of the plants in the film are notably realistic. An azalea bush, which has nothing to do with the action in the film, is lovingly rendered, with lush, dark pink blossoms fairly bursting off the screen. It's obvious that making his film look beautiful is just as important to Miyazaki (if not more so) as telling his story.

Chihiro is a suitably plucky heroine. Sure, she can conquer lots of monsters and pass many difficult tests, but it's a nice touch that when the movie begins she is whiney and frightened. Even after she's in the new world, she spends quite a bit of time crying and feeling scared.

The critics enjoyed themselves thoroughly. The *Boston Globe*'s Wesley Morris described the film as "a surrealist picture book that renders obsolete a shopworn term like 'cartoon.'" "You could dream for years on the visual grace notes hiding in this movie," he continued. Elvis Mitchell of the *New York Times* called *Spirited Away* "epic and marvelous," while the *San Francisco Examiner*'s Jeffrey M. Anderson describes it "as gently frightening and superbly enchanting as any movie I can remember." Lou Lumineck of the *New York Post* considered the film praiseworthy enough to describe it as "such a landmark in animation that labeling it a masterpiece seems almost inadequate."

—*Jill Hamilton*

CREDITS

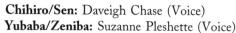

Chihiro/Sen: Daveigh Chase (Voice)
Yubaba/Zeniba: Suzanne Pleshette (Voice)
Haku: Jason Marsden (Voice)
Lin: Susan Egan (Voice)

Kamaji: David Ogden Stiers (Voice)
Chihiro's mother: Lauren Holly (Voice)
Chihiro's father: Michael Chiklis (Voice)
Assistant Manager: John Ratzenberger (Voice)
Boh: Tara Strong (Voice)

Origin: Japan
Released: 2001
Production: Toshiro Sunzuki, Donald W. Ernst, Tokuma Shoten; Studio Ghibli, Dentsu; released by Buena Vista
Directed by: Hayao Miyazaki
Written by: Hayao Miyazaki
Music by: Joe Hisaishi
Sound: Shuji Inoue
Editing: Takeshi Seyama
Art Direction: Youji Takeshige
Production Design: Norchu Yeshida
MPAA rating: PG
Running time: 124 minutes

REVIEWS

Chicago Sun-Times Online. September 20, 2002.
Los Angeles Times Online. September 20, 2002.
New York Times Online. September 20, 2002.
San Francisco Chronicle. September 20, 2002, p. D5.
Variety Online. September 18, 2002.
Washington Post. September 20, 2002, p. WE47.

QUOTES

Zeniba (Suzanne Pleshette): "Nothing that happens is ever forgotten, even if you can't remember it."

AWARDS AND NOMINATIONS

Oscars 2002: Animated Film.

Spun

The sun rises and sets a handful of times on a grungy group of crystal meth addicts in L.A. in Swedish director Jonas Akerlund's frenetic feature debut. Renowned music video director for the likes of Madonna, Prodigy, and Ozzy Osbourne, Akerlund underscored the jumped up world of speed aficionados in post-production, making

5,435 film cuts, earning him a world record amid comparisons to the arguably superior *Requiem For A Dream*. Topping the constant cutting are graphic animations, souped-up sound effects, and bleached-out images that add to the drugged out experience lived by the equally animated cast of characters. The existence of these varied group—who go days on crank without sleep—is best embodied by the constant images of the never-closing eye that crop up everywhere in the film. Like the unblinking eye that sees all but never comments, Akerlund wisely never judges his characters but manages to honestly portray the gritty underground meth world that avoids becoming too bleak thanks to a healthy, and ultimately necessary, dose of humor.

With her green dog, evoking an Irma La Douce-like decadent innocence, Brittany Murphy's Nikki is a stripper whose boyfriend is The Cook (Mickey Rourke). A sort of amoral alchemist, The Cook spins over-the-counter medications into crank and casually migrates from motel room to motel room after accidentally torching them in the process. An equally decadent couple, the aptly tattooed Spider Mike (John Leguizamo) and his girlfriend Cookie (Mena Suvari) sell the Cook's stuff and among their motley cohorts is the pock-marked, video-game addicted Frisbee (Patrick Fugit). Good-boy-gone-bad Ross (Jason Schwartzman) gets caught in the undertow of their meth world when he drops by looking to score one day and, due to the fact he is the only one with a running car, ends up becoming chauffeur and escort for Cook and Nikki.

While Ross ventures off on endless, and often aimless, meth-fueled trips with Nikki in his broken down Volvo through the pouring sun of the L.A. Valley to procure the myriad of non-prescription pills for Cook, pieces of his current and former life begin to unspool in various ways. Ross's current girlfriend April (Chloe Hunter) is also a stripper and co-worker of Nikki's whom he leaves tied up and gagged with heavy metal music blaring in his own seedy motel room while on his drug-related sojourns, sometimes for days at a time. Though adding a highly disturbing edge, it is clear Ross isn't actually all that sadistic but merely absent-minded, which enrages the helpless April even further. It isn't April that preoccupies most of Ross's thoughts anyway, however, as he is still in love with his ex-girlfriend Amy (Charlotte Ayana), to whom he owes money and who clearly left him as his addiction grew. Other than snorting crank, most of Ross's time is spent futilely obsessing about how to get Amy back while leaving her rambling, incoherent phone messages. Ross's fantasy world and real life blend during sometimes pornographic and definitely disturbing animated sequences that appear when Ross is inhaling lines of meth.

The plot mainly revolves around Ross's desperate descent into addiction, while also chronicling the lives of the lost souls in his orbit. Interesting subplots include the varied relationships of the characters and their quest for sex and drugs, not necessarily in that order. Cook and Nikki argue when her beloved green Taco inhales too many meth fumes and has to be rushed in Ross's bedraggled Volvo to the vet. Alternating between WWF wrestling and his very specific taste in porn while mixing up the meth in his tubes and beakers, Cook both barks gruffly and mumbles incoherently while warning Ross against fooling around with Nikki, as the two are apparently growing closer. Meanwhile, Spider Mike is engrossed in his semi-paranoid fantasies about being ripped off and watched by the cops while his slovenly girlfriend complains about their lack of intimacy. During a particularly hyper-realistic bathroom scene with a long-constipated Cookie, Spider Mike's timing is perfectly off when he is finally able to rouse a bodily reaction of his own and where, comically, a black sock takes the place of the missing Cookie, now locked out of their bedroom.

Another humorous subplot involves the reticent Frisbee, who lives in a trailer with his morbidly obese mother and becomes the unwitting target of two strung-out narcotics policeman (Alexis Arquette and Peter Stormare) whose movements are being filmed by a reality cop show. The two inept detectives strap a wire on the frightened teenager who reluctantly goes back to Spider Mike's lair where a lascivious and fuming Cookie, reeling from her near miss at satisfaction with her boyfriend who remains besocked in the bedroom, aims to seduce the unsuspecting and very miked Frisbee.

The film winds to a close as Ross is dispatched on a mission to bring Cook into downtown Los Angeles to meet the Man (Eric Roberts), who finances Cook's operation. While in the city, Ross wangles a face-to-face meeting with Amy, who agrees to see him merely because he promises her the money he owes her. Whatever Ross's romantic fantasies about seeing Amy again, they quickly unravel when she gets a load of the now seriously strung-out Ross who hands her a mere one hundred of the four hundred dollars she is owed. While many of the characters continue to spin their wheels at the film's close, Nikki actually manages to leave, boarding a bus headed out of town, albeit for Las Vegas.

Among the more meaty of the amusing cameos is Debbie Harry's lesbian phone sex operator and next-door neighbor of Ross who manages to come to April's rescue. Roberts also shines as the highly flamboyant man's Man. In the music arena, Rob Halford of Judas Priest turns up as a porn shop clerk who drops the dime on steady customer Cook while Billy Corgan, who also provided original music for the soundtrack, makes an appearance as a doctor. Ubiquitous porn legend Ron Jeremy may be seen as a bartender.

More importantly, *Spun* brings back Rourke in a major way with an effortlessly cool performance that is easily the film's best. Although far from a character stretch, Rourke's baddie here is much less calculated or self-consciously detached than some of his previous heavies and he seems to slide into this perfectly worn-in character as easily as the battered, white cowboy boots he wears throughout the film.

Lead Schwartzman manages to completely divorce himself from the long shadow of *Rushmore*'s precocious Max Fischer, and he plays the college dropout with a bad habit to a tee, conveying the schizophrenic nature of the user who talks about quitting even while shooting up, his urgent longings for his old girlfriend and dying Volvo the only discernable connections to his previous, middle-class life. Even while losing his tenuous ties with decency—duct taping his stripper girlfriend's eyes and mouth shut while she's bound to the bed—Schwartzman manages to make Ross sympathetic, seemingly almost unaware of the harm he's doing to April. Murphy glides through the film lightly, providing an appealing, upbeat performance and a surprisingly sane point of view. Nikki likes Ross because he seems a decent sort in their decadent world and indeed the two seem almost kindred spirits—that is until she finds out about what he admitted doing to April. Then it is Las Vegas stripper Nikki who finds she has the moral high ground and informs baby-faced, one-time college student Ross that although she once thought so, he is indeed not "normal" after all. The two also provide an undeniable, offbeat chemistry in their many scenes together.

Leguizamo could not be more perfectly cast, his manic energy providing all the reality necessary to portray a meth junkie/dealer. The actor is also credited with the creative idea to use a black sock in his solo bedroom scene. However, both Suvari, with her greasy hair, brown teeth and grungy pajamas, and Fugit, as a pizza-faced near-idiot, are perfectly cast against type with just as wonderful results.

Shot in Los Angeles in a mere 22 days, the $2.8 million independent film was originally intended to be a documentary and is based on the true story of the film's writer (with co-writer Creighton Vero) and former meth addict Will De Los Santos who acted as the driver of a methamphetamine cook for three days in Eugene, Oregon. Much of the film's bleak moodiness came during the laborious post-production process of adding the myriad cuts, special effects, and innovative soundtrack. Akerlund seems adept at these technical aspects, but they add little to the pitch perfect performances of the characters that litter the bleached L.A. landscape.

—Hilary White

CREDITS

Ross: Jason Schwartzman
Spider Mike: John Leguizamo
Cookie: Mena Suvari
Frisbee: Patrick Fugit
Nikki: Brittany Murphy
The Cook: Mickey Rourke
Mullet Cop: Peter Stormare
Moustache Cop: Alexis Arquette
The Man: Eric Roberts

Origin: USA, Sweden
Released: 2002
Directed by: Jonas Akerlund
Written by: Will De Los Santos, Creighton Vero
Cinematography by: Eric Broms
Music by: Billy Corgan
MPAA rating: Unrated
Running time: 96 minutes

REVIEWS

Chicago Sun-Times Online. April 4, 2003.
Entertainment Weekly. March 12, 2003.
Washington Post. March 28, 2003.

Spy Kids 3-D: Game Over

3rd Mission. 3rd Dimension.
—Movie tagline

Box Office: $111 million

Robert Rodriguez, the director behind *Desperado*, has developed a critical favorite and successful franchise with his *Spy Kids* movies. Rodriguez is a fast worker and has managed to pop out a new version each year. The first one, 2001's *Spy Kids* was wacky, funny, and inventive and introduced the world to the Cortez family. Dad Gregorio (Antonio Banderas) and mom, Ingrid (Carla Gugino) were spies, but young Juni (Daryl Sabara) and his big sister, Carmen (Alexa Vega) quickly got into the action and did some spying of their own. In 2002's *Spy Kids 2: Island of Lost Dreams,* grandfather (Ricardo Montalban) and grandmother (Holland Taylor) were put to work, too, solving a crime on an island populated by weird hybrid animals created by mad scientist, Romero (Steve Buscemi). Reviewers felt the film was not quite as spunky as the first, but still good fun. With *Spy Kids 3-D: Game Over,* the critics are less enthralled. The consensus is that the 3-D process was too gimmicky (or too hard to watch) and the story wasn't as zippy as the ones before.

Other non-critics, and many kids, disagreed and helped make *Spy Kids 3-D: Game Over* the number one movie of the week it debuted. Perhaps compared to the other *Spy Kids* films, the third one is not up to speed, but compared to a lot of other kids' fare (and plenty of adult fare) in the summer of 2003, it was fine stuff indeed. And yes, the 3-D parts of the film are kind of hard to watch, but they also look pretty darned cool.

In this film, Juni is in a funk. He has quit the spy business and is working on solving private cases for a $4.99 fee. He refuses to be drawn back in until the president of the United States (George Clooney) summons him in for a meeting. It seems that Juni's sister Carmen, who has been missing for over a year, is actually stuck inside a video game. Her body is physically present in the lab run by Donnagan Giggles (Mike Judge) and wife, Cesca (Salma Hayek) but her mind is caught on Level 4 of a video game created by the villainous Toymaker (Sylvester Stallone). Juni must go into the game, rescue Carmen, then shut down the game. There is something about the Toymaker wanting to trap America's youth in the game then control their minds. It's all kind of hard to understand but the basic idea is that the Toymaker is a bad guy who must be stopped and the way to do that is for Juni to go inside the game.

This is the point at which the movie goes 3-D and viewers must don their special glasses. The glasses are that old-fashioned kind with one red lens and one blue one. And yes, some things look like they're popping out of the screen, among them: a cream pie, nuts and bolts, and boxing gloves. But the problem is that the glasses don't seem to work very well; the 3-D effects always seem a bit off. Parts of the screen are blurry and sometimes it seems like the glasses need adjusting. And because of the nature of this sort of technology, when the movie is in 3-D, the color becomes muted and indistinct. This is too bad because one of Rodriquez's trademarks is the over-the-top look of his films. (Rodriquez was able to create most of the film's effects using inexpensive computer techniques.)

Even with the technological limitations, *Spy Kids 3-D* is still a neat looking film. Most of the action takes place inside a video game and Rodriquez has captured the feel of one of these games. There are several sequences that are just as fun to watch as they would be to play. There is a high-speed race inside the game that's exhilarating and exciting. And there's another good scene when players surf through a field of lava. When Juni gets hurt, the life indicator on his chest bursts to the front of the screen and counts down one or more lives. Graphics announcing new levels or particular challenges bound to the front of the screen with great fanfare.

Once inside the game, Juni meets up with some other kids who are beta testers (beta testers are the people who use the software first to check for glitches). There is the cool kid Rez (Robert Vito), strong Arnold (Ryan Pinkston), and smart Francis (Bobby Edner.) Juni is particularly interested in pretty and tough Demetra (Courtney Jines). The other players think that Juni might be The Guy, that is the guy on the box who will lead them to victory. Juni doesn't think

that's true, but he goes along with it because he only has a limited amount of time to save Carmen and can use all the help he can get.

Before entering the game, Juni is allowed to choose someone to take along to help. He passes over the rest of his family in order to take his grandfather who is confined to a wheelchair. Grandfather turns out to have some sort of history with the Toymaker. The best part of all of this is that once inside the game, Grandfather manages to get a magic token called Superlegs. When he uses it, he is instantly given a brawny plastic body that gives him back all his old mobility and more. It's a poignant thought. "This is what I feel like in here," says Montalban stabbing his finger into his chest with typical dramatic flair.

Through it all, Rodriquez still shows his trademark humor. At one point when Juni is addressing the audience, he has to pause and take a call on his cell phone. And when the beta testers appear in their real bodies back in the regular world, they reveal themselves to be not so cool, smart, or strong but rather nerdy. And Montalban, who manages to look suave even in 3-D glasses, makes a reference to "rich Corinthian leather."

The last scenes provide a treat for *Spy Kids* fans when Rodriquez trots out the heroes of the past two films. Besides mom and dad Cortez, there's Uncle Felix (Cheech Marin), Dinky Winks (Bill Paxton), and Uncle Machete (Danny Trejo). It would have been nice if these folks could have had more screen time, since they were already on the set and all, but if you're whipping out one new movie a year like Rodriquez, maybe you don't have enough time to think everything through.

Critics were split about evenly on *Spy Kids 3-D: Game Over*. Owen Gleiberman of *Entertainment Weekly* gave the film a B and commented, "It's *The Matrix* meets *TRON* meets *Jimmy Neutron*, with all the cheery (if not cheesy) evanescence of a Jolly Rancher commercial. I mean that as a compliment." Kevin Thomas of the *Los Angeles Times* described the film as "a good example of complex Hollywood wizardry placed in the service of sharp, intelligent family entertainment." Roger Ebert of the *Chicago Sun-Times,* who was of the opposite opinion, concluded, "I wasn't excited, I wasn't amused, and although 3-D didn't help, the movie wouldn't work in 2-D either." Wesley Morris of the *Boston Globe* declared that the movie "snaps, crackles and pops with wit and color, but the 3-D simulates the experience of watching a movie through an ashtray."

—*Jill Hamilton*

CREDITS

Gregorio Cortez: Antonio Banderas
Ingrid Cortez: Carla Gugino

Juni Cortez: Daryl Sabara
Carmen Cortez: Alexa Vega
Grandfather: Ricardo Montalban
Toymaker: Sylvester Stallone
Grandmother: Holland Taylor
Machete: Danny Trejo
Donnagon Giggles: Mike Judge
Gertie Giggles: Emily Osment
Gary Giggles: Matt O'Leary
Cesca Giggles: Salma Hayek
Felix Gumm: Richard "Cheech" Marin
Francis: Bobby Edner
Demetra: Courtney Jines
Fegan Floop: Alan Cumming
Alexander Minion: Tony Shalhoub
Romero: Steve Buscemi
Dinky Winks: Bill Paxton
Devlin: George Clooney
The Guy: Elijah Wood

Origin: USA
Released: 2003
Production: Elizabeth Avellan, Robert Rodriguez;
Troublemaker Studios; released by Dimension Films
Directed by: Robert Rodriguez
Written by: Robert Rodriguez
Cinematography by: Robert Rodriguez
Music by: Robert Rodriguez
Sound: Stacy Brownrigg
Editing: Robert Rodriguez
Art Direction: Jeanette Scott
Costumes: Nina Proctor
Production Design: Robert Rodriguez
MPAA rating: PG
Running time: 85 minutes

REVIEWS

Chicago Sun-Times Online. July 25, 2003.
Entertainment Weekly. August 1, 2003, p. 61.
Los Angeles Times Online. July 25, 2003.
New York Times Online. July 25, 2003.
People. August 4, 2003, p. 32.
USA Today Online. July 25, 2003.
Variety Online. July 20, 2003.
Washington Post. July 25, 2003, p. WE37.

AWARDS AND NOMINATIONS

Golden Raspberries 2003: Worst Support. Actor
(Stallone).

The Statement

*At the end of World War II, many of those
involved in war crimes were prosecuted. Some got
away. Until now.*
—Movie tagline

It's hard to know just what to make of *The Statement*.
There are so many things it seems like it's going to be: a
thriller about a chase, a psychological study of a war
criminal, an expose of Catholic Church war secrets. But the
movie is only sort of some of these things. It either can't
decide what it wants to do or can't be bothered. Reviewers
described the film using such words as "vagueness,"
"incoherence," and "lumbering."

That the film is so lackluster comes as a surprise because
it has a pretty fine pedigree. The film stars seemingly can't-
miss actors like Michael Caine, Tilda Swinton, and Jeremy
Northam. It's directed by Norman Jewison (*The Hurricane*)
and adapted by Ronald Harwood (*The Pianist*). The idea
came from Brian Moore's best-selling novel, which was
based on a true incident. In 1944, during World War II,
Touvier, a Vichy commander, killed seven Jewish people. In
grainy black-and-white footage, *The Statement* begins by
showing the incident.

Fast forward and Touvier, now called Pierre Brossard
(Caine), is living in Provence in the early 1990s. In one of
the film's first missteps, it is a Provence where everyone
speaks English. Brossard has been in hiding for years. He
stays with sympathetic sects of the Roman Catholic Church.
One sect, the Chevaliers du Ste. Marie, is particularly helpful to Brossard.

Even though Brossard is now an older man who has to
take heart pills and spends his days reading the papers and
drinking beer, he still has the instincts of a killer. When he is
driving back to the monastery after having a beer, he comes
upon an assassin posing as a hapless guy whose car has
broken down. Just as the man is preparing to kill him,
Brossard whips out a gun and kills him first. Brossard coldly
and matter-of-factly, dons gloves, steals the man's money
and disposes of the body.

It seems that a shadowy group of people are trying to
assassinate Brossard. After they kill him, they plan to leave
on his body a statement which reads: "This man is Pierre
Brossard. He has been executed for being a Nazi collaborator." So this would be the thriller part. Stephen Holden of
the *New York Times* described it as a "prolonged, largely
suspense-free manhunt, in which Brossard scurries like a
weary hunted animal from one monastery to the next as the
net closes around him." The chase is made less interesting by
the fact that it's hard to care whether or not Brossard is
caught or not. Aside from his heinous crimes, his character is

not the kind of over-the-top hateful person that audiences would cheer to see captured. But he isn't a hero either. It's hard to believe that anyone would be rooting for this criminal to escape.

Brossard is also being hunted by Annemarie Livi (Swinton), a judge who is investigating his case. She is interested in exposing the power forces in the Church who have been abetting Brossard for so long. She is repeatedly warned by various folks, including a powerful family friend that she shouldn't dig too deep into the case, otherwise her life might be in danger. We hear this a lot, yet Livi's life never seems to be in any kind of actual danger. But then, that might provide a jarring moment of excitement next to the dull proceedings that are the rest of the film. Livi is the kind of person who is sharp and tenacious. In case we don't get this by her quick movements and obvious dedication to the case, Harwood has her say it several times. When that is not deemed to be enough for us to get the idea, Harwood has other characters say it, too. Livi is assisted in her quest for Brossard by Colonel Roux (Northam). He helps Livi discover some information, and otherwise is there so that she can tell him that she is tenacious. There is no romantic tension between Livi and Roux, which is a shame.

Thus we have the chase which ends up being a sort of slow-motion, nothing ever happens, kind of chase. The character study part of the film suffers much the same fate. The mind of a Nazi war criminal is surely interesting territory to explore, but here there are only two sides we see. On one hand, Brossard is a cold-blooded killer, evading would-be assassins and living on his survival instincts. On the other hand, he is a weak old man who goes to confession and weeps for forgiveness. Brossard seems to take the whole forgiveness thing pretty seriously. He respects the elders in the church so much that when they give him forgiveness, he seems to forgive himself, too. Despite Caine's best efforts, the whole character of Brossard turns out to be frustrating because it is so under-explored.

Another under-explored aspect of the film is Brossard's relationship with his ex-wife, Nicole (Charlotte Rampling). The two seem to have a fascinating past (this is based on their acting more than the script), and it would be interesting to learn about it; but here Brossard just insists on hiding at Nicole's house, threatening to kill her dog if she disobeys.

The one bright spot in the film is that, with a cast like this, at least the actors will be interesting to watch. Even though he never quite gets it, it's fun to watch Caine try to get a handle on his character. Swinton is interesting to watch because of her forceful androgynous presence. Women in today's Hollywood films don't look or act like her. And Northam, who has somehow escaped from one of his usual British period pieces, brings his usual easy charm.

Critics were left cold by the film. Owen Gleiberman of *Entertainment Weekly* gave the film a C and complained, "If any actor could reveal the squirmy soul of a war criminal, it's Caine, so it feels like a cheat when *The Statement* gives him nothing to portray but self-condemnation." Holden of the *New York Times* said of the film: "A cat-and-mouse thriller with delusions of grandeur, *The Statement* arrives wrapped in an intimidating mystique of high-minded solemnity that makes its vagueness and incoherence all the more disappointing when the pieces don't add up." Charles Taylor of *Salon.com* stated, "Michael Caine is brilliant as a French Nazi collaborator hidden by the Catholic Church. Too bad Norman Jewison's film is a stiff, limping bore." *Newsday's* John Anderson described the film as "a surprisingly mild thriller, one that meanders and spasms dramatically, and that, despite its occasional outburst of violence, wastes a cast of ordinarily superb actors." And Kenneth Turan of the *Los Angeles Times* concluded, "As the good guys try to figure out who the bad guys are and both sides try and figure out where Brossard is, we're left trying against all odds to minimally care about any of the above. The characters are not finely drawn enough to be involving, and without a firm directing hand nothing feels at stake."

—*Jill Hamilton*

CREDITS

Pierre Brossard: Michael Caine
Anne Marie Livi: Tilda Swinton
Roux: Jeremy Northam
Bertier: Alan Bates
Nicole: Charlotte Rampling
Old Man: John Neville
Pochon: Ciaran Hinds
Commissaire Vionnet: Frank Finlay
Le Moyne: William Hutt
David: Matt Craven
Michael: Noam Jenkins
Cholet: Peter Wight
Patrice: Colin Salmon
Dom Andre: David de Keyser

Origin: Canada, Great Britain, France
Released: 2003
Directed by: Norman Jewison
Written by: Ronald Harwood
Cinematography by: Kevin Jewison
Music by: Normand Corbeil
Sound: Bruce Carwardine
Editing: Stephen E. Rivkin, Andrew S. Eisen
Costumes: Carine Sarfati
Production Design: Jean Rabasse
MPAA rating: R
Running time: 120 minutes

Chicago Sun-Times Online. January 16, 2004.
Entertainment Weekly. December 12, 2003.
USA Today Online. December 12, 2003.

The Station Agent

 Box Office: $5.5 million

A little movie with a big heart, *The Station Agent* marks the writing-directing debut of Tom McCarthy, whose deeply felt characterizations and acute observations about loneliness and friendship make his work a joy. Focusing on three characters thrown together by chance, the script explores the unlikely ways new bonds can form among people who seem to share very little in common.

Peter Dinklage plays Finbar McBride, a dwarf who works at a model train store, a two-man shop where he does the repairs. It is the perfect job for a man with a fascination for trains and an aversion to social interaction. When his boss suddenly dies, Fin, as he is called, inherits a train station and a small plot of land in a secluded part of Newfoundland, New Jersey, which should suit Fin's personality just fine. Indeed, with an economy of scenes and dialogue, McCarthy lets us understand the isolation of not only being different but being regarded as something of a freak, a curiosity for people to jeer at or, at best, stare at. When Fin goes to the local grocery store to pick up a few items for his new home, for example, the woman behind the counter snaps a photo, and we can surmise from his look of resignation that he has encountered similar incidents before.

Fin begins to set up his home in the old depot, which has not been used in years and is in need of serious repair, a metaphor, perhaps, for some of the people he will encounter. There is a food wagon nearby run by Joe (Bobby Cannavale), who is outgoing and cannot stand to be alone. He is constantly chattering away and practically begging to be part of his new neighbor's life, while Fin does his monosyllabic best to keep his distance.

Fin also runs into a woman named Olivia (Patricia Clarkson)—or rather she nearly runs into him twice with her SUV as he dodges out of the road in the nick of time. She feels terrible and tries to offer her friendship, but the already wary Fin is more reticent to get to know someone who nearly killed him.

Content to spend time reading about trains or waiting in a designated spot for a train to pass by, Fin is very comfortable in his solitude. Such activities are foreign to Joe, who needs to learn to sit still for a few moments. But while Fin teaches his neighbor to relax a bit and enjoy the quiet of an afternoon, Joe also brings Fin out of his shell, offering a camaraderie that he has probably not encountered before.

Still grieving from the accidental death of her son, Olivia is undergoing a separation from her husband and is ignoring all of his attempts to talk to her. A painter whose contact with the world is limited, she is gradually drawn into companionship with these guys, and the three make an unlikely alliance borne out of a mutual affection and need that each would probably not be able to articulate.

The performances in *The Station Agent* could be considered the epitome of ensemble acting, so wonderfully do the three leads play off each other while bringing depth and nuance to their roles. Cannavale, for example, could have played Joe as the annoying neighbor, good-looking and brash, full of the confidence that Fin lacks. But instead Joe is endearing and gleeful like a teenager trying desperately to fit in. The character also has a softer side that Cannavale tenderly reveals when Joe is expressing concern for his sick father or pausing to say grace before a meal. Clarkson gives yet another wonderful performance, gradually revealing the depth of hurt in Olivia so we understand that her need for friendship is just as great as Joe's, even if she is not as obvious or vocal in expressing it. Dinklage is the film's discovery, not because he outshines his costars but because his Fin is the anchor of the film, the character who touches so many different people and ever so gradually discovers that they are decent and can see him for who he is and not focus on his size.

The Station Agent has a relaxed, leisurely pace in which the three friends just take time walking on the train tracks or sitting around enjoying each other's company. Sometimes the silent moments are as profound as anything they could say to one another. But there are also funny, lighthearted moments, as when Joe and Fin do some train chasing, a favorite activity of enthusiasts whereby they follow a train and film its journey. Fin could never do this on his own. He does not drive or own a video camera, so he needs other people. With a camera supplied by Olivia and Joe driving his wagon, he and Fin enjoy a little adventure together and then later share their movie with Olivia.

No matter how hard he tries to resist, then, Fin finds himself being drawn into a community. People seem to take an instant liking to him; they are, of course, initially curious, but they also find something appealing in him. A little girl named Cleo (Raven Goodwin) observes him inspecting his train, and she gradually tries to make friends. Perhaps it is because they are roughly the same height or because she too is fascinated by the railroad. He gradually warms up to her but cannot bring himself to accept an invitation to speak at her school.

More intriguing is the relationship between Fin and Emily (Michelle Williams), the cute librarian who is having some tough times facing a pregnancy by a boyfriend who does not treat her very well. Fin is the first person she confides her secret to, and, while he cannot provide any pat solutions, the episode speaks volumes about the kind of trust he inspires. While she obviously has a crush on him, it is not clear what kind of relationship will develop between them, but at least Fin is able to open his heart to a woman.

The emotional high point of the film revolves around Olivia. When she learns that her husband is having a baby with another woman, the news sends her into a tailspin. She isolates herself from her new friends, forcing the concerned Fin into the role of caretaker, checking on her to see if she is all right. Finally, he finds her on her kitchen floor, having finished off a bottle of pills. Fin holds her in his arms in the film's most poignant scene—it is powerful yet also simple—as one human being reaches out to another when she needs it the most.

McCarthy's screenplay subtly plays on the American mythology of trains, hearkening back to simpler times when a public form of transportation united the country just as Fin's little depot becomes the focal point for a group of people who would not otherwise have a sense of belonging. Peppered throughout *The Station Agent* are bits of train folklore and the history of the railroad in the United States. We learn, for example, that the station agent once played a pivotal role in a community. Not only did he run the train depot but also delivered mail, sold groceries, and cut hair as well. Fin follows in the footsteps of the old-time agents in spirit, giving direction in life and relationships by being there when people need him.

Indeed, his new role is an extension of his original job, but rather than fixing models in a simulated world, Fin has moved on to making repairs in the real world. The irony, of course, is that this is not a role he relishes or wants, but, perhaps it is one that he needs. Fin gains the confidence to speak in front of Cleo's class, and when an insensitive student questions him about his height and it seems that things might go badly, Fin handles the situation with an even temper and gracefully segues into a historical reference to the first train, the Tom Thumb. Still small in size, Fin has grown in character by learning what it means to depend on others and, in turn, have them depend on him.

While the film has an upbeat ending, McCarthy does not feel bound to tie up all the loose threads. For example, Olivia has recovered but will still have to come to terms with her husband's new life, and we never learn what happens to the pregnant Emily. It is enough to know, however, that at least these characters have taken small but important steps toward forming a community, even if that was never their intention. It is a tribute to McCarthy's writing that *The Station Agent*, at 88 minutes, leaves the audience wanting more time with all of these people, so warm and genuine and so much of a pleasure to get to know.

—*Peter N. Chumo II*

CREDITS

Finbar McBride: Peter Dinklage
Olivia Harris: Patricia Clarkson
Joe Oramas: Bobby Cannavale
Cleo: Raven Goodwin
Henry Styles: Paul Benjamin
Emily: Michelle Williams

Origin: USA
Released: 2003
Production: Mary Jane Skalski, Robert May, Kathryn Tucker; SenArt Films, Next Wednesday; released by Miramax Films
Directed by: Tom McCarthy
Written by: Tom McCarthy
Cinematography by: Oliver Bokelberg
Music by: Stephen Trask
Sound: Damian Canelos
Music Supervisor: Mary Ramos, Michelle Kuznetsky
Editing: Tom McArdle
Art Direction: Len X. Clayton
Costumes: Jeanne Dupont
Production Design: John Paino
MPAA rating: R
Running time: 88 minutes

REVIEWS

Boxoffice. April, 2003, p. 83.
Chicago Sun-Times Online. October 17, 2003.
Entertainment Weekly. October 10, 2003, p. 100.
Los Angeles Times Online. October 3, 2003.
New York Times Online. October 3, 2003.
People. October 13, 2003, p. 32.
Vanity Fair. October, 2003, p. 102.
Variety Online. January 22, 2003.
Washington Post. October 17, 2003, p. WE47.

QUOTES

Finbar (Peter Dinklage): "It's really funny how people see me and treat me, since I'm really just a simple, boring person."

AWARDS AND NOMINATIONS

Ind. Spirit 2004: First Screenplay
Natl. Bd. of Review 2003: Support. Actress (Clarkson)
Natl. Soc. Film Critics 2003: Support. Actress (Clarkson)
Nomination:
Ind. Spirit 2004: Actor (Dinklage)

Screen Actors Guild 2003: Actor (Dinklage), Actress (Clarkson), Cast
Writers Guild 2003: Orig. Screenplay.

Step Into Liquid

No special effects. No stuntmen. No stereotypes. No other feeling comes close.
—Movie tagline

 Box Office: $3.6 million

With the stunning surfing documentary *Step Into Liquid,* writer-director Dana Brown follows in the footsteps of his father Bruce Brown, director of the legendary 1964 surfing documentary, *The Endless Summer* and its 1994 sequel. Much as his father did, the younger Brown travels the globe to profile surfers from such diverse regions as Sheboygan, Wisconsin; Galveston, Texas; County Donegal, Ireland; Vietnam; and Australia. Alternating between spectacular wave footage and human-interest stories, Brown's entertaining film has definite mainstream appeal.

Narrated by Brown in the same casual, self-deprecating style that his father adopted in the *Endless Summer* films, *Step Into Liquid* presents a comprehensive overview of the contemporary world of surfing. Although surfing has grown into a highly lucrative industry, Brown focuses on the joys of this addictive sport and what draws so many surfers to endlessly pursue the perfect wave. Brown's inspiration in making the documentary was reportedly to delve below the surface of the sport, to get past the stereotype and preconception and show surfing as a multi-dimensional activity. His main goal was to show the commonality that surfers around the world have, and in this he's succeeded beautifully.

Many of the sport's top competitors are shown here, including pros Laird Hamilton, Kelly Slater, Rob Machado, Mike Parsons, and Taj Burrow. There's also amazing footage of a few stars on the women's circuit—Keala Kennelly, Rochelle Blanchard, and Layne Beachley—although the film would have benefited from showing more female wave riders. However, *Liquid* resonates the most when it focuses on regular folks like the middle-aged, Midwestern guys from Sheboygan, Wisconsin, who have been surfing the small waves of Lake Michigan for over 20 years. Another interesting story spotlights a group of Texans who chase down oil tankers and then ride the wakes of the ships on their longboards. Subjects like 54-year-old Dale Webster, who has surfed every day for the past three decades at Salmon Creek Beach in Bodega Bay, California, portray the passion

and relentless desire to catch a wave. "It's gone from a streak to a quest to a mission," says Webster of his goal to be the first man ever to surf waves caused by the moon in all its calendar phases.

One poignant segment involves military veteran Jim Knost returning to Vietnam with his son, Alex, to surf and socialize with the ten members of the Da Nang Surfing Club. With very little wave action, the group must eventually resort to surfing sand dunes. Although sand is no substitute for awesome surf, the camaraderie shared among the men is evident. Surfing's universal allure is further exhibited when the Ojai pro-surfing brothers Dan, Chris, and Keith Malloy give lessons at an Irish surf school, while Catholic and Protestant children happily play together in the freezing water. Another engaging story showcases surfer Robert August (the star of the original *Endless Summer*) and his family surfing in the waves off Costa Rica.

For the most breathtaking visuals and daredevil thrills, Brown captures the exploits of Laird Hamilton and Derrick Doerner, big-wave, tow-in surfers from Hawaii's North Shore. Towed into a monstrous wave by a Jet Ski, Hamilton rides a "foil board," which allows him to glide just above the water on an aluminum hydro-wing. It makes for an extraordinary scene—especially when Hamilton drops down the face of a gigantic wave off a deep-water reef at Maui. Riding humongous waves is about being "in harmony with the sea at its most dynamic moment," explains Hamilton.

Without a doubt, though, the most wild, mind-blowing ride portrayed in *Liquid* comes courtesy of the action caught at Cortes Bank, part of an underwater mountain range located 100 miles west of San Diego, which can produce giant open-ocean reef waves in excess of 60 feet. In January of 2001, pros and first-rate tow-in surfers Brad Gerlach and Mike Parsons made surfing history when Gerlach towed Parsons into a 66-foot wave, the largest wave ever ridden by man. Two months later, Parson's accomplishment at Cortes Bank earned him first place ($60,000) in the Swell XXL Big Wave Awards.

With gorgeous photography, authentic vignettes, and a light narrative, critics found much to like about Dana Brown's positive take on the surfing lifestyle. Noting the remarkable surf footage shot by cinematographer John-Paul Beeghly, *Variety* critic Scott Foundas called the documentary "an awe-inspiring survey of global surf culture, with the power to crush the post 'Gidget' decades of Hollywood stereotyping of surfers and surfing." Kenneth Turan of the *Los Angeles Times* commented that Brown's surfing movie is "an enticing invitation to get your feet wet in the world of surfing, to experience the beauty and feel the rush of this most addictive of pastimes." Perhaps Dave Kehr best described the film's appeal when he wrote in the *New York Times,* "Like his father, Mr. Brown has the magical ability to take his public on a two-hour vacation. It's the next best thing to being there, and you don't need to worry about sand in your beer."

Watching the mesmerizing swells of *Step Into Liquid* in a packed Southern California theater, this reviewer has to agree with the rest of the critics. You don't need to hang ten to appreciate Brown's refreshing and compelling film—you just need to appreciate life.

—*Beth Fhaner*

CREDITS

Narrator: Dana Brown

Origin: USA
Released: 2003
Production: John-Paul Beeghly; Top Secret; released by Artisan Entertainment
Directed by: Dana Brown
Written by: Dana Brown
Cinematography by: John-Paul Beeghly
Music by: Richard Gibbs
Music Supervisor: Joe Fischer, George Acogny
Editing: Dana Brown
MPAA rating: Unrated
Running time: 87 minutes

REVIEWS

Entertainment Weekly. August 15, 2003, p. 53.
Los Angeles Times Online. August 8, 2003.
New York Times Online. August 8, 2003.
People. August 18, 2003, p. 35.
San Diego Union-Tribune Online. August 14, 2003.
Variety Online. February 18, 2003.

QUOTES

Keala Kennelly: "The best surfer in the world is the one having the most fun."

Stone Reader

A movie for anyone who has ever loved . . . a book.
—Movie tagline

Mark Moskowitz's documentary, *Stone Reader*, takes the film of fact onto a terrain where it often fears to tread. As a maker of film commercials by profession, he boldly turns the camera upon himself, more specifically, upon his restless, idealistic self. Like the noted Frederick Wiseman, he allows reality to speak for itself, including within it his subjective biases his failings as a documentary filmmaker, his inability to obtain relevant material from his subjects and most important, his willingness to abandon the project altogether. Thus, the more than two-hour film that emerges imparts a double joy: one, that the film has come into existence and, two, the triumph of an impossible wish shared by readers everywhere.

Unlike Wiseman, it should be noted, Moskowitz keeps reminding us that we are watching a film, and a clumsily made one at that. This is not to detract from the film's lyrical cinematography or its plaintive guitar score, but to stress its ontological aspect as a documentary. We are kept as much in the dark about the future as those we are watching. In this, *Stone Reader* imparts the same brand of excitement as *startup.com* (2001) by Chris Hegedus and Jehane Noujaim, in which we share the jubilation of the film's get-rich-quick millionaires, while remaining as ignorant as they are that their bubble of success will eventually burst.

Moskowitz's winning unassuming stance becomes clear in the film's first sequence in which in the midst of the bustle created by a roomful of film technicians, he explains to his cinematographer, Joseph Vandergast, and, by extension, to us the aim of the film we are about to see. Way back in 1972, he picked up a doorstop of a novel entitled *The Stones of Summer*, by an unknown writer named Dow Mossman. The book was hailed in a review as the "definitive" work of and for the new generation. Moskowitz couldn't get beyond the first section of the book and so abandoned it, only to pick it up again much later. This time, he was inspired to read it through, then hunt for more books by the author. When he found that it was in fact the only book Mossman had ever written, he felt he had to answer one overriding question for himself: "What kind of writer writes a giant tome like that and then just disappears?" Vandergast is immediately won over to the project, and the opening titles roll.

The next sequence shows Moskowitz accessing as many copies of the book as he can find, as well as any information on it. We are as shocked as he is to learn that the *Book Review Digest*, that venerable compendium of respected literature, makes no mention of the book. All Moskowitz can gather from his reference sources are a review in the *New York Times*, from which he must have got the adjective "definitive," and a few sketchy articles about Mossman; hardly the material on which to float a documentary film project. Moskowitz then decides to broaden his inquiry to include other books he has loved and why their authors faded away.

With that template in mind, he goes to visit the famous literary critic Leslie Fiedler, author of the radical *Love and Death in the American Novel*. Fiedler in his advancing years emerges as gaunt and almost infirm. He inspires Moskowitz by recounting how he helped a little-known novel (*Call It Sleep* by Henry Roth) become a bestseller after he wrote about it. It so happens that the phenomenon of "one-book writers" has always fascinated Fiedler. We learn that he places J. D. Salinger (*Catcher in the Rye*) and Margaret Mitchell (*Gone with the Wind*) in that category. Then comes the shock: even Fiedler hasn't heard of *The Stones of Summer*. At this point, Moskowitz admits in a voiceover that he felt all hope vanish.

That doesn't mean Moskowitz is prepared to give up. His next target is John Seelye, the critic who wrote the review in the *Times*. To prepare for his meeting in Eastport, Maine, Moskowitz selects certain volumes to take along and discuss. He doesn't tell us the reason for his selections; his intellectually arrogant stance assumes we would know. We see Moskowitz motoring across a lush countryside, an interview with Mario Puzo playing on his car radio. Clearly, here is a man who lives and breathes literature.

Seelye, within the summer retreat he shares with his wife, looks the epitome of the aged literati, with his vibrant countenance and short thick white beard. For all his willingness to cooperate, he, too, knows little about where Mossman could be now, or why the author never wrote another book. He recalls *The Stones of Summer* as "a multi-textual mosaic," very much in the "inventive" tradition of Kerouac. He adds that his review, however, elicited no reaction, and that last he heard of Mossman, the author was working as a trucker. Moskowitz admits in a voiceover that he realized at that point that what was propelling his inquiry was more than just curiosity, and it made his need to find Mossman that much more compelling.

The film then intercuts this search with an autobiographical segment in which Moskowitz and his teenaged son wander through an amusement park as the filmmaker's voiceover relates how he got hooked on reading. "One book can turn a kid into a reader for life," Mossman muses. For him, it was Joseph Heller's *Catch-22*, which appealed to his "subversive self." After that, "everything else smacked of suburbia." Moskowitz ends his soliloquy with the words, "Heller died today."

Moskowitz then rushes headlong into an interview with the editor of *Catch-22*, Robert Gottlieb, and gets him to discuss what lay behind the phenomenal success of the Heller novel. Gottlieb, who was an editor at Simon and Schuster at the time, claims it was the post-Vietnam sensibility. When Moskowitz asks him about *The Stones of Summer*, Gottlieb replies he hasn't heard of it, adding that perhaps the publisher was responsible for letting the book go "falling through the cracks." Gottlieb's closing words: "Publishing is a crap shoot."

As we see Moskowitz lost in the drudgery of cleaning a pool on his estate, his voiceover recounts that a year went by and nothing happened. Then, he manages to locate an author, Robert C. Downs, who attended the Writer's Workshop at the University of Iowa with Mossman, and "Bingo!"

Once Moskowitz gets to Iowa, the mystery that has preoccupied him, and us, starts to unravel, but not right away. While discussing "one-book authors," Downs on his own mentions Mossman and *The Stones of Summer*. We can relate to Moskowitz's excitement, though his voiceover tells us that Mossman, for all we know, could be dead. As if foregrounding the masochistic aspect of researching, Moskowitz seemingly takes a number of detours before providence leads him to Mossman's home turf.

It is when Moskowitz finds Mossman's papers, unearthed from the Special Collections at the University of Iowa, that the nitty-gritty behind all the abstractions that have been bandied around in the film hits home. We see boxes and boxes of drafts and redrafts of *The Stones of Summer,* some with editorial notations, twelve versions in all that resulted in the 1,200 typewritten pages that finally made it into print. In relation to all that we have come to know up to that point, it is a heartbreaking sight.

The man who leads Moskowitz to Mossman is the aged but hardy William Cotter Murray, an Iowa resident to whom Mossman dedicated his book. From Murray, we learn that Mossman is alive and well and living in Cedar Rapids, and that he spent time in a psychiatric ward after the book was published. Very sheepishly, Murray adds words to the effect, "Don't tell him I told you!"

When Dow Mossman finally does appear onscreen, he looks every bit the downhome hero. His rotund face, curly mop, and thick moustache make him look the archetypal frontiersman, in contrast to Moskowitz's balding pate and urban pace. "The whole book was a poem," Mossman admits, one that he originally wrote in longhand. The two men then hunt around in the attic and basement of Mossman's house for his publishing contract in order to read "the reversion clause" related to reprinting the work. But that is a matter left to another film, Moskowitz seems to say.

When Moskowitz appears in the same frame as Mossman, his humble stance is akin to that of a disciple for his guru. Though armed with his hi-tech information armada, he doesn't question what Mossman says, either for our benefit, as the audience of his completed film, or as Mossman's interviewer. That adulatory stance remains his film's only real drawback.

As if to compensate for the injustice done to Mossman's opus, critics have showered unanimous praise on the film. In the *Los Angeles Times,* Kevin Thomas calls *Stone Reader* "stunning" and describes the film as "a literary suspense tale" that is "also a celebration of nature and of literature." *Newsday*'s John Anderson calls the film "enormously affectionate, gloriously self-indulgent, and unhesitatingly heroic in its championing of good books." Elvis Mitchell concludes his rave in the *New York Times* by noting that the "best thing about [the film] . . . is that it will provoke discussions of the alarming number of authors . . . who lighted a single fire in their lifetimes."

—*Vivek Adarkar*

CREDITS

Origin: USA
Released: 2002
Production: Mark Moskowitz; released by Jet Films
Directed by: Mark Moskowitz
Written by: Mark Moskowitz
Cinematography by: Mark Moskowitz, Joseph Vandergast, Jeffrey Confer
Music by: Michael Mandrell
Editing: Mark Moskowitz, Kathleen Soulliere
MPAA rating: PG-13
Running time: 128 minutes

REVIEWS

Chicago Sun-Times Online. July 11, 2003.
Entertainment Weekly. February 28, 2003, p. 60.
Los Angeles Times Online. May 2, 2003.
New York Times Online. February 12, 2003.
Newsday. February 12, 2003.
Pages. May/June, 2003, p. 72.
Variety Online. January 27, 2002.
Washington Post. May 9, 2003, p. WE41.

Stuck On You

A Farrelly outrageous comedy.
—Movie tagline
Brothers stick together.
—Movie tagline

 Box Office: $33.7 million

S *tuck on You*, the latest film by Peter and Bobby Farrelly, aka the Farrelly Brothers, defies expectations. Its storyline, involving conjoined twins Bob (Matt Damon) and Walt (Greg Kinnear) Tenor who decide to move to Hollywood to follow their dreams, seems like it's quickly going to lead to typically non-politically-correct Farrelly jokes. The surprise is that *Stuck on You* is actually quite a mild, gentle comedy. There are some of the usual twinge-inducing jokes, such as when Walt, working a crossword puzzle, asks Bob for a four-letter word for snatch. (The answer, "grab," is not along the lines of what Walt had been thinking of.) But, overall, the film is a sweet ode to brotherly love.

One thing that is unusual about the Farrelly brothers' films is the way that disability is handled in them. Their films are populated with characters that have disabilities. In *There's Something About Mary*, Mary's brother was mentally handicapped. In *Stuck on You*, there's the obvious condition of the stars, and one of their coworkers, Rocket, is played by an actor (Ray "Rocket" Valliere) who is apparently mentally challenged. The next film by the Farrellys is set to be *The Ringer*, which involves someone faking their way into the Special Olympics. In our culture, we keep disabilities at a distance. In Hollywood films, we are taught to look upon people with differing abilities either with pity or to treat them as heroic. In the Farrellys' films, such folks are just there mixing with the "regular" people.

It's easy to see why the subject of conjoined twins would be interesting to the Farrellys. After all, they are famous as brothers, not as Peter Farrelly and Bobby Farrelly. They share directing, producing and writing duties. (By contrast, in Coen Brother films, one writes and one directs.) Like the Tenors, if the Farrellys were to separate—professionally, at least—it's unclear if they would each survive alone.

If Walt and Bob were to separate, Walt would only have a 50 percent chance of survival. Given such poor odds, the two decide to stick together and make a life for themselves. They've done a pretty good job of it, too. They live in Martha's Vineyard and run a short-order restaurant. So speedy are the brothers behind the grill that they offer anyone a free meal if their food isn't ready in three minutes. To watch the brothers cook the food is to watch a type of intricate ballet. One flips the burgers to the other, the other catches them in hamburger buns. Damon and Kinnear are so graceful and natural together, this cooking sequence alone must have involved hours of practice.

The brothers, who share a liver and are joined by a swatch of flesh at their waists, are fraternal twins. (Originally the Farrellys wanted to cast Woody Allen and Jim Carrey.) Walt, who, oddly, appears to be older, is the "cool" one. He is smooth with the ladies and has a confident and sunny personality. Bob is sweet, shy, and given to panic attacks. Whenever he tries to talk to women, he quickly strikes out—not because of his physical condition, but because he starts tripping over his words. Whenever Walt is with another of his conquests, Bob sits on the other side of the bed, shielded by a sheet and writes to his pen pal, May (Wen Yann Shih). Bob considers May to be his girlfriend, even though the two have never met and he has neglected to tell her about Walt.

Walt's great passion, besides women, is acting. He is well respected in his small town for his yearly one-man shows. When he performs *Tru,* the one-man play about Truman Capote, Bob crouches behind him, dressed in black and sweating. While Walt lives for the stage, Bob suffers from severe stage fright. Bob isn't thrilled then when Walt announces that he wants to move to Hollywood to try to make it big. Not only will Bob have to subject himself to the nightmare of being onstage, but he will also have to give up the job he loves at the restaurant. Perhaps worst of all is that May lives in Hollywood. If they go, he will have to meet her face-to-face. But Bob eventually agrees because he wants to give his brother the chance to follow his dream.

When the brothers arrive in Hollywood and Walt starts auditioning, the two are laughed at. The brothers decide that surely the problem must be that Walt doesn't have an agent, so they enlist the help of Morty O'Reilly (Seymour Cassel of *Rushmore*), an old-timer who lives in a retirement home and still thinks that Walter Cronkite is the preeminent newscaster of the day.

No thanks to Morty's nonexistent efforts, Walt scores a role on a TV sitcom starring Cher (playing herself, or what we would hope is a parody of herself). When Cher was not busy sleeping with her teenaged boyfriend (Frankie Muniz of TV's "Malcolm in the Middle") or yelling at her manager, she is to star in a bad network series, *Honey and the Beaze.* Cher hates the project and is desperate to get out of her contract. She hopes that if she insists upon hiring Walt as her co-star, the network will refuse to air the show.

But the show does air. Director Griffin Dunne (playing himself) hides Bob behind potted plants and the like. Still word leaks that Walt is a conjoined twin and the news makes *Honey and the Beaze* a top-rated hit. Walt is a Hollywood success, indicated by the scene in which he makes the requisite appearance on Jay Leno's show. Things are not going as well for Bob, who still hasn't told May his important secret. He goes on dates with her, but explains Walt's constant presence as a kind of excessive brotherly love.

Stuck on You is intermittently funny, but the film isn't nearly as filled with humor as *There's Something About Mary.* Still, some of the jokes are quite clever. When Walt needs to sign a contract for the TV show, Morty comes in with all kinds of absurdly low demands. He asks for the same sweet deal that he once got for Kitty Carlisle and it involves the actor's dressing room being stocked with Folgers Crystals. Other jokes are quite lowbrow: for example, a porn star is called Phil Rupp. Certainly mixing different kinds of humor in a film is fine and even desirable, but the stuff here is not sharp enough or plentiful enough. Different people with different senses of humor will all find a laugh or two here but that's all. Those wanting the raunchier humor will find the gaps between such gags to be rather large. Those liking the more intellectual humor will have a similar experience.

What's left is the bond (both physical and emotional) between the brothers. If different actors had played the roles, it might not have worked as well. Damon and Kinnear appear to take their roles very seriously and their acting is the main thing the movie has going for it. Damon, especially, does his darnedest. In a scene in which Walt is golfing, Bob is the caddie. Walt swings, and as he does, Bob moves out seamlessly to the front, bringing his hand up to shield his eyes from the sun as he follows the shot. Like the cooking scene, it has a certain effortless grace.

Critics were receptive to the film. *Entertainment Weekly's* Owen Gleiberman gave the film an A– and wrote, "*Stuck on You* has a fractured fairy-tale charm, even if it isn't a nonstop laugh riot." Manohla Dargis of the *Los Angeles Times* wrote, "Sweeter and softer than their early comedies, and largely devoid of gags about bodily functions, *Stuck on You* has the vibe of a transitional work, as if the brothers were trying to see how a post-scatological Farrelly comedy could play." In the *Chicago Sun-Times* Roger Ebert wrote, "The subjects of [the Farrellys] comedies are defiantly non-P.C., but their hearts are in the right place, and it's refreshing to see a movie that doesn't dissolve with embarrassment in the face of handicaps." Stephanie Zacharek summed up on *Salon.com:* "The jokes in *Stuck on You* are easy and relaxed, and the picture ambles along amiably. It's a friendly, unpretentious little thing—at times it's a bit too muted and indistinct, but then, you have to at least give the Farrellys credit for not making the mistake of trying too hard."

—*Jill Hamilton*

CREDITS

Bob: Matt Damon
Walt: Greg Kinnear
April: Eva Mendes
May: Wen Yann Shih
Mimmy: Pat Crawford Brown
Morty: Jean-Pierre Cassel
Herself: Cher
Rocket: Ray "Rocket" Valliere
Himself: Jay Leno (Cameo)

Origin: USA
Released: 2003
Production: Charles B. Wessler, Bradley Thomas, Bobby Farrelly, Peter Farrelly; Conundrum Entertainment; released by 20th Century-Fox
Directed by: Bobby Farrelly, Peter Farrelly
Written by: Bobby Farrelly, Peter Farrelly
Cinematography by: Dan Mindel
Sound: Jonathan Earl Stein
Music Supervisor: Manish Raval
Editing: Christopher Greenbury, Dave Terman
Art Direction: Arlan Jay Vetter, Richard Fojo
Costumes: Deena Appel

Production Design: Sidney J. Bartholomew Jr.
MPAA rating: PG-13
Running time: 118 minutes

the best, the film still survives and is a fun ride the entire two hours.

—Laura Abraham

REVIEWS

Chicago Sun-Times Online. December 12, 2003.
Entertainment Weekly. December 19, 2003, p. 54.
Los Angeles Times Online. December 12, 2003.
New York Times Online. December 12, 2003.
People. December 22, 2003, p. 28.
USA Today Online. December 12, 2003.
Variety Online. December 6, 2003.
Washington Post. December 12, 2003, p. WE48.

Suspended Animation

Will chill you to the bone.
—Movie tagline

Suspended Animation, directed by John D. Hancock, may not be the next great piece of American cinema, and, in fact, many would call it nothing but trash. But it's fun trash! Once in a while a film comes along that reminds us that not all cinema need be heartfelt and sincere, and sometimes entertainment can be just about that: entertaining.

Tom Kempton (Alex McArthur), a Hollywood animator, is attacked by some women on a snowmobile trip and is exposed to horrible torture by the two ladies. Laura Esterman and Sage Allen are wonderfully psychotic as the sisters. At first it seems as though this film will be nothing more than a rip off of the tons of films about kidnapping and torture, but within a short period of time it is clear this film is a bit more than that.

Tom's friends attempt a daring rescue and succeed after a very bloody snowmobile chase. The torture and subsequent rescue are quick paced and interesting. Many times films such as this get bogged down with too many details making the action drag and leading to a pretty lame conclusion. This is not the case with *Suspended Animation* as it bolts towards the finish line with the ease of a winner.

Physically Tom is fine after all this, but he is not exactly mentally all there. He can't escape from the thoughts in his head even though the sisters were killed. He directs an animation show using the daughter of one of the sisters in an attempt to work through his trauma. The craziness that follows is pretty out there and really does deserve a viewing. While the dialogue seems contrived and the direction is not

CREDITS

Tom Kempton: Alex McArthur
Ann Boulette: Sage Allen
Hilary Kempton: Rebecca Harrell
Vanessa Boulette: Laura Esterman
Clara Hansen: Maria Cina

Origin: USA
Released: 2002
Production: John Hancock; Filmacres; released by First Run Features
Directed by: John Hancock
Written by: Dorothy Tristan
Cinematography by: Misha (Mikhail) Suslov
Music by: Angelo Badalamenti
Music Supervisor: Chris Ussery
Editing: Dennis O'Connor
Costumes: Richard Donnelly
Production Design: Don Jacobson
MPAA rating: Unrated
Running time: 114 minutes

REVIEWS

Boxoffice. November, 2003, p. 105.
Entertainment Weekly. November 7, 2003, p. 54.
Los Angeles Times Online. October 31, 2003.
New York Times Online. October 31, 2003.
Variety Online. November 10, 2002.

S.W.A.T.

Even cops dial 911.
—Movie tagline

 Box Office: $116.6 million

Little is remembered today from the short-lived 1970s television cop drama *S.W.A.T.* except the theme song, which, once heard, sticks with you. There is also little to

remember after viewing the adequate but generic and flawed film based on the series, except maybe the ringing ears from a deafening soundtrack.

From the start, the filmmakers turn up the volume as the LAPD turns up the heat on robbers holed up in a bank full of hostages. Kinetic editing helps create a sense of tumult and excitement. Amidst all the commotion, a call goes out to S.W.A.T. The elite S.W.A.T. (Special Weapons and Tactics) units are called into some of the most dangerous and daunting situations. A good job is done here of showing how these special forces must work with amazing composure, focus, and precision in horribly tense situations if they are to succeed. They succeed in snuffing out the problem within the Valley Trust, but when a hotshot member of the team and his partner disobey their superior's orders, a female hostage almost gets snuffed out as well.

Feeling that Brian Gamble (Jeremy Renner of 2002's *Dahmer*) as well as the disapproving but nevertheless loyal Jim Street (Colin Farrell of last year's *Phone Booth*) gambled with innocent lives, doughy and unpleasant Captain Fuller (Larry Poindexter) throws them out of the unit. Although faced with the less-than-exciting prospect of sitting around manning the gun cage for months on end, Street nonetheless agrees to the demotion with professional calm and an eye on earning the chance to someday get back on the team. The impetuous and tempestuous Gamble, however, rages against his superiors and his partner (who Gamble suspects of fingering him as the actual source of trouble to help his own situation), and stalks off the force entirely. Before doing so, he smashes Street into a mirror, the shattering perhaps meant to symbolize the breaking up of their relationship as well as the effect this demotion has had on their senses of self. We get the definite sense that Gamble will be heard from again.

S.W.A.T. then jumps forward six months, and we see that Street is working out rigorously to keep in shape should an opportunity for advancement appear. It materializes in the form of legendary Sergeant Dan "Hondo" Harrelson (Samuel L. Jackson of 2002's *XXX*). Referred to as the "S.W.A.T. gold standard," he has been brought back by the Chief against his former colleague Fuller's wishes. Hondo's mission is to bring back some of the luster which the unit has lost due to bad press from the recent events. His job will include choosing a group of "young pups" and molding them into an extra-special special unit. The obvious antagonism between Fuller and Hondo is exacerbated by Hondo's picks for the squad—especially Street—and Fuller pettily forecasts failure. Hondo finds that he and Street have an immediate rapport and respect for each other, finding they have much in common, including their military training. An even greater bond, however, is that both are now going to get a much hoped for second chance at doing the work they are best at and love the most.

S.W.A.T. then offers up a series of scenes in which we get cursory introductions to the other members of Hondo's new unit. There is sinewy Deke Kaye (LL Cool J of 2002's *Rollerball*, billed as James Todd Smith), tough and tenacious on his beat but a loving and gentle family man at home. Thrice-rejected sole female candidate Chris Sanchez (Michelle Rodriguez, memorable in 1999's *Girlfight*) is a devoted single parent and as tender with her offspring as Deke is with his but tough enough to shrug off being painfully slashed while on duty. Also added are S.W.A.T. vets T. J. McCabe (Josh Charles), a sharpshooter who bristles when Street bests him at the firing range, and Michael Boxer (Brian Van Holt of 2002's *Windtalkers*). Some of the most interesting sequences in *S.W.A.T.* are those in which we watch the group train and gel into a cohesive unit. They shine, Fuller's grudging admiration is hidden below his bitterness and resentment of their success, and Hondo smiles a broad, contented, victorious smile.

Perhaps the biggest thing that hobbles *S.W.A.T.* is that it is about half over before it really begins. That is when the police realize that they have lucked into capturing ice-cold, European mobster Alex Montel (Olivier Martinez of last year's *Unfaithful*), long of hair and short on morals. As he is led off in cuffs after an initial attempt to transfer him goes horribly wrong, the cutthroat (literally) killer looks into a sea of television cameras and brazenly offers $100 million to anyone who helps him get away. Hondo's unit is given the task of transporting Montel to a secure federal facility without any further incident (or embarrassment). All sorts of deadly, money-hungry mischief-makers come out of the woodwork and test the team's ability to successfully carry out their mission.

As they drive along with Montel, we sense that something big is about to happen. The close-ups of an edgy T. J. lend an expectant air, so it is hardly shocking when he pulls his gun on his colleagues to spring Montel. That Gamble is in on this escape plan, getting part of the fortune as well as his foreshadowed retribution against S.W.A.T. and Street comes as little surprise, as well. The hunt is on amidst a good use of dramatic, pulse-pounding music that adds to the sense of urgency. The expertly trained, heroic squad pursues Montel and his expertly trained, villainous assistants through shadowy subway tunnels and storm drains, while Fuller fumes and doubts a successful outcome. Hondo and his officers are determined to prevail, which is a good thing since they must stop a hijacked Lear jet that has landed along a 3000-foot-high bridge to pick up the treacherous trio. The plausibility of this overheated scene is debatable. The plane careens and crashes amidst gunfire, while a female hostage screams and carries on. T. J. opts to blow his own brains out, and Montel is apprehended. And, finally, Street has a showdown with Gamble in what turns out to be a rather brief and—after the whole plane spectacle—anticlimactic battle in which good triumphs over evil.

Many previous films have focused on police in general and the LAPD in particular, and *S.W.A.T.* comes off as merely the latest—more of the same, but nothing particularly new, remarkable, or memorable. Obviously, the S.W.A.T. members' specialized skills prevent loss of life, and their exhaustive training helps to ensure that they meet with few surprises. Unfortunately, while being able to anticipate what happens next is laudable and even lifesaving in their line of work, it can be highly injurious and even lethal to a film. *S.W.A.T.* offers few surprises, suffers from too-sketchy characterization, and has an uninspired air about the whole proceedings. In general, it plays out merely like an extended television episode, shooting for something exceptional but never quite hitting its target. It is simply a standard issue police action drama. Filmed on a budget of $80 million, *S.W.A.T.* grossed almost $115 million and received mixed reviews. *S.W.A.T.* was directed by Clark Johnson, who got the job helming this production based upon his past work in gritty television police dramas like *Homicide: Life on the Street* and *NYPD Blue,* among numerous others. *S.W.A.T.* was written by David McKenna and David Ayer, the latter of whom had better and more interesting things to say pertaining to law enforcement in earlier films (2001's *Training Day* and last year's *Dark Blue*). While the scenes in which the team trains are worthwhile, they also, in retrospect, point to some of the film's weaknesses. As the officers have fun shooting at targets representing bad guys or deal with a simulated hijacking/hostage situation, their juices are clearly flowing and they are yearning for the exciting and challenging real deal. It comes along for them, but it never fully materializes on the screen for us. The acting is adequate (Rodriguez is the most memorable), and we like or hate who we are supposed to. Unfortunately, our feelings for the characters, like those for the film in general, are never as deep or intense as a better film might have elicited. People familiar with the television show will take note of the old *S.W.A.T.* theme song when it appears on the soundtrack, reworked but certainly not better. The same can be said for the film based on the series.

—*David L. Boxerbaum*

CREDITS

Sgt. Dan "Hondo" Harrelson: Samuel L. Jackson
Jim Street: Colin Farrell
Deacon "Deke" Kaye: L.L. Cool J.
T.J. McCabe: Josh Charles
Chris Sanchez: Michelle Rodriguez
Alex Montel: Olivier Martinez
Brian Gamble: Jeremy Renner
Michael Boxer: Brian Van Holt
Lt. Greg Velasquez: Reg E. Cathey

Capt. Thomas Fuller: Larry Poindexter
GQ: Domenick Lombardozzi
Kathy: Lucinda Jenney
Officer Burress: Reed Edward Diamond
Deke's Handsome Partner: Clark Johnson (Cameo)
SWAT truck driver: Steve Forrest (Cameo)

Origin: USA
Released: 2003
Production: Neal H. Moritz, Dan Halstead; Original Film, Camelot; released by Columbia Pictures
Directed by: Clark Johnson
Written by: David Ayer, David McKenna
Cinematography by: Gabriel Beristain
Music by: Elliot Goldenthal
Sound: Steve Nelson
Music Supervisor: Evyen Klean
Editing: Michael Tronick
Art Direction: Gershon Ginsburg
Costumes: Christopher Lawrence
Production Design: Mayne Berke
MPAA rating: PG-13
Running time: 111 minutes

REVIEWS

Chicago Sun-Times Online. August 8, 2003.
Entertainment Weekly. August 15, 2003, p. 50.
Los Angeles Times Online. August 8, 2003.
New York Times Online. August 8, 2003.
People. August 18, 2003, p. 35.
USA Today Online. August 8, 2003.
Variety Online. August 8, 2003.
Washington Post. August 8, 2003, p. WE41.

QUOTES

Hondo (Samuel L. Jackson): "You know what they say, you're either SWAT or you're not."

Sweet Sixteen

Life . . . it's about to hit the fan!
—Movie tagline

The film's title contains a hideous irony. The film's main character, a potentially decent and ambitious youngster named Liam, is looking forward to his sixteenth birthday, because that is the day his mother is to be released from prison. Liam is optimistic. He plans to build a home for his mother, along with his sister and her son Colum. But it's difficult to make plans for other people. Stan's mother is a junkie, who apparently has kept "clean" in prison, but old habits die hard. Liam's sister has never forgiven the mother for her irresponsible habits. She won't even visit her in prison.

The film is set in a one-time shipbuilding center called Greenock, on the Clyde, downriver from Glasgow. Since this is a Ken Loach film, written by Loach regular Paul Laverty, the economy is depressed, unemployment is a problem, and dead-enders are more than recreationally interested in drugs. Despite appearances—a rainbow in evidence over the city early in the film, for example—Greenock has "one of the highest incidences of drug use in Europe," according to critic Roger Bromley's *Cineaste* review. In other words, this is a typical Ken Loach film, involved, as A. O. Scott described in the *New York Times,* with "the grim lot of the British working class—in particular the effects of work, poverty, and the putatively benevolent intervention of the state on proletarian family life." The juvenile lead, Martin Compston, who plays a sixteen-year-old Liam, grew up in Greenock, bringing the best kind of authenticity to the project, including a very thick accent that requires subtitles. His performance won the London Critics Circle Film Award for best newcomer of the year 2002. The film premiered at the Cannes International Film Festival.

Liam's stepfather, Stan (Gary McCormack) is a drug dealer who should be serving time in prison, but the cad has arranged it so that Liam's mother, Jean (Michelle Coulter), is serving time instead. Since Stan is a loser and a worthless slacker, Liam plots to make money to provide for his family. He hopes to buy his mother a caravan (house trailer) on the banks of the Clyde, but where will he find that kind of money? His no-good stepfather has him transporting drugs, just as he wants Liam's mother to sell drugs in prison. Maybe Liam could cadge his Stan's stash of heroin and sell it himself?

Liam refuses to cooperate in Stan's plan to get drugs to his mother in prison. He is instructed to keep a filled packet in his mouth, which he is supposed to transfer to his mother by kissing her in the prison reception room while, Stan creates a diversion in the visitor's room by dropping a cup of coffee. After Liam refuses, he is later beaten and kicked by Stan and his grandfather, Rab (Tommy McKee). Liam then moves in with his sister, Chantelle (Annmarie Fulton) and her infant son Calum. She dresses his wounds and recites a litany of things that she will not allow in her flat. Chantelle is well disciplined and determined not to become like her mother, whom she has essentially rejected and disowned. Liam wants them to be reconciled so that his mother may enjoy her grandson and all of them may live together as a happy family.

In order to raise money to buy the caravan, Liam becomes a drug dealer, working with his friend, "Pinball" (William Ruane). He builds his drug inventory by stealing Stan's stash, hidden under the floorboards of an outbuilding. Liam's advantage is that he is not himself a user. Although not yet sixteen, he is wise and tough beyond his years. When three thugs attempt to steal his drugs, he fights back and will not give up, though clearly outnumbered. He keeps coming back after he has been beaten and kicked, until he finally reclaims what is his. His extreme determination is driven by his desire to purchase the caravan for his mother in order to keep her away from Stan.

Liam is so successful as a pusher that he comes to the attention of Douglas, the local drug kingpin, who operates behind the "front" of a respectable health spa. Liam becomes Douglas's middleman, organizing his distribution process. Douglas sets him up in the pizza business that delivers more than just pizza. Liam has to provide reliable delivery boys on scooters and works out a smooth procedure. Though Douglas respects Liam for his organizational skills and efficiency, he wants nothing at all to do with Pinball, Liam's sidekick, who gets ignored and is both angry and disappointed, to the extent that he steals Douglas's car and crashes it into the show window of Douglas's health club. Meanwhile, the caravan that Liam wanted for his mother and had placed a deposit on is mysteriously burned to the ground. When Douglas sends Liam out to punish Pinball, Pinball claims credit for the arson, but, then, so does Stan in another confrontation later on. One gets the sick feeling that this story cannot end well, and in fact it does not.

Douglas makes it clear that he will take care of Liam, so long as Liam is useful to him. He wants Pinball punished (which turns out to be, unbeknownst to Douglas, a matter of self-punishment, but an ambulance needs to be called), and in return he gives Liam the keys to a well-appointed apartment on the better side of town, with a balcony and a nice view of the Clyde. When Jean is released from prison on Liam's birthday, he takes her to the new apartment, where she is welcomed with a house-warming party. Chantelle even comes to share in the festivities and perhaps to stay, willing to give her mother a second chance. It looks like everything is going according to Liam's plan—at least until the next morning.

When Liam wakes up the next morning, Chantelle tells him that their mother has gone to live with Stan. So on his birthday, Liam goes across town to retrieve his mother, but she prefers to stay with Stan and presumably go back to her old habits. Liam argues with her, and with Stan, and, when Stan gets physical with him, Liam knifes him in the stomach. The last shot of the film resembles François Truffaut's *The 400 Blows* (1958), when Antoine Doinel is standing by the sea after having escaped from reform school. Liam is also at the water's edge. He has just spoken to his sister on his cellular telephone, telling her that he does not know where he is, though she tells him that the police are looking for him. In the film's last shot, Liam is seen walking toward the water.

Washington Post reviewer Stephen Hunter praised Loach for "making tough working-class dramas in England for nearly 30 years" and called the film "a wee masterpiece." That's rather too cute a dismissal for a film as serious as this one. Elvis Mitchell was nearer the mark in his *New York Times* review when he noted that Loach's sense of purpose "leaves no room for sentimentality." *Sweet Sixteen*, Mitchell concluded, shows that Loach is "as capable of anger as his protagonist and just as eager to draw attention to an unchanging problem: the blight of generational poverty." One wonders, however, if it is not just as surely a matter of spiritual poverty. The story is by turns hopeful and grim as Liam's hopes are dashed by the reality of the situation. The film recalls *Trainspotting* (1995) to a degree, without descending to quite the same surreal levels of degradation.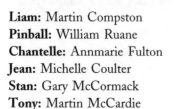

—*James M. Welsh*

CREDITS

Liam: Martin Compston
Pinball: William Ruane
Chantelle: Annmarie Fulton
Jean: Michelle Coulter
Stan: Gary McCormack
Tony: Martin McCardie
Suzanne: Michelle Abercromby
Rab: Tommy McKee

Origin: Great Britain, Germany, Spain
Released: 2002
Production: Rebecca O'Brien; Road Movies, Tornasol Films SA, Alta Films SA, BBC Films, Scottish Screen; released by Lions Gate Films
Directed by: Ken Loach
Written by: Paul Laverty
Cinematography by: Barry Ackroyd
Music by: George Fenton
Sound: Ray Beckett
Editing: Jonathan Morris
Art Direction: Fergus Clegg
Costumes: Carole K. Millar
Production Design: Martin Johnson
MPAA rating: R
Running time: 106 minutes

REVIEWS

Boxoffice. July, 2002, p. 79.
Chicago Sun-Times Online. June 13, 2003.
Entertainment Weekly. May 23, 2003, p. 54.
Los Angeles Times Online. May 23, 2003.
New York Times Online. May 16, 2003.
People. May 26, 2003, p. 37.
Sight and Sound. October, 2002, p. 54.
Variety. May 27, 2002, p. 29.
Washington Post. June 6, 2003, p. WE44.

AWARDS AND NOMINATIONS

Cannes 2003: Screenplay.

Swimming Pool

On the surface, all is calm.
—Movie tagline

 Box Office: $10.2 million

"You must have mistaken me with someone else. I'm not the person you think I am," best-selling mystery writer Sarah Morton (Charlotte Rampling) tells an adoring fan when she is spotted on the London underground in the opening minutes of François Ozon's *Swimming Pool.* Sarah is weary of the recognition she receives for her popular series of Inspector Dorwell books and would rather be left alone. But her words hint at something else as well, a deep yearning within herself to be someone new, to shed her stale persona and regain the sense of creativity she has lost. *Swimming Pool,* however, is not just a sly character study of a writer's transformation; it is also a cool, elegant puzzler of a mystery, a kind of game between filmmaker and audience in which everything we see takes on a whole new meaning in the film's last few minutes.

When Sarah visits her publisher, John Bosload (Charles Dance), she becomes jealous of a young, up-and-coming writer he is spending time with. The fact that the writer tells her how much his mother likes the Dorwell series only makes Sarah feel like a dinosaur, though the real problem seems to be her frustration with the police procedural genre that bores her despite its financial rewards. John offers her his home in the south of France as a retreat where she can clear her head and allow the change of setting to inspire her to write something new.

Sarah takes up residence in his beautiful villa, complete with swimming pool. She meets Marcel (Marc Fayolle), the groundskeeper, and then settles in and begins work. She sets up her laptop computer, buys a few items for the refrigerator, visits the local café, and calls John to tell him how pleased she is that she accepted his offer. It is a tribute to Rampling's talent that even when she is alone performing seemingly menial tasks, she is riveting to watch. We anticipate that something is going to poke a hole in her steely reserve. Indeed, we know that it will happen, and we know that she wants it to happen so she can challenge herself.

That night, in fact, Sarah is awakened when a car comes barreling into the driveway, and she goes downstairs to discover a young blonde girl in the living room. She is Julie (Ludivine Sagnier), John's French daughter, and it is apparent from her bags that she plans to stay for a while. Despite Julie's initial attempts to be friendly, they have a very tense relationship. Julie is very forward and obviously wants to see if she can push Sarah's buttons, asking at the outset if Sarah is her father's latest conquest.

Basking in her youth and sexual allure, Julie is very promiscuous, bringing home different men and having loud, wild sex in the living room while Sarah is trying to sleep. Julie also lounges around topless and swims in the pool. Sarah, while she acts repulsed by this hedonistic creature, is clearly fascinated by her and grows increasingly curious about her past.

Sarah's imagination is waiting to be stimulated and explored like the initially covered, dormant pool, which is strewn with leaves and needs to be cleaned and refreshed. When Julie, her sexy sprite of a muse, lifts the tarp and has Marcel clean the pool, it becomes a symbol of Sarah's reawakening and a reflection for her new writing life. It will also become the scene of the crime for her new book, thus linking her own baptism into a new creativity with the product of her imagination.

For much of *Swimming Pool*, not a lot happens in terms of plot, but the film is never boring because we are constantly wondering where the Sarah-Julie relationship is going. The film could be seen as a languorous mood piece charting how a classically repressed, older Englishwoman falls under the spell of French culture and indulges the physical pleasures of youth. The young girl is clearly a catalyst sparking Sarah's imagination and getting her to live more adventurously, even though she does her best to remain aloof and not be friends. Ozon and co-screenwriter Emmanuèle Bernheim use the accumulation of details, even in small things like diet, to flesh out this shift. Sarah is only too happy, for example, to forego her Spartan diet of yogurt and enjoy secretly the rich delicacies of cheese and meat that Julie brings home.

Inspired to write about Julie, Sarah copies directly out of her housemate's journal and even asks her out to dinner to gather material. Surprisingly enough, Julie does not mind talking about her past. Sagnier is not only a pleasure to look

at but suggests that there is more to Julie than the oversexed nymphet. Stories of her father's abandonment and her first true love let us see a deep-seated vulnerability and a certain sadness, which usually is masked by her toughness and sexual adventurism. Later, Sarah also reveals the person she once was, mentioning her wild times in "swinging London." Under Julie's influence, perhaps this seemingly staid writer could be that person again.

Since the narrative is very simple, the performances are crucial to our enjoyment of *Swimming Pool*, and the interplay of Rampling and Sagnier is perfect. It is not the obvious clash of opposites, as we might at first think, but rather a devious exploration of how a writer finds inspiration in the most unexpected of places.

The story takes a major turn when Julie discovers that Sarah has been writing about her and then, as if to fulfill the role of temptress, brings back Franck (Jean-Marie Lamour), the hunky waiter from the local café whom Sarah likes. When he takes more of an interest in Sarah, a jealous Julie coaxes him to the pool for a sexual encounter that ends in violence.

The next day Sarah searches the town for Franck, only to have Julie confess that she killed him. The two women bury the corpse, and, given all of her experience in writing detective fiction, Sarah is confident that they will get away with the crime. Admittedly, all of these plot turns tend to feel arbitrary. After all, in a matter of hours, the two women go from being antagonists to uneasy friends to accomplices in a murder. Julie's only explanation for killing Franck is that she thought it would be good for Sarah's book, an odd justification that can be understood only in the context of the conclusion.

Indeed, we are left to ponder why the narrative flow is odd and why character motivations seem inconsistent until the end when all of these events take on a logic of their own. From the film's last sequence, which takes place back in England, we understand that everything that happened in France took place in Sarah's mind. Julie, Franck, and the murder are all pieces of a story Sarah imagined and turned into *Swimming Pool*, a book she publishes without John's help because she guesses correctly that he would not like it. After she shows it to him and is leaving his office, Sarah sees Julia, John's real daughter, coming to visit her father. Blonde like the fictional Julie, this girl could be a younger version of the woman Sarah created. As a hint of a smile crosses her lips, Sarah seems to feel a certain satisfaction, as if she were happy that she had come close in guessing what John's daughter might look like.

It is, ultimately, a very simple twist but one that makes us reexamine everything we have seen from a fresh perspective. When we do, the film's narrative illogic makes sense. Even Sarah's brief encounter with a dwarf who looks old enough to be Marcel's wife but is really his daughter now has a surreal edge, as if Sarah the writer were playing with her audience, creating a mysterious character to add color to her story. And other strange scenes, including one of Franck appearing out of nowhere and standing over Julie seemingly unnoticed at poolside and another of Marcel gazing at Sarah in the same way, can now be interpreted as the blurring of fantasy and reality in Sarah's mind.

Audiences may remember *Swimming Pool* for Ozon's narrative gamesmanship in telling a story through his protagonist's imagination, but his cleverness should not obscure the film's achievement as a meditation on the writing life itself. Through her art, a burned-out Sarah writes herself into one of her mysteries, even allowing herself the fantasy of being desired by Franck along the way, and emerges rejuvenated with a piece of fiction she is proud of. Ozon may employ the mechanics of suspense films to keep us intrigued, but he also paints a unique portrait of an artist transforming herself through her fiction.

—Peter N. Chumo II

CREDITS

Sarah Morton: Charlotte Rampling
Julie: Ludivine Sagnier
John Bosload: Charles Dance
Marcel: Marc Fayolle
Franck: Jean-Marie Lamour

Origin: France, Great Britain
Released: 2003
Production: Olivier Delbosc, Marc Missionier; Fidelite Productions; released by Focus Features
Directed by: Francois Ozon
Written by: Francois Ozon, Emmanuele Bernheim
Cinematography by: Yorick Le Saux
Music by: Philippe Rombi
Sound: Lucien Balibar
Editing: Monica Coleman
Costumes: Pascaline Chavanne
Production Design: Wouter Zoon
MPAA rating: R
Running time: 102 minutes

REVIEWS

Boxoffice. September, 2003, p. 124.
Chicago Sun-Times Online. July 2, 2003.
Entertainment Weekly. July 11, 2003, p. 62.
Los Angeles Times Online. July 2, 2003.
New York Times Online. July 2, 2003.
People. July 21, 2003, p. 35.
Premiere. July/August, 2003, p. 25.
Variety Online. May 18, 2003.
Washington Post. July 2, 2003, p. C9.

Sylvia

Life was too small to contain her.
—Movie tagline
Uncover the truth behind the century's most powerful voice and the fall's most passionate and provocative love story.
—Movie tagline

 Box Office: $1.3 million

Because of the quality of her poetry, Sylvia Plath (1932-1963) is considered a major American poet. Because of the chaos of her personal life, which led to her suicide, she has attained almost mythological status among poetry lovers, feminists, and those, in the words of John Keats, "half in love with easeful death." *Maclean's* film critic Brian D. Johnson calls Plath "the Che Guevara of feminist martyrs." Her turbulent marriage to English poet Ted Hughes (1930-1998) is the subject of several books and dozens of articles. Then there is *The Birthday Letters* (1998), Hughes's own poetic account of his marriage; Kate Moses's *Wintering* (2003), a fictional account of Plath's final months; another novel; a play; and even an opera. Plath, Keats, F. Scott Fitzgerald, and a handful of other writers who died young are the literary equivalent of James Dean, Marilyn Monroe, and Janis Joplin. Poet Anne Sexton, also a suicide, termed her friend's death as a great career move. *Sylvia* attempts to dramatize Plath's tortured soul and succeeds up to a point.

The film opens with Plath (Gwyneth Paltrow) meeting Hughes (Daniel Craig) at a University of Cambridge party in 1956. (She received a Fulbright scholarship after graduating from Smith College.) Partly because he has written a negative review of one of her poems in a student literary journal, Plath is intrigued by Hughes, and there is an instant animal attraction between the two. This meeting, one of several effective scenes, has Plath, after a kiss, biting Hughes on the cheek; the action is well handled by screenwriter John Brownlow, director Christine Jeffs, and the actors.

After a brief courtship, they marry and move to the United States to take up teaching positions. (Although the film is vague about locations, Plath taught at her alma mater and Hughes at the University of Massachusetts.) Hughes meets Plath's rather icy widowed mother, Aurelia (Blythe Danner, Paltrow's real-life mother), who seems suspicious of him from the very beginning. At a welcoming party, the rugged Hughes almost has to fight off advances from his mother-in-law's friends. Plath later uneasily observes wide-eyed co-eds hovering around her husband. Her jealousy leads to their return to England.

From this point on, the film alternates between Plath's increasing jealousy and the impediments to her writing created by her family life, which eventually includes a daughter and a son. Because all the lust aimed at Hughes seems unreciprocated, *Sylvia* implies that Plath's suspicions drive her husband to adultery. During production, the film was entitled *Sylvia and Ted,* and a film alternating between their points of view would have presented a more complete picture. (The title may very well have been changed because the original sounds like a comedy.) As it is, Hughes remains rather enigmatic, and the focus on Plath heightens her isolation, as Jeffs and Brownlow no doubt intend.

The film's dramatic highlight comes with a very tense dinner party for another couple. Plath grows increasingly self-pitying and unstable during the meal and almost drives Hughes and Assia Wevill (Amira Casar) together. Soon, Hughes leaves Plath for Wevill. During a brief reconciliation, Plath and Hughes have sex, and she asks him to come back to her only to have him reveal that his lover is pregnant. Her suicide follows, thankfully off screen. The film's postscript fails to disclose that Wevill killed her daughter by Hughes and committed suicide in 1969.

While it is relatively easy to dramatize the lives of painters and composers, writers present a unique dilemma because watching someone scribble or pound on typewriter keys conveys little. Even Fred Zinnemann, in *Julia* (1977), one of the few good films about writers, can find no other means of conveying Lillian Hellman at work.

Something else, however, seems to be missing from Sylvia because the sudden revelations that Plath has been writing, despite all the cooking, cleaning, baby tending, and worrying about Hughes, seem to come out of nowhere. Hughes's casual reference to his wife's novel *The Bell Jar* (1963) is especially startling. To this point, the audience thinks she is a poet only. Where has this novel come from? And how did she find the time to write it? Are her complaints about marriage and motherhood keeping her from working merely a self-delusional pose? Obviously not, but the film certainly leaves this interpretation open. Any cinematic treatment of artists is necessarily superficial to a certain degree, but Sylvia seems much more interested in its protagonists as a troubled couple than as writers, resembling an adaptation of a Margaret Drabble novel. Brownlow has said that the ultimate battling couple drama, Edward Albee's play *Who's Afraid of Virginia Woolf?* (1962), is a major influence on his screenplay. The most literary parts of the film come at the beginning: a small gathering of Cambridge poets reciting their works and responding to the poems of their friends; Plath and Hughes reciting poetry while punting on the Cam, with her arising to declaim Chaucer to cows standing on the riverbank. These early scenes offer a convincing portrait of the protagonists' literary fervor.

Some omissions or seeming superficialities are justified. Before they are married, Plath tells Hughes that she once attempted suicide, but the filmmakers provide little more clinical information beyond the impact of her father's death when she was eight. Her psychiatric treatment is never mentioned. Jeffs and Brownlow clearly do not want Plath reduced to a too-easily-understood case study.

Casting Paltrow aids greatly in this approach. It is easy to see how an admirer of the Geraldine Page, Gena Rowlands, or Sandy Dennis schools of self-conscious tics would have presented Plath, but Paltrow refrains from Method acting. As a result, some might see her as inadequate to the task, but she, as well as Jeffs, knows it is best to trust the material and not try to underscore the character's obvious neuroses. Paltrow is best at conveying Plath's complexity economically and often silently, as when she is kneeling naked on a sofa after Hughes's disclosure of his pregnant mistress. This is one of the few shots in which Plath appears in the center of the frame. Most of the time, she is hovering on the edge of the frame, as on the margin of a tenuous existence.

There are several scenes, well-framed and well-lit by cinematographer John Toon, combining Plath's beauty, sexuality, sadness, loneliness, and resolve. Likewise is the film's final shot, with a forlorn Hughes framed within a window seen from outside Plath's apartment during a light snowfall. The shot encompasses both Hughes's complicity and sense of loss.

While the real Hughes was the son of a carpenter, he had an upper-class mien, so the more roughhewn Craig at first seems too working-class. But as Jeffs presents the character, Craig's more pronounced maleness supports the view that the poet had to fight women off. Best known as the murderous monk in *Elizabeth* (1998), painter Francis Bacon's lover in *Love Is the Devil* (1998), and Paul Newman's villainous weasel of a son in *The Road to Perdition* (2002), Craig, like Paltrow, underplays the part while capturing Hughes's combination of charisma, weakness, and sadness.

There are also good performances by Jared Harris as Al Alvarez, the journalist who became Plath's confidante and who has written extensively about her; the great Michael Gambon in a small role as Plath's kindly neighbor (and unwitting accomplice in her suicide); and Danner, worlds away from her wacky mom in *Meet the Parents* (2000). As with her daughter's performance, Danner conveys Aurelia's coldness with subtle strokes to avoid turning her into a clichéd mother-as-monster.

Jeffs' first film, *Rain* (2001), also focuses on a dysfunctional family and infidelity (this time in the early 1970s), with alcoholism, rather than mental instability, as an attendant problem. Both films feature good performances, atmospheric photography (both by Toon), and period detail. Production designer Maria Djurkovic, as she does in *The Hours* (2002), helps convey the moral confusion of the characters by creating drab, claustrophobic settings for their misery.

As a portrait of a complex, suicidal poet, *Sylvia* is inferior to *Stevie* (1978), with Glenda Jackson's wonderful performance as Stevie Smith, but it is more consistent in its tone than the somewhat similar *The Hours* and much easier to take than *The Bell Jar* (1979), the dreary adaptation of Plath's novel. The film also avoids the easy trap of becoming a feminist tract; the audience is never hit over the head with sexual politics, unlike, say, in *The Hours*. Thanks to Jeffs, Brownlow, and the cast, what could easily have been off-putting, even depressing, is a calm, compassionate, if slightly superficial treatment of its subject.

—*Michael Adams*

CREDITS

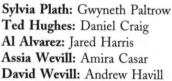

Sylvia Plath: Gwyneth Paltrow
Ted Hughes: Daniel Craig
Al Alvarez: Jared Harris
Assia Wevill: Amira Casar
David Wevill: Andrew Havill
Tom Hadley-Clarke: Sam Troughton
Michael Boddy: Anthony Strachan
Doreen: Lucy Davenport
Aurelia Plath: Blythe Danner
Professor Thomas: Michael Gambon
Morecambe: David Birkin
Charles Langridge: Michael Mears

Origin: Great Britain
Released: 2003
Production: Alison Owen; BBC Films, Capitol Films, Ruby Films; released by Focus Features
Directed by: Christine Jeffs
Written by: John Brownlow
Cinematography by: John Toon
Music by: Gabriel Yared
Sound: David Crozier
Editing: Tariq Anwar
Art Direction: Jane Cecchi
Costumes: Sandy Powell
Production Design: Maria Djurkovic
MPAA rating: R
Running time: 110 minutes

REVIEWS

Chicago Sun-Times Online. October 24, 2003.
Entertainment Weekly. October 24, 2003, p. 82.
Los Angeles Times Online. October 17, 2003.
Maclean's. October 27, 2003, p. 93.
New Republic. November 10, 2003, p. 24.
New York Times. October 17, 2003, p. E1.
New York Times Online. October 19, 2003.
New Yorker. October 20, 2003, p. 206.
Newsweek. October 20, 2003, p. 57.
People. October 27, 2003, p. 32.
Rolling Stone. November 13, 2003, p. 106.
USA Today. October 17, 2003, p. E5.
Variety Online. October 3, 2003.
Washington Post. October 24, 2003, p. WE33.

QUOTES

Aurelia (Blythe Danner) to Ted (Daniel Craig): "I think you frightened her. That's why she likes you."
Syliva (Gwyneth Paltrow) to Ted (Daniel Craig): "You go for a bike ride and come back with an epic in hexameter. I try to write, and I get a bake sale."

Taking Sides (Der Fall Furtwangler)

Celebrated master Hungarian filmmaker Istvan Szabo's *Taking Sides* goes beyond the structure of the traditional whodunit to ask a moral question: did the "who" in question have to do it? Set during the American Occupation of a Germany devastated by the Second World War, the film's protagonist, the irascible, aging Major Arnold (Harvey Keitel), must investigate how a popular orchestra conductor of the time, Wilhelm Furtwangler (Stellan Skarsgard), became a national treasure, and more, an artistic embodiment of Nazi rule.

Szabo, for his part reveals an ideological complexity noticeably missing in Nazi-bashing epics, including last year's *The Pianist* by Roman Polanski, which ironically was also scripted by Ronald Harwood. *Taking Sides* raises the question of how much blame can be placed on a serious artist if a repressive regime chooses to exploit his success. Furtwangler was the charismatic conductor of the Berlin Philharmonic; his artistic achievement in getting his orchestra to play as he wanted, and, at the same time, being able to develop a huge following among the German masses, mirrored the power of Hitler himself. On an even deeper level, Szabo's film embodies a self-reflexivity having to do with his own work as a film director under the stern noses of the Party bosses during the Soviet domination of his country.

It is important to note that Szabo, a graduate of the Bela Balazs Film Academy, has allowed the Balazsian ideal of film storytelling to permeate not just the form but also the content of his films. Balazs, writing in the heyday of the silent film, believed that the film medium, among all of man's art forms, was uniquely equipped to lay bare the workings of the human soul, as evident in the filmic device of the facial close-up. For Balazs, this had to go hand-in-hand with film stories that had to be intimate and that looked inward, as opposed to, say, stories of adventures in the great big world out there. Hungarian films have used the Balazsian ideal to their advantage and thereby achieved universal recognition.

Thus, on one level, *Taking Sides* remains an intimate drama. Those being questioned by Arnold have to come to his office, rather than being sought out. Their overt confrontations become ideological battles embellished through their facial expressions. As gripping dramatic entertainment, however, what the film lacks is a sense of mystery and surprise. Adopting the template of Furtwangler's real-life story, what the Major suspects all along is merely fleshed out, as part of a case being built for a trial that we never get to see. Nothing is revealed, of a climactic nature, that anyone wouldn't have suspected. This remains the film's chief drawback.

What redeems the film, however, is Furtwangler's silent mask of guilt mixed with the self-righteousness of an artist, and Arnold's equally powerful and virulent countenance, which remains accusatory and militaristic. The Major is already foreshadowing the rise of the military as a dominant force in American politics. The film's narrative thus shows how Arnold's monomaniacal pursuit of the truth also reveals the moral ambivalence of the artist trapped in such a situation, an ambivalence that Arnold himself refuses to acknowledge.

The film begins with the somber grandeur of the opening notes of Beethoven's Fifth Symphony as it is being conducted by an out-of-focus conductor. In fact, as the main titles roll, the orchestra playing the music remains deliberately blurred in the background. When the titles end, Szabo presents the conventional view of the orchestra playing in an ornate hall designed very much like a church, with the packed audience seated in pews. In keeping with the sweep of the music, Szabo's camera roams freely above their heads, then tracks pew by pew, as if to convey a macrocosmic view of German society—including the Nazis, who are prominent in military uniform—all stock-still and enraptured. As searchlights intrude upon the scene, along with the roar of aircraft above, we see Furtwangler conducting with a worried expression. The camera then captures the second violinist, Helmut Rode (Ulrich Tukur), who will provide the most telling testimony on Furtwangler. With the sound of bombs dropping, the lights go off, and the film's introductory sequence is complete, depicting the inextricable bond between music, politics, and war.

As in his earlier work, Szabo bolsters his fictional reenactment with the truth of documentary reality. In this case, it is footage of the Nuremberg rallies showing Hitler raising his arm to acknowledge a multitude of Nazi salutes as he is driven by. As the camera pulls back from a makeshift screen in a darkened room, a voice in a thick American accent comments, "Boy, did they love him!" The voiceover then argues that Hitler touched something that has to be "rooted out". With simplistic wisdom, the voice concludes: "You know what I think? I think we're all Nazis!" Arnold is then acquainted with the strategic underpinnings of his project. "Now we can't take every Nazi in this country to trial," his superior intones, "so we're going for the big boys in industry, education, law and culture." Unfortunately, the film doesn't take as expansive a view, and decides instead to close in on Arnold's particular project, with the result that it too begins to appear as monomaniacal as the Major.

For the hard-boiled Arnold, however, who is made to sit through films of Nazi bombings, it is just so much more of war's atrocities. But even he has his sleep disturbed by scenes of corpses bulldozed into a mass grave. Thus, with his historical antinomies forcefully in place, Szabo is ready to start his story of the investigation proper.

As Arnold sets up his office within a former Nazi fortress, now a vacant baroque mansion, he has two soft-spoken assistants to kick around: Lieutenant Wills (Moritz Bleibtrau), an American of German origin, as his liaison officer, and Emmi Straube (Birgit Minichmayr), a concentration camp survivor, as his personal secretary. From his initial interviews with the former orchestra members, Arnold encounters only vociferous denial of any involvement with the Nazi party, along with admiration for their conductor, who they maintain was a great artist, one the Fuhrer chose to idolize, instead of the other way around. In his defense, they cite the one incident that according to them proved that Furtwangler did not kowtow to Hitler: after a performance he walked up to the Fuhrer with a baton in his hand, and, very cleverly, avoided having to give the Nazi salute. Rode, in fact, claims that it was he who gave Furtwangler the idea.

For Arnold, all this is straddling the fence. The narrative of the film at this stage also becomes repetitive and, like Arnold, seems to be getting nowhere. Wisely, Szabo adopts an omniscient stance, We see Furtwangler traveling alone in a trolley car, dressed in a black coat, black gloves and a black hat, all serving to highlight the facial expression of a man racked by a deep sense of guilt. This refreshing omniscience, however, doesn't last long. We are shunted back to Arnold's oppressive, obsessive German-bashing. "I'll make you listen to Beethoven!" he threatens Wills at one point.

Furtwangler's testimony, whose stages structure the film's narrative from this point on, remains centered on his conscience rather than his actions. The latter, however, become the basis of Arnold's nagging accusations, which he crudely, and cruelly, hurls at him. As Arnold, assisted by Wills and Emmi, conducts his research, Szabo's narrative falls into yet another trap. We get to know some of the facts before Arnold confronts Furtwangler with them. A resulting undertow of tedium sets in, one that cannot be offset by the film's subplots. In one, Wills, quite independently, prepares a case in Furtwangler's defense. In the other, the shy Emmi gives in to her co-worker's burgeoning romantic advances.

Taking Sides is basically a film about ideas rather than character. Its real payoff is the climactic confrontation between its two archetypal opponents in terms of what they represent. On that level, it is Furtwangler who triumphs. His cry from a wounded spirit speaks of how the music he was celebrating for the Fuhrer was, for Furtwangler, the only Germany, a metaphysical entity of far greater inspirational force than the political monster it had become. Arnold's voiceover informs us that Furtwangler, who was to die in 1954, was acquitted by the American tribunal, and was able to resume his career, but he was never allowed to conduct in the U.S.

But Szabo, the master, has one final lesson for film storytellers the world over: it is only documentary film reality that can provide a substratum of truth, read ambivalence, for the fiction film. In the film's closing moments, we see the real-life Furtwangler receiving a standing ovation, then bowing to Hitler and walking up to shake hands with him.

Szabo's own reluctance to "take sides" seems to have counted the most among the film's American critics. *Newsday*'s Jan Stuart in finds a "tantalizing inconclusiveness" in his stance, while Leslie Camhi, in the *Village Voice*, notes Szabo's "courage (and sense) to leave the film's compelling questions unresolved." Stuart goes on to conclude: "As we grapple now with our renewed identity as a liberating, occupying nation, *Taking Sides* registers with a timeliness that is properly unnerving."

—*Vivek Adarkar*

CREDITS

Major Steve Arnold: Harvey Keitel
Wilhelm Furtwangler: Stellan Skarsgard
Lt. David Wills: Moritz Bleibtreu
Emmi Straube: Birgit Minichmayr
Col. Dymshitz: Oleg Tabakov
Helmut Rode: Ulrich Tukur
Rudolf Werner: Hanns Zischler
Captain Ed Martin: August Zirner
General Wallace: R. Lee Ermey
Captain Vernay: Robin Renucci

Origin: France, Germany
Released: 2001
Production: Yves Pasquier; Little Big Bear Film, Maecenas Film, Studio Babelsberg, Paladin Productions; released by New Yorker Films

Directed by: Istvan Szabo
Written by: Ronald Harwood
Cinematography by: Lajos Koltai
Sound: Brian Simmons
Music Supervisor: Ulrich Trimborn
Editing: Sylvie Landra
Art Direction: Anja Mueller
Costumes: Gyorgyi Szakacs
Production Design: Ken Adam
MPAA rating: Unrated
Running time: 105 minutes

REVIEWS

Boxoffice. December, 2001, p. 56.
Chicago Sun-Times Online. October 17, 2003.
Entertainment Weekly. September 12, 2003, p. 131.
Los Angeles Times Online. September 19, 2003.
New York Times Online. August 31, 2003.
New York Times Online. September 5, 2003.
Newsday Online. September 5, 2003.
Variety. September 24, 2001, p. 24.
Village Voice Online. September 3, 2003.

Tears of the Sun

He was trained to follow orders. He became a hero by defying them.
—Movie tagline

Box Office: $42.8 million

Tears of the Sun is yet another Bruce Willis action adventure, but this is not the *Die Hard* Bruce but a glum, monosyllabic Bruce in the tradition of Clint Eastwood and Sylvester Stallone. The film is adequately if unimaginatively directed by Antoine Fuqua, but the script by Patrick Cirillo and Alex Lasker is strictly by the numbers.

The democratically elected president of Nigeria has been murdered by Muslim rebels during a military coup, and the rebels are swarming the country engaged in what the film repeatedly calls "ethnic cleansing." In immediate danger is Dr. Lena Kendricks (Monica Bellucci), the Italian widow of an American doctor, working in a clinic at a Catholic mission deep in the jungle. Captain Bill Rhodes (Tom Skerritt) sends Lieutenant A. K. Waters (Bruce Willis) and his team of Navy SEALS to rescue the doctor and the three European religious-aid workers at the mission.

At first, Dr. Kendricks refuses to leave, but she changes her mind after Waters agrees to take some of her "people" with them. The priest and two nuns decide to stay behind even though rebel forces are closing in. The decision to take villagers with them is slightly confusing. It's unclear whether by "my people" the doctor means patients or clinic workers, but most of the group is fit enough to trek through miles of jungle. Fuqua's shots of those left behind, who seem relatively tranquil, raise questions (completely ignored by the filmmakers) about how Dr. Kendricks decided who would stay and who would go. What matters is that there is a manageably small group for the drama ahead.

Waters and his men lead the group to a spot where they meet transport helicopters, but mean old Waters has tricked them, leaving the able adults behind because there is no room for them. A few minutes later, after witnessing from the air the bloodbath back at the mission, he changes his mind because, you see, despite his gruff exterior, he's really a mushy old humanitarian at heart. Waters, the SEALS, and the good doctor then reunite with the discarded citizens to continue their journey to the Cameroon border. On the way, there's a narrow escape from the rebels, the discovery of a traitor, and, finally, a fierce battle. As time passes, Waters and Dr. Kendricks evolve from animosity to understanding to friendship.

There is, however, no romance, and that's one of the few clichés *Tears of the Sun* avoids. (According to the *Los Angeles Times*, a kissing scene was shot.) It's almost as if Lasker, whose credits include *Firefox* (1982) and *Beyond Rangoon* (1995), and Cirillo, who wrote *Homer & Eddie* (1989), had taken that screenwriting class Brian Cox teaches in *Adaptation* (2002). Dr. Kendricks resists coming with Waters before giving in. Those who stay behind are slaughtered. Waters does something bad but changes his mind and redeems himself. The pilgrims march through the jungle for a few minutes and then stop and chat for a few minutes and so on until the bullets start flying. They must hide and keep quiet the first time the rebels are near, and naturally there's a baby so that all can worry that its cries will give them away. A rebel almost walks into a hiding SEAL before he's called back, a narrow escape. The men resent putting their lives at risk against Captain Rhodes's orders but gradually come to understand Waters's motivation. Those who avoid death in one battle live on to die in another.

The latter is good, however, for the poor actors playing the SEALS because they have little chance to stand out until they are killed. Except for the African-American Silk (Charles Ingram), it's hard to tell them apart until over halfway through the film. It doesn't help that all have one-syllable names (Doc, Flea, Red, Slo, Zee) that are difficult to match to the grimy faces. Others in the large cast fare little better. Just after being outstanding as the servant in *The Others* (2001), Fionnula Flanagan has only a few lines as a nun. Even worse, Malick Bowens, so wonderful as Karen

Blixen's loyal servant Farah in *Out of Africa* (1985), has no lines as a rebel officer.

Cirillo and Lasker do a few things right. There's no explanation for why Waters is the oldest lieutenant in the navy. (The men call him L.T.) There are several hints that his stoicism has been erected to hide from the emotional wounds of the past, but what exactly has happened to him is never spelled out. (The original screenplay explained Waters's bitter experience in Bosnia.) Without this enigmatic mystery, there would be no character for Willis to play. Explanations for such tortured souls always diminish them. On the other hand, Dr. Kendricks is simply underwritten. She's a good woman trying to do the right thing against great odds, and that's it.

Best known for sexy roles in films such as *Malena* (2000) and *Irreversible* (2002), Bellucci is to be applauded for trying something different. Dr. Kendricks is decidedly unglamorous: Her face is constantly dirty and her hair matted and wild. Wearing little makeup, Bellucci bravely exposes the defects in her complexion, especially an apparent scar on her nose. There is plenty of time to contemplate the flaws and virtues of her face and body because there's so little else in *Tears of the Sun* to engage the attention.

Because Willis has a closely shaved skull, viewers can also concentrate on the size, shape, and defects of his head. It's hard to imagine how someone so charmingly lively as Willis was as David Addison on *Moonlighting* (1985-1989) could so completely abandon light comedy and become a humorless action star. He has never looked so glum as here. About all he's called upon to do is scowl. When Kendricks finally gets Waters to admit he is damaged, Willis utters a sensitive response in such a squeaky adolescent voice that the scene is almost comical. After reaching his peak in the mid-1990s with *Pulp Fiction* (1994), *Nobody's Fool* (1994), and *Twelve Monkeys* (1995), Willis has done little noteworthy work, with the exception of *The Sixth Sense* (1999).

Fuqua gave his previous film, *Training Day* (2001), a sense of gritty style and energy, but he seems to be pacing himself here. The jungle scenes are reminiscent of films about the Vietnam war, and as Owen Gleiberman observed in *Entertainment Weekly*, the director seems to have studied the looks and pacing of *Platoon* (1986) and *Rambo: First Blood Part II* (1985) in particular. The result is competent direction but nothing remarkable.

As with *Training Day*, Mauro Fiore provides good cinematography. The final sequence, in particular, has a distinctive look, with the yellows and reds capturing both the physical and emotional heat of the situation as the survivors straggle into Cameroon. This washed-out look shows a debt to the style of Janusz Kaminski, for whom Fiore worked as a gaffer on *Schindler's List* (1993).

One of the reasons *Tears of the Sun* looks so much like a Vietnam film is that it was made not in Africa but in Hawaii. The scenery, especially some of the shots from helicopters, is beautiful, but it doesn't look like Africa and distracts from the film's main points. And what are these, after all? Are the filmmakers criticizing the American government for not intervening in the recent periods of ethnic cleansing in Rwanda and Bosnia? Because the film opened days before the American attacks on Iraq, it can also easily be seen as a right-wing rabble-rouser. Or does it have anything at all on its mind? Are the fictional coup and the tropical setting nothing more than excuses to get manly Bruce and sexy Bellucci out there in the jungle? While at times *Tears of the Sun* recalls films such as *The Seven Samurai* (1954), *The Professionals*, (1966), and *Three Kings* (1999), it pales in comparison. Instead of raising the audience's humanitarian or militaristic concerns, *Tears of the Sun* merely elicits a shrug.

—Michael Adams

CREDITS

Lt. A.K. Waters: Bruce Willis
Dr. Lena Kendricks: Monica Bellucci
James "Red" Atkins: Cole Hauser
Capt. Bill Rhodes: Tom Skerritt
Ellis "Zee" Pettigrew: Eamonn Walker
Michael "Slo" Slowenski: Nicholas Chinlund
Sister Grace: Fionnula Flanagan
Col. Idris Sadick: Malick Bowens
Danny "Doc" Kelley: Paul Francis
Kelly Lake: Johnny Messner
Patience: Akosua Busia
Terwase: Peter Mensah
Jason "Flea" Mabry: Chad Smith
Demetrius "Silk" Owens: Charles Ingram

Origin: USA
Released: 2003
Production: Mike Lobell, Arnold Rifkin, Ian Bryce; Revolution Studios, Cheyenne Enterprises; released by Columbia Pictures
Directed by: Antoine Fuqua
Written by: Alex Lasker, Patrick Cirillo
Cinematography by: Mauro Fiore, Mauro Fiore
Music by: Hans Zimmer
Sound: Willie Burton
Editing: Conrad Buff
Art Direction: David Lazan
Costumes: Marlene Stewart
Production Design: Naomi Shohan
MPAA rating: R
Running time: 121 minutes

REVIEWS

Chicago Sun-Times Online. March 7, 2003.
Entertainment Weekly. March 14, 2003, p. 42.
Los Angeles Times Online. March 7, 2003.
New York Times Online. March 7, 2003.
People. March 17, 2003, p. 35.
USA Today Online. March 7, 2003.
Variety Online. March 2, 2003.
Washington Post. March 7, 2003, p. WE41.

QUOTES

Waters (Bruce Willis): "It's been so long since I've done a good thing—the right thing."

Ten

In *Ten*, the celebrated Iranian master filmmaker Abbas Kiarostami offers a family melodrama, what could be called a "woman's picture," in the form of ten segments, each a conversation taking place in real time, and each set in the front seat of one car, a setting from which the film never strays. Historically, Kiarostami's minimalism has its antecedents: Jean Eustache's *The Mother and the Whore* (France, 1973) is three-and-a-half hours comprising a mere handful of scenes in which the characters bare their souls, while Eustache's camera holds them in its unflinching gaze; and R. W. Fassbinder's *The Bitter Tears of Petra Von Kant* (Germany, 1973), in which the entirety of the action takes place within the bedroom of a cramped apartment. While Kiarostami's minimalism is far more extreme, what sets it apart from its forebears is not its uncompromising filmic style, but its national origin.

As such, *Ten*, through its radical form, challenges the Iranian state apparatus as much as its content portrays the repression of Iranian women at all levels of that country's society. Beyond that, however, what makes the film a masterwork is that on a more universal plane, it emerges as a comment on the cybernetic hold on lives lived in hi-tech societies everywhere.

Kiarostami's nameless heroine (Mania Akbari) is a glamorous, recently divorced member of post-revolutionary Iran's nouveau elite. She has found liberation from an oppressive marriage only to realize, as we slowly come to know, that it does not spell freedom to pursue her own happiness. While she remains the film's ostensible narrative lynchpin, the one closer to the film's heart is Amin (Amin Maher), her son from her first marriage, a precocious, globally tuned-in lad in his early teens. Like his slightly older counterparts in the recent Iranian films *Djomeh* and *Baran* the inexperience of youth does not prevent Amin from spouting truths about adult relationships.

The film pays tribute to the kid's enlightening simplicity by keeping its camera focused solely on him during its first 16 minutes. As his Mother harangues him, attempting to justify her divorce of his father, her voice is reduced to a mere voiceover, even though she is seated right next to him. Only those viewers who are prepared to accept this formal conceit will be rewarded with the emotional realism of the sequence.

When the Mother pleads that she needs someone to talk to, we see it as the cry of a woman repressed by male orthodoxy. Amin however covers his ears. In the guise of domestic bickering, Kiarostami shows tomorrow's generation criticizing those in power today. Moreover, it becomes clear that Amin belongs to a generation that has found its self-empowerment via cyberspace. He knows of flying cars from satellite TV. As the son of divorced parents, Amin is content living with his grandmother and spending time with each of his parents in turn. But the kid has plans. Once his Father remarries, Amin is looking forward to living with him. He tells his Mother to her face, "You will never amount to anything!" For her part, she tries to make him see that he "belongs" to the world, and not to his Father. He retorts, with maturity one would never suspect: "Once I grow up, I'll belong to myself!" "Who taught you to talk like that?" his mother asks. "I taught myself!" Amin shoots back. He then comes forth with his main beef, which is that she lied at the trial about his father being a drug addict so that she could get a divorce. The mother defends herself by arguing that a woman in such a society must lie in order to acquire any rights at all. She wins our sympathy when she rages, "A woman has to die in order to live!" Amin merely gets out when the car stops.

It is only then that the shot changes to show us the mother at the wheel, an attractive woman in her thirties, dressed in colorful traditional attire. She has her head covered by a white silk scarf, as proscribed by the state, but at the same time she sports a fashionable pair of sunglasses. At one glance, she would appear to embody the contradictions among today's Iranian elite. Cleverly, Kiarostami cuts to her just as we begin to sympathize with her, precisely because her son doesn't.

Remarkably, our sympathy for her only grows in the scenes, or rather segments, that follow even though we remain locked in, as it were, the front seat of her car. Kiarostami gives his film's title a double meaning by preceding each sequence with numbers from a film leader. A leader ordinarily accompanies each film reel, and runs backward from the "10" as a cue for the projectionist. Kiarostami uses this practice to introduce each segment. Thus, segment nine, which follows, introduces the mother's nameless sister, a large stocky woman dressed in the traditional black *chador* but one revealing a rustic face. The camera merely holds on

her as she sits waiting in the front seat by herself. The film then cuts to the mother as she returns after shopping for fruits. Here, as in the segments to follow, after listening to the woes of the women she picks up, the mother offers advice. In this case, it has to do with bondage to one's husband as being unhealthy. In this segment, the camera freely cuts from one character to the other. When the Mother stops at a baker to buy a cake for her second husband's birthday, the sister is again by herself. There is a troubled look on her face, which vanishes when the mother returns. At one point, the mother offers a lift to a hunchbacked old woman, who turns it down. "I'll be like her one day," the mother says.

When the sister gets out, the film cuts to leader number "8," which introduces the mother at the wheel, driving through an affluent neighborhood, which we glimpse only from the car window. In this segment, she gives a lift to a woman who again remains a voiceover. We can gather that she's a traditional woman dressed in the religiously prescribed *chador*. From her own admission, she has given away everything after her husband died. All she has in the world are her beads. When she offers the mother a rosary, the latter does not accept it, saying that she has no time to pray.

Starting with the above segment, an undertow to our emotional involvement begins to take effect, and one that keeps growing until it almost risks our losing interest in the character of the mother, as we have come to know her. We can relate to the mother's compassion as she picks up various women; what proves repetitive, and puts a strain on the film's length, is her playing an amateur psychotherapist. During these conversations, as the mother spouts platitudes, we don't know enough about her to see what lies behind those abstractions. What is remarkable though, and keeps us riveted, is the mother being able to strike an instant rapport with those belonging to lower social classes. This speaks volumes for post-revolutionary Iranian society.

The woman in segment seven is an unseen prostitute the mother picks up at night. Here, it is the stranger who turns the tables on her. "I'm a woman and you're a woman," the mother says. "No. I'm smart and you're dumb!" the prostitute replies. While remaining a voiceover, she proves to the mother that she, too, is a prostitute for trading sex for expensive gifts. "You're the wholesalers and we're the retailers," the woman of the night concludes. When she gets out, the film provides its only exterior shot, taken from behind, of her soliciting customers in cars.

Segment six takes us into the next day. The mother is dressed in black and without her sunglasses because it is a Friday. Here, she gives a lift to a thin woman with an angular facial beauty. This stranger came to pray at the mausoleum so that she would get married. During this segment, we come to know that despite the mother's modern outlook, religion has been a source of comfort to her.

This again is an example of how basic contradictions can be bridged as a society is thrust, unprepared, into the future.

In the fifth segment, Amin returns. This time, we see his father's jeep in the background. In a more cheerful frame of mind, he speaks of learning computer programming. He and the mother joke about the kind of wife he would like. He then lets his mother in on a secret: his father watches the "sexy scenes" on the locked channels on satellite TV at night by himself. This bit of incidental dialogue provides an incisive comment on how the religious orthodoxy that seized power in Iran with the Islamic Revolution has been unable to prevent the intrusions of global technologies.

In segment four, the mother, driving through downtown Tehran at night, gives a lift to a sobbing young woman, whom she consoles with the words, "Love is an illusion. You only hurt yourself." In the third segment, Amin gets in, looking cheerful but no less recalcitrant. "You don't know what a mother is," he barks at her. Segment two shows the woman from the sixth, who has now shaved her head because her man rejected her proposal of marriage. She too allows herself to cry openly.

Then, the number "1" introduces the final, and shortest, segment. Amin gets into the front seat after getting out of from his Father's jeep. With a knowing half-smile, he orders his mother to take him to his grandmother's, as the film fades out.

Critics receptive to Kiarostami's austere formalism have tried to explain it in relation to the filmmaker's earlier work. In the *New York Times*, A. O. Scott calls Kiarostami "among the world masters of automotive cinema . . . [who] understands the automobile as a place for reflection, observation and, above all, talk." He says that *Ten* is "a movie whose greatest virtue is its wry, compassionate precision . . . a work of inspired simplicity." In a similar vein, *Newsday*'s Jan Stuart asserts that "Kiarostami liberates the possibilities of narrative film" and that "once you get past the claustrophobia . . . you should be swept away by the spectacle of life playing out before your eyes with so much astonishing insight."

—*Vivek Adarkar*

CREDITS

Driver: Mania Akbari
Amin: Amin Maher

Origin: France
Language: Farsi
Released: 2002
Production: Marin Karmitz, Abbas Kiarostami; MK2; released by Zeitgeist Films
Directed by: Abbas Kiarostami
Written by: Abbas Kiarostami
Cinematography by: Abbas Kiarostami
Music by: Howard Blake
Editing: Abbas Kiarostami
MPAA rating: Unrated
Running time: 94 minutes

REVIEWS

Boxoffice. April, 2003, p. 106.
Chicago Sun-Times Online. April 11, 2003.
Entertainment Weekly. March 14, 2003, p. 46.
New York Daily News Online. March 5, 2003.
New York Times Online. September 28, 2002.
Newsday Online. March 5, 2003.
Sight and Sound. October, 2002, p. 30.
Variety Online. May 19, 2002.
Washington Post. April 18, 2003, p. C5.

Terminator 3: Rise of the Machines

The Machines Will Rise.
—Movie tagline

Box Office: $150.3 million

Terminator 3: Rise of the Machines could be a study in the folly of betting a lot of money on unrealistic expectations. In 1984, James Cameron's *The Terminator* was a surprise hit. Made on a relatively modest budget of just over $6 million, the combination science fiction/horror film grossed $40 million and helped propel Arnold Schwarzenegger to stardom. The 1991 sequel, *Terminator 2: Judgment Day*, was a bigger movie on every level—budget, special effects, story—and ultimately grossed over $200 million. Twelve years later, evidently believing that the return of Schwarzenegger's famous Terminator character would again draw business far surpassing its predecessor, Warner Brothers sank over $175 million into *Terminator 3: Rise of the Machines*, betting on a huge return even though the film was not directed or written by Cameron, whose skills had made the first two movies so successful. In retrospect, the investment in the new film probably seemed like unwise overkill. Though *Terminator 3* drew enough of an audience to earn $145 million domestically, the movie failed to live up to expectations.

It's been ten years since the events of *Terminator 2,* and the adult John Connor (Nick Stahl) is now a construction day laborer living "off the grid." He has no address and no phone. "Judgment Day" has apparently been avoided.

The T-X Terminator (Kristanna Loken), or Terminatrix, arrives naked in Beverly Hills. The T-X kills a woman before she can put up any protest, takes her red leather pant suit, adopts her hairstyle, and drives off through the busy streets of Los Angeles in her Lexus. She uses the woman's cell phone to tap into the computer system of the Los Angeles Unified School District and obtain the pictures and addresses of eight students.

We meet Kate Brewster (Claire Danes) and her fiancé, Scott (Mark Famiglietti), as they attempt to complete their bridal registry. When the hand-held scanner malfunctions, Kate flatly states her dislike of machines. She then gets a cell phone call from her father, Lt. General Robert Brewster (David Andrews), who begs out of meeting Scott that night because of a computer problem at work; a computer virus has infected half of the civilian internet and some of the secondary military applications, but all of the military's primary systems are safe.

The T-101 Terminator (Arnold Schwarzenegger) arrives much the way he did in the first film of the franchise: naked and in the desert near a roadhouse. He strides into the bar for clothes and what he finds is familiar: black leather pants and jacket.

Meanwhile, after a motorcycle accident, John Connor breaks into a veterinary clinic and downs several painkillers. Elsewhere, Kate receives an emergency call and must open her veterinary clinic. When she arrives, she discovers that someone has broken into the drug cabinet. John comes out of hiding to reveal himself to her, and she recognizes him, calling him by name. She identifies herself as one of his junior high classmates. However, their "reunion" is cut short by the arrival of the Terminatrix, who guns down the owner of one of Kate's patients. Kate then flees from the clinic but only makes it out to the clinic's truck before being assaulted by the Terminatrix. The T-X demands to know where John Connor is. The questioning is halted abruptly when the T-X is run down and slammed into the walls of the clinic by a truck driven by the T-101. John and Kate escape while the T-101 confronts the T-X. The battle is short-lived, however, when she incapacitates him with one plasma blast that sends him through several walls of the clinic.

After a wild and destructive chase, John and Kate find a temporary haven with the T-101. John demands that Kate be freed, but the T-101 refuses to comply. The cyborg explains that the T-X was sent back to kill John Connor's lieutenants when John could not be located. Then the Terminator delivers the really bad news: Judgment Day was only postponed. The Terminatrix that pursues them is equipped with an onboard weapons arsenal that includes nanotechnological injectors, meaning it can control other machines, and it has polynemetic properties and can assume the form of anything it touches. Back in Los Angeles, Kate's fiancé is awakened and killed by the Terminatrix. Moments later, "Scott" answers the door for the LAPD.

The Terminator takes John and Kate to Sarah Connor's grave. The T-101 destroys the grave and removes the coffin. He explains that Sarah was cremated, but her will gave instructions to leave a weapons cache in her coffin. When the coffin is opened, Kate grabs a pistol and shoots him in the face. He catches the bullet in his mouth and spits out the slug. A bullhorn sounds, announcing that the mausoleum is surrounded by police. As gas canisters come through the door, Kate escapes. The Terminator then tells John that they must reacquire Kate. When John wants to know why she is so important, the T-101 informs him that Kate will be his wife.

Meanwhile, Kate believes she is safe when she sees "Scott" emerge from a police car and come toward her, but her relief melts into horror as the Terminatrix reverts to its female form. Before the T-X can kill Kate, T-101 and John pull up in a hearse and rescue her. The chase is on again and the Terminatrix cuts through the roof of the hearse just before the Terminator rams the car underneath a semi-truck. The force of this impact damages one of her weapon-loaded arms.

When John asks the Terminator how many more people are on the T-X's hit list, the T-101 begins rattling off a list of names of secondary targets. Kate has an outburst at hearing the name of General Robert Brewster. The T-101 tells that General Brewster is the Program Director for Cyber Research Systems (i.e., SkyNet). The Terminator goes on to reveal that today is Judgment Day. The bombs will begin falling at 6:18 pm.

At CRS, the virus has broken through the firewalls of primary military systems. CRS cannot trace the virus because it keeps growing and changing, as if it had a mind of its own. The Chairman of the Joints Chiefs of Staff orders General Brewster to bring SkyNet online. However, the T-X has infiltrated CRS and reprograms the experimental robotic soldiers. When SkyNet is brought online, it suddenly achieves sentience.

When the General is mortally wounded, he orders Kate and John to take him to his office where the SkyNet access codes are kept in his wall safe. CRS dissolves into chaos as the robotic soldiers begin shooting everyone in sight. The General informs Kate that she must go to Crystal Peak in the Sierra Nevada mountains where the SkyNet central core is housed. While John and Kate escape, the two Terminators engage in a battle that culminates with the T-X injecting the T-101 with nanotechnology to override his original programming.

John and Kate find her father's plane and are about to escape when the Terminator arrives and tells John his programming has been compromised. As the Terminator starts to attack him, John asks the machine to recall its original mission. Unable to resolve the conflict, the Terminator shuts himself down, and the duo escapes.

They locate Crystal Peak, where they use the General's codes to open the doors. The T-X appears, followed shortly by the T-101. An explosion causes the blast doors to begin closing. The Terminator dives under the emergency closure to prevent it from sealing and beckons John and Kate to slip under it. As John begins to crawl under the door, the T-X goes after John. The Terminator sacrifices himself and self-terminates with the T-X in his clutches.

John and Kate take the elevator down, but it is not what they expect to find. There is no central computer core here. The Terminator led them down here to live. His dream of preventing Judgment Day shattered, John considers allowing the explosives he is carrying to go off, but when he hears voices over a radio calling for help, he deactivates his bomb and answers the calls. John Connor realizes that Judgment Day was inevitable. By the time SkyNet became self-aware, it had spread to millions of ordinary computers throughout the world. It was software in cyberspace; there was no system core. Now the real battle for John Connor has just begun.

Terminator 3 is the weakest movie in the trilogy. It never reaches the chilling desperation of the other two films. It is a shame that Schwarzenegger did not spend the same amount of time learning to articulate his lines as he did getting his body into the same shape as when he appeared in the first movie twenty years ago. Kristanna Loken is certainly the most attractive Terminator, but she never inspires fear the way Robert Patrick managed to do in the second film even though he used the same unemotional delivery as Loken. Nick Stahl makes John Connor a likeable character. He has lived his whole life with the weight of the world on his shoulders, yet Stahl makes him meek without being too remorseful. Claire Danes brings strength and spunk to the role of Kate. One would never guess that she was literally cast the day before shooting began. Only because of her solid acting ability is she able to give Kate dignity while uttering lines like, "Go to hell, you bastard" and "Just die, you bitch!" Likeability and strength, though, are not enough to save the thin plot.

—*David Flanagin and Donna Wood-Martin*

CREDITS

Terminator T-101: Arnold Schwarzenegger
John Connor: Nick Stahl
Kate Brewster: Claire Danes
T-X: Kristanna Loken
Robert Brewster: David Andrews
Scott Petersen: Mark Famiglietti

Origin: USA
Released: 2003
Production: Mario Kassar, Andrew G. Vajna, Joel B. Michaels, Hal Lieberman, Colin Wilson; Intermedia Films, IMF, C-2 Pictures; released by Warner Bros.
Directed by: Jonathan Mostow
Written by: John Brancato, Michael Ferris
Cinematography by: Don Burgess
Music by: Marco Beltrami
Sound: William B. Kaplan
Editing: Neil Travis, Nicolas De Toth
Art Direction: Mark Zuelzke, Beat Frutiger, Andrew Menzies, Shepherd Frankel
Costumes: April Ferry
Production Design: Jeff Mann
MPAA rating: R
Running time: 110 minutes

REVIEWS

Chicago Sun-Times Online. July 1, 2003.
Entertainment Weekly. July 11, 2003, p. 59.
Los Angeles Times Online. July 2, 2003.
New York Times Online. July 1, 2003.
People. July 14, 2003, p. 35.
Rolling Stone Online. July 2, 2003.
USA Today Online. July 2, 2003.
Variety Online. June 30, 2003.
Washington Post. July 2, 2003, p. C1.

QUOTES

John Connor (Nick Stahl): "My destiny was never to stop Judgment Day, it was only to survive it."

The Texas Chainsaw Massacre

Inspired by a true story.
—Movie tagline

What you know about fear . . . doesn't even come close.
—Movie tagline

 Box Office: $80.1 million

The original *Texas Chainsaw Massacre* horrified audiences in 1974 with its vicious portrayal of realistic violence with no purpose or rational cause. This slickly directed update fails to capture the brutal tone or shock value of its predecessor, but it is a crowd pleaser due to the presence of a strong heroine (played by Jessica Biel).

The film begins in the same manner as the original with a group of teenagers traveling across Texas by van. They pick up a hitchhiker and things quickly go from bad to worse. The kids eventually find themselves tangling with an obviously psychotic sheriff (R. Lee Ermey), saddled with a dead body, exploring a dilapidated farmhouse, discovering an inbred hillbilly family that enjoys the fine art of killing, and every other cliché associated with what Roger Ebert of the *Chicago Sun-Times* calls the "formula of a Dead Teenager Movie." The kids are dispatched one after another by increasingly gruesome means until young Erin (Biel) is left alone to grapple with Leatherface (the infamous antihero of the franchise) for the remainder of the film.

Mike Clark described the film in *USA Today* as "junky and disposable . . . but fast most of the time." That is precisely what is simultaneously both wrong and right with it. The original *Texas Chainsaw Massacre* festered and took its time to scare the hell out of you by letting its unfathomable horror reveal itself piecemeal before you. This new, modernized-version wants to shock the thrill out of you and isn't really all that interested in genuinely terrifying you. Screenwriter Scott Kosar (working from the original screenplay by Tobe Hooper and Kim Henkel) is not inclined to allow things to sink in and would rather get to Leatherface's rampage. But, while the film sacrifices this under-your-skin type of horror, it does succeed in delivering a very audience-friendly action/adventure. First-time director Marcus Nispal deserves most of the credit for this. His music video background is evident in the frenzied action (particularly in Erin's chase scene with Leatherface, during which the camera rarely remains motionless) and the quick pacing of the film. Producer Michael Bay's knack for providing audience-compatible fare is evident here as well. But, the biggest reason for the film's popular success is the character of Erin. As the main, levelheaded character, she is the one the audience identifies with from the onset. She is the one not interested in drugs, sex, or any other offshoots of teen debauchery that usually foreshadow a bloody end in a film such as this. Erin fights bravely against Leatherface, displays empathy by ending the suffering of one of her companions when she is unable to save him, and then saves a baby from being brought up by the murderous family deep in the heart of Texas, all the while wearing a wet t-shirt. In this way, she functions as both mother and whore—a sort of archetype for strong female characters (like Sigourney Weaver's macho Ellen Ripley in *Aliens*). The audience easily takes to her and panics when she is in trouble and cheers voraciously when she lets loose on Leatherface and his sadistic clan.

While not as successful on a psychological level as its forbearer, the remade *Texas Chainsaw Massacre* is a crowd pleaser primarily due to the presence of a strong female lead. However, that seems to be a trait of many modern horror films and has become a sort of crutch within the genre for films short in other areas. Still, this film succeeds by being enjoyable while still somewhat insignificant, historically speaking, when compared to its namesake.

—*Michael J. Tyrkus*

CREDITS

Erin: Jessica Biel
Morgan: Jonathan Tucker
Pepper: Erica Leerhsen
Andy: Mike Vogel
Leatherface/Thomas Hewitt: Andrew Bryniarski
Sheriff Hoyt: R. Lee Ermey
Jedidiah: David Dorfman
Kemper: Eric Balfour
Old Monty: Terrence Evans
Narrator: John Larroquette

Origin: USA
Released: 2003
Production: Michael Bay, Mike Fleiss; Radar Pictures, Platinum Dunes, Next Entertainment; released by New Line Cinema
Directed by: Marcus Nispel
Written by: Scott Kosar
Cinematography by: Daniel Pearl
Music by: Steve Jablonsky
Sound: Stacy Brownrigg
Editing: Glen Scantlebury
Art Direction: Scott Gallagher
Costumes: Bobbie Mannix
Production Design: Gregory Blair
MPAA rating: R
Running time: 98 minutes

REVIEWS

Chicago Sun-Times Online. October 17, 2003.
Entertainment Weekly. October 24, 2003, p. 83.
Los Angeles Times Online. October 17, 2003.
New York Times Online. October 17, 2003.
People. October 27, 2003, p. 32.
Rolling Stone. November 13, 2003, p. 106.
USA Today Online. October 17, 2003.
Variety Online. October 17, 2003.

Thirteen

She's not your little girl anymore.
—Movie tagline
It's happening so fast.
—Movie tagline

 Box Office: $4.6 million

Thirteen doesn't bill itself as being "inspired by a true story," but it was. It was a true story that was very close to home. The film was based on the experiences of Nikki Reed, a 13 year-old who started having trouble with her parents and hanging out with what used to be called a "fast" crowd. At 15, Reed and family friend Catherine Hardwicke, a production designer who worked on *Three Kings* and *Laurel Canyon,* wrote a script about a teen in a similar situation. Reed ended up playing one of the lead roles in the film.

Hardwicke and Reed first met when the production designer was dating Reed's father. In an interview with the two in the *Los Angeles Times,* Scarlet Cheng wrote, "As Reed entered sixth grade, Hardwicke noticed a dramatic and disturbing change—the girl was dressing up way beyond her years and was often angry toward her mother, with whom she had been close." Even after Hardwicke and Reed's father broke up, Hardwicke and the girl continued to see each other. Reed would stay at Hardwicke's house for long stretches of time and Hardwicke served as the adult that Reed was willing to talk to. *Thirteen* started as something for Reed to do that would be a constructive activity.

After writing the script, the two sought out funding, found people willing to be in the movie and had to stick to a 24-day shooting schedule. The cast only had a week to rehearse and the sets were stocked with things the filmmakers had in their own houses. The results look nothing like anything that could have been co-written by a fifteen year-old, shot in 24 days, and held together by the skills of a debuting actress and first-time director. The film looks good, has a kinetic style and a keen eye for the details of modern teenage life. Most amazing are the dead-on performances by Reed, Holly Hunter, and Evan Rachel Wood. The three exactly capture the nuances of teen-adult relations

at this tumultuous time. There is no hint that Reed hadn't done any acting before this. She captures the screen like she belongs there.

The 13 year-old in the film is Tracy (Wood of *Once and Again*). She lives with her single mother, Melanie (Hunter), a still sexy ex-hippie who works as a hairdresser out of their ramshackle house. She's a recovering alcoholic with a soft spot for friends who need a meal or a place to sleep. She's not a terrible mother; she has flaws, like not taking time to talk to her daughter when her daughter needs it, but nothing that would automatically turn a teen's life to ruin. Tracy is a good student with a group of nice, somewhat nerdy girlfriends. When she gets to a new school, she realizes that she wants to be in the group with the most popular girl, Evie (Reed). Tracy is thrilled when Evie invites her to go shopping.

When Tracy arrives on Melrose for the shopping date, Evie and her friend ignore Tracy and make fun of her. She makes a quick decision to steal a woman's handbag so that she can prove herself to her would-be friends. Evie is impressed by the theft (and happy to take the money off of Tracy's hands) and accepts Tracy into her inner circle.

Tracy is so excited to be in the group that she does everything Evie suggests without question. Tracy, who already had been dealing with her problems by making cuts on her arm, finds herself eagerly getting various piercings and shoplifting. She gets a new, sexy-beyond-her-years wardrobe of barely there tops and low-slung, tight pants. Drugs and indiscriminate sex are now part of her new lifestyle, too. Evie and Tracy wile away afternoon hours by sniffing an aerosol can, then hitting each other. "I can't feel a thing!" they laugh. "Hit me harder!" Tracy quickly ditches her old group of friends.

Naturally this kind of behavior doesn't go over very well with Melanie, though Melanie's more tolerant than a lot of mothers would be. Melanie would be considered by most girls to be a "cool mom." She still dresses in hip clothing and is the kind of mom who suggests that her daughter could wear body glitter. She loves her daughter fiercely and the two have always been close. It is a mystery to her why Tracy has suddenly turned so cold and abusive. "Before she met you, she was playing with Barbie dolls!" yells Melanie at Evie in one heated exchange.

Tracy rails against any attempt her mother makes to get involved with her life. She has switched her devotion to Evie and wants to make that perfectly clear to her mom. Joining a rough crowd in this day and age can be especially dangerous, and Tracy finds herself wandering Hollywood Blvd., taking weird drugs, and hanging out with questionable people. Coaxed on by the images of what Hollywood and the media present as a suitable lifestyle for kids, Tracy transforms herself into a sexual creature. At one point, she and Evie instigate a threesome with an older neighbor (Kip Pardue).

Evie is a more confusing character. While urging Tracy to rebel against her family she simultaneously seems to want to be taken in by it. Evie coaxes an invitation to stay by telling Melanie that she is being sexually abused at home. It's a lie. Evie is a smart girl and is expert at manipulating all the people in her life.

The style of the film reflects the hyper-kinetic world Tracy has entered. The film stock changes in various scenes. In a scene where Tracy is lost on Hollywood Blvd., it's shot in a green tone, making everything look even more alien. Hardwicke makes the shots of the teens having fun look even more dizzy and intoxicated by quickly whipping the camera around.

Critics liked *Thirteen. Entertainment Weekly*'s Owen Gleiberman gave the film an A, claiming, "*Thirteen* feels like a dramatized documentary, yet it has the grip of a thriller." Elvis Mitchell of the *New York Times* enthused, "Ms. Wood's performance bounces with mood swings from anxiety to exhilaration in a movie with moments so realistically painted that your eyes will sting from the fumes. Ms. Hardwicke's directing approach echoes the chemical surges of its little-girl star, bounding and lunging as if it were in the back seat of a car hurtling down bumpy roads without a seat belt." Jami Bernard of the *New York Daily News* praised the reality of the film: "Shot with the urgency and claustrophobia of a hand-held camera, and going for a bleaching effect as Tracy loses herself, *Thirteen* is packed with genuine incidents. Any female who is now or has ever been that age will recognize them—peer pressure, the tyranny of fashion, the pinpricks of feeling and the exquisite thrill of being wild."

—*Jill Hamilton*

Tracy: Evan Rachel Wood
Evie Zamora: Nikki Reed
Melanie: Holly Hunter
Brady: Jeremy Sisto
Brooke: Deborah Kara Unger
Luke: Kip Pardue
Mason: Brady Corbet
Birdie: Sarah Clarke
Travis: D.W. Moffett

Origin: USA
Released: 2003
Production: Michael London, Jeff Levy-Hinte; Working Title Productions, Antidote Film; released by Fox Searchlight
Directed by: Catherine Hardwicke
Written by: Nikki Reed, Catherine Hardwicke
Cinematography by: Elliot Davis
Music by: Mark Mothersbaugh
Sound: Steve Weiss, Steve Morantz

Music Supervisor: Michelle Norell, Amy Rosen
Editing: Nancy Richardson
Art Direction: Johnny Jos
Costumes: Cindy Evans
Production Design: Carol Strober
MPAA rating: R
Running time: 95 minutes

REVIEWS

Boxoffice. April, 2003, p. 76.
Chicago Sun-Times Online. August 29, 2003.
Entertainment Weekly. September 5, 2003, p. 54.
Los Angeles Times Online. August 22, 2003.
New York Times Online. August 10, 2003.
New York Times Online. August 20, 2003.
People. September 1, 2003, p. 37.
Premiere. July/August, 2003, p. 40.
Variety Online. January 29, 2003.
Washington Post. August 29, 2003, p. WE34.

AWARDS AND NOMINATIONS

Ind. Spirit 2004: Debut Perf. (Reed)
Sundance 2003: Director (Hardwicke)
Nomination:
Oscars 2003: Support. Actress (Hunter)
Golden Globes 2004: Actress—Drama (Wood), Support. Actress (Hunter)
Ind. Spirit 2004: First Screenplay
Screen Actors Guild 2003: Actress (Wood), Support. Actress (Hunter).

Till Human Voices Wake Us

Passion. Attraction. Dreams. Memory. Desire. Sometimes the mysteries of your past find a way into your future.
—Movie tagline

When we first meet Dr. Sam Franks (Guy Pearce) in writer-director Michael Petroni's *Till Human Voices Wake Us,* he is teaching a psychology class about memory and the two kinds of forgetting. Contrasting active forgetting with passive forgetting, he focuses on the former, which he equates with repression, and, in an obvious bit of irony, we will see that the wise yet sad doctor suffers from this exact ailment. It is an easy setup that is all too indicative of the predictable trajectory the script will take.

A psychological ghost story with poetic overtones, *Till Human Voices Wake Us* is a slow, deliberate film about making contact with a deceased loved one and freeing oneself from the memory of a painful past—potentially gripping themes that are undermined by consistently lackluster execution. A dull story, static characters, and an anticlimactic payoff prove to be a disastrous combination, leaving the talented Guy Pearce and Helena Bonham Carter unable to redeem this anemic tale of love lost and found.

Pearce, who was extraordinary playing tormented, driven characters in *L.A. Confidential* and *Memento,* is straitjacketed as a character who is so disconnected from the world that it takes the death of his father to initiate the events that will change his life. Living in Melbourne, Australia, Sam learns that his father wanted to be buried in the outback town of Genoa, where Sam spent a memorable summer during his youth. On the train ride, Sam encounters the mysterious Ruby (Bonham Carter), who disappears only moments after he meets her. Returning to Genoa brings back memories of his boyhood, specifically the time young Sam (Lindley Joyner) shared with Silvy (Brooke Harman), and the film intercuts Sam's present with the story of his younger self that fateful summer.

The flashback scenes are sweet, youthful recollections of a first romance, bathed in a nostalgic glow. Silvy wears braces on her legs, although her disability is not specified, and she and Sam ride together through the country on his bicycle. They engage in activities befitting the pastoral setting and their own fascination with the world around them—observing a dead bird that someone has carefully buried under a rock, speculating on whether the town's crazy old woman is really a witch, and simply enjoying lazy days at the river. Silvy's parents are very welcoming to young Sam and take more of an interest in him than his cold, distant father. Silvy's father gives Sam a job helping out on the farm, where he witnesses a cow giving birth. From this episode, Silvy's father teaches him the lesson that it is important to embrace life in all its variety instead of hiding from it, a heavy-handed comment that foreshadows the way Sam will later withdraw from the world.

After he buries his father, the adult Sam stays at his childhood home. One night during a rainstorm, he saves a woman who has taken a plunge into the river, resuscitates her, and brings her to his home to recuperate. The woman is Ruby, who suffers from amnesia, and Sam soon makes it his mission to help her recover her memory and identity. Unfortunately, their scenes together, which make up the heart of the film, are very dull. Their long conversations do not add up to much, and Pearce and Bonham Carter do not have much chemistry. Sam and Ruby take a long walk through town, but moving the story from Sam's home to the streets feels like an attempt to disguise the mundane nature of their

discussion, filled with ethereal ruminations on the moonlight and speculation on dreams. In an ironic plot device, Sam thinks that he is helping Ruby discover herself when he is in fact the one who needs help coming to terms with his own past.

The story of young Sam and Silvy is more engaging than Sam's adult story, even if the tale of doomed adolescent love mines familiar territory. Sam and Silvy go to a dance one night, but, because of her disability, she does not feel comfortable going in. So instead they go out to the river, where they enjoy a beautiful reverie in the water until Sam lets go of Silvy's hand and she drowns. It was, we soon learn, the key event in the shaping of Sam's life. From that day forward, he closed himself off to the world, making him the repressed man we see as an adult.

Ruby, it turns out, is some kind of incarnation of the late Silvy. Perhaps she is the ghost of Silvy, or maybe she is a creation of Sam's imagination conjured up so that he can heal his past and move on with his life. Clues to her identity are revealed gradually, but it is not hard to figure out long before Sam does. During their long talk, he plays a word association game with her that mirrors one he played with Silvy, and Ruby quotes T.S. Eliot's "The Love Song of J. Alfred Prufrock," a poem that Silvy was fond of. Ruby even spontaneously visits a town dance and twirls around among the dancing couples, something her teenage self was not able to do.

Only when Sam puts Ruby under hypnosis does he discover her identity. Meeting the spirit of one's first love could elicit a variety of responses, from fear and anxiety to joy and wonder, but Sam's reaction is flat. Pearce exhibits little range as Sam, even when he realizes that he is facing the embodiment of Silvy, which makes it hard to care what happens to him. Moreover, once Ruby is revealed to be a psychological prop for Sam's redemption, we no longer see her as an individual—she is reduced to being an aid in his recovery. Bonham Carter projects an otherworldly, haunted air as Ruby and does her best to convey the sense of an adolescent in a woman's body, especially in a cute scene in which Ruby scoops cherries from a jar right into her mouth. But Bonham Carter cannot overcome the fact that Ruby is a mere projection of Sam's troubled psyche and thus an almost impossible character to play with any depth. Because the reunited lovers are ciphers even when they are rediscovering each other, they never connect emotionally. As a result, their story remains inert and never matches the warmth embodied in the scenes of young Sam and Silvy.

The movie takes its title from the last line of "The Love Song of J. Alfred Prufrock," and the poem is clearly meant to be a touchstone for the film, but it does not work. Like Prufrock, Sam may be cut off from the world, but his stunted emotional growth from the death of Silvy is very different from Prufrock's inability to seduce a woman or break free of his isolation. Petroni's use of the poem ends up feeling like an attempt to imbue the film with a heightened grandeur that it does not have on its own, especially in the way the poem echoes the film's sense of romantic longing, melancholy mood, and drowning imagery. Just before she dies, Ruby asks Sam to read her the last stanza: "We have lingered in the chambers of the sea/By sea-girls wreathed with seaweed red and brown/Till human voices wake us, and we drown." While these lines may give poetic voice to Ruby's own nebulous state, they do not deepen Sam's character or comment on his story.

In the end, Sam puts Ruby's body in a boat and sends it off on the river only to climb inside moments later and discover that her body is gone. As he lies in the boat with a hint of a smile on his face, it seems that he is ready to get on with living, that he has been healed through the experience of encountering his lost love and putting her away. But since we have witnessed no breakthrough suggesting how the experience has made him a new man or has helped him achieve closure, the ending is not very persuasive. Indeed, we are treated only to the obligatory promise of a new beginning—not a happy ending that has been earned.

Because the notion of a love that transcends death is a powerful theme, one of the most poignant in all of literature, it is particularly disappointing that *Till Human Voices Wake Us* should be so unimaginative. Instead of exuding a sense of enchantment and wonder befitting the magic of a supernatural love story, Petroni's stilted script and direction present Sam's journey as a slow, cerebral exercise that finally leads nowhere.

—*Peter N. Chumo II*

CREDITS

Sam Franks: Guy Pearce
Ruby: Helena Bonham Carter
Maurie Lewis: Frank Gallacher
Young Sam: Lindley Joyner
Silvy Lewis: Brooke Harman
Dr. David Franks: Peter Curtain
Dorothy Lewis: Margot Knight
Russ: Anthony Martin
Mrs. Sarks: Dawn Klingberg

Origin: Australia
Released: 2002
Production: Shana Levine, Dean Murphy, Nigel Odell, David Redman, Matthias Emcke; Instinct Entertainment; released by Paramount Classics
Directed by: Michael Petroni
Written by: Michael Petroni
Cinematography by: Roger Lanser
Music by: Dale Cornelius

Sound: John Wilkinson, Michael Slater, Scott Findlay
Editing: Bill Murphy
Art Direction: Adele Flere
Costumes: Jeanie Cameron
Production Design: Ralph Moser
MPAA rating: R
Running time: 97 minutes

REVIEWS

Boxoffice. April, 2003, p. 106.
Chicago Sun-Times Online. February 28, 2003.
Los Angeles Times Online. February 21, 2003.
New York Times Online. February 21, 2003.
People. March 10, 2003, p. 39.
Variety Online. September 13, 2002.
Washington Post. March 14, 2003, p. C5.

TRIVIA

The film's title is taken from the last line of T.S. Eliot's "The Love Song of J. Alfred Prufrock": "Till human voices wake us, and we drown."

Timeline

A rescue mission will begin and history will hang in the balance.
—Movie tagline

 Box Office: $19.4 million

A man wearing medieval clothing is found dying in the woods of New Mexico. As if that weren't odd enough, x-rays taken of his body show that it is totally out of alignment, as if he were a paper doll cut up and badly pasted back together. What puzzles the doctors who treated the dying man is his last word: "Castlegard." His body is picked up without explanation by Frank Gordon (Neal McDonough) of ITC, the International Technology Corporation, which is run by Robert Doniger (David Thewlis), the most powerful man in technology.

Meanwhile, at an archeological dig in France, we learn of a battle that took place during the 100 Years' War. The English held the French Castle of La Roque, situated up on a high hill, but they eventually lose it because of their arrogance: When the English hang the body of the popular

French aristocrat Lady Claire over the castle walls, the French are inflamed and spurred on to victory. This archeological endeavor, headed by Professor Edward Johnston (Billy Connolly), is having incredible success, especially while digging at the base of La Roque's hill in the ruins of a monastery and at the site of the castle's town, Castlegard. What a coincidence that Professor Johnston's dig is sponsored by Doniger's company, ITC, and Johnston is being fed tips on where to dig. But how is Doniger getting his information?

Visiting the dig is the professor's son, Chris (Paul Walker), who really isn't all that interested in the past, but who does have a crush on one of the professor's students, Kate Ericson (Frances O'Connor). Kate, however, loves history and archeology more than she loves Chris.

While the professor is off visiting Doniger, Kate is exploring the monastery looking for tunnels that link it to the castle ruins above. Imagine her complete surprise when, after a cave-in exposes some tunnels, she finds a pair of modern-day bifocals. Even more surprising is a note she finds saying simply, "Help Johnston. November 2, 1357." Professor Johnston is sending them notes from the Middle Ages? Chris and Karen and several others from the dig travel to ITC headquarters in Silver City, New Mexico, to either talk to Professor Johnston, who seems to be MIA, or to confront Doniger about what exactly his hi-tech outfit has to do with the dig in France.

The group learns that ITC's latest invention allows three-dimensional objects to be "faxed" through space. Doniger's intention is to put UPS and FedEx out of business. However, a slight problem has developed. It seems that when objects are broken into a stream of electrons and then reassembled, they don't end up at their desired destination, they end up somewhere else, and it's always the same place: France . . . during the Middle Ages. It's as if a permanent wormhole has opened up between present day New Mexico and medieval Castlegard, and no one knows why or how. That's why Doniger has been able to help with the dig—he's been sending people back in time to France. One of those people is Chris's father, who, for some reason, seems to be trapped there.

Leaving behind the physicist amongst them, Stern (Ethan Embry), to stay at ITC and watch their backs, Chris and Karen and two other members of the dig, Francois (Rossif Sutherland, son of Donald and brother of Kiefer) and Andre (Gerard Butler), along with ITC employee Gordon (Neal McDonough) and two marines travel back in time to rescue Johnston. To return to the present, they need only activate a special medallion they all wear, but the hitch is that they only have six hours before the medallion can no longer do its job. This is made painfully obvious by the way the pendants continually indicate the time remaining.

Their difficult task is further complicated when one of the marines takes a modern hand grenade with him back to the Middle Ages. He comes under attack, is shot by arrows, activates his homing device and his hand grenade at the same time, and the resulting explosion severely damages the ITC machine. Now everyone is trapped in 14th century France unless Stern and the ITC staff can get it up and running again . . . as the clock quickly counts down the remaining hours.

As improbable luck would have it, our intrepid gang of archeologists has landed in Castlegard on the exact day the English burn the town to the ground and Lady Claire is murdered. The group is caught by surprise and ultimately captured by the English, led by the cruelly evil Lord Oliver (Michael Sheen). Eventually they do manage to escape after enlisting the help of a woman, clad in men's garb, who turns out to be Lady Claire (Anna Friel).

Needless to say Lady Claire will eventually fall into the hands of the English, but not before, predictably, one of the archaeologists falls in love with her and risks changing history by trying to save her life. The others, with the aid of Lady Claire's brother (Lambert Wilson), attempt to free the professor from the castle where he is being kept prisoner until he gives the English a new weapon known as Greek fire.

The disregard for the effects on history shown by the travelers with their constant tampering may be one of the most annoying things about *Timeline*. Haven't these guys ever watched *Star Trek?* They violate the laws of time travel at every opportunity and—especially in the case of the archeologists among them whose vocation it is to uncover and preserve history—seem little interested in the time they're suddenly plunged into.

Timeline is based on the 1999 Michael Crichton bestseller of the same name. Typical of Crichton, its primary plot has to do with the misuse of science and technology. (It's been said that Crichton asked for no money up front for the rights to his book, instead taking 15 percent of the grosses—up to $15 million.) Crichton's basic plot has been retained, but some changes were made in the film: the actual timeline has been shortened from a few days to a few hours; some characters who were women in the book appear here as men; a ridiculously thin romantic subplot has been added; and the English are decidedly portrayed as the bad guys, while the French have inexplicably become the good guys.

Films based on Crichton books have an uneven track record. There have been hits, including the blockbuster *Jurassic Park,* but others have been less than stellar (*Congo* comes to mind). His stories are well researched and usually fast paced, and this comes across in *Timeline,* but the plot itself is extraordinarily witless when interpreted by screenwriters Jeff Maguire (*Line of Fire*) and first-timer George Nolfi.

While the general story itself is filled with groaners and a lack of imagination, what's worse are the thin characters and the embarrassingly campy dialogue they have. Of course misunderstandings inevitably occur as the modern English language is much like a foreign tongue to people of the Middle Ages—for example, when Andre asks Lady Claire if she's "seeing anyone."

Besides failing to provide a thoughtful script, *Timeline* also has a problem with its casting. David Thewlis and Billy Connolly portray archetypes of, respectively, the genius verging on madness and the job-obsessed professor. The rest of the cast is as nondescript as their characters and could have been played by virtually anyone.

The real clinker, however, is Paul Walker. Just for starters this California Valley-boy seems so alien to Billy Connolly's eccentric British scholar that it's inconceivable one would have sired the other. Walker, best known for the *Fast and Furious* movies is, at this point in his career, just another one of the pretty, young, slightly-talented actors who ooze out of teen movies. Here he plays the standard hotheaded teen hero in such an artificial, if earnest, way, that his casting seems less about choosing the right actor for the role than about marketing. One can't help but wonder what a different movie this might have been if it hadn't catered to the younger set; if it had been thoughtful and imaginative, omitting the silly romance and transporting back to medieval Castlegard only adults with a sincere interest in history. Thank heavens at least the women are able to hold their own in the story. Frances O'Connor and Anna Friel climb and battle with the best of them.

Although the battle of Castlegard/La Roque is a fictional one, it must be admitted that *Timeline* does do an interesting job of portraying Medieval warfare. The armaments used are well researched and effectively presented on the screen with, extraordinary for today, a minimum of special effects

As seen through the lens of cinematographer Caleb Deschanel (*The Natural, The Right Stuff*), medieval France is distinctive and atmospheric. Although shooting originally involved European locations, ensuing difficulties (the outbreak of foot and mouth disease shut down shooting in Wales, then the 9/11 attacks made shooting in Berlin a security risk) prompted the filmmakers to shoot scenes of 14th century Dordogne Valley in Montreal, Canada. Not only were La Roque and Castlegard built there, but also the monastery—used for one night of shooting, then taken apart and replaced with its 21st-century ruins.

Montreal also proved a boon to the filmmakers in casting convincing extras to play the French and British armies. The Company Medieval, people from the Montreal area who reenact jousts and battles from the Middle Ages, proved to be versatile enough to play French soldiers one day and English the next, their ranks beefed up with extras and strategically placed stuntmen.

However, even these few pluses can't overcome the basically silly and childish story, the questionable casting and the feeble characters. Director Richard Donner (*Ladyhawke, Lethal Weapon, Maverick,* and *Superman*) keeps the action

moving quickly, but the flimsy characters, the stiff dialogue, and the casting of Paul Walker make the movie feel more like a spoof than a serious entry in the time travel genre. Too bad the script wasn't funnier.

—*Beverley Bare Buehrer*

CREDITS

Chris Johnston: Paul Walker
Kate Ericson: Frances O'Connor
Andre Marek: Gerard Butler
Professor Johnston: Billy Connolly
Robert Doniger: David Thewlis
Lady Claire: Anna Friel
Frank Gordon: Neal McDonough
Steven Kramer: Matt Craven
Josh Stern: Ethan (Randall) Embry
Lord Oliver: Michael Sheen
Lord Arnaut: Lambert Wilson
De Kere: Marton Csokas

Origin: USA
Released: 2003
Production: Richard Donner, Lauren Shuler-Donner, Jim Van Wyck; Donners' Company, Artists Production Group, Paramount Pictures, Cobalt Media Group, Mutual Film Corporation; released by Paramount Pictures
Directed by: Richard Donner
Written by: Jeff Maguire, George Nolfi
Cinematography by: Caleb Deschanel
Music by: Brian Tyler
Sound: Patrick Rousseau
Editing: Richard Marks
Art Direction: Caroline Alder, Real Proulx, David Sandefur
Costumes: Jenny Beavan
Production Design: Daniel T. Dorrance
MPAA rating: PG-13
Running time: 116 minutes

REVIEWS

Chicago Sun-Times Online. November 26, 2003.
Entertainment Weekly. December 5, 2003, p. 68.
Los Angeles Times Online. November 26, 2003.
New York Times Online. November 26, 2003.
People. December 8, 2003, p. 37.
Variety Online. November 21, 2003.
Washington Post. November 26, 2003, p. C10.

Together
(He Ni Zaiyiqi)

*An impossible dream . . . an incredible journey . . .
and a boy who holds his destiny in his hands.
Some lessons can only be learned by heart.*
—Movie tagline

 Box Office: $1.1 million

When we first meet Xiaochun (Tang Yun), the 13-year-old violin prodigy at the heart of Chen Kaige's *Together* (written by Chen and Xue Xiaolu), he is preparing to make the journey from his small provincial town to Beijing to further his talent. Accompanying him is his peasant father, Liu Cheng (Liu Peiqi), who is proud of his son's accomplishments and eager to do whatever it takes to make him a success. A simple, goodhearted story of family, ambition, and discovery in the big city, *Together* is imbued with such warmth and inspires such affection for all of its characters—and especially for the father-son relationship—that the film is quite moving despite its sometimes melodramatic plot twists and the familiar story line. The drama is played out against a cultural moment in contemporary China that may be especially foreign to many Western viewers: a post-Cultural Revolution clash between old-world, peasant values and modern, consumeristic impulses (of which Chen is especially suspicious).

The odds seem stacked against Xiaochun the minute he arrives in Beijing. He places fifth in a competition for entrance into a prestigious music school but would have finished first if bribery did not trump outright talent. Ever the scrappy hustler, Liu secures private lessons for his son from Professor Jiang (Wang Zhiwen), even though Jiang is skeptical that success is possible without money or the right connections. He is the classic rumpled, eccentric professor who shuffles around in old clothes, has a cigarette dangling from his mouth, and lives in a cluttered studio with his cats as his only companions. A lifelong bachelor, he still pines for the girl he lost many years ago at the conservatory because he was too timid to try to win her from his rival. A positive influence on his teacher, Xiaochun tidies up his home between lessons and inspires him to improve his appearance.

Meanwhile, Xiaochun becomes friends with Lili (Chen Hong, the director's wife), a slightly older girl who lives nearby and is the classic gold digger, dating men who can spend large sums of money on her. She is the glamorous face of the new China, seduced by the materialism of the bur-geoning capitalist culture. But she also has a good heart and becomes a kind of mother figure or big sister for a boy whose real mother abandoned him when he was little. Lili appreciates Xiaochun's musical talent and becomes his first crush and his ideal of big-city beauty, which stirs his adolescent imagination. (It is interesting to note that some reviews of the film refer to her as a prostitute, although the film is not clear on what she does for a living.)

Life in the big city is hard for father and son. Liu loses his knit hat where he hid all of his money and takes a job as a delivery boy. On one of his deliveries, he learns about a famous violin teacher, Professor Yu (Chen Kaige), who has an acclaimed performer for a student. Thinking that Xiaochun should be destined for the same kind of fame, Liu is quick to fire Jiang and curry favor with Yu. Liu may seem like an old-world hick (even his son considers him a country bumpkin), but he exhibits great determination and savvy in seeking out the best teacher for his son.

Xiaochun is so upset that his lessons with Jiang have come to an end that he sells his violin, which his mother left him, to buy an expensive coat for Lili. Unfortunately, Xiaochun leaves the coat with Lili's philandering boyfriend when she is not home, and he takes credit for the gift, which she allows him to return since she knows he is low on funds.

Selling the violin creates a great rift between Liu and Xiaochun, who has essentially been lured away from his pure dream of music to win the affection of a materialistic party girl. He also embarrasses his father in front of Professor Yu by refusing to audition for him. But ultimately Lili comes to understand what Xiaochun did for her; when she cannot find her errant boyfriend, she seeks out Yu to explain her culpability, finally bringing Yu and Xiaochun together for an audition. Lili thus exhibits a depth of character that perhaps she herself did not realize she possessed, but, in the world of *Together,* just about everyone is capable of a moment of grace. Indeed, Xiaochun seems to bring out the best in people like Jiang and Lili, who grow under his tutelage.

The audition goes well, and Professor Yu consents to take Xiaochun as a student, but this new relationship threatens the bond between father and son. Unlike Jiang, who emphasizes consummate musicianship, Yu is a star maker who gives Xiaochun a haircut and new wardrobe and has the boy live with him, all of which separates Xiaochun from his father. Professor Yu also pits Xiaochun against another student, a girl named Lin Yu (Zhang Qing), for a coveted spot in an international competition.

While the film's strength is its focus on the intimate yet fragile bonds that connect people—a father and son exchanging a triumphant high five, a student mastering a difficult piece of music as his teacher looks on proudly—Chen also makes some social commentary about China's past and future. While Jiang represents traditional values such as art for the sake of art, Yu is the teacher for the new consumeristic mindset that sees art as a means to fame and fortune. He has a sophisticated wife and lives in a beautifully appointed apartment with all the modern amenities. Even a seemingly small detail like an orange juice squeezer in his kitchen suggests the technology of the modern world that threatens the old ways.

The screenplay is very smart in the subtle way it shows the dream that unites father and son ultimately breaking them apart just when it seems close to being realized. Liu begins feeling superfluous to his son's new life and contemplates returning home, and even the violin, the symbolic link to their old life, seems gone forever when Liu discovers that someone has purchased it from the store where Xiaochun sold it. When Xiaochun begins thinking about rejoining his father, Professor Yu reveals a secret that he believes will encourage the boy to stay and pursue his goal and thereby make his father happy: Liu is not Xiaochun's natural father but rather the man who found him as an infant in a train station with the violin next to him. When Xiaochun learns his true origins, he runs to his father to apologize for his disobedience.

Xiaochun eventually returns to Professor Yu's home, where he receives yet another startling revelation: Yu has chosen him over Lin Yu for the competition. She is so angry that she shows Xiaochun his old, beloved violin and tells him that Professor Yu purchased it from the store with the intention of giving it back to him only if he were to emerge victorious in the competition. Thus, Yu would have Xiaochun's loyalty forever, but, if he were to lose, he would never again see the violin. Upon hearing this, Xiaochun grabs his violin and runs to the train station to catch his father before he leaves. Intercut with Xiaochun's flight is a flashback of Liu finding him as a baby. Chen thus pulls out all the stops to give us a sentimental, heart-tugging finale.

To complete the all-around feelings of goodwill, the screenplay has Xiaochun meet not only his father but also Lili and Professor Jiang, who have accompanied Liu on his trip to the station. Why Professor Jiang would miraculously resurface after all this time is hard to fathom—after all, Liu did fire him!—but, on a symbolic level, it makes sense that a representative of the old world should be present for the return home. It also adds to the conclusion's sentimental uplift when Xiaochun gives an impromptu concert in the station and strangers gather all around to hear him play. In a musical variation on *It's a Wonderful Life*, Xiaochun discovers that he did not need success for happiness; he had everything he needed all along from the people who loved him. Unlike Lin Yu, who is performing on the concert stage when we last see her, Xiaochun has decided that his dream does not revolve around fame and fortune, which are suspect because they pull a person away from his roots.

Chen's own background may provide some insight into this ending. The production notes mention that, during China's Cultural Revolution, he was ordered to denounce his father as a counterrevolutionary, and he complied. It was

a painful decision that haunted him for many years, so perhaps a resolution in which a son chooses to remain loyal to his father, even at the cost of his own worldly achievement, is a way for Chen to exorcise his demons. Whatever Chen's motives may be, the rousing, celebratory ending works emotionally, even if the proposition behind it is questionable. After all, everyone who succeeds artistically does not reject his family or focus on the superficialities of show business over the craft itself. One is left wondering if the cultural divide is really so deep that family loyalty, artistic excellence, and professional recognition cannot be reconciled for a boy who possesses such immense talent.

—*Peter N. Chumo II*

CREDITS

Liu Xiaochun: Yun Tang
Liu Cheng: Peiqi Liu
Prof. Jiang: Zhiwen Wang
Lili: Hong Chen
Prof. Yu Shifeng: Chen Kaige

Origin: China
Language: Chinese
Released: 2002
Production: Hong Chen, Joo-ik Lee; China Film, 21st Century Hero Film Investment, China Movie Channel, Big Bang Creative; released by United Artists
Directed by: Chen Kaige
Written by: Chen Kaige, Xiaolu Xue
Cinematography by: Hyung-koo Kim
Music by: Lin Zhao
Sound: Danrong Wang
Editing: Ying Zhou
Art Direction: Luyi Liu
Costumes: Yeong-su Ha
Production Design: Cao Jiuping
MPAA rating: PG
Running time: 116 minutes

REVIEWS

Chicago Sun-Times Online. June 6, 2003.
Entertainment Weekly. June 6, 2003, p. 56.
Los Angeles Times Online. May 30, 2003.
New York Times Online. May 30, 2003.
Time. May 26, 2003, p. 75.
Variety Online. September 16, 2002.
Washington Post. June 6, 2003, p. WE38.

The Triplets of Belleville (Les Triplettes de Belleville) (Belleville Rendez-Vous)

Box Office: $4.4 million

"Every so often," wrote Ty Burr of the *Boston Globe,* "the far fringes of animation cough up something so unique that it's almost beyond criticism." Such is the case with the very-French animated feature, *The Triplets of Belleville.* Not only is the film beyond criticism, it's almost beyond description. It's like nothing that's come before it. It looks odd, it sounds odd, and there is barely any dialogue.

Whatever it is, exactly, it's well-liked by critics. It drew a hearty response when it was shown at the Cannes Film Festival, even though it wasn't an official entry. According to the *Los Angeles Times,* one French reviewer was so upset that the film wasn't competing that the critic wrote, "It's the most inventive, the most droll, the best-directed film and it's not in competition? Scandale!" On the *RottenTomatoes.com* website, which compiles critical opinions, *The Triplets of Belleville* received a nearly unanimous thumbs up, or in Rotten Tomatoes parlance, a "fresh" rating.

The film is the work of Sylvain Chomet, a Frenchman who lives in Montreal. He won an Oscar in 1988 for a short called *The Old Lady and the Pigeons* and is a writer and illustrator of book-length comics. He cites as his influences *The Jungle Book, The Aristocats,* and *101 Dalmatians,* but it's difficult to see how they've affected his work.

The first bit in the film is done in the style of an old Max Fleisher (of Betty Boop fame) cartoon. It's in black and white and the film looks scratched and damaged. We see an old nightclub where the triplets of the title are performing. The sisters are draped in fur coats that nearly obscure their faces and perform their hit ditty, which incorporates a raucous finger-snapping, clapping rhythm. Also on hand to perform is Josephine Baker, who wears a banana skirt and nothing else. Django Reinhart plays his guitar with such skill that he starts playing with his feet, too. Fred Astaire gets so caught up in his dance that he is unaware when his shoes come alive and gobble him up. It's a rollicking scene to be sure.

The camera pulls back and we realize that it's all just a TV show. We are in the apartment of an old grandmother, Madame Souza, and her orphaned grandson, Champion. Madame Souza, whose wide eyes carefully watch her grandson from behind her huge thick glasses, is a tiny woman with a fierce determination. Champion is a small, chubby boy with large, round, blankly sad eyes. The grandmother tries to spark an interest in her young grandson by giving him a train and a puppy, Bruno. Finally, she gives Champion a tricycle and his eyes finally show a tiny spark of interest.

Cut to years later. Bruno is now a fat dog whose tiny legs can barely support his huge girth. His only exercise is running up the stairs to bark at the commuter trains that rumble by their old apartment. We get a peak into Bruno's inner life during some of his dreams. One of them, in black and white, shows Bruno riding the train while various commuters sit in the apartment window barking wildly. It is a very happy dream for the dog.

Champion is now a sad-eyed grown-up bike rider. His life consists only of training for races, and he seems to accept this without question. Instead of a fat little boy, he is now an extremely gaunt young man whose angular body is punctuated only by absurdly gigantic calves and thighs.

During the day, Champion pedals, followed by his grandmother riding behind blowing a whistle rhythmically. Tweet. Tweet. Tweet. Madame Souza doesn't seem to notice that while her grandson is training at a champion's level, she is doing the very same thing. (It somehow hasn't affected her body shape.)

Chomet never passes up an opportunity to follow where his whimsical ideas lead him. In one scene, Champion eats the special dinner that his grandmother has prepared for him. Champion is rigged up to a scale so that Madame Souza can tell when he's eaten exactly the right amount of the icky goop that's she made. While he takes his slow, measured bites, grandma spins a bicycle wheel, hitting it with a mallet and testing it for balance. At Champion's feet, Bruno pants and begs. The scene is all about rhythm, repetition and sound. Champion eats, and there are the sounds of his chewing and the scale's needle creeping up. Grandma spins the wheel and hits it. Bruno begs. The sequence continues on and on, until it becomes something of its own.

When Champion is riding in the Tour de France, he collapses and is picked up by what he thinks is the medical van. It is, instead, being driven by some members of the French mafia. The kidnappers are two looming guys whose bodies look like big blocky rectangles. Champion and two other riders are hooked up to some kind of weird mechanical contraption involving stationary bikes. The three men are placed in an auditorium where men bet on who will pedal fastest. As with everything else in his life, Champion simply seems to accept this fate.

But Madame Souza, of course, cannot let this stand. She and Bruno are hot on the trail. When the Mafia members take Champion on an ocean liner across the Atlantic, the tiny grandmother rents a paddleboat and pedals across the ocean, too. Chomet contrasts the tiny boat with the huge ship and the equally giant waves.

Once in the new city, which is somewhat of a cross between New York City and Montreal, Madame Souza meets up with the Triplets of Belleville. The three women, now old, take the grandmother into their apartment. Chomet focuses on the strangeness of their existence, including a scene in which the sisters eat frogs for dinner. If the visuals in this scene aren't nausea-inducing enough, the sound effects will do the trick.

In a scene which almost makes up for the dinner sequence, the Triplets and grandma create a song out of objects in the apartment. One plays the refrigerator, for example, while one plays the newspaper. The results, wrote Burr of the *Boston Globe,* "sound like dinner music for cavemen."

Along the way, Chomet delights in digressions. In one scene at a restaurant, the waiter is so obsequious that he literally bends over backwards to please his customers. Another quick shot of the Statue of Liberty shows Lady Liberty eating a hamburger and looking quite a bit more hefty than usual. When Champion finishes a long ride and needs his calves to be massaged, Madame Souza takes an egg beater to them.

Critics were united in their approval of the film. A. O. Scott of the *New York Times* wrote that the film "may be the oddest movie of the year, by turns sweet and sinister, insouciant and grotesque, invitingly funny and forbiddingly dark. It may also be one of the best, a tour de force of ink-washed, crosshatched mischief and unlikely sublimity." The *Boston Globe's* Burr claimed, "All you really need to enjoy *Triplets* is a taste for the weird and the wonderful." C. W. Nevius of the *San Francisco Chronicle* said of the film, "Impossible to describe, impossible to forget, *The Triplets of Belleville* sends audiences tottering out of the theater, dazed and delighted, and wondering what it is they have just experienced." Kenneth Turan of the *Los Angeles Times* concluded, "Hearing about a film this special isn't enough. It demands to be seen, and it generously rewards those who, like Madame Souza, let nothing stand in their way."

—*Jill Hamilton*

CREDITS

Origin: France, Belgium, Canada
Language: French
Released: 2002
Production: Didier Brunner, Paul Cadieux; Les Armateurs; released by Sony Pictures Classics
Directed by: Sylvain Chomet
Written by: Sylvain Chomet
Music by: Benoit Charest

Editing: Chantel Colibert Brunner
Production Design: Evgeni Tomov
MPAA rating: PG-13
Running time: 91 minutes

REVIEWS

Boxoffice. November, 2003, p. 96.
Chicago Sun-Times Online. December 26, 2003.
Entertainment Weekly. December 5, 2003, p. 66.
Los Angeles Times Online. November 26, 2003.
New York Times Online. November 2, 2003.
New York Times Online. November 26, 2003.
People. December 15, 2003, p. 32.
Sight and Sound. September, 2003, p. 40.
Variety Online. May 17, 2003.

AWARDS AND NOMINATIONS

L.A. Film Critics 2003: Animated Film, Score
Nomination:
Oscars 2003: Animated Film, Song ("Belleville Rendez-Vous")
Ind. Spirit 2004: Foreign Film.

Tully (What Happened to Tully) (The Truth About Tully)

Tully is the kind of film that mainstream Hollywood—with its big budgets and big boxoffice needs—can't seem to afford to make anymore. A film that's quiet and character-driven, given to taking its time and presenting adult (if occasionally melodramatic) situations. This first feature from director, co-writer Hilary Birmingham is adapted from Tom McNeal's 1992 prize-winning short story "What Happened to Tully." And what does happen to Tully Coates Jr. (Anson Mount) is life and love and death and coming to terms with adulthood. The twenty-something Tully lives with his taciturn father, Tully Sr. (Bob Burrus), and his quiet younger brother Earl (Glenn Fitzgerald) on the family's Nebraska farm where they moved after their mother's death 15 years before. Tully's handsome face and muscled body easily seduce all the local girls, without his needing to get emotionally close to any of them, while Earl is too shy to even ask out a girl he likes. Earl, however, is friends with Ella Smalley (Julianne Nicholson), a neighbor studying to be a vet who's just returned from college for the summer to do an internship at the local animal hospital.

Ella is a red-haired, freckled tomboy type who's kind, generous, and too levelheaded to be taken in by Tully's obvious charms—or so she thinks. Tully wants to know why she would come back to their uneventful small town and, though one reason is that her widowed grandfather has been incapacitated by a stroke, Ella tells Tully that she wanted to come back simply because she likes it there. She enjoys mocking Tully about his prowess with the local ladies, including April Reece (Catherine Kellner), a slightly older woman who works as a stripper in a nearby town. She wants Tully for sex and he's happy to oblige. April does have one demand though, that no other girl of Tully's makes it with him on the hood of his old car or she'll do something drastic. Tully agrees, teasing her that that still leaves him the back seat.

Meanwhile, Tully Sr. gets a letter from a collection agency that there is a lien on his property for $300,000 and that the farm is in foreclosure unless he can pay. Confused, the man consults local attorney Burt Hodges (V. Craig Heidenreich) who says the matter is probably a case of mistaken identity and he'll look into it. Tully Sr. doesn't tell his sons about their financial troubles, angering his name-sake who knows something is up and who believes his dad doesn't trust him. Tully may sometimes be reckless but he's also a hard worker and is resentful when his father doesn't include him in making decisions about running the farm.

When Ella stops by, Tully invites her to keep him company while he runs errands and, in return, she takes him to her favorite swimming spot at the river bend. Tully can't resist making a pass, which a disgusted Ella rejects. Tully doesn't understand when Ella says she wants to be friends and returns to April's more apparent charms. April tells him Ella is the kind of girl who wants to settle down, get married, and have children. Concepts Tully can't seem to consider.

The brothers learn of the family's financial problems when they can't pick up an order on credit because the bank has frozen their assets. Tully Sr. still refuses to explain anything to his sons. He does learn from Burt that the debts are medical bills run up by someone claiming to be Tully's wife. He's forced to admit that his wife isn't dead: "She left me. She just walked away one day . . ." Because they never divorced, he's legally obligated to pay. Burt can only suggest that Tully Sr. try to get in touch with his wife and see what's going on, so he mails a letter to her last known address.

Ella's upset that her grandfather is going to be placed in a nursing home and to comfort her, Tully takes her driving out to the pasture where it's quiet so they can talk. They also go back to the river bend, a favorite spot of her grandparents,

and she tells Tully that her (now-deceased) grandmother would look at her grandfather "like the two of them knew the secret of everything that mattered." It's what Ella wants in her life and something even the emotionally adrift Tully can understand is worth having. Both Earl and his father warn Tully that Ella is too good for him to just be playing around with.

It's Ella who happens to give Tully the return-to-sender letter his father mailed to Irene Duffy. Tully goes off without explaining why he's upset but Ella learns from Earl that their mother's name was Irene. She finds Tully at the river and says "I thought you might want someone to talk to." Instead of merely talking, she kisses Tully, which leads to them having sex (unseen) in the backseat of his car. When they're done, Tully refuses to look at Ella. Later, he won't answer her phone calls and pushes her away when she comes to see him. Angry and humiliated, Ella tells him "you don't want to care about anything!"

Still trying to reach Irene before the bank forecloses, Tully Sr. puts in a call to Mal "Mac" MacAvoy (John Diehl), who shows up unexpectedly and talks to Tully Jr. He tells the young man that he knew his mother back in Kansas and he'd like to speak to his brother. Earl sees MacAvoy and hides out listening to the conversation. When Tully Sr. spots the man, he orders him off the property but Mac insists he wants to speak to his son—Earl—which Tully won't allow. Tully Sr. thinks Irene has sent MacAvoy, but Mac informs him that he hasn't seen Irene in years and that she really is dead—she spent most of the last year in the hospital and died from cancer: "I thought you would have known al-ready." The younger Tully runs the man off.

Later, Earl spots his father sitting in his truck, looking at the farm. The older man says it's Irene's birthday and they reminisce for a moment before Earl assures him: "You're my father. I don't care about that guy. . . . You done good by us, Pop." Tully Jr. isn't so forgiving about the deception. When he confronts his father, he says he doesn't understand how he could still care about the woman so much. His father does blame himself for his wife abandoning them but also says that Irene threatened to take the boys from him unless he told the children that she was dead. Although not demon-strative, it's obvious that Tully Sr. is willing to do anything for his sons.

Still shaken, Tully gets drunk and shows up at the local bar where Ella and Earl are sitting with friends. He tries to get Ella to talk to him but she walks out. When Tully further makes a fool of himself, Earl pushes his brother into the men's room so they can talk. He tells Tully that he knew about MacAvoy because he's seen him before. He didn't say anything because he didn't want to hurt their father. The next day, Tully finds Ella at the river, swimming, and tries to apologize again. She brushes him off saying she's meeting someone. Before leaving, Tully explains his behavior: " I got scared. I never loved anyone before."

After dinner, their normally reserved father informs his sons that he's bought ice cream for desert because they deserve something sweet. He also tells Tully that the hydraulics on their flatbed truck, which is parked in one of the far fields, is still a problem but refuses the younger man's offer to help him the next day. When Tully does go out to the field, he discovers his father crushed beneath the bed of the truck. After a wake at the farm, Tully finds his father's life insurance policy for $500,000. Ella's come by to help and a suspicious Tully takes her with him to look at the truck. It's clear that he believes his father planned his death as a way to clear up his debts and leave the boys the farm. Ella consoles Tully and the film ends with them sitting together on the porch the next morning, having coffee.

Tully fell victim to the not-unknown vagaries of the independent film scene. Filmed on a small budget in five weeks in 1999, the film was shown at the 2000 Toronto Film Festival. A couple of distribution deals fell apart and the film underwent a name change before its limited 2002 release when its original title—*The Truth About Tully*—was changed to avoid any confusion with the 2002 film *The Truth About Charlie.*

Tully is unhurried storytelling. In fact, the pace is sometimes as slow as a lazy summer day at the ole swimming hole. This isn't necessarily a bad thing but it takes some getting used to. At the beginning, the story would seem to be about a wild young man who learns how to handle adult situations with the help of a more emotionally-open young woman. And it does have that aspect. But it is also about the ties that bind a family together and how secrets keep them apart. The death of Tully's father does not turn out to be that unexpected—it's clear something will happen. (Always beware of a faulty truck.) Nor is the fact that there's a life insurance policy that will cover all the farm's debts.

Performances help overcome any of the clichés. Bob Burrus, who has had a long stage career, conveys sadness, stubbornness, guilt, and love with the way he hunches his shoulders and looks at, and away from, his sons. Anson Mount may be better recognized as "that guy" from the Britney Spears movie *Crossroads* (2002) but he's more than a Hollywood pretty boy. He convincingly portrays a character who knows he's missing out on something important and is not too macho to admit it, even if he doesn't know how to get what he wants. On the other hand, Nicholson, a face not-unfamiliar from the TV shows *Ally McBeal* and *Presidio Med,* is no standard Hollywood babe. Besides the freckles, she has a lanky body, and a manner that says she won't be anybody's fool. *Tully* may not be blockbuster material but it manages to stay with you long after the popcorn movie is forgotten.

—*Christine Tomassini*

CREDITS

Tully Coates Jr.: Anson Mount
Ella Smalley: Julianne Nicholson
Earl Coates: Glenn Fitzgerald
Tully Coates Sr.: Bob Burrus
April Reece: Catherine Kellner
Claire: Natalie Canerday
Mal MacAvoy: John Diehl
Burt Hodges: V. Craig Heidenreich

Origin: USA
Released: 2000
Directed by: Hilary Birmingham
Written by: Hilary Birmingham, Matt Drake
Cinematography by: John Foster
Music by: Marcelo Zarvos
Sound: Brad Bergbom
Music Supervisor: Matthew Abbott
Editing: Affonso Goncalves
Art Direction: Nathan Carlson
Costumes: Christine Vollmer
Production Design: Mark White
MPAA rating: R
Running time: 107 minutes

REVIEWS

Chicago Sun-Times Online. November 8, 2002.
Los Angeles Times Online. November 1, 2002.
New York Times. November 1, 2002, p. E14.
San Francisco Chronicle. November 8, 2002, p. D5.
Seattle Post-Intelligencer Online. March 28, 2003.
Variety Online. May 20, 2000.

QUOTES

Ella (Julianne Nicholson) to Tully (Anson Mount): "I don't really like thinking of people as types. I think it's lazy. I like thinking people can surprise you."
Ella (Julianne Nicholson) teases Tully (Anson Mount): "What's it like to drive women crazy?"

AWARDS AND NOMINATIONS

Nomination:
Ind. Spirit 2000: Film, Screenplay, Support. Actress (Nicholson), Debut Perf. (Burrus).

21 Grams

*They say we all lose 21 grams at the exact moment
of our deaths . . . everyone. The weight of a stack
of nickels. The weight of a chocolate bar. The
weight of a hummingbird. . . .*
—Movie tagline

How much does life weigh?
—Movie tagline

How much does love weigh?
—Movie tagline

How much does revenge weigh?
—Movie tagline

How much does guilt weigh?
—Movie tagline

 Box Office: $15.4 million

Writing in the *New York Times,* Elvis Mitchell called *21
Grams* "tantamount to the discovery of a new country"—a bold declaration one might think is being
directed at a groundbreaking classic like *Citizen Kane.* Yet
Mitchell was not the only major critic to fall under the spell
of the most overrated movie of the year. Indeed, many critics
heaped lavish plaudits on a film that uses elaborate narrative
gimmickry to disguise its shallowness.

Directed by Alejandro González Iñárritu and written by
Guillermo Arriaga, the creative team behind the vastly superior *Amores Perros, 21 Grams* revolves, like the previous film,
around a car accident and the disparate lives it touches. But
Amores Perros told three distinct stories, each one detailing
how people are affected by the tragedy. *21 Grams* tells one
big story involving three lives that collide in tragedy, but the
timeframe has been so juggled that it feels like the filmmakers threw bits of film into the air and started splicing
together adjacent pieces. In the space of any given few
minutes, we can see, for no discernible reason, a succession
of scenes showing the same character at very different parts
of his life. At first, the technique is confusing, leaving the
audience unable to gain its bearings. (Of course, sometimes
making the audience work operates to a film's benefit, as in
Memento, in which the backward chronology served as a
thematic counterpoint to the protagonist's short-term memory loss.) Once the pieces begin to fall into place, the editing
becomes irritating and plays like a desperate attempt to
impart depth to what is essentially a mundane melodrama.

To untangle the narrative, Sean Penn plays Paul, a
mathematics professor awaiting a heart transplant. His wife,
Mary (Charlotte Gainsbourg), has remained loyal despite

some marital problems, including Paul's infidelities. Meanwhile, Jack (Benicio Del Toro), an ex-con and recovering
substance abuser, has gone straight with the help of his
newfound belief in Jesus. Indeed, Jack attributes everything
to a divine hand and dedicates lots of time to the local
church. His wife, Marianne (Melissa Leo), is devoted to her
husband but cannot help looking somewhat askance at his
fanaticism and wondering if she still knows the man she
married. Cristina (Naomi Watts) is a one-time drug addict
now happily married with two little daughters.

Their fates converge one night when Jack accidentally
runs down Cristina's husband and daughters and then flees
the scene. All three are killed, but Paul gets a new lease on
life when he receives the husband's heart. Over Marianne's
protests, Jack decides to turn himself in. He believes that
everything is predestined and now thinks that God has
abandoned him and rewarded his faith with the horrible
guilt of having killed three people. The tragedy sends Cristina back to a life of drugs and sets Paul on a mission to find
out who saved his life. He begins stalking her and tentatively
makes friends, keeping secret their connection until an acknowledged mutual attraction forces him to tell the truth,
and they become lovers anyway.

The essential story, then, is fairly straightforward, but
the editing is so random that there is no logical order. We
know fairly early on that the three main characters will
ultimately converge in a motel room where Paul will suffer a
gunshot wound, but only gradually does it become clear that
Paul is on a mission to kill Jack at Cristina's behest. It is an
odd turn in her character that she goes from not even caring
to press charges to ordering Paul to kill the man who
destroyed her family. She suddenly comes to the conclusion
that Paul owes it to her now that he has become her lover.

The acting by all three principals was roundly applauded, and certainly they all demonstrate an intensity and
concentration that is unflagging. But it always feels like they
are acting. Watts was brilliant in her breakthrough role in
2001's *Mulholland Drive* because the character was startling
in her many dimensions and incarnations. Her Cristina is a
more obvious creation—a tortured soul barely able to keep
her life together. She screams and cries and rages against the
cruel hand fate has dealt her, and, while Watts's work is
believable, it is not very moving. Penn is perpetually withdrawn and seems to carry the weight of the world on his
shoulders in practically every scene. He is the protagonist,
yet he remains vague at best. In one scene, Paul explains the
beauty of math to Cristina, which is our only glimpse into
his professional life and intellectual passion, and yet this
speech seems out of place for him. Del Toro gives the most
sympathetic performance because we have some inkling of
the hard road he has traveled to put his life in order, and he
seems, in his sometimes odd way, to be trying to lead a
decent life. But his character is ultimately very simplistic—

going from a devout believer to a Job-like figure utterly abandoned by his Savior.

The main problem, however, lies not with the actors so much as it does with the filmmakers. The nonlinear cutting actually sabotages the performances because it does not allow the audience to appreciate the development of a character, to understand how each person is affected by the tragedy and responds to it. Because we could be anywhere at any time, the actors could be doing just about anything, and it might seem plausible. In essence, we are distanced from the characters when we want to be drawn in and made to feel an empathy with their plights. We should share their grief and trials, but instead the artificial narrative technique is constantly pulling us out of the moment, giving us no time to feel anything as we try to guess where we are in the scattered time frame.

Central plot points like Paul falling for Cristina feel arbitrary, as does Mary's overriding desire to freeze Paul's sperm so she can later have his child. After Paul disappears for a few days, spending time with Cristina, Mary finally walks out, and we never find out what happens to her. And although Jack gets released from prison, he ends up moving out of his home, leaving his family's future unclear. Meanwhile, Paul, having learned that his heart will soon give out, chooses to spend his remaining time out in the world rather than die more comfortably in a hospital room waiting for another heart transplant that will probably never happen. Pulling a gun on Jack and marching him into the desert, Paul seemingly acquiesces to Cristina's demand for revenge, but he changes his mind at the last minute and instead orders Jack to go away forever.

That night, however, Jack barges into Paul and Cristina's motel room for a final confrontation. While Cristina is able to pummel Jack repeatedly with a lamp, Paul gets hold of his gun and shoots himself in the chest, which now explains scenes we have seen throughout the film of Paul bleeding in the back seat of a car while Jack is driving to a hospital. But now we know that it was not Jack who shot him, as we might have expected; it was Paul who chose to end his life rather than die a painful death from a deteriorating heart. This resolution, however, is not very profound, and neither is a last-minute revelation that Cristina is pregnant.

What is worse, as Paul lays dying, we hear him in a voiceover, ruminating on the notion that everyone loses 21 grams at the exact moment of death, as if this were an illuminating fact with far-reaching philosophical implications, especially when he speculates on what is lost and gained. We see a montage of shots that suggest the other characters are moving on with their lives (Cristina, for example, is finally able to enter her daughters' room), but Paul's deathbed reverie comes across as pretentious and ultimately meaningless. The film introduces this weight metaphor at the very end as if it provided a context for these three tortured lives, but it feels like an afterthought designed to imbue the story with a resonance it has not earned on its own. Perhaps, as some religious people believe, 21 grams is the weight of the soul as it leaves the body, but this idea is not explicitly stated by Paul, and, even if it were, it would not shed new light on what we have seen.

Indeed, if *21 Grams* were told in linear fashion, it would not receive the accolades heaped upon it by so many critics—"[the film] may well be the crowning work of this year," Elvis Mitchell raved—but instead clearly be understood as a standard melodrama with a *noir* turn in the final act. Giving the film a grainy, washed-out look and presenting the story in a haphazard fashion does not turn this material into an intellectual exercise. Moreover, pretending the story has metaphysical or spiritual import actually weighs it down and is ultimately no substitute for solid storytelling and characters we can care about. If the filmmakers had concentrated on these areas, then perhaps deeper themes would have emerged naturally, and not have to be added awkwardly at the end.

—*Peter N. Chumo II*

CREDITS

Paul: Sean Penn
Jack: Benicio Del Toro
Cristina: Naomi Watts
Mary: Charlotte Gainsbourg
Marianne: Melissa Leo
Claudia: Clea DuVall
Michael: Danny Huston
Brown: Paul Calderon

Origin: USA
Released: 2003
Production: Robert Salerno, Alejandro Gonzalez Inarritu; This Is That, Y Productions; released by Focus Features
Directed by: Alejandro Gonzalez Inarritu
Written by: Guillermo Arriaga
Cinematography by: Rodrigo Prieto
Music by: Gustavo Santaolalla
Sound: Jose Antonio Garcia
Editing: Stephen Mirrione
Art Direction: Deb Riley
Costumes: Marlene Stewart
Production Design: Brigitte Broch
MPAA rating: R
Running time: 125 minutes

REVIEWS

Boxoffice. November, 2003, p. 94.
Chicago Sun-Times Online. November 26, 2003.
Entertainment Weekly. November 21, 2003, p. 58.
Los Angeles Times Online. November 21, 2003.
New York Times Online. October 18, 2003.
People. December 1, 2003, p. 31.
Rolling Stone. December 11, 2003, p. 213.
Sight and Sound. June, 2003, p. 12.
USA Today Online. November 21, 2003.
Vanity Fair. November, 2003, p. 128.
Variety Online. September 7, 2003.
Washington Post. November 26, 2003, p. C1.

AWARDS AND NOMINATIONS

L.A. Film Critics 2003: Actress (Watts)
Natl. Bd. of Review 2003: Actor (Penn)
Nomination:
Oscars 2003: Actor (Del Toro), Actress (Watts)
Screen Actors Guild 2003: Actress (Watts), Support. Actor (Del Toro).

28 Days Later

Your Days Are Numbered.
—Movie tagline

Box Office: $45 million

The "darkly clever" *28 Days Later,* an apocalyptic British horror thriller from a relatively unexpected source, reunited producer Andrew Macdonald and director Danny Boyle, who had first successfully collaborated on *Shallow Grave* (1994), then on *Trainspotting* (1995), *A Life Less Ordinary* (1997), and *The Beach* (2000) and teamed them with novelist Alex Garland, who had written the source story for *The Beach.* Expectations were that Boyle and Garland might conjure up a spoof horror film featuring post-apocalyptic zombies transformed by a so-called "Rage" virus loosed upon humanity by animal-rights activists trying to liberate infected chimps; but, as Glenn Kenny pointed out in his *Premiere* review, *28 Days Later* was not a spoof but "the genuine article." It turned out to be a cautionary tale disguised as a horror film.

The film begins with a prologue: A group of animal activists bursts into an animal testing laboratory. Against the frantic pleas of the workers, the activists release a horde of diseased monkeys. The creatures then dispatch their liberators within seconds. Some "28 days later," bicycle courier Jim (Cillian Murphy) wakes up from a coma in a deserted hospital. In a daze, he wanders outside to encounter London's empty, deserted streets, bridges, and buildings. There are a few corpses scattered about and a strange quiet hangs over the decimated scene.

These opening moments are eerily effective as Jim wanders past familiar London landmarks that are now wholly deserted and have fallen into a state of ruin. Then come the zombies. More specifically, gangs of gesticulating, spasmodic creatures that have been infected with a strange, blood-related virus. They blindly pursue any human being that comes within their ken. Their bloodlust is relentless, and a mere drop of blood will transmit the virus to the victim within seconds.

Accompanied by two other survivors he finds, Selena (Naomie Harris) and Mark (Noah Huntley), Jim seeks safety in a high-rise apartment belonging to Frank (Brendan Gleeson), a cab driver, and his daughter, Hannah (Megan Burns). He learns that the infection set in 28 days ago, that contact with the blood of a victim transforms anyone into this zombie-like state in a matter of seconds, and that there's no cure. All of London is gone and maybe all of the United Kingdom as well. But what about other countries across the sea? No one knows. Perhaps England itself is under some sort of quarantine.

Alerted by a radio signal promising the remaining human survivors a haven and a cure for the infection in Manchester, the group leaves London in Frank's taxi. They unwisely take an underpass across the river Thames, where a flat tire leaves them momentarily at the mercy of the approaching zombies. A tense scene follows. Even the rats are fleeing from these infected creatures. The group escapes in the nick of time. Near Manchester they stop at a road barrier. Frank looks around. A crow devouring a corpse above him deposits a single drop of blood in his eye. In seconds he's a raving maniac begging his friends to "stay away." He's shot dead on the spot by an arriving squad of soldiers. The soldiers, under the command of Major Henry West (Christopher Eccleston), live in an armed and barricaded camp, and they are on 24-hour alert against the nightly encroachments of the zombies. At first Jim and Selena think they have found a safe haven. But quickly they sense something is wrong. There's a zombie creature in chains in the back yard. "We're keeping him to see how long it takes one of them to starve to death," says Major West, calmly. Discipline is slack, there's no sign of the promised cure, and at dinner one night it's revealed that Major West has promised his men that women will come. Selena and Frank's 15-year old daughter are sure to become victims of the mindless lust of these starved men. The horrified Jim manages to rescue them, but not before the marauding zombies outside burst the barriers and slaughter all the soldiers.

The film ends with an epilogue. Jim and Selena and the young girl have pitched camp in the country. They hear the sounds of an airplane overhead and quickly spell out a huge H-E-L-L-O. "It seems the main British Isle is effectively under global quarantine," Dr. Harold Varmus concluded in his *New York Times* piece on the film, adding that after "another 28-day interval, everyone who was infected [will be] presumed dead." He concluded that the small plane, "dipping its wings to acknowledge a colorful 'hello' spelled out in bedspreads" should remind us "that the rest of the world, apparently spared from the epidemic, is now ready to pick up the pieces cheerfully."

Well, perhaps, but director Danny Boyle and his screenwriter Alex Garland had problems with the conclusion. The DVD version released at the end of the year included two other alternative endings, one of which, according to *Premiere* magazine was so radical that it was never filmed but is represented on the DVD with storyboards and voiceovers.

Glenn Kenny predicted that Boyle's "punk rock zombie" film would "scare the stuffing" out of viewers, "both viscerally and existentially." Many reviewers were in agreement on this point, but the reviews were mixed. For his part Stephen King was "intrigued" by *28 Days Later* and even "liked" the film, but he was ultimately disappointed because it offered nothing "that came back to haunt me later that evening, after the bedroom light was out." For King the film fell short of the "bottom line," which is simply "to scare you silly." In his *New Yorker* review Anthony Lane also noted "a serious shortage of fright." Though the "setup is gruesome enough," Lane wrote, Boyle "cannot hope to horrify" unless he learns to linger, "to pause patiently while monstrosity looms." Lane also lamented "a shortage of superior zombies" in the film's design. Others were indeed "scared silly," if not disgusted by the film. The *Washington Post*'s Ann Hornaday, for example, was repulsed by Boyle's "post-apocalyptic necropolis," judging it to be "detestable, not just because its action is so vile or its technique so crude, but because its moral imagination is so impoverished." Varmus, President of the Memorial Sloan-Kettering Cancer Center, was far more positive. One of Boyle's accomplishments, he thought, was that the film "makes us think about [the] insidious plagues that now afflict us," including AIDS, the Ebola virus, and SARS. Even so, *28 Days Later* managed to compete head-on with the would-be summer blockbuster *Charlie's Angels 2*. After seven weeks in release, *28 Days Later* had grossed over $42 million.

The film is eerily unnerving with its scenes of a deserted London, and it is shocking in the outbursts of violence in the soldiers' camp. Shot on gritty digital video by Anthony Dod Mantle (under the obvious influence of Lars von Trier and other *Dogma 95* disciples), *28 Days Later* for some reviewers looked convincingly and even urgently post-apocalyptic. Of course, the film strongly recalls the work of George Romero,

since, like Romero's horror classic, *Night of the Living Dead* (1968), *28 Days Later* reveals how humanity under stress can behave in a bestial, destructive manner fully the equal of the disease-ravaged creatures menacing them. For some critics, Boyle's film even surpasses Romero's. "The infected, with their surprising virus-induced hyperkinesis, are every bit as frightening as the spookily revitalized ghouls" of Romero's classic horror film, Varmus wrote in the *New York Times*, though he went on to criticize the film's "lack of microbial verisimilitude," since no known virus could produce symptoms so quickly as the film suggests.

Ordinary viewers were not so demanding about "microbial verisimilitude," however, and in Britain *28 Days Later* was credited with having "reanimated" Boyle's career. After the film opened in the United Kingdom in October of 2002, it marked the first time one of the director's films made it to the top of the releases The film succeeded without stars and was cheaply made with handheld digital cameras on a budget of $8.7 million. The production costs were recovered over the film's opening weekend in the United States, when it grossed $9.7 million from 1,260 screens, according to *Entertainment Weekly*. "I wasn't looking to make a zombie movie," Boyle told Benjamin Svetkey, "but five pages into the script, I knew I wanted to make the movie." Boyle knew what he wanted and he got what he wanted.

—James M. Welsh and John C. Tibbetts

CREDITS

Jim: Cillian Murphy
Hannah: Megan Burns
Frank: Brendan Gleeson
Selena: Naomie Harris
Major Henry West: Christopher Eccleston
Mark: Noah Huntley

Origin: Great Britain, USA
Released: 2002
Production: Andrew Macdonald; DNA Films Ltd.; released by Fox Searchlight
Directed by: Danny Boyle
Written by: Alex Garland
Cinematography by: Anthony Dod Mantle
Music by: John Murphy
Sound: John Rodda
Editing: Chris Gill
Art Direction: Mark Digby
Costumes: Rachel Fleming
Production Design: Mark Tildesley
MPAA rating: R
Running time: 108 minutes

REVIEWS

Boxoffice. April, 2003, p. 75.
Entertainment Weekly. June 27, 2003, p. 114.
The Guardian Online. November 1, 2002.
Premiere. July/August, 2003, p. 22.
Sight and Sound. December, 2002, p. 59.
Variety Online. October 24, 2002.

QUOTES

Selena (Naomie Harris) to Jim (Cillian Murphy): "Staying alive is as good as it gets."

2 Fast 2 Furious

How fast do you like it?
—Movie tagline
Cross the line one more time.
—Movie tagline
The new models are in.
—Movie tagline

Box Office: $122.5 million

2 *Fast 2 Furious,* the follow-up to the 2001 surprise hit, *The Fast and the Furious* came to theaters without most of the people from the first film. Director Rob Cohen, some of the writers, and stars Vin Diesel and Michelle Rodriguez went on to other things. Diesel, who demanded too much money, went on to work with Cohen on the poorly received *XXX.* To have such a talent drain—though perhaps talent isn't exactly the right word—has a big effect on this film. As Manohla Dargis of the *Los Angeles Times* put it, it's "a triple whammy that is, loosely speaking, akin to a second *Godfather* movie minus Al Pacino, Francis Ford Coppola and Mario Puzo, never mind Robert De Niro."

Luckily for this movie, the people aren't so important. What is important is made clear in the first few moments of the film. Director John Singleton (*Shaft*) shows one of those illegal street gatherings that peppered the first film. There are a lot of shots of women's well-toned bottoms and an equal number of open hoods on souped-up cars. The crowd is multicultural, the better to appeal to a wider demographic. There are cars with all kinds of tacky accessories, a pounding soundtrack and a race that climaxes with cars jumping over an open drawbridge.

Unfortunately, Singleton, who is relying heavily on the cars to carry the movie, isn't as good as Cohen at conveying the excitement of the race. Cohen used a quick cutting style that made his races and car stunts viscerally exciting and immediate. Even if you didn't care for car racing, Cohen's action sequences were undeniably engaging. Singleton doesn't have that same gift. Singleton repeatedly shows each competitor shifting their gears and swearing at the other racers while the engines roar.

And it's too bad because Singleton has nothing in his star. Paul Walker, who returns from the first movie, is Brian O'Conner. Brian is as bland as his name. The blonde-haired, blue-eyed California boy is supposed to be a bad dude that's down with all the homeboys. He gamely tacks "bro" onto the end of his sentences, but Walker can't seem to make it believable. The more he tries, the more nerdy he seems. He's ill suited for his role as a tough guy, and he doesn't begin to have the acting ability to fake it.

Tyrese Gibson, the singer/model, who is teamed up with Walker plays Roman Pearce. Walker suffers further by being paired with Tyrese, who actually is cool. He looks great (at one screening, women cheered when he took off his shirt), and manages to be tough, funny, and charming. Tyrese (who also worked with Singleton on *Baby Boy*) does a great job here and shows that he has what it takes to be a movie star. He does the street thing without breaking a sweat, but also does a killer imitation of bad guy Carter Verone (Cole Hauser). It's possible that Tyrese just seems good in comparison to the stiff Walker, but it sure seems like the man's got talent.

The only thing more ridiculous than Walker as a tough street punk is the plot that puts him there. Brian, as fans of the first film will probably not remember, was working for the LAPD but screwed them when he decided to let truck hijacker Diesel go free. Even though he's a proven flake, the FBI decides that it would be a good idea to have him go undercover again. Brian is reluctant, but since he's in trouble for jumping that open drawbridge, he agrees.

To help him in his mission, Brian chooses Roman, a childhood friend and ex-con who thinks that Brian's the reason he's in jail. This allows for the verbal sparring that buddy films thrive on, as well as some homoerotic fighting. Their job is to get close to a Miami crime lord, Verone. Verone is shacked up with Monica (Eva Mendes), a customs official who may or may not have "flipped" on the force. Apparently the sexy Monica is so devoted to her job that she is perfectly willing to sleep with criminals in order to bring them down. Monica seems to like Brian, though their relationship ends up being as chaste as that of Marcia Brady and Davy Jones. In matters sexual, *2 Fast* is all talk and no action.

Brian and Roman need to get a job working for Verone. Instead of having potential employees fill out an application or something, Verone has his applicants race each other to recover a package. Naturally, Brian and Roman win, but first they do the shifting gears, whirring engines, muttered trash talk sequence.

Their job will be to deliver some big bags of money across town to Verone. During fifteen police-free moments, they are to speed through the streets in their race cars to get to the delivery site. As A. O. Scott of the *New York Times* put it, "The kingpin is eager to hire street racers to ferry his ill-gotten gains from one place to another, perhaps because brightly painted flame-shooting cars traveling at double the speed limit are unlikely to attract the attention of law enforcement. He might have done better with Buick-driving retirees, or carrier pigeons, but that would have been a different movie." Roger Ebert of the *Chicago Sun-Times* had a different problem with this scene. He wondered about the $100,000 the guys were to make for their journey. "Hell," mused Ebert, "For 10 Gs, I'd rent a van at the Aventura Mall and deliver the goods myself."

For such a boneheaded movie, *2 Fast* is more politically correct than it has to be. There's the whole multicultural aspect, for one. In this world of street racing, black, Latino, Asian, and the one white guy, Brian, all join hands as gearheads. And there's even a girl driver, Suki (model Devon Aoki). She doesn't win, of course, but at least she's there.

Critics knew *2 Fast* was meant as a lightweight summer movie and took it as such. Ebert wrote, "It doesn't have a brain in its head, but it's made with skill and style and, boy, is it fast and furious." Scott's assessment differed from Ebert's: "*2 Fast 2 Furious* is among the most lethargic action movies I have ever seen: when Mr. Walker and Tyrese are not driving, it might as well be called *2 Slow 2 Tedious,* since the script shows all the energy and sophistication of an old episode of *TJ Hooker.*" Lou Lumenick of the *New York Post* wrote, "*2 Fast 2 Furious* is a lark for anyone who's willing to check their brains at the concession stand for 100 minutes." Leah Rozen of *People* said of the film, "It's loud, fast, saturated with a fluorescent Florida palette and matters not a whit. Hey, it must be summer."

—Jill Hamilton

Brian O'Connor: Paul Walker
Roman Pearce: Tyrese Gibson
Carter Verone: Cole Hauser
Monica Fuentes: Eva Mendes
Tej: Ludacris
Suki: Devon Aoki
Agent Markham: James Remar
Agent Bilkins: Thom Barry
Slap Jack: Michael Ealy
Detective Whitworth: Mark Boone Jr.

Origin: USA
Released: 2003
Production: Neal H. Moritz; released by Universal Pictures
Directed by: John Singleton
Written by: Derek Haas, Michael Brandt
Cinematography by: Matthew F. Leonetti
Music by: David Arnold
Sound: Walter Anderson
Editing: Bruce Cannon, Dallas S. Puett
Art Direction: Lawrence A. Hubbs
Costumes: Sanja Milkovic Hays
Production Design: Keith Brian Burns
MPAA rating: PG-13
Running time: 94 minutes

REVIEWS

Chicago Sun-Times Online. June 5, 2003.
Entertainment Weekly. June 13, 2003, p. 69.
Los Angeles Times Online. December 10, 2002.
Los Angeles Times Online. June 6, 2003.
New York Times Online. June 6, 2003.
People. June 16, 2003, p. 39.
Rolling Stone. June 26, 2003, p. 87.
USA Today Online. June 6, 2003.
Variety Online. June 6, 2003.
Washington Post. June 6, 2003, p. WE37.

AWARDS AND NOMINATIONS

Nomination:
Golden Raspberries 2003: Worst Remake/Sequel.

Tycoon
(Oligarch)

Pavel Lounguine's disturbing political satire from Russia, *Tycoon,* proposes a dictum of alarmingly universal proportions for the early years of the new millennium: the only true democracy is a corrupt democracy. Lounguine sets about to prove this theory by showing how corporate aggrandizement—bordering on gangsterism—propped up by government decrees, can result in not only a restructuring of economic power within a country, by decentralizing it, but in also providing a source of pride for the masses.

Lounguine thus seems to have intentionally chosen a generic term for the title of his film, thereby stressing the universal aspects of his narrative. On the surface, *Tycoon* is ostensibly about the peculiarly post-Soviet phenomenon of the Oligarchs, businessmen who came to wield such enormous power that they could topple ministers. The chronology of the tale Lounguine is telling extends over a 15-year period beginning roughly around 1985, with the eponymous character created as a composite of real-life figures.

Wisely, Lounguine draws upon the template adopted by Orson Welles for the classic *Citizen Kane* (1941), in which the narrative shuffles around the events in the life of Charles Foster Kane so as to show his fall as a person coinciding with his rise as a public figure. Like Welles, Lounguine adopts the framing device of a "story within a story." Chapter headings intentionally keep his audience at a distance, as he keeps his tale moving at a fast clip.

For example, the film's opening titles are underscored by jazz music, suggesting intimacy and decadence, in contrast with the music of patriotism linked to Russia's historical past. As if to show the weakening power of the State, the film opens in the present, that is, in the year 2000. A title announces: "The Day of Plato's Death," but we see instead the middle-aged, asthmatic special investigator, Chmakov (Andrei Krasko), waking up in his cramped quarters on a rainy morning in Moscow. A live TV broadcast announces a raid on the headquarters of the corporate giant, Infocar. An attractive female reporter is explaining its importance. The State does not like Oligarchs, she says, especially rebellious ones, the foremost amongst them being Plato Makovski, the founder of Infocar.

As Chmakov arrives on the scene, he looks surprised by the sudden turn of events. On hand, celebrating in the street, are the Communists, dressed in their traditional red, applauding the action of the State. They are shouting at the unseen villain: "Pack your bags! Go Live in Israel!" Inside, Chmakov wants to know from a junior officer who ordered the raid. He receives an answer shrouded in bureaucratic mystery. Worse, he's told: "The less you know, the better you'll sleep!"

When we finally see Plato (Vladimir Mashkov), he's spectacled, slightly balding but handsome. He looks strained and withdrawn as the female reporter is hounding him. "*Forbes* calls you one of the 100 richest men in the world with a fortune of five billion," she says, "yet you are not spared these humiliations." Plato mutters that the charges against him are all a "tissue of lies."

Lounguine immediately widens his socio-political perspective to show the mood in the country. Muckraking seems to have taken over the airwaves. A TV expose shows the governor of Northern Siberia lolling around half-nude at home, while female lovelies are giving him a rubdown. The lascivious images in stark black-and-white are interrupted by the announcement of Plato's assassination. From a barstool,

Chmakov watches, stunned, as the remnants of Plato's Mercedes are shown after an attack from several anti-tank missiles.

Here the film introduces Plato's archrival in many spheres, the equally charismatic but blond Koretski (Alexandre Baluev), a State lackey. Toward the end of the film, he will confide to Chmakov his role in the conspiracy to kill Plato, and then add that he belongs to an aristocracy whose hereditary power stretches all the way back to the Czars. When we first see him, he's shown gloating over the news of the success of the thirteenth attempt on Plato's life. He then consults with his subordinates in a sauna. Like decadent Romans in their togas, they're shown feasting by a pool. Through their conversation, we come to know that Chmakov was really a judge from the provinces sent for by Moscow to investigate Plato's business scams. Koretski vows to find Plato's killer and, in the same breath, wants Chmakov to be demoted.

The next brief chapter, "The Day After Plato's Death," shows a TV interview in which a dashing Plato speaks of his country's willingness to massacre an entire people, but that killing an individual was way beyond them. With a smile, he hedges his bets, adding that he himself believes in eternal life since he was baptized a Christian. Chmakov is shown admiring Plato's cunning, as the subordinate seen earlier, now his boss, remarks that Plato was smart enough to "put his soul into a Swiss bank along with his gold." Chmakov, on his part, plans to explore three fields related to Plato's life: his friends, his business, and the underworld.

The next chapter, "15 Years Before Plato's Death" introduces Plato as embodying the iconography of machismo. In a train passageway, he is holding up skewers of kebabs, while attempting to charm the ravishing blond Maria (Maria Mironova), Koretski's wife. It is a joyous occasion as Plato and his cohorts are on their way to an academic conference, where one of them, Viktor (Sergei Oshkevich), plans to read a paper that will shake the State's economic foundations. Also present in the compartment is the fat, curly-topped Moussa (Alexandre Samoilenko), Plato's close friend and business associate. Lounguine uses this segment to drive home his point that the roots of the Oligarchs did not lie so much in criminal behavior, as much as in poetry and intellectual derring-do. At one point, as Plato swigs vodka from a bottle, Maria looks up at him in admiration and remarks that he looks like a trumpeter.

The introduction of the intellectual factor into the equation can be seen to cut both ways. It certainly gives Lounguine an opportunity to veer his narrative onto an ideological track in order to show just where the thinking of the Oligarchs stood in relation to the dominant values at the time. Viktor's presentation—which he claims is a mathematical, as opposed to an ideological, justification for economic growth unfettered by State control—flies in the face of the Marxism-Leninism championed by Koretski, who tries to nail Viktor down as a traitor. Ironically, at that very moment, Maria, in full frontal glory, is cavorting with Plato in bed. When the latter is urgently summoned to defend Viktor, he turns the tables on Koretski by arguing that his economic principles are an oversimplification, akin to assuming that the underbelly of a crocodile is also green.

As Lounguine proceeds to tell his tale of developing business and political machinations, his film hits a snag that the *Kane* template manages to avoid. As Pauline Kael points out in her monumental *The "Citizen Kane" Book,* Herman J. Mankiewicz's original screenplay was a sprawling work, containing scenes of the kind that were to surface decades later in Fellini's three-hour *La Dolce Vita* (1960). Welles, the prodigy, as Kael refers to him, revamped Mankiewicz's screenplay to focus it on the character of Charles Foster Kane, and without writing one line of dialogue himself. What Kael is not prepared to admit, however, and what Lounguine's film makes clear, is that in so doing, Welles in fact saved *Citizen Kane.* This becomes clear when we see how Lounguine adopts Welles's narrative form, right down to the climactic childhood flashback, but it is his honest urge to convey the complex business and political reality he is handling that eventually does his film in.

For Lounguine, the character of Plato provides a center of gravity for his narrative, which breezes along at a dizzy pace, shuffling time periods, but lacking a dramatic center with which the audience can become involved. This becomes evident as *Tycoon* charts Plato's various scams, from writing theses for others to using government decrees under Gorbachev and Yeltsin to expand into car retailing and even the eventual acquisition of an Infocar TV channel. Among the political forces that Plato draws upon, and one that eventually does in his cohorts, is that of regional power in Russia. As Plato negotiates with the retired Colonel Belinki, a war veteran still bloodthirsty from the Afghan campaign, and the ruthless governor of Northern Siberia, whose electoral campaign Plato supports, Lounguine's film offers its starkest insights.

At the end of it all, we learn that on that fateful day, Plato got into the female reporter's car and so escaped the attack, unbeknownst to Chmakov, who is conveniently sent packing back to the Urals. The film's final shot shows Plato's battered head, bloody but unbowed, heading back to Moscow after his gang has been decimated. The superimposed title reads: "A New Russian."

Critics appear to have uniform praise for how much Lounguine's film reveals about, what Stephen Kotkin calls in the *New York Times,* "the phantasmagoria of the late Soviet Union." For Kotkin, the film is "a smart political whodunit" on one level, but also one that can "indeed be enjoyed strictly as entertainment." This could explain how, despite its lack of patriotism, *Tycoon* went on to become the highest grossing film of 2002 on its home turf. Kotkin's expert knowledge leads him to point out that Lounguine's film is full of "sly

touches" that work as inside jokes. A tennis racket hanging on a wall beside an official photograph of Yeltsin, could be taken as reference to the leader's notorious tennis coach, who not only had an office in the Kremlin but "was responsible for the giveaway of a private television network."

—*Vivek Adarkar*

CREDITS

Platon Makovski: Vladimir Mashkov
Andrei Krasko: Andrei Krasko
Maria: Maria Mironova
Viktor: Sergei Oshkevich
Moussa: Alexandre Samoilenko
Larry: Levani Uchaineshvili
Koretski: Alexandre Baluev
Mark: Mikael Vasserbaum

Origin: Russia, France
Language: Russian
Released: 2002
Production: Catherine Dussart, Vladimir Grigoriev; Arte France Cinema, France 2 Cinema, Gimages Films, CDP, Magnat; released by New Yorker Films
Directed by: Pavel (Lungin) Lounguine
Written by: Pavel (Lungin) Lounguine, Alexandre Borodianski, Yuli Dobov
Cinematography by: Alexey Federov, Oleg Dobronravov
Music by: Leonid Diesyatnikov
Sound: Alain Curvelier
Editing: Sophie Brunet
Production Design: Pavel (Lungin) Lounguine
MPAA rating: Unrated
Running time: 128 minutes

REVIEWS

Chicago Sun-Times Online. September 12, 2003.
Los Angeles Times Online. August 8, 2003.
New York Daily News. June 13, 2003.
New York Times. June 15, 2003, p. AR22.
Variety Online. August 6, 2002.
Washington Post. July 25, 2003, p. WE35.

QUOTES

Platon (Vladimir Mashkov): "I am a politician and jail is part of the game."

Under the Tuscan Sun

Life offers you a thousand chances . . . all you have to do is take one.
—Movie tagline

 Box Office: $41.3 million

Under the Tuscan Sun, the screen adaptation of Frances Mayes's 1996 best-selling memoir, features gorgeous Italian scenery and the always appealing Diane Lane. Writer-director Audrey Wells (*Guinevere*) has crafted a visually pleasing film, although one that is short on dramatic tension. With a literary travelogue serving as the film's inspiration, the movie doesn't feature much of a plot besides the ongoing renovation of a Tuscan villa—and really, how exciting can that be onscreen?

Basically, *Under the Tuscan Sun* exists as a showcase for the talented, luminous Lane (*Unfaithful, A Walk on the Moon*). The actress plays Frances, a heartbroken divorcee and writer from San Francisco who finds herself on a recuperative trip to Italy—compliments of her pregnant lesbian friend Patti (Sandra Oh of HBO's *Arliss*) who presents her with a ticket to Tuscany. Traveling through the lush Italian countryside, Frances impulsively falls for and decides to buy Bramasole, a centuries-old villa in Cortona.

Living alone in her rundown country house, Frances hires some illegal workers from Poland to renovate the place, and as the villa is transformed, so is Frances. As the charming heroine settles into her new life, she has the opportunity to get acquainted with several of the colorful locals, including Mr. Martini (Vincent Riotta), a kind, married real estate agent; and Katherine (Lindsay Duncan), an intriguing Englishwoman who was an actress in Fellini films. Of course, this romance pic wouldn't be complete without a gorgeous, Italian lover; a sexy antiques dealer named Marcello (Raoul Bova) steals Frances's heart but ends up being too young and noncommittal for her.

In addition to the eccentric village residents Frances welcomes into her life, a very pregnant Patti also shows up at Bramasole and decides to stay on indefinitely, so Frances ultimately finds herself surrounded by an extended family in her adopted country. On a quest for self-fulfillment, Frances is triumphant at the film's finale, exuding happiness and hope while a celebration takes place at her villa.

As a travelogue, *Under the Tuscan Sun* glows with beautiful scenes of Cortona, Siena, Monteulciano, and several locations in Rome and Positano. Life in sun-dappled Tuscany does indeed look inviting, whether the characters are serving up dinners of pasta and wine or Lane is riding up a hill in Positano on the back of a Vespa. In postcard-perfect Italy, magical moments abound and *Under the Tuscan Sun* does make its audience feel as if they're actually experiencing firsthand the sights and sounds of Tuscany.

This breezy chick flick is writer-director Wells's second directorial effort and her first book adaptation. She wrote and directed *Guinevere* (1999), and wrote *The Truth About Cats and Dogs* (1996), *Disney's The Kid* (2000), and the U.S. remake of the Japanese film *Shall We Dance?*, which is currently in production. While adapting Mayes's bestseller for the screen, Wells decided to spice up the story and implemented a few changes—most notably making Frances a divorcee and providing her with new friendships. Adding interesting supporting characters does round out the story more, but it's not enough to compensate for a lack of plot in the book.

For a romantic-comedy about second chances, *Under the Tuscan Sun* is easy to look at and succeeds as escapist entertainment. However, some detractors characterized it as a spiritless adaptation. The film's main flaw is that nothing much happens. Besides the restoration of Bramasole, there are a few other subplots, but none of them are all that compelling. Even Marcello, the love interest, is relegated to a very small role. His character could have benefited from further development. What redeems this movie is Lane's expressive performance. The movie clearly belongs to her and she makes a refreshing heroine.

Most reviewers agreed that the movie, with its stunning scenes of the Italian countryside, works as pure Hollywood escapism. Critics were also overwhelmingly positive in their reviews of Lane's performance. In the *Chicago Sun-Times*, Roger Ebert writes, "Diane Lane involves us, implicates us. We don't stand outside her performance, and neither does she." Kim Williamson of *Boxoffice* comments, "Diane Lane and her compatriots are right on the mark. They strike every note with a resonance that carries through to the heart.". Perhaps *Entertainment Weekly*'s Lisa Schwarzbaum says it the best: "The camera showers Diane Lane with victory kisses in *Under the Tuscan Sun*. The role is a glamour gig, a love hug for an actress in a revival of stardom."

Distaff moviegoers who go along for the ride will enjoy this lighthearted fare flavored with Italian culture. Others may find it slow-going. Although director Wells and the cast certainly give it their best effort, the subject of Mayes's memoir just doesn't seem suited for the big screen and the film fails to live up to its potential. Special kudos go to Lane, however, for her radiant portrayal of a woman taking a risk on a new life. Let's hope to see more of this lovely actress in the near future.

—*Beth Fhaner*

Underworld

When the battle begins which side will you choose?
—Movie tagline

 Box Office: $51.4 million

CREDITS

Frances: Diane Lane
Patti: Sandra Oh
Katherine: Lindsay Duncan
Marcello: Raoul Bova
Mr. Martini: Vincent Riotta
Chiara: Guilia Steigerwalt
Pawel: Pawel Szajda
Jerzy: Valentine Pelka
Sasa: Sasa Vulicevic
Ed: David Sutcliffe

Origin: USA
Released: 2003
Production: Tom Sternberg, Audrey Wells; Timnick Films, Blue Gardenia; released by Touchstone Pictures
Directed by: Audrey Wells
Written by: Audrey Wells
Cinematography by: Geoffrey Simpson
Music by: Christophe Beck
Sound: Aaron Glascock, Curt Schulkey
Editing: Andrew Marcus, Arthur Coburn
Costumes: Nicoletta Ercole
Production Design: Stephen McCabe
MPAA rating: PG-13
Running time: 113 minutes

REVIEWS

Boxoffice. November, 2003, p. 106.
Chicago Sun-Times Online. September 26, 2003.
Entertainment Weekly. October 3, 2003, p. 49.
Los Angeles Times Online. September 7, 2003.
Los Angeles Times Online. September 26, 2003.
New York Times Online. September 26, 2003.
People. October 6, 2003, p. 33.
Rolling Stone. October 16, 2003, p. 95.
USA Today Online. September 26, 2003.
Variety Online. September 14, 2003.
Washington Post. September 26, 2003, p. WE48.

AWARDS AND NOMINATIONS

Nomination:
Golden Globes 2004: Actress—Mus./Comedy (Lane).

Set in a dark world where vampires and werewolves are fighting a seemingly neverending war, Len Wiseman's *Underworld* is a classic case of too much and not enough at the same time. It offers up lots of stylish yet deafening gunplay, convoluted plot turns, and endless backstory to fill us in on characters we have no genuine emotional investment in. Indeed, the plot is so confusing that it becomes a chore just to figure out all of the basic relationships, let alone digest the betrayals and rivalries stretching back through vampire-werewolf history. For fans of the horror genre, *Underworld*'s premise is promising, but the execution is a major disappointment.

Kate Beckinsale stars as Selene, a vampire who, in the opening scenes, is stalking some werewolves (more commonly known as lycans) when a protracted gun battle erupts in a subway station. The confrontation is impressively staged and shot, even if we have seen similar set pieces in better films like *The Matrix*. With her rain-soaked hair falling seductively over her face, Selene is a stoic, coolly sexy presence, decked out in shiny, black latex and firing two guns at once. But while Beckinsale's Selene is riveting in battle, her aloof demeanor between skirmishes renders her a thin, remote character.

Selene figures out that the lycans were actually trailing a human named Michael Corvin (Scott Speedman), and she is determined to find out why they considered him such an important target. The leader of her group, the aptly named Kraven (Shane Brolly), would rather that she put the episode behind her. Being the plucky heroine, however, she ignores orders and seeks out Michael in his apartment, but arriving there as well are the lycans. Another battle ensues, but it is hard to care about the outcome since we hardly know the participants and have no idea for whom we should be rooting. Selene rescues Michael but not before the lycan leader bites him.

Feeling frustrated by Kraven's dismissal of her investigation, Selene does some secret research and discovers that the lycan who bit Michael is in fact Lucian (Michael Sheen), the werewolf leader supposedly killed centuries ago, and that Kraven and Lucian are really in cahoots with each other. Wanting answers to all of her questions, she awakens one of the vampire elders, her mentor Viktor (Bill Nighy). The elders lie comatose in the heart of the mansion and are supposed to take turns ruling every hundred years. By awakening Viktor, Selene is breaking the proper order of vampire succession, but she feels a special kinship to him; when she was a child, lycans devoured her family, and Viktor turned her into a vampire so that she could spend her life exacting revenge. Selene tries to explain to Viktor that Lucian is alive and is plotting with Kraven, but Viktor passes judgment on her for breaking the chain and says she must be punished.

If all of this seems confusing, it is. The screenplay is an overstuffed mess, constantly introducing arcane vampire customs and history and expecting us to grasp it all while we keep track of so many characters whose identity, motivations, and relationships to each other are as murky as the gray night in which they travel.

But all of the plot machinations, intricate though they may seem, are merely rest stops on the way to more mind-numbing action. Amelia, the reigning vampire elder, and her entourage are killed by lycans, and her blood is removed. Meanwhile, Michael is experiencing what appear to be hallucinations but which are really Lucian's memories transmitted through his bite. Selene's efforts to protect Michael fail, and he is kidnapped and taken to the lycan laboratory, but she is able to apprehend the lycan doctor and bring him back to Viktor to validate all of her suspicions.

Thus begins more back story as the doctor reveals Lucian's plot, which is to combine the bloodlines of the rival species. Michael is a descendant of an ancient family called Corvinus, and his blood allows for this union, which would be fatal to other humans. Lucian's plan is to inject Michael's blood along with the blood of Amelia into himself to create a species half vampire and half lycan but stronger than both.

If the lycan plot is not complicated enough, we are soon filled in on Lucian's background, which he narrates to the captive Michael. The lycans were once slaves to the vampires, and Lucian fell in love with Sonja, Viktor's daughter. But Viktor feared a blending of the species, so, to punish them for their transgression, Viktor had Sonja killed and forced Lucian to watch her die. This should be a very emotional moment in the film; after all, it deals with a thwarted love and a father's murder of his own daughter, but, since we barely know Lucian and only catch fleeting glimpses of the suffering Sonja via Michael's memory flashes, the tragic story just feels like one more extended digression.

Is *Underworld* meant to be a commentary on race mixing or ethnic cleansing? If so, it could have been a unique use of the horror genre, but the screenplay by Danny McBride does not tap into this compelling subtext for a larger purpose. He just ladles on more action and empty vampire-lycan confrontations. Likewise, class issues are raised obliquely but are not developed. The vampire world is populated by sexy Goth types who live like royalty in a cavernous mansion, while the werewolves seem to hide out in the

sewers and never clean up, let alone dress up. In short, the seeds of a provocative movie lie just below the surface, if only the filmmakers had chosen to focus on substance as well as style.

Kraven, whose betrayal of the vampires is now known to Viktor, flees the mansion and meets up with Lucian in his underground hideout. Apparently, Kraven was going to wrest control of both covens by entering into league with the lycans. But with Viktor awake, that is now impossible, so Kraven ends up shooting Lucian with silver nitrate ammunition designed to effect a quick death in lycans. At the same time, the vampire warriors have arrived and are waging a great battle in the sewers.

During the battle, the special bullets are fired at Michael as well, and, when Selene resists running off with Kraven, he assumes that she is attracted to Michael. Perhaps this is indeed the impetus for her overriding dedication to him, but, because there is no chemistry or even the hint of an emotional spark between Selene and Michael—they hardly have a conversation or even share a meaningful glance in their brief time together—the movie also fails miserably as a love story.

Stung by yet another rejection, the jealous Kraven reveals the true story of Selene's origins as a vampire. It was Viktor, not the lycans, who slaughtered her family, but he spared Selene because she reminded him of Sonja. Apparently, Viktor has a soft spot for the daughter he killed, which makes about as much sense as anything else in this film. Once again, the screenplay inundates us with potentially serious, weighty issues and then treats them as if they did not matter. Moreover, because so many key events took place long before the action of the movie, each of them has to be explained by some of the least convincing actors in any movie this year. Brolly as Kraven is especially bad; he seems to think that wearing a perpetual sneer is the way to build a character. Maybe these passages would have been bearable if great actors were relaying the ancient stories. Or perhaps it would have been better simply to make a movie about the history itself, especially Lucian and Sonja's doomed romance, instead of the half-baked Selene-Michael relationship that hardly feels like a relationship at all.

Even if we were touched by the tragedy of Selene's childhood, the film gives us no time to feel anything. Kraven is about to kill Selene when Lucian, who should be dead by now after being shot with the supposedly lethal ammunition, stabs Kraven in the leg and then tells Selene to bite Michael. He will become the super creature Lucian wanted to be. Before escaping, Kraven finishes Lucian off, but Selene follows his last request and sucks Michael's blood, thus making Lucian's plan a reality.

Viktor, who looked like a rotting corpse when he was first awakened, is now rejuvenated and has the strength to do battle with Michael, who metamorphoses into a hulking creature with superhuman power. After a lengthy showdown, Selene finally uses Viktor's sword to slash his head in two. Selene and Michael leave the sewer, and the movie ends on an inconclusive note—Selene says that the age-old war will continue and, in one of the film's typically hokey lines, declares that "a tide of anger and retribution will spill out into the night." She will now become the hunted.

Lacking the energy and excitement befitting an epic struggle between rival supernatural forces, *Underworld* is unable to muster much interest in its one-dimensional characters, increasingly tiresome action sequences, and exhausting explanations of vampire-werewolf history. The filmmakers succeed only in focusing our gaze on striking surfaces (all photographed to great effect by Tony Pierce-Roberts), from the grungy lycan hideouts, to the stony, ornate architecture of the vampire mansion to Selene's skintight, slick garments. *Underworld* could have been a fast-paced, scary, comic-book-style adventure, but instead it is a hollow love letter to Goth style and fashion.

—*Peter N. Chumo II*

 CREDITS

Selene: Kate Beckinsale
Michael Corvin: Scott Speedman
Lucian: Michael Sheen
Kraven: Shane Brolly
Viktor: Bill Nighy
Singe: Erwin Leder
Erika: Sophia Myles
Kahn: Robbie Gee
Dr. Adam: Wentworth Miller

Origin: USA, Great Britain, Germany, Hungary
Released: 2003
Production: Tom Rosenberg, Gary Lucchesi, Richard Wright; Screen Gems, Lakeshore Entertainment; released by Sony Pictures
Directed by: Len Wiseman
Written by: Danny McBride
Cinematography by: Tony Pierce-Roberts
Music by: Paul Haslinger
Sound: Claude Letessier
Music Supervisor: Danny Lohner
Editing: Martin Hunter
Art Direction: Kevin Phipps
Costumes: Wendy Partridge
Production Design: Bruton Jones
MPAA rating: R
Running time: 121 minutes

 REVIEWS

Chicago Sun-Times Online. September 19, 2003.
Los Angeles Times Online. September 7, 2003.
Los Angeles Times Online. September 19, 2003.
New York Times Online. September 19, 2003.
Variety Online. September 8, 2003.

Uptown Girls

They're about to teach each other how to act their age.
—Movie tagline

Box Office: $36.6 million

Uptown Girls is a trite formula movie, and given the predictability, it would be easy to dismiss this film immediately. However, there is something worthwhile in the film. It's not Shakespeare, but it is a heart-warming, well-meaning film.

Molly Gunn (Brittany Murphy) is not just any socialite. She is a rock-n-roll princess. Her father, the late Tommy Gunn, immortalized his daughter in his popular ballad "Molly Smiles." As rock-n-roll royalty, she lives atop her palace, an uptown flat, with her precious pet pig, Mu (meaning "pork" in Thai). The film opens on the eve of Molly's twenty-second birthday. At a party thrown by her best friend, Ingrid (Marley Shelton), her perpetual buddy, Huey (Donald Faison), arranges for Molly to be serenaded by Australian Neal Fox (Jesse Spencer). Huey also arranges that the live performance be an audition for Neal with A&R executive Roma Schleine (Heather Locklear). Here Molly first encounters Roma Schleine's daughter, Ray (Dakota Fanning), in the ladies' restroom. Ray is an uptight, precocious eight-year-old who goes through nannies like Spinal Tap goes through drummers.

Molly literally throws herself on Neal in an attempt to seduce him. Her charms and her parentage entice Neal to accompany her home. Once inside, Neal discovers Molly's treasure: a collection of her father's guitars. He grabs up an acoustic and begins to sing the ballad her father wrote about her. Even though Neal explains that as part of his sobriety pact, he is not supposed to have romantic entanglements for a year after becoming sober, he falls for Molly. Twenty-four hours later, she is starting to feel suffocated by his company, but as soon as Neal announces his intention to leave, Molly becomes clingy and needy.

Meanwhile, Ingrid is horrified at the state of Molly's flat. While picking up trash, Ingrid finds a couple of bills marked "Final Notice." She snaps Molly to attention and demands to know who handles Molly's finances. They soon learn that her accountant has absconded with all of her money.

Ingrid gets her a job. Still unable to come to grips with reality, Molly spends $1,300 on 900-count Egyptian cotton sheets for Neal. Because he has a recording session the next day, Neal asks if Molly has seen his lucky jacket that he forgot at her place. The next morning Ingrid and Huey find Molly wrapped in 900-count cotton sheets—at her place of employment. Molly is promptly fired.

Huey comes through with the perfect new job for Molly: Ray Schleine's nanny. The first day, however, does not go well. Ray is shocked that this immature woman is her new caretaker. In one of the rooms of Ray's home, Molly encounters a comatose man, but Ray quickly shuts the door and says nothing about it (Molly later learns that it is Ray's father, who had a massive stroke). Later, after a mishap, Ray keenly states that her mother is not around until three in the morning unless you make an appointment with her. Tired of being treated like she is the young girl needing a nanny, Molly finally quits in disgust.

However, when Molly arrives back home, she learns that she has been thrown out of her apartment because of the back rent and utilities owed. Molly moves in with Ingrid and realizes that she must make some changes in her life. The next day, Molly asks for her position back, and she and Ray find themselves discussing their contrasting outlooks on life. Molly explains that when she took ballet, she liked to dance her own steps. Ray's mantra is encapsulated by a quote from Baryshnikov: "Fundamentals are the building blocks of fun." When the discussion climaxes, Molly finally asserts herself and demands some respect from Ray.

More trouble for Molly lies ahead. At "Baking Night" with Ingrid's friends, Molly creates a chocolate chip inferno. In a panic, she smothers the flames with Neal's lucky jacket. Molly tries to disguise the damage with shoe polish, spray paint, and grommets. The final product is unrecognizable. Later, Neal asks Molly out for dinner and reveals that he has signed a record deal with Schleine Records. He plays the recording of the song he was having difficulty writing when they first met. The song was inspired by her and is entitled "Sheets of Egyptian Cotton." She is his muse, and she is devastated when he breaks up with her.

With Molly's world crashing down, Ray admonishes Molly to grow up, but Molly does not take the words to heart. After Molly sets up a date (with a guy who holds a regular job) that conflicts with one of Ingrid's planned events, the best friends break up over Molly's refusal to acquiesce to Ingrid. Molly moves in with Huey, who takes her clubbing, where Molly spots Roma. Molly asks Roma who is taking care of Ray because this is the night of Ray's dance recital. As Roma explains that she has sent a car to pick her up, Molly realizes the impact this will have on Ray. Indeed, Ray is crushed.

The next day Molly takes her to Coney Island to ride in the giant teacups at the amusement park. But when they get there, they find that it is one week shy of the open season. Molly spills her heart to Ray. After her parents died, she ran away to Coney Island, and the teacups ride was the only one the operators would let her on. Molly got on the ride and began spinning, and she still feels as if she is on that ride. She confesses to Ray that she is scared, but she also points out that Ray is scared, too.

Molly then tells the girl about the positive effects of family members speaking to their comatose loved ones. For the first time, Ray completely lets her guard down as she tells her comatose father about her life. Later, Molly arrives at her employer's to find a perfectly composed Ray at her ballet barre. Molly is then escorted in to see Roma, who hands her two checks: one for the last week's pay and the other for a month's severance. Molly will not leave without an explanation, so Roma tells her that Ray has made it perfectly clear that she never wants to see Molly again. When Molly expresses concern for Ray's emotional state, Roma says her daughter is taking her father's death well. Molly rips up both checks and reminds Roma that Ray is "eight, not twenty-eight."

Once outside, Molly encounters Neal, but she is in no mood to deal with him. He pleads that he needs his muse back in his life, but she turns him down. He lashes out at her, saying that when he wasn't ready, she hunted him down. Now that he is ready to make it work, she is not interested. Molly retorts that it is his selfishness that is the problem, and she has nothing left to give. With no income, Molly plays her last card: she arranges to auction her father's guitar collection at Christie's. Just when it appears that Tommy Gunn's beloved acoustic is going to sell for a meager $2,600, an anonymous telephone bidder offers $75k for the entire collection.

A mature Molly shows Huey her new, tiny flat. As Huey is trying to absorb this new reality, he receives a phone call from Roma, asking if he knows where Ray is. Molly grabs the phone. Roma begs for Molly's help. Molly instantly knows where to find Ray and goes to Coney Island. When Molly finds her, Ray physically lashes out at Molly but eventually collapses into her arms. Things start to look up when Molly and Ingrid make up. Ray offers Molly her job back but Molly declines, saying that they will be friends instead.

The movie ends with Ray's year-end ballet recital. In the final number, Ray is the featured dancer and is being accompanied by special guest Neal, who is playing Tommy Gunn's acoustic. As Neal begins playing "Molly Smiles," the other dancers come on stage, each holding one of Tommy Gunn's electric guitars.

Brittany Murphy's performance, though not robust, is sweet and charming. In the few moments when Molly must really assert herself, Murphy takes the role to a whole new level of determined grit worthy of the audience's appreciation. However, the role of Molly also calls for pratfalls that Murphy has yet to master. She is not Lucille Ball, but she does show promise. Dakota Fanning is already known in the industry as a little adult. The telltale sign that an actress may be hiding in that kid's suit, however, is when she struggles to maintain her composure upon realizing that she does not have a guest in the audience at her first recital.

Director Boaz Yakin did not seem to know what kind of film he wanted to make. *Uptown Girls* is too hokey for teenagers and too horny for children. The story would have been perfectly suited to a younger audience, but instead Yakin settled for a cheap thrill. He could have made a solid movie about friendship, both between Molly and Ray and between Molly and Neal. Yakin, winner of the Filmmakers' Trophy at the 1994 Sundance Film Festival, has shown himself capable of handling emotionally intense plots like those of *Fresh* (1994) and *A Price Above Rubies* (1998). The director had the makings of a solid film, but squandered it by going for the PG-13 rating in an apparent search for the teenage audience share.

—*David Flanagin and Donna Wood-Martin*

CREDITS

Molly Gunn: Brittany Murphy
Ray Schleine: Dakota Fanning
Roma Schleine: Heather Locklear
Huey: Donald Adeosun Faison
Ingrid: Marley Shelton
Mr. McConkey: Austin Pendleton
Neal: Jesse Spencer

Origin: USA
Released: 2003
Production: John Penotti, Fisher Stevens, Allison Jacobs; Greenstreet; released by MGM
Directed by: Boaz Yakin
Written by: Mo Ogrodnik, Julia Dahl, Lisa Davidowitz
Cinematography by: Michael Ballhaus
Music by: Joel McNeely
Sound: Bob Hein
Music Supervisor: Maureen Crowe
Editing: David Ray
Art Direction: Frank White III
Costumes: Sarah Edwards
Production Design: Kalina Ivanov
MPAA rating: PG-13
Running time: 93 minutes

REVIEWS

Chicago Sun-Times Online. August 15, 2003.
Entertainment Weekly. August 22-29, 2003, p. 110.
Los Angeles Times Online. August 15, 2003.
New York Times Online. August 15, 2003.
People. August 25, 2003, p. 53.
USA Today Online. August 15, 2003.
Variety Online. August 13, 2003.
Washington Post. August 15, 2003, p. WE37.

Veronica Guerin

Why would anyone want to kill Veronica Guerin?
—**Movie tagline**

 Box Office: $1.6 million

Veronica Guerin's life story is a heroic saga that deserves to be told. A courageous Irish journalist who almost single-handedly broke the backs of Irish drug lords in the 1990s, Guerin is an icon of modern Ireland, but her story isn't well known outside the Irish Republic. Remarkably, it's blow-'em-up blockbuster magnate, producer Jerry Bruckheimer, who has brought her tale to the big screen. And not only that, he's done so under the imprimatur of Touchstone Pictures, the Disney subsidiary.

There's nothing Disneyesque about the grim world that Guerin enters in 1994, when she sets off on the trail of heroin pushers who have brought a plague of crime, youth violence, and drug addiction onto the Emerald Isle. Director Joel Schumacher (*Phone Booth*) is unsparing as he follows Guerin (Cate Blanchett) into the mean streets of Dublin. Needles litter the sidewalks and toddlers play with syringes. Preteen boys and girls sit zombie-like on tenement steps, half-dead already, and try to sell their bodies to strangers for sex so they can score another hit. Pushers patrol the streets in broad daylight, ruling their turf with little opposition.

The gritty scene makes an effective opener for Guerin's harrowing saga—or would have. Schumacher instead makes the puzzling choice of showing us Guerin's fate and explaining the entire story in an unnecessary opening scene and a series of titles. We don't need to start from the end and then go back to the beginning of the story, because doing so robs the film of its suspense. Maybe the filmmakers were so involved in the story that they came to believe, inexplicably, that the rest of the world already knew too much about Guerin and what happened to her, so it was useless to attempt to hide the climax to the story. If so, they were badly mistaken.

Blanchett leads the way to help us try to recover the story's momentum after this fatal opening misstep. She is all cool and sassy, hard-bitten yet charming, another Hollywood version of a star reporter. Journalists don't really act this way; few of them are quite so defiant and forthright and charming, but Blanchett is a pro, and her performance is delightful. She almost makes us believe Guerin is so cocky and feels so invulnerable that she can stride right up to the bad guys and face them down. Certainly, hers is a heroism that is admirable, but the script also makes her seem a bit naïve, as if she never suspects she could be placing herself in harm's way.

But the script—by Agnes Donoghue and Carol Doyle—does hew closely to the actual details of Guerin's case, and it shows us how thoroughly absorbed she is in her work, so much so that she can forget her own son's bedtime. Blanchett portrays Guerin both as a tough-as-nails student of realpolitik and an idealistic do-gooder who truly believes that if she can expose the criminals, she can help the children they've turned into prostitutes and drug addicts. And this is entirely believable, because most journalists are a remarkable combination of cynic and true believer. Guerin is driven by her desire to expose the truth, no matter what the cost to herself, and she, like many of her peers, refuses to believe she's that important to the scheme of things that she would be placing herself at risk. Perhaps she believes that as a pseudo-public figure, she's not likely to be tampered with.

Whatever the reasons for her character's blitheness, Blanchett makes the best of it. She's an angel of mercy and a devil of an interviewer at the same time, bold and brassy. Yet a few important scenes allow audiences to see that Guerin, in private moments, knew fear and confusion. She just refused to let those emotions interfere with her bravery in the line of fire, or with her persistence in doing her job.

The most important of the changes that were made in fictionalizing Guerin's story was to consolidate several of her sources into the compelling character of John Traynor, nicknamed the Coach (Ciaran Hinds). Guerin has traded favors with the Coach for awhile, and she trusts him, but that proves to be a mistake. Each is using the other, but Guerin has no idea how much she's being used until it's too late. Hinds makes the Coach into a nearly sympathetic figure despite his treachery; he's a man caught in a trap of his own devising.

Equally effective in his role is Gerard McSorley as drug kingpin John Gilligan—about as icy and despicable a screen villain as is imaginable—a slimeball who wants to be hidden from public view and is ruthless in the face of defiance. Almost as odious is his wife (Maria McDermottroe), who has used the drug money to buy herself a fine stable of horses and pretends to be a bona fide member of the horsey set.

Some of the first part of the film is confusing, as a panoply of crooks jostle for power and for Guerin's attention. It might have been easier to follow if more of them

stood out from the scenery, and it's not always easy, either, to cut through the Irish brogue and slang to follow all the dialogue. But there is nothing so tricky about the plot that all this needs to be understood. Even if you don't recognize that the word "gardai" means policemen or that the Irish pronounce a common expletive as "sheet," you can get the gist of what's happening.

Schumacher is effective in allowing audiences to glimpse just the right amount of Guerin's home life. Her husband is believable and effective, and her bond to her son is both realistic and heartfelt without crossing over into excess sentimentalism. Brenda Fricker plays Guerin's mother with a quiet solidity.

This is a realistic Irish landscape, gritty and difficult, across which Guerin parades—a bleak land of dashed dreams and elusive justice. At some points the plot hints that law enforcement agencies aren't doing their utmost to catch the drug kingpins, but any suspicions of a conspiracy eventually lead to a presumption that the police are just underbudgeted, hamstrung by lenient laws that favor the criminals, and in some cases simply overworked and incompetent. But none of these conclusions emerges full-blown.

In fact, it would have been more effective if one of the supporting characters—the police detective Guerin works with, her husband, her boss, the prime minister, the Coach, or any of the criminals—were to have emerged from the crowd and become a standout in the plot. Instead, Guerin touches each of these characters and moves on.

Because it follows so closely a messy, real story, the film doesn't have the tight, gripping feel of a typical movie drama. The director chose not to highlight any of the other characters, but simply gave everyone a background role as Guerin skates on ever thinner ice. In some respects this makes the film more believable and more powerful, but there's nothing beyond Blanchett to really latch onto. And that's why the power of Blanchett's customarily magnificent acting is so crucial to the success of *Veronica Guerin*. Blanchett makes her into a character who manages to love life and love justice without ever being cloying, a woman who pours herself into the work she loves and is dedicated to improving the lot of mankind. It's important to have a scene in which Guerin confesses to her husband that she's never felt that anything she's done—and she's already had a long career covering important religious and social issues—has really made a difference. Her longing to have an impact is deeply felt; it is the force that drives her into situations where she seems to be in over her head. But she always learns to swim; she shares the journalist's fatal flaw that she thinks herself invincible.

Despite the opening of the movie giving too much away, the power of the closing scenes of this film will stay with audiences a long time. Schumacher treats the climax with reverence and awe, slowing down the film to a crawl and emphasizing the iconic nature of what has happened.

Guerin's story, at this point, achieves a universal resonance, a kind of shorthand for the global battle against the injustice of crime and societal indifference to its victims. It's a powerful and unifying message, delivered without a signal snippet of preaching.

Yet it's doubtful that *Veronica Guerin* will have the kind of impact the story deserves. Schumacher or whoever is responsible for the near-fatal misstep of the film's giveaway beginning has squandered an opportunity to make a film of real import. He has failed to lift out of this complicated story, which doesn't have a trajectory except downward, a handle for audiences to grab onto, any familiar signposts to guide their way through. He has put the entire burden on Blanchett, but while she is up to the task, this isn't her most compelling performance. All this said, however, filming the story of Veronica Guerin is still an admirable achievement, and keeping it true to its source is laudatory.

—*Michael Betzold*

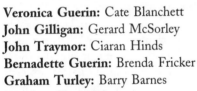

CREDITS

Veronica Guerin: Cate Blanchett
John Gilligan: Gerard McSorley
John Traymor: Ciaran Hinds
Bernadette Guerin: Brenda Fricker
Graham Turley: Barry Barnes
Bowden: David Murray
Holland: Joe Hanley
Peter "Fatso" Mitchell: David Herlihy
Martin "The General" Cahill: Gerry O'Brien
Chris Mulligan: Don Wycherley
Spanky McSpank: Colin Farrell
Gerry "The Monk" Hutch: Alan Devine

Origin: USA
Released: 2003
Production: Jerry Bruckheimer; released by Touchstone Pictures
Directed by: Joel Schumacher
Written by: Carol Doyle, Mary Agnes Donoghue
Cinematography by: Brendan Galvin
Music by: Harry Gregson-Williams
Sound: Kieran Horgan
Editing: David Gamble
Art Direction: Patrick Lumb
Costumes: Joan Bergin
Production Design: Nathan Crowley
MPAA rating: R
Running time: 98 minutes

REVIEWS

Chicago Sun-Times Online. October 17, 2003.
Entertainment Weekly. October 24, 2003, p. 84.
Los Angeles Times Online. October 17, 2003.
New York Times Online. September 7, 2003.
New York Times Online. October 17, 2003.
People. October 27, 2003, p. 30.
Rolling Stone. October 30, 2003, p. 100.
Sight and Sound. October, 2003, p. 70.
USA Today Online. October 17, 2003.
Variety Online. July 30, 2003.
Washington Post. October 17, 2003, p. C5.

AWARDS AND NOMINATIONS

Nomination:
Golden Globes 2004: Actress—Drama (Blanchett).

View from the Top

Taking comedy to a whole new altitude.
—Movie tagline
Don't stop till you reach the top.
—Movie tagline

 Box Office: $15.5 million

Stewardess Donna Jensen, the somewhat ditzy heroine of *View From the Top*, wants nothing more than to rise above her less than promising trailer trash upbringing, yearning for more out of life than what the daughter of a much-married ex-showgirl can expect in dusty, small-town Nevada. Unfortunately, she has no idea what to shoot for nor how to go about getting it, quite similar to the quandary in which those who brought this film to the screen seem to have found themselves. They appear to have been unclear about exactly what type of film they wanted to make, and while Donna eventually figures out what she needs in order to soar, the filmmakers clearly did not.

When we first meet Donna (Gwyneth Paltrow, who filmed this before her much better turn in 2001's *The Royal Tennenbaums*), she does not seem to be going anywhere, but sells luggage to those who are at the local Big Lots discount store. She is cruelly left behind by her newly-promoted boyfriend, who throws her over on her birthday and whisks another coworker off to the excitement of the big city (Tucson, in this case). Donna, he explains, is just not meant for life outside of their tiny town, while Barb in barbeques apparently has bigger things to offer. Sitting at a bar, rejected and dejected, Donna's ears perk up to the inspirational words of best-selling author, motivational speaker, and former stewardess Sally Westin (Candice Bergen) on the television. The assurance of this glamorous lady with the glamorous lifestyle is that you can be who you want to be no matter where you are from or who other people think you are. Donna, clearly mesmerized, decides then and there to purchase Sally's book, *My Life in the Sky,* and it becomes her guidebook to getting above and beyond her prosaic, dead-end existence.

Aiming high but realizing she must start out low, a newly-motivated Donna gets a job as a flight attendant for a small, bargain-basement commuter named Sierra Airlines, which has standards as low as its stewardesses' skirts are high. It looks like Sierra does all its recruiting at Hooters, and its leggy, buxom flight attendants are barely contained by their gaudy outfits. (Sierra's slogan: "Big hair, short skirts, and service with a smile.") The classier stewardesses from the better airlines openly ridicule the Sierra sirens. Donna learns the ropes from Sherry (Kelly Preston) and soon gets her own trainee, Christine (Christina Applegate, not too far removed from the character she played on TV's *Married . . . With Children*), and becomes fast friends with both. Donna's first flight on Sierra is her first flight ever and an utter disaster: she freaks out, bolting up the aisle and shrieking hysterically to the startled passengers that they are all about to perish. Still, her morale is boosted by the attentions of dashing pilot Steve (Rob Lowe), and then sparks fly with Ted (Mark Ruffalo), a sweet former law student from Cleveland who Christine would like for herself.

Aspiring to greater heights, Donna urges Sherry and Christine to go with her to interview with prestigious Royalty Airlines, where Sally Westin still serves as a mentor. While the stewardesses may have met many a man with a roving eye before, the right eye of their peculiar interviewer John (Mike Myers) literally does have a disconcerting tendency to cross. Donna is torn as she pursues the opportunity, knowing that this chance to further her career will mean moving to Texas and leaving Ted behind. Still, Donna, along with Christine, accepts a job offer from Royalty. There, determined and focused, Donna is delighted to be taken under Sally's wing, her idol turning out to be a kindred spirit. Donna is exhilarated by Sally's words and enchanted by the woman's wondrous wardrobe. We see Donna, energized and confident, listening intently in class and taking copious notes, only to have the prized international flights go to thickheaded Christine while Donna is relegated to the airline's Cleveland express hub. Donna is baffled by this development, sure that there must have been some mistake, but she resigns herself to at least a year of seeing sights she deems far less enchanting than those in cities like London and Paris.

In Cleveland, Donna once again runs into Ted (who had returned home to re-enroll in law school), and as they grow closer than ever before she nervously anticipates the day when she will once again have to decide between love and all she has worked so hard to attain in her career. At this point, it is revealed that Christine had deviously stabbed Donna in the back by switching their tests. (What is more, she is stealing company freebies by the purseful.) Donna gets a perfect score when she is re-tested and opts once again to leave Ted for the coveted position Christine had cheated her out of. (There is a rough-and-tumble catfight between the two women in which a loaf of bread comes in handy for Donna, a zany moment and probably the film's most lasting image.)

We get a shot of Donna coming into view as she rises up an escalator on her way to working in first class on an international flight, a newly-crowned queen ascending to her throne. Long-gone is the bigger hair, the less attractive attire, and the straining to reach the top. She is now elegantly coiffed and stylishly outfitted, beaming as she is now saluted by her colleagues. Donna has finally arrived, and the view from the top is pretty grand—except that she has no one to enjoy it with. She sees couples and families as she crisscrosses the globe and begins to feel that perhaps her longstanding push to move onward and upward has left something essential behind. With Sally's help, Donna is able to reunite with Ted in Cleveland, which will become their home-sweet-home base. Apparently anticipating that those with a more feministic point of view might have a problem with Donna's choice, a false and wholly unbelievable note is tacked on to the end, as she is shown flying into Cleveland—but now as a pilot. A slew of outtakes wrap up the proceedings, which only serve to point out how *View From the Top* was much more of a hoot to shoot than to watch.

The film completed principal photography about six months before the events of September 11th, 2001. Concerns about airline-related humor pushed back its initial release date, but then additional trepidation about its quality kept its release up in the air until it finally landed in theaters in March of 2003. By then, re-shoots and extensive (and sometimes sloppy) editing had been ordered in an attempt to fashion the material into a more acceptable form. From the finished product, it is hard to put your finger on the initial intent of director Bruno Barreto (showing much less skill than in 1978's *Dona Flor and Her Two Husbands* or 1997's *Four Days in September*) and screenwriter Eric Wald (in his feature film debut). The tone jerks back and forth throughout the film, like a plane desperately out of control. The film is part sweet inspirational/empowerment tale, part satire, part farce, and part romantic comedy reminiscent of old films starring actresses like Rosalind Russell and Barbara Stanwyck in which women charging ahead in their careers decide that absolute fulfillment can only be achieved after a walk down the aisle.

View is as confused as Donna is about how best to proceed. Wherever it intended to go, it never really makes any of those destinations. There are only a few brief flashes of successful comedy in this harmless, anemic film, which never quite gains enough momentum to get off the ground. (Clever little touches like having pictures of ocularly-challenged Sammy Davis Jr., Marty Feldman, and Peter Falk in John's office are welcome but may not register with many viewers.) It is not that *View* amounts to something horrible but that it fails to amount to much of anything, as poofy as the women's initial hairstyles and as insubstantial as their various skimpy getups.

It is certainly a waste of an undeniably talented group of actors, some of whom (Preston and Lowe, in particular) make less of an impression than one would hope due to poor character development and/or the cuts that abbreviated the film to less than an hour and a half. Trailers made many expect that Myers played a more prominent role in the proceedings than he actually does, his cockeyed shtick growing tiresome long before his screen time is up. What keeps this film from being completely out of fuel is Paltrow, who, one hopes, envisioned a far different end result when signing onto the project. As Donna, she comes off as sweet and endearing enough to make us wish her well, even though we never aggressively root for her as the filmmakers were doubtlessly counting on. With material as thin as the air up there, the vast majority of critics were decidedly unimpressed with *View From the Top*, Roger Ebert being the only prominent critic who gave it a thumbs up. The film grossed just over $15 million. *View* is like a seat in coach: serviceable, but not nearly as enjoyable as if it were first class.

—*David L. Boxerbaum*

CREDITS

Donna: Gwyneth Paltrow
Christine: Christina Applegate
Ted: Mark Ruffalo
Sally Weston: Candice Bergen
Sherry: Kelly Preston
Pilot Steve: Rob Lowe
Randy: Joshua Malina
John: Mike Myers

Origin: USA
Released: 2003
Production: Brad Grey, Matthew Baer, Bobby Cohen; released by Miramax Films
Directed by: Bruno Barreto
Written by: Eric Wald
Cinematography by: Alfonso Beato
Music by: Theodore Shapiro

Sound: Stephen Halbert
Music Supervisor: Randy Spendlove
Editing: Christopher Greenbury
Art Direction: Elizabeth Lapp
Costumes: Mary Zophres
Production Design: Dan Davis
MPAA rating: PG-13
Running time: 87 minutes

REVIEWS

Chicago Sun-Times Online. March 21, 2003.
Entertainment Weekly. March 28, 2003, p. 45.
Los Angeles Times Online. March 21, 2003.
New York Times Online. March 21, 2003.
People. March 31, 2003, p. 29.
USA Today Online. March 21, 2003.
Variety Online. March 21, 2003.
Washington Post. March 21, 2003, p. WE37.

QUOTES

Flight attendant Donna (Gwyneth Paltrow): "Why can't all choices be simple? Why can't they all be window or aisle?"

Washington Heights

Washington Heights . . . where roots run deep.
—Movie tagline

Despite the contemporary hip-hop setting, *Washington Heights* comes from the Old School: a father-son melodrama tailor-made for Al Jolson and company. Director and co-writer Alfredo de Villa serves up not one, but two father-son stories, plus other assorted subplots in what purports to be a realistic view of life today in the Latino (mainly Dominican) community of New York's Washington Heights (near the famous George Washington Bridge).

First there is Carlos (Manny Perez), a cartoonist who yearns to be a serious artist but feels compelled to work in his father's bodega after papa, Eddie (Tomas Milian), is shot in a hold-up and confined to a wheelchair. Then there is Mickey (Danny Hoch), a hot-shot bowler who wants to compete in a Las Vegas tournament, but who fails to get the money or support of his father, Sean (Jude Ciccolella). Adding to the plot twists and family tensions, Eddie is in debt to Sean, making Carlos resentful, Carlos's girlfriend Maggie (Andrea Navedo) has issues with Carlos and his aspirations, and Maggie's drug-dealing brother Angel (Bobby Cannavale) complicates life for everyone.

If de Villa's tale (co-written with Nat Moss, from a story by Perez, the film's star) sounds familiar, that's because *Washington Heights* steals from everywhere. Carlos's dilemma to stay in the family business or break free as his own person could be straight from *The Jazz Singer* (1927) or maybe *It's a Wonderful Life* (1946). In any case the narrative is nothing new or surprising, particularly the contrived way the central conflict results (from Eddie's shooting).

There are more plusses than minuses to the presentation of the hackneyed material, so much so, it becomes an ironic disparity. *Washington Heights* looks and feels "authentic," but gets mired in unnecessary plot formula. It's as if John Cassavetes were directing a script by William Goldman.

Credit goes to nearly all the actors, particularly Manny Perez as the intense, uptight artist-hero, Carlos. Even in the melodramatic scenes with Tomas Milian (as the overly generous, weak-willed Eddie), Perez remains convincing and persuasive. Perez gets more than adequate, even engaging support from the rest of the cast, although ubiquitous performance artist Danny Hoch (as Mickey) can't help trying to steal a few scenes.

In other areas, *Washington Heights* delivers solid professionalism: highly colorful but natural production design (by Charlotte Bourke), exemplary camerawork and lighting (by Claudio Chea), non-intrusive but suitably lively salsa music (by Leigh Roberts), and sharp, clean editing (by Tom Donahue), the last of which is particularly effective during a montage of Carlos being inspired while working on an illustration. In terms of sheer style and presentation, *Washington Heights* does at least as well as the much-praised *Raising Victor Vargas*, which is also set in a Latino community and deals with similar issues of identity, assimilation and independence.

Like *Raising Victor Vargas*, critical reaction to *Washington Heights* was generally favorable. After all, it is hard not to admire such a sincere, well-meaning effort. But oddly (given the above), David Noh of *Film Journal International* thought is was "amateurishly filmed." John Anderson in *Newsday* countered, "What makes you keep watching *Washington Heights* isn't so much the tale as the way de Villa makes it so alive and electric." And Evan Henerson of the *Los Angeles Daily News* saw the pros and cons: "*Washington Heights* is an often engaging sleeper that merits audience appreciation [but] the plotting feels largely by the numbers." *Washington Heights* can't quite overcome its limitations (a parallel dilemma for the story's hero), but also like Manny, it's not such a bad catch, either. 🎞️

—*Eric Monder*

CREDITS

Carlos Ramirez: Manny Perez
Eddie Ramirez: Tomas Milian
Mickey Kilpatrick: Danny Hoch
Maggie: Andrea Navedo
Sean Kilpatrick: Jude Ciccolella
Angel: Bobby Cannavale
Daisy: Judy Reyes
Raquel: Callie (Calliope) Thorne
David: David Zayas

Origin: USA
Released: 2002
Production: Luis Dantas, Tom Donahue; Samy Boy Entertainment; released by Mac Releasing
Directed by: Alfredo de Villa
Written by: Alfredo de Villa, Nat Moss
Cinematography by: Claudio Chea
Music by: Leigh Roberts
Sound: Andre Bellware
Editing: Tom Donahue
Art Direction: Sandra Goldmark
Production Design: Charlotte Bourke
MPAA rating: R
Running time: 85 minutes

REVIEWS

Boxoffice. July, 2003, p. 46.
Los Angeles Times Online. July 11, 2003.
New York Times Online. May 9, 2003.
Variety Online. May 20, 2002.

The Weather Underground

The Weather Underground is an important documentary, coming as it does at a time when the U.S. faces the threat of subversive attacks, both from within and without. However, the filmic form—adopted by director-producer-editor Sam Green and Bill Siegel, who is credited as co-director and producer—along with the film's subversive stance, leaves a lot to be desired. Even so, their film deserves to be analyzed in terms of the radical political issues it raises, as well as the equally radical views on those very paradoxes that still remain unexpressed.

What remains the film's chief drawback is that the views espoused by some of the members of the Underground as they look today—mature, responsible, middle-aged Americans—remain for the most part confined to their actions thirty years ago. These "talking heads" (no pun intended) do not speak to what is happening in the U.S. today. This allows Green and Siegel to side with them, as filmmakers, and at the same time, to safely historicize the revolutionary, anti-capitalist ideals being spouted as belonging to a distant past.

Which is not to say that *The Weather Underground* cannot prove electrifying viewing for those already converted, as it were, to its brand of discourse. More simply put, the film seems to cater to those prepared to accept the Underground's basic platform: the violent overthrow of the government of the United States was the only ideological solution for stopping the war in Vietnam.

This is also not to imply that the film has no redeeming value for others. As often happens in the non-fiction film, owing to the photographic realism of the medium, the filmmaker proposes; the medium disposes. As the German film theorist Siegfried Kracauer would argue, the artistic impact of such a documentary lies in the extent to which it is able to reveal the unrehearsed, the fortuitous, and the accidental.

A good example of such a starkly revelatory moment occurs at the very start of the film. We are shown "raw" footage, in crude black-and-white, of dollar bills on fire being held up by young people with hopeful smiles. A filmmaker, also smiling, holds up his camera as if to get a close-up of the burning bills, while a female voice on the soundtrack intones that war has been declared on the U.S. by the Weather Underground, a group identified in the film's opening shot as the militant wing of the Students for a Democratic Society.

In a flashing instant, the shot reveals more than what Green and Siegel would perhaps want it to. We can see that despite the serious nature of the Underground's threat to bomb public buildings, these so-called young radicals seem to be animated by a spirit of fun. It is socio-political protest as weekend bash. The ambivalent truth that has riddled even peaceful protests in the U.S. surfaces in that one shot: joining movements for civil and political reform was the easiest way to find sex.

This riveting opening then goes on to wallow in its own crudity. Black and white photographs fill the screen, each a kind of mug shot of prominent members of the Underground, unidentified, but linked by a common cause spelled out by the voiceover. Beyond the credo of "smoking dope and making love," looms the commitment to undo the injustices of the American legal system. "Within the next 14 days," the voice states coldly, "we will attack an institution of American injustice."

The film cuts to bomb blasts on the soundtrack punctuating images of small-scale destruction to what looks like an office building. The place remains unidentified. We see

President Ford looking at the damage, his face expressing more curiosity than alarm. The film then cuts to a TV reporter saying that, according to the FBI, the group responsible is the same one behind the bombing of the U.S. Capitol in 1971 and the Pentagon in 1972. In this brief pre-credit sequence, before the opening titles flash on, the film has also managed to get its audience to consider a truth pertaining to all documentaries, a proposition that might not appeal to their tastes: unlike a story film, a documentary can be as crude and unimaginative as it wishes, it can commit every sin in the book except one—it cannot fail to be timely.

As the film then introduces some of the members of the Underground, it sets up, perhaps without intending to, an antinomy between their identities today and their 1970's personas. Most notable in this parade is the still beautiful Bernadine Dohrn, photographed against the sunlit hills of San Francisco. She is forthright in identifying herself and the years of her involvement with the movement. She then allows her face to express whatever regret she now feels. The film cuts to black-and-white footage of a young and darkly beautiful Bernadine in 1969 as she expounds on the credo of violence used for political reasons: "There's no way to be committed to non-violence in the middle of the most violent society history has created."

Also notable is the still charismatic Mark Rudd, famous for his role in the takeover of Columbia University. Now silver-haired and a teacher in a community college, he admits that his students think he's from another planet when he speaks of his days with the Underground. Then, while young blacks are making faces at the camera behind him, we see the young Rudd speaking in the street of the need for Americans to find a common cause with blacks, the Vietnamese, and others around the world, presumably to fight the injustices of American capitalism.

Remarkable for his unblinking honesty is Brian Flanagan, now a bartender, who expresses more by what he claims he cannot say. He accepts his guilt. "Armed robberies, terrorism . . . there were all kinds of things that went down," he confesses. "I'll tell you we did them," he says, then adds with a grin, "but I'm not going to tell you which ones I did, or who did what." Clearly, he's one member who ostensibly still feels linked to his compatriots, if by no other bond than that of secrecy.

After this parade, Green and Siegel put into motion a third strand of filmic discourse: "raw" footage of American brutality in Vietnam, including material already seen in the Academy Award winning documentary *Hearts and Minds* (1974) by Peter Davis. While historically truthful, the footage seems to belong more to the Davis film, which explores the paradox of American involvement in Vietnam, rather than to the Green-Siegel effort, which takes that very paradox as a given. The way Green and Siegel use these harrowing images, the senseless violence depicted therein appears merely sensational.

What comes to light, once the film's subversive tinge wears off, is that it appears repetitive and even monomaniacal. Green and Siegel do little, given the complex interplay of protest across various media at that time, to vary their presentation. Worse, only the voice of Todd Gitlin is featured as the "dissent-within-the-dissent." He boldly claims, bewildered, that the Weathermen usurped the power base established by the Students for a Democratic Society, before they became notorious as the Underground.

Similarly, there is only one sequence that should make audiences sit up. As a bomb, intended for Fort Dix, is shown being built in a townhouse in Greenwich Village, ominous music on the soundtrack evokes the mood of a thriller. We then learn a short circuit in the device resulted instead in the death of three Underground members.

What becomes clear through the selected events and the interviews linked to this filmic history—from scenes of group sex to the Underground finding a common cause with Dr. Timothy Leary—is that these self-styled revolutionaries never really thought out the political stance they adopted in response to the horrors of the Vietnam War. They allowed themselves to be carried along by the manic fervor of the times into killing innocent people. This explains why, when America withdrew from Vietnam, members of the Underground surrendered and were even absorbed into the Establishment.

Thus, what remains unexpressed, but clearly evident from the footage and interviews linked to that war, is the equally radical notion that the Vietnam War was really a war between generations. One would have expected these radicals to argue that that war never really ended, but was merely transposed onto American soil. One would have expected, instead of smug, middle-aged contentment, a semblance of protest at how, even today, young Americans are sent out to die on foreign soil to preserve American interests, often for corporate dictatorships.

It is only Bill Flanagan who, toward the end of the film, sees the Underground as no different from those who brought down the World Trade Center, "believing Allah was on their side." In an amusing closing note, Flanagan is shown winning his way to more than $23,000 on the TV game show, *Jeopardy*.

Critics seem to have forgiven the film's homespun approach to its subject matter. In the *The New York Times* Elvis Mitchell calls it a "terrifically smart and solid piece of filmmaking . . . that captures a movement in motion . . . a revolt so accelerated and noisy, there was no time for reflection during its heyday." J. Hoberman of the *Village Voice*, while admiring the film's "pleasingly rough-hewn quality," cannot accept "the filmmakers' unwillingness to ask their subjects any really tough questions." He concludes, "[O]ne leaves with barely a clue as to how this group was able to orchestrate a successful string of terror bombings."

—*Vivek Adarkar*

CREDITS

Origin: USA
Released: 2002
Production: Sam Green, Bill Siegel, Carrie Lozano, Marc Smolowitz; Upstate Films; released by Shadow Distribution
Directed by: Sam Green, Bill Siegel
Cinematography by: Andrew Black, Federico Salsano
Music by: Dave Cerf, Amy Domingues
Sound: David Westby
Editing: Sam Green, Dawn Logsdon
MPAA rating: Unrated
Running time: 92 minutes

REVIEWS

Chicago Sun-Times Online. August 1, 2003.
Entertainment Weekly. July 11, 2003, p. 62.
Los Angeles Times Online. August 29, 2003.
New York Times Online. June 4, 2003.
Variety Online. February 19, 2003.
Village Voice Online. June 4, 2003.
Washington Post. August 15, 2003, p. WE33.

QUOTES

Brian Flanagan: "When you feel you have right on your side, you can do some pretty horrific things."

TRIVIA

Onetime Weather Underground member Kathy Boudin was released from prison in 2003 after serving 22 years for a 1981 armored car heist in which three men were killed.

AWARDS AND NOMINATIONS

Nomination:
Oscars 2003: Feature Doc.
Directors Guild 2003: Feature Doc.

Whale Rider

In the ways of the ancients she found a hope for the future.

—Movie tagline

 Box Office: $20.7 million

A moving coming-of-age tale set among the Maori of New Zealand, *Whale Rider* received accolades at several prominent film festivals long before it became one of the best-reviewed movies of the summer. Niki Caro, who adapted the screenplay from Witi Ihimaera's children's novel and directed the film, has created a majestic piece of entertainment, a work that manages to be almost mythic in its updating of an ancient legend while capturing the intimate details of a complex grandfather-granddaughter relationship. Filmed in Whangara, *Whale Rider* is also a visual triumph, capturing the austere beauty of this small coastal village.

The movie opens with the most primal of scenes—underwater images of whales intercut with a woman in childbirth. A little girl's voiceover informs us that her people are waiting for a leader, a new successor to their founder, Paikea, who, according to legend, arrived long ago on their shores on the back of a whale. But as the voiceover continues, we see that all has not gone well: "There was no gladness when I was born. My twin brother died and took our mother with him," the girl laments. She survives, but, since leadership can be passed down only to a male child, her grandfather, Koro (Rawiri Paratene), is devastated. He wants his son, Porourangi (Cliff Curtis), to try again, but, having just lost a wife and son at the same time, he is too distraught to think about starting over with a new family. Porourangi names his daughter Paikea (played as a young girl by Keisha Castle-Hughes), which infuriates Koro, the tradition-bound patriarch who believes that name should be reserved for the male heir apparent, not given to a girl.

The novel is narrated by the little girl's uncle, who traces Paikea's early childhood years and tells his own story as well, whereas Caro's screenplay judiciously cuts his story and condenses the time frame, beginning Paikea's story when she is twelve. She has developed a close bond with her grandfather—there are lovely scenes of him taking her to and from school on his bicycle—even though he stubbornly ignores the signs that she is destined to be the rightful leader of the tribe. In one scene loaded with symbolism, he draws an analogy between a piece of rope and their ancestry, suggesting that the various threads are like their ancestors coming together. When Paikea ties the rope and uses it to start an outboard motor that had been bedeviling Koro, it is a clever piece of foreshadowing—she is the one who can link the past and the future and will regenerate the motor of her people.

Porourangi leaves home after his wife's death and visits sporadically. Koro holds out hope that his son will produce a future chief, but, once he is committed to a different life in Europe—he is an artist and has a pregnant girlfriend in Germany—Koro must look elsewhere. He decides to start a school for the village's first-born boys to teach them the old traditions and discover a leader. In the novel, because Porourangi does not flee the tribe, the crisis of leadership is not as pressing, but his absence here gives Caro's script a sense of urgency and a stronger narrative drive.

Seeing how disappointed her grandfather is in her being a girl and overhearing him tell Porourangi that "she's no use to me," Paikea accepts her father's invitation to live with him in Germany. However, as they are driving away, she seems to feel some natural pull from the whales in the ocean drawing her back. It is not explained rationally, but it is one of the signs that she is meant to be the leader, even if no one else, especially Koro, can see it right now. There is a heartbreaking scene when she returns home and barges in on her grandfather, who is in a meeting with the elders. She proudly announces, "I'm back," but he is not interested, brushing her off with a curt "Not now, Pai" and clearly irritated that he is being interrupted. "But I'm back. I'm back," she continues, not understanding why he is not happy to see her.

The relationship between Paikea and Koro is at the heart of *Whale Rider*. While his strict adherence to tradition renders him unable to recognize Paikea's true gifts, they nonetheless share an underlying warmth and mutual affection. Without this love, Koro could have become an unbearable, one-dimensional patriarch who bullies people. But Paikea never gives up on him, and Castle-Hughes, in a stunning debut performance—she was only eleven when the film was made—conveys Paikea's sadness and pensiveness along with her determination to prove herself without ever sliding into bitterness or hostility. Although Paikea yearns for her grandfather's complete acceptance, she does not allow his rejection to stop her from immersing herself in their cultural traditions, especially the songs and dances she leads at school.

When the training for the boys begins, Paikea eavesdrops on the lessons and incurs Koro's wrath when she is caught. Her grandmother, Nanny Flowers (Vicky Haughton), however, is sympathetic—she shrewdly regards her husband with the wry sense that he is in charge only because she lets him think he is—and tells Paikea to see her Uncle Rawiri (Grant Roa) for some private lessons. Before he got fat and lazy, Rawiri won a trophy for his fighting skills. While the film does not dwell on the apathy and neglect into which the tribe has fallen, Rawiri, napping in the afternoon with marijuana and a pipe close by, is a gentle reminder of why the tribe needs a leader to point the way to a better future. Rawiri, however, is not a tragic figure—on the contrary, he provides some great comic relief when he enthusiastically demonstrates some fighting moves to Paikea.

The novel's Rawiri, on the other hand, is a central figure, not the apathetic uncle who surprisingly turns mentor but rather a guy who hangs out with his biker buddies and then spends some time abroad because he wants to see some of the world. Much of the novel actually deals with his life, and he interprets his niece's story for us. The film, however, makes Paikea the focus from beginning to end—a key change that streamlines the narrative and strengthens her character arc.

For his class's final test, Koro takes his students out in a boat and throws into the ocean his sacred whale-tooth necklace for them to retrieve. Calling it "a test of your spirit" and seeing it as the way of finding his leader, Koro is crushed when no one is able to bring it back. Later, however, when Paikea is out with her uncle, she boldly jumps in the water and brings back the whale tooth. Rawiri gives it to Nanny, who knows that Koro is not ready to acknowledge that Paikea is the one meant to lead them.

On the night of a special school performance, Paikea, dressed splendidly in full Maori garb, receives an award and gives a poignant speech dedicated to her grandfather, who is supposed to be present as her special guest. But as his front-row chair remains empty, poor Paikea is unable to fight back tears as she speaks proudly of her heritage. Even at her most vulnerable, the luminous Castle-Hughes displays the fortitude, resilience, and charisma to show that Paikea has the authority to be chief.

Koro, intending to go to the performance and having put on his best clothes, heads out for the school. He doesn't get far, however, before he discovers the whales stranded along the beach and dying. Paikea had called to the ancestors for help, and the whales came, but now they are in trouble.

The community comes together to try to save these creatures, which are inextricably linked to the tribe's past and future. Koro believes that, if the village can lead one back to the ocean, then the others will follow, but their efforts are fruitless. Finally, Paikea fulfills her destiny in this moment of crisis. Like her namesake, she climbs on the back of one of the whales, which magically revives, and she rides the whale out into the ocean, with the others following. It is rare for a film grounded in the reality of everyday village life to make a leap to a spiritual plain, but, when *Whale Rider* boldly plunges into the transcendent, it feels like the inevitable conclusion and culmination of all that has come before. Paikea rides the whale underwater and finally lets go, ending up unconscious in a hospital room, with her grandfather, who has finally had a change of heart, begging for forgiveness.

Paikea recovers, and, in the triumphant final scene, a grand ceremony portending rebirth takes place on the beach. Tribe members are wearing native attire and chanting as a grand canoe is pushed out into the water. Paikea has assumed the role of leader and, in her concluding voiceover, speaks of her people "going forward, all together, with all of our strength," and the enthusiasm of the participants confirms the renewal and hope she has brought to her tribe.

It is a marvelous, optimistic ending that reconciles the ancient and the modern, which, in a way, is the essence of the film. Are old ways relevant in the modern world, the film seems to ask, and, if so, can they adapt? *Whale Rider* simultaneously embraces tradition while also persuasively showing that flexibility and change must be a part of that tradition, here, in order to see the gifts of a leader no one was expecting. In the end, this is not just a coming-of-age story for Paikea, but for her grandfather and the tribe as well, who are stepping into a new world on the shoulders of a little girl.

—*Peter N. Chumo II*

CREDITS

Pai: Keisha Castle-Hughes
Koro: Rawiri Paratene
Nanny Flowers: Vicky Haughton
Porourangi: Clifford Curtis

Origin: New Zealand, Germany
Released: 2002
Production: John Barnett, Tim Sanders, Frank Hubner; Apollomedia, Pandora Film, Forest Whitaker; released by Newmarket Films
Directed by: Niki Caro
Written by: Niki Caro
Cinematography by: Leon Narbey
Music by: Lisa Gerrard
Sound: David Madigan
Editing: David Coulson
Art Direction: Grace Mock
Costumes: Kirsty Camerson
Production Design: Grant Major
MPAA rating: PG-13
Running time: 105 minutes

REVIEWS

Boxoffice. April, 2003, p. 76.
Chicago Sun-Times Online. June 20, 2003.
Entertainment Weekly. June 13, 2003, p. 73.
Los Angeles Times. May 4, 2003, p. E31.

Los Angeles Times Online. June 6, 2003.
New York Times Online. May 11, 2003.
New York Times Online. June 6, 2003.
People. June 16, 2003, p. 42.
Rolling Stone. June 26, 2003, p. 88.
USA Today Online. June 6, 2003.
Variety Online. September 18, 2002.
Washington Post. June 20, 2003, p. WE37.

AWARDS AND NOMINATIONS

Ind. Spirit 2004: Foreign Film
Nomination:
Oscars 2003: Actress (Castle-Hughes)
Screen Actors Guild 2003: Support. Actress (Castle-Hughes).

What a Girl Wants

Trying to fit in. Born to stand out.
—Movie tagline

Box Office: $36 million

This modern day Cinderella story stars the Nickelodeon channel's Amanda Bynes, of *The Amanda Show*. An appealing young woman, Bynes's previous big screen efforts include a decent turn in the tween comedy *Big Fat Liar* with another small screen star, Frankie Muniz. *Girl* will appeal to the same pre-teen audience, but mostly of the female variety. Feeling like a knock-off of 2001's *The Princess Diaries,* this contemporary fairytale actually has its roots in Vincente Minnelli's 1958 comedy with Sandra Dee, *The Reluctant Debutante,* which was written by William Douglas Home and based on a 1956 play of the same name. While Dee was merely a supporting actor in that film, Bynes takes center stage here as a girl of rather humble means living with her mother in New York City, and who discovers the father she has never met is a wealthy English lord.

Bynes's Daphne Reynolds lives with her single mother in a small apartment above a restaurant in the decidedly unglamorous Chinatown section of New York. Libby Reynolds (Kelly Preston) is a rock musician now relegated to playing mostly weddings in Long Island. It seems Daphne is the result of a meeting between Sir Henry Dashwood (Colin Firth) and her mum in Morocco some 15 years ago. The pair fell in love and hastily participated in a marriage ceremony performed by a Bedouin prince, which unfortunately, was not legal. The "newlyweds" then headed to London to meet Henry's hoity-toity family who rather coldly disapproved of his free-spirited new bride. Mere disapproval won't deter the lovestruck Henry, however; every fairytale needs a villain, and Jonathan Pryce turns up to fill that role. Pryce is Alastair Payne, Sir Henry's nefarious advisor, who quickly schemes to break up the happy couple, being averse to his master's "marriage" to someone so far beneath him and an American, no less. Payne successfully convinces Libby that the dashing Sir Dashwood is not really in love her, and the American commoner flees to New York along with, unbeknownst to him, Henry's unborn child.

While Daphne is busy becoming a perky teenager on the other side of the pond, Sir Henry, in the meantime, has renounced his seat in the House of Lords to run for the House of Commons. The titled English politician is in for a big surprise when Daphne suddenly decides to meet her father, hopping a jet to London-town and popping in for a surprise visit. Having scaled the walls of the vast Dashwood estate, Daphne wins over her father and even her very stiff-upper-lipped British grandmother ("No hugging, dear. I'm British, we only show affection to dogs and horses.") played by Eileen Atkins. She has a much harder time, however, with Dad's new fiancée, Alastair's snooty daughter, Glynnis Payne (Anna Chancellor, playing the heavy once again), and her like-minded daughter Clarissa (Christina Cole), not to mention Alastair himself, who worries that the election for Sir Henry may be jeopardized by Daphne's very existence. Indeed, the rambunctious American girl's free-wheeling attitude causes a number of minor catastrophes that have even Henry frowning and reminding his daughter of what it means to be a Dashwood. This fish out of water bit carries the humor for much of the film, with Daphne trying to fit in and not make waves while, naturally, teaching the uptight Brits a thing or two in the process (Firth later shows up in leather pants playing air guitar). Trying to fit in while retaining one's individuality is ultimately the movie's message, one that is perfectly appropriate for its audience.

Bynes is pleasing as the American charmer but comes off a little too cutesy at times. Supports, especially of the British variety, are strong despite a lack of strong material. While the characters are pretty much one-dimensional and the requisite stereotyping abounds (Brits are stuffy, Americans are spontaneous and free), there are some exceptions, notably Daphne's British hipster musician boyfriend Ian (Oliver James) who encourages her to be herself. The plot has its share of inconsistencies and is a bit too pat, down to the ending, a la *Parent Trap,* that will no doubt please the children of divorce but that doesn't exactly reflect reality. However, this is a fairy tale and the material is perfectly suited for writers Jenny Bicks and Elizabeth Chandler, who also penned the similar, *A Little Princess.* Director Dennie Gordon (*Joe Dirt*) makes this likable fantasy a more mainstream offering with broad swaths of humor, yet little appeal outside its pre-teen, female audience.

—*Hilary White*

CREDITS

Daphne Reynolds: Amanda Bynes
Sir Henry Dashwood: Colin Firth
Libby Reynolds: Kelly Preston
Lady Jocelyn Dashwood: Eileen Atkins
Glynnis Payne: Anna Chancellor
Alistair Payne: Jonathan Pryce
Ian Wallace: Oliver James
Clarissa Payne: Christina Cole
Princess Charlotte: Sylvia Syms
Armistead Stuart: Ben Scholfield

Origin: USA
Released: 2003
Production: Denise DiNovi, Hunt Lowry, Bill Gerber; Gaylord Films; released by Warner Bros.
Directed by: Dennie Gordon
Written by: Elizabeth Chandler, Jenny Bicks
Cinematography by: Andrew Dunn
Music by: Rupert Gregson-Williams
Sound: Colin Charles, Brian Simmons
Music Supervisor: Debra Baum
Editing: Charles "Chuck" McClelland
Art Direction: Karen Wakefield
Costumes: Shay Cunliffe
Production Design: Michael Carlin
MPAA rating: PG
Running time: 104 minutes

REVIEWS

Chicago Sun-Times Online. April 4, 2003.
Entertainment Weekly. April 11, 2003.
Los Angeles Times Online. April 4, 2003.
New York Times Online. April 4, 2003.
People. April 14, 2003, p. 37.
USA Today Online. April 4, 2003.
Variety Online. March 28, 2003.
Washington Post. April 4, 2003, p. WE47.

QUOTES

Lady Jocelyn (Eileen Atkins) to her American granddaughter Daphne (Amanda Bynes): "No hugs, dear. I'm British. We only show affection to dogs and horses."

Willard

A new breed of friendship.
—Movie tagline
From small things . . . comes great power.
—Movie tagline

 Box Office: $6.8 million

A remake of the 1971 film *Willard* is probably something that should never have come to fruition. All the original had going for it was cult status and a questionable subtext of the disaffected worker versus queen bee. It was campy, suffered from dated special effects, and was really a rather dubious horror film at best. Still, the thought of Crispin Glover taking over the role of Willard must have been the driving force behind the belief that a remake of such a cult classic was warranted.

The 2003 edition of *Willard* follows the original narrative to a tee. Willard is a disassociated young man. He lives with his invalid yet domineering mother whom he dotingly cares for (his father committed suicide some years earlier). Willard's life away from home isn't any better. He works at the company his father founded with Mr. Martin (played to the hilt by a constantly barking R. Lee Ermey). Like his mother, Mr. Martin affords Willard little respect. In fact, Willard is constantly told he has his job only because of a promise Martin made to Willard's father. It's not until Willard befriends a white rat whom he cannot bring himself to kill that his character starts to emerge. He names the rat Socrates and they become the best of friends. With the help of his clever friend (and another more brutish rat named Ben), Willard exacts a small amount of revenge on Mr. Martin and begins to enjoy a certain amount of societal worth. For a short time it looks as though he might even have himself a girlfriend. However, Willard's situation takes several tragic turns and he eventually uses his horde of rats for diabolical purposes until they eventually turn on him in a macabre enactment of the cycle of life.

With the pedigree of their past success (*The X-Files* and *Final Destination*), the team of James Wong and Glen Morgan seemed able enough to deliver an acceptable update of this cult classic. However, the ambitious amalgamation of elements of *The Birds* and *Psycho* and the apparent desire to not make a "camp" film overwhelmed what should have been a simple story about Willard's empowerment and destruction. As the embodiment of the creepy Willard, Crispin Glover is flawless. He infests the role with such vigor that it's hard to believe the film wasn't originally written as a vehicle for him alone. However, Glover's manifestation of Willard, like the film itself, is as Michael Rechtshaffen writes in *The Hollywood Reporter*, "alternately creepy and crappy." While Morgan's infusion of Hitchcockian elements aids the film in its "creepy" look and mood, it fails it miserably with regards to the main character. Since, as Rechtshaffen notes, Willard has apparently been "recast as [*Psycho*'s] Norman Bates," the character elicits absolutely no sympathy. Whereas you were never supposed to feel for Norman Bates (you just weren't supposed to suspect him), you should be able to feel empathy for Willard as an ostracized everyman. As portrayed by Glover, Willard is an outcast, but that's because he's just plain scary (even before he finds his special gift). Since Willard needs to be sympathetic for the rest of the story to be successful, this becomes the film's major flaw. He isn't and the film is ultimately a slick and silly monster show that goes nowhere.

Character development notwithstanding, the look of the film is quite impressive. The gothic design of Willard's house is extremely frightening and it even threatens to take on a character of its own in a few scenes. However, its claustrophobic and suffocating effect on Willard isn't played to its fullest potential and the set is yet another squandered opportunity. The camera work in the film includes wild angles and moody close-ups and it plays like early Sam Raimi. This would be fine if the film wanted to be *Evil Dead* (or even *Darkman*). But, the film so often begs to be taken seriously and then forces a cutesy in-joke or inappropriate sequence into the story (Michael Jackson's theme song for *Ben*—the sequel to the original *Willard*—playing over the rats stalking and devouring a house cat is an example of this unwarranted excess) which ultimately leads the narrative nowhere. To borrow a line from *This Is Spinal Tap*, with a film like *Willard* there is a fine line between clever and stupid and too often *Willard* falls on the side of the latter. All of these elements combined with the creepy/cool character of Willard make the film, as Rechtshaffen summarized, "an unsuccessful mix of sci-fi horror and a highly exaggerated filmmaking approach that borders on unintentional parody."

—Michael J. Tyrkus

CREDITS

Willard Stiles: Crispin Glover
Frank Martin: R. Lee Ermey
Catherine: Laura Elena Harring
Mrs. Stiles: Jackie Burroughs
Detective Boxer: David Parker

Origin: USA
Released: 2003

Production: Glen Morgan, Gurinder Chadha; Hard Eight Pictures; released by New Line Cinema
Directed by: Glen Morgan
Written by: Glen Morgan
Cinematography by: Robert McLachlan
Music by: Shirley Walker
Sound: Patrick Ramsay
Editing: James Coblentz
Art Direction: Catherine Ircha
Costumes: Gregory Mah
Production Design: Mark Freeborn
MPAA rating: PG-13
Running time: 95 minutes

REVIEWS

Chicago Sun-Times Online. March 14, 2003.
Entertainment Weekly. March 21, 2003, p. 86.
Los Angeles Times Online. March 14, 2003.
New York Times Online. March 14, 2003.
USA Today Online. March 14, 2003.
Variety Online. March 9, 2003.
Washington Post. March 14, 2003, p. WE41.

TRIVIA

Bruce Davison, who played the lead in the original film, is shown in an oil painting as the current Willard's deceased father.

Winged Migration (Le Peuple Migrateur) (Traveling Birds)

 Box Office: $10.7 million

On the website *RottenTomatoes.com*, a site that compiles critics' movie reviews, the film *Winged Migration* scored 93 percent positive reviews. Among critics for the major publications, the tally was 100 percent positive. *Winged Migration* also was nominated for an Oscar for best documentary (it lost to Michael Moore's *Bowling for Columbine*). What did it take for a film to do this well? Birds.

Winged Migration had no big stars, no car chases, nary a plot and barely any narration. And at the beginning of the film there's a notice that no special effects were used in the filming of the movie. What's left? Birds. Birds flying, birds eating, birds being eaten and birds flying some more.

The film was the project of Jacques Perrin. Perrin has had a long career in film, beginning with a stint as an actor in the 1960s in the Costa-Gavras films *The Sleeping Car Murders* and *Z*. Even though Perrin was only 28 at the time, he was also a producer on *Z*. He is probably best known for his 1996 film *Microcosmos*. That film examined the world of bugs, up close and personal.

Winged Migration is less like one of the TV nature documentaries, than a free-flowing, impressionistic picture of birds. The film is sparsely narrated by Perrin, who gives only the smallest of informational tidbits. He briefly states, for example, that birds know their migration route by looking for landmarks and feeling magnetic fields, but doesn't explain how any of that works. There are also some occasional text messages, but these are brief and usually only explain which bird we are looking at, how far they will fly and where the start and finish points are on their route. The furthest flyers are the Arctic terns, which fly 12,500 miles, between the Arctic and Antarctica, twice a year. The action of the birds is punctuated by the natural sounds of their environment or by the birds' own squawks, squeaks and caws. Drifting in and out of the soundtrack are new agey compositions by Bruno Coulais (who also scored *Microcosmos*), using vocals from Nick Cave, Robert Wyatt, and a Bulgarian children's choir.

This leaves a lot of time for a contemplation of the birds. A large part of the film is devoted to the sight of birds in flight. Here, Perrin has some amazing footage, which he spent over three years compiling, using a crew of more than 450 people. There were five crews, including 17 pilots and 14 cinematographers who traveled to more than 40 countries and all of the continents. For every foot of film that made it into the movie, 225 feet were shot. The film contains probably the most amazing footage of birds ever shot. There are numerous shots taken from the bird formations themselves. The effect is nothing less than dazzling. It's as though the viewer is another bird in the formation, an extra member of the flock. It is unforgettable.

The notice about no special effects being used in the film is definitely necessary. The shots are so stunning and so groundbreaking that it's difficult to believe that they are real. Perrin captured the images using a variety of techniques. Some of the shots were taken from hot air balloons, some were shot from ultralight aircraft and some from remote-controlled gliders. In some cases, the birds were exposed to the sounds of ultralight airplanes while they were still in the shell so they would be used to it. Such techniques helped the young birds to treat the machines as adult members of the flock.

The real drama of the film is the meditation on life that comes from watching birds soaring above the vastness of the world. They fly by the Eiffel tower, over the Amazon and in front of a pre-9/11 New York City. They ride on ice chunks and search for scarce water in the Sahara. The birds truly have a God's-eye view upon all of nature and all that man has made.

The rest of the drama comes from what is inherent in a bird's life. The twice-yearly migrations are a matter of survival and the trip is fraught with peril. The movie shows some of these dangers, but doesn't focus on them in an unsavory manner. The most disturbing scene is of a bird with a broken wing that is cornered by crabs, clicking their claws together. (Reportedly, the bird was actually rescued by the film crew just in time.) The birds' biggest problems come from man. One bird, following his flock through an industrial district in Eastern Europe, gets caught in some sludge and is unable to fly out. And, in North America, some birds are flying gracefully over a field when shots ring out and they start falling from the sky one by one. Their plunge to the ground is balletic, yet horrifying.

The birds seem alien as they go through their specific rituals. Why does this bird make this particular sound? Why does this species puff up their chest? Why do these others clack their beaks together? Perrin doesn't offer any answers; he just shows us what's happening. Despite their otherness, it's difficult not to anthropomorphize them. In one scene, a pair of penguins is watching their fuzzy baby toddling around when a bird comes near to steal the baby. The parents squawk and try to warn the bird away, but the bird closes in and eventually gets the baby. The parents seem to wail mournfully to the heavens, then hang their heads in defeat.

Perrin switches between flocks and terrains without much logic. We stay with some birds for a few minutes then move on to others. Some of the birds we watch are bald eagles, sage grouse, white storks, and Clark's grebes. We see birds looking for bits of food to put in their eager young babies' open mouths and we see a newborn bird inadvertently push the egg of his not-yet born brother or sister out of their high nest. We see birds migrating over the ocean set down to take a well-deserved rest on the deck of a military ship at sea. Most of it is fascinating.

Winged Migration is not a perfect film. It would have been nice if there could have been a bit more information in Perrin's narration. For example, he says, "Staying out of bad weather is a necessity," but he doesn't say how they avoid such weather or what happens when they get into it. There are also parts of the film that seem slow. Although it was surely a gargantuan task winnowing those 225 feet of film into each foot, they might have edited down even more. Still, it is a rare film that manages to dazzle its audience in such a basic, fundamental way.

Reviewers were enchanted. Megan Lehmann of the *New York Post* described the film as "a thrillingly vicarious experience that answers a primal urge to join our feathered friends as they soar and glide in the blue beyond." Michael Wilmington of the *Chicago Tribune* gave the film four out of four stars and wrote, "A movie of awesome beauty and innovation, *Winged Migration* reveals a piece of the world we've glimpsed from afar but have never seen before with such stunning clarity." Roger Ebert of the *Chicago Sun-Times* explained, "It wants to allow us to look, simply look, at birds—and that goal it achieves magnificently. There are sights here I will not easily forget." And Stephen Holden of the *New York Times* concluded that "it may sound facetious, but *Winged Migration* provides such an intense vicarious experience of being a flapping airborne creature with the wind in its ears that you leave the theater feeling like an honorary member of another species."

—*Jill Hamilton*

CREDITS

Narrator: Jacques Perrin

Origin: France, Germany, Spain, Italy, Switzerland
Language: English, French
Released: 2001
Production: Jacques Perrin; France 2 Cinema, France 3 Cinema, BAC Films Ltd.; released by Sony Pictures Classics
Directed by: Jacques Perrin
Written by: Jacques Perrin, Stephane Durand
Cinematography by: Bernard Lutic, Thierry Machado, Olli Barbe, Michel Benjamin, Sylvie Carcedo, Laurent Charbonnier, Luc Drion, Laurent Fleutot, Philippe Garguil, Dominique Gentil, Stephane Martin, Fabrice Moindrot, Ernst Sasse, Michel Terasse, Thierry Thomas
Music by: Bruno Coulais
Sound: Gerard Lamps, Philippe Barbeau, Laurent Levy
Editing: Marie-Josephe Yoyotte
Production Design: Regis Nicolino
MPAA rating: G
Running time: 89 minutes

REVIEWS

Chicago Sun-Times Online. May 2, 2003.
Los Angeles Times Online. May 2, 2003.
Sight and Sound. July, 2003, p. 60.
Time. June 16, 2003, p. 69.
Variety Online. December 14, 2001.
Washington Post. June 12, 2003, p. WE35.

AWARDS AND NOMINATIONS

Nomination:
Oscars 2002: Feature Doc.

Wonderland

The 80's—unplugged. The murders—unveiled. The legend—unzipped.
—Movie tagline

Sex, guns, money and murder. Welcome to L.A.
—Movie tagline

 Box Office: $1 million

Wonderland is more than a little misleading. For one thing, it duplicates the title of a very different British film directed by Michael Winterbottom a few years ago. This *Wonderland* concerns porn star John Holmes (played by Val Kilmer), but not in his pornographic splendor. In this respect it runs parallel to Paul Thomas Anderson's *Boogie Nights* (1997), based on the legend of a well-endowed porn star who seemed to resemble John Holmes. The text that begins the film whets the audience's prurient appetites. The audience is informed, as Anthony Lane wrote in his *New Yorker* review, that "the late Mr. Holmes, as preeminent in the trouser department as his namesake Sherlock had been in the cerebellum, was the leading pornographic star of his time," rumored "to have slept with fourteen thousand women, though not all on the same evening." But this movie is not exactly a sleeper.

Instead, *Wonderland* is about spectacular violence rather than spectacular sex. In fact, the film's central event is an investigation of the so-called "Wonderland Murders" in 1981, a repulsive multiple homicide case that took place on Wonderland Avenue in Los Angeles. John Holmes was one of the main suspects being investigated, a sorry junkie whose word could not be trusted and a has-been celebrity of sleaze. His main agenda seemed to be scoring and stealing drugs. The film follows his every move leading up to the murders he might or might not have committed. (Holmes was brought to trial, but acquitted the next year. He later died of AIDS complications in 1988.)

In the film Holmes spends time hanging out on Wonderland Avenue in Laurel Canyon with a strange assortment of low-lifes led by the hyperactive and presumably dangerous Ron Launius (Josh Lucas) and including Billy Deverell (Tim Blake Nelson) and ex-convict biker David Lind (actor

Dylan McDermott, cast against type). Holmes hatches a scheme for them to rob local crime kingpin and nightclub owner Eddie Nash (Eric Bogosian). Later on, he rats out his friends and helps Eddie take revenge.

As a result of the robbery and deception, five people are attacked on Wonderland Avenue and four of them are bludgeoned to death with lead pipes. David Lind survives, as does John Holmes. Both of them are interrogated by police detectives Sam Nico (Ted Levine) and Louis Cruz (Franky G.); each blames the other, but both are unreliable narrators. It is not the business of this film, however, to sort out the truth of the situation, but merely to exploit the ambiguity and the spectacular violence. Absolutely nothing is settled here, which makes the film appear to be merely a pointless stylistic exercise, directed flamboyantly by James Cox and written by Cox and others. "With its flashbacks, split-screen montages, decade-jumping soundtrack, sped-up action, and frequent shifts of light and color," A. O. Scott wrote in the *New York Times*, *Wonderland* "feels like *Law & Order* on crack." The *Washington Post* dismissed the film as being "overblown, overheated, overdirected, overacted, [and] overlong." Overstated, perhaps, but accurate on all counts.

The only characters presumably worth caring about in this film are the women in Holmes's life: Dawn Schiller (Kate Bosworth), a pathetic 15-year-old drifter who carries with her a purse and a pet Chihuahua; and Holmes's estranged wife, Sharon (Lisa Kudrow), a professional woman who hates what her husband represents but still seems to care about him and the younger woman, whom she seems to mother. Kudrow's "unglamorous, unsexy, [and] unfunny turn as a woman of solid virtue," in the words of *Washington Post* critic Stephen Hunter, is by far the film's "strongest performance." Three other actresses—Christina Applegate, Natasha Gregson Wagner, and Janeane Garofalo—are also in the film but tend to get lost amongst the clutter of the incoherent plot. All of the other characters, aside from the investigating cops, are "psychologically transparent" criminals and addicts, not developed in any interesting depth and not worth caring about. Val Kilmer, who played Jim Morrison memorably for Oliver Stone in *The Doors* (1991) is essentially wasted here, as is his character, John Holmes, all the way through this movie. 🎞

—*James M. Welsh*

John Holmes: Val Kilmer
Dawn Schiller: Kate (Catherine) Bosworth
Sharon Holmes: Lisa Kudrow
David Lind: Dylan McDermott
Eddie Nash: Eric Bogosian
Ron Launius: Josh(ua) Lucas

Susan Launius: Christina Applegate
Billy Deverell: Tim Blake Nelson
Sam Nico: Ted Levine
Barbara Richardson: Natasha Gregson Wagner
Joy Miller: Janeane Garofalo
Louis Cruz: Franky G.
Bill Ward: M.C. Gainey
Sally Hansen: Carrie Fisher
Greg Diles: Faizon Love

Origin: USA
Released: 2003
Production: Mike Paseornek, Holly Wiersma; released by Lions Gate Films
Directed by: James Cox
Written by: James Cox, Captain Mauzner, Todd Samovitz, D. Loriston Scott
Cinematography by: Michael Grady
Music by: Michael A. Levine
Sound: Steve Morrow
Editing: Jeff McEvoy
Art Direction: John R. Zachary
Costumes: Kte Healey
Production Design: Franco-Giacomo Carbone
MPAA rating: R
Running time: 99 minutes

Boxoffice. November, 2003, p. 97.
Chicago Sun-Times Online. October 17, 2003.
Entertainment Weekly. October 10, 2003, p. 101.
Los Angeles Times Online. January 26, 2003.
Los Angeles Times Online. October 3, 2003.
New York Times Online. September 7, 2003.
New York Times Online. October 3, 2003.
People. October 13, 2003, p. 32.
USA Today Online. October 3, 2003.
Variety Online. September 10, 2003.
Washington Post. October 17, 2003, p. WE47.

Wrong Turn

Wrong Turn . . . It's the last one you'll ever take.
—Movie tagline

Box Office: $15.4 million

Not that its potential audience would notice or care, but there was not a lot of pride behind the teen slash flick, *Wrong Turn*. The filmmakers didn't offer advance screenings to the press and the distributors of *Wrong Turn*, 20th Century Fox and Regency, took their names off the movie. Unfortunately, the actors in the film can't be afforded the same luxury.

Like similar movies that have come before, *Wrong Turn* involves good-looking teens, girls wearing skimpy clothing, and lots of gory deaths. If you're not a person who appreciates this particular formula, it's difficult to understand its appeal. Kevin M. Williams, who reviewed the film for the *Chicago Tribune* wrote, "There is something so lovely, so Darwinian about slasher flicks, even forgettable nonsense as *Wrong Turn*. The TV commercials make you anticipate seeing young, cute people getting murdered in the woods of West Virginia, and a choppin' and a hackin' we go."

It's doubtful that this film earned any fans in the West Virginia tourism department because it shows the state as a breeding ground for toothless, inbred murdering freaks. In the movie, Chris Finn (Desmond Harrington of *Ghost Ship*) is an attractive young medical student who is running late for a big job interview. The main freeway is backed up with a big traffic jam so he decides to take a back road. This is the "wrong turn."

As he's speeding on his way, he smacks into an SUV stopped in the middle of the road. He is unhurt, as are the five more attractive young people from the SUV. They tell Chris that they were stopped by some barbed wire that someone deliberately strung across the road. Since these kids are in a slasher flick, their first order of business is to separate. Newly single Jessie Burlingame (Eliza Dushku of *Buffy the Vampire Slayer*) and Chris walk with recently engaged couple, Carly (Emmanuelle Chriqui of *On the Line*) and Scott (Jeremy Sisto of *Six Feet Under*) to find a phone. (At least the filmmakers bothered to explain that cell phones aren't getting reception in the mountains.)

Evan (Kevin Zegars) and Francine (Lindy Booth) are the ones who decide to stay back, thus ensuring that their immediate future is not going to be so rosy. Further sealing their fate, the two decide to smoke pot and have sex. Of course they must be killed. Evan goes quickly. He is yanked away soundlessly offscreen. Francine has long enough to notice that he is gone, then she too is offed. She's grabbed by a big snorting guy who seems barely human. This guy and his buddies, the movie informs us, are the product of inbreeding. (As one critic pointed out, where are their womenfolk? It seems plausible that they would have difficulty finding dates.) So removed from humanness are these guys that they don't speak English but rather communicate in a series of grunts and hysterical laughs. They are supposedly mentally retarded, but they seem awfully clever in tracking down and outwitting groups of teens.

After Evan and Francine are killed, it's just a matter of waiting to see who will be next. The killing is so rote and emotionless, that it's easy to cold-heartedly start rooting for characters that you don't like to be the next to go. Carly would be a good candidate, but, alas, it is intelligent and talkative Scott who goes next. This is a pity because he is the only character who has any interesting lines. When Carly whines that she has to use the restroom and wants to go into a scary shack to do so, Scott says, "I need to remind you of a little movie called *Deliverance*."

Of course they go into the scary shack anyway and find lots of gross stuff in there. There are decapitated dolls all around and a pot of human body parts simmering on the stove. In the bathroom, Carly finds jars of human jaws and similar decor. Maybe using the restroom outside wouldn't be so gross after all. Most people would see this stuff and leave immediately, but the kids linger and poke around more, giving the freaky bad guys ample time to return. In the movie's creepiest scene, Chris and Jessie hide under the bed while one of the creepy guys saws off the leg of their dead friend, Francine. Francine's blood creeps along the floor and pools by their arms, while Jessie weeps noiselessly. Hey, that's entertainment.

The movie drags on, while we wait for Carly to be offed. We know that she is next because Jessie and Chris are the most attractive and have a budding romance going. While we wait for her demise, Chris gets a hurt leg, the kids get caught in a burning watchtower and they exhibit the ability to jump down 20 feet into a tree. All the while, they battle these inbreds, who—conveniently for the sequel—seem to be extremely difficult to kill. One of these freaks gets burned and an ax planted in his shoulder, but he seems like he's going to be okay.

The film was directed by Rob Schmidt (*Crime and Punishment in America*) and written by Alan McElroy (the poorly titled *Ecks vs. Sever*). These are not the most promising credentials, but horror fans were surely cheered by the fact that the film was produced by Stan Winston, the make-up artist who did *Aliens*, *Terminator 2*, and *Jurassic Park*. Unfortunately, the creatures in this film are much more scary when they remain unseen. When they eventually come into the light, they look like they are guys wearing rubber masks.

The studios were right about one thing: critics did not like the film. Lou Lumineck of the *New York Post* did not have high hopes for the film: "*Wrong Turn* is low-end schlock that will likely land with a dull thud in the video remainder bin before the frost is on the pumpkin." Wesley Morris of the *Boston Globe* wrote, "A stultifying blend of *The Texas Chainsaw Massacre*, boot camp, and maybe *The Blair Witch Project*, *Wrong Turn* is profoundly less than the sum of its influences." And C. W. Nevius of the *San Francisco Chronicle* concluded, "This is standard hack-and-giggle fare, with a few wisecracks mixed in with the gore."

—*Jill Hamilton*

CREDITS

Jessie Burlingame: Eliza Dushku
Scott: Jeremy Sisto
Carly: Emmanuelle Chriqui
Chris Finn: Desmond Harrington
Francine: Lindy Booth
Evan: Kevin Zegers
Three Finger: Julian Richings
One-Eye: Garry Robbins
One-Eye: Ted Clark
Halley: Yvonne Gaudry
Trooper: David Huband
Rich: Joel Harris
Old Man: Wayne Robson
Trucker: James Downing

Origin: USA
Released: 2003
Production: Erik Feig, Robert Kulzer, Stan Winston, Brian Gilbert; Summit Entertainment, Constantin Film, Newmarket Capital Group; released by 20th Century-Fox
Directed by: Rob Schmidt
Written by: Alan B. McElroy
Cinematography by: John Bartley
Music by: Elia Cmiral
Sound: David Lee
Music Supervisor: Randy Gerston
Editing: Michael Ross
Art Direction: Elis Lam
Costumes: Georgina Yarhl
Production Design: Alicia Keywan
MPAA rating: R
Running time: 85 minutes

 REVIEWS

Detroit Free Press. May 31, 2003, p. 2A.
Entertainment Weekly. June 13, 2003, p. 75.
Los Angeles Times Online. June 2, 2003.
New York Times Online. May 31, 2003.
San Francisco Chronicle. May 31, 2003, p. D1.
Variety Online. June 1, 2003.

 QUOTES

Scott (Jeremy Sisto): "We are never going into the woods again!"

X2: X-Men United (X-Men 2)

Evolution Continues.
—Movie tagline
The time has come for those who are different to stand united.
—Movie tagline
First, they were fighting for acceptance. Now, they're battling for survival.
—Movie tagline

 Box Office: $214.9 million

The film opens with a sonorous narration by Professor Charles Xavier (Patrick Stewart) before the credits: "Mutants. Since the discovery of their existence, they have been regarded with fear, suspicion, often hatred. Around the world the debate rages: Are mutants the next step in the evolutionary chain or simply a new species of humanity fighting for its share of the world? Either way, one fact has been historically proven: Sharing the world is not humanity's most defining attribute." And some humans (and mutants) are worse about sharing than others.

Then the action starts. Teleporting, blue-skinned Nightcrawler (Alan Cumming)—who also has a nifty tail and the ability to spring about like an acrobatic monkey on steroids—enters the White House and forces his way into the Oval Office. He grips a knife to kill President McKenna (Cotter Smith) before being shot by one of the Secret Service agents and disappearing into a puff of smoke. The knife he leaves behind has a ribbon that reads "Mutant Freedom Now."

The story then switches to Logan/Wolverine (Hugh Jackman) somewhere in the snowy reaches of Canada, looking at an apparently abandoned military base at Alkali Lake. This is where he was subjected to the experiments that gave him his adamantine skeleton and claws. But his mysterious past appears as elusive as ever. [Although the sequel might have taken some three years to reach the screen from *The X-Men*'s 2000 debut, this story is set only a few months later.]

Meanwhile, Jean Grey (Famke Janssen), Scott Summers/Cyclops (James Marsden), and Ororo Munroe/Storm (Halle Berry) are escorting a bunch of the younger mutants on a field trip to the natural history museum. Jean is having trouble with her powers—they're stronger than ever but harder to control. She feels that something terrible is about to happen. We also are subjected to the interplay between teens Marie/Rogue (Anna Paquin), good guy and would-be boyfriend Bobby Drake/Iceman (Shawn Ashmore), and the sullen troublemaker John Allerdyce/Pyro (Aaron Stanford).

Back at White House, the President is listening to the advice of former Colonel William Stryker (a smoothly menacing Brian Cox), who wants the President to approve an attack on a "mutant training facility" AKA Xavier's school. Also present at the meeting, and in opposition to Stryker, is Senator Kelly (Bruce Davison)—yes, he died in the first film but Mystique (Rebecca Romijn-Stamos) is still impersonating him. The President agrees to let Stryker go ahead as long as his mission is just to "enter, detain, question." He doesn't want any dead mutant children appearing on the six o'clock news. Stryker, of course, has more devious and lethal intentions.

Xavier has been using Cerebro (the machine that can mentally connect him to every human and mutant on the planet) to track the would-be mutant assassin and is sending Jean and Storm to Boston to seek him out. The gals are leaving just as Wolverine returns to the school. Wolverine is pining for Jean but she wants him to know that she and Scott are still a couple. This pining is too bad since the clawed one has more chemistry with the teenaged Rogue (who is ecstatic to have her protector back) than with the glum Grey. (And even more with Mystique, but that's another scene.)

Stryker comes to visit Magneto (Ian McKellen) in his plastic prison and drugs him to get him to tell Stryker everything that Magneto knows about Cerebro. Wolverine has been left behind at the school as a babysitter while Xavier and Scott also go to visit Magneto. Meanwhile, a suspicious Mystique has transformed herself into Stryker's mutant assistant Yuriko (Kelly Hu) in order to break into his office and discover his plans. She learns that Stryker's invasion of Xavier's school is intended to let him acquire Cerebro for his own purposes.

In Boston, Jean and Storm discover the German-accented, former circus performer Kurt Wagner/ Nightcrawler in an abandoned church. Nightcrawler is big on religion: He informs Storm that his intricate tattoos are a form of archaic language passed down by the archangel Gabriel. He's etched one for each of his supposed sins. Nightcrawler is also prone to reciting the rosary when agitated. He tells Jean that he remembers nothing about his attack on the President but he has the same mark on the back of his neck that Magneto has, the place where Stryker injected him with drugs. (When Jean reads Nightcrawler's mind, he remembers being tortured at the same lab where Wolverine was held prisoner.)

Xavier discovers that Magneto has told Stryker everything he knows about Cerebro but Xavier and Scott are captured by Stryker's men before they can tell any of the X team. Meanwhile, Stryker and his men execute a military assault on the school and capture some of the students. Others get away thanks to a series of tunnels while Wolverine battles the bad guys. And he also sees Stryker for the first

time in 15 years. Stryker gets the parts of Cerebro that he needs while Bobby, Rogue, Pyro, and Wolverine get away (in a brand-new metallic blue Mazda RX-8) and head towards Boston, which is where Bobby's unsuspecting family live.

Mystique manages to help free Magneto from his prison at last and the twosome decide to meet up (somehow) with their fellow mutants to defeat Stryker. Stryker has taken Xavier to his underground base at Alkali Lake and is using a neural inhibitor to prevent the professor from using his telepathic abilities. It turns out it's personal between them since Stryker's son Jason (Michael Reid MacKay) is a mutant and was once one of Xavier's students. Jason is a great illusionist and has the ability to project any kind of vision into one's mind. He tormented his parents when they couldn't accept his abilities and his mother eventually killed herself. Stryker blames all mutants for his personal tragedy.

Meanwhile, Bobby and company have shown up at his parents' house and Bobby has revealed he's a mutant. They don't take the news well and Bobby's resentful brother Ronny (James Kirk) calls the cops since the mutants are considered dangerous. When the police surround the house, Pyro uses his fire controlling abilities to attack them, leaving an appalled Rogue to use her abilities to stop *him*. Wolverine has managed to contact Storm and Jean and they come to the rescue (along with Nightcrawler) in the X plane. However, when they're finally airborne, the plane is attacked by a couple of fighter jets and Storm and Jean must both use their abilities to save everyone. But when the X plane nearly crashes, it's Magneto who prevents it. He explains that Stryker was once a military scientist who has decided to deal with the mutant problem once and for all by building a second Cerebro.

Before everyone heads off to Stryker's base to prevent disaster, various new teammates discuss their feelings: Nightcrawler wants to know why Mystique doesn't stay in a disguise all the time but she replies that she shouldn't have to just to be accepted. Wolverine makes his feelings clear to Jean but she tells him: "Girls only flirt with a dangerous guy, they don't take them home. They marry the good guy." She doesn't believe him when Wolverine says "I could be the good guy." And shape-shifting Mystique decides to mess with Wolverine's mind by invading his tent disguised as a lascivious Jean, and then shifting into Rogue and Storm. The young Pyro is intrigued by Magneto and says of his own abilities: "I can only manipulate fire. I can't create it." Magneto replies: "You are a god among insects. Never let anyone tell you differently."

Stryker's base is located under a dam and the entrance is through a spillway. Mystique transforms herself into Wolverine in order to enter and manages to seal herself into Stryker's command center to learn his operations. The others enter and head in various directions: Wolverine goes after Stryker, Storm and Nightcrawler go after the imprisoned mutant children, and Jean tries to find Scott, while Magneto and Mystique go after Xavier. Rogue, Bobby, and Pyro have been left behind with the X plane.

Stryker is using a crippled Jason to control Xavier by projecting himself in the form of a helpless little girl who encourages Xavier to use Cerebro to locate all the mutants. Stryker knows that Xavier's mental link can kill them if he concentrates enough. When Jean finds Scott, he's been drugged by Stryker and attacks her. She uses so much force to repel him that she causes a breach in the dam and water begins to enter. Wolverine has found the lab where he was experimented on and a vat of liquid adamantine. He has a fight with Yuriko, who also has an adamantine skeleton, and he discovers that each of her fingertips sprout nine-inch nails, which is probably why her mutant name is Lady Deathstrike. Wolverine manages to defeat her by shooting her full of the liquid adamantine, which then hardens.

When Magneto discovers Jason is manipulating Xavier's mind, he reconfigures things so that Xavier is now finding all humans instead of mutants and leaves his old friend to destroy them. Jean senses what's happening: "Magneto's reversed Cerebro. It's not targeting mutants—it's targeting everyone else." Nightcrawler teleports himself and Storm into the chamber where they find the little girl alone. Storm knows she's an illusion and forces Jason to stop while Nightcrawler rescues Xavier.

Wolverine has found Stryker trying to get away in his helicopter. He prevents him and tries to get some answers about his past: "Who am I?" Stryker replies: "You are just a failed experiment. . . . You were an animal then, you're an animal now. I just gave you claws." Logan ties Stryker up and heads back to rescue the others as the dam begins to burst.

Magneto and Mystique come upon the helicopter and use it to escape, taking Pyro with them (and leaving Stryker behind). Wolverine has managed to get everyone out of the base but now the helicopter is gone. The inexperienced Rogue pilots the X plane to where everyone is but they lose power and can't take off as a wall of water heads their way. Jean leaves the plane and uses her powers to stop the water from flooding over them and give the plane power enough to take off. But then she's lost in the flood waters. (In the comic books, Jean will be resurrected, appropriately enough, as the Phoenix.)

Xavier has them fly to Washington, where the President is about to give a press conference. He shows the President Stryker's secret files and persuades him not to repeat past mistakes but to realize that mutants are here to stay and humans and mutants must learn to survive together. Later, at the school, Xavier, Scott, and Logan mourn Jean even as the students come in for their lessons and things try to go back to normal. Over the ending narration, Jean's voice is heard: "Mutation: it is the key to our evolution. This process is slow. . . . But every few hundred millennia, evolution leaps forward." Nice set-up to the eventual *X-Men 3*.

X2 is as packed with characters and stories as the first film, so some naturally fall by the wayside. Scott/Cyclops get short shrift except for acknowledging his love for Jean and his rivalry with Wolverine. Wolverine, probably the most charismatic of the characters both in and out of the comic books, gets additional screen time and Jackman is more than capable of handling the action and the emotional elements of his role. Jean's amazingly boring for a woman in a leather catsuit but Storm gets to use her abilities a bit more and even express a passing personal interest in Nightcrawler. Cumming, along with Romijn-Stamos, must be given praise for simply surviving their extensive makeup requirements but both play intriguing characters. Cox is appropriately meglomaniacal and righteously menacing while McKellen is sly and Stewart calm and grave.

The sequel earned a healthy $85.8 million at the box office during its opening weekend and director Bryan Singer not only introduced new characters but showed rather obvious set-ups ready to be explored in a second sequel. It will be interesting to see how many of his cast decide to return; Wolverine may be the focus of either a separate film or the next *X-Men* adventure if Jackman is available. Since Singer had a healthy increase in his budget, the sequel's action sequences are bolder and bigger with Wolverine's battle against Stryker's men at the school a highlight. Rather like those other heavily-populated franchise pictures—*The Lord of the Rings* and *The Matrix*—it's sometimes hard to follow just who is doing what to whom and why. It's best to have some previous knowledge than to go in cold to this action viewing experience.

—*Christine Tomassini*

CREDITS

Professor Charles Xavier: Patrick Stewart
Eric Lensherr/Magneto: Ian McKellen
Jean Grey: Famke Janssen
Logan/Wolverine: Hugh Jackman
Scott Summers/Cyclops: James Marsden
Ororo Munroe/Storm: Halle Berry
Mystique: Rebecca Romijn-Stamos
Marie/Rogue: Anna Paquin
Bobby Drake/Iceman: Shawn Ashmore
General William Stryker: Brian Cox
Kurt Wagner/Nightcrawler: Alan Cumming
Yuriko Oyama/Lady Deathstrike: Kelly Hu
Senator Kelly: Bruce Davison
John Allerdyce/Pyro: Aaron Stanford
Kitty Pryde: Katie Stuart
President McKenna: Cotter Smith

Peter Rasputin/Colossus: Daniel Cudmore
Lyman: Peter Wingfield
Jason Stryker: Michael Reid MacKay
Little Girl: Keely Purvis
Mrs. Drake: Jill Teed
Mr. Drake: Alf Humphreys
Ronny Drake: James Kirk

Origin: USA
Released: 2003
Production: Lauren Shuler-Donner, Ralph Winter;
Marvel Enterprises, Donners' Company, Bad Hat Harry;
released by 20th Century-Fox
Directed by: Bryan Singer
Written by: Michael Dougherty, Daniel P. "Dan" Harris
Cinematography by: Newton Thomas (Tom) Sigel
Music by: John Ottman
Sound: Rob Young
Editing: John Ottman
Art Direction: Helen Jarvis
Costumes: Louise Mingenbach
Production Design: Guy Hendrix Dyas
MPAA rating: PG-13
Running time: 134 minutes

REVIEWS

American Cinematographer. April, 2003, p. 36.
Chicago Sun-Times Online. May 2, 2003.
Detroit Free Press. May 2, 2003, p. D1.
Detroit News. May 2, 2003, p. E1.
Entertainment Weekly. October 25, 2002, p. 46.
Los Angeles Times Online. May 2, 2003.
Los Angeles Times Online. May 4, 2003.
New York Times Online. May 2, 2003.
New York Times Online. May 5, 2003.
People. May 12, 2003, p. 37.
San Francisco Chronicle. May 2, 2003, p. D1.
Sight and Sound. June, 2003, p. 59.
USA Today Online. May 2, 2003.
Variety Online. April 28, 2003.
Washington Post. May 2, 2003, p. WE51.

QUOTES

Professor Xavier (Patrick Stewart) to the amnesiac Wolverine (Hugh Jackman): "Sometimes the mind needs to discover things for itself."

Mrs. Drake (Jill Teed) to Bobby (Shawn Ashmore): "Have you ever tried not being a mutant?"

Storm (Halle Berry): "Sometimes anger can help you survive."
Nightcrawler (Alan Cumming): "So can faith."

XX/XY

There's no place for honesty in a healthy relationship.
—Movie tagline

In the funniest yet oddest scene in first-time writer-director Austin Chick's *XX/XY*, Coles Burroughs (Mark Ruffalo), a failed independent filmmaker, finds himself confronted by a man who long ago saw his one and only film and hated it. Believing that Coles should be held accountable despite the fact that he made no money from the project, the man asks for and receives a refund. It is an amusing but ludicrous scene since no filmmaker would agree to such a preposterous request. But if filmmakers were forced to give refunds to disgruntled moviegoers, Chick himself would probably face a few for *XX/XY*. His unfocused storytelling and lazy characterizations would most likely elicit a feeling of indifference, if not anger and frustration, in an audience expecting to see a film touted as a serious exploration of contemporary relationships. Not much happens among the central characters, and the thin story hinges on a protagonist who never figures out what he really wants and finally does not grow or even learn anything.

The movie begins in the fall of 1993 at Sarah Lawrence College, where Coles first encounters the beautiful Sam (Maya Stange) on the subway. They coyly avoid making eye contact and then later meet at a party, but before they have barely gotten to know each other even a little bit, they are in bed together, and Sam has invited her wild friend, Thea (Kathleen Robertson), to join them for a ménage à trois. Obviously uncomfortable, Sam gets out of bed first; perhaps she has feelings for Coles and does not like sharing him with her friend, although, as in so much of the film, the characters' true emotions are never spelled out very clearly. The incident, however, does not stop the three from remaining friends, and Coles and Sam even become a couple of sorts, with Thea hanging out on the perimeter of their relationship.

Although Coles and Sam are attracted to each other, their relationship is based in non-communication. No matter how hard she tries to get Coles to open up about his feelings and ambitions, he remains vague about what he wants. Ultimately, he is just one of those stereotypical guys who cannot commit to one woman or honestly face himself, choosing instead to deflect inquiries with a smile and an ironic reply. When Sam playfully asks him what he wants to be when he grows up, he deadpans, "I'm never growing up," which literalizes what is already obvious about the character, that he is in a state of arrested adolescence.

Just as murky as Coles's motivation is Chick's filmmaking, which is disjointed and random in this early section as he jumps from scene to scene without telling a coherent story or developing his characters. For example, Coles, Sam, and Thea dance around in the street and shoot off fireworks in a silly sequence that was probably more fun to shoot than it is to watch. Moreover, Chick indulges a penchant for camera tricks that reek of a first-time director showing off. From the freeze-frame to the jump cut, slow motion and fast, Chick dabbles in different filmic styles that serve no thematic purpose—the same way Coles dabbles in women just because he can.

Mistrust and betrayal define Coles and Sam's relationship. Both cheat on each other, but when Sam walks in on Coles and Thea having sex, it is too much for her to bear, and she ends the relationship. The film then shifts to the present day. Coles is living with his girlfriend of five years, Claire (Petra Wright), an attractive woman who seems too mature for him. Having abandoned his dreams as a filmmaker, Coles is working as an animator for an advertising firm and is creating an embarrassing commercial that features a dancing taco. (It is, of course, a clichéd, shorthand way of suggesting that a character has sold out his creative ideals by having him debase his talents in advertising and work for an unctuous boss he despises.)

Coles bumps into Sam, and the old spark is reignited, but since their original relationship was marked more by lust than any deep emotional connection like love, it is hard to muster up much interest in their reunion. Sam has been in touch with Thea, and, in a funny twist, it turns out that the cocaine-snorting, wild girl of the group is married to a restaurateur and has become the most settled and the most successful.

The scenes of the old friends reconnecting are not very revealing. When Coles and Claire go out to dinner with Thea and her husband, Miles (David Thornton), and Sam and her young boyfriend, the highlight of the dinner is Sam's boyfriend showing off his knowledge of the Old English origin of the word "rife," which Coles finds rude. But as in so much of the movie, a seemingly big issue at the moment ends up meaning nothing, especially since Sam soon dumps her boyfriend and we never see him again. The only significant outcome of the dinner is that Claire picks up on the feeling that Coles is still attracted to Sam.

Later, Sam asks Coles to help her pick out a new car, and Coles goes with her on a test-drive. He drives the car like a wild man, something no one would do in real life, but perhaps the scene suggests that he test-drives a car the way he recklessly test-drives the women in his life. Afterwards, they give in to temptation and have sex in his living room but are jolted out of the moment when they hear a noise. Claire comes in moments later, and it is clear that she can sense what has happened, but nobody confronts what everyone is thinking.

Ultimately, however, this potentially explosive love triangle just sputters along in an extended sequence at Thea's

beach house, where she has invited everyone for the weekend. When Sam does not show up, Coles confides to Thea that he is in love with Sam, although it is never made clear why, which makes it impossible for us to feel that anything is really at stake. Coles and Sam exhibit very little chemistry, but maybe she represents the carefree youth that he cannot have living with the more stable, adult Claire, who actually comes across as more of a mother figure to the childish Coles.

Mark Ruffalo gave an incredible breakthrough performance three years ago as the ne'er-do-well brother in *You Can Count on Me*. *XX/XY* represents a step sideways more than a step forward for him. He is playing yet another adult shunning grownup responsibilities, but this character is not nearly as well written. Moreover, Ruffalo is running the risk of repeating himself, even in the details of his performance, relying on the same mannerisms and facial expressions to suggest a young fellow out of sorts with the world around him and always trying to hide from himself.

Instead of building to a climax, the already limp story finally fizzles out. Sam appears at the beach house, and, in a completely arbitrary plot turn that makes no sense, announces that she just married the man she had been engaged to in London a short time ago. Her decision settles Coles's dilemma for him but takes away his chance to choose for himself. Realizing that Claire is all he has left, he begs her to marry him (just one more example of Coles not having a clue as to what he wants). Claire, it turns out, has known everything about him and Sam, and, when she confronts him, she scolds him as a mother would a little boy who has to be put in his place. She had seen Coles and Sam having sex that day in the living room but walked away, hoping his betrayal meant that he was finally making a choice and would be honest with her. But ultimately he did not make a choice—Sam did—and Claire, realizing that Coles is just settling for her instead of choosing her, now has been reduced to a mere consolation prize.

But in the last scene, a pretentious slow-motion shot, as Coles watches Sam leave the house with her new husband, Claire closes the door. It is fitting that, in a film in which so many characters are, metaphorically speaking, keeping doors open, the climactic act is the shutting of a door and consequently the closing of a chapter in Coles's life. Claire, it seems, has made her decision to accept Coles, but, like a mother, will have to take a firm hand to keep him in line and force him into adulthood. Why a smart, attractive woman such as Claire would settle for Coles is another of the film's infuriating puzzles, unless she simply enjoys mothering a wayward adolescent.

The very title *XX/XY* suggests grandiose ambitions—this is a film with supposedly so much to say about men and women that the characters are emblematic of their respective genders the same way the chromosomes are. According to the production notes, Chick also liked the way the letters looked graphically, a statement that just happens to sum up his main problem as a filmmaker—his tendency to focus on surfaces when he could be digging deeper. If the screenplay offered fresh insights into the psychology of a man in prolonged adolescence, *XX/XY* could have been a provocative film. But Chick is as indecisive about what he wants to say as Coles is about which woman he should choose, and, in trotting out the familiar clichés about men who refuse to grow up and the women who love them anyway, Chick ends up saying nothing new about modern relationships.

—*Peter N. Chumo II*

CREDITS

Coles: Mark Ruffalo
Sam: Maya Stange
Thea: Kathleen Robertson
Claire: Petra Wright
Miles: David Thornton
Sid: Kel O'Neill
Jonathan: Joshua Spafford
Nick: Zach Shaffer

Origin: USA
Released: 2002
Production: Mitchell B. Robbins, Isen Robbins, Aimee Schoof; released by IFC Films
Directed by: Austin Chick
Written by: Austin Chick
Cinematography by: Uta Briesewitz
Sound: Jose Torres
Music Supervisor: Lynne Geller
Editing: William A. Anderson, Pete Beaudreau
Art Direction: Terrence Dunlop
Costumes: Sarah Beers
Production Design: Judy Becker
MPAA rating: R
Running time: 91 minutes

REVIEWS

Boxoffice. April, 2002, p. 172.
Boxoffice. March, 2003, p. 21.
Chicago Sun-Times Online. April 25, 2003.
Entertainment Weekly. April 18, 2003, p. 47.
Los Angeles Times Online. April 11, 2003.
New York Times Online. April 11, 2003.
Variety. February 11, 2002, p. 46.
Washington Post. April 25, 2003, p. C5.

QUOTES

Sam (May Stange) asks Coles (Mark Ruffalo): "Where are we going? What do you want out of this?"

Zus & Zo
(This and That)
(Hotel Paraiso)

A comedy about love, family and other discomforts.
—Movie tagline

Imitation may be the sincerest form of flattery, but Woody Allen couldn't be too pleased with *Zus & Zo*, only the latest film farce to ape the Allen style. Like several Allen films, *Zus & Zo* (which translates as "This and That") models itself after Anton Chekhov's *Three Sisters*, with a narrative that could have been lugubrious but turns out sitcomic. Writer-director Paula van der Oest bases her tale in contemporary Holland, where three sisters, Wanda (Anneke Blok), Michelle (Sylvia Poorta), and Sonja (Monic Hendrickx) join forces against their gay brother, Nino (Jacob Derwig), when they learn he plans to marry the decidedly female Bo (Halina Reign).

The sisters try to prevent the nuptials, not out of concern with Nino's future happiness, or confusion over his sexual orientation, but rather out of fear of a clause in their father's will that allows Nino to sell off the family's beach-front hotel in Portugal if he gets married. For Wanda, the hotel is the place where she dreams of having an art show. For Sonja, a journalist, the hotel represents a getaway spot to rekindle her troubled marriage to the philandering Hugo (Theu Boermans). For Michelle, the hotel creates a peaceful refuge from her tiring work as a humanitarian foundation director.

Nino's past desire for TV chef Felix Delicious (Pieter Embrechts) only helps the sisters' scheme to undermine the wedding, though one plan that backfires places Hugo in the position of seducing Bo. In the end, the principals get what they want (more or less), but not without a lot of crying and reconciliation.

The critics were uniformly unkind to this light retread of Woody's terrain. Bill Muller of the *Arizona Republic* focused on the "profoundly unlikable characters doing selfish, underhanded things, all the while generating nary a giggle." Perhaps Muller would prefer Allen's *Hannah and Her Sisters* (1986), where most of the characters exhibited guilt over their transgressions, though it should be noted that Allen's classic three-sister comedy also had an occasional attack of the cutes.

V.A. Musetto of the *New York Post* gave the film one star—out of a four-star rating—and added, "The Dutch entry for the foreign-language Oscar, *Zus & Zo* proves that dumb sex comedies aren't restricted to Hollywood. In fact, English-language rights to the cliché-ridden story have already been sold. I expect to read any day now that Jennifer Lopez and the ever-obnoxious Hugh Grant will star."

Indeed, what *Zus & Zo* shares with Hollywood (and more recent Woody Allen films, too) is a lack of inspiration mixed with a slickly professional veneer. It may even surprise those who've avoided the film—because of the many negative reviews—that *Zus & Zo* is quite well made, from Bert Pot's sturdy widescreen camerawork to Harry Ammerlaan's colorful production design to Fons Merkies' jaunty score.

What is missing, sadly, is any kind of an original story (or even a formula story with a few original twists). *Four Weddings and a Funeral* and *My Best Friend's Wedding* were both overrated films of this type but seem fresh and charming by comparison. Further, one could forgive the selfishness of the characters more if they were funnier or if they received a better comeuppance, but Paula van der Oest seems content with relying on the story conflict to provide both belly laughs and touching sentiment. Somehow, in the process, she turns her characters into caricatures from a pre-enlightened era, despite respectable work from the ensemble cast (so much for the idea of a woman making a more feminist or less homophobic version of a Woody Allen movie).

In the end, *Zus & Zo*'s bad reviews and poor box office may hurt the distribution of future, hopefully better, sex farces, which is too bad, though there is no denying the hollowness of the particular venture. With so many good little films that never make it to the big screen, one has to wonder why *Zus & Zo* was "picked up" at all. Does the film industry really believe that a professional "look" is all that matters? Yes, some funeral homes do wonders with dressing up corpses, but everyone knows the bodies are still dead.

—*Eric Monder*

CREDITS

Michelle: Sylvia Poorta
Wanda: Anneke Blok
Sonja: Monic Hendrickx
Nino: Jacob Derwig
Bo: Halina Reijn
Hugo: Theu Boermans
Jan: Jaap Spijkers
Felix Delicious: Pieter Embrechts
Mother: Annet Nieuwenhuyzen

Origin: Netherlands
Language: Dutch
Released: 2001
Production: Jacqueline de Goeij; Filmprodukties De Luwte; released by Lifesize Entertainment
Directed by: Paula van der Oest
Written by: Paula van der Oest
Cinematography by: Bert Pot
Music by: Fons Merkies
Sound: Ben Zijlstra
Editing: Sander Vos
Costumes: Mariella Kallenberg
Production Design: Harry Ammerlaan
MPAA rating: Unrated
Running time: 100 minutes

REVIEWS

Arizona Republic Online. June 13, 2003.
Film Journal International Online. February, 2003.
New York Post Online. February 7, 2003.
New York Times Online. February 7, 2003.
Variety Online. October 12, 2001.

AWARDS AND NOMINATIONS

Nomination:
Oscars 2002: Foreign Film.

List of Awards

Academy Awards

Film: *The Lord of the Rings: The Return of the King*

Animated Film: *Finding Nemo*

Director: Peter Jackson (*The Lord of the Rings: The Return of the King*)

Actor: Sean Penn (*Mystic River*)

Actress: Charlize Theron (*Monster*)

Supporting Actor: Tim Robbins (*Mystic River*)

Supporting Actress: Renee Zellweger (*Cold Mountain*)

Original Screenplay: Sofia Coppola (*Lost in Translation*)

Adapted Screenplay: Phillippa Boyens, Peter Jackson, Frances Walsh (*The Lord of the Rings: The Return of the King*)

Cinematography: Russell Boyd (*Master and Commander: The Far Side of the World*)

Editing: Jamie Selkirk (*The Lord of the Rings: The Return of the King*)

Art Direction: Grant Major, Dan Hennah, Alan Lee (*The Lord of the Rings: The Return of the King*)

Visual Effects: Jim Rygiel, Joe Letteri, Randall William Cook, Alex Funke (*The Lord of the Rings: The Return of the King*)

Sound: Christopher Boyes, Michael Semanick, Michael Hedges, Hammond Peek (*The Lord of the Rings: The Return of the King*)

Makeup: Richard Taylor, Peter King (*The Lord of the Rings: The Return of the King*)

Costume Design: Ngila Dickson (*The Lord of the Rings: The Return of the King*)

Original Score: Howard Shore (*The Lord of the Rings: The Return of the King*)

Original Song: "Into the West" (Frances Walsh, Howard Shore, Annie Lennox, *The Lord of the Rings: The Return of the King*)

Foreign Language Film: *Les Invasions barberes (The Barbarian Invasions)*

Documentary, Feature: *Fog of War: Eleven Lessons from the Life of Robert S. McNamara*

Directors Guild of America Award

Director: Peter Jackson (*The Lord of the Rings: The Return of the King*)

Writers Guild of America Awards

Original Screenplay: Sofia Coppola (*Lost in Translation*)

Adapted Screenplay: Shari Springer Berman, Robert Pulcini (*American Splendor*)

Golden Globes

Film, Drama: *The Lord of the Rings: The Return of the King*

Film, Musical or Comedy: *Lost in Translation*

Director: Peter Jackson (*The Lord of the Rings: The Return of the King*)

Actor, Drama: Sean Penn (*Mystic River*)

Actor, Musical or Comedy: Bill Murray (*Lost in Translation*)

Actress, Drama: Charlize Theron (*Monster*)

Actress, Musical or Comedy: Diane Keaton (*Something's Gotta Give*)

Supporting Actor: Tim Robbins (*Mystic River*)

Supporting Actress: Renee Zellweger (*Cold Mountain*)

Screenplay: Sofia Coppola (*Lost in Translation*)

Score: Howard Shore (*The Lord of the Rings: The Return of the King*)

Song: "Into the West" (Howard Shore, Fran Walsh, Annie Lennox; *The Lord of the Rings: The Return of the King*)

Foreign Language Film: *Osama*

Independent Spirit Awards

Film: *Lost in Translation*

First Film: *Monster*

Director: Sofia Coppola (*Lost in Translation*)

Debut Performance: Nikki Reed (*Thirteen*)

Actor: Bill Murray (*Lost in Translation*)

Actress: Charlize Theron (*Monster*)

Supporting Actor: Djimon Hounsou (*In America*)

Supporting Actress: Shohreh Aghdashloo (*House of Sand and Fog*)

Screenplay: Sofia Coppola (*Lost in Translation*)

First Screenplay: Thomas McCarthy (*The Station Agent*)

Cinematography: Declan Quinn (*In America*)

Foreign Language Film: *Whale Rider*

Documentary: *The Fog of War: Eleven Lessons from the Life of Robert S. McNamara*

Los Angeles Film Critics Awards

Film: *American Splendor*

Director: Peter Jackson (*The Lord of the Rings: The Return of the King*)

Actor: Bill Murray (*Lost in Translation*)

Actress: Naomi Watts (*21 Grams*)

Supporting Actor: Bill Nighy (*AKA, I Capture the Castle, Lawless Heart, Love Actually*)

Supporting Actress: Shohreh Aghdashloo (*House of Sand and Fog*)

Screenplay: Shari Springer Berman, Robert Pulcini (*American Splendor*)

Cinematography: Eduardo Serra (*Girl With a Pearl Earring*)

Score: Benoit Charest, Mathieu Chedid (*The Triplets of Belleville*)

Animated Film: *The Triplets of Belleville*

Foreign Language Film: *Man on a Train*

Documentary: *The Fog of War: Eleven Lessons from the Life of Robert S. McNamara*

National Board of Review Awards

Film: *Mystic River*

Director: Edward Zwick (*The Last Samurai*)

Actor: Sean Penn (*Mystic River, 21 Grams*)

Actress: Diane Keaton (*Something's Gotta Give*)

Supporting Actor: Alec Baldwin (*The Cooler*)

Supporting Actress: Patricia Clarkson (*Pieces of April, The Station Agent*)

Foreign Language Film: *The Barbarian Invasions*

Documentary: *The Fog of War: Eleven Lessons from the Life of Robert S. McNamara*

National Society of Film Critics Awards

Film: *American Splendor*

Director: Clint Eastwood (*Mystic River*)

Actor: Bill Murray (*Lost in Translation*)

Actress: Charlize Theron (*Monster*)

Supporting Actor: Peter Sarsgaard (*Shattered Glass*)

Supporting Actress: Patricia Clarkson (*Pieces of April, The Station Agent*)

Cinematography: Russell Boyd (*Master and Commander: The Far Side of the World*)

Foreign Language Film: *The Man Without a Past*

New York Film Critics Awards

Film: *The Lord of the Rings: The Return of the King*

Director: Sofia Coppola (*Lost in Translation*)

Actor: Bill Murray (*Lost in Translation*)

Actress: Hope Davis (*American Splendor, The Secret Lives of Dentists*)

Supporting Actor: Eugene Levy (*A Mighty Wind*)

Supporting Actress: Shohreh Aghdashloo (*House of Sand and Fog*)

Screenplay: Craig Lucas (*The Secret Lives of Dentists*)

Cinematography: Harris Savides (*Elephant, Gerry*)

Foreign Language Film: *City of God*

Documentary: *Capturing the Friedmans*

Animated Film: *The Triplets of Belleville*

Screen Actors Guild Awards

Actor: Johnny Depp (*Pirates of the Caribbean: The Curse of the Black Pearl*)

Actress: Charlize Theron (*Monster*)

Supporting Actor: Tim Robbins (*Mystic River*)

Supporting Actress: Renee Zellweger (*Cold Mountain*)

Ensemble Cast: *The Lord of the Rings: The Return of the King*

Obituaries

Rod Amateau (December 20, 1923–June 29, 2003). Born in New York City, the writer, director, and producer moved to Los Angeles with his family when he was 13. He began his career as a staff writer for CBS radio and was later hired by 20th Century Fox. Amateau co-wrote and made his directorial debut with 1952's *The Bushwhackers* and also directed *Monsoon* the same year. He wrote *Hook, Line & Sinker* (1969); directed *The Statue* (1970); wrote and directed *Pussycat, Pussycat, I Love You* (1970); co-wrote, directed, and produced *Where Does It Hurt?* (1972); and co-wrote, directed, and produced *The Garbage Pail Kids Movie* (1987). Amateau also worked extensively in television, including *The George Burns and Gracie Allen Show, Private Secretary, The Many Loves of Dobie Gillis, Mister Ed, The Patty Duke Show, My Mother the Car,* and *The Dukes of Hazzard.*

Royce Applegate (December 25, 1939–January 1, 2003). Born in Midwest City, Oklahoma, Applegate was a veteran character actor of film and television, including his co-starring role as Chief Manilow Crocker in the 1993–96 TV series *seaQuest DSV.* Screen credits include *Splash; History of the World: Part I; The Getaway; Gettysburg; Gods and Generals; O Brother, Where Art Thou?; The Rookie;* and *Talking in Your Sleep.*

George Axelrod (June 9, 1922–June 21, 2003). The writer was born in New York City and found work in summer stock productions as a stage manager and actor. He wrote scripts for radio and television after serving in World War II and found success as a playwright with *The Seven Year Itch, Will Success Spoil Rock Hunter?* and *Goodbye Charlie,* all of which were later filmed for the screen. Axelrod wrote the screenplay for 1956's *Bus Stop* and received an Academy Award nomination for 1961's *Breakfast at Tiffany's.* He was also the screenwriter and co-producer of 1962's *The Manchurian Candidate.* Axelrod also wrote and directed *Lord Love a Duck* (1966) and *The Secret Life of an American Wife* (1968). In 1971, Axelrod published his memoirs, *Where Am I Now When I Need Me?*

Alan Bates (February 17, 1934–December 27, 2003). Born in Allestree, Derbyshire, England, the actor studied at the Royal Academy of Dramatic Arts. After serving in the Royal Air Force, Bates made his stage debut in 1955 and later joined the English Stage Company where he had his first success with John Osborne's *Look Back in Anger* (1956). Bates made his film debut in 1960's *The Entertainer.* Other screen credits included *Whistle Down the Wind* (1961); *A Kind of Loving* (1962); *Zorba the Greek* (1964); *Georgy Girl* (1966); *King of Hearts* (1966); *Far from the Madding Crowd* (1967); *The Fixer* (1968), for which Bates received an Oscar nomination; *Women in Love* (1969); *The Go-Between* (1971); *Butley* (1973); *An Unmarried Woman* (1978); *The Rose* (1979); *An Englishman Abroad* (1983); *Hamlet* (1990); *Gosford Park* (2001); *The Mothman Prophecies* (2002); *The Sum of All Fears* (2002); *Evelyn* (2002); and *The Statement* (2003). Bates also continued his successful stage career, appearing in some 60 productions, and received Tony awards for *Butley* (1972) and *Fortune's Fool* (2002).

George Baxt (June 11, 1923–June 28, 2003). The novelist and screenwriter was born in Brooklyn, New York. After working as a casting agent, Baxt moved to London in the mid-1950s to work on the television series *Sword of Freedom.* His first screenplay was 1960's *City of the Dead* (released in the U.S. as *Horror Hotel*). Other screen credits included *Circus of Horrors* (1960), *The Shadow of the Cat* (1961), *Payroll* (1962), and *Night of the Eagle* released as *Burn, Witch, Burn* in the U.S. (1962). After returning to the U.S., Baxt published the first in a series of Pharoah Love detective novels, 1966's *A Queer Kind of Death.* He also wrote a series of mysteries featuring celebrities, beginning with 1984's *The Dorothy Parker Murder Case.*

Earl Bellamy (March 11, 1917–November 30, 2003). Born in Minneapolis, Minnesota, the director's family moved to Hollywood in 1920. After high school, Bellamy began working at Columbia Studios, eventually becoming an assistant director. His first directorial credit was 1955's *Seminole Uprising* and among Bellamy's other credits were *Blackjack Ketchum, Desperado, Incident at Phantom Hill,* and *Fluffy.* Bellamy was also a prolific television director with more than 1,600 episodic credits, including *Wagon Train, Rawhide, Daniel Boone, The Virginian, McHale's Navy, Leave It to Beaver, I Spy, The Mod Squad, Starsky and Hutch, Hart to Hart,* and *M*A*S*H.*

Fred W. Berger (July 9, 1908–May 23, 2003). Born in New York City, Berger's career as a film and television editor spanned almost 60 years. He attended the University of Michigan and entered the brokerage business, transferring to Los Angeles in 1930. At the suggestion of his brother-in-law, film director/editor Eddie Mann, Berger entered the film industry as an assistant editor at Walter Wanger Productions in 1937. He received his first credit as an editor at Paramount for the Hopalong Cassidy western, *False Colors* (1943). Berger edited some 40 films and received an Academy Award nomination for *The Hot Rock* (1972). Berger was an early editor for television beginning in the late 1940s, including four years of *Gunsmoke* and 11 years on *Death Valley Days*. He received a 1975 Emmy for his work on *M*A*S*H*, which he edited from 1972 to 1976. Berger's last work as an editor was the TV movie *Dallas: J.R. Returns* (1996). Fred Berger was an original member of the Editors Guild and a founding member of the American Cinema Editors, from which he received the Career Achievement Award in 1997.

Lyle Bettger (February 22, 1915–September 24, 2003). Born in Philadelphia, Pennsylvania, the actor was frequently cast as the heavy in a series of supporting roles. Bettger made his film debut with *No Man of Her Own* (1950) and was also featured in *Union Station, The Greatest Show on Earth, Gunfight at the O.K. Corral,* and *Nevada Smith.* Bettger starred in the 1950s NBC crime series *The Court of Last Resort.*

Mel Bourne (February 22, 1923–January 14, 2003). The production designer, who was born in Chicago, Illinois, was nominated for three Academy Awards for art direction for *Interiors* (1978), *The Natural* (1984), and *The Fisher King* (1991). Besides *Interiors,* Bourne collaborated with director Woody Allen on *Annie Hall, Manhattan, Stardust Memories, A Midsummer Night's Sex Comedy, Zelig,* and *Broadway Danny Rose.* Bourne's other film credits included *F/X, Cocktail, Indecent Proposal,* and *Fatal Attraction.*

Stan Brakhage (January 4, 1933–March 9, 2003). A leading figure in American experimental cinema, Brakhage made nearly 400 films ranging in length from nine seconds to four hours, beginning in the early 1950s. He was born Robert Sanders in a Kansas City, Missouri, orphanage and adopted by the Brakhages, who named him James Stanley. He made his first film, *Interim,* in 1952. Films included *Desistfilm* (1955); *Anticipation of the Night* (1958); *Window Water Baby Moving* (1959); *Mothlight* (1963); *Dog Star Man* (1964), which is on the Library of Congress's National Film Registry; *23rd Psalm* (1966); *The Act of Seeing With One's Own Eyes* (1971); and *The Text of Light* (1974).

Jonathan Brandis (April 13, 1976–November 12, 2003). Born in Danbury, Connecticut, the actor began his career as a model at the age of two, later doing commercials and appearing in the daytime series *One Life to Live.* He became a teen heartthrob on the series *seaQuest DSV,* which ran from 1993 to 1995. Film credits included *The NeverEnding Story II: The Next Chapter, Sidekicks, Ladybugs, Stephen King's It, Outside Providence, The Year That Trembled,* and *Puerto Vallarta Squeeze.* The actor committed suicide by hanging.

Charles Bronson (November 3, 1921–August 30, 2003). Born Charles Buchinsky, the tough-guy actor grew up in the coal-mining town of Ehrenfield, Pennsylvania. He worked in the mines as a teenager before being drafted in 1943. After his discharge, Bronson held a variety of jobs before working with a Philadelphia theatrical company. In 1949, he moved to Los Angeles and enrolled in the Pasadena Playhouse, making his movie debut as a sailor in 1951's *You're in the Navy Now.* More substantial roles followed in *Pat and Mike, The House of Wax,* and in 1954's *Drum Beat* where he was credited for the first time as "Charles Bronson." His first lead was Roger Corman's *Machine Gun Kelly* (1958). Bronson continued his career with supporting roles in three of his best-known films: *The Magnificent Seven* (1960), *The Great Escape* (1963), and *The Dirty Dozen* (1967). A cult figure in Europe, he become a top star with such films as *Adieu, l'Ami* (*Farewell Friend*), *Once Upon a Time in the West, Rider on the Train, You Can't Win 'Em All, Chato's Land, Red Sun,* and *The Valachi Papers.* Bronson finally achieved U.S. stardom with his breakout role in *Death Wish* (1974), which was followed by several sequels. Additional screen credits included *The Sandpiper, This Property is Condemned, Mr. Majestyk, The Mechanic, Hard Times, From Noon Till Three, Breakheart Pass, St. Ives, Ten to Midnight,* and *The Indian Runner.* He starred with his second wife, Jill Ireland, in 15 films. Bronson, who began working in television in the 1950s, returned to television late in his career in films and miniseries (*Raid on Entebbe, Act of Vengeance,* and *Family of Cops*).

Rand Brooks (September 21, 1918–September 1, 2003). Born in St. Louis, Missouri, Brooks moved to Los Angeles with his mother when he was four. He was signed to an MGM contract after graduating from Beverly Hills High School and played a bit part in 1938's *Love Finds Andy Hardy.* But Brooks achieved his most enduring claim to fame with the role of Charles Hamilton, Scarlett O'Hara's first husband, in 1939's *Gone With the Wind.* He appeared in dozens of Hopalong Cassidy films as sidekick Lucky Jenkins in the 1940s and '50s as well as such films as *Babes in Arms, Ladies of the Chorus, Northwest Passage, Requiem for a Gunfighter,* and *The Cimarron Kid.* Brooks was also featured in the television series *The Adventures of Rin Tin Tin* (1954–59). Brooks left acting in the mid-1960s and began a private ambulance service.

Robert Brown (July 23, 1921–November 11, 2003). Born in Swanage, Dorset, England, the character actor played spy boss M in four James Bond films: *Octopussy* (1983), *View to a Kill* (1985), *The Living Daylights* (1987), and *License to Kill* (1989). He took over the role after the death of Bernard Lee, with whom Brown had worked in the 1960s British TV series *King of the River*. Brown also appeared in another role in the Bond film *The Spy Who Loved Me* (1971). The actor began his career after serving in the Royal Navy during World War II and was frequently cast in historical adventures, including *Helen of Troy, Billy Budd,* and *The 300 Spartans*. Brown also worked previously with Roger Moore in the 1950s TV series *Ivanhoe*.

Horst Buchholz (December 4, 1933–March 3, 2003). Born in Berlin, Germany, the actor was dubbed the James Dean of German films for his rebellious teen roles. He began his career on stage at 15 in *Emil and the Detectives* in 1948. Buchholz's film debut was for French director Julien Duvivier in *Marianne de me Jeunesse/Marianne—My Youthful Love* (1955), and he earned a Cannes film festival award for *Himmel Ohne Steme/Sky Without Stars* (1956), followed by *Die Halbstarken/The Hooligans* (1956), *The Confessions of Felix Krull* (1957), and *Tiger Bay* (1959). He moved to the United States and made his Hollywood debut with the 1960 western *The Magnificent Seven*. Screen credits included *Fanny* (1961), *One, Two, Three* (1961), *Nine Hours to Rama* (1962), *From Hell to Victory* (1979), and *Life Is Beautiful* (1997).

Art Carney (November 4, 1918–November 9, 2003). Born Arthur William Matthew Carney in Mount Vernon, New York, the award-winning actor will always be remembered for his role as sewer worker Ed Norton in the television series *The Honeymooners*. After graduating from A.B. Davis High School, Carney went on the road doing impersonations and novelty songs with the Horace Heidt Orchestra, later trying his luck with vaudeville, nightclubs, and radio parts. After service in World War II, Carney made his TV debut in 1948. In 1950, he began his work with Jackie Gleason, the host of DuMont's *Cavalcade of Stars,* which introduced *The Honeymooners* sketches in 1951. Carney then continued the role on *The Jackie Gleason Show,* which had two different runs and earned Carney five Emmy awards. Carney and Gleason later teamed up for the 1985 TV movie *Izzy and Moe*. Carney also acted on stage, beginning with 1957's *The Rope Dancers,* and originated the role of Felix Ungar in Neil Simon's *The Odd Couple* in 1965. In 1974, Carney received a best actor Oscar for his first leading role in the film *Harry and Tonto*. Other screen credits included *The Late Show, Going in Style, The Muppets Take Manhattan,* and *Last Action Hero*.

Johnny Cash (February 26, 1932–September 9, 2003). The country music legend, known as "The Man in Black," was born John R. Cash in Kingsland, Arkansas, and grew up on a cotton farm. His music career spanned five decades, beginning at Sun Records in Memphis in 1955; Cash recorded more than 1,500 songs and won 11 Grammys. Cash had his own television series, *The Johnny Cash Show,* on ABC from 1969–71. He took guest-star roles in such series as *Columbo* and *Dr. Quinn, Medicine Woman* and also appeared in films and television movies, including *A Gunfight, Five Minutes to Live, The Night Rider, Murder in Coweta County, The Baron and the Kid, The Last Days of Frank & Jesse James,* and *Stagecoach*. Cash wrote two autobiographies: *Man in Black* (1975) and *Cash: The Autobiography* (1997).

June Carter Cash (June 23, 1929–May 15, 2003). Born Valerie June Carter in Maces Spring, Virginia, the singer and sometime actress was the second of three daughters born to Mother Maybelle Carter of the famed country music Carter Family. In 1943, the original Carter Family group disbanded and June, her sisters, and her mother toured and recorded as Mother Maybelle and the Carter Sisters, becoming regulars at Nashville's Grand Ole Opry by 1950. In the mid-50s, Carter Cash studied acting with Lee Strasberg and Sanford Meisner at the Neighborhood Playhouse in New York. In 1956, June Carter met Johnny Cash and the Carters became part of Cash's touring shows. The duo married in 1968. She was a part of ABCs *The Johnny Cash Show* and took roles on *Gunsmoke, Little House on the Prairie,* and *Dr. Quinn, Medicine Woman* as well as in the 1997 film *The Apostle*. Carter Cash published her memoirs, *Among My Klediments,* in 1979 and a book of autobiographical vignettes, *From the Heart,* in 1987.

Anthony Caruso (April 7, 1916–April 4, 2003). Born in Frankfort, Indiana, the actor appeared in more than 120 films and 110 television shows, frequently as a bad guy. He was raised in Long Beach, California, and enrolled at the Pasadena Playhouse where he befriended Alan Ladd. Caruso would appear in 11 films with Ladd, beginning with 1942's *The Glass Key*. He made his screen debut (as a villain) in 1940's *Johnny Apollo*. Other screen credits included *Tarzan and the Leopard Woman* (1946), *The Asphalt Jungle* (1950), *The Iron Mistress* (1952), *Cattle Queen of Montana* (1954), *Drum Beat* (1954), *The Big Land* (1957), and *Zebra Force* (1976). Caruso's last film was *The Legend of Grizzly Adams* (1990).

Leslie Cheung (September 12, 1956–April 1, 2003). Born in Hong Kong, the popular Asian actor/singer committed suicide by falling to his death from the 24th floor of a Hong Kong hotel, a fate that echoed some of his film roles. He first achieved success as a pop star with the 1981 album *The Wind Blows On*. His big-screen debut was in 1982's *Nomad,* but Cheung's breakthrough film role was as a rookie cop in John Woo's *A Better Tomorrow* (1986). He also collaborated with the director on *Once a Thief* (1990). Cheung worked with director Wong Kar-wai in the films *Days of Being Wild* (1990), *Ashes of Time* (1994), and *Happy Together* (1997). Other credits included *Rouge* (1988), director Chen Kaige's *Farewell, My Concubine* (1993) and *Temptress Moon* (1996), and *Inner Senses* (2003).

Peggy Conklin (November 1, 1906–March 18, 2003). Best known for her stage work, the actress was born Margaret Eleanor Conklin in Dobbs Ferry, New York. She made her stage debut in the chorus line of 1928's *Treasure Girl* and went on to play a number of both comedic and dramatic roles, including Gabby Maple in the 1935 production of *Petrified Forest* opposite Leslie Howard and Humphrey Bogart. (Bette Davis played the role in the 1936 film version). Conklin made only five films, all in the 1930s: *The President Vanishes*, *The Devil Is a Sissy*, *One-Way Ticket*, *Her Master's Voice*, and *Having a Wonderful Time.*

Fielder Cook (March 9, 1923–June 20, 2003). Born in Atlanta, Georgia, Cook began his career in New York directing numerous live television dramas on such programs as *Lux Video Theater*, *Kraft Television Theater*, *Playhouse 90*, and *The Kaiser Aluminum Hour.* The Rod Serling-scripted TV drama *Patterns*, which Cook directed for NBC in 1955, became his feature film debut when it was remade in 1956. Cook also directed the TV movie *The Homecoming: A Christmas Story*, which became the basis for the series *The Waltons*, as well as *Teacher, Teacher, Miracle on 34th Street, I Know Why the Caged Bird Sings*, and *The Member of the Wedding.* Among his other films were *A Big Hand for a Little Lady, Prudence and the Pill, How to Save a Marriage (and Ruin Your Life)*, and *Seize the Day.*

Jeanne Crain (May 25, 1925–December 14, 2003). Born in Burbank, California, the actress, who was primarily known for lightweight romances and comedies, received an Academy Award nomination as best actress for the controversial drama *Pinky* (1949). Crain began winning beauty contests as a teenager, which attracted the attention of 20th Century-Fox, who signed her to a contract. She made her debut (in a bathing suit) in 1943's *The Gang's All Here*, but was soon playing leading roles in such films as *Home in Indiana, In the Meantime, Darling, Winged Victory*, and *State Fair.* Other screen credits included *Margie, You Were Meant for Me, An Apartment for Peggy, A Letter to Three Wives, People Will Talk, Cheaper by the Dozen*, and *Belles on Their Toes.*

Richard Crenna (March 30, 1926–January 17, 2003). Born in Los Angeles, Richard Donald Crenna began his career on radio as part of the *Boy Scout Jamboree.* He worked on numerous radio shows as a teenager and while attending the University of Southern California. After serving with the Army, Crenna resumed his radio career in 1948 as teenager Walter Denton on *Our Miss Brooks* with Eve Arden, a role he continued after the show moved to television in 1952. He

even played the role in the movie version of *Our Miss Brooks* in 1956. He starred opposite Walter Brennan on the CBS comedy *The Real McCoys* (1957–63). Crenna also began his career as a TV director with episodes from that series. His television work continued to 2002 with his recurring role as Jared Duff in the CBS series *Judging Amy.* Crenna received an Emmy Award for his role as a cop who is sexually assaulted in the 1985 TV movie, *The Rape of Richard Beck*, and starred as another cop, Det. Lt. Frank Janek, for the 1985 TV movie *Doubletake* and its six sequels. His screen credits included *The Pride of St. Louis* (1953), *The Sand Pebbles* (1966), *Wait Until Dark* (1967), *Breakheart Pass* (1975), *Body Heat* (1981), and *The Flamingo Kid* (1984). Crenna memorably appeared as Col. Trautman, opposite Sylvester Stallone, in the 1980s action movies *First Blood, Rambo: First Blood Part II*, and *Rambo III.*

Hume Cronyn (July 18, 1918–June 15, 2003). Born in London, Ontario, Canada, the actor/writer/director's career lasted for more than 60 years. After briefly studying at McGill University, Cronyn enrolled in the American Academy of Dramatic Arts in 1932 and made his Broadway debut in 1934's *Hipper's Holiday.* Cronyn often played opposite his wife of 52 years, Jessica Tandy (who died in 1994), including the plays *The Fourposter* (1951), *The Gin Game* (1977), and *The Petition* (1986), and in the films *Honky Tonk Freeway* (1981), *Cocoon* (1985), *Batteries Not Included* (1987), and *Cocoon: The Return* (1988), as well as the TV film *Foxfire* (1987). One of their last joint appearances was the 1991 TV movie *To Dance With the White Dog*, for which both received Emmy nominations; only Cronyn won. He also received an Emmy for 1989's *Age-Old Friends.* His first film role was for Alfred Hitchcock's *Shadow of a Doubt* (1942); he also wrote the adaptations for the Hitchcock films *Rope* (1948) and *Under Capricorn* (1949). Cronyn was nominated for an Academy Award for *The Seventh Cross* (1944). Screen credits included *Phantom of the Opera* (1943), *Lifeboat* (1944), *The Green Years* (1946), *The Postman Always Rings Twice* (1946), *The Beginning of the End* (1947), *People Will Talk* (1951), *Sunrise at Campobello* (1960), *There Was a Crooked Man* (1969), and *Marvin's Room* (1996). Cronyn published his autobiography, *A Terrible Liar*, in 1991.

Richard Cusack (August 25, 1925–June 2, 2003). Born in New York City, Cusack left a successful advertising career to become a screenwriter and actor, forming his own film production company in 1970. Cusack received an Emmy for the documentary *The Committee* in 1971. Acting credits included parts in *My Bodyguard, The Fugitive*, and *Return to Me.* He wrote the 1995 cable film *The Jack Bull*, starring son John; children Joan, Susan, Ann, and William are also actors.

Jacques Deray (February 19, 1929–August 9, 2003). Born Jacques Desrayaud in Lyon, France, the director first studied acting in Paris before working behind the camera. He directed some 24 films and specialized in gangster, police detective, and film noir themes. After working as an assistant for Luis Bunuel and Jules Dassin, among others, Deray made his directorial debut with 1960's *Le Gigolo*. The director made nine films with actor Alain Delon, beginning with 1968's *Le Piscine/The Swimming Pool*. Among Deray's other films were *Rififi a Tokyo*, *Flic Story/Cop Story*, *Borsalino*, *Un Papillon sur l'Epaule/Butterfly on the Shoulder*, *Un Homme est Mort/The Outside Man*, and his final film, 1994's *L'Ours en Peluch/The Teddy Bear*.

Ellen Drew (November 23, 1914–December 3, 2003). Born Esther Loretta Ray in Kansas City, Missouri, the actress began her career as a contract player at Paramount. After playing a number of bit parts (under the name Terry Ray), Drew finally received a more substantial role in 1938's *Sing, You Sinners*. It was at this point Drew changed her name—first to Erin Drew and later to Ellen Drew. Among her other films were *Christmas in July*, *If I Were King*, *Buck Benny Rides Again*, *Reaching for the Sun*, *Man in the Saddle*, *The Baron of Arizona*, *Davy Crockett*, *Indian Scout*, *The Great Missouri Raid*, and her last film, 1957's *Outlaw's Son*. Drew later appeared in a number of television shows, including *Perry Mason*, *Ford Television Theatre*, and *Schlitz Playhouse of Stars*.

John Gregory Dunne (May 25, 1932–December 30, 2003). Born in Hartford, Connecticut, the writer graduated from Princeton and, after serving in the Army, moved to New York to work in an ad agency and, later, as a staff writer for *Time* magazine. He married fellow writer Joan Didion in 1964 and the duo moved to Los Angeles, working as freelancers. Their first screenplay was *The Panic in Needle Park* (1971) and they also collaborated on the remake of *A Star is Born* (1976) and on *Up Close and Personal* (1996). They also collaborated on the screenplays for his novel *True Confessions* (filmed 1981) and her novel *Play It As It Lays* (filmed 1972).

Buddy Ebsen (April 2, 1908–July 6, 2003). Born Christian Rudolph Ebsen Jr. in Belleville, Illinois, the actor had a long career and found particular success on television. His father, who owned a dance school, moved the family to Orlando, Florida, and Ebsen originally was a pre-med student at the University of Florida. But a loss of the family's money had Ebsen leaving school to become a chorus boy in New York in 1928. He and his younger sister Vilma became dance partners and toured the vaudeville circuit, also appearing on Broadway in various revues. Their only film together was their debut in *Broadway Melody of 1936*, after which Vilma retired. Ebsen continued to work on such 1930s films as *Born to Dance*, *The Girl of the Golden West*, *My Lucky Star*, and (dancing with Shirley Temple) 1936's *Captain January*. He had to give up the role of the Tin Man in *The Wizard of Oz* after developing a severe allergy to the silver makeup. He turned down an

MGM contract and was essentially blacklisted by studio head Louis B. Mayer, so Ebsen returned to the stage. After serving in WWII, Ebsen found work at Republic Pictures on several Rex Allen westerns and in the mid-1950s, Disney studios co-starred Ebsen with Fess Parker in TV's *The Adventures of Davy Crockett*, making him a household name. Character roles in the 1961 films *Breakfast at Tiffany's* and *The Interns* led producer Paul Henning to cast Ebsen as Jed Clampett in the CBS comedy series *The Beverly Hillbillies*, an unexpected hit that ran from 1962 to 1971. He then starred as the title detective in *Barnaby Jones* (1973–80) and co-starred in *Matt Houston* (1984). Among his other films were *They Met in Argentina*, *Sing Your Worries Away*, *Red Garters*, *Night People*, *Attack*, *Mail Order Bride*, and *The One and Only Genuine, Original Family Band*. In addition, Ebsen was also a playwright, songwriter, painter, and the author of the romance *Kelly's Quest*, published in 2001.

Anthony Eisley (January 19, 1925–January 29, 2003). Born Frederick Glendinning Eisley in Philadelphia, Pennsylvania, the actor starred as half of a dashing detective team, opposite Robert Conrad, on the TV series *Hawaiian Eye* (1959–63) while under contract to Warner Bros. He studied drama at the University of Miami and worked in a stock company and in touring stage productions before finding television work in the early 1950s. Eisley began his film career with supporting roles in *Fearless Fagan* and *Operation Secret* (both 1952). Eisley also starred in a number of B genre movies, including *The Wasp Woman* (1959), *The Naked Kiss* (1964), *The Navy vs. the Night Monsters* (1966), *They Ran for Their Lives* (1968), *The Witchmaker* (1969), *Dracula vs. Frankenstein* (1971), *The Doll Squad* (1973), *Monster* (1979), *Deep Space* (1987), and *Evil Spirits* (1990).

Jack Elam (November 13, 1916–October 20, 2003). Born in Miami, Arizona, the character actor appeared in some 100 films and many television roles. His wandering left eye, which made him appear menacing, was the result of an accident at the age of 12. Elam worked as an accountant for Samuel Goldwyn Studios and William "Hopalong Cassidy" Boyd's production company. He offered to arrange financing for a producer's western in exchange for a role as a heavy and made his debut with 1950's *The Sundowners*. Other screen credits included *Rawhide*, *The Man from Laramie*, *The Comancheros*, *Gunfight at the O.K. Corral*, *Vera Cruz*, *Rio Lobo*, *Once Upon a Time in the West*, *Support Your Local Sheriff!*, *Support Your Local Gunfighter*, and *The Cockeyed Cowboys of Calico County*. His last credit was the 1995 TV movie *Bonanza: Under Fire*. Elam's birth year may be as late as 1920; according to his family the actor added years to his age to get work in his youth.

Mary Ellis (June 15, 1897–January 30, 2003). Born May Belle Elsas in New York City, the actress was best known for her work on the London stage although she also appeared in movies and on television until the age of 97. Ellis joined the Metropolitan Opera at the age of 18, leaving to act on Broadway. Rudolf Friml wrote the operetta *Rose-Marie* for Ellis in 1924 and she played the role for more than a year, but after a falling out with producer Arthur Hammerstein, she never sang on the American stage again. Ellis moved to London after her marriage to British matinee idol Basil Sydney in 1929, later starring in the Ivor Novello shows *Glamorous Night* and *The Dancing Years,* which Novello wrote for her. Ellis continued to act on stage until 1970. Her first film was 1934's *Bella Donna;* other credits included *All the King's Horses* (1934), *Glamorous Night* (1951), and *Three Worlds of Gulliver* (1961). Ellis's last role was a part in the Jeremy Brett Sherlock Holmes series for television in 1993. Her autobiography, *Those Dancing Years,* was published in 1982.

Nick Enright (December 22, 1950–March 30, 2003). Born in Maitland, Australia, the playwright shared an Oscar nomination with director George Miller for the screenplay of *Lorenzo's Oil* in 1993. Enright primarily wrote for the stage and had a long association with Australia's National Institute of Dramatic Art. He adapted his play *Blackrock* for film and also wrote the television miniseries *Come in Spinner.*

Jean-Yves Escoffier (July 12, 1950–April 4, 2003). Born in Lyon, France, the cinematographer studied at L'Ecole Louis Lumiere and began his career with short films and documentaries. His first feature was *Simone Barbes, ou la Vertu/Simone Barbes or Virtue* (1980). Other credits included *Boy Meets Girl* (1984), *Mauvais Sang* (1986), *Les Amants du Pont-Neuf* (1991), *Dream Lover* (1994), *Good Will Hunting* (1997), *Rounders* (1998), *Cradle Will Rock* (1999), *Nurse Betty* (2000), *Possession* (2002), and *The Human Stain* (2003). Escoffier received a Cesar Award for 1985's *Trois Hommes et un Couffin/Three Men and a Cradle.*

Adam Faith (June 23, 1940–March 8, 2003). Born Terence Nelhams-Wright in London, the singer/actor was playing in a skiffle group and made his debut on the BBC pop show *Six-Five Special,* where producer Jack Good gave the singer his stage name. Faith's solo career was launched in 1959 with "What Do You Want If You Don't Want Money?" and he had more than 20 British pop hits in the pre-Beatles era. Film credits included *Beat Girl, Never Let Go, Mix Me a Person, Stardust, McVicar,* and *Minder on the Orient Express.* Faith also played the title role in the 1971 series *Budgie* and co-starred in the comedy-drama *Love Hurts* in 1992.

Jinx Falkenburg (January 21, 1919–August 27, 2003). Born Eugenia Lincoln Falkenburg in Barcelona, Spain, the model and actress was also a pioneer of radio and TV talk shows. She signed a contract with Warner Brothers at the age of 16 and, because of her fluency in Spanish, was given

parts in films to be distributed to the Spanish-language market. While at MGM, Falkenburg began her association with photographer Paul Hesse and made her first cover appearance in 1937, appearing on the cover of more than 60 magazines. After marrying Tex McCrary in 1945, the duo started the New York radio program "Hi Jinx" in 1946 and an NBC TV interview show, *At Home,* in 1947 as well as a second radio program, *Meet Tex and Jinx.* Falkenburg worked on a number of films in the 1940s, including *Sing for Your Supper, Sweetheart of the Fleet, Lucky Legs, Laugh Your Blues Away, She Has What It Takes, Two Senoritas from Chicago,* and *Cover Girl.*

Marjorie Fowler (July 16, 1920–July 8, 2003). The daughter of screenwriter Nunnally Johnson, film editor Fowler was nominated for an Oscar for her work as co-editor of the 1967 film *Doctor Doolittle.* Born in Los Angeles, she began her career as a contract player at 20th Century-Fox before moving onto story analysis and work as an editor. Fowler edited her father's film, *The Three Faces of Eve,* which won star Joanne Woodward an Oscar in 1957. Other screen credits included *Elmer Gantry, Separate Tables,* and *Lover Come Back.* Fowler was awarded the Lifetime Career Achievement Award from the American Cinema Editors association in 2000 and received their Eddie Award for 1981's television movie *The Marva Collins Story.*

Fred Freiberger (February 19, 1915–March 2, 2003). Born in New York City, the film and television writer and producer studied at the Pace Institute of Films. After serving in World War II, Freiberger went to Hollywood and worked as a publicist. He later wrote for such TV series as *Zane Grey, Fireside Theatre, Have Gun, Will Travel, Bonanza, Rawhide, The Big Valley, Ben Casey, Starsky and Hutch,* and *The Dukes of Hazard.* Freiberger also produced the science fiction cult classic *The Beast From 20,000 Fathoms* (1953) as well as *The Weapon* (1956) and *Crash Landing* (1958).

Kinji Fukasaku (July 3, 1930–January 12, 2003). Born in Mito, Japan, the director made more than 60 films and was best known in his native country for a series of yakuza, or gangster, films, including *Cops vs. Thugs* (1975), *Yakuza Graveyard* (1976), and *Graveyard of Honor* (1976). Fukasaku studied cinema at Tokyo's Nihon Univeristy and began his career in 1953 as a screenwriter and assistant director at Toei. Among Fukasaku's other credits were the Japanese scenes from *Tora! Tora! Tora!* (1970), *Battle Without Honor and Humanity* (1973) and *The Geisha House* (1999). His last film was the provocative and graphic *Battle Royale* (2000); at his death, the director was working on a sequel, which is expected to be completed by his son.

Herb Gardner (December 28, 1934–September 24, 2003). Born Herbert George Gardner in Brooklyn, New York, the playwright started his career in the 1950s with the syndicated cartoon, "The Nebbishes," which was published for eight years. His first play was 1962's *A Thousand Clowns*. Gardner wrote the screenplay for the 1965 film version, which earned him an Oscar nomination for best adapted screenplay. Gardner's short story, "Who Is Harry Kellerman and Why Is He Saying Those Terrible Things About Me?" was filmed in 1971, and he wrote the screenplay for 1977's *Thieves* from his 1974 Broadway show. Gardner made his directorial debut in 1984 with the film version of his 1968 play, *The Goodbye People*. Gardner also wrote and directed the 1996 film version of his 1985 play, *I'm Not Rappaport*. Gardner received a Tony Award for his last play, *Conversations with My Father* (1991).

Massino Girotti (May 18, 1918–January 5, 2003). Born in Mogliano, Italy, the actor made his film debut in 1939's *Dora Nelson*. Screen credits included *A Pilot Returns* (1942), *Door of the Sky* (1943), *Obsession* (1943), *Last Tango in Paris* (1972), and *The Monster* (1994).

Trevor Goddard (October 14, 1962–June 7, 2003). The professional boxer-turned-actor was born in Perth, Australia, and began his career in a series of beer commercials. His first film was 1994's *Men of War* and other credits included *Mortal Kombat* (1985), *Deep Rising* (1998), *Gone in 60 Seconds* (2000), and *Pirates of the Caribbean: The Curse of the Black Pearl* (2003). Goddard also played the recurring role of Lt. Cmdr. Michael "Mic" Brumby in the television series *JAG* from 1998 to 2001.

Ron Goodwin (February 17, 1925–January 8, 2003). Born in Plymouth, England, Goodwin composed some 60 film scores during his 50-year career as well as touring as a conductor and working as a musical director and recording artist. He began his career in 1943 as an arranger and joined Parlophone (EMI) Records in 1950 as musical director. Goodwin began his movie career in the mid-1950s by writing scores for documentaries. His first film score was for 1959's *Whirlpool*. Other film scores included *Village of the Damned*, *The Day of the Triffids*, *Where Eagles Dare*, *633 Squadron*, *The Battle of Britain*, *Operation Crossbow*, *Force 10 From Navaronne*, *Those Magnificent Men in Their Flying Machines*, and *Frenzy*.

David Greene (February 22, 1921–April 7, 2003). The four-time Emmy-winning director was born in Manchester, England. He began his career as an actor at the Old Vic and later toured the U.S. and Canada, eventually working for the Canadian Broadcasting Co. Greene earned his first Emmy for the TV movie *The People Next Door* (1969). He also earned Emmys for the TV miniseries *Rich Man, Poor Man* (1975), the first episode of *Roots* (1977), and the TV movie *Friendly Fire* (1979), and received a nomination for the

miniseries *Fatal Vision* (1984). Other TV credits included *Madame Sin* (1972), *The Trial of Lee Harvey Oswald* (1977), *The Betty Ford Story* (1987), *Willing to Kill: The Texas Cheerleader Story* (1992), and *Bella Mafia* (1997). Greene earned a Writers Guild Award nomination for the screenplay of 1973's *Godspell*, which he also directed. He also directed *The Shuttered Room* (1967), *Sebastian* (1968), *I Start Counting* (1969), *Gray Lady Down* (1978), and *Hard Country* (1981).

Anne Gwynne (December 10, 1918–March 31, 2003). Born Marguerite Gwynne Trice in Waco, Texas, the actress first studied drama at Stephens College in Missouri and began modeling after moving to Los Angeles with her family. She began acting on stage as Anne Gwynne and was signed to a contract at Universal Studios in 1939, where she was a leading lady in B movies, including westerns and horror films. She also appeared in Buster Crabbe's Flash Gordon serials, including *Flash Gordon Conquers the Universe* (1940). Among Gwynne's Universal horror pictures were *Black Friday*, *The Black Cat*, *House of Frankenstein*, *The Strange Case of Doctor Rx*, *Weird Woman*, *Murder in the Blue Room*, and *Dick Tracy Meets Gruesome*. Other films included *Ride 'Em Cowboy* and *Men of Texas* (both 1942) and her last film *Adam at 6 A.M.* (1970).

Buddy Hackett (August 31, 1924–June 30, 2003). The short and rotund comedian, born and raised in Brooklyn, New York, as Leonard Hacker, was admired for his improvisational skills and (often) blue routines, which he honed at New York's Catskills resorts and in Las Vegas. He made an early debut on TV in 1948's *School House* for the DuMont Network and as the voice of the talking camel in the film *Slave Girl* (1947). Hackett finally appeared on camera in 1953's *Walking My Baby Back Home*, after signing a contract with Universal. Hackett was a regular performer on *The Tonight Show*, *Hollywood Squares*, *Rowan & Martin's Laugh-In*, and made his final television appearance as a celebrity judge on the NBC reality series *Last Comic Standing* (2003). Screen credits included *It's a Mad Mad Mad Mad World*, *All Hands on Deck*, *Everything's Ducky*, *The Music Man*, *The Love Bug*, *Scrooged*, and as the voice of Scuttle in *The Little Mermaid*. Hackett also starred as comedian Lou Costello in the telepic *Bud and Lou*.

Conrad L. Hall (June 21, 1926–January 4, 2003). Born in Papeete, Tahiti, the cinematographer had a nearly 50-year career and received three Oscars, including his posthumous award for 2002's *Road to Perdition*. He was the son of James Norman Hall, the co-author of *Mutiny on the Bounty*, and entered the University of Southern California to study journalism. After doing poorly in a writing class, Hall switched to film and, after graduation, formed the production company Canyon Films with two other USC graduates, working on all types of films and honing his early career in television. In 1954, Hall shot his first film for Canyon, *My Brother*

Down There. He received a co-photography credit for the studio film *Edge of Fury* (1958) and his first full credits for 1965's *The Wild Seed* and *Morituri,* which earned Hall his first Oscar nomination. Other nominations were for *The Professionals* (1966), *In Cold Blood* (1967), *The Day of the Locust* (1975), *Tequila Sunrise* (1988), *Searching for Bobby Fischer* (1993), and *A Civil Action* (1998). In addition to his win for *Perdition,* Hall also received Academy Awards for *Butch Cassidy and the Sundance Kid* (1969) and *American Beauty* (1999). Other film credits included *Harper* (1966), *Cool Hand Luke* (1967), *Hell in the Pacific* (1968), *Tell Them Willie Boy Is Here* (1969), *Fat City* (1972), *Electra Glide in Blue* (1973), *Marathon Man* (1976), *Black Widow* (1987), *Love Affair* (1994), and *Without Limits* (1998). Conrad Hall received the lifetime achievement award from the American Society of Cinematographers in 1994.

Edmund Hartmann (September 24, 1911–November 28, 2003). Born in St. Louis, Missouri, the screenwriter and producer's film and television career spanned more than 60 years. Hartmann worked at several Hollywood studios beginning in 1934, including Paramount, where he wrote five comedies that starred Bob Hope: *Paleface* (1948), *Sorrowful Jones* (1949), *Fancy Pants* (1950), *Lemon Drop Kid* (1951), and *Casanova's Big Night* (1954). Other screen work included *Ali Baba and the Forty Thieves, Sherlock Holmes in Washington, The Scarlet Claw,* and *The Caddy.* In the late 1950s, Hartmann began working on television, including producing *My Three Sons* from 1960 to 1972 as well as *Family Affair, To Rome With Love,* and *The Smith Family.*

Anthony Havelock-Allan (February 28, 1904–January 11, 2003). Anthony James Allan Havelock-Allan was born near Darlington, England, and educated at Charterhouse and schools in Switzerland. The screenwriter and producer began working in films as a casting director in 1933. Working for British & Dominions film studios, Havelock-Allan produced more than 20 low-budget films between 1935 and 1937. His first feature productions for Pinewood began with *This Man is News* (1938) and its sequel *This Man in Paris* (1939). In 1943, Havelock-Allan founded Cineguild and went on to produce *This Happy Breed* (1944), *Blithe Spirit* (1945), *Brief Encounter* (1946), and *Great Expectations* (1946); he received Academy Award nominations as co-screenwriter on both of the 1946 releases. Other film credits included *In Which We Serve* (1942), *The Small Voice* (1948), *The Young Lovers* (1954), *Orders to Kill* (1958), *Romeo and Juliet* (1968), and *Ryan's Daughter* (1970).

Lowell S. Hawley (1909–May 6, 2003). The screenwriter was born in Lynden, Washington and began writing for a radio station in Bellingham, Washington. After moving to Los Angeles in 1942, Hawley spent a decade writing for radio KFI. He was a writer for Walt Disney Studio from

1957 to 1969 and worked on the *Zorro* television series as well as the films *Zorro, the Avenger* (1960), *The Swiss Family Robinson* (1960), and *Babes in Toyland* (1961).

David Hemmings (November 18, 1941–December 3, 2003). The actor and director, who was born in Guildford, England, died of a heart attack while filming *Samantha's Child* in Romania. Hemmings began his career as a night-club singer and his early film roles generally cast him as a rebellious teen. He achieved international success with Michelangelo Antonioni's 1966 classic *Blow-Up.* Screen credits included *Camelot* (1967), *Barbarella* (1968), *The Charge of the Light Brigade* (1968), *Islands in the Stream* (1977), *Murder by Decree* (1979), *The Rainbow* (1989), *Gladiator* (2000), *Last Orders* (2001), *Mean Machine* (2001), *Spy Game* (2001), *Gangs of New York* (2002), and *The League of Extraordinary Gentlemen* (2003). In the 1970s, Hemmings began focusing on directing, primarily for television.

Katharine Hepburn (May 12, 1907–June 29, 2003). Born Katharine Houghton Hepburn in Hartford, Connecticut, the actress received 12 Academy Award nominations and won a record four Best Actress Oscars (for *Morning Glory* [1933], *Guess Who's Coming to Dinner* [1967], *The Lion in Winter* [1968], and *On Golden Pond* [1981]). She attended Bryn Mawr College and made her stage debut in Baltimore in *The Czarina* and on Broadway in *These Days* (both 1928). Hepburn signed a contract with RKO Pictures and director George Cukor signed her to play John Barrymore's daughter in *A Bill of Divorcement* (1932). The director and actress would work on a total of 10 films together, including *Little Women* (1933). After several film flops, Hepburn was labeled "box office poison" by theater owners; she decided to buy out her RKO contract and return to the stage with the Philip Barry play *The Philadelphia Story,* in a role written specifically for her. Hepburn optioned the successful play and sold the film rights to MGM with the stipulation that she star, which she did opposite Cary Grant and Jimmy Stewart in the hit 1940 adaptation. Well-known for her angular looks, idiosyncratic diction, strong and sometimes eccentric personality, Hepburn also managed to keep her 25-year relationship with actor Spencer Tracy a private matter in a public profession. The two co-starred in nine films beginning with 1942's *Woman of the Year* and ending with 1967's *Guess Who's Coming to Dinner,* completed shortly before Tracy's death. Among her many film credits were *Christopher Strong, Sylvia Scarlett, Holiday, Bringing Up Baby State of the Union, The African Queen, Summertime, Suddenly Last Summer, Long Day's Journey Into Night, Grace Quigley, Love Affair,* and *This Can't Be Love.* The actress also received a Tony nomination for her portrayal of designer Coco Chanel in the musical *Coco* and an Emmy for the telepic *Love Among the Ruins,* opposite Laurence Olivier and directed by Cukor. The confusion over Hepburn's birth date (also cited as November 8) was created by Hepburn herself; the November birthday was that of her older brother Tom, who committed suicide when the actress was 14. Hepburn revealed this in her autobiography, *Me: Stories of My Life,* which was published in 1991.

Wendy Hiller (August 15, 1912–May 14, 2003). Born in Bramhall, England, the actress joined the Manchester Repertory Theater after her secondary education and worked for five years as an actor in increasingly important roles, including the heroine of *Love on the Dole* (1934). George Bernard Shaw saw her in that part and cast her as Eliza Doolittle in his *Pygmalion* (1936); Hiller played the same role in the 1938 film version. Screen credits included *Major Barbara* (1941), *I Know Where I'm Going!* (1948), *Outcast of the Islands* (1952), *Something of Value* (1957), *Sons and Lovers* (1960), *A Man for All Seasons* (1966), *Murder on the Orient Express* (1974), *Voyage of the Damned* (1976), *The Elephant Man* (1980), and *The Lonely Passion of Judith Hearne* (1987). Her last film was the title role in the television movie *The Countess Alice* (1992). Hiller received a best supporting actress Oscar for 1958's *Separate Tables.*

Earl Hindman (October 20, 1942–December 29, 2003). Although the character actor also did films and stage work, Hindman was probably best-known as next-door neighbor Wilson, whose face was always partially obscured, in the hit television series *Home Improvement.* Born in Brisbee, Arizona, Hindman studied at the University of Arizona before moving to New York and finding success off-Broadway with *Dark of the Moon* and *The Basic Training of Pavlo Hummel.* Before appearing on *Home Improvement,* Hindman played Detective Lt. Bob Reid on the soap opera *Ryan's Hope* for 16 years. Among his film credits were *Silverado; The Taking of Pelham One, Two, Three; Three Men and a Baby; The Ballad of the Sad Café;* and *Final.*

Gregory Hines (February 14, 1946–August 9, 2003). Born in New York City, he began studying dance at the age of three along with his elder brother Maurice. The duo began performing as the Hines Kids two years later; they became a trio when their father, Maurice Sr., joined them on drums in an act billed as Hines, Hines and Dad. The brothers also danced together in the 1984 film *The Cotton Club.* Hines's first non-dancing roles came with the 1981 films *The History of the World, Part I* and *Wolfen.* Screen credits included *Deal of the Century* (1983), *The Muppets Take Manhattan* (1984), *White Nights* (1985), *Running Scared* (1986), *A Rage in Harlem* (1991), *Renaissance Man* (1994), *Waiting to Exhale* (1995), *The Preacher's Wife* (1996), and *The Tic Code* (1998). He also directed the 1994 film *Bleeding Hearts* and the 2001 television drama *The Red Sneakers.* Hines starred in his own TV series, *The Gregory Hines Show,* in 1997 and had a recurring role on the series *Will & Grace.*

In 2001, he was nominated for an Emmy for the title role in the Showtime film *Bojangles.* Hines earned Tony nominations for *Eubie!* (1979), *Comin' Uptown* (1980), and *Sophisticated Ladies* (1981); he won for best actor in a musical in *Jelly's Last Jam* (1992).

Al Hirschfeld (June 21, 1903–January 20, 2003). The caricaturist, famous for his drawings of stage and screen stars, was born Albert Hirschfeld in St. Louis, Missouri, studied at the Art Students League in New York, and began working for Selznick Pictures as an art director at the age of 18. His first drawing, a sketch of French actor Sacha Guitry, was printed in the *New York Herald Tribune* in 1926 and he also began working for the *New York Times* in the same year. After the birth of daughter Nina in 1945, Hirschfeld included her name in his drawings and readers strove to find the hidden term; the artist listed the number next to his signature in each drawing. Hirschfeld even inserted his trademark into the drawings he did for a booklet of five 29-cent stamps honoring comedians Laurel and Hardy, Edgar Bergen and Charlie McCarthy, Jack Benny, Fanny Brice, and Abbott and Costello with the permission of the United States Postal Service (whose policy forbade secret marks). The artist wrote about the theater in 1951's *Show Business Is No Business* and published collections of his caricatures in *The American Theater as Seen by Hirschfeld* (1961) and *The World of Hirschfeld* (1970). Hirschfeld was the subject of Susan W. Dryfoos's 1996 documentary *The Line King.*

David Holt (August 14, 1927–November 15, 2003). Born in Jacksonville, Florida, Holt began his career as a child actor in 1934's *You Belong to Me.* He also appeared in *The Adventures of Tom Sawyer* (1938), *Beau Geste* (1939), *Pride of the Yankees* (1942), *What's Cookin'?* (1942), *The Human Comedy* (1943), and *Courage of Lassie* (1946). Holt later had a career as a jazz musician and songwriter, including co-writing "The Christmas Blues" with Sammy Cahn.

Bob Hope (May 29, 1903–July 27, 2003). Born Leslie Townes Hope in London, England, the entertainer's family moved to Cleveland, Ohio, when he was four. He began working in vaudeville in 1924, changing his name from Les to Bob while on the theater circuit. Hope moved to New York and began working on Broadway in 1927 and made his radio debut on the *Capitol Family Hour* in 1932. By 1938 he had his own radio show sponsored by Pepsodent. Hope made 54 films, beginning with *The Big Broadcast of 1938.* It featured him dueting with Shirley Ross on "Thanks for the Memories," which became the comedian's theme song. He made seven *Road* movies with Bing Crosby, beginning with 1940's *Road to Singapore.* Among his other films were *The Cat and the Canary* (1939); *My Favorite Blonde* (1942); *The Princess and the Pirate* (1944); *Monsieur Beaucaire* (1946); *My Favorite Brunette* (1947); *The Paleface* (1948); *The Seven*

Little Foys (1955); *Beau James* (1957); *Call Me Bwana* (1963); *Boy, Did I Get a Wrong Number!* (1966); and his final starring role in *Cancel My Reservation* (1972). Hope began his television career in 1950 by hosting the NBC variety show *The Star Spangled Revue*, with his last special airing in 1997. Hope also began touring military bases with the USO in 1941 and began his annual Christmas show for the troops in 1948; his military appearances lasted until 1990.

Sebastien Japrisot (July 4, 1931–March 4, 2003). Born Jean-Baptiste Rossi in Marseille, France, the writer and director studied philosophy at the Sorbonne. He wrote his first novel *The False Start* at 17. The story, about a boy who has a love affair with a nun, created a scandal when it was published in 1950. Japrisot wrote screenplays for many of his novels, including *The Sleeping Car Murders,* which became Costa-Gavras' directorial debut in 1965, as well as *The Lady in the Car with Glasses and a Gun* and *One Deadly Summer.*

Graham P. Jarvis (August, 25, 1930–April 16, 2003). The longtime character actor was born in Toronto, Ontario, Canada and studied acting at the American Theater Wing in New York in the early 1950s. He had recurring roles in the 1970s television series *Mary Hartman, Mary Hartman* and in *7ᵗʰ Heaven.* Screen credits included *Alice's Restaurant* and *Silkwood.*

Michael Jeter (August 26, 1952–March 30, 2003). Born in Lawrenceburg, Tennessee, the actor earned a Tony Award for the musical *Grand Hotel* (1990) and an Emmy for his role of Herman Stiles on the series *Evening Shade* (1992). In 1998, Jeter began playing the role of Mr. Noodle on *Sesame Street.* Jeter made his film debut in *Hair* (1979); other screen credits included *The Fisher King, Sister Act 2, Drop Zone, Waterworld, Mouse Hunt, The Green Mile, Jurassic Park III, Open Range,* and *The Polar Express,* which will be released in 2004.

Michael Kamen (April 15, 1948–November 18, 2003). The composer was born in New York City and began learning to play the piano at the age of two. He studied at the Juilliard School of Music, where he formed the New York Rock and Roll Ensemble for which Kamen wrote the orchestrations. Kamen wrote the scores for 28 films, including *Polyester, Brazil,* the remake of *101 Dalmatians, Mr. Holland's Opus, X-Men,* and *Open Range.* He was also the composer on the *Lethal Weapon* and *Die Hard* films. Kamen received co-writer Oscar nominations for the songs "(Everything I Do) I Do It For You" from the film *Robin Hood: Prince of Thieves* and "Have You Ever Really Loved a Woman?" from *Don Juan DeMarco.*

Elia Kazan (September 7, 1909–September 28, 2003). The director's career was long overshadowed by his testimony before the House Un-American Activities Committee in 1952 where he acknowledged his two-year membership in the Communist Party and gave the names of eight other members. Born Elia Kazanjoglous in Constantinople, his Greek immigrant family moved to New York when Kazan was four. He began acting and directing while studying at Yale University's School of Drama. He joined the Group Theater in 1932 and went to Hollywood after it dissolved in 1940, where he acted in the films *City of Conquest* (1940) and *Blues in the Night* (1941); his first film as a director was 1945's *A Tree Grows in Brooklyn.* Kazan received Academy Awards for directing *Gentleman's Agreement* (1947) and *On the Waterfront* (1954) and a Lifetime Achievement award in 1999. Among his other films were *Boomerang!* (1947), *Pinky* (1949), *Panic in the Streets* (1950), *Viva Zapata!* (1952), *East of Eden* (1955), *Baby Doll* (1956), *A Face in the Crowd* (1957), *Splendor in the Grass* (1961), *America America* (1963), *The Arrangement* (1969), and his final film, *The Last Tycoon* (1976). The director made his Broadway debut with 1942's *The Skin of Our Teeth.* Among his other productions was 1947's *A Streetcar Named Desire,* (he also directed the 1951 film version), *All My Sons* (1947), *Death of a Saleman* (1949), *Tea and Sympathy* (1953), *Cat on a Hot Tin Roof* (1955), *Sweet Bird of Youth* (1959), and *After the Fall* (1964). He co-founded the Actors Studio with Cheryl Crawford and Robert Lewis in 1947. Kazan also wrote an autobiography *Elia Kazan: A Life.*

Stacy Keach Sr. (May 29, 1914–February 13, 2003). Born in Milwaukee, Wisconsin, the character actor, director, and producer taught acting at the Pasadena Playhouse in the early 1940s and was signed to a contract at Universal Studios. In 1946, Keach formed a company that produced industrial films and he also formed Kaydan Records, which produced spoken-word recordings. He also produced and directed the radio series *Tales of the Texas Rangers,* starring Joel McCrea. Keach played recurring roles on the television series *Get Smart* and *Dr. Quinn, Medicine Woman* and appeared as Clarence Birdseye in a series of commercials for General Foods' Birds Eye frozen foods. His film work included *Pretty Woman* (1990) and *Cobb* (1994). Sons Stacy and James both followed him into acting.

William Kelley (May 27, 1929–February 3, 2003). Born in Staten Island, New York, the film and television writer shared a screenwriting Oscar with longtime friend Earl W. Wallace for the 1985 film *Witness.* After serving in the Air Force and receiving degrees from Brown and Harvard, Kelley joined Doubleday as an editor, later working for McGraw-Hill and Simon & Schuster. The first of his six novels, *Gemini,* was published by Doubleday in 1959. Kelley began writing for television in the late 1960s and had more than 150 credits, including episodes of *Gunsmoke, Bonanza, Judd for the Defense,* and *Kung Fu.* He also wrote for the miniseries *How the West Was Won* and the TV movies *The*

Winds of Kitty Hawk, The Blue Lightning, and *The Demon Murder Case.*

Rachel Kempson (May 28, 1910–May 24, 2003). The matriarch of the Redgrave acting family was born in Dartmouth, England, studied at the Royal Academy of Dramatic Arts, and made her stage debut in 1932. She married actor Michael Redgrave in 1935—a marriage that lasted until his death in 1985. Best-known for her stage work, Kempson appeared in a number of television dramas, including *Jane Eyre* (1971), *Lady Randolph Churchill* (1975), *The Jewel in the Crown* (1984), and *Camille* (1984). Her films included *Tom Jones* (1963), *Georgy Girl* (1966), and *Out of Africa* (1985). Kempson published her memoirs, *Life Among the Redgraves: A Family and Its Fortunes,* in 1986.

Andrea King (February 1, 1919–April 22, 2003). Born Georgina Andre Barry in Paris, France, her mother was an American who returned to the U.S. shortly after King's birth and she grew up on Long Island as Georgette McKee after her mother's remarriage. King made her Broadway debut in 1933 and appeared in other stage roles until her 1940 film debut in the March of Time documentary-drama *The Ramparts We Watch.* She signed a contract with Warner Bros. (who changed her name to King) in 1944 and had an uncredited role as a nurse in the 1944 Bette Davis film *Mr. Skeffington.* An alleged feud with Davis over the starring role in 1945's *Hotel Berlin* (which King got), lead to trouble with the studio although King continued her career, often in the role of the "other woman." King's film credits included *The Very Thought of You, God Is My Co-Pilot, The Man I Love, The Beast with Five Fingers, My Wild Irish Rose, Mr. Peabody and the Mermaid, Darby's Rangers The Lemon Drop Kid, Red Planet Mars, Buccaneer's Girl, Daddy's Gone A-Hunting, Blackenstein,* and *The Color of Evening.*

Elem Klimov (July 9, 1933–October 26, 2003). Born in Stalingrad, USSR, the filmmaker was known for his satires of Communist rule and the ravages of war. He graduated from the State Institute of Cinematography in 1964. Among Klimov's films were *Welcome, No Trespassing, The Dentist's Adventures, Agony,* and *Come and See.* He completed his director wife Larissa Shepitko's film *Farewell* after her death in a 1979 car crash and made the 1980 documentary *Larissa* in her memory. Klimov later served as the president of the USSR Cinema Association and the secretary of the Soviet Filmmakers Union.

Hope Lange (November 28, 1931–December 19, 2003). The actress was born Hope Elise Ross Lange in Redding Ridge, Connecticut, into a showbiz family that moved to Greenwich Village when Lange was a child. She made her Broadway debut in *The Patriots* at the age of 12 and later worked as a model before making her film debut in 1956's *Bus Stop.* Lange earned an Oscar nomination for her third film, *Peyton Place* (1957), and received two Emmy awards for the television series *The Ghost and Mrs. Muir;* she also co-starred in the series *The New Dick Van Dyke Show.* Other screen credits included *The Young Lions* (1958), *The Best of Everything* (1959), *Wild in the Country* (1961), *Death Wish* (1974), *Blue Velvet* (1986), and *Clear and Present Danger* (1994).

William Marshall (August 19, 1924–June 11, 2003). Born in Gary, Indiana, the actor studied at the Actors Studio and the Neighborhood Playhouse in New York, combining acting with his commitment to African American heritage. Marshall toured with his one-man show, *Enter Frederick Douglass,* in the early 1990s and played the abolitionist for the PBS special *Frederick Douglass, Slave and Statesman* in 1983. His best-known film role was a variation of the Count Dracula character in the films *Blacula* (1972) and *Scream, Blacula, Scream* (1973). Other screen credits included *Demetrius and the Gladiators* (1954) and *Something of Value* (1957).

Addie McPhail (July 15, 1905–April 14, 2003). Born Addie Dukes in White Plains, Kentucky, her family relocated to Hollywood in 1925 and McPhail (the name came from her first marriage) signed a contract with the Stern Brothers, who produced short comedies distributed by Universal, including the comedy series *The Newlyweds* and *Keeping Up with the Joneses.* In 1930, she met famed (and disgraced) silent screen comedian Roscoe "Fatty" Arbuckle, who was directing low-budget comedies under a pseudonym; he directed McPhail in the short *Up a Tree* and they toured in a vaudeville act. The two married in 1932 but Arbuckle died shortly after their first wedding anniversary. After Arbuckle's death, McPhail only appeared in bit parts in a few films, including a last uncredited role in 1940's *Northwest Passage.*

Paul Monash (June 14, 1917–January 7, 2003). Born in New York City, the producer and writer began writing for television in the 1950s and wrote, directed and produced the series *Peyton Place* (1964–69). He also wrote the pilots for the TV series *The Untouchables, The Asphalt Jungle,* and *Twelve O'Clock High,* and served as the executive producer for the series *Judd, for the Defense.* Monash won a Golden Globe for the telepic *All Quiet on the Western Front* (1980) and received Emmy nominations for *Stalin* (1972) and *George Wallace* (1997). Film producer credits included *Deadfall* (1968), *Butch Cassidy and the Sundance Kid* (1969), *Slaughterhouse-Five* (1972), *The Friends of Eddie Coyle* (1973, for which Monash also co-wrote the screenplay), *The Front Page* (1974), *Carrie* (1976), *Big Trouble in Little China* (1986), and *Carrie 2: The Rage* (1999).

Karen Morley (December 12, 1909–March 8, 2003). Born Mildred Litton in Ottumwa, Iowa, the actress moved with her adoptive family to Hollywood at the age of 14. She studied at the Pasadena Playhouse and changed her name when she signed an MGM contract. Her first credited role was in 1931's *Inspiration* and she played gun moll Poppy in *Scarface* (1932). After marrying her first husband, director Charles Vidor, Morley left MGM in 1934 and worked freelance. She became involved in politics after marrying actor Lloyd Gough and was blacklisted in 1952 after refusing to answer questions from HUAAC. Screen credits included *Arsene Lupin* (1932), *The Mask of Dr. Fu Manchu* (1932), *Mata Hari* (1932), *Dinner at Eight* (1933), *Gabriel Over the White House* (1933), *Our Daily Bread* (1934), *Black Fury* (1935), *The Littlest Rebel* (1935), *Pride and Prejudice* (1940), and *M* (1951).

Anita Mui (October 10, 1963–December 30, 2003). Born Yim-Fong Mui in Hong Kong, the pop singer/actress began her career at the age of four singing in amusement parks. She launched her professional singing career after winning a local talent contest in 1982 and recorded nearly 40 albums, selling 10 million records. Mui appeared in some 50 films, including *Rumble in the Bronx*, *Drunken Master II*, *Black Dragon*, *Rouge*, *The Enforcer*, and *Top Bet*.

Brianne Murphy (April 1, 1933–August 20, 2003). The cinematographer was born in London, England, to American parents who moved back to the U.S. in 1939. Murphy studied acting at the Neighborhood Playhouse in New York and moved to Hollywood in the mid-1950s where she got a job working for low-budget horror film producer Jerry Warren. She was admitted to the International Cinematographers Guild in 1973 and became the first women director of photography on a major studio feature with 1980's *Fatso* as well as being the first woman admitted to the American Society of Cinematographers that same year. She also worked on television for such series as *Little House on the Prairie*, *Breaking Away*, *Highway to Heaven*, and *In the Heat of the Night*.

N!xau (1944?–July 2, 2003). Born in Namibia, the bushman, a member of the nomadic San tribe, was discovered by director Jamie Uys and starred in his South African film *The Gods Must Be Crazy* (1980), which became an international hit, as well as its sequel *The Gods Must Be Crazy II*. He also appeared in several Hong Kong action films, *Crazy Safari*, *Crazy Hong Kong*, and *The Gods Must Be Funny in China*. N!xau's exact age was unknown but he was estimated to be 59 at the time of his death.

David Newman (February 4, 1937–June 27, 2003). Born in New York City, the screenwriter was nominated (along with Robert Benton) for an Academy Award for 1967's *Bonnie and Clyde*. He began his career as a writer and editor for *Esquire* magazine in 1960. Additional credits included *There Was a Crooked Man; Bad Company; What's Up, Doc?;*

Superman; Superman II; Superman III; Jinxed; and *Santa Claus: The Movie.*

Cliff Norton (March 21, 1918–January 25, 2003). Character actor Norton was born in Chicago, Illinois, and began his career on radio in 1937. He became a regular on Dave Garroway's live television variety series *Garroway at Large* (1949–51). Norton followed Garroway to New York in 1952 and worked on numerous TV shows as well as doing standup on *The Ed Sullivan Show* and *The Tonight Show*. Among the actor's screen credits were *It's a Mad Mad Mad Mad World; Frankie and Johnny; The Russians Are Coming, the Russians Are Coming; The Ghost and Mr. Chicken; Harry and Tonto;* and *Funny Lady.*

Albert Nozaki (January 1, 1912–November 16, 2003). The art director was born in Tokyo, Japan; his family moved to Los Angeles when he was three. Nozaki began as a draftsman for Paramount Pictures in 1934 and worked at the studio until his retirement in 1969. However, his employment was interrupted when he was interned in the Manzanar internment camp in 1942; Nozaki returned to Paramount after the end of World War II. Among his credits were *The War of the Worlds, When Worlds Collide, The Big Clock, Sorrowful Jones, Appointment with Danger, Pony Express, Houdini, The Buccaneer,* and *Loving You*. He received an Oscar nomination for color art direction for *The Ten Commandments* (1956).

Donald O'Connor (August 28, 1925–September 27, 2003). The song-and-dance comedian, who made more than 70 films, was born in Chicago, Illinois, to parents who worked in vaudeville. O'Connor began his own career doing acrobatics at the age of 13 months. He made his film debut with 1937's *Melody for Two* and was signed by Paramount a year later. He was a child actor in such films as *Tom Sawyer—Detective* and *Beau Geste* and a popular performer in a series of low-budget musicals in the 1940s for Universal, including *Something in the Wind; Feudin', Fussin', and A-Fightin';* and *Yes, Sir, That's My Baby*. He also starred in the popular series *Francis the Talking Mule* and its five sequels from 1950 to 1956. Among his other films were *I Love Melvin, Call Me Madam, Anything Goes, There's No Business Like Show Business, The Buster Keaton Story, Ragtime, Toys,* and his last film, 1997's *Out to Sea*. O'Connor may be best known for his rendition of "Make 'Em Laugh" in the 1952 MGM classic *Singin' in the Rain*.

Norman Panama (April 21, 1914–January 13, 2003). Born in Chicago, Illinois, Panama began a three-decade long writing partnership with Melvin Frank in the 1930s. They frequently collaborated with Bob Hope, beginning when Hope hired the duo to write for his *Pepsodent Hour* radio show in 1938. Their first screen credit was the Hope comedy *My Favorite Blonde* (1942). The duo received an Oscar nomination for the Hope-Crosby film *The Road to Utopia* (1945) and also for their films *Knock on Wood* (1954) and *The Facts of Life* (1960). Among their other dual credits were *Happy Go Lucky* (1943), *Thank Your Lucky Stars* (1943), *And the Angels Sing* (1944), *Monsieur Beaucaire* (1945), *Mr. Blandings Builds His Dream House* (1948), *White Christmas* (1954), and *The Court Jester* (1956). Panama and Franks also wrote and directed *The Reformer and the Redhead* (1950), *Calloway Went Thataway* (1951), *Strictly Dishonorable* (1951), *Above and Beyond* (1952), and *That Certain Feeling* (1956). The duo split amicably in 1966. Panama's solo directing credits included *The Trap* (1959); *The Road to Hong Kong* (1962); *Not With My Wife, You Don't!* (1966); *How to Commit Marriage* (1969); *The Maltese Bippy* (1969); *I Will, I Will . . . for Now* (1975); and *Barnaby and Me* (1977).

Suzy Parker (October 28, 1933–May 3, 2003). Born Cecelia Anne Rene Parker in Long Island City, New York (some sources say San Antonio, Texas), the beautiful redhead began modeling at the age of 14, following her older sister Dorian Leigh into the profession. She was the highest-paid model and cover girl during her heyday in the 1950s and her fame led to a brief acting career. Fashion photographer Richard Avedon introduced Parker to director Stanley Donen, who used her as one of three Paris models in his 1957 musical *Funny Face*. Parker also appeared in *Kiss Them for Me* (1957), *Ten North Frederick* (1958), *The Best of Everything* (1959), *Circle of Deception* (1960), *The Interns* (1961), and *Chamber of Horrors* (1966) as well as guest-starring in a number of television series. Parker retired from acting after moving with actor husband Bradford Dillman to Montecito, California in 1968.

Gregory Peck (April 5, 1916–June 12, 2003). Born Eldred Gregory Peck in La Jolla, California, the actor studied English and was in the drama club at the University of California Berkeley. He moved to New York and worked as a barker in the 1939 World's Fair and then studied at the Neighborhood Playhouse. Peck, who was disqualified for military service because of a spinal injury, made his film debut in 1944's *Days of Glory*. Peck earned his first Academy Award nomination for 1944's *The Keys of the Kingdom*, his second for *The Yearling* (1946), a third for 1947's *Gentleman's Agreement*, and a fourth for *Twelve O'Clock High* (1949). He finally won for probably his best-known role, that of Southern lawyer Atticus Finch in *To Kill a Mockingbird* (1962). Additional screen credits included *Spellbound* (1945), *Duel in the Sun* (1946), *The Gunfighter* (1950), *Captain Horatio Hornblower* (1951), *The Snows of Kilimanjaro* (1952), *Roman Holiday* (1953), *Moby Dick* (1956), *The Man in the Grey Flannel Suit* (1956), *Designing Woman* (1957), *On the Beach* (1959), *Pork Chop Hill* (1959), *The Guns of Navarone* (1961), *Cape Fear* (1961; Peck also had a cameo in the 1991

remake), *Arabesque* (1966), *The Omen* (1976), *MacArthur* (1977), *The Boys from Brazil* (1978), *Old Gringo* (1989), and *Other People's Money* (1991). Peck was president of the Academy of Motion Pictures Arts & Sciences (AMPAS) from 1967 to 1970 and received the Academy's Jean Hersholt Humanitarian Award in 1967 and the American Film Institute's Life Achievement Award in 1989.

Maurice Pialat (August 31, 1925–January 11, 2003). Born in Cunlhat, France, the director grew up in Paris and studied at the Ecle des Arts Decoratifs and Ecole des Beaux Arts. He began making short films in the 1950s and spent much of the 1960s directing for French television and making documentaries. Films included *L'Enfance Nue/Naked Childhood* (1969), *We Will Not Grow Old Together* (1972), *Mouth Agape* (1974), *Passe Ton Bac D'Abord* (1978), *Loulou* (1979), *A Nos Amours/To Our Loves* (1983), *Police* (1985), *Van Gogh* (1991), and *Le Garcu* (1995). Pialat won the Palme d'Or at the Cannes Film Festival for *Sous le Soleil de Satan/Under the Sun of Satan* (1987).

George Plimpton (March 18, 1927–September 25, 2003). The urbane writer and editor was born in New York City and graduated from Harvard University. He was a founding editor of the *Paris Review* literary magazine in 1953 and wrote about his participatory adventures in such fields as football (with *Paper Lion*, which was filmed in 1968), boxing, baseball, basketball, hockey, and professional golf. Plimpton also had small roles in a number of films, including *Rio Lobo*, *Reds*, *Good Will Hunting*, *Nixon*, and *Little Man Tate*.

Vera Hruba Ralston (June 12, 1921–February 9, 2003). Born in Prague, Czechoslovakia, the actress began figure skating as a child, skating in the 1936 Olympics and in the Ice Capades. It was there that Herbert J. Yates, head of Republic Pictures, saw Hruba and featured her in the 1941 musical *Ice-Capades*, which was followed by a 1942 sequel. She signed a contract with Republic and added the surname Ralston because Americans had difficulty pronouncing Hruba. Over 14 years, Ralston appeared in more than 20 Republic films, including *The Lady and the Monster; Lake Placid Serenade; Storm Over Lisbon; I, Jane Doe; Dakota; The Fighting Kentuckian; The Plainsman and the Lady;* and *Fair Wind to Java*. Ralston married Yates in 1952 and retired from the screen in 1958 when Yates left Republic.

Maurice Harry Rapf (May 19, 1914–April 15, 2003). Born in New York City, the screenwriter moved with his family to Hollywood at age seven where his father, Harry Rapf, was a pioneering producer at MGM Studios. He attended Dartmouth and, after a visit to Russia to attend the Anglo-American Institute in 1934, became a supporter of the Communist Party. He began working as a screenwriter after graduating in 1935 with *They Gave Him a Gun, The Bad Man of Brimstone,* and 1939's *Winter Carnival.* Rapf worked for Disney on *Song of the South* and *So Dear to My Heart,* as well as contributing to *Cinderella,* before leaving the studio in 1947. A member and supporter of the Screen Writers Guild, Rapf was blacklisted in 1947 and later moved back to New York, where he worked as a writer, director, and producer of more than 60 commercial and industrial films. He also contributed to films and television shows under a pseudonym and was a film reviewer for several publications. In 1966, Rapf began lecturing on film at Dartmouth, where he had earlier co-founded the Dartmouth Film Society. Rapf was also the author of *All About the Movies: A Handbook for the Movie-Loving Layman* and *Back Lot: Growing Up With the Movies.*

Gene Anthony Ray (May 24, 1962–November 14, 2003). Born in Harlem, the actor starred as Leroy Johnson in the 1980 film *Fame* and the subsequent series which ran on NBC in 1982 and in syndication from 1983 to 1987. Other film credits included *Out of Sync* (1995) and *Eddie* (1996). Ray also participated in the 2003 reunion documentary *Fame Remember My Name.* He died of complications from a stroke.

Leni Riefenstahl (August 22, 1902–September 7, 2003). Born Helene Bertha Amalie Riefenstahl in Berlin, Germany, the filmmaker was denounced as a propagandist for Hitler for her documentaries *Triumph of the Will* (1934), the official commemoration of the Nazi party rally in Nuremburg, and *Olympia* (1936), which covered the Berlin Olympic Games. She began acting in 1924 and starred in seven so-called "mountain films" for director Arnold Fanck. In 1932, Riefenstahl directed her first movie, *The Blue Light,* and also made the 1944 film *Tiefland/Lowlands.* She later turned to photography and made a documentary on marine life, *Impressions Under Water,* in 2002. Riefenstahl also wrote an autobiography, *Leni Riefenstahl: A Memoir,* which was published in 1987.

Dorothy Fay Ritter (April 4, 1915–November 5, 2003). Born Dorothy Fay Southworth in Prescott, Arizona, the actress appeared under the name Dorothy Fay in a series of B-movie westerns from 1938 to 1941, beginning with *Law of the Texan,* and in the serials *White Eagle* and *The Green Archer.* She also made four westerns with her future husband Tex Ritter, including *Song of the Buckaroo,* retiring shortly after their marriage in 1941.

John Ritter (September 17, 1948–September 11, 2003). Born in Burbank, California, the actor graduated from the University of Southern California and began his career with a recurring role as a minister on the TV series *The Waltons.* However, Ritter was best known for his starring role in the

series *Three's Company,* which ran from 1977 to 1984 and earned him an Emmy and a Golden Globe. After a couple of unsuccessful tries, Ritter had a modest hit with *Hearts Afire* (1992–95) and was working on his ABC sitcom *8 Simple Rules for Dating My Teenage Daughter,* when he was stricken by a previously unknown heart problem. Film credits included *Problem Child* (1990), *Sling Blade* (1996), *Panic* (2000), *Tadpole* (2002), *Bad Santa* (2003), and *Manhood* (2003).

Carlos Rivas (September 16, 1928–June 16, 2003). Born in El Paso, Texas, the character actor appeared in more than 40 films, beginning with a series of films shot in Mexico, before being signed to a contract with 20th Century-Fox. Screen credits included *The King and I* (1956), *The Deerslayer* (1957), *The Unforgiven* (1960), *True Grit* (1969), *Gas Food Lodging* (1992), and *Mi Vida Loca* (1994). He also guest-starred in numerous television series and had a recurring role in *Zorro.*

Patricia Roc (June 7, 1915–December 30, 2003). Born Felicia Herold in London, England, the actress was a top movie star in Britain in the 1940s and 50s. After studying at the Royal Academy of Dramatic Arts, Roc made her stage debut in 1938 in *Nuts in May.* She was spotted by movie mogul Alexander Korda, who hired Roc for his 1938 costume adventure, *The Rebel Son.* Roc made some 40 films during her career, including *Millions Like Us, The Wicked Lady, The Brothers, When the Bough Breaks,* and *Canyon Passage.*

Robert Rockwell (October 15, 1920–January 25, 2003). Born in Chicago, Illinois, the actor studied at the Pasadena Playhouse and began his film career as a contract player for Republic Pictures. He made more than 30 films, including *War of the Worlds.* But Rockwell was best known for his 50-year career in television, including co-starring as biology teacher Mr. Boynton in the CBS series *Our Miss Brooks,* which ran from 1952 to 1956. He and star Eve Arden also starred in the 1956 movie based on the series. Rockwell was also featured in some 200 commercial and voice-over spots.

Janice Rule (August 15, 1931–October 17, 2003). Born in Norwood, Ohio, the actress started her career as a dancer and made her debut on Broadway in 1953 in *Picnic.* Among her films were *Goodbye, My Fancy* (1951); *Bell, Book and Candle* (1958); *The Subterraneans* (1960); *The Chase* (1966); *The Swimmer* (1968); and *3 Women* (1977). Rule guest-starred on television in the 1980s but later studied psychoanalysis, earning a doctorate from the Southern California Psychoanalytic Institute and starting a private practice.

Walter Scharf (August 1, 1910–February 24, 2003). Born in New York City, the film score composer and arranger moved to Los Angeles in 1934 and worked as an arranger for Rudy Vallee's orchestra, also writing incidental music for dozens of films. Scharf received 10 Academy Award nominations, including *Mercy Island* (1942), *Hans Christian Andersen* (1953), *Funny Girl* (1968), *Willy Wonka and the Chocolate Factory* (1972), and *Ben* (1973). Scharf also worked on numerous television shows, including *The Man from U.N.C.L.E.* and *Mission: Impossible*. Scharf retired from Hollywood in the mid-1970s but continued composing, including the symphony "The Tree Stands Still."

John Schlesinger (February 16, 1926–July 25, 2003). Born in London, England, the director won an Oscar for the X-rated *Midnight Cowboy* in 1969. Schlesinger studied English at Oxford University and also joined the Oxford University Dramatic Society. During the 1950s, he made a series of documentaries for the BBC before making his feature film debut with 1962's *A Kind of Loving*. Other films included *Billy Liar* (1963), *Far from the Madding Crowd* (1967), *The Day of the Locust* (1975), *Marathon Man* (1976), *Yanks* (1979), *The Falcon and the Snowman* (1987), *Madame Sousatzka* (1988), *Cold Comfort Farm* (1995), and *The Next Best Thing* (2000). Schlesinger also received Oscar nominations for 1965's *Darling* and 1971's *Sunday Bloody Sunday*.

Martha Scott (September 22, 1912–May 28, 2003). Born in Jamesport, Missouri, the actress earned a degree in drama from the University of Michigan in 1934. While living in New York, Scott saw her first success originating the part of Emily in Thornton Wilder's play *Our Town* in 1938. Scott recreated the role for her film debut in 1940, earning a best actress Oscar nomination. Other screen credits included *The Howards of Virginia, One Foot in Heaven, In Old Oklahoma, The Desperate Hours, Sayonara, The Ten Commandments,* and *Ben-Hur*. Scott also remained active onstage until her last role in 1991's *The Crucible*.

Albert Sendrey (December 26, 1911–May 18, 2003). Born in Chicago, Illinois, the studio film orchestrator, arranger, and composer contributed (often uncredited) to more than 170 films and television shows. Educated at the Leipzig Conservatory and Trinity College of Music, he received his first credit for a French film in 1933. Sendrey worked at MGM in the 1940s and '50s on such films as *Neptune's Daughter, Guys and Dolls, Easter Parade, High Society, The Yearling, Thoroughly Modern Millie,* and *Finian's Rainbow*.

Richard "Dick" Simmons (August 19, 1913–January 11, 2003). Born in St. Paul, Minnesota, the actor moved to Los Angeles in the late 1930s, working odd jobs and taking bit film parts until being signed to a contract at MGM in 1942. He had small roles in such films as *Love Laughs at Andy Hardy, Lady in the Lake, The Three Musketeers,* and *Angels in the Outfield*. But Simmons became best known for his title role in the CBS television series *Sergeant Preston of the Yukon,* which ran from 1955 to 1958. His last role was in the 1977 television movie, *Don't Push, I'll Change When I'm Ready*.

Penny Singleton (September 15, 1908–November 12, 2003). Born Dorothy McNulty in Philadelphia, Pennsylvania, the actress was best known for her role as Blondie Bumstead in 28 movies from 1938 to 1950. She performed in vaudeville as a child and later had small roles on Broadway before moving to Hollywood and changing her name for films. Singleton's credits included *Good News* (1930), *After the Thin Man* (1936), *Boy Meets Girl* (1938), and *The Best Man* (1964). She also voiced the character of Jane Jetson in the animated TV series, *The Jetsons*.

Michael Small (May 30, 1939–November 25, 2003). Born in New York City, the composer scored more than 50 feature and TV movies, beginning with 1969's *Out of It*. Credits included *Klute, The Parallax View, Marathon Man, The Stepford Wives, The China Syndrome, Brighton Beach Memoirs, Comes a Horseman, Night Moves, The Postman Always Rings Twice, Black Widow,* and *Mountains of the Moon*.

Jack Smight (March 9, 1925–September 1, 2003). The director, who was born in Minneapolis, Minnesota, was a drama major at the University of Minnesota. After moving to Hollywood, Smight found work instead as a stage manager and, eventually, a director. Films included *I'd Rather Be Rich* (1964), *Harper* (1966), *The Secret War of Harry Fig* (1968), *No Way to Treat a Lady* (1968), *The Illustrated Man* (1969), *Airport 1975* (1974), *Midway* (1976), *Fast Break* (1979), *Number One with a Bullet* (1987), and *The Favorite* (1989). Smight also worked extensively in television, beginning in the 1950s, and directed a number of TV films, which included *Columbo: Dead Weight* (1971), *The Longest Night* (1972), *Double Indemnity* (1973), *Frankenstein: The True Story* (1973), *Roll of Thunder, Hear My Cry* (1978), and *Remembrance of Love* (1982).

Albert Sordi (June 15, 1919–February 24, 2003). Born in Rome, Italy, the actor made more than 160 films over a 50-year career. Sordi began his career dubbing comedian Oliver Hardy's voice for Italian screenings of Laurel and Hardy films in the 1930s. Screen credits included *White Sheik* (1952), *I Vitelloni* (1953), *An American in Rome* (1954), *Count Max* (1957), *The Great War* (1959), *The Best of Enemies* (1961), *Complexes* (1965), *Those Magnificent Men in Their Flying Machines* (1965), and *An Average Little Man* (1977). Sordi also directed some films, beginning with 1965's *Smoke over London*.

Robert Stack (January 13, 1919–May 14, 2003). Born Robert Langford Modini in Los Angeles, Stack made his movie debut in 1939's *First Love*, where he received attention for giving teenaged star Deanna Durbin her first screen kiss. Stack appeared in more than 70 films and received a best supporting actor Oscar nomination for *Written on the Wind* (1956). Other screen credits included *To Be or Not to Be* (1942), *The*

Bullfighter and the Lady (1951), *Bwana Devil* (1952), *The High and the Mighty* (1954), *House of Bamboo* (1955), *1941* (1979), and *Airplane!* (1980). In 1959, Stack starred as Eliot Ness in the series *The Untouchables,* which ran until 1963. He earned an Emmy for his role in 1960 and later played the role for a 1991 TV movie *The Return of Eliot Ness.* Stack also starred in the TV series *The Name of the Game* (1968–71), *Most Wanted* (1976–77), and *Strike Force* (1981–82), and was the host of *Unsolved Mysteries* (1987–2002).

Peter Stone (February 27, 1930–April 26, 2003). Born in Los Angeles, the writer attended Bard College and the Yale School of Drama and worked in Paris as a writer and news reader for CBS. His first credit was a 1956 episode of the *Studio One* TV series. Stone's first screenplay was 1963's *Charade* and he won an Oscar for another Cary Grant film, 1964's *Father Goose.* Other screen credits included *Mirage* (1965); *Arabesque* (1966); *Sweet Charity* (1969); *The Skin Game* (1971); *The Taking of Pelham One, Two, Three* (1974); *Who is Killing the Great Chefs of Europe?* (1978); and *Just Cause* (1995). Stone used the pseudonym Peter Joshua for his contributions to the screenplay of the 2002 *Charade* remake *The Truth About Charlie.* Stone also received an Emmy for a 1962 episode of *The Defenders* and three Tony awards for *1776* (1969), *Woman of the Year* (1981), and *Titanic* (1997).

Daniel Taradash (January 29, 1913–February 22, 2003). Born in Louisville, Kentucky, the screenwriter, who studied law at Harvard, won a playwriting contest in 1938 and was then signed by Columbia Pictures. His first credit was co-writing 1939's *Golden Boy.* Taradash won a screenwriting Oscar for 1953's *From Here to Eternity.* Other writing credits included *The Noose Hangs High* (1948); *Knock on Any Door* (1949); *Don't Bother to Knock* (1952); *Rancho Notorious* (1952); *Desiree* (1954); *Picnic* (1955); *Bell, Book and Candle* (1958); *Hawaii* (1966); *Doctors' Wives* (1971); and *The Other Side of Midnight* (1977). Taradash also co-wrote and directed the 1956 film *Storm Center.*

Lynne Thigpen (December 22, 1948–March 12, 2003). Born in Joliet, Illinois, the actress made her New York stage debut in 1973's *Godspell,* which she reprised for the film. In 1997, Thigpen received a Tony Award for *American Daughter.* She also played the part of Chief on the PBS series *Where in the World Is Carmen Sandiego?* and received an Emmy for the role in the second series *Where in Time Is Carmen Sandiego?* She also had regular roles on the series *All My Children; Love, Sidney;* and *The District.* Screen credits included *The Insider, Shaft, Tootsie, Lean on Me, Bob Roberts, The Paper, Random Hearts,* and *Anger Management.*

Marie Trintignant (January 21, 1962–August 1, 2003). Born in Boulogne-Billancourt, France, the actress was the

daughter of actor Jean-Louis Trintignant and director Nadine Trintignant. Her first role was at the age of five, working with her parents in *Mon Amour, Mon Amour.* Screen credits included *Serie Moire, Une Affaire de Femme,* and *Betty.*

Michael Wayne (November 23, 1934–April 2, 2003). Born Michael Anthony Morrison in Los Angeles, the eldest son of actor John Wayne, Michael Wayne worked for his father's Batjac Productions company, beginning as an associate producer on 1960's *The Alamo.* He also produced *McLintock!* (1963), *The Green Berets* (1968), *Big Jake* (1971), *Cahill U.S. Marshall* (1973), and *Brannigan* (1975). Wayne also started Wayne Enterprises, which controlled the use of his father's name and image, and was the president of the John Wayne Foundation and chairman of the John Wayne Cancer Institute.

Sheb Wooley (April 10, 1921–September 9, 2003). Born Shelby F. Wooley in Erick, Oklahoma, the singer and character actor began his career onscreen in 1950 with the film *Rocky Mountain.* Credits included *High Noon, The Outlaw Josey Wales, The War Wagon, Distant Drums, Man Without a Star, Giant,* and *Hoosiers.* In 1958, Wooley had a No. 1 pop hit with the novelty tune "The Purple People Eater" and later acted in the 1988 movie of the same name. Wooley also appeared in a number of television series, including the role of trail scout Pete Nolan on the series *Rawhide* from 1959 to 1965.

Philip Yordan (April 1, 1914–March 24, 2003). The writer and producer, who was born in Chicago, Illinois, began his career in the 1930s working for director William Dieterlie. He received an Oscar for his original story for 1954's *Broken Lance* and was nominated for *Dillinger* (1945) and *Detective Story* (1951). Among his other writing credits were *House of Strangers, The Man from Laramie, Blowing Wild, The Harder They Fall,* and *55 Days to Peking.* Yordan also acted as a front for blacklisted colleagues during the McCarthy era, which later resulted in the Writers Guild of America correcting writing credits on some films to restore the names of blacklisted writers, including *Johnny Guitar, El Cid,* and *The Day of the Triffids.* Among Yordan's producer credits were *The Battle of the Bulge, The Royal Hunt of the Sun, El Cid, Circus World,* and *Krakatoa, East of Java.*

Paul Zindel (May 15, 1936–March 27, 2003). The playwright and successful young adult novelist was born in Staten Island and wrote plays and sketches in high school. He received his bachelor's and master's degrees in chemistry and was a high school chemistry teacher when his play, *The Effect of Gamma Rays on Man-in-the-Moon Marigolds,* won an Obie Award in 1970 and a Pulitzer in 1971. Zindel wrote the screenplay for the 1972 film version; other screen credits included *Up the Sandbox* (1972), *Mame* (1974), *Maria's Lovers* (1984), and *Runaway Train* (1985).

Vera Zorina (January 2, 1917–April 9, 2003). Born Eva Brigitta Hartwig in Berlin, Germany, she began studying ballet at the age of six. Zorina moved to London in 1933 and joined the Ballets Russes de Monte Carlo in 1934; it was the director of that company who changed her name. In 1937, Samuel Goldwyn gave her a contract and she made her film debut in 1938's *The Goldwyn Follies.* Zorina made only six more films: *On Your Toes* (1939), *I Was an Adventuress* (1940), *Louisiana Purchase* (1941), *Star-Spangled Rhythm* (1942), *Follow the Boys* (1944), and *Lover Come Back* (1946). Zorina continued her career as a dancer and comedic actress on the stage and as a narrator of concert works. She published her autobiography, *Zorina,* in 1986.

Selected Film Books of 2003

Alexander, George. *Why We Make Movies: Black Filmmakers Talk About the Magic of Cinema.* Harlem Moon, 2003.

Interviews with more than 35 African-American filmmakers, including Gordon Parks, Melvin Van Peebles, Ossie Davis, Spike Lee, Lee Daniels, and others.

Armstrong, Kent Byron. *Slasher Films: An International Filmography, 1960 through 2001.* McFarland & Company, Inc., 2003.

Covers more than 250 genre films, including such information as major cast and production credits, plot synopsis, and short critique. Filmographies are provided for directors, actors, writers, and composers.

Berg, A. Scott. *Kate Remembered.* Putnam, 2003.

The biographer describes his 20-year friendship with Katharine Hepburn.

Blottner, Gene. *Universal Sound Westerns, 1929–1946: A Complete Filmography.* McFarland & Company, Inc., 2003.

Includes entries for some 180 feature films and serials released by Universal.

Boorman, John. *Adventures of a Suburban Boy.* Faber & Faber, 2003.

The British film director offers a memoir of his life and career.

Briggs, Joe Bob. *Profoundly Disturbing: The Shocking Movies That Changed History.* Universe, 2003.

An analysis of some 20 cult films from *And God Created Woman* to *The Texas Chainsaw Massacre*.

Bruck, Connie. *When Hollywood Had a King: The Reign of Lew Wasserman, Who Leveraged Talent into Power and Influence.* Random, 2003.

A look at the life and career of the man who transformed MCA from a talent agency into a powerful and influential film and television studio.

Buhle, Paul and David Wagner. *Hide in Plain Sight: The Hollywood Blacklistees in Film and Television, 1950–2002.* Palgrave, 2003.

Study of the impact of the Hollywood blacklist on the arts in both America and Europe and the careers of such individuals as Joseph Losey, Carl Foreman, Jules Dassin, Dalton Trumbo, and others.

Burt, Jonathan. *Animals in Film.* Reaktion Books, 2003.

Examines the roles animals have played from Disney to avant-garde cinema, including shift in contemporary attitudes towards animals and animal rights activists.

Buscombe, Edward. *Cinema Today.* Phaidon, 2003.

An analysis of international cinema from 1970 to the present and the influence of American movies worldwide.

Capua, Michelangelo. *Vivien Leigh: A Biography.* McFarland & Company, Inc., 2003.

Biography of the British star that details her development and career as a stage and film actress as well as her private life.

Cary, Diana Serra. *Jackie Coogan: The World's Boy King.* Scarecrow Press, Inc., 2003.

Biography of the first major Hollywood child star and his subsequent career and personal troubles.

Chace, Reeve. *The Complete Book of Oscar Fashion: Variety's 75 Years of Glamour on the Red Carpet.* Reed Press, 2003.

Showcases Oscar fashions from the 1920s to 2003 organized by decade as well as information on top designers and looks.

Chierichetti, David. *Edith Head: The Life and Times of Hollywood's Celebrated Costume Designer.* HarperCollins, 2003.

The author details Head's life and 40-year career at Paramount studios, including her eight Oscar wins.

Clagett, Thomas D. *William Friedkin: Films of Aberration, Obsession and Reality.* Silman-James Press, 2003.

A behind-the-scenes look at the director's works, including *The Exorcist* and *The French Connection.*

Curtis, James. *W.C. Fields: A Biography.* Knopf, 2003.

Warts-and-all biography of the acerbic comedian from his vaudeville days to his screen career.

Early, Emmett. *The War Veteran in Film.* McFarland & Company, Inc., 2003.

Examines more than 125 films that feature the war veteran in various eras and themes.

Elder, Jane Lenz. *Alice Faye: A Life Beyond the Silver Screen.* University Press of Mississippi, 2003.

Biography of the actress on- and off-screen.

Erickson, Gunnar, Harris Tulchin and Mark Halloran. *The Independent Film Producer's Survival Guide.* Schirmer Trade Books, 2003.

Presents business and legal advice in layman's terms and includes a comprehensive set of legal forms.

Ferrer, Sean Hepburn. *Audrey Hepburn, An Elegant Spirit: A Son Remembers.* Atria, 2003.

Memoir of the actress from her deprivations growing up in Belgium in World War II to her career, home life, and work with UNICEF.

Fishgall, Gary. *Gonna Do Great Things: The Life of Sammy Davis Jr.* Scribner, 2003.

Portrait of the performer's life and work on stage as well as his recording, film and television careers, his involvement in the civil rights movement, and his tumultuous private life.

Fraser-Cavassoni, Natasha. *Sam Spiegel.* Simon & Schuster, 2003.

Biography of the Oscar-winning producer; includes a filmography and bibliography.

Gehring, Wes D. *Carole Lombard: The Hoosier Tornado.* Indiana Historical Society, 2003.

Biography of the screen siren/comedian, born in Indiana and raised in California, whose premature death at the age of 33 in a plane crash made her a Hollywood legend.

Giesen, Rolf. *Nazi Propaganda Films: A History and Filmography.* McFarland & Company, Inc., 2003.

Focuses on feature films and feature-length documentaries made in Germany between 1933 and 1945 that were released to the public. Included are cast and production credits as well as brief biographies of actors, directors, producers, and others involved in the making of the films.

Gilbey, Ryan. *It Don't Worry Me: The Revolutionary American Films of the Seventies.* Faber & Faber, 2003.

Examines the careers of 10 influential directors, including Martin Scorsese, Francis Ford Coppola, Woody Allen, Brian De Palma, and George Lucas.

Haines, Richard W. *The Moviegoing Experience, 1968–2001.* McFarland & Company, Inc., 2003.

Examines the American moviegoing experience, including the way in which movies are made and regulated; the changes in various technical aspects of film, including computerized special effects; and how home video and cable have affected the content of films.

Halpern, Leslie. *Dreams on Film: The Cinematic Struggle Between Art and Science.* McFarland & Company, Inc., 2003.

Part One discusses the history of dream theory and filmic use of sleeping and dreaming. Part Two investigates the psychology of dream interpretation, altered states of consciousness, reality versus illusions, and an analysis of dream sequences and their use in film.

Hansberry, Karen Burroughs. *Bad Boys: The Actors of Film Noir.* McFarland & Company, Inc., 2003.

Provides information on more than 90 actors who starred in the film noirs of the 1940s and 50s from James Cagney and Edward G. Robinson to Gene Lockhart and Moroni Olsen.

Haygood, Wil. *In Black and White: The Life of Sammy Davis Jr.* Knopf, 2003.

Biography of the entertainer examines his career from vaudeville to Vegas as well as his desire to be accepted by white America.

Henderson, Sanya Shoilevska. *Alex North, Film Composer.* McFarland & Company, Inc., 2003.

A biography with musical analyses of North's film scores for *A Streetcar Named Desire, Spartacus, The Misfits, Under the Volcano,* and *Prizzi's Honor.* Appendices include a filmography, information on other compositions, a discography, and a list of awards.

Hoberman, J. *The Dream Life: Movies, Media, and the Mythology of the Sixties.* New Press, 2003.

The *Village Voice* critic offers a historical, political, and cinematic view of the era.

Hodges, Graham Russell Gao. *Anna May Wong: From Laundryman's Daughter to Hollywood Legend.* Palgrave, 2003.

Biography of the Asian-American actress, a third-generation Californian, who could only find film work in stereotypical Asian roles in pre- and post-WWII Hollywood.

Hoffmann, Henryk. *Western Film Highlights: The Best of the West, 1914–2001.* McFarland & Company, Inc., 2003.

For each year, the author offers information on outstanding films in such categories as picture, screenplay, direction, cinematography, music, and performance.

Holley, Val. *Mike Connolly and the Manly Art of Hollywood Gossip.* McFarland & Company, Inc., 2003.

A look at the career of the flamboyant writer for *The Hollywood Reporter* from 1951 to 1966.

Horton, Andrew. *Henry Bumstead and the World of Hollywood Art Directors.* University of Texas Press, 2003.

An assessment of Bumstead's seven–decade career as a production designer.

Hunter, Jack, editor. *Search and Destroy: An Illustrated Guide to Vietnam War Movies.* Creation Books, 2003.

Essays cover some 300 movies, including documentaries, depicting the Vietnam War.

Jacobson, Laurie. *Dishing Hollywood: The Real Scoop on Tinseltown's Most Notorious Scandals.* Cumberland House, 2003.

Part gossip, part cookbook as Jacobson includes information on some 40 Hollywood scandals with recipes connected to each one, from griddle cakes to salads to cocktails.

Joshi, Lalit Mohan *Bollywood: Popular Indian Cinema.* Weatherhill, 2003.

Examines the success of Hindi cinema.

Kaufman, Lloyd, with Adam Jahnke and Trent Haaga. *Make Your Own Damn Movie: Secrets of a Renegade Director.* St. Martin's Press, 2003.

Troma Studios' writer/producer/director offers a memoir of his career in low-budget filmmaking.

Keaney, Michael F. *Film Noir Guide: 743 Films of the Classic Era, 1940–1959.* McFarland & Company, Inc., 2003.

Reference guide to the genre that provides film title, release date, main performers, screenwriter, director, type of noir, themes, brief summary, and rating.

Kuhn, Michael. *One Hundred Films and a Funeral.* Thorogood Publishing, 2003.

An account of the rise and fall of Polygram Films, which produced *Four Weddings and a Funeral* and *Notting Hill,* among other movies.

Lanzoni, Remi Fournier. *French Cinema, From its Beginnings to the Present.* Continuum, 2003.

An examination of French filmmaking from the late 19th century to the present, including the silent era and the Nouvelle Vague.

Leider, Emily W. *Dark Lover: The Life and Death of Rudolph Valentino.* Farrar, Strauss and Giroux, 2003.

Biography of the silent-screen star.

Lennig, Arthur. *The Immortal Count: The Life and Films of Bela Lugosi.* University Press of Kentucky, 2003.

Biography of the actor who made his name with *Dracula* and found himself typecast in the horror genre.

Lentz, Robert J. *Korean War Filmography.* McFarland & Company, Inc., 2003.

Examines 91 films that were made about the conflict, with credits, synopsis, and comments.

Levy, Emanuel. *All About Oscar: The History and Politics of the Academy Awards.* Continuum, 2003.

Survey of the Academy Awards, including how genres have been represented, how popularity figures in, what winning means, and references to various Oscar ceremonies.

Lewis, C. Jack. *White Horse, Black Hat: A Quarter Century on Hollywood's Poverty Row.*
Scarecrow Press, Inc., 2003.

Autobiography of the screenwriter and stunt performer who worked in low-budget westerns.

Lisanti, Tom. *Drive-In Dream Girls: A Galaxy of B-Movie Starlets of the Sixties.*
McFarland & Company, Inc., 2003.

Profiles of some 50 actresses, including a biography, filmography, and the actresses' comments.

Louvish, Simon. *Keystone: The Life and Clowns of Mack Sennett.*
Faber & Faber, 2003.

Looks at the life and career of silent film mogul Mack Sennett and the Keystone studio, which he founded in 1912, and which featured the Keystone Kops, Fatty Arbuckle, Mabel Normand, Ben Turpin, Charlie Chaplin, and Gloria Swanson, among others.

Lyman, Rick. *Watching Movies: The Biggest Names in Cinema Talk About the Films That Matter Most.*
Times Books, 2003.

Collection of interviews that the film critic and industry reporter conducted with 21 film professionals for his *New York Times* column.

MacCabe, Colin. *Godard: Portrait of the Artist at Seventy.*
Farrar, Strauss & Giroux, 2003.

An annotated chronology of the film and video work of director Jean-Luc Godard.

McGilligan, Patrick. *Alfred Hitchcock: A Life in Darkness and Light.*
Regan Books, 2003.

Scholarly appraisal of the director from his London East End boyhood to his successful career.

McGrath, Declan and Felim MacDermott.
Screenwriting.
Focal Press, 2003.

The authors offer a short biography and extensive interview with some 13 screenwriters, including William Goldman, Ruth Prawer Jhabvala, Jim Sheridan, Robert Towne, and others.

Nott, Robert. *He Ran All the Way: The Life of John Garfield.*
Limelight Editions, 2003.

Biography of the actor, from his work with the Group Theater to Hollywood films, and his troubles with HUAAC and the blacklist.

O'Connell, Pat Hitchcock. *Alma Hitchcock: The Woman Behind the Man.*
Berkley, 2003.

Memoir of the famed director's wife by their daughter. Alma, who was a silent-screen actress and film editor, served as her husband's collaborator on scripts, casting, and directing. The narrative is structured around a filmography of Alfred Hitchcock's movies.

O'Connor, Garry. *Alec Guinness: A Life.*
Applause, 2003.

Biography of the chameleon-like British actor's long theater and film career.

Parish, James Robert, editor. *The Encyclopedia of Ethnic Groups in Hollywood.*
Facts on File, Inc., 2003.

Highlights movies, TV shows, themes, and people within five ethnic groups: African-Americans, Hispanic-Americans, Asian-Americans, Native-Americans, and Jewish-Americans.

Rainey, Buck. *The Strong, Silent Type: Over 100 Screen Cowboys, 1903–1930.*
McFarland & Company, Inc., 2003.

Provides biographical information and a complete filmography for more than 100 screen cowboys who starred in silent westerns.

Rensin, David. *The Mailroom: Hollywood History from the Bottom Up.*
Ballantine, 2003.

An oral history of working in the mailroom of various talent agencies, including William Morris, and CAA.

Roeper, Richard. *Ten Sure Signs a Movie Character is Doomed, and Other Surprising Movie Lists.*
Hyperion, 2003.

Humorous collection of movie-related lists.

Rollins, Peter C. and John E. O'Connor, editors.
Hollywood's White House: The American Presidency in Film and History.
University Press of Kentucky, 2003.

Explores the accuracy of the presidency as portrayed in film and television.

Rose Marie. *Hold the Roses.*
University Press of Kentucky, 2003.

Autobiography of the comedian and her career in vaudeville, film, and television, including *The Dick Van Dyke Show* and *Hollywood Squares.*

Schickel, Richard.   *Good Morning, Mr. Zip Zip Zip: Movies, Memory, and World War II.*
Ivan R. Dee, 2003.

Schickel, a 20-year film critic for *Time*, offers a memoir of his Wisconsin childhood, his interest in movies (which began at the age of five), and how both were shaped by WWII.

Schilling, Mark.   *The Yakuza Movie Book: A Guide to Japanese Gangster Films.*
Stone Bridge Press, 2003.

A look at actors and directors associated with the genre.

Seger, Linda and Edward J. Whetmore.   *From Script to Screen: The Collaborative Art of Filmmaking.*
Lone Eagle, 2003.

Devotes chapters to each element of making films from the idea to completion, including music, actor's research, and special effects.

Segrave, Kerry.   *Piracy in the Motion Picture Industry.*
McFarland & Company, Inc., 2003.

Includes a discussion of some early cases of piracy and how the problem has continued to grow as well as measure taken to prevent piracy over the years.

Shaw, Jeffrey and Peter Weibel, editors.   *Future Cinema: The Cinematic Imaginary After Film.*
MIT Press, 2003.

An investigation of new cinematic forms that incorporate electronic media to transform the traditional relationship between producer and audience.

Soares, Andre.   *Beyond Paradise: The Life of Ramon Navarro.*
St. Martin's Press, 2003.

Biography of the gay actor's career and life, including an examination of his murder.

Stevens, Brad.   *Monte Hellman: His Life and Films.*
McFarland & Company, Inc., 2003.

Biography of the actor/director that includes a study of his films.

Stevens, Michael G.   *Reel Portrayals: The Lives of 640 Historical Persons on Film, 1929 through 2001.*
McFarland & Company, Inc., 2003.

Reference guide provides a brief biography of non-fictional personages of historical or social importance who have been portrayed in at least two films. Also included are the film's title, information on the actor portraying the real person, cast credits, and other information.

Stidworthy, David.   *High on the Hogs: A Bike Filmography.*
McFarland & Company, Inc., 2003.

Provides information on some 58 biker movies, including credits, synopsis, and comments.

Stine, Scott Aaron.   *The Gorehound's Guide to Splatter Films of the 1980s.*
McFarland & Company, Inc., 2003.

Provides a brief overview of the genre plus a filmography that includes technical information, cast and production credits, plot synopsis, reviews, and other information on each film.

Vieira, Mark A.   *Hollywood Horror: From Gothic to Cosmic.*
Abrams, 2003.

An examination of the horror film genre from 1923 through 1968, including plot synopsis and anecdotes from actors, writers, directors, and producers.

Wayne, Jane Ellen.   *The Golden Girls of MGM: Greta Garbo, Joan Crawford, Lana Turner, Judy Garland, Ava Gardner, Grace Kelly and Others.*
Carroll & Graf, 2003.

Looks at the private and public lives of the ladies of Metro-Goldwyn-Mayer studio.

Wolper, David L.   *Producer: A Memoir.*
Scribner, 2003.

Autobiography covers the long career of the producer whose work encompasses corporate films, documentaries, television miniseries (including *Roots*), sitcoms, and feature films.

Magill's Cinema Annual 2004
Indexes

Director Index

KARIM AINOUZ
Madame Sata *284*

JONAS AKERLUND
Spun *419*

DAN ALGRANT
People I Know *359*

WOODY ALLEN (1935-)
Anything Else *19*

JON AMIEL (1948-)
The Core *91*

DENYS ARCAND (1941-)
The Barbarian
  Invasions *28*

OLIVIER ASSAYAS (1955-)
Demonlover *111*

FENTON BAILEY
Party Monster *356*

RANDY BARBATO
Party Monster *356*

M. NEEMA BARNETTE
Civil Brand *81*

BRUNO BARRETO (1955-)
View from the Top *477*

ANDRZEJ BARTKOWIAK
  (1950-)
Cradle 2 the Grave *93*

MICHAEL BAY (1965-)
Bad Boys 2 *23*

RICHARD BENJAMIN
  (1938-)
Marci X *299*

ROBERT BENTON (1932-)
The Human Stain *203*

PETER BERG (1964-)
The Rundown *389*

SHARI SPRINGER
  BERMAN
American Splendor *9*

CLAUDE BERRI (1934-)
A Housekeeper *194*

TROY BEYER (1965-)
Love Don't Cost a
  Thing *277*

HILARY BIRMINGHAM
Tully *459*

AARON BLAISE
Brother Bear *50*

DANNY BOYLE (1956-)
28 Days Later *464*

MARTIN BREST (1951-)
Gigli *157*

DANA BROWN
Step Into Liquid *427*

TIM BURTON (1960-)
Big Fish *39*

REGGIE ROCK
  BYTHEWOOD
Biker Boyz *42*

MARS CALLAHAN (1972-)
Poolhall Junkies *373*

MARTIN CAMPBELL
Beyond Borders *38*

JANE CAMPION (1954-)
In the Cut *215*

CHRISTIAN CARION
The Girl from Paris *159*

NIKI CARO
Whale Rider *483*

STEVE CARR
Daddy Day Care *98*

ROBERT CARY
Anything But Love *17*

CLAUDE CHABROL (1930-)
The Flower of Evil *146*

GURINDER CHADHA
Bend It Like Beckham *35*

GORDON CHAN (1960-)
The Medallion *313*

LARRY CHARLES
Masked and
  Anonymous *302*

AUSTIN CHICK
XX/XY *495*

LISA CHOLODENKO
Laurel Canyon *250*

SYLVAIN CHOMET (1963-)
The Triplets of
  Belleville *458*

JOEL COEN (1954-)
Intolerable Cruelty *221*

ILAN DURAN COHEN
Confusion of Genders *88*

ISABEL COIXET
My Life Without Me *330*

NIGEL COLE
Calendar Girls *61*

LAETITIA COLOMBANI
He Loves Me . . . He Loves
  Me Not *180*

SOFIA COPPOLA (1971-)
Lost in Translation *273*

GERALD CORMIER
See Alan Rudolph

DON A. COSCARELLI
  (1954-)
Bubba Ho-Tep *54*

CONSTANTIN COSTA-
  GAVRAS (1933-)
Amen *7*

KEVIN COSTNER (1955-)
Open Range *348*

JAMES COX
Wonderland *489*

EMANUELE CRIALESE
Respiro *381*

DAVID CRONENBERG
  (1943-)
Spider *415*

RICHARD CURTIS
Love Actually *275*

JOE DANTE (1946-)
Looney Tunes: Back in
  Action *267*

ANDREW DAVIS (1946-)
Holes *185*

JAN DE BONT (1943-)
Lara Croft Tomb Raider:
  The Cradle of Life *243*

PHILIPPE DE BROCA
  (1933-)
On Guard! *341*

ALFREDO DE VILLA
Washington Heights *479*

MARK DECENA
Dopamine *121*

TED (EDWARD) DEMME
  (1964-2002)
A Decade Under the
  Influence *107*

CLAIRE DENIS (1948-)
Friday Night *153*

DANNY DEVITO (1944-)
Duplex *130*

MATT DILLON (1964-)
City of Ghosts *77*

DAVID DOBKIN
Shanghai Knights *404*

ROGER DONALDSON
  (1945-)
The Recruit *380*

RICHARD DONNER (1939-)
Timeline *453*

DENNIS DUGAN (1946-)
National Security *334*

FRANCOIS DUPEYRON
Monsieur Ibrahim *324*

ROBERT DUVALL (1931-)
Assassination Tango *21*

JESSE DYLAN
American Wedding *11*

ERIC EASON
Manito *297*

CLINT EASTWOOD (1930-)
Mystic River *332*

DAVID R. ELLIS
Final Destination 2 *140*

JOHN ENG
Rugrats Go Wild! *385*

JIM FALL
The Lizzie McGuire
Movie *265*

BOBBY FARRELLY (1958-)
Stuck On You *430*

PETER FARRELLY (1957-)
Stuck On You *430*

JON FAVREAU (1966-)
Elf *134*

MIKE FIGGIS (1948-)
Cold Creek Manor *82*

GARY FLEDER (1963-)
Runaway Jury *386*

ANDREW FLEMING
The In-Laws *213*

JAMES FOLEY
Confidence *86*

ANNE FONTAINE
How I Killed My
Father *196*

CARL FRANKLIN (1949-)
Out of Time *352*

STEPHEN FREARS (1941-)
Dirty Pretty Things *116*

JUAN CARLOS
FRESNADILLO
Intacto *220*

WILLIAM FRIEDKIN
(1939-)
The Hunted *205*

KEITH FULTON
Lost in La Mancha *271*

ANTOINE FUQUA (1966-)
Tears of the Sun *442*

TIM FYWELL
I Capture the Castle *207*

MATTEO GARRONE
The Embalmer *136*

EMILE GAUDREAULT
Mambo Italiano *291*

BAHMAN GHOBADI
Marooned in Iraq *300*

PATRICK GILMORE
Sinbad: Legend of the Seven
Seas *410*

FRANCIS GLEBAS
Piglet's Big Movie *368*

DELPHINE GLEIZE
Carnage *67*

DENNIE GORDON
What a Girl Wants *485*

KEITH GORDON (1961-)
The Singing
Detective *412*

TODD GRAFF (1959-)
Camp *63*

F. GARY GRAY (1970-)
The Italian Job *227*
A Man Apart *292*

DAVID GORDON GREEN
All the Real Girls *5*

SAM GREEN
The Weather
Underground *480*

CHRISTOPHER GUEST
(1948-)
A Mighty Wind *314*

JOHN HANCOCK (1939-)
Suspended Animation *432*

GARY HARDWICK
Deliver Us from Eva *109*

CATHERINE HARDWICKE
Thirteen *450*

PETER HEDGES (1962-)
Pieces of April *365*

CHRIS HEGEDUS
Only the Strong
Survive *346*

BRIAN HELGELAND
(1961-)
The Order *350*

CHARLES HERMAN-
WURMFELD
Legally Blonde 2: Red,
White & Blonde *260*

JOHN HOFFMAN
Good Boy! *165*

P.J. HOGAN (1962-)
Peter Pan *361*

RON HOWARD (1954-)
The Missing *317*

PETER HOWITT (1957-)
Johnny English *232*

LI-KONG HSU
Fleeing by Night *145*

TOM HUNSINGER
Lawless Heart *252*

NEIL HUNTER
Lawless Heart *252*

PAUL HUNTER
Bulletproof Monk *58*

ALEJANDRO GONZALEZ
INARRITU
21 Grams *462*

JAMES IVORY (1928-)
Le Divorce *256*

PETER JACKSON (1961-)
The Lord of the Rings 3:
The Return of the
King *269*

BENOIT JACQUOT (1947-)
Sade *391*

ANDREW JARECKI
Capturing the
Friedmans *65*

CHRISTINE JEFFS
Sylvia *438*

PATTY JENKINS
Monster *326*

NORMAN JEWISON (1926-)
The Statement *423*

ZHANG-KE JIA
Platform *372*

CLARK JOHNSON (1954-)
S.W.A.T. *432*

MARK STEVEN JOHNSON
Daredevil *101*

TIM JOHNSON
Sinbad: Legend of the Seven
Seas *410*

GREGOR JORDAN
Buffalo Soldiers *56*

NEIL JORDAN (1950-)
The Good Thief *167*

CHEN KAIGE (1952-)
Together *456*

LAWRENCE KASDAN
(1949-)
Dreamcatcher *124*

MATHIEU KASSOVITZ
(1967-)
Gothika *169*

ABBAS KIAROSTAMI
(1940-)
Ten *444*

CLARE KILNER
How to Deal *197*

CEDRIC KLAPISCH (1961-)
L'Auberge Espagnole *248*

CHRIS KOCH
A Guy Thing *174*

ANDREI KONCHALOVSKY
(1937-)
House of Fools *190*

WAYNE KRAMER
The Cooler *89*

MARTINA KUDIACEK
In the Mirror of Maya
Deren *217*

RICHARD
KWIETNIOWSKI
(1957-)
Owning Mahowny *354*

CASEY LA SCALA
Grind *171*

NEIL LABUTE (1963-)
The Shape of Things *405*

RICHARD LAGRAVENESE
(1959-)
A Decade Under the
Influence *107*

PATRICE LECONTE
(1947-)
The Man on the
Train *294*

ANG LEE (1954-)
Hulk *200*

CLAUDE LELOUCH (1937-)
And Now Ladies and
Gentlemen *13*

FERNANDO LEON DE
ARANOA (1968-)
Mondays in the Sun *321*

SHAWN LEVY
Cheaper by the Dozen *75*
Just Married *237*

JONATHAN LIEBESMAN
Darkness Falls *105*

JUSTIN LIN
Better Luck Tomorrow *36*

CAROLINE LINK
Nowhere in Africa *338*

RICHARD LINKLATER
(1961-)
School of Rock *394*

KEN LOACH (1936-)
Sweet Sixteen *434*

TODD LOUISO (1970-)
Love Liza *278*

PAVEL (LUNGIN)
LOUNGUINE
Tycoon *467*

KATIA LUND
City of God *79*

JONATHAN LYNN (1943-)
The Fighting
Temptations *139*

JOHN MALKOVICH (1953-)
The Dancer Upstairs *100*

JAMES MANGOLD (1964-)
Identity *209*

GREGORY MARS MARTIN
See Mars Callahan

MELISSA MARTIN
The Bread, My Sweet *47*

GUS VAN SANT (1952-)
Elephant *132*
Gerry *156*

GORE VERBINSKI
Pirates of the Caribbean: The
Curse of the Black
Pearl *369*

NORTON VIRGIEN
Rugrats Go Wild! *385*

ANDY WACHOWSKI
(1967-)
The Matrix Reloaded *308*
The Matrix
Revolutions *311*

LARRY WACHOWSKI
(1965-)
The Matrix Reloaded *308*
The Matrix
Revolutions *311*

ROBERT WALKER
Brother Bear *50*

MARK S. WATERS (1964-)
Freaky Friday *150*

PETER WEBBER
Girl with a Pearl
Earring *160*

PETER WEIR (1944-)
Master and Commander:
The Far Side of the
World *303*

SAM WEISMAN
Dickie Roberts: Former
Child Star *112*

BO WELCH
Dr. Seuss' The Cat in the
Hat *119*

AUDREY WELLS
Under the Tuscan
Sun *470*

JOHN WHITESELL
Malibu's Most
Wanted *289*

LEN WISEMAN
Underworld *471*

JOHN WOO (1948-)
Paycheck *358*

BILLE WOODRUFF
Honey *188*

BOAZ YAKIN (1944-)
Uptown Girls *473*

ZHANG YIMOU (1951-)
Hero *184*

CHI YIN
Fleeing by Night *145*

RONNY YU
Freddy vs. Jason *152*

ROB ZOMBIE (1966-)
House of 1000
Corpses *191*

DAVID ZUCKER (1947-)
My Boss's Daughter *328*

JERRY ZUCKER (1950-)
Scary Movie 3 *392*

HARALD ZWART
Agent Cody Banks *1*

EDWARD ZWICK (1952-)
The Last Samurai *244*

TERRY ZWIGOFF (1948-)
Bad Santa *25*

Screenwriter Index

JOHN COLLEE
Master and Commander:
The Far Side of the
World *303*

LAETITIA COLOMBANI
He Loves Me . . . He Loves
Me Not *180*

MICHAEL COONEY
Identity *209*

SOFIA COPPOLA (1971-)
Lost in Translation *273*

CHRIS CORSO
Poolhall Junkies *373*

DON A. COSCARELLI
(1954-)
Bubba Ho-Tep *54*

JEAN COSMOS
On Guard! *341*

CONSTANTIN COSTA-
GAVRAS (1933-)
Amen *7*

JAMES COX
Wonderland *489*

EMANUELE CRIALESE
Respiro *381*

RICHARD CURTIS
Love Actually *275*

JULIA DAHL
Uptown Girls *473*

MATT DAMON (1970-)
Gerry *156*

LISA DAVIDOWITZ
Uptown Girls *473*

WILLIAM DAVIES
Johnny English *232*

PHILIPPE DE BROCA
(1933-)
On Guard! *341*

WILL DE LOS SANTOS
Spun *419*

ALFREDO DE VILLA
Washington Heights *479*

MARK DECENA
Dopamine *121*

EDWARD DECTER (1959-)
The Lizzie McGuire
Movie *265*

IGNACIO DEL MORAL
Mondays in the Sun *321*

CLAIRE DENIS (1948-)
Friday Night *153*

MATT DILLON (1964-)
City of Ghosts *77*

LESLIE DIXON
Freaky Friday *150*

YULI DOBOV
Tycoon *467*

MARY AGNES
DONOGHUE
Veronica Guerin *475*

DAVID DORFMAN
Anger Management *15*
My Boss's Daughter *328*

MICHAEL DOUGHERTY
X2: X-Men United *492*

CAROL DOYLE
Veronica Guerin *475*

LARRY DOYLE
Duplex *130*
Looney Tunes: Back in
Action *267*

DENNIS DRAKE
Down With Love *122*

MATT DRAKE
Tully *459*

FRANCOIS DUPEYRON
Monsieur Ibrahim *324*

STEPHANE DURAND
Winged Migration *487*

ROBERT DUVALL (1931-)
Assassination Tango *21*

ERIC EASON
Manito *297*

CAROLINE ELIACHEFF
The Flower of Evil *146*

TED ELLIOTT
Pirates of the Caribbean: The
Curse of the Black
Pearl *369*

BOBBY FARRELLY (1958-)
Stuck On You *430*

PETER FARRELLY (1957-)
Stuck On You *430*

JOHN FASANO
Darkness Falls *105*

LI FENG
Hero *184*

CRAIG FERANDEZ
Biker Boyz *42*

MICHAEL FERRIS
Terminator 3: Rise of the
Machines *446*

GLENN FICARRA
Bad Santa *25*

JACQUES FIESCHI
How I Killed My
Father *196*
Sade *391*

JASON FILARDI
Bringing Down the
House *49*

TIM FIRTH
Calendar Girls *61*

ANNE FONTAINE
How I Killed My
Father *196*

RENE FONTAINE
Masked and
Anonymous *302*

ERNESTO M. FORONDA
Better Luck Tomorrow *36*

MICHAEL FRANCE
Hulk *200*

PAUL FRASER
Once Upon a Time in the
Midlands *344*

JUAN CARLOS
FRESNADILLO
Intacto *220*

RON J. FRIEDMAN
Brother Bear *50*

KEITH FULTON
Lost in La Mancha *271*

OLIVIER GAL
Fellini: I'm a Born
Liar *137*

STEVE GALLUCCIO
Mambo Italiano *291*

ALEX GARLAND
28 Days Later *464*

MATTEO GARRONE
The Embalmer *136*

MASSIMO GAUDIOSO
The Embalmer *136*

EMILE GAUDREAULT
Mambo Italiano *291*

BART GAVIGAN
Luther *283*

DEAN GEORGARIS
Lara Croft Tomb Raider:
The Cradle of Life *243*
Paycheck *358*

BAHMAN GHOBADI
Marooned in Iraq *300*

BARRY GIFFORD
City of Ghosts *77*

MITCH GLAZER
The Recruit *380*

DELPHINE GLEIZE
Carnage *67*

GREG GLIENNA
A Guy Thing *174*

MICHAEL GOLDENBERG
Peter Pan *361*

WILLIAM GOLDMAN
(1931-)
Dreamcatcher *124*

ALFRED GOUGH
Shanghai Knights *404*

TODD GRAFF (1959-)
Camp *63*

DAVID GORDON GREEN
All the Real Girls *5*

NICHOLAS GRIFFIN
Matchstick Men *305*

TED GRIFFIN
Matchstick Men *305*

DAVID GRIFFITHS
The Hunted *205*

PETER GRIFFITHS
The Hunted *205*

J. MACKYE GRUBER
Final Destination 2 *140*

JEAN-CLAUDE
GRUMBERG
Amen *7*

CHRISTIAN GUDEGAST
A Man Apart *292*

KARL GUERS
The Jungle Book 2 *234*

CHRISTOPHER GUEST
(1948-)
A Mighty Wind *314*

SEBASTIAN GUTIERREZ
Gothika *169*

DEREK HAAS
2 Fast 2 Furious *466*

HEATHER HACH
Freaky Friday *150*

FRANK HANNAH
The Cooler *89*

GARY HARDWICK
Deliver Us from Eva *109*

CATHERINE HARDWICKE
Thirteen *450*

SAM HARPER
Cheaper by the Dozen *75*
Just Married *237*

DANIEL P. "DAN" HARRIS
(1979-)
X2: X-Men United *492*

JOE HARRIS
Darkness Falls *105*

RONALD HARWOOD
(1934-)
The Statement *423*
Taking Sides *440*

PETER HEDGES (1962-)
Pieces of April *365*

KAREN MONCRIEFF
(1963-)
Blue Car *43*

ART MONTERSATELLI
The Hunted *205*

SUSANNA MOORE
In the Cut *215*

GLEN MORGAN
Willard *486*

MARK MOSKOWITZ
Stone Reader *428*

NAT MOSS
Washington Heights *479*

PETER MULLAN (1954-)
The Magdalene
Sisters *286*

TAB MURPHY
Brother Bear *50*

MORT NATHAN
Boat Trip *45*

GASPER NOE
Irreversible *223*

MARIE NOELLE
Love the Hard Way *280*

GEORGE NOLFI
Timeline *453*

JOHN O'BRIEN
Cradle 2 the Grave *93*

STEVE OEDEKERK (1961-)
Bruce Almighty *52*

MO OGRODNIK
Uptown Girls *473*

MARK O'KEEFE
Bruce Almighty *52*

SHAWN OTTO
House of Sand and
Fog *192*

FRANCOIS OZON (1967-)
Swimming Pool *436*
Criminal Lovers *95*

SALADIN PATTERSON
The Fighting
Temptations *139*

RANDY PEARLSTEIN
Cabin Fever *60*

LOUIS PEPE
Lost in La Mancha *271*

VADIM PERELMAN
House of Sand and
Fog *192*

SERGEI PEROV
Masked and
Anonymous *302*

JACQUES PERRIN (1941-)
Winged Migration *487*

BOB PETERSON
Finding Nemo *142*

MICHAEL PETRONI
Till Human Voices Wake
Us *451*

DAMIAN PETTIGREW
Fellini: I'm a Born
Liar *137*

TODD PHILLIPS
Old School *339*

MARK POLISH (1972-)
Northfork *336*

MICHAEL POLISH (1972-)
Northfork *336*

DENNIS POTTER (1935-94)
The Singing
Detective *412*

DONNA POWERS
The Italian Job *227*

WAYNE POWERS
The Italian Job *227*

GREG PRITKIN
Dummy *129*

PAT PROFT
Scary Movie 3 *392*

ALEX PROYAS (1965-)
Garage Days *155*

ROBERT PULCINI
American Splendor *9*

NEAL PURVIS
Johnny English *232*

ROBERT RAMSEY
Intolerable Cruelty *221*

CHARLES RANDOLPH
The Life of David
Gale *263*

BILLY RAY
Shattered Glass *408*

NIKKI REED
Thirteen *450*

BRIAN REGAN
How to Lose a Guy in 10
Days *199*

ETHAN REIFF
Bulletproof Monk *58*

JOHN REQUA
Bad Santa *25*

DAVE REYNOLDS
Finding Nemo *142*

MIKE RICH
Radio *376*

SCOTT ROBERTS
The Hard Word *176*

JAMES ROBINSON
The League of Extraordinary
Gentlemen *257*

CHRIS ROCK (1966-)
Head of State *182*

GEOFF RODKEY
Daddy Day Care *98*

ROBERT RODRIGUEZ
(1968-)
Once Upon a Time in
Mexico *342*
Spy Kids 3-D: Game
Over *421*

JOHN ROGERS
The Core *91*

ALEXANDER
ROGOZHKIN
The Cuckoo *97*

DAVID RONN
National Security *334*

ISABEL ROSE
Anything But Love *17*

SCOTT ROSENBERG
Kangaroo Jack *239*

MARK ROSENTHAL
Mona Lisa Smile *319*

GARY ROSS
Seabiscuit *396*

TERRY ROSSIO
Pirates of the Caribbean: The
Curse of the Black
Pearl *369*

ELI ROTH
Cabin Fever *60*

PAUL RUDNICK
Marci X *299*

LOUIS SACHAR
Holes *185*

RALPH SALL
Grind *171*

VICTOR SALVA (1958-)
Jeepers Creepers 2 *229*

TODD SAMOVITZ
Wonderland *489*

ELIZABETH SARNOFF
Chasing Papi *74*

JOHN SAYLES (1950-)
Casa de los Babys *68*

JEFF SCHAFFER
Dr. Seuss' The Cat in the
Hat *119*

JAMES SCHAMUS
Hulk *200*

JAY SCHERICK
National Security *334*

PAUL SCHEURING
A Man Apart *292*

PAUL SCHNEIDER
All the Real Girls *5*

ROLF SCHUEBEL (1942-)
Gloomy Sunday *161*

PETE SCHWABA
A Guy Thing *174*

D. LORISTON SCOTT
Wonderland *489*

PETER SEHR
Love the Hard Way *280*

ANTONIO SERRANO
Lucia, Lucia *281*

COLINE SERREAU (1947-)
Chaos *69*

NICHOLAS
SHAKESPEARE
The Dancer Upstairs *100*

DAMIAN SHANNON
Freddy vs. Jason *152*

RON SHELTON (1945-)
Bad Boys 2 *23*
Hollywood Homicide *186*

JIM SHERIDAN (1949-)
In America *211*

KIRSTEN SHERIDAN
In America *211*

NAOMI SHERIDAN
In America *211*

LAURA ANGELICA
SIMON
Chasing Papi *74*

ADAM SMALL
Malibu's Most
Wanted *289*

ALEC SOKOLOW
Cheaper by the Dozen *75*

PETER SOLLETT
Raising Victor Vargas *377*

EDWARD SOLOMON
The In-Laws *213*
Levity *262*

ROBERT SOUZA
Hollywood Homicide *186*

DAVID SPADE (1964-)
Dickie Roberts: Former
Child Star *112*

JERRY STAHL
Bad Boys 2 *23*

ANDREW STANTON
Finding Nemo *142*

BURR STEERS (1966-)
How to Lose a Guy in 10
Days *199*

Cinematographer Index

THOMAS ACKERMAN
The Battle of Shaker
Heights *32*
Dickie Roberts: Former
Child Star *112*

BARRY ACKROYD
Sweet Sixteen *434*

LANCE ACORD
Lost in Translation *273*

REMI ADEFARASIN
The Haunted
Mansion *178*
Johnny English *232*

LLOYD AHERN, II (1942-)
American Wedding *11*

PIERRE AIM
He Loves Me . . . He Loves
Me Not *180*

**JOSE LUIS ALCAINE
(1938-)**
The Dancer Upstairs *100*

JAMIE ANDERSON
Bad Santa *25*

SHAHRIAR ASADI
Marooned in Iraq *300*

JOHN BAILEY (1942-)
How to Lose a Guy in 10
Days *199*

IAN BAKER
It Runs in the Family *225*

FLORIAN BALLHAUS
The Secret Lives of
Dentists *402*

**MICHAEL BALLHAUS
(1935-)**
Something's Gotta
Give *414*
Uptown Girls *473*

OLLI BARBE
Winged Migration *487*

JOHN BARTLEY
Wrong Turn *490*

MARC ANDRE BATIGNE
Divine Intervention: A
Chronicle of Love and
Pain *117*

ALFONSO BEATO
The Fighting
Temptations *139*
View from the Top *477*

DION BEEBE
In the Cut *215*

JOHN-PAUL BEEGHLY
Step Into Liquid *427*

MICHEL BENJAMIN
Winged Migration *487*

GABRIEL BERISTAIN
S.W.A.T. *432*

STEVEN BERNSTEIN
Monster *326*

ADRIAN BIDDLE
Shanghai Knights *404*

ANDREW BLACK
The Weather
Underground *480*

PATRICK BLOSSIER
Amen *7*
Jet Lag *231*

SEAN BOBBITT
Lawless Heart *252*

KIP BOGDAHN
Camp *63*

OLIVER BOKELBERG
The Station Agent *425*

RUSSELL BOYD
Master and Commander:
The Far Side of the
World *303*

BRIAN J. BREHENY
The Hard Word *176*

UTA BRIESEWITZ
XX/XY *495*

ERIC BROMS
Spun *419*

JONATHAN BROWN
Cheaper by the Dozen *75*
Just Married *237*

DON BURGESS
Radio *376*
Terminator 3: Rise of the
Machines *446*

SHARON CALAHAN
Finding Nemo *142*

ANTONIO CALVACHE
Prey for Rock and
Roll *374*

GARY CAPO
Final Destination 2 *140*

SYLVIE CARCEDO
Winged Migration *487*

RUSSELL CARPENTER
Charlie's Angels: Full
Throttle *71*

JAMES L. CARTER
The Shape of Things *405*

WALTER CARVALHO
Madame Sata *284*

ROBERT CHAPPELL
The Fog of War: Eleven
Lessons from the Life of
Robert S.
McNamara *148*

LAURENT CHARBONNIER
Winged Migration *487*

CESAR CHARLONE
City of God *79*

CLAUDIO CHEA
Washington Heights *479*

REMY CHEVRIN
Monsieur Ibrahim *324*

**PATRICE LUCIEN
COCHET**
Better Luck Tomorrow *36*

CHUCK COHEN
Love Don't Cost a
Thing *277*

DOMINIQUE COLIN
L'Auberge Espagnole *248*

JEFFREY CONFER
Stone Reader *428*

ERICSON CORE
Daredevil *101*

MICHAEL COULTER
Love Actually *275*

JEFF CRONENWETH
Down With Love *122*

DENIS CROSSAN
Agent Cody Banks *1*

RICHARD CRUDO
Grind *171*

DEAN CUNDEY
Looney Tunes: Back in
Action *267*

OLIVER CURTIS
Owning Mahowny *354*

STEFAN CZAPSKY
Bulletproof Monk *58*

ELLIOT DAVIS
Legally Blonde 2: Red,
White & Blonde *260*
Thirteen *450*

JOHN DE BORMAN
The Guru *173*

ROGER DEAKINS (1949-)
House of Sand and
Fog *192*
Intolerable Cruelty *221*
Levity *262*

HENRI DECAE
Le Cercle Rouge *254*

BENOIT DELHOMME
Sade *391*

PETER DEMING (1957-)
People I Know *359*

JIM DENAULT
City of Ghosts *77*

**CALEB DESCHANEL
(1941-)**
The Hunted *205*
Timeline *453*

JAMES DESMOND
Only the Strong
Survive *346*

OLEG DOBRONRAVOV
Tycoon *467*

PETER DONAHUE
The Fog of War: Eleven
Lessons from the Life of
Robert S.
McNamara *148*

NICK DOOB
Only the Strong
Survive *346*

ADOLFO DORING
Capturing the
Friedmans *65*

CHRISTOPHER DOYLE
(1952-)
Hero *184*

JEAN-MARIE DREJOU
The Man on the
Train *294*

LUC DRION
Winged Migration *487*

STUART DRYBURGH
(1952-)
The Recruit *380*

GUY DUFAUX
The Barbarian
Invasions *28*
Love the Hard Way *280*

SIMON DUGGAN
Garage Days *155*

ANDREW DUNN
What a Girl Wants *485*

ERIC ALAN EDWARDS
How to Deal *197*

FREDERICK ELMES
Hulk *200*

ROBERT ELSWIT
Gigli *157*
Runaway Jury *386*

JEAN-YVES ESCOFFIER
(1951-2003)
The Human Stain *203*

KELLY EVANS
Die Mommie Die! *114*

JEAN-MARC FABRE
How I Killed My
Father *196*

DON E. FAUNTLEROY
Jeepers Creepers 2 *229*

ALEXEY FEDEROV
Tycoon *467*

GAVIN FINNEY
Alex & Emma *3*

MAURO FIORE
Tears of the Sun *442*

LAURENT FLEUTOT
Winged Migration *487*

JOHN FOSTER
Tully *459*

CRYSTAL FOURNIER
Carnage *67*

ROBERT FRAISSE
Luther *283*

BRENDAN GALVIN
Veronica Guerin *475*

GREG GARDINER
Biker Boyz *42*
Elf *134*

PHILIPPE GARGUIL
Winged Migration *487*

ERIC GAUTIER
A Housekeeper *194*

DOMINIQUE GENTIL
Winged Migration *487*

DIDIER GERTSCH
Manito *297*

PIERRE WILLIAM GLENN
And Now Ladies and
Gentlemen *13*

JAMES GLENNON (1942-)
Good Boy! *165*

AGNES GODARD
Friday Night *153*

MICHAEL GRADY
Wonderland *489*

RICHARD GREATREX
I Capture the Castle *207*

JACK N. GREEN
A Man Apart *292*
Secondhand Lions *400*

ROBBIE GREENBERG
A Guy Thing *174*
Marci X *299*

XAVIER PEREZ GROBET
Chasing Papi *74*
Lucia, Lucia *281*

ALEXANDER GRUSYNSKI
Deliver Us from Eva *109*
The In-Laws *213*

NICK HAY
Manic *296*

ANTOINE HEBERLE
The Girl from Paris *159*

CHRIS HEGEDUS
Only the Strong
Survive *346*

ROBERT HUMPHREYS
Dopamine *121*

MARK IRWIN
Malibu's Most
Wanted *289*
Old School *339*
Scary Movie 3 *392*

ADAM JANEIRO
Bubba Ho-Tep *54*

ANTHONY JANELLI
A Decade Under the
Influence *107*

KEVIN JEWISON
The Statement *423*

XAVIER JIMENEZ
Intacto *220*

SCOTT KEVAN
Cabin Fever *60*

DARIUS KHONDJI (1955-)
Anything Else *19*

ABBAS KIAROSTAMI
(1940-)
Ten *444*

HYUNG-KOO KIM
Together *456*

JEFFREY L. KIMBALL
Paycheck *358*

EDWARD KLOSINSKI
Gloomy Sunday *161*

MARK KNOBIL
The Bread, My Sweet *47*

LAJOS KOLTAI (1946-)
Taking Sides *440*

SERGEI KOZLOV (1964-)
House of Fools *190*

SERGE LADOUCEUR
Mambo Italiano *291*

ROGER LANSER
Till Human Voices Wake
Us *451*

JEANNE LAPOIRIE
Confusion of Genders *88*

JEAN-CLAUDE LARRIEU
My Life Without Me *330*

JEREMY LASKY
Finding Nemo *142*

DAN LAUSTSEN
Darkness Falls *105*
The League of Extraordinary
Gentlemen *257*

YORICK LE SAUX
Swimming Pool *436*

WOLFGANG LEHNER
In the Mirror of Maya
Deren *217*

DENIS LENOIR
Demonlover *111*

JOHN R. LEONETTI
Honey *188*

MATTHEW F. LEONETTI
(1941-)
2 Fast 2 Furious *466*

ANDREW LESNIE
The Lord of the Rings 3:
The Return of the
King *269*

PIERRE LHOMME
Le Divorce *256*

MATTHEW LIBATIQUE
(1969-)
Gothika *169*
Phone Booth *363*

JONG LIN
Bend It Like Beckham *35*

JOHN LINDLEY
The Core *91*

EMMANUEL LUBEZKI
Dr. Seuss' The Cat in the
Hat *119*

BERNARD LUTIC
Winged Migration *487*

JULIO MACAT
Bringing Down the
House *49*

THIERRY MACHADO
Winged Migration *487*

TEODORO MANIACI
Party Monster *356*

ANTHONY DOD MANTLE
(1955-)
28 Days Later *464*

HORACIO MARQUINEZ
Anything But Love *17*
Dummy *129*

STEPHANE MARTIN
Winged Migration *487*

STEVE MASON
Basic *30*

JOHN MATHIESON
Matchstick Men *305*

SHAWN MAURER
Boat Trip *45*

ALFREDO MAYO
Mondays in the Sun *321*

DONALD MCALPINE
Anger Management *15*
Peter Pan *361*

TIM MCCANN
Revolution #9 *383*

MARTIN MCGRATH
My Boss's Daughter *328*

ROBERT MCLACHLAN
Willard *486*

PHIL MEHEUX
Beyond Borders *38*

DARIUS WOLSKI
Pirates of the Caribbean: The
Curse of the Black
Pearl *369*

ARTHUR WONG
The Medallion *313*

OLIVER WOOD
Freaky Friday *150*
National Security *334*

LIK-WAI YU
Platform *372*

FABIO ZAMARION
Respiro *381*

ANDREI ZHEGALOV
The Cuckoo *97*

JERZY ZIELINSKI
The Lizzie McGuire
Movie *265*

MARCEL ZYSKIND
In This World *219*

Editor Index

DOUG ABEL
The Fog of War: Eleven
Lessons from the Life of
Robert S.
McNamara *148*

SANDRA ADAIR
School of Rock *394*

CHUCK AIKMAN
The Bread, My Sweet *47*

JOHN DAVID ALLEN
Le Divorce *256*

TIM ALVERSON
Darkness Falls *105*

WILLIAM A. ANDERSON
XX/XY *495*

TARIQ ANWAR
Sylvia *438*

MICK AUDSLEY
Dirty Pretty Things *116*
Mona Lisa Smile *319*

JOHN AXNESS
Boat Trip *45*

ZENE BAKEL
All the Real Girls *5*

LUC BARNIER
Demonlover *111*
Sade *391*

CLIVE BARRETT
Luther *283*

ROGER BARTON
Bad Boys 2 *23*

MARIO BATTISTEL
The Dancer Upstairs *100*

DAVID BEATTY
Civil Brand *81*

PETE BEAUDREAU
XX/XY *495*

NICHOLAS BEAUMAN
Beyond Borders *38*

ALAN EDWARD BELL
Alex & Emma *3*

PETER BESTON
Once Upon a Time in the
Midlands *344*

IVAN BILANCIO
Piglet's Big Movie *368*

LARRY BOCK
Down With Love *122*

ROGER BONDELLI
Dickie Roberts: Former
Child Star *112*

DEREK G. BRECHIN
Cradle 2 the Grave *93*

DAVID BRENNER
Identity *209*

JACOB BRICCA
Lost in La Mancha *271*

DANA BROWN
Step Into Liquid *427*

ROBERT BROWN
A Man Apart *292*

SOPHIE BRUNET
Tycoon *467*

**CHANTEL COLIBERT
BRUNNER**
The Triplets of
Belleville *458*

JOHN BRYANT
Rugrats Go Wild! *385*

CONRAD BUFF
Tears of the Sun *442*

SHAWNA CALLAHAN
How to Deal *197*

JACQUELINE CAMBAS
Marci X *299*

MALCOLM CAMPBELL
Scary Movie 3 *392*
Shanghai Knights *404*

BRUCE CANNON
2 Fast 2 Furious *466*

PO-WEN CHEN
Fleeing by Night *145*

PETER CHRISTELIS
In This World *219*

LISA ZENO CHURGIN
House of Sand and
Fog *192*

JAMES COBLENTZ
Willard *486*

ARTHUR COBURN
The Cooler *89*
Monster *326*
Under the Tuscan
Sun *470*

DAVID CODRON
Love Don't Cost a
Thing *277*

MONICA COLEMAN
Swimming Pool *436*

ANNIE COLLINS
The Lord of the Rings 3:
The Return of the
King *269*

RICHARD COMEAU
Mambo Italiano *291*

JESS CONGDON
Dopamine *121*

MARTIN CONNOR
The Hard Word *176*

DAVID COULSON
Whale Rider *483*

JOEL COX
Mystic River *332*

GARTH CRAVEN
Peter Pan *361*

SAM CRAVEN
My Boss's Daughter *328*

RAUL DAVALOS
Dreamcatcher *124*

**ALEXANDRE DE
FRANCHESCHI**
In the Cut *215*

HELENE DE LUZE
And Now Ladies and
Gentlemen *13*

NICOLAS DE TOTH
Terminator 3: Rise of the
Machines *446*

ISABELLE DEDIEU
The Barbarian
Invasions *28*

NICOLAS DETOTH
See Nicolas De Toth

TOM DONAHUE
Washington Heights *479*

DODY DORN (1955-)
Matchstick Men *305*

VICTOR DU BOIS
The Last Samurai *244*

MARIE-SOPHIE DUBUS
Le Cercle Rouge *254*

AMY DUDDLESTON
Laurel Canyon *250*

MICHAEL J. DUTHIE
Open Range *348*

CORKY EHLERS
Gods and Generals *163*

ANDREW S. EISEN
The Statement *423*

SUZY ELMIGER
People I Know *359*

KATE EVANS
Girl with a Pearl
Earring *160*

MONIQUE FARDOULIS
The Flower of Evil *146*

DOMINIQUE FAYSSE
Monsieur Ibrahim *324*

TOM FINAN
Sinbad: Legend of the Seven
Seas *410*

RICK W. FINNEY
Looney Tunes: Back in
Action *267*

SARAH FLACK
Lost in Translation *273*

GEORGE FOLSEY, JR.
Basic *30*
Cabin Fever *60*
Cheaper by the Dozen *75*

RYAN FOLSEY
Cabin Fever *60*

JEFFREY FORD
Shattered Glass *408*

RICHARD FRANCIS-
BRUCE
The Italian Job *227*

DAVID GAMBLE
Veronica Guerin *475*

JORGE GARCIA
Lucia, Lucia *281*

MADELEINE GAVIN
Manic *296*

FRANCOIS GEDIGIER
A Housekeeper *194*

CHRISTOPHER GEE
The Jungle Book 2 *234*

NAOMI GERAGHTY
In America *211*

CHRIS GILL
28 Days Later *464*

SCOTT J. GILL
Bubba Ho-Tep *54*

MARK GOLDBLATT
Bad Boys 2 *23*

WILLIAM GOLDENBERG
Seabiscuit *396*
Kangaroo Jack *239*

MIA GOLDMAN
The In-Laws *213*

SHANNON GOLDMAN
Revolution #9 *383*

AFFONSO GONCALVES
Tully *459*

STEVEN GONZALES
All the Real Girls *5*

MARGARET GOODSPEED
The Lizzie McGuire
Movie *265*

JEFF GOURSON
Anger Management *15*

BRUCE GREEN
Freaky Friday *150*
The Guru *173*

SAM GREEN
The Weather
Underground *480*

JERRY GREENBERG
Bringing Down the
House *49*

CHRISTOPHER
GREENBURY
Daddy Day Care *98*
Stuck On You *430*
View from the Top *477*

OLGA GRINSHPUN
House of Fools *190*

JOELLE HACHE
The Man on the
Train *294*

GERRY HAMBLING
The Life of David
Gale *263*

JANICE HAMPTON
How to Deal *197*

RICHARD HANKIN
Capturing the
Friedmans *65*

DAN HANLEY
The Missing *317*

PHILIP HARRISON
Die Mommie Die! *114*

MARSHALL HARVEY
Looney Tunes: Back in
Action *267*

CHRIS HEGEDUS
Only the Strong
Survive *346*

MARK HELFRICH
Honey *188*

BILL HENRY
Dummy *129*

KYLE HENRY
Manito *297*

CRAIG P. HERRING
Good Boy! *165*

AUGIE HESS
The Hunted *205*

EMMA E. HICKOX
Honey *188*

MIKE HILL
The Missing *317*

SCOTT HILL
Bruce Almighty *52*
Just Married *237*

HENRY HILLS
In the Mirror of Maya
Deren *217*

KATHRYN HIMOFF
House of 1000
Corpses *191*

PAUL HIRSCH
The Fighting
Temptations *139*

URSULA HOEF
Gloomy Sunday *161*

ROBERT HOFFMAN
Bad Santa *25*

CHAN KI HOP
The Medallion *313*

MAYSIE HOY
Chasing Papi *74*

WILLIAM HOY
A Man Apart *292*

MARTIN HUNTER
Underworld *471*
Below *33*

JOE HUTSHING
Something's Gotta
Give *414*

MICHAEL JABLOW
Old School *339*

RODERICK JAYNES
Intolerable Cruelty *221*

ALLYSON C. JOHNSON
Prey for Rock and
Roll *374*

LAWRENCE JORDAN
Dumb and Dumberer: When
Harry Met Lloyd *127*

MICHAEL KAHN
Lara Croft Tomb Raider:
The Cradle of Life *243*
Peter Pan *361*

ANDY KEIR
The Secret Lives of
Dentists *402*

YANNICK KERGOAT
Gothika *169*
Amen *7*

MYRON KERSTEIN
Camp *63*
Raising Victor Vargas *377*

ABBAS KIAROSTAMI
(1940-)
Ten *444*

LYNZEE KLINGMAN
Duplex *130*

JING-LEI KONG
Platform *372*

CAROLE KRAVETZ
Out of Time *352*

JUSTIN KRISH
Bend It Like Beckham *35*

JANE KURSON
Monster *326*

ANGIE LAM
Hero *184*

ROBERT K. LAMBERT
Bulletproof Monk *58*
House of 1000
Corpses *191*

SEAN LAMBERT
House of 1000
Corpses *191*

SYLVIE LANDRA
Jet Lag *231*
Taking Sides *440*

VERONIQUE LANGE
Divine Intervention: A
Chronicle of Love and
Pain *117*
Alias Betty *4*

HENRI LANOE
On Guard! *341*

EREZ LAUFER
Only the Strong
Survive *346*

TONY LAWSON
The Good Thief *167*

RICHARD LEAROYD
Garage Days *155*

DAN LEBENTAL
Elf *134*

CHRIS LEBENZON
Big Fish *39*
Radio *376*

GUY LECORNE
How I Killed My
Father *196*

ROBERT LEIGHTON
Alex & Emma *3*
A Mighty Wind *314*

ALISA LEPSELTER
Anything Else *19*

STUART LEVY
Confidence *86*

JUSTIN LIN
Better Luck Tomorrow *36*

CAROL LITTLETON
Dreamcatcher *124*

MARK LIVOLSI
Pieces of April *365*

DAWN LOGSDON
The Weather
Underground *480*

PETER N. LONSDALE
The Jungle Book 2 *234*

PATRICK LUSSIER
My Boss's Daughter *328*

STEPHEN MACK
Assassination Tango *21*

ANDREW MARCUS
Under the Tuscan
Sun *470*

RICHARD MARKS
Timeline *453*

ED MARX
Jeepers Creepers 2 *229*

TOM MCARDLE
The Station Agent *425*

TIM MCCANN
Revolution #9 *383*

KATHLEEN SOULLIERE
Stone Reader *428*

MARCO SPOLETINI
The Embalmer *136*

TIM SQUYRES
Hulk *200*

ZACH STAENBERG
The Matrix Reloaded *308*
The Matrix
Revolutions *311*

ANN STEIN
Love Liza *278*

WILLIAM STEINKAMP
Runaway Jury *386*

MARK STEVENS
Freddy vs. Jason *152*
Phone Booth *363*

KEVIN STITT
The Order *350*

ERIC STRAND
Grind *171*

CHRISTOPHER
TELLEFSEN
The Human Stain *203*

DAVE TERMAN
Stuck On You *430*

PETER TESCHNER
Legally Blonde 2: Red,
White & Blonde *260*

SCOTT THOMAS
Lawless Heart *252*

DYLAN TICHENOR
Cold Creek Manor *82*

JAMES TOOLEY
Poolhall Junkies *373*

NEIL TRAVIS
Terminator 3: Rise of the
Machines *446*

LEO TROMBETTA
Northfork *336*

MICHAEL TRONICK
S.W.A.T. *432*

GUS VAN SANT (1952-)
Elephant *132*

GLORIA ROSA VELA
Manic *296*

DENNIS VIRKLER
Daredevil *101*

SANDER VOS
Zus & Zo *497*

WAYNE WAHRMAN
Charlie's Angels: Full
Throttle *71*

TREVOR WAITE
Once Upon a Time in the
Midlands *344*

EARL WATSON
Deliver Us from Eva *109*

BILLY WEBER
Gigli *157*

KATE WILLIAMS
It Runs in the Family *225*

JEFF WISHENGRAD
The Singing
Detective *412*

JEFFREY WOLF
Holes *185*

CRAIG WOOD
Pirates of the Caribbean: The
Curse of the Black
Pearl *369*

MIKLOS WRIGHT
Open Range *348*

TOBY YATES
Blue Car *43*

MARIE-JOSEPHE
YOYOTTE
Winged Migration *487*

YING ZHOU
Together *456*

DON ZIMMERMAN
Dr. Seuss' The Cat in the
Hat *119*
Just Married *237*

PAUL ZUCKER
Gerry *156*

Art Director Index

MICHELE ABBE
Chaos *69*
Jet Lag *231*

CAROLINE ADLER
The Barbarian
    Invasions *28*

CAROLINE ALDER
Timeline *453*

GEORGE ALLISON
It Runs in the Family *225*

KRISTAN ANDREWS
Masked and
    Anonymous *302*

MICHAEL ATWELL
Biker Boyz *42*

BRANIMIR BABIC
The Order *350*

MARIA BAKER
Freaky Friday *150*

LAURA BALLINGER
Party Monster *356*

CATHRYE BANGS
The Fighting
    Temptations *139*

PATRICK BANISTER
A Guy Thing *174*
The Lizzie McGuire
    Movie *265*

GUY BARNES
The Missing *317*

JEFFREY BARROWS
All the Real Girls *5*

HUGH BATEUP
The Matrix Reloaded *308*
The Matrix
    Revolutions *311*

(PETER) JOE BLEAKLEY
The Lord of the Rings 3:
    The Return of the
    King *269*

GREGORY BOLTON
Gods and Generals *163*

PAULO BONFINI
The Embalmer *136*

PETER BORCK
Bad Santa *25*

DREW BOUGHTON
House of Sand and
    Fog *192*

DANIEL BRADFORD
Kill Bill: Vol. 1 *240*

SIMON BRIGHT
The Lord of the Rings 3:
    The Return of the
    King *269*

MAX BRISCOE
Old School *339*

BRIGITTE BROCH
Lucia, Lucia *281*

DAVID BROER
Manic *296*

ANDREW MAX CAHN
Holes *185*

NATHAN CARLSON
Tully *459*

AMANDA CARROLL
Dummy *129*

CRISTINA CASALI
Lawless Heart *252*

JANE CECCHI
Sylvia *438*

LEK CHAIYAN
City of Ghosts *77*

SUE CHAN
Gigli *157*

SYLVAIN CHAUVELOT
How I Killed My
    Father *196*
Sade *391*

LEN X. CLAYTON
The Station Agent *425*

FERGUS CLEGG
Sweet Sixteen *434*

SANDY COCHRANE
Paycheck *358*

TIM COHN
Love Liza *278*

CHRIS CORNWELL
Daddy Day Care *98*

SUSAN CULLEN
In America *211*

MARC DABE
Dickie Roberts: Former
    Child Star *112*

DENNIS DAVENPORT
The In-Laws *213*
The Recruit *380*

ARNAUD DE MOLERON
Criminal Lovers *95*

ROSS DEMPSTER
Freddy vs. Jason *152*

JOHN DEXTER
Hulk *200*

MARK DIGBY
28 Days Later *464*

TERRENCE DUNLOP
XX/XY *495*

FRANCOISE DUPERTUIS
Confusion of Genders *88*

BRIAN EDMONDS
Kangaroo Jack *239*

KENDELLE ELLIOT
Dreamcatcher *124*

DAVID ELLIS
Love Don't Cost a
    Thing *277*

FRANCOIS EMMANUELLI
L'Auberge Espagnole *248*

JULIO ESTEBAN
Mondays in the Sun *321*

TONY FANNING
Intolerable Cruelty *221*

JAMES FENG
How to Lose a Guy in 10
    Days *199*

JOHN FENNER
Lara Croft Tomb Raider:
    The Cradle of Life *243*

ADELE FLERE
Till Human Voices Wake
    Us *451*

RICHARD FOJO
Stuck On You *430*

ANDRE FONSNY
Carnage *67*

SHEPHERD FRANKEL
Terminator 3: Rise of the
    Machines *446*

JOHN FRANKISH
Johnny English *232*

BEAT FRUTIGER
The Haunted
    Mansion *178*
Terminator 3: Rise of the
    Machines *446*

**ELINOR ROSE
GALBRAITH**
The League of Extraordinary
    Gentlemen *257*

SCOTT GALLAGHER
The Texas Chainsaw
    Massacre *448*

JOHANN GEORGE
And Now Ladies and
    Gentlemen *13*

BAHMAN GHOBADI
Marooned in Iraq *300*

STEPHANIE GILLIAM
Laurel Canyon *250*

GERSHON GINSBURG
S.W.A.T. *432*

SANDRA GOLDMARK
Washington Heights *479*

JESS GONCHOR
Identity *209*

BRANDT GORDON
How to Lose a Guy in 10
    Days *199*

CAROLINE GREBBELL
The Magdalene
    Sisters *286*

T. ARRINDER GREWAL
Bulletproof Monk *58*

Music Index

ARMAND AMAR
Amen *7*

SACHA AMBAK
Madame Sata *284*

CRAIG ARMSTRONG
Love Actually *275*
The Magdalene
Sisters *286*

DAVID ARNOLD (1962-)
2 Fast 2 Furious *466*

EDUARD ARTEMYEV
House of Fools *190*

PIERRE AVIAT
The Barbarian
Invasions *28*

CHRIS BABIDA
Fleeing by Night *145*

LUIS BACALOV
Assassination Tango *21*

ANGELO BADALAMENTI
(1937-)
Suspended Animation *432*

KLAUS BADELT
Basic *30*
Pirates of the Caribbean: The
Curse of the Black
Pearl *369*
The Recruit *380*

THOMAS BANGALTER
Irreversible *223*

TYLER BATES
City of Ghosts *77*

CHRISTOPHE BECK
American Wedding *11*
Cheaper by the Dozen *75*
Dickie Roberts: Former
Child Star *112*
Just Married *237*
Under the Tuscan
Sun *470*

MARCO BELTRAMI
Terminator 3: Rise of the
Machines *446*

DAMON BLACKMAN
Cradle 2 the Grave *93*

DAVID "DJ QUIK" BLAKE
Head of State *182*

HOWARD BLAKE
Ten *444*

TERENCE BLANCHARD
(1962-)
Dark Blue *103*
People I Know *359*

FREDERIC BOTTON
A Housekeeper *194*

BT (BRIAN TRANSEAU)
(1971-)
Monster *326*

CARTER BURWELL (1955-)
Intolerable Cruelty *221*

DAVID CARBONARA
The Guru *173*

TEDDY CASTELLUCCI
Anger Management *15*
My Boss's Daughter *328*

DAVE CERF
The Weather
Underground *480*

MATTHIEU CHABROL
The Flower of Evil *146*

BENOIT CHAREST
The Triplets of
Belleville *458*

ELIA CMIRAL
Wrong Turn *490*

PHIL COLLINS (1951-)
Brother Bear *50*

NORMAND CORBEIL
The Statement *423*

BILLY CORGAN
Spun *419*

DALE CORNELIUS
Till Human Voices Wake
Us *451*

ED CORTES
City of God *79*

ELVIS COSTELLO (1954-)
The Shape of Things *405*

BRUNO COULAIS
Winged Migration *487*

JEROME COULLET
He Loves Me . . . He Loves
Me Not *180*

DOUGLAS J. CUOMO
Revolution #9 *383*

MIRIAM CUTLER
Lost in La Mancha *271*

DARIEN DAHOUD
Love the Hard Way *280*

MYCHAEL DANNA (1958-)
Shattered Glass *408*

MASON DARING (1949-)
Casa de los Babys *68*

IVA DAVIES
Master and Commander:
The Far Side of the
World *303*

DON DAVIS
The Matrix Reloaded *308*
The Matrix
Revolutions *311*

ERIC DE MARSEN
Le Cercle Rouge *254*

ALFONSO DE
VILLALONGA
My Life Without Me *330*

JOHN DEBNEY (1957-)
Bruce Almighty *52*
Elf *134*

GARY DEMICHELE
The Secret Lives of
Dentists *402*

ALEXANDRE DESPLAT
Girl with a Pearl
Earring *160*

LEONID DIESYATNIKOV
Tycoon *467*

ROBERT DIGGS
See The RZA

AMY DOMINGUES
The Weather
Underground *480*

PATRICK DOYLE (1953-)
Calendar Girls *61*
Secondhand Lions *400*

ANNE DUDLEY (1956-)
A Man Apart *292*

TAN DUN
Hero *184*

BOB DYLAN (1941-)
Masked and
Anonymous *302*

CLINT EASTWOOD (1930-)
Mystic River *332*

RANDY EDELMAN (1947-)
Gods and Generals *163*
National Security *334*
Shanghai Knights *404*

CLIFF EIDELMAN (1967-)
The Lizzie McGuire
Movie *265*

DANNY ELFMAN (1953-)
Big Fish *39*
Hulk *200*

DAMON ELLIOTT
Malibu's Most
Wanted *289*

EMILIO ESTEFAN, JR.
Chasing Papi *74*

PASCAL ESTEVE
The Man on the
Train *294*

MARK OLIVER EVERETT
Levity *262*

GEORGE FENTON
Sweet Sixteen *434*

MIKE FIGGIS (1948-)
Cold Creek Manor *82*

ROBERT FOLK
Boat Trip *45*

GAVIN FRIDAY
In America *211*

JOHN (GIANNI) FRIZZELL
(1966-)
Cradle 2 the Grave *93*
Gods and Generals *163*

LISA GERRARD
Whale Rider *483*

RICHARD GIBBS
Love Don't Cost a
Thing *277*
Step Into Liquid *427*

PHILIP GLASS (1937-)
The Fog of War: Eleven
Lessons from the Life of
Robert S.
McNamara *148*

RICHARD GLASSER
Poolhall Junkies *373*

LUCIO GODOY
Intacto *220*
Mondays in the Sun *321*

ELLIOT GOLDENTHAL
The Good Thief *167*
S.W.A.T. *432*

JERRY GOLDSMITH
(1929-)
Looney Tunes: Back in
Action *267*

MICHAEL J. GONZALES
Better Luck Tomorrow *36*

CHRISTOPHER GORDON
Master and Commander:
The Far Side of the
World *303*

PAUL GRABOWSKY
It Runs in the Family *225*

RICHARD GRASSBY-
LEWIS
Owning Mahowny *354*

HARRY GREGSON-
WILLIAMS
Phone Booth *363*
The Rundown *389*
Sinbad: Legend of the Seven
Seas *410*
Veronica Guerin *475*

RUPERT GREGSON-
WILLIAMS
What a Girl Wants *485*

YOSHIHIRO HANNO
Platform *372*

JIMMY HARRY
Party Monster *356*

SUSAN HARTFORD
The Bread, My Sweet *47*

RICHARD HARVEY
Luther *283*

PAUL HASLINGER
Underworld *471*

JOHN MICHAEL HIGGINS
(1962-)
A Mighty Wind *314*

HILMAR ORN
HILMARSSON (1958-)
In the Cut *215*

DICKON HINCHLIFFE
Friday Night *153*

JOE HISAISHI
Spirited Away *418*

ERIC HOLLAND (1933-)
Dopamine *121*

ANDREW HOLLANDER
Anything But Love *17*

DAVID HOLMES
Buffalo Soldiers *56*

JAMES HORNER (1953-)
Beyond Borders *38*
House of Sand and
Fog *192*
The Missing *317*
Radio *376*

JAMES NEWTON
HOWARD (1951-)
Dreamcatcher *124*
Peter Pan *361*

SCOTT HUMPHREY
House of 1000
Corpses *191*

ALBERTO IGLESIAS
The Dancer Upstairs *100*

MARK ISHAM (1951-)
The Cooler *89*

STEVE JABLONSKY
The Texas Chainsaw
Massacre *448*

JIMMY JAM (1959-)
The Fighting
Temptations *139*

JAY-JAY JOHANSON
Confusion of Genders *88*

CARL JOHNSON
Piglet's Big Movie *368*

ADRIAN JOHNSTON
Lawless Heart *252*

TREVOR JONES (1949-)
The League of Extraordinary
Gentlemen *257*

CAMARA KAMBON
Biker Boyz *42*

MICHAEL KAMEN (1948-
2003)
Open Range *348*

ROLFE KENT (1963-)
Freaky Friday *150*
Legally Blonde 2: Red,
White & Blonde *260*

JOHN KIMBROUGH
A Decade Under the
Influence *107*

DAVID KITAY
Bad Santa *25*
How to Deal *197*

ARSALAN KOMKAR
Marooned in Iraq *300*

NATHAN LARSON
Dirty Pretty Things *116*

ADRIAN LEE
The Medallion *313*

MICHEL LEGRAND (1932-)
And Now Ladies and
Gentlemen *13*

MICHAEL A. LEVINE
Wonderland *489*

EUGENE LEVY (1946-)
A Mighty Wind *314*

TERRY LEWIS (1956-)
The Fighting
Temptations *139*

MICHAEL LINNEN
All the Real Girls *5*

JOHN LUNN
Once Upon a Time in the
Midlands *344*

STEVEN LUTVAK
Anything But Love *17*

MARK MANCINA
Brother Bear *50*
The Haunted
Mansion *178*

MICHAEL MANDRELL
Stone Reader *428*

MANDRILL
Civil Brand *81*

DARIO MARIANELLI
I Capture the Castle *207*

NATHAN MARR
Cabin Fever *60*

RICHARD (RICK) MARVIN
The Battle of Shaker
Heights *32*

NACHO MASTRETTA
Lucia, Lucia *281*

STUART MATTHEWMAN
Northfork *336*

DENNIS MCCARTHY
Die Mommie Die! *114*

DAVID MCCORMACK
Garage Days *155*

MICHAEL MCKEAN
(1947-)
A Mighty Wind *314*

JOEL MCNEELY
Holes *185*
The Jungle Book 2 *234*
Uptown Girls *473*

FONS MERKIES
Zus & Zo *497*

STEPHEN MERRITT
Pieces of April *365*

MARCUS MILLER (1959-)
Deliver Us from Eva *109*
Head of State *182*

ANDREA MORRICONE
Capturing the
Friedmans *65*

MARK MOTHERSBAUGH
(1950-)
Good Boy! *165*
A Guy Thing *174*
Rugrats Go Wild! *385*
Thirteen *450*

JOHN MURPHY
28 Days Later *464*

ROY NATHANSON
Raising Victor Vargas *377*

LUDOVIC NAVARRE
Chaos *69*

ERIC NEVEUX
Carnage *67*

DAVID NEWMAN (1954-)
Daddy Day Care *98*
Dr. Seuss' The Cat in the
Hat *119*
Duplex *130*
How to Lose a Guy in 10
Days *199*

RANDY NEWMAN (1943-)
Seabiscuit *396*

THOMAS NEWMAN
(1955-)
Finding Nemo *142*

CATHERINE O'HARA
(1954-)
A Mighty Wind *314*

JIM O'ROURKE
Love Liza *278*

BANDA OSIRIS
The Embalmer *136*

ANNETTE O'TOOLE
(1953-)
A Mighty Wind *314*

JOHN OTTMAN (1964-)
Gothika *169*
X2: X-Men United *492*

ALEX PARKER
The Life of David
Gale *263*

Performer Index

AXELLE ABBADIE
A Housekeeper *194*

MICHELLE ABERCROMBY
Sweet Sixteen *434*

JON ABRAHAMS (1977-)
My Boss's Daughter *328*

BRYAN ADAMS
House of Fools *190*

MARK ADDY (1963-)
The Order *350*

PAUL ADELSTEIN
Intolerable Cruelty *221*

ISABELLE ADJANI (1955-)
Monsieur Ibrahim *324*

BEN AFFLECK (1972-)
Daredevil *101*
Gigli *157*
Paycheck *358*

CASEY AFFLECK (1975-)
Gerry *156*

NICOLE AFFLERBACH
School of Rock *394*

SHOHREH AGHDASHLOO
House of Sand and Fog *192*

DAVID AGRANOV
Just Married *237*

JONATHAN AHDOUT
House of Sand and Fog *192*

LIAM AIKEN (1990-)
Good Boy! *165*

MANIA AKBARI
Ten *444*

JOE ALASKEY
Looney Tunes: Back in Action (V) *267*

JESSICA ALBA (1981-)
Honey *188*

JOHN ALDERTON (1940-)
Calendar Girls *61*

TOM ALDREDGE (1928-)
Cold Mountain *84*

Intolerable Cruelty *221*

ERIKA ALEXANDER
Love Liza *278*

KHANDI ALEXANDER (1957-)
Dark Blue *103*

MARY ALICE (1941-)
The Matrix Revolutions *311*

ALANA ALLEN
Camp *63*

ALEISHA ALLEN
School of Rock *394*

KRISTA ALLEN (1972-)
Anger Management *15*

PARRY ALLEN
See Parry Shen

SAGE ALLEN
Suspended Animation *432*

SASHA ALLEN
Camp *63*

WOODY ALLEN (1935-)
Anything Else *19*

MARIA CONCHITA ALONSO (1957-)
Chasing Papi *74*

SUMMER ALTICE
Grind *171*

BRUCE ALTMAN
Matchstick Men *305*

CARLOS ALVAREZ-NOVOA
Lucia, Lucia *281*

VINCENZO AMATO
Respiro *381*

AMIDOU (1942-)
And Now Ladies and Gentlemen *13*

ANDY ANDERSON
Garage Days *155*

ANTHONY ANDERSON (1970-)
Cradle 2 the Grave *93*
Kangaroo Jack *239*

Malibu's Most Wanted *289*
Scary Movie 3 *392*

PAMELA ANDERSON (1967-)
Scary Movie 3 *392*

STANLEY ANDERSON (1945-)
Runaway Jury *386*

DAVID ANDREWS (1952-)
Terminator 3: Rise of the Machines *446*

GIUSEPPE ANDREWS (1979-)
Cabin Fever *60*

RUSSELL ANDREWS
The In-Laws *213*

SHAWN ANDREWS
City of Ghosts *77*

JENNIFER ANISTON (1969-)
Bruce Almighty *52*

KATHLEEN ANTONIA
Dopamine *121*

CAS ANVAR
Shattered Glass *408*

DEVON AOKI
2 Fast 2 Furious *466*

SHIRI APPLEBY (1978-)
The Battle of Shaker Heights *32*

CHRISTINA APPLEGATE (1971-)
View from the Top *477*
Wonderland *489*

ROYCE D. APPLEGATE (1939-2003)
Gods and Generals *163*
Intolerable Cruelty *221*
Seabiscuit *396*

MANUEL ARANGUIZ
Levity *262*

SEAN ARBUCKLE
Anything But Love *17*

LEE ARENBERG (1962-)
Pirates of the Caribbean: The Curse of the Black Pearl *369*

GEOFFREY AREND
It Runs in the Family *225*

CARMEN ARGENZIANO (1943-)
Identity *209*

VICTOR ARGO (1934-)
Anything But Love *17*

PEDRO ARMENDARIZ, JR. (1930-)
Once Upon a Time in Mexico *342*

REGAN ARNOLD
Blue Car *43*

TICHINA ARNOLD
Civil Brand *81*

TOM ARNOLD (1959-)
Cradle 2 the Grave *93*

ALEXIS ARQUETTE (1969-)
Spun *419*

PATRICIA ARQUETTE (1968-)
Holes *185*

KATE ASHFIELD
Beyond Borders *38*

SHAWN ASHMORE (1979-)
X2: X-Men United *492*

ED ASNER (1929-)
Elf *134*

MACKENZIE ASTIN (1973-)
How to Deal *197*

SEAN ASTIN (1971-)
The Lord of the Rings 3: The Return of the King *269*

WILLIAM ATHERTON (1947-)
The Last Samurai *244*

KATE ATIKINSON
The Hard Word *176*

FEODOR ATKINE (1948-)
Carnage *67*

EILEEN ATKINS (1934-)
Cold Mountain *84*
What a Girl Wants *485*

ESSENCE ATKINS (1972-)
Deliver Us from Eva *109*

FINN ATKINS
Once Upon a Time in the
Midlands *344*

ROWAN ATKINSON
(1955-)
Johnny English *232*
Love Actually *275*

YVAN ATTAL (1965-)
And Now Ladies and
Gentlemen *13*

DANIEL AUTEUIL (1950-)
On Guard! *341*
Sade *391*

ERIK AVARI (1952-)
Daredevil *101*

MILI AVITAL (1972-)
The Human Stain *203*

CHARLOTTE AYANNA
Love the Hard Way *280*

NICKI AYCOX
Jeepers Creepers 2 *229*

JOHN AYLWARD
Down With Love *122*

HANK AZARIA (1964-)
Shattered Glass *408*

MICHAEL BACALL
Manic *296*

KEVIN BACON (1958-)
In the Cut *215*
Mystic River *332*

JEAN-PIERRE BACRI
(1951-)
A Housekeeper *194*

EDOUARD BAER
Alias Betty *4*

GIACOMO BAESSATO
Dreamcatcher *124*

VLADAS BAGDONAS
House of Fools *190*

DAVID BAILIE
Pirates of the Caribbean: The
Curse of the Black
Pearl *369*

SCOTT BAIO (1961-)
The Bread, My Sweet *47*

HELMUT BAKAITIS
The Matrix Reloaded *308*
The Matrix
Revolutions *311*

DYLAN BAKER (1958-)
Head of State *182*
How to Deal *197*

KATHY BAKER (1950-)
Assassination Tango *21*
Cold Mountain *84*

ROBERT BAKER
Out of Time *352*

SIMON BAKER (1969-)
The Missing *317*

BOB BALABAN (1945-)
A Mighty Wind *314*

ALEC BALDWIN (1958-)
The Cooler *89*
Dr. Seuss' The Cat in the
Hat *119*

CHRISTIAN BALE (1974-)
Laurel Canyon *250*

ERIC BALFOUR
The Texas Chainsaw
Massacre *448*

JEANNE BALIBAR
Sade *391*

ALEXANDRE BALUEV
Tycoon *467*

GERRY BAMMAN (1941-)
Runaway Jury *386*

ERIC BANA (1968-)
Finding Nemo (V) *142*
Hulk *200*

CAMERON BANCROFT
(1967-)
Anything But Love *17*

ANTONIO BANDERAS
(1960-)
Once Upon a Time in
Mexico *342*
Spy Kids 3-D: Game
Over *421*

ELIZABETH BANKS
Seabiscuit *396*

REGGIE BANNISTER
(1945-)
Bubba Ho-Tep *54*

CHRISTINE BARANSKI
(1952-)
The Guru *173*
Marci X *299*

JAVIER BARDEM (1969-)
The Dancer Upstairs *100*
Mondays in the Sun *321*

JOSH BARKER
Northfork *336*

BARRY BARNES
Veronica Guerin *475*

JEAN-MARC BARR (1960-)
Le Divorce *256*

JACINDA BARRETT
The Human Stain *203*

CHRIS (CHRISTOPHER)
BARRIE (1960-)
Lara Croft Tomb Raider:
The Cradle of Life *243*

JUNE BARRIE
Lawless Heart *252*

RAYMOND J. BARRY
(1939-)
Just Married *237*

THOM BARRY
2 Fast 2 Furious *466*

DREW BARRYMORE
(1975-)
Charlie's Angels: Full
Throttle *71*
Duplex *130*

JUSTIN BARTHA
Gigli *157*

JAMIE BARTLETT
Beyond Borders *38*

J BARTON
Legally Blonde 2: Red,
White & Blonde *260*

ALAIN BASHUNG
Confusion of Genders *88*

KIM BASINGER (1953-)
People I Know *359*

ANGELA BASSETT (1958-)
Masked and
Anonymous *302*

LINDA BASSETT
Calendar Girls *61*

ALAN BATES (1934-2003)
The Statement *423*

KATHY BATES (1948-)
Love Liza *278*

FLAVIO BAURAQUI
Madame Sata *284*

NATHALIE BAYE (1948-)
The Flower of Evil *146*

JENNIFER BEALS (1963-)
Runaway Jury *386*

SEAN BEAN (1959-)
The Lord of the Rings 3:
The Return of the
King *269*

JIM BEAVER (1950-)
The Life of David
Gale *263*

ERICA BECK
Finding Nemo (V) *142*

GRAHAM BECKEL (1955-)
Northfork *336*

KUNO BECKER
Lucia, Lucia *281*

ROLF BECKER (1935-)
Gloomy Sunday *161*

TYSON BECKFORD
Biker Boyz *42*

KATE BECKINSALE (1974-)
Laurel Canyon *250*
Underworld *471*

ED BEGLEY, JR. (1949-)
A Mighty Wind *314*

CATHERINE BELL
Bruce Almighty *52*

DREW TYLER BELL
Jeepers Creepers 2 *229*

MARSHALL BELL (1944-)
Identity *209*
Northfork *336*

MICHAEL BELL
Rugrats Go Wild! (V) *385*

MARIA BELLO (1967-)
The Cooler *89*

MONICA BELLUCCI
(1968-)
Irreversible *223*
The Matrix Reloaded *308*
The Matrix
Revolutions *311*
Tears of the Sun *442*

PAUL BEN-VICTOR
Daredevil *101*

ROBERTO BENIGNI
(1952-)
Fellini: I'm a Born
Liar *137*

ANNETTE BENING (1958-)
Open Range *348*

MAX BENITZ
Master and Commander:
The Far Side of the
World *303*

PAUL BENJAMIN (1938-)
The Station Agent *425*

RICHARD BENJAMIN
(1938-)
Marci X *299*

JEFF GLENN BENNETT
Looney Tunes: Back in
Action (V) *267*

ABRAHAM BENRUBI
(1969-)
Open Range *348*

CANDICE BERGEN (1946-)
The In-Laws *213*
View from the Top *477*

CHARLES BERLING
(1958-)
Demonlover *111*
How I Killed My
Father *196*

MARC BERMAN
The Girl from Paris *159*

A.J. BUCKLEY
Blue Car *43*

CELSO BUGALLO
Mondays in the Sun *321*

CARA BUONO (1974-)
Hulk *200*

ZLATKO BURIC
Dirty Pretty Things *116*

DELTA BURKE (1956-)
Good Boy! (V) *165*

KATHY BURKE (1964-)
Once Upon a Time in the
Midlands *344*

EDWARD BURNS (1968-)
Confidence *86*

MEGAN BURNS
28 Days Later *464*

JACKIE BURROUGHS
(1938-)
A Guy Thing *174*
Willard *486*

SAFFRON BURROWS
(1973-)
Peter Pan (N) *361*

BOB BURRUS
Tully *459*

STEVE BUSCEMI (1957-)
Big Fish *39*
Spy Kids 3-D: Game
Over *421*

CHARLES BUSCH
Die Mommie Die! *114*

JAKE BUSEY (1972-)
Identity *209*

TIMOTHY BUSFIELD
(1957-)
National Security *334*

AKOSUA BUSIA (1968-)
Tears of the Sun *442*

GERARD BUTLER (1969-)
Lara Croft Tomb Raider:
The Cradle of Life *243*
Timeline *453*

JOSEPHINE BUTLER
Lawless Heart *252*

TOM BUTLER
Freddy vs. Jason *152*

VIKTER BYCHKOV
The Cuckoo *97*

AMANDA BYNES (1986-)
What a Girl Wants *485*

GABRIEL BYRNE (1950-)
Spider *415*

ROSE BYRNE (1979-)
City of Ghosts *77*
I Capture the Castle *207*

JAMES CAAN (1939-)
City of Ghosts *77*
Elf *134*

CHRISTINA CABOT
The Italian Job *227*

MANUEL CABRAL
Manito *297*

NICOLAS CAGE (1964-)
Matchstick Men *305*

DEAN CAIN (1966-)
Out of Time *352*

MICHAEL CAINE (1933-)
Secondhand Lions *400*
The Statement *423*

PAUL CALDERON
21 Grams *462*

SERGIO CALDERON
(1945-)
The Missing *317*

MONICA CALHOUN
Civil Brand *81*

JAMES CALLAHAN (1930-)
Freddy vs. Jason *152*

MARS CALLAHAN (1972-)
Poolhall Junkies *373*

VANESSA BELL
CALLOWAY (1957-)
Biker Boyz *42*
Cheaper by the Dozen *75*
Love Don't Cost a
Thing *277*

BILLY CAMPBELL (1959-)
Gods and Generals *163*

BRUCE CAMPBELL (1958-)
Bubba Ho-Tep *54*

BRUNO CAMPOS (1974-)
Dopamine *121*

RON CANADA
The Human Stain *203*
The Hunted *205*

NATALIE CANERDAY
Tully *459*

BOBBY CANNAVALE
(1971-)
The Station Agent *425*
Washington Heights *479*

NICK CANNON (1980-)
Love Don't Cost a
Thing *277*

ION CARAMITRU
Amen *7*

CLAUDIA CARDINALE
(1939-)
And Now Ladies and
Gentlemen *13*

LENA CARDWELL
Jeepers Creepers 2 *229*

STEVEN CARELL
Bruce Almighty *52*

MATTHEW CAREY
Old School *339*

GEORGE CARLIN (1937-)
Scary Movie 3 *392*

JODI CARLISLE
Rugrats Go Wild! (V) *385*

ROBERT CARLYLE (1961-)
Once Upon a Time in the
Midlands *344*

FRANCESCO
CARNELUTTI
The Order *350*

LESLIE CARON (1931-)
Le Divorce *256*

DAVID CARRADINE
(1936-)
Kill Bill: Vol. 1 (V) *240*

ROBERT CARRADINE
(1954-)
The Lizzie McGuire
Movie *265*

ISABELLE CARRE
He Loves Me . . . He Loves
Me Not *180*

JIM CARREY (1962-)
Bruce Almighty *52*

MATTHIEU CARRIERE
(1950-)
Luther *283*

KEVIN CARROLL
The Secret Lives of
Dentists *402*

TERRENCE "T.C."
CARSON
Final Destination 2 *140*

MARCELLA CARTAXO
Madame Sata *284*

ALEX CARTER
Out of Time *352*

SARAH CARTER
Final Destination 2 *140*

NANCY CARTWRIGHT
(1959-)
Rugrats Go Wild! (V) *385*

VERONICA
CARTWRIGHT (1950-)
Just Married *237*

AMIRA CASAR
How I Killed My
Father *196*
Sylvia *438*

FRANCESCO CASISA
Respiro *381*

JEAN-PIERRE CASSEL
(1932-)
Sade *391*

Stuck On You *430*

VINCENT CASSEL (1967-)
Irreversible *223*

KEISHA CASTLE-HUGHES
Whale Rider *483*

MIGUEL CASTRO
Holes *185*

REG E. CATHEY (1958-)
S.W.A.T. *432*

BRIGITTE CATILLON
A Housekeeper *194*

JESSICA CAUFFIEL
Legally Blonde 2: Red,
White & Blonde *260*

EMMA CAULFIELD
Darkness Falls *105*

HENRY CAVILL
I Capture the Castle *207*

CEDRIC THE
ENTERTAINER (1964-)
Intolerable Cruelty *221*

CLEMENTINE CELARIE
(1957-)
Lawless Heart *252*

LACEY CHABERT (1982-)
Daddy Day Care *98*
Rugrats Go Wild! (V) *385*

THOMAS CHABROL
The Flower of Evil *146*

JACKIE CHAN (1954-)
The Medallion *313*
Shanghai Knights *404*

KIM CHAN
Shanghai Knights *404*

ANNA CHANCELLOR
(1965-)
What a Girl Wants *485*

STOCKARD CHANNING
(1944-)
Anything Else *19*
Le Divorce *256*

ROSALIND CHAO (1949-)
Freaky Friday *150*

KEVIN CHAPMAN
Mystic River *332*

LONNY (LONNIE)
CHAPMAN (1921-)
The Hunted *205*

JOSH CHARLES (1971-)
S.W.A.T. *432*

MELANIE CHARTOFF
(1955-)
Rugrats Go Wild! (V) *385*

CHERYL CHASE
Rugrats Go Wild! (V) *385*

DAVEIGH CHASE (1990-)
Spirited Away (V) *418*

MARTON CSOKAS (1966-)
Garage Days *155*
Kangaroo Jack *239*
The Lord of the Rings 3:
The Return of the
King *269*
Timeline *453*

DANIEL CUDMORE
X2: X-Men United *492*

MACAULAY CULKIN
(1980-)
Party Monster *356*

RORY CULKIN (1989-)
It Runs in the Family *225*

BRETT CULLEN (1956-)
National Security *334*

PETER CULLEN
Piglet's Big Movie (V) *368*

ALAN CUMMING (1965-)
Spy Kids 3-D: Game
Over *421*
X2: X-Men United *492*

JIM (JONAH) CUMMINGS
(1953-)
Piglet's Big Movie (V) *368*

TONY CURRAN
The League of Extraordinary
Gentlemen *257*

CHRISTOPHER CURRY
City of Ghosts *77*

TIM CURRY (1946-)
Rugrats Go Wild! (V) *385*

PETER CURTAIN
Darkness Falls *105*
Till Human Voices Wake
Us *451*

CLIFFORD CURTIS (1968-)
Runaway Jury *386*
Whale Rider *483*

JAMIE LEE CURTIS (1958-)
Freaky Friday *150*

PIERRE CURZI (1946-)
The Barbarian
Invasions *28*

JOAN CUSACK (1962-)
Looney Tunes: Back in
Action *267*
School of Rock *394*

JOHN CUSACK (1966-)
Identity *209*
Runaway Jury *386*

SINEAD CUSACK (1948-)
I Capture the Castle *207*

ELISHA CUTHBERT
Old School *339*

DA BRAT (1974-)
Civil Brand *81*

LEANDRO FIRMINO DA
HORA
City of God *79*

MARK DACASCOS (1964-)
Cradle 2 the Grave *93*

WILLEM DAFOE (1955-)
Finding Nemo (V) *142*
Once Upon a Time in
Mexico *342*

VERONICA D'AGOSTINO
Respiro *381*

AMER DAHER
Divine Intervention: A
Chronicle of Love and
Pain *117*

JAMEL DAHER
Divine Intervention: A
Chronicle of Love and
Pain *117*

NAYEF FAHOUM DAHER
Divine Intervention: A
Chronicle of Love and
Pain *117*

ELIZABETH (E.G.
DAILEY) DAILY
Rugrats Go Wild! (V) *385*

TIMOTHY DALTON
(1944-)
Looney Tunes: Back in
Action *267*

TIMOTHY DALY (1956-)
Basic *30*

NICK DAMICI
In the Cut *215*

MATT DAMON (1970-)
Gerry *156*
Stuck On You *430*

CHARLES DANCE (1946-)
Swimming Pool *436*

CLAIRE DANES (1979-)
Terminator 3: Rise of the
Machines *446*

ERIN DANIELS
House of 1000
Corpses *191*

JEFF DANIELS (1955-)
Gods and Generals *163*

BLYTHE DANNER (1944-)
Sylvia *438*

JAMES D'ARCY
Master and Commander:
The Far Side of the
World *303*

GERARD DARMON (1948-)
The Good Thief *167*

JACK DAVENPORT (1973-)
Pirates of the Caribbean: The
Curse of the Black
Pearl *369*

LUCY DAVENPORT
Sylvia *438*

KEITH DAVID (1954-)
Agent Cody Banks *1*
Head of State *182*
Hollywood Homicide *186*

LOLITA (DAVID)
DAVIDOVICH (1961-)
Dark Blue *103*
Hollywood Homicide *186*

OLIVER FORD DAVIES
Johnny English *232*

AREE DAVIS
The Haunted
Mansion *178*

DEAUNDRE "DOUBLE D"
DAVIS
Jeepers Creepers 2 *229*

ESSIE DAVIS
Girl with a Pearl
Earring *160*
The Matrix Reloaded *308*
The Matrix
Revolutions *311*

HOPE DAVIS (1964-)
American Splendor *9*
The Secret Lives of
Dentists *402*

MATTHEW DAVIS
Below *33*

NATHAN DAVIS
Holes *185*

OSSIE DAVIS (1917-)
Bubba Ho-Tep *54*

BRUCE DAVISON (1946-)
Runaway Jury *386*
X2: X-Men United *492*

ROSARIO DAWSON (1979-)
The Rundown *389*
Shattered Glass *408*

JAMES DE BELLO
See James DeBello

CECILE DE FRANCE
L'Auberge Espagnole *248*

XAVIER DE GUILLEBON
L'Auberge Espagnole *248*

ROBIN DE JESUS
Camp *63*

DAVID DE KEYSER
The Statement *423*

CHRISTIAN DE LA
FUENTE
Basic *30*

DREA DE MATTEO (1973-)
Prey for Rock and
Roll *374*

MARIA DE MEDEIROS
(1965-)
My Life Without Me *330*

NIEVE DE MEDINA
Mondays in the Sun *321*

JAMES DEBELLO (1980-)
Cabin Fever *60*

ANTONIO DECHENT
Intacto *220*

ELLEN DEGENERES
(1958-)
Finding Nemo (V) *142*

DAVID DEKEYSER
See David de Keyser

BENICIO DEL TORO
(1967-)
The Hunted *205*
21 Grams *462*

BRIAN DELATE
Buffalo Soldiers *56*

MARIEH DELFINO
Jeepers Creepers 2 *229*

ALAIN DELON (1935-)
Le Cercle Rouge *254*

REBECCA DEMORNAY
(1962-)
Identity *209*

MARIANNE (CUAU)
DENICOURT (1966-)
Sade *391*

DAVID DENMAN
Big Fish *39*

GERARD DEPARDIEU
(1948-)
City of Ghosts *77*

JOHNNY DEPP (1963-)
Once Upon a Time in
Mexico *342*
Pirates of the Caribbean: The
Curse of the Black
Pearl *369*

EMILIE DEQUENNE
(1981-)
A Housekeeper *194*

BO DEREK (1956-)
Malibu's Most
Wanted *289*

BRUCE DERN (1936-)
Masked and
Anonymous *302*
Monster *326*

JACOB DERWIG
Zus & Zo *497*

ZOOEY DESCHANEL
(1980-)
All the Real Girls *5*
Elf *134*
Manic *296*

ERIC DEULEN
Elephant *132*

ALAN DEVINE
Veronica Guerin *475*

R. LEE ERMEY (1944-)
Taking Sides *440*
The Texas Chainsaw
Massacre *448*
Willard *486*

MIKE ERWIN (1978-)
Hulk *200*

DANA ESKELSON
Cold Creek Manor *82*

EILEEN ESSELL
Duplex *130*

LAURA ESTERMAN
Suspended Animation *432*

TREVA ETIENNE
Pirates of the Caribbean: The
Curse of the Black
Pearl *369*

LEE EVANS (1965-)
The Medallion *313*

TERRENCE EVANS
The Texas Chainsaw
Massacre *448*

MARILYNE EVEN
Carnage *67*

CHRISTOPHER FAIRBANK
Below *33*

**DONALD ADEOSUN
FAISON (1974-)**
Good Boy! (V) *165*
Uptown Girls *473*

FRANKIE FAISON (1949-)
Gods and Generals *163*

BRIAN FALDUTO
School of Rock *394*

JIMMY FALLON (1974-)
Anything Else *19*

SIOBHAN FALLON (1972-)
Holes *185*

**MARK FAMIGLIETTI
(1979-)**
Terminator 3: Rise of the
Machines *446*

ROGER FAN
Better Luck Tomorrow *36*

DAKOTA FANNING (1994-)
Dr. Seuss' The Cat in the
Hat *119*
Uptown Girls *473*

ANNA FARIS
Lost in Translation *273*
Scary Movie 3 *392*

VERA FARMIGA (1973-)
Dummy *129*

DUEL FARNES
Northfork *336*

COLIN FARRELL (1976-)
Daredevil *101*

Phone Booth *363*
The Recruit *380*
S.W.A.T. *432*
Veronica Guerin *475*

JOEY FATONE
The Cooler *89*

JAMES FAULKNER (1948-)
I Capture the Castle *207*

JON FAVREAU (1966-)
Daredevil *101*
Elf *134*
Something's Gotta
Give *414*

MARC FAYOLLE
Swimming Pool *436*

BRENDAN FEHR (1977-)
Biker Boyz *42*

**FEDERICO FELLINI (1920-
93)**
Fellini: I'm a Born
Liar *137*

COLM FEORE (1958-)
National Security *334*
Paycheck *358*

JUAN FERNANDEZ
A Man Apart *292*

WILL FERRELL (1968-)
Boat Trip *45*
Elf *134*
Old School *339*

CLAUDIA FERRI
Mambo Italiano *291*

LOU FERRIGNO (1952-)
Hulk *200*

JOHN FIEDLER (1925-)
Piglet's Big Movie (V) *368*

SALLY FIELD (1946-)
Legally Blonde 2: Red,
White & Blonde *260*

JOSEPH FIENNES (1970-)
Luther *283*
Sinbad: Legend of the Seven
Seas (V) *410*

RALPH FIENNES (1962-)
The Good Thief *167*
Spider *415*

**HARVEY FIERSTEIN
(1954-)**
Duplex *130*

**DENNIS FIMPLE (1940-
2002)**
House of 1000
Corpses *191*

RHONDA FINDLETON
The Hard Word *176*

CARRIE FINKLEA
Elephant *132*

FRANK FINLAY (1926-)
The Statement *423*

JOHN FINN (1952-)
The Hunted *205*

ALBERT FINNEY (1936-)
Big Fish *39*

COLIN FIRTH (1961-)
Girl with a Pearl
Earring *160*
Love Actually *275*
What a Girl Wants *485*

JONATHAN FIRTH (1967-)
Luther *283*

**LAURENCE "LARRY"
FISHBURNE (1963-)**
Biker Boyz *42*
The Matrix Reloaded *308*
The Matrix
Revolutions *311*
Mystic River *332*

CARRIE FISHER (1956-)
Charlie's Angels: Full
Throttle *71*
Wonderland *489*

FRANCES FISHER (1952-)
Blue Car *43*
House of Sand and
Fog *192*

GREGOR FISHER
Love Actually *275*

THOMAS FISHER
Shanghai Knights *404*

GLENN FITZGERALD
Buffalo Soldiers *56*
Tully *459*

**TARA FITZGERALD
(1968-)**
I Capture the Castle *207*

JOE FLAHERTY (1941-)
National Security *334*

**FIONNULA FLANAGAN
(1941-)**
Tears of the Sun *442*

FLEA (1962-)
Rugrats Go Wild! (V) *385*

JASON FLEMYNG (1966-)
Below *33*
The League of Extraordinary
Gentlemen *257*

**BRENDAN FLETCHER
(1981-)**
Freddy vs. Jason *152*

**DEXTER FLETCHER
(1966-)**
Below *33*

SUZANNE FLON (1918-)
The Flower of Evil *146*

NINA FOCH (1924-)
How to Deal *197*

SCOTT FOLEY (1973-)
Below *33*

ABEL FOLK
The Dancer Upstairs *100*

HARRISON FORD (1942-)
Hollywood Homicide *186*

TRENT FORD
How to Deal *197*

CLAIRE FORLANI (1972-)
The Medallion *313*
Northfork *336*

STEVE FORREST (1924-)
S.W.A.T. *432*

ROBERT FORSTER (1941-)
Charlie's Angels: Full
Throttle *71*
Confidence *86*

JOHN FORSYTHE (1918-)
Charlie's Angels: Full
Throttle (V) *71*

JOHN FORTUNE
Calendar Girls *61*

BEN FOSTER (1980-)
Northfork *336*

**GLORIA FOSTER (1936-
2001)**
The Matrix Reloaded *308*

RICK FOX
Holes *185*

VIVICA A. FOX (1964-)
Boat Trip *45*
Kill Bill: Vol. 1 *240*

JON FRANCIS
See Jon(athan) Gries

PAUL FRANCIS
Tears of the Sun *442*

JACQUES FRANTZ
A Housekeeper *194*

BRENDAN FRASER (1968-)
Dickie Roberts: Former
Child Star *112*
Looney Tunes: Back in
Action *267*

MARTIN FREEMAN
Love Actually *275*

**MORGAN FREEMAN
(1937-)**
Bruce Almighty *52*
Dreamcatcher *124*
Levity *262*

STEPHANE FREISS
Alias Betty *4*

BRENDA FRICKER (1944-)
Veronica Guerin *475*

JUDAH FRIEDLANDER
American Splendor *9*

ANNA FRIEL (1976-)
Timeline *453*

ALEX FROST
Elephant *132*

HEATHER GRAHAM
(1970-)
Anger Management *15*
The Guru *173*

LAUREN GRAHAM (1967-)
Bad Santa *25*

MARCELLA GRANITO
The Embalmer *136*

BETH GRANT (1949-)
Matchstick Men *305*

HUGH GRANT (1960-)
Love Actually *275*

MACY GRAY
Scary Movie 3 *392*

SPALDING GRAY (1941-
2004)
Revolution #9 *383*

JORDAN-CLAIRE GREEN
School of Rock *394*

SETH GREEN (1974-)
The Italian Job *227*
Party Monster *356*

BILLOAH GREENE
Levity *262*

ELLEN GREENE (1952-)
The Cooler *89*

BRUCE GREENWOOD
(1956-)
Below *33*
The Core *91*
Hollywood Homicide *186*

PASCAL GREGGORY
(1954-)
Confusion of Genders *88*

DORIAN GREGORY (1971-)
Deliver Us from Eva *109*

ADRIAN GRENIER (1976-)
Anything Else *19*

PAM GRIER (1949-)
Love the Hard Way *280*

JON(ATHAN) GRIES (1957-)
Northfork *336*
The Rundown *389*

EDDIE GRIFFIN (1968-)
Scary Movie 3 *392*

KHAMANI GRIFFIN (1998-)
Daddy Day Care *98*

RACHEL GRIFFITHS
(1968-)
The Hard Word *176*

REUBEN GRUNDY
Dopamine *121*

AH-LEH GUA
Fleeing by Night *145*

CHRISTOPHER GUEST
(1948-)
A Mighty Wind *314*

CARLA GUGINO (1971-)
The Singing
Detective *412*
Spy Kids 3-D: Game
Over *421*

ROBERT GUILLAUME
(1937-)
Big Fish *39*

SOPHIE GUILLEMIN
He Loves Me . . . He Loves
Me Not *180*

STEPHANE GUILLON
How I Killed My
Father *196*

SIENNA GUILLORY
Love Actually *275*

TOM GUIRY (1981-)
Mystic River *332*

BOB GUNTON (1945-)
Boat Trip *45*

KICK (CHRISTOPHER)
GURRY
Garage Days *155*

ALTAGRACIA GUZMAN
Raising Victor Vargas *377*

LUIS GUZMAN (1956-)
Anger Management *15*
Confidence *86*
Dumb and Dumberer: When
Harry Met Lloyd *127*

MAGGIE GYLLENHAAL
(1977-)
Casa de los Babys *68*
Mona Lisa Smile *319*

KIM GYNGELL
The Hard Word *176*

JOHNATHAN
HAAGENSEN
City of God *79*

PHELIPE HAAGENSEN
City of God *79*

WILLIE HAAPSALO
The Cuckoo *97*

KEVIN MICHAEL
HABERER
Secondhand Lions *400*

MATTHIAS HABICH
(1940-)
Nowhere in Africa *338*

GENE HACKMAN (1930-)
Runaway Jury *386*

JONATHAN HADARY
Intolerable Cruelty *221*

ELLIE HADDINGTON
Lawless Heart *252*

JUSTIN HAGAN
Party Monster *356*

JULIE HAGERTY (1955-)
A Guy Thing *174*

KATHRYN HAHN
How to Lose a Guy in 10
Days *199*

SID HAIG (1939-)
House of 1000
Corpses *191*

CAITLIN HALE
School of Rock *394*

BRADLEY HALL
Spider *415*

DOMINIC HALL
Lawless Heart *252*

MICHAEL C. HALL (1971-)
Paycheck *358*

PHILIP BAKER HALL
(1931-)
Bruce Almighty *52*
Die Mommie Die! *114*

REGINA HALL (1971-)
Malibu's Most
Wanted *289*
Scary Movie 3 *392*

JOHNNY HALLYDAY
(1943-)
The Man on the
Train *294*

MARK HAMMER
It Runs in the Family *225*

DARRELL HAMMOND
Agent Cody Banks *1*

MARINA HANDS
The Barbarian
Invasions *28*

JOE HANLEY
Veronica Guerin *475*

DARYL HANNAH (1960-)
Casa de los Babys *68*
Kill Bill: Vol. 1 *240*
Northfork *336*

ALYSON HANNIGAN
(1974-)
American Wedding *11*

MASATO HARADA
The Last Samurai *244*

MARCIA GAY HARDEN
(1959-)
Casa de los Babys *68*
Mona Lisa Smile *319*
Mystic River *332*

KADEEM HARDISON
(1965-)
Biker Boyz *42*

CHRIS HARDWICK
House of 1000
Corpses *191*

DORIAN HAREWOOD
(1950-)
Gothika *169*
Levity *262*

SHALOM HARLOW (1973-)
How to Lose a Guy in 10
Days *199*

BROOKE HARMAN
Till Human Voices Wake
Us *451*

ANGIE HARMON
Agent Cody Banks *1*

MARK HARMON (1951-)
Freaky Friday *150*

FRANK HARPER
Bend It Like Beckham *35*

REBECCA HARRELL
Suspended Animation *432*

WOODY HARRELSON
(1962-)
Anger Management *15*

LAURA ELENA HARRING
(1964-)
Willard *486*

DESMOND HARRINGTON
(1976-)
Wrong Turn *490*

DANIELLE HARRIS (1977-)
Rugrats Go Wild! (V) *385*

ED HARRIS (1949-)
Buffalo Soldiers *56*
The Human Stain *203*
Masked and
Anonymous *302*
Radio *376*

ESTELLE HARRIS (1926-)
Brother Bear (V) *50*

JARED HARRIS (1961-)
Dummy *129*
Sylvia *438*

JOEL HARRIS
Wrong Turn *490*

NAOMIE HARRIS
28 Days Later *464*

SHAWNTAE HARRIS
See Da Brat

STEVE HARRIS
Bringing Down the
House *49*

DEBORAH HARRY (1945-)
My Life Without Me *330*

RONA HARTNER
Le Divorce *256*

JOSH HARTNETT (1978-)
Hollywood Homicide *186*

STEVE HARVEY
The Fighting
Temptations *139*

JASON ISAACS (1963-)
Peter Pan *361*

MARGARITA ISABEL
Lucia, Lucia *281*

KATHARINE ISABELLE
(1982-)
Freddy vs. Jason *152*

SULTAN ISKAMOV
House of Fools *190*

MARCEL IURES
Amen *7*

DANA IVEY (1942-)
Legally Blonde 2: Red,
White & Blonde *260*

BOB IVY
Bubba Ho-Tep *54*

JA RULE (1976-)
Scary Movie 3 *392*

MICHAEL JACE (1965-)
Cradle 2 the Grave *93*

HUGH JACKMAN (1968-)
X2: X-Men United *492*

MEL JACKSON
Deliver Us from Eva *109*

SAMUEL L. JACKSON
(1948-)
Basic *30*
S.W.A.T. *432*

YVES JACQUES
The Barbarian
Invasions *28*

SAKINA JAFFREY
Revolution #9 *383*

JAMAU
In This World *219*

GERALDINE JAMES (1950-)
Calendar Girls *61*

OLIVER JAMES
What a Girl Wants *485*

THOMAS JANE (1969-)
Dreamcatcher *124*

ALLISON JANNEY (1960-)
Finding Nemo (V) *142*
How to Deal *197*

FAMKE JANSSEN (1964-)
X2: X-Men United *492*

TONY JAY
The Jungle Book 2
(V) *234*

BRENDAN JEFFERSON
Holes *185*

MARC JOHN JEFFRIES
The Haunted
Mansion *178*

NOAM JENKINS
The Statement *423*

RICHARD JENKINS
Cheaper by the Dozen *75*
The Core *91*
Intolerable Cruelty *221*

LUCINDA JENNEY
S.W.A.T. *432*

JUANITA JENNINGS
Runaway Jury *386*

MICHAEL JETER (1952-
2003)
Open Range *348*

COURTNEY JINES
Spy Kids 3-D: Game
Over *421*

SCARLETT JOHANSSON
(1984-)
Girl with a Pearl
Earring *160*
Lost in Translation *273*

AARON JOHNSON
Shanghai Knights *404*

CLARK JOHNSON (1954-)
S.W.A.T. *432*

DWAYNE "THE ROCK"
JOHNSON (1972-)
The Rundown *389*

BOB JOLES
The Jungle Book 2
(V) *234*

ANGELINA JOLIE (1975-)
Beyond Borders *38*
Lara Croft Tomb Raider:
The Cradle of Life *243*

ANGUS T. JONES
Bringing Down the
House *49*

EDDIE JONES
Seabiscuit *396*

GEMMA JONES (1942-)
Shanghai Knights *404*

JANUARY JONES
American Wedding *11*
Anger Management *15*

MARK LEWIS JONES
Master and Commander:
The Far Side of the
World *303*

ORLANDO JONES (1968-)
Biker Boyz *42*

RICHARD T. JONES (1972-)
Phone Booth *363*

TAMALA JONES (1974-)
Head of State *182*

TOMMY LEE JONES
(1946-)
The Hunted *205*
The Missing *317*

SEU JORGE
City of God *79*

JENNIFER JOSTYN
House of 1000
Corpses *191*

MILLA JOVOVICH (1975-)
Dummy *129*

ELLA JOYCE
Bubba Ho-Tep *54*

LINDLEY JOYNER
Till Human Voices Wake
Us *451*

MIKE JUDGE (1962-)
Spy Kids 3-D: Game
Over *421*

PATRICIA KAAS
And Now Ladies and
Gentlemen *13*

CHEN KAIGE (1952-)
Together *456*

CHRISTIAN KANE (1974-)
Just Married *237*
Secondhand Lions *400*

TOM KANE
Rugrats Go Wild! (V) *385*

SUNG KANG
Better Luck Tomorrow *36*

PHILIPP KARNER
The Battle of Shaker
Heights *32*

TCHEKY KARYO (1953-)
The Core *91*
The Good Thief *167*

MAX KASCH
Holes *185*

MATHIEU KASSOVITZ
(1967-)
Amen *7*

NICKY KATT (1970-)
School of Rock *394*
Secondhand Lions *400*

JONATHAN KATZ
Daddy Day Care *98*

BILLY KAY
The Battle of Shaker
Heights *32*

LAINIE KAZAN (1942-)
Gigli *157*

JAMES KEANE
Assassination Tango *21*

DIANE KEATON (1946-)
Something's Gotta
Give *414*

SALIM KECHIOUCHE
Criminal Lovers *95*

MONICA KEENA (1979-)
Freddy vs. Jason *152*

JACK KEHLER
Love Liza *278*

HARVEY KEITEL (1947-)
Taking Sides *440*

DAVID KEITH (1954-)
Daredevil *101*

SHEILA KELLEY (1964-)
Matchstick Men *305*

CATHERINE KELLNER
Tully *459*

BRENDAN KELLY
The Lizzie McGuire
Movie *265*

BRETT KELLY
Bad Santa *25*

SEREYVUTH KEM
City of Ghosts *77*

ANNA KENDRICK
Camp *63*

JAMIE KENNEDY (1970-)
Malibu's Most
Wanted *289*

LEILA KENZLE
Identity *209*

JOEY KERN
Cabin Fever *60*
Grind *171*

PAUL KERSEY (1970-)
Hulk *200*

IRWIN KEYES (1952-)
Intolerable Cruelty *221*

MANAL KHADER
Divine Intervention: A
Chronicle of Love and
Pain *117*

SHAHEEN KHAN
Bend It Like Beckham *35*

WAKEEL KHAN
In This World *219*

ANUPAM KHER
Bend It Like Beckham *35*

GEORGE KHLEIFI
Divine Intervention: A
Chronicle of Love and
Pain *117*

SANDRINE KIBERLAIN
(1968-)
Alias Betty *4*

KID ROCK (1971-)
Biker Boyz *42*

NICOLE KIDMAN (1966-)
Cold Mountain *84*
The Human Stain *203*

LAURA KIGHTLINGER
(1969-)
Down With Love *122*

ERICA LEERHSEN
Anything Else *19*
The Texas Chainsaw
Massacre *448*

JOHN LEGUIZAMO (1964-)
Spun *419*

RON LEIBMAN (1937-)
Dummy *129*

**JENNIFER JASON LEIGH
(1963-)**
In the Cut *215*

VALERIE LEMERCIER
Friday Night *153*

ALEXANDRA LENCASTRE
The Dancer Upstairs *100*

HARRY J. LENNIX
The Human Stain *203*
The Matrix Reloaded *308*
The Matrix
Revolutions *311*

THOMAS LENNON (1969-)
A Guy Thing *174*
How to Lose a Guy in 10
Days *199*
Le Divorce *256*

JAY LENO (1950-)
Calendar Girls *61*
Stuck On You *430*

MELISSA LEO (1960-)
21 Grams *462*

**MARCO LEONARDI
(1971-)**
Once Upon a Time in
Mexico *342*

TEA LEONI (1966-)
People I Know *359*

MICHAEL LERNER (1941-)
Elf *134*

JALIL LESPERT
Sade *391*

MATT LETSCHER (1970-)
Gods and Generals *163*
Identity *209*

DANIEL LETTERLE
Camp *63*

**TONY LEUNG CHIU-WAI
(1962-)**
Hero *184*

ILANA LEVINE
Anything But Love *17*

TED LEVINE (1958-)
Wonderland *489*

EUGENE LEVY (1946-)
American Wedding *11*
Bringing Down the
House *49*
Dumb and Dumberer: When
Harry Met Lloyd *127*
A Mighty Wind *314*

DAMIAN LEWIS
Dreamcatcher *124*

JULIETTE LEWIS (1973-)
Cold Creek Manor *82*
Old School *339*

SHAZNAY LEWIS
Bend It Like Beckham *35*

VICKI LEWIS (1960-)
Finding Nemo (V) *142*

**THIERRY LHERMITTE
(1957-)**
And Now Ladies and
Gentlemen *13*
Le Divorce *256*

JET LI (1963-)
Cradle 2 the Grave *93*
Hero *184*

JING-DONG LIANG
Platform *372*

CODY LIGHTNING
Manic *296*

LIL' ROMEO (1989-)
Honey *188*

ANDREW LINCOLN
Love Actually *275*

DELROY LINDO (1952-)
The Core *91*

VINCENT LINDON (1959-)
Chaos *69*
Friday Night *153*

REX LINN (1956-)
Cheaper by the Dozen *75*
The Hunted *205*

LAURA LINNEY (1964-)
The Life of David
Gale *263*
Love Actually *275*
Mystic River *332*

LIO (1962-)
Carnage *67*

RAY LIOTTA (1955-)
Identity *209*

EUGENE LIPINSKI (1956-)
The Recruit *380*

**(LISA RAY MACCOY)
LISARAYE (1967-)**
Civil Brand *81*

TOMMY (TINY) LISTER
Confidence *86*

GORDON LIU
Kill Bill: Vol. 1 *240*

LUCY ALEXIS LIU (1968-)
Charlie's Angels: Full
Throttle *71*
Kill Bill: Vol. 1 *240*

PEIQI LIU
Together *456*

RENE LIU
Fleeing by Night *145*

JOHN LIVINGSTON
Dopamine *121*

RON LIVINGSTON (1968-)
The Cooler *89*

L.L. COOL J. (1968-)
Deliver Us from Eva *109*
Rugrats Go Wild! (V) *385*
S.W.A.T. *432*

SABRINA LLOYD (1970-)
Dopamine *121*

**HEATHER LOCKLEAR
(1962-)**
Looney Tunes: Back in
Action *267*
Uptown Girls *473*

BRET LOEHR
Identity *209*

MUZZI LOFFREDO
Respiro *381*

DONAL LOGUE (1966-)
American Splendor *9*
Confidence *86*

LINDSAY LOHAN (1986-)
Freaky Friday *150*

ALISON LOHMAN (1979-)
Big Fish *39*
Matchstick Men *305*

KRISTANNA LOKEN
Terminator 3: Rise of the
Machines *446*

LOUIS LOMBARDI
Confidence *86*

**DOMENICK
LOMBARDOZZI**
S.W.A.T. *432*

JASON LONDON (1972-)
Grind *171*

JEREMY LONDON (1972-)
Gods and Generals *163*

TONY LONGO (1962-)
The Cooler *89*

JENNIFER LOPEZ (1970-)
Gigli *157*

JULISSA LOPEZ
Manito *297*

MONICA LOPEZ
Intacto *220*

SERGI LOPEZ (1965-)
Dirty Pretty Things *116*
Jet Lag *231*

SOPHIE LORAIN
Mambo Italiano *291*

JONATHAN LOUGHRAN
Anger Management *15*

FAIZON LOVE
Elf *134*
Wonderland *489*

JON LOVITZ (1957-)
Dickie Roberts: Former
Child Star *112*

ROB LOWE (1964-)
View from the Top *477*

JOSH(UA) LUCAS (1972-)
Hulk *200*
Secondhand Lions *400*
Wonderland *489*

FABRICE LUCHINI (1951-)
On Guard! *341*

THAD LUCKINBILL
Just Married *237*

**WILLIAM LUCKING
(1942-)**
The Rundown *389*

LUDACRIS
2 Fast 2 Furious *466*

DEREK LUKE (1974-)
Biker Boyz *42*
Pieces of April *365*

DIEGO LUNA (1979-)
Open Range *348*

JANE LYNCH
A Mighty Wind *314*

**JOHN CARROLL LYNCH
(1963-)**
Confidence *86*
Gothika *169*

SUSAN LYNCH (1971-)
Casa de los Babys *68*

MEREDITH SCOTT LYNN
Hollywood Homicide *186*

**MELANIE LYNSKEY
(1977-)**
Shattered Glass *408*

NATASHA LYONNE (1979-)
Die Mommie Die! *114*
Party Monster *356*

BERNIE MAC (1958-)
Bad Santa *25*
Charlie's Angels: Full
Throttle *71*
Head of State *182*

JAMES MACDONALD
Hollywood Homicide *186*
Phone Booth *363*

JUSTINA MACHADO
Final Destination 2 *140*

GABRIEL MACHT (1972-)
The Recruit *380*

MICHAEL REID MACKAY
X2: X-Men United *492*

BRUCE MCGILL (1950-)
Legally Blonde 2: Red,
White & Blonde *260*
Matchstick Men *305*
Runaway Jury *386*

JOHN C. MCGINLEY
(1959-)
Identity *209*

ELIZABETH MCGOVERN
(1961-)
Buffalo Soldiers *56*

EWAN MCGREGOR (1971-)
Big Fish *39*
Down With Love *122*

MATTHEW MCGRORY
Big Fish *39*

EITHNE MCGUINNESS
The Magdalene
Sisters *286*

MICHAEL MCKEAN
(1947-)
The Guru *173*
A Mighty Wind *314*

LONETTE MCKEE (1954-)
Honey *188*

TOMMY MCKEE
Sweet Sixteen *434*

IAN MCKELLEN (1939-)
The Lord of the Rings 3:
The Return of the
King *269*
X2: X-Men United *492*

RAY MCKINNON
The Missing *317*

KEVIN MCNALLY
Johnny English *232*
Pirates of the Caribbean: The
Curse of the Black
Pearl *369*

IAN MCSHANE (1942-)
Agent Cody Banks *1*

GERARD MCSORLEY
Veronica Guerin *475*

MICHAEL MEARS
Sylvia *438*

JULIO OSCAR MECHOSO
Assassination Tango *21*

GILBERT MELKI
Monsieur Ibrahim *324*

EVA MENDES (1978-)
Once Upon a Time in
Mexico *342*
Out of Time *352*
Stuck On You *430*
2 Fast 2 Furious *466*

PETER MENSAH
Tears of the Sun *442*

IAN MERCER
Master and Commander:
The Far Side of the
World *303*

S. EPATHA MERKERSON
(1952-)
Radio *376*

LUCK MERVIL
Alias Betty *4*

DANIEL MESGUICH
Le Divorce *256*

JOHNNY MESSNER
Tears of the Sun *442*

DOMINIQUE MICHEL
The Barbarian
Invasions *28*

MICHAEL MICHELE
(1966-)
Dark Blue *103*
How to Lose a Guy in 10
Days *199*

DASH MIHOK (1974-)
Basic *30*
Dark Blue *103*
The Guru *173*

ALYSSA MILANO (1972-)
Dickie Roberts: Former
Child Star *112*

CHRISTINA MILIAN
(1981-)
Love Don't Cost a
Thing *277*

TOMAS MILIAN (1937-)
Washington Heights *479*

BEN MILLER
Johnny English *232*

KATHERINE MICHEAUX
MILLER
Assassination Tango *21*

LARRY MILLER (1953-)
A Mighty Wind *314*

PETER MILLER
Mambo Italiano *291*

WENTWORTH MILLER
The Human Stain *203*
Underworld *471*

LEO MINAYA
Manito *297*

ELVIRA MINGUEZ
The Dancer Upstairs *100*

BIRGIT MINICHMAYR
Taking Sides *440*

KRISTIN MINTER
The Bread, My Sweet *47*

PIA MIRANDA (1973-)
Garage Days *155*

MARIA MIRONOVA
Tycoon *467*

HELEN MIRREN (1946-)
Calendar Girls *61*

JIMI MISTRY (1973-)
The Guru *173*

DONNA MITCHELL
Mona Lisa Smile *319*

RADHA MITCHELL (1973-)
Phone Booth *363*

RHONA MITRA
The Life of David
Gale *263*

MATTHEW MODINE
(1959-)
Le Divorce *256*

D.W. MOFFETT (1954-)
Thirteen *450*

FA-EQ MOHAMMADI
Marooned in Iraq *300*

GRETCHEN MOL (1973-)
The Shape of Things *405*

BRITTANY MOLDOWAN
Good Boy! *165*

ALFRED MOLINA (1953-)
Identity *209*
Luther *283*
My Life Without Me *330*

ANGELA MOLINA (1955-)
Carnage *67*

RAPHAELLE MOLINIER
Carnage *67*

JORDI MOLLA
Bad Boys 2 *23*

SLOANE MOMSEN (1997-)
Daddy Day Care *98*

DOMINIC MONAGHAN
(1976-)
The Lord of the Rings 3:
The Return of the
King *269*

MICHELLE MONAGHAN
It Runs in the Family *225*

LUCIA MONIZ
Love Actually *275*

RICARDO MONTALBAN
(1920-)
Spy Kids 3-D: Game
Over *421*

YVES MONTAND (1921-91)
Le Cercle Rouge *254*

SHERI MOON
House of 1000
Corpses *191*

ALICIA MOORE
See Pink

DEMI MOORE (1962-)
Charlie's Angels: Full
Throttle *71*

MANDY MOORE (1984-)
How to Deal *197*

MELBA MOORE (1945-)
The Fighting
Temptations *139*

ROGER MOORE (1928-)
Boat Trip *45*

TIRIEL MORA
Garage Days *155*

JESSICA MORALES
Manito *297*

RICK MORANIS (1954-)
Brother Bear (V) *50*

LAURA MORANTE
The Dancer Upstairs *100*

MARGUERITE MOREAU
(1977-)
Runaway Jury *386*

JOSE ELIAS MORENO
Lucia, Lucia *281*

RITA MORENO (1931-)
Casa de los Babys *68*

TRACY MORGAN (1968-)
Head of State *182*

JENNY MORRISON
Grind *171*

ROB MORROW (1962-)
The Guru *173*

VIGGO MORTENSEN
(1958-)
The Lord of the Rings 3:
The Return of the
King *269*

JOE MORTON (1947-)
Paycheck *358*

SAMANTHA MORTON
(1977-)
In America *211*

MOS DEF
See Dante "Mos Def" Beze

DAVID MOSCOW (1974-)
Honey *188*
Just Married *237*

BILL MOSELEY (1957-)
House of 1000
Corpses *191*

CARRIE-ANNE MOSS
(1970-)
The Matrix Reloaded *308*
The Matrix
Revolutions *311*

ELISSABETH (ELISABETH,
ELIZABETH, LIZ)
MOSS (1983-)
The Missing *317*

BILLY MOTT
The Bread, My Sweet *47*

TERRY O'NEILL
The League of Extraordinary
Gentlemen *257*

SIDEDE ONYULO
Nowhere in Africa *338*

TERRY O'QUINN (1952-)
Old School *339*

LELAND ORSER (1960-)
Confidence *86*
Daredevil *101*
Runaway Jury *386*

HECTOR ORTEGA
Lucia, Lucia *281*

**HOLMES OSBORNE
(1952-)**
Cheaper by the Dozen *75*
Identity *209*

SERGEI OSHKEVICH
Tycoon *467*

EMILY OSMENT (1992-)
Spy Kids 3-D: Game
Over *421*

**HALEY JOEL OSMENT
(1988-)**
The Jungle Book 2
(V) *234*
Secondhand Lions *400*

CHERI OTERI
Dumb and Dumberer: When
Harry Met Lloyd *127*

MIRANDA OTTO (1967-)
The Lord of the Rings 3:
The Return of the
King *269*

CLIVE OWEN (1965-)
Beyond Borders *38*

AL PACINO (1940-)
Gigli *157*
People I Know *359*
The Recruit *380*

DAVID PAETKAU
Final Destination 2 *140*

JOANNA PAGE
Love Actually *275*

DIDIER PAIN
On Guard! *341*

JOSH PAIS
Phone Booth *363*

**GEOFFREY PALMER
(1927-)**
Peter Pan *361*

JOEL PALMER
Dreamcatcher *124*

**CHAZZ PALMINTERI
(1952-)**
Poolhall Junkies *373*

**GWYNETH PALTROW
(1973-)**
Sylvia *438*
View from the Top *477*

ARCHIE PANJABI
Bend It Like Beckham *35*

JOE PANTOLIANO (1951-)
Bad Boys 2 *23*
Daredevil *101*

ANNA PAQUIN (1982-)
Buffalo Soldiers *56*
X2: X-Men United *492*

IMRAN PARACHA
In This World *219*

RAWIRI PARATENE
Whale Rider *483*

KIP PARDUE (1976-)
Thirteen *450*

JUDY PARFITT (1935-)
Girl with a Pearl
Earring *160*

ANNIE PARISSE
How to Lose a Guy in 10
Days *199*

DAVID PARKER
Willard *486*

**NATHANIEL PARKER
(1963-)**
The Haunted
Mansion *178*

PAULA JAI PARKER
Phone Booth *363*

MICHAEL PARKS (1938-)
Kill Bill: Vol. 1 *240*

PASCAL PARMENTIER
The Man on the
Train *294*

ADAM PASCAL (1970-)
School of Rock *394*

ADRIAN PASDAR (1965-)
Secondhand Lions *400*

ANGELA PATON
American Wedding *11*

ROBERT PATRICK (1959-)
Charlie's Angels: Full
Throttle *71*

RUBEN PAUL
Deliver Us from Eva *109*

SARAH PAULSON
Down With Love *122*

BILL PAXTON (1955-)
Spy Kids 3-D: Game
Over *421*

DAVID PAYMER (1954-)
Alex & Emma *3*

GUY PEARCE (1967-)
The Hard Word *176*

Till Human Voices Wake
Us *451*

LUCIANA PEDRAZA
Assassination Tango *21*

AMANDA PEET (1972-)
Identity *209*
Something's Gotta
Give *414*

HARVEY PEKAR
American Splendor *9*

VALENTINE PELKA (1956-)
Under the Tuscan
Sun *470*

**MARK PELLEGRINO
(1965-)**
The Hunted *205*

MICHAEL PENA
Buffalo Soldiers *56*

**AUSTIN PENDLETON
(1940-)**
Finding Nemo (V) *142*
Uptown Girls *473*

KAL PENN
Love Don't Cost a
Thing *277*

SEAN PENN (1960-)
Mystic River *332*
21 Grams *462*

LARRY PENNELL (1928-)
Bubba Ho-Tep *54*

PIPER PERABO (1977-)
Cheaper by the Dozen *75*

MANNY PEREZ
Washington Heights *479*

VINCENT PEREZ (1964-)
On Guard! *341*

**FRANCOIS PERIER (1919-
2002)**
Le Cercle Rouge *254*

**ELIZABETH PERKINS
(1960-)**
Finding Nemo (V) *142*

MAX PERLICH (1968-)
The Missing *317*

JACQUES PERRIN (1941-)
Winged Migration
(N) *487*

HAROLD PERRINEAU, JR.
The Matrix Reloaded *308*
The Matrix
Revolutions *311*

**BERNADETTE PETERS
(1948-)**
It Runs in the Family *225*

BOB PETERSON
Finding Nemo (V) *142*

**ISABELLE PETIT-
JACQUES**
The Man on the
Train *294*

LORI PETTY (1964-)
Prey for Rock and
Roll *374*

**MICHELLE PFEIFFER
(1957-)**
Sinbad: Legend of the Seven
Seas (V) *410*

MEKHI PHIFER (1975-)
Honey *188*

REGIS PHILBIN (1934-)
Cheaper by the Dozen *75*

**LOU DIAMOND PHILLIPS
(1962-)**
Hollywood Homicide *186*

**JOAQUIN RAFAEL (LEAF)
PHOENIX (1974-)**
Brother Bear (V) *50*
Buffalo Soldiers *56*

**DAVID HYDE PIERCE
(1959-)**
Down With Love *122*

FREDERIC PIERROT
The Girl from Paris *159*

**TIM PIGOTT-SMITH
(1946-)**
Johnny English *232*

ALISON PILL
Pieces of April *365*

PINK (1979-)
Charlie's Angels: Full
Throttle *71*

**JADA PINKETT SMITH
(1971-)**
The Matrix Reloaded *308*
The Matrix
Revolutions *311*

MARCUS JEAN PIRAE
Bulletproof Monk *58*

MAX PIRKIS
Master and Commander:
The Far Side of the
World *303*

GRANT PIRO
Darkness Falls *105*

BRAD PITT (1963-)
Sinbad: Legend of the Seven
Seas (V) *410*

JEREMY PIVEN (1965-)
Old School *339*
Runaway Jury *386*
Scary Movie 3 *392*

SCOTT PLANK (1958-2002)
Holes *185*

OLIVER PLATT (1960-)
Pieces of April *365*

ROBIN RENUCCI
Taking Sides *440*

SIMON REX
Scary Movie 3 *392*

ERNIE REYES, JR. (1972-)
Poolhall Junkies *373*
The Rundown *389*

JUDY REYES
Washington Heights *479*

DOMINIQUE REYMOND
Demonlover *111*

RYAN REYNOLDS (1976-)
The In-Laws *213*

VING RHAMES (1961-)
Dark Blue *103*

JOHN RHYS-DAVIES
(1944-)
The Jungle Book 2
(V) *234*
The Lord of the Rings 3:
The Return of the
King *269*
The Medallion *313*

JONATHAN RHYS
MEYERS (1977-)
Bend It Like Beckham *35*

GIOVANNI RIBISI (1976-)
Basic *30*
Cold Mountain *84*
Lost in Translation *273*

CHRISTINA RICCI (1980-)
Anything Else *19*
Monster *326*

NATHALIE RICHARD
Confusion of Genders *88*
Le Divorce *256*

DENISE RICHARDS (1972-)
Love Actually *275*
Scary Movie 3 *392*

DAMIEN RICHARDSON
The Hard Word *176*

DEREK RICHARDSON
Dumb and Dumberer: When
Harry Met Lloyd *127*

KEVIN M. RICHARDSON
The Matrix
Revolutions *311*

LATANYA RICHARDSON
The Fighting
Temptations *139*

MIRANDA RICHARDSON
(1958-)
Spider *415*

SALLI RICHARDSON
(1967-)
Biker Boyz *42*

WILLIAM RICHERT
Manic *296*

JULIAN RICHINGS
My Life Without Me *330*
Wrong Turn *490*

PETER MARK RICHMAN
(1927-)
Poolhall Junkies *373*

ANDY RICHTER (1966-)
Elf *134*
My Boss's Daughter *328*

ALAN RICKMAN (1946-)
Love Actually *275*

MARIA RICOSSA
The In-Laws *213*

TERENCE RIGBY (1937-)
Mona Lisa Smile *319*

JACK RILEY (1935-)
Rugrats Go Wild! (V) *385*

VINCENT RIOTTA
Under the Tuscan
Sun *470*

KELLY RIPA (1970-)
Cheaper by the Dozen *75*

LEON RIPPY
The Life of David
Gale *263*

MICHAEL RISLEY
Revolution #9 *383*

BOB RITCHIE
See Kid Rock

JASON RITTER
Freddy vs. Jason *152*

JOHN RITTER (1948-2003)
Bad Santa *25*

SARA RIVAS
Manic *296*

KEVIN RIVERA
Raising Victor Vargas *377*

LINUS ROACHE (1964-)
Beyond Borders *38*

ANDREW ROBB
Dreamcatcher *124*

GARRY ROBBINS
Wrong Turn *490*

TIM ROBBINS (1958-)
Mystic River *332*

DORIS ROBERTS (1930-)
Dickie Roberts: Former
Child Star *112*

ERIC ROBERTS (1956-)
National Security *334*
Spun *419*

JULIA ROBERTS (1967-)
Mona Lisa Smile *319*

KATHLEEN ROBERTSON
(1973-)
XX/XY *495*

LUKE ROBERTSON
Levity *262*

JOHN ROBINSON
Elephant *132*

LEON ROBINSON (1962-)
Buffalo Soldiers *56*

SMOKEY ROBINSON
Hollywood Homicide *186*

WAYNE ROBSON
Wrong Turn *490*

ELISABETTA ROCCHETTI
The Embalmer *136*

KALI ROCHA
Gods and Generals *163*

JEAN ROCHEFORT (1930-)
The Man on the
Train *294*

ROCK, THE
See Dwayne "The Rock"
Johnson

CHRIS ROCK (1966-)
Head of State *182*

SAM ROCKWELL (1968-)
Matchstick Men *305*

KAREL RODEN
Bulletproof Monk *58*

MICHAEL RODRICK
Revolution #9 *383*

FREDDY RODRIGUEZ
(1975-)
Chasing Papi *74*

KRYSTAL RODRIGUEZ
Raising Victor Vargas *377*

MICHELLE RODRIGUEZ
(1978-)
S.W.A.T. *432*

ALEXANDRE RODRIQUES
City of God *79*

DANIEL ROEBUCK (1963-)
Agent Cody Banks *1*

MIMI ROGERS (1956-)
Dumb and Dumberer: When
Harry Met Lloyd *127*

HENRY ROLLINS (1961-)
Bad Boys 2 *23*

REBECCA ROMIJN-
STAMOS (1972-)
X2: X-Men United *492*

STEPHEN (STEVE) ROOT
(1951-)
Finding Nemo (V) *142*

ISABEL ROSE
Anything But Love *17*

MICHAEL ROSENBAUM
(1972-)
Bringing Down the
House *49*

Poolhall Junkies *373*

EMMY ROSSUM
Mystic River *332*

CECILIA (CELIA) ROTH
(1958-)
Lucia, Lucia *281*

ELI ROTH
Cabin Fever *60*

GIUSEPPE ROTUNNO
(1923-)
Fellini: I'm a Born
Liar *137*

RICHARD ROUNDTREE
(1942-)
Boat Trip *45*

MICKEY ROURKE (1955-)
Once Upon a Time in
Mexico *342*
Spun *419*

STEPHANE ROUSSEAU
The Barbarian
Invasions *28*

JEAN-PAUL ROUSSILLON
The Girl from Paris *159*

KELLY ROWLAND
Freddy vs. Jason *152*

RICHARD ROXBURGH
(1962-)
The League of Extraordinary
Gentlemen *257*

WILLIAM RUANE
Sweet Sixteen *434*

SAUL RUBINEK (1949-)
The Singing
Detective *412*

ALAN RUCK (1960-)
Cheaper by the Dozen *75*

PAUL RUDD (1969-)
The Shape of Things *405*

MAYA RUDOLPH (1972-)
Duplex *130*

MARK RUFFALO (1967-)
In the Cut *215*
My Life Without Me *330*
View from the Top *477*
XX/XY *495*

DEBORAH RUSH
American Wedding *11*

GEOFFREY RUSH (1951-)
Finding Nemo (V) *142*
Intolerable Cruelty *221*
Pirates of the Caribbean: The
Curse of the Black
Pearl *369*

KURT RUSSELL (1951-)
Dark Blue *103*

JAMES RUSSO (1953-)
Open Range *348*

GARY SINISE (1955-)
The Human Stain *203*

SISQO
Pieces of April *365*

JEREMY SISTO (1974-)
Thirteen *450*
Wrong Turn *490*

TOM SIZEMORE (1964-)
Dreamcatcher *124*

STELLAN SKARSGARD
(1951-)
City of Ghosts *77*
Taking Sides *440*

TOM SKERRITT (1933-)
Tears of the Sun *442*

JOHN SLATTERY (1963-)
Mona Lisa Smile *319*

LINDSAY SLOANE
The In-Laws *213*

AMY SMART (1976-)
The Battle of Shaker
Heights *32*

JEAN SMART (1959-)
Bringing Down the
House *49*

ANNA DEAVERE SMITH
(1950-)
The Human Stain *203*

BRITTA SMITH
The Magdalene
Sisters *286*

CHAD SMITH
Tears of the Sun *442*

COTTER SMITH (1949-)
X2: X-Men United *492*

JACLYN SMITH (1947-)
Charlie's Angels: Full
Throttle *71*

JACOB SMITH
Cheaper by the Dozen *75*

JAKE M. SMITH
Holes *185*

JAMES TODD SMITH
See L.L. Cool J.

KEVIN SMITH (1970-)
Daredevil *101*

RILEY SMITH (1978-)
Radio *376*

SUKIE SMITH
Lawless Heart *252*

WILL SMITH (1968-)
Bad Boys 2 *23*

SONJA SMITS (1958-)
How to Deal *197*
Owning Mahowny *354*

VICTORIA SMURFIT
(1974-)
Bulletproof Monk *58*

SNOOP DOGG (1971-)
Malibu's Most Wanted
(V) *289*
Old School *339*

CLAYTON SNYDER
The Lizzie McGuire
Movie *265*

PAUL SONKKILA
The Hard Word *176*

MIRA SORVINO (1967-)
Gods and Generals *163*

PAUL SORVINO (1939-)
The Cooler *89*
Mambo Italiano *291*

SHANNYN SOSSAMON
(1979-)
The Order *350*

KATH SOUCIE
Piglet's Big Movie (V) *368*
Rugrats Go Wild! (V) *385*

STEPHEN SPACEK
Gods and Generals *163*

KEVIN SPACEY (1959-)
The Life of David
Gale *263*

DAVID SPADE (1964-)
Dickie Roberts: Former
Child Star *112*

JOSHUA SPAFFORD
XX/XY *495*

TIMOTHY SPALL (1957-)
The Last Samurai *244*

SCOTT SPEEDMAN (1975-)
Dark Blue *103*
My Life Without Me *330*
Underworld *471*

BRUCE SPENCE (1945-)
Finding Nemo (V) *142*
The Matrix
Revolutions *311*

JESSE SPENCER
Uptown Girls *473*

JAAP SPIJKERS
Zus & Zo *497*

CHRIS STACK
School of Rock *394*

NICK STAHL (1979-)
Terminator 3: Rise of the
Machines *446*

SYLVESTER STALLONE
(1946-)
Spy Kids 3-D: Game
Over *421*

TERENCE STAMP (1940-)
Fellini: I'm a Born
Liar *137*

The Haunted
Mansion *178*
My Boss's Daughter *328*

AARON STANFORD
X2: X-Men United *492*

MAYA STANGE
Garage Days *155*
XX/XY *495*

FLORENCE STANLEY
(1924-2003)
Down With Love *122*

ANDREW STANTON
Finding Nemo (V) *142*

HARRY DEAN STANTON
(1926-)
Anger Management *15*

ROBERT STANTON
Head of State *182*

SULLIVAN STAPLETON
Darkness Falls *105*

JASON STATHAM (1972-)
The Italian Job *227*

MARY STEENBURGEN
(1952-)
Casa de los Babys *68*
Elf *134*

LESLIE STEFANSON
(1971-)
The Hunted *205*

ROD STEIGER (1925-2002)
Poolhall Junkies *373*

GUILIA STEIGERWALT
Under the Tuscan
Sun *470*

JEAN-FRANCOIS
STEVENIN (1944-)
On Guard! *341*
The Man on the
Train *294*

GARY STEVENS (1963-)
Seabiscuit *396*

CYNTHIA STEVENSON
(1963-)
Agent Cody Banks *1*

JULIET STEVENSON
(1956-)
Bend It Like Beckham *35*
Mona Lisa Smile *319*

KRISTEN STEWART
(1990-)
Cold Creek Manor *82*

PATRICK STEWART
(1940-)
X2: X-Men United *492*

DAVID OGDEN STIERS
(1942-)
Spirited Away (V) *418*

JULIA STILES (1981-)
A Guy Thing *174*

Mona Lisa Smile *319*

BEN STILLER (1965-)
Duplex *130*

BRETT STILLER
Garage Days *155*

SARA STOCKBRIDGE
Spider *415*

DEAN STOCKWELL
(1936-)
Buffalo Soldiers *56*

ANDRE STOJA
Piglet's Big Movie (V) *368*

SHARON STONE (1958-)
Cold Creek Manor *82*

ALYSON STONER (1993-)
Cheaper by the Dozen *75*

DIRK STORM
See Kevin Nealon

PETER STORMARE (1953-)
Bad Boys 2 *23*
Spun *419*

ANTHONY STRACHAN
Sylvia *438*

DAVID STRATHAIRN
(1949-)
Blue Car *43*

KADEE STRICKLAND
Anything Else *19*
Something's Gotta
Give *414*

RIDER STRONG
Cabin Fever *60*

TARA STRONG
Rugrats Go Wild! (V) *385*
Spirited Away (V) *418*

KATIE STUART (1985-)
X2: X-Men United *492*

ANNE SUAREZ
Monsieur Ibrahim *324*

JEREMY SUAREZ
Brother Bear (V) *50*

DAVID SUCHET (1946-)
The In-Laws *213*

SHUN SUGATA
The Last Samurai *244*

ELIA SULEIMAN
Divine Intervention: A
Chronicle of Love and
Pain *117*

ERIK PER SULLIVAN
(1991-)
Finding Nemo (V) *142*

CREE SUMMER
Rugrats Go Wild! (V) *385*

JEREMY SUMPTER
Peter Pan *361*

ETHAN SUPLEE
Cold Mountain *84*

DAVID SUTCLIFFE
Under the Tuscan
Sun *470*

DONALD SUTHERLAND
(1934-)
Cold Mountain *84*
Fellini: I'm a Born
Liar *137*
The Italian Job *227*

KIEFER SUTHERLAND
(1966-)
Phone Booth *363*

MENA SUVARI (1979-)
Spun *419*

HILARY SWANK (1974-)
The Core *91*

D.B. SWEENEY (1961-)
Brother Bear (V) *50*

TILDA SWINTON (1961-)
The Statement *423*

AMANDA SWISTEN (1978-)
American Wedding *11*

PETER SYMONDS
Lawless Heart *252*

SYLVIA SYMS (1934-)
What a Girl Wants *485*

PAWEL SZAJDA
Under the Tuscan
Sun *470*

OLEG TABAKOV
Taking Sides *440*

YUTAKA TADOKORO
Lost in Translation *273*

SAID TAGHMAOUI (1973-)
The Good Thief *167*

LI-JEN TAI
Fleeing by Night *145*

JEFFREY TAMBOR (1944-)
Malibu's Most
Wanted *289*
My Boss's Daughter *328*

YUN TANG
Together *456*

LARENZ TATE (1975-)
Biker Boyz *42*
A Man Apart *292*

AUDREY TAUTOU (1978-)
Dirty Pretty Things *116*
He Loves Me . . . He Loves
Me Not *180*
L'Auberge Espagnole *248*

JAY TAVARE
The Missing *317*

DANIEL TAY
Elf *134*

HOLLAND TAYLOR
(1943-)
Spy Kids 3-D: Game
Over *421*

JORDAN TAYLOR
Elephant *132*

LILI TAYLOR (1967-)
Casa de los Babys *68*

NATASCHA TAYLOR
See Natascha (Natasha)
McElhone

NOAH TAYLOR (1969-)
Lara Croft Tomb Raider:
The Cradle of Life *243*

RIP TAYLOR (1934-)
Alex & Emma *3*

ROBERT TAYLOR
The Hard Word *176*

TIFFANY TAYLOR
Camp *63*

JILL TEED
X2: X-Men United *492*

LEE TERGESEN (1965-)
Monster *326*

SCOTT TERRA
Daredevil *101*

**BERNARDINO
TERRACCIANO**
The Embalmer *136*

SCOTT TESSA
Dickie Roberts: Former
Child Star *112*

TIA TEXADA
Phone Booth *363*

CHARLIZE THERON
(1975-)
The Italian Job *227*
Monster *326*

JUSTIN THEROUX (1971-)
Charlie's Angels: Full
Throttle *71*
Duplex *130*

DAVID THEWLIS (1963-)
Timeline *453*

**LYNNE THIGPEN (1948-
2003)**
Anger Management *15*

DAVE THOMAS (1949-)
Brother Bear (V) *50*

EDDIE KAYE THOMAS
(1980-)
American Wedding *11*

HENRY THOMAS (1971-)
I Capture the Castle *207*

JAKE THOMAS (1990-)
The Lizzie McGuire
Movie *265*

KHLEO THOMAS
Holes *185*

MARSHA THOMASON
(1976-)
The Haunted
Mansion *178*

AL THOMPSON
Love Don't Cost a
Thing *277*

EMMA THOMPSON (1959-)
Love Actually *275*

KENAN THOMPSON
(1978-)
Love Don't Cost a
Thing *277*
My Boss's Daughter *328*

REECE THOMPSON
Dreamcatcher *124*

**CALLIE (CALLIOPE)
THORNE**
Revolution #9 *383*
Washington Heights *479*

BILLY BOB THORNTON
(1955-)
Bad Santa *25*
Intolerable Cruelty *221*
Levity *262*
Love Actually *275*

DAVID THORNTON
XX/XY *495*

CYRILLE THOUVENIN
Confusion of Genders *88*

DAVID THRELFALL
(1953-)
Master and Commander:
The Far Side of the
World *303*

UMA THURMAN (1970-)
Kill Bill: Vol. 1 *240*
Paycheck *358*

RACHEL TICOTIN (1959-)
Something's Gotta
Give *414*

JENNIFER TILLY (1963-)
The Haunted
Mansion *178*

JASON J. TOBIN
Better Luck Tomorrow *36*

STEPHEN TOBOLOWSKY
(1951-)
Freaky Friday *150*
Love Liza *278*
National Security *334*

HALLIE TODD
The Lizzie McGuire
Movie *265*

TONY TODD (1954-)
Final Destination 2 *140*

LAUREN TOM (1961-)
Bad Santa *25*

MARISA TOMEI (1964-)
Anger Management *15*
The Guru *173*

RICKY TOMLINSON
(1939-)
Once Upon a Time in the
Midlands *344*

AMANULLAH TORABI
In This World *219*

JAMAL UDIN TORABI
In This World *219*

MIRWAIS TORABI
In This World *219*

GINA TORRES (1969-)
The Matrix Reloaded *308*
The Matrix
Revolutions *311*

GUY TORRY
Runaway Jury *386*

LUIS TOSAR
Mondays in the Sun *321*

TOM TOWLES (1950-)
House of 1000
Corpses *191*

STUART TOWNSEND
(1972-)
The League of Extraordinary
Gentlemen *257*

IAN TRACEY (1964-)
Owning Mahowny *354*

**KEEGAN CONNOR
TRACY**
Final Destination 2 *140*

STACEY TRAVIS
Intolerable Cruelty *221*

JOHN TRAVOLTA (1954-)
Basic *30*

DANNY TREJO (1944-)
Once Upon a Time in
Mexico *342*
Spy Kids 3-D: Game
Over *421*

**JOHANNE-MARIE
TREMBLAY**
The Barbarian
Invasions *28*

KATE TROTTER
Beyond Borders *38*

SAM TROUGHTON
Sylvia *438*

ROBERT TSAI
School of Rock *394*

STANLEY TUCCI (1960-)
The Core *91*

JONATHAN TUCKER
(1982-)
The Texas Chainsaw
Massacre *448*

ULRICH TUKUR
Amen *7*
Taking Sides *440*

ROBIN TUNNEY (1972-)
The In-Laws *213*
The Secret Lives of
Dentists *402*

TED TURNER
Gods and Generals *163*

JOHN TURTURRO (1957-)
Anger Management *15*

LIV TYLER (1977-)
The Lord of the Rings 3:
The Return of the
King *269*

TYRESE
See Tyrese Gibson

NATHAN TYSON
Elephant *132*

ALANNA UBACH (1977-)
Legally Blonde 2: Red,
White & Blonde *260*

LEVANI UCHAINESHVILI
Tycoon *467*

BLAIR UNDERWOOD
(1964-)
Malibu's Most
Wanted *289*

DEBORAH KARA UNGER
(1966-)
Thirteen *450*

GABRIELLE UNION (1973-)
Bad Boys 2 *23*
Cradle 2 the Grave *93*
Deliver Us from Eva *109*

KARL URBAN (1972-)
The Lord of the Rings 3:
The Return of the
King *269*

JAMES URBANIAK
American Splendor *9*

ANNI-KRISTINA USSO
The Cuckoo *97*

PETER USTINOV (1921-
2004)
Luther *283*

WILMER VALDERRAMA
Party Monster *356*

AMBER VALLETTA
Duplex *130*

RAY "ROCKET" VALLIERE
Stuck On You *430*

BRIAN VAN HOLT (1969-)
Basic *30*
Confidence *86*
S.W.A.T. *432*

YORICK VAN
WAGENINGEN
Beyond Borders *38*

STANISLAV VARKKI
House of Fools *190*

MIKAEL VASSERBAUM
Tycoon *467*

VINCE VAUGHN (1970-)
Old School *339*

EMMANUELLE VAUGIER
(1976-)
Secondhand Lions *400*

YUL VAZQUEZ
Bad Boys 2 *23*

ALEXA VEGA (1988-)
Spy Kids 3-D: Game
Over *421*

JACI VELASQUEZ
Chasing Papi *74*

EDDIE VELEZ (1958-)
The Hunted *205*

LENNY VENITO
Gigli *157*

EDUARDO VERASTEGUI
Chasing Papi *74*

SOFIA VERGARA
Chasing Papi *74*

ARIE VERVEEN
Cabin Fever *60*

CHRISTINA VIDAL
Freaky Friday *150*

LISA VIDAL (1965-)
Chasing Papi *74*

VINCE VIELUF
Grind *171*

GERARDO VIGIL
Once Upon a Time in
Mexico *342*

ENRIQUE VILLEN
Mondays in the Sun *321*

PRUITT TAYLOR VINCE
(1960-)
Identity *209*
Monster *326*

CERINA VINCENT
Cabin Fever *60*

MIKE VOGEL
Grind *171*
The Texas Chainsaw
Massacre *448*

JON VOIGHT (1938-)
Holes *185*

GIAN MARIE VOLONTE
(1933-94)
Le Cercle Rouge *254*

MAX VON SYDOW (1929-)
Intacto *220*

LARK VOORHIES
Civil Brand *81*

ARNOLD VOSLOO (1962-)
Agent Cody Banks *1*

SASA VULICEVIC
Under the Tuscan
Sun *470*

JULIA VYSOTSKY
House of Fools *190*

NATASHA GREGSON
WAGNER (1970-)
Wonderland *489*

ROBERT WAGNER (1930-)
Hollywood Homicide *186*

DONNIE WAHLBERG
(1969-)
Dreamcatcher *124*

MARK WAHLBERG (1971-)
The Italian Job *227*

ROBERT WAHLBERG
Mystic River *332*

LOUDON WAINWRIGHT,
III
Big Fish *39*

CHRISTOPHER WALKEN
(1943-)
Gigli *157*
Kangaroo Jack *239*
Poolhall Junkies *373*
The Rundown *389*

EAMONN WALKER
Tears of the Sun *442*

PAUL WALKER (1973-)
Timeline *453*
2 Fast 2 Furious *466*

EILEEN WALSH
The Magdalene
Sisters *286*

MARY WALSH
Mambo Italiano *291*

JESSICA WALTER (1940-)
Dummy *129*

LISA ANN WALTER
Bruce Almighty *52*

JULIE WALTERS (1950-)
Calendar Girls *61*

MELORA WALTERS
(1968-)
Cold Mountain *84*

HONG-WEI WANG
Platform *372*

ZHIWEN WANG
Together *456*

ESTELLA WARREN (1978-)
The Cooler *89*
Kangaroo Jack *239*

DENZEL WASHINGTON
(1954-)
Out of Time *352*

ISAIAH WASHINGTON, IV
(1963-)
Hollywood Homicide *186*

KERRY WASHINGTON
(1977-)
The Human Stain *203*

KEN(SAKU) WATANABE
(1959-)
The Last Samurai *244*

DINA WATERS
The Haunted
Mansion *178*

SAM WATERSTON (1940-)
Le Divorce *256*

ROYALE WATKINS
Deliver Us from Eva *109*

LEONOR WATLING
My Life Without Me *330*

NAOMI WATTS (1968-)
Le Divorce *256*
21 Grams *462*

DAMIEN DANTE
WAYANS
Malibu's Most
Wanted *289*

DAMON WAYANS (1960-)
Marci X *299*

BLAYNE WEAVER
Manic *296*

SIGOURNEY WEAVER
(1949-)
Holes *185*

HUGO WEAVING (1959-)
The Lord of the Rings 3:
The Return of the
King *269*
The Matrix Reloaded *308*
The Matrix
Revolutions *311*

MARK WEBBER (1980-)
People I Know *359*

JIMMIE RAY WEEKS
Buffalo Soldiers *56*

RACHEL WEISZ (1971-)
Confidence *86*
Runaway Jury *386*
The Shape of Things *405*

FREDERICK WELLER
The Shape of Things *405*

PETER WELLER (1947-)
The Order *350*

TOM WELLING (1977-)
Cheaper by the Dozen *75*

TITUS WELLIVER (1961-)
Biker Boyz *42*

Subject Index

SMUGGLING OR SMUGGLERS
Bad Boys 2 *23*
City of God *79*
A Man Apart *292*
Party Monster *356*
Spun *419*
Sweet Sixteen *434*
Veronica Guerin *475*

SOCCER
Bend It Like Beckham *35*

SOUTH AMERICA
Assassination Tango *21*
Casa de los Babys *68*
The Dancer Upstairs *100*

SPAIN
Carnage *67*
Intacto *220*
L'Auberge Espagnole *248*
Mondays in the Sun *321*

SPIES AND ESPIONAGE
Agent Cody Banks *1*
The In-Laws *213*
Once Upon a Time in Mexico *342*
The Recruit *380*

SPORTS—GENERAL
Bend It Like Beckham *35*
Radio *376*
Seabiscuit *396*

STEPPARENTS
The Flower of Evil *146*
I Capture the Castle *207*
Kangaroo Jack *239*
Love Actually *275*

STORYTELLING
Big Fish *39*

SUBMARINES
Below *33*
The League of Extraordinary Gentlemen *257*

SUBWAYS
Bulletproof Monk *58*
The Italian Job *227*

SUICIDE
Love Liza *278*
Sylvia *438*

SUPER HEROES
Daredevil *101*
Hulk *200*
The League of Extraordinary Gentlemen *257*
X2: X-Men United *492*

SUPERNATURAL HORROR
Darkness Falls *105*
The Order *350*

SURFING
Step Into Liquid *427*

SURVIVAL
Cold Mountain *84*
The Core *91*
Gerry *156*

Intacto *220*
Marooned in Iraq *300*
28 Days Later *464*

SWASHBUCKLERS
On Guard! *341*
Pirates of the Caribbean: The Curse of the Black Pearl *369*

TEACHING OR TEACHERS
Blue Car *43*
Dumb and Dumberer: When Harry Met Lloyd *127*
Mona Lisa Smile *319*
School of Rock *394*

TECHNOLOGY
Demonlover *111*
The Matrix Reloaded *308*
The Matrix Revolutions *311*
Terminator 3: Rise of the Machines *446*

TEENAGERS
Agent Cody Banks *1*
All the Real Girls *5*
The Battle of Shaker Heights *32*
Bend It Like Beckham *35*
Better Luck Tomorrow *36*
Blue Car *43*
Criminal Lovers *95*
Freaky Friday *150*
How to Deal *197*
The Lizzie McGuire Movie *265*
Love Don't Cost a Thing *277*
Manic *296*
Raising Victor Vargas *377*
Sweet Sixteen *434*
Swimming Pool *436*
Thirteen *450*
Together *456*
What a Girl Wants *485*
X2: X-Men United *492*
Television
Bruce Almighty *52*
A Mighty Wind *314*
Stuck On You *430*

TERMINAL ILLNESS
The Barbarian Invasions *28*
Big Fish *39*
The Bread, My Sweet *47*
In America *211*
My Life Without Me *330*
Pieces of April *365*
21 Grams *462*

TERRORISM
The Dancer Upstairs *100*
The Weather Underground *480*

THANKSGIVING
Pieces of April *365*

THEATER
Platform *372*

TIME TRAVEL
Terminator 3: Rise of the Machines *446*
Timeline *453*

TOKYO, JAPAN
Kill Bill: Vol. 1 *240*
Lost in Translation *273*

TORONTO, ONTARIO
Owning Mahowny *354*

TRAINS
The Station Agent *425*

TRUE CRIME
Capturing the Friedmans *65*
City of God *79*
Monster *326*
Owning Mahowny *354*
Party Monster *356*
Veronica Guerin *475*
Wonderland *489*

TRUE STORIES
Calendar Girls *61*
The Magdalene Sisters *286*
Radio *376*
Shattered Glass *408*
Taking Sides *440*

TWINS
The Good Thief *167*
Looney Tunes: Back in Action *267*
Stuck On You *430*

VACATIONS
A Housekeeper *194*
Raising Victor Vargas *377*
Rugrats Go Wild! *385*
Swimming Pool *436*

VAMPIRES
The League of Extraordinary Gentlemen *257*
Underworld *471*

VENICE, ITALY
The Italian Job *227*
The League of Extraordinary Gentlemen *257*

VENTRILOQUISTS OR VENTRILOQUISM
Dummy *129*

WAR—GENERAL
House of Fools *190*

WEDDINGS
American Wedding *11*
Bend It Like Beckham *35*
The Bread, My Sweet *47*
Confusion of Genders *88*
Freaky Friday *150*
The In-Laws *213*
Intolerable Cruelty *221*
Kill Bill: Vol. 1 *240*
Old School *339*

WEREWOLVES
Big Fish *39*
Underworld *471*

WESTERNS
The Missing *317*
Open Range *348*

WIDOWS AND WIDOWERS
Calendar Girls *61*
The Human Stain *203*
Love Liza *278*
A Man Apart *292*
21 Grams *462*

WILD KINGDOM
Brother Bear *50*
Carnage *67*
Finding Nemo *142*
The Jungle Book 2 *234*
Piglet's Big Movie *368*

WOMEN
Lucia, Lucia *281*
Monster *326*
Ten *444*
Veronica Guerin *475*

WORK
Dirty Pretty Things *116*
The Human Stain *203*
Mondays in the Sun *321*
My Boss's Daughter *328*
Revolution 9 *383*

WORLD WAR II
Below *33*
The Cuckoo *97*
Gloomy Sunday *161*
Taking Sides *440*

WRITERS
Alex & Emma *3*
Alias Betty *4*
American Splendor *9*
Anything Else *19*
Cheaper by the Dozen *75*
Down With Love *122*
Duplex *130*
The Human Stain *203*
I Capture the Castle *207*
In the Cut *215*
Lucia, Lucia *281*
Mambo Italiano *291*
The Singing Detective *412*
Something's Gotta Give *414*
Stone Reader *428*
Swimming Pool *436*
Sylvia *438*
Under the Tuscan Sun *470*

YAKUZA
Kill Bill: Vol. 1 *240*

YOGA
Hollywood Homicide *186*

ZOMBIES
Cabin Fever *60*
28 Days Later *464*

Title Index

This cumulative index is an alphabetical list of all films covered in the volumes of the *Magill's Cinema Annual*. Film titles are indexed on a word-by-word basis, including articles and prepositions. English and foreign leading articles are ignored. Films reviewed in this volume are cited in bold with an Arabic number indicating the page number on which the review begins; films reviewed in past volumes are cited with the *Annual* year in which the review was published. Original and alternate titles are cross-referenced to the American release title. Titles of retrospective films are followed by the year, in brackets, of their original release.

A corps perdu. *See* Straight for the Heart.
A. I.: Artificial Intelligence 2002
Á la Mode (Fausto) 1995
A Ma Soeur *See* Fat Girl.
A nos amours 1984
Abandon 2003
ABCD 2002
Abgeschminkt! *See* Making Up!.
About a Boy 2003
About Adam 2002
About Last Night . . . 1986
About Schmidt 2003
Above the Law 1988
Above the Rim 1995
Abre Los Ojos. *See* Open Your Eyes.
Abril Despedacado *See* Behind the Sun.
Absence of Malice 1981
Absolute Beginners 1986
Absolute Power 1997
Absolution 1988
Abyss, The 1989
Accidental Tourist, The 1988
Accompanist, The 1993
Accused, The 1988
Ace in the Hole [1951] 1991, 1986
Ace Ventura: Pet Detective 1995
Ace Ventura: When Nature Calls 1996
Aces: Iron Eagle III 1992
Acid House, The 2000
Acqua e sapone. *See* Water and Soap.
Across the Tracks 1991
Acting on Impulse 1995
Action Jackson 1988
Actress 1988
Adam Sandler's 8 Crazy Nights 2003
Adam's Rib [1950] 1992
Adaptation 2003
Addams Family, The 1991
Addams Family Values 1993
Addicted to Love 1997
Addiction, The 1995
Addition, L'. *See* Patsy, The.
Adjo, Solidaritet. *See* Farewell Illusion.
Adjuster, The 1992
Adolescente, L' 1982

Adventure of Huck Finn, The 1993
Adventures in Babysitting 1987
Adventures of Baron Munchausen, The 1989
Adventures of Buckaroo Banzai, The 1984
Adventures of Elmo in Grouchland, The 2000
Adventures of Felix, The 2002
Adventures of Ford Fairlane, The 1990
Adventures of Mark Twain, The 1986
Adventures of Milo and Otis, The 1989
Adventures of Pinocchio, The 1996
Adventures of Pluto Nash, The 2003
Adventures of Priscilla, Queen of the Desert, The 1995
Adventures of Rocky and Bullwinkle, The 2001
Adventures of Sebastian Cole, The 2000
Adventures of the American Rabbit, The 1986
Advocate 1995
Aelita 1995
Affair of Love, An 2001
Affair of the Necklace, The 2002
Affaire de Femmes, Une. *See* Story of Women.
Affaire de Gout, Un *See* Matter of Taste, A.
Affengeil 1992
Affliction 1999
Afraid of the Dark 1992
Africa the Serengeti 1995
After Dark, My Sweet 1990
After Hours 1985
After Life 2000
After Midnight 1989
After the Rehearsal 1984
Afterglow 1979
Against All Odds 1983
Age Isn't Everything (Life in the Food Chain) 1995
Age of Innocence, The 1993
Agent Cody Banks pg. 1
Agent on Ice 1986
Agnes Browne 2001

Agnes of God 1985
Aid 1988
Aileen Wuornos: The Selling of a Serial Killer 1995
Air America 1990
Air Bud 1997
Air Bud: Golden Receiver 1999
Air Force One 1997
Air Up There, The 1995
Airborne 1993
Airheads 1995
Airplane II: The Sequel 1982
Akai Hashi no Shita no Nurui Mizo *See* Warm Water Under a Red Bridge.
Akira Kurosawa's Dreams 1990
Aladdin (Corbucci) 1987
Aladdin (Musker & Clements) 1992
Alamo Bay 1985
Alan and Naomi 1992
Alan Smithee Film, An 1999
Alarmist, The 1999
Alaska 1996
Alberto Express 1992
Albino Alligator 1997
Alchemist, The 1986
Alex & Emma pg. 3
Alfred Hitchcock's Bon Voyage & Aventure Malgache. *See* Aventure Malgache.
Ali 2002
Alias Betty pg. 4
Alice (Allen) 1990
Alice (Svankmajer) 1988
Alice et Martin 2001
Alien Nation 1988
Alien Predator 1987
Alien Resurrection 1997
Alien3 1992
Aliens 1986
Alive 1993
Alive and Kicking 1997
All About My Mother 2000
All About the Benjamins 2003
All Dogs Go to Heaven 1989
All Dogs Go to Heaven II 1996
All I Desire [1953] 1987
All I Want for Christmas 1991
All of Me 1984
All or Nothing 2003
All Over Me 1997

All Quiet on the Western Front [1930] 1985
All the Little Animals 2000
All the Pretty Horses 2001
All the Rage. *See* It's the Rage.
All the Real Girls pg. 5
All the Right Moves 1983
All the Vermeers in New York 1992
All's Fair 1989
All-American High 1987
Allan Quatermain and the Lost City of Gold 1987
Alley Cat 1984
Alligator Eyes 1990
Allnighter, The 1987
Almost an Angel 1990
Almost Famous 2001
Almost Heroes 1999
Almost You 1985
Aloha Summer 1988
Alone. *See* Solas.
Along Came a Spider 2002
Alphabet City 1983
Alpine Fire 1987
Altars of the World [1976] 1985
Always (Jaglom) 1985
Always (Spielberg) 1989
Amadeus 1984, 1985
Amanda 1989
Amantes. *See* Lovers.
Amants du Pont Neuf, Les 1995
Amateur 1995
Amateur, The 1982
Amazing Grace and Chuck 1987
Amazing Panda Adventure, The 1995
Amazon Women on the Moon 1987
Ambition 1991
Amelie 2002
Amen pg. 7
America 1986
American Anthem 1986
American Beauty 2000
American Blue Note 1991
American Buffalo 1996
American Chai 2003
American Cyborg: Steel Warrior 1995
American Desi 2002
American Dream 1992

American Dreamer 1984
American Fabulous 1992
American Flyers 1985
American Friends 1993
American Gothic 1988
American Heart 1993
American History X 1999
American in Paris, An [1951] 1985
American Justice 1986
American Me 1992
American Movie 2000
American Ninja 1985
American Ninja II 1987
American Ninja III 1989
American Ninja 1984, 1991
American Outlaws 2002
American Pie 2000
American Pie 2 2002
American Pop 1981
American President, The 1995
American Psycho 2001
American Rhapsody, An 2002
American Stories 1989
American Splendor pg. 9
American Summer, An 1991
American Taboo 1984, 1991
American Tail, An 1986
American Tail: Fievel Goes West, An 1991
American Wedding pg. 11
American Werewolf in London, An 1981
American Werewolf in Paris, An 1997
American Women. See The Closer You Get.
America's Sweethearts 2002
Ami de mon amie, L'. See Boyfriends and Girlfriends.
Amin-The Rise and Fall 1983
Amistad 1997
Amityville II: The Possession 1981
Amityville 3-D 1983
Among Giants 2000
Among People 1988
Amongst Friends 1993
Amor brujo, El 1986
Amores Perros 2002
Amos and Andrew 1993
Amour de Swann, Un. See Swann in Love.
Anaconda 1997
Analyze That 2003
Analyze This 2000
Anastasia 1997
Anchors Aweigh [1945] 1985
And God Created Woman 1988
... And God Spoke 1995
And Life Goes On (Zebdegi Edame Darad) 1995
And Nothing but the Truth 1984
And Now Ladies and Gentlemen pg. 13
And the Ship Sails On 1984
And You Thought Your Parents Were Weird 1991
And Your Mother Too. See Y Tu Mama Tambien.

Andre 1995
Android 1984
Âne qui a bu la lune, L'. See Donkey Who Drank the Moon, The.
Angel at My Table, An 1991
Angel Baby 1997
Angel Dust 1987
Angel Dust (Ishii) 1997
Angel Eyes 2002
Angel Heart 1987
Angel 1984
Angel III 1988
Angel Town 1990
Angela's Ashes 2000
Angelo My Love 1983
Angels and Insects 1996
Angels in the Outfield 1995
Anger Management pg. 15
Angie 1995
Angry Harvest 1986
Anguish 1987
Angus 1995
Angustia. See Anguish.
Anima Mundi 1995
Animal, The 2002
Animal Behavior 1989
Animal Factory 2001
Animal Kingdom, The [1932] 1985
Anna Karamazova 1995
Anna 1987
Anna and the King 2000
Anne Frank Remembered 1996
Année des meduses, L' 1987
Années sandwiches, Les. See Sandwich Years, The.
Annie 1982
Annihilators, The 1986
Anniversary Party, The 2002
Another Day in Paradise 2000
Another 48 Hrs. 1990
Another Stakeout 1993
Another State of Mind 1984
Another Time, Another Place 1984
Another Woman 1988
Another You 1991
Anslag, De. See Assault, The.
Antarctica (Kurahara) 1984
Antarctica (Weiley) 1992
Antigone/Rites of Passion 1991
Antitrust 2002
Antonia and Jane 1991
Antonia's Line 1996
Antwone Fisher 2003
Antz 1999
Any Given Sunday 2000
Any Man's Death 1990
Anything But Love pg. 17
Anything Else pg. 19
Anywhere But Here 2000
Apache [1954] 1981
Apartment, The [1960] 1986
Apartment Zero 1988
Apex 1995
Apocalypse Now Redux 2002
Apollo 13 1995
Apostle, The 1997
Apple, The 2000

Appointment with Death 1988
Apprentice to Murder 1988
Apres l'amour. See Love After Love.
April Fool's Day 1986
April Is a Deadly Month 1987
Apt Pupil 1999
Arabian Knight 1995
Arachnophobia 1990
Ararat 2003
Arashi Ga Oka 1988
Arch of Triumph [1948] 1983
Archangel 1995
Architecture of Doom, The 1992
Argent, L' 1984
Aria 1988
Ariel 1990
Arlington Road 2000
Armageddon 1999
Armageddon, The. See Warlock.
Armed and Dangerous 1986
Armed Response 1986
Army of Darkness 1993
Arrangement, The [1969] 1985
Arrival, The 1996
Art Blakey 1988
Art Deco Detective 1995
Art of Cinematography, The. See Visions of Light.
Art of War, The 2001
Artemisia 1999
Arthur 1981
Arthur II 1988
Arthur's Hallowed Ground 1986
Article 99 1992
As Good As It Gets 1997
Ashik Kerib 1988
Aspen Extreme 1993
Assassination 1987
Assassination Tango pg. 21
Assassins 1995
Assault, The 1986
Assault of the Killer Bimbos 1988
Assignment, The 1997
Associate, The 1996
Astonished 1989
Astronaut's Wife, The 2000
Asya's Happiness 1988
At Close Range 1986
At First Sight 2000
At Play in the Fields of the Lord 1991
Atame. See Tie Me Up! Tie Me Down!.
Atanarjuat, the Fast Runner 2002
Atlantic City 1981
Atlantis 1995
Atlantis: The Lost Empire 2002
Atraves da Janela. See Through the Window.
Attention Bandits. See Warning Bandits.
Au Revoir les Enfants 1987
August 1996
August 32nd on Earth 1999

Austin Powers in Goldmember 2003
Austin Powers: International Man of Mystery 1997
Austin Powers: The Spy Who Shagged Me 2000
Author! Author! 1981
Auto Focus 2003
Autumn in New York 2001
Autumn Tale 2000
Avalon (Anderson) 1988
Avalon (Levinson) 1990
Avanti [1972] 1986
Avengers, The 1999
Avenging Angel 1985
Avenging Force 1986
Aventure Malgache 1995
Aviator, The 1985
Awakenings 1990
Awfully Big Adventure, An 1995
Ayn Rand: A Sense of Life 1999
Ayneh. See The Mirror.

B. Monkey 2000
Ba Mua. See Three Seasons.
Babar 1989
Babe: Pig in the City 1999
Babe, The 1992
Babe, the Gallant Pig 1995
Babette's Feast 1987
Baby 1985
Baby Boom 1987
Baby Boy 2002
Baby Geniuses 2000
Baby, It's You 1982
Baby's Day Out 1995
Babyfever 1995
Babysitter's Club 1995
Bacheha-Ye aseman. See The Children of Heaven.
Bachelor, The 2000
Bachelor Mother [1939] 1986
Bachelor Party 1984
Back Door to Hell [1964] 1995
Back to School 1986
Back to the Beach 1987
Back to the Future 1985
Back to the Future Part II 1989
Back to the Future Part III 1990
Backbeat 1995
Backdraft 1991
Backfire 1987
Backstage 1988
Backstage at the Kirov 1984
Bad Behaviour 1993
Bad Blood 1989
Bad Boy, The 1985
Bad Boys 1982
Bad Boys 1995
Bad Boys 2 pg. 23
Bad Company (Harris) 1995
Bad Company (Schumacher) 2003
Bad Dreams 1988
Bad Girls 1995
Bad Guys 1986

Black Hawk Down 2002
Black Joy 1986
Black Knight 2002
Black Lizard 1995
Black Mask 2000
Black Moon Rising 1986
Black Peter [1964] 1985
Black Rain (Imamura) 1990
Black Rain (Scott) 1989
Black Robe 1991
Black Sheep 1996
Black Stallion Returns, The
   1983
Black Widow 1987
Blackboard Jungle [1955]
   1986, 1992
Blackout 1988
Blackout. *See* I Like It Like
   That.
Blade 1999
Blade II 2003
Blade Runner 1982
Blair Witch Project, The 2000
Blame It on Night 1984
Blame It on Rio 1984
Blame It on the Bellboy 1992
Blank Check 1995
Blankman 1995
Blassblaue Frauenschrift, Eine.
   See Woman's Pale Blue
   Handwriting, A.
Blast 'em 1995
Blast from the Past 2000
Blaze 1989
Bless the Child 2001
Bless Their Little Hearts 1991
Blessures Assassines, Les. *See*
   Murderous Maids.
Blind Date 1987
Blind Fairies *See* Ignorant
   Fairies
Blind Fury 1990
Blink 1995
Bliss 1997
Bliss 1986
Blob, The 1988
Blood and Concrete 1991
Blood and Wine 1997
Blood Diner 1987
Blood in Blood Out 1995
Blood, Guts, Bullets and
   Octane 2001
Blood Money 1988
Blood of Heroes, The 1990
Blood Salvage 1990
Blood Simple 1985
Blood Wedding 1982
Blood Work 2003
Bloodfist 1989
Bloodhounds of Broadway
   1989
Bloodsport 1988
Bloody Sunday 2003
Blow 2002
Blow Dry 2002
Blow Out 1981
Blown Away 1995
Blue (Jarman) 1995
Blue (Kieslowski) 1993
Blue Car pg. 43
Blue Chips 1995
Blue City 1986

Blue Crush 2003
Blue Desert 1991
Blue Ice 1995
Blue Iguana, The 1988
Blue in the Face 1995
Blue Kite, The 1995
Blue Monkey 1987
Blue Skies Again 1983
Blue Sky 1995
Blue Steel 1990
Blue Streak 2000
Blue Thunder 1983
Blue Velvet 1986
Blue Villa, The 1995
Bluebeard's Eighth Wife
   [1938] 1986
Blues Brothers 2001 1999
Blues Lahofesh Hagadol. *See*
   Late Summer Blues.
Boat, The. *See* Boot, Das.
Boat is Full, The 1982
Boat Trip pg. 45
Bob le Flambeur [1955] 1983
Bob Marley: Time Will Tell.
   See Time Will Tell.
Bob Roberts 1992
Bodies, Rest, and Motion 1993
Body, The 2002
Body and Soul 1982
Body Chemistry 1990
Body Double 1984
Body Heat 1981
Body Melt 1995
Body of Evidence 1993
Body Parts 1991
Body Rock 1984
Body Shots 2000
Body Slam 1987
Body Snatchers 1995
Bodyguard, The 1992
Bodyguards, The. *See* La Scorta.
Boesman & Lena 2001
Bogus 1996
Bohème, La [1926] 1982
Boiler Room 2001
Boiling Point 1993
Bolero (Derek) 1984
Bolero (Lelouch) 1982
Bollywood/Hollywood 2003
Bon Plaisir, Le 1984
Bon Voyage 1995
Bone Collector, The 2000
Bonfire of the Vanities, The
   1990
Bongwater 1999
Bonne Route. *See* Latcho
   Drom.
Boogie Nights 1997
Book of Love 1991
Book of Shadows: Blair Witch
   2 2001
Boomerang 1992
Boost, The 1988
Boot, Das 1982
Boot Ist Voll, Das. *See* Boat Is
   Full, The.
Bootmen 2001
Booty Call 1997
Booye Kafoor, Atre Yas. *See*
   Smell of Camphor, Fragrance
   of Jasmine.
Bopha! 1993

Border, The 1982
Boricua's Bond 2001
Born American 1986
Born in East L.A. 1987
Born on the Fourth of July
   1989
Born Romantic 2002
Born to Be Wild 1996
Born to Race 1988
Born Yesterday 1993
Borrowers, The 1999
Borstal Boy 2003
Bossa Nova 2001
Bostonians, The 1984
Bottle Rocket 1996
Boum, La 1983
Bounce 2001
Bound 1996
Bound and Gagged 1993
Bound by Honor 1993
Bounty, The 1984
Bourne Identity, The 2003
Bowfinger 2000
Box of Moonlight 1997
Boxer, The 1997
Boxer and Death, The 1988
Boxing Helena 1993
Boy in Blue, The 1986
Boy Who Could Fly, The
   1986
Boy Who Cried Bitch, The
   1991
Boyfriend School, The. *See*
   Don't Tell Her It's Me.
Boyfriends 1997
Boyfriends and Girlfriends
   1988
Boys 1996
Boys, The 1985
Boys and Girls 2001
Boys Don't Cry 2000
Boys from Brazil, The [1978]
   1985
Boys Next Door, The 1986
Boys on the Side 1995
Boyz N the Hood 1991
Braddock 1988
Brady Bunch Movie, The 1995
Brady's Escape 1984
Brain Damage 1988
Brain Dead 1990
Brain Donors 1995
Brainstorm 1983
Bram Stoker's Dracula 1992
Branches of the Tree, The
   1995
Brandon Teena Story, The
   2000
Brassed Off 1997
Brat. *See* Brother.
Braveheart 1995
Brave Little Toaster, The 1987
Brazil 1985
Bread and Roses 2002
Bread and Salt 1995
Bread and Tulips 2002
Bread, My Sweet, The pg. 47
Break of Dawn 1988
Breakdown 1997
Breakfast Club, The 1985
Breakfast of Champions 2000
Breakin' 1984

Breakin' II: Electric Boogaloo
   1984
Breaking In 1989
Breaking the Rules 1992
Breaking the Sound Barrier. *See*
   Sound Barrier, The
Breaking the Waves 1996
Breaking Up 1997
Breath of Life, A 1993
Breathing Room 1996
Breathless 1983
Brenda Starr 1992
Brewster McCloud [1970]
   1985
Brewster's Millions 1985
Brian Wilson: I Just Wasn't
   Made for These Times
   1995
Bride, The 1985
Bride of Chucky 1999
Bride of Re-Animator 1991
Bride of the Wind 2002
Bride with White Hair, The
   1995
Bridge of San Luis Rey, The
   [1929] 1981
Bridge on the River Kwai, The
   [1957] 1990
Bridges of Madison County,
   The 1995
Bridget Jones's Diary 2002
Brief Encounter [1946] 1990
Brief History of Time, A 1992
Bright Angel 1991
Bright Lights, Big City 1988
Brighton Beach Memoirs 1986
Brimstone and Treacle 1982
Bring It On 2001
Bring on the Night 1985
Bringing Down the House
   pg. 49
Bringing Out the Dead 2000
Brittania Hospital 1983
Broadcast News 1987
Broadway Damage 1999
Broadway Danny Rose 1984
Brokedown Palace 2000
Broken April *See* Behind the
   Sun.
Broken Arrow 1996
Broken Blossoms [1919] 1984
Broken English 1997
Broken Hearts Club, The 2001
Broken Rainbow 1985
Broken Vessels 1999
Bronx Tale, A 1993
Brother (Balabanov) 1999
Brother (Kitano) 2001
Brother Bear pg. 50
Brother from Another Planet,
   The 1984
Brother of Sleep 1996
Brotherhood of the Wolf 2003
Brothers, The 2002
Brother's Keeper 1993
Brother's Kiss, A 1997
Brothers McMullen, The 1995
Brown Sugar 2003
Browning Version, The 1995
Bruce Almighty pg. 52
Bruce Lee Story, The. *See*
   Dragon.

Musketeer, The 2002
Mustang: The Hidden Kingdom 1995
Musuko. *See* My Sons.
Mutant on the Bounty 1989
Mute Witness 1995
Mutiny on the Bounty [1962] 1984
My African Adventure 1987
My American Cousin 1986
My Apprenticeship. *See* Among People.
My Beautiful Laundrette 1986
My Best Fiend 2000
My Best Friend Is a Vampire 1988
My Best Friend's Girl 1984
My Best Friend's Wedding 1997
My Big Fat Greek Wedding 2003
My Blue Heaven 1990
My Boss's Daughter pg. 328
My Boyfriend's Back 1993
My Chauffeur 1986
My Cousin Rachel [1952] 1981
My Cousin Vinny 1992
My Crazy Life. *See* Mi Vida Loca.
My Dark Lady 1987
My Demon Lover 1987
My Dinner with André 1981
My Family (Mi Familia) 1995
My Father Is Coming 1992
My Father, the Hero 1995
My Father's Angel 2002
My Father's Glory 1991
My Favorite Martian 2000
My Favorite Season 1996
My Favorite Year 1982
My Fellow Americans 1996
My First Mister 2002
My First Wife 1985
My Foolish Heart (1949) 1983
My Giant 1999
My Girl 1991
My Girl II 1995
My Heroes Have Always Been Cowboys 1991
My Left Foot 1989
My Life 1993
My Life and Times with Antonin Artaud 1996
My Life as a Dog [1985] 1987
My Life in Pink. *See* Ma Vie en Rose.
My Life So Far 2000
My Life Without Me pg. 330
My Life's in Turnaround 1995
My Little Pony 1986
My Mom's a Werewolf 1989
My Mother's Castle 1991
My Mother's Courage
My Name is Joe 2000
My Neighbor Totoro 1993
My New Gun 1992
My New Partner 1985
My Other Husband 1985
My Own Private Idaho 1991
My Reputation [1946] 1984, 1986

My Science Project 1985
My Son the Fanatic 2000
My Sons 1995
My Stepmother Is an Alien 1988
My Sweet Little Village 1986
My True Love, My Wound 1987
My Tutor 1983
My Twentieth Century 1990
My Uncle's Legacy 1990
My Voyage to Italy 2003
My Wife Is an Actress 2003
Mystery, Alaska 2000
Mystery Date 1991
Mystery of Alexina, The 1986
Mystery of Rampo 1995
Mystery of the Wax Museum [1933] 1986
Mystery Men 2000
Mystery Science Theater 3000: The Movie 1996
Mystery Train 1989
Mystic Masseur, The 2003
Mystic Pizza 1988
Mystic River pg. 332
Myth of Fingerprints, The 1997

Nadine 1987
Nadja 1995
Naked 1993
Naked Cage, The 1986
Naked Gun, The 1988
Naked Gun 2 1/2, The 1991
Naked Gun 33 1/3: The Final Insult 1995
Naked in New York 1995
Naked Lunch 1991
Name of the Rose, The 1986
Nanou 1988
Napoleon [1927] 1981
Napoleon 1997
Narc 2003
Narrow Margin 1990
Nasty Girl, The 1990
Nate and Hayes 1983
National Lampoon's Christmas Vacation 1989
National Lampoo's Class Reunion 1982
National Lampoon's European Vacation 1985
National Lampoon's Loaded Weapon I 1993
National Lampoon's Senior Trip 1995
National Lampoon's Vacation 1983
National Lampoon's Van Wilder 2003
National Security pg. 334
National Velvet [1944] 1993
Native Son 1986
Natural, The 1984
Natural Born Killers 1995
Navigator, The 1989
Navy SEALs 1990
Near Dark 1987
Nebo nashevo detstva. *See* Sky of Our Childhood, The.

Necessary Roughness 1991
Needful Things 1993
Negotiator, The 1999
Neil Simon's Lost in Yonkers 1993
Neil Simon's The Odd Couple 2 1999
Neil Simon's The Slugger's Wife 1985
Nell 1995
Nell Gwyn [1934] 1983
Nelly & Mr. Arnaud 1996
Nemesis 1993
Nenette et Boni 1997
Neon Bible, The 1995
Nervous Ticks 1995
Net, The 1995
Nettoyoge a Sec. *See* Dry Cleaning.
Never Again 2003
Never Been Kissed 2000
Never Cry Wolf 1983
Never Say Never Again 1983
Never Talk to Strangers 1995
Never too Young to Die 1986
Neverending Story, The 1984
Neverending Story II, The 1991
New Adventures of Pippi Longstocking, The 1988
New Age, The 1995
New Babylon, The [1929] 1983
New Eve, The 2001
New Guy, The 2003
New Jack City 1991
New Jersey Drive 1995
New Kids, The 1985
New Life, A 1988
New Nightmare. *See* Wes Craven's New Nightmare.
New Rose Hotel 2000
New Year's Day 1989
New York in Short: The Shvitz and Let's Fall in Love 1995
New York, New York [1977] 1983
New York Stories 1989
Newsies 1992
Newton Boys, The 1999
Next Best Thing, The 2001
Next Big Thing, The 2003
Next Friday 2001
Next Karate Kid, The 1995
Next of Kin 1989
Next Stop Greenwich Village [1976] 1984
Next Stop Wonderland 1999
Next Summer 1986
Next Year if All Goes Well 1983
Niagara Falls 1987
Niagara, Niagara 1999
Nice Girls Don't Explode 1987
Nicholas Nickleby 2003
Nick and Jane 1997
Nick of Time 1995
Nico and Dani 2002
Nico Icon 1996

Niezwykla podroz Balthazara Kobera. *See* Tribulations of Balthasar Kober, The.
Night and Day 1995
Night and the City 1992
Night at the Roxbury, A 1999
Night Crossing 1982
Night Falls on Manhattan 1997
Night Friend 1988
Night Game 1989
Night in Heaven, A 1983
Night in the Life of Jimmy Reardon, A 1988
'night, Mother 1986
Night of the Comet 1984
Night of the Creeps 1986
Night of the Demons II 1995
Night of the Hunter, The [1955] 1982
Night of the Iguana, The [1964] 1983
Night of the Living Dead 1990
Night of the Pencils, The 1987
Night of the Shooting Stars, The 1983
Night on Earth 1992
Night Patrol 1985
Night Shift 1982
Night Song [1947] 1981
Night Visitor 1989
Night We Never Met, The 1993
Nightbreed 1990
Nightcap. *See* Merci pour le Chocolat.
Nightfall 1988
Nightflyers 1987
Nighthawks 1981
Nighthawks II. *See* Strip Jack Naked.
Nightmare at Shadow Woods 1987
Nightmare Before Christmas, The 1993
Nightmare on Elm Street, A 1984
Nightmare on Elm Street: II, A 1985
Nightmare on Elm Street: III, A 1987
Nightmare on Elm Street: IV, A 1988
Nightmare on Elm Street: V, A 1989
Nightmares III 1984
Nightsongs 1991
Nightstick 1987
Nightwatch 1999
Nil by Mouth 1999
9 1/2 Weeks 1986
9 Deaths of the Ninja 1985
Nine Months 1995
Nine Queens 2003
976-EVIL 1989
1918 1985
1969 1988
1990: The Bronx Warriors 1983

Salsa 1988
Salt of the Earth [1954] 1986
Salt on Our Skin. See Desire.
Salton Sea, The 2003
Saltwater 2002
Salvador 1986
Sam and Sarah 1991
Sam's Son 1984
Samantha 1995
Samba Traore 1995
Same Old Song 2000
Sammy and Rosie Get Laid 1987
Sandlot, The 1993
Sandwich Years, The 1988
Sang for Martin, En. See Song for Martin, A.
Sans toit ni loi. See Vagabond.
Santa Claus 1985
Santa Clause, The 1995
Santa Clause 2, The 2003
Santa Fe 1988
Santa Sangre 1990
Sara 1995
Sarafina! 1992
Satan 1995
Satisfaction 1988
Saturday Night at the Palace 1987
Saturday Night, Sunday Morning: The Travels of Gatemouth Moore 1995
Sauve qui peut (La Vie). See Every Man for Himself.
Savage Beach 1989
Savage Island 1985
Savage Nights 1995
Savannah Smiles 1983
Save the Last Dance 2002
Save the Tiger [1973] 1988
Saving Grace (Young) 1986
Saving Grace (Cole) 2001
Saving Private Ryan 1999
Saving Silverman 2002
Savior
Say Anything 1989
Say It Isn't So 2002
Say Yes 1986
Scandal 1989
Scandalous 1984
Scanners III: The Takeover 1995
Scarface 1983
Scarlet Letter, The [1926] 1982, 1984
Scarlet Letter, The 1995
Scarlet Street [1946] 1982
Scary Movie 2001
Scary Movie 2 2002
Scary Movie 3 pg. 392
Scavengers 1988
Scenes from a Mall 1991
Scenes from the Class Struggle in Beverly Hills 1989
Scent of a Woman 1992
Scent of Green Papaya, The (Mui du du Xanh) 1995
Scherzo del destino agguato dietro l'angolo come un brigante di strada. See Joke of Destiny, A.
Schindler's List 1993

Schizopolis 1997
School Daze 1988
School of Flesh, 432
School of Rock pg. 394
School Spirit 1985
School Ties 1992
Schtonk 1995
Scissors 1991
Scooby-Doo 2003
Scorchers 1995
Score, The 2002
Scorpion 1986
Scorpion King, The 2003
Scorta, La 1995
Scotland, PA 2003
Scout, The 1995
Scream 1996
Scream 2 1997
Scream 3 2001
Scream of Stone 1995
Screamers 1996
Screwed 2001
Scrooged 1988
Sea of Love 1989
Sea Wolves, The 1982
Seabiscuit pg. 396
Search and Destroy 1995
Search for Signs of Intelligent Life in the Universe, The 1991
Searching for Bobby Fischer 1993
Season of Dreams 1987
Season of Fear 1989
Season of Men, The 2003
Seasons 1995
Second Best 1995
Second Sight 1989
Second Skin 2003
Second Thoughts 1983
Secondhand Lions pg. 400
Secret Admirer 1985
Secret Garden, The 1993
Secret Life of Walter Mitty, The [1947] 1985
Secret Lives of Dentists, The pg. 402
Secret Love, Hidden Faces. See Ju Dou.
Secret of My Success, The 1987
Secret of NIMH, The 1982
Secret of Roan Inish, The 1995
Secret of the Sword, The 1985
Secret Places 1985
Secret Policeman's Third Ball, The 1987
Secretary 2003
Secrets 1984
Secrets & Lies 1996
Seduction, The 1982
See No Evil, Hear No Evil 1989
See Spot Run 2002
See You in the Morning 1989
Segunda Piel. See Second Skin.
Selena
Self Made Hero, A
S'en Fout la Mort. See No Fear, No Die.
Sender, The 1982

Sensations 1988
Sense and Sensibility 1995
Sense of Freedom, A 1985
Senseless 1999
Sentimental Destiny 2002
Seppan 1988
September 1987
Serendipity 2002
Serial Mom 1995
Series 7: The Contenders 2002
Serpent and the Rainbow, The 1988
Servants of Twilight, The 1995
Serving Sara 2003
Sesame Street Presents: Follow That Bird 1985
Session 9 2002
Set It Off 1996
Set Me Free 2001
Seto uchi shonen yakyudan. See MacArthur's Children.
Seunlau Ngaklau See Time and Tide.
Seven 1995
Seven Hours to Judgement 1988
Seven Men from Now [1956] 1987
Seven Minutes in Heaven 1986
Seven Women, Seven Sins 1987
Seven Year Itch, The [1955] 1986
Seven Years in Tibet
Seventh Coin, The 1993
Seventh Sign, The 1988
Severance 1989
Sex and Lucia 2003
sex, lies and videotape 1989
Sex, Drugs, and Democracy 1995
Sex, Drugs, Rock and Roll 1991
Sex: The Annabel Chong Story 2001
Sexbomb 1989
Sexy Beast 2002
Sgt. Bilko 1996
Shades of Doubt 1995
Shadey 1987
Shadow Conspiracy, The
Shadow Dancing 1988
Shadow Magic 2002
Shadow of the Raven 1990
Shadow of the Vampire 2001
Shadow of the Wolf 1993
Shadow, The 1995
Shadowlands 1993
Shadows and Fog 1992
Shadrach 1999
Shaft 2001
Shag 1988
Shakedown 1988
Shakes the Clown 1992
Shakespeare in Love 1999
Shaking the Tree 1992
Shall We Dance? 1997
Shallow Grave 1995
Shallow Hal 2002

Shame 1988
Shanghai Knights pg. 404
Shanghai Noon 2001
Shanghai Surprise 1986
Shanghai Triad 1995
Shape of Things, The pg. 405
Sharky's Machine 1981
Sharma and Beyond 1986
Shatterbrain. See The Resurrected.
Shattered 1991
Shattered Glass pg. 408
Shaunglong Hui. See Twin Dragons.
Shawshank Redemption, The 1995
She Must Be Seeing Things 1987
She's All That 2000
She's Gotta Have It 1986
She's Having a Baby 1988
She's Out of Control 1989
She's So Lovely 1997
She's the One 1996
She-Devil 1989
Sheena 1984
Sheer Madness 1985
Shelf Life 1995
Sheltering Sky, The 1990
Sherlock Holmes [1922] 1982
Sherman's March 1986
Shiloh 2: Shiloh Season 2000
Shine 1996
Shining, The [1980]
Shining Through 1992
Shipping News, The 2002
Shipwrecked 1991
Shiqisuide Danche. See Beijing Bicycle.
Shirley Valentine 1989
Shoah 1985
Shock to a System, A 1990
Shocker 1989
Shoot the Moon 1982
Shoot to Kill 1988
Shooting Fish 1999
Shooting Party, The 1985
Shooting, The [1966] 1995
Shootist, The [1976] 1982
Short Circuit 1986
Short Circuit II 1988
Short Cuts 1993
Short Film About Love, A 1995
Short Time 1990
Shot, The 1996
Shout 1991
Show, The 1995
Show Me Love 2000
Show of Force, A 1990
Showdown in Little Tokyo 1991
Shower, The 2001
Showgirls 1995
Showtime 2003
Shrek 2002
Shrimp on the Barbie, The 1990
Shvitz, The. See New York in Short: The Shvitz and Let's Fall in Love.
Shy People 1987

Siberiade 1982
Sibling Rivalry 1990
Sicilian, The 1987
Sick: The Life and Death of
  Bob Flanagan,
  Supermasochist 1997
Sid and Nancy 1986
Side Out 1990
Sidekicks 1993
Sidewalk Stories 1989
Sidewalks of New York, The
  2002
Siege, The 1999
Siesta 1987
Sign o' the Times 1987
Sign of the Cross, The [1932]
  1984
Signal Seven 1986
Signs 2003
Signs & Wonders 2002
Signs of Life 1989
Silence, The 2001
Silence After the Shot, The See
  Legend of Rita, The.
Silence at Bethany, The 1988
Silence of the Lambs, The
  1991
Silencer, The 1995
Silent Fall 1995
Silent Madness, The 1984
Silent Night 1988
Silent Night, Deadly Night II
  1987
Silent Night, Deadly Night III
  1989
Silent Night, Deadly Night
  1984
Silent Rage 1982
Silent Tongue 1995
Silent Touch, The 1995
Silent Victim 1995
Silk Road, The 1992
Silkwood 1983
Silver City 1985
Silverado 1985
Simon Birch 1999
Simon Magus 2002
Simon the Magician 2001
Simone 2003
Simpatico 2000
Simple Men 1992
Simple Plan, A 1999
Simple Twist of Fate, A 1995
Simple Wish, A 1997
Simply Irresistible 2000
Sin Noticias de Dios. See No
  News from God.
Sinbad: Legend of the Seven
  Seas pg. 410
Sincerely Charlotte 1986
Sinful Life, A 1989
Sing 1989
Singin' in the Rain [1952]
  1985
Singing Detective, The pg. 412
Singing the Blues in Red 1988
Single White Female 1992
Singles 1992
Sioux City 1995
Sirens 1995
Sister Act 1992
Sister Act II 1993

Sister, My Sister 1995
Sister, Sister 1987
Sisters. See Some Girls.
Sitcom 2000
Six Days, Seven Nights 1999
Six Days, Six Nights 1995
Six Degrees of Separation
  1993
Six Pack 1982
Six-String Samurai 1999
Six Ways to Sunday 2000
Six Weeks 1982
Sixteen Candles 1984
Sixteen Days of Glory 1986
Sixth Day, The 2001
Sixth Man, The 1997
Sixth Sense, The 2000
Sixty Glorious Years [1938]
  1983
'68 1987
Ski Country 1984
Ski Patrol 1990
Skin Deep 1989
Skins 2003
Skipped Parts 2002
Skulls, The 2001
Sky Bandits 1986
Sky of Our Childhood, The
  1988
Skyline 1984
Slacker 1991
Slackers 2003
Slam 1997
Slam Dance 1987
Slap Shot [1977] 1981
Slapstick 1984
Slate, Wyn, and Me 1987
Slave Coast. See Cobra Verde.
Slave Girls from Beyond
  Infinity 1987
Slaves of New York 1989
Slaves to the Underground
  1997
Slayground 1984
SLC Punk 2000
Sleazy Uncle, The 1991
Sleep With Me 1995
Sleepers 1996
Sleeping with the Enemy 1991
Sleepless in Seattle 1993
Sleepwalkers. See Stephen King's
  Sleepwalkers.
Sleepy Hollow 2000
Sleepy Time Gal, The 2002
Sliding Doors 1999
Sling Blade 1996
Slingshot, The 1995
Sliver 1993
Slugs 1988
Slums of Beverly Hills 1999
Small Faces 1996
Small Soldiers 1999
Small Time Crooks 2001
Small Wonders 1996
Smash Palace 1982
Smell of Camphor, Fragrance of
  Jasmine 2001
Smile Like Yours, A 1997
Smiling Fish and Goat on Fire
  2001
Smilla's Sense of Snow 1997
Smithereens 1982, 1985

Smoke 1995
Smoke 1995
Smoke Signals 1999
Smokey and the Bandit-Part 3
  1983
Smoking/No Smoking [1995]
  2001
Smooth Talk 1985
Smurfs and the Magic Flute,
  The 1983
Snake Eyes. See Dangerous
  Game.
Snake Eyes 1999
Snapper, The 1993
Snatch 2002
Sneakers 1992
Sniper 1993
Snow Day 2001
Snow Dogs 2003
Snow Falling in Cedars 2000
Snows of Kilimanjaro, The
  [1952] 1982
S.O.B. 1981
So I Married an Axe Murderer
  1993
Soapdish 1991
Sobibor, October 14, 1943, 4
  p.m. 2002
Society 1992
Sofie 1993
Soft Fruit 2001
Soft Shell Man 2003
Softly Softly 1985
Sokhout. See The Silence.
Sol del Membrillo, El. See
  Dream of Light.
Solarbabies 1986
Solaris 2003
Solas 2001
Soldier 1999
Soldier, The 1982
Soldier's Daughter Never Cries,
  A 1999
Soldier's Story, A 1984
Soldier's Tale, A 1988
Solid Gold Cadillac, The
  [1956] 1984
Solo 1996
Solomon and Gaenor 2001
Some Girls 1988
Some Kind of Hero 1982
Some Kind of Wonderful 1987
Some Like It Hot [1959]
  1986, 1988
Some Mother's Son 1996
Someone Else's America 1996
Someone Like You 2002
Someone to Love 1987, 1988
Someone to Watch Over Me
  1987
Something to Do with the Wall
  1995
Something to Talk About
  1995
Something Wicked This Way
  Comes 1983
Something Wild 1986
Something Within Me 1995
Something's Gotta Give
  pg. 414
Sommersby 1993
Son, The 2003

Son of Darkness: To Die For II
  1995
Son of the Bride 2003
Son of the Pink Panther 1993
Son-in-Law 1993
Sonatine 1999
Song for Martin 2003
Songcatcher 2001
Songwriter 1984
Sonny 2003
Sonny Boy 1990
Sons 1989
Sons of Steel 1988
Son's Room, The 2002
Sontagsbarn. See Sunday's
  Children.
Sophie's Choice 1982
Sorority Babes in the Slimeball
  Bowl-o-Rama 1988
Sorority Boys 2003
Sorority House Massacre 1987
Sotto Sotto. See Softly Softly.
Soul Food 1997
Soul Man 1986
Soul Survivors 2002
Sound Barrier, The [1952]
  1984, 1990
Sour Grapes 1999
Source, The 2000
Soursweet 1988
Sous le Sable See Under the
  Sand.
Sous le Soleil de Satan. See
  Under the Sun of Satan.
Sous Sol 1997
South Central 1992
South of Reno 1987
South Park: Bigger, Longer &
  Uncut 2000
Southern Comfort 1981
Souvenir 1988
Space Cowboys 2001
Space Jam 1996
Spaceballs 1987
Spacecamp 1986
Spaced Invaders 1990
Spacehunter: Adventures in the
  Forbidden Zone 1983
Spalding Gray's Monster in a
  Box. See Monster in a Box.
Spanish Prisoner, The 1999
Spanking the Monkey 1995
Spartacus [1960] 1991
Spawn 1997
Speaking in Strings 2000
Speaking Parts 1990
Special Day, A 1984
Special Effects 1986
Specialist, The 1995
Species 1995
Species 2 1999
Specter of the Rose [1946]
  1982
Speechless 1995
Speed 1995
Speed 2: Cruise Control 1997
Speed Zone 1989
Spellbinder 1988
Spellbound [1945] 1989
Sphere 1999
Spice World 1999
Spices 1989